A

GENEALOGICAL DICTIONARY

OF

THE FIRST SETTLERS OF NEW ENGLAND,

SHOWING

THREE GENERATIONS

OF

THOSE WHO CAME BEFORE MAY, 1692,

ON THE

BASIS OF FARMER'S REGISTER.

BY

JAMES SAVAGE,

FORMER PRESIDENT OF THE MASSACHUSETTS HISTORICAL SOCIETY AND EDITOR OF WINTHROP'S
HISTORY OF NEW ENGLAND.

WITH TWO SUPPLEMENTS

IN FOUR VOLUMES.

VOL. IV.

Originally Published
Boston, 1860-1862

Reprinted with
"Genealogical Notes and Errata,"
excerpted from
*The New England Historical
and Genealogical Register,*
Vol. XXVII, No. 2, April, 1873,
pp. 135-139

And

*A Genealogical Cross Index
of the Four Volumes
of the Genealogical Dictionary
of James Savage,*
by O. P. Dexter, 1884.

Genealogical Publishing Co., Inc.
Baltimore, 1965, 1969, 1977, 1981, 1986, 1990, 1994, 1998

Library of Congress Catalogue Card Number 65-18541
International Standard Book Number: 0-8063-0963-6
Set Number: 0-8063-0759-5

CLOSING ADDRESS.

THE task, that, near twenty years since, was assumed by me, is now ended; and no regret is felt for the time devoted to it. Pleasure and duty have been equally combined. In the result some exultation might be felt, if success rewarded diligence, and proficiency had always followed patience; but in parts of so wide a range around genealogy, as this of New England, frequent failures ought to be anticipated, since the triumphs even within the narrow space traversed, in their long campaigns, by Bond or Shattuck, Judd or Goodwin, proved imperfect. Gleaners may find reward in following even their footsteps.

For a partial indication of the ample assistance from modern copious correspondence, a reference to my preface in Vol. I. may seem sufficient; yet it appears requisite, in this valedictory obeisance to subscribers, to desire their forgiveness for the awkwardness they may discover, that among the ten or twelve thousand items of improvement in or increase upon the first text, as herein set forth, not a few hundred additions to additions with a score or two of corrections for corrections are interspersed. Of such materials the History of Watertown has subjoined 303 pages to its first 672; and parallel to such overflow might always be expected in a larger work, though not in exact proportion to its size. To exhaust the vocabulary of a civilized nation in a living tongue would appear impossible, for we all know, that new streams are constantly flowing into it from sources before unknown; and similar supplies, by analogy, in a dictionary to set forth the origin of our families subsisting one hundred and seventy years ago, may naturally arise. Una-

voidable omissions in these two thousand five hundred closely
marshalled pages ought, therefore, to be expected ; but if neither
residence nor time were given, no right to a place for a new
surname on my page would be yielded, though popular opinion
traced the pretender to a Plantagenet, or his veins swelled with
all the blood of all the Howards.   Half a million, I presume, of
those incidents may be found in this work.   Blanks, not above
two or three in the thousand, I believe, may remain in the myr-
iads of names of family or baptism, and, I hope, the erroneous
may only slightly outnumber the deficient.

   Some notes of events and of men have been lost, probably,
though only a single instance, but of half a line, occurs to my
recollection, and this is more cause of sorrow, than surprise,
when I remember how many hundred have been written twice,
thrice, and even four times over.   To a few, who consult these
volumes, such vacancies may give no disquiet, as thereby room
was gained for a little general biography or historical criticism
in place of the multitudinous ocean of numerals, or names as
little discriminated as *fortemque Gyan, fortemque Cloanthum.*
But never was such occasion made, however easily found by
one who will feel pleasant surprise at a rare deviation from
predominant dulness.   I have dared to express, in a very few
instances, my sense of the need of correction in old contempo-
rary statements of history, either public or private, and more
gladly to detect the modern adoption of idle traditions that
kept long out of sight, when their small value would not have
saved, the perpetuation of trifling fictions.

   May not some degree of favor be extended to my departure
from the narrow circle of universal genealogy to snatch a few
additional lines for some and sentences for others bearing prominent names like Bellingham, Burrows, Chauncey, Clark, Davenport, Dudley, Eaton, Endicott, Goffe, Hoar, Hopkins, Hull,
Jackson, Johnson, Leverett, Mather, Osgood, Paddy, Parker,
Phips, Pratt, Rogers, Saltonstall, Scroop, Sherman, Smith,
Temple, Welde, Whalley, Wigglesworth, Williams, Wilson,
and Winthrop.

   The prosecution of this work has continued without inter-
ruption in this long course of years, except twice, in both cases
from illness, first, short but severe, more than fourteen years

ago, next, lighter and longer, less than four years since; yet from the time printing of the volumes began, Dec. 1858, no day has passed without progress, except the legal holidays. By the majority who in careless hours may turn over these columns, the scrupulous diligence of the printer will justly be more observed than the research of the author, who should feel sufficient reward, if his countrymen acknowledge they have no further claim to use of his pen after the owner's reaching so near the age of fourscore. Still my rejoicing should be rather, that my service is finished, than that I have no more to do.

No slight vexation arose from defeat of my utmost vigilance in gathering the desired additions to this immense array of names, collected while the volumes have been passing under the press; but it was soothed by reflecting how many would show no regard to the defect, and better still how liberal would be the allowance of the few that duly weighed the excuse by making the suffering their own. I desire the reader in

Vol. I. p. 277, l. 12, aft. 1701. add, Perhaps his d. Hannah m. William Punchard.

Vol. IV. p. 160. l. 3, at the end, add, He was s. of Thomas, and m. 28 Nov. 1677, Priscilla Buckley, had Priscilla, b. 10 Oct. foll. and d. next yr.; William, 21 July 1680, d. young; Thomas, 28 Mar. 1682; Sarah, 17 Jan. 1684; William, again, 25 Dec. 1686; Priscilla, again, 3 Aug. 1689, prob. d. soon; for next is Priscilla, 1 May 1690; and Simon, 1 Mar. 1695.

MAY 17, 1862.

GENEALOGICAL DICTIONARY

OF THE

FIRST SETTLERS OF NEW ENGLAND.

SABIN, BENJAMIN, Rehoboth 1670, perhaps s. of William, had Benjamin, b. 2 Dec. 1673, call. on for contribut. of money in the war of 1675, rem. to Roxbury, prob. to escape nearer evils, there had Mehitable, 7 Sept. 1677. Early next yr. his w. d. and he m. 5 July 1678, Sarah Parker, had Sarah, 1 Aug. 1679; Nehemiah, 10 Jan. 1681; Patience, 3 May 1682; Jeremiah, 11 Mar. 1684; Experience, Feb. 1685; and Experience, 1686, if we believe the rec. JOSEPH, Rehoboth, perhaps s. of William, had Jonathan, b. 12 July 1674; Abigail, 16 Aug. 1678; Experience, 14 Mar. 1681, d. soon; Joseph, 18 Nov. 1682, d. soon. JONATHAN, Rehoboth, wh. serv. 1675 and 6 in the gr. Ind. war, may have been br. of Benjamin, but I kn. no more. NEHEMIAH, Rehoboth, perhaps br. of the preced. had David, b. 10 Nov. 1674, d. soon. In Col. Rec. a name of one bur. at R. in the latter pt. of May 1676, print. Nathaniel Sahen, perhaps a ch. I think may mean one of this fam. NOAH, a soldier in Gallop's comp. 1690, perhaps of Rehoboth. SAMUEL, Rehoboth, s. of William, I suppose, was a soldier in the war begun by Philip both yrs. at differ. times, had Israel, b. 16 June 1673; Experience, 5 Oct. 1676, wh. prob. d. next yr.; and Mary, 4 Mar. 1679. He was a serj. in Gallop's comp. 1690 for Phips's crusade against Quebec. * WILLIAM, Rehoboth 1643, sign. the combina. or compact of 1644, was oft. a selectman, rep. 1657 and sev. yrs. more; had Mehitable, b. 10 May 1673, unless she were ch. of one of his s. He was liberal in contribut. for Philip's war, and prob. two, if not more of his ch. render. personal serv. What number of ch. he had is unkn.

nor is the date of either giv. but seven appear with some distinctness, and the names are thot. to be Mercy, in add. to the five foregoing, and William, beside, perhaps, ano. s. whose wid. gave of her mite to the cause. WILLIAM, Rehoboth, s. perhaps of the preced. had Mary, b. 18 Sept. 1675; and Margaret, 10 Apr. 1680. Easi. this name gains final *e*.

SABLE, or SABLES, JOHN, Hartford 1639, rem. prob. bef. 1650, to some other town of uncert. name, perhaps Wethersfield, and was freem. 1658. WILLIAM, Braintree, a soldier of Johnson's comp. 1675.

SACKET, JOHN, New Haven, m. 20 May 1652, Agnes Tinkham, had John, b. 30 Apr. 1653; Jonathan, 6 June 1655; Mary, 24 Sept. 1657; Joseph, 3 May 1660; Martha, 19 Sept. 1662; and d. 3 Sept. 1684. His wid. d. 1707. JOHN, Northampton, had John, b. 1660; William, 1662; Abigail, 1663; Mary, wh. d. 1667; and Hannah, 1669; rem. to Westfield, there had Mary, again, 8 June 1672; Samuel, 18 Oct. 1674; Eliz. 28 Aug. 1677, wh. d. at 5 yrs. His ho. was burn. by the Ind. 1675; his w. d. 9 Oct. 1690; and he m. 1691, Sarah, the only d. of John Stiles, wid. of John Stewart of Springfield; and d. 8 Apr. 1719. He was prob. s. of the first Simon, and may have been brot. from Eng. Abigail m. 13 Sept. 1682, John Noble; and Mary m. 2 Oct. 1689, Benjamin Morley. All his other ch. were m. also; but William, Samuel, and Abigail d. bef. their f. JOHN, New Haven, eldest s. of John of the same, was a propr. 1685. JOHN, Westfield, eldest s. of John of the same, by w. Deborah had John, b. 3 Mar. 1688; Abigail, 16 Oct. 1690; Daniel, 14 Aug. 1693; David, 7 July 1696; Benjamin, 30 Oct. 1698; and Deborah, 16 Nov. 1701. His w. d. 4 days aft. and he m. ano. w. had sev. ch. and d. 20 Dec. 1745. JOSEPH, Newtown, L. I. s. of the sec. Simon, had, says Riker, three ws. Eliz. d. of capt. Richard Betts; the next, Ann; and last, 1711, Mercy, wid. of Thomas Betts, d. of Daniel Whitehead. He had large est. was lieut. and capt. d. 1719. The ch. were Simon, Joseph, Richard, John, William, Samuel, Eliz. and Sarah; but the hist. of Newtown gives no dates of their bs. nor does he appropr. the mos. SIMON, Cambridge 1632, came with w. Isabel, and, prob. both s. Simon and John, all, perhaps, in the Lion, that brot. in Sept. of that yr. sev. sett. of C.; had sh. in the div. of ld. Aug. 1635, and d. soon aft. since admin. of his goods was giv. by the Ct. of Assist. to his wid. 3 Nov. foll. as our Col. Rec. I. 155, shows. Perhaps she m. again. SIMON, Springfield 1654, s. prob. of the preced. b. in Eng. m. Sarah, d. of William Blomfield, had only Joseph, b. 23 Feb. 1656; and d. 9 July 1659. WILLIAM, Westfield, s. of John of the same, m. 27 Nov. 1689, Sarah Cram, had Joseph, b. 25 July 1690; Hannah, 15 Aug. 1692; Rebecca, 16 Sept. 1694; Jonathan, 20 Mar. 1696; and d. 28 Mar. 1700.

SADD, JOHN, Hartford, a tanner, with good est. from Earl's Colne, Co. Essex, purch. ho. and ld. 1674, had left s. John in Eng. here m. a. 1690, as sec. w. Hepzibah, wid. of John Pratt, the third of that name, had Thomas, b. 1691 ; and d. 20 Dec. 1694. THOMAS, Windsor, s. of the preced. had Thomas, wh. d. 8 May 1728, a. 10 yrs. old ; Hannah, b. 2 Dec. 1719; Thomas, 3 Aug. 1723 ; Hepzibah, 20 Mar. 1725 ; Matthew, 11 July 1729 ; and John, 22 Nov. 1734.

SADLER, ABIAL, Gloucester 1689, had been a soldier, Babson says, in the Col. serv. ; by w. Rebecca had a ch. b. 13 Mar. 1693 ; and the f. d. 15 Sept. 1697. ANTHONY, Newbury, came from Southampton in the Confidence, as serv. to Stephen Kent, 1638, as the rec. has it, 9 yrs. old, the fig. on the left hand being lost, would, perhaps, be supplied by 2, for he was adm. freem. 6 Sept. 1639 ; was a shoemak. m. Martha, d. of John Cheney, had only ch. Abiel, b. 2 Nov. 1650; rem. to Salisbury, and was drown. 23 Feb. 1651. His wid. next yr. m. prob. the sec. Nicholas Busbee. JOHN, Gloucester, freem. 19 May 1642, and select-man the same yr. ; had been, with other inhabs. of G. 1640, at Marsh-field, was capt. and had s. Robert. He gave that s. ho. and ld. went home, and sent for his w. to come to him ; prob. s. Robert foll. bef. many yrs. as his atty. Hugh Caulkins, in 1651, convey. the est. JOHN, Wethersfield 1643, on Glastonbury side of the riv. is found in the list of freem. 1669, had w. Deborah, but no ch. prob. for all his prop. was giv. to her by the will of 8 July 1673, and he d. next mo. RICHARD, Lynn, freem. 14 Mar. 1639, had come in 1636, it is said, from Worcester, Eng. in 1639 had charge, with John Oliver and Robert Keayne, of run. line between that town and Boston ; was made clk. of the writs, i. e. town clk. with addit. function, in Dec. 1641, but went home in 1646, as fellow-passeng. with John Leverett, Gov. Sayles of Bermuda, and many others, of wh. were the malcontent doctor Child, Thomas Fowle, and William Vassall. See the curious tract, New England's Salamander, by Gov. Winslow, in 3 Mass. Hist. Coll. II. 130–3. He bec. a preach. ord. 16 May 1648, at the little chapel of Whixall, in the N. pt. of Shropshire, adj. Flint, says Calamy ; and was eject. aft. the restorat. from a better living at Ludlow, but d. at W. 1675, aged 55. Lewis, in his Hist. Ed. 2d, p. 92, would instr. us, that he had s. Richard, b. 1610, wh. was the min. then ord. and eject. wh. is wide. from Calamy, by mak. the s. b. ten yrs. bef. the suppos. f.

SAFFERY, SOLOMON, a mathemat. employ. with Nathaniel Woodward to run the S. line of the Col. in 1642. See Hutch. Hist. II. 263.

SAFFIN, or SAFFYN, ‡ * JOHN, Scituate, a lawyer, selectman 1653, m. 2 or 3 Dec. 1658, Martha Willet, d. of capt. Thomas of Plymouth, had John, b. 13 Sept. foll. d. at 2 yrs. ; John, again, 14 Apr. 1662 ; Thomas,

18 Mar. 1664; Simon, 4 Apr. 1666; Josiah, 30 Jan. 1668; Joseph, 2 Feb. 1670, d. young; Benjamin, 15 June 1672, d. soon; and Joseph, again, 24 Jan. 1676. His w. with two of the ch. d. 1678, of smallpox; and the rest of the ch. all d. young. Soon aft. m. he rem. to Boston, join. the first ch. and took freem.'s o. 1671, was rep. 1684 to 6, in the latter yr. being chos. speaker, had large interest in the Narraganset or King's Prov. 1683, and at the first pop. elect. of counsel. in 1693, was chos. one of the ten by the peop. prefer. to ten others, dictat. to k. William in the chart. by Increase Mather, and made one of the judges in Sup. Ct. 1701, from wh. place Gov. Dudley rem. him, and two yrs. later negat. him as counsel. For sec. w. he took, 1680, Eliz. wid. of Peter Lidget, Esq. and she made her will 14 Apr. 1682, prob. hav. such power by her contr. of m. and in July foll. attempt. to destr. hers. as by the diary of Noadiah Russell, in Geneal. Reg. VII. 56, is seen. He had third w. Rebecca, d. of Rev. Samuel Lee of Bristol, whither he rem. a. 1690, and was appoint. the first judge of Pro. in the new Co. then pt. of Mass. since assign. to R. I. From this w. aft. long disagr. he separat. hims. and very curious matter a. the affair may be read in Baylies, IV. 56–61; but far more interest is found in the letter to S. from Cotton Mather, 3 Mass. Hist. Coll. I. 137, writ. only ten days bef. d. of S. prob. therefore never rec. It is one of the happiest of the eccentric writer's productions; and highly piquant would have been the reply of the judge to his ghostly adviser, had he liv. to offer one. The will, made two days bef. pro. two days aft. his d. in wh. nothing is giv. to his w. and £5 to Cotton Mather, confirms this conject. He d. at B. 29 July 1710, and Hutch. II. 136, refers to the interm. of his last surv. s. wh. d. 18 Jan. 1687, immortaliz. by the epitaph in Addison's Spectator, as in the judicious memoir to be read in Geneal. Reg. IV. 109. His wid. m. 26 July 1712, Rev. Joseph Baxter of Medfield.

SAFFORD, JOHN, Ipswich 1665, perhaps br. perhaps s. of Thomas. JOHN jr. took o. of alleg. at Ipswich 1683. JOSEPH, Newtown, L. I. 1655. JOSEPH, Ipswich, s. of Thomas, freem. 1682. THOMAS, Ipswich 1641, d. 1667, leav. wid. s. Joseph, b. prob. 1633, and three ds.

SAGE, DAVID, Middletown, freem. 1667, m. Eliz. Kirby, wh. d. 1670, had David, b. 1 Feb. 1665; John, 5 Mar. 1668; and by w. Mercy, wh. d. 7 Dec. 1711, had Mary, 15 Nov. 1672; Jonathan; and Timothy, 14 Aug. 1678; all nam. exc. Mary, with his w. in the will short. bef. he d. 31 Mar. 1703; beside ds. Eliz. 6 June 1666, wh. m. a Bull; Mary, w. of Samuel Johnson; and Mercy, without surname, so may be presum. unm. Good est. he left to wid. Mary, and these seven ch. Descend. are num.

SALE, SEALE, or SAILE, EDWARD, Salem, was prob. that passeng.

1635, aged 24, in the Elizabeth and Ann from London, freem. 2 Nov. 1637, but he must have belong. to ano. ch. than S. In June preced. his w. Margaret was charg. for adultery with more than one, and banish. next yr. See Col. Rec. I. 198, and Winth. II. 349. He was of Rehoboth 1644. ‖ EPHRAIM, Boston, s. of Edward, ar. co. 1674, was its lieut. and d. 2 Dec. 1690. By w. Alice he had Samuel, b. 11 Feb. 1678; Nathaniel, 21 Oct. 1679; and by w. Mary, d. of Hopestill Foster, had Mary, 21 Aug. 1681; Hepzibah, 24 Dec. 1684; John, 17 Jan. 1687; and Thankful, 18 May 1689. His wid. m. 10 Dec. 1691, Samuel Ward. OBADIAH, Boston, freem. 1681, by w. Sarah had John, b. 23 July 1680; Abigail, 6 Aug. 1681; Sarah, 3 Mar. 1683; and Sarah, again, 27 Aug. 1684.

SALISBURY, JOHN, Swanzey, perhaps s. of William, k. by the Ind. 24 June 1675, perhaps the first victim of the gr. war. JOHN, Boston, prob. s. of Nicholas, perhaps b. in Eng. by w. Annabel had John, b. 5 Jan. 1690; Nicholas and James, tw. 20 Aug. 1694, both prob. d. with the mo. soon; and by w. Bridget had Nicholas, again, 28 Oct. 1697; Benjamin, 7 Nov. 1699; was a mariner, and, perhaps, d. abroad. His inv. was tak. 5 June 1708, and the wid. appoint. adminx. 6 July, and brot. in the docum. 4 Oct. foll. by the name of Bridget Gooding, late Salisbury. NICHOLAS, Boston, had w. Eliz. wh. d. 17 Feb. 1688, aged 53, perhaps was f. of John, and the com. ancest. of sev. disting. fams. WILLIAM, Swanzey 1671, was, perhaps, f. of John bef. ment. certain. of that William, prob. k. by the Ind. 24 June 1675 in Philip's war, the first blast of wh. utter. scatter. this town. Admin. on *his* est. was giv. to his wid. 17 Sept. of that yr. and 11 Nov. 1684 the f. took admin. de bonis non. But he was of Milton, had w. Susanna; and from Hist. of Dorchester, 59, I learn that he had been there bef. 1656.

SALLOWS, BENJAMIN, Salem 1637. Felt. JOHN, Salem 1668, s. prob. of Michael, was a petitnr. against imposts. MICHAEL, Salem 1635, in his will of 14 Nov. 1646, pro. 31 Dec. foll. names Michael, his youngest s. d. Martha, beside s. Thomas, Robert, John, and Samuel, with s.-in-law Edward Wilson, made Wilson and s. Robert excors. both of wh. declin. to serve. ROBERT, Salem, s. of the preced. d. 1663, prob. in June, as his inv. was brot. in 1 July. THOMAS, br. of the preced. wh. d. 1663, perhaps at the same time with his br. it may be by shipwreck, or in a distant ld. at least the Ct. of Pro. rec. his inv. two days aft. that of Robert, and from differ. apprais. He was f. perhaps, of the ch. Hannah, Mary, Sarah, and Robert, all bapt. 5 June 1664.

SALLS, SAMUEL, Lynn, m. 4 Aug. 1663, Ann Lenthall. Perhaps the name should be Sallows, and he s. of Michael.

SALLY, or SALLEE, MANES, Charlestown, adm. of the ch. 3 May

1647, freem. the same mo. Of so unusual a name of bapt. or surname, I should be slow in acknowl. but Mary, prob. his w. join. the ch. 9 July next yr. his d. Rebecca m. John Jones, so there are three places of rec. and the potential authori. of Frothingham, 152, shows " Sarah Sallee's ho." in 1658. The classic Manes bec. Manus on his adm. in Col. rec.

SALMON, SALMONDS, or SAMMON, CLEMENT, Boston, m. 13 June 1660, Joanna Riland, had Mary, b. 12 Jan. 1663; Eliz. 26 Feb. 1666; and Samuel, 5 Apr. 1668. DANIEL, Lynn 1630, serv. in the Pequot war 1636 or 7, had Daniel, b. 2 May 1665; in 1681 gave testim. a. the iron works, in wh. he had labor. near 40 yrs. bef. GEORGE, Salem 1668. JOHN, Newport, one much esteem. d. 1676. JOHN, New Haven 1682. SAMUEL, Salem 1660, prosecut. as a Quaker. THOMAS, Northampton 1659, by w. Mary had Mary, b. 1660; Ruth, 1666; Eliz. 1673; beside two ch. that d. young; and Thomas, posthum. Mar. 1676; was k. by the Ind. 29 Oct. preced. His wid. Mary m. 1676, Joseph Phelps of Windsor, but prob. aft. his rem. to Simsbury. Ruth m. 1684, William Hulbert the sec.; and Eliz. m. 1693, Caleb Root. WILLIAM, Amesbury, took o. of alleg. 1677.

SALTER, CHARLES, Boston, by w. Eliz. had Benoni, b. 17 July 1685; and from rec. of B. I gain no more. ENEAS, Boston, a mason, by w. Joan had Eneas, b. 17 Apr. 1673; John, 24 Sept. 1674; Sarah, 1 Aug. 1676; Peter, 13 Feb. 1679; and Benjamin, 8 May 1682. HENRY, Charlestown, by w. Hannah had John, b. 6 Jan. 1656; Henry; Richard; and Nicholas; all bapt. 26 Oct. 1673, in right of the mo. wh. join. the ch. four wks. bef. One Thomas, without surname, is found in the rec. of b. at C. 20 Oct. and I presume he was this man's s. and that he d. young; but I do not see the name of f. among householders there 1658 or 1678. || JABEZ, Boston, s. of William, ar. co. 1674, by w. Eliz. had Eliz. b. 6 Oct. 1671; Mary, 28 Jan. 1673; Jabez, 8 July 1678, d. soon; William, 5 Jan. 1680; Jabez, again, 4 July 1682, d. soon; Jabez, again, 1 June 1683; Elisha, 22 Sept. 1685, d. soon; Elisha, again, 9 Oct. 1686; Richard, 3 Feb. 1689; and Samson, 21 Mar. 1692. He d. 31 Dec. 1720; and his wid. Eliz. d. 29 Oct. 1726, near 75 yrs. old. MATTHEW, Marblehead 1674. SAMSON, Newport 1639, came in the James 1635, from Southampton, then call. a fisherman in the custom-ho. docum. yet of Caversham, wh. is in Co. Oxford. SAMUEL, a soldier in Gallop's comp. 1690, against Quebec. THEOPHILUS, Ipswich 1648, of Salem 1654, acc. Felt. WALTER, Boston 1658, sett. short. aft. on L. I. as may be infer. from certain queries by him propound. to Conn. See Trumbull, Col. Rec. I. 423. WILLIAM, Boston, shoemak. by w. Mary had Peleg, b. 15 Mar. 1634, but bapt. 25 Mar. 1638, wh. makes me doubt the date in rec. of b.; Eliz. 16 Apr. 1639, bapt. 26 Apr. 1640;

Mary, 10 Aug. 1642, bapt. 30 Oct. foll. as "a 3 days old," that shows
wh. rec. is wrong; Jabez, bapt. 17 Aug. 1645, wh. perhaps d. soon; yet
possib. the next town rec. Jabez, b. Sept. 1647 is wrong; Elisha, 7 Mar.
1654, d. next yr.; and Lydia, 24 Mar. 1656. He kept the prison in
this yr. and long aft. was witness to the will of wretch. Mrs. Hibbins,
wid. of the Assist. execut. as a witch, when she was only a scold; and
he d. 10 Aug. 1675, aged 68. His will of 11 May preced. names s.
Jabez, and John, wh. was gone away, but if he came back, should have
five acres on Spectacle isl.; ds. Mehitable, that should have half his
dwel.-ho.; and d. Beck, wh. had rec. her portion, prob. on m.; and
gr.ch. are refer. to, and w. Mary made extrix. On Boston rec. appears
m. of Nicholas Phillips with Hannah S. 4 Dec. 1651, but of wh. she
was d. is unkn.

SALTONSTALL, ‖ HENRY, Watertown, s. of Sir Richard, b. in Eng.
brot. prob. by his f. 1630, ar. co. 1639, gr. in the first class of H. C. 1642,
went soon aft. to Eng. was in Holland 1644, stud. med. and in Oct. 1649
had degr. of M. D. at the Univ. of Padua, and 24 June 1652, at Oxford,
by order of the Long Parliam. and was made fellow of New Coll. as
was, with less regard to rules, our William Stoughton; but place of his
later resid. or date of his d. is unkn. See Wood's Athenæ Oxon.
‡ * NATHANIEL, Haverhill, s. of Richard the sec. was prob. the first male
of this disting. fam. b. on our side of the ocean, freem. 1665, rep. 1666,
8–71, Assist. 1679 and until the vacat. of our old chart. 1686, but again
on overthrow of Andros, tho. the k. had made him one of the counc. to
Dudley; yet was nam. again in the new chart. and a judge of the Sup.
Ct. in 1692, when he refus. participat. in the monstrous trials for witchcr.
leav. his seat to be occup. by Jonathan Corwin, br. of the sheriff that
was call. to hang so many innocent victims. But many yrs. he was
head of the Essex militia. He m. 28 Dec. 1663, Eliz. d. of Rev. John
Ward, had Gurdon, b. 27 Mar. 1666, H. C. 1684, the disting. min. of
New London, and Gov. of Conn. (so nam. for Brampton Gurdon the
Suff'k. patriot M. P. whose d. was his mo.); Eliz. 15 Sept. 1668;
Richard, 25 Apr. 1672; Nathaniel, 5 Sept. 1674; both H. C. 1695;
and John, 14 Aug. 1678, wh. d. at 3 yrs.; and d. 21 May 1707. His
wid. d. 29 Apr. 1741, as Bond, 921, tells; but the yr. should be 1714.
Of his hon. descend. large acco. may be read in 2 Mass. Hist. Coll. IV.
154, and 3 M. H. C. IX. 119, but more in Bond's copious Hist. of
Watertown. ‖ PETER, by the hist. of the Ancient and Hon. Art. Co.
made one of the corps 1644, is prob. a name without right giv. by Whitman, as if he were s. of Sir Richard, for no such person is ever heard of
elsewhere, and Bond rejects it as any of our N. E. stock. Orig. rec. of
that famous milit. band have been lost above a hundred and fifty yrs.

‡ RICHARD, Watertown, the knight, s. of Samuel, and neph. of Sir Richard, mayor of London in the time of Queen Eliz. was from the neighb. of Halifax, in the W. Riding of Co. York, in the royal chart. of 4 Mar. 1629 first nam. of the 18 Assist. came 1630 in the fleet bring. all his fam. with Gov. Winth. but prob. his w. had d. some yrs. bef. With two ds. Rosamond and Grace, and one of his younger s. prob. Samuel, he left N. E. for home 1 Apr. 1631, hav. attend. eight of the nine sess. of the Ct. of Assist. and was fin. for abs. at that of 7 Sept. preced. Earnest. he befriend. our country in Eng. by thought, word, and deed; and was active, with the Lords Brooke, Say and Seal and other puritans in the first settlem. of Conn. By his first w. Grace, d. of Robert Kaye, Esq. of Yorksh. he had four s. Richard, b. 1610 ; Robert; Samuel; and Henry ; two ds. Rosamond, perhaps the eldest ch. and Grace. By uncert. tradit. he is giv. two other ws. one said to be d. of the Earl of Delawarr, for wh. in Collins's Peerage no support can be seen, and the other, less improb. Martha Wilford ; but no ch. is ascrib. to either. He was, with s. Henry, in Holland 1644, perhaps min. to the States, and there was paint. the likeness of wh. engrav. is seen in the sec. vol. of Mass. Hist. Soc. Proceed. His will was made 1658, at the age of 72.
‡ * RICHARD, Ipswich, s. of the preced. by his f. brot. 1630, hav. left the Univ. of Cambridge, where he was enter. at Emanuel Coll. as a fellow commoner, 18 Apr. 1627, from Yorksh. and matricula. 14 Dec. foll. adm. freem. of Mass. 18 Oct. 1631, and next mo. went home, by circuitous voyage of six wks. to Virg. and m. in Eng. a. 1633, Meriel, d. of Brampton Gurdon of Assington, Co. Suff'k. near the ancestr. resid. of our first Gov. Winth. and emb. on return in the Susan and Ellen 1635, with that w. aged 22, and d. of the same name, was rep. in Mar. 1636 and foll. sess. until chos. an Assist. in May 1637, and in 1641 made first offic. under Endicott, of the Essex regim. when only two were in the Col. went home again, perhaps for the health of his w. 1649, as told in the anecdote relat. of Rev. John Cotton in note to Hutch. I. 94. For many yrs. he was not chos. Assist. but in 1664 in hope of his com. again, the honor was renew. and it was erron. assert. that he had been aft. in the country, bec. in 1672 he gave £50. to relief of Goffe and Whalley, the regicides. In 1680, however, he was once more in Mass. and in May organizat. made an Assist. tak. the o. in Aug. wh. was renew. in 1681 and 2, but in this latter yr. he went home again, as the hope of preserv. liberty under the old chart. evapora. and d. 20 or 29 Apr. 1694, at Hulme, in Lancashire, at the ho. of Sir Edward Morley, wh. m. his eldest d. Other ch. were Richard, wh. d. young, prob. unm. certain. and Nathaniel, bef. ment. also Abigail, wh. m. Thomas Harley, s. of Sir Robert, and uncle to the famous Robert, prime min. of

Queen Anne, the friend of Pope and Swift, well kn. as Earl of Oxford (see Collins's Peerage, IV. 244, Ed. 5, and correct the slight error there) ; beside Eliz. wh. m. Hercules Horsey, Esq. Instruct. may be got as to the just value of tradit. from a note in Hutch. II. 122, in wh. is read the story of a letter from Mrs. Harley to her sis. in N. E. that was many yrs. preserv. aft. the d. of that disting. statesman, for this passage in it: "I am now going to carry Bob. up to the inns of ct. to make a man of him," and Hutch. wh. seldom falls into such an error, makes the mo. "gr.d. of Sir Richard S." and this H. introduc. by refer. to "a tradit. that Harley had some N. E. blood in him, his mo. being a gr.d. of Sir Richard S." Now beside that *this* gr.d. of Sir Richard S. had no sis. here to write unto, the tale is false in the most vital pt. as usual, for she, being w. of his uncle, not of his f. could transmit no blood to the Lord High Treasurer. ‖ ROBERT, Watertown, br. of the preced. ar. co. 1638, was prob. at Windsor 1640–2, engag. for his f. or elder br. but allow. Francis Stiles to lead him into gr. useless expense, from wh. both suffer. inconven. to their dying day. He d. 1650, unm. ; in his will of 13 June, pro. 15 Aug. nam. only relat. his f. brs. Richard, Samuel, and Henry, sis. Rosamond and Grace, and made John Clark excor. wh. forthwith renounc. his office. See Geneal. Reg. VII. 334. SAMUEL, Watertown, br. of the preced. of wh. we would glad. kn. more than Farmer told of his d. 21 Jan. 1696. Even in the gr. Hist. of W. Bond could add only that admin. was tak. in Oct. foll. by his neph. Nathaniel, saying that he had no active participat. in munici. concerns, nor is w. or ch. found in the rec. But in that vol. p. 918, amends are made by one of the finest letters of that age from his sis. Rosamond, 22 Apr. 1644. She was then resid. in conseq. of the loss of his prop. by her f. in the family of the puritan Earl of Warwick, Ld. High Adm. and her sis. with the lady of the Earl of Manchester, one of the ch. command. in the civil war. Of descend. of Sir Richard, in the male line, thirteen had, in 1834, been gr. at Harv. and six at Yale.

SAMFIELD, AUSTIN, Fairfield 1658, d. 1661, leav. small prop. to wid. and no ch. heard of.

SAMPSON, ABRAHAM, Duxbury 1638, perhaps br. of Henry, m. a d. of Samuel Nash, and Windsor says, he had a sec. w. His ch. were Abraham, Isaac, Samuel, wh. was k. by the Ind. in Philip's war, and George, b. 1655. ABRAHAM, Duxbury, s. of the preced. m. Sarah, d. of Alexander Standish, had Abraham, b. 1686 ; Miles, 1690 ; Ebenezer ; Rebecca ; Sarah ; and Grace. CALEB, Duxbury, s. perhaps youngest, of Henry, m. Mary, d. of Alexander Standish, had, says Winsor, Rachel and Lora. GEORGE, Duxbury, or Plympton, s. of the first Abraham, by w. Eliz. had Joseph, b. 14 July 1679; Abigail, 22 Jan. 1681;

Judith, 3 Mar. 1683; Ruth, 22 Dec. 1684; Benjamin, 19 Sept. 1686; Martha, 25 Oct. 1689; George, 10 Mar. 1691; Eliz. 22 Dec. 1692; William, 8 July 1693; and Seth, 22 Dec. 1697. His w. d. 27 May 1727, in her 70th yr. and he d. 26 July 1739, in his 84th yr. as Winsor tells. HENRY, Plymouth 1620, came in the Mayflower, of the fam. of his uncle, Edward Tilley, a youth too small to sign the immortal compact of Nov. at Cape Cod; but whether, or not, entit. in the div. of lds. he was certain. in the div. of cattle, 1627, enumerat. in the comp. of Elder Brewster, liv. on Duxbury side, m. 6 Feb. 1636, Ann Plummer, had Stephen, John, James, Caleb, Eliz. Hannah, Mary, and, perhaps, Dorcas, but when Bradford wrote, 1650, only seven ch. and d. 24 Dec. 1684. Eliz. m. Robert Sproat; Hannah m. Josiah Holmes; Mary m. John Summers; Dorcas m. Thomas Bonney; and one d. it is said, m. John Hammond, but he is not of my acquaint. ISAAC, Duxbury, s. of Abraham, m. Lydia, d. of Alexander Standish, had Isaac, b. 1688; Jonathan, 1690; Josiah, 1692; Lydia, 1694; Ephraim, 1698; Priscilla, 1702; and Barnabas, 1705. JAMES, Dartmouth 1686. JOHN, Boston, merch. rem. perhaps, to Beverly 1671, there m. a d. of Richard Haynes, and bef. the begin. of Ind. war, 1675, may have liv. at Scarborough. Ano. JOHN, at New London, m. aft. 1672, not long bef. 1676, the wid. mo. of John Stodder, or Stother, a youth of only 16, wh. possess. by a malice almost incredib. murder. with an axe, 6 June 1678, Zipporah, w. of Thomas Bolles, with two of her ch. Joseph, and Mary, and soon aft. murder. John Sampson, s. of his mo. aged betw. one and two yrs. as by his own confess. is seen in the rec. of his trial at Hartford. For the soundness of the maxim in common law, malitia supplet ætatem, I believe, no stronger proof can be found, since the creation, in the stories of juven. depravity. He acknowl. that he k. his br. with a hatchet "bec. he cried, and bec. he did not love the ch. nor his f." and was execut. 9 Oct. foll. RICHARD, by Farmer call. of Boston, the freem. of 1674, I dare not accept, but think, was rather appropr. by New Hampsh. ROBERT, Boston 1630, came in the same sh. with Gov. Winth. wh. calls him cous. in a let. to his w. Apr. bef. depart. from Isle of Wight. His fam. was ancient. in the rank of knights, resid. at Sampson's Hall, in the parish of Kersey, adj. Groton, where W. was patron as well as lord of the manor. He was s. of John, by Bridget Clopton, sis. of the sec. w. of our Gov. W. By Whitman he is count. a memb. of the ar. co. 1639; but it seems far more prob. (as we never hear of him aft.) that he was some yrs. gone home. ROGER, Ipswich 1654. STEPHEN, Duxbury, s. of Henry, had Benjamin; Cornelius; Hannah; Mary; Eliz.; John, b. 17 Aug. 1688; Dorcas; and Abigail.

SAMS, or SAMMES, CONSTANTINE, Boston, by w. Eliz. had Richard,

b. 7 Oct. 1678 ; Mary, 2 Dec. 1684; Mercy, 3 July 1687, d. soon; and
Mercy, again, 12 Jan. 1689. JOHN, Roxbury 1640, went to Eng. and
at Coggeshall, in Co. Essex, was success. in the pulpit of celebr. John
Owen, D. D. says Calamy, from wh. he was eject. 1675 ; and the eccles.
hist. tells, that he was educat. in N. E. Very strange it seems, that no
more is kn. of him here, but that in R. he purch. lds. of Rev. Thomas
Weld, of capt. John Johnson, and of Joseph Weld, a. 1640, to amount,
in aggreg. of £134., and that in Sept. 1642, Gov. Thomas Dudley, on
ex'con. for £51. got the whole, in pt. satisfact. thereof, by appraisem. at
£42, 17, 8½, so that little benefit of his acres was enjoy. by the poor
scholar, wh. could not redeem his est. See Dudley's investit. in Reg. of
Suff 'k. Deeds, I. 37. RALPH, Dorchester, a tailor, rem. to Boston bef.
1659 ; and was liv. 1663. THOMAS, Salem, had gr. of ld. in 1638, as
Felt tells, and liv. at Marblehead 1648. Yet he may have been of
Roxbury 1637, and one of the appraisers on inv. of Edward Blackley.

SAMUEL, JOHN, Boston, wh. m. 24 Dec. 1652, wid. Lucy Wight, is
call. mariner in 1656 ; and he d. 8 Dec. 1662, or his inv. was then made.

SAMWAYS, SAMWAYES, SAMOIS, or SAMWIS, JOHN, Huntington, L. I.
adm. freem. of Conn. 1664, perhaps was s. of the foll. RICHARD,
Windsor 1640, had one ch. wh. d. 1648, and he d. 1650, leav. wid.
Esther, and, perhaps, two ch. But the name was not long in W. so
that, by var. spell. Hinman, 71, made two out of him.

SANBORN, ancient. SAMBORNE, BENJAMIN, Hampton, s. of the first
John, by first w. Sarah, wh. d. 29 June 1720, had Mary, b. 27 Oct.
1690; Joanna, 1 Dec. 1692; Sarah, 30 Sept. 1694 ; Theodate, 1696;
Dorothy, 27 Oct. 1698 ; Abigail, 21 July 1700 ; Jemima, 17 May
1702 ; Susanna, 20 Sept. 1704 ; Benjamin, 1 June 1706, d. young;
Judith, 26 Oct. 1708; Benjamin, again, 7 Nov. 1712. He next m.
Meribah Tilton, a wid. and had Ebenezer, 10 Oct. 1723 ; and this w. d.
15 Dec. 1740 ; and he had third w. Abigail Dalton, perhaps wid. of the
sec. Philemon, and d. of Edward Gove. *JOHN, Hampton 1643, by
tradit. said to have come from Co. Derby, and more prob. to be s. of
John by a d. of Rev. Stephen Bachiler, wh. left three s. John, William,
and Stephen, to the care of their gr.f. by wh. they were brot. in the
William and Francis, arr. at Boston from London, 5 June 1632.
For first w. he took Mary, d. of Robert Tuck of H. wh. d. 30 Dec.
1668, hav. borne him John, 1649 ; Mary, 12 Apr. 1651, d. young; Abigail, 23 Feb. 1653 ; Richard, 4 Feb. 1655 ; Mary, again, 19 Mar. 1657,
d. young ; Joseph, 13 Mar. 1659 ; Stephen, 12 Nov. 1661, d. soon;
Ann, 20 Dec. 1662 ; Nathaniel, 27 Jan. 1666 ; Benjamin, 20 Dec.
1668 ; and by sec. w. wid. Margaret Moulton, d. of Robert Page, had
Jonathan, 25 May 1672 ; was freem. 1666 ; lieut. rep. 1684 and 5 ; and

d. 20 Oct. 1692. His wid. d. 13 July 1699. JOHN, Hampton, eldest s. of the preced. m. 19 Nov. 1674, Judith Coffin, prob. d. of the sec. Tristram, had Judith, b. 8 Aug. 1675; Mary, 2 July 1677; Sarah, 8 May 1679; Deborah, 1681; John, 1683; Enoch, 1685; Lydia, 24 Feb. 1687; Peter; Tristram; and Abner, 27 Apr. 1694. JONATHAN, Hampton, youngest s. of John the first, m. Eliz. Sherburne, perhaps d. of John, had Eliz. b. 27 Dec. 1692; Samuel, 7 Sept. 1694; Achaicus, (?) 1696; Margaret, 20 Mar. 1698; Jonathan, 28 Apr. 1700; Love, Aug. 1702; Dorothy, 20 Aug. 1704, d. next yr.; Dorothy, again, 22 Aug. 1706, d. young; Sarah, 18 Apr. 1708; John, 19 Dec. 1710, d. soon; Benjamin, 22 Jan. 1712, d. young; and Mary, 7 Dec. 1713; and d. 20 June 1741, leav. wid. and eight ch. JOSEPH, Hampton, br. of the preced. m. 28 Dec. 1682, Mary Gove, d. of that Edward, wh. was not hang. for treason, had Abigail, b. 1 Apr. 1686; Huldah, 3 May 1688; Reuben, 18 May 1692; Edward, 7 Apr. 1694; Abraham, 10 Mar. 1696; Mary, 28 July 1697; Joseph, 22 July 1700; and David, 16 Jan. 1702. JOSIAH, Hampton, s. of William of the same, m. 25 Aug. 1681, Hannah Moulton, had William, b. 2 Mar. 1682; Hannah, 1684; and Sarah, 1686. He m. 1690, Sarah, wid. of Jonathan Perkins, had Jabez, Mar. 1691; Keziah, 15 Mar. 1693; Rachel, 13 Mar. 1695; Jonathan, 27 Apr. 1697; Reuben, 10 Apr. 1699; Abner, 9 Sept. 1702; and Richard, 9 Aug. 1705. His w. or wid. d. 1 Sept. 1748, aged 85. MEPHIBOSHETH, Hampton, br. of the preced. m. Lydia Leavitt, had Mary, b. 24 Feb. 1695; Lydia, 11 June 1697; Sarah, 1699; Nathan, 8 Aug. 1701; Abigail, 23 Oct. 1704; James, 1706; and Rachel, 15 Feb. 1708; and d. 5 Feb. 1749. NATHANIEL, Hampton, s. of the first John, m. 3 Dec. 1691, Rebecca Prescott, had Richard, b. 27 Feb. 1693; James, 6 Aug. 1696; Rachel, 4 Oct. 1698; Jeremiah, 10 Feb. 1701; Abigail, 22 Feb. 1703; Nathan, 27 June 1709; Jacob, 7 May 1711; Eliphaz, 10 Dec. 1712; Nathaniel, 10 Nov. 1714; Judith, 10 June 1717; and Daniel, 31 Dec. 1719; and d. 9 Nov. 1723. But in the fam. geneal. when we read that he had sec. w. Sarah, it would be agreeable to discern what portion of these eleven ch. all liv. in 1721, were b. respective. by ea. as great unwillingness must be felt at inflict. the whole on either. RICHARD, Hampton, br. of the preced. m. 5 Dec. 1678, Ruth Moulton, had Mary, b. 30 Sept. 1679; John, 6 Nov. 1681; and Ruth; but by sec. w. m. 20 Dec. 1693, wid. Mary Boulter, he had Shubael, b. next yr. STEPHEN, Hampton, br. perhaps youngest, of the first John, went home, it is said, with his gr.f. Bachiler, wh. had brot. him, of course, in his youth. STEPHEN, Hampton, s. of William of the same, m. 26 July 1693, Hannah Philbrick, had Stephen, b. 1 May 1694; James, 20 June 1697; Ann, 10 Sept. 1699; Hannah, 23 June 1701;

Phebe, 20 June 1703 ; Abiathar, 25 Feb. 1705 ; Zadok, 1 June 1707 ; Amy, 10 Dec. 1710 ; Abigail, 15 June 1712 ; Mary, 17 July 1715 ; and Jonathan, 16 Mar. 1718 ; and d. 21 July 1750. * WILLIAM, Hampton, was brot. from Eng. by his gr.f. Bachiler, says the fam. tradit. in June 1632, by w. Mary Moulton, had William, b. 1650 ; Josiah, bef. ment. ; Mary, 19 July 1660; Mephibosheth, 5 Nov. 1663; Sarah, 12 Feb. 1667 ; and Stephen, 4 Sept. 1671 ; was selectman, rep. and d. 18 Sept. 1692. WILLIAM, Hampton, eldest s. of the preced. m. 1 Jan. 1680, Mary Marston, had John, b. 6 Nov. foll. ; Mary, 1683 ; and a d. 21 Sept. 1685, wh. d. next yr. as had his w. some wks. bef. but he liv. to 9 Dec. 1744.

SANBROOKE, THOMAS, Boston, whose will of 16 May 1649, pro. 6 Feb. foll. is seen in Geneal. Reg. VII. 227, could not be other than a trans. trader here.

SANDERBANT, JOHN, the freem. of 10 May 1643, is, I doubt not, blunder of Mr. Secr. for Sunderland, as shall in that place be explain.

SANDON, ARTHUR, Salem 1639, on Marblehead side, had license to keep an inn, and in 1645 to sell wine ; d. a. 1667.

SANDS, or SANDES, JAMES, Block Isl. now call. New Shoreham, was b. it is said, 1622, at Reading, Co. Berks, came with w. Sarah, and, per-haps, was of Taunton 1658, but among first sett. at the Isl. bef. 1672 ; had Sarah, wh. m. prob. bef. 1673, Nathaniel Niles, and tradit. tells, that he had been as early as 1643, of Portsmouth, R. I. and freem. 1655. See Niles, in 3 Mass. Hist. Coll. VI. 192. In Hist. of New London, 293, Caulkins ment. that his d. Mercy m. 29 Apr. 1683, Joshua Ray-mond ; and that she was incident. connect. with the famous pirate, Wil-liam Kidd. Beside that Mercy he had John, James, Samuel, and ano. s. and d. 13 Mar. 1695. James and Samuel liv. at Cowneck, on L. I. JOHN, Charlestown, d. 28 June 1659 ; but as this surname is not seen in the rec. of ch. or of town resid. 1654, he may have been only trans. inhab.

SANDY, or SANDIE, sometimes SAND, JOHN, Boston, m. 7 July 1653, Ann Holmes, had Eliz. b. 15 Oct. 1654 ; and Mary, 24 Oct. 1656.

SANDYS, HENRY, Boston, merch. adm. of the ch. with w. Sybil, 20 Dec. 1638, and on 6 Jan. foll. had d. bapt. Deliverance, wh. d. young ; but in Nov. foll. was with others dism. to form new ch. at Rowley ; freem. 7 Oct. 1640, when the clk. call. him Sand ; had Samuel, b. 1640 ; Deliverance, again, Aug. 1644 ; rem. back to B. and had John, 28 Aug. 1646, and d. Dec. 1651. His d. Mary d. 14 Oct. 1654.

SANFORD, oft. SAMFORD, or SANDFORD, ANDREW, Hartford 1651, freem. 1657, rem. to Milford 1667, and there d. 1684, leav. ch. Andrew ; Mary, wh. d. unm. 1689; Ezekiel ; Hannah ; Martha ; Eliz. ; Abigail ;

and Sarah. One d. had d. bef. her f. ANDREW, Milford, s. of the preced. m. 8 Jan. 1668, Mary, d. of Henry Botsford, had Mary, bapt. Nov. 1668; Samuel, 1672, d. soon; Andrew, 16 July 1673; Samuel, again, 1675; and Esther, 1677. He was liv. in 1700, and date of d. is unkn. EPHRAIM, Milford, s. of Thomas of the same, m. 1669, at New Haven, Mary Powell, prob. d. of Thomas of the same, had Mary, b. there, but he d. at M. In Nov. 1692 his est. was div. to wid. Mary and ch. Mary, Samuel, Ephraim, Thomas, Nathaniel, and Zechariah. EZEKIEL, Fairfield, freem. 1669, was eldest s. of Thomas, as is thot.; had good est. 1670, and d. late in 1683, leav. wid. Rebecca, s. Ezekiel, and Thomas, ds. Sarah, w. of Cornelius Hull; Mary, w. of Theophilus Hull, Rebecca, w. of John Seely, beside Martha, and Eliz. then unm. as by agreem. 1697, for partitn. of est. we learn. EZEKIEL, Milford, s. of the first Andrew, d. 1685 or 6, leav. wid. and, perhaps, one ch. HENRY, Charlestown, m. 23 Jan. 1677, Mary, d. of John Long. JAMES, Boston, m. 1656, Eliz. d. of Francis Smith of the same, wh. had first liv. at Roxbury. He d. 2 Nov. 1661. § ‡ JOHN, Boston 1631, wh. is No. 115 on the list of ch. memb. was sw. freem. 3 Apr. 1632, and the same yr. made cannoneer at the fort; had John, bapt. 24 June 1632; Samuel, 22 June 1634; Eliphal, Dec. 1637, when he was disarm. as a support. of Wheelwright. He went with Coddington, Hutchinson, and others, to purch. R. I. and liv. at Portsmouth, the N. end of the isl. is in the list of freem. there 1655, was constable, treasr. Secr. Assist. 1647, and chos. head of the Colo. as Presid. in May 1653. One or more of his ch. were tak. by the Ind. when they k. Mrs. Hutchinson, it is said; and the friend. visit from a distance of a hundred and thirty miles, shows the intimacy the poor wid. kept up with old acquaint. When he d. is not heard. JOHN, Boston, by w. Bridget had Ann, wh. d. 26 Aug. 1654, as prob. the f. had good time bef. and the wid. m. lieut. William Phillips of B. who gave security, 10 Mar. 1657, to four ch. of said John, for portions of his est. in conform. with his will. But wh. those ch. were, is not ascertain. JOHN, Portsmouth, R. I. eldest s. of the first John, m. 17 Apr. 1663, Mary, d. of Samuel Gorton, wid. of Peter Greene, as is thot. by wh. he had Mary, b. 3 Mar. foll.; Eliphal, 20 Feb. 1656; John, 18 June 1670; and Samuel, 5 Oct. 1677; but he had been adm. freem. 1653, and m. 8 Aug. 1654, Eliz. eldest d. of Henry Spatchurst of Bermuda, wh. d. 6 Dec. 1660, and had, as the Portsmouth rec. tells, Eliz. b. 11 July 1655; Mary, 18 Aug. 1656; Susanna, 31 July 1658; and Rebecca, 23 June 1660. JOHN, Boston, the sch.master, wh. I rejoice to say, taught writ.; m. 19 Feb. 1657, Sarah, wid. of Robert Potter, was, perhaps, the freem. of 11 Oct. 1670, and d. 10 Feb. 1677. His will, of 19 Jan. preced. pro. 24 Apr. foll. ment. no ch. but gives all est. to w. Sarah for life, and

aft. devise to the third ch. his sch.ho. and ld. adj. one half of other est.
to childr. of his br. Robert, they to pay aft. entry upon d. of the wid.
£20. to Hannah Potter, if she liv. with her until 18 yrs. old, and other
half to childr. of Edward Turner of Middletown, they to pay, as soon as
they rec. and enter upon it £10. to John Potter of R. I. and £10. to
Stephen Coppock of L. I. The excors. were nam. w. Sarah and capt.
Timothy Wheeler, but he renounc. the office. Wh. Coppock was, or
how he or Turner were relat. to testator is unkn. but I hazard the
conject. that he was br. of Turner's w. NATHANIEL, Hartford 1655, d.
1687, leav. good est. to wid. Susanna, wh. m. John Buttolph of Wethersfield, and only ch. Mary, wh. many yrs. bef. had m. Phineas Wilson.
§ PELEG, Newport, s. of the first John, Gov. of the Col. 1680–2, call.
by Gov. Brenton, in his will, s.-in-law, as he m. Mary, d. of B. bef.
1665. His ch. were Ann, Bridget, and Eliz. He declin. reëlect. in
1683, but was oft. honor. with commiss. from Eng. as judge in the admiralty, and was liv. 1699. RICHARD, Boston 1640, laborer, whose w.
Margery d. that yr. was adm. of the ch. 30 Jan. 1641, and freem. 2 June
foll. had possib. s. John and Robert, and certain. d. Mary, wh. m. 25
Oct. 1656, Edward Turner. ROBERT, Hartford 1645, d. June 1676,
leav. w. Ann, d. of Jeremy Adams, wh. d. 1682. His ch. were, as in
order nam. on the Pro. rec. Zachary; Eliz. b. 19 Feb. 1646, wh. m.
Joseph Collier; Ezekiel, 13 Mar. 1648; Mary, w. of John Camp;
Sarah; Robert; Hannah; and Abigail. ‖ ROBERT, Boston, br. of the
third John, freem. 1652, ar. co. 1661, by w. Eliz. had John, wh. d. 23
Nov. 1654; Eliz. 5 Dec. 1655; Bathshua, 6 Jan. 1659 ; Sarah, 23 Nov.
1661 ; Mary, 22 Sept. 1664 ; Robert, 15 Apr. 1667; Richard, 27 Mar.
1670 ; and Thomas, 27 Apr. 1673. At Scarborough, in 1663, may have
been one of this name, unless erron. giv. in Geneal. Reg. V. 264, as
may well be suspect. from the many mistakes in that list. ROBERT,
Hartford, prob. youngest s. of Robert of the same, had a fam. but details
have not reach. me. SAMUEL, Milford, s. of Thomas, propound. for
freem. 1669, d. 1691, leav. wid. Hannah, and ch. Hannah, aged 16 ;
Samuel, 12 ; Sarah, 9; Mary, 6 ; and Thomas, 4; as on the inv. return.
18 Dec. SAMUEL, Portsmouth, R. I. prob. s. of John of the same, m.
Oct. 1662, Sarah, d. of William Waddel, had Eliz. b. 3 Oct. 1663;
John; Jane, 1668; Bridget, 27 June 1671 ; and Mary, 27 Apr. 1674.
THOMAS, Dorchester 1634, freem. 9 Mar. 1637, aft. few yrs. rem. prob.
to Milford a. 1639, was a householder 1646, there, and freem. bef. 1669 ;
by w. Sarah he had, bef. rem. from Mass. Ezekiel, and Sarah, and at
Milford had Samuel, b. Apr. 1643 ; Thomas, Dec. 1644 ; Ephraim,
1646; and Eliz. 1648 ; beside Mary, bapt. Feb. 1642, wh. prob. did not
live to be nam. as all the others were, in his will. His w. d. 14 May

1681, and he d. in Sept. or Oct. foll. His d. Sarah m. 14 Aug. 1656,
Richard Shute ; and Eliz. m. 28 Oct. 1669, Obadiah Allyn of Middletown. THOMAS, New Haven, perhaps s. of the preced. m. 11 Oct.
1666, Eliz. Paine, perhaps d. of John, had Samuel, b. 13 Sept. 1668 ;
Eliz. Sept. 1671 ; Thomas, 13 Oct. 1673, d. soon ; Ann, 19 Feb. 1675 ;
Thomas, again, 25 May 1677 ; William, 29 Nov. 1679 ; Sarah, 26 Nov.
1682 ; and, perhaps, more ; was freem. 1669, and a propr. contin. 1685.
THOMAS, Scarborough 1663, subject to the same suspic. as attach. to the
name of Robert there. * ZACHARY, Saybrook 1651, was, perhaps, first
at Hartford, m. a d. of John Rockwell of Windsor, had Zachary, b.
1653, d. young; Hannah, 1656; Ruth, 1659 ; Ezekiel, 1663 ; Deborah,
Jan. 1666; Sarah and Rebecca, tw. Nov. 1668 ; was freem. 1658, rep.
1657 and 8, and d. 23 Dec. 1668. His wid. was inhab. there 1672 ; d.
Hannah m. 16 Jan. 1680, Abraham Chalker ; and Ruth m. 17 Apr.
1684, Samuel Bushnell. ZACHARY, Hartford, s. of Robert the first,
freem. 1669, m. Sarah, d. of Nathaniel Willet, had Sarah, b. 15 Nov.
1681 ; Zachary, 26 Apr. 1686; Ann and Rebecca, tw. 27 Aug. 1689 ;
and Abigail, 11 Oct. 1692. He kept that inn, where the Cts. sat, and d.
early in 1714, leav. only ch. Sarah, and Abigail. This name is spell.
with much variat. in early days the first syl. was Samp, and aft. d was the
end of that syl. Farmer found at the N. E. coll. sixteen gr. in 1828
half at Yale, three at Harv.

　　SANGER, JOHN, Watertown, s. of Richard, blacksmith, m. 1685, Rebecca, d. of Thomas Park, had John, b. 19 Dec. 1685 ; Rebecca, 7
Mar. 1689 ; Mary, 1 Mar. 1694 ; David, 21 Mar. 1697 ; Isaac, 9 Nov.
1699 ; and Eliz. 21 June 1703 ; and he d. Jan. 1705. NATHANIEL,
Sherborn, br. of the preced. blacksmith, m. Mary, d. of Richard Cutter
of Cambridge, had Mehitable, b. 1680, at S. says Barry, but at Roxbury had Mary, 30 Jan. 1682 ; a s. 9 Dec. 1684, d. soon ; Nathaniel,
Dec. 1685 ; and Jane, 14 May 1688 ; rem. to Woodstock, a new planta.
there d. a. 1735, leav. wid. Ruth, and ch. beside those ment. bef. says
Barry, David, Eliż. Jonathan, and Eleazer. RICHARD, Hingham 1636,
of wh. no more is heard. RICHARD, Sudbury 1646, said to have emb.
at Southampton, Apr. 1638, in the Confidence, of London, as serv. of
Edmund Goodenow of Dunhead, Co. Wilts, was a blacksmith, rem. to
Watertown, in the autumn of 1649, there, by w. Mary, d. of Robert
Reynolds the first of Boston, had Mary, b. 26 Sept. 1650 ; Nathaniel,
14 Feb. 1652 ; John, 6 Sept. 1657 ; and by sec. w. Sarah had Sarah, 19
Jan. 1662, d. soon; Sarah, again, 31 Mar. 1663 ; Richard, 22 Feb.
1667 ; Eliz. 23 July 1668 ; and David, 21 Dec. 1670, wh. d. at 24 yrs.
prob. unm. and d. 20 Aŭg. 1691. His d. Mary m. 20 Sept. 1670, John
Harris. RICHARD, Sherborn, s. of the preced. blacksmith, m. Eliz. d.

of the sec. Daniel Morse, had Eliz. b. 2 Apr. 1693; Mary, 11 Apr. 1695; Hannah, 7 Feb. 1697; Esther, 20 Oct. 1698; Deborah, 5 Aug. 1701; Sarah, 10 Feb. 1705; Richard, 4 Nov. 1706; Abigail, 3 July 1709; and David, 22 Feb. 1712; and d. 1731.

SANKEYS, * ROBERT, Saco, came in the Increase from London, Apr. 1635, aged 30, sent by Robert Cordell, a goldsmith of Lombard street, says the rec. at custom-ho. appears as a witness with Cleves and Tucker, to the import. deed of 30 Mar. preced. from Richard Vines, agent of Sir Ferdinando Gorges, to Arthur Mackworth. Mr. Willis, in Hist. of Portland, I. 32, recit. the docum. makes it 1635, as " in the eleventh yr. of Charles," keeping in mind, that the tenth yr. of that reign end. 27 Mar. 1635, of course three days later was within the eleventh. Now this witness was then in London, and so, I suppose, tho. dated in 1635, the indent. was not actually deliver. for some months aft. Possib. eleventh may be error of the instrum. for twelfth. But I leave the solution to the perspicacity of so good a judge. He was appoint. by Gorges, in 1640, Provost Marshal, and sat in the *first* Gen. Ct. of that Province, with other dignitaries, 25 June of that yr. Willis, I. 47. Of the doings of that Ct. I employ. an amanuensis to take large extr.

SANSOM, RICHARD, Nantucket, a tailor, emb. at London, May 1635, in the Elizabeth and Ann, aged 28, m. a. 1658, Jane, wid. of the sec. Thomas Mayhew, lost in his voyage to Eng. 1657.

SARGENT, SEARGEANT, SARGEANT, SERGEANT, or SERJENT, ED-WARD, Newbury, by w. Eliz. had Edward, and Eliz. b. 2 Dec. 1684; Nathaniel, 16 Jan. 1687, all at Saco; Eliz. again, 3 Oct. 1689, at Portsmouth; Elisha, 24 Oct. 1695; Rachel, 10 Oct. 1698; Ichabod, 5 Aug. 1701; and Abigail, 26 June 1704; as Coffin distrib. them. * EPES, Gloucester, s. of the sec. William of the same, m. 1 Apr. 1720, Esther Maccarty, had Epes, b. 1721; Esther, 1722; Ignatius, 1724; James, 1726, d. next yr.; Winthrop, 1728; Sarah, 1729; Daniel, 1731; William, 1734; and Benjamin, 1736. He took sec. w. 10 Aug. 1744, wid. Catharine Brown of Salem, had Paul Dudley, and John; was rep. 1740; rem. to Salem, and d. 6 Dec. 1762. JOHN, Barnstable, s. of William of the same, m. 19 Mar. 1663, Deborah, d. of Hugh Hillier, had Joseph, b. 18 Apr. 1663; John, 16 Feb. 1665; Mary; Jabez, Apr. 1669; rem. a. that time to Malden, and was selectman six yrs. His w. d. 20 Apr. 1669, and he m. 3 Sept. foll. Mary Bense, unless this name be wrong, wh. had no ch. and d. Feb. 1671. By third w. Lydia, d. of Elder John Chipman, he had Hannah, Dec. 1675; Jonathan, 17 Apr. 1677; William, 20 Nov. 1680; Ruth, 26 Oct. 1686; Samuel, 15 Sept. 1688; Ebenezer, 25 Sept. 1690; Mehitable, 5 Sept. 1696; beside Lydia, Deborah, Hope, and Sarah, whose dates are not seen. He d. 9

2 *

Sept. 1716, near. 77 yrs. old; and his wid. d. 2 Mar. 1730. All the
fifteen ch. are ment. in his will of 20 May 1708. JOHN, Gloucester,
eldest s. of the first William of the same, m. 24 Dec. 1679, Hannah
Howard, had Hannah, b. 30 Mar. 1681; John, 1683; Thomas, 1685;
Andrew, 1691; Joseph, 1702; and ano. s. and six more ds. * JOHN,
Saco, was lieut. 1680, and at a Gen. Ct. held by Presid. Danforth, 1684,
was rep. JONATHAN, Branford 1646, had tak. o. of fidel. 1644, at New
Haven, where he had also four ch. bapt. at once, 10 Aug. 1651, nam.
Jonathan, Hannah, Thomas, and John, most, perhaps all, able to walk to
N. H. I suppose, some it may be adult. He d. 12 Dec. foll. and his
wid. d. in seven days, and in few yrs. the fam. was extinct in Conn. by
John's d. a. 1675, at Guilford, without issue, as did Thomas, at Branford,
1700, and Jonathan, with his sis. wh. had m. Benjamin Baldwin, hav.
rem. to Newark, N. J. at the great migrat. Of this fam. was the celebr.
missiona. to the Stockbridge Ind. JOSEPH, Gloucester, youngest s. of
the first William of the same, m. 1712, Martha Baker of Topsfield, had
Joseph, b. 16 May 1713, and she d. few days aft. He m. 16 Sept. 1717,
Hannah Haraden, and d. a. 1750. NATHANIEL, Gloucester, sixth s. of
the first William of the same, m. 24 Jan. 1695, Sarah Harvey, wh. d. 5
Feb. 1706; and next m. 26 Mar. 1710, Mary Stevens, had five s. and
seven ds. but in Babson no names are ment. exc. of Nathaniel, b. 1702,
and Daniel, 1714; and he d. 12 Dec. 1732. ‡ PETER, Boston, merch.
came, 1667, from London, was a strenuous oppon. of Andros, and chos.
on his overthrow, to be one of the com'tee of safety, freem. 1690, was
nam. of the counc. in the new chart. His w. whose name I hear not,
d. 10 Nov. 1700, and he m. 9 Oct. foll. Mary, the wid. of Sir William
Phips, wh. first was wid. of John Hall, and d. of capt. Roger Spencer.
Next, he m. 19 Dec. 1706, Mehitable, wid. of Thomas Cooper, d. of
James Minot, and d. 8, was bur. 13 Feb. 1714. His will, of 17 Jan.
preced. ment. dec. brs. Joseph, and Henry, two surv. sis. beside nephs.
and nieces of dec. brs. and sis. but no ch. nor do I find that he ever had
one. His wid. m. 12 May 1715, Simeon Stoddard. SAMUEL, Gloucester, br. of Joseph, m. 24 May 1689, Mary, d. of Francis Norwood,
had Samuel, b. 1690; William, 1692; four ds. and four more s. of wh.
Solomon, the youngest, was b. 1708. The f. was liv. 1746, but time of
his d. is unkn. STEPHEN, Boston, by w. Dorothy had Eliz. b. 12 Apr.
1670; Margaret, 10 Mar. 1675; and Mary, 5 July 1677. THOMAS,
Branford 1667. THOMAS, Amesbury, prob. s. of William of the same,
m. 2 Mar. or by ano. story, 2 Apr. 1668, Rachel, d. of William Barnes,
had sev. ch. as a careful hand writes in Geneal. Reg. X. 184, whose pen
gives no name but Thomas, b. 15 Nov. 1676; but this s. perpet. the
success. He was freem. 1690. WILLIAM, Ipswich, one of the first sett.

Mar. 1633, when John Winthrop, jr. plant. there, and short. aft. join. to sett. Newbury, and with Rev. Stephen Bachilor, began Hampton planta. 1638, lov. the pioneer's life so much, Coffin says, as to help build Amesbury, and there he found his final rest, a. 1673, aged 75. His w. was Eliz. d. of John Perkins, and ch. Thomas, b. 11 June 1643 ; William, 2 Jan. 1646 ; Mary ; Eliz. 22 Nov. 1648 ; and Sarah, 29 Feb. 1652. His will, of 1671, names w. and ch. Thomas, William, Mary, w. of Philip Challis, and her ch. William, Eliz. Mary, Philip, and Watson, beside his d. Eliz. w. of Samuel Colby, and her ch. Dorothy and Eliz. and his br.-in-law Thomas Bradbury, wh. had m. the sis. of his w. WILLIAM, Charlestown 1638, adm. to the ch. 10 Mar. 1639, as was, on the next Sunday, his w. Sarah, may be the freem. of 22 May foll. had John, bapt. 8 Dec. 1639 ; Ruth, b. 25 Oct. 1642 ; Samuel, 3 Mar. 1645 ; and, perhaps, others. Farmer thot. him the preach. at Malden 1648–50, of wh. slight ment. is seen in Johnson's W. W. Providences, Book III. cap. 7 ; yet as the min. is not nam. by Mather, he might be suppos. to have gone home, but he was never ord. acting only as lay preach. This William had long puzzled me much, but my final infer. was that he rem. to Barnstable, where a will of one William, 9 Mar. 1680, names w. Sarah, s. John, and Samuel, ds. Ruth Bourne (wh. had been wid. of Jonathan Winslow of Marshfield, m. Richard B. of Sandwich, July 1677, and had third h. John Chipman of the same town), and Hannah Felch, beside gr.s. Samuel Bill, whose mo. Eliz. had been wid. Nichols, when she m. 14 June 1653, Thomas Bill ; but this d. Eliz. must have been b. in Eng. and she d. 5 Mar. 1658. Abundant proof of all this is obtain. by the diligence of Aaron Sargent, of the eighth generat. with success admira. exhibit. in the fam. geneal. print. 1858. Hannah m. Henry F. of Reading. * WILLIAM, Gloucester, had gr. of ld. 1649, m. 10 Sept. 1651, Abigail, d. of Edmund Clark, had John, b. 1653 ; Andrew, 1655 ; William, 16 Aug. 1658 ; Samuel, 22 Mar. 1662 ; Nathaniel, 30 Oct. 1663, d. soon ; Abigail, 8 May 1665 ; Nathaniel, again, 28 May 1671 ; Joseph, 27 Mar. 1675 ; and Mary, 24 Nov. 1678, was rep. 1671, 90, and 1, and his w. d. 8 Mar. 1711, aged 79. He d. 19 Feb. 1717, aged 92. Abigail m. 15 June 1682, the sec. William Stevens. WILLIAM, Amesbury, s. of William of the same, took o. of fidel. 20 Dec. 1677, m. 23 Sept. 1668, Mary, d. of Anthony Colby, had William, and, prob. sev. more ch. WILLIAM, Gloucester, call. sec. to disting. him from the other, was b. in Bristol, Eng. m. 21 June 1678, Mary, d. of Peter Duncan, had Fitz William, b. 6 Jan. 1680 ; and Mary, 19 Dec. 1681 ; Andrew, 1683 ; Daniel, 1686 ; Jordan, 1688 ; Epes, 1690, the ancest. of most of the disting. men of this name ; Ann, 1692 ; Samuel, 1694, d. young ; Fitz John, 1696, d. soon ; one, with an out of the way name, 1699, d. the same yr.; Jabez, 1700, d. the same yr.; Fitz William, 1701; and Winthrop, 1704. WILLIAM, Gloucester, s. of the first William of the same, m. 26 Oct. 1681, Naomi Stanwood, perhaps d. of Philip, wh. d. 13 Mar. 1702, and he m. 14 Sept. 1703, Hannah Short, perhaps d. of the sec. Henry; and by the two ws. he had eleven ch. but Babson ment. no names, and thinks he rem. bef. 1721. Glad. would I learn, wh. was f. of that Nathaniel, gr. at Harv. 1707, by the catal. mark. as d. 1762, for to him Stephen Glover of G. gave all his prop. requir. that he should be "bred up to learn." Of this name eighteen had been, in 1843, gr. at Harv. nine at Dart. and two at Yale.

SATCHELL, SATCHWELL, or SETCHELL. See Shatswell.

SATTERLY, or SHATTERLY, BENEDICT, New London, there liv. but few yrs. d. a. 1689, leav. perhaps, a s. and two ds. Sarah, wh. m. Joseph Wickham of Killingworth; and Rebecca, m. Joseph Swasey of L. I. NICHOLAS, Westerly 1680.

SAULE, THOMAS, New Haven, or some pt. of that Col. 1639.

SAUNDERS, sometimes SANDERS, CHRISTOPHER, Windsor 1671, came short time bef. as seems prob. had Daniel, wh. d. 22 Dec. 1675, at 11 days old; Susanna, b. 20 Nov. 1676; Daniel, again, 27 Oct. 1678; and Eliz. 30 Apr. 1681; and it may be he was unsuccess. in trade, and rem. to Rehoboth, for one of this name was there 1690. DANIEL, Cambridge, d. 27 Feb. 1640, and no more is kn. of him. EDWARD, Portsmouth 1639, may be the man punish. at Watertown, 1654, for abuse of Ruth Parsons. See Col. Rec. III. 364. GEORGE, Windsor, br. of Christopher, propound. for freem. 1667, when he was ens. at Killingworth, m. bef. 1674, Mary, d. of George Saxton, had George, perhaps by former w. old eno. at least to be tax. with his f. 1675; and d. 16 Nov. 1690, leav. Mary, then 13 yrs. old, and Abiah, a. 6. GEORGE, Windsor, br. of Christopher, acc. Stiles, 770, rem. to Simsbury, m. 17 Dec. 1691, Abigail, perhaps d. of Nathaniel Bissell, wh. Stiles prints Russell, had, he says, Hannah, b. 23 May previous, and he d. 5 Dec. 1697. Very much confusion a. this name exists, and it may not be wholly dissipat. by reducing two Georges to one. JAMES, Haverhill, took the o. of alleg. 1677. JOHN, Weymouth 1622, sent by Weston as gov. or overseer of his planta. gave up next yr. the undertak. and prob. went home. JOHN, prob. at Ipswich 1635, freem. 25 May 1636, was permit. with Samuel Dudley and others, to found Colchester, soon call. Salisbury, perhaps was f. of that Sarah, wh. m. 3 Apr. 1641, Robert Pike of S. Yet possib. JOHN of Newbury sev. yrs. later, might be thot. her f. and even it might seem that these two were only one man. But he of S. had w. Esther, d. of John Rolfe, and by her had Esther, b. 5 Sept. 1639; John, 1 July 1641, wh. d. in few wks.; Ruth, 16 Dec. 1642; and John, again, 10 Dec. 1644; and he went home, own. an est. in Wiltsh. leav. his br.-in-law Richard Dole of Newbury, his atty. To prevent confus. of the two Johns, we may further note, that one of the name came in the Confidence of London, aged 25, husbandman of Longford, also in Co. Wilts, with w. Sarah, emb. at Southampton 24 Apr. 1638; and if we accept him as the John to wh. (with w. Sarah) Coffin gives ch. Sarah, b. 20 Aug. 1647; Mary, 12 June 1649; Abigail, 12 Apr. 1651; Joseph, 1653, d. soon; and Eliz. 26 Jan. 1655; we may feel sure that Pike's w. was not his d. It may indeed seem that she might have been sis. of either of the two. JOHN, Salem 1637, mem. of the ch. had m. a d. of the first Joseph Grafton, in his will of 28 Oct. 1642, pro. Dec. 1643, ment. s. John, and f. Grafton. JOHN, Wells 1645, had been of Hampton bef. 1643, was freem. 1653, lieut. 1658, and of the gr. jury 1660, then call. sen. His will, of 13 June 1670, pro. 3 Aug. foll. names w. Ann, and s. Thomas, to wh. all the homestead was giv. to s. John a thousand acres 8 or 9 miles "above Cape Porpus riv. falls," wh. means, I judge, the Saco riv. and to all the resid. of his ch. equal sh. The whole est. was £139. JOHN, Braintree, perhaps s. of Martin, b. in Eng. m. 9 Oct. or 8 Nov. 1650, Mary Munjoy, sis. of George the first, had Mary, b. 12 Dec. 1653; John, 23 Nov. 1657, d. in few days; Judith, 28 Feb. 1663, d. very soon; Rachel, 4 Feb. 1664, d. in few days; Judith, again, 23 Jan. 1665, d. very soon; and John, 1 Sept. 1669. JOHN, Billerica 1679. JOHN, perhaps of Salem, and possib. s. of John of the same, m. 14 Sept. 1688, Return, d. of Samuel Shattuck, wh. rec. that name on acco. of happy com. from Eng. of her f. in 1662, bef. her b. with royal rescript for lenity to the Quakers. JOSEPH, Dover 1656, was k. by the Ind. in the night betw. 27 and 28 June 1689, at the same time, says Mr. Quint, when Waldron's garrison ho. was destroy. MARTIN, Boston, currier, came in the Planter from London, in the spring of 1635, aged 40, with w. Rachel, 40, and ch. Leah, 10; Judith, 8; and Martin, 4; beside Mary, prob. older than either. Here his w. join. our ch. 8 Nov. of that yr. but as they liv. at the Braintree planta. he was one of the found. of that ch.; kept the inn in 1639, was adm. freem. 13 Mar. 1640. His d. Judith d. 7 July 1651, and his w. d. 15 Sept. foll. For sec. w. he took, 23 May 1654, Eliz. Bancroft, wid. of Roger, and d. 4 Aug. 1658, hav. made his will 5 July preced. His wid. m. deac. John Bridge of Cambridge, and had fourth h. Edward Taylor; d. Mary m. bef. 1641, Francis Eliot; Leah, m. perhaps, Robert Parmenter; and ano. d. Rachel, is also giv. to P. MARTIN, Braintree, s. of the preced. brot. from Eng. by his f. was freem. 1651, and m. 1 Apr. of the same yr. Lydia, d. of Richard Hardier; had Joseph, wh. d. 17 May 1657; Joseph, again, b. 3 Oct. 1657; Eliz. 2

Oct. 1663 ; Jonathan, 3 Nov. 1672, bapt. 5 Jan. foll. d. soon ; and
Lydia, b. 17 Feb. 1675, d. at 2 yrs. and he d. 4 Sept. 1706, aged
78. Eliz. m. 23 Nov. 1680, Solomon Veazie. ‖ ROBERT, Cambridge
1636, ar. co. 1638, freem. 23 May 1639, rem. it is thot. to Boston
soon, and aft. to Dorchester, where, in 1680, he was a poor man. To-
BIAS, Taunton 1643, rem. to Newport, there was one of the freem. in
1655, and of Stonington 1669, yet on the R. I. side of the riv. now
Westerly, and had to sustain many yrs. the claim against Conn. usurpat.
His w. was Mary, d. of the first Joseph Clark of Newport. WILLIAM,
Hampton, a carpenter, had been in this country 2 or 3 yrs. bef. he went
to plant there, Sept. 1638, with Rev. Stephen Bachiler and others. Of
this name, oft. spell. without *u*, Farmer says, eight had, in 1829, been
gr. at N. E. coll. of wh. six were of Harv.

SAUNDERSON, BENJAMIN, Watertown, s. of Robert, by w. Mary had
Mary, b. 29 Nov. 1677 ; and Bond tells no more. EDWARD, Watertown, m. 15 Oct. 1645, Mary Eggleston, by Bond thot. to be eldest d. of
Bigod, but she was not (for that d. was only 4 yrs. old), and prob. was
his sis. had Jonathan, b. 15 Sept. 1646 ; and Esther, call. strange. a
young person, when bapt. 20 Mar. 1687, Bond constr. the phrase to
mean only unm. But he may have had other ch. bef. or aft. rem. to
Cambridge, and, perhaps, went home. In the vicin. of W. num. descend.
are found. HENRY, Sandwich 1643. JONATHAN, Watertown, s. of Edward, perhaps the only one, m. 24 Oct. 1669, Abia, youngest d. of Thomas
Bartlett of W. had Abia and Jonathan, tw. b. 28 Oct. 1673 ; Thomas,
10 Mar. 1675 ; John, 25 Mar. 1677 ; Benjamin, 28 May 1679 ; Samuel,
28 May 1681 ; Edward, 3 Mar. 1684 ; and Hannah, 31 May, bapt. at
W. 14 July 1689 ; was constable 1695, selectman, and deac. many yrs.
His w. d. 13 Sept. 1723, and he d. 3 Sept. 1735. JOSEPH, Boston, s.
perhaps, of Robert the first, by w. Mary had Mary, b. 6 July 1666.
JOSEPH, Groton, s. of William, m. 30 July 1714, Sarah, d. of Samuel
Page of Concord, had David, b. 5 Sept. 1715 ; Sarah, 19 Jan. 1717 ;
William, 17 July 1718 ; Hannah, 5 Apr. 1720 ; Joseph, 17 Mar. 1722,
d. soon ; Susanna, 18 May 1723 ; Gideon, 19 Feb. 1725 ; Joseph, again,
5 Mar. 1727 ; Sarah, again, 15 Oct. 1729 ; and John, 13 Dec. 1731.
ROBERT, Hampton 1638, freem. 7 Sept. 1639, by w. Lydia had Mary,
bapt. 27 Oct. 1639 ; rem. to Watertown 1642, prob. aft. m. Mary, wid.
of John Cross of H. and had Joseph, b. 1 Jan. 1643 ; Benjamin, bapt.
29 July 1649 ; Sarah, 19 Jan. 1651 ; Robert, perhaps 3 Oct. 1652 ;
and John, wh. d. 17 Sept. 1658 ; rem. next yr. to Boston, and was
partner in gainful business, with John Hull, the mint master. He had,
also, eldest ch. by first ♥. perhaps b. in Eng. Lydia, wh. was m. (by
Gov. Bellingham), 13 Dec. 1654, to Thomas Jones ; but as no more is

told of either of the young couple, I conject. they went to Eng. He
had sec. w. Eliz. was deac. and d. 7 Oct. 1693, not 6, as Farmer gave
it. By his will, of 18 July, pro. 20 Oct. his w. was made extrix. and in
her will of 15 Sept. 1694, pro. 21 Nov. 1695, is evid. proof, that ch. and
gr.ch. nam. in the will of her h. were not his, but hers. No blood relat.
of his, exc. br. Edward, and s. Robert can with confid. be found in his
own will. ROBERT, Cambridge, s. of the preced. by w. Eliz. had
Joseph, b. 10 Oct. 1684 ; and he took sec. w. in Boston, 21 Dec. 1693,
Sarah Crow. WILLIAM, Watertown, perhaps s. of the first Robert,
says Bond, but prob. was not, old eno. to sw. fidel. 1652, by w. Sarah, m.
18 Dec. 1666, had John, b. 13 Oct. 1667 ; Sarah, 17 Mar. 1669 ; William, 6 Sept. 1670 ; Mary, 30 Nov. 1671 ; Hannah, 3 May 1674, at
Groton, whence he was driv. next yr. again to W. and had Lydia, 21
Apr. 1679 ; and Joseph, 28 Aug. 1680. WILLIAM, Watertown, s. of
the preced. m. 14 May 1702, Abigail, d. of John Traine, wh. d. soon ;
and he m. (if Bond has right dates) 14 May 1704, Ann, d. of Philip
Shattuck, had Lydia, b. 17 Dec. foll. ; William, 10 Apr. 1706 ; and
rem. to Sudbury, there had Amos ; Isaac ; and, Barry says, others.
This name is sometimes abbrev. of its last syllab. and oft. is without *u*.

SAVAGE, ‖ EBENEZER, Boston, s. of the first Thomas, was of ar. co.
1682, m. Martha, d. of capt. Bozoan Allen, had Mary, b. 15, bapt. 19
Aug. 1683, and he d. next yr. EDWARD, Dorchester, if it be truly giv.
1664, as sign. the petitn. to the Gen. Ct. in vindicat. of our liberties.
See Hist. of D. 200. But I doubt the name is wrong, and the writer in
Geneal. Reg. V. 395, giv. the same list, in wh. this is No. 40, when he
aft. publ. acco. of all the subscrib. to that docum. on p. 465, omits him.
Of such a man in other connex. nothing is kn. and the same Hist. 38,
gather. 134 first sett. of the town, includes but one Edward, and his surname was Raymond. * ‖ EPHRAIM, Boston, s, of the first Thomas, by
w. Mary, eldest d. of the sec. Edmund Quincy of Braintree, had Mary,
b. 19 Nov. 1671, d. soon ; Mary, again, 8, bapt. 13 Apr. 1673 ; John, 30
Nov. bapt. 6 Dec. 1674, H. C. 1694 ; and Hannah, 7, bapt. 13 Aug.
1676, wh. d. early. By sec. w. m. 26 Feb. 1678, Sarah, d. of Rev.
Samuel Hough of Reading, had Sarah, b. 27 Oct. foll. as by rec. of
Boston and Roxbury both ; Mary, 10 Nov. 1680 ; Richard, 15, bapt. 17
Sept. 1682 ; Eliz. 8, bapt. 11 Jan. 1685 ; and Hannah, again, 17 Jan.
1687, when the mo. d. For third w. Eliz. wid. of Timothy Symmes, d.
of capt. Francis Norton of Charlestown, the ceremo. of m. 12 Apr.
1688, was perform. by Rev. Charles Morton, being one of the earliest
instances of cleric. not civ. officiat. but this was during the period of
Andros's usurpa. She d. 13 Apr. 1710, and for fourth w. he m. 8 Jan.
1713, Eliz. d. of Abraham Brown of B. wid. of Peter Butler of the

same; but had no issue by the two later ws. and all the ch. by the first
w. d. young; but of the sec. w. three ds. were m. and liv. long. He was
freem. 1672, ar. co. 1674, its capt. 1683, and was many yrs. town clk. and
in that period the rec. were careful. kept, exc. when he was engag. with
his f. in Philip's war, and serv. in the unhappy expedit. of Sir William
Phips, 1690, then hav. command of one of the fleet, was rep. 1703 and
six yrs. more, and took the head of a comp. of the force draft. and sent
on serv. to Nova Scotia in the abortive campaign, 1707. He d. 1731,
his will of 3 Dec. 1730, pro. 22 Mar. foll. giv. to wid. Eliz. and to ea.
of *her* three ch. a gold ring, beside rememb. *his* ds. Sarah, w. of Joshua
Wells, Mary, w. of Zechary Trescott, wh. had been w. of Bernard
Jenkinson, and Hannah, w. of . . . . . Parmenter, wh. had been w. of
John Butler, perhaps s. of the w. of her f. || HABIJAH, Boston, eldest
br. of the preced. m. 8 May 1661, Hannah, d. of capt. Edward Tyng,
had Joseph, b. 15 Aug. 1662, d. soon; Thomas, 17 Aug. 1664 (the
freem. of 1690, wh. d. 3 Mar. 1721, and progenit. of the fam. in
Charleston, S. C.); Hannah and Mary, tw. 27 Aug. 1667; was freem.
1665, ar. co. capt. of a comp. but d. on trade in Barbados, 1669. Male
descent fail. here, but his ds. both diffus. the blood; Hannah, by m. with
Rev. Nathaniel Gookin of Cambridge, and Mary, by m. with Rev.
Thomas Weld of Dunstable. HENRY, Haverhill 1644, may be the man
wh. m. Eliz. d. of Thomas Walford of Portsmouth. JOHN, Middletown,
freem. 1654, m. 10 Feb. 1652, Eliz. Dubbin, at Hartford, if we may
rely on the delightful vol. of "Hartford in the olden time;" to wh.
objection is rais. on read. the rec. in Geneal. Reg. XIII. 142, of m. of
the same w. on the same day to James Wakely. However the ch. giv.
to him (whoever was his w.) are John, b. 2 Dec. 1652; Eliz. 3 June
1655; Sarah, 30 July 1657; Thomas, 10 Sept. 1659, d. soon; Hannah,
6 or 16 Apr. 1661, d. next mo.; Mary, 25 June 1663; Abigail, 10 July
1666; William, 26 Apr. 1668; Nathaniel, 7 May 1671; Rachel, 15
Apr. 1673; and Hannah, again, 16 July 1676; and he d. 6 Mar. 1685.
His will, of 22 Nov. preced. names three s. and six ds. liv. and his est.
was good. Mary m. 1 Apr. 1686, as sec. w. John Whitmore; and Abigail m. 14 Apr. 1687, Edward Shepard. JOHN, Rehoboth, m. 16 May
1668, Sarah Bowen, perhaps d. of Richard of the same, had Eliz. b.
1673, d. soon; Sarah, 10 Mar. 1674; Eliz. again, 11 Jan. 1676; and
Mary, 5 June 1678; and d. 22 Aug. of that yr. His wid. m. 29 Sept.
1681, Joseph Brooman, if Col. rec. gives the name right. JOHN, Nantucket 1672, drawn thither by the gener. offer for settlem. as print. in
Geneal. Reg. XIII. 311, had Susanna, b. 23 Mar. 1673; and John, 24
June 1674; but, perhaps, he rem. and may have been of Portsmouth,
N. H. 1689–1732. JOHN, Chatham, was constable 1681, as Plymouth rec.

tells. JOHN, Middletown, eldest s. of John of the same, m. 30 May 1682, Mary Ranney, d. of Thomas of the same, had John, b. 20 Feb. 1683, d. in few days; Thomas, 21 Aug. 1684; John, again, 30 Jan. 1686, d. in few mos.; John, again, 7 Aug. 1688; Mary, 11 Feb. 1691; William, late in July 1693; Eliz. 1696; Abigail, Dec. 1698, d. at 3 mos.; Sarah, late in Sept. 1700; Rachel, 15 Jan. 1704; and Mercy, or this may be Mary, again, 10 Apr. 1706; was a capt. and d. 31 Oct. 1726. His wid. d. 19 Aug. 1734. NATHANIEL, Middletown, youngest s. of the first John of the same, m. 3 Nov. 1696, Esther, d. of Thomas Ranney, had Esther; Nathaniel, wh. d. soon; Abigail; Susanna; Mary; Eliz.; John; and Nathaniel, again; and d. 4 Jan. 1735. His wid. d. 1 Apr. 1750, aged 76. PEREZ, Boston, s. of the first Thomas, ens. of Moseley's comp. "a noble, heroic youth," as the great Ind. warrior, capt. Church, marks him, bad. wound. at Swansey in the first week of Philip's war, 29 June 1675, and again wound. in the hard swamp fight, 19 Dec. foll. where the concentra. power of the enemy was brok. when he was lieut. of the same corps. He was never m. and might have been omit. in this place, but for the events of his life, and chief. the curious incid. grow. out of his wills. Bef. go. to London, from wh. he carr. on trade to Spain, he made one, 8 Sept. 1690, nam. brs. Thomas (made excor.), Ephraim, and Benjamin, with sis. Hannah Sylvester, Mary Thacher, Dyonisia Ravenscroft, and Sarah Higginson, giv. to ea. £10., to Thomas, wid. sis. Thacher's s. wh. accomp. him in his voyages, £50., and resid. of his prop. to oldest surv. br. Thomas. This was pro. 18 Apr. 1695, aft. his d. at Mequinez, in Barbary, had been ascertain. See Vol. XIII. of Pro. rec. Contrib. to redeem from the Turks him and his neph. Thacher, as well as many others, had in former yrs. been made, as for more, in later yrs. by gen. concert of town and country chhs. and for young Thacher they were not too late. But in the Prerogat. Ct. of the Archbp. of Canterbury, at London, 11 May 1702, was brot. in a later will of 24 May 1694, by the same testat. "made in my sick bed," at Mequinez, whereby (aft. small money presents to Robert Carver, or Carew, and four others, prob. his compan. in the sad slavery, to wh. one of the two witness. was the same Carver), all his prop. in hds. of Richard Hill of Cadiz, merch. or in London, or in N. E. is bequeath. to the neph. then under 21 yrs. old, his companion, I suppose, in that Algerine misery. This instrum. may be read in Vol. XVII. together with revocat. by our Judge Addington, 10 Nov. 1708, of the former admin. gr. by Judge Stoughton, when A. had been the Reg. But in Vol. XVIII. subseq. proceed. mov. in the Ct. of Arches, bef. Sir Charles Hedges, by Eliz. wid. of Thomas, excor. of the Boston will, wh. was aunt of the devisee in the Barbary will, show a reversal of the former decree in support of the Mequinez will, and set up the right of the appellant under the Boston will, perhaps with concur. of Thacher. All may read the curious law Latin abbreviat. Mr. Justice Story, of the U. S. Sup. Ct. once ask. me, if the form of Eng. proceedings in litigat. testament. cases were to be seen in our country, and the yr. aft. his d. I could have answ. his desire. ‡ * ‖ THOMAS, Boston, merch. s. of William of Taunton, Co. Somerset, blacksmith, where the name prevails in the parish reg. for the whole reign of Eliz. had been apprent. at Merchant Tailors, London, as the comp. rec. prove, in the 18th yr. of James, 9 Jan. 1621, came in the Planter from London, Apr. 1635, aged 27, was adm. of the ch. Jan. and freem. 25 May foll. ar. co. 1637. He m. a. 1637, Faith, d. of William Hutchinson, and for receiv. the revelat. of her mo. or entertain. the opin. of Rev. John Wheelwright, he was disarm. Nov. of that yr. and driv. to unite with Gov. Coddington and others in purch. of R. I. where in 1638 he sett. but for short time. Ret. to B. he had Habijah, bef. ment. b. 1, bapt. 12 Aug. 1638, H. C. 1659; Thomas, bapt. 17 May 1640, tho. by stupid town rec. copy (orig. long lost), not b. bef. 28 of that mo.; Hannah, 28 June, bapt. 2 July 1643; Ephraim, bapt. 27, a. six days old, says ch. rec. (when the copy of town rec. makes him b. 2 July) 1645, H. C. 1662; Mary, bapt. 6 June 1647; Dyonisia, 30 Dec. 1649, one day old, the two last not on town book; Perez, b. 17, bapt. 22 Feb. 1652, idly call. a d. on rec. of the ch. The mo. d. 20 Feb. the same week, and he m. 15 Sept. foll. Mary, d. of Rev. Zechariah Symmes of Charlestown, had eleven more ch. Sarah, b. 25, bapt. 26 June foll.; Richard, bapt. 27 Aug. 1654, not found among the bs. yet rec. as d. 22 Sept. of next yr. on town list; Samuel, b. 16, bapt. 25 Nov. 1656, d. Aug. foll.; Samuel, again, 22 Aug. 1657, d. very soon; Zechariah, bapt. 4 July 1658, not found on town's list; Ebenezer, 22, bapt. 27 May 1660; John, 15, bapt. 18 Aug. 1661; Benjamin, bapt. 12 Oct. 1662, but not found on town's list; Arthur, 26, bapt. 28 Feb. 1664; Eliz. b. 8 Nov. 1667, d. very soon; and Eliz. again, 24, bapt. 28 Feb. 1669; and, I believe, no descend. has equal. that num. of ch. He was capt. of ar. co. 1651, and some later yrs. rep. 1654, and sev. yrs. more for B. beside var. yrs. for Hingham and Andover, speaker 1659, 60, 71, 7, and 8, had ch. command of the forces in Philip's war at its opening, and serv. with reput. E. and W. chos. Assist. 1680, to his d. 14 Feb. 1682. His will, of 28 June 1675, the day of march. to Philip's war, was so well arrang. that in the resid. of his life no change was suggest. and it was pro. 9 Mar. 1682. The sermon on his d. by Willard, of O. S. ch. was print. and a copy was held by John Farmer of Concord, until he prefer. with his usual liberality, to bestow it on me. His wid. m. Anthony Stoddard; and four of the ds. (three by the first w.) were m. the eldest, Hannah, 26 Oct. 1660, to Benjamin Gillam, and next, to Giles Sylvester; Mary, to Thomas Thacher, s. of the Rev. Thomas, first min. of the O. S. or 3d ch. in the format. of wh. and bring. the pastor from Weymouth to B. her f. was much engag. and she, as his wid. outliv. him more than forty-four yrs. d. 22 July 1730; Dyonisia m. Samuel Ravenscroft, and Sarah m. 9 Oct. 1672, John Higginson of Salem. ‖ THOMAS, Boston, s. of the preced. m. a. 1664, Eliz. d. of Joshua Scottow, had Thomas, b. 20 July 1665, d. soon; Thomas, again, 2 Aug. 1668, bapt. 19 June 1670; Scottow, 4, bapt. 12 Feb. 1671; Habijah, 10, bapt. 13 Sept. 1674; Eliz. 4, bapt. 5 Aug. 1677; Arthur, 29 Mar. bapt. 4 Apr. 1680; Faith, 11, bapt. 13 Aug. 1682, d. soon; Faith, again, 3, bapt. 7 Oct. 1683; and Lydia, 6, bapt. 12 Sept. 1686; was of ar. co. 1665, serv. short time in Philip's war, was freem. 1690, in wh. yr. he head. one of the three regim. for the wild expedit. of Sir William Phips against Quebec, and was the first field officer that land. Of that brief and blasted campaign, a suffic. acco. may be read in a letter from him to his br. Perez in London, that was by his majesty's officer licens. and print. Apr. 1691. He d. 2 July 1705, and his wid. d. 29 Aug. 1715. WILLIAM, Middletown, s. of the first John, by w. Christian, m. 6 May 1696, had Sarah, and d. 25 Jan. 1727. Of this name, thirteen, all descend. of the first Thomas, had been gr. at Harv. in 1854, and four at Yale.

SAVIL, SAVEL, SAVILS, or SAVALLS, BENJAMIN, Braintree, s. of William the first, had w. Lydia, and was liv. 13 Dec. 1700, nam. in the will of his br. Samuel. EDWARD, Weymouth, had Obadiah, b. 20 July 1640. JOHN, Braintree, s. of William the first, may have been at Woburn, when freem. 1684. His will, of 8 Nov. 1687, pro. 2 Feb. 1691, names w. Mehitable, s. John, and Mehitable. SAMUEL, Woburn, perhaps br. of the preced. freem. 1684, yet it may be prob. that neither was of W. but of Braintree. He m. 10 Apr. 1672, Hannah, eldest d. of the first Joseph Adams, had Hannah, b. 13 July 1674; Abigail, 14 Feb. 1678; William and Deborah, tw. 19 Feb. 1680, both prob. d. early; Bethia, 17 Oct. 1681; beside eldest s. Samuel, and later b. John, Sarah, and Mary, nam. in his will of 13 Dec. 1700, as well as their mo. wh. was nam. extrix. until Samuel attain. full age. He d. 14 Dec. 1700. WILLIAM, Braintree 1640, by w. Hannah had John, b. 22 Apr. 1642; Samuel, 30 Oct. 1643; Benjamin, 28 Oct. 1645; and William, 17 July 1652; beside ds. Hannah, 11 Mar. 1648; and Sarah, 1 Oct. 1654, but the last of ea. sex was by sec. w. m. 9 Aug. 1655, Sarah Gamitt, as the rec. has it, wh. by Mr. Vinton, 311, is read Jarmill, and in neither form is accessib. to any search of mine, yet in his will of 18 Feb. 1669 made extrix. Vexat. from contradict. rec. is frequent in these inquir. and much refinem. will be need. to reconcile that m. as print, in Geneal.

Reg. XII. 347, with the bs. in same Vol. 110 and XI. 334, "evident.
the sec. w.'s childr." says Vinton, 298. His wid. m. 5 Sept. 1670,
Thomas Faxon, and d. 1697. WILLIAM, Braintree, s. of the preced.
m. 1 Jan. 1680, Deborah, d. of Thomas Faxon the sec. and had sec. w.
Experience, youngest d. of the sec. Edmund Quincy, and d. early in
1700. He serv. in brave capt. Johnson's comp. Dec. 1675, but Geneal.
Reg. VIII. 242, makes him Sable. Only from his will of 31 Jan. pro.
7 Mar. foll. in wh. w. is made extrix. until his eldest s. William should
be of age, do we learn names of other ch. Joseph, Benjamin, Deborah,
and Judith; by wh. w. or when b. respective. is unkn. Yet I venture
to conject. that the last nam. alone was by the Quincy w. wh. outliv. him
six or seven yrs. His brs. Samuel and Benjamin also are ment. in that
instrum.

SAVORY, SAVORIE, or SAVARY, ANTHONY, Dartmouth 1686, then a
townsman, may not be the one by Farmer said to come, 1640, from
Slade, in Devonshire, with Thomas S. Yet no such place was found
by me. But if Thomas be he so unfavo. ment. in our Col. Rec. I. 248,
sub an. 1638 refer. to the Ct. at Ipswich for one offence, and Ib. 297,
sentenc. to be whip. for ano. 1640, and sold as a slave, our ign. may not
be lament. ROBERT, Newbury, m. 8 Dec. 1656, Mary, wid. of William Mitchell, had Sarah, b. 12 Nov. foll.; William, 15 Sept. 1659;
Samuel, 18 Mar. 1662; Richard, 20 Jan. 1664; and Robert, 8 Aug.
1666. SAMUEL, Plymouth, perhaps s. of Thomas of the same, was aft.
at Rochester, there had Mary, b. 3 Jan. 1678; Judah, 10 Jan. 1680;
Susanna, 19 May 1690; and Samuel, 16 Nov. 1695; perhaps more ch.
THOMAS, Plymouth, was in that serv. under Howland at Kennebeck, in
Apr. 1634, when one of his compan. was k. by Hocking, wh. was forthwith k. by the Plymouth men. See the evid. in Geneal. Reg. IX. 80,
and full relations by the Govs. Bradford of Plymouth and Winth. of
Mass. He was, I suppose, of Plymouth in 1643, had Moses, b. 22 Jan.
1650, d. soon; Samuel, 4 June 1651; Jonathan, or Thomas, 4 Mar.
1653; Mary, 7 Apr. 1654; and, perhaps, others. Either he or his s.
Thomas is rememb. in the will of Timothy Hatherley, Sept. 1664.
THOMAS, a passeng. in the Mary and John from London, with William,
perhaps his br. perhaps f. or s. hav. tak. o. of suprema. and alleg. 24
Mar. 1634, may have sat down first at Ipswich, but on our side of the
sea was of narrower, perhaps, or wider faith than his fellows, and so
driv. to Newport 1639, perhaps next to Sandwich, unless the Plymouth
man had right to that place. THOMAS, Scituate, s. perhaps of Thomas
of Plymouth, was in the employm. of Hatherley, and a doz. yrs. aft.
d. of H. was k. by the Ind. 26 Mar. 1676, as one of the comp. of capt.
Peirce. He was unm. Of WILLIAM, that fellow-passeng. with Thomas

from London, 1634, in the Mary and John, it is equal. hard to follow any footstep.

SAWDY, JOHN, Boston, cordwainer, by w. Ann had Eliz. b. 15 Oct. 1654; Mary, 24 Oct. 1656; John, 14 Oct. 1658, d. young; Joseph, 5 Dec. 1660; Benjamin, 7 Aug. 1663; John, again, Apr. 1666.

SAWIN, JOHN, Watertown 1641, s. of Robert of Boxford, Co. Suffk. was prob. brot. from Eng. by his mo. Abigail, a wid. sold his est. at home in 1651, was freem. 1652, m. Abigail, d. of George Munning, had John, whose b. is not told; Munning, 4 Apr. 1655; and Thomas, 27 Sept. 1657. He m. sec. w. 16 Feb. 1667, Judith, youngest ch. of Anthony Pierce, as Bond tells, 423; but my suspic. is very strong, that the m. was with John, the s. for she was under 17 yrs. at that time, and p. 932, he gives countenance to that conject. for he makes John jr. have w. of that name. He was selectman 1664 and 72, and d. 2 Sept. 1690. MUNNING, Watertown, s. of the preced. m. 15 or 18 Dec. 1681, Sarah, eldest d. of deac. John Stone, had Sarah, b. 25 May 1684; Abigail, 27 Nov. 1686; John, 13 Aug. 1689; Joseph, 1 Mar. 1692, d. young; Mary, 14 Feb. 1695; George, 2 Apr. 1697; Samuel, 7 Feb. 1700; Deborah, 5 Sept. 1702; Eliz. 6 May 1705; Joseph, again, 27 Nov. 1707; and Mercy, June 1710, wh. d. next yr. He was many yrs. town clk. treasr. and selectman, and d. 8 Nov. 1722. THOMAS, Sherborn, br. of the preced. m. 23 Jan. 1685, Deborah, d. of Matthew Rice, had Ruth, b. 24 July 1686; John, 26 June 1689; beside Deborah, 4 Apr. 1696, and, perhaps, others.

SAWKYN, WILLIAM, came July 1635, a passeng. aged 25, in the Defence from London; but no more is told of him.

SAWTELL, SARTELL, SATTELL, or SAUTELL, ENOCH, Watertown, s. of Richard of the same, a weaver, by w. Susanna, d. of John Randall, had Susanna, bapt. 2 Oct. 1687·; Richard, 21 Apr. 1689; Mary, wh. d. 13 Apr. 1696; Eliz. bapt. 8 Oct. 1699; and Mary, again, 6 Oct. 1700. HENRY, Newtown, L. I. 1669–86. JONATHAN, Groton, br. of Enoch, by w. Mary, m. 3 July 1665, had Mary, b. 16 Oct. 1667; Eliz. 3 Feb. 1669; Hannah, 6 Oct. 1670; Abigail, 5 Mar. 1672; Sarah, 24 Feb. 1674; Jonathan, 6 Apr. 1676; and his w. d. in few days aft. He was adm. freem. 1672, and d. 6 Jan. 1691. OBADIAH, Groton, eldest br. of the preced. by w. Hannah, d. of George Lawrence, had Abigail, b. 13 Mar. ,1666; and prob. Obadiah. RICHARD, Watertown 1636, had Eliz. b. 1 May 1638, wh. prob. d. bef. her f.; Jonathan, 24 Aug. 1639; Mary, 19 Nov. 1640; Hannah, 10 Dec. 1642; and Zechariah, 25 July 1645, unless the last fig. be wrong; beside Enoch, John, Ruth, and Bethia; was one of the early proprs. of Groton, and town clk. there, perhaps driv. back to W. by Ind. and there d. 21 Aug. 1694; in his will of 16 May 1692, names w. Eliz. wh. d. 18 Oct. aft. him, and ch. Obadiah, Enoch, Bethia, John, Hannah, wh. had m. 13 July 1665, Increase Winn, and Ruth, wh. had m. 9 Mar. 1677, John Hewes, beside childr. of s. Jonathan, of s. Zechariah, and of d. Mary Sterling. THOMAS, Boston, br. of the preced. on adm. of the ch. 17 Apr. 1647, call. "one of our teacher's serv." freem. 1649, when the word is by Shurtleff or Pulcifer in Col. Rec. II. giv. Sacetell, wh. must be an impossib. name, but Sawtell by Paige; d. unm. 14 July 1651, or at least, made that day his nuncup. will, pro. 18 Nov. foll. ZECHARIAH, Groton, s. of Richard, m. at Boston, Apr. 1668, Eliz. Harris, perhaps d. of Robert, had Eliz. b. Dec. 1671 ; and by w. Mary, that d. 2 Dec. 1699, had Ann, 14 Mar. 1674, as giv. by Butler, but by Bond one yr. earlier, and he also thinks a s. Nathaniel. Aft. the dispers. by the Ind. wars, there may have been others. At G. this fam. name has been large. diffus.

SAWYER, EDMUND, Ipswich 1636, rem. bef. 1661 to York. EDWARD, Rowley 1643, had w. Mary, and s. John. EZEKIEL, a soldier of "the flower of Essex," k. by the Ind. at Bloody brook, 18 Sept. 1675. HENRY, Haverhill 1646, perhaps next yr. of Hampton, and of York 1676. JAMES, Ipswich 1669, may have rem. to Gloucester, and by w. Sarah, d. of Thomas Bray, had Nathaniel, b. 1677 ; Abraham, 1680 ; Sarah, 1683 ; Isaac, 1684 ; Jacob, 1687 ; James, 1691 ; beside Thomas, John, and Mary, b. earlier, as Babson thinks, as also, that he was s. of William of Newbury. He d. 31 May 1703 ; but his wid. liv. long. JAMES, Lancaster, s. of Thomas, m. 4 Feb. 1678, Mary Marble. JOHN, Marshfield, m. Nov. 1666, Mercy Little, perhaps d. of Thomas, wh. was bur. 10 Feb. 1693, had Ann, bur. 1 Sept. 1682 ; and he m. 23 Nov. 1694, Rebecca, wid. of Josiah Snow, and d. 28 Apr. 1711. JOHN, Haverhill 1670, perhaps the s. of William, wh. m. 18 Feb. 1676, Sarah Poor, perhaps d. of John of Hampton, had Ruth, b. Sept. 1677 ; William, 29 Apr. 1679 ; Sarah, 20 May 1681 ; John, 25 Apr. 1683, d. young ; Jonathan, 4 Mar. 1685 ; Daniel, 13 June 1687 ; John, again, 10 Sept. 1688, d. next yr. was, perhaps, the freem. of 1681, print. in Paige's list, Sanyde, and in Shurtleff's Col. Rec. Sauyer. In the Paige catal. he is call. of Rowley, and there was tax. 1691, but he d. 30 May 1689. Prob. his est. had not been admin. as all the ch. were too young. JOSHUA, Woburn, s. of Thomas of Lancaster, m. 2 Jan. 1678, Sarah Potter, had Abigail, b. 17 May 1679 ; Joshua, 20 June 1684; Sarah, 4 July 1687 ; Hannah, 15 Nov. 1689 ; Martha, 26 Apr. 1692 ; and Eliz. 7 Nov. 1698 ; was adm. freem. 1690. RICHARD, Hartford, in employm. of John Cullick, there d. unm. 24 July 1648. ROBERT, Hampton 1640. STEPHEN, Newbury, s. of William, by w. Ann had Ann, b. 1 Aug. 1687 ; Daniel, 28 Jan. 1689 ; and Enoch, 22

June 1694. THOMAS, Lancaster 1647, one of the first six sett. had been, I think, of Rowley 1643, freem. 1654, by w. Mary, d. of John Prescott, had Thomas, b. July 1649 ; Ephraim, 2 Jan. 1651, wh. was k. by the Ind. 10 Feb. 1676 ; Mary, 7 Jan. 1653 ; Eliz. 7 Jan. 1654 ; Joshua, Mar. 1655 ; James, Mar. 1657 ; Caleb, Apr. 1659 ; John, Apr. 1661 ; and Nathaniel, Nov. 1670. Descend. are very num. tho. of the sec. generat. we are quite ign. WILLIAM, Salem 1643, Wenham 1645, rem. to Newbury, by w. Ruth had John, b. 24 Aug. 1645 ; Samuel, 22 Nov. 1646 ; Ruth, 10 Sept. 1648 ; Mary, 7 Feb. 1650, d. soon ; Sarah, 20 Nov. 1651 ; Hannah, 23 Feb. 1654, d. young ; William, 1 Feb. 1656 ; Francis, 24 Mar. 1658, d. in 2 yrs. ; Mary, again, 29 July 1660 ; Stephen, 25 Apr. 1663 ; Hannah, again, 11 Jan. 1665, d. at 18 yrs. ; and Francis, again, 3 Nov. 1670. Perhaps he had sec. w. Sarah, wid. of John Wells of Wells, parents of Rev. Thomas. His d. Mary m. 13 June 1683, John Emery third of N. WILLIAM, Newbury, s. of the preced. m. 10 Mar. 1671, Mary, d. of John Emery the sec. had Mary, b. 20 Jan. 1672 ; Samuel, 5 June 1674 ; John, 15 Mar. 1676 ; Ruth, 20 Sept. 1677 ; Hannah, 12 Jan. 1679 ; and Josiah, 20 Jan. 1681. Oft. this name seems Sawer, and Sayer. Ten are among gr. at Harv. ten at Dart. and one at Yale.

SAXTON, or SEXTON, DANIEL, Westfield, perhaps s. of George, m. 28 Dec. 1680, Sarah, d. of John Bancroft, had Nathaniel, b. 22 Dec. foll. d. in 3 days ; and Sarah, 6 Mar. 1683. GEORGE, Windsor, had John, b. there 26 May 1673, went back to Westfield, where he had liv. bef. and had Benjamin, a. 1667, said to be the first white b. in that place, wh. also liv. to old age, but Joseph bef. him, and prob. George earlier still, bef. W. was plant. and in 1688 sold to Joseph and Benjamin his est. there for £160., his w. Catharine join. in the deed, and he d. a. 1690. GEORGE, Westfield, s. prob. eldest of the preced. had, by w. that d. 19 Sept. 1689, Charles, b. 9 Sept. 1680 ; and Nathaniel, 5 Dec. 1682 ; and rem. to Newtown, L. I. GILES, Boston or Charlestown, prob. arr. in the fleet with Winth. for on 18 Sept. 1630, he was a witness bef. the coroner as to d. of William Bateman in the harb. near Pullen point, and on 28 of same serv. on inq. at Charlestown on the case of Austin Bratcher, k. by Walter Palmer ; req. adm. as freem. 19 Oct. foll. when the title Mr. is bef. his name, and was sw. 18 May next without that prefix. My conject. is that he soon went home, and that Deane was wrong in suppos. him the min. to wh. the Magnalia, III. 214, could not give Christian name, or tell time of com. or go. Better informa. is now enjoy. JAMES, Westfield, perhaps s. of George the first, or of Richard, by w. Hannah had John, b. 28 Jan. 1681 ; Hannah, 29 Oct. 1683 ; Phebe, 7 Jan. 1687 ; Eliz. 5 Feb. 1689, wh. d. at 3 mos. ; Mary, or

Mercy, 26 Dec. 1695; and James, 9 Nov. 1702; and d. 12 Dec. 1741. His w. was d. of the first Ambrose Fowler. JOHN, Windsor, eldest s. of Richard, m. 30 July 1677, Mary Hill,, d. of Luke, had Mary, b. 4 May foll. rem. to Simsbury, and had Richard and John. JOSEPH, Stonington, m. Hannah, d. of capt. George Denison of the same, had Jerusha, and Mercy; but of him I hear no more, exc. that he was a capt. JOSEPH, Westfield, s. of George the first, m. 1690, Hannah, d. of the first Abel Wright of the same, had Gershom; Hannah, b. 1692; Joseph, 1694; Mindwell, 1696; Daniel, 1700, and Ezekiel, 1704; rem. to Enfield, and had Charles, 1708; and d. 1742, says Dr. Pease in the careful contribut. to Hinman, aged 76. PETER, Scituate 1640, aft. rem. of Lothrop, was from Yorksh. bred at Trinity Coll. Cambridge, where he proceed. A. M. 1603, adm. by Archbp. Hutton bef. 1606 to holy orders, liv. but few mos. in our country, and was not ord. yet may well be thot. one of the four min. that went home with dep.-gov. Humfrey, Dec. 1641, whose pious exclama. in the storm is so well told by Mather. Considera. offer was tender. him of good liv. in Kent; but, prefer. his native shire, he gain. the valua. vicarage of Leeds, to wh. the triumph of his party sent him in Apr. 1646, and there he d. 1 Oct. 1651. When here, his d. Silence m. capt. Samuel Pool. See Brook's Lives of the Puritans, III. 139. RICHARD, Windsor 1643, not early eno. to have been at Dorchester, yet said to have come in the ship Blessing, but the more important fact would have been a date, m. 16 Apr. 1646, Sarah Cook, perhaps sis. of Nathaniel, had Sarah, b. 23 Mar. 1648; John, 4 Mar. 1650; Mary, 27 Feb. 1652; Richard, 1 Mar. 1655, wh. fell in the gr. battle of Narraganset, 19 Dec. 1675; Patience, 28 June 1658, or Jan. 1659; Francis, 11 or 17 Jan. 1662, d. at 4 yrs. He d. 3 May 1662, and his wid. d. 13 June 1674; but in Stiles's Hist. 770, the ds. of h. and w. are exchang. in date. Sarah had m. bef. the latest date, perhaps Oct. 1668, Robert Roath of Norwich; and Mary m. George Saunders. THOMAS, Boston, miller, by w. Lucy had Mary, b. 2 Jan. 1645; and John, 29 June 1647. He m. 10 Mar. 1652, as sec. w. Ann, wid. of Herman Atwood, d. of William Copp, had Samuel, 8 Oct. 1653, whose gr.st. tells his d. 21 July 1693; Joseph, 9 May 1656; Nathaniel, 29 Nov. 1658, wh. d. at 19 yrs.; and Eliz. 8 June 1661; and his w. d. 2 wks. aft. By a third w. Mary, he had Benjamin, 18 May 1664; and Mary, 9 Jan. 1666; and he d. 31 July 1686.

SAYER, SAYERS, or SAYRE, DANIEL, JOB, and FRANCIS, at Southampton, L. I. 1673, had, perhaps, rem. from Lynn, at least one Job was there 1635, and the others may have been his brs. or s. ICHABOD, New London, s. of Francis, m. 1697, Mary, d. of Hugh Hubbard, and this was the first m. says Miss Caulkins, solemniz. by Gov. Saltonstall.

JAMES, from Northbourne, Co. Kent, came, 1635, in the Hercules from Sandwich, but we kn. not where he sat down. JAMES, Gloucester, by w. Sarah had Nathaniel, b. 29 Dec. 1677 ; and Abraham, 5 Nov. 1680. JOHN, Falmouth, sold, 1655, to Isaac Walker of Boston, that isl. call. Long Isl. in Casco Bay. THOMAS, Lynn 1635, one of the purch. 1640, of Southampton, L. I. may be the freem. of 22 May 1639, giv. on rec. Say or Says ; and also may be f. of one or more of the first nam. sett. at S. Conject. is unsatisfact. when Shurtleff and Paige differ in spell. of the names, and confid. is still less indulg. as to the surname of *two* syl. when ano. THOMAS is found in the will of Stephen Lincoln, at Hingham, 1658. See Geneal. Reg. IX. 38.

SAYLE, or SAYLES, JOHN, Providence 1645, in list of freem. 1655, next yr. town clk. by w. Mary had Mary, b. 11 July 1652 ; and John, 17 Aug. 1654 ; and prob. others ; in May 1666, sw. alleg. to Charles II. JOHN, Providence, s. prob. of the preced. took the o. of alleg. May 1682, m. Eliz. Comstock, perhaps d. of the first Daniel, had Mary, b. 30 May 1689 ; John, 10 Jan. 1692 ; Richard, 24 Oct. 1695 ; Daniel, 13 Dec. 1697 ; and Thomas, 9 Feb. 1699 ; and d. 2 Nov. foll. WILLIAM, Boston, a trans. visit. in 1646, wh. had been Gov. at Bermuda, was so happy as to attend Cotton's lecture on Thursday, 5 Nov. in that yr. and soon aft. sail. for London. Out of incid. in that Thursday lecture advert. to, sprang two tracts of antagonist spirit, " N. E.'s Jonas cast up at London," by Dr. Child, and " N. E.'s Salamander," by Edward Winslow, and this latter appeal. to Gov. Seyle as a witness against the story told by·C. Five yrs. later he was sent by the Eng. governm. to plant at Eleutheria, one of the Bahamas, as is told by Winth. II. 334, and I presume the same gent. was, in 1670, Gov. in Carolina, under royal commiss. of 26 July 1669, where prob. he d. 1671.

SAYWARD, or SAYWORD, EDMUND, Ipswich 1635. HENRY, Hampton 1646, Portsmouth 1650, soon aft. at York, there was constable 1664, perhaps had s. John, and Samuel, wh. there took o. of alleg. 1681, and long perpet. the name. He d. 1679, and his wid. Mary had admin. RICHARD, New Hampsh. 1662.

SAYWELL, DAVID, Boston, perhaps s. of Robert, m. 15 Aug. 1660, Abigail, d. of Thomas Buttolph ; was freem. 1666, and d. 1672. His wid. m. next yr. Thomas Bingley. ROBERT, Boston, came in the Blessing, 1635, aged 30, with Susan, prob. his w. 25, and James, prob. their s. 1 and ½ yrs. had Eliz. wh. m. 7 May 1662, Joseph Davis.

SCADDING, WILLIAM, Taunton 1638. Baylies, I. 289.

SCADLOCK, WILLIAM, Saco 1636, freem. 1653, of gr. jury 1654, and 1660, had William, Susanna, John, Rebecca, Samuel, and Sarah. He d. 1662, in his will of 7 Jan. nam. w. Elinor, and these six ch. Samuel was liv. 1719, aged 73; but John d. 1664; and William d. four yrs. aft. his f. hav. lost a s. William, it is said of lawful age, the yr. preced. but this seems rather strange. The name is Chaddock, in Folsom, wh. perhaps, foll. Sullivan in Hist. 218 and 19.

SCALES, JOHN, Rowley 1648. MATTHEW, k. by the Ind. at Hatfield, 25 Aug. 1675, may not have been an inhab. but a soldier from the E. WILLIAM, Rowley, freem. 13 May 1640.

SCAMMON, SCAMMAN, or SCAMMOND, HUMPHREY, Kittery, or Saco, perhaps both, m. Eliz. d. of the first Dominicus Jordan, had Humphrey, b. 10 May 1677; Eliz.; Mary; Rebecca; and Samuel. JOHN, Kittery, perhaps s. of William, certain. br. of Humphrey and of Richard, as also of Eliz. w. of Peter Lidgett, had Eliz. but wh. was his w. the diligence of Quint has not discov. RICHARD, Dover, br. of the preced. perhaps s. of William, m. Prudence, only d. of William Waldron, had Richard; William, b. 29 Feb. 1664; Jane, 21 June or July 1667; Prudence, 29 Aug. 1669; Eliz. 22 Apr. 1671; and Mary, 31 May 1673. He escap. the Ind. war by liv. at Exeter 1677; and both h. and w. were there 21 Apr. 1691. Jane m. Thomas Deane of Boston, and d. 9 Oct. 1726. WILLIAM, Boston 1640, prob. rem. soon, may have been ancest. of the disting. fam. but nothing can be ascertain.

SCAMP, ROBERT, Gloucester, m. 25 Dec. 1661, Joan, d. of John Collins, had Mary, b. 25 Nov. foll. and his w. d. next 9 Nov. and he d. 23 Apr. 1691. I suggest, that possib. this name may have been Stamp, for in old rec. t and c are much alike.

SCANT, WILLIAM, Braintree, m. 29 Mar. 1654, Sarah Brown, had William, b. 16 Mar. foll.; Thomas, 11 Apr. 1657; Sarah, 5 Sept. 1660; Joseph, 4 June 1662, d. at 2 yrs.; Susanna, 30 Jan. 1664; and ano. d. 27 May 1665, with a strange or undecypher. name; and he d. Sept. 1684. His will, of 8 Aug. pro. 30 Oct. names w. and refers to ch. without nam. them.

SCARBOROUGH, or SCARBARROW, JOHN, Roxbury 1639, freem. 13 May 1640, unless the Col. rec. of Shurtleff, I. 377, justify an earlier date of four days, wh. must seem very improb. for the regular day of open. Gen. Ct. was 13, and, of course, the 9th was Saturday; by w. Mary, prob. sis. of Robert Smith of Boston, had John, b. 10, bapt. 24 July 1642, d. next mo.; Hannah, 3 Dec. 1643, bapt. same day; Samuel, 20 Jan. bapt. 1 Feb. 1646; and was k. 9 June foll. by casualty in charg. a gr. gun. His wid. m. 1 Oct. 1647, Philip Torrey. SAMUEL, Roxbury, s. of the preced. by first w. wh. d. 1679, had prob. no ch. but by w. Bethia had prob. Samuel, b. 1681, wh. d. of smallpox, 2 Nov. 1721; Joseph, Feb. 1683; Jeremiah, 31 July 1685, wh. d. in few wks.; Deborah, 16 July 1687, wh. d. at six yrs.; and he d. 18 Mar. 1715. His wid. d. 10 Sept. 1728, aged 75.

SCARLET, BENJAMIN, Salem 1635, s. prob. of Mary, wh. bound him apprent. that yr. aged only 11 yrs. to capt. Endicott, and he contin. the Gov.'s man 1651, and was liv. 1678. A wid. Scarlet, early memb. of Salem ch. in her will of 2 Mar. 1640, pro. June 1643, nam. Joseph Grafton excor. calls him br. as also James Lind, and br. Browning, and his w. and sis. Dennis. All these, I think, refer to Christian soc. but she ment. her own ch. Mary, Margaret, and Joseph; and when she nam. br. Samuel in Eng. she means, I suppose, kinsm. and he may have been f. of this apprent. Yet, as to the fam. of the testator, I see no more light. JOHN, Springfield 1640, was then constable, rem. to Boston 1650, by w. Thomasine had Mary and Jane, tw. b. 21 Sept. 1653; perhaps John, 1657, wh. d. young; Thomasine, 18 May 1660; John and Samuel, tw. 16 Apr. 1664; and Eliz. 18 Nov. 1667; and by Farmer, in MS. geneal. was, I think, mistak. for his br. Samuel. His will, of 16 Feb. 1688, pro. 21 Mar. foll. gives to his w. to d. Thomasine Taylor, and to gr.s. James Fryer; so that my conject. is, that ano. of his ds. had m. James, only s. of Hon. Nathaniel F. ROBERT, Salem 1635, perhaps br. of Benjamin, was that yr. sentenc. to be whip. for run. from his master. SAMUEL, Boston 1664, br. of John, master of a sh. from London to B. with his w. join. Mather's ch. 1672, was freem. and constable 1673, and was mort. inj. by explos. of a sh. in the harbor, 4 May 1675, dy. in a few hours. He was b. in Kersey, Co. Suffk. he says in his will, made that day, pro. 26 May foll. by wh. he dispos. of good amt. of prop. but left no ch.

SCATE, JOHN, Boston, by w. Sarah had John, b. 14 Apr. 1659.

SCATHE, JOHN, Hingham, with Ann, perhaps a sis. are ment. in the wills of John Merrick and of his wid. Eliz. 1647 and 9. Prob. they were serv. but he was in Boston, prob. 1674, a cordwainer, and in 1678 sold lds. at H. to William Hersey, writ. his name John Skeath.

SCHRICK, PAULUS, Hartford, one of the little colo. of Dutch from New York, that had plant. bef. the Eng. went thither. He m. 30 Dec. 1658, Mary, wid. of Josephus Ambeck, d. of Caspar Varleet; but no issue is ment.

SCILIAN, BENJAMIN, and JOSEPH, unless surname be mistak. as I suspect, were of Ipswich 1683.

SCOFIELD, SCOVIL, SCOVEL, SCHOFEL, or SKOFIELD, ARTHUR, Middletown, a propr. 1671, by w. Rachel, m. 17 Dec. 1690, at Lyme, had Arthur, b. 13 Jan. 1692; and James, 9 Jan. 1694, wh. d. in few wks. and the f. d. 24 June foll. ARTHUR, Middletown, s. of the preced. by w. Eliz. m. Feb. 1711, had James, b. 18 Jan. 1712; and Eliz. 26 July 1715. BENJAMIN, Haddam, perhaps s. of John, by w. Ann had Edward, b. 9 Apr. 1704; Sarah, 9 Oct. 1706; and Amie, 14 Mar. 1709.

DANIEL, Stamford 1641, one of the first sett. d. 1671, leav. ch. Daniel, John, Richard, Joseph, Sarah, w. of John Pettit; and Mary or Mercy. His wid. Sarah bec. third w. of Miles Merwin, and is nam. in his will. His two eldest s. liv. many yrs. at Stamford, and left num. progeny; but their br. Joseph d. 1676, in serv. or by the hardships of Philip's war, leav. no fam. yet some est. to brs. and sis. EDWARD, Haddam, m. Hannah, d. prob. youngest, of Andrew Benton of Hartford, d. 1703, leav. wid. and two ds. but I miss any early date. JOHN, Farmington, m. 29 Mar. 1666, Sarah Barnes, d. of Thomas, rem. to Waterbury, next to Haddam, there d. 1712, had John, William, and Benjamin. JOHN, Middletown, m. 9 Feb. 1698, Mary Lucas, d. prob. of William, had Joanna, John, Mary, Eliz. William, and Ebenezer, and d. 12 Dec. 1712. RICHARD, Ipswich 1648, came in the Susan and Ellen, aged 22, from London, may have been of Stamford 1650, and d. 1671, and the same, whose wid. m. Robert Penoyer. He was prob. f. of Richard, propound. for freem. 1670, a trader at S. 1689–1701; and, perhaps, other ch. Great vexation has attend. my desire to avoid confus. of families under such various spell. and it would not be easy for a congress of those with so hard a name, in our days, to make out the derivat. of the mem.

SCOLLEY, or SCHOLLEY, JOHN, Malden 1674, then 33 yrs. old, had liv. at Charlestown, m. Hannah, d. of James Barrett, had John, b. 20 June 1665; Hannah, 3 Apr. 1669; James, Oct. 1671; Mary, Feb. 1675; and Sarah, wh. m. 16 Nov. 1699, Jonathan Eustis.

SCOON, or SCONE, JOHN, Westfield, m. Sarah, d. of Edmund Hart, had William, b. 15 Nov. 1676; Sarah, 7 Mar. 1678; Eliz. 14 June 1680; and Joseph, 16 Apr. 1683; and d. 19 Aug. 1684.

SCOTCHFORD, JOHN, Concord, was town clk. m. Susanna, perhaps d. of George Meriam, had no ch. says Shattuck, and d. 10 June 1696. His wid. d. 2 Feb. 1707.

SCOTT, BENJAMIN, Braintree, had, perhaps b. in Eng. Hannah, wh. m. Christopher Webb; John, b. 25 Dec. 1640, d. soon; rem. to Cambridge, there, by w. Margaret, had Joseph, 14 July 1644; Benjamin, 5 July 1646; John, again, 2 July 1648; Eliz. 27 May 1650, wh. d. in one wk.; rem. to Rowley bef. 1652, there had Samuel, 1655, and two ds.; was freem. 1665, and d. 1671. Of ano. BENJAMIN of Braintree, we kn. only, that his will of 7 Oct. 1683, pro. 29 Apr. foll. refers to no w. or ch. but gives all his est. to br. Peter until the eldest s. of Peter come of age. BENJAMIN, Rowley, s. of the first Benjamin, m. Susanna Searle, had John, b. 1681; Joseph, 1682; Benjamin, 1687; Samuel, 1692. EDMUND, Farmington 1649, by first w. had seven ch. was freem. 1669, had two more ch. by sec. w. Eliz. wid. of Thomas Upson, but the date of ms. or bs. for neither is told. From his will of 11 June

1690, we gain the names of all, Edmund; Samuel, b. 1660; Jonathan; George; David; Robert; Joseph; Eliz. Davis; and Hannah, w.
of John Brunson; yet we shall not be justif. in suppos. this to be the
order of success. exc. that the two s. last nam. were by sec. w. nor will
conject. be reasona. to determine the priority of the d. whose h.'s name
is not seen. Positive informat. however, is afford. on two points, that he
was an orig. propr. of Waterbury, and there d. 1691. EDMUND, Waterbury, s. of the preced. by w. who d. 17 Jan. 1749, had a s. b. Oct. 1690,
wh. d. in few wks.; Sarah, 29 Jan. 1692; Samuel, Sept. 1694; Eliz. 1
Mar. 1697; Hannah, June 1700; Edmund, 10 May 1703; John, 21
Sept. 1707; and Jonathan, 4 Aug. 1711; and d. 20 July 1746. ED-
WARD, ask. for gr. at New London 1651, yet did not impr. it, when giv.
not however tempt. towards Hadley, where he first is heard of as serv.
of Joseph Kellogg 1662, and where was ano. EDWARD, wh. was he
prob. that m. 1670, Eliz. Webster, perhaps d. of Gov. John, had Eliz.
b. 1671; Sarah, 1674; Thomas, 1675; John, 1677; Ebenezer, 1681;
Bridget and Ann, tw. 1682; and Hannah, 14 Mar. 1689. His w. d.
two days aft. aged 40; and he rem. perhaps to New Haven, where one
Edward was excus. in 1703 from train. in the milit. so leav. us to infer,
that he was over 60 yrs. of age. GEORGE, New Haven, a gunsmith,
in 1690, had not, nor any other of this surname, been propr. 1685.
GEORGE, Waterbury, s. of Edmund, m. Aug. 1691, Mary, d. of Obadiah
Richards, had Obadiah, George, and William; and d. 26 Sept. 1724.
JOHN, the freem. in Mass. of 22 May 1639, then spelt in Secr.'s list with
a k, and JOHN, the freem. of 10 May 1643, aft. many hours of very dilig.
scrutiny, elude my skill in search. for the resid. of either; but strong
reasons lead me to believe that neither of them was of the three foll.
JOHN, Salem, 1648, serv. of Lawrence Southwick, the Quaker, may have
gone to Providence, and by w. Rebecca there had Sarah, b. 29 Sept.
1662; John, 14 Mar. 1664; Mary, 1 Feb. 1666; Catharine, 20 May
1668; Deborah, 24 Dec. 1669; and Sylvanus, 10 Nov. 1672. He took
o. of alleg. to Charles II. in 1668. JOHN, Charlestown 1658, d. 25 Jan.
1682, aged 75, says the gr.st. JOHN, Springfield, m. 20 July 1659, Sarah,
d. of Thomas Bliss, had Sarah, b. 19 Oct. 1663; John, 4 Jan. 1666, perhaps, but the last fig. is uncert.; Hannah, 16 Oct. 1668; Margaret, 8
Feb. 1671; Ebenezer, 3 Aug. 1673; William, 8 Aug. 1676; Mary, 29
Dec. 1678; rem. to Suffield, there had Eliz. 2 Sept. 1683; and he d. 2
Jan. 1690. His wid. m. the same yr. Samuel Terry, and d. 27 Sept.
1705. Of the s. William only, one of the first sett. at Palmer, had ch.
Sarah m. 9 Feb. 1680, Benjamin Leonard; Hannah m. 31 Oct. 1695,
John Fowler; Margaret m. but the name of her h. is not kn.; Mary m.
July 1701, Ebenezer Nash; and Eliz. m. 1708, Jonathan Worthington.

JOHN, of Newtown, Southold, or other L. I. town, was very active for
the honor of the k. in 1663, but in Apr. or May 1664, was tak. by Conn.
officers and carr. to prison at Hartford, heavi. fined, and disfranchis. as
a defamer of his majesty, &c., &c. JOHN, Roxbury, m. 29 May 1672,
Hannah Duncan, or Dunkin, perhaps d. of Samuel, had Hannah, b. 24
July 1674, d. soon; John, 11 Nov. 1675, d. soon; Sarah, d. soon; Hannah, agam, 18 Aug. 1678; Mary, 28 July 1679, d. in two days; Margaret, 6 Jan. 1691, d. soon; Joseph, 27 Mar. 1682; John, again, 8 Nov.
1683, d. soon; Sarah, 9 Nov. 1684, d. next day; and John, again, 9
July 1686. Perhaps he was of Johnson's comp. in the Narraganset
campaign, Dec. 1675. His w. d. 1 Jan. 1706, if the rec. that calls her
Sarah, be good. JONATHAN, Waterbury, s. of Edmund, m. Nov. 1694,
Hannah, d. of John Hawks of Deerfield, had a d. b. and d. Aug. 1695;
Jonathan, 29 Sept. 1696; John, 5 June 1699; Martha, 9 July 1701;
Gershom, 6 Sept. 1703; Eleazer, 31 Dec. 1705; and Daniel, 20 Sept.
1707. His w. d. 7 Apr. 1744; and he d. 15 May 1745. JOSEPH,
Rowley, s. of the first Benjamin, was, perhaps, of Ipswich 1683. Jo-
SEPH, Farmington, s. of Edmund, d. 1708, leav. s. John. PETER,
Braintree, br. of the sec. Benjamin, by w. Abigail had Benjamin, b.
24 Sept. 1674; Peter; and John; was freem. 1685. RICHARD, Boston, shoemaker, join. our ch. 28 Aug. 1634, yet his w. Catharine, d.
of Rev. Edward Marbury (as Bishop, in N. E. Judged tells), did not
unite, nor either of the ch. Richard, John, Mary, or Patience, tho.
Ann Hutchinson, their aunt, and her sis. had so great sway in it. To
this w. Gov. Winth. I. 293, ascribes much power in giv. light on
believers' bapt. to Roger Williams, 1638, at Providence, where he was
rem. 1637, bef. the time of disarm. heretic favorers of Hutchinson.
He is on the list of freem. 1655, and was among the Quaker converts
1658, and his w. "an ancient woman," was imprison. and whip. at
Boston for benevol. serv. in diffus. her opinions, and her ds. Mary and
Patience also were imprison. by equal impolicy. Mary m. 12 Aug.
1660, Christopher Holder; Patience m. 28 Sept. 1668, Henry Beere;
and Deliverance, prob. a younger d. m. 30 Aug. 1670, William Richardson. ROBERT, Boston, join. to the ch. 15 Dec. 1633, then stil. "serv. to
our br. John Sanford," so that he prob. was a passeng. in the fleet with
Winth. 1630, was adm. freem. 7 Dec. 1636, by w. Eliz. had Nathaniel,
bapt. 19 Aug. 1638; Eliz. b. 10, bapt. 13 Dec. 1640; Mary, 28 Feb.
bapt. 5 Mar. 1643; John, bapt. 24 Aug. 1645, d. very soon; Redemp-
tion, 2 Mar. 1653; and Eleazer, posthum. 10 July 1654, wh. d. in few
days; and the f. d. in Feb. preced. Mary m. 16 Aug. 1660, Samuel
Emmons. ROBERT, Ipswich 1638. ROBERT, Hartford, s. of Edmund,
prob. d. unm. aft. 1725. ROGER, Lynn 1642. SAMUEL, Farmington,

s. of Edmund, m. Feb. 1687, Mary, d. of George Orvis, had Martha, b. 7 Dec. foll.; Ebenezer, 10 Aug. 1694; Samuel, 7 Oct. 1696; Mary, 1 Mar. 1700; and Hezekiah, Sept. 1703; and d. 30 June 1745; and his w. d. 28 Nov. 1748; ea. aged 85. THOMAS, Ipswich, came in the Elizabeth from Ipswich 1634, aged 40, with w. Eliz. 40; and ch. Eliz. 9; Abigail, 7; and Thomas, 6; was freem. 4 Mar. foll. made his will 8 Mar. 1654, names ea. of these ch. as liv. but that Thomas was at Stamford, and ment. younger ch. Hannah, Sarah, and Mary. In the same ship came Martha, aged 60, prob. mo. of this Thomas, and Richard Kimball, 39, by Scott, in his will, 20 yrs. later, call. br. At Boston, Co. Lincoln, in 1630, was one Thomas Scott, that may have been the same as the preced. or the foll. THOMAS, Hartford 1637, had been, perhaps, of Cambridge, was k. 6 Nov. 1643, careless. by John Ewe, for wh. he was fin. £5. to the Col. and £10. to the wid. Aft. being wound. he made nuncup. will, held good, tho. incomplete, as not nam. overseers, provid. for wid. Ann, s. Thomas, and three ds. That s. was infirm in body, or mind, perhaps both, and liv. not long; and the wid. m. 7 Nov. 1644, Thomas Ford; and d. at Northampton, 5 May 1675. One d. Mary m. at the same time with her mo. Robert Porter; ano. Sarah, m. 5 Dec. 1645, John Stanley; and the other, Eliz. m. 3 or 6 Feb. 1649, John Loomis of Windsor. THOMAS, Stamford, s. of Thomas the first, had m. at Ipswich, Margaret, d. of William Hubbard the first, sis. of the histo. had Thomas, and d. 1657. His wid. m. Ezekiel Rogers. THOMAS is the name of a soldier, k. by the Ind. at Northfield, 2 Sept. 1675. WILLIAM, Hatfield, m. 1670, Hannah, d. of William Allis, had Josiah, b. 1671; Richard, 1673; William, 1676; Hannah, 1679; Joseph, 1682; John, 1684, d. at 8 yrs.; Mary, 1686; Mehitable, 1687, d. soon; Jonathan, 1688, d. soon; and Abigail, 1689. Num. are descend. Josiah and Joseph cont. at H. but Richard and William were of early sett. in Sunderland.

SCOTTOW, or SCOTTAWAY, JOHN, Boston, s. of Thomas, by w. Rebecca had John, b. 25 June 1668; Rebecca, 27 June 1672, d. young; Joshua, 22 Feb. 1675; Rebecca, again, 1 Mar. 1677, d. soon; and Rebecca, again, 21 June 1678. ‖ JOSHUA, Boston, merch. brot. by his mo. Thomasine, a wid. wh. join. our ch. 21 Sept. 1634, and he, with br. Thomas, join. it 19 May 1639; was never sw. freem. yet appoint. by the Gen. Ct. a commissnr. for regulat. the export of powder. By his w. Lydia, wh. join. the ch. 23 May 1641, and d. 9 May 1707, aged 86, had Joshua, b. 30 Sept. 1641, d. very soon; Joshua, again, 12, bapt. 20 Aug. 1643; Lydia, bapt. 29 June 1645, tho. the poor substit. for town rec. says b. 30 of that mo.; Eliz. 1 Aug. 1647, 2 days old; Rebecca, 10 Oct. 1652; Mary, b. 11, bapt. 18 May 1656; Thomas, 30

June, bapt. 10 July 1659, H. C. 1677 ; and Sarah ; was of ar. co. 1645, its ens. 1657, and capt. later. He was confident. agent for La Tour in transact. with our governm. 1654–7, and a great propr. aft. Philip's war at Scarborough, capt. of the garrison and magistr. in that region. He was heedless. or cruel. charg. with murder of Nathan Bedford, 1681, shown to be casual. drown. as in the Maine Hist. Coll. III. may be read. As author of two very curious tracts a. the early hist. of N. E. publish. 1691 and 4, he is oft. quot. and, at the age of 83, he d. 20 Jan. 1698, as tells the gr.st. that was transfer. from the early bur. yd. to the inside of the tower of the O. S. or 3d ch. See Genealog. Reg. V. 78. His d. Eliz. m. a. 1664, Thomas Savage ; Rebecca m. 1 Apr. 1675, Benjamin Blackman ; and Mary m. capt. Samuel Checkley, as by his will of 23 June 1696, pro. 3 Mar. 1698, is seen ; beside wh. it gives adeq. provis. to w. Lydia, to s. Thomas a doub. portion, rings to ds. Mary Checkley and Sarah, w. of Samuel Walker, and to ea. of sixteen gr.ch. then liv. and made Judge Sewall and s. Savage and Checkley excors. His eldest d. Lydia, wh. first m. Benjamin Gibbs, and next m. 1678, Anthony Checkley, the atty.-gen. that d. 18 Oct. 1708, had, no doubt, been long bef. set out with her full sh. and for third h. she took, 6 Mar. 1712, William Colman, f. of the disting. Benjamin Colman, then min. of Brattle st. ch. D. D. JOSHUA, prob. s. of the first Thomas, m. 25 May 1697, Sarah, eldest d. of the sec. Zechariah Symmes ; but where he liv. when he d. or any further acco. of him, is beyond my power to tell. THOMAS, Boston, br. perhaps elder, of the first Joshua, a joiner, by w. Joan, wh. was adm. of the ch. 19 Sept. 1641, had Thomas, b. says the stupid town rec. Jan. 1640, when the ch. rec. shows bapt. 8 Dec. preced. wh. d. soon ; Thomas, again, bapt. 10 Apr. 1641, one day old, tho. town rec. gives b. in Mar.; John, 2, bapt. 5 May 1644; Thomas, again, 3, bapt. 7 Mar. 1647 ; and Mehitable, bapt. 11 Feb. 1649 ; and by sec. w. Sarah had Joshua, 3, bapt. 9 Dec. 1655; Sarah, 27 Sept. bapt. 4 Oct. 1657 ; Thomasin, 14, bapt. 15 Aug. 1659, d. soon; and Thomasin, again, 18 Aug. 1660. His will, of 9 May 1660, pro. 18 Dec. 1661, names aged mo. Sandford (tho. wh. she was is beyond my conject.), w. Sarah, s. John, and other ch. without naming. THOMAS, Scarborough, s. of Joshua the first, sw. alleg. 1681.

SCOVIL, SCOVALL, SCOVEL, or SCOVELL, * JOHN, Waterbury, s. of that John, under Scofield, 4 pages bef. m. 6 Feb. 1694, Hannah, d. of Obadiah Richards, had John, b. 12 Jan. foll. perhaps others; was constable, and rep. 1714. His w. d. 5 Mar. 1720; and he d. 26 Feb. 1727. WILLIAM, Haddam, sett. there soon aft. 1668, says Field, 65, to wh. Hinman, 231, adds, that he d. 1712. That may refer to first John. See Scofield, with wh. name I have been much embarrass. to disting. one from ano. and can but fear, that little success has foll. my perplexity.

SCRANTON, DENNIS, New Haven 1660, gave informat. perhaps rather minute, than trustworthy, about Whalley and Goffe, to Gov. Endicott's pursuivants in 1661. See Hutch. Coll. 335 for the curious docum. But they mistook the name, and should have writ. Crampton. JOHN, Guilford 1650, whose w. Joanna d. 1651, is among freem. of 1669. For sec. w. he took Adeline, wid. in 1663 of Robert Hill, as in 1661 she had been of Robert Johnson; but prob. had no ch. by her, and d. 27 Aug. 1671, leav. ch. Thomas, John, and Sarah; and his wid. d. 1685. Sarah m. 15 May 1665, John Bushnell. JOHN, Guilford, s. of the preced. m. Mary Seward, d. prob. of William of the same, had Mary, John, and Mehitable, was propound. for freem. 1670; and by sec. w. Eliz. Clark, perhaps d. of Thomas, had Mercy, b. 1688; Eliz. 4 Nov. 1692; Ann, 23 Dec. 1693; Ebenezer, 16 Mar. 1696; and Deborah, 3 Dec. 1697. John d. young; but other seven ch. were liv. 1703, at d. of the f. NATHANIEL, Guilford, may have been s. of Thomas of the same, and d. at Wethersfield, 13 Mar. 1693, in his will giv. prop. to William Goodrich, as Hinman, 232, tells; yet it is more prob. that there was no such Nathaniel S. and that the testator's name was Crampton. THOMAS, Guilford, s. of the first John, was propos. for freem. 1676, and next yr. accept.; had two ws. first, Deborah Thompson, wid. of Ebenezer, and sec. Eliz. Goodrich; but had only two ch. that grew up to mature life, Samuel, and Hannah.

SCRIBNER, or SCRIVENER, BENJAMIN, Norwalk, m. 5 Mar. 1680, Hannah, d. of John Crampton, had Thomas, b. 31 Mar. 1681; and John; perhaps others. JOHN, Exeter 1689. JOHN, Norwalk, s. of Benjamin, m. 9 Mar. 1710, Deborah, d. of William Lees of the same, had Mary, b. Mar. 1711; and Rebecca, 12 Oct. 1712.

SCRIPTURE, SAMUEL, Groton, by w. Eliz. had Samuel, b. 4 Oct. 1675; Mary, 7 Feb. 1681; Abigail, 28 Jan. 1687; Ruth, 2 Feb. 1697; and Lydia, 28 June 1700. SAMUEL, Groton, s. of the preced. by w. Mary had Sarah, b. 16 Dec. 1700; Jemima, 19 Apr. 1702, wh. d. at 21 yrs.; Samuel, 25 Apr. 1705, d. at 18 yrs.; and James, wh. d. 28 Sept. 1723. His w. d. 3 days bef. and by sec. w. Eliz. he had Samuel, again, 27 Apr. 1727.

SCRIVEN, SCREVEN, SCRIEVEN, or SCRIVINE, JOHN, Dover 1662, d. 2 Oct. 1675, says Quint, in Geneal. Reg. VIII. 65, tho. in the same l. he makes his will of 24 Nov. 1674, pro. 27 June foll. that date of its mak. not of his d. Some error, wh. is seldom found in so careful a writer, must here demand correct. It ment. w. Mary, and ch. John, Edward, Thomas, and Eliz. all minors. The d. perhaps m. 1686, Samuel Eastman. * WILLIAM, Kittery, had w. Bridget in 1680, was rep. 1681, found. of a Bapt. ch. there 1682, in wh. he was teacher, but aft. some yrs. went to South Carolina, and d. 1713, aged, as is said, 84.

SCROOP, ADRIAN, Hartford, witness to execut. of a deed of 31 Mar. 1665, and again, 8 May 1667 sign. as witness, his name, in a very elegant hand, to deed of Simon Wolcott to Richard Loud of three parcels of ld. wh. was put on rec. 3 days aft. yet no more is ever told of him. Curiosity to a high pitch naturally is felt on two points in this case, when did he come to our country, and what did he do aft. sign. that rare name. One Adrian Scrope, we kn. had been execut. in London, 17 Oct. 1660, for hav. sat on the pretend. trial of k. Charles I. and sign. the warrant for his d. In Noble's Regicides the rep. of his trial is very full, much more than most of the others. Strong prob. from union of such giv. name and surname arises, that this man was s. or near relat. of the regicide; and Dr. Stiles, in the latter part of his extraord. book relative to the three judges, that found shelter at New Haven, appeals to proof from hd.writ. in the fac-simile of the death warrant of Charles and the rec. of this deed at Hartford, for, strange as it seems, the attestation of the deed is by the witnesses on the rec. itself as well as on the docum. The Doctor's eye saw more than mine, and he appears almost satisf. with the identity of the writing, as if Col. Scrope were in person at H. six yrs. and a half aft. his head was cut off. Between 29 Jan. 1649, when he affix. his hd. and seal to that writ, order. the subord. officer at such an hour next day to put the k. to d. and this Hartford act 8 Mar. 1667, I would not affirm, that Col. Scrope's writing could not vary much, had not the solemn execution of the 17 Oct. 1660 interven. Stiles was a man of wonderful capacity of belief, and the estimate of his judgment in this matter is reduced by a mistake of the name of the other witness in this very docum. writ. Reeve, but by the President made Robert Pierce. Beside, the difference of names between the London sufferer, wh. used but one *o*, and our Hartford witness that doubled the letter, is not ment.

SCRUGGS, * THOMAS, Salem, came with the few companions of Endicott in the Abigail, 1628, says Felt, yet this relies solely on tradit. and might seem too early, for he did not take o. of freem. until 2 Sept. 1635; but he was esteem. eno. to be chos. to three Gen. Cts. next yr. also authoriz. with others to hold special Ct. for the vicinage, and was a selectman. But for his heretic. pravity he was next yr. supersed. and in Nov. disarm. as a danger. man, like the majority of Boston ch. I suppose he had w. Margery, and that he d. early in 1652; and that Felt mistook his name as if it were William; and that, as the wid. gave up to her s.-in-law John Raymond in June 1652 her est. in dower, she may have gone home, or perhaps was the woman that d. 26 Jan. 1663. See Hist. Coll. of Essex Inst. I. 11.

Scudder, James, Woburn, had Deborah, b. 26 July 1647, tho. the name is not clear. legib. and may be mistak. John, Charlestown 1639, came in the James from London, 1635, aged 16, was of Salem 1640 prob. for among memb. of ch. that yr. is Eliz. and he had Mary, bapt. 11 June 1648; Eliz. Mar. 1649; and Hannah, 19 Aug. of the same yr. In 1654 he rem. to Southold, as Felt assur. Farmer; yet Riker, wh. gives him s. Samuel, and John, makes the resid. bef. 1660, at Newtown, quite to the W. of his first habitat. John, Newtown, L. I. s. of the preced. m. Joanna, d. of capt. Richard Betts, had John, and d. 1732. John, Barnstable 1640, bore arms 1643, had a sis. Eliz. dism. from Boston ch. 10 Nov. 1644, with recommenda. and she m. 28 of the same Samuel Lothrop, s. of the Rev. John, at his f.'s house. He had, by w. whose name is not kn. ds. Eliz. and Sarah, bapt. 10 May 1646; Mary, bur. 3 Dec. 1649, prob. very young; and Hannah, bapt. 5 Oct. 1651, wh. m. 1 Dec. 1669, Joshua Bangs. John, Barnstable, perhaps s. of the preced. m. 31 July 1689, Eliz. d. of James Hamlin, had John, b. 23 May 1690, bapt. 6 Sept. 1691; Experience, b. 28 Apr. 1692; James, bapt. 13 Jan. 1695; Ebenezer, 23, bapt. 26 Apr. 1696; Reliance, 10 Dec. 1700, bapt. Feb. foll.; and Hannah, 7 June 1706. Samuel, Newtown, L. I. s. of the first John, m. Phebe, d. of Edmund Titus, had Samuel, and d. 1689; and his wid. m. next yr. Robert Field. Thomas, Salem, had gr. of ld. 1648, and, perhaps, w. Rachel that was adm. of the ch. 1649. But ano. w. Eliz. is nam. in his will of 30 Sept. 1657, pro. 29 June foll. and the ch. ment. are John, Thomas, Henry, William, and Eliz. perhaps w. of Henry Bartholomew, beside gr.s. Thomas, s. of dec. s. William. Thomas, Huntington, L. I. accept. as freem. of Conn. 1664. William, Salem, s. of Thomas, had gr. of ld. 1650.

Scullard, or Skullard, Samuel, Newbury 1637, at Hampton next yr. but soon back to N.; by w. Rebecca, d. of Richard Kent, had Mary, b. 9 Jan. 1642; Rebecca, 4 Feb. 1644; Sarah, 18 June 1645; and prob. the oldest ch. Martha d. 6 Mar. 1645; and he d. 1647. In Oct. of this yr. his wid. m. John Bishop, and his d. Mary m. 4 Dec. 1656, rather young, John Rolf.

Seaborn, or Sibborne, John, Boston. See Sebborn.

Seabrook, Robert, Stratford, had sev. ds. of wh. one m. William Preston, and one m. Thomas Fairchild; and much ld. he own. there, for in 1668 are rec. half a doz. persons' shares set off from gr.f. R. S. est.

Seabury, John, Boston, by w. Grace, wh. was adm. of the ch. 15 May 1642, had Samuel, b. 10 Dec. 1640, and no more on our rec. is seen, but prob. he had elder s. John, that went to Barbados, bef. d. of his f. Samuel, Duxbury, s. of the preced. m. at Weymouth, 9 Nov. 1660, Patience, d. of William Kemp of D. had Eliz. b. 16 Sept. 1661;

Sarah, 18 Aug. 1663; Samuel, 20 Apr. 1666; Hannah, 7 July 1668; John, 7 Nov. 1670, d. young; Grace and Patience, tw. 1 Mar. 1673, both d. soon; and his w. d. 29 Oct. 1676. He m. 4 Apr. 1677, Martha, d. of William Peabody, and had Joseph, 8 June 1678; Martha, 23 Sept. 1679; John, again, and a posthum. ch. and d. 5 Aug. 1681. For him and br. John est. in Boston of their f. John, claim was made 16 Apr. 1662, as may be read in Vol. III. 523 of our regist. of deeds.

SEAGER, SEEGER, or SEGER, HENRY, Newton, m. Apr. 1671, Sarah Bishop, had Job, b. 1 Feb. 1675, d. young; Sarah, 2 Mar. 1677; Ebenezer, 2 May 1679; Eliz. 28 Jan. 1683; Henry, 25 Sept. 1686; Mary, 31 Jan. 1690; Job, again, 1691; Margaret, 22 Aug. 1692; Mercy; Thankful, 24 Apr. 1695; but the order may be uncert. for one or two. He had sec. w. Eliz. and m. third, 1709, Sarah Wheeler of Dedham. Ebenezer was k. by the Ind. 21 July 1706, at Groton. Butler, in Hist. 96, gives the name Leger, but that is only mistake of the author's handwrit. by the print. LAWRENCE, came to Boston in the James from Southampton, 1635, a youth of 17, and no more is kn. of him. RICHARD, Hartford 1650, had Eliz. b. in June of that yr.; also had Richard, John, and Ebenezer, wh. was drown. 1669. He was adm. freem. of Conn. May 1657, and may have been of Stonington, for a goodw. S. is ment. in 1668, as adher. of the jurisdict. of R. I. and the Conn. (Stonington) freem. of 1669 has not his name. His w. Eliz. was indict. 1663 for "familiarity with Sathan," and practis. witchcr. but tho. the jury found her in Mar. guilty of the familiarity, the wiser Ct. set her free in May 1666, "the verdict of the jury not answer. to the indictm. legally." Aft. this prob. the fam. rem. to R. I. where, I presume, the devil had less power or impudence. To Eliz. S. in his will of 25 July 1655, John Moody of Hartford gave £25., and it may be suppos. therefore, that the mo. of this ch. was his sis. The time of his d. is unkn. RICHARD, Windsor 1672, perhaps s. of the preced. rem. bef. 1683, to Simsbury, where he d. 14 Mar. 1698. Next mo. at the pro. office his ch. were nam. Eliz. aged 14; John, 12; Joseph, 7; and Abigail, 1.

SEAILES, JAMES, Rowley, freem. 1684.

SEALE, EDWARD, Salem or Marblehead 1638. See Sale.

SEALIS, or SELLICE (as Lothrop writes it) RICHARD, Scituate 1635, by first w. whose name is unkn. had ds. b. in Eng. Hannah, wh. m. 15 Oct. 1638, John Winchester of Hingham, and Esther, wh. m. 20 Nov. 1639, Samuel Jackson; join. the ch. 24 Dec. 1637, was deac. m. sec. w. Eglin Hanford, that had twice been wid. mo. of Rev. Thomas H. and sis. of good Timothy Hatherly, the founder of the town; and d. prob. 1656, at least his inv. is of 26 Mar. in that yr. but the date of his will 17 Sept. 1653. In that he gave, beside his own ds. to Eglin H. d. of his w.

SEAMAN, CALEB, New Haven 1646, rem. soon. JOHN, Wethersfield, rem. to Stamford 1641, and thence in few yrs.

SEARCH, JOHN, Boston, a weaver, adm. inhab. 3 May 1641, of the ch. 19 Sept. foll. as was his w. Catharine, 29 Jan. next, freem. 18 May 1642, and liv. 1662. Ano. w. Ann, says Farmer, d. 11 May 1674, in 85th yr.

SEARLE, ANDREW, Ipswich, or Rowley, perhaps both, b. it is said, a. 1616, was of Kittery 1668, there clk. of the writs, went back to R. and there d. 7 Nov. 1670. ANDREW, Kittery, prob. s. of the preced. dwelt there 1674, 6, and aft. DANIEL, Boston, a gent. of large est. m. Deliverance, d. of Edward Tyng, had Daniel, b. 29 Oct. 1666, bapt. 2 June foll. d. young; and Samuel, b. 16 Oct. 1668; rem. to Barbados 1669, where, I suppose, his prop. lay. He is scrupulous. call. Col. or Esq. both in rec. of town and ch. and in priv. corresp. Gov. EDWARD, Warwick, m. wid. Joan White, sis. of Edmund Calverly, had Edward, and was liv. 1679. A s. of his w. by her former h. went home prob. to Eng. EDWARD, Warwick, s. of the preced. m. 21 Feb. 1671, Ann, wid. of John Lippit the sec. rem. to Cranston, and prob. had a fam. as the name there is com. EPHRAIM, Boston, freem. 1672, was a lieut. JOHN, Springfield, m. 19 Mar. 1639, Sarah Baldwin, had John, b. 30 Mar. 1641; and d. 11 Aug. foll. His wid. m. 28 Apr. next, Alexander Edwards; his will, of 21 Dec. 1640, being pro. 8 days bef. this m. JOHN, Boston, m. 16 Nov. 1661, Catharine Warner, wid. perhaps of Thomas, had John, b. 19 Nov. 1664; may have rem. 1668 to Dover, or been of Stonington 1670, freem. of Conn. 1673, yet not join. to ch. bef. 1677. JOHN, Northampton, s. of the first John, m. 3 July 1667, Ruth, d. of William Jones, wh. d. 20 Nov. 1672, had a ch. that d. 25 Mar. 1668, without name on the rec.; John, b. 11 Mar. foll. wh. d. in few days; John, again, 6 Aug. 1670; beside ano. b. the day of its mo.'s d. wh. d. very soon. Sec. w. Mary, d. of John North, he took 10 or 30 May 1675, had James, 12 Feb. 1676; Mary, a. 1678; Ebenezer, 9 Jan. 1680; Ruth, 17 Dec. 1681; Sarah, 28 Feb. 1684; Nathaniel, 3 May 1686; Lydia, 22 Aug. 1688; was freem. 1690, and d. 3 Oct. 1718. His wid. d. 5 Nov. 1726. RICHARD, Providence 1638. ROBERT, Dorchester, adm. an inhab. 9 June 1662, by w. Deborah, wh. d. 2 Mar. 1714, had Nathaniel, b. 9 June 1662; Salter, 26 June 1664; Esbon, 24 Feb. 1669, d. young; Robert, 2 July 1671; Esbon, again, 18 Mar. 1674; Deborah, 4 Apr. 1677; and Jabez, 13 Mar. 1679, was town clk. Blake says, 16 yrs. and d. 7 Feb. 1717. WILLIAM, Kittery, perhaps br. of the first Andrew, may have been the town clk. instead of A. WILLIAM, Rowley 1689, prob. s. of the preced. by w. Deborah had William, b. 1690. Of this name, in 1829, two had been gr. at Harv. two at Yale, and six at other N. E. coll.

SEARS, DANIEL, Boston, mariner, had w. Mary, on whose d. when he was abroad, admin. was giv. Feb. 1652 to John Sunderland for him. JOHN, Woburn, had been of Charlestown 1639, and was one of the earliest at W. 1640, freem. 2 June 1641 ; had first w. Susanna, wh. was adm. of the ch. 2 Feb. 1640, and d. at W. 29 Aug. 1677 ; and in less than three mos. he m. Esther Mason, wh. d. 14 Aug. 1680, and 80 days aft. he m. Ann, wid. of the first Jacob Farrar ; but he had no ch. Early as 1654 he was engag. in E. settlem. and next yr. sold Long isl. in the beautiful bay of Casco. KNYVETT, Yarmouth, s. thot. to be eldest, of Richard of the same, m. Eliz. Dimmock, perhaps d. of Thomas of Barnstable, had Daniel, and d. in Eng. 1686, says fam. tradit. PAUL, Yarmouth, br. of the preced. m. Deborah Willard, prob. d. of George of Scituate, and d. 1707. RICHARD, Yarmouth, said, in fam. tradit. to have come to Plymouth 1630, there, certain. was tax. 1633, and Felt gives him gr. of ld. 1638 at Salem ; but there he did not long stop, if he ever liv. ; by w. Dorothy had Knyvett, b. 1635 ; Paul, 1637 ; and Silas, 1639, prob. others ; and d. 1676. Deborah, prob. his d. m. 1659, Zechariah Paddock. * SILAS, Yarmouth, s. perhaps youngest, of the preced. had Thomas, b. 1664 ; Hannah, Dec. 1672 ; liv. then at Eastham, and prob. had other ch. ; was rep. 1685, 6, and, aft. the over-throw of Andros, 1689, 90, and 1, and d. by fam. tradit. 1697. THOM-AS, Newbury, m. 11 Dec. 1656, says Coffin, Mary Hilton, alias Downer, wh. I do not understand, had Mary, b. 30 Oct. 1657; and Rebecca, posthum. 5 Nov. 1661 ; and he d. 16 or 26 May preced.

SEAVER, CALEB, Roxbury, s. of Robert of the same, m. 15 Dec. 1671, Sarah Inglesby, or Ingoldsby, wh. d. 31 Jan. 1709, had Caleb, b. 31 Mar. 1673 ; Eliz. 20 Jan. 1676 ; Nathaniel, 6 Oct. 1677, d. at 11 yrs.; Nicholas, 15 Apr. 1680, H. C. 1701 ; Thomas, 10 Mar. 1682 ; Sarah, 1 Aug. 1686; and d. 6 Mar. 1713. JOSHUA, Roxbury, tw. br. of the preced. m. 28 Feb. 1678, Mary, wid. of Joseph Pepper, had Joshua, b. 18 Feb. 1679 ; and Mary, 29 Mar. 1683 ; and his w. d. 22 May foll. ; and by ano. w. Mary, had Mary, 15 Aug. 1684 ; and Eben-ezer, 1 Aug. 1687 ; was freem. 1690. NATHANIEL, Roxbury, br. of the preced. had John, b. 18 Aug. 1671 ; and Sarah, wh. d. soon ; and he fell at Sudbury fight, 21 Apr. 1676. ROBERT, Roxbury, took o. of suprem. 24 Mar. 1634, at London, and came in the Mary and John that yr. and here m. 10 Dec. foll. Eliz. Allard as the town rec. says, call. Ballard in ch. rec. (unless we should read Bullard), had Shubael, b. 31 Jan. 1640 ; Caleb, and Joshua, 31 Aug. 1641 ; wh. all were bapt. no doubt, since f. and mo. were memb. of the ch. but the earliest bapt. on its rec. is of 26 Dec. 1641 ; Eliz. bapt. 19 Nov. 1643 ; Nathaniel, 8 Feb. 1646 ; Hannah, 6 Feb. 1648, d. soon ; and Hannah, again, 13 Oct.

1650, wh. d. at 3 yrs.; and his w. d. 6 June 1657. Ano. w. d. 1669 and he d. 13 May 1683, aged 74. SHUBAEL, Roxbury, s. of the preced. m. 7 Feb. 1669, Hannah, d. of Nathaniel Wilson, had Robert, b. 7 June 1670; Joseph, 1 June 1672; Hannah, 1 Sept. 1674; Abigail, 23 July 1677; Shubael, 10 Oct. 1679; and Thankful, 6 Apr. 1684. His w. d. 13 Feb. 1722, and he d. 18 Jan. 1730, aged 90, the gr.st. says. Oft. this name was writ. without *a*, and Hon. Nicholas and Hon. William were by Farmer call. of this fam. but I see not evid. Nine of this name had been gr. at Harv. in 1818, and one at Dart.

SEAVERNS, SEAVERN, or SEBORN, ‖ JOHN, Boston, tailor, by w. Mary had Eliz. b. 21 Oct. 1642, bapt. in Aug. 1644, when the mo. join. the ch.; Mary, 15, bapt. 22 Sept. 1644; Deborah, 26 Feb. 1646, bapt. 11 Mar. foll. d. in few days; was of ar. co. 1654. SAMUEL, Charlestown, m. 23 Feb. 1666, Sarah, d. of Christopher Grant, was a mariner, sold his ld. in Boston 1672; but no more of him is kn. SAMUEL, Watertown, brot. from Eng. prob. by a wid. mo. wh. offer. him to bapt. 28 Nov. 1686, m. 20 Dec. 1699, Rebecca, d. of John Stratton, had Eliz. b. 20 Oct. 1700; Sarah, 19 Jan. 1703; Samuel, July 1706; Rebecca, 21 Feb. 1710; and Abigail, 7 Mar. 1712; and he d. 10 Nov. 1714. Eliz. m. 23 Oct. 1719, Jonas Warren; and Rebecca m. 6 May 1730, Peter Ball.

SEAVY, JOHN, Portsmouth, perhaps s. of William, m. 29 July 1686, Hannah, wid. of Joseph Walker, d. of John Philbrook of Hampton. NATHANIEL, and THOMAS, were, perhaps, brs. of the preced. and unit. with him and f. in praying, 1690, for jurisdict. of Mass. THOMAS, Newcastle, N. H. perhaps br. of the preced. at Isle of Shoals in 1663, d. 15 Mar. 1708. WILLIAM, Portsmouth, one of the comp. by Mason sent over in 1631, was constable at Isle of Shoals 1655, much engag. in the fishery, and selectman 1657, and d. 1671. His prop. was large, by inv. of 13 Dec. amount. to £631, 7, 8, and in Apr. foll. his wid. Eliz. had admin.

SEBBORN, SIBBORNE, SEBORNE, or SEABORN, JOHN, Boston, by w. Mary, wh. join. our ch. 10 Aug. 1644, had Eliz. bapt. next day; Mary, 22 Sept. foll. a. 7 days old; and Deborah, 1 May 1646, a. 4 days old.

SECCOMB, PETER, Medford, perhaps s. of the first Richard, m. 25 Feb. 1702, Hannah Willis, d. of Stephen, had Willis, b. 30 Apr. 1704, d. under 21 yrs.; John, 30 July 1706, d. next yr.; John, again, 25 Apr. 1708, H. C. 1728, min. of Harvard; Charles, 15 Jan. 1710, d. under 21 yrs.; Thomas, 16 Aug. 1711; and Joseph, H. C. 1731, min. of Kingston, a celebr. wit; and d. 8 Sept. 1756. His wid. d. 15 Dec. 1760. RICHARD, Lynn 1660, d. 1694, had Noah; Richard; Peter, b. 1678; and Susanna. RICHARD, Medford, s. prob. of the preced. by w.

Ann had Jonathan, b. 17 Sept. 1710; Ann, 17 Sept. 1712; and Dorothy, 24 Jan. 1715. THOMAS, br. prob. of the preced. m. Rebecca, d. of Stephen Willis, may have liv. at Lynn.

* ‖ SEDGWICK, ROBERT, Charlestown 1636, prob. came 1635 in the Truelove, aged 24, tho. in the custom-ho. rec. the name appears Jo. inst. of Ro. join. the ch. with w. Joanna, on 27 Feb. 1637, and was made freem. 9 Mar. foll. when he was appoint. capt. for the town by our Ct. and chos. next mo. rep. and aft. for sixteen Cts. more. His neighb. capt. Edward Johnson, in Wonder work. Provid. c. 26 of book ii., the most valua. of that curious vol. assures us, that he was "nurst up in London's Artil. garden;" and our rec. show, that he was one of the found. of our art. co. 1638, its capt. 1640, command. of the castle 1641, head of the regim. of Middlesex 1643, and last. maj.-gen. of the Col. soon aft. call. by O. Cromwell to milit. serv. with John Leverett (aft. our Gov.) for his sec. and bef. long time sent to Jamaica, recent. conquer. There he d. 24 May 1656. Joanna, the Gen.'s wid. was liv. 1667 at Stepney, near London. By her he had Samuel, bapt. 31 Mar. 1639; and Hannah, 14 Mar. 1641; beside William, and Robert, wh. prob. were his ch. and Sarah, b. certain. in Eng. as may have been these s. Certainty is beyond our reach, bec. the rec. of town is imperfect, and the ch. rec. of bapt. from 20 Sept. 1642 to 4 July 1658 is a total. sad blank space. Our Charlestown soldier, in letters of Nov. 1655, pray. leave to come from Jamaica to London, recommends his w. and five ch. to the kindness of the Lord Protector, and we have only to regret, that his pathetic appeal was disregard. Frothingham, 135-9, is copious and correct. Sarah bec. sec. w. of Gov. Leverett. Whether she were sis. or d. might be disput. and this point that Mather ought to have elucidat. is confus. by him. Yet high is the prob. if her d. 2 Jan. 1705 is accomp. with correct statem. that she was 74 yrs. old, that she was b. in Eng. and was eldest ch. of the disting. soldier. ROBERT, Charlestown, s. of the preced. as confident. is presum. b. prob. in Eng. by w. Sarah had William, b. 9 June 1676; and Sarah, 19 Dec. 1677. He d. on a return voyage from Jamaica, leav. trifl. est. of wh. admin. was giv. to his wid. Sarah, 26 Apr. 1683. SAMUEL, br. of the preced. was of Charlestown not long, but chief. liv. at London, had w. Eliz. prob. hoped to obt. some reward for serv. of his f. but long bef. his m. he was witness to the will, 17 June 1657, of Jonathan Wade of our Ipswich, then at L. and it is curious, that his signature was pro. in Eng. by his wid. 1 Dec. 1683, then aged only 33 yrs. and she says he was her h. six yrs. "Citizen and clothworker of London," he calls hims. in a deed of 20 May 1667, whereby he sold his ho. and ld. in C. to Francis Willoughby. SAMUEL, Hartford, only ch. of William of the same, m. 1689, Mary, d.

of Stephen Hopkins of the same, had Samuel, b. 22 Aug. 1690; Jonathan, 29 Mar. 1693; Ebenezer, 25 Feb. 1695; Joseph, 16 May 1697; Stephen, 17 Mar. 1701; Abigail, 23 Feb. 1703; Mary, 1 July 1705; William, 29 June 1707; Eliz. 10 Dec. 1708; Thankful, 3 Nov. 1710, d. under 10 yrs.; Mercy, 18 Jan. 1713; and Benjamin, 7 Nov. 1716; and d. 24 Mar. 1735. His wid. d. 4 Sept. 1743. He was gr.f. of the Hon. Theodore, speaker of the Ho. of Rep. in Congr. of the U. S. a. 65 yrs. since, and aft. a judge of S. J. C. in Mass. and progenit. of many amiab. and disting. writers that have adorn. the name in our country. WILLIAM, Hartford, s. of the first Robert, may have been b. in Eng. m. Eliz. youngest d. of Rev. Samuel Stone, had Samuel, b. 1667; but he had prob. been ruin. in morals by serv. in the army of Eng. and aft. many yrs. of abandonm. of his w. as she alleg. in petitn. for div. May 1673, the Gen. Ct. of Conn. Oct. 1674, releas. her from the "unchristian bondage." She m. John Roberts, but tho. she had s. John, was not much better sort. with the new h. yet liv. with him, 1695, on L. I. Of S. little more is kn. exc. that he sold, 7 Sept. 1668, all right in est. of his f. to Francis Willoughby. Yet an obscure report was circulat. that he d. on return from the W. I. to Boston.

SEDLEY, JAMES, was, says Farmer, early sett. at Weymouth; but I kn. nothing of him.

SEELEY, JOHN, Isle of Shoals 1647, was, perhaps, aft. at Newbury. JOHN, Fairfield, perhaps s. of Robert, m. bef. 1691, Sarah, d. of George Squire. NATHANIEL, New Haven 1646, s. of Robert, m. at Fairfield, 1649, or earlier, Mary, d. of Benjamin Turney, rem. to F. was freem. 1657; m. sec. w. late in 1674, or early next yr. Eliz. wid. of Obadiah Gilbert, former. wid. of Nehemiah Olmstead, serv. as lieut. in Philip's war, 1675, and was k. at the head of his comp. in the gr. swamp fight, 19 Dec. A gr. was made next yr. to his wid. Nine ch. all, I presume, by first w. were left, Nathaniel, Robert, Benjamin, Joseph, John, Mary, Sarah, Phebe, and Rebecca. OBADIAH, Stamford, prob. s. of Robert, m. the wid. of John Miller of S. but d. 1657, leav. wid. and ch. Obadiah, Cornelius, and Jonas. ROBERT, Watertown, prob. came in the fleet with Winth. for his req. of adm. was in Oct. 1630, and he took the o. of freem. 18 May foll. was employ. as surveyor 1634, and in 1636 rem. to Wethersfield, was next yr. a lieut. in the Pequot war, perhaps short time at New Haven 1639, and in 1646 had leave to go home, but in few yrs. was again here, and in 1654 led the force of N. H. rais. for serv. under Sedgwick and Leverett against the neighb. prov. of New Netherlands, that was happi. prevent. by restor. of peace in Europe. He was at Saybrook 1662, Stratford 1663, and the same yr. at Huntington, on L. I. in the head of the milit. but at New York aft. its conq. and

there d. His wid. Mary had admin. 19 Oct. 1668. WILLIAM, Isle of
Shoals, perhaps br. of John of the same, was of gr. jury 1656, d. at
Saco, 1672, says Folsom, 188, wh. tells, that his d. Emma m. John Ruel,
and Dorcas m. James Gibbins, jr. in 1668.

SEKER, or SECKER, HENRY, a youth of 8 yrs. wh. came in the Speedwell from London, arr. at Boston 27 July 1656, perhaps was he that
sett. at Newton with name of Seager.

SELDEN, or SELDON, JOSEPH, Hadley, s. of Thomas the first, m.
1677, Rebecca Church, d. of deac. Edward of Hatfield, had Rebecca, b.
1678; Esther, 1680, d. next yr.; Joseph, 1682; rem. to Deerfield, there
had Thomas, 1684; and Hannah; but in few yrs. was back at Hadley,
and had Mary, 5 Mar. 1689; Esther, again, 2 May 1691; Samuel, 17
May 1695; rem. once more to Lyme, there purchas. large est. and
part. in Haddam, had Sarah, bapt. 20 July 1712; and d. bef. 1 Feb.
1725, when this est. was div. by their own act to three s. Joseph and
Thomas of H. and Samuel of L. with five ds. Rebecca, w. of James
Wells; Mercy, w. of Isaac Spencer; Esther, w. of Jabez Chapman;
Hannah, w. of Daniel Brainard, all of H. and Sarah Selden of L.
THOMAS, Hartford 1639, freem. 1640, had Thomas, bapt. 31 Aug.
1645; John, wh. d. May 1650; Mary, 26 Mar. 1648 or 9; Esther, 3
Mar. 1650, d. next yr.; Joseph, 2 Nov. 1651; Hannah; and Sarah;
and d. bef. the end of 1655. His will, of 14 Aug. names wid. Esther,
wh. m. Andrew Warner, and all the five ch. rem. to Hadley. The mo.
d. 1693; Hannah, infirm, d. 1695; and Mary m. 12 Dec. 1666, John
Taylor. THOMAS, Hadley, s. of the preced. m. Felix, d. of William
Lewis the sec. of Farmington, had John, b. 16 June 1675; Thomas, 12
Nov. 1677, wh. was k. on that terrib. 29 Feb. 1704, at Deerfield; and
Ebenezer, 2 Mar. 1679 or 80; and d. at honora. age, 24 Nov. 1734.
His wid. was liv. 1738. Sometimes this name, of wh. twelve had been
gr. at Yale, two at Dart. none at Harv. in 1848, is seen under pervers.
as Selding.

SELLAN, or SELLEN, THOMAS, Ipswich, allow. as inhab. by the Gen.
Ct. 11 June 1633, tho. they had order, 1 Apr. preced. that no person
should go to plant there exc. those already gone. Possib. he rem. bef.
1638 to Braintree, at least no more at I. can be heard of him; and at B.
a rec. of d. is seen, 3 Dec. 1642, of Thomas Sellein, wh. may seem to
be this man.

SELLOCK, SELLICK, SILLECK, or SELLECK, DAVID, Boston, soapboiler, by w. Susanna had David, b. 11 Dec. 1638; Jonathan, 20 May
1641; John, 21, bapt. 23 Apr. 1643; Nathaniel, 18, bapt. 27 July
1645; Joanna, 11 Dec. 1647; Eliz. 1 Feb. 1652; and Susanna, 1653,
wh. d. soon; and he d. 1654, in Virg. His inv. of 6 Dec. in that yr.

shows fair est. in sum, yet very little beyond debts. DAVID, Boston, merch. eldest s. of the preced. trad. to Barbados 1663. JOHN, Stamford, br. of the preced. freem. 1670, was rich and enterpris. master of a vessel to Eng. tak. May 1689 by the French, and never came home, yet his est. was not administ. bef. 5 Mar. 1700. By w. Sarah, d. of Richard Law, he had Sarah, b. 22 Aug. 1669; David, 27 Dec. 1672; Nathaniel, 7 Apr. 1678; John, 7 June 1681; Susanna, 2 Feb. 1683; and Joanna, 31 May 1686. His wid. d. 8 Nov. 1732. * JONATHAN, Stamford, elder br. of the preced. m. Abigail, d. of Richard Law, had Jonathan, b. 11 July 1664; David, 27 Jan. 1666; and John, H. C. 1690, but he and the other ch. with the mo. all d. bef. the f. wh. d. 10 Jan. 1713. By his will he gave "the Latin, Greek, and Hebrew books" to Rev. John Davenport, wh. had m. 1695, Martha, the wid. of his s. John, d. of Nathan Gould. He had been active in business, was innholder 1665, freem. 1667, lieut. capt. and at last major, rep. 1670, and again 1675. NATHANIEL, Boston, youngest br. of the preced. was apprent. to David Evans, wh. in his will of 30 June 1663, left him £10. if he faithful. discharg. his indent. My conject. is, that this is the name giv. as Lellock by the careless penman wh. copied the book used as a rec. of births in Boston bef. 1690.

SELMAN, JOHN, Pemaquid, took o. of fidel. to Mass. 1674.

SEMOND, WILLIAM, Boston, by w. Ann, d. of George Barrell, had Hannah, b. Sept. 1640, wh. is nam. in the will of gr.f. B.

SENDALL, SAMUEL, Boston, first was at Newbury, as in his will he says, " Edward Rawson brot. me into this country." By w. Joanna had Joanna, bapt. 21 Sept. 1651, wh. m. John Hunlock; and Mary, b. 13 Mar. 1653, wh. d. young. Ano. w. Eliz. in his will of 29 Sept. 1684, pro. 8 Oct. next, describ. as " singular. comfortable, and good w. and yokefellow," was provid. for by the contract of m. 4 Oct. 1684; yet he gave something to her and also to her d. Abigail W. tho. most, of course, to his d. Hunlock and ch. The wid. had been third w. of John Warren, and found ano. h. in John Hayward, the notary, and a fourth in Phineas Wilson of Hartford.

SENDEN, SAMUEL, Marblehead, a petitnr. 1668, against imposts, freem. 1684.

SENNOT. See Sinnett.

SENSION, SENTION, SENCHION, or ST. JOHN, JAMES, Norwalk, s. prob. of the first Matthew, m. 31 Dec. 1673, Rebecca, d. of John Picket of Stratford, propound. as freem. 1674, d. prob. bef. 1688, yet may have had sev. ch. * MARK, Norwalk, s. of Matthew the first, suppos. eldest, perhaps b. in Eng. m. Eliz. youngest d. of Timothy Stanley, had Eliz. b. 6 Dec. 1656; Sarah, 18 Jan. 1659; perhaps others; was freem. 1664, constable 1669, rep. 1672. He took sec. w. prob. in Jan. 1693, Dorothy, wid. of Francis Hall, d. of Rev. Henry Smith, and had been wid. of John Blakeman; and d. 12 Aug. foll. For her fourth h. the wid. took deac. Isaac Moore, first of Farmington, aft. of Norwalk. MATTHEW, or MATTHIAS, Dorchester 1634, freem. 3 Sept. of that yr. rem. prob. in 1638 to Windsor, was one of the first sett. at Norwalk, a. 1654, there d. 1669, aft. 11 Oct. the date of certific. by the constable (wh. was his s..Mark), mak. return of the freem. of the town. Beside him, he left Matthew, Samuel, James, and sev. ds. MATTHEW, Norwalk, s. of the preced. in 1672 had sev. ch. of wh. one was Matthew, and he, I believe, gave the same name to one in the fourth generat. NICHOLAS, Windsor, thot. to be younger br. of the first Matthew, came, at the age of 13, in the Elizabeth and Ann from London, 1635, was of W. in 1640, so that we may suppose, he had been at Dorchester, and rem. with him. He was adm. freem. 1657, and d. 1689, leav. no ch. SAMUEL, Norwalk, br. of James, m. Sept. 1663, Eliz. d. of Walter Haite, had Sarah, b. Jan. 1665, wh. d. at 20 yrs.; Thomas, Oct. 1666; and Eliz. Apr. 1673; was propound. for freem. 1667, and d. 14 Jan. 1684.

SENTER, JOHN, Boston, m. 27 Mar. 1651, Mary Muzzey, possib. mean. Matthews.

SESSIONS, ALEXANDER, Andover, freem. 1677, m. 24 Apr. 1672, Eliz. d. prob. of John Spofford of Rowley, had John, b. 1674; Alexander; Timothy; Samuel; Nehemiah; Josiah; and Joseph; and d. 26 Feb. 1689.

SEVER. See Seaver.

SEVERANCE, oft. writ. SEVERNS, as sound. EPHRAIM, Salisbury, s. of John, m. 9 Nov. 1682, Lydia, d. of Abraham Morrill, had Abigail, b. 29 Aug. 1683; Mary, 2 July 1685; Lydia, 15 Jan. 1687; Ephraim, 2 Dec. 1689; Dinah, 3 Sept. 1692; Ebenezer, 9 Nov. 1694; Sarah, 7 Feb. 1698; and Jonathan, 21 Apr. 1700. JOHN, Salisbury, one of the orig. proprs. freem. 17 May 1637, bef. that town was sett.; by first w. Abigail had Samuel, b. 19 Sept. 1637, wh. d. young; Ebenezer, 7 Mar. 1639 (wh. d. 1667, unm. in his will of 22 Aug. 1665 giv. three brs. and two sis. all his est.); Abigail, 7 Jan. 1641, d. in few wks.; Abigail, again, 25 May 1643; Mary, 5 Aug. 1645; John, 24 Nov. 1647; Joseph, 14 Feb. 1650; Eliz. 8 Apr. 1652, d. soon; Benjamin, Jan. 1654; Eliz. again, 17 June 1658, d. at four yrs.; and his w. d. 17 June 1658, as did a tw. d. five days aft. His sec. w. was Susanna, wid. of Henry Ambrose, and he d. 9 Apr. 1682, hav. made his will two days bef. Mary m. Dec. 1663, James Coffin of Nantucket. JOHN, Salisbury, s. of the preced. by w. Mary had Ebenezer, b. 19 Sept. 1673; Abigail, 6 May 1675; John, 22 Sept. 1676; and Daniel, 3 June 1678; rem. to

Suffield, there had Mary, 14 July 1681; and Joseph, 26 Oct. 1682; rem. to Deerfield, where Abigail d. 1691, and Daniel was k. by the Ind. 1694; and he rem. to Bedford bef. 1709, giv. his D. lds. to s. Joseph.

SEWALL, or SEWELL, EDWARD, Exeter 1677, d. 1684. HENRY, Newbury 1635, had liv. 1623 at Manchester, Eng. it is said, as also that he was eldest s. of Henry, Mayor of Coventry, and bapt. 8 Apr. 1576. His w. Coffin calls Ann Hunt, but in Col. rec. her name is Ellen, and his only ch. was Henry, old eno. to be sent over a yr. bef. his f. but perhaps he was s. of an earlier w. than this brot. from Eng. No doubt the s. would better have been pleas. had the f. contin. at home, for he was dissatisf. with every body and thing, soon separat. from his w. disturb. the ch. of Ipswich bef. he mov. to N. thence he rem. to Rowley, there d. 1657, more than 80 yrs. old. That he was insane, is the natur. conclusion, and the acts of governm. were injudic. See Col. Rec. I. 163, 233, and 286, beside the full relat. in Coffin, 61. HENRY, Newbury, only s. of the preced. came, at the age of 20, in the Elizabeth Dorcas, 1634, was first at Ipswich, but with early sett. went to N. next yr.; m. 25 Mar. 1646, Jane, eldest ch. of Stephen Dummer, had gone home with f. and mo. of his w. and resid. short time at Warwick, next at Tunworth, 4 miles from Basingstoke, in Hants, where was b. his first ch. Hannah, 10 May 1649, and near B. had Samuel, 28 Mar. 1652, bapt. there 4 May foll. H. C. 1671, the venerab. Ch. J. Bef. the rite was solemniz. Rashley, wh. had, a doz. yrs. earlier, been a memb. of our Boston ch. preach. a sermon, tho. it was on a Tuesday, as in his autobiog. the Judge delights to tell. Rem. to Baddesly, in the same shire, a. 4 miles from Rumsey, he had John, 10 Oct. 1654, bapt. Wednesday, 22 Nov. foll.; Stephen, 10 Aug. 1657; and Jane, 25 Oct. 1659. He had, however, made ano. voyage to N. E. to look aft. his f. and bef. the b. of this last nam. ch. came on his third visit, and next yr. sent for his fam. The w. with her five ch. land. at Boston, July 1661, aft. six wks. pass. in the Prudent Mary, capt. Woodgreen, and all were carr. five days aft. to N. There he had Ann, 3 Sept. 1662; Mehitable, 8 May 1665; and Dorothy, 29 Oct. 1668. He was a min. in Eng. but I do not so mark him, for he never officiat. here; but a let. to our Gov. from the Lord Protector, Richard, the wiser son of Oliver, during his brief exalta. 23 Mar. 1659, fully proves it; and grow. from personal acquaint. it is well worth perus. in Hutch. I. appx. xii. He d. 16 May 1700, and his wid. d. 13 Jan. foll. Near all that have borne the name in our land are descend. Hannah m. 24 Aug. 1670, Jacob Toppan, and d. 12 Nov. 1699; Jane m. 24 Sept. 1677, Moses Gerrish, and d. 29 Jan. 1717; Ann m. 10 Nov. 1678, William Longfellow, and next, Henry Short, had both Longfellows and Shorts; Mehitable m. 15 Nov. 1684, William

Moody, and d. 8 Aug. 1702; and Dorothy m. 10 Sept. 1691, Ezekiel
Northend. HENRY, Newbury, s. of John, m. 1 Jan. 1707, Eliz. d. of
Benaiah Titcomb, had Sarah, b. 20 Sept. 1708, d. soon; Stephen, H. C.
1731; Sarah, again, 21 Aug. 1711; Mary, 25 Aug. 1713; Eliz. 4 Aug.
1715; and Hannah; and d. 29 June 1760. JOHN, Newbury, s. of
Henry the sec. b. in Eng. m. 27 Oct. 1671, Hannah Fessenden of
Cambridge, prob. sis. of the first Nicholas, had Hannah, b. 21 Dec.
1675, d. soon; Hannah, again, 26 Dec. 1677, wh. m. Rev. Samuel
Moody of York; John, 10 Apr. 1680; Henry, 7 Sept. 1682; Stephen,
17 Jan. 1685; Samuel, 9 Apr. 1688; Nicholas, and a tw. ch. wh. d.
soon, 1 June 1690; and Thomas, 5 Mar. 1693, wh. d. at coll. 18 July
1716, as by Harris's Epit. 52. He d. 8 Aug. 1699, and his wid. m.
Jacob Toppan, wh. had been h. of the sis. of her h. and d. 4 Apr. 1723.
JOHN, Newbury, s. of the preced. m. Esther, d. of Rev. Michael
Wigglesworth, had prob. no ch. and d. 25 Feb. 1712. His wid. m. 21
Oct. 1713, Abraham Toppan. JONATHAN, Boston, merch. s. of the first
Stephen, d. in early life, but was f. of that Jonathan, disting. as adher. of
the royal cause in 1774, author of Massachusettensis, whose mo. was his
sec. w. Mary Payne; by her also he had two ds. and by his first w.
Eliz. Alford, d. prob. of Benjamin, wh. d. 11 Sept. 1723, had two ds.
and d. Nov. 1731. JOSEPH, Boston, s. of Samuel the first, ord. 16 Sept.
1713, collea. with Rev. Ebenezer Pemberton at the O. S. ch. m. 29 Oct.
foll. Eliz. d. of Hon. John Walley, had Samuel, b. 2, bapt. 8 May 1715,
H. C. 1733; Joseph, 13, bapt. 19 July 1719, d. next mo. That Samuel
was f. of the excellent Samuel, b. 11 Dec. 1757, H. C. 1776, the third
Ch. J. giv. by this fam. to the Ct. of highest civ. and crim. jurisdict. in
Mass. His w. d. 27 Oct. 1756, and he d. 27 June 1769, aft. hav. the
opportunity for declin. 1724, to be Presid. of H. C. the honor of wh.
election was ascrib. to his *piety* by a competitor of more learning than
decency or discretion, who solaced his mortificat. in defeat by the
happiness of his sneer. MITCHELL, Salem, br. of Jonathan, m. 10
May 1729, Mary, d. of John Cabot, had Catharine, Margaret, and
Mary; and by sec. w. m. 10 June 1743, Eliz. Price, had Eliz. Stephen,
and Jonathan M. NATHANIEL, Newbury, a pauper youth, murder.
1644, by his master, William Franklin, wh. met the just reward. See
Winth. II. 184. NICHOLAS, York, s. of John the first, m. Mehitable, d.
of Samuel Storer, had Samuel, b. 8 Nov. 1714; John, 6 July 1716;
Hannah, 12 Feb. 1719, wh. d. a wid. 25 Jan. 1810; Thomas, 2 May
1721; William, 26 Apr. 1723; Mehitable, 13 Mar. 1725; Henry, 26
Mar. 1727; Jane, 29 May 1729; Sarah, 1 July 1731; and Stephen, 24
Mar. 1734, H. C. 1761, profess. of Hebr. &c. at the same. He was a
tanner, and d. a. 1740. ‡ ‖ SAMUEL, Boston, eldest s. of the sec. Henry,

b. in Eng. at Horton, near Basingstoke, Co. Hants, was bapt. at the ch. of B. taught his rudim. at Rumsey sch. and came with his mo. at 9 yrs. of age to our country, adm. freem. 1678, ar. co. 1679, of wh. he was capt. 1701, a supervis. of the press 1681, and print. with his own hand the catechism, chos. an Assist. 1684 to 6, when chart. was abrogat. and again, on its restora. 1689 to 92, and nam. of the counc. in new chart. by k. William and Mary under adv. of Increase Mather, of wh. list he was the last surv. when he withdrew 1725; was made a judge of Sup. Ct. 1692, and one of a special, but unlawful, commiss. with others under dep.-gov. Stoughton for trial of the witches; sev. yrs. judge of pro. and d. 1 Jan. 1730. For his partak. in the doleful delusion of that monstrous tribunal at Salem, that caus. the d. of so many innocents, he suffer. remorse for long yrs. with the highest Christian magnanim. supplicat. for mercy on the Lord's day, in the open congregat. tho. less tenderness of conscience was shown by a very relig. magistr. the chief in that cause. See Hutch. II. 61. He may also claim the honor of being one of the earliest in exertions against domestic slavery, and in answ. to him one of his assoc. judges publish. defence. By his first w. Hannah, only surv. ch. of John Hull, the mintmaster, m. 28 Feb. 1676, he had John, b. 2, bapt. 8 Apr. 1677, wh. d. next yr.; Samuel, 11, bapt. 16 June 1678; Hannah, 3, bapt. 8 Feb. 1680, wh. d. unm. at 44 yrs.; Eliz. 29 Dec. 1681, bapt. 1 June foll.; Hull, 8, bapt. 13 July 1684, d. young; Henry, 8, bapt. 13 Dec. 1685, d. in few days; Stephen, 31 Jan. bapt. 6 Feb. 1687, d. in few mos. Joseph, 15, bapt. 19 Aug. 1688, H. C. 1707; Judith, 13, bapt. 24 Aug. 1690, d. soon; Mary, 28 Oct. bapt. 1 Nov. 1691, ano. ch. 7, bapt. 13 Aug. 1693, d. soon; Sarah, 21, bapt. 25 Nov. 1694, d. young; one more, in 1696, d. very soon; and Judith, again, 2, bapt. 4 Jan. 1702; so that only six of the fourteen ch. grew to maturity. A sec. w. Abigail, d. of Jacob Melyen, wh. was wid. of William Tilley, as she had been of James Woodmansey, m. 29 Oct. 1719, d. 26 May foll. and a third w. m. 29 Mar. 1722, Mary, d. of Henry Shrimpton, wid. of Robert Gibbs, outliv. him; but neither had brot. him ch. Eliz. m. 17 Oct. 1700, Grove Hirst, and d. 10 July 1716; Mary m. Samuel Gerrish, and d. 16 Nov. 1710; and Judith, m. 12 May 1720, Rev. William Cooper, and d. 23 Dec. 1740. Folly has never been gratif. by any tradit. more than the story of the m. of this Judge S. as Hutch. I. 178, tells, that he rec. with his first w. "as common. report. thirty thousand pounds in N. E. shillings." Easy was it for credulity to accept the addit. to that tale, that she was put into the scales against an equal load of her f.'s coin. Slight arithmetic would prove, that f. and d. together would scarce. balance one tenth of the silver; so that if we strike out one of the cyphers from that 30000, and assume that dollars were the

true read. instead of pounds, it might be less marvel. if equal. ridiculous.
Prob. he was the richest man in the Prov. at his d. yet he left no will,
and his admors. saw no use in return of inv. Amicable partition, no
doubt, was suffic. for the heirs. SAMUEL, Brookline, s. of the preced. m.
15 Sept. 1702, Rebecca, eldest d. of Gov. Joseph Dudley, had Hull, b.
19 July 1703, d. in few mos.; Rebecca, 30 Dec. 1704, tho. Boston rec.
then gives Samuel, wh. foll. and Hannah, Mary, Henry, and John, but
all d. bef. their f. wh. liv. to 27 Feb. 1751. His wid. d. 14 Apr. 1761.
SAMUEL, York, s. of the first John, by w. Lydia, not Sarah (as Alden
calls her) Storer, had John, b. 14 Aug. 1712, d. at 3 yrs.; Dummer, 12
Feb. 1715, d. at 21 yrs.; Lydia, 24 Jan. 1717; Mary, 30 May 1718, d.
soon; Mary, again, 29 Feb. 1720; and Hannah, 22 Jan. 1722; and by
sec. w. m. 28 Nov. 1723, wid. of Joseph Titcomb of Newbury, d. of
Samuel Batchelder of Reading, whose bapt. name is not seen, had seven
s. Samuel, b. 14 Sept. 1724, wh. liv. unm. to gr. age; John, again, 5 May
1729; Joseph, 3 Sept. 1731; Moses, 22 July 1733; David, 7 Oct. 1735,
H. C. 1755; Dummer, 17 Dec. 1737; Henry, 7 Feb. 1740; Sarah and
Jane, tw. that d. young, and he d. 28 Apr. 1769. His wid. d. 4 Feb.
1790, aged 92. * SAMUEL, Boston, eldest s. of Stephen the first, a
merch. m. 1 Jan. 1717, Catharine, wid. of Henry Howell, d. of Rev.
Samuel Lee, prob. had no issue. But her two young ch. by H. were
drown. 8 Jan. 1727, thro. break. of the ice on the riv. while S. was in
Eng. and he prob. req. celebr. Dr. Watts to write a let. of condolence
to his w. that has been print. in Geneal. Reg. I. 191. Poor Cotton
Mather had m. their aunt and was made admor. on est. of their f.
thereby caus. gr. trouble to hims. and unjust delay to the orphans. S.
was rep. sev. times aft. coming home, and d. 5 May 1757. STEPHEN,
Newbury, youngest s. of Henry the sec. b. in Eng. m. 13 June 1682,
Margaret, d. of Jonathan Mitchell, the matchless, had, Eliot says, 17 ch.
tho. I see acco. of only ten, Margaret, b. 7 May 1687; Samuel, 24 Nov.
1689; Susanna, 24 Oct. 1691; Jonathan, 7 Feb. 1693; Jane, 10 Feb.
1695; Mehitable, 21 May 1697; Mitchell, 29 Oct. 1699, H. C. 1718;
Henry, 25 Oct. 1701, d. under 20 yrs.; Stephen, 18 Dec. 1704, H. C.
1721, the Ch. J. wh. d. unm. 10 Sept. 1760; and Benjamin, 6 Apr.
1708; d. 17 Oct. 1725; and his wid. d. 20 Jan. 1736. Of his ds.
Margaret m. 11 Nov. 1714, as his sec. w. John Higginson; Susanna m.
22 Oct. 1713, Rev. Aaron Porter; Jane m. Rev. William Cooke; and
Mehitable m. Thomas Robie. Gr. serv. this Stephen render. in 1704,
as head of the volunt. in a successf. expedit. against the pirate Quelch,
wh. with five of his comp. were hang. THOMAS, Springfield, had a d.
b. 5 Jan. 1649, wh. d. in 3 wks.; and Abigail, 14 Mar. 1650, and rem.
soon aft. but to what place is hard to decide, perhaps was at Wickford

1674; and wholly uncert. whence he came; and the spell. on rec. is Sewill. Wide. spread the name has not been in our country, tho. none more honor. for gr. in 1849 at Harv. count. twenty-two, none at Yale, and one at Dart.

SEWARD, CALEB, Guilford, s. of William, m. 14 July 1686, Lydia, d. of the sec. William Bushnell of Saybrook, had Daniel, b. 1687, d. next yr.; Lydia, 1689; Caleb, 1692; Thomas, 1694; Noadiah, 1697; rem. to Durham, and had Ephraim, 6 Aug. 1700, the first b. of that town; and Ebenezer, 1703. He d. 2 Aug. 1728; and his wid. d. 1753. EDWARD, Ipswich 1637, may have gone home, and been a soldier in the gr. civil war 1643, and was serv. in the garrison of Chichester, Co. Sussex, when he made his will, giv. prop. to kinsm. and friends at Selsey and Chichester, but he came to our country again, in 1650 was of Guilford, and d. a few yrs. aft. GEORGE, Guilford 1651, was one of the orig. covenant. 1668 at Branford, rem. it is suppos. last to Newark, N. J. Perhaps he was br. of William. JOHN, Guilford, eldest s. of William, m. 25 June 1679, Abigail, eldest d. of the sec. William Bushnell, had Abigail, b. 1680, d. young; John, 1682; William, 1684; Hezekiah, 1687; Abigail, again, 1689; Daniel, 1692; Deborah, 1694; Jedediah, 1696; and Temperance, 1698; and he d. 5 Dec. 1748, near. 95 yrs. old. His wid. d. 1750. JOSEPH, Guilford, br. of the preced. m. 5 Feb. 1681, Judith, d. of the sec. William Bushnell, had Joseph, b. 1682, d. soon; Judith, 1684; Mary, 1686, d. soon; Joseph, again, 1687; and Mary, again, 1690; was a physician at Durham, and d. 14 Feb. 1731. His wid. d. 1740. RICHARD, Portsmouth, d. 1663, leav. ch. and gr.ch. ROBERT, Exeter 1639, perhaps was br. of the preced. and resid. of Portsmouth 1649. ROGER, Boston 1655, a mariner. *WILLIAM, Taunton 1643, whose name is by Baylies, II. 267, call. Edwards, was of New Haven 1651, and m. 2 Apr. of that yr. Grace, d. of Thomas Norton of Guilford, had Mary, b. 28 Feb. 1652; and soon aft. rem. to G. there had John, 14 Feb. 1654; Joseph, 1655; Samuel, 20 Aug. 1659, d. young; Caleb, 14 Mar. 1662; Stephen, 6 Aug. 1664; Samuel, again, 8 Feb. 1667, d. at 22 yrs. in few days aft. his f.; Hannah, 8 Oct. 1670; and Ebenezer, 13 Dec. 1672; was a lieut. and rep. 1673 and 4, had good est. and d. early in 1689, aged a. 62. His will was of 29 Mar. of that yr. Mary m. John Scranton, but d. bef. her f. leav. three ch.; Hannah m. Joseph Hand. Stephen outliv. his f. but d. without ch. bef. his youngest br. wh. d. 19 Oct. 1701, by kick of a horse. Sometimes this name is Seaward.

SEXTON. See Saxton.

SEYLE, FRANCIS, as giv. by Farmer for the freem. of 13 May 1640, so print. by me in the earlier Ed. of Winth.'s Hist. and thus approv. by

Paige and Shurtleff in their lists, was not satisfact. and with gr. confid.
I chang. the letters to Lyle in the Ed. of Winth. 1853, aft. severe
scrutiny of the orig. writ. in the rec. It seems almost certain, that it
stands for Fr. Lyall, the surgeon. See that name.

SEYMOUR, SEIMOR, SEAMOR, or SEAMER, JOHN, Hartford, s. of Richard, freem. 1667, m. Mary Watson, d. of John of H. had John, b. 12
June 1666 ; Thomas, 12 Mar. 1669 ; Mary, Nov. 1670 ; Margaret, 17
Jan. 1675 ; Richard, 11 Feb. 1677 ; Jonathan, 10 Jan. 1679 ; Nathaniel,
6 Nov. 1680 ; and Zechary, 10 Jan. 1685. MATTHEW, Norwalk, s. of
Thomas, was a lieut. 1718. RICHARD, Hartford 1639, but not an orig.
propr. rem. 1652 to Farmington, next to Norwalk, there was a selectman
1655, and d. 25 Nov. leav. Thomas, Richard, John, and Zechariah,
perhaps Mary, and Eliz. b. June 1650 ; and wid. Mercy, wh. m. 22
Nov. 1656, John Steele, as his sec. w. In Geneal. Reg. XII. 197, this
name is mistak. for Seger, as Mr. Porter says. I presume his sis. Mary
m. 29 Sept. 1644, Thomas Gridley. RICHARD, s. of the preced. was of
Farmington in the list of freem. 1669, by w. Hannah, d. of Anthony
Howkins, had Samuel ; Ebenezer ; Jonathan, bapt. 17 Apr. 1687 ; and
ds. Hannah ; and Mercy, bapt. 14 Jan. 1683. THOMAS, Norwalk, s. of
Richard the first, was prob. b. in Eng. m. Jan. 1654, Hannah, d. of
Matthew Marvin, had Hannah, b. 12 Dec. foll. ; Abigail, Jan. 1656,
wh. m. 16 Nov. 1676, Thomas Picket of Stratford ; Mary and Sarah,
tw. Sept. 1658 ; Thomas, Sept. 1660 ; Mercy, Nov. 1666 ; Matthew,
May 1669 ; Eliz. Dec. 1673 ; and Rebecca, Jan. 1676 ; was freem. 1668.
ZECHARIAH, Hartford, br. of the preced. was of Farmington, among
freem. of 1669, had ds. Mary, b. 1689 ; Eliz. and Abigail, tw. 1692 ;
and Ruth, 1699 ; d. 1702, aged 60. Of this name, in 1834, Farmer
notes in MS. eleven had been gr. at Yale, and five at other N. E. coll.
but none at Harv. or Dart.

SHACKFORD, or SHACKFORTH, WILLIAM, Dover 1662-72, was of the
gr. jury 1682, and a capt. prob. 1696, perhaps had a fam.

SHADDUCK, or CHADDOCK, ELIAS, Windsor, m. Hannah, d. of John
Osborn, had only ch. Hannah, wh. m. 14 Mar. 1692, Benjamin West,
and d. 26 May 1676. His wid. m. 6 Mar. 1678, Benjamin Eggleston.

SHAFLIN, MICHAEL, Salem, a tailor, from Salisbury, Co. Wilts, emb.
Apr. 1635 at Southampton in the James, may first have been of ano.
town, but in 1637 had gr. of ld. at S.; freem. 18 May 1642, had Catharine and Sarah by w. Eliz. wh. is among memb. of the ch. 1639, and
she may be not the same, call. Alice in his will of 5 Apr. 1686, pro. 19
May 1687, made extrix. with gift of his est. in fee, pay. in four yrs. aft.
his d. (that occur. in Dec. 1686), six pounds to ea. of the ds. Catharine
King, and Sarah Stone ; but wh. were hs. of those ds. is not kn.

SHAKESPEAR, ISAAC, may be the name of a soldier, k. by the Ind. at Northampton, 28 Sept. 1675, as in that acco. of Rev. Mr. Russell to our Gen. Ct. of which Coffin's valua. Hist. 389, 90, gives copy. Uzackabee Shacksbee is the name on town rec. as Mr. Judd assur. me, and he is designat. as Praisever Turner's man. Possib. he was a friend. Indian, not a few of wh. enjoy. the advantage of bear. arms in our cause; but certain it is very unlike an Eng. or even Christian name.

SHALER, SHALLOR, SHALIER, SHAILER, SHAYLER, or SHALLER, MICHAEL, Boston, freem. 1690. THOMAS, Haddam, propound. for freem. 1671, rem. to Killingworth, there had Nathaniel, b. 16 Dec. 1677 ; went back to H. and had more, and Goodwin (wh. makes him m. 1673, Alice, d. of Jared Spencer, wid. of Thomas Brooks), gives other ch. as Thomas, a. 1674 ; Abel; Timothy ; and Ann; but does not name Nathaniel. However he says, he sail. for the W. I. 1692, and was lost at sea.

SHANNON, RICHARD, Portsmouth 1689, m. Abigail, d. of William Vaughan, had Cutt, and Nathaniel, and descend. of distinct. are num.

SHAPLEIGH, spell. sometimes as sound. SHARPLEY, more oft. SHAP-LEY, ALEXANDER, Kittery 1642, had some yrs. bef. been agent, prob. of Sir Ferdinando Gorges, and so may be thot. to have come from Devonsh. had Catharine, wh. m. perhaps in Eng. James Treworthy ; Nicholas, and other ch. ; all, it may be, b. in his native ld. He soon went home, and d. there bef. 1650. BENJAMIN, New London, mariner, s. of Nicholas, m. 10 Apr. 1672, Mary, eldest d. of John Picket, had Ruth, b. 24 Dec. foll. ; Benjamin, 20 Mar. 1675 ; Mary, 26 Mar. 1677 ; Joseph, 15 Aug. 1681, wh. d. young; Ann, 31 Aug. 1685 ; Daniel, 14 Feb. 1690; Jane, 1696 ; and Adam, 1698, d. young; and d. 3 Aug. 1706, in 56th yr. if the credit of the gr.st. leads us to believe he was the *sec.* not *first* Benjamin of his f. JOHN, Kittery, perhaps s. of Alexander, was serg. 1659 ; k. by the Ind. 29 Apr. 1706, as Penhallow tells, when his s. was tak. by them to Canada, and treat. very cruel. Niles relates the same matter with slight differ. of date. See 3 Mass. Hist. Coll. VI. 275. NICHOLAS, Boston, perhaps br. of Alexander, had Benjamin, b. Sept. 1645, perhaps his youngest, liv. aft. at Charlestown, was a capt. and d. 15 Feb. 1663. His will, of 21 Jan. 1662, pro. 7 Sept. 1663, gave to his w. "the ho. in wh. Mr. Roswell lives," wh. was, of course, one of the best in that town, ment. three s. Nicholas, Joseph, and Benjamin, and made Hon. Richard Russell an overseer. For bequest of a sh. in his est. to s. Joseph, is attach. a curious condition — "in case he m. Sarah, d. of Randall Nichols." His wid. Ann d. 26 Mar. 1687, in 80th yr. She and her s. Joseph act. as excors. NICHOLAS, Kittery, s. of Alexander, b. in Eng. a man of emin. was first of Portsmouth, sold his est. there in Dec. 1644, chos.

Treasr. of the Province of Maine 1649, capt. in 1653, major in 1656,
supersed. in 1663 by William Phillips, being in 1662 a magistr. next to
the right worshipf. Henry Josselyn. He had w. Alice, no ch. went home
prob. seven yrs. later, and liv. long, yet came not again to our side of the
ocean, I presume, but d. in Eng. 1681 or 2. His name is not includ.
with those the royal commissnrs. honor. in giv. office, wh. might seem to
prove his abs. tho. special reason may be, his tenderness for Quakers.
* NICHOLAS, Charlestown, s. of Nicholas the first, was a major, dism. in
July 1669, by the County Court, from that office, as a Quaker, but his
nearer neighb. contin. to trust his goodness, made him rep. 1696, and he
prob. had s. of the same name, and no little hesitat. is felt in distinguish.
one from the other.

      SHARP, CHARLES, New Hampsh. 1684. JOHN, Dover 1663. JOHN,
Westerly 1668. JOHN, Boston, by w. Martha had Robert, b. 1665;
and prob. others. He was s. of Robert, liv. at Muddy riv. now Brookline, was lieut. of that comp. of Wadsworth at Sudbury fight, Apr. 1676,
that was near. cut off to a man. A let. of his, writ. few wks. bef. his d.
in Geneal. Reg. X. 65, is worth read. Dr. Pierce, in his Hist. of the
town, says, "the s. of this lieut. S. afterwards lost his life in an expedit.
against the Ind. in Canada." JOHN, Cambridge, merch. had w. Eliz. wh.
d. 9 Mar. 1699, in her 59th yr. as the inscr. of her gr.st. is giv. by Harris,
wh. tells no more of him. RICHARD, Boston, freem. 1674, d. 5 Aug.
1677. ROBERT, Braintree, came in the Abigail, perhaps, 1635, from
London, aged 20, had John, b. 12 Mar. 1643, and may have been at
Rehoboth the same yr. but certain. bot. in 1650, with Peter Aspinwall,
the large farm of William Colborn at Muddy riv.; had Mary, bapt. at
Roxbury, 5 Dec. 1652, and elder d. Abigail, b. a. 1648. He d. Jan.
1655, his inv. in Geneal. Reg. VIII. 276, being of 19th of that mo. tho.
Farmer had it July 1653; and his wid. Abigail, bec. sec. w. of Nicholas
Clap. SAMUEL, Salem 1629, came, with Rev. Samuel Skelton, in the
George Bonadventure, emb. in Apr. of this yr. with a duplicate of the
chart. of the Col. by the Gov. and Assist. of Mass. betrusted to him, and
they appoint. him to be of the counc. to capt. John Endicott, Gov. of
their planta. with three min. Higginson, Skelton, and Bright, beside the
two Browns, John, and Samuel, and Thomas Graves, the engineer.
But as they were requir. to be under oath, and that was prob. never
admin. (see Endicott); and as he was chos. an Assist. at the Gen. Ct. in
London, 20 Oct. foll. (when Winth. was chos. Gov. in lieu of Cradock
then resign.) but never took the o. of qualificat. being on our side of the
water, and Ludlow was chos. in his place, at the Ct. 10 Feb. aft. I have
not giv. him the ‡ designat. of that rank. Aft. the governm. was transfer.
hither, he desir. adm. as freem. 19 Oct. 1630, and was adm. 3 July 1632,

but had been made rul. elder, prob. in 1630, aft. d. of Houghton. By w. Alice he had Elias, bapt. 1 Jan. 1637; Edward, 14 Apr. 1639; Mary, 28 June 1640; Experience, a d. 19 Sept. 1641; Nathaniel, 10 Nov. 1644; and Hannah, 1647; beside the eldest, Abigail (perhaps by a former w.), wh. m. Oct. 1647, Thomas Jeggles. He d. says Bentley, 1658; but Felt thinks, 1656; and his wid. d. 1667. ‡ THOMAS, Boston, chos. an Assist. 20 Oct. 1629, in London, when the new Gov. Winth. was chos. and they came together in the fleet of 1630. On 3 Jan. foll. his only d. (as from the lang. of Gov. Dudley may be infer.) was tak. from him, and his ho. burn. 16 Mar. aft. so that we may not blame, however we regret, his leav. our country forever, emb. 1 Apr. with Sir Richard Saltonstall and his fam. to go home.

SHARSWOOD, GEORGE, New London 1666, had George, and William, perhaps not tw. bapt. 2 Apr. 1671; Mary, 1672; and Catharine, 1674. He d. 1 May of that yr. and his wid. m. 1678, George Darrow; and Mary m. Jonathan Hill. WILLIAM, New London, s. of the preced. by w. Abigail had Jonathan, George, and Abigail, all bapt. Sept. 1700; and he d. bef. 1705, when George Polly of Philadelphia had m. his wid. Yet he had other s. William, and James.

SHATSWELL, SHOTSWELL, SATCHWELL, or SATCHELLS, JOHN, Ipswich 1633, was fined, 3 Sept. by our Gen. Ct. for distemper in drink, but 5 yrs. aft. half of the fine was remit. and he was much more correct in deportm. d. 1647, and his will was pro. 30 Mar. It names w. Joanna, s. Richard, br. Theophilus, br. Curwin, and sis. Mary Webster, w. of John. His wid. m. John Green of Charlestown, outliv. him, and d. 17 Apr. 1673. JOHN, Ipswich, s. of Richard, m. 20 June 1684, Sarah Younglove, d. of the sec. Samuel of the same, had John, b. 1 Apr. 1685, d. soon; John, again, 17 Mar. 1687, d. young. RICHARD, Ipswich, s. of the first John, b. prob. in Eng. by w. Rebecca, perhaps, had Mary, wh. d. Sept. 1657; Sarah, b. 19 Aug. 1658; Richard, wh. d. 28 Jan. 1664; Ann, b. 21 Feb. 1666; Richard, again; John; and Hannah, or Joanna, perhaps both; and he d. 13 July 1694. Sarah m. a Rindge. RICHARD, Ipswich, s. of the preced. d. 16 May 1698, leav. w. Elinor, wh. was d. of Daniel Cheney, and only ch. Richard. THEOPHILUS, Ipswich 1642, was at Haverhill 1646, but back to I. in 1648, had w. Susanna, and d. 1668. He may have been f. of a William, wh. d. there a. 1663.

SHATTON, SAMPSON, as in the valua. Hist. of R. I. by Arnold this name is giv. four times out of five to the man common. nam. Shotten, wh. see.

SHATTUCK, JOHN, Watertown, eldest s. of William the first, m. 20 June 1664, Ruth, eldest d. of John Whitney of the same, had John, b.

4 June 1666, wh. was, with his first b. ch. John, k. by the Ind. at Groton,
8 May 1709; Ruth, 24 Jan. 1668; William, 11 Sept. 1670; and Samuel.
He was in capt. Beers's comp. at Squakeag fight, 4 Sept. 1675, and ten
days aft. was drown. in cross. Charlestown ferry; and his wid. m. 6 Mar.
1677, Enoch Lawrence of Groton. PHILIP, Watertown, br. of the
preced. physician, m. 9 Nov. 1670, Deborah, d. of William Barstow of
Dedham, had Deborah, b. 11 Oct. 1671, d. in few days; Philip, 26 Jan.
1673, d. young; Susanna, 6 Aug. 1675; Ann, 8 Dec. 1677; and his w.
d. 4 or 24 Nov. 1679. On 11 Feb. foll. he m. Rebecca Chamberlain,
had Joseph, 12 Aug. 1681, d. at 2 yrs.; Rebecca, 10 Mar. 1683; Benjamin, 17 Mar. 1685; Joseph, again, 6 Mar. 1687; Nathaniel, 14 Jan.
1689; Isaac; Amos, 19 Mar. 1695; Sarah, 26 Oct. 1696; Theophilus;
and Philip, again, 19 Oct. 1699, both bapt. 14 (not 15, as Bond tells, wh.
was Monday) Apr. 1700; and d. 26 June 1722. His will, of 29 Jan.
pro. 30 Aug. foll. made Isaac excor. names both of his s. Philip, and
other ch.; and his wid. d. 1728. SAMUEL, Salem, a feltmaker, s. of that
wid. Damaris, wh. m. Thomas Gardner the sec. was b. in Eng. a. 1620,
adm. of the ch. 1642, but excommun. aft. many yrs. for a Quaker, and
fin. 1669 for entertain. Thomas Maule, ano. of that sect, and banish. on
pain of death; went home, and came back with order, I exult in saying,
from Charles II. for cessat. of such prosecut. Wh. was his w. is unkn.
but he had ch. Samuel, b. 7 Oct. 1649; Hannah, 28 Aug. 1651;
Damaris, 11 Nov. 1653; Mary, 14 Mar. 1655; Priscilla, 1 May 1658;
Return, 16 Aug. 1662; Retire, 28 Mar. 1664; and Patience, 18 Nov.
1666. Six ds. were m. Hannah to John Somes of Boston; Damaris to
Benjamin Pope of Salem; Mary, to Benjamin Trask, of Beverly; Priscilla, 26 Apr. 1694, to Hugh Nichols of Salem; Return, 14 Sept. 1688,
to John Saunders; and Patience, 29 July 1689, to John Smith of Salem.
SAMUEL, Salem, eldest ch. of the preced. hatter, m. 24 July 1676, Sarah,
d. of the first William Bucknam of Malden, had Samuel, b. 7 Sept. 1678,
wh. d. bef. his f. John, 13 Mar. 1680; and Margaret; and d. aft. mak. his
will, 22 Dec. 1722, pro. 25 Mar. foll.   SAMUEL, Watertown, youngest s.
of William, by w. Abigail had Abigail, b. 17 Oct. 1686; Samuel, 16 Feb.
1689; and Martha, 11 Apr. 1694. WILLIAM, Watertown 1642, by w.
Susanna had Susanna, b. 1643; Mary, 25 Aug. 1645; John, 11 Feb.
1647; Philip, 1648; Joanna; William, 1653; Rebecca, 1655; Abigail,
1657; Benjamin, d. young; and Samuel, 28 Feb. 1666. He d. 14 Aug.
1672, aged 58, in his will of 11 days preced. spell. his name Shathock,
names all the ten ch. His wid. m. 18 Nov. 1673, Richard Norcross, as
his sec. w. and d. 11 Dec. 1686. Descend. are very num. Susanna m.
12 Apr. 1661, Joseph Morse, and next, 5 July 1678, John Fay, and for
third h. William Brigham; Mary m. 14 Feb. 1662, Jonathan Brown;
Joanna d. 4 Feb. 1673, unm.; Rebecca m. 7 Feb. 1672, Samuel Church;

and Abigail m. 17 Oct. 1678, Jonathan Morse, and next, Joshua Parker of Groton. WILLIAM, Boston, shoemak. adm. an inhab. 1652, by w. Hannah had Hannah, b. 8 July 1654; and Exercise, 12 Nov. 1656; bec. a Quaker, and aft. fail. to be instruct. by whip. and prison, was banish. and went to Shrewsbury, N. J. There his d. Hannah m. 6 Nov. 1674, Restore Lippincot, and had num. ch. WILLIAM, Watertown, s. of the first William, weaver, m. Susanna, d. of Stephen Randall, had Eliz. b. 3 Nov. 1684; William, a. 1686; Benjamin, 30 July 1687, H. C. 1709; Joanna; Mary, bapt. 13 Apr. 1690; Abigail; Joseph, b. 9 Oct. 1694, d. next wk.; Jonathan, 16 Oct. 1695; Robert, 1 Jan. 1698; and Moses, 1 Nov. 1703. His w. d. 8 May 1723, and he d. 19 Oct. 1732. Farmer notes, that four of this name had, in 1829, been gr. at Harv. and three at Dart.

SHAVELIN, GEORGE, Charlestown 1635, but not inhab. next yr. Frothingham, 84.

SHAW, ABRAHAM, Dedham 1638, had prob. liv. at Watertown some yrs. bef. at least his ho. and goods were burn. there Oct. 1636, as told in Winth. I. 200, was freem. 9 Mar. 1637. He had that yr. gr. of half the coal and iron to be found in common lds. and this would more stimulate his curiosity than incr. his wealth, had he not d. the next yr. and in 1639 his admors. sold the est. at D. Of ch. we hear the names, Joseph, John, Mary, and Martha; and to Joseph, with Nicholas Byram, wh. had m. one of the ds. was entr. the admin. under the will, of wh. the abstr. is giv. in Genealog. Reg. II. 180. Descend. perhaps thro. both s. are found in the neighb. ANDREW, Salem 1691. ANTHONY, Boston, m. 8 Apr. 1653, Alice Stonard, perhaps d. of John, had William, b. 21 Jan. 1654, d. at 2 mos.; William, again, 24 Feb. 1655; and Eliz. 21 May 1656; but no descend. is kn. BENJAMIN, Weymouth, s. of John the first, by w. Hannah had Susanna, b. 6 Feb. 1699; and, perhaps, if our rec. did not fail soon aft. that date, we might read sev. more. BENONI, Plympton, s. of Jonathan, m. Lydia, d. of John Waterman, had Lydia, b. 1697; John, 1699; Mary, 1700; Margaret, 1701; Elkanah, 1703; Jonathan, 1704; Moses, 1705; Benoni; Benjamin and Hannah, tw. 1715; Rebecca and Abigail, tw.; Phebe; and a d. without name; and he d. 5 Mar. 1751; and his wid. d. 25 July 1657. EDWARD, Duxbury 1632, acc. Winsor, may be the same, as Folsom found at Saco, where his w. Jane was whip. for slander, and the yr. bef. was of Scarborough, acc. Southgate, 26; and there in few yrs. he d. for his s. Richard, aft. resid. some yrs. as heir, sold his est. 1662. FEARNOT, Boston, blacksmith 1671, s. of Joseph the first of Weymouth, m. Bethia, d. of Jacob. Leager, had Jacob, b. 6 Nov. 1672; and John, 30 Mar. 1678. GEORGE, Eastham, s. perhaps, of Jonathan, m. 8 Jan. 1690, Constance, d. of Dan-

iel Doane of the same, had Elkanah, Rebecca, George, Hannah, John,
and Jonathan; and d. 2 May 1720. ISRAEL, Salem, s. of William,
claim. sh. of com. lds. in right of proprs. of 1661, so late as 1713, and
no more is kn. of him. JAMES, Plymouth 1643, s. of the first John,
prob. b. in Eng. m. 24 Dec. 1652, Mary, d. of Experience Mitchell, had
James, b. 6 Dec. 1654, and two ds. JOHN, Plymouth 1632, or some yrs.
bef. brot. from Eng. w. Alice and ch. John, James, Jonathan, and Abigail,
wh. m. Stephen Bryant, and d. 24 Oct. 1694. He was one of the purch.
of Dartmouth 1652; his w. d. 6 Mar. 1655, at P. and he bec. one of the
first sett. at Middleborough 1662. His s. John went unm. to Eng.
JOHN, Boston, a butcher, ar. co. 1646, by w. Martha had John, b. 16
May 1646, prob. d. soon; John, again, 1648; Samuel, 4 Nov. 1651, d.
at 10 mos.; Martha, 16 Sept. 1655; and Joseph, 11 Nov. 1657; made
provis. for annuity to hims. and w. Eliz. 1670, and d. 23 July 1687.
He may be the same, wh. was call. a fisherman in the list of contribut.
1657 to build the "town house" of B. JOHN, Weymouth, s. of Abraham, b. in Eng. by w. Alice, wh. outliv. him, had Eliz. b. 26 Feb. 1656;
Abraham, 10 Oct. 1657; Mary, 24 Mar. 1660; Nicholas, 23 Mar.
1662; Joseph, 15 Apr. 1664; Alice, 6 July 1666; Hannah, 7 Apr.
1668; Benjamin, 16 June 1670; Abigail, 15 July 1672; and Ebenezer,
24 Apr. 1674; beside John, prob. his first b. bef. the date of perfect rec·
I ought to ment. that some slight uncert. is felt, whether this man were
s. of Abraham, since Weymouth rec. show, that one JOHN there m. 7
June 1658, Sarah Waters, and he may have been s. of Abraham, and
this h. of Alice have been br. of Abraham. However, as he nam.
his eldest, or sec. s. Abraham (wh. serv. as a soldier on Conn. riv.
Mar. 1676), my assumpt. may be good. JOHN, Malden, a tailor, had
John, b. 16 Dec. 1667; and w. in 1670, Hannah, wh. d. 8 Apr. 1674;
and he m. 12 Aug. foll. Eliz. Ramsdell. JOHN, Stonington 1670, prob.
eldest s. of Thomas of the same, was b. at Charlestown, and join. the ch.
of Rev. James Noyes at S. 1677. JOHN, Rehoboth, had Priscilla, b. 22
June 1680; and Ann, 15 Mar. 1682. Prob. he rem. from Weymouth
aft. 1676, for none of this name is earlier found at R. JOHN, Weymouth,
s. prob. eldest ch. of John of the same, yet may have been s. of Joseph,
freem. 1681, by w. Hannah had John, b. 16 Dec. 1679, wh. prob. d.
young; Abraham, 14 Feb. 1685; Hannah, 26 Apr. 1687; John, again,
20 Jan. 1690; Mary, 5 May 1691; and Benjamin, 25 July 1693.
JOHN, Weymouth, perhaps cous. ger. of John the sec. of the same, and
s. of John or Joseph, but of wh. I am ign. by w. Judith had Eliz. b. 26
Sept. 1687; Joseph, 11 Jan. 1692; Judith, 4 May 1693; and Abigail,
17 July 1695; perhaps others. Whatever doubt of identi. as to one or
ano. John of Weymouth is felt, it is indisput. that Rev. John, gr. gr.s. of

Abraham, H. C. 1729, had four s. wh. were min. viz.: Oakes, H. C. 1758, f. of Hon. Lemuel, H. C. 1800, thirty yrs. Ch. Just. of Mass. ; Bezaleel, H. C. 1762; William, H. C. 1762, min. of Marshfield, and f. of other min.; beside John, H. C. 1772, f. of the late William S. Shaw, the large-hearted founder of the Boston Athenæum. JONATHAN, Plymouth 1654, s. of the first John, by him brot. from Eng. m. 22 Jan. 1657, Phebe, d. of George Watson, had Hannah; Jonathan, b. 1663 ; Phebe ; Mary ; George ; Lydia; Benjamin and Benoni, tw. 1672, of wh. the former d. young; but whether all, or how many, of these were b. by that w. or when she d. we are ign. Yet it is kn. that he had sec. w. Persis, wid. of Benajah Pratt, and d. of deac. John Dunham. He may have liv. at Duxbury, or Eastham, pt. of his days. Hannah m. 5 Aug. 1678, Thomas Paine, jr. of Eastham; Phebe m. John Morton; Mary m. 1687, Eleazer Ring ; and Lydia m. 4 Apr. 1689, Nicholas Snow. JONATHAN, s. of the preced. by first w. Mehitable Pratt had Jonathan, Phebe, Persis, Mehitable, James, Hannah, Eliz. Priscilla, Abigail, and Samuel, it is said, and this w. d. 1712. By sec. w. Mary Darling, m. 16 Nov. 1715, he had Rebecca, b. 1718 ; and tho. his resid. or date of d. are unkn. his wid. we are told, d. 9 Mar. 1754, aged 80. JOSEPH, Dedham 1636, s. of Abraham, brot. from Eng. by his f. freem. 22 May 1639, rem. soon aft. d. of his f. to Weymouth, had Joseph, b. 14 July 1643 ; John; and others, not nam. of wh. Fearnot was one ; d. 1653 at W. bef. rec. of that town are visib. His will is abstr. in Geneal. Reg. V. 303. JOSEPH, Boston, cooper, m. 1 Dec. 1653, Mary, d. of Nathaniel Souther, and d. 12 days aft. and the wid. m. 16 Aug. foll. John Blake. JOSEPH, Hampton, s. of Roger, m. 26 June 1661, Eliz. d. of William Partridge of Salisbury, had Abiel, b. Oct. 1662, wh. m. Thomas Brown, and prob. others. JOSEPH, Charlestown, m. 16 Dec. 1664, Sarah Patten, perhaps d. of William ; but nothing more is kn. of him, and it may be that he rem. JOSEPH, Weymouth, prob. s. of John first of the same, freem. 1691, by w. Judith had Judith, b. 4 May 1693 ; Abigail, 17 July 1695 ; and, perhaps, others aft. our transcr. stops. NICHOLAS, Weymouth, prob. br. of the preced. by w. Deborah had Alice, b. 13 Apr. 1687.; Nicholas, 7 May 1689 ; Joshua, 18 Mar. 1692 ; John, 31 Mar. 1696 ; Zechary, 7 May 1699 ; and, perhaps, more. * ROGER, Cambridge 1636, freem. 14 Mar. 1639, by w. Ann had Esther, b. June 1638 ; Mary, wh. d. 26 Jan. or Feb. 1640 ; Mary, again, 29 Sept. 1645 ; rem. to Hampton, there had sec. w. Susanna, wid. of William Tilton of Lynn, was rep. 1651 and 2, and d. 29 May 1662, leav. s. Joseph, Benjamin, and four ds. prob. all by first w. THOMAS, Hingham 1637, rem. bef. 1643, to Barnstable, tho. he did not sell his est. at H. bef. 1665, may have had no w. or ch. at least his will, of 25 June 1672, refers to none. Some have writ. the name Shave. THOMAS, Charlestown, perhaps had w. Mary, adm. of the ch. July 1645; had John, b. 4 Mar. 1648, whose bapt. would fail to be found in the ch. rec. hav. large gap aft. 1642; rem. 1656 to New London, and in 1658 was of Stonington, made freem. 1666, in the town list of 1669 call. sen. wh. permits us to suppose he had s. of the name. The governm. of Conn. in 1675 gr. to his w. a hundr. acres, so that we may presume he was late. d. THOMAS, Concord 1663. WILLIAM, Salem 1657, then was a serv. of Thomas Palmer, m. 23 Nov. 1668, Eliz. d. of George Fraile of Lynn, had Samuel, b. 19 Feb. 1670, d. soon; William, 25 Sept. 1672; Eliz. perhaps Jan. 1677; Israel, July 1680; and in his will of 1 Jan. 1722, pro. 30 Dec. 1726, he names ano. w. Mary, and other ch. beside those three, viz. Ebenezer, Daniel, Benjamin, and Margaret. Eliz. had m. a Stockwell. Of this name, the gr. in 1834 were mark. by Farmer as fourteen at Harv. one at Yale, and ten at the other N. E. coll. The first eight at Harv. were min.

SHAWSON, GEORGE, Duxbury 1638, says Winsor, rem. bef. 1640, to Sandwich.

SHEAFFE, EDMUND, Boston, came from Cranbrook, Co. Kent, but when is unkn. nor is any thing told of him, but that he m. Eliz. d. of Sampson Cotton of London, had Rebecca, Eliz. and Sampson, but no dates of b. are giv. exc. 1650 for the last nam. ch. aft. d. of his f. ‖ JACOB, Boston, came with his mo. and Rev. Henry Whitfield, wh. m. one of his sis.; went first to Guilford, where he was one of the seven pillars for constitut. the ch. wh. to us appears strange, as he was so young, and unm. yet his relat. with the pastor will expla. if not justify, this distinct. He was b. at Cranbrook, in Kent, on the ch. reg. there call. s. of Edmund, b. 4 Aug. 1616, and prob. cous. ger. of the preced. In 1643 he rem. to Boston, and was engag. soon to m. the only ch. of Henry Webb; and in the rec. of our Gen. Ct. II. 46, we read this unusu. favor: "Jacob S. and Margaret Webbe are permit. to join in m. tho. but twice publish." He had Eliz. b. 1 Oct. 1644; Sarah, 14 Sept. 1652; Ebenezer, 4 Feb. 1654; a ch. whose name is not told, 25 July 1655; Mehitable, 28 May 1658; and Jacob, posthum. 23 July 1659. In 1648 he was chos. to the ar. co. and the inscript. on his tomb in the old gr.yd. tells, that he d. 22 Mar. 1659, aged 42, only ch. then liv. being Eliz. and Mehitable. His wid. m. Rev. Thomas Thacher of Boston, long outliv. him, and d. 23 Feb. 1694, in 68th yr.; Eliz. m. 7 Sept. 1660, then under 16 yrs. Mr. Robert Gibbs, and 20 Mar. 1675, m. Jonathan Curwen, and d. 29 Aug. 1718; and Mehitable m. Sampson Sheaffe. He seems to have the largest est. of any that hitherto had d. at B. His mo. Joanna d. at Guilford, July 1659. ‡ SAMPSON, Boston 1672, merch.

wh. in indent. of Apr. 1673 calls hims. of London, m. Mehitable, d. of Jacob Sheaffe, had Jacob, b. 1677; and Sampson, 1681, H. C. 1702, went, aft. 1685, to Newcastle, N. H. and in that Prov. was collector of the customs, memb. of the counc. 1698, and Secr. and Judge of the Sup. Ct. but came back to B. and d. 1724. From him most of the name in N. H. descend. WILLIAM, Charlestown, m. 15 Aug. 1672, Ruth Wood, perhaps d. of Josiah, had Mary, b. 31 May 1673, bapt. 14 Dec. 1684; Edward; William; and Mary, all bapt. 13 Jan. 1689; but why some were not earlier, I am ign. Of the s. Edward, I think, had Edward; and the gr.st. shows d. of his w. Mary, 1 Nov. 1748, aged 70; and William d. 17 May 1718, and his s. William d. in Oct. foll. Among the early memb. of the ch. at Roxbury was a wid. S. and Ellis, in Hist. gives the name as of a man, with supply of goats and kids, prob. bef. 1640, yet no light has been shed on either. She may have been mo. of Jacob the first. Of this name, in 1839, ten had been gr. at Harv. and two at Yale.

SHEARER, sometimes SHERWOOD, THOMAS, Boston, tailor, m. 18 Apr. 1659, Hannah, d. of Thomas Bumstead.

SHEARS, or SHEERES, JEREMIAH, prob. of York, m. Susanna, wid. of Nicholas Green, and no more is told of him, but that he d. 1664. SAMUEL, Dedham, m. 15 Aug. 1658, wid. Ann Grosse of Boston, prob. as sec. w. and resid. in that pt. wh. bec. Wrentham, where he liv. 1691, aged 64. SAMUEL, Wrentham, s. perhaps, of the preced. by w. Mary had Mary, b. 1664; John, 1666; Mehitable, 1 Feb. 1668; Solomon, 20 Feb. 1670, wh. d. at 19 yrs.; Grace, 29 Feb. 1672; and Judith, 17 June 1675; and his w. d. 26 Apr. 1704. Ano. SAMUEL of W. m. 27 Oct. 1683, Eliz. d. of Isaac Heath of Roxbury. WILLIAM, Boston 1657, may have gone home, and come again in 1671, then print. Shoars.

SHEATHER, JOHN, Guilford 1650, had John, b. 15 Aug. 1651; Mary, 14 Mar. 1654; Samuel, 3 Feb. 1658; Eliz. 8 Jan. 1660; and Hannah, wh. m. 1685, Thomas Hall; and he was bur. 1 June 1670. JOHN, Killingworth, s. of the preced. m. 9 Jan. 1679, Eliz. Wellman, had Eliz. b. 20 Nov. foll.; Hannah, 25 Nov. 1681; John, 23 Mar. 1685; Susanna; and Rachel. His w. d. 5 Feb. 1718, and he d. 12 May 1721. SAMUEL, Killingworth, br. of the preced. by w. Mary had Mary, b. 1689; and Deborah, 1691. His wid. m. 29 Oct. 1694, Robert Chapman of Saybrook.

SHED, DANIEL, Braintree 1646, by w. Mary had Mary, b. 8 Mar. 1648; Daniel, 30 Aug. 1649; Hannah, 7 Sept. 1651; John, 2 Mar. 1655; Eliz. and Zechariah, tw. 17 June 1656; Sarah, 30 Oct. 1658; and rem. a. 1660 to Billerica, there had Samuel, 13 Aug. of that yr.; and Nathan, 5 Feb. 1668. His younger ds. Susanna and Eunice, per-

haps one, if not both of the younger s. were b. by w. Eliz. wh. d. 17
Jan. 1700, and he d. 27 July 1708. In the Col. Rec. this name is print.
Shode. DANIEL, Billerica, s. of the preced. freem. 1690, m. 5 July
1670, Ruth, d. of Golden Moore, had seven ch. and d. 24 Dec. 1690, of
smallpox. JOHN, Billerica, br. of the preced. m. 1677, Sarah, d. prob.
of William Chamberlain, had eleven ch. and d. 31 Jan. 1737. ZECHA-
RIAH, Billerica, br. of the preced. had w. Ann, and two ch. Hannah and
Agnes, all k. by the Ind. 1 Aug. 1692.

SHEDER, JOHN, Guilford, by Ruggles call. an early sett. 1 Mass. Hist.
Coll. X. 92, is the same as Sheather, wh. see.

SHEFFIELD, EDMUND, Roxbury 1641, m. 17 Apr. 1644, Mary, d. of
the first Richard Woody, had John, b. 6, bapt. 23 Mar. 1645, rem. to
Braintree, there had Edmund, b. 15 Dec. 1646; Ann, 1 Apr. 1649;
Isaac, 15 Mar. 1651; Mary, 14 June 1653, wh. d. at 7 yrs.; Matthew,
26 May 1655; Samuel, 26 Nov. 1657; and Sarah, 6 June 1660; was
freem. 1644; m. sec. w. 5 Sept. 1662, Sarah, d. of John Beal, wid. of
Thomas Marsh of Hingham, and had Mary, 26 June 1663; Nathaniel,
16 Jan. 1666; and Deborah, 23 June 1667, wh. d. 8 Jan. 1691. Morse
gave no acco. of the childr. FREDERICK, Portsmouth, R. I. was, perhaps, s. of Joseph, but certain. among freem. 1655. ICHABOD, Dover
1658, may have rem. to Portsmouth, R. I. and m. Mary, d. of George
Parker of the same, had Joseph, b. 22 Aug. 1661; Mary, 30 Apr. 1664;
Nathaniel, 8 Nov. 1667; Ichabod, 6 Mar. 1670; and Amos, 25 Jan.
1673. JOSEPH, Portsmouth, R. I. 1643, was, perhaps, br. of the preced.
and prob. d. bef. 1655, as his name is not seen on the list of freem.
‡JOSEPH, Portsmouth, R. I. s. of Ichabod, m. 12 Feb. 1685, Mary
Shrieve, perhaps d. of Thomas, had Joseph, b. 2 Nov. foll.; Mary, 8
Nov. 1687; Eliz. 15 Nov. 1689, d. soon; Benjamin, 18 June 1691;
Edward, 5 Apr. 1694; William, 30 Mar. 1696; and Eliz. 1 June 1698,
was an Assist. 1699. JOSEPH, Dover, s. of William, so late as 1735 had
ld. laid out by metes and bounds that had been gr. to his f. in 1658; and
d. unm. leav. good est. NATHANIEL, Sherborn, youngest br. of the
preced. by w. Mary had Nathaniel, b. 3 Feb. 1727; Rachel, 30 Mar.
1732; Ann, 15 Mar. 1734, d. at 9 yrs.; Catharine, 13 June 1737, d. at
6 yrs.; and Mary. He made his will 8 Dec. 1752, d. next mo. and his
wid. d. 25 Jan. 1754, aged a. 53. THOMAS, Boston, mariner, of wh. I kn.
nothing but that in Apr. 1663 he sold ld. to Edward Cartwright, and bot.
more next yr. WILLIAM, Boston, mariner 1653. WILLIAM, Dover
1658, had rem. to Hingham in Philip's war, and aft. to Sherborn, there
d. 6 Dec. 1700. In Hist. of Framingham, Barry gives his progeny, at
Braintree, by w. Mary, he had Rachel, b. 24 May 1660, wh. d. young;
and prob. at Dover all these, Hannah, 18 Apr. 1663; Daniel, 3 Mar.

1665; William, 19 Mar. 1667; Martha, 8 Jan. 1669; Joseph, 3 Mar. 1671; Tamosin, 25 May 1673; but at Hingham, Susanna, 11 Dec. 1675; and prob. at S. Eliz. 28 Nov. 1678; Nathaniel, 7 Mar. 1681; Mary; and Rachel, again. He does not ment. any sec. w. Tamosin m. Jonathan Adams; Susanna m. 1 Sept. 1697, Zuriel Hall; Mary m. John Clark; and Rachel m. and had fam. not ment. WILLIAM, Sherborn, s. of the preced. m. 30 May 1692, Hannah, prob. d. of Jonathan Bullard, had Hannah, b. 24 Nov. 1693; Isaac, 3 Mar. 1697; William, 28 Feb. 1699; Rachel, 12 Oct. 1702; Sarah, 18 June 1708; and Mary, 27 Nov. 1710.

SHELDON, or SHELDEN, EBENEZER, Northampton, seventh s. of the first Isaac, m. 16 Dec. 1701, Mary Hunt, prob. d. of Jonathan, had Ebenezer, b. 14 Sept. 1702, k. by the Ind. 27 June 1724; Miriam, 6 Mar. 1704; Noah, 20 Mar. 1706; Stephen, 2 Feb. 1709; Catharine, 7 Mar. 1711, d. young; Aaron, 4 Mar. 1713; Israel, 15 May 1715; Moses, Nov. 1716; Esther, 12 Mar. 1719; Elias, 13 Mar. 1721; Jemima, 16 Oct. 1722; and Mary, 8 Dec. 1724; and d. 18 Mar. 1755. His wid. d. 12 Nov. 1767, in 88th yr. GODFREY, Scarborough 1660, had William, and John, and d. 1671. He was aged 65 when he made his will of 13 Mar. 1664. Most of his prop. he gave to s. William, and his w. Alice, with charge to pay small sums to his br. John, ea. of his sis. as also to testator's w. Rebecca (therefore prob. not mo. of his s.) and to her br. Samuel Scarlet. ISAAC, Windsor 1640, perhaps not com. from Dorchester, where Dr. Harris thot. he saw him in 1634. Earlier than 1652 he may not be found at W. by Stiles, in Hist. 54, but in 1653 he m. Mary, d. of Thomas Woodford of Hartford, had Mary, b. 1654; rem. with his f.-in-law and sett. at Northampton a. 1655, had Isaac, 4 Sept. 1656; John, 5 Dec. 1658; Thomas, 6 Aug. 1661; Ruth and Thankful, tw. 27 Aug. 1663; Mindwell, 24 Feb. 1666; Joseph, 1 Feb. 1668; Hannah, 29 June 1670; Eleazer, 4 Aug. 1672, wh. d. at six mos.; Samuel, 9 Nov. 1675; Ebenezer, 1 Mar. 1678; and Mercy, wh. d. but few days old, 24 Feb. 1682; and his w. d. 17 Apr. 1684. He m. sec. w. 1685, Mehitable, d. of Thomas Gunn, the divorc. w. of David Ensign, and had Jonathan, 29 May 1687; and d. 27 July 1708, aged 79, when twelve of his ch. were liv. Stiles, 771, has not ment. the early items, but sunk the names of ch. Mary m. 11 Dec. 1670, John Bridgeman; Ruth m. 6 Nov. 1679, Joseph Wright, and next, 28 Oct. 1698, Samuel Strong; Thankful m. 23 Feb. 1681, Benjamin Edwards; Mindwell m. 30 Apr. 1684, John Pomeroy, and next, 19 Apr. 1687, John Lyman; and Hannah m. 24 Dec. 1690, Samuel Chapin of Springfield. ISAAC, Northampton, eldest s. of the preced. m. 25 Nov. 1685, Sarah, d. of Daniel Warner of Hatfield, had Isaac, b. 26 Aug. 1686; Sarah, 16 July 1688;

Mary, 18 Sept. 1690 ; Mindwell, 22 Mar. 1693 ; Daniel, 14 Apr. 1696,
d. young; Thankful, 6 June 1698; and Hannah, 30 Oct. 1701 ; and he
d. 29 Mar. 1712. JOHN, Billerica, m. 1 Feb. 1659, Mary Thompson,
perhaps d. of Simon, had John, b. 24 Apr. 1660, and, perhaps, more.
JOHN, Providence, sw. alleg. May 1682, may have m. Joanna Vincent,
perhaps d. of William. JOHN, Northampton, sec. s. of ,Isaac the first,
m. 5 Nov. 1679, Hannah, d. of John Stebbins, then less than 15 and ½
yrs. old, had John, b. 19 Sept. 1681; Hannah, 9 Aug. 1683; rem. to
Deerfield, there had Mary, 24 July 1687 ; Abigail, 21 Nov. 1689, d. in
few mos.; Ebenezer, 15 Nov. 1691; Remembrance, 21 Feb. 1693;
Mercy, 25 Aug. 1701, wh. with her mo. was k. by the Fr. and Ind. 29
Feb. 1704. He had built that ho. at D. call. few yrs. since, the Hoyt
ho. whose door we saw, as it was cut by tomahawks, and pierc. by bullets
on the morn. of the onslaught. Aft. that desolat. of the town, he rem.
to Hartford, m. 1708, Eliz. Pratt, a young wid. whose former h. is unkn.
by me, had Abigail, 8 Sept. 1710; and John, 8 Mar. 1718, and d. a.
1734, at least in Mar. of that yr. his inv. was tak. JONATHAN, Northampton, youngest br. of the preced. m. 30 Dec. 1708, Mary, d. of William Southwell, had Mehitable, b. 4 Nov. 1709; Jonathan, 13 Apr.
1711; Rebecca, 18 Apr. 1714; Daniel, 12 Dec. 1715; Phineas, 27
June, 1717; Elijah, 2 Nov. 1719; Silence; Asa; dates of either of
wh. are not seen; he rem. to Suffield, and had Gershom, 11 July 1724;
and Mary, 27 Nov. 1725. His w. d. 11 Jan. 1768, aged 80, and he d.
10 Apr. 1769, aged 83. *JOSEPH, Northampton, br. of the preced. m.
Mary, d. of Joseph Whiting of Hartford or Westfield, had Joseph, wh.
d. Dec. 1694; Joseph, again, b. 13 June 1695, wh. d. young; Mary ;
Ary; whose dates are unkn.; rem. to Suffield, there had Joseph, again,
26 Dec. 1700; Rachel, 1703 ; and Benjamin, 1705 ; was rep. and d. at
Boston 1708, when the Gov. and both branch. of the legislat. attend. his
funeral. The wid. m. John Ashley of Westfield. NICHOLAS, Provi-
dence, sw. alleg. May 1682, m. Abigail, d. of the first Pardon Tillinghast.
SAMUEL, Northampton, sixth s. of Isaac the first, by w. Mary had Sam-
uel, b. 26 Jan. 1700; Mary, 13 July 1702 ; Martha, 11 Jan. 1709; and
Eunice, 14 July 1713 ; and d. on a visit, at Boston, 31 Mar. 1745.
THOMAS, Billerica, freem. 1680. THOMAS, Northampton, third s. of
the first Isaac, m. 1685, Mary Hinsdale, had Thomas, b. June 1688 ;
Mary, 26 July 1690 ; Rebecca, 1693, d. at 10 yrs.; Josiah, Dec. 1695 ;
Benjamin, 1697; Rachel, 22 Feb. 1701; Jemima, 31 May 1703; and
Elisha, 2 Sept. 1709, Y. C. 1730 ; was deac. and d. 7 June 1725; and
his wid. d. Sept. 1738. TIMOTHY, Providence, sw. alleg. 1 May 1682.
WILLIAM, Billerica 1659. WILLIAM, Scarborough, s. of Godfrey, had
been of Saco 1664, m. Rebecca Scarlet, was driv. away by the Ind. war

1675, and liv. at Salem, where his s. Nathaniel d. 30 Nov. that yr. aged 10. He went back to S. aft. that war, and in 1690 was again driv. off by the same evil. Farmer says, in 1834, 19 of this name had been gr. at N. E. coll. of wh. 7 at Yale, none at Harv.

SHELLEY, ROBERT, Scituate, came to Boston in the Lion, 1632, arr. 16 Sept. rem. 1640 to Barnstable, m. Judith Garnett of Boston, 26 Sept. 1636, at S. where he join. Lothrop's ch. 14 May 1637, had Hannah, bapt. 2 July foll.; Mary, 3 Nov. 1639 ; John, 31 July 1642 ; and other ch. it may be. Hannah m. 9 Mar. 1653, David Linnell ; and Mary m. 25 Jan. 1666, William Harlow, and next, Ephraim Morton. ROBERT, Barnstable, perhaps s. of the preced. had Joseph, b. 24 Jan. 1669 ; Shubael, 25 Apr. 1674 ; and Benjamin, 12 Mar. 1679. Sometimes the name is Sherley or Shirley.

SHELSTONE, ROBERT, Boston, by w. Ann had Eliz. b. 19 Nov. 1676 ; Mary, 1 June 1678 ; Ann, 22 Feb. 1680 ; Susanna, 12 Feb. 1682 ; and Prudence, 3 May 1684.

SHELTON, DANIEL, Stratford, merch. m. 4 Apr. 1692, Eliz. youngest d. of the first Samuel Welles, had Eliz. b. 2 Jan. 1694 ; Sarah, 2 Jan. 1696 ; and Joseph, 24 June 1698 ; and d. a. 1728.

SHEPARD, SHEPPARD, SHEPHEARD, or SHEPHERD, ABRAHAM, Concord, s. of Ralph, m. 2 Jan. 1673, Judith Sill, d. perhaps, of John, had Sarah, b. 10 Sept. 1674 ; Abraham, 25 Mar. 1677 ; Judith, 11 Jan. 1679 ; Hepzibah, 9 May 1681 ; Thanks, 30 Jan. 1683 ; Mary, 3 Jan. 1686 ; and Hannah, 13, bapt. 15 Sept. 1689, at Charlestown, in right, perhaps, of his w. ANDREW, Boston, merch. d. with his w. 1676, leav. John Scottow, and John Endicott, excors. of his will, and sis. Martha Emery to inherit his little prop. EDWARD, Cambridge, freem. 10 May 1643, brot. from Eng. ch. John, Eliz., Abigail, and Deborah, with w. Violet, wh. d. 9 Jan. 1649. He had also, Sarah, bapt. at Braintree, says Farmer, so that we may infer, that he liv. there some time, but in 1650 call. hims. of C. By sec. w. Mary, wid. of Robert Pond of Dorchester, he prob. had no ch. and made his will 1 Oct. 1674. Abigail m. Daniel Pond ; and Deborah m. Jonathan Fairbanks of Dedham ; Sarah m. by one rec. 25 Apr. or by ano. 14 Sept. 1656, Samuel Tomson, and d. 15 Jan. 1680, aged 43 ; Eliz. m. and had ch. it is said, but name of h. or any dates are not seen by me. EDWARD, Middletown, s. of John of Hartford, m. 14 Apr. 1687, Abigail, d. of John Savage, had John, b. 19 Feb. 1688 ; Edward, 18 Dec. 1689 ; and Samuel, 18 Apr. 1692. FRANCIS, Charlestown 1677, had bapt. 3 Mar. 1695, ds. Sarah, aged 20, and Ann, 16. GEORGE, Providence 1646, adm. freem. May 1658. ISAAC, Concord, s. of Ralph, m. 10 Dec. 1667, Mary Smedley, and was k. by the Ind. 12 Feb. 1676. His wid. m. Nathaniel Jewell. ISAAC,

Concord, s. of the yeoman Thomas of Charlestown, m. 31 Dec. 1702, Eliz. Fuller, and d. 4 June 1724. JACOB, Wrentham, br. of the preced. m. 22 Nov. 1699, Mercy, d. of John Chickering of Charlestown, had Jacob, b. 22 Aug. 1700, d. young; John, 25 Feb. 1704, wh. d. 3 Apr. 1809; Thomas, 24 Mar. 1706; Joseph, 9 Feb 1708; and Benjamin, 24 Dec. 1710; and d. 1717. The centenarian had three ws. hav. liv. with the last, wh. d. 9 yrs. bef. him, for sixty-nine yrs. See Daggett, in Geneal. Reg. VI. 128. *JEREMIAH, Lynn, youngest s. of the first Rev. Thomas, preach. at Rowley and Ipswich bef. sett. at L. by w. Mary, d. of Francis Wainwright, had Hannah, b. 1676; Jeremiah, 1677, wh. d. at 23 yrs.; Mehitable, d. young; Nathaniel, 16 June 1681; Margaret, d. soon; Thomas, 1687, d. at 22 yrs.; Francis, d. soon; Mary; John; and Mehitable, again; and these last three liv. to m. He was freem. 1680, ord. 6 Oct. of the same yr.; ardent patriot, and rep. 1689. His w. d. 28 May 1710, aged 53, and he d. 2 June 1720. JOHN, Braintree, br. of Edward, had Samuel, wh. d. 29 Aug. 1641; was freem. 10 May 1643, in 1645 was one of the 32 petitnrs. desiring to plant at Narraganset. Happi. that project, caus. some trouble by adverse claim of Plymouth, and more by the iniquit. pursuit of the poor Gortonists, to drive them from Warwick, was overthrown by the Charter giv. to Roger Williams; and both the unjust pretensions were abandon. See Winth. II. 252. To support the Mass. claim, and defeat the R. I. chart. of 14 Mar. 1644, a fictitious gr. of that territory bear. date 10 Dec. preced. that is earlier by 94 days, was brot. out from the files in our Secretary's office by Mr. Felt, and aft. slumber of two hundred and thirteen yrs. innocent. publ. in Geneal. Reg. XI. 41, 2, 3. I have examin. the orig. parchm. and have no doubt of its worthless character, as several of the signatures, if not all, are pretty evident forgeries; and scrupulous history would be content with the declarat. of the Earl of Warwick, whose name is the first sign. of course, as he was the first man in the Parliament's commiss. for the N. E. Planta. He (as Roger Williams wrote to John Mason of Conn.) said that he had not sign. any such patent *bef.* that of 14 Mar. "and he was sure, that chart. wh. the Mass. Englishmen pretend. had never passed the table." In 1645 Dudley was our Gov. and we may be sure, he had no belief in it, or he would have relied on its absolute grant when writing to the governm. of Plymouth. He makes no refer. to it. Endicott, the Gov. of 1644, and Winthrop, the ch. ruler of 1646, 7, and 8, must despise it, aft. they knew it was denounc. as no act of the signers in Eng. How, and by wh. this docum. was fabricat. may be a curious question. Not a single seal of the pretend. nine signers is attach. but three of them, Rudyard, Vassal, and Bond, in their solemn order of 15 May 1646, giv. in full by Winth. II. 280–2; — four of them, Heselrige and Corbet, in equal. solemn act of 22 July 1647, with the two Earls of Warwick and Manchester, Winth. II. 319 ; — and the same four in a prior letter of 25 May 1647, Winth. II. 320, implicit. deny any such grant to Mass. So that we have seven of the nine denounc. the spurious act, and four of them twice over, and the two Earls even thrice. Prob. the parchm. was sent by one or both of the former Mass. agents, Hugh Peter and Thomas Welde ; but I ought not to charge on either of them an intent to deceive, unless a false date led irresitab. to such deduct. It was only a draft or *project* of a patent, it *might* be said; but that 10 Dec. 1643 was a Sunday. A judicial blindness seems to have attend. base or childish attempts at forgery in the remarka. instances of tak. the Lord's day for date of the magnific. grant of all New Hampsh. 17 May 1629, usual. call. the Wheelwright deed, — the petty convey. to Brewster of only eighty acres at Portsmouth, 6 Dec. 1629, — and this charter or patent to rob R. I. of all the territo. both E. and W. of Narraganset Bay, 10 Dec. 1643. SIC SEMPER INJUSTIS. A subsequent or aft. thot. was, indeed, the contrivance of Welde in his famous issue of "Antinomians and Familists, &c." near. a. the same time. But such jugglery is more to be expect. in a controversial pamphlet, than a solemn State docum. Rogues must always dread the sun, and sometimes the almanac. * The w. of S. was Margaret, and he d. Sept. 1650, she surv.

---

* A brief note (on the first word of the last sentence of this invalua. docum. " Yeouen"), by Mr. Felt, is very significant. It proves that Chaucer, wh. d. 244 yrs. bef. employ. the term for Given. Aft. Chaucer it was not prob. used in many cases ; but between the time of bloody Queen Mary, and booby King James,,it must have given way to our modern word. The use of it proves too much by a great deal, if intend. to indicate the issue of the deed Dec. 1643 bef. that of Mar. 1644. In those 94 days our language did not so rapid. improve ; but near twelve times as many months, I suppose, our *generous* had supersed. the *barbarous* term, at least in solemn acts of States ; and we all feel, that the right of existence in a large community should not be sett. by a point of verbal criticism.

Since the foregoing was written, I have gained the benefit of the sec. Vol. of the Hist. of N. E. and find that Dr. Palfrey (whose inspection nothing escapes) had felt more than one difficulty on this subject. A valua. note on p. 217 states, " respect- ing this patent," " there are some things obscure." He then adopts the suggest. that " it was prob. obt. by Welde," concur. with the presumpt. express. in the Rec. of R. I. II. 162 ; but aggravates the *palpable obscure* by a most reasona. conject. that it was " without authority from Mass." Yet it would seem very odd, that a solemn patent conveying jurisdict. from the sovereign power of Eng. to the colony of Mass. over the whole of the present State of R. I. should be solicit. by a private man for her without any commiss. thereunto. Next, the acumen of the historian observes, that " Williams's patent CONFLICTS with it ; and we are left without informat. as to the cause wh. could have led to *such an inconsistency on the part of the Commissnrs.*" Certain. that act of the E. of Warwick, Sir Arthur Heselrige, Samuel Vassal, Miles

JOHN, Cambridge, prob. br. of Edward, m. 4 Oct. 1649, Rebecca, d. of Samuel Greenhill, had Rebecca; Sarah, b. 5 Mar. 1656; John, 22 Jan. 1658; Violet; Eliz. bapt 29 July 1660; Edward, b. 31 July 1662; Samuel, bapt. 3 July 1664; Thomas, b. 30 Apr. 1666; Deborah; Abigail; and Hannah. His w. d. 22 Dec. 1689, and he m. Martha, wid. of Arthur

Corbet, and Wm. Spurstowe on 14 Mar. 1644, *conflicts* with the possibility of their having on 10 Dec. preced. grant. and convey. similar, aye the same, power and authority to an antagonist. comp. Still, it is not only the *conflict* we inquire about, but the ease with wh. the weaker side prevail. ; and so the persevering scrutiny next finds rêmarka. "the forbearance of Mass. to found any practical claim upon it." Great sagacity is observa. in suggest. of the reason by the elaborate writer, — "to have been *the caution of her magistr. a. involv. thems. in an admissn. of the lawfulness of the authty.* intrusted to the Parliamenta. Commissnrs." Here seems much more refinement than solidity ; but all need of such exercise of skill was taken away very soon, when it was found that the pretended patent was only a flimsy fabrication. Dr. Palfrey had on the former p. refer. to a letter in Gov. Winth's. Hist. II. 193, from the E. of Northumberland and eleven others of the princip. leaders in affairs, of wh. eight were *not* Commissnrs. of plantations, and took notice that only three whose names are sign. to the spurious parchm. as Commissnrs. unit. with that recommend. of Ro. Williams to friend. treatm. and therefore puts an inquiry — Were the Commissnrs. cautious a. *compromis. their dignity* by demand. of Mass. *what she was not unlikely to deny ?* I can ascribe no such exquisite craft to our friends in Eng. especial. bec. in Nov. 1646 the Commissnrs. Order of 15 May preced. (relat. to Gorton and Holden), so clear. asserts the wrong in views of Mass. "We find withal that the tract of ld. call. the Narraganset Bay (concerning wh. the questn. is arisen), was divers yrs. since inhab. by those of Providence, Portsmouth, and Newport, wh. are int·rest in the compl. and that the same is *wholly without the bounds of the Mass. patent gr. by his Majesty.*" This is on the page in Winth. II. 281, *next* to that quoted by the modern hist. to explain *why* Mass. would *not* take a charter.

Deep. as is felt the shame for such deception, that led our governm. to inform Williams of the recent reception (27 Aug. 1645) of a charter, dat. 10 Dec. 1643, giv. to Mass. the Narraganset Bay, and a certain tract of ld. wherein Providence and the isl. of Quidy were includ. as in Palfrey II. 217 is plainly told, we may well exult at the speedy triumph of equity and right in R. I. and Providence Plantations (feeble as that side seem.) over the formidab. array of the four provinces confederat. Fiat justitia.

Connecticut and Plymouth, wh. were each stimulat. to claim part of this territo. that now forms one of the glorious old thirteen U. S. (at least, the greater part by one and the remainder by the other) seem easi. to have discern. the futili. of such claims ; and I believe that Gov. Bradford has not permit. even a word on the right of his col. over R. I. to appear in his copious Hist. The love of justice and a true sense of honor soon brought Gov. Winth. to relinquish the whole jurisdict. E. of the Pawcatuck riv. It is curious to read the modesty of statement by the recent hist. of R. I. in the instructive pages 118 and 119 of Gov. Arnold. The sanctity of that parchm. was assumed at Providence, in 1859, as it had been in 1645, at Boston ; but henceforward I hope, that neither patriotism nor timidity will be called to believe a lie.

Henbury, aft. Aug. 1697. Rebecca m. Jonathan Bigelow; Sarah m. Benajah Stone; Violet m. John Stedman; Eliz. m. William Goodwin; Deborah m. Jacob White; Abigail m. 6 Aug. 1691, Thomas Butler; and Hannah m. 1 Dec. 1692, Thomas Ensign. * JOHN, Lynn, prob. br. of the first Rev. Thomas, was rep. 1689. JOHN, Hartford, s. of John of Cambridge, m. 12 May 1680, Hannah, d. of Paul Peck, wh. d. bef. Dec. 1695; and he m. third w. 18 May 1712, Mary Bigelow, wid. of Jonathan, was deac. and d. 1736. His wid. d. 23 Dec. 1752. By his first w. he had John, b. 1 Nov. 1681; Samuel, 2 Feb. 1684; Hannah, 29 Jan. 1688; Joseph, 29 Apr. 1689; and by sec. w. whose name is not found, had Timothy, 7 June 1697, wh. d. young; and Rebecca, 20 May 1698. By ano. acco. Rebecca was b. 20 May 1695, and Timothy, 7 June 1698; and both d. young. JOHN, Charlestown, s. of Thomas of Malden, was, I suppose, of Moseley's comp. Dec. 1675, by w. Persis, d. perhaps, of Benjamin Pierce, wh. he m. 26 May 1690, had only ch. Persis, bapt. 9 Aug. 1691, aft. d. of the f. wh. had been wound. in the mad expedit. of Phips against Quebec, and d. of it 9 Mar. foll. JOHN, Rowley 1691. JOHN, Concord, freem. 1690. RALPH, Dedham, came in the Abigail from London, 1635, aged 29, with w. Thanks, 23, and d. Sarah, 2; first sat down, prob. at Watertown, but by Farmer is call. of Weymouth, when he had there Isaac, b. 20 June 1639; and Trial, a d. 19 Dec. 1641; but had, also, Abraham; Thanks, 10 Feb. 1651; and Jacob, June 1653. Shattuck makes him live some time at Concord; but earlier he was of Rehoboth, perhaps in 1644; and yet more prob. to me appears his resid. at Malden, where one of the not freq. name was bur. 11 Sept. 1693, aged 90, with moderate allow. for usual exaggera. See Geneal. Reg. IV. 66. Trial m. 11 Mar. 1661, Walter Power. RALPH, Milton, s. of Thomas of Malden, liv. at Brookline 1697–1712, had w. Mary, but no ch. is kn. Prob. his f. d. under his roof, and he d. 26 Jan. 1722. * SAMUEL, Cambridge, came from London, 1635, in the Defence, aged 22 by the custom-ho. rec. wh. may then deserve more trust than when it calls him serv. of Herlakenden (to deceive the governm. prob.), arr. 3 Oct. was one of the first memb. of a new ch. gather. 1 Feb. foll. by his br. Thomas, Gov. Haynes, Herlakenden, and others, freem. 3 Mar. 1636, rep. 1639, 40, 4, and 5, ar. co. 1640, went home, and was a major in Ireland 1658. His w. was Hannah, and ch. Thomas, b. 5 Nov. 1638, wh. d. 9 Feb. 1650; Samuel, Feb. 1640, d. at 5 yrs.; Hannah, 20 June 1642; and Jane, 16 May 1645. SAMUEL, Rowley, s. of Rev. Thomas of Cambridge, ord. 15 Nov. 1665, m. 30 Apr. 1666, Dorothy, youngest d. of Rev. Henry Flint, had only Samuel, b. 10 or 19, bapt. 25 Aug. 1667, H. C. 1685; and his w. d. 12 Feb. 1668, and he d. 8 wks. aft. SAMUEL, Haverhill, took o. of alleg. 1677. SOLOMON, Salisbury, freem. 1690,

m. 4 Aug. 1684, Sarah, wid. of Joseph French, d. of Roger Eastman,
had Sarah, b. 25 June 1686 ; Bethia, 13 Mar. 1688 ; Solomon, 18 Apr.
1691 ; Israel, 7 Mar. 1694 ; and Jeremiah, 10 Aug. 1698. *THOMAS*,
Cambridge, s. of William, b. at Towcester, Co. Northampton, on 5
Nov. 1605 (gunpowder-plot day), bred at Emanuel, where he was matric.
1619, and had his degr. 1623, and 1627, preach. at Earls Colne in
Essex, fail. of success in first attempt to come hither in 1634, but next
yr. arr. 3 Oct. in the Defence from London, with w. Margaret Touteville
(a relat. of Sir Richard Darley), wh. had b. one ch. that d. soon ; and
Thomas, b. at London, 5 Apr. 1635, bapt. Feb. aft. reach. Boston, H. C.
1653 ; but the mo. d. 1 Feb. bef. this solemnity. He m. next, Joanna,
eldest d. of Rev. Thomas Hooker, had Samuel, b. Oct. 1641, H. C.
1658 ; and John, 2 Apr. 1646 ; and this w. d. 28 of the same mo. He
m. 8 Sept. 1647, Margaret Boradale, had Jeremiah, 11 Aug. 1648, H.
C. 1669 ; was freem. 3 Mar. 1636, and d. 25 or 28 Aug. 1649. So well
employ. had been his short life, that no loss of a publ. man in our country
was more lament. exc. that of Gov. Winth. a few mos. bef. His wid. m.
Jonathan Mitchell, his successor in the pulpit. *THOMAS*, Charlestown, s.
of the preced. b. in Eng. just bef. emb. of his parents, ord. 13 Apr. 1659,
collea. of Rev. Zechariah Symmes, had m. 3 Nov. 1656, Hannah, d. of
William Tyng, had Thomas, b. 3, bapt. 4 July 1658, H. C. 1676 ; William, 24 June 1660, wh. d. bef. his f. ; Hannah, 13 Sept. 1663 ; and
Margaret, 26 Aug. 1666 ; and d. 22 Dec. 1677, of smallpox. His d.
Hannah m. 9 Nov. 1682, Daniel Quincy. THOMAS, Charlestown 1657,
b. in Eng. s. perhaps, of Ralph, liv. some yrs. at Medford or Malden,
and again at C. ; m. 19 Nov. 1658, Hannah, d. of Thomas Ensign of
Scituate, had Thomas ; Ralph, b. 1667 ; John ; Jacob ; Hannah ; Isaac,
May, bapt. 23 July 1682 ; and, perhaps, others ; but none, exc. Isaac,
prob. the youngest, was there bapt. for goodman Thomas did not join the
ch. bef. 2 Sept. 1677. His w. d. 14 Mar. 1698 ; and he in few yrs. had
sec. w. Joanna, wh. outliv. him, and he d. at Milton, 29, as gr.st. tells, but
town rec. says 26 Sept. 1719, aged 87. See Geneal. Reg. VI. 128.
His d. Hannah m. 13 Apr. 1681, Joseph Blanchard. *THOMAS*, Charlestown, s. of Rev. Thomas of the same, began to preach 19 May 1678,
and was ord. success. to his f. 5 May 1680, freem. same yr. ; m. 27 July
1682, wid. Mary Lynde, d. of John Anderson, but of wh. she was wid.
aft. dilig. inq. I am unable to discov. had Hannah, bapt. 29 Apr. 1683,
d. soon ; and Hannah, again, 1 Feb. 1685; and he d. 8 Jan. foll. His
wid. m. next yr. Samuel Hayman, Esq. THOMAS, Charlestown, s. of
goodman Thomas, of the same, m. 7 Dec. 1682, Hannah, d. of George
Blanchard, had Hannah, bapt. 12 Aug. 1683; Sarah, 17 May 1685 ;
Mary, 13 Feb. 1687 ; Abigail, 17 Feb. 1689 ; Ruth, 11 May 1690 ;

and Thomas, 27 Nov. 1692 ; rem. to Bristol, bef. 1700, to Branford 1709, and last to New Haven, there d. 18 Apr. 1726. But if Dodd is right, p. 148, he had, also, John, and Eliz. aft. leav. Charlestown. THOMAS, Hartford, br. of Samuel of the same, m. 5 Sept. 1695, Susanna Scott, had Thomas, b. 2 Apr. 1697 ; Susanna, 24 Aug. 1698 ; Violet, 14 May 1700 ; Ebenezer, 21 Feb. 1702 ; Daniel, 11 Jan. 1704 ; Zebulon, 16 Oct. 1705 ; Rebecca, 16 Mar. 1707 ; and by sec. w. m. 12 Oct. 1710, Jane North, had Jane, 20 July 1711 ; Deborah, 18 Dec. 1713 ; and Sarah, 15 May 1717. WILLIAM, Dorchester, a serv. of William Sumner, order. by Ct. in Apr. 1636, to be whip. for steal. from his master, and in no other instance is the name found in Mass. for the first quarter of a centu.; so that Farmer, in giv. one to ar. co. 1642, was, no doubt, misled by read. Mr. as abbreviat. for William ; but in Conn. 1677 was a WILLIAM, perhaps the thief from Mass. whose w. was that yr. divorc. for his desertion. Nineteen had been gr. in 1834 at the N. E. coll. says Farmer, of wh. I find five at Harv. a century and a half bef.

SHEPARDSON, DANIEL, Charlestown 1632, blacksmith, by w. Joanna had Lydia, bapt. 24 July 1637 ; Daniel, 14 June 1640 ; and Joanna, 13 Mar. 1642, wh. m. Nov. 1661, Roger Kennicut ; and d. 26 July 1644, his will of 16th bef. provid. for w. and those three ch. The wid. m. Thomas Call, and her d. Lydia m. 22 July 1657, his s. Thomas. Our Gen. Ct. as in the Col. rec. II. 194, appears, had act. for care of the est. in May 1647. DANIEL, Charlestown, s. of the preced. took o. of fidel. 15 Dec. 1674, m. 11 Apr. 1668, Eliz. d. of Thomas Call, wid. of Samuel Tingley of Malden, had Daniel, b. June 1669 ; John, Jan. 1671 ; and Nathaniel, 28 Oct. 1680, perhaps others. The s. Daniel was a soldier in the fleet to Canada 1690.

SHEPLEY, or SHIPLEY, JOHN, Salem 1637, Felt says had then gr. of ld. but tells no more. He was in that pt. wh. bec. Wenham, had John, b. a. 1637 ; Nathaniel, 1639 ; and Lydia, a. 1641 ; and rem. with Fiske, his min. to Chelmsford, there liv. long. Perhaps his w. in 1644 was Ann.

SHEPWAY, or SHIPWAY, JOHN, Portsmouth, by w. Ann had John, b. 26 July 1662, was one of the petitnrs. to the k. 1683, against his Gov. Cranfield, constable 1688, and d. 1690, leav. wid. wh. was prob. his sec. w. and d. of major Frost.

SHERBURNE, GEORGE, Portsmouth 1650. * HENRY, Portsmouth 1632, came in the James, arr. 12 June in 8 wks. from London, m. 13 Nov. 1637, as fam. rec. tells, Rebecca, only d. of Ambrose Gibbons, had Samuel and. Eliz. tw. b. 4 Aug. 1638 ; Mary, 20 Nov. 1640 (and fam. tradit. says these two ds. were bapt. by Rev. Mr. Gibson) ; Henry, 11

Jan. 1642 ; John, 3 Apr. 1647 ; Ambrose, 3 Aug. 1649 ; Sarah, 10 Jan.
1652 ; Rebecca, 21 Apr. 1654; Rachel, 4 Apr. 1656, wh. d. Dec. foll. ;
Martha, 4 Dec. 1657, d. Nov. foll. ; and Ruth, 3 June 1660 ; was rep. 1660,
and his w. d. 3 June 1667. For sec. w. he had Sarah, wid. of Walter Abbot, and d. 1680. No account of any of the ch. exc. Samuel, John, Mary,
and Eliz. can be obtain. Eliz. m. 10 June 1656, Tobias Langdon, and
next, 11 Apr. 1667, Tobias Lear, had Eliz. b. 11 Feb. 1669 ; Mary m. 21
Oct. 1658 Richard Sloper. ‡ HENRY, a counsell. of N. H. appoint. 1728,
wh. d. 1757, aged 83, may have been neph. or more prob. gr.s. of the preced.
JOHN, Portsmouth 1643, perhaps a br. of the first Henry, of the gr.
jury 1650, m. Eliz. d. of Robert Tuck of Hampton, had Henry, John,
Mary, and Eliz. pray. for jurisdict. of Mass. 1653, and sw. alleg. 1656.
JOHN, Portsmouth 1683, perhaps s. of the first Henry, sign. addr. to
the k. against his Gov. Cranfield. SAMUEL, Hampton, prob. s. of the
first Henry, m. 15 Dec. 1668, Love, d. of John Hutchins of Haverhill,
had John, and, perhaps, other ch. beside d. Love ; sw. alleg. 1678, and
join. the petitn. against Cranfield in 1683 ; rem. to Portsmouth, and in
1691 was a capt. and k. 4 Aug. that yr. by the Ind. at Maquoit, near
Brunswick. His wid. Love d. at Kingston 1739, aged 94. WILLIAM,
Portsmouth 1644.

SHERIN, ROBERT, came from London in the Elizabeth, 1634, aged
32, perhaps sitt. down first with other fellow-passeng. Sherman, Kimball,
Underwood, and others, at Watertown, but may soon have rem. to Ipswich, and prob. is the same as Sherwin.

SHERLOCK, ‡ JAMES, Portsmouth, a counsell. appoint. 1684, was
made by Andros, the royal Gov. of N. E. Sheriff of Suffk. 1687, and
imprison. by the patriots on overthr. of A.

SHERMAN, ABIAH, Watertown, s. of Rev. John, freem. 1690, d. without issue, says Cothren. BENJAMIN, Stratford, s. of the first Samuel of
the same, had, says Cothren, Job, Nathaniel, Enos, Benjamin, Samuel,
Timothy, and James ; but C. gives no date to either, nor tells the name
of mo. nor d. of f. From more careful glean. I obt. some facts, as foll.
He m. 1683, Rebecca Phippeny, perhaps d. of James of S. wh. d. 1739,
and he d. 1741. BEZALEEL, Watertown, s. of Rev. John, prob. eldest,
aft. leav. coll. was m. and Bond marks his d. bef. 1685, leav. childr.
Perhaps his m. was in the East Indies, engag. in trade there, and mak.
his resid. abroad, as I infer from let. of Rev. John Higginson to his s.
Nathaniel, at Madras, Aug. 1697, ask. " what has bec. of Bezaleel S.'s
w. and ch." See 3 Mass. Hist. Coll. VII. 200. As no more is ever
heard of him, I conject. that he was *then* d. at least in the Catal. 1698
of the Magn. he is among the stars. DANIEL, New Haven, br. of the
preced. among the freem. in 1669, m. 28 Sept. 1663, Abiah, or Abigail,

d. of Rev. Nicholas Streete, had Abigail, b. 5 Sept. 1665; ano. d. b.
1667, d. very soon; Daniel, 5 Sept. 1668; Mary, 28 Oct. 1670; John,
Nov. 1673; Eliz. 20 Sept. 1676; Samuel, 27 Jan. 1679; Eunice, 10
Nov. 1682; was ens. of the milit. 1676, and there liv. a propr. 1685.
DAVID, Stratford, youngest s. of the first Samuel (miscall. Daniel by
Cothren), m. Mercy, perhaps d. of Jeremiah Judson, was one of the found.
of ch. in Stratfield, now Bridgeport, in 1695, and deac. in it, and d. 1753.
EDMUND, Watertown, br. or more prob. Mr. Judd thot. f. of Rev.
John, a clothier; was one of the selectmen 1636, adm. freem. 25 May of
that yr. went home, and liv. at Dedham, Eng. 1648, and 66, says Bond.
EDMUND, Stratford, s. of the first Samuel, by w. Susanna, says Cothren,
had Bezaleel, b. 11 Apr. 1676, wh. is error for 1 Jan. 1674; Sarah,
bapt. Aug. 1678; Samuel, b. 8 Jan. 1679; Edmund, 20 Mar. 1680;
and Matthew, 8 Jan. 1683; and d. in that yr. EDWARD, perhaps
rather, Edmund, Wethersfield 1636, is said to have foll. his s. Rev. John,
to N. E. prob. the yr. preced. and was an orig. propr. of W. but gave
his ld. to s. Samuel, being well advanc. in yrs. when he rem. to New
Haven, was adm. freem. 29 Oct. 1640, and d. 1641. HENRY, Boston,
perhaps, but I kn. nothing of him, exc. that in the inv. of John Mills,
1651, this man's name appears among debtors. *JAMES*, Sudbury, s. of
Rev. John, there began to preach 1677, m. 1680, Mary, d. of Thomas
Walker, had John, and Thomas, was very unhappy in his place, so as in
July 1705 to be strip. of his functions, "deposed from his pastoral
office," is the exact phrase of 1 Mass. Hist. Coll. X. 87, but for the
cause of such unusual proceed. I have less anxious. sought, than to learn
how he went to Elizabethtown in N. J. and aft. to Salem, there d. 1718.
See Mather's Hecatompolis. * *JOHN*, Watertown, prob. s. of Edmund,
b. at Dedham, in Essex, 26 Dec. 1613, bapt. 4 Jan. foll. bred at Trinity
Coll. tho. Mather (wh. so common. is wrong in minute matters), says
Emanuel; but that is of far less importance than his elaborate error
a. subscription, as by king James's rules exacted, bef. the University
honors: "When his turn came to be a grad." says the Magnalia, "he
serious. consider. the *subscript.* requir. of him, and upon invincib. argum.
bec. so dissatisf. therewithal, that, advis. with Mr. Rogers, Dr. Preston,
and other emin. persons, wh. commend. his conscient. consider. counsel,
he WENT AWAY under the persecut. charact. of a COLLEGE PURITAN."
Now I testify to the contra. for 12 July 1842, I saw at the Univ. of
Cambridge, in the origin. the subscript. of John Sherman on tak. his
A. B. 1629–30, and repeat. on commenc. A. M. 1633.   It is needless to
ask how such a fiction was impos. on the credulity of Mather, as it is
prob. no answer can be found.   The yr. aft. tak. his sec. degr. a. the end
of Apr. 1634, S. emb. in the Elizabeth at Ipswich, where he had fam.

relat. and reach. Boston in June. At Watertown he resid. near a yr.
and was dism. with others from the ch. at W. 29 May 1635, says Bond,
to form a new one on the Conn. riv. tho. we read in the Magn. " not
many wks. at W. bef. he rem. upon mature adv. unto New Haven."
Now instead of *not many wks.* we know New Haven was not sett. until
more than four yrs. after he arr. at W. Such is the perpetual laxity of
narrative in the ecclesiast. histori. of N. E. Beside this, it was not to
New Haven that he first went, but to Hartford and Wethersfield, where
the attractions of Hooker or Smith were strong eno. and at the latter he
obt. gr. of a house lot alongside of that giv. by Rev. Henry Smith to
his s. Samuel. Prob. no work in the ch. was early desir. or at least
gain. for he was releas. from serv. of watch and ward not until 1640 at
May sess. of Gen. Ct. Soon aft. he sold to Thomas Bunce his Wethersfield lot, and rem. to Milford, join. the ch. there, yet acting only in civ.
life, rep. 1643, and preach. for short season in 1645 for the early days
of Branford. There he was desir. to sett. as their min. but no ch. was
then gather. By first w. Mary (wh. d. says the ch. rec. at M. 8 Sept.
1644), he had, says Mather, six ch. wh. is liable to doubt (tho. we are
igno. of the date of m. as well as the parents of w.) for it is not prob.
that he was m. in Eng. nor in our country bef. 1638, then 24 yrs. old.
Four ch. are ment. Mary, b. perhaps in 1639 ; Bezaleel, bapt. at M. 15
Nov. 1640, H. C. 1661 ; Daniel, 27 Mar. 1642 ; and Samuel, 14 Apr.
1644, wh. prob. d. soon. At New Haven he m. sec. w. Mary Launce,
late in 1645, a maiden in the fam. of Gov. Eaton, and glad eno. must
she have been to escape the perpetual trouble grow. from the unhap.
temper of the w. of the Gov. full report of wh. is giv. in Appx. to the
charm. Hist. Discours. of Rev. Dr. Bacon. By her he had Samuel,
again, bapt. at N. H. 23 Aug. 1646, and next yr. he rem. to Watertown,
wh. on req. obt. his dismis. from Milford ch. 8 Nov. 1647. With more
than his usual exuberance of invent. Mather makes it " upon the d. of
Phillips" (that was in July 1644), Watertown offer. a call and he
accept. tho. he adds, " at the same time one of the chhs. at Boston used
their endeav. to bec. the owner of so well *talented* a person, and sev.
chhs. in London also by lett. much urged him to come over and help
them." If this be true (wh. is quite unlike.) for London, we kn. it must
be false for B. since there was only one ch. many yrs. later, and in that
Cotton and Wilson could wish or rec. no collea. Our sec. ch. where
Mather was all his days a min. was not gather. bef. 5 June 1650, and
could sett. no pastor bef. Nov. 1655. Stranger than such inexcusa.
carelessn. however, is what he tells of this w. call her mo. d. of Darcy,
Earl Rivers, one of the Popish Counsellors of Charles I. wh. had no d.
that m. a Launce ; and next, in mak. this w. bring "no less than twenty

ch. add. unto the number of six, wh. he had bef." Authority for such improb. he design. his reader should infer, I suppose, from tell. in the begin. of the sentence, " by the d. of that Mr. Launce, *wh. is yet liv. among us,* Sherman had no less than, &c." To this fable full credit was long giv. bec. it obt. the sober sanction of Hutch. I. 19, a relative of Mather, more than once misled by him. But in our day, a descend. of Sherman by this w. aft. bestow. large investigat. with adequate critical skill, puts the result, 1851, with " special wonder" in Geneal. Reg. V. 307, as *not* " establ. the Darcy lineage." The writer refers to an emin. Eng. antiquary, wh. had been very slow to reject the tale even of Mather, or to distrust so judicious an auth. as Hutch. but pursu. the inq. long, and wrote me the issue, three yrs. later, "aft. all the attent. I have paid to Mr. Willard's point, there is no satisfacto. conclus. arr. at; and I am inclin. to think, that there was real. no particle of truth in the report wh. Mather had receiv. and has giv. circul. to." Equal distrust is more natur. felt a. the number of ch. that led our ecclesiast. hist. to dilate in eight and twenty lines on " such a Polytokie," as he tersely or foolishly calls it. Suspicion arises from this fact, that exactly one less than half of the twenty-six ch. giv. to both ws. have never found a name either in rec. or benevol. tradit. See Bond, 432. Yet one more, Benjamin, was prob. lost from the rec. (by wearing out the paper) of b. 23 Apr. 1661, and d. 14 Oct. 1662. By the sec. w. wh. long outliv. him, d. 9 Mar. 1710, we see, then, ten ch. or at most eleven, instead of twenty, were b. and whence could the error arise ? Aft. the b. of the first ch. the f. was always at Watertown, there as min. he would make rec. of bapt. of his own, as well as of others; but the rec. is lost, and we have to seek in town rec. for entry of births ; and fortunate. his cous. of the same name was many yrs. the clk. Five only are thus found, Abigail, 3 Feb. 1648; Joanna, 3 Sept. 1652; Mary, 5 Mar. 1657 ; Grace, 10 Mar. 1659 ; and John, 17 Mar. 1660 ; but with more or less confidence, beside Benjamin, five more can be read in Bond (tho. the first two are count. by him as of first w.), James, bef. ment. Abiah, Eliz. Esther, and Mercy. Sometimes I have suspect. that the ch. of *both* contempo. Johns were count. for *one* by the informant of Mather, and very exact is the rec. of seven of capt. John, part. bef. part. aft. he bec. clk. and so by office bound to kn. bs. ds. and ms. No weight can be denied to such surmise from the fact of differ. names of the ws. of Rev. John and capt. John, for the prefix of respect in h. is less likely to be omit. than the bapt. name in w. With all his assidu. Bond could not satisfy hims. How Mather got this story of the *fruitful vine,* conject. would be various, if anyways reasona. The eldest d. of this sec. w. could not have told it to him, for she d. the yr. of Mather's bachelor's degr. 20 yrs. bef. his book was writ. and her mo. (wh. was liv. aft. the light of the immortal author had shone upon the readers of Magnalia a dozen yrs.) could not be so monstrous. wrong in the tale of her own childr. But if she did give him these myths of her noble descent and prolific felicity, either she was insane, wh. he had not sanity eno. to discov. or she was irreverent. playing on his bottomless credulity. More prob. however, seems this solution, that much of what he had heard about Sherman was forgotten, and sev. stories turn. into one, and he tax. his fancy (that was always lively, especial. at a marvel), for some incidents, and confus. the whole. Sherman was adm. freem. of Mass. 1669, and was struck with fever and delirium in the pulpit of his s. at Sudbury where he preach. his last sermon, 5 July 1685 (as, in his diary, is told by Sewall), made his will 6 Aug. and d. two days aft. He made James excor. and (includ. two dec.) names twelve other ch. Mary, the ch. of first w. m. a. 1658, Daniel Allen; Abigail m. 8 Aug. 1661, Rev. Samuel Willard; Mary, of sec. w. m. 27 May 1679, Ellis Barron, jr; and Mercy m. 4 Apr. 1700, Samuel Barnard. * JOHN, Watertown, cous. of the preced. b. at Dedham, Co. Essex, freem. 17 May 1637, by w. Martha, d. of William Palmer (whose wid. hav. m. Roger Porter, by this means came the error, that she wh. m. S. was d. of Porter), had John, b. 2 Nov. 1638; Martha, 21 Feb. 1641; Mary, 25 Mar. 1643; Sarah, 17 Jan. 1648, d. at 19 yrs.; Eliz. 15 Mar. 1649; Joseph, 14 May 1650; and Grace, 20 Dec. 1653, acc. Bond; but Cothren, 680, omits Eliz. and makes Grace 1655. He was capt. selectman 1637, and oft. aft.; town clk. many yrs. from 1648, rep. 1651, 3, and 63, d. 25 Jan. 1691, aged 76. His wid. d. 7 Feb. 1701. Martha m. 26 Sept. 1661, Francis Bowman; Mary m. 18 Jan. 1667, Timothy Hawkins, jr. and d. 6 Nov. foll.; Eliz. m. 20 July 1681, Samuel Gaskell, or Gascoyne of Charlestown. JOHN, Watertown, eldest ch. of the preced. was k. as Bond says (but I presume only so bad. wound. as to d. soon) in the gr. Narraganset bat. with the Ind. 19 Dec. 1675, being of Mosely's comp. left. no issue, prob. never m. JOHN, Marshfield, s. prob. of the first William, m. at Boston, perhaps as sec. w. 25 Oct. 1677, Jane, d. of Walter Hatch, had sev. ch. by ea. w. it is thot. but dates or names are not seen. He may be the man, wh. took o. of fidel. at Dartmouth 1684. ‡* JOHN, Stratford, s. of the first Samuel of the same, was disting. in Conn. speaker of the ho. made an Assist. in 1713, for ten yrs.; by w. Eliz. had Ichabod; Hannah, bapt. July 1680; Samuel, Aug. 1682; Eliz. Oct. 1684; John, June 1687; Sarah, Jan. 1690; Mary, Mar. 1692; and Susanna, Nov. 1693. He rem. early, perhaps 1673, to Woodbury, where he was town clk. capt. and deac. and d. 13 Dec. 1730. His wid. d. 1 Oct. 1744. JOSEPH, Wethersfield 1639, or earlier, had Samuel, to wh. he gave his ld. at W. and rem. to

Stamford 1641, says Chapin, Hist. 163, 4, tho. Mr. Judd (wh. had bestow. much research on rec. of W., does not agree that the name of Samuel's f. was Joseph, for in the first two generat. he says there was no Joseph in Conn. and Hinman, 72, and prob. Chapin mistook Jo. (the perpet. abbreviat. for John) as Joseph. The *fifth* lot was, he is confid. set out to Edward, easi. read Edmund. * JOSEPH, Watertown, youngest s. of capt. John, a blacksmith, m. 18 Nov. 1673, Eliz. d. of Edward Winship of Cambridge, had John, b. 11 Jan. 1675; Edward, 2 Sept. 1677; Joseph, 8 Feb. 1680; Samuel, 28 Nov. 1681; but Cothren makes it 1682; Jonathan, 24 Feb. 1684; Ephraim, 16 Mar. 1685, d. soon; Ephraim, again, 20 Sept. 1686; Eliz. 15 July 1687, unless 1689 be the true yr.; William, 28 July 1692; Sarah, 2 June 1694; and Nathaniel, 19 Sept. 1696; and d. 20 Jan. 1731. William, the youngest but one of these s. was a shoemak. at Newton, and m. at Watertown, 3 Sept. 1715, Mehitable Wellington, had as third s. Roger, b. 19 Apr. 1721 at N. forever to be honor. as one of the framers, with Franklin, of the Declarat. of Independ. and of the most sagacious men ever produc. by N. E. MATTHEW, Stratford, br. of Benjamin, had w. Hannah, and d. 1698, leav. David, b. 1692; and Hannah, perhaps more. NATHANIEL, Boston, perhaps s. of Samuel of the same, by w. Grace had Nathaniel, b. 19 Dec. 1659; and by w. Mary had Mary, 28 Mar. 1665. NATHANIEL, Stratford, br. of Matthew, m. 1680, Mary, perhaps d. of James Phippeny, and d. 1712. PELEG, Portsmouth, R. I. m. 25 July 1657, Eliz. d. of Thomas Lawton, had Thomas, b. 8 Aug. 1658; William, 3 Oct. 1659; Daniel, 15 June 1662; Mary, 11 Dec. 1664; Peleg, 8 Oct. 1666; Ann, 30 Apr. 1668; Eliz. 25 Nov. 1670; Samuel, 15 Oct. 1672; Eber, 20 Oct. 1674; John, 28 Oct. 1676; Benjamin, 15 July 1677; Sarah, 25 Jan. 1680; Isabel, 3 June 1683; and George, 18 Dec. 1687. * PHILIP, Roxbury, came in 1633, a single man, freem. 14 May 1634, first on the list aft. Gov. Haynes, m. Sarah Odding, d. of John Porter's w. by former h. went home early, but soon came again, and was led away, says the ch. rec. to familism by Porter, disarm. Nov. 1637, and banish. next yr. went to R. I. there sign. the compact of civil governm. Mar. 1638, was Secr. or Recorder of the Col. 1648, and was rep. 1656. See Callender, 30. As Secr. he was happy eno. to have a descend. in 1857, prob. in seventh generat. fill. the same post; but I can hardly indicate the line. He had Samson, and Samuel, perhaps more. PHILIP, Boston, " apprent. of John Blower," but it will not easi. be learn. wh. was his f. He d. 12 Dec. 1655. RICHARD, Boston, merch. by w. Eliz. had Eliz. b. 1 Dec. 1635, had two ds. Ann, and Priscilla in Eng. of wh. the latter was m. two liv. here, Martha Brown, and Abigail Duncan; all wh. is learn. from his will of 7 Apr. pro. 31 July 1660, as

abstr. in Geneal. Reg. IX. 227, wh. ment. also, gr.ch. Mary, and Eliz.
Spawle, wh. Bond read Sprawle, so that he must have had five ds. if
not six. If it be very diffic. to find any thing of the fam. in other rec.
his terrib. lawsuit against Capt. Keayne a. his w.'s sow, wh. much
convuls. the col. and led to a radical change in its constitut. of governm.
supplies the place abundant. as told in Winth. II. 69–72. He d. 30
May. SAMSON, Portsmouth, R. I. s. of Philip, m. 4 Mar. 1675, Isbel,
d. of John Tripp, had Philip, b. 16 Jan. foll.; Sarah, 24 Sept. 1677;
Alice, 12 Jan. 1680; Samson, 28 Jan. 1682; Abiel, 15 Oct. 1684; and
Job, 8 Nov. 1687. SAMUEL, Ipswich 1636, of importance eno. to be
disarm. with only one more of that town, Nov. 1637, as danger. heretic,
d. bef. 1660, leav. ch. Samuel, Nathaniel, and Mary Clark, but wh. was
the w. is not seen. SAMUEL, Boston, husbandman, perhaps br. of Philip,
by w. Grace had Philip, b. 31 Dec. 1637; Martha, 5 Sept. 1639; both
bapt. 8 Mar. 1640; Nathaniel, 19 Dec. 1642; Jonathan, 11 Feb. 1644,
a. 3 days old; and Philip, d. young. He had join. the ch. 1 Mar. and
was adm. freem. 13 May 1640; and his w. join. the ch. 29 Aug. 1641;
he d. early in 1645, and in 1652 the Gen. Ct. interfer. in admin. of his
est. by the deacons of Boston ch. ‡ SAMUEL, Stratford, br. of Rev.
John, perhaps did not come so early as 1634, wh. Cothren, 60, assumes,
but was aft. 1640 some yrs. at Wethersfield, there had houselot, giv. by
his f.; was among first resid. at Stamford, and had sev. ch. b. there; was
chos. an Assist. 1662, 3, 4, and aft. the union of the Cols. of Conn. and
N. H. 1665–7, but tho. nominat. for 1668, he fail. of the elect. and is no
more heard of, exc. in project. with others, 1672, settlem. of Woodbury.
Cothren says he m. in Eng. Sarah Mitchell, and brot. her hither; but
this is to the last degr. improb. for he brings him in 1634, then only 19
yrs. old at most, perhaps only 18, and in the mo. country very few so
young were m. beside wh. he calls this w. sis. of Rev. Jonathan, wh.
does not seem to have had such sis. at least we kn. that Richard Mather,
a fellow-passeng. with Mitchell's f. in 1635, has no refer. to a d. then m.
on our side of the water, and f. Mitchell in his will of 1646 names ds.
only Susanna and Hannah, no Sarah; and beyond that, our Sherman
tribe was from the E. part of Essex, while the Mitchells were of the W.
Riding of Yorksh. on the edge of Lancash. opposite sides of the kingdom, between wh. two hundred and thirty yrs. ago intercourse was very
rare. Reconciliat. of the principal fact (if it be true) may be gain. by
a reasona. conject. that the m. tho. it could hard. have occur. in Eng. was
some yrs. aft. com. of the parties hither. The dates of b. of their ch.
give further evid. as Cothren hims. furnish. them, of his error, as the
earliest is 1641, and the latest 1665, wh. is beyond the usual result of a
m. in 1634. His roll, with slight corrections, is: Samuel, b. 19 Jan.

1641; Theophilus, 28 Oct. 1643; Matthew, 21 Oct. 1645; Edmund, 4 Dec. 1647; John, 8 Feb. 1651; Sarah, 8 Feb. 1654; Nathaniel, 21 Mar. 1657; Benjamin, 29 Mar. 1662; and Daniel (wh. careful Mr. Judd made David) 15 Apr. 1665. Some ground for support of the tradit. of m. with the d. of Mitchell may appear in two of the names of these ch. Matthew and Sarah; but I must adhere to my conject. a. the time. When he d. might seem as hard to settle, as his date of m. Cothren tells, that he d. bef. Oct. 1684, but it was prob. fifteen yrs. later, at least we kn. that div. of his est. among heirs, whose lang. implies recent dec. of their ancest. was made Sept. 1700, and deeds by him as late as 1694 can be read. SAMUEL, Boston, s. perhaps, of Samuel of Ipswich, by w. Naomi had Nathaniel, b. 19 Dec. 1659; Samuel, 3 Oct. 1661, d. soon; and Samuel, again, 24 Apr. 1664. SAMUEL, Stratford, eldest s. of Samuel of the same, m. 19 June 1665, Mary, d. of Daniel Titterton, had Mary, b. 7 May 1666; Daniel, 23 Mar. 1669; Susanna, 22 July 1670; Sarah, bapt. May 1673; Grace, b. 8 July 1676; and Eliz. 1 Jan. 1679. He had sec. w. m. Aug. 1695, Abigail, d. of John Thompson, wid. of Nicholas Huse, wh. had been wid. of Jonathan Curtis, and d. Feb. 1719. His wid. d. 1731. SAMUEL, Portsmouth, R. I. s. of Philip, m. 3 Feb. 1681, Martha, d. of John Tripp, had Sarah, b. 10 Apr. 1682; Mary, 1 Dec. 1683; Mehitable, 18 Aug. 1685; Samuel, 12 June 1687; and Othniel, 29 Jan. 1690. Perhaps he had former w. Sarah, that d. at Marshfield July 1680. THEOPHILUS, Stratford 1669, was br. of the sec. Samuel of the same, and a man of distinct. d. early in 1712; but Cothren gives him no w. or ch. THOMAS, Ipswich 1638. WILLIAM, Plymouth 1632, may have come in 1629, for to one of the name was giv. by our Gov. and Comp. in London, liberty to bring in his kine from Northampton in fourteen days from 26 Feb. doubtless to be emb. in the fleet with Higginson. He m. 1639, Prudence Hill, whose f. is unkn. to me, was of Duxbury and Marshfield 1643, had prob. John, b. 1646, and William; but Winsor may have confus. f. and s. The f. d. or was bur. 25 Oct. 1679. WILLIAM, Marshfield, prob. s. of the preced. m. 25 Dec. 1667, not 26 Dec. 1677, both dates being giv. in Geneal. Reg. VI. 348, Desire, d. of Edward Dotey, had Hannah, b. 1668; Eliz. 1670, wh. d. young; William, 1672; Patience, 1674; and Experience, 1678; and d. perhaps, early in 1681. His wid. m. 24 Nov. of that yr. Israel Holmes, and next, Alexander Standish. WILLIAM, Portsmouth, R. I. s of Peleg, m. 12 May 1681, Martha, d. of William Wilbor, had William Thomas, Eleanor, Mary, Eliz. Peleg, Benjamin, Sarah, and Hannah. He m. it is said, sec. w. in 1697, Mercy, d. of Peregrine White. Most of fams. of this name in R. I. write it with a aft. e but in early days it was usual.

as now, sometimes Sharman. Of this name, twelve had, in 1834, been gr. at Yale, and two at Harv.

SHERRITT, SHARRATT, SHEROTT, or SHERROT, HUGH, Ipswich 1634, freem. 4 Mar. 1635, rem. bef. 1647, to Haverhill, there had license to sell wine, may have been at Dover short time, in 1659, but d. at H. 5 Sept. 1678, of gr. age, as tradit. tells, of course, a. 100 yrs. His w. Eliz. wh. had been wid. of Humphrey Griffin, in her will, of 30 July 1670, names her five ch. by the former h. but nothing is heard of any issue of S.

SHERWIN, JOHN, Ipswich, m. 25 Nov. 1667, Frances, d. of Edward Loomis, had Mary, b. Aug. 1679; Frances, 27 Jan. 1682; Sarah, 7 Oct. 168. the last fig. being lost from the rec. He m. sec. w. 30 Sept. 1691, Mary, eldest d. of William Chandler of Andover, had John; Alice, 21 Jan. 1694; Abigail, 4 May 1695; Elinor, 28 June 1696; William, 27 July 1698; and Jacob, 17 Oct. 1699; and d. 15 Oct. 1726, aged 82. Mary m. 9 June 1702, Caleb Foster.

SHERWINGTON, or SHERRINGTON, THOMAS, propound. for freem. of Conn. 1672; but his resid. is not told, nor any thing more kn. to me.

SHERWOOD, GEORGE, New London, d. 1 May 1674. MATTHEW, Fairfield 1664, then adm. freem. was ens. in 1673. STEPHEN, Greenwich, a propr. in 1672, had been adm. freem. in 1664, m. Rebecca, d. of the first Benjamin Turney, was prob. s. of Thomas, br. of preced. THOMAS, Stratford, or Fairfield, first at S. 1645, had come to Boston, 1634, in the Francis from Ipswich, aged 48, with w. Alice 47; and ch. Ann, 14; Rose, 11; Thomas, 10; and Rebecca, 9; and may be thot. to have had others, b. bef. or aft. or both, was, perhaps, freem. 1664, and prob. d. soon aft. THOMAS, Fairfield, or Stratford, s. of the preced. b. in Eng. was, perhaps, rather than his f. the freem. of 1664; and prob. had that Thomas, propound. for freem. 1672. Of this name, eleven had been gr. at Yale 1846.

SHESTELL, or SHESTEN, THOMAS, Boston 1665, lighterman, was a householder 1695; and I kn. no more of so strange a name, but that he made mortg. of his est. in 1666, wh. soon was dischg.

SHETHER, SHEATHER, or SHEDAR, JOHN, Guilford 1650, in the list of freem. 1669, rem. to Killingworth, there d. leav. John, and, perhaps, other childr. bef. May 1677, when his wid. Susanna, on her petitn. was empower. to make deed. JOHN, Killingworth, s. I presume of the preced. m. 9 Jan. 1679, Eliz. d. of William Wellman of the same, had Eliz. b. 20 Nov. 1679; Hannah, 25 Nov. 1681; John, 23 Mar. 1685; Rachel; and Susanna. His w. d. 5 Feb. 1718; and he d. 12 May 1721.

SHILLINGSWORTH, THOMAS, Plymouth 1643, freem. 1644, must be

thot. the same man under the more valua. and venera. name of Chillingworth, wh. see.

SHINE, THOMAS, Malden, when call. to take o. of fidel. 15 Dec. 1674,
mark. junr. and he may have br. John in Boston; but the name
is strange.

SHIPLEY. See Shepley.

SHIPMAN, EDWARD, Saybrook, m. Jan. 1651, Eliz. Comstock, had
Eliz. b. says the rec. cop. in Geneal. Reg. IV. 140, May foll.; Edward,
Feb. 1654; William, June 1656; and his w. d. July 1659. He m. 1
July 1663, Mary Andrews, had John, 5 Apr. 1664; Hannah, Feb. 1666;
Samuel, 25 Dec. 1668; Abigail, Sept. 1670; and Jonathan, Sept. 1674;
was propound. for freem. Oct. 1667, as Shipton, acc. the town rec. and
tho. all the ch. stand with the old name, his name at d. as rec. 15 Sept.
1697, is in the new form. In the will of the Ind. sachem Uncas, 29
Feb. 1676, he is one of three devisees to ea. of wh. testator gave 3000
acres, and this "within sight of Hartford," when in that clause of the
instrum. the aggreg. gr. reach. to 83,000 acres to only 28 persons. Eliz.
m. 3 (but ano. acco. says 9) Dec. 1672, John Hobson. WILLIAM, Saybrook, s. of the preced. m. 26 Nov. 1690, Alice Hand, had Edward, b.
20 Mar. 1692; and, perhaps, more.

SHIPPEN, ‖ EDWARD, Boston, ar. co. 1669, then a. 30 yrs. old, m. a.
1671, Eliz. whose surname appears Lybrand, a Quaker, not long resid.
here, had Francis, b. 2 Feb. 1671, wh. d. next yr.; Edward, 2 Oct.
1674, d. in few wks.; William, 4 Oct. 1675, d. soon; Eliz. Aug. 1676,
d. very soon; Edward, again, 10 Dec. 1677; Joseph, 28 Feb. 1679;
Mary, 6 May 1681, d. young; and Ann, 17 June 1684. When his first
w. d. is not kn. but he m. 15 July 1688, at Newport, Rebecca, wid. of
Francis Richardson of New York, as the Friends' rec. show, and had
Eliz. 1690, wh. d. as did her mo. soon aft. and he went, on invita. of
Penn, a. 1693, to Philadelphia, was there the first mayor under chart. of
1701, and found. of a fam. of much distinct. He was rich, early chos.
to the Assemb. was Speaker 1695, head of the Counc. 1704, m. third w.
Eliz. wid. of Thomas James of Bristol, Eng. had John, wh. d. young;
and last ch. William, wh. d. 1731, prob. unm.; and d. 2 Oct. 1712.
JOSEPH, Boston, s. of the preced. m. 28 July, or, Boston rec. says, 5
Aug. 1702, Abigail, d. of Thomas Grosse, had Edward, b. 9 July 1703,
f. of Edward, the Ch. J. of Pennsylv. and rem. to Phila. next yr. there
by her had five more ch. and had a sec. w.

SHIPPEY, SHEPPY, or SHIPPIE, THOMAS, Charlestown 1637, by w.
Grace had Thomas, b. 27 Sept. 1656, d. in three mos.; Grace, 30 Dec.
1658; Mary; Thomas, again; and Sarah; these four bapt. 21 June
1668, the mo. hav. join. the ch. on Sunday preced.; John, 25 July 1669 ·

Richard, 4 Dec. 1670, d. soon; Richard, again, 1 Sept. 1672, d. at 15 yrs.; and the f. d. 17 Oct. 1683. Eliz. S. wh. join. Charlestown ch. in Apr. 1650, may have been his mo. and Thanklord S. the asserter of Matthews' right in the ch. at Malden, 1651, against our Gen. Ct. may have been his first w. THOMAS, Charlestown, s. of the preced. m. 17 Apr. 1690, Mabel Mitchell, had Grace; Mabel, bapt. 14 July 1695; his w. hav. join. the ch. 23 June preced.; Margaret, 27 Sept. 1696, d. young; Mary, 30 Oct. 1698; and Margaret, again, 19 May 1701. His wid. m. 13 Aug. 1707, Nicholas Hoppin.

SHIPWAY. See Shepway.

SHOOTER, PETER, Braintree, by w. Hannah had Hannah, b. 3 Mar. 1655; and he d. 15 July foll.

SHORE, JAMES, Boston, s. of the first Sampson, was, perhaps, b. in Eng. JONATHAN, Lynn, br. of the preced. m. 15 Jan. 1669, Priscilla Hathorne, d. of John, had Jonathan, b. 14 Dec. foll.; Phebe, 20 Apr. 1674; and Samuel, 1 Feb. 1684. SAMPSON, Boston 1641, a tailor, join. our ch. 29 Jan. 1642, freem. 18 May foll.; by w. Abigail had Jonathan, prob. b. 12, certain. bapt. 18 June 1643, a. 7 days old, perhaps d. soon, unless unusual carelessness is imput. as prob. is just. due, to the town rec. that he was b. 16 May 1644, and bur. the same mo.; Sampson, 26 Jan. 1645, a. 14 days old; and James, beside Abigail, wh. m. Dec. 1674, Samuel Hudson; Eliz. b. 25 June 1657, d. soon; Susanna, bapt. 20 May 1660; and Ann, 16 Aug. 1663. SAMPSON, Hull, s. of the preced. m. Mary, d. of capt. Bezaleel Payton, was freem. 1673. For the first hundred yrs. I find not this surname in our Suffk. Prob. Such deficiency is not to be regret. or credit should be allow. to the scrupul. town rec. that tells of ——

SHOREBORNE, SAMPSON, Boston, by w. Abigail had Jonathan, b. 12 June 1643. Eheu!

SHORT, ABRAHAM, Pemaquid 1628, may have been sixty yrs. aft. the town clk. unless a namesake had the office. A mortge. to him of the isl. of Monhegon by Thomas Elbridge, 1650, may be read in Vol. I. of our Suffk. rec. Oft. it is writ. Shurd. ANTHONY, Newbury 1635, had, the yr. bef. been at Ipswich, of course, was one of the first sett. of ea. may have had w. Ann, but d. without ch. 4 Apr. 1670. CLEMENT, Boston, m. 21 Nov. 1660, Faith, d. of Thomas Munt, rem. to Newichwannuck, now Berwick, bef. 1666; was k. by the Ind. as Niles tells, 3 Mass. Hist. Coll. VI. 210, with w. and three ch. * HENRY, Ipswich, br. of Anthony, came in the Mary and John, 1634, was adm. 3 Sept. that yr. claim. to be adm. as rep. in Mar. foll. but as "unduly chos." was reject. rem. to Newbury, was rep. 1644; had w. Eliz. wh. d. 22 Mar. 1648, and he, 9 Oct. foll. m. Sarah Glover, had Sarah, b. 18 Dec. 1649, wh. d. in few mos. ; Henry, 11 Mar. 1652 ; John, 31 Oct. 1653, d. soon; and Sarah, again, 28 Jan. 1660; and he d. 5 May 1673. His wid. m. 6 Feb. 1678, Robert Adams, and d. 24 Oct. 1697. HENRY, Newbury, s. of the preced. freem. 1677, m. 30 Mar. 1674, Sarah Whipple, had Mary, b. 22 Aug. 1675 ; Sarah, 1 Aug. 1677 ; John, 14 Dec. 1679, d. young; Hannah, 28 Mar. 1682 ; John, again, 13 Oct. 1685; Matthew, 14 Mar. 1688, H. C. 1707 ; Lydia, 7 May 1690, d. next yr. ; and his w. d. 28 Dec. 1691. He m. 11 May 1692, Ann, d. of Henry Sewall, wid. of William Longfellow, and had Jane, 4 Mar. 1693; Samuel, 18 Nov. 1694, d. young; Mehitable, 12 Jan. 1696; Samuel, again, 16 Feb. 1698, d. soon; Samuel, again, 22 Feb. 1699 ; Hannah, 2 Mar. 1701, d. soon ; and Joseph, 8 Apr. 1702 ; d. 23 Oct. 1706. LUKE, Marblehead, mariner, came from Dartmouth, Co. Devon, rem. to Middleborough, had fam. of wh. Luke was name of one ch. He was of so gr. age, when he join. the ch. 1731, that, at his d. 1746, his yrs. were count. 116, if any will believe it.

SHORTHOSE, SHORTHUS, or SHORTUS, ROBERT, Charlestown 1634, by w. Catharine had John, b. 13 Sept. 1637 ; Eliz. 7 Sept. 1640 ; but among householders in 1658 his name is not seen ; nor was he a valua. inhab. we judge, for three times in as many yrs. Ct. proceed. against him.

SHORTRIDGE, or SHORTRIGGS, RICHARD, Portsmouth, freem. 1672, m. Esther, d. of Godfrey Dearborn of Hampton, had Richard, or, more prob. Robert, and Ann, wh. m. 18 Nov. 1686, George Wallis. ROBERT, Portsmouth, perhaps s. of Richard, m. 16 May 1687, one, whose name is not clear. made out in Geneal. Reg. VII. 128.

SHOTTEN, or SHATTON, SAMPSON, Newport 1638, was rec. as freem. 1640, but disfranchis. Mar. foll. and with Gorton, Holden, and others, purch. Shaomet from the Ind. Jan. 1643, and escap. the holy vengeance of the Mass. governm. by d. in Sept. next bef. their forces for the conquest arr. He left only Rachel (d. of his wid. Alice) that m. Robert Hodgson ; and the mo. m. Ralph Cowland of Portsmouth, R. I. wh. in her will gave all the prop. of her f. to the ch. then, Nov. 1664, presum. to be unm. and she d. Aug. 1666. See Winth. II. 121.

SHOVE, EDWARD, Bristol, s. of George, by w. Lydia had George and Mary tw. b. 2 June 1705 ; Lydia, 31 July 1707 ; Ruth, 10 Sept. 1709 ; Eliz. 10 Mar. 1711 ; Theophilus, 7 Apr. 1715 ; Edward, 21 Dec. 1716 ; Hannah, 19 June 1719 ; and Nathaniel, 9 May 1723, d. 12 Oct. 1746. GEORGE, Taunton, perhaps s. of a wid. Margery, 1643, at Rowley, tho. Baylies, II. 211, thot. he was b. at Dorchester, that seems improb. ord. 16 Nov. 1665, not 19 as Dr. Harris, in Hist. of Dorch. gave it, wh. was Sunday, m. 12 July 1664, Hopestill, d. of Rev. Samuel Newman, had Edward, b. 28 Apr. 1665, d. soon ; Eliz. 10 Aug. 1666;

Seth, 10 Dec. 1667, H. C. 1687; Nathaniel, 29 Jan. 1669, d. in Braintree, at 25 yrs.; Samuel, 16 June 1670; and Sarah, 30 July 1671.
His w. d. 7 Mar. 1674, and he m. 18 Feb. 1675, Hannah, prob. d. of
Rev. Thomas Walley, and had Mary, 11 Aug. 1676; Joanna, 28 Sept.
1678; Edward, again, 3 or 6 Oct. 1680; and the whimsical. bapt.
Yetmercy, 7 Nov. 1682. This w. d. 22 Dec. 1685, and for third w.
he took, 8 Dec. 1686, Sarah, wid. of Thomas Farwell, and d. 21 Apr.
foll. *SETH*, Danbury, s. of the preced. aft. leav. Coll. taught sch. for
some yrs. at Newbury and prob. other places, was ord. 13 Oct. 1697,
may have had w. and ch. and d. 3 Dec. 1735.

SHREVE, or SHERIVE, JOHN, Portsmouth, R. I. perhaps s. of Thomas,
m. late in Aug. 1686, Jane, d. of John Havens, had John, b. 10 June
1687; Thomas, 24 Dec. 1691; Eliz. 16 Nov. 1693; Mary, 9 June
1696; Caleb, 12 Apr. 1699; Daniel, 16 Jan. 1702; and William, 3
May 1705. THOMAS, Plymouth 1643–51, had w. or d. Martha, and,
perhaps, others, certain. Thomas, b. 2 Sept. 1649. A Jeremiah submit.
1652, at Kittery, to Mass. jurisdict.

SHRIMPTON, EPAPHRAS, Boston, by w. Rebecca had Samuel, bapt. 17
July 1687, at Charlestown, but why there, I see not; and all .I hear of
him, is, that he was s. of Edward of London. HENRY, Boston, br. of
Edward of Bednal Green, Co. Middlesex, had been a brazier in London,
join. our ch. 15 Sept. 1639, by w. Elinor had Eliz. bapt. 3 Oct. 1641,
a. 10 days old, wh. d. under 18 yrs.; Samuel, 25 June 1643, a. 26 days
old; Mary, 10 Aug. 1645, a. 13 days, wh. d. I presume, 9 Mar. 1652,
tho. blunder. town rec. calls her Elinor, d. of H. S. and his w. Mary;
John, 28 May 1648, a. 6 wks. wh. I dare to adopt; Sarah, b. 1649, wh.
was not bapt. for eleven yrs.; Henry, 26 Apr. 1653, says one of the
copies of town rec. but an older one, 1654, and he, I suppose, d. young;
Mehitable, wh. d. 29 July 1657; Jonathan, 18 Nov. 1656, wh. d. 22 July
1657; Abigail, 3 Jan. 1658; Bethia, 30 Jan. 1659; Eliz. again, 10 Apr.
1660, bapt. at 5 days, with three sis. bef. ment. He m. 27 Feb. 1662,
sec. w. Mary, wid. of capt. Robert Fenn (wh. had first been wid. of
capt. Thomas Hawkins, and m. F. 26 June 1654); and d. July 1666.
His will, of 17 of that mo. pro. 4 Aug. foll. aft. provid. for his w. made
dispos. of large prop. to ch. Samuel, Sarah, Abigail, Bethia, and Eliz.
and provides for Eliz. wid. of his br. Edward of London, and the seven
ch. Jonathan, Mary, Ebenezer, Epaphras, Silas, Eliz. and Lydia, large
pt. of whose est. he held in tr.; gave £50. to the ch. and £50., with this
curious proviso, for "leave that I may be bur. in the tomb wherein
my former w. Elinor S. was bur. otherwise I give nothing." A
better proof of his sense is a bequest of £10., "token of my love," to
Gold, Osborn, and others, of the Bapt. ch. worship. at Noddle's isl. A

copy of the will of his br. Edward, that sheds some light on our side of
the water, sent from the Prerogative Ct. of the Archbp. of Canterbury,
may be read in our Prob. rec. I. 390. ‖JONATHAN, Boston 1648, eldest
s. of Edward of Bednal Green, wh. was elder br. of the preced. m.
Mary, d. of Peter Oliver, had Mary and James tw. b. 30 Oct. 1667 ;
Sarah, 29 Nov. 1669 ; and Samuel, 10 Dec. 1671 ; ar. co. 1665 ; d.
1673. His wid. m. Nathaniel Williams ; d. Sarah m. John Clark, Esq.
ROBERT, Boston, had John, bapt. 28 May 1648, "a. six wks. old," says
the ch. rec. but tho. the ancient *copy* calls him " s. of our br. Robert S."
I feel compell. aft. long investigat. to say, that it seems to be a mistake,
inasmuch as there was no br. Robert S. of our ch. nor does the town rec.
give any such person. To be sure the ch. and town rec. in the orig. for
many early yrs. are both lost, and the copies are of various value ; that
of the ch. very far superior to the town copy, especially as gaps in 1647,
8, and 9 are num. Now, since the name of f. is not seen in any time
bef. nor for a long success. of yrs. aft. if ever, my conject. is, that John,
the ch. bapt. on that day, was s. of Henry, and d. soon. That this may
not appear too hazardous a guess, I beg the student of our early manners
to obs. that Henry had brot. to bapt. his three ch. in a short time aft.
their sev. births ; but of six succeed. ch. no one was brot. up to the font
bef. the fifth day aft. b. of a seventh, and then the rec. has this strange
relat.: on 15 Apr. 1660, were bapt. ch. of our br. Henry Shrimpton,
Sarah, aged eleven yrs. ; Abigail, two yrs. ; Bethia, one yr. ; and Eliz.
at five days. The three intermed. were, I presume, d. and my excuse
for omission of such ordinance in the six cases, is, that the f. was too
much impress. with the d. of his s. John. If in opposit. to this conject.
it be suggest. that Henry had deriv. prejudice against the ceremony of
inf. bapt. the inq. natural. springs up, if his conscient. scruple restrain.
him in 1649, and 1653, and 1654, and 1656, and 1658, and 1659, why
should it have relax. in 1660 ? Still, if my disesteem of the copy in the
old engrossing hand that serves for first ch. rec. seem too confident, I
must be excus. from abundant experience of the errors in such docum.
Our town rec. as it is call. (I mean the oldest MS. venerat. by me, as
the County Recorder's Copy from the lost transcript of the lost orig. rec.
of the town clk. of the writs) asserts falsely, that " Elinor, the d. of
Henry Shrimpton and of his w. Mary, dec. 9 Mar. 1652," on p. 128,
whereas Mary was the ch. not the w. and Elinor was the w. wh. had
three or four ch. aft. that date of d. and there was no ch. nam. Elinor,
that we hear of. ‡ ‖ SAMUEL, Boston, s. of Henry, freem. 1673, got off
by fine of £10. from serv. same yr. as constable, to wh. office he was
then chos. ; had by w. Eliz. d. of wid. Eliz. Roberts of London, Mary, b.
4 Dec. 1666 ; Martha, 21 Jan. 1671 ; Samuel, 20 Apr. 1673 ; and Eliz.

again, 21 Apr. 1674 ; yet, perhaps, Samuel is the only ch. that liv. long.
He was of ar. co. 1670, and its capt. 1694, one of the Counc. to Andros
1687, but not a partaker in his tyranny ; one of the Counc. of Safety
1689, and head of the regim. of Suffk. and d. 9 Feb. 1698, of apoplexy.
What is meant by the statement in Sewall's Diary, that lieut.-gov. Usher
was commit. to prison, 4 Dec. 1694, on the examinat. of col. S. is
uncert.   His large est. by will of 5 June 1697, pro. 17 Feb. foll. pass.
to his s. Samuel, wh. m. 7 May 1696, Eliz. Richardson, niece of his mo.
had only ch. Eliz. and d. 1703, insolv.

SHURD, ABRAHAM. See Short.

SHURTLIFF, SHIRTLEY, or SHETLE, ABIEL, youngest s. of William
the first, was of Plymouth, there m. 14 Jan. 1696, Lydia, d. of Jonathan
Barnes of the same, had James, b. 16 Nov. 1696; Eliz. 6 Dec. 1698 ;
Lydia, 28 Feb. 1701; David, 1 June 1703 ; Hannah, 31 July 1705 ;
John, 8 Nov. 1707 ; Benjamin, 11 Apr. 1711 ; William, 8 Sept. 1713 ;
Joseph, 22 Jan. 1716 ; and Abiel, 23 Oct. 1717.   He liv. in that part of
the town wh. bec. Plympton, where his w. d. 10 Sept. 1727 ; and he d.
28 Oct. 1732.   THOMAS. Plympton, s. of William the first, tho. some
doubt is felt, whether he were not s. of the sec. ; m. 21 May 1713,
Sarah Kimball, but it is not kn. what ch. if any, he had, or the time of
his or her d.   WILLIAM, Marshfield, had liv. at Plymouth, where he was
apprent. to Thomas Clark, a carpenter, but not, prob. brot. by him, m.
18 Oct. 1655, Eliz. d. of Thomas Lettice, had William, b. 1657 ;
Thomas ; and Abiel, in June 1666, the same mo. in wh. the f. was k. by
lightning on 23 ; and, Miss Thomas instr. us, the s. was b. aft. that event,
but there is reasonab. tradit. that the ch. was b. bef. the d. of his f.   His
wid. m. 18 Nov. 1669, Jacob Cooke ; and, next, 1 Jan. 1689, Hugh
Cole of Swansey ; and she d. 31 Oct. 1693.   WILLIAM, Plymouth,
eldest s. of the preced. m. Oct. 1683, Susanna, d. of Barnabas Lothrop
of Barnstable, had Jabez, b. 22 Apr. 1684; Thomas, 16 Mar. 1687 ;
Jacob, bapt. at B. 11 Aug. 1698; William, 4 Apr. 1689, H. C. 1707,
min. of Portsmouth ; Susanna, bapt. 1691 ; John, b. June 1693 ; Barnabas, 19 Mar. 1696 ; Ichabod, 8 Nov. 1697 ; Eliz. 28 May 1699 ;
Mary, 22 Dec. 1700 ; Sarah, 8 June 1702 ; Samuel ; Abigail ; and Nathaniel, 2 Dec. 1707.   His w. d. 9 Aug. 1726, and he d. 4 Feb. 1730.

SHUTE, ENOCH, Weymouth 1636.   RICHARD, Milford 1642, perhaps
rem. to Pemaquid bef. 1651 ; may be the mariner wh. bot. a small lot of
ld. in Boston, June 1670, wh. by w. Eliz. had William, b. 1 Oct. 1670,
yet this more prob. appears to be the man wh. d. at B. 2 Oct. 1703, aged
72.   The mariner, Richard, in his will of 11 Sept. 1703, pro. 6 Oct.
foll. speaks of his farm at Malden, on wh. he had charg. in fav. of his
present w. Catharine, a jointure by the contr. of m. and as by this will

that sum is incr. the est. shall. also enure to the good of his ch. Michael,
Richard, and Joanna, wid. of Joseph Buckley, late of Boston, and to
Eliz. Nichols, and Hannah Mountfort, ds. of said Joanna, by her first h.
Nichols, and to his other twelve gr.ch. viz.: five ds. of Michael, four ch.
of Richard, and three s. of Joanna; beside £3. to his kinsman, William S. RICHARD, Milford, m. 14 Aug. 1656, Sarah, eldest d. of
Thomas Sandford, had Thomas, b. 5 Aug. 1659, and in 1665 was resid.
at East Chester, in N. Y. jurisdict. RICHARD, Malden, s. of Richard,
by w. Lydia had John, b. 26 Mar. 1693; Lydia, 14 July 1696; and
Eliz. and Joanna, tw. 20 Feb. 1699. ROBERT, Boston, prob. unm. as no
w. or ch. is ment. in his will of 24 Mar. 1651, pro. 29 Apr. foll. but he
names br. Richard, liv. near Pemaquid, br. Thomas, sis. Mary, and sis.
Sarah Holly's childr.; had fair est. of wh. to Richard Russell, his excor.
he gives £10., and legac. to Rev. Messrs. Cotton, Wilson, Symmes, and
Allen, the pastors and teachers of Boston and Charlestown. Perhaps
THOMAS had fam. as well as Richard, and liv. at East Chester in
later yrs. WILLIAM, Boston, m. 1 July 1659, Hopestill, d. of John
Viall, wh. gave him, 1665, ho. and ld. in Boston; perhaps was of
Jamaica 1671.

SHUTER, or SHOOTER, PETER, Braintree, d. 15 July 1654, says
Farmer. He was prob. not that Mr. S. by the Assist. ord. of 1 Mar.
1631 sent home.

SIBBORNE, JOHN, Boston. See Sebborn.

SIBLEY, SEBLEY, or SYBLEY, JOHN, Salem, came with Higginson,
1629, says Felt, of wh. I would gladly see the evid.; freem. 3 Sept.
1634, yet was prob. unm. for sev. yrs.; had there bapt. Sarah, 18 Sept.
1642; Mary, 8 Sept. 1644; Rachel, 3 May 1646; John, 14 May 1648;
Hannah, 22 June 1651; William, 8 Sept. 1653; Samuel, 12 Apr. 1657;
and Abigail, 3 July 1659; was selectman 1636, had ld. at Manchester,
then call. Jeffery's creek, 1637, and in 1640, with other Salem men,
pray. the Gen. Ct. to give leave to rem. there. Perhaps he had ano. w.
Rachel, d. of John Pickworth, and by her Joseph; but he d. at M.
1661, leav. wid. Rachel, four s. five ds. Mary m. 26 Jan. 1665, Jonathan Walcot; Rachel m. a Bishop; and Hannah m. Stephen Small.
JOHN, Charlestown 1634, with w. Sarah was adm. of the ch. 21 Feb.
1635, freem. 6 May foll. then spell. with e in the first syl. d. 30 Nov.
1649. * JOHN, Beverly, or Manchester, prob. both, s. of the first John,
was capt. selectman, and rep.; m. says the scrupul. descend. librar. at
the Univ. Rachel, d. of Amariah Pickworth, had Mary, b. 21 Mar. 1677;
Eliz. 4 Mar. 1679; John, 7 Sept. 1680; and Hannah, 18 Feb. 1682;
and he d. early in 1710. JOSEPH, Salem, perhaps br. of the preced.
m. 4 Feb. 1684, Susanna Follet, wh. may have been d. of William of

Dover, had Joseph, b. 9 Nov. 1684; John, 18 Sept. 1687; Jonathan, 1 May 1690; Hannah, bapt. May 1695; Samuel, 1697; William, 7 Apr. 1700; and Benjamin, 19 Sept. 1703. RICHARD, Salem 1656, by w. Hannah had Samuel, b. 10 Mar. 1659; Hannah, 20 Sept. 1661; Sarah, 20 Dec. 1663; Damaris, 26 Aug. 1666; John, Apr. 1669; Mary, 25 Jan. 1672; and Eliz. He was a traymaker, and d. early in 1676, his inv. being of 30 June, when all the ch. and wīd. were liv. SAMUEL, Salem, s. of the first John, by w. Mary had Samuel, b. 7 Jan. 1686; Mary; Benjamin; William; Rebecca; and Lydia. He liv. in that unhàppy village where the Rev. Mr. Paris, in his ch. rec. says his w. raised the devil, by advis. John, an Ind. (wh. with w. Tituba, were, I suppose, slaves of Paris) how to make a cake. See 3 Mass. Hist. Coll. III. 170; also copious and curious ch. rec. a. sis. Sibly's confess. Geneal. Reg. XI. 133. We may rejoice in read. Felt, II. 476, how easily she got off, by confess. of her *innocence* in the folly. SAMUEL, Salem, prob. eldest s. of Richard, m. 13 Sept. 1695, Sarah Wells, had Hannah, b. 17 May 1696; Richard, Jan. 1698; Sarah, 27 Mar. 1699; Jonathan, 25 Nov. 1701; Samuel, July 1704, d. soon; and Samuel, again, 5 May 1705; was k. by the Ind. 29 Aug. 1708, in their assault on Haverhill. WILLIAM, Salem, s. of John the first, m. 1 Nov. 1676, wid. Ruth Small, had Ruth, John, Joseph, Nathaniel, and Rachel.

SICKLERDAM, JOHN, Boston, a pirate, tak. in the Sound, Oct. 1689. In Geneal. Reg. II. 393, a full acco. is giv. tho. the command. capt. Pease, was k. in the fight. We may not fear to call him a trans. person, perhaps a Dutch mariner, looking out for any serv. to favor the Prince of Orange; but execut. for not find. better employm.

SIDALL, FRANCIS, is the name print. as one of the soldiers in Moseley's comp. Dec. 1675, but I suppose it a misspell.

SIGOURNEY, SIGOURNAY, SEGOURNE, or SIGOURNIE, ANDREW, Boston, came prob. in 1686, from devotion to the cause of relig. truth, as one of the noble Huguenot confessors, bring. s. Andrew, d. Susanna, perhaps other ch. Their first settlem. was at Oxford, whence aft. 7 or 8 yrs. with most of the other French emigr. he came to B. but aft. the peril of Ind. invasion pass. away shortly, once more he tried the country resid. I think prob. for few yrs. but d. at B. 16 Apr. 1727, aged 88, acc. gr.st. Susanna m. John Johnson, wh. with three ch. was k. by the Ind. 1696, at Oxford, and she m. 18 Apr. 1700, her cous. Daniel Johonnot of Boston. ANDREW, Boston, s. of the preced. brot. from France, in youth, by his f. m. Mary Germaine, also a native of France, had Andrew, b. 30 Jan. 1702; Susanna, 27 Dec. 1704; Peter, 1 Mar. 1707, not 6, as the fam. geneal. gives it; Mary, 1 Aug. 1709; Charles, 27 Apr. 1711, wh. d. unm. at 40 yrs.; Anthony, 17 Aug. 1713; Daniel,

17 Nov. 1715 ; Rachel, 5 Mar. 1718, d. next yr.; and Hannah, 27 Feb.
1719 ; but of the place of b. assign. by fam. geneal. for the first nam.
five or six I entertain strong doubt. The print. vol. prepar. with
exempla. devot. makes them all to be b. at Boston, but a fair infer. is
against it, as no rec. is found bef. 1714, and then the whole six are
brot. into our town rec. He made his will 20 May 1736, but it was
not pro. bef. 7 July 1748, soon aft. his d. and his wid. d. 20 Mar.
1763 or 4, the uncertain. of fam. geneal. rais. a suspicion that the author
had confus. old and new style so many yrs. aft. d. of " Mr. Old Style."
Susanna m. 24 Oct. 1726, Martin Brimmer; Mary m. 20 Feb. 1734,
John Baker; and Hannah m. 23 June 1748, Samuel Dexter, the celebr.
patriot. ANDREW, Boston, s. of the preced. m. 7 Oct. 1731, Mary, only
d. of John Ronchon, had Mary, b. 14 Aug. 1732 ; Andrew, 14 Feb.
1734, both d. young; Mary, 26 Nov. 1735 ; Andrew, again, 22 May
1737, d. young ; John Ronchon, 29 May 1740; Andrew, again, 22 May
1742, d. young; Eliz. 17 Aug. 1743 ; Susanna, 13 Oct. 1744 ; Andrew,
again, 27 Mar. 1746, d. at 21 yrs. ; Charles, 4 Mar. 1748 ; Martin Baker,
3 Sept. 1751, d. young; and Hannah, 30 Apr. 1754. He d. 4 Nov.
1762 ; and his wid. d. 28 Feb. 1772. ANTHONY, Boston, br. of the
preced. m. 10 Apr. 1740, Mary Waters of Salem, had Mary, b. 23 Mar.
1741 ; Susanna, 11 Jan. 1743 ; Peter, 8 Dec. 1745 ; and by sec. w.
Eliz. Breed, b. Whittemore, wh. d. at Oxford, 18 May 1804, had Anthony, 12 May 1751; and Andrew, 30 Nov. 1752; and d. 1761.
DANIEL, Boston, youngest br. of the preced. m. Mary, d. of James
Varney, had Mary, b. 31 Aug. 1736 ; Andrew, 11 Feb. 1738 ; Daniel, 1
Oct. 1739, d. soon ; James, 22 May 1741 ; Charles, 21 Aug. 1744 ; and by
sec. w. Joanna Tileston, wh. d. 19 Sept. 1770, had Elisha, 21 Oct. 1747,
d. next yr.; Thomas Tileston, 31 Dec. 1749, d. soon ; Joanna, of wh.
date of b. I doubt the fam. geneal. has error ; Jane, 13 Nov. 1751; and
Elisha, again, 14 Apr. 1753 ; and third w. he had, m. 13 Feb. 1780,
Rebecca Tileston, wh. d. 14 Jan. 1807, aged 87, says the print. vol. but
he d. 7 July 1787.

SIGSWORTH, GEORGE, Boston, by w. Esther had Isabel, b. 23
Sept. 1679.

SIKES, SYCKES, or SYKES, INCREASE, Springfield, eldest s. of Richard, m. 17 Mar. 1671, Abigail, d. of Ambrose Fowler, had John, b. 23
Apr. 1672 ; Nathaniel, 7 July 1673 ; Increase, 1 Jan. 1675 ; Abigail,
16 Mar. 1676 ; Rebecca, 17 Sept. 1678 ; and Samuel, 27 Mar. 1680 ;
beside Phebe, 27 Feb. 1682 ; James, 14 Mar. 1683 ; James, again, 27
Mar. 1684 ; and Benjamin, 5 Dec. 1685, wh. last four d. soon ; was
freem. 1684, and d. 24 Mar. 1712 ; his wid. d. 19 June 1733. JAMES,
Springfield, youngest br. of the preced. wh. d. on the same day with him,

had no w. or ch. NATHANIEL, Springfield, br. of the preced. m. 3 Feb.
1681, Hannah, d. prob. of John Bagg of the same, had Hannah, b. 27
June 1682, d. young; Hannah, again, 14 July 1685; and Nathaniel, 22
Aug. 1686. He d. 15 Sept. foll. and his wid. in her widowhood, 13 May
1740. RICHARD, Springfield, freem. 13 May 1640, when, I suppose,
by the names above and below his in the list, he was of Dorchester, next
yr. rem. to S. there, by w. Phebe, had Experience, b. 5 Nov. 1642, d.
young; Increase, 6 Aug. 1644; Nathaniel, 30 Oct. 1646; and Victory,
or as Col. Rec. reads, Vicary, 3 Mar. 1649; and James, 11 June 1651;
and d. Mar. 1676, in his will nam. w. Phebe, and these ch. All four s.
sw. alleg. at S. on the last day of Dec. 1678, or the next day. VICARY,
or VICTORY, Springfield, s. of the preced. m. 29 Jan. 1673, Eliz. d. of
Jonathan Burt, had Jonathan, b. 16 Dec. 1673, d. soon; Jonathan, again,
17 July 1675; Elizur, 11 Dec. 1677, d. in few days; Abel, 24 Feb.
1679, d. in few days; Samuel, 3 Mar. 1680; Benjamin, 16 Oct. 1682,
d. soon; rem. to Suffield, had there Ebenezer, 24 Sept. 1683; and his
w. d. next mo. and this ch. not long aft. He m. next, 16 July 1684,
Eliz. d. of Lancelot Granger, had John, 18 May 1685, d. next yr.;
Vicary, 9 Nov. 1686, d. soon; Vicary, again, 5 Sept. 1689; and his w.
d. 20 Mar. 1692. For third w. 22 Dec. foll. he had Mary, wid. of
Judah Trumbull; and d. 1708, only three of his ten ch. being left alive.

SIKY, DENNIS, an unkn. or misprint. name of one of Moseley's
soldiers in Dec. 1675, clk. of the comp.

SILL, SYLL, or SCILL, JOHN, Cambridge 1637, brot. from Eng. says
the fam. tradit. w. Joanna, ch. Eliz. and Joseph; was freem. 2 May
1638, perhaps had other ch. but d. prob. bef. 1653. His wid. had gr. of
ld. 1662, but of her d. the exact date is unkn. yet her will was pro. in
Oct. 1671. Eliz. m. 28 Oct. 1652, Zechariah Hicks, and d. 12 Sept.
1730. JOSEPH, Cambridge, s. of the preced. b. in Eng. came with his
f. in inf. m. 5 Dec. 1660, Jemima, d. of Andrew Belcher the first of the
same, wh. d. a. 1675, had sev. ch. of wh. I kn. only Andrew, b. 5 Feb. 1665,
that d. soon; Joseph, bapt. 11 Mar. 1666; and Jemima, b. 21 Sept. as the
town rec. proves to Mr. Paige's satisfact. tho. the ch. reg. says, bapt. 31 Mar.
1667; and Eliz. b. 12 Sept. 1668; and the rec. of b. has no others.
But others there were, as the fam. tradit. makes two s. lost at sea; and
fully confirm. is it by the fact, that aft. the d. of w. in the begin. of
Philip's war, and aft. m. of sec. w. he made deed of trust, 7 Nov. 1681,
to Andrew Belcher, their uncle, in favor of his s. Andrew, and Thomas.
He was much disting. for serv. in that war, espec. at Groton, where he
had com. and at Dover, aid. with Hawthorne in the surpr. of the Ind.
at maj. Waldron's. On the close of it, rem. to Lyme, there m. 12 Feb.
1677 or 8, Sarah, d. of George Clark, wid. of Reynold Marvin, and

had Joseph, b. 6 Jan. 1678 or 9; and Zechariah, 1 Jan. 1682; and, perhaps, others, but d. 6 Aug. 1696, in 60th yr. Jemima, m. 2 Dec. 1687, John Hall of Medford; and Eliz. m. 18 Nov.1685, Samuel Green, jr. of Boston. In Milford a Joseph is nam. 1648; but I think it may be a mistake for 1678. JOSEPH, Lyme, s. of the preced. m. Phebe, d. of Richard Lord, had Lucy, b. Feb. 1706; Eliz. 20 Nov. 1707; John, 14 Feb. 1710; Phebe, 10 Feb. 1713; Joseph, 25 Apr. 1715; Thomas, 25 Aug. 1717; Lucy, again, 1 Dec. 1719; Jabez and Richard, tw. 4 Aug. 1722; Elijah, 8 Nov. 1724; Sarah, 2 Jan. 1728; and Elisha, 6 Apr. 1730; and d. 10 Nov. 1765. His wid. d. 4 Jan. 1774, aged 86. ZECHARIAH, Lyme, br. of the preced. m. Eliz. d. of Richard Mather of the same, had Andrew; Zechariah, b. 1717; David; Sarah; Eliz.; and Joanna; but dates are unkn. of the b. of most of his ch. or of d. of hims. or w. Eight of this name had, in 1852, been gr. at Yale.

SILLIMAN, DANIEL, Fairfield 1658, had, it is said, for first w. Peaceable, wid. of John Egleton, (wh. d. 1659); and tho. she d. bef. 5 July 1661, yet tradit. tells that there were no ch. of the sec. m. with Hannah, wid. of Hendrick Hendrickson. His ch. Daniel, Thomas, and Robert, were all Peaceable's; and he d. 1690, it is thot. bec. admin. of his est. was grant. 13 Jan. 1691. DANIEL, Fairfield, s. of the preced. by w. Abigail had Daniel, Peaceable, Abigail, John, Jemima, and Mary; but no dates of b. can be found; and he d. 1697. ROBERT, Fairfield, s. of the first Daniel, had by Sarah, d. of Cornelius Hull, it is said, Nathaniel, b. 20 Aug. 1696; Sarah; Robert; Martha; Rebecca; and Ebenezer, 1707, Y. C. 1727, whose descend. have confer. gr. honor on the State; and d. 1748. Fam. tradit. makes the first Daniel come from Holland; and the derivat. is quite distinct from the city of Lucca, in Italy, in the early day of the Protestant reformat. thro. Geneva, where had sett. the f. of one Daniel. This Daniel was chos. 1575 into the Council of 200 for that Republic. Sometimes in fam. tradit. there is a basis of truth, however distort.

SILLIS. See Sealis.

SILLIVANT, or SELEVANT, DANIEL, New Haven 1654, had m. bef. 1652, Abigail, only d. of James Cole of Hartford; but we kn. not the date, nor whether she d. early; but one Daniel S. at N. H. m. 17 Oct. 1654, Eliz. Lamberton, d. of the trad. capt. George L. wh. was lost in a voyage to London, Jan. 1646. Pro. rec. shows that he d. in Virg. 1655, leav. a will, pro. June in that yr. nam. wid.; but there have been doubts, however indistinct, if the name were not the same with the (Daniel Silliman) man's in the former article. We read in the New Haven rec. that William Trowbridge m. 9 Mar. 1657, at Milford, Eliz. wid. of Daniel Sillevant, d. of George Lamberton. But bef. this m.

and aft. the d. of Sillevant, his wid. Eliz. had, Oct. 1655, convey. to John Cole of Hartford the ho. and ld. giv. to her h. and his former w. Abigail, by James Cole, her f. in his will. See Goodwin, Geneal. Notes, p. 48, in note, for the curious testam.

SILSBEE, oft. SILSBY, EPHRAIM, Lynn, s. of Henry, by w. Rachel had Henry, b. 15 Nov. 1694. HENRY, Salem 1639, Ipswich 1647, Lynn 1658, had Henry, John, Ephraim, and three ds. beside Samuel. His w. Dorothy d. 27 Sept. 1676, and he m. 18 Nov. 1680, Grace Eaton perhaps wid. of Jonas of Reading. One of the ds. was Hannah, wh. m. 2 Dec. 1680, Thomas Laighton. His will of Mar. 1698, pro. 16 Dec. 1700, names three s. three gr. s., John March, Henry Collins, John Laighton, beside gr. d. Mary S. JOHN, Salem, prob. s. of the preced. m. 16 Feb. 1674, Bethia Pitman, had only ch. John, b. 7 Feb. foll. and d. early, his inv. being of 26 June 1676. JONATHAN, Lynn, s. of Henry, m. 1 Jan. 1674, Bethia March, had Sarah, b. 5 Dec. foll. ; a ch. 16 Feb. 1677, d. same day ; Jonathan, 16 Mar. 1678 ; and Bethia, 12 Apr. 1680, d. at one yr.; Eliz. 2 Aug. 1685 ; and Hannah, 3 Oct. 1687 ; was freem. 1684. NATHANIEL, Salem, br. of the preced. m. 5 Nov. 1671, Deborah Tompkins, had Henry, b. 12 Apr. 1674 ; Nathaniel, 11 Apr. 1676, d. in few days ; Nathaniel, again, 23 Oct. 1677 ; Samuel, 30 Jan. 1679 ; John, 20 Mar. 1682 ; and Margaret, 20 Mar. 1684. SAMUEL, Lynn, s. of Henry, m. 4 July 1676, Mary Biscoe, had Mary, b. 20 June 1677 ; and he was bur. 18 Oct. 1687. Six of this name, says Farmer, had gr. at Harv. in 1834, and one at Dart.

SILVER, SAMUEL, Rowley, 1691, s. of Thomas the first, had then a fam. THOMAS, Newbury, had first been of Ipswich 1637, by first w. had Mary, b. 1645 ; and by sec. w. Catharine, m. 18 Aug. 1649, had Eliz. and Martha, tw. b. 14 Mar. 1651 ; Thomas, 26 Mar. 1653, d. at 3 yrs.; Hannah and Sarah, tw. 18 Oct. 1655 ; Thomas, again, 26 Mar. 1658 ; John, 24 Aug. 1660 ; Samuel, 16 Feb. 1662 ; and his w. d. 23 July 1665. Mary, it is said, m. a Robinson; Martha m. 20 Dec. 1669, Francis Willet ; Sarah m. 9 Feb. 1672, Thomas Alley ; and Hannah m. 13 Mar. 1677, Henry Akers. THOMAS, Newbury, not s. of the preced. but call. jr. was b. Coffin says, 1652, but not in N. of course, or he would have nam. his f. ; m. 4 Jan. 1682, Mary Williams, had Sarah, b. 2 Oct. 1682. He d. 1695, and his wid. m. Simon Wainwright of Haverhill.

SILVERWOOD, JOSHUA, may be only a nickname, borne on the roll, however, of Moseley's comp. Dec. 1675.

SILVESTER, or more properly, SYLVESTER, BENJAMIN, Scituate, youngest of eleven ch. of Richard, m. 1684, Lydia Standlake. CONSTANT, a merch. from London, at Barbados 1657, may never have been in N. E. yet as he and his br. Nathaniel, with two others purchas. 9

June 1651, of Stephen Goodyear, grantee of the Earl of Stirling, the gr. est. of Shelter Isl. in the Sound, on our coast, it should be presum. that he knew what he was buying, and his will in Doctor's Commons, 1671, proves that he contin. to value it. Thompson's Hist. of L. I. 234, shows how the right of Constant was confiscat. and sold to his br. Nathaniel, by the Dutch Gov. 1674, as, also, how the Gov. compel. payment. Descend. are very num. either of him, or his br. or both. GILES, Boston, perhaps s. of Nathaniel, m. Hannah, d. of the first Thomas Savage, wid. of Benjamin Gillam, in Sept. 1685; but I have no further acco. of him. Perhaps he dwelt on Shelter Isl. the manorial est. of his f. ISRAEL, Scituate, br. of Benjamin, had Israel, b. 28 Sept. 1675; Silence, 1677; Richard, 1679; Lois, 1680; Martha, 1682; Mary, 1683; Elisha, 1685; Peter, 1687; Zebulon, 1689; Barshua, 1692; and Deborah, 1696. * JOHN, Scituate, eldest br. of the preced. had Sarah, b. 1671; John, 1672; Joseph, 1674; Samuel, 1676; and Lydia, 1679; was rep. 1689. JOSEPH, Scituate, third s. of Richard of the same, by w. Mary had Joseph, b. 11 Nov. 1664; Mary, 24 Dec. 1666; Naomi, 5 Mar. 1668; Ann, 5 May 1669; and, possib. by sec. w. Benjamin, 11 Dec. 1680; David, 20 Apr. 1683; and Amos, 15 Nov. 1685; was a brave soldier, capt. under Col. Church in his expedit. 1689 in Maine, and in the disastrous one of Sir William Phips, next yr. against Quebec. In that serv. with very many others of the best spirit of N. E. he d. leav. nuncup. will, pro. by three of his soldiers. His liv. s. were Joseph, Benjamin, Amos, and David. NATHANIEL, Shelter Isl. on E. end of L. I. 1659, wh. with his br. Constant he purch. 9 June 1651, from Stephen Goodyear, was h. of Grizzle, d. of Thomas Brinley of Datchett, in Co. Bucks, the parish well kn. to the million readers of Shakespeare's Merry Wives of Windsor, one of the gr. fam. lords param. of that est. as the Gardiners were of Gardiner's, and the Winthrops of Fisher's isl. in the early days; d. 1680. He had, beside d. Grizzle, five s. Giles, Nathaniel, Constant, Peter, and Benjamin, of wh. are many descend. Griselda m. James Lloyd of Boston, as his first w. There is no slight reason to believe this Nathaniel to be s. of the celebr. poet, Joshua Sylvester, translat. of the divine rhapsodies of Du Bartas, of whose fame, in the age of Eliz. and James, the puritans were anxious guardians. The relig. bard was aged 54 at his d. 1618. But if the ancestr. honors of literary glory are denied, the more enduring worth of bold serv. in the higher cause of humanity shall be accord. to him wh. gave protect. and shelter to the Shattuck and Southwick fugitives from the bloody persecut. in Mass. under the successive rule of Govs. Endicot and Bellingham, whose zeal for the honor of God exterminat. all tenderness for their fellow creatures. RICHARD, Weymouth, prob.

came in the fleet with Winth. desir. adm. as freem. 19 Oct. 1630, and
was sw. 1 Apr. 1634, m. a. 1632, Naomi Torrey, perhaps sis. of William,
had Lydia, b. 8 Dec. 1633; John, 14 Mar. 1635; Peter, 1637, d. at 5
yrs. by casualty, as Winth. II. 77, relates; Joseph, 12 Apr. 1638;
Dinah, 2 Apr. 1642; Eliz. 23 Jan. 1644; Richard, 1648; Naomi,
1649; Israel, 1651; Esther, 1653; and Benjamin, 1656. He had
trouble with the col. governm. in 1639, about gather. a ch. or sett. a
min. and sold his est. next yr. of wh. rec. is on p. 16 of Vol. I. but did
not rem. bef. 1642 or 3, then fix. his abode at Scituate, in the freer col.
of Plymouth, there d. 1663. His inv. is of 24 Sept. and his will names
w. and the ten liv. ch. His wid. d. Nov. 1668. Lydia m. 4 Sept. 1652,
Nathaniel Rawlins; Eliz. m. 24 Jan. 1659, John Lowell, d. aft. hav.
three ch.; and Naomi m. 1666, the same John Lowell. RICHARD,
Milton 1678, s. of the preced. m. Hannah, d. of James Leonard of
Taunton. THOMAS, Watertown, m. Sarah, d. of Christopher Grant,
and d. 27 Nov. 1696, leav. her alive; but Bond has not furnish. any
further acco. nor his usual affluence of dates.

SIMMONS, SYMONS, SIMONES, or SYMONDSON, JOHN, Rowley 1671,
Haverhill 1678, then said to be 38 yrs. old, may have intermed. been at
Dover a few yrs. unless, as seems more prob. this were an older man,
and one sent by capt. Mason very early to his patent at Piscataqua, wh.
liv. at Dover, and was a juryman 1673. JOHN, Taunton 1679, had w.
Martha, eldest s. John, eldest d. Mary. MICHAEL, Dover 1665, tax.
there next yr. MOSES, Plymouth, one of the first comers, arr. in the
Fortune 1621, b. at Leyden, and bearing the Dutch name of Symonson
or Simonson, but early shorten. his name to the first two syllab.; prob.
brot. w. but no ch. is kn. exc. Moses, and Thomas, wh. may both have
been b. here. He sett. at Duxbury, was one of the orig. purch. of
Dartmouth and proprs. of Bridgewater, and of Middleborough, but did
not rem. to either. MOSES, Duxbury, s. of the preced. or perhaps his
gr.s. for one of the name is ment. wh. may, however, have been s. of
Thomas; by w. Sarah had John, Aaron, Mary, Eliz. and Sarah, wh. all
m. and he d. 1689. RICHARD, Salem 1668. SAMUEL, Haverhill 1669,
may be the same wh. d. at Lynn, 26 July 1675. SAMUEL, Newbury,
casual. k. 18 June 1682. THOMAS, Braintree, sold his ho. and ld. Mar.
1640. THOMAS, Scituate 1646, s. of Moses the first, had Moses and
Aaron. WILLIAM, Boston, prob. by w. Ann had Hannah, b. a. Aug.
1640, and he d. in short time aft. for his wid. had bec. w. of Abel
Porter, and brot. this Hannah to bapt. 30 Apr. 1643, call. 2 yrs. and 8
mos. old, the mo. join. the ch. on Sunday bef. WILLIAM, Woburn
1662, may have been first of Charlestown 1639, but rather may this
name be Simonds. WILLIAM, Haverhill 1657.

SIMPKINS, ‖ NICHOLAS, Boston, a tailor, made the first capt. at the castle, one of his success. Roger Clap says, a. 1634, seems in 1636 to have giv. dissatisfact. by being indebt. to the governm. and rem. 1638 to Yarmouth, aft. some yrs. came again to B. bef. 1649, and was of ar. co. 1650; beside Deborah, wh. m. George Burrill, I think he had by w. Isabel prob. Pilgrim, and Rebecca, perhaps both, b. at Yarmouth. Rebecca m. 29 Jan. 1655, William Therrell or Tirrell. PILGRIM, Boston, prob. s. of the preced. by w. Miriam, wh. d. 10 Nov. 1660, had Nicholas, b. 22 Oct. preced. He m. 27 Mar. 1661, Catharine Richardson, had William, b. 3 Oct. 1662, d. I suppose, bef. his f.; Rebecca, 14 Mar. 1665; Sarah, 21 Sept. 1668; and Thomas, 30 May 1671; beside John and Miriam, prob. by former w. His will, of 19 Nov. 1714, pro. 2 Jan. 1721, provides for w. Catharine, wh. is made extrix. and marks s. Nicholas for "five shil. and no more, if he come for it;" but for resid. of est. directs equal partit. betw. his ch. John, Miriam Tyler, Rebecca Kilby, and Sarah Kilby, and childr. of s. Thomas, dec. VINCENT, Stamford 1641, m. a d. of Henry Ackerly of the same, had Daniel, John, and, perhaps, other ch. and d. bef. 1671. We kn. of the two s. only that Daniel liv. in the adjoin. town of Bedford, d. there 1699; and that John, soon aft. d. of his f. sold his est. and rem.

SIMSON, SYMSON, or SIMPSON, ALEXANDER, Boston 1659, Scotchman, call. a brickmaker, was a householder, liv. 1695. FRANCIS, Salem or Marblehead 1648, in Nov. 1659 was worried as a Quaker. HENRY, York, d. bef. 1655. HENRY, York, s. of the preced. ens. of the milit. comp. 1680, sw. alleg. 22 Mar. 1681, tak. by the Ind. car. to Canada. JOHN, Watertown, came in the Truelove, 1635, aged 30, by w. Susanna, wh. prob. came with him in this as in a former voyage, had Sarah, b. 28 May 1634, wh. perhaps, d. young; Hannah, 25 July 1636; John, 20 Nov. 1638; Jonathan, 17 Dec. 1640; and Eliz. 3 Mar. 1642 or 3; and he d. or was bur. 10 June 1643. The wid. in Nov. foll. sold the est. and m. the same yr. George Parkhurst. JOHN, Charlestown, perhaps s. of the preced. by w. Abigail had John, Joseph, Benjamin, Jonathan, Abigail, Susanna, and Deborah, all bapt. 1 Mar. 1685, both h. and w. hav. the Sunday bef. been adm. of the ch. JONATHAN, Charlestown, br. of the preced. by w. Wait, d. of capt. Roger Clap, had Jonathan, bapt. 1 Mar. 1685; and Wait, 5 Apr. foll. the parents join. the ch. on the last Sunday of Feb. preced. PETER, Milford 1654, as by Lambert is erron. stat. certain. more than twenty yrs. too early; there d. in 1685. He had fam. no doubt, for his home-lot, ho. and barns are fully ment. in 1678. THOMAS, Salisbury, had Mary, b. 2 June 1664.

SINCLAIR, ST. CLAIR, or SINKLER, JAMES, and JOHN, Exeter, 1677,

9 *

took o. of alleg. 30 Nov. of that yr. but as John, whose w. was Mary, had been there 16 yrs. at least, the other may be his s.

SINGLETARY, or SINGLETERY, AMOS, Haverhill, perhaps s. of Richard, took o. of alleg. Dec. 1677. BENJAMIN, Haverhill, s. of Richard, perhaps his youngest, sw. alleg. the same day with Amos, m. 4 Apr. 1678, Mary Stockbridge, had Susanna, b. 27 Jan. foll.; Richard, 16 Mar. 1681; Jonathan, 28 Aug. 1683; John, 6 July 1686; Broughton, 25 Mar. 1689; Joseph, 9 Feb. 1693; and Mary, 14 July 1695. JONATHAN, Haverhill, prob. br. of the preced. in 1663 had w. Mary. NATHANIEL, Haverhill, br. of Benjamin, sw. alleg. the same day with him, m. 22 Dec. 1673, Sarah Belknap, perhaps d. of Abraham the first, had John, b. 7 May 1675; Jonathan, 18 Nov. 1678, d. in few days; Sarah, 23 Oct. 1679; Susanna, 19 Sept. 1681; Richard, 5 Aug. 1683, perhaps that one k. by the Ind. 19 Aug. 1707, at Lancaster; Hannah, 23 May 1685; Ebenezer, 18 June 1687; and ano. 20 Aug. 1689; but the f. was k. by the Ind. 7 days bef. RICHARD, Salem 1637, rem. bef. join. the ch. to Newbury, there was freem. 7 Sept. 1638, may have had sev. ch. b. there bef. rem. to Salisbury in 1645 or aft. but there are rec. by w. Susanna, Jonathan, b. 17 Jan. 1640; Eunice, 7 Jan. 1642; Nathaniel, 28 Oct. 1644; Lydia, 30 Apr. 1648; and Amos, Apr. 1651. He was a selectman in 1650, tax. decently for the supp. of min. yet gone in 1652 to Haverhill, there, by w. Susanna Cooke, says Barry, had Benjamin, b. 4 Apr. 1656. Coffin says, he had John, that is perhaps the same as Jonathan. Eunice m. at Andover, 6 Jan. 1659, Thomas Eaton. His w. d. 11 Apr. 1682, and he d. 25 Oct. 1687, in the 102d yr. if the repts. may be accept. RICHARD, New London 1686, wh. may have been s. or gr.s. of the preced. d. 16 Oct. 1711, leav. nine ch. some of wh. were in Carolina, but the only kn. names are Richard, William, Waitstill, and beside a d. wh. m. Samuel Latham.

SINNET, SENNOT, or SENNITT, JOHN, Boston, mariner, s. of Walter, appears to own est. from 1667 to 1676. WALTER, Boston, by w. Mary, wh. join. our ch. 23 May 1647, had Mary, b. 19 Nov. 1640; Eliz. 23 June 1642, d. soon; John, 10 July 1643; and on Sunday aft. the adm. of his w. had bapt. Mary, John, and Stephen, the last "being 1 yr. 6 mos. and a. 18 days old," and he d. at 10 yrs.; Joseph, 12 Mar. 1648, a. 9 days; Sarah, 28 Apr. 1650; Thomas, 28 Mar. 1652; and Isaac, b. 22 Sept. bapt. 1 Oct. 1654, d. in few days. Mary m. 26 Nov. 1661, John Sparke.

SISSON, GEORGE, Portsmouth, R. I. m. 1 Aug. 1667, Sarah, d. of Thomas Lawton, had Eliz. b. 18 Aug. 1669; Mary, 18 Oct. 1670; Ann, 17 Feb. 1672; Hope, 24 Dec. 1674; Richard, 10 Sept. 1676; Ruth, 5 May 1680; George, 23 Mar. 1683; Abigail, 23 Mar. 1685;

Thomas, 10 Sept. 1686; John, 26 June 1688; and James, 26 July 1690; his w. d. 17 July 1718; and he d. 10 Sept. foll. aged 74. His eldest d. Eliz. m. Jeremiah Clark. JAMES, Dartmouth 1684, was, perhaps, br. of the preced.

SIVERNS, JOHN, Lynn, had John, b. 22 Mar. 1684. Perhaps this may be Severance of Salisbury.

SKATE, JOHN, Weymouth 1658, is nam. by Farmer; but I find no such name, unless it mean the next.

SKEATH, JOHN, Boston 1674, liv. long, as from his will of 6 May 1700, pro. 22 Jan. 1708, is clearly discern. It gives to w. Sarah, ds. Sarah Bradshaw, Rebecca Allen, Mary, and Joanna S. beside gr.ch. Joseph, and Hannah, and makes w. and d. Mary excors. See Scathe.

SKEEL, JOHN, Stratford, m. Hannah, d. of Roger Terrill of the same, had John, and Hannah, bapt. 10 Nov. 1678, of wh. John d. soon; John, again, Nov. 1679; Thomas, 23 Apr. 1682; Eliz. 20 Apr. 1683; Abigail, 9 May 1686; and Ephraim, July 1689; had rem. to Woodbury 1682; perhaps even bef. any of these ch. Hannah m. 3 Mar. 1697, Benjamin Hicock.

SKEETH, WILLIAM, of Charlestown, or Woburn, d. a. 1672, for his inv. was then ret. in Middlesex by Lawrence Dowse and Josiah Convers, wh. were of those two towns.

SKELLING, THOMAS, Salem 1643, had then, says Felt, a gr. of ld. But prob. that was inadeq. inducem. to leave Gloucester where he had liv. some yrs. and by w. Deborah had Deborah, b. 22 Aug. 1640, or 1648, rem. perhaps, to Falmouth 1651, and own. est. in Maine; but was soon back, yet d. at F. 1667; in his will, of 14 Nov. 1666, nam. s. Thomas and John. See Skilling. THOMAS, Falmouth, eldest s. of the preced. says Babson, m. 1654, Mary Lewis, d. of George of the same, had John, and Benjamin, and d. at Salem, 30 Dec. 1676. His wid. m. Jotham Lewis; and next a. Wilkins, says Mr. Willis, and in 1732 was of Salem 78 yrs old.

SKELTON, BENJAMIN, Salem, nam. 1639, when his s. John was bapt. and NATHANIEL, Salem 1648, when his s. John was bapt. are in the list of sett. but not ch. mem. Strange as it seems, no more is told of either; and to larger or less credulity must be left the opin. whether one or both were ch. of Rev. Samuel. SAMUEL, Salem, came from Co. Lincoln, in 1629, arr. with w. and ch. three or four, in the George, 29 June, in co. with Samuel Sharpe, hav. sail. 4 May from Isle of Wight. He was b. 1584, bred at Clare Hall, Cambr. Univ. where he had his degr. 1611 and 1614; nam. by the Gov. and Comp. at London to be of the Counc. to Capt. Endicot, wh. they appoint. Gov. of the Planta. as they heard that E. had "formerly receiv. much good by his ministry;"

but prob. he never was sw. for the arrest of his assoc. the Browns, bef. com. of the commiss. would prevent organiz. or action. But in the pulpit his right as pastor, as well as that of Higginson, for teacher, was fix. 6 Aug. 1629. Desir. adm. as freem. 19 Oct. 1630, he was rec. 18 May foll. His w. d. 15 Mar. 1631, and prob. he took ano. w. if the ord. of Court, June 1638, with the consent of Mrs. Baggerly," that the incr. of his " cattle shd. b. div. acc. to Mr. Skelton's will; and that the goods and household stuff wh. belong to the three eldest ch. shd. be div. by some of the ch." be constr. to mean, that he left a younger ch. and we might infer, that his wid. had tak. new h. Mr. Baggerly. But no such name is found in Felt's list of ch. memb. of Salem, nor indeed does any Skelton appear there, but the pastor. He rec. in July 1632 gr. of four lots of ld. of various quantity, from the Col. besides what the town may have gr. if any, tho. no such benefact. to either him or Higginson, or any ch. of either is ment. He d. 2 Aug. 1634, and much do we regret the loss of his will, that perhaps would have nam. the childr. In his Ann. II. 568, Mr. Felt explains the denial to Gov. Winthrop, Isaac Johnson, and compan. of liberty, to unite in the Lord's supper, or to have a ch. bapt. for wh. Cotton, then at home, express. his surpr. and regr. No wonder the Browns were driv. away, when these later comers could not by Mr. Skelton be adm. to *his* communion as " not memb. of reformed chhs." The great master of us all would gladly have rec. these men ; but the rigid separatists had sterner sense of duty. So extreme was their repugn. to the formulary, wh. they had once used in their weekly worsh. that they would not longer believe in the communion of saints. SAMUEL, Salem, s. prob. of the preced. b. in Eng. sold ld. in* S. Feb. 1644, to lieut. Richard Davenport.

SKERRY, FRANCIS, Salem 1637, freem. 17 May of that yr. ; was, it is said, aged near 84 at his d. 1692. HENRY, Salem, perhaps br. of the preced. came from Yarmouth, in Co. Norfk. Apr. 1637, cordwainer, aged 31, with w. Eliz. 25, one ch. Henry, and one apprent. Edmund Towne, aged 18. See 4 Mass. Hist. Coll. I. 97, or Geneal. Reg. XIV. 325. He was adm. freem. Mar. 1638 ; had Eliz. bapt. that mo. ; Mary, Sept. 1640 ; Ephraim, 26 Mar. 1643 ; and John, 3 June 1649 ; he car. a prisoner, 1649, to Boston, prob. as a constable, and was liv. 1696, then call. 89 yrs. old ; and in Felt's ch. list of 1645 is Bridget, wh. may have been w. of him or Francis. HENRY, Salem, s. of the preced. was freem. 1677.

SKIDMORE, or SKIDMER, JAMES, Boston 1636, appears as agent for John Winthrop of Conn. JOHN, perhaps of Cambridge, was fin. 1641, for sale of strong water to Ind. THOMAS, Cambridge 1642, had, in 1636, been engag. for John Winthrop in his prepar. for plant. at Saybrook ; by w. Ellen had John, b. 11 Apr. 1643 ; and Joseph ; may have been at Lancaster at its early sett. 1653, but certain. bef. and aft. that date at New London, and prob. 1672 at Huntington, L. I. He had also, Dorothy, wh. m. 20 July 1652, Hugh Griffin.

SKIFF, * JAMES, Sandwich 1643–63, had come from Lynn a. 1637, was rep. 1645 and 13 yrs. more, had Bathshua, b. 21 Apr. 1648, wh. m. perhaps in 1666, Shearjashub Bourne ; Mary, 24 Mar. 1650; perhaps that Patience wh. m. 26 Oct. 1675, Elisha Bourne. * STEPHEN, Sandwich 1667, was rep. 1676 and sev. yrs. aft. See Baylies. An Eliz. Skaffe, the Col. Rec. says, was bur. at Rehoboth, 25 June 1676. I suppose it means Skiff.

SKILLING, SKILLIN, or SKILLINGS, JOHN, Falmouth 1651, may have been s. of Thomas. His wid. rem. 1688, to Portsmouth. THOMAS, Salem 1643, may have belong. rather to Gloucester, where he was in 1642, there, perhaps, had Thomas, b. Nov. 1643 ; and Abigail, wh. m. 18 Nov. 1670, John Curney, Carney, or Gurney. Perhaps both f. and s. were of Falmouth in 1665.

SKILLINGER, or STILLINGER, JACOB, a Dutchman, at New London 1661, had been at New Haven, was liv. 1666, and had a w.

SKINNER, ABRAHAM, Malden, s. of the first Thomas, by w. Hannah had Abraham, b. 8 Apr. 1681 ; Thomas, 7 Dec. 1688 ; and Mary, Sept. 1690. His wid. d. 14 Jan. 1726. EDWARD, Cambridge, d. early, perhaps in 1639, perhaps in 1641, as the articles in Geneal. Reg. II. 103, and III. 81, seem discord. By his will he gave half of his est. to the ch. of C. and half to Mr. Robert Ibbit of Cambridge, in Old Eng. but calls no w. ch. or other relat. so that we may infer that he was a bach. if not, also, that he came from Co. Cambridge. FRANCIS, was command. of the fort at Pemaquid, May 1683, as in Geneal. Reg. XI. 33. JOHN, Hartford 1639, had w. Mary, wh. m. 13 Nov. 1651, Owen Tudor, prob. by her had JOHN ; is among freem. of 1669. JOHN, Hartford, s. of the preced. had Mary, b. 1 Dec. 1664 ; John, 1 Mar. 1667 ; Joseph, 26 Aug. 1669 ; Nathaniel, 5 Apr. 1672 ; Richard, 16 Jan. 1674 ; Sarah, 4 Nov. 1677 ; and Thomas, 15 Nov. 1680. JOSEPH, Windsor, m. 5 Apr. 1666, Mary, d. of William Filley of the same, had Mary, b. 22 Sept. 1667 ; and Eliz. 23 Jan. 1669 ; was freem. 1669, and next yr. of Simsbury. RICHARD, perhaps of Hartford 1648, may have been f. or br. of John and Joseph. Perhaps his was that wid. Mary S. wh. m. 13 Nov. 1651, Owen Tudor. THOMAS, Malden, came from Chichester, in Co. Sussex, where by w. Mary, were b. his s. Thomas, 25 July 1645 ; and Abraham, 29 Sept. 1649 ; and soon aft. prob. for first time, he arr. here. His w. Mary d. 9 Apr. 1671. THOMAS, Boston, baker, bot. est. 1673, near the Exchange, was freem. 1690. THOMAS, Malden, s. of the first Thomas, b. in Eng. by w. Mary, d. of Richard Pratt of the same, had Thomas, b. Nov. 1668 ; and he m. 22 Dec. 1669, Mary, d.

of Thomas Gould, had John, Apr. 1673; Richard, 3 Jan. 1676; beside Nathaniel, 27 Mar. 1686, I presume, for the transcrib. from the rec. of b. in Geneal. Reg. VI. 336, has Jan. and here, prob. as in most of the dates, has mistak. the meaning of the numeral for the month; and Abigail, 17 Feb. 1691, was freem. 1690, and d. 2 Mar. 1704. WALTER, Salem 1680. Of this name, Farmer says, there had been gr. in 1829, five at Yale, three at Harv. and six at other N. E. coll.

SKIPPER, or SKEPPAR, THEOPHILUS, Lynn, a minor, hav. demand of £51. against Benjamin Keayne, payab. on his com. of age, and Rev. John Cotton and Rev. Thomas Cobbett, his guardians in 1646, interfer. for his security. A Jane S. of Boston, spinster, in Jan. 1652, obt. secur. for £50. from Valentine Hill of Dover in comp. with Rev. Thomas Cobbett and Joshua Scottow, so that I infer a relat. betw. this maiden and Theophilus, prob. br. and sis. She m. 19 Aug. 1653, Abraham Brown.

SKOULING, ROBERT, Hingham, came 1638, from old Hingham, with Thomas Cooper, and his fam. perhaps as serv. in the Diligent, but certain. he had no gr. of ld. there, nor is his name ever found again.

SKULLARD. See Scullard.

SLACK, WILLIAM, Weymouth, by w. Mary had Thomas, b. 5 July 1690.

SLADE, WILLIAM, Newport, adm. freem. 1659. See R. I. Hist. Coll. III. 251.

SLAPUM, PETER, if the strange name be correct, was a selectman of Fairfield 1669.

SLATER, JOHN, Marblehead 1665, had w. Eliz. when he d. that yr.

SLAUGHTER, JOHN, Simsbury, propound. for freem. 1674, had m. 15 July 1669, Abiah, wid. of Elisha Bartlett.

SLAWSON, ELEAZER, Stamford, s. of George, had a fam. but the names are unkn. GEORGE, Lynn 1637, rem. to Sandwich, yet is not found among men able to bear arms in 1643; prob. went to Stamford bef. 1644, where were, 1669, propound. for freem. he with s. Eleazer, and John. He had a d. wh. m. John Gould, and these three ch. seem to be all he had when his will was made. He d. 17 Feb. 1695. JOHN, Stamford, s. of the preced. m. 12 Nov. 1663, Sarah, d. of William Tuttle of New Haven, had John, b. 1664; Sarah, 1667; and Jonathan, 1670. His w. was k. 17 Nov. 1676, with an axe, by her br. Benjamin T. wh. tho. prob. insane, was execut. for it, 13 June foll. He m. sec. w. Eliz. Benedict, had Mary, Thomas, and, perhaps, more ch. and d. 1706. JOSIAH, Marshfield, possib. but not prob. s. of George, m. 12 Mar. 1679, Mary Williamson. THOMAS, Stamford, had gr. of houselot in 1641, but did not contin. there to enjoy it. Sometimes this name is Slason, and oft. Slosson.

SLEEPER, AARON, Hampton, took o. of alleg. 1678, by w. Eliz. had Moses, b. 22 Jan. 1685; and Thomas, 3 Nov. 1686. JOHN, Hampton 1678, Exeter 1682, perhaps s. of Thomas, charg. with high treason in 1683, aft. convict. was set free. THOMAS, Hampton 1645, bot. that yr. ho. in Boston from Christopher Lawson, but did not rem. had w. Joanna, and by her prob. Aaron and John, certain. Eliz. wh. m. 27 Aug. 1668, Abraham Perkins the sec.; and he d. 30 July 1696, in 80th yr.

SLEY, or SLYE, CHRISTOPHER, Boston, his w. Eliz. d. 10 Aug. 1696, and he d. 25 Nov. 1697. ROBERT, in Conn. was fin. in Apr. 1649, for exchang. a gun with an Ind.

SLINNINGS, RICHARD, in Geneal. Reg. XII. 12, is error for STIN-NINGS, as the Plymouth rec. and Gov. Bradford 362–4, show.

SLOCUM, or SLOCOME, ANTHONY, Taunton 1639, one of the first purch. and early sett. at Dartmouth, where his s. all m. he says, and the name is preserv. Baylies, I. 286; II. 282. They were, as I presume, Eleazer, Giles, and Peleg, wh. were proprs. 1694. Ib. IV. 92. GILES, Portsmouth, R. I. perhaps br. of the preced. among the freem. of 1655, had (as his will, made 1680, teach.) Giles, wh. was b. 25 Mar. 1647; Ebenezer, 25 Mar. 1650; Nathaniel, 25 Dec. 1652; Peleg, 17 Aug. 1654; Eleazer; Mary; and Joanna, wh. was b. 16 May 1642. His w. was Joan, wh. d. 31 Aug. 1679, and she had John, b. 1645, prob. d. young; and Mary, 3 July 1660. GILES, Portsmouth, R. I. s. of the preced. by w. Ann, d. of Thomas Lawton, wh. he m. 26 May 1669, had Eliz. b. 8 Sept. 1671; Joanna, 9 Oct. 1672; Mary, 31 Jan. 1676; Sarah, 1 Mar. 1679; Giles, 8 Dec. 1680; and John, 22 Sept. 1682. PELEG, Dartmouth, br. of the preced. was one of the early sett. there.

SLOMAN, SLUMAN, or SLOWMAN, SIMON, Newbury, by w. Hannah had Simon, b. 14 July 1691. THOMAS, Norwich 1663, m. Dec. 1668, Sarah, d. of Thomas Bliss of the same, had Sarah, b. 13 Mar. 1670; Mary, 13 Feb. 1672; Thomas, 19 Dec. 1674; Eliz. 23 July 1677; Abigail, 14 Mar. 1680; and Rebecca, 3 Oct. 1682; was constable 1680.

SLOPER, RICHARD, Dover 1657, b. Nov. 1630, was aft. of Ports-mouth, m. 21 Oct. 1658, Mary, d. of Henry Sherburn, had Bridget, b. 5 Aug. 1659; John, 13 Jan. 1661; Mary, 11 Feb. 1663; Sarah, 26 July 1667; Susanna, 21 Mar. 1669; Eliz. 26 June 1671; Rebecca, 29 Oct. 1673; Martha, 26 Dec. 1676; Tabitha, 17 Dec. 1679; Richard and Henry, tw. 19 June 1682; and Ambrose, 20 Jan. 1684; and d. 16 Oct. 1716. His wid. d. 22 Sept. 1718.

SLOUGH, SLOW, or SLOFF, JOHN, Newport 1639. WILLIAM, New Haven 1644, rem. next yr. to Milford, and join. the ch. 1648; m. Eliz. d. of James Prudden, had Hasadiah, a d. bapt. that yr.; and James, b. Jan. 1650, d. next mo. He was excom. says the rec. for horrid offence,

and put to d. at New Haven. His wid. m. 18 Dec. 1653, Roger Prichard of M. wh. soon rem.

SLOWE, THOMAS, Providence, among freem. 1655, unless the name
be Stowe.

SMALL, BENJAMIN, Salem 1674, a sailmaker, was, perhaps, s. of John
of the same. EDWARD, Kittery 1640, was that yr. on the gr. jury, and
in 1645 had commiss. as a magistr. FRANCIS, Dover 1648, Falmouth
1658, freem. that yr. and aft. the Ind. incurs. rem. to Portsmouth, where
he was 1685, aged 65. JOHN, Salem 1643, had come, as serv. of Edmund Batter, maltster, of Salisbury, in Co. Wilts, Apr. 1635, in the
James of London, from Southampton, arr. at Boston 3 June; perhaps
had Stephen, and Benjamin; was troubl. in 1658 for a Quaker, but
soon was permit. to go to R. I. JOHN, Braintree, rem. perhaps, to
Mendon, 1662. THOMAS, Salem 1670, may have been that inhab. of
Marblehead 1674, print. in Geneal. Reg. VII. 76, Smace, wh. seems an
impossib. name. From rec. of Pro. it seems, that he had w. Ruth,
wh. pray. 25 Mar. 1676, for admin. and benefit of est. for s. William, ds. Lydia, Hannah, and Ann; but one of these ch. was d. bef.
30 Nov. foll. when the Ct. gr. her petitn. See Hist. Coll. of Essex Inst.
II. 183, 4.

SMALLEY, JAMES, Concord, freem. 1690. JOHN, Plymouth, came in
the Francis and James, 1632, with Edward Winslow, arr. from London,
at Boston, 5 June, rem. 1644 to Eastham, with first sett. there, had
Hannah, b. 14 June 1641; John, 8 Sept. 1644, both at P.; Isaac and
Mary, tw. 11 Dec. 1647, bapt. at Barnstable, 27 Feb. 1648; and was
liv. in 1655. Hannah m. 23 Jan. 1661, John Bangs; and Mary, wh. is
call. Small, perhaps, m. 19 Sept. 1667, John Snow.

SMALLIDGE, or SMALLEDGE, WILLIAM, Ipswich 1650, Boston 1653,
by w. Mary had Johanna, b. 15 Apr. of that yr., and Abigail, 28 May
1657.

SMART, CHARLES, Marblehead 1668. JOHN, Hingham 1635, came
with w. and two s. from Co. Norfolk, drew his house lot there in
Sept. of this yr., was of Exeter 1642–53, prob. was f. of Richard, or
James, or Robert, or of all, or he or his s. of the same name may have
been at Edgartown 1663. James was a capt. 1668, at E. Richard has
the prefix of resp. 30 Nov. 1677, when he, with serj. ROBERT, and
Robert junr. all sw. alleg. at Exeter. The younger Robert had m.
25 Sept. 1674, acc. the County rec. as print. in Geneal. Reg. VIII.
224, but the bride's name must be erron. since it was never heard in
N. E.

SMEAD, SMEED, or SMED, RICHARD, Windsor 1672, of wh. no more
is kn. SAMUEL, Deerfield, s. of William, had w. and two ch. k. by Fr.

and Ind. when the town was destroy. 29 Feb. 1704. WILLIAM, Dorchester, prob. one of the ch. b. in Eng. of wid. Judith Smead, sis. of Israel Stoughton, wh. had join. the ch. a. 1636, and on whose est. he was appoint. 1639, to admin. acc. her will, for the good of them, was tak. to be brot. up by John Pope, wh. in his will, call. him little boy, gave his looms and tackling of them, to the val. of £3. provid. he would live with his w. aft. his time was out, and willing to learn his trade. This was in 1646. He m. 31 Dec. 1658, Eliz. d. of Thomas Lawrence, and was freem. 1680, at Northampton, whither he rem. a. 1660, had William; Eliz. b. 20 May 1663; Judith, 18 Feb. 1665; Mehitable, 2 Jan. 1667; Samuel, 27 May 1669; John, 27 Aug. 1671, d. soon; John, again, 1673; Ebenezer, bapt. 9 May 1675; Thankful, 13 May 1677; and Waitstill, a d. b. 15 Mar. 1679. He rem. a. 1684 to Deerfield, and there d. but the time is not kn. His wid. with sev. of the same name, ch. or gr. ch. were slain by the French and Ind. 29 Feb. 1704. The first ch. William, b. prob. at D. was k. 18 Sept. 1675, with the flower of Essex under Capt. Lothrop at Bloody Brook; but Samuel, John, and Ebenezer had fams. at D. and the name has been well perpet.

SMEDLEY, SMEADLY, or SMEEDLY, BAPTIST, or BAPTIZE, as the Col. Rec. gives it, Concord 1639, freem. 1644, had Samuel, b. 1646; Mary; and James; and d. 16 Aug. 1675 in 68th yr. His d. Mary m. 10 Dec. 1667, Isaac Shepard; Samuel was k. 2 Aug. 1675, at Quaboag, by Ind in ambush, when Capt. Hutchinson was treacherously surpris. as our his tory tells. *JOHN, Concord, br. prob. elder, of the preced. freem. 1644, had John, and perhaps other ch. was rep. 1667 and 70, and senior selectman 1680. JOHN, Concord, s. of the preced. m. 1669, Sarah, d. of Thomas Wheeler, and was freem. in 1677. SAMUEL, Fairfield 1690, may have been s. of the first John.

SMIKING, VINCENT, is among emigr. a. 1641 from Wethersfield to Stamford, but nothing else is kn. to me.

SMITH, ABIEZER, possib. Charlestown, print. Abzar, by Frothingham, 181, in his list of the freem. 1677, but I feel doubt of the character, and think it refers only to those call. to take the o. of alleg., for Paige's list of freem. has not that name, nor any like it, a. that yr., and beside the ch. rec. contains no evid. of adm. of such an one. Prob. it stands for Abraham. ABRAHAM, Watertown 1660, was aft. of Charlestown, and join. the ch. 6 Jan. 1667, as did his w. Martha, 3 Apr. 1670, there had bapt. John, 19 May 1667; and Mary, 9 Aug. 1668; but he certain. was a householder in C. 1658, and may have soon aft. been at Salem bef. W. freem. 1670; yet it may be there were two of this name at the same hour in C. for the list of freem. sw. 1671 repeats it, tho. he may have renew. the solemnity, or one of the two may have been of Roxbury, where Ellis claims an Abraham without date, and he d. 5 Sept. 1683. Martha his wid. admin. ABRAHAM, Middletown, m. 13 Feb. 1678, Hope Stow, prob. d. of Rev. Samuel, had Samuel, b. 2 Nov. foll. wh. d. at ten days, as did the mo. in five more. ARTHUR, Hartford 1640, was engag. on a salary for the col. to cease that yr., had w. Margaret, and sev. ch. perhaps Mary, b. and bapt. Feb. 1645, wh. d. young, was one; eldest s. John; Arthur, bapt. 20 Apr. 1651; and perhaps Eliz. in the will of her mo. call. Thompson, w. of Thomas. He d. bef. 1655, and the wid. m. Stephen Hart, and d. 1693. ARTHUR, Southold, L. I. 1659, was sent over to New Haven for trial, as a Quaker, sentenc. to be whip. and give large bonds for good behav. ARTHUR, Hartford, not s. prob. of either of the preced. by w. Sarah had Sarah, b. 14 Apr. 1684; and Hannah, 4 Oct. 1688; and by w. Phebe had Phebe, 4 Sept. 1701; and d. 1713, in his will nam. only these ds. ASAHEL, Dedham 1642. ASAHEL, Dorchester, perhaps s. of the preced. was a young man in 1669, and may be the freem. 1690. BATHOLOMEW, Dover 1640. BENJAMIN, Providence 1645, or earlier, one of the first hundred adm. inhab. had Joseph, perhaps others. BENJAMIN, the freem. of 2 June 1641, may have been, as Coffin thot., of Lynn, b. a. 1612, and ar. co. 1643; but at Dedham was BENJAMIN, also, hav. there bapt. Benjamin, 18 Oct. 1646. BENJAMIN, Boston 1650. ‡ BENJAMIN, Providence, came a. 1660, one of the many, as to the cause of whose coming tradit. is happy to repeat many foolish stories. Either he was a parliam. man or a support. of Cromwell, so that it was good for him to escape at the restorat. "losing the bulk of his est." and as he was rather young, this prob. was not much. However he m. Lydia, d. of William Carpenter of Pawtuxit, had Benjamin, b. a. 1661; Joseph; William; Simon; Lydia, wh. it is said, m. a Fones; and Eliz. wh. m. 28 Feb. 1699, Israel Arnold. He was an Assist. 1696, his w. d. 1 Oct. 1711, and he d. 13 Dec. 1713. BENJAMIN, Reading, perhaps s. of Benjamin of Lynn, by w. Jehoidan m. 27 Mar. 1661, had Benjamin, b. 27 Jan. foll. and his w. d. 5 Nov. aft. He d. Eaton says, 1691. BENJAMIN, Milford, s. of William, of Huntington, L. I. m. 21 Oct. 1660, Mary, eldest d. of Timothy Baldwin, had Mary, b. 1662; Hannah, 1664; Benjamin, 1666; Abigail, 1668, d. soon; Timothy, 1669; Sarah, 1671; and Samuel, 1678; and his w. d. 23 Aug. 1680. He was in the list of freem. 1669, and he m. a. 1682, Sarah, wid. of Robert Haughton, d. of Gamaliel Phippen, and was liv. 1700. BENJAMIN, Farmington, s. of William of the same, m. Ruth, d. of Samuel Loomis of Westfield, had William, rem. to Westfield, there had Ruth, b. 8 Feb. 1685; Benjamin, 14 Feb. 1687; Samuel, 24 Aug. 1689; Eliz. 14 Feb. 1693; Rachel, 1694; Jonathan, 1697; Job, 1700, and Mary, 1703. He had sec. w.

Hannah, rem. to West Springfield, there d. 1738. BENJAMIN, Sandwich, by w. Eliz. had Elkanah, b. 7 Mar. 1685; Ruth, 17 Dec. 1687; Hannah, 10 March 1689; Elisha, 26 Feb. 1692; Bathsheba, 13 June 1694; Eliz. 4 Aug. 1696; Penninah, 19 Apr. 1699; Ichabod, 27 June 1702; and Ebenezer, 4 Sept. 1704. CHILIAB, or CHILEAB, Hadley, s. of Samuel of the same, m. 2 Oct. 1661, Hannah, d. of Luke Hitchcock of Wethersfield, had Hannah, b. 7 July 1662; Samuel, 9 Mar. 1664; Luke, 16 Apr. 1666; Ebenezer, 11 July 1668; Nathaniel, 2 Jan. 1670, d. soon; John, 8 Oct. 1671; one in 1673, d. very soon; Esther, 31 Mar. 1674; one in 1677, d. very soon; Eliz. 2 Feb. 1678; Mary, 16 Aug. 1681; one in 1682, d. soon; Chiliab, 18 Feb. 1685; and Sarah, 26 Apr. 1688; was freem. 1673, and d. 7 Mar. 1731, aged almost 96. His wid. d. 31 Aug. 1733, aged 88, by the gr. stone. CHRISTOPHER, Dedham 1642, freem. 10 May 1643, m. 2 Aug. 1654, Martha, d. of Michael Metcalf the first, wid. of William Brignall, perhaps as sec. w. and d. soon aft., when the Metcalf pedigree in Geneal. Reg. VI. 173, says she took 3d h. a Stow. CHRISTOPHER, Providence, in the list of freem. there 1655, had d. Susanna wh. m. Lawrence Wilkinson; engag. for alleg. to Charles II. June 1668. In 1672, his w. was Alice; but what was her fam. name, or whether she were first, sec. or later w. is unkn. CHRISTOPHER, Dedham, perhaps s. of the first Christopher, m. Mary, d. of Jonathan Fairbanks, and no more is kn. of him, unless he be, wh. is not very prob., that CHRISTOPHER of Hartford perhaps first, one of four brs. whose only sis. Mary was there w. of William Partridge, and wh. rem. to Northampton, early, where he had w. Sarah, adm. of the ch. 1664, but no ch. there sw. alleg. 8 Feb. 1679, and d. 13 Feb. 1692. His wid. was liv. in 1706, neph. Samuel Partridge, Esqr. of Hatfield, s. of his only sis. Mary, wh., by contr. had support. him and his w. in old age, had the est. DANIEL, Watertown, by w. Eliz. prob. d. of Thomas Rogers, had Daniel, b. 27 Sept. 1642; and he d. 14 July 1660, wh. is the date of his will, mak. w. Eliz. Extrix. names s. Daniel, and br. Abraham, wh. with Rev. John Sherman, and others, he made overseers. ‡ * DANIEL, Rehoboth 1650, nam. in the will of that date of his mo. Judith, was prob. s. of Henry, m. 20 Oct. 1659, Esther, d. of Francis Chickering of Dedham; rep. 1672, an Assist. 1679, had Nathaniel, b. 7 Aug. 1674; Ebenezer, 29 July 1676; Judith, 7 Feb. 1679; Rebecca, 20 Apr. 1680. He was made one of the Counc. for governm. of N. E. under Sir Edmund Andros, 1687. DANIEL, Watertown, s. of the first Daniel, m. 22 or 27 Feb. 1668 (Dr. Bond gives both dates), Mary, d. of Christopher Grant, had Daniel, b. 15 Mar. 1669; Grace, 13 Jan. 1671; John, 13 July 1672; Eliz. 15 Jan. 1674; Sarah, 27 Dec. 1675; Abigail, 3 Dec. 1678; and Joseph, 8 June 1680; beside

Susanna; and he d. 7 June 1681, in his will made eight days bef. nam. only the w. and three s. Perhaps the youngest three ds. d. soon. DAN-IEL, Greenwich 1672–97. DANIEL, Charlestown, a householder 1678, had w. Eliz. wh. join. the ch. 23 Jan. 1676. DANIEL, Eastham, perhaps s. of the first John, m. 3 Mar. 1677, Mary, d. of John Young of the same, had Daniel, b. 8 Jan. 1679; Content, 8 June 1680; Abigail, 30 Apr. 1683; James, Apr. 1685; Nathaniel, Oct. 1687; May, or Mary, more likely, 8 Jan. 1693, wh. d. at 13 yrs. DELIVERANCE, Dartmouth, 1686. EBENEZER, New Haven, s. of George of the same, was a propr. 1685. EDWARD, Weymouth, had Phebe, b. 15 Aug. or Nov. 1642, may have been of Providence 1645, Rehoboth where he was with his w. indict. 1650 for not going to ch. to worship on Sunday; was perhaps of Newport, on the list of freem. 1655. His d. Sarah m. 24 Nov. 1646, Stephen Arnold of Providence. Another EDWARD was of Providence, when he engag. alleg. June 1668, and was publish. 1669, to Amphyllis, d. of Thomas Angell of the same, by wh. I suppose, he had Edward, and Joseph; among those wh. did not rem. in the perils of 1676; d. Jan. 1703, without a will. EDWARD, Boston 1655. ED-WARD, New London 1669, then propound. for freem.; had m. 7 June 1663, Eliz. d. of Thomas Bliss of Norwich, had John, wh. d. at 15 yrs. in July 1689, as did his mo. in two days, and this f. four days aft. her, leav. beside six ds. Obadiah, wh. was b. 5 Feb. 1677. EDWARD, Exeter, m. 13 Jan. 1669, Mary Hall, perhaps d. of Ralph, took the o. of alleg. 30 Nov. 1677, and was one of the address. to the king 1683, against his Gov. Cranfield. ELEAZER, Fairfield 1669, s. of Giles of the same, m. Rebecca, d. of Henry Rowland of the same. ELIEZER, Dartmouth 1686. ELISHA, Warwick perhaps, more prob. of Newport, m. Mary, d. of James Barker, d. early, and his wid. m. 16 Apr. 1677, Israel Arnold of Providence. EPHRAIM, Milford, s. of the first John of the same, propos. for freem. 1669; and rem. to Derby. EPHRAIM, Farmington, s. of Joseph of Hartford, m. Apr. 1686, Rachel, d. of John Cole, had Ephraim, b. 16, bapt. 21 Dec. 1690; Rachel 10, bapt. 17 Feb. 1695; Lydia, 20 Nov. 1697; Sarah, 6 Aug. 1700; Mary, 11 Apr. 1703; Benjamin, 10 Apr. 1706; and John, 16 Apr. 1709; and d. 5 Apr. 1751. FRANCIS, the freem. of 17 Apr. 1637, was a propr. Bond thinks, in Watertown, that yr. but not in 1642, and in my opin. prob. that Reading man, wh. d. 20 Mar. 1651, then call. sen. wh. was first, perhaps, of Lynn. His will, made six days bef. ment. without nam. w. s. John, and Benjamin, and gr. d. Mary S. FRANCIS, Roxbury, one of the first mem. of the ch. freem. 18 May 1631, so that we may infer, that he came in one of the fleet with Winth. and, as the town rec. ment. that his s. Andrew, d. or was bur. 15 Mar. 1640, whose b. is not told, it is thot. he brot. w. and fam. but no more can be deriv. as unhap. the ch. rec. of bapt. or d. begin. in Dec. 1641, more than nine yrs. aft. its orig. He serv. 28 Sept. 1630 on the first inq. held by a coroner, and by their find. Walter Palmer was chged. with manslaughter, for death of Austen Bratcher, of wh. he was acq. He liv. most of his days in Boston, prob. to practise better his trade of cardmaker, and by twelve sev. deeds to or from him of ld. in B. I have tracked him down to Jan. 1667. It may be very difficult to determine, whether F. the glazier, had any ch. or how old he was, when he d. but his br. Joseph, the saddler, had admin. of his est. 12 Aug. 1690. His w. Eliz. (by wh. in B. he had John, b. 30 Aug. 1644; Joseph, 24 Aug. 1646; Mercy, wh. d. 4 Sept. 1652; Sarah, b. 6 May 1655; Benjamin 10 Apr. 1658; and Mary, 18 July 1663); join. Boston ch. 31 May 1646, and his d. Eliz. m. 1656, James Sanford. But ano. FRANCIS, prob. s. of this Roxbury man, may have been f. of the two last ment. ch. as I presume; and had earlier, in R. Sarah, b. 6 May 1655; tho. it is not impossib. that one was f. of all. FRANCIS, Hingham, drew his house lot, 18 Sept. 1635, freem. 13 May 1640, rem. says Lincoln, to Taunton, where his w. d. 6 Jan. 1666. There he, or one of this name was liv. 1679. Inscript. at T. on gr. st. are seen of Eliz. "aged 40, d. 31 Jan. 1687;" and of Damaris "aged 21, d. 29 Oct. 1689." FRANCIS, Reading, perhaps s. of the first Francis of the same, freem. 1691, and not prob. that deac. wh. d. says Eaton, 1744. GEORGE, Salem 1635, had then gr. of ld. of wh. or other he contin. propr. perhaps was of Ipswich 1648, and soon back to S. bef. 1663. GEORGE, New Haven 1639–47, was not on the list of freem. there 22 yrs. aft. At N. H. by w. Sarah he had Sarah, and Martha, perhaps tw. b. 1642; Hannah, 1644; but all three, in the right of their mo. bapt. 14 Dec. 1645; Mercy, 22 Feb. 1646; John, 18 Apr. 1647; Eliz. 16 Sept. 1649; Samuel, b. 4 Dec. 1651; Ebenezer, 15 Nov. 1653; Joseph, 14 Aug. 1655; and Nathan, 27 Dec. 1656. He d. 17 May 1662, and descend. have been num. and hon. Sarah m. 1661, John Clark; Hannah m. 1663, Stephen Bradley of Guilford; Mercy m. 1669, John Benham; and Eliz. m. 13 Nov. 1669, John Hall of Guilford. Yet some uncert. attends the filiation of sev. of these ch. bec. ano. Sarah, w. of Nehemiah, was engag. in the same pious work of bring. ch. to bapt. in the same yr. nearly. GEORGE, Dover 1645, came, perhaps, from the city of Salisbury, a tailor, in the James, from Southampton, Apr. arr. June 1635, unless this array of circumstance pertain rather to the Salem man, for a fam. tradit. says, this man came from Plymouth, in Devon, to "Boston, when there were only a few huts, and not one cellar dug;" was town clk. in 1646 had commiss. from Mass. and at the head of the tax list 1648; had Joseph, b. 1640; and, as Mr.

Quint thinks, John, and James. His wid. he says, m. Monday, perhaps Henry of Salisbury, and next Mason. GILES, Hartford 1639, had Joanna, bapt. there 25 Mar. 1649; was of the earliest sett. at New London, but his gr. of 1648 was soon sold or forfeit. by non. resid. and he was of Fairfield 1651, there d. 1669. He left sec. w. Eunice, not mo. of his ch. wh. had been wid. of Jonathan Porter of Huntington, L. I.; three s. Samuel, Eleazer, and John; three ds. Elian, if that be a possib. name; Eliz. Jackson; and Joanna Gray, nam. in his will of 10 Sept. 1669. * HENRY, Dorchester, came in the fleet with Winth. perhaps req. adm. as freem. 19 Oct. 1630, and was rec. 18 May foll. may be thot. the gent. wh. with Ludlow, Pynchon, and others, was commis. in Mar. 1636 by Mass. to govern the first sett. on Conn. and act. at Hartford 1638. See Mass. Col. Rec. I. 170, with Conn. Col. Rec. I. 17; but whether he was or not, the Rev. HENRY, first min. of Wethersfield, I cannot confidently decide. On the whole, I conclude, since Mather puts the Wethersfield min. into his first classis (as of those, in the actual exercise of their min. bef. they left Eng.), that this man was only in civ. life, for he is not dignif. with the prefix Mr. and would never seem to be looked on as cleric. in Mass., and prob. the min. of Wethersfield came not for five, or even six, yrs. more. See Winth's. letter of June 1636 to his s. John, Gov. of the new planta. in Hist. I. Appx. A. 60 of the Ed. 1853. He, in 1636, rem. to Springfield with Pynchon; was s. by a former h. of that wid. Sanford wh. had m. Pynchon, and this s. had m. his P's. d. Ann, I suppose bef. the m. of his mo. with the f. of his w. possib. bef. they, any of them, came from Eng. to confound the two, if there were not three (wh. seems improb.) Henry Smiths. I design always to put the names in the order of their com. to our country, so that Rev. Henry, tho. older, must follow the Springfield man. Felt has, in his Eccles. Hist. of N. E. 253, made the min. wh. was receiv. of the ch. of Charlestown in midsum. of 1637, one of the commission to govern the Conn. planta. in 1636, with Ludlow, Steele, Pynchon and others, when we may feel sure, that it was Pynchon's s. in law wh. had that honor; as also, that the Wethersfield min. was at the date of 1636 in his native land, had Ann, and Mary, wh. were b. bef. his rem. the latter, bur. at S. 15 Nov. 1641; Martha, b. 31 July 1641; Mary, again, 7, bapt. 12 Mar. 1643; Eliz. 22, bapt. 27 Oct. 1644; Margaret, 26 Apr. 1646, d. at two yrs.; Sarah, 6 Oct. 1647, d. soon; Margaret, again, 1 Nov. 1648; Rebecca, 1 Apr. 1650; Samuel, 23 June 1651, d. next yr.; and Abigail, 10 Feb. 1653; was rep. 1651, and, with his min. Rev. George Moxon, prob. in disgust at the proceed. against his f.-in-law, went home 1653. Prob. most of the ch. went with the f. but Mary perhaps contin. here with her uncle Pynchon, and m. 15 Apr. 1665, Richard Lord of Hartford;

and Ann, wh. we may be sure, was the first b. m. 9 Nov. 1651, John Allyn of Hartford, the famous Secr. Other ch. he may have had, either
bef. or aft. leav. S. but where Farmer found his Elisha, is hard to guess.
He seems to be as well entit. as the Watertown Henry, to be thot. the
freem. of 18 May 1631, prob. better. Since reach. the conclus. that my
Dorchester Henry is the same as he, wh. Farmer in MS. had thot. of
Watertown, and by his two lines drove me to many wks. research, I
have the gratification of ascertain. from Dr. Bond's untir. investigat.
that at Watertown was no Henry Smith at all. *HENRY*, Charlestown, join.
the ch. with w. Dorothy, 10 July 1637, prob. rem. soon. He may have been
passeng. in the Elizabeth, 1635, without wishing his name to appear at
the custom ho. as no min. could be suf. to emb. at least we kn. that ship
brot. Dorothy, aged 45; d. Mary 15, and John, 12; most likely he was
the Wethersfield min. Very critical caution, however, is requisite, about
the concomitants of the rev. gent. whose will, of 8 May 1648, refers,
without nam. them, to two ds. m. Of course they were b. in Eng. It
also names s. Peregrine, wh. may not have been b. on this side of the
water, certain. was older than Samuel, but whether s. of the w. Dorothy,
or not, is uncert. Of that Dorothy, the w. we may be very sure, that
she was his sec. w. not mo. of Mary, or John, fellow passeng. with her.
For the elder ds. we are not sure of the h.'s, unless of Rebecca we judge
her w. of Samuel Smith of New London. See Caulkin's Hist. of N. L.
151. She was divorc. for his desertion, and m. 1669, Nathaniel Bowman. At least the age of this w. at Charlestown, if she be the passeng.
in the Elizabeth, is very much overrat. perhaps fifteen yrs. if not more;
for bef. his rem. to W. he had Dorothy, b. 1636, or 7; and at W. had
Samuel, 27 Jan. 1639; Joanna, 25 Dec. 1641; Noah, 25 Feb. 1644, d.
young; and Eliz. perhaps posthum. 25 Aug. 1648. The min. of W.
had a long controv. with a part of his people, whereby the peace of that
whole commonwealth was disturb. See Trumbull, Col. Rec. I. 97 and
98. It seems only to have terminat. by his d. 1648. In his will, Ib. 502,
he speaks of his large fam. ment. only s. Samuel, Perigrine, wh. was d.
Noah and two ds. m. with every one of their childr. as a part. His wid.
m. John Russell in 1649, and ten yrs. aft. rem. to Hadley; there made her
will, 1682, but it was not pro. bef. 22 Dec. 1694, so that we may presume her life was long protract. It disposes a decent est. to her s. Samuel, and d. Dorothy Hall, wh. had first been w. of John Blakeman, next
of Francis Hall; and late in life was so happy as to have ano. h. Mark
Sension, and fourth partner Isaac Moore. Joanna m. Philip Russell, 4
Feb. 1664, but with inf. Joanna d. 29 Dec. foll. Both of the m. ds. of
Rev. Henry were, no doubt, d. long bef. the will of his sec. w. It is
very easy to fall into confus. betw. contempo. persons of the same Chris-

tian and surnames. Aft. many hours, and days, study, I had the satisfact. of learn. that my conclus. as to the first Wethersfield min. concur.
with those of the scrupulous Mr. Goodwin of Hartford bef. his d. in
June 1855, so far as his had been writ. out. They were aft. publ.
1856, and have excel. illustrat. pp. 100 and 1. * HENRY, Hingham,
was from Co. Norfk. came in the Diligent 1638, with w. three s. two ds.
three men and two maid serv. freem. 13 Mar. 1639, rep. 1641, rem. to
Rehoboth 1643, there d. 1649. Of his will, 3 Nov. 1647 (in wh. his w.
is made Extrix. and ch. Henry, Daniel, and Judith, with br. Thomas
Cooper are nam.) abstr. is giv. in Geneal. Reg. IV. 319 ; and the will of
Judith, his wid. 24 Oct. 1650, abstr. on the next page, enlarges our acquaint. with the fam. by refer. to others ; but she may have been a sec.
w. HENRY, Dedham, came, I presume, from New Buckenham in Co.
Norfk. 1637, aged 30, call. a husbandman, with w. Eliz. 34, and two ch.
John, and Seth, arr. from Great Yarmouth at Boston, 20 June ; and by
w. Eliz. had Daniel, b. 13 Oct. 1639, d. young; Samuel, 13 Oct. 1641 ;
and Joseph, b. and bapt. 20 Aug. 1643; was freem. 13 May 1640; and
liv. in what bec. Medfield. A Mary, wh. d. at D. 2 Dec. 1641, may
have been his ch. but more likely his sis. one Mary hav. come in the
Planter, aged 18 ; ano. in the Susan and Ellen, 21 ; and a third in the
Elizabeth, 15, all in 1635, and all from London ; but this last is in the
London custom ho. call. d. of Dorothy, aged 45. HENRY, Boston 1652,
nam. in the will of Rev. John Cotton, wh. calls him cous. mean. neph.
HENRY, Rowley 1656. * HENRY, Rehoboth, s. of Henry of the same,
was ens. rep. 1662, and sev. yrs. aft. had Henry, b. 4 Dec. 1673 ; Eliz.
bur. 1 Mar. 1676 ; Abiel, 24 Dec. 1676 ; and the f. was bur. that day, if
Col. Rec. be correct. HENRY, Stamford, propound. for freem. 1670,
had been one of the first sett. at that planta. 1641, and went from Wethersfield, d. 1687, in his will names only s. John ; but he had d. Rebecca,
wh. m. 2 July 1672, Edward Wilkinson of Milford, and Hannah, wh.
m. a Lawrence ; and perhaps others. HENRY, Cambridge, m. 3 Mar.
1673, Lydia Buck, perhaps d. of Roger, had Lydia, b. 20 July 1677 ;
Henry, 17 Oct. 1679 ; and Ebenezer, 19 Mar. 1689 ; perhaps more ;
was freem. 1690, d. 21 Aug. 1720, says the gr. st. aged a. 75 yrs. HEZ-
EKIAH, Dartmouth 1686. HUGH, Rowley, freem. 18 May 1642 ; by w.
Mary had Edward, b. 1654, and prob. earlier, John, Samuel, and four
ds. and he d. 1656. His wid. m. 2 Dec. 1657, Jeremiah Ellsworth.
ICHABOD, Hadley, youngest s. of Philip the first, m. 19 July 1698, Eliz.
d. of Capt. Aaron Cook, had Philip, b. 2 May 1699 ; Aaron, 20 Sept.
1700 ; Nathaniel, 16 Feb. 1702 ; Rebecca, 9 Nov. 1703 ; Moses, 30
Apr. 1706 ; Bridget, 15 Mar. 1708 ; Miriam, 22 Aug. 1710 ; Eliz. 10
Sept. 1712 ; Samuel, 4 Aug. 1715 ; Experience, 27 Jan. 1717 ; and Eli-

sha, 23 Jan. 1721; was deac. and d. 6 Sept. 1746; and his wid. d. 10
Oct. 1751. ISRAEL, Boston 1672, a carpenter. JAMES, Salem 1653,
liv. in the part that bec. Marblehead in 1648, one wh. attend. the min.
serv. of Rev. William Walton, and prob. had gr. of ld. at Gloucester
1642; had w. Mary, and d. Catharine, wh. m. Samuel Eburne, and s.
James, liv. at Bristol, O. E. to wh. by deed, 13 June 1656, as his only
s. he gave his Salem est. prob. d. a. 1661. His will, of 9 Nov. 1660,
was pro. 27 June foll. and his est. was good. JAMES, Boston, a shipmaster, was admin. of our ch. 13 Oct. 1644, was next yr. engag. in the
infam. steal. of blacks on the coast of Guinea, and bring. them here, two
being brot. and a hundred k. He had his w. with him on his voyage at
Barbados. See Winth. II. 243, with the addr. of Richard Saltonstall,
Ib. Appx. M. and large proceed. in Col. rec. For other foul play with
the w. of Isaac Gross here he was excom. 4 July 1647. JAMES, Rehoboth, d. 1653, and admin. of his est. was giv. to Amos Richardson of
Boston, perhaps as a creditor. JAMES, Weymouth, had Nathaniel, b. 8
June 1639, may have been freem. 1654. JAMES, Salem, or Marblehead, prob. s. of James of the same, had James, and others; in 1659
was persecut. as a quaker, but liv. at M. 1674. JAMES, Newtown, L. I. 1642–86. JAMES, Weymouth, perhaps the freem. of 1681,
by w. Mary had Mary, b. 22 Mar. 1663; Eliz. 14 Sept. 1667; Hannah, 1 Mar. 1670; perhaps Sarah, 25 May 1672, for wh. see Geneal.
Reg. III. 270; and Sarah, again, 1684. JAMES, Newbury, s. of Thomas,
m. 26 July 1667, Sarah, d. of Robert Coker, had Sarah, b. 12 Sept. 1668;
James, 16 Oct. 1670; Thomas, 9 Mar. 1673; Hannah, 23 Mar. 1675;
Joseph, 8 June 1677, d. in few wks.; John, 1 Nov. 1678; Samuel, 31
Jan. 1680; Benjamin, 21 Aug. 1681; and Mary, 27 Feb. 1684, d.
young; was freem. 1671, a lieut. in the crusade of Phips against Que-
bec, on ret. from wh. in Oct. 1690 he perish. by shipwreck on Anticosti.
JAMES, Danvers, a man of some distinct. 1692, had Tabitha, wh. d. 11
Mar. 1689, aged 3 yrs. JAMES, Dover 1669, was perhaps s. of George
of the same, m. Sarah, d. of John Davis, had John; James; Samuel;
May or Mary, wh. m. a Dean; Sarah, wh. m. a Freeman; and two, wh.
d. young. He was an innholder, and d. from over-exert. in going to join
Capt. Floyd, 1690, against the Ind. wh. not long after k. his wid. and s.
Samuel. JAMES, Charlestown, s. of the first Thomas of the same, was a
householder 1678, by w. Mary had Mary, bapt. 12 Oct. 1684. JAMES,
Watertown, eldest s. of the first Thomas of the same, m. 1680, Hannah,
d. of John Goodenow, and by Dr. Bond is suppos. to have d. at Lancaster, leav. wid. Hannah, to wh. with ch. James, Samuel, Hannah,
John, Sarah, Joseph, Benjamin, and Daniel, his est. was distrib. 8 Apr.
1701. One JAMES, possib. the preced. was of Moseley's comp. Dec.

1675. JAMES, New London, s. prob. eldest ch. of Richard of the same, m. Eliz. d. of Jonathan Rogers, had childr. of wh. descend. to this day reside there.· JEREMIAH, Eastham, m. 3 Jan. 1678, Hannah Astwood, perhaps d. of Stephen, had Mercy, b. 17 Feb. 1679; Abigail, 1 June 1681; Jeremiah, 18 Aug. 1685; and Hannah, Sept. 1691. He d. 29 Apr. 1706, and his wid. d. 29 Mar. 1729. JOBANNA, Farmington, a young soldier, s. of William of the same, in Capt. Newberry's comp. in Philip's war, k. by the Ind. at Hatfield 30 May 1676. JOHN, Dorchester 1630, came in the Mary and John, a man of distinct. no doubt from Co. Devon, brot. fam. prob. s. John, perhaps Lawrence, possib. d. Mary, wh. m. first Nathaniel Glover, and next Gov. Thomas Hinckley, as most of the people of D. said, tho. it is evid. eno. to me, that this high matched Mary was d. of a later John; is com. call. the quarter-master, bec. he had serv. in the Netherlands in that rank, was, perhaps, the freem. of 4 Mar. 1633, or of 7 Dec. 1636. Mr. Clap thinks he was past mid. age, when he came, and my inq. are unsatisf. a. him. JOHN, Maine 1640, one of the gr. jury at the *first* Gen. Court of Sir Ferdinando Gorges, in that yr. "sw. to inq. for our Sovereign Lord the K. and the Lord of this Province." Perhaps he was of Kittery, aft. as we kn. he was, in 1635, of Saco. § ‡ JOHN, Providence, one of the hundred first purch. may have been of Salem 1631 or 2, one of the friends of Roger Williams, wh. calls him a merch. perhaps, but not very likely the freem. of 4 Mar. 1633, and banish. at the Court Sept. 1635, for "divers dangerous opin. wh. he holdeth and hath divulg." His name is always Smyth, and he bec. one of the heads of the Col. of R. I. aft. rem. to Warwick, the presid. of R. I. chos. to succeed Williams in 1649. In the new chart. of the k. July 1663, he is nam. of the counc. but d. bef. its arr. leav. wid. Ann, wh. had been w. of . . . . . . Collins, and had s. Elizur C. b. a. 1622, and the est. of S. went to them. See 3 Mass. Hist. Coll. IX. 286. But betw. other Johns of the neighb. my power of discrimin. fails. In Providence alone were four Johns among the first hundred purch. One *JOHN*, if not two, was of Newport, in 1640. JOHN, Watertown 1631, perhaps the freem. of 25 May 1636 (whose w. Isabel d. or was bur. 12 July 1639, aged 60, as Dr. Bond says), may have been f. of John, Thomas, and Francis, sometimes nam. of W. perhaps of others, but all b. in Eng. and, as Bond thinks, rem. to Lancaster, and d. there, yet I think it more prob. that it was a younger man. JOHN, Taunton, one of the first purch. 1637. JOHN, Plymouth 1643, then call. senr. was one of the first sett. at Eastham; but we ask in vain as to his fam. or time of d. and are left to infer that, tho. he was sen. in the list of those able to bear arms, John jun. was not his s. as he did not accomp. the sen. to Eastham, and it may equally be doubt. whether he was f. of either the sec. or third John of Eastham, or of Samuel of the same. JOHN, Weymouth, may have been the freem. of 17 Apr. 1637, caus. gr. trouble a. ch. matters, at the captious time of antinom. schism, favor Rev. Robert Lenthall 1638, for wh. he was fin. £20. and imprison. and as L. soon withdrew to Newport, I suppose S. follow. him. JOHN, Taunton, wh. had John, Eliz. and Samuel, bef. 1643, rem. to Newtown, L. I. and his ch. dispers. to Hempstead and Jamaica on that isl. See Riker's Hist. 20. JOHN, Boston, a tailor, adm. of the ch. 6 Feb. 1639, and his w. Mercy or Mary, 14 Apr. 1644, was freem. 22 May 1639. His w. d. 11 Jan. 1659; and he d. 1674, in his will, of 23 Sept. 1673, pro. 13 June foll. aft. giv. ld. to Robert and Nathaniel Woodward, his gr. ch. (on wh. they had already built new houses), to be enjoy. in fee, he devis. to his d. Rachel, their mo. now w. of Thomas Harwood, all other est. and made her Extrix. She had been wid. of Robert W. JOHN, Medford 1638. JOHN, Newport 1639, may have cont. there and be found on their list of freem. 1655; but may be the one at Providence, disting. as the miller, wh. had Joseph, and engag. his alleg. June 1668 and did not rem. during the perils of 1676, in Philip's war. * JOHN, Barnstable 1640, join. the ch. 13 Oct. 1644, and his w. Susanna d. of the first Samuel Hinckley, join. 13 June 1652; but whether she was mo. of all the ch. is not cert. but he had Samuel, b. Apr. bapt. 20 Oct. 1644; Sarah, bapt. 11 May 1645; Ebenezer, 22 Nov. 1646, d. next mo.; Mary, 21 Nov. 1647; Dorcas, 18 Aug. 1650; John, 22 Feb. 1652; bur. in two days; Shubael, 13 Mar. 1653; John, again, b. Sept. 1656; Benjamin, Jan. 1659; Ichabod, Jan. 1661; Eliz. Feb. 1663; Thomas, Feb. 1665; and Joseph, 6 Dec. 1667; was rep. 1656 and 7. In 1659 being allow. by the Ct. to hear what the Quakers could say in their defence, was wise eno. with Isaac Robinson, s. of blessed John of Leyden, to advise repeal of the laws against them. * JOHN, Lynn, rem. early to Reading, may be he wh. m. at Roxbury, 1 Aug. 1647, Catharine, d. of Isaac Morrill of R. had Sarah, b. 14 Apr. 1654, d. next mo. ; Isaac, 20 June 1655; Benjamin, 8 Aug. 1657, d. in 3 days; Francis, 23 Dec. 1658; and Abraham, 10 Apr. 1661; beside John and Mary, elder than any, as from abstr. of Morrill's will, Geneal. Reg. XI. 35, is plain. His w. Catharine d. 12 Sept. 1662; and he was rep. in 1669. JOHN and John jr. of Stamford among the first sett. 1641, both rem. to Hempstead, L. I. The younger, in 1675, gave a depon. call. hims. 60 yrs. old, in wh. he says that formerly at S. they call. him Rock John S. for distinct. JOHN, Sudbury, a. 1647 had w. Sarah. JOHN, Guilford 1643, a blacksmith, said to have come from Boston, and ano. John was there at the same time. JOHN, Charlestown, by Farmer call. ship carpenter ; had Zechariah, b. by w. Sarah, 29 Mar. 1656, and prob. sev. bef. as Benoni,

his s. d. 15 June 1646; and she was adm. of the ch. 23 Sept. 1652, and
he and they may have been bapt. as the rec. for many yrs. bef. 1659 is
wholly defic. and 5 Feb. 1660 appears Rebecca, d. of sis. S. His will
of 8 Mar. 1672, of wh. w. Sarah, s. John, and ano. were Excors. names
her, and ch. John, James, Josiah, Eliz.; Sarah, and Mary, and he d. 6
Mar. foll. JOHN, Providence, call. the mason for distinct. m. bef. 1661,
a d. of Samuel Comstock had Leonard, d. young; John, d. young; and
Joseph; rem. to Warwick, there d. without will, and the municipal governm. supplied the want, 14 Sept. 1668. He was useful as a surveyor.
JOHN, Watertown, may have been that youth, aged 13, wh. came from
London in the Planter, 1635, prob. s. of Alice, 40, in the same sh. In
his will of 12 Apr. 1665, pro. 27 Sept. 1669, names ch. John, Richard,
Alice, and Ann, w. of John Moore, wh. is made Ex'cor. and may have
been his fellow-passeng. JOHN, Dedham, by w. Margaret had John, b.
5 July 1644, and the next entry is, John, d. 14 Aug. 1645, says the rec.
but he may have been the ch. and the f. liv. 1660. JOHN, Milford
1640; and ano. JOHN was there 1646, both sen. and jun. freem. in
1669; but tho. not f. and s. are easily disting. The elder, wh. d. 1684,
by w. Grace, wh. join. the ch. 1642, had there bapt. Ephraim, 13 Oct.
1644; John, b. 27 Aug. 1646; Mary, 1648; Ebenezer, 10 Nov. 1651,
d. young; Mercy, bapt. 5 Dec. 1652, d. at 18 yrs.; and Mehitable, 25
Mar. 1655. Only four of these liv. to maturity, viz. Ephraim; John;
Mary, wh. m. Abel Gunn of Derby; and Mehitable, wh. m. 1674, Edward Camp. His wid. d. 1690. Of the younger John, not s. of the
preced. we learn, that he was a blacksmith, m. 19 July 1665, Sarah, d.
of Lieut. William Fowler of the same, had Joseph; John, b. 1669, d.
young; Jonathan, 5 Sept. 1671; and John, again, 18 June 1674, wh. d.
young. For sec. w. he m. 1694, Clemence, wid. of Jonathan Hunt of Northampton, and d. 1704. JOHN, Hampton 1644, was, prob. the progenit. of
a line of Smiths in that town, and his d. Deborah was first w. of Nathaniel Bachiler. JOHN, wh. by Farmer is nam. of Boston, com. from Ireland, and adm. of the ch. 1640, must be look. at as a supernum. for the
ch. rec. in the yr. foll. giv. only this foundat. for such a statem. " 21 of
the 12th 1640 Mrs. Hannah S. the w. of one Mr. John Smyth in Ireland" and it may seem as prob. (no more being heard of her) that she
went to him, as that he came to her. The gr. rebellion in I. broke out
the same yr. JOHN, Dorchester, came in 1635 with w. and d. Mary (in
the James of Bristol), the ch. brot. from Warrington, Lancash. on a horse
in a pannier, balanc. by young Nathaniel, s. of Rev. Richard Mather,
then five yrs. old, as a decent tradit. relates; and in that voyage partook
the vexat. and dangers so well relat. by Mather, in Young's Chron.
Here he was prob. freem. 7 Dec. 1636, and had by w. Catharine other

ch. for wh. the will gives us some light, slightly confus. by the artic. in Geneal. Reg. V. 465, mak. the d. some mos. earlier than the will, and one ch. b. less than 3 mos. after a former. The heroine of the pannier m. Nathaniel Glover, and next, Gov. Hinckley, and d. 29 July 1703, in her 73d yr. Her f.'s will made 28 Dec. 1676, some mos. aft. the date ment. in Geneal. Reg. for his d. with a codic. was pro. 25 July 1678. JOHN, Watertown 1640, s. of Adrean, the w. of Jeremiah Norcross, had w. Mary. JOHN, Rowley, s. perhaps, of Hugh, m. Faith, d. prob. of Francis Parrott, had, says Gage, John, and Jonathan, tw. b. 1659. Perhaps both d. and he d. 1661, leav. d. Sarah. His wid. I think, m. Ezekiel Jewett. JOHN, Saco, freem. 1653, had been there from 1636, and we would gladly learn more of him. JOHN, Plymouth, usually call. jr. able to bear arms 1643, was not, perhaps, s. of the first John of the same, m. 4 Jan. 1649, Deborah, d. of Arthur Howland of Marshfield, had Hasadiah, b. 11 Jan. 1650; John, 1 Oct. 1651; Josiah, 16 Apr. 1652; Eleazer, 20 Apr. 1654; and Hezekiah, 8 Feb. 1656. JOHN, Eastham, call. sen. had w. Lydia, wh. d. 21 July 1672, and he m. 15 Nov. foll. Jael Packer, or Packard, of Bridgewater. ‡ * JOHN, Hingham, freem. 1647, as to me seems more prob. tho. Farmer decid. for 1654, m. May 1645, Sarah, d. of Ralph Woodward of the same, had, perhaps, sev. ch. besides John, b. 19 Sept. 1653, was lieut. 1661, rep. 1683 and aft. till chos. Assist. 1686, in wh. he contin. to serve until the new Chart. and d. May 1695. JOHN, Providence, call. for distinct. Jamaica John, perhaps bec. he came from there, was d. bef. 20 May 1685, when his s. John executes a deed, in wh. he styles hims. s. and heir. JOHN, Taunton, had Eliz. b. 7 Sept. 1663; Henry, 27 May 1666; perhaps others. JOHN, Salem 1659, was a tailor; and Felt names ano. John, Salem 1660, a malster, who had w. Ann. Ano. JOHN, of Salem, was a mason in 1671. One of these Salem Johns, at the ord. of Rev. John Higginson, in 1660, rais. a disturb. Perhaps his w. Margaret and her ch. were then in prison at Boston, as quakers. See Hutch. I. 203. JOHN, Dorchester, had James, and Mary, wh. were adult when they were bapt. in right of their mo. 10 June 1683, she then being w. of Ellis Wood as the ch. rec. tells. But very curious rec. of bapt. is found few mos. preced. as follows: "The childr. of Miriam, the w. of Ellis Smith, were bapt. 19 Nov. 1682, viz. Ann, Miriam, Sarah, and David." Who was f. of these ch. is on the face of the rec. doubtful. No such man as Ellis Smith can be heard of, and easy eno. might the scribe mistake this name for Wood, if we may assume that the w. of Wood was bring. up to the font offspring of her former h. John Smith, wh. d. 1682. JOHN, New London 1658, call. "nailor Smith" had come from Boston (where he liv. in 1653), with w. Joanna, and only ch. Eliz. made collector of the imposts, 1659, freem.

1666; was deac. and d. 4 Oct. 1670. His wid. d. 1687, aged a. 73; and Eliz. m. a Way of Lyme. Caulkins, 323. JOHN, Dedham 1661, may be the h. of a d. of Philip Eliot of Roxbury, nam. in his will. JOHN, Watertown, s. of the first Thomas of the same, m. 1 Apr. 1665, Mary, d. of Anthony Beers, had Mary, b. 15 June 1667; John, 8 Aug. 1668; Abigail, 29 June 1670; Hannah, 27 Dec. 1672; Sarah, 7 June 1675; and, perhaps, but not prob. Samuel, whose day of b. as giv. by Bond, 10 Mar. 1700, excites suspic. of error. JOHN, Eastham, m. 24 May 1667, Hannah Williams, had Eliz. b. 24 Feb. 1669; Sarah, 27 Mar. 1672; perhaps Mercy, 17 Sept. 1676; and Ebenezer, 16 Jan. 1680; yet some uncertainty arises as to the names and births of some. Ano. JOHN, Eastham, m. 30 Nov. 1668, Mary Eldridge, perhaps d. of Robert of the same, had John, b. 18 Oct. 1669; Jeremiah, 27 Dec. 1670; William, 2 Aug. 1672; a d. 10 Feb. 1675; Mary, 30 Nov. 1676, d. soon; Mary, again, 15 Jan. 1678; Beriah, 2 Mar. 1680; Bethia, 16 Jan. 1682; and Mehitable, 1 May 1691; but some confus. is appar. in the assignm. of the ch. to these two Johns in Geneal. Reg. VII. 279. JOHN, Boston, mason, in his will of 27 Oct. 1678, pro. 8 Nov. foll. aft. giv. £4. ea. to his f. and mo. and relinq. half of their debts to his serv. Mungo Craford, and John Wilson, names his two ch. Jeremiah, wh. should have $\frac{2}{3}$ of his est. and Joseph $\frac{1}{3}$, as ea. reach. 21 yrs. JOHN, Hampton, a tailor, and JOHN, Hampton, a cooper, ea. took o. of alleg. 1678, of wh. one may have been f. and one s. but it is not very prob. and I am ign. of the priority; only the cooper, it is said, by w. Huldah had Abigail, b. 24 Feb. 1688. One of them was s. of JOHN, late of the Vineyard, but I find in Geneal. Reg. VIII. 52, no mark of time, to inform what late refers to. JOHN, Providence, call. junr. in May 1671, when he engag. alleg. JOHN, Newbury, perhaps s. of Thomas of the same, freem. 1671, m. 26 Nov. 1667, Rebecca, d. of the first Samuel of the same, had John, b. 14 Sept. 1668, d. in a mo. Rebecca, 1 Aug. 1669; John, again, 20 Oct. 1671, d. young; Mary, 20 Dec. 1673; John, again, 17 Mar. 1678; Samuel, 31 Jan. 1680, d. young; Josiah, 28 Mar. 1687; Hannah, 27 Jan. 1690; and Dorothy, 20 Aug. 1692. JOHN, Hadley, s. of lieut. Samuel of the same, m. 12 Nov. 1663, Mary, d. of William Partridge, had John, b. 15 May 1665, perhaps freem. of 1690; Samuel, 7 Dec. 1667, wh. was k. by lightning in his 14th yr.; Joseph, 1670; Benjamin, 1673; and Mary, early in 1677, posthum. for her f. was k. by the Ind. 30 May 1676. See Capt. Newbury's despatches in Conn. Rec. II. 450. His s. Joseph was ancest. of the late Oliver S. wh. had gain. the largest est. of any person in all the neighb. of Hatfield, and by his will design. to favor that and the adjoin. towns. JOHN, Fairfield, s. of Giles of the same, of wh. no more is kn. but only that he d. 1690. JOHN, Boston, bricklayer, m. 1671, Sarah, the young wid. of John Wilmot. JOHN, Taunton, call. jun. may have had Deborah, b. 7 Mar. 1676; Hannah, 22 Mar. 1678; and John, 6 Dec. 1680. But, in so common a name, sen. and jun. are very inadeq. to express distinct. betw. two hav. the same bapt. name, when the order of time may be uncert. JOHN, Milford, s. of the first John of the same, m. a. 1669, Phebe Campfield, perhaps d. of Matthew, or Thomas. JOHN, Charlestown 1674, a mason, householder in 1678, was perhaps he, wh. m. at Woburn, 7 May 1674, Abigail, d. of Rev. Thomas Carter; but no ch. appear in bapt. at C. and perhaps they were carr. to W. for bapt. by the gr.f. JOHN, York, call. jr. when he sw. alleg. 1681, wh. may lead us to presume that an elder John liv. there, tho. he may have been s. of the John of Saco, óne of the chief men. JOHN, Dover 1675, perhaps s. of George of the same, rem. to Little Compton, there m. says tradit. and had two ds. JOHN, Newport, by w. Susanna had Rebecca, b. 14 Oct. 1678. JOHN, Hingham, prob. s. of John of the same, freem. 1679, then call. jun. JOHN, Dartmouth 1686. JOHN, Hadley, sec. s. of Philip the first of the same, m. 29 Nov. 1683, Joanna, d. of Joseph Kellogg, had John, b. 3 Dec. 1684; Joanna, 7 Sept. 1686; Rebecca, 5 Aug. 1688; Joseph, 19 July 1690; Martin, 15 Apr. 1692; Eleazer, 25 Sept. 1694; Sarah, 18 Nov. 1696, d. next yr.; Sarah, again, 9 Nov. 1698; Prudence, 15 Mar. 1701; Experience, 19 Apr. 1703; Eliz. 12 Oct. 1705; and Mindwell, 25 May 1708; and he d. 16 Apr. 1727. JOHN, York, call. junr. on sw. alleg. 1680, to the k. JOHN, Cambridge vil. or Newton, a tanner, by w. Sarah, prob. d. of Henry Prentice of the same, m. 8 June 1676, had Sarah, b. 31 Mar. foll. d. next mo.; John, 2 Mar. 1678; Sarah, again, 17 Aug. 1681; Thankful; Rachel, 19 Dec. 1685; and Joseph, 9 Aug. 1687; and by sec. w. Susanna had Jerusha, b. 8 May 1695; Margaret, 29 July 1698; Daniel, 16 Aug. 1700; Esther, 20 July 1703; Ephraim, 5 Oct. 1704; Josiah, 27 May 1707; and Silas, wh. was drown. 1729. See Jackson's Newton. JOHN, New Haven, s. of George, was a propr. 1685. JOHN, Charlestown, s. of Thomas, the butcher, was a mariner, d. at Jamaica, 22 July 1688. One JOHN, at Dartmouth, took o. of fidel. in 1684. JOHN, Gloucester, by w. Abigail had Miriam, b. 20 Aug. 1689, and prob. more ch. by ano. w. See Babson, 159. JOHN, Salem, m. 29 July 1689, Patience, youngest d. of Samuel Shattuck of the same. JOHN, Eastham, youngest s. of Samuel first of the same, m. 14 May 1694, Bethia, d. of Stephen Snow, had James, b. 13 Feb. 1695, d. next yr.; and Samuel, 25 May 1696. Ano. JOHN, of Eastham, I think was s. of John the third of the same, and by w. Sarah he had Hannah, b. 18 Mar. 1696; Joseph, 28 Dec. 1697; Sarah, 6 Nov. 1699; William, 6 Sept. 1702; Lydia, 24 Apr. 1704;

Seth, 28 Jan. 1706; Eliz. Mar. 1708; Rebecca, Mar. 1710; and John, 13 Mar. 1713. After assid. attent. I am unable to give distinct. to any more Johns, tho. beyond doubt there were sev. wh. would be embrac. by my plan; yet the ingenuity of any single antiquary would be oft. at fault, even if his patience were not exhaust. in pursuit of the local habitat. of all. In Boston alone were four tax payers of the name in 1695. JON-ATHAN, Wethersfield, s. of Richard the first of the same, made freem. 1657, m. 1 Jan. 1664, Martha, d. of Francis Bushnell, prob. had sev. ch. bef. rem. to Middletown, where he had Gershom, b. Nov. 1679; and Deborah, 23 Sept. 1682; went back to W. where, tho. he sold part of his est. he held other lds. on the E. side of the gr. riv. and join. with his neighb. in obtain. incorpo. of Glastenbury, liv. 1698. JONATHAN, Exe-ter, took the o. of alleg. 30 Nov. 1677. JONATHAN, Farmington 1678, eldest s. of William of Wethersfield, m. Mary, d. of Joseph Bird, had Eliz. Samuel, Jonathan, Mary, Mehitable, wh. was bapt. 11 Oct. 1691; Sarah, 24 Dec. 1693; Abigail, 29 Dec. 1695; William, perhaps 30 June 1700; and Eleazer, perhaps 20 Sept. 1702. But whether all were by first w. is unkn. as are dates of b. of four earliest ch. He had sec. w. Rachel, d. of Samuel Steele; and third w. Sarah, he took in 1714, and d. 5 Apr. 1721; and his wid. m. Thomas Bird. JONATHAN, Water-town, youngest s. of Thomas, first of the same, m. 16 Mar. 1683, Jane Peabody, had Jonathan, b. 4 May 1684; Zechariah, 16 May 1687; Eliz. bapt. 7 Apr. 1689, d. soon; Eliz. again, 19 May 1691; Elisha, b. 11 Jan. 1692; Jonas, 7 Jan. 1693; Dinah, 25 Jan. 1695; Abigail, 7 July 1697; and Nathaniel, 15 Nov. 1701; was freem. 1690, and d. prob. 1724. JONATHAN, Hatfield, s. of Philip the first, m. 14 Nov. 1688, Abigail, d. of Joseph Kellogg, had Jonathan, b. 10 Aug. 1689; Daniel, 3 Mar. 1692; Abigail, 20 Apr. 1695; Stephen, 5 Dec. 1697; Prudence, 16 May 1700; Moses, 8 Sept. 1702; Elisha, 10 July 1705; Eliz. 8 May 1708; Ephraim, 24 Mar. 1711; and Aaron, 7 Feb. 1715; and d. a. 1737. Ano. JONATHAN at Wethersfield 1690, was s. of Joseph of the same. JOSEPH, Wethersfield, freem. 1657, had been of Middletown, but m. Lydia, d. of Thomas Wright, of W. and had Lydia, b. 1654; Joseph, Mar. 1660; Jonathan; and Samuel, Aug. 1663; and d. 1673 or 4 leav. wid. wh. m. William Harris of M. JOSEPH, Hartford, br. of Christopher of Northampton, m. 10 or 20 Apr. 1656, Lydia, d. of Rev. Ephraim Huitt, had Joseph, b. Mar. 1657; Samuel, May 1658, d. young; Ephraim, 8 Sept. 1659; Lydia, Apr. 1661, d. young; Simon, 2 Aug. 1662; Nathaniel, Oct. 1664; Lydia, again, 14 Feb. 1666; Susanna, June 1667; Mary, Nov. 1668; Martha, Mar. 1670; Benjamin, 21 July 1671; Eliz. Nov. 1672; Sarah, Apr. 1674; Edward, 19 June 1677; and Mercy, 16 Nov. 1679; but the last two prob. d. bef. 1715, when their f.'s heirs unit. in a lawsuit, and eleven of the fifteen ch. were then alive. Benjamin then was in London. He was freem. 1667, and made his will 13 June 1689, and d. Jan. foll. His wid. liv. 21 yrs. aft. Of the ds. we kn. that Mary was unm. in 1715; that Lydia m. Lanerick Flowers; Susanna m. John Dickinson; Martha m. Barnabas Hinsdale, s. of Barnabas; Eliz. m. 8 May 1695, Joseph Gilbert; and Sarah m. 4 Oct. 1693, John Spencer. JOSEPH, Dover, s. of George of the same, by w. Eliz. had John, b. 9 Jan. 1669 or 70; Mary; Eliz.; and Samuel, wh. was b. in June 1687; was a leader among the quakers. His w. d. 25 May 1726; and he d. 15 Dec. 1727. JOSEPH, Norwalk 1675, from Long Isl. purchas. ld. that yr. but is not found there in 1688. JOSEPH, Providence, s. of Benjamin of the same, m. Lydia, d. of the first William Carpenter of the same, sw. alleg. May 1682. JOSEPH, Watertown, s. of Thomas first of the same, m. 1 Dec. 1674, Hannah Tidd, had Joseph, b. 19 Apr. 1677; John, 5 Apr. 1678; Daniel, 26 Sept. 1681; Hannah, and Rebecca, perhaps not tw. yet both bapt. 4 Dec. 1687. ‡ * JOSEPH, Hampton, took the o. of alleg. in Apr. and, perhaps, again in Dec. 1678, had m. Dorothy, d. of Rev. Seaborn Cotton, wh. d. 20 Dec. 1706, was in 1683 petitnr. to the K. against his Gov. Cranfield, rep. 1688, maj. or col. in the milit. and of the Counc. 1698, d. 9 or 24 Nov. 1717, aged 64. JOSEPH, New Haven, s. of George of the same, m. 1680, Lydia, d. of Henry Bristol, had Joseph, b. 1681; Lydia, 1683; Hannah, 1686; Esther, 1689; Daniel, 1693; and d. 1697, leav. w. and her five ch. JOSEPH, Farmington, s. of William, by first w. Lydia had Joseph, b. a. 1681; Lydia; both bapt. prob. 17 Aug. 1684, tho. the rec. as giv. in Geneal. Reg. XII. 147, says 18, wh. was Monday; Jobanna, 12 Apr. 1685; Mary, 30 Jan. 1687; Eliz. 16 Feb. 1690; Joanna, b. 15, bapt. 16 Oct. 1692; Ruth, bapt. 1 Dec. 1694; Susanna, b. 20 Apr. 1698; Thankful, 4 Nov. 1700; Mercy, 6 Aug. 1702; Esther, 30 Oct. 1705; Experience, bapt. prob. 11 July 1708; and Zephaniah, b. 16 Feb. 1710, d. young; but prob. the last two were b. by a sec. w. Joanna Loomis. JOSEPH, Hartford, eldest s. of Joseph of the same, rem. a. 1680, to Hadley, freem. 1690, m. 11 Feb. 1681, Rebecca, d. of John Dickinson, first of the same, had Joseph, b. 3 Nov. 1682; John, 24 Oct. 1684, d. young; John, again, 5 June 1686, d. soon; Rebecca, 11 June 1689; Jonathan, 28 Oct. 1691; Lydia, 15 Sept. 1693; Benjamin, 22 Jan. 1696; and Eliz. 22 Dec. 1701; and his w. d. 16 Feb. 1731; and he d. 1733. JOSEPH, New Haven, a propr. 1685. JOSEPH, Dartmouth 1686. JOSEPH, Wethersfield, s. of Joseph of the same, d. 1687, leav. only Joseph, 9 mos. old. JOSEPH, Haddam, perhaps s. of Simon of the same, a merch. d. at Barbados, 1694, gave his prop. to mo. brs. and sis. yet nam. only br. John. JOSEPH, Barnstable, m. 29 Apr. 1689, Ann Ful-

11 *

ler, perhaps d. of Mathew, had Susanna, b. 12 Jan. 1690; Joseph, 28
Oct. 1691; James, 18 Dec. 1693; Ann, 8 Nov. 1695; Matthew, 10
July 1697; Ebenezer, 21 Mar. 1699, d. at 2 mos.; Daniel, 11 Apr.
1700; David, 24 May 1702; Eliz. 19 Apr. 1704; Thomas, 6 Feb.
1706; Mary, 22 Dec. 1707, d. near 21 yrs.; Jemima, 9 Nov. 1709;
Benjamin, 5 Dec. 1711; Ebenezer, again, 26 Sept. 1714; and his w. d.
2 July 1722. JOSEPH, Middletown, had taught a sch. at Hadley, and
Springfield, m. 15 Sept. 1698, Esther, d. of Joseph Parsons, had Martha, b. 17 Sept. 1699; Joseph, 1704; and Mary, 1709. He went in
1708 to N. J. and was ord. as a Presbyt. min. but left in a. 2 yrs. preach.
short time at Brookfield, and was instal. over the new, sec. ch. at M. 15
Jan. 1715, d. 8 Sept. 1736, and his wid. d. 30 May 1760. JOSHUA,
Weymouth, by w. Ruth had James, b. 14 Dec. 1668. JOSIAH, Taunton,
m. 25 May 1687, Mary Pratt of Dartmouth. || LAWRENCE, Dorchester,
wh. Mr. Clapp thot. s. of John, the quarter-master, by w. Mary had
Mary, b. 28 Feb. 1643; ar. co. 1642, freem. 10 May 1643, oft. a select-
man, d. 3 Oct. 1665. In his will ment. is found of w. and ch. but names
of none are seen, exc. w. Mary. His w. Mary was Extrix. LEONARD,
Providence, of wh. I see nothing, but that he was among those wh. in
June 1668, engag. alleg. LESTER, Boston, came in the Speedwell from
London, arr. 27 July 1656, aged 24; but no more is kn. of him. MAR-
MADUKE, Rye, then claim. as belong. to Conn. was in 1669 a sort of
preacher to the people there, but not to the satisfact. of the governm.
See Trumbull, Col. Rec. II. 120. MARTIN, Northampton, took the o. of
alleg. 8 Feb. 1679. He may be the man k. 29 Feb. 1704 at Deerfield,
by the Fr. and Ind. MATTHEW, Charlestown, a cordwinder, came, 1637,
from Sandwich, Co. Kent, with w. Jane and four ch. and was that yr.
adm. inhab. of C. tho. Felt shows, that Salem made him gr. of ld. perhaps conditional. His w. was rec. by the ch. 22 Dec. 1639; but no
bapt. is ment. on the rec. nor can the names of those brot. from Eng. be
ascertain. He was a householder in 1658, and perhaps in 1678, under
the title of goodman. MATTHEW, Watertown, wh. sw. fidel. in 1652,
may be the man claim. by Eaton among early sett. of Reading, but the
Boston rec. of d. call. him "of W. and s. in law of Thomas Cooper of
B." shows that he was "drown. at Noddle's isl. 21 May 1658." He was,
I presume, a young man, whose mo. the wid. S. of W. had m. Cooper.
MATTHEW, Woburn, prob. s. of Matthew of Charlestown, b. in Eng.
had Eliz. b. 15 Sept. 1658; Matthew, 2 Sept. 1659; John, 19 Jan.
1661, d. young; Samuel, 29 Apr. 1662, d. soon; Samuel again, 26 July
1663; Hannah, 21 Oct. 1664; and John, again, 28 Mar. 1667. MAT-
THEW, Woburn, s. of the preced. m. 20 June 1684 (tho. ano. rec. has it
2 Mar. 1682), Mary, d. of John Cutler of the same. MICHAEL, Charles-

town 1644, liv. on the Malden side, adm. of the ch. 1 July 1645; had been fin. for voting unduly, but the tender mercy of the Gen. Court in May 1647, when he was made freem. extend. to him, as "being poor and of an harmless disposition, and the act done in simplicity." He prob. had sev. ch. and Farmer names Samuel, b. 19 July 1648, but this is aft. the sad vacuity in our ch. rec. of bapt. Yet aft. the blessed restorat. not of Charles II. but of the writing down of ch. brot. to the font, I find Sarah, "d. of our br. M. S. (of Malden side)" on 4 Aug. 1661; was a householder 1658. MORRIS, Gloucester, m. 4 Nov. 1681, Sarah Millet, perhaps d. of Thomas, or, as Babson thinks more prob. wid. of John. By her he had Sarah, b. 1683; and Morris, 1686. He was sexton of the ch. and in that office was succeed. by Stephen Robinson, wh. m. his d. Sarah. NATHAN, New Haven, s. of George of the same, was a propr. 1685, then had w. Esther, d. prob. of John Goodyear, wh. he m. 10 Aug. 1682. NATHANIEL, Charlestown, a householder in 1658. NATHANIEL, Haverhill, m. 14 May 1663, Eliz. Ladd, perhaps d. of Daniel, was freem. 1668. NATHANIEL, Weymouth, by w. Experience had John, b. 26 Aug. 1679; and Hannah, 29 Mar. 1687; was freem. 1681. NATHANIEL, Hampton, took o. of alleg. Dec. 1678; and NATHANIEL, Hadley, took the same o. in Feb. foll. NATHANIEL, Hartford, m. 9 July 1686, Esther Dickinson, d. of Thomas, had Nathaniel, b. 20 Jan. 1698; Susanna, 1699; Jerusha; Abigail, 1704; Gideon; and Joseph; beside perhaps some earlier, or some of these may have been; but these six were liv. 1715. He was s. of Joseph, and his wid. Esther m. Hezekiah Porter. NATHANIEL, Hatfield, s. of Philip the first, m. 6 Feb. 1696, Mary, d. of Nathaniel Dickinson of the same, had Nathaniel, b. 1 July 1698; Mary, 11 Dec. 1700; Joshua, 2 Nov. 1702; Rebecca, 4 Apr. 1705; Hannah, 7 Mar. 1707; Martha, 31 Jan. 1709; Lydia, 16 Mar. 1711; and Jerusha, 9 Jan. 1713; his w. d. 16 Aug. 1718; and he d. 1740. NEHEMIAH, by Miss Thomas thot. to be first relig. teach. at Marshfield, I hear no more of, exc. that in an eminent. confus. obitua. on p. 82 of Geneal. Reg. XIV. Ann, a d. of the first Thomas Bourne, is said to m. Rev. Nehemiah S. in 1639. NEHEMIAH, New Haven, had Sarah, and Mary, b. 1642; Hannah, 1644, all bapt. 14 Dec. 1645; Mercy and Eliz. 1645, both bapt. 22 Feb. 1646; and Nehemiah, bapt. not (as in Geneal. Reg. IX. 362) 24 Oct. but 25, 1646; all in right of his w. Sarah; kept the sheep of the town 1644–9 and rem. soon aft. to New London, and a. 1660 to Norwich, freem. 1669, d. 1686, leav. w. Ann and four ds. Mary, w. of Samuel Raymond; Ann, w. of Thomas Bradford; Eliz. w. of Joshua Raymond; and Experience, wh. m. 1 Nov. 1677, Joshua Abel. NEHEMIAH, New London, only s. of the preced. m. 24 Oct. 1669, Lydia, d. of Alexander Winchester of Rehoboth, had Lydia,

b. 29 Oct. 1670; Nehemiah, 14 Nov. 1673; Samuel, 2 June 1676; Martha, 15 Oct. 1678; Daniel, 29 Oct. 1680; and Margaret, 1683; was in very high esteem, and d. 8 Aug. 1727; his w. d. 1725. NEHEMIAH, Exeter, d. says Farmer, 1673. He thinks him s. of William of Weymouth. NICHOLAS, Exeter 1658, perhaps f. of that young Nicholas, wh. was k. by the Ind. 5 July 1697. Comp. Magn. VII. 91 with Storer's despatch in Geneal. Reg. III. 165. NICHOLAS, Milford, m. 12 July 1664, Mary, or Mercy Tibbals, d. of Thomas had Samuel, b. 1665; Andrew, 1670; Sarah, 1672; John, 1674; and Cornelius, 1676. OBADIAH, Dorchester 1661, as Farmer says, undoubt. by error for Swift. PELATIAH, Malden, freem. 1680, by w. Sarah, wh. d. 1 Mar. 1688, had Eleanor, b. 17 Feb. 1684; Ruhamah, 21 Dec. 1685; and Sarah, 25 Oct. 1687. * PHILIP, Wethersfield, sec. s. of Samuel, brot. at one yr. old by his f. from Eng., made freem. 1654, m. 1657, Rebecca, youngest d. of Nathaniel Foote, soon rem. and is the same wh. in Hadley, among its new sett. took the freem.'s o. for Mass. 26 Mar. 1661; was rep. for Hadley 1677, 80–4, aft. wh. last he d. 10 Jan. foll. was selectman, lieut. of horse, and deac. yet " murder. with an hideous witchcraft, that fill. all those parts of N. E. with astonishment," as most minutely is told in the Magn. VI. 70. Still the wonder did not so far outrun conscience and common sense, as to prevail on the trial of Mary Webster, charg. for such clear malignities not only against Smith, the hypochondriac suffer. but others; even tho. she was before a jury at Boston, then peculiar. expos. to false impress., she was acquit. and d. peaceably at Hadley. Years more were need. for the full triumph of the devil and Cotton Mather. His ch. were Samuel, b. Jan. 1659; John, 18 Dec. 1661; Jonathan, 1663; Philip, 1665; Rebecca, 1668; Nathaniel, 1671; Joseph, 1674, H. C. 1695; and Ichabod, 11 Apr. 1675 or 6; all the eight are ment. in his will. His wid. m. 2 Oct. 1688, Major Aaron Cook, of Northampton, wh. d. 6 Sept. 1690, and she d. at H. 6 Apr. 1701. His only d. Rebecca early in 1686, m. George Stillman of H. PHILIP, Newport 1676, in the will of John Clark nam. a trustee. PHILIP, Hadley, s. of Philip of the same, m. 8 July 1687, Mary, d. of Samuel Bliss of Springfield, had Philip, b. 1 May 1689; David, 23 Apr. 1691; tw. ds. 11 June 1693; and Martha, 27 Sept. 1694; rem. to Springfield, and had Aaron, 14 Feb. 1697; Mary, 23 Feb. 1699; Samuel, 1702; and Rebecca; rem. to Hartford, there had Ebenezer, 1 Jan. 1707. His w. d. 23 Dec. foll. and he m. Sept. 1708, Mary Robinson, had Nehemiah, 17 July 1709; and Hannah, 20 Nov. 1711; and d. 26 Jan. 1725. His wid. d. 17 May 1733. *RALPH*, Plymouth, came, in 1629, with Higginson in the Talbot, for supply of the Pilgrims from Leyden, as their first min. He had been bred at Christ's coll. Cambridge, where he had his A. B. 1613, but our Gov. and comp. felt some distrust of his tendency to separat. and his success in various stations seems abundant. to confirm their judgment. He m. perhaps in 1634, Mary, wid. of Richard Masterson, and for a time gave up his office in 1635, when a hope of obtain. Norton was felt, but prob. resum. it, and was active in opposit. to Gorton, 1638; but dismiss. bef. 1645, when he preach. to the small body at Manchester, was of Salem ch. 1647, and perhaps with w. Mary, wh. join. in 1650; but in 1655 was among the early sett. at Eastham, (unless this man was ano. Ralph); but out of office he d. at Boston 1 Mar. 1661, the rec. proves, not 2 as Farmer had been told. Among his many wanderings, he may have found trans. resid. 1657, at New London, and again in 1659. Caulkins, 322. RALPH, Hingham, from Hingham, Co. Norf. came, it is said by Lincoln, 1633, and sat down at our Hingham 1635; prob. went to Eastham, there had Deborah, b. 8 Mar. 1654, and prob. other ch. Yet in this much doubt is felt, for Roxbury rec. of d. in 1672 has RALPH, aged 95, of wh. more strange is it, that nothing else was ever heard, so that I fear error in this Roxbury rec. tho. he may have been the Hingham man. RICHARD, Taunton 1638, one of the first purch. was from Gloucestersh. may be the man, wh. went to R. I. the next yr. and some yrs. aft. was the promin. man on the main, hav. a large trad. ho. in the Narraganset land, perhaps two, North Kingston and Wickford, purch. of the sachem in 1641, and this, in my opin. led to tak. side against Gorton and his assoc. wh. bot. of other sachems a principality of Showamet, or Warwick, to the Northward of Smith, wh. made Arnold and comp. of Providence cry out against G. and his friends, wh. preach. bad doctrines in the judgment of Mass. people, and thence in the summer came the cruel, if not perfidious, slaughter of Miantinomo, head of both parties of the Ind. and next the relig. war of 1643 against Gortonism. For his knowledge Smith was employ. with others, in Oct. 1643 " to fetch the cattle from Providence," being the plunder our forces took with the misbelieving prisoners. Comp. Col. Rec. II. 48 with Winth. II. 84 and 142–8. In that wide estate, aft. a brief trial at Newtown, L. I. he enjoy. gr. esteem forty yrs. as sovereign of all Misquamicuck, Caucumsquissic, and Pettaquamscut, was honor. with a commiss. as chief magistr. from Conn. 1671, as he had support. their rights against the claims of Providence, wh. were favor. by the royal commiss. in 1665. His s. of the same name was made constable there 1663, when the Conn. Counc. dignif. his neighborhood with the town rights of Wickford; but the ultimate decision of the disput. title, in the highest tribunal at home, went contrary to both Mass. and Conn. RICHARD, Wethersfield 1648, then hav. full grown childr. of wh. Mary m. that yr. Matthias Treat, was involv. in the controv. with his min.

Russell, that caus. the rem. 1659, of many of the parish, and founda.
(by R. and his friends) of Hadley; but if not d. he was too old to rem.
and contin. at W. His s. Richard's name is on the list of freem. 1669,
and his d. Esther m. John Strickland; Beriah m. Richard Fox; and
Bethia m. 15 Aug. 1684, Joshua Stoddard. Other ch. were Jonathan,
wh. he estab. in est. as early as 1662 ; Samuel; Joseph; and Benjamin.
But I ought to add, that these ch. are by Chapin reckon. gr. ch. of the
first sett. of 1648, and progeny of his s. Richard. With him I agree,
tho. not to receive the result of his testim. in 1684 when he tells of coming from the Vineyard "30 or 40 yrs. ago," yet ment. no f. Perhaps we
may resolve that Richard jr. whose ch. are here refer. to, and whose
will of 1680 could not have effect bef. 4 July 1690, when is notic. the
first d. in W. of any Richard, was s. of the chief man of the town. But,
for a season, sev. yrs. bef. 1673, there was only one, tho. three bef. R. S.
at W. and of wills or est. in prob. there is only one exc. the insolv.
R. S. call. of Hartford. RICHARD, Ipswich 1642, as Farmer's MS.
has it, without a word of add. but it is kn. there was one of the name
there 1678. He may have been s. of Richard of Shropham, Co. Norf.
short dist. from E. Harling. RICHARD, New London 1652, came from
the Vineyard, but soon rem. to Wethersfield, there, says Caulkins, call.
senr. and we can hardly doubt that he is the promin. Richard of W.
RICHARD, Watertown, sw. fidel. 1652, perhaps was of Lancaster, and
m. 2 Aug. 1654, Joanna Quarles. RICHARD, Boston, came in the
Speedwell, July 1656, aged 43, may be the man wh. had (with cons. of
their f.) bound to him ch. Edward Phillips for ten yrs. and Deborah P.
for 13 yrs. on 12th May 1671, whose indent. on 21 July foll. he assign.
to Henry Green of Rumney Marsh, now Chelsea, or perhaps Malden.
He was prob. a bricklayer. RICHARD, Wethersfield, call. jun. prob. not
s. of Richard of the same, yet, like him, had been of New London, in
1655, was adm. freem. 1658, and is on the list of W. with the other.
Difficult as it is to attain certainty, it seems highly prob. that he is the
same person, wh. at Hartford, 1665 and 6, is call. junr. yet had s.
Samuel well grown, and may be he wh. d. at H. 1689 insolv. Still the
opin. of Mr. Chapin is entit. to gr. weight, and aft. fluctuat. long, my
friend, Sylvester Judd, concluded, that the Richard Smiths are more
confus. than the John S. RICHARD, Lyme, propound. for freem. 1671,
had d. Eliz. wh. m. John Lee. RICHARD, Salisbury, m. 17 Oct. 1666,
Sarah Chandler, had Lucy, b. 17 Sept. 1667 ; Richard, 30 Oct. 1669 ;
William, 10 Mar. 1673 ; Mary, 13 Mar. 1676; and his d. w. d. 6 July,
1682. He took the o. of alleg. 1677, and was freem. 1690. RICHARD,
New London, m. 4 Mar. 1670, Bathsheba, d. of James Rogers, had
James, bapt. 12 Apr. 1674; Eliz.; John; and Bathsheba; d. 1682,

and his wid. m. Samuel Fox. RICHARD, Wickford, call. jun. 1663, s. of Richard the first, purch. Hog Isl. in Narraganset Bay, was one of the Counc. of Sir Edmund Andros. See Hutch. I. 354 in note. His will, of 16 Mar. 1691, call. hims. of Rochester in the King's Prov. at Narraganset, allows us to suppose, that he had no ch. for it gives all the income of his various est. to his w. "for her natural life, and no longer, aft. wh. the whole to kinsmen, Lodowick and Daniel Updike," &c. &c. for wh. we may care less than to obs. the fact, that the instrum. was pro. by our Gov. Sir William Phips, 12 July 1692, only two or three days prior to devolv. that office upon Stoughton. RICHARD, Falmouth, by w. Mary had Thomas, b. 1684; rem. to Marblehead, and had Richard, 1689, rem. again to Gloucester, where Babson notes those bs. were rec. RICHARD, Salisbury, s. of Richard of the same, by w. Eliz. had Joanna, b. 22 May 1686; and James, 26 Jan. 1692. ROBERT, Boston, a wine cooper, a. 1637, had w. Mary, went home, and kept the Lion tav. in Fetter lane, as Felt inf. Farmer, and add. that he brot. two sis. Ann, wh. m. John Kenrick, and Mary, wh. m. Philip Torrey. But Mary had first m. John Scarborough. ROBERT, Exeter, one of the formers of the compact 1639 with Wheelwright and others, may have been of Boston the yr. bef. ROBERT, Ipswich 1648. ROBERT, Boston, a mariner, m. betw. 1662 and 1666, Eliz. wid. of David Kelly, as is shown by deeds of her and her s. David K. ROBERT, Hampton 1657, took the o. of alleg. Dec. 1678, d. 1706, aged perhaps 95. ROBERT, Charlestown, m. 15 Aug. 1687, Margaret Swilloway of Malden. ROWLAND, Marblehead 1648, may have been br. of James. SAMUEL, Lynn 1630, was a farmer at Swampscot, and Lewis somewhere says he d. 1642. SAMUEL, Salem 1637, when, Felt says, he had gr. of ld. is perhaps the same wh. d. at Wenham 1642, in his will, of that date 5 Oct. pro. 27 Dec. foll. names w. Sarah; s. Thomas; and his ch. William, and Mary; and d. Mary, w. of William Brown, mo. of William and John B. * SAMUEL, Wethersfield, came in the Elizabeth 1634, from Ipswich, then by the custom-ho. rec. aged 32, with w. Eliz. 32, and ch. Samuel, 9; Eliz. 7; Mary, 4; and Philip, 1; was adm. freem. 3 Sept. 1634; was first, perhaps, at Watertown, where most of the passeng. of that sh. plant. but in few yrs. rem. with many of them to the banks of the Conn. was rep. 1641-53 almost all the sess. more than any other man, was in 1658 exempt. from train. Next yr. he rem. with many of Rev. Henry Smith's opponents (wh. support. his success. Rev. John Russell's side of the Hartford controv.), to Hadley, where he was in very high repute, rep. oft. from 1661 to 73, lieut. in com. of the milit. from 1663 to 78, then hon. disch. and his s. Philip made lieut. and a capt. was appoint. for the first time; made a magistr. for the town, and d. in Dec. 1680, or next mo. Of the four ch. he bro't three are nam. in his will, tho. he gave the eldest only 5s. no doubt for suffic. reason, yet not express. Mary, not nam. had prob. d. young. Chiliab, and John, his s. are ment. in that docum. the former, b. a. 1636, and the other some yrs. aft. His wid. d. 16 Mar. 1685; and his d. Eliz. m. 1646, Nathaniel Foote, and next, William Gull, wh. d. 1701, and she outliv. him. SAMUEL, New London, s. of the preced. brot. from Eng. by his f. 1634, in the Eliz. from Ipswich, Co. Suffolk, came from Wethersfield, there prob. m. Rebecca, d. of Rev. Henry Smith; was lieut. in 1657, and much betrust. in all town concerns, yet beyond any reason kn. for such conduct, abandon. his w. early in 1664, and went to Roanoke, on the borders of Virg. and N. C. His w. wh. had borne him no ch. was divorc. for such desert. and in 1669 m. Nathaniel Bowman of W. The runaway picked up, it was thot. ano. w. and left descend. at the S. See Caulkins' Hist. SAMUEL, Boston, m. 13 Dec. 1659, Susanna, d. of William Read. SAMUEL, Eastham, m. 3 Jan. 1665, Mary Hopkins, had a ch. b. and d. Mar. 1667; Samuel, 26 May 1668; Mary, 3 Jan. 1670; Joseph, 10 Apr. 1671, d. at 21 yrs.; John, 26 May 1673; Grace, 5 Sept. 1676, d. at 15 yrs.; and Rebecca, 10 Dec. 1678; and he d. 22 Mar. 1697, aged 55. Ano. SAMUEL liv. at Taunton, there had Hannah, b. 17 Sept. 1662; Sarah, 25 Jan. 1664; Sarah, again, 18 July 1665; Samuel, 15 Oct. 1666; Susanna, 20 July 1669; Esther, 6 Jan. 1672; Nathaniel, 26 July 1675. SAMUEL, Northampton, s. of the Rev. Henry, and the only one, wh. reach. mature life, the freem. of 1676, had m. a. 1662, Mary, d. of James Ensign, and had Samuel, and Sarah bef. his rem. from Conn. to N. where he had Dorothy, bapt. 1667; Ebenezer, 1668; beside Ichabod, b. 24 Jan. 1670; Mary, 18 Jan. 1673; James, 12 June 1675; and Preserved, Aug. 1677. Aft. the d. of John Russell, at Hadley, h. of his mo. he rem. to Hadley, to take care of her, and d. 10 Sept. 1703. Of his five s. three, viz. the eldest, sett. at Suffield, where Ichabod, the youngest of them had Samuel, b. 1700, wh. m. Jerusha, d. of Atherton Mather, and had Cotton M. Smith. Ludicrous perversity in modern days of this genealogy, so as to make the blood of the Mathers follow thro. wrong f. and wrong m. beside sinking in the male line one generat. yet grasp. in the female at one too old. See p. 34 in the valua. Centen. of Rev. Alonzo B. Chapin, where all the error is giv. for truth. His Excellency, John Cotton Smith, Y. C. 1783, late Gov. of Conn. was thus, it is said, misdirect. by his f. Rev. Cotton Mather S. Y. C. 1751, wh. seems to have partak. in one ill habit of his illustr. namesake. How he should exchange the name of his mos. f. for that of her gr.f. is less strange, however, than it might seem, if we suppose the reference being oft. made to the famous Dr. M. in the youth's hearing, he always assoc.

the Presid. of the Coll. at Cambridge with that rare title, and thot. more of Increase, than of the humble neph. Atherton Mather, from wh. his own prefix came. Good substitution the f. made in the child's name by enrich. him with an honor. designat. tho. no Cotton blood ran in his veins, as had heedless. been assum. SAMUEL, Fairfield, propound. for freem. 1670, perhaps m. Sarah, d. of Daniel Frost. SAMUEL, Medfield 1670, had w. Eliz. SAMUEL Norwalk 1672, perhaps s. of Thomas, propound. for freem. 1674, m. Rachel, youngest ch. of Matthew Marvin, the first of the same, and had from him gift 20 Aug. 1674. of half his home lot and orchard (Hall, 27); was selectman 1702. SAMUEL, Ipswich, a propr. 1678. SAMUEL, Farmington, s. of William of the same, m. 24 Mar. 1687, Ruth, d. of Thomas Porter, had William, b. 8 Jan. 1688; Sarah, 2 Aug. 1690; Ruth, 24 Feb. 1693, d. soon; Samuel, 26 Feb. 1694; Martha, 20 Jan. 1697; Thomas, 12 Oct. 1699; John, 4 Feb. 1702; James, 10 Oct. 1704; Stephen, 3 Apr. 1707; Ruth, again, 12 Jan. 1710; and Eliz. 15 July 1713. He d. 1725, and his wid. m. 3 May 1727, Joseph Root. SAMUEL, Hadley, or Northampton, took o. of alleg. at the former 8 Feb. 1679, m. 1685, Joanna Macklathlin, perhaps d. of Robert, and was adm. freem. 1690, as inhab. of the latter. SAMUEL, New Haven, s. of George, a propr. 1685, had w. Obedience, d. of George Lamberton, wh. he m. 1676. SAMUEL, Hadley, eldest s. of Philip, the first of the same, one of the four of this name at that town, wh. took the o. of alleg. 8 Feb. 1679, of wh. not one was adm. freem. as of H. while three freem. of 1668, 76, and 90, call. of Northampton, show not one to take there the o. of alleg. on the same day as the H. men were sw. He m. 16 Nov. 1682, Mary, d. of Samuel Church of H. had Mary, b. 28 Dec. 1689; Rebecca, 20 Nov. 1691; Samuel, 18 Dec. 1694; Mehitable, 9 May, 1696; and Benoni, 12 June 1700. His w. d. a few d. aft. and he m. 24 Jan. foll. Mary Smith, had Timothy, 1 June 1702; Edward, 17 Nov. 1704, d. young; rem. to Hartford, had Mercy, was deac. there, and d. 1707. SAMUEL, Eastham, s. of Samuel of the same, m. 26 May 1690, Bathshua Lothrop, prob. d. of Barnabas, had Samuel, b. 13 Feb. 1691; and Joseph, posthum. 9 Oct. 1692; the f. d. 17 days bef. SAMUEL, Reading, freem. 1691. SETH, Medfield 1662, had w. Mary. SHUBAEL, Sandwich, m. 8 Feb. 1678, Mary Swift, had Mercy, b. 3 Feb. 1679; Susanna, 16 Jan. 1681; and Abigail, 2 Feb. 1683. His w. d. 6 Mar. 1689. SIMON, Hartford, br. of Christopher of Northampton, adm. freem. 1677, may be the same wh. in 1646 was fin. for a misdemean. prob. then a youth, perhaps serv. of William Gibbins. Hinman, 236, says he was one of the 28 orig. sett. of Haddam, and had s. Simon, but tho. he copiously tells of the descend. to fourth generat. the only date in his paragr. is 1830, when one of the 4th d.

aged 93, leav. 250 descend. Still it is true, that he liv. at Haddam, in 1684 call. hims. 56 yrs. old; and Dr. Field thinks he had Benjamin, Simon, Joseph, and John. SIMON, Hadley, s. of Joseph of Hartford, m. 1689, Hannah, wid. of John Haley, d. of Samuel Bliss, had at H. Hannah, b. 1690; Lydia, 1691; rem. to Springfield, had there Simon, 1693; Eliz. 1697; and Margaret, 1699; and last rem. to Hartford, there had Ebenezer, 1702; Martha, 1704, d. young; Elisha, 1706; Jemima, 1708; and Martha, again, 1710. He was liv. at H. 1715. STEPHEN, prob. of Roxbury, m. 7 Dec. 1666, Decline, d. of Thomas Lamb. SOLOMON, the ensign of Gallop's comp. 1690, in Sir William Phipps' rash attempt upon Quebec, was prob. of Rehoboth. *THOMAS, Lynn, freem. 11 June 1633, rep. 1635, of wh. we ought to kn. more. THOMAS, Saco, was in 1640 of the gr. jury at the first Gen. Ct. held by Vines and others under warrant from the Ld. Propr. of the Prov. Sir Ferdinando Gorges. THOMAS, Salem, had Benjamin, bapt. 17 Feb. 1637; and Nathaniel, 24 Mar. 1639; but in whose right this benefit was bestow. is not seen, for neither f. nor mo. is in the list of ch. mem. tho. Felt tells that he had gr. of ld. that yr. Farmer thinks he was of Lynn 1649, and I think he may have been s. of the preced. Of one Thomas of S. prob. the same, the Hist. Coll. of Essex Inst. I. 144, shows, that inv. was tak. 17 June 1662, and that he had w. and childr. THOMAS, Watertown, perhaps s. of the first John of the same, b. in Eng. freem. 17 May 1637, m. Mary, d. of the first William Knapp, had James, b. 18 Sept. 1637; John, 1639, bur. 26 Nov. of that yr.; Thomas, 26 Aug. 1640; John, again, 10 Dec. 1641; Joseph, 10 June 1643; Mary; Ephraim; Jonathan; and Sarah; d. 10 Mar. 1693, aged 92, but he had made his will, says Bond, 16 Mar. 1688. Of one of his s. Thomas, or John, the remarka. preserv. from drown. in pass. thro. the wheel pit of his f.'s mill is relat. in Winth. II. 267. THOMAS, Newbury, from Romsey, Co. Hants, came in from Ipswich, says Coffin, was a weaver, arr. at Boston in the James from Southampton, 3 June 1635, by w. Rebecca had Thomas, b. 1639, prob. at Hampton, drown. at 9 yrs.; Rebecca, 20 Feb. 1641; James, 10 Sept. 1645; John, 9 Mar. 1648; Matthias, 27 Oct. 1652; Thomas, 7 July 1654, the serg. k. 18 Sept. 1675, by the Ind. at Bloody brook, with the flower of Essex, under Lothrop; and the f. d. 22 Apr. 1666. Rebecca m. 4 Aug. 1663, Stephen Swett, and d. 1 Mar. 1670. THOMAS, Ipswich, 1641, is, perhaps, the same wh. had w. Joanna in 1655, and there is call. sen. 1679. THOMAS, Gloucester, had Thomas, b. 29 Sept. 1643; and Deborah, 22 Aug. 1648; had commiss. to end small causes in 1644 and 5; possib. is he wh. d. as Coffin tells, at Newbury, 14 May 1653. THOMAS, Braintree, call. serv. of Thomas Gatline, was drown. 7 June 1654. THOMAS, Nor-

walk, bef. 1657, may have been f. of Joseph, or Samuel, or both, of the
same. THOMAS, Boston, builder, as he calls hims. in his deed, 1671,
to his s. in law, Francis Lyford; by w. Eliz. had Eliz. b. 6 Nov. 1646;
and Samuel, 20 Apr. 1659. THOMAS, Boston, mariner, m. Rebecca, d.
of Habakkuk Glover, bef. 1656, was perhaps, the freem. of 1674.
THOMAS, Branford, blacksmith, m. 10 July 1656, Hannah, d. of Samuel
Nettleton, had perhaps, one or more ch. bef. he rem. to Guilford 1659,
there had Hannah, b. 15 Mar. 1661; and Samuel, earlier or aft.; rem.
1663 to Killingworth, there had Thomas, 1 Feb. 1665; Margaret, 6
Mar. 1668; Ebenezer, 15 Feb. 1670; Thomas, 3 Jan. 1673; and Eliz.
1 Dec. 1676. THOMAS, Roxbury, 1660. THOMAS, Providence, m.
Ruth, d. of William Wickenden, had John, b. 4 Aug. 1661; Thomas, 9
Aug. 1664; William, 10 Jan. 1667; and Joseph, 18 Feb. 1669; if the
memory of the aunt Plain was correct, when she testif. to their age 14
Mar. 1670. Both he and his w. were drown. in Patuxet riv. THOMAS,
New Haven, perhaps eldest s. of George of the same, m. Eliz. only ch.
of Edward Patterson, had John, b. 13 Mar. 1664, d. soon; Ann, 1 Apr.
1665; a ch. 1667, d. soon; John, again, 14 June 1669; Thomas, 1 Aug.
1671, d. soon; Thomas, again, 31 Jan. 1673; Eliz. 11 June 1676;
Joanna, 17 Dec. 1678; Samuel, 24 May 1681; Abigail, 17 Aug. 1683;
Lydia, 24 Mar. 1686; and Benjamin, 21 Nov. 1690, d. young; was
propound. for freem. 1669, and the propr. of this name 1685; but of the
other five proprs. call. Smith that yr. neither was prob. his s. THOMAS,
Haddam 1663, one of the first sett. d. 1674, had no w. nor ch. and gave
prop. to friends; but ano. THOMAS, of Haddam, had, it is said, a d.
Lydia, wh. m. 1681, Nathaniel Spencer. THOMAS, Newbury, had John,
b. 14 Sept. 1668, says Coffin. THOMAS, Charlestown, butcher, by w.
Sarah, d. of Thomas Boylston, Watertown, had Sarah, b. 22 July 1664,
d. in few days; Thomas, 1 July 1665; William, 24 Mar. 1667; both
bapt. 3 Mar. 1668, she hav. join. the ch. on the Sunday preced.; Sarah,
again, bapt. 3 May 1668; John, 12 Feb. 1671, prob. d. young; a
s. 12 Feb. 1682, whose name was omit. in the rec. and John,
again, bapt. 10 Feb. 1689; and d. 14 Feb. 1691. His wid. d. 18
Aug. 1711. THOMAS, Concord, s. of Thomas the first of Watertown,
m. Mary, d. of James Hosmer, the first of the same, had Thomas,
James, and John, b. there, rem. to Lexington, and had Samuel, wh. d. 22
Apr. 1670; Samuel, again; Joseph, b. 4 Mar. 1681; and Benjamin, 24
Sept. 1689; the last three bapt. 24 Nov. foll. at W. His w. d. 1 Oct.
1719 aged 67. THOMAS, Marblehead 1674. THOMAS, Eastham, per-
haps s. of Ralph, by w. Mary had Ralph, b. 23 Oct. 1682; Rebecca, 31
Mar. 1685; Thomas, 20 Jan. 1688; David, Mar. 1691; Jonathan, 5
July 1693; Isaac, 3 June 1695, d. at 9 yrs.; Jesse, 30 June 1704; and

his w. d. 22 Mar. 1727. THOMAS, Suffield, prob. from some pt. of Mass. m. 1685, Joanna Barber, d. prob. of John of Springfield, had John, b. 18 June 1688. His w. d. that yr. and he m. Mary Younglove, had Thomas, 26 Aug. 1690; Mary, 3 Nov. 1692; and sev. more. THOMAS, Sandwich, had Samuel, b. 18 Jan. 1688; John, 7 Feb. 1690; Thomas, 25 Dec. 1691; Isaac, 11 Feb. 1694; Abigail, 17 Jan. 1696; Rebecca, 7 Nov. 1697; and Shubael, 20 Nov. 1699; and d. 9 Dec. 1700. THOMAS, Charlestown, s. of Thomas of the same, mariner, d. at sea, 8 Sept. 1690. WALTER, Milford, m. 1 Apr. 1677, Rebecca Prime, perhaps d. of James of the same; but he had m. only 26 Sept. preced. Eliz. Farrand, prob. d. of Nathaniel, wh. very shortly d. He d. 1709, leav. William, Rebecca, Thomas, Mary, James, John, Joseph, Dorothy, Eliz. and Samuel, neither of the ds. were then m. * WILLIAM, Weymouth, freem. 2 Sept. 1635, had Ruth, bur. 20 May 1640; and Nehemiah, b. 2 Oct. 1641; rep. 1636 and 7, was oft. aft. commiss. to end small causes, and rem. to Rehoboth 1643. WILLIAM, Charlestown, adm. an inhab. 1638, by w. Ann had Ann, b. 27 Sept. 1639, bapt. 27 Sept. 1640, his w. join. the ch. on Sunday preced. Nathaniel, 25, bapt. 31 Jan. 1641; Mary, b. 20 Dec. 1642; and Hepzibah, 28 Feb. 1645; whose bapt. and others we kn. not, perhaps, bec. rec. fail us in the mid. of 1642 for many yrs. He join. the ch. 8 July 1643, was made freem. next yr. and d. a. 1653, as did his w. and their inv. was tak. 1 Apr. 1654. WILLIAM, Wethersfield 1644, br. of Christopher of Northampton, where prob. he did not seat hims. till ten or a dozen yrs. later, but must have been here at W. with William, or at Hartford with the other brs. Joseph, and Simon, and sis. Mary Partridge; m. 16 Aug. 1644, Eliz. Standley, perhaps d. of Timothy, made clk. of the milit. comp. next yr. perhaps was of Middletown 1649, for there are rec. b. of his first six ch. tho. prob. the first two were b. at W. viz. Jonathan, 20 Jan. 1647; Jobanah, 2 Jan. 1649; Susanna, 20 Mar. 1651; Eliz. and Mehitable, tw. 20 May 1653; and Joseph, 25 Aug. 1655; rem. to Farmington soon aft. join. the ch. and brot. Joseph to bapt. 15 Mar. 1657, and there had Benjamin, bapt. prob. 11 (not 14, as in Geneal. Reg. XI. 325) Apr. 1658; William, b. Apr. 1661; and Samuel, May 1664; was in the list of freem. 1669, and d. early next yr. His wid. Eliz. d. 1678, and three of the nine ch. d. in the interval, viz. Eliz. William, and Jobanah, wh. was a soldier in Capt. Newberry's comp. in Philip's war, k. by the Ind. Three of his s. Jonathan, Joseph, and Samuel, liv. at F. but nothing is kn. of their condit. WILLIAM, Ipswich 1654. WILLIAM, Falmouth, or Cape Elizabeth, where he was constable 1636, on 4 July 1663, then 74 yrs. old, unit. with many others of Scarborough and F. in declar. of readiness to obey the K. His will was of 25 Sept. 1661, yet he liv. to Mar. 1676, prob. unm. It gave

most of his prop. to br. Richard, sis. Eliz. and Mary, all in Eng. WIL
LIAM, Lynn, m. 28 Jan. 1666, Hannah Graves, perhaps d. of Samuel
the first, had William, b. 14 Feb. 1667; Hannah, 27 Jan. 1669;
Thomas, 25 Apr. 1671; Sarah, 10 June 1673, d. at 3 yrs.; Mary, 15
Aug. 1675; Sarah, again, 24 Feb. 1678, d. next yr.; and Eliz. 25 Apr.
1680, was freem. 1684. WILLIAM, Boston 1662, witness to will of
Robert Clark, was adm. freem. 1672. WILLIAM, Salisbury, s. of Richard, m. 21 Apr. 1693, Abigail Page. WILLIAM, Lynn, s. prob. of William of the same, was freem. 1690. WILLIAM, Charlestown, may have
been that youngest s. of Thomas, whose bapt. 12 Feb. 1682, is rec. in
the ch. vol. without the name. He m. Abigail, d. of Isaac Fowle, had
Abigail, bapt. 20 Apr. 1701; William, 19 July 1702, d. young; Sarah,
30 Jan. 1704; and William, again, 2 Feb. 1706, H. C. 1725, min. of
Weymouth, f. of Abigail, the mo. of first Presid. Adams. This name
Farmer truly calls, "the most freq. of any in N. E. and perhaps in the
U. S." In 1834, he says, 214 had been gr. at N. E. coll. of wh. 74 are
found at Yale, 35 at Dartmouth, and only 38 at Harv.

SNAWSELL, ABRAHAM, Marblehead 1672. ‖ THOMAS, Boston, merch.
1663, ar. co. 1665.

SNELL, CHRISTOPHER, Dover 1671, in this yr. was tax. GEORGE,
New Hampsh. 1689, a mariner, favor. Mass. jurisdict. d. 1708, may
have been s. of the preced. JOHN, Boston 1669. THOMAS, Bridgewater, had Thomas, b. 1671, was the largest ld. holder in the town.

SNELLING, JOHN, Saco 1653, s. of Thomas of Chaddlewood, in
Plympton St. Mary, Co. Devon, may have rem. to Boston 1657, and d.
1672, leav. s. Joseph, perhaps also John, and Benjamin, these three
being tax payers in Boston 1695; and Joseph perpet. the fam. dying 15
Aug. 1726, aged 59, leav. eleven ch. NICHOLAS, Gloucester, m. 8 Nov.
166 , (the fourth figure for the yr. is lost), Mary Hibbert, prob. d. of
Robert of Salem. WILLIAM, Newbury 1651, a physician, s. of Thomas
of Plympton, St. Mary, had purch. 1654, est. in Boston, wh. he sold in
1657, but purchas. ano. in B. 1660; and here his w. Margery, eldest d.
of Giles Stagg of Southwark, wh. he m. 5 July 1648, d. 18 June 1667,
aged 46 yrs. By her he had William, b. 24 June 1649; Ann, 2 Mar.
1652, wh. prob. d. young; and Ann, again, 7 May 1654, bapt. next Sunday. Coffin, p. 55, furnishes some amusing story of his short resid.
at Newbury. WILLIAM, Boston, prob. s. of the preced. m. Margaret,
wid. of William Rogers, had Mary, b. 20 June 1677; but, it is said by
Farmer, that no descend. remain.

SNOOKE, JAMES, Weymouth, by his will, of 22 June 1655, pro. 19
July foll. of wh. he made his w. Margaret Extrix., he seems to have
come from Fifehead Magdalen near Shaftesbury, Co. Dorset, nam. two

12 *

sis. and a sis. in law in that sh. His wid. made her will 9 Apr. 1660.
The name was not, I think, perpet.

SNOW, * ANTHONY, Plymouth 1638, Marshfield 1643, was rep. aft.
1656 for 20 yrs. He had w. Abigail, d. of Richard Warren, m. 1639,
and ch. Josiah, Lydia, Sarah, Alice, and Abigail, wh. m. 12 Dec. 1667,
Michael Ford. JABEZ, Eastham, by w. Eliz. had Jabez, b. 6 Sept.
1670; Edward, 26 Mar. 1672; Sarah, 26 Feb. 1674; Grace, 1 Feb.
1676; and Thomas, wh. d. young; and he d. 27 Dec. 1690. JAMES,
Woburn, whose f. or w. is not kn. had James, b. 10 Oct. 1671; Abigail,
2 May 1674; Lydia, 7 Nov. 1676; and Sarah, 18 Apr. 1679. JOHN,
Woburn, prob. br. of the preced. had John, b. 13 May 1668; Zerubabel,
14 May 1672; Timothy, 16 Feb. 1675; Hannah, 6 June 1677; Mary,
4 Aug. 1680; Ebenezer, 6 Oct. 1682; and Nathaniel, 17 Nov. 1684.
JOHN, Eastham, perhaps s. of Nicholas, m. 19 Sept. 1667, Mary Small,
had Hannah, b. 26 Aug. 1670; Mary, 10 Mar. 1672; Abigail, 14 Oct.
1673; Rebecca, 23 July 1676; John, May 1678; Isaac, 10 Aug. 1683;
Lydia, 29 Sept. 1685; Elisha, 10 Jan. 1687; and Phebe, 27 June
1689. JOSEPH, Eastham, perhaps br. of the preced. had Joseph, b. 24
Nov. 1671; Benjamin, 9 June 1673; Mary, 17 Oct. 1674; Sarah, 30
Apr. 1677; Ruth, 14 Oct. 1679; Stephen, 24 Feb. 1682; Lydia, 20
July 1684; Rebecca, 4 Dec. 1686; James, 31 Mar. 1689; Jane, 27
Mar. 1692; and Josiah, 27 Nov. 1694; was a lieut. and d. 3 Jan. 1723.
JOSIAH, Marshfield, m. 1669, Rebecca Baker, had, as Miss Thomas
teaches us, Lydia, b. 1672; Mercy, 1675; Deborah, 1677, d. young;
Sarah, 1680; Susanna, 1682; and Abiah, the youngest; but Winsor
says, he had eight ds. He d. Aug. 1692; and his wid. m. 23 Nov.
1694, John Sawyer. * MARK, Eastham, s. of Nicholas, prob. eldest (if
he had more than two), count. among those fit to bear arms 1643, at
Plymouth, m. 18 Jan. 1655, Ann, d. of Josiah Cook, had Ann, b. 7
July 1656, and his w. d. few days aft. He m. 9 Jan. 1661, Jane, d. of
Gov. Thomas Prence, had Mary, b. 30 Nov. foll.; Nicholas, 6 Dec.
1663; Eliz. 9 May 1666, d. young; Thomas, 6 Aug. 1668; Sarah, 10
May 1671; Prence, 22 May 1674; Eliz. again, 22 June 1676, d. young;
and Hannah, 16 Sept. 1679; was town clk. rep. 1675, 86, and 9, and d.
a. 1695. * NICHOLAS, Plymouth, one of the first comers, being passeng. in the Ann 1623, m. Constance, d. of Stephen Hopkins, one of the
blessed comp. of the Mayflower, had Mark, b. 9 May 1628; and eleven
other ch. s. and ds. bef. 1650. He rem. to Eastham in 1654, was
rep. 1650, and 2, and aft. rem. 1657. Date of his d. is 15 Nov. 1676,
and of his wid. Oct. 1677. RICHARD, Woburn, had Daniel, b. 4 Feb.
1645, d. soon; Samuel, 28 May 1647; and Zechariah, 29 Mar. 1649.
SAMUEL, Boston 1671, a shoemaker. SAMUEL, Woburn, s. of Richard,

by w. Sarah had Samuel, b. 8 Feb. 1670; Sarah, 28 May 1672; Daniel,
9 July 1674; Abigail, 4 Apr. 1677; Richard, 10 Dec. 1683, and Hannah, 8 June 1686. His w. d. next wk. and, in one day, short of eight
wks. aft. he m. Sarah, d. of John Parker of Newton, had Deborah, b.
Oct. 1687, d. in 2 mos.; Joanna, 10 Feb. 1689; Ebenezer, 7 Oct. 1691;
and his w. d. 28 Jan. 1695. STEPHEN, Eastham, m. 28 Oct. 1663,
Susanna, wid. of Joseph Rogers jun. d. of Stephan Deane, had Bathshua, b. 25 July 1664; Hannah, 2 Jan. 1667; Micajah, 22 Dec. 1669;
and Bethia, 1 July 1672. THOMAS, Boston 1636, a barber, by w. Mil-
cah had Meletiah, b. 30 Sept. 1638; was adm. of our ch. 5 Sept. 1641,
and had Melita, bapt. Sunday foll. a. 3 wks. old; Hannah, 21 Apr.
1644, a. 5 days old, prob. d. young; Abigail, and Hannah, tw. b. 10
Mar. 1652; Mehitable, 8 Feb. 1655; was freem. 18 May 1642; in
1667, was an innholder at the sign of the dove. WILLIAM, Plymouth
1643, came prob. in the Susan and Ellen from London 1635, aged 18,
was apprent. of Richard Derby, was of Bridgewater 1682, m. Rebecca,
d. of Robert Barker, and had William, James, Joseph, Benjamin, Mary,
Lydia, Hannah, and Rebecca. WILLIAM, Bridgewater, s. prob. of the
preced. m. Naomi, d. of Thomas Whitman. Of this name, in 1829,
Farmer says three had been gr. at Brown Univ. of wh. was Caleb H.
the dilig. and lament. hist. of Boston.

SNUFFENE, GEORGE, if such a name be true, was propound. 1670, for
freem. in Conn.

SOLART, or SALART, JOHN, Wenham 1656, had w. Sarah, nam. in
his will of 26 Sept. 1672; but perhaps she was then in Eng. certain. in
1676, when he went for her, was back here in 1679. JOSEPH, perhaps
of Ipswich, was br. of the preced. ROBERT, in some pt. of Essex, had
recent. d. when his inv. was made 1663.

SOLEY, or SOLLY, JOHN, Charlestown 1686, by w. Abigail wh. was
bapt. 9 Jan. 1687, had Mary, bapt. 12 Feb. 1688; and Abigail, 19 June
1692. MANUS, Charlestown, had Rebecca, b. 20 Oct. 1646. MAT-
THEW, Charlestown, perhaps br. of John, had w. Sarah, bapt. 20 Mar.
1681, with John, and Matthew (perhaps not tw.), their ch. at the same
time; a ch. whose name is omit. on the rec. 2 Apr. 1682; and Sarah, 22
June 1684. May not these persons have been Huguenots?

SOLLENDEN, or SALINDINE, JOHN, Dunstable, m. 2 Apr. 1679, or 2
Aug. 1680 (by the rec. of Middlesex or Fox's Hist. respectiv.), Eliz.
Usher, and F. gives the names and dates of the ch. Sarah, b. Apr. 1682;
John, May 1683; and Alice, Jan. 1686. He was a selectman, liv.
1695.

SOMERBY, ABIEL, Newbury, s. of Anthony, freem. 1669, m. 13 Nov.
1661, Rebecca, d. of deac. Richard Knight, had Henry, b. 13 Nov.

1662; Eliz. 20 Dec. 1664; Abiel, 2 Aug. 1667; Abigail, 25 Jan. 1670; and Anthony and Rebecca, tw. posthum. 2 June 1672 ; for he d. 27 Dec. 1671. From him descends Horatio G. Somerby, the assid. enquir. for geneal. in Eng. ANTHONY, Newbury, s. of Richard, gr. s. of Henry of Little Bytham, 8 ms. from Stamford, in Co. Linc. where he was bapt. 16 Aug. 1610, came in the Jonathan, 1639, was freem. 18 May 1642, the first sch. master, town clk. from 1648 to his d. at the end of July 1686, aged 76. By w. Abigail, wh. d. 3 June 1673, he had Abiel only, b. 8 Sept. 1641. HENRY, Newbury, br. of the preced. with wh. he came, was bapt. 17 Mar. 1612, m. Judith, d. of Capt. Edmund Greenleaf, had Sarah, b. 10 Feb. 1645; Eliz. Nov. 1646 ; John, 24 Dec. 1648, d. within 2 yrs.; and Daniel, 18 Nov. 1650, wh. d. on serv. in Philip's war 1676; was freem. on 18 May 1642, and d. 2 Oct. 1652. His wid. m. 2 Mar. 1653, Tristram Coffin. Eliz. m. 25 Nov. 1663, Nathaniel Clark; and next, 8 Aug. 1698, Rev. John Hale of Beverly.

SOMERS, JOHN, Marshfield, by w. Eliz. had Eliz. b. 1686; John, 1688 ; Mary, 1691; and Nathan, 1693. That the fam. rem. to Rochester, is told by Miss Thomas, but neither she, nor others, give the much more interesting fact, where it came from.

SOMES, JOHN, Boston, s. of Morris of Gloucester, m. Hannah, eldest d. of Samuel Shattuck of Salem, the happy messeng. of Charles II. who brot. the order to stop the execrable policy of persecut. the Quakers; made his will 13 Nov. 1687, pro. in 1700, when of sev. ch. only Benjamin was liv. to settle the est. MORRIS, Gloucester, by w. Margery had Mary, b. 1 Mar. 1642 ; and Sarah, 15 June 1643. His w. d. 22 Jan. 1647 ; and he m. 26 June foll. Eliz. d. of John Kendall of Cambridge, had John, 22 Apr. 1648 ; Lydia, 3 Oct. 1649 ; and some others, of wh. Hannah, 3 Sept. 1658. He d. 1689. Mary m. 17 Oct. 1660, John Hammond, and Sarah m. 15 June 1665, Henry Witham. TIMOTHY, Gloucester, perhaps s. of the preced. m. 2 Jan. 1672, Jane Stanwood, perhaps d. of Philip, had Timothy, b. 27 July 1673 ; Jane, 1 Dec. 1674; Alice, 11 Mar. 1677 ; Joseph, 26 Aug. 1679 ; and William, 24 Jan. 1682.

SOPER, JOSEPH, Boston, m. 6 May 1656, Eliz. d. of Thomas Alcock; but I see no more of him.

SOULE, SOLE, or SOUL, * GEORGE, Plymouth, came in the Mayflower 1620, under protect. of Edward Winslow, sign. the Cape Cod compact in Nov. was tax. in 1633 and 4 independ. of W. had rem. to Duxbury bef. 1643, by w. Mary Becket had George ; Zechariah ; John, b. 1632 ; Nathaniel; Benjamin, but the order is unk. as also Patience, Eliz. and Mary, wh. m. John Peterson ; all as Bradford says, bef. 1650. He was rep. 1645, and some yrs. later; an orig. propr. of Bridgewater, as in 1652, he had been among the purch. of Dartmouth. His w. d. 1677 and he d. 1680 ; in 1668 gave est. in Middleborough to John Haskins and Francis Walker, wh. m. respectiv. Patience and Eliz. GEORGE, and NATHANIEL, s. of the preced. were of Dartmouth 1686, but no acco. of either is gain. JOHN, Duxbury, s. of the first George, when his f. made his will, was the oldest, by w. Esther had John; Joseph, b. 31 July 1679 ; Joshua, 12 Oct. 1681 ; Josiah, 1682 ; Benjamin ; and two ds. ZECHARY, Duxbury 1643, perhaps br. more prob. as Weston says, s. of the preced. d. 1663, his wid. Margaret gave inv. on 11 Dec. Winsor thinks, he had s. of the same name, wh. perish. in the unhappy expedit. of Phips, 1690 ; and tells one of his cous. James, of Middleborough, wh. was fin. £5 for refus. to go.

SOUTH, JOHN, Dorchester, if the name spell. Sougth in the ret. of d. 1635, may thus be writ. Yet no such name is heard of at D. exc. in this list of d. and it may be he was only trans. WILLIAM, Mass. sentenc. by Court of Assist. 4 Sept. 1638, and by the Gen. Ct. few days aft. to be banish. on pain of d. but the rec. names not the offence.

SOUTHCOATE, or SOUTHCOT, RICHARD, Dorchester 1630, came in the Mary and John, req. adm. as freem. 19 Oct. of that yr. and perhaps 18 May foll. was adm. under designat. of Capt. If so, had leave 26 July next to go to Eng. promis. to return with conven. speed; but came not. Yet he may have been short time at Piscataqua in 1639. THOMAS, Dorchester, prob. br. of the preced. an orig. patentee under the Great Plymouth Comp. but not ment. in royal chart. came perhaps in the Mary and John, and req. adm. as freem. 19 Oct. 1630, and as he is never ment. again, it is believ. that he went home that autumn.

SOUTHER, SOUTER, or SOWTHER, JOHN, Boston, m. 11 Jan. 1661, Hannah, d. of Robert Read, may not be the same, wh. took o. of alleg. at Hampton, Dec. 1678, was keep. of the prison here 1683, perhaps had sec. w. and d. at B. 2 Jan. 1697. JOSEPH, prob. of Boston, m. 22 Oct. 1657, Eliz. d. of Daniel Fairfield, had Joseph, b. 20 Aug. 1658 ; John, 5 Sept. 1660 ; Hannah, 31 Aug. 1663 ; Paul, 30 Jan. 1666 ; Samuel, 9 Dec. 1670; Daniel, 12 Aug. 1674; and Dinah, 13 Apr. 1677 ; was freem. 1684. NATHANIEL, Plymouth 1636, clk. of the Court, rem. to Boston 1649, was freem. 1653, and a notary. His w. Alice d. 27 Sept. 1651 ; and he m. 5 Jan. 1654, wid. Sarah Hill, and d. 27 June 1655. His wid. sold his est. in Feb. foll. His d. Mary m. 1 Dec. 1653, Joseph Shaw, and next, 16 Aug. foll. John Blake.

SOUTHMEAD, or SOUTHMAYD, JOHN, New London 1668, s. of William, the first, was a mariner and soon rem. WILLIAM, Gloucester, mariner and shipwright, m. 28 Nov. 1642, Milicent d. of William Addis, had William, b. 12 Sept. 1643 ; John, 26 Oct. 1645, d. soon; and

John, again, 31 Dec. 1646. Soon aft. he d. for his inv. is found at Pro. Ct. 20 Feb. 1649, wh. I regret to add, shows little prop. and his wid. m. William Ash, wh. rem. a. 1650 to New London, and had 3d h. Thomas Beebee, prob. was happy to give ch. to ea. WILLIAM, New London, mariner and ship owner, eldest s. of the preced. rem. to Middletown, m. Oct. 1673, Esther, d. of Giles Hamlin, had William, b. 1674, d. young; John, 1676, H. C. 1697, min. of Waterbury; William, again, 1679, d. young; Giles, 1680; and Esther, 1682, d. soon; by sec. w. Margaret, d. of Hon. John Allyn of Hartford, had Allyn, b. 1685; Daniel, 1687, d. at 16 yrs.; Margaret, 1691; Ann, 18 Jan. 1693; Joseph, 1695; William, again, 1698; and Milicent, 1700, wh. d. at 17 yrs. and he d. 4 Dec. 1702. His wid. wh. d. 16 Mar. 1733, in her will of 5 Dec. 1728, names only four of her ch. Margaret Gaylord, Ann Stillman, Joseph, and William. The name is well perpet. in Conn.

SOUTHWELL, EBENEZER, Northampton, s. of William of the same, m. Eliz. d. of Samuel Judd, had Eliz. b. 28 June 1721; and he rem. to Suffield. ENOCH, Northampton, br. of the preced. m. 1732, but Mr. Judd omit. the w's. name, tho. he add. that he had ch. until 1743. WILLIAM, Northampton, m. 24 Feb. 1687, Sarah, d. of John Stebbins of the same, was freem. 1690, had Mary, b. 25 Feb. 1688; Enoch, 1689, d. soon; Sarah, 19 Nov. 1690; Ebenezer, 17 Jan. 1694; Abigail, Apr. 1696, d. young; Hannah, 16 Sept. 1698; Enoch, again, 26 Apr. 1700; and John, b. and d. 1703. No gain has follow. the search for this man's origin; and perhaps one of the very few instances of emigrat. from Eng. to our country, later than 1670, may be this of Southwell. More than the proportion of ninety-five in the hundr. of the populat. of N. E. in 1775, had descend. I think, from the sett. wh. came at least 25 yrs. bef. that earlier date.

SOUTHWICK, LAWRENCE, Salem 1639, with. w. Cassandra join. the ch. and was adm. freem. 6 Sept. of that yr. I presume, and on 6 Dec. foll. had John, Josiah, Daniel, and Provided bapt. at once. Other ch. were Mary, w. of Henry Trask, and Deborah. He was, I suppose, a glass blower, had gr. of ld. for house lot of two acres; but in the dark days of delus. against the quakers, 1658 and 1659, the whole fam. suffer. much, fines and imprison. fell on all, and the d. Clarissa was subj. to gr. severity. When the fines of Daniel and Provided were unpaid, the tender-hearted Gen. Court, with intent to magnify the glory of God, order. them to be sold for slaves to any Christians in Virg. or Barbados. We are permit. to rejoice, that the sentence was not enforc. and the f. with his flock found refuge at Shelter isl. near the East end of L. I. where in peace he made his will of 10 July 1659, allow. in 1660; names the ch. Daniel, Provided, John, Josiah, and ds. Mary, w. of Henry

Trask, and Deborah; and his w. and hims. d. within three days of ea. other, it is said. See Felt, II. 580–2, and Col. Rec. IV. part first, pp. 349, 366, 7, and 410. Much as they might love their native ld. the danger from their opin. requir. banishm. it seem. with a proviso, that they should suffer death for return.

SOUTHWORTH, ‡* CONSTANT, Plymouth, s. of Constant, or Thomas, b. 1615, was not brot. in the Ann 1623, by his wid. mo. when she came to m. Gov. Bradford, but came, it is presum. in 1628, was made freem. of the col. and m. 2 Nov. 1637, Eliz. d. of William Collier, resid. in Duxbury, was rep. in 1647 and 22 yrs. foll. and on the d. of his br. Capt. Thomas, was chos. an Assist. till his own d. 11 Mar. 1679, and once was a Commiss. for the Unit. Col. He left s. Edward; Nathaniel, b. 1648; and William, 1659; ds. Mercy, wh. m. 12 May 1658, Samuel Freeman; Alice, wh. m. 26 Dec. 1667, famous Benjamin Church; Mary, wh. m. David Alden; Eliz. m. William Fobes; and Priscilla. * EDWARD, Duxbury, eldest s. of the preced. m. 16 Nov. 1669, Mary, d. of William Peabody, had Thomas; Eliz. b. 1672; Constant; Mercy; Benjamin; Priscilla; and John; but their dates of b. are unkn. was rep. 1689 and 91 at Plymouth, and under the new chart. at Boston 1692 and 3. * NATHANIEL, Plymouth, br. of the preced. m. 10 Jan. 1672, Desire, d. of Edward Gray, wh. d. 4 Dec. 1690, had Constant, b. 12 Aug. 1674; Mary, 3 Apr. 1676; Ichabod, Mar. 1678; Eliz.; Nathaniel, 10 May 1684; and Edward, 1688. He liv. at Middleborough, was a lieut. rep. 1696, and d. 14 Jan. 1711. ‡ THOMAS, Plymouth, br. of Constant, prob. younger, came with him, was a milit. lieut. and capt. an Assist. 1652 and twelve times aft. until 1667, d. 8 Dec. 1669, in his 53d yr. He and his br. Constant were among the purch. of Dartmouth. He m. Sept. 1641, Eliz. d. of Rev. John Reyner, had only d. Eliz. wh. m. 7 Dec. 1664, lieut. Joseph, s. of John Howland of the Mayflower's glorious comp. WILLIAM, Little Compton, s. prob. youngest of Constant, by w. Rebecca, wh. d. 3 or 23 Dec. 1702, in her 43d yr. had Benjamin, b. 18 Apr. 1681; Joseph, 1 Feb. 1683; Edward, 23 Nov. 1684; Eliz. 23 Sept. 1686; Alice, 14 July 1688; Samuel, 26 Dec. 1690; Nathaniel, 31 Oct. 1692; Thomas, 13 Dec. 1694; and Stephen, 31 Mar. 1696; and by sec. w. had Gideon, 21 Mar. 1707; and Andrew, 12 Dec. 1709; and d. 25 June 1719. The name is not now seen at Little Compton, but is well diffus. in other parts of N. E. It was sometimes Southwood, in the early days, and belong. to "eminently a Basset-Law fam." by wh. I am constrain. to doubt the deduct. of pedigree, as print. in Winsor, 316. Sir Gilbert, Sir John, Sir Thomas, Sir Christopher, may well have flourish. in Lancash. on the West Coast of the kingdom, but Constant, the h. of Alice Carpenter, wh. bec. w.

of our Gov. Bradford, liv. on the E. side; and of a line, however humble, long estab. there, so would not prob. draw his blood from them. Much benefit to thousands of inquirers on our side of the ocean may be deriv. from wise use of a few words in the note of Mr. Hunter, on pp. 6 and 7 of "The founders of New Plymouth," Ed. 1854: "mere possess. of a surname wh. coincides with that of an Eng. fam. is no proof of connex. with that fam. Claims of alliance found. on this basis are not the legitimate offspring of laborious genealog. inquiry, but of self-love and the desire to found a reputa. for ancestorial honor where no such honor is really due." Well is the topic explain. in further remarks, found. on experience of more than one gross case of indecent pretension.

SOWDEN, THOMAS, Marblehead, 1674.

SOWELL, THOMAS, Boston, by w. Eliz. had Hannah, b. 2 Nov. 1652, d. young; and Thomas, 13 July 1653; in wh. the rec. is, of course, less worthy of belief, than in ment. of his d. 7 Dec. 1654.

SPARHAWK, or SPARROWHAWK, JOHN, Cambridge, d. 21 Sept. 1644. JOHN, Bristol, s. of the sec. Nathaniel, m. Eliz. Poole, and had two more ws. yet d. under 45 yrs. 29 Apr. 1718, leav. two s. John, b. 1713, H. C. 1731, min. of Salem; and Hon. Nathaniel, 4 Mar. 1715, wh. m. 10 June 1742, Eliz. eldest d. of the first Sir William Pepperrell, and the only ch. wh. surv. him, and by her was f. of the late Sir William, permit. by the k. to assume the name of gr.f. Pepperrell, H. C. 1766. * NATHANIEL, Cambridge 1638, wh. may have been br. of first John, or his f. brot. perhaps from Braintree, or Dedham, Co. Essex, most of his ch. prob. with w. Mary, and here had Samuel, b. 27 Oct. 1638, d. in Oct. foll. He was freem. 23 May 1639, and at the same Court licens. to sell wine, deac. and rep. 1642-7. His w. d. 25 Jan. 1644, and by a sec. w. Catharine wh. outliv. him only 7 days, he had Nathaniel; Ann; Mary; Esther; and Eliz., whose gr.-stone says she d. 9 Nov. 1692, aged a. 47 yrs.; but certain. Ruth, wh. d. 9 May 1645, was by the first w. He d. 28 June 1647, and beside his w. there d. a serv. of his, Mary Peirce, a week aft. so that we may well suppose some epidem. His other ch. were Ann wh. m. deac. John Cooper; Nathaniel; both certain. b. in Eng. as may have been Esther; and Mary, wh. m. 8 Oct. 1673, William Barrett, as his 3d w. NATHANIEL, Cambridge, s. of the preced. b. in Eng. m. 3 Oct. 1649, Patience, d. of Rev. Samuel Newman, had Nathaniel, wh. d. 12 Feb. 1651; Mary; Sybell; both bapt. at C.; Esther, bapt. 5 May 1661; Samuel, 5 Feb. 1665; Nathaniel; and John, H. C. 1689; was deac. and oft. selectman. His w. d. 3 Feb. 1690. Sybell m. Rev. Michael Wigglesworth. NATHANIEL, Cambridge, s. of the preced. m. Abigail Gates, eldest ch. of Simon, had Abigail; Nathaniel, H. C. 1715, min. of Lynnfield; Noah; and Simon; was deac. freem. 1690; and d. 8 Nov. 1734, aged 67. SAMUEL, Cambridge, br. of the preced. freem. 1690, m. Sarah Whiting, had Joseph, Thomas, Samuel, and John, and d. 2 Nov. 1713, aged 49. His wid. d. 8 Dec. 1752 in her 85th yr. Above seventy yrs. ago, eleven of this fam. had been gr. at H. C. but I kn. not any more.

SPARK, or SPARKS, EDWARD, came, 1635, aged 22, as a serv. to Thomas Page, from London, in the Increase, and prob. was of Saco. JOHN, Boston, m. 26 Nov. 1661, Mary, d. of Walter Sinnet, was of Ipswich 1655, may have been of Saco; and here may have been f. of Thomas, certain. of Eliz. wh. m. 15 Oct. 1684, Jacob Perkins, third of the name in that town.

SPARRELL, CHRISTOPHER, Wells, freem. 1653.

SPARROW, JOHN, Eastham, s. of Jonathan, m. 5 Dec. 1683, Apphia Freeman (but this 'name is by my conject. suppl. for the d. of Samuel of Eastham), had Rebecca, b. 23 Dec. 1684; John, 24 Aug. 1687; Eliz. 19 Jan. 1689; and Stephen, 6 Sept. 1694. His w. d. 15 Dec. 1739. *JONATHAN, Eastham, s. of Richard, m. 26 Oct. 1654, Rebecca, d. of Edward Bangs, wh. d. bef. her f.; had Rebecca, b. 30 Oct. 1655; John, 2 Nov. 1656; Priscilla, 13 Feb. 1658; Mary, 10 Mar. 1659; Apphia, 11 Dec. 1660, d. at 2 mos.; Jonathan, 9 July 1665; Richard, 17 Mar. 1670; and he m. 2d w. Hannah, wid. of Nathaniel Mayo, d. of Gov. Thomas Prence; for third w. had Sarah, wid. of James Cobb, d. of George Lewis, m. 23 Nov. 1698; was capt. rep. 1668, and 18 yrs. foll. and under new chart. 1692. *RICHARD, Plymouth, 1632, rem. to Eastham 1653, brot. from Eng. Jonathan and prob. other ch. was rep. 1655 and 6, and d. 8 Jan. 1660. His will of 19 Nov. preced. names w. Pandora, and s. Jonathan, Excors.; and gr.ch. John, Priscilla, and Rebecca.

SPAULDING, SPAULDEN, SPOLDEN, SPARLDEN, or SPALDEN, ANDREW, Chelmsford, s. of Edward the first, was a deac. perhaps had fam. and d. 5 May 1713. BENJAMIN, Chelmsford, br. of the preced. m. 30 Oct. 1668, Olive, d. of Henry Farwell, had, beside sev. others, Edward, b. 1672, and Benjamin, 1685. EDWARD, Braintree, by w. Margaret, prob. had John, b. a. 1633; Edward, a. 1635; and Grace, the latter bur. May 1641. His w. d. Aug. 1640, and by ano. w. he had Benjamin, b. 7 Apr. 1643; Joseph, 25 Oct. 1646; Dinah, 14 Mar. 1649; and Andrew, 19 Nov. 1652; was freem. 13 May 1640, rem. to Wenham 1654, hav. nine yrs. bef. project. with other Braintree people the settlem. in the domain of Pomham and other Ind. friends in R. I. thence soon aft. to Chelmsford, there d. 26 Feb. 1670. His will of 13 Feb. 1667, in wh. Benjamin is not ment. made w. Rachel Extrix. but she d. soon aft. him, and on prob. of the will 5 Apr. 1670, admin. was giv. to John and Edward. *EDWARD, Chelmsford, s. of the preced. m. 6 July 1663, Priscilla Underwood, d. of William, had Dorothy, b. 1664; Deborah, 1667; and Edward, 1674; was freem. 1690, and rep. 1691. JOHN, Chelmsford, s. prob. the eldest, of Edward the first, m. 18 May 1658, Hannah Hale, had Eunice, b. 27 July 1660, says the rec. in Middlesex; but Farmer MS. beside sev. ds. not nam., gives him John, b. 28 Feb. 1661; Edward, 16 Sept. 1663; Samuel, 6 Mar. 1668; and Joseph, 22 Oct. 1673; was freem. 1690. Descend. of the first Edward have been very num. much scatter. and highly respectab. Nine of this name had in 1834 been gr. at Yale, two at Harv. and eighteen at other N. E. coll. acc. Farmer's MS.

SPAULE, SPOWELL, or SPAUL, THOMAS, Boston, by w. Alice had Mary, b. Sept. 1644; and for sec. w. had Mary, wh. brot. him Eliz. 29 Sept. 1646; if the rec. be true; and yet ano. w. Eliz. d. of Thomas Buckminster of Muddy riv. and by her two ch. ment. in the will of their gr.f. Sept. 1656; but the rec. of Boston m. has 18 Aug. 1653 his union with Mary Guttridge, of wh. I am ign. whether she was wid. or maid; so that we ought to hesitate, whether Spaul and Spowell be the same. Mary his w. by his will of 23 Feb. 1671, was devisee of his ho. ld. and personal est. while a wid. but aft. his d. Mary, w. of Joseph Knight, to enjoy in perpet. and failing issue, then to his kinswom. Eliz. d. of Edmund Brown of Dorchester. So that it may seem almost certain, that he had not m. the Buckminster. WILLIAM, Boston, by w. Eliz. had Thomas; and Mehitable, the latter b. 31 Mar. 1652; and William, 18 Jan. 1655; all bapt. 21 July 1661; and by the style of William Spowell sen. conveys by deed of 19 Jan. 1675 all his right of commonage in B. to John Marion sen. cordwainer of B.

SPEAR, EBENEZER, Braintree, s. of George the first, m. 16 July 1679, Rachel, d. of Samuel Deering, had Ebenezer, b. 24 June 1680; Mary, 10 June 1682; Samuel, 18 May 1684; Rachel, 10 Apr. 1686; Joseph, 25 Feb. 1689; Nathaniel, 18 May 1693; Abigail, 7 Nov. 1695; Benjamin, 12 Feb. 1699; and Deering, 6 Mar. 1700; and d. 27 Mar. 1719. GEORGE, Braintree, had first been of Dorchester, says fam. tradit. but against evid. of the negat. kind, freem. 29 May 1644, when the name is spelt Spere, by w. Mary, wh. d. 7 Dec. 1674, had George; Sarah, b. 11 May 1647; Richard; Samuel, b. 18 Oct. 1651, d. soon; Hannah, 30 Mar. 1653, d. soon, but the rec. in Geneal. Reg. XII. 110, must be wrong; Ebenezer, 3 Aug. 1654; Samuel, again, 16 Jan. 1659; Nathaniel, 15 May 1665; and Hannah, again. Sarah m. 19 June 1672, George Witty; and Hannah m. 28 Dec. 1694, Simeon Bryant. GEORGE, Braintree, s. of the preced. m. 27 Apr. 1669, Mary, d. of

Samuel Deering, had Mary, b. 3 June, 1676; and Ebenezer, 24 Feb. 1679, and d. the same yr. as also her mo. d. NATHANIEL, Braintree, youngest s. of George the first, m. 8 Aug. 1689, Hannah Holman, perhaps d. of Thomas, had Hannah, b. 30 Sept. 1690; Nathaniel, 25 Sept. 1692; John, 11 Nov. 1694; Mary, 18 Feb. 1697; Daniel, 27 Mar. 1699; Joseph, 24 May 1701; Nathan, bapt. 19 Sept. 1703; Thomas, 28 Sept. 1707, d. only one day less than 16 yrs. aft. stud. at Harv. Coll.; Margaret, 16 Aug. 1710; and Lydia, 5 Feb. 1713. His w. d. 9 Apr. 1725, and he d. 12 Sept. 1728. RICHARD, Braintree, br. of the preced. had Rebecca, Benjamin, Richard, John, James, Mary, and Deborah, all bapt. 11 Apr. 1698. SAMUEL, Braintree, br. of the preced. had Samuel, b. 6 July 1696, H. C. 1715, min. of Provincetown; Daniel, 25 Aug. 1698; Eliz. 19 June 1700; Mehitable, 28 Sept. 1702; Dorothy; Hannah, bapt. 4 Aug. 1706; William, b. 8 July 1708; John, 8 Apr. 1710; Mary, bapt. 23 Mar. 1712; and Benoni, 23 July 1714, posthum. for his f. d. 24 Dec. preced.

SPENCER, or SPENSER, ABRAHAM, Boston, 1677, m. Abigail, d. of the first Theodore Atkinson. * JARED, GERRET, GARADE, or GARRETT, Cambridge 1634, rem. to Lynn, freem. 9 Mar. 1637, in Mar. 1639, had gr. of the ferry at L. rem. to Haddam bef. 1660, was propound. for freem. of Conn. 1672, was ens. of the milit. rep. 1674 and 5; had w. Hannah, s. John; Thomas; Samuel; William; Nathaniel; Timothy; and ds. Hannah, wh. m. a. 1665, Daniel Brainard, gr.f. of the celebr. missiona. to the Ind.; Mehitable m. Daniel Cone; Alice m. early in 1662, Thomas Brooks, and, next, 1673, Thomas Shaler; Rebecca m. a. 1682, John Kennard, and, next, John Tanner; and Ruth m. Joseph Clark; and he d. 1685. JARED, Hartford, s. of Thomas the first, m. 22 Dec. 1680, Hannah, d. of John Pratt the third of the same, wh. d. 22 Oct. 1692, and he d. 1712, hav. had Hannah, b. 12 Oct. 1681; Jared, 15 Jan. 1683; Nathaniel, 2 Feb. 1685, d. soon; John, 25 Oct. 1686; Sarah, and Eliz. tw. 16 Feb. 1688; Nathaniel, again, 21 Dec. 1690; and Mary, 8 Sept. 1692. * JOHN, Ipswich, came from London in the Mary and John 1634, hav. tak. the o. of suprem. and alleg. 26 Mar. in London; and was freem. 3 Sept. foll. and the first rep. 1634 and 5, rem. to Newbury with the first sett. and was rep. for that town 1635, and the same yr. allow. to build with Mr. Dummer, chos. capt. by the Gen. Ct. Mar. 1637, but two mos. aft. turn. out for his heresy in favor. Wheelwright, and Nov. foll. ord. to surrender his arms. See Winth. I. 248. He went home next yr. and d. it is thot. in 1648, for in Mar. 1649, his will of 1 Aug. 1637, was pro. at Salem. In it he ment. neph. John S. his heir, br. Thomas Spencer, and cous. Ann Knight. JOHN, Haddam, s. perhaps eldest, of the first Jared, was a propr. 1660, offer. as freem.

1669, m. a. 1665, Rebecca, d. of Robert Howard, had Rebecca, b. Mar. 1666; Jared, Jan. 1669; Benjamin, Mar. 1671; Lydia, 1673; and Grace, Feb. 1677; and he d. 3 Aug. 1682. JOHN, E. Greenwich, in his later days, had brot. fam. to that town, as in the rec. we find " Thomas, the seventh s. of John and Susanna Spencer, was b. in E. G. 22 July 1679, a. 5 o'clock in the morn. and was the first Eng. ch. b." there. But he had liv. in some part of the Col. a dozen yrs. bef. for he was freem. 1668, yet since no trace of him is earlier seen, or any report of progenit. my conject. is that he is one of the few that came over aft. the restorat. of Charles II. and had w. and some ch. soon aft. Perhaps his w. was d. of John Greene the sec. of Warwick. He had sec. w. and d. 1684, as the will made by the town governm. ment. her and the ch. in the order, prob. of age, John, Michael, Benjamin, William, Robert, Abner, Thomas, Peleg, and Susanna. MICHAEL, Cambridge 1634, br. of Jared the first, rem. to Lynn 1637, freem. Mar. 1638, m. the wid. of Thomas Robbins of Salem, and d. 1653, leav. two ch. perhaps by a former w.; Susanna, b. 1643, wh. m. 1 Aug. 1664, Daniel Bacon of Salem; and MICHAEL, then aged 6 yrs. wh. under care of his gr.f. Robbins, bec. a shipwright, and liv. at Cambridge, it is said, in 1670, there m. Rebecca, d. of Thomas Sweetman. Porter claims the elder Michael as an inhab. of Hartford, on Mill str. 1645; but I conject. that his eye mistook Mr. for this name. NATHANIEL, Haddam, s. of Jared, m. 1681, Lydia, d. of Thomas Smith, had Lydia, b. 10 Aug. 1682; Nathaniel, 15 July 1684; Eliz. 18 Jan. 1686; John, 30 Mar. 1688; Mary, 9 June 1692; Daniel, 20 Aug. 1694; Susanna, 8 Nov. 1696; Dorothy, 8 Mar. 1699; and Phineas, 20 Mar. 1701. A sec. w. brot. him no ch. and d. more than 20 yrs. aft. him, 20 Feb. 1742. OBADIAH, Hartford, s. of Thomas the first, made freem. 1658, m. Mary, d. of Nicholas Disbrow, had Obadiah, b. 1666; Thomas, 1668; Samuel; Ebenezer; John; Disbrow; and Mary; and d. 1712. ROBERT, East Greenwich, s. of John of the same, m. 15 July 1697, Theodosia Waite, had Joanna, b. 1711. ROGER, Saco 1652, submit. then to Mass. came up to Charlestown 1653, mariner, was a capt. at Saco the same yr. perhaps, and aft. until 1669. His d. Mary m. John Hull of Boston, not the mintmaster, and next, Sir William Phips, wh. was made Gov. of Mass. and last, Hon. Peter Sargent; ano. d. Rebecca m. Dr. David Bennet, and was mo. of Spencer, him wh. took the name of Spencer Phips, and was Lieut.-Gov. of Mass. and ano. as I think, the eldest, was w. of Freegrace Norton. See Folsom, 182, 3. SAMUEL, Hartford, s. of William, b. in Eng. and the only one nam. in the will of 4 May 1640, wh. gave him, then under 20 yrs. old, a third of his est. He was, may be, instead of his cous. Samuel, s. of Thomas, the one meant in the ret.

1669, of freem. of H. by w. Sarah had Samuel, b. a. 1668; Sarah, wh. m. Joseph Easton; perhaps Hannah, wh. m. 13 May 1696, Caleb Stanley ; Eliz. m. Nathaniel Marsh ; Rachel, m. Joseph Cook; Mary a. 1681, m. Cyprian Nichols; Abigail, m. Joseph Symonds; and Agnes, m. Nathaniel Humphreys, and, next, John Hubbard. His w. d. 24 Apr. 1706; and he d. a. ten yrs. later. SAMUEL, East Haddam, s. of Jared of the same, m. a. 1663, the wid. of Thomas Hungerford, and next m. Hannah, d. of Isaac Willey, wid. of Peter Blatchford. SAMUEL, Hartford, br. of Obadiah, perhaps freem. bef. 1669, rem. to Windham, there d. 1728, aged 88, by sec. w. Sarah, d. of Nathaniel Bearding, wh. d. 24 Apr. 1706, he had five ds. and one s. SAMUEL, Hartford, s. of Samuel the first, m. 16 Sept. 1696, Hepzibah Church, d. of deac. Edward of Hatfield, had William, b. 9 Feb. 1698, d. young; Hepzibah, 28 Dec. 1701; Samuel, 8 Mar. 1705; William, again, 9 Aug. 1708; Edward, 29 Apr. 1711; Sarah, 4 Sept. 1714; Caleb, 28 June 1718 ; Job, 1722 ; and Philip, 30 Apr. 1724; this last in Bolton, Conn. where his w. d. 13 Sept. 1745, and he d. 26 Mar. 1748. STEPHEN, Boston 1661. THOMAS, Piscataqua 1630, sent by Mason, the patentee, perhaps liv. first on the W. side, but in 1652 was on Kittery side, and in 1654 liv. at Saco, and in 1651, 3 and 6 was of the gr. jury, of only eight, in this last yr. He m. a d. of William Chadbourne. His wid. Patience kept an inn at Saco in 1662, and was d. 1683. The ch. were William, Humphrey, and Moses, beside two ds. wh. may have m. Ephraim Joy, and Thomas Chick, respectiv. THOMAS, Cambridge 1632, br. of Jared and John, freem. 14 May 1634, rem. 1638 to Hartford, was serj. of the milit. and had, in 1671, a gr. for serv. d. 11 Sept. 1686. By his first w. he had Obadiah, Thomas, Samuel, and Jared; but he m. sec. w. 11 Sept. 1645, Sarah, only ch. of Nathaniel Barding or Bearding of H. and by her had Sarah; Eliz. bapt. 26 Mar. 1648; Hannah, b. 25 Apr. 1653 ; Mary, 29 May 1655 ; and Martha, 19 May 1657 ; of wh. Sarah m. Thomas Huxley ; Eliz. m. Samuel Andrews; and Martha m. a Benton. THOMAS, Concord, 1666, by Farmer was thot. to be the freem. of 1681; tho. as the rec. calls him of Suffield, it seems to me equal. prob. that the foll. was he. THOMAS, Hartford, s. of Thomas of the same, on the list of freem. 1669, adm. 1658, with br. Obadiah, m. Esther, d. of William Andrews, had Abigail, wh. d. young; Thomas; Eliz. ; Esther; William; Samuel; and Ann, this last b. June 1680 ; liv. for most of his days at Suffield, and d. 23 July 1689, and his wid. d. 6 Mar. 1698. THOMAS, Haddam, s. of Jared of the same, rem. to Saybrook, d. bef. 1703, had a w. but we kn. no more. THOMAS, East Greenwich, s. of John of the same, was a physician, and d. 25 Apr. 1752. TIMOTHY, Haddam, s. perhaps youngest, of Jared, had Timothy,

Sarah, Hannah, Deborah, to neither of wh. could Goodwin give date, nor name of mo. nor m.; beside Ruth, b. 1689; and Jonathan, 1692; and d. 1704. *WILLIAM, Cambridge 1631, br. of Thomas, was much betrust. one of that Comtee. appoint. 9 May 1632, at the gen. meet. of the whole people, to confer with the Assist. a. rais. common stock, wh. soon led to erect. of ho. of reps. of wh. he was at the first, 1634, and most succeed. ones until 1638, but previously made freem. 4 Mar. 1633, was of the Com. to form body of fundam. laws, Mar. 1638, and lieut. of the milit. one of the found. of the Anc. and Hon. Artil. Co. being fourth nam. in its chart. Mar. 1639, rem. to Hartford that yr. was rep. in Apr. Aug. Jan. foll. beside Apr. 1640; and d. 1640. His will of 4 May of that yr. pro. 4 Mar. foll. part. his est. to w. one third, Samuel his s. one third, Sarah, and Eliz. his ds. one third. Sarah m. a. 1657, John Case of Windsor, and Eliz. m. 1649, William Wellman, and, next, 23 May 1672, Jacob Joy. The wid. Agnes m. William Edwards, and so was the happy instrum. of diffus. that illustr. name; of wh. Farmer MS. says eleven had in 1834 been gr. at N. E. coll. six at Yale alone. WILLIAM was the name of a passeng. in the John and Mary 1634, from London, with John, aforement. and may have been his br. but where he sat down is unkn. Yet one William was of Kittery 1663. WILLIAM, Haddam, s. of Jared of the same, m. Sarah, d. of Nicholas Ackley, had Joseph, Eliz. James, Micajah, Margaret, Hezekiah, William, Jonathan, and Ichabod; but no date is found for either of them.

SPENNING, or SPINNING, in earliest rec. SPINAGE, HUMPHREY, New Haven 1639, liv. on the Delaware afterwards; there by a w. dec. had £200, and a d. Mary, came back to N. H. made his will, 20 June 1649 (intending a voyage to Boston, wh. he outliv. and came safe back), in wh. he gave half his prop. to Mary, wh. m. . . . . Rice of Stratford, and a quarter ea. to Edward, and Lettice, ch. of his w. whose surname is not told; and what he had at Delaware to his neph. Humphrey Spenning. Aft. his ret. from the Bay, he d. bef. 29 Sept. 1656. HUMPHREY, New Haven, neph. and legatee of the preced. m. 14 Oct. 1657, Abigail, d. of George Hubbard of Guilford, had John, b. 11 Feb. 1659; and Daniel, 5 Feb. 1662, wh. perhaps d. young; and so may have both f. and mo. bec. the gr.f. George Hubbard names John, gr.s. as a legatee, without more.

SPERRY, RICHARD, New Haven 1643, sw. freem. 1644, had Ebenezer, b. July, bapt. 30 Aug. 1663; and Daniel, 1665; beside Esther, wh. m. 21 June 1683, Daniel Hotchkiss; had liv. on the W. side of the rock, a. one mile from the cave, where Goffe and Whalley, the regicides, enjoy. their hiding, and he had supplied them with food; was a propr. 1685, as were JOHN, RICHARD Jun. NATHANIEL, and THOMAS, perhaps his s. Mary, prob. his d. m. 29 Mar. 1670, Benjamin Peck. JOHN m. Eliz.

wh. next m. Benjamin Bunnell; and THOMAS m. 18 Nov. 1684, Eliz. d. of Samuel Fernes.

SPICER, PETER, New London 1666, rem. to Norwich, d. prob. in 1695, or 6, his inv. being offer. in latter by w. Mary, d. of Peter Busicot, m. 15 Dec. 1670. His ch. were Edward, Samuel, Peter, William, Joseph, Abigail, Ruth, Hannah, and Jane. THOMAS, Newport, sign. the compact, at the same time with Nicholas Easton, 16 July 1638.

SPICK, or SPECK, JARED, Windsor, m. Mary, d. of John Purchase, or Purkas of Hartford.

SPIGHT, JAMES, Charlestown, had James, b. 1 Jan. 1647.

SPINKE, or SPINK, ROBERT, Newport, among the freem. on the list 1655, is found at Wickford 1674. His d. Margaret, I suppose, m. 26 July 1680, George Vaughan of Greenwich.

SPINNEY, THOMAS, Kittery 1652, submit. then to Mass. was constable 1656, d. 31 Aug. 1701.

SPOFFORD, or SPAFFORD, FRANCIS, Rowley, youngest s. of the first John, m. Mary Leighton, d. prob. of Richard of the same; but we learn no more. JOHN, Rowley 1643, by w. Eliz. had Eliz. b. 15 Dec. 1646; John, 24 Oct. 1648; Thomas, 4 Nov. 1650; Samuel, 31 Jan. 1653; Hannah, 1655; Mary, 1656; Sarah, 15 Jan. 1658, d. young; Sarah, again, 24 Mar. 1662; and Francis, 24 Sept. 1665. The youngest d. m. Richard Kimball, and Eliz. the eldest m. 24 Apr. 1672, Alexander Sessions, perhaps, of Andover. His will of 7 Oct. pro. 6 Nov. 1678, names these four s. and ds. Eliz. Hannah, Mary, and Sarah. An uncommon anecdote of his intrepid tongue is preserv. by tradit. in Geneal. Reg. IX. 318. JOHN, Rowley, s. of the preced. m. Sarah Wheeler, had John, b. 12 June 1678; Mary, 9 Mar. 1680; David, 23 Nov. 1681; Jonathan, 28 May 1684; Martha, 16 May 1686; Ebenezer, 14 June 1690; Nathaniel, 10 Sept. 1691; and Sarah, 20 Dec. 1693. He d. 22 Apr. 1696, and his wid. m. 12 June 1701, Caleb Hopkinson, and d. 24 Oct. 1732, aged 80. SAMUEL, Rowley, br. of the preced. was freem. 1684, m. 5 Dec. 1676, Sarah Birkbee, had Samuel, b. 12 Sept. 1677, d. in few days; Thomas, 6 June 1678; Sarah, 16 Sept. 1680; Mary, 7 Aug. 1682; Hannah, 12 Feb. 1685; Ruth, 18 Nov. 1687; Samuel, again, 27 Apr. 1690; Abigail, 9 Mar. 1694; Mehitable, bapt. 10 May 1698; Lydia, 7 July 1700; and Eliz. b. 5 July 1702. His w. d. 18 Nov. 1729; and he d. 1 Jan. 1743, aged almost 90 yrs. THOMAS, Rowley, br. of the preced. m. 22 Sept. 1668, Abigail Hagget, perhaps d. of Henry; but the fam. geneal. furnishes no more detail.

SPOORE. See Spurr.

SPOONER, EBENEZER, Marshfield, perhaps youngest s. of William

the first by his sec. w. was freem. of Plymouth Col. June 1691, m.
Mercy, d. prob. youngest, of John Branch, had Thomas, b. 1694;
Ephraim; John; Bethia; and Susanna; and he d. 5 Feb. 1718.
ISAAC, Dartmouth, s. of the first William, had Simpson, b. 12 Jan.
1700; Edward, 27 Dec. 1701; and Mercy, 27 Apr. 1707. JOHN,
Dartmouth, eldest s. of the first William, and his only ch. by first w. wh.
d. Apr. 1648; but he was prob. b. sev. yrs. bef. tho. the fam. geneal.
gives no precise informat. exc. that he had John, b. 2 July 1668; and
that by ano. w. (the bapt. or fam. name of either is not seen) he had
William, 11 May 1680; Jonathan, 24 Aug. 1681; Eliz. 19 June 1683;
Eleanor, 1 Feb. 1685; Phebe, 11 May 1687; Nathan, 21 Sept. 1689;
Rebecca, 8 Oct. 1691; Deborah, 10 Aug. 1694; and Barnabas, 5 Feb.
1699. His brs. Samuel and William are nam. with hims. and s. John
in the orig. deed to the fifty-six grantees of the town, from William
Bradford, 13 Nov. 1694. SAMUEL, Dartmouth, s. prob. eldest by the
sec. w. of William, took o. of alleg. 1686, by w. Experience had William, b. 13 Feb. 1688; Mary, 4 Jan. 1690; Samuel, 4 Feb. 1692;
Daniel, 28 Feb. 1693; Seth, 31 Jan. 1694; Hannah, 27 Jan. 1696;
Joseph, or Jabesh, as one rec. has it, 13 June 1698; Ann, 18 Apr.
1700; Experience, 19 June 1702; Beulah, 27 June 1705; and Wing,
30 Apr. of yr. not ment. He d. 1737, or, at least, his will was pro. that
yr. THOMAS, Salem 1637, freem. Mar. 1638, prob. had w. Ann, as her
name stands among early ch. mem. was of Wenham 1657, by sec. w.
Eliz. had Hannah, wh. m. John Ruck, and possib. others. He got
involv. with the Quakers 1659; and d. prob. 1664, for his inv. is found
of 19 Nov. 1664. His wid. Eliz. in her will, pro. 26 Mar. 1677 (see
Essex Inst. Hist. Coll. II. 236), made Excor. John Ruck, h. of her
d. Hannah S. and names his five ch. Eliz. Sarah, Hannah, John, and
Thomas, beside other gr. ch. Eliz. and John Osborn Jr. and perhaps ch. of
John Osborn of Boston, and some others. WILLIAM, Plymouth 1643,
is by fam. tradit. said to have come from Colchester, Co. Essex, had in
Mar. 1637 been serv. or apprent. to John Combe, and aft. d. of C. was
by the Ct. in 1645 made guardn. of the childr. of C. By w. Eliz. wh.
d. 28 Apr. 1648, he had only ch. John, bef. ment. aft. wh. he m. 18 Mar.
1652, Hannah Pratt, had Sarah, b. 5 Oct. 1653; Samuel, 14 Jan. 1655;
William; Isaac; Ebenezer; Martha; Hannah, and Mercy; but these six
of unkno. dates or order; was propound. in June 1653 for freem. and
adm. next June; was good public serv., surveyor of highways, gr. juror
1657, and aft. in 1670 liv. at Dartmouth, and. d. 1684. WILLIAM, Dartmouth, s. of the preced. is nam. with other proprs. in the gr. of Bradford
for the town 1694, and sw. alleg. two yrs. aft. by w. whose name is not
seen, had Benjamin, b. 31 Mar. 1690; Jabesh, 18 Feb. 1692; Joshua,

16 Mar. 1693 ; Sarah, 6 Oct. 1700; and Abigail, 6 Dec. 1702. Five of this name had in 1835 been gr. at Harv.

SPOWELL, THOMAS, nam. in the will, Sept. 1656, of Thomas Buckminster, of Muddy riv. as the h. of his d. Eliz. hav. two ch. I conject. to have liv. in Boston. WILLIAM. See Spaule.

SPRAGUE, ANTHONY, Hingham, eldest s. of William of the same, m. 26 Dec. 1661, Eliz. d. of Robert Bartlett of Plymouth, had Anthony, Benjamin, John, Eliz. Samuel, Sarah, James, Josiah, Jeremiah, Richard, and Matthew, as in the Sprague Geneal. rank. ; but some d. young, and his w. d. Feb. 1713. In his will of 21 July 1716, pro. 12 Oct. 1719, in our rec. XXI. 245 are nam. Anthony with Anthony his s. and other s. Richard, James, Samuel, Matthew, Josiah, and Jeremiah, beside d. Sarah Bates, w. of Caleb. He d. 3 Sept. 1719. His house was burn. 20 Apr. 1676 by the Ind. in Philip's war. Of this branch, of Anthony, thro. Jeremiah, the seventh s. is the celebr. poet, Charles, descend. EDWARD, Malden, youngest s. of the first John m. 24 Nov. 1693, Dorothy, d. of Job Lane of the same, had William, b. 4 Sept. 1695 ; Ann, 20 Mar. 1697 ; Dorothy, 9 Sept. 1698 ; and d. 13 Apr. 1715. FRANCIS, Plymouth, came with w. and a d. in the Ann 1623, but the names, Ann, and Mercy, are all that are giv. in 1627, at the div. of cattle, so that it is infer. that he left other ch. abroad, perhaps had John, or more b. here ; and at P. was tax. 1633 and 4, but aft. was of Duxbury. He was liv. in 1666, as Winsor says, and he names the ch. John, Ann, Mary, and Mercy. This last, he tells, m. 9 Nov. 1637, William Tubbs ; and one of the others m. Robert Lawrence ; but I kn. no such man, and casually turn. (three yrs. aft. writ. this maledict.) from p. 317 to 275, of Winsor, obs. that he calls him William. He was one of the orig. purch. of Dartmouth. * JOHN, Malden, eldest s. of Ralph, b. in Eng. freem. 1653, m. 2 May 1651, Lydia, d. of Edward Goffe of Cambridge, brot. from Eng. had John, b. 9 Mar. 1651 ; Lydia ; Jonathan, b. Oct. 1656 ; Samuel, 21 Feb. 1659 ; and Mary, 13 Apr. 1661 ; Phineas, Feb. 1666 ; Edward ; Deborah, 21 Sept. 1670 ; Sarah, Feb. 1673 ; and d. 16 Dec. 1703. The wid. d. 11 Dec. 1715. A will of his br. Richard, wh. outliv. him, in 1703, gives to five s. of this John, wh. was rep. 1689, 90, and 1. JOHN, Duxbury, only s. of Francis, liv. first at Marshfield, but d. in D. ; m. 1655, Ruth, d. of William Bassett, had John ; William ; Samuel ; Ruth, b. 12 Feb. 1659 ; Eliz. ; Desire ; and Dorcas ; was k. in Philip's war, 26 Mar. 1676, under Pierce, at the fierce fight of Pawtucket. JOHN, Plymouth and Duxbury, in Hutch. I. 354 call. one of the counc. to Sir Edmund Andros, was perhaps s. of William, and if this be true, he m. 13 Dec. 1666, Eliz. Holbrook, and Hosea S. in his Geneal. tells no more, but that he sold in 1682 his est. at Hingham, and d.

at Mendon 1690. Yet there is, in my opin. very slight reason for think. the s. of William of Hingham to be the counsellor. Judge Mitchell refers to the will of the Hingham man, of 1683, as it ment. his ch. John, William, Ebenezer, Eliz., Hannah, Milicent, and Persis. JOHN, Malden, eldest s. of John of the same, by w. Eliz. had John, b. 28 July 1685; Abiah, 21 Aug. 1687; Mary, 27 Nov. 1689; was freem. 1690; and he d. June 1692. JONATHAN, Weymouth, s. of William of Hingham, by w. Eliz. had Eliz. b. 21 July 1670 ; rem. to R. I. by fam. tradit. and may be the same, wh. at Providence had preach. in the early part of 18th centu. was town clk. in 1722, and perhaps d. at Smithfield, Jan. 1741, aged 92. JONATHAN, Malden, s. of the first John of the same, by w. Mary had Richard, b. 28 June 1686; John, 7 May 1689; Joseph, 24 Oct. 1691; Nathan, 2 Feb. 1694; Hannah, and Mary, tw. 25 May 1696; David, 15 Aug. 1698 ; and was freem. 1690. PHINEAS, Malden, youngest s. of Ralph, freem. 1690, m. 11 Dec. 1661, Mary Carrington, perhaps d. of Edward, wh. brot. him no ch. and d. 7 Dec. 1667 ; but by sec. w. m. 5 Jan. 1670, Sarah Hasey, perhaps d. of William, had Phineas, b. 27 Dec. foll. William, 21 Nov. 1672; Ralph, Nov. 1674; Sarah, 23 Apr. 1686 ; Joanna, 17 Apr. 1688; and Abigail, 2 Mar. 1690. But my suspicion is strong, that the three last belong to the other man of the same name in that town. He took the o. of fidel. 15 Dec. 1674, and was rep. 1689 and 90. PHINEAS, Malden, prob. s. of the first John, by w. Eliz. had Eliz. b. 11 Oct. 1691 ; Mary, 15 Oct. 1693 ; Tabitha, 19 Oct. 1696 ; and I find nothing more of him. * ‖ RALPH, Charlestown 1629, came prob. with w. Joan, and s. John and Richard, that yr. in the fleet with Higginson, certain. with brs. Richard, and prob. William. They were s. of Edward prob. of Upway in Devonshire. Sometimes it has been thot. that these gent. were passeng. in 1628, with Endicott, but to me it seems more likely that, as they came, paying their own charges, they were in the fleet of 1629. With Endicott, in the Abigail, beside his fam. and serv. there were not, I suppose, over twenty, includ. men, women, and ch. and most of them sent by the adventurers in London, as the *first* sh. for the planta. would naturally be occup. in transport. of persons wh. they should wholly control. The much larger exped. aft. gr. of the chart. in 1629 had, also, wider views of policy, and in obedience to the direct. of the officers of the comp. at home the Spragues, wh. came at their own charge, were sent by Endicott to take up the lands at C. but we kn. that the compiler of the Charlestown rec. threw back his narra. of early transact. by one yr. mak. Winth. and the gr. body of our early sett. come in 1629. As the Spragues came one yr. bef. Winth. Mr. Green, the compiler of that MS. compliment. by Prince and most of us as the first rec. of C. natural. gave them the date 1628, and on the same premises our confidence reposes, that the true yr. was 1629. He had w. Joan, and the Nos. of hims. and her on our ch. list are 102 and 3. He had Samuel, bapt. 3 June 1632, but he may have been b. many mos. for this was the sixth ch. nam. in our list, and the rite had not been perform. since Nov. 1630, by reason of the abs. of Wilson the pastor, wh. came back from Eng. the wk. bef. this bapt. He and his w. were of the 33, wh. had desir. dismiss. from the congr. of Boston "to enter into a new ch. body at C." and were dismiss. 14 Oct. 1632 ; and his d. Mary was bapt. 14 Sept. 1634; s. Phineas, 31 July 1637. He had sprung, I imagine, from Dorsetsh. and own. lds. in Upway of that Co. as by let. of 25 Mar. 1651 from his f.-in-law, John Corbin, at that parish, appears. On 19 Oct. 1630 he req. adm. and 18 May foll. was sw. as freem. made constable at the Gen. Ct. Oct. 1630, serg. lieut. and capt. in regular success. rep. May 1635, being the third time of such an assemb. and very freq. aft. ; ar. co. 1639 ; but I believe that in later days he liv. on Mistick side, or Malden, for his name is in a commiss. to sett. bounds there, and he d. Nov. 1650, and his s. Jonathan next mo. and the name of his wid. is the sec. on the women's memo. to the Gen. Ct. 1651 in favor of Matthews; and she may have m. eleven yrs. later Edward Converse of Woburn. Mary, his d. m. Daniel Edmunds, oft. writ. Edmands, and in the will of her br. Capt. Richard has good provis. * ‖ Richard, Charlestown, came, no doubt, with the preced. wh. was elder br. bring. w. Mary, and on the Boston list of ch. mem. stands bef. his br. being No. 79, adm. freem. 18 May 1631, was with w. dismiss. Oct. 1632, to form new ch. at C. in 1637 took side with Wheelwright, and sign. the remonstr. against the proceed. of the Ct. but on express. his regret, the signa. was eras. ; was of ar. co. 1639, capt. rep. 1659 and sev. yrs. more, prob. had no. ch. and d. 25 Nov. 1668, aged 63. His will of 15 Sept. preced. names w. Mary, Richard, John, Samuel, and Phineas, s. of his br. Ralph, his br. William of Hingham, and gave to Harv. Coll. 30 ewes with their lambs. By the will of his wid. 12 Nov. 1671, pro. 16 June 1674, we gain a fine fam. crop. It names kinsmen, lieut. John, Samuel, and Phineas Sprague ; kinsman Nathaniel Rand, and his s. Nathaniel ; kinsman, Lawrence Dowse and his two ds. Eliz. and Mary ; childr. of Thomas Rand, and Lawrence Dowse ; Jonathan, s. of Daniel Edmands ; br. William Sprague, and his childr. sis. Alice Rand ; kinsmen Thomas Rand, Nathaniel Rand, Lawrence Dowse, Abraham Newell, Nathaniel Brewer, and Thomas Lord ; Mary Dowse, d. of Lawrence ; made Excors. Nathaniel Rand, and lieut. John Sprague. His inv. summed up well. * ‖ Richard, Charlestown, s. of Ralph, b. in Eng. m. 25 Feb. (but Goodwin says 1 Feb.) 1673, Eunice, d. of Leonard Chester, wh. d. 27 May 1676 ; in 1674 dur. the Dutch war, he command. an arm. vessel òf 12 guns to cruise in Long Isl. sound, for secur, of the coast. trade. He took sec. w. Catharine Anderson, on whose gr. stone appears, that she d. 23 July 1701, aged 45 ; but prob. had no ch. by either w. as none is heard of. He was ar. co. 1681, capt. rep. 1681, and aft. ; and was bur. 13 Oct. 1703, hav. d. 7, two days bef. wh. he made his will of unusual and judicious liberality to relatives, to clerg. to ch. and £400 to Harv. Coll. See Budington, 192, wh. in his valua. work had miscal. him s. of Richard, 33, but correct. the error on last page. SAMUEL, Malden, s. of Ralph, m. in Boston, 23 Aug. 1655, Recuba Crawford, says our rec. perhaps mistak. the name (for the Malden rec. gives her name Rebecca), had Rebecca, wh. d. 15 Aug. 1658 ; Samuel, 4 May 1660 ; Samuel, again, May 1662 ; Rebecca, again, Sept. 1666 ; and perhaps sev. more, for by the will of Capt. Richard his elder br. 1703, est. was giv. to two s. of this Samuel, wh. d. 3 Oct. 1696. He was lieut. and town clk. freem. 22 Mar. 1690, when his s. Samuel, and three other Malden Spragues took the o. His wid. Rebecca m. Capt. John Brown, and d. 8 July 1710, in her 77th yr. * SAMUEL, Marshfield, s. of William the first, m. a. 1666, Sarah, d. of Thomas Chillingworth, had Samuel, b. 1674 ; John ; Nathan ; James ; Sarah ; Mary ; Joanna ; and Hannah. Of this branch of Samuel, thro. the eldest s. is the disting. Judge, Peleg, descend. He was rep. 1682, and 3 yrs. more, was reg. of deeds, and the last Secr. of the Col. WILLIAM, Hingham 1636, br. prob. youngest, of Ralph, and perhaps brot. by him in 1629, m. 1635, Milicent Eames, prob. d. of Anthony, and rem. to Marshfield early, but back to H. in few yrs. had Anthony, bapt. says the rec. of Charlestown ch. 23 May 1636 ; John, b. 1638 ; Samuel, 1640 ; Jonathan, 1643, d. at 4 yrs. ; Jonathan, again, 1648 ; William, 7 May 1650, beside ds. Eliz. 1641 ; Persis, 1643 ; Joanna, 1644 ; Mary, 1652 ; and Hannah, 25 Feb. 1655. He d. 26 Oct. 1675, and his wid. d. 8 Feb. 1696. Of his ds. Persis m. John Doggett ; Joanna m. 16 Dec. 1667, Caleb Church ; and Mary m. Thomas King of Scituate. WILLIAM, Hingham, youngest s. of the preced. m. 30 Dec. 1674, Deborah, d. of Andrew Lane, had William, b. 24 Dec. 1675 ; Deborah, 24 May 1678 ; Joanna, 15 Feb. 1680 ; Jonathan, 24 July 1686 ; Abiah, a d. 27 Jan. 1689 ; John, 13 Sept. 1692 ; and Benjamin, 3 Jan. 1695. He took convey. by his f. of the est. in H. on condit. was selectman sev. yrs. but final. rem. to Providence. His s. Jonathan sett. at Bridgewater. Seventeen of this name had in 1834 been gr. at the var. coll. in N. E. of wh. ten were at Harv.

SPRING, HENRY, Watertown, eldest s. of John, brot. by his f. in the Elizabeth from Ipswich 1634, aged 4, freem. 1660, m. 7 Jan. 1658, Mehitable, d. of Thomas Bartlett, had Eliz. b. 13 Oct. 1659 ; Henry, 11 or 30 Mar. 1662; Mehitable; Thomas; Abiah; and Ann, 21 Sept. 1671. He m. sec. w. 12 Sept. 1691, Susanna, wid. of Gregory Cook, and d. prob. 1697, in his will of 29 June 1695, nam. this new w. and those five ch. but perhaps he had others wh. d. young. Eliz. m. 27 Sept. 1677, John Gale, and next John Mellen; Ann m. 18 Mar. 1691, Jonathan Park; and Mehitable m. 21 Mar. 1699, Jonathan Stimpson, and next, 17 Feb. 1730, Gershom Brigham. HENRY, Watertown, s. of the preced. m. Lydia, d. of Richard Cutting, had Lydia, b. 12 Aug. 1686; Ann, 10 July 1691; Henry, 19 July 1692; Sarah, 5 Sept. 1695; Eliz. bapt. 6 Apr. 1701; Mehitable, b. 2 Apr. 1702; and Susanna, 15 Mar. 1706. He was freem. 1690, and d. 24 Nov. 1749. JOHN, Watertown 1634, came in the Elizabeth from Ipswich, Co. Suffk. that yr. aged 45, with w. Elinor, 46; and ch. Mary, 11; Henry, 6; John, 4; and William, 9 mos.; emb. late in Apr. arr. in June, aft. very pleasant pass.; took o. of fidel. 1652. From the rec. we hear of no other ch. * JOHN, Cambridge vil. now Newton, s. of the preced. brot. from Eng. by his f. 1634, cross. the riv. from the Watertown side, when Eliot, the first min. was sett. and built his ho. next to E's.; m. 19 Dec. 1656, Hannah, d. of William Barsham of W. had Hannah, b. 1 Oct. 1657; Mary, 10 June 1659; Susanna, 16 Apr. 1661, d. young; Sarah, 6 Feb. 1663; Rebecca, 10 Feb. 1665; Abigail, 20 Feb. 1667; Susanna, again, 18 Aug. 1670, d. young; Mary, again, 19 Feb. 1673; Eliz. 7 Apr. 1675; and John, 1678; was freem. 1690, lieut. selectman 8 yrs. and rep. 1704, 6 and 7. His w. d. 18 Aug. 1710, and he d. 18 May 1717 in his 87th yr. Mary m. 30 Nov. 1681, John Ward; Abigail m. 31 Dec. 1689, William Ward; and Eliz. m. 18 Oct. 1699, John Mason, eldest s. of John of Newton, and gr. s. of Hugh. JOHN, Watertown, s. of William, went to Barbados, a. 1698, as soon as he was compet. to make a will, to look aft. the est. of his f. and never came back. He gave his est. to Jonathan Greene. JOHN, Newton, youngest of nine ch. and only s. of John of the same, call. ens. m. 8 Mar. 1703, Joanna Richards of Dedham, had William, b. 24 Dec. 1704; John, 1706; Ephraim, 30 May 1708, H. C. 1728; Mary, 20 Nov. 1709; Hannah, Feb. 1712; Deborah, 27 Feb. 1714; Nathaniel, 26 Aug. 1715; and Samuel, 17 June 1723; and d. 5 May 1754. THOMAS, Watertown, s. of the first Henry, m. 20 Nov. 1701, Eliz. d. of John Traine, had Mary, b. 19 Jan. 1703; Eliz. 10 Sept. 1705; Thomas, 5 July 1708; and Henry, 2 Feb. 1710. He d. early and the wid. m. a Bullard. WILLIAM, Watertown, brot. by the first John, his f. had only s. John, b. a. 1677; went to Barbados, and there d. a. 1695. Three of this name have been gr. at Harv. and as many at Yale.

SPRINGFIELD, EMANUEL, Boston, m. 13 Sept. 1655, Mary, d. of Oliver Mellows, and no more is ever heard of him.

SPROAT, ROBERT, Scituate 1660, m. Eliz. d. of Henry Sampson of Duxbury, had Mercy, b. 1661; Eliz. 1664; Mary, 1666; Robert, 1669; Ann, 1671; James, 1673; Ebenezer, 1676; and Hannah, 1680. Robert perish. in Phips' crusade 1690. Mercy m. 1683, Thomas Oldham Jr. and Ann m. a Richmond.

SPURR, SPOURE, SPOOER, and SPORE, JOHN, Boston 1638, join. our ch. with w. Eliz. 14 Apr. 1639, was adm. freem. 22 May foll. had Mary, bapt. next Sunday, 21, wh. was b. 20 Mar. 1638; Ebenezer, b. 3, bapt. 8 May 1642; Eliz. bapt. 30 Mar. 1645, a. six days old; Martha, 26 Mar. 1648, d. soon; and John, b. 16, bapt. 22 Dec. 1650. ROBERT, Dorchester 1654, freem. 1666, or 1671, both yrs. being giv. in the rec. had Eliz. b. 4 Jan. 1659; and Robert, 21 Apr. 1661; beside Mary, wh. m. Teague Crehore; Waitstill; John; and Patience; of wh. Mr. Clapp, the indefatig. hist. of his native town, can supply no dates; d. 16 Aug. 1703, aged 93. * ROBERT, Dorchester, s. of the preced. m. 24 Oct. 1684, Eliz. Tilestone, wh. d. 27 July 1738, had Thomas, Eliz. and Robert, and d. 16 Jan. 1739; had been selectman, lieut. col. and 4 yrs. a rep.

SPYERS, JOHN, Boston, was prob. only trans. person, made his will 25 July 1655, pro. 6 Aug. foll. as in Geneal. Reg. V. 442. He direct. Evan Thomas, his Excor. to send proceeds to his w. and ch. perhaps in Eng.

SQUIRE, or SQUIER, GEORGE, Concord 1642, had a s. b. 11 Mar. 1643; rem. to Fairfield where he d. 1691. By his will of 7 Aug. in that yr. he gave est. to s. Thomas, John, Jonathan, Samuel, gr.s. George, s. of George dec. and s.-in-law, John Seely, h. of his d. Sarah. In 1672 is GEORGE jun. propound. for freem. but he d. 1674, leav. s. George, rememb. in the will of his gr.f. JOHN, Boston, freem. 1686; may have come in from, or gone to, Reading, where he was town clk. JOHN, Cambridge, freem. 1690. JONATHAN, Woodbury 1682, may be s. of George the first, and may have liv. at Stratford bef. PHILIP, Boston 1670, distiller, or, in one deed, nam. brewer, m. Rachel, d. of George Ruggles, was freem. 1690. PHILIP, Newbury, perhaps s. of the preced. by w. Mary had Mary, b. 10 Mar. 1687; and Thomas, 31 Oct. 1694. ‖ THOMAS, Charlestown 1630, prob. came with Gov. Winthrop, is number 83 on the Boston list of ch. mem. and was of those dismiss. in Oct. 1632, to found the new ch. at C. freem. 14 May 1634, ar. co. 1646. Whether he had ch. is unkn. I think his w. was Bridget; and he of Boston 1659, but perhaps rem. THOMAS, s. of George the first of Fairfield, was, in 1672, with his br. George, propound. for freem. liv.

prob. first at Stratford, next Woodbury, and d. 9 Apr. 1712, leav. many ch. as Thomas, Samuel, Ebenezer, John, Hannah, Martha, Sarah, and Eliz. wh. all were bapt. Aug. 1697; beside Joseph, b. 25 Dec. 1698, as Cothren tells. WILLIAM, Stamford, sold out his est. 1666, perhaps was never resid.

STACKHOUSE, RICHARD, Salem 1638, had, as I judge, w. Susanna, wh. join. the ch. 1648, had Jonathan, Hannah, and Abigail, bapt. May of that yr.; Ruth, 8 July 1649; Samuel, 13 Feb. 1653; and Mary, 25 June 1654; was, says Felt, in 1653, gr. the ferry to Beverly side, wh. he enjoy. till 1686, and prob. he liv. in the town of B.

STACY, STACE, STACIE, or STACEY, sometimes STASY, HENRY, Marblehead 1648, may have been of Salem in 1677, and perhaps f. of Mary, wh. m. a. 1667, John Parnell, and of the foll. HENRY, Lynn, m. 2 May 1673, Hannah Ingalls, had Ephraim, b. late in Aug. 1673; William, 3 Jan. 1675; Henry, 1 Apr. 1677; Sarah, 3 Jan. 1679; Ebenezer, 4 Jan. 1681; John, 30 Oct. 1682, d. in few days; and his w. d. June 1684, when perhaps he rem. to Ipswich. HUGH, Plymouth 1621, came in the Fortune, rem. to Dedham, where his w. and d. Hannah were adm. of the ch. 1640, and the d. soon aft. d. as I infer from the town rec. of Hannah, b. 17 Feb. 1641; rem. soon aft. and was of Lynn or Salem, where he had gr. of ld. in 1640, says Felt, was made freem. 28 Feb. 1643, and Farmer says, his w. was adm. of Salem ch. 1659. Possib. it was ano. of the same bapt. name; and he may have gone home, for one Hugh Stacey was of the Congr. ch. with Rev. John Philip, wh. went from our country, and organiz. that dissent. form at Wrentham, in Co. Suffk. 1650. JOHN, Lynn or Marblehead 1641, prob. br. of the first Henry, had John, bapt. at Salem 9 Oct. 1642; Deborah, 22 Oct. 1643; and John, 29 Mar. 1646. He d. a. 1672, and admin. on his est. was giv. to his wid. Elinor, wh. brot. inv. to Ct. 27 June. JOHN, Salem 1692, prob. s. of the preced. kept the Ship tavern 1692. MARK, of Exeter, perhaps, in 1689, I kn. not any more of. RICHARD, Taunton 1643, d. 1687, and 7 Dec. of that yr. Thomas Lincoln Jr. had adm. of his est. SAMUEL, Salem 1678. * SIMON, Ipswich 1641, freem. 1668, a capt. rep. 1685, 6, 9, and 90, d. 27 Oct. 1699. THOMAS, Ipswich 1648, had William; Thomas; John, b. 1658, d. young; Joseph, 1661; Simon, 1664; John, again, 1666; beside Eliz. Mary, and Susanna. This is found by Barry; but ano. THOMAS, wh. m. 4 Oct. 1653, Susanna Worcester, wh. must have been eldest ch. of Rev. William, and had Thomas, b. 6 July 1654; William, 21 Apr. 1656; Rebecca, 7 Dec. 1657; Eliz. 10 Apr. 1659; Joseph, 27 June 1660; and Mary, 7 Nov. 1661, Coffin tells of, in his Extr. from old Norfolk rec. Of his est. sett. in 1692, he says w. Susanna, and ch.

were partak. William, John, Eliz. w. of John Woodwell, and Susanna, w. of John Marston Jr. wh. was perhaps the miller of Salem in 1679. WILLIAM, Salem 1678, freem. 1680.

STAFFORD, JOSEPH, Warwick, s. prob. youngest, of Thomas, m. Sarah, fourth d. of Randall Houlden, had three s. and four ds. certain. for the wills of hims. and of his w. give the names of Stukely, Joseph, and John, beside ds. Francis Congdon, Eliz. Case, Margaret Place, and Sarah Smith. ‡ * SAMUEL, Warwick, s. of Thomas of the same, m. Mercy, d. of Stukely Westcott; had, as in Friend's rec. at Newport is seen, Stukely, b. 7 Nov. 1661; Amos, 8 Nov. 1665; Mercy, 8 July 1668; Sarah, 18 Apr. 1671; and Samuel, 19 Nov. 1673; but other ch. he had, as nam. in his will, where the first, third, and fifth of that rec. are not seen, leav. us the right of conject. that those were d. bef. him. Substitutes for them appear in Thomas, the youngest, Patience, w. of Howland, Freelove, w. of Tillinghast, and Eliz. w. of Devotion. Amos is call. the eldest s. and Sarah, eldest d. nam. Scranton. Gr. ch. too, are found, Mercy Thurbar, and Mary Stafford, claim. the testator's regard. He was oft. rep. in 1674 was chos. an Assist. and d. 20 Mar. 1718, aged 82. THOMAS, Newport or Portsmouth 1638, said to have been b. 1605, and to have come to Plymouth 1626, and to have built there the first mill for grind. corn by water, but this seems very loose rep. and the Col. rec. that refer to the first mill aft. June 1635, do not ment. him. He is found at Warwick 1652, among the freem. there 1655, rem. I presume to Conn. whose Gen. Ct. gr. him, 1674, fifty acres; but he had been at New London as early as 1662, and was at W. to end his days 1677. He made his will 4 Nov. 1677, and d. soon aft. had Sarah, wh. m. 13 July 1667, and Deborah, wh. m. 9 June 1670, both to Amos Westcott; Samuel; and Joseph. His will names w. Eliz. eldest s. Thomas, and d. Hannah, w. of Luke Bromley, beside the others. Claim was assert. by him to be " of the blood of *the* Stafford," but of wh. Stafford is less clear, and prob. unimport. tho. he perhaps had a coat of arms. THOMAS, Warwick, s. of the preced. m. 28 Dec. 1671, Jane Dodge, had Thomas, and William, but no dates are told, either of their or his own b. nor can the f. of w. be trac.

STAGPOLE, JAMES, Dover, had a gr. as Mr. Quint tells, 1694, but he says that he was b. 1653, meaning, I suppose, in Eng. Possib. this name has become Stackpole.

STAINES, RICHARD, Boston 1654, sailmaker, had w. Joice, and ch. Sarah, b. 16 Nov. 1655; Thomas, 16 Aug. 1658; Richard, 3 Dec. 1660; Rebecca, 26 Dec. 1662; and Ann, 29 Jan. 1664; for wh. in his will of 24 Oct. 1672, pro. 1 Nov. foll. he made provis. The wid. m. John Hall. Richard was a soldier in Philip's war, at Hatfield 1675.

STAINWOOD, or STAINEWOOD. See Stanwood.

STAIRES, THOMAS, Windsor, nam. in the will of Rev. Ephraim Huit, Oct. 1644, is prob. the same man call. serj. S. in the Conn. Rec. 1638.

STALLION, EDWARD, New London 1650, had, by w. Margaret, Deborah, wh. m. James Avery Jr.; Sarah, m. 9 Feb. 1674, John Edgecombe; and Margaret, m. 30 Nov. 1678, Pasco Foote; and by sec. w. Eliz. d. of George Miller, m. 1685, had two. ch. of wh. one prob. was Edward; and in 1693 m. third w. Christian, wid. of William Chapell, wh. surv. him. This name has singular mutations. It first appears as Stanley, changes to Stallon, Stolion, or Stallion, and subsides, as Caulkins shows, into Sterling.

STAMFORD, THOMAS, at Scarborough, or Saco, sw. fidel. to Mass. 1658.

STANBURY, STANBERRY, or STANBOROUGH, JOSIAH, Lynn 1639, rem. to Southampton, L. I. had prob. s. Josiah, and d. there 1659. See Trumbull, Col. Rec. I. 348. JOSIAH, Southampton, L. I. went to New Haven, m. 1657, Alse, wid. of Thomas Wheeler Jr. of N. H. and ret. to L. I. THOMAS, Boston, by w. Martha had Thomas, b. 15 Oct. 1642, wh. as his mo. join. our ch. 29 Nov. 1645, was bapt. the day foll. being Sunday, with John, 1 yr. and 11 wks. old; but the careless town rec. says b. 15 Sept. 1645. He had, also, Nathan, b. 25 Dec. 1646; and Martha, bapt. 11 Mar. 1649; and d. 27 Sept. 1652. His wid. was bur. 28 Sept. 1685, says Sewall in his Diary. Yet this is giv. by my conject. only, for there was WILLIAM of Boston, wh. had Sarah bapt. in right of his w. 1 June 1651, if the rec. be trust., wh. is not in my opin. clear.

STANCLIFFE, JAMES, Middletown, had, says Mr. Parsons, betw. 1686 and 1712, William, Martha, James, Sarah, William, again, and James, again; but no date to either is seen. He d. 3 Oct. 1712, and his wid. of whose bapt. or fam. name knowl. is not gain. d. 30 Dec. foll. JAMES, Middletown, s. of the preced. m. 8 Apr. 1714, Abigail Bevans, prob. d. of Arthur, had Abigail; Mary; Martha; Sarah; James; Sibbil; and Benoni, wh. d. 5 Mar. 1727. WILLIAM, Middletown, br. of the preced. m. 30 Mar. 1710, Olive, wid. of Jonas Wright, had James, b. 30 Sept. 1712. His w. d. 7 Nov. 1719, and he m. 5 Oct. 1721, Esther Adams of Hartford, had William, 1722; Samuel, 1724; Oliver, 1726; Esther, 1727; Jerusha, 1730; Solomon, 1732; Josiah, 1734; Olive, 1737; and Joseph, 1739, as in Geneal. Reg. XIV. 133.

STANDISH, * ALEXANDER, Duxbury, eldest s. of Capt. Miles, m. Sarah, d. of John Alden, had Miles; Ebenezer, b. 1672; Lora; Lydia; Mercy; Sarah; Eliz. and perhaps David. By sec. w. Desire, d. of Edward Doty, wh. had been wid. of Israel Holmes, and first of William

Sherman, he had Thomas, in 1687; Desire, 1689; and Ichabod. JAMES, Salem 1638, freem. 13 May 1640, when the name is writ. Standige, prob. had w. Sarah, and was one of the petnrs. 1640 for grant at Jeffery's creek, now Manchester, but of Lynn 1642. * JOSIAH, Duxbury, br. of Alexander, m. 19 Dec. 1654, Mary Dingley, d. perhaps of John, wh. was bur. 1 July 1665, as was her br. John eight days aft.; had sev. ch. by her and also by sec. w. Sarah, d. of Samuel Allen of Braintree, Miles, Josiah, Samuel, Israel, Mary, Lois, Mehitable, Martha, and Mercy, tho. we can never assign the respect. ch. to ea. w. was lieut. rep. 1665 and sixteen yrs. more. He rem. a. 1686 to Preston, where he d. 1690. His wid. Sarah and s. Miles had admin. of his est. His d. Mercy m. 30 Sept. 1726, Ralph Wheelock, as his sec. w. and was not mo. of Rev. Eleazer, the first Presid. of Dartmouth Coll. (as oft. said in books) inasmuch as he was b. more than fifteen yrs. bef. that m. and his mo. was Ruth, d. of the sec. Christopher Huntington. Equal. unsound is the derivat. of that more disting. Presid. Kirkland of Harv. Univ. from the same Mercy (as told in many places), for his gr.mo. was Sarah, d. of Ruth, first w. of the said Ralph, not of the sec. w. Mercy Standish. See full illustrat. by Weaver, in Geneal. Reg. XIV. 376. ‡ MILES, or MYLES, Duxbury, the celebr. capt. of the pilgr. of the Mayflower, was b. in Lancashire, being a cadet, it was said, of the old house of Standish, long estab. with good landed possess. at Duxbury, a town of the parish of Standish in that Co. close to Wigan, 9 ms. from Bolton, and a. 20 ms. N. E. of Liverpool. He had been at Leyden some yrs. bef. the emb. 1620, but we are ign. whether he had ch. at that time, tho. certain that he brot. nobody, beside w. Rose, wh. d. 29 Jan. one mo. aft. the land. His next w. Barbara, came in the Ann 1623, and was prob. the mo. of some that were d. and of all his ch. as nam. in his will of 7 Mar. 1656, Alexander, Miles, Josiah, and Charles, beside d. Lora. Of these last two, we kn. nothing, and if indulg. in conject. we might assume only, that both were old eno. to have been notic. in the ensuing days. He was constant. engag. in public serv. and for 19 yrs. was an assist. and had a mission to London in 1625, where he could effect little on acco. of the raging of the plague, and early in the spring foll. he came back. Of his character, wh. partook, in no small degree, of the ancient heroic, Belknap in Americ. Biog. furnishes excellent illustr. and just analysis. He d. 3 Oct. 1656. A copy of his will and inv. may be seen in Geneal. Reg. V. 335–8. MILES, Boston, s. of the preced. m. 19 July 1660, Sarah, d. of John Winslow, had no ch. and d. on a voyage to London, the sh. never heard of. His wid. m. 1665, Tobias Paine, and last Richard Middlecot, wh. she surv. THOMAS, Wethersfield, a soldier in the Pequot war 1637, had gr. of ld. on that acco. 1671, is on the list of freem. 1669, and his d. Eunice m. 7 Dec. 1693, Nathaniel Stoddard. He d. 1692, aged 80, and Susanna, his w. d. the same yr. aged 68. Perhaps she was sec. w. but prob. mo. of Eunice. He had, also, s. Thomas, and perhaps more ch.

STANDLAKE, DANIEL, Scituate 1636, bur. 7 May 1638, leav. only s. Richard and a d. Prob. he d. sudden, for his will was nuncup. See Geneal. Reg. IV. 36. His d. d. next yr. RICHARD, Scituate, only s. of Daniel, m. 1677, Lydia, wid. of Jeremiah Barstow. Deane says the name has bec. Stanley, prob. by degr.

STANDY, ROBERT, a passeng. from London 1635, aged 22, in the Elizabeth and Ann, whose setting down is unkn.

STANFORD, ROBERT, Marshfield, m. 22 Jan. 1680, wid. Mary Williamson, had, perhaps, been of Scituate 1670, and at M. had Robert, b. 1693, and prob. others.

STANHOPE, STANAPE, or STANUP, JONATHAN, Sudbury, m. at Charlestown, 16 Apr. 1656, Susanna Ayer, had Jonathan, b. 2 Feb. foll. ; Sarah, 25 Mar. 1658 ; Hannah ; Joseph, 13 Sept. 1662 ; Jemima, 1665; Mary, 1667 ; and Rebecca, 1670 ; and he d. 25 Oct. 1702, aged 70. JONATHAN, Sudbury, s. of the preced. m. 11 May 1674, Sarah Griffin, had Isaac, b. 1675 ; and Jonathan, d. young. JOSEPH, Sudbury, br. of the preced. m. 1 Jan. 1685, Hannah Bradish, prob. d. of Joseph, had Susanna, b. 1685 ; Jonathan, 1687 ; Jemima, 1691 ; and Isaac, 1696.

STANIELL, STANIARD, or STONIARD, ANTHONY, wh. I presume is call. Stannion, a glover, passeng. in the Planter from London 1635, was of Exeter 1644, one of so much distinct. as to be empow. by the Gen. Ct. of Mass. next yr. to decide small controv.

STANIFORD, or STANIFORTH, JOHN, Ipswich, m. bef. 1680, Margaret, d. of Thomas Harris, had prob. ch. for the name was long kn. there. THOMAS, Concord 1644, of wh. I have nothing, exc. a suggest. on Farmer's interleav. copy, that he may have been at Casco 1658. THOMAS, Charlestown, had David, Richard, Rebecca, and Eliz. all bapt. 19 Aug. 1688, when he ent. into covenant with that ch. and is styl. "the blind man," wh. was suffic. descript. at the time, it may be, tho. for our distant day, it would have been equally good, had we got the name of the mo. Of those ch. the ages were 8, 5, 2, and 1 ; and aft. he had bapt. Samuel, 8 June 1690 ; and Martha, 26 Feb. 1693. Perhaps this was the same as Stanford, for so Morton, the min. of C. wrote it, but as he was lately come from Eng. it is uncert. Wid. Sarah S. d. at C. 11 Dec. 1707.

STANLEY, or STANDLEY, ‡ CALEB, Hartford, s. of Timothy, eldest that liv. to adult yrs. freem. 1665, was serj. 1669, and a capt. in later yrs. m. a. 1665, Hannah, d. of John Cowles, by wh. was b. Hannah, 13 Oct. 1666 ; Eliz. 24 Oct. 1669, wh. m. William Pitkin the sec. He had

also Caleb, 6 Sept. 1674. His w. d. 4 or 7 Feb. 1690, aged 44; and he
m. 24 Sept. foll. Sarah, wid. of Zechary Long of Charlestown, and had
Ann, and Mary, tw. b. 14 June 1692, of wh. Mary d. young; Abigail,
24 Feb. 1695; and Ruth, 1 July 1696. His w. d. 30 Aug. 1698, aged
44; and he m. 1699, Lydia Wilson. He was made an Assist. 1691, as
Farmer in MS. says; and he d. 5 May 1718, aged 76. His will of
Mar. 1716, names w. Lydia, four ds. and four childr. of his s. Caleb, wh.
was dec. and Roger Pitkin, h. of his d. Hannah, dec. CHRISTOPHER,
Boston, came in the Elizabeth and Ann, from London 1635, aged 32,
with w. Susanna, 31, join. our ch. 16 May 1641, and was adm. freem.
2 June foll. He is call. taylor, wh. in my opin. means a mem. of the
gr. comp. of Merch. Taylors of London; was a capt. and d. early in
1646, leav. good est. to his wid. beside sev. legacies and devises, but
names no ch. Of his will, 27 Mar. in that yr. abstr. is in Geneal. Reg.
IV. 52, and therein it appears not to have been brot. to pro. until 19 Jan.
1650. His wid. m. William Phillips, and 10 Sept. 1650, with assent of her
new h. made her will of the est. that came from Stanley pro. 2 Aug. 1655.
See Phillips, or a larger abstr. in Geneal. Reg. V. 447. GEORGE, perhaps
of Beverly, m. a. 1680, Bethia Lovett, perhaps d. of John. JOHN, br.
of Thomas, d. on his passage to N. E. in 1634, leav. three ch. of wh.
the youngest was d. bef. the order of Gen. Ct. in 3 Mar. 1635 as to
dispos. of his goods and chattels, the whole being of the val. of £116,
£58 to ea. See Coll. Rec. I. 134. The others, John, and Ruth, were
several. commit. to uncles Thomas and Timothy. Ruth m. 5 Dec. 1645,
Isaac Moore of Farmington. * JOHN, Farmington, s. of the preced. b.
in Eng. brot. in 1634, by his f. wh. d. on the pass. m. 5 or 15 Dec. 1645,
Sarah, d. of Thomas Scott, had John, b. 3 Nov. 1647, at Hartford;
Thomas, 1 Nov. 1649; Sarah, 18 Feb. 1652; Timothy, 17 Mar. 1654;
Eliz. 1, bapt. 5 Apr. 1657, d. young; Isaac, 22 Sept. 1660; all at F. His
w. d. 26 June 1661; and he m. 20 Apr. 1663, Sarah, d. of John
Fletcher of Milford, and had Abigail, 25 July, bapt. 1 Aug. 1669; and
Eliz. b. 28 Nov. 1672; was freem. 1665, a lieut. and capt. in Philip's
war in active serv. up. the riv. many yrs. rep. says Porter, d. 19 Dec.
1705, hav. made his will Apr. preced. in wh. he names all the s. and d.
Sarah, w. of Joseph Gaylord of Windsor; Abigail, w. of John Hooker;
and Eliz. w. of John Wadsworth the sec. The wid. d. 15 May 1713.
* JOHN, Waterbury, s. of the preced. m. 1669 Esther, d. of Thomas
Newell of Farmington, had Esther, b. 2 Dec. 1672; and John, 9 Apr.
1675, wh. d. next yr. both bapt. at F. (where he had m.); Samuel, 1677;
Nathaniel, 1679; John, again, bapt. not (as in Geneal. Reg. XII. 38)
25 May, wh. was Thursday, but 28 May 1682; Thomas, 25 May 1684;
Sarah, 4 July 1686; and Timothy, b. 1689, bapt. 11 May 1690; was

rep. 1690 and 3, but rem. to Farmington a. 1696; and d. 23 May
1718. MATTHEW, Lynn 1646, was of Topsfield 1664. ‡ * NATHAN-
IEL, Hartford, only s. of Thomas of the same, m. 2 June 1659, Sarah,
d. of James Boosey, had Nathaniel, b. 5 June 1664, at Hadley, d.
young; Sarah, 24 Aug. 1669, at Hartford, d. at 20 yrs.; Joseph, 20
Feb. 1672, d. young; Hannah, 30 Sept. 1674, d. at seven yrs.; Mary,
8 Oct. 1677; Susanna, 13 Apr. 1681, d. at two yrs.; and Nathaniel,
again, 9 July 1683, wh. d. 1755; and Sarah, 28 Nov. 1689. He was
freem. 1669, or earlier, rep. 1678 to 89, then an Assist. to his d. 14
Nov. 1712, in 74th yr. His will, made three days bef. names w. Sarah,
and the two ch. Nathaniel and Mary, w. of Nathaniel Hooker, wh. had
been betroth. to his br. Roger, dec. The wid. m. 8 Dec. 1713, John
Austin. ONESIPHORUS, Roxbury, was of Moseley's comp. in Dec.
1675. SAMUEL, Topsfield 1661, perhaps s. of Matthew, was freem.
1690. * THOMAS, Lynn, freem. 4 Mar. 1635, and rep. in Sept. foll.
perhaps of ar. co. 1640; but I think a few days aft. ano. THOMAS of
more consequence, br. of the first John and Timothy, is found on the
rec. of London custom ho. aged 16, as Mr. Drake cop. the fig. in Geneal.
Reg. XIV. 307, precisely like mine in 3 Mass. Hist. Coll. VIII. 257;
and the spell. of the surname is Stansley, as shown in the Index of that
series of the Mass. Hist. Coll. but in the Index of Geneal. Reg. vol. it is
alter. to Stanley, and so justifies the construct. I had many yrs. since giv.
He emb. in the Planter 1635, for N. E. from that port, and was among
the first sett. of Hartford 1636, had Nathaniel, b. 1638, and three ds. rem.
1659 to Hadley, d. 30 Jan. 1663. Of his ds. Hannah m. Samuel Porter;
Mary m. John Porter; and Sarah m. John Wadsworth. His wid. Bennet m. Gregory Wilterton as his sec. w. the same yr. and d. the next,
aged 55. THOMAS, Farmington, prob. s. of John of the same, had, late
in life, m. May 1690, Ann, d. of Rev. Jeremiah Peck, and had Thomas,
b. 31 Oct. 1696; and Ann, 14 May 1699; and he d. 14 Apr. 1713. His
wid. d. 23 May 1718. TIMOTHY, Cambridge, br. of the first John, came
to N. E. in May 1634, with w. Eliz. and s. Timothy, b. Jan. 1633, and
as his mo. testif. not weaned on their passage, but he d. soon; freem. 4
Mar. 1635, rem. to Hartford, an orig. propr. and there d. in Oct. 1648,
his inv. in Trumbull, Col. Rec. I. 489 hav. that date. The est. was distrib. in Dec. foll. but his elder s. Caleb was then minor, and of the other
Isaac I hear nothing, but that he was b. 10 Mar. 1648, and d. 22 Sept.
1671 at Hadley unm. Of the ds. one, Lois, b. prob. 23 Aug. 1645, m.
Thomas Porter; Abigail m. 1661, Samuel Cowles; and Eliz. m. Mark
Sension. His wid. m. Andrew Bacon. * TIMOTHY, Farmington 1687,
rem. to Waterbury, was s. of Capt. John, m. 1676 Mary, d. of John
Strong, rep. 1694, and oft. aft. had no ch. but gave his prop. to Thomas

Clark, d. 12 Nov. 1728, and his w. Mary d. six yrs. bef. The name was commonly in early days writ. with *d* in the first syl. and more recent. is not; as in the catal. of Yale Coll. in 1852 is found the list of ten gr. Stanley.

STANNARD, or STANARD, JOSEPH, Haddam, an early sett. Field, 67. See Stonard.

STANNION, ANTHONY. See Staniel.

STANTLEY, JOHN, came in the Abigail from London 1635, aged 34; but where he sat down, or any thing else a. him, is unkn.

STANTON, DANIEL, Stonington, s. of the first Thomas, may first have liv. at Westerly 1669, by w. Eliz. had, as the rec. of Friends at Newport shows, Eliz. b. 20 June 1676; Martha, 3 June 1678; Sarah, 27 Feb. 1680; Daniel, 19 Apr. 1683; and Ruth, 8 Apr. 1687; m. prob. in Barbados, there d. leav. wid. and one ch. * JOHN, Stonington, s. of Thomas the first, was wish. by the Conn. governm. to be educ. for an Ind. interpret. and teacher, and sent by his f. to Harv. Coll. 1661, but not long eno. stud. there to partake in the honors. He prob. learn. more by practice and exper. of acquaint. with the unlet. natives; was freem. 1666, liv. at S. 1670-9, prob. had s. of the same name, as he was call. sen. a capt. in Philip's war, and much employ. in every thing relat. to the Ind. By w. Hannah he had John, b. 22 May 1665; Joseph, 22 Jan. 1668; Thomas, Apr. 1670; Ann, 1 Oct. 1673; Theophilus, 16 Jan. 1676; and Dorothy, wh. d. 28 Apr. 1699. * JOHN, prob. s. of Robert of Newport, had by Mary, d. of John Harndel of Newport, Robert, b. 4 May 1667; Benjamin; Mary, 4 June 1668; and Hannah, 7 Nov. 1670, as in the will of their gr.f. 9 Feb. 1685, may be seen; beside these, Patience, b. 10 Sept. 1672; Joseph; John, 22 Apr. 1674; and Content, 20 Dec. 1675; wh. may all have been d. when the will was made. He was rep. 1690; and d. 3 Oct. 1713, at the age of 72. JOSEPH, Stonington, younger br. of the preced. was yet old eno. to be propound. for freem. 1669, may be, tho. not prob. that s.-in-law of William Mead of Roxbury, in whose will of 1683 he is nam. "tho. undutiful," for we can hardly doubt, that our Stonington man had some yrs. bef. m. Hannah Lord, or even third w. a Prentice. But no ch. is giv. him. ROBERT, Newport, adm. an inhab. early in 1639, on the freem.'s list 1655, by w. Avis had John b. Aug. 1645. He was perhaps br. of the elder Thomas, yet we must not be too confident, for Farmer ment. a ROBERT of Dorchester wh. as I find had Thomas, and whose d. Prudence was b. 14 June 1659; but he was of town's poor 1689. ROBERT, s. of the first Thomas his youngest but one, the ch. mem. of 1677, was that youthful soldier, 1676, to wh. the Ind. capt. prince Nanunteno made reproachf. ansr. as Hubbard tells. He d. 25 Oct. 1724, aged 70, had Robert, b. 7 Dec. 1689,

H. C. 1712. But other ch. bef. and aft. he had, as he m. 12 Sept. 1677, Joanna Gardner, and issue were Joanna, b. 5 Jan. 1679; Lucy, 16 Sept. 1681; Ann, 26 Oct. 1684; Mary, 3 Feb. 1687; Thomas, 9 Jan. 1693; Lucy, again, 3 May 1696; and Gardner, 27 May 1701. SAM-UEL, Stonington, younger ch. of the first Thomas, m. 15 June 1680, Borrodel, d. of Capt. George Denison, had Samuel, b. 16 June 1683; Daniel, 4 Nov. 1685; and Ann, 2 July 1688. * THOMAS, Stonington, came from Virginia, whither, in 1635, he had gone from London, at the age of 20, was one of the orig. proprs. of Hartford, and there resid. many yrs. for it is thot. that all of his nine ch. were b. at that place; yet with a traveller's spirit learn. the lang. of the Ind. and so was of prime import. as an interp. He seems to have shown his ability first in this kind 1637, when Stoughton, in his advice of Aug. on the first exped. ment. his serv. Perhaps a. 1658 he sett. at S. with w. Ann, d. of Thomas Lord the first, by wh. as is inferr. by Miss Caulkins, aft. dilig. inq. he had Thomas, b. prob. 1639; John, 1641; Hannah; Mary; Joseph, bapt. 21 Mar. 1647; Daniel, or David; Dorothy, 1652; Robert, 1653; Samuel, and Sarah, a. 1655. Hannah m. 20 Nov. 1662, Nehe-miah Palmer; Mary m. 17 Nov. 1664, tho. in ano. p. Caulkins says 1662, Samuel Rogers; Dorothy m. 11 Sept. 1674, Rev. James Noyes, and d. 19 Jan. 1742, aged 90; Sarah m. first Thomas Prentice, and next, Capt. William Denison, and d. 1713, aged 59. He was rep. 1666, and aft. the chief inhab. active in the founda. of ch. 3 June 1674, and obtain. ordina. of Rev. Mr. Noyes in Sept. foll. his name being first, and that of Thomas Jr. sixth, and of addit. to the ch. in 1675, is sec. name of Mrs. Ann his w. wh. d. 1688. He d. 1678, his will being pro. in June of that yr. THOMAS, Stonington, eldest s. of the preced. had shown bef. the rem. of his f. from Hartford such an aptn. for the lang. of the Ind. as to be desir. 1654, by the Commissnrs. of the Unit. Col. of N. E. from his f. with younger br. John to be empl. in the pub. serv. by train. up at Harv. Coll. for interpr. and sev. yrs. the Col. made gr. of money, and lds. to the f. for the benefit of him and them. See Haz. II. 322. He had by w. Sarah, eldest d. of Capt. George Denison, other ch. Dorothy, Sarah, Mary, William, and Samuel; tho. instead of William, one acco. gives Ann; beside Thomas, prob. eldest, wh. d. at age of 18 in 1683; but the f. d. 1718, aged 80.

STANWOOD, or STAINWOOD, JOHN, Gloucester, s. of the first Philip, m. 9 Dec. 1680, Lydia Butler, whose f. is not kn. had John, b. 26 Sept. 1681; Jonathan; James; and six other ch. and d. 25 Jan. 1706. Babson thinks two of those s. were set. at Falmouth. JONATHAN, Gloucester, br. of the preced. prob. youngest, m. 17 Dec. 1688, Mary Nichols, and had ten ch. of wh. Ebenezer, David, and Nehemiah, are all that Babson ment. PHILIP, Gloucester, by w. Jane had Philip; John, b. 1653; Jane, 1655; Samuel, 5 Jan. 1658; Jonathan, 29 Mar. 1661; Naomi, 29 Apr. 1664; Ruth, 10 Mar. 1667; and Hannah, 16 Sept. 1670. He d. 7 Aug. 1672, and his wid. m. 12 Sept. 1673, John Pearce, as his sec. w. and d. 18 Aug. 1706. His s. Philip, John, and Samuel had grs. of ld. for serv. in Ind. wars bef. 1679. PHILIP, Gloucester, s. of the preced. m. 22 Nov. 1677, Mary Blackwell, wh. d. 3 Jan. 1679; and he m. 30 Oct. 1683, Esther, d. of Thomas Bray, and had Philip, b. 1690; and other ch. David, both of wh. m. and had fams. SAMUEL, Gloucester, br. of the preced. m. 16 Nov. 1686, Hannah, whose surname Babson saw not, had bef. 1695 five ch. of wh. only Ebenezer is nam. and in that yr. he rem. to Amesbury.

STANYAN, STANNYAN, STANIAN, or STANION, ANTHONY, Boston, had been of Exeter, by w. Mary, says our town rec. had John, b. 16, bapt. 24 July 1642, our ch. rec. show. that he was mem. of the ch. of E.·and thither he soon went back, had there Mary, wh. m. 10 Jan. 1666, John Pickering jr. and perhaps more there or at Hampton, where he was in 1654, m. sec. w. 1 Jan. 1656, Ann, wid. of William Partridge of Salisbury, and took the o. of alleg. 1678. In his MS. Farmer says he was freem. 1644, wh. does not mean of Mass. but of E. where he was town clk. 1647, and rep. of H. in 1654. JOHN, Hampton, s. of the preced. m. 17 Dec. 1663, Mary, d. of Thomas Bradbury of Salisbury. Descend. are found in N. H.

STAPLES, or STAPLE, ABRAHAM, Weymouth, m. 17 Sept. 1660, Mary, d. of Robert Randall of the same, rem. soon aft. and prob. was one of the first sett. of Mendon 1663. His wid. is nam. in the will of her f. 27 Mar. 1691. ABRAHAM, Dorchester 1658, rem. to Weymouth 1660, thence to Mendon, was freem. 1673, by w. Hannah had Ephraim, b. 2 Sept. 1678; and Mary, 8 Feb. 1681; by w. Mary had Benjamin, 27 Dec. 1682; and Hannah, 13 May 1686; but by a third w. Mehitable, perhaps, he had Mehitable, 19 Dec. 1689, d. soon; Mehitable, again, 20 May 1692; Isaac, 10 June 1699; Abraham, 12 Apr. 1702, and Abraham, again, 3 Apr. 1706. If it be object. that these three ws. hav. ch. seem too much for one man's felicity, conject. may be indulg. that the h. of the last w. may have been s. of the former Abraham. EDWARD, Braintree, early, says Farmer. JEFFREY, Weymouth, had Martha, wh. was bur. 17 Feb. 1640. JOHN, Weymouth, freem. 1648, had Rebecca, b. 27 Nov. 1639, and Joseph, 19 Feb. 1642. Farmer names, also, Increase, of wh. no other report is found. But prob. he had, also, John; and d. in 1658, or bef. I guess the name of his w. was Margery, for a deed of two parcels of ld. in W. 10 Jan. 1659 is found in our Vol. III. of the registr. convey. to James Priest of W. by Margery Staples, wid. of W. JOHN, Weymouth, prob. s. of the preced. by w. Sarah had John, b. 3 Nov. 1672; and Thomas, 19 Apr. 1674; and perhaps he rem. across the brook that div. W. from Braintree, where one John d. 30 Aug. 1692, and ano. John d. 5 Nov. 1700. JOSEPH, Taunton, prob. s. of John the first of Weymouth, had John, b. 28 Jan. 1671; Amy or Ann, 13 Apr. 1674; Mary, 26 Jan. 1678; Joseph, 12 Mar. 1680; Hannah, 17 May 1682; and Nathaniel, 22 Mar. 1685. SAMUEL, Braintree, m. 30 Aug. 1652, Mary Coles, had Mary, b. 24 Sept. 1655; Rachel, 31 Oct. 1657; and Sarah, 10 July 1660. THOMAS, Fairfield 1645, is on freem.'s list 1669. He had by w. Mary, Thomas; Mary, wh. m. Josiah Harvey; ano. d. m. John Beach; Mehitable; and John; but the order of success. is not kn. He d. bef. 1688; was a man of import. and spirit eno. to prosecute Dept. Gov. Ludlow, not long bef. his rem. to Virg. for defam. in report. that the w. of S. was a witch. The trial for satisfact. of both parties was in the neighb. Col. of New Haven, where the Court wisely held, "that there was no proof that goodw. S. was a witch," mulct. L. to pay £10 to the h. for repar. of his w's. name, and £5 for his trouble and cost. Happily in a later day the New Haven Col. pass. unharm. by the doleful delus. spread in Mass. by rampant vanity and insane apprehension. Four of this name had, in 1834, been gr. at Yale, and three at some other N. E. coll. says Farmer.

STAPLETON, SAMUEL, Newport, came from London, hav. m. Mary White of Newport Pagnel, Co. Bucks, and here had Mary, b. 7 Feb. 1679; Ann, 20 Jan. 1680; Mary, and Eliz. tw. 7 June 1681; and Samuel, 28 Sept. 1682.

STAR, or STARR, BENJAMIN, New Haven, may have been s. of Thomas of Charlestown, perhaps of N. Hampsh. 1673, m. 23 Dec. 1675, Eliz. d. of the sec. Isaac Allerton, had Allerton, b. 6 Jan. 1677. He d. 1678, and his wid. m. 22 July 1679, Simon Eyre the third. COMFORT, Cambridge, surgeon, or physician, of Ashford in Co. Kent, came in the Hercules 1635, from Sandwich, with three ch. and three serv. and prob. w. Eliz. perhaps had one or more ch. in this country; was of Duxbury 1638, or by dif. rep. 1642, thence to Boston aft. 1643, and his w. d. 25 June 1658, aged 63. He d. 2 Jan. 1660, and left s. John excor. of his will made 22 Apr. 1659, pro. 2 Feb. foll. In it, beside to John and his three ch. he gives to five ds. of d. Maynard dec. £10 ea. as they come to 16 yrs. of age; to the childr. of s. Thomas dec. £10 apiece, as they come to 18 yrs. of age, as also to the four youngest of them, an addit. legacy; to his gr.ch. Simon Eyre £6 per an. until he came to 18 yrs. to help him to learning in the tongues, &c. to d. Eliz. Ferniside, w. of John, a resid. dev. to be div. betw. her three ch. to d. Hannah, if she wd. come to N. E. such a piece of plate, but all his

debts in O. E. and £50 out of his rents in Ashford, or as he spelt it,
Eshitisford, to s. Comfort, and his heirs, the ho. and ld. at Ashford ; and
to d. Eliz. the ld. on wh. her present dwel. ho. is built, from the hi. way
back to the mill pond, and to his d.-in-law, wid. of Thomas. Of this will
Mr. Trask has pub. much larger abstr. than mine, in Geneal. Reg. IX.
223, 4. COMFORT, Boston, s. of the first Comfort, brot. by his f. from
Eng. where he was b. a. 1624, educ. at Harv. Coll. where he took his
A. B. 1647, in the Catal. call. Consolantius, is one of the five fellows
nam. in the Chart. of H. C. in 1650, and soon went home, and was
benefic. at Carlisle, Co. Cumberland, and from that liv. eject. by the
Act of Uniform. 1662, retn. to a preach. station at Lewes, Co. Sussex,
where he d. says Calamy, 1711. COMFORT, Middletown, s. of Thomas
of Charlestown, m. Rachel Harris, had Comfort, b. 1670 ; Mary, 1672 ;
Hannah, 24 Mar. 1674; Joseph, 1676; Benjamin, 1679; Rachel,
1681 ; Thomas, 1684; and Daniel, 1689; Hinman, 239, mak. his wid.
Mary, when he d. 18 Oct. 1693. But I judge, that he was first of Boston, here by w. Mary, prob. d. of Joseph Weld, as more exactly our
rec. show, bef. his rem. had Comfort, b. 15 Nov. 1666 ; Joseph, 7 Mar.
1668, perhaps d. soon ; Mary, 14 Mar. 1669, d. soon ; and Mary, again,
18 Jan. 1672. Of course this Comfort of Boston might be thot. a
differ. man from him of M.; yet he could hardly be that Comfort, the
gr. of Harv. But he may, in spite of Hinman, well be the Middletown
man. COMFORT, Dedham, prob. s. of John of Boston, m. Mary, d. of
the sec. Simon Stone of Watertown, had a ch. bapt. 20 Feb. 1687 ;
Lydia, 7 June 1688; and Hannah, 6 July 1690; all at Watertown, as
Bond, in Hist. 585, correct. on p. 951, exhibits. ELEAZER, Boston
1664, cooper, s. of the sec. John, by w. Martha had Abigail, b. 26 Nov.
1681 ; Joseph, 26 Aug. 1687 ; and Benjamin, 7 Mar. 1692. Of the
earlier w. and a d. that Winsor names, I find no trace. JOHN, Boston,
s. of the first Comfort, prob. b. in Eng. had, says Winsor, been at Duxbury 1643, and Bridgewater 1645, by w. Martha had Comfort, b. 4 Feb.
1662 ; John, 7 Dec. 1664; Comfort, again, 15 Nov. 1666 ; and Benjamin, 19 Aug. 1667, prob. rem.; may have had others earlier, and ano.
JOHN, of Boston, a housewright, d. in the winter of 1703–4, and admin.
of his small est. was in Jan. 1704 giv. to his s. Eleazer, and I kn. no
more of him. JOSIAH, Danbury, s. of Thomas the sec. prob. the youngest, had, says Hinman, Benjamin and Comfort. ROBERT, Salem, m. a
d. of the first Richard Hollingsworth, was a sea capt. ROBERT, wh.
was k. by the Ind. in Philip's war, may have been s. of William of
Lynn, and his inv. was pro. at Essex prob. Ct. on 24 June 1679.
SAMUEL, New London 1663, m. 25 Dec. 1664, Hannah, d. of Jonathan
Brewster, had Samuel, b. 11 Dec. 1665 ; Thomas, 27 Sept. 1668 ;

Comfort, bapt. Aug. 1671; Jonathan, 1674; and Benjamin, 1679. Miss Caulkins, with good reason, thinks him eldest s. of Thomas, and that he d. early in 1688, for his wid. execut. a deed 2 Feb. of that yr. He prob. is that kinsman, to wh. his gr.f. gave the "Book of Martyrs." His s. Thomas, Jonathan, and Benjamin contin. the name at N. L. and Norwich. The progeny of Jonathan have been not. for longev. THOMAS, Boston, younger br. of the first Comfort, a surgeon, had come prob. soon aft. or even with him, from Canterbury, Co. Kent, and brot. w. Susan, and one ch. serv. as our Col. rec. shows, in the Pequot war, 1637, and d. perhaps 1640, for in Mar. 1641, his w. Susan had gr. of admin. by our Gen. Ct. THOMAS, Duxbury 1639, s. of the first Comfort, b. in Eng. had serv. in the Pequot war, and rem. early from D. and liv. at Scituate, where his s. Comfort was b. in 1644, and Eliz. in 1646; but rem. again to Yarmouth, where he had former. been, for he was there fin. with others, as a scoffer at religion [Felt, Eccles. Hist. I. 496], and there had Benjamin, 6 Feb. 1648; and Jehosaphat, 12 Jan. 1650. By his profess. it was diffic. to live in so sm. towns, and he rem. to Charlestown, there was clk. of the writs 1654, in wh. yr. his d. Constant d. and William was b. wh. d. 13 Dec. 1657; Josiah had been 1 Sept. bef. that, by w. Rachel, as the rec. of C. tells; and he was a householder, with small income, 1658, and d. in this yr. 26 Oct. leav. w. Rachel. Neither he nor his w. was mem. of the ch. Winsor says right. that he d. bef. his f. while Thacher, whose Med. Biog. has many similar errors, extends his life to 1670. Gr. of 400 acres to his desolate wid. and eight small ch. will be found in Vol. IV. pt. I. p. 355 of our Col. Rec. WILLIAM, Lynn, d. 5 Feb. 1666, and admin. was giv. to Robert S. on 12 of same mo. but the rec. titles him late sojourner in Boston, of Devonsh. wh. depart. this life on his going to Salem on 6th inst. Fifteen of this name had, says Farmer, MS. been gr. in 1834, at the N. E. coll. of wh. eight were of Yale alone, and four of Harv.

STARBOARD, or STARBIRD, THOMAS, perhaps of Dover, m. 4 Jan. 1688, Abigail Dam, wh. may have been d. of John, had Jethro, b. 28 Aug. 1689; Thomas, 19 Oct. 1691; Agnes, 4 Oct. 1693; Abigail, 29 Sept. 1695; Eliz. 15 Feb. 1699; John, 10 Mar. 1701; and Samuel, 22 Apr. 1704.

STARBUCK, *EDWARD, Dover 1640, came from Derbysh. as is said, m. Eunice or Catharine Reynolds, said to be from Wales, had s. Nathaniel, b. 1636, and Jethro, ds. Sarah, Abigail, and Esther, beside Dorcas, wh. went to Nantucket, and m. William Gayer; was Elder of the ch. rep. 1643, and rem. with his ch. 1660, aft. hav. been prosecut. for his relig. 1648, as a Bapt. and in short course bec. a

Quaker. He was long happy at the new sett. in wh. he was the chief promoter, a. 1660, of Nantucket, and d. by one report, 12 June 1690, in 86th yr. or by ano. 4 Feb. 1691, aged 86. Sarah m. at D. first William Story, wh. d. a. 1658; next Joseph Austin, wh. d. a. 1663; and, third, m. as his sec. w. Humphrey Varney; Abigail m. Peter Coffin; and his youngest d. Esther m. Humphrey Varney. JETHRO, Nantucket, s. of the preced. d. 27 May 1663, by a cart run. over him; but whether he had been m. or what was his age, are unkn. JETHRO, Nantucket, s. of Nathaniel, m. 6 Dec. 1694, his cous. Dorcas, d. of William Gayer. NATHANIEL, Nantucket, s. of Edward, b. prob. in Eng. had sold to Peter Coffin in 1661 his est. at Dover, and rem. to N. prob. with his f. m. Mary, d. of Tristram Coffin, a woman of super. power of mind, wh. d. 13 Nov. 1717, aged 72; and he d. 6 Aug. 1719. They had Mary, b. 30 Mar. 1663, call. the first b. at N.; Eliz. 9 Sept. 1665; Nathaniel, 9 Aug. 1668; Jethro, 14 Dec. 1671; Eunice, 11 Apr. 1674; Hepzibah, 2 Apr. 1680; and Paul. Mary m. James Gardner; Eliz. m. 15 Aug. 1682, Peter Coffin jr. and next, Nathaniel Barker; Eunice m. George Gardner, and is said to have d. 26 Oct. 1772; and Hepzibah m. Thomas Hathaway.

STARKE, or START, AARON, Hartford 1639, or Windsor 1643, an unpromis. youth, subject. by sentence of Court to whip. rem. to New London 1655, near Stonington, freem. 1669; d. a. 1685, leav. s. Aaron, John, William, and had ds. wh. m. John Fish and Josiah Haynes. JOHN, Boston, "Scottish-man," serv. to Lieut. William Hudson, d. 22 May 1652;" was one of the unhappy prisoners, prob. tak. on the bloody field of Dunbar, 3 Sept. 1650, sent over here next yr. to be sold for such a term of yrs. that left no hope to the suffer. ROBERT, Concord, d. 1646. See Geneal. Reg. VIII. 57. WILLIAM, Lynn 1641.

STARKEY, GEORGE, H. C. 1646, may have been of Lynn, or Malden, but very little ground in favor of either is discernab. Nor is any knowl. likely to be got, other than of his d. in London, Sept. 1665, where he had bestow. his serv. dur. the terrible plague, hav. made hims. acquaint. with medicine, as is relat. in the letters of Allin, the reverend grad. of 1643. For the credit of the new-born Harv. Coll. at Cambridge in N. E. the metropolis of their native ld. in its most dismal visitat. was indebt. to a grad. of its sec. yr. and to ano. of its fifth yr. of bestow. such honors, when the time-honor. university, so many thousand miles nearer, perhaps, gave far less contrib. of educ. skill to her relief.

STARKWEATHER, JOHN, Ipswich 1684, s. of Robert, had w. Ann, and ch. John, b. 16 Sept. 1680; Robert, 12 Nov. 1684; and Richard, 25 Dec. 1686. All these ch. were of Stonington 1705, and in that town or neighb. m. and perpetua. the name. His s. John was gr.f. of the late

Hon. Ezra S. of Worthington, one of the most valua. men in Hampsh.
ROBERT, Roxbury, had w. Jennet, a mem. of the ch. and ch. Eliz. bapt.
23 July 1643 ; Lydia, 23 June 1644 ; John, 1646 ; Deborah, 27 Aug.
1648 ; he sold his est. at R. and rem. to Ipswich 1651, there d. 1674,
and 4 Nov. of that yr. his wid. had admin. By tradit. four other ch. are
ment. but not nam.

STARLING, or STERLING, WILLIAM, freem. 1681, liv. at Haverhill
1677, m. Ann, wid. of the sec. John Neal, perhaps as sec. or third w.
and rem. to Lyme.

START, EDWARD, York 1655, in Farmer's MS. by me presum. to be
that freem. of 1652, call. Stirt. He d. 19 May 1671, leav. sev. ch. of
wh. only Thomas is nam. and wid. Willmott, wh. m. William Roanes.

STAWERS. See Stowers.

STEARNS, CHARLES, Watertown, freem. 1646, bot. 1648, est. of
Edward Lamb, by w. Hannah had Samuel, b. 2 June 1650. His w. d.
July 1651, and he m. 22 June 1654, Rebecca, d. of John Gibson of
Cambridge, had Shubael, 20 Sept. 1655 ; John, 24 Jan. 1657 ; both at
C. but at W. Isaac, Charles, Rebecca, and Martha ; soon aft. 1681 was
of Lynn, there d. bef. 1695. His s. Charles d. in the army bef. his f.
Rebecca m. 25 Jan. 1693, Thomas Stearns ; and Martha m. a Hutchinson. ISAAC, Watertown 1630, came prob. with Sir Richard Saltonstall
in the fleet, was adm. freem. 18 May of next yr. tho. he may have been
drawn thither as much by regard for Winthrop, since he was not a dist.
neighb. of the Gov. in their native ld. He was of Neyland, Co. Suff'k.
where his two eldest ch. were bapt. ; Mary, 6 Jan. 1627 ; and Ann, 5
Oct. 1628. Here by w. Mary (tho. Dr. Cogswell in Geneal. Reg. I. 43,
calls Sarah mo. of John) had John, b. perhaps the first yr. ; Isaac, 6
Jan. 1633 ; Sarah, 22 Sept. 1635 ; tho. this by Pulsifer in Geneal. Reg.
VII. 159 is giv. careless. as ch. of I. and M. *Storie ;* Samuel, 24 Apr.
1638 ; Eliz. and Abigail. He d. 19 June 1671, and his will of 14 of
that mo. provides for w. Mary, for ch. of his s. John ; for the ch. of his
d. Mary, dec. besides special remem. of Isaac and Mary ; for the ch. of
ds. Sarah, Eliz. and Abigail sever. ment. his kinsman Charles S. and
makes his own s. Isaac, and Samuel excors. His wid. d. 2 Apr. 1677.
Prob. he is the ancest. of near. all of his nam. sev. thousand in number,
in Mass. but sure. Farmer should have qualif. his universality. He
was on the first jury that tr. civ. cause in N. E. when large dams. were
giv. against Endicott for assault on Thomas Dexter in May 1631. His
d. Mary m. 9 July 1646, Isaac Learned, and d. bef. her f. Ann m. 25
Dec. 1650, Henry Freeman ; Sarah m. 7 June 1655, deac. Samuel Stone ;
Eliz. m. 13 Apr. 1664, Samuel Manning ; and Abigail m. 27 Apr. 1666,
deac. John Morse. ISAAC, Cambridge, s. of the preced. liv. in that part,

call. the Farms, now Lexington, m. 24 June 1660, Sarah, d. of Capt. Richard Beers, had Sarah, b. 14 Jan. 1662; Mary, 8 Oct. 1663; Isaac, 26 Aug. 1665; Samuel, 11 Jan. 1668; Abigail; and John, 1675; and d. 2 Aug. 1676. His wid. m. 23 July 1677, Thomas Wheeler; of ds. Sarah m. 27 Dec. 1678, John Wheeler; Mary m. 1 Jan. 1694, John Cutler; and Abigail m. 29 Nov. 1692, Samuel Hartwell. ISAAC, Salem, s. of Charles, by w. Hannah had Rebecca, b. 15 Jan. 1685; Isaac, 28 July 1687; and John, 20 Dec. 1690; and d. soon aft. His wid. m. Dec. 1694, John Chapman. JOHN, Billerica, s. of the first Isaac, one of the first sett. of B. m. Sarah, only d. of Isaac Mixer, had John, b. May 1654, first b. of the town rec. and Isaac, wh. d. young. His w. d. 18 June 1656, and he m. Dec. foll. at Barnstable, Mary, d. of Thomas Lothrop, had Isaac, again, 17 Apr. 1658, wh. d. young; Samuel, 3 Sept. 1659; Isaac, again, 23 Dec. 1661; Nathaniel, 30 Nov. 1663, d. young; and Thomas, 6 Dec. 1665. He d. 5 Mar. 1669, and his wid. m. 6 May foll. Capt. William French, and in 1684 bec. third w. of Isaac Mixer, and long outliv. him. JOHN, Malden, a capt. m. Joanna, wid. of Jacob Parker, and she d. 4 Dec. 1737, aged 78. JOHN, Watertown, s. of Charles, m. a. 1681, Judith d. of George Lawrence, of the same, had Rebecca, b. 21 Mar. 1683; Judith; Sarah; George; and Benjamin, wh. were all bapt. 22 June 1690; John; Thomas; Daniel; Isaac; Mary; Eliz.; and Abigail; this last b. 12 May 1700; all bapt. 11 May 1701; and Charles, 20 Oct. 1702, bapt. 28 Feb. foll. He was freem. 1690, unless it be that this adm. is of the foll. John, as seems more prob. This Watertown man m. sec. w. 2 Apr. 1713, Mary, d. of Richard Norcross, and d. 22 Feb. 1722. JOHN, Billerica, s. of John the first wh. d. 26 Oct. 1728, aged 74, was, I think, the freem. of 1690, and the found. of a very num. line much diffus. * NATHANIEL, Dedham 1647, freem. 2 May 1649, had Samuel, bapt. 25 Nov. 1666; Nathaniel, 6 Dec. 1668; and James, 28 May 1671. Yet I doubt, from the lateness of these dates, that not the freem. of 1649, but ano. Nathaniel of D. perhaps his s. was f.; was a lieut. rep. 1684, 9, 90, and 1. SAMUEL, Watertown, s. of Isaac the first, m. 1 Feb. 1663, Hannah, eldest d. of William Manning, had Samuel, b. 4 May 1664, wh. d. at 7 yrs.; Hannah, 8 Dec. 1666; Nathaniel, 13 Dec. 1668; Sarah, 23 Apr. 1671; Samuel, again, 29 Mar. 1673; Isaac, 31 Dec. 1674; John, 24 June 1677; Mary, 5 Apr. 1679; Abigail, 16 Apr. 1680; and Joseph, 11 Dec. 1682, d. in few mos. He d. 1683, and his wid. d. 16 Feb. 1724, aged near 82 yrs. SAMUEL, Watertown, s. of Charles, by w. Mehitable had Joseph, bapt. 7 Aug. 1698, more than four yrs. after d. of his f. and Samuel, b. 27 Feb. 1686, bapt. 21 Aug. 1698. He d. bef. 6 June 1694, the date of his inv. SHUBAEL, Lynn, eldest s. of Charles, serv. in Philip's war, had Shubael, b. 19 Aug. 1683; Samuel; Hannah; John, 1691; Mary; and perhaps one or two others. In 1834 Farmer notes, that of this name eighteen had been gr. at Harv. two at Yale, and three at other N. E. coll.

STEBBINS, STEBBIN, or STEBBING, in early rec. oft. STIBBIN, STEBBONS, and STUBBING, BENJAMIN, Springfield, s. of Thomas of the same, took o. of fidel. 1678, freem. 1690, m. 9 Oct. 1682, Abigail Denton, perhaps d. of Rev. Richard, but more prob. of Daniel, by first w. wh. may have been s. of Richard; had Abigail, b. 13 Aug. 1683; and Mercy, 29 Oct. 1685. His w. d. 24 or 28 Aug. 1689; he m. 11 Apr. 1690, Mary, wid. of Samuel Ball, had no. ch. by her. He d. 12 Oct. 1698, and his wid. m. 29 Dec. 1704, James Warriner the elder. BENJAMIN, Northampton, youngest s. of John of the same, m. 1709, Mary, d. of David Ashley of Westfield, had Benjamin, b. 15 Sept. 1711; and Gideon, 30 June 1714, wh. d. at 20 yrs. With the other s. he rem. to Belchertown 1741, and there are descend. BENONI, Northampton, s. of John, first of the same, took o. of fidel. 1678, and was adm. freem. 1684, m. Mary, wid. of James Bennet, wh. had been m. only the yr. preced. and whose h. was k. in the morning aft. the Falls fight, 19 May 1676, had Ebenezer, b. 1677; and was tak. by the Ind. 19 Sept. of that yr.; Thankful, 10 Mar. 1680; Abigail, a. 1683; Mindwell, 20 Jan. 1686; rem. to Deerfield, there had Joseph, and Esther, tw. Feb. 1689; and the mo. d. 2 Aug. foll. He m. a. 1691, Hannah, wid. of Joseph Edwards, and had Benjamin, 1692; and Esther, 1695. He was k. 29 Feb. 1704 at the assault by the Fr. and Ind. his wid. m. Thomas French, wh. had lost most of his fam. in the same assault; but most of the ch. d. young. DANIEL, New London, s. of John of same, m. Bethia, d. of Daniel Comstock. *EDWARD, Cambridge 1633, freem. 14 May 1634, rem. with the early sett. to Hartford, was rep. oft. aft. 1639 to 56; had sev. ch. but no s. He d. 1663; and his wid. whose name was Frances, d. ten yrs. later. His d. Mary m. 29 Apr. 1648, Walter Gaylord; Eliz. m. first Robert Wilson, and next, Thomas Cadwell in 1658; Lydia m. deac. John Wilson; and ano. d. m. in Eng. John Chester. He call. Elizur Holyoke his br.-in-law and speaks of dear sis. H. EDWARD, Springfield, s. of Thomas of the same, freem. 1690; m. Apr. 1679, Sarah Graves, d. of Isaac or John, had Sarah, b. 20 Feb. 1682; Thomas, Oct. 1685, d. soon; Thomas, again, 7 Mar. 1687; Mary, 11 Sept. 1689, d. soon; John, 10 Jan. 1693; Mary, again, 2 Jan. 1696, d. at 2 yrs. His w. d. 12 June 1700, and he m. 18 Oct. 1701, Mary, wid. of Isaac Colton, and d. 31 Oct. 1712. Increase is nam. by Farmer, as of Springfield 1650, but I fear it is an error. JOHN, Watertown, by w. Mary or Margaret had John b. 25 Mar. 1640; and Mary, 6 Aug. 1641, may as Miss Caulkins suppos. have rem. to New London in its earliest day ; but his w. was Margaret wh. d. 1 Jan. 1679. He was constable 1660, and d. a. 1685. Three ch. are ment. John, Daniel, and the w. of John Marshall of Hartford, of wh. all may have been b. as we are sure John was, bef. sett. of N. L. JOHN, Roxbury, a baker, freem. 1647, m. 17 Apr. 1644, Ann Munke, of wh. all that is kn. is unpleas. as Ellis quotes from the venerab. ch. rec. "She was of so violent passion, that she offer. violence to her h. wh. being of such infamy, she was cast out of the ch." But she d. 3 Apr. 1680, aged 50 ; and he improv. his freedom by m. 4 June foll. wid. Rebecca Hawkins, and d. 4 Dec. 1681, aged 70. JOHN, Northampton, s. of Rowland, b. in Eng. m. 14 May 1646, a wid. Ann, and had John, b. 28 Jan. 1647 ; Thomas, wh. d. 24 Apr. 1649 ; Ann, 10 Apr. 1651, d. at two yrs.; Edward, 12 July 1653, d. at 3 mos.; Benoni, 23 June 1655 ; had liv. prob. at Springfield until 1656. The d. of his w. is not found on rec. at S. or N. but at N. he m. 17 Dec. 1657, sec. w. Abigail, d. of Robert Bartlet, had Samuel, 21 Jan. 1659 ; Abigail, 24 Sept. 1660 ; Thomas, 6 May 1662, d. at 27 yrs.; Hannah, 8 July 1664 ; Mary, 10 Sept. 1666 ; Sarah, 4 June 1668 ; Joseph, 17 Jan. 1670, d. at 11 yrs.; Deborah, 5 Mar. 1672 ; Benjamin, bapt. 3 May 1674 ; Rebecca, bapt. 20 Feb. 1676 ; and Thankful, b. 11 May 1678. He d. 7 Mar. 1679, leav. twelve ch. His wid. m. 28 Dec. 1681, Jedediah Strong, had two or more ch. and d. 15 July 1689. All the 7 ds. m. well, and some very young. Abigail m. 1678, William Phelps ; Hannah m. 5 Nov. 1679, being not much over 15 yrs. John Sheldon, of N.; Mary m. 17 Nov. 1683, Thomas Strong; Sarah m. 1687, William Southwell; Deborah m. a. 1690, Benjamin Alvord; Rebecca m. 1697, Nathaniel Strong, of N. ; and Thankful m. 10 July 1700, Jerijah Strong. Oft. this man is call. Edmund, as by Farmer, and in the list of freem. appears as abbrev. Edm. but the real name was as here giv. JOHN, New London, s. of the first John, m. a. 1663, Deborah, by Caulkins thot. to be d. of Miles Moore. JOHN, a soldier of Maudsley's comp. 9 Dec. 1675, may have been of Boston, but no acco. of him is gain. JOHN, Deerfield, eldest s. of John of Northampton, m. Dorothy Alexander, sis. of Robert, wh. to her and brs. and sis. div. his est. had John, and Abigail, of whose b. the date is not found ; Samuel, b. 1688 ; Thankful, 1691 ; Ebenezer, 1694 ; and Joseph, 1699. He suffer. from the French and Ind. when they destroy. D. 29 Feb. 1704, when his w. and the six ch. were car. away to Canada, whence exc. f. mo. and s. John they came not back. He died 20 yrs. aft. the captiv. in his will, giv. all his est. to John, but ea. of the five in Canada should have a share, if he came to live in N. E. JOSEPH, Springfield, s. of Thomas the first, took o. of fidel. 1678, was freem. 1681, m. 27 Nov. 1673, Sarah, d. of Anthony

Dorchester of the same, had Joseph, b. 4 Oct. 1674; Benjamin, 23 Jan.
1677; Thomas, 13 July 1679 ; John, 22 Sept. 1681, k. casual. at 5 yrs.;
Mehitable, 27 Nov. 1683; Ebenezer, 8 June 1686; Sarah, 8 June
1688; John, again, 8 Nov. 1690; Hannah, 9 Nov. 1692; and Martha,
28 June 1697; and d. 15 Oct. 1728. His wid. d. 18 Aug. 1746, aged
almost 93. The late sagacious Gov. Strong descend. from Mehitable.
MARTIN, Roxbury, a brewer, m. 25 Dec. 1639, Jane Green, had Hannah, b. 23 Oct. 1640; Mary, 1, bapt. 5 Feb. 1643; and Nathaniel, bapt.
23 Mar. 1645; rem. soon to Boston, and there his w. d. 24 July 1659.
ROWLAND, Springfield, came from Ipswich, Co. Suff'k. in the Francis,
1634, aged, as the custom ho. rec. says, 40, with w. Sarah, 43, and four
ch. Thomas, 14; Sarah, 11; John, 8; and Eliz. 6; beside Mary Winch,
perhaps a relat. The fam. Memoir says, he first sett. at Roxbury, where
however is no ment. of him, but he prob. went with Pyncheon, found.
of S. the next yr. aft. land. at Boston in June. At S. his w. d. 4 Oct.
1649; and he some yrs. later rem. to Northampton, there d. 14 Dec.
1671. In his will of 1 Mar. 1670 he names only the ch. brot. from
Eng. Sarah had m. 14 Jan. 1641, Thomas Merrick; and Eliz. m. 2
Mar. 1647, John Clark, both of Springfield. SAMUEL, Springfield,
eldest s. of Thomas, m. 22 July 1679, Joanna, d. of John Lamb, had a
s. b. and d. 1680; Thomas, b. 26 Dec. 1681, d. soon; and Samuel, 13
May 1683. His w. d. 8 Aug. foll. and he m. 10 Dec. 1685, Abigail
Brooks, had John, 13 Feb. 1687; Ebenezer, 30 Nov. 1688; William,
27 July 1693; Abigail, 30 Nov. 1695; Joanna, 4 Mar. 1697; Thomas,
again, 10 Aug. 1698; Benjamin, 10 Dec. 1700; and Mercy, 19 June
1705; was adm. freem. 1690, and d. 13 July 1708, leav. wid. and the
last nine of the eleven ch. SAMUEL, Northampton, s. of John, m. 4
Mar. 1678, Mary, d. of John French of the same, had Mercy, b. 1683;
and Samuel, 1689; both prob. d. bef. the mo. wh. was aband. this last
yr. by her h. He rem. to Boston, or R. I. or both, and on 14 Mar.
1692, was m. in R. I. by a clerg. of the Episc. communion to Sarah
Williams, but whether by her he had any issue is not kn. His w. sought
for divorce in 1695, and alleg. that he had sev. ch. by that woman ; but
perhaps she obt. divorce only by her d. 26 Jan. 1697. He came back to
Mass. aft. few yrs. sat down 1727 at Belchertown, there d. 3 Sept. 1732.
THOMAS, Springfield, eldest s. of Rowland, b. in Eng. m. Nov. 1645,
Hannah, d. of deac. Samuel Wright, had Samuel, b. 19 Sept. 1646;
Thomas, 31 July 1648; Joseph, 18 May 1650, d. next yr.; Joseph,
again, 24 Oct. 1652; Sarah, 18 Aug. 1654; Edward, 14 Apr. 1656;
Benjamin, 11 Apr. 1658; Hannah, 1 Oct. 1660, d. a. 17 yrs. and tw.
Rowland, 2 Oct. 1660, d. next yr. His w. d. 16 Oct. 1660, and he m. 14
Dec. 1676, Abigail, wid. of Benjamin Mun, d. of Henry Burt, wh. had

been wid. of Francis Ball. He was a lieut. and d. as says the fam.
mem. in Geneal. Reg. V. 352, 15 Sept. and Farmer says 25 Sept. 1683.
THOMAS, Springfield, s. of the preced. m. 21 Dec. 1672, Abigail, d. of
Benjamin Mun, had Thomas, b. 28 Jan. 1674, d. next yr. ; Abigail, 27
May 1675, d. young; Hannah, 29 Dec. 1677, d. soon ; Hannah, again,
22 Dec. 1680 ; Thomas, again, 13 Nov. 1682, d. in two yrs.; a d. b. and
d. 1685 ; Sarah, 17 Apr. 1686; Mary, 1 Nov. 1688 ; and Abigail, again,
b. and d. 1692. His w. d. 5 Feb. 1692 or 3, and he m. 12 Apr. 1694,
Mary, wid. of Samuel Ely. He sw. fidel. 1678, was freem. 1690, and
d. 7 Dec. 1695. Next yr. 11 Dec. his wid. m. deac. John Coleman of
Hatfield. THOMAS, Northampton, s. of John of the same, m. 16 Sept.
1684, Eliz. d. of . . . . . Wright, had Eliz. 31 Oct. 1685 ; Thomas, 2
June 1689 ; Josiah, Sept. 1694 ; Hannah, whose date of b. is not found;
Joseph, 30 Mar. 1697 ; Experience, 14 Mar. 1699, d. young; Asahel,
10 Apr. 1701 ; Experience, again, 18 Mar. 1703 ; and Mary, 26 Dec.
1705. He d. 28 Apr. 1712, and his wid. m. 1715, John Hannum.
Under date of 3 Nov. 1685, in his Diary, Sewall notes, that one S. of
Watertown was fin. with James Bigelow, "for insult. Lt. Gov. Stoughton
and Dudley." No doubt this was a political offence. But in Dr. Bond's
Geneal. Reg. of W. tho. he notes this suffering of Bigelow, the name of
Stebbins for many yrs. bef. had disapp. Of this name, in 1816, there
had been gr. six at Yale, and one at Harv.

STEDMAN, ancient. STUDMAN, AUGUSTINE, Newbury 1678, sw.
alleg. that yr. then aged 40. GEORGE, Charlestown, m. 4 Apr. 1674,
Hannah Coburn, had William, b. 20 Mar. 1675 ; Hannah, 16 Oct.
1677; Sarah, 13 Aug. 1683 ; and Mary, 27 May 1686; all bapt. 17
Apr. 1687, his w. join. the ch. 25 Sept. foll. and the rec. says the bapt.
was by mistake. ISAAC, Scituate, came from London in the Elizabeth
1635, aged 30, tho. his name is not seen in the print. list, with w. Eliz.
26; and s. Nathaniel, 5; and Isaac, 1, join. Lothrop's ch. 17 July
1636, had at S. Eliz. bapt. 26 Nov. 1637; Thomas ; and Sarah; rem.
1650, to Boston, liv. at Muddy riv. was a merch. d. 1678, says Deane.
His will of 2 Oct. in that yr. provides for s. Nathaniel, and Thomas, ds.
Eliz. Haman, i. e. Hammond, w. of the sec. Thomas ; Hannah, w. of
Samuel Hyde; and Sarah, w. of Thomas Perry. JOHN, Cambridge,
came, in 1638, with Rev. Josse Glover, wh. d. on the voyage, freem. 13
May 1640. His w. Alice, prob. brot. from Eng. d. 6 Mar. 1690, aged
as gr. stone says, a. 80, and he d. 16 Dec. 1693, aged 92. He was oft.
selectman betw. 1640 and 76, and ensign 1645, had ds. Eliz. Sarah, b.
11 Jan. 1644; and Martha, 3 June 1646; all bapt. at C. Eliz. m. 5
Mar. 1662, Nathaniel Upham, wh. d. 15 days aft.; and she m. 27 Apr.
1669, Henry Thompson of Boston; and last, John Sharp ; outliv. him,

and d. 9 Mar. 1700, aged 58. Sarah m. 23 Aug. 1662, John Bracket of Boston, and sec. m. Dr. Samuel Alcock, and next Thomas Graves, and fourth, Hon. John Phillips, outliv. him, and d. 1 Mar. 1731 ; and Martha m. 4 Dec. 1665, Joseph Cooke, the younger. JOHN, Hartford, had John, b. 5 Apr. 1651 ; Mary, 24 Sept. 1653 ; Thomas, 9 Oct. 1655 ; Robert, 1 Feb. 1658 ; Samuel, 27 Feb. 1660 ; and Eliz. 9 Nov. 1665. He was few yrs. at Wethersfield, made freem. 1654, yet I find not his name in the list of 1669, was a lieut. and in the early part of Philip's war com. the dragoons, but d. in Dec. 1675. JOHN, Cambridge, s. of Robert, m. 14 May 1666, Eliz. Remington, d. of the first John, had John, b. 22 Aug. 1668 ; and Eliz. wh. d. 15 July 1676 ; and he d. of smallpox, 24 Nov. 1678. His wid. m. 14 July 1679, Samuel Gibson. NATHANIEL, Cambridge, s. prob. of Isaac, b. in Eng. m. it is suppos. Sarah, d. of the first Thomas Hammond, had Sarah, and Eliz. provid. for by the will of gr.f. Hammond, wh. ment. that his d. their mo. was d. bef. 30 Sept. 1675, when that will, without date, says Jackson, was brot. in. ROBERT, Cambridge 1638, freem. 14 Mar. 1639, by w. Ann had a d. b. 14 Sept. 1638, d. young; John, 27 Dec. 1642; Mary, 27 Apr. 1645, wh. m. 1 Apr. 1674, Daniel Thurston; and Thomas, wh. d. 9 Apr. 1659, prob. quite young ; and d. 20 Jan. 1666. His wid. liv. beyond 10 Dec. 1674, but d. bef. Nov. 1676. THOMAS, New London 1649, of wh. Caulkins was unable to find more but that he soon disapp. may have been f. of the sec. John, and of Thomas, whether he d. at N. L. or rem. THOMAS, Boston, of that pt. call. Muddy riv. now Brookline, m. Mary, d. of John Watson of Roxbury, bef. 1671, had Thomas, Joshua, Joseph, and Mary, all nam. with legacies in the will of their uncle John W. 1693. THOMAS, New London, mariner, perhaps s. of Thomas of the same, certain. br. of John of Wethersfield, m. 6 Aug. 1668, Hannah, d. of Robert Isbell, had John, b. 25 Dec. 1669 ; and Ann ; and d. 1701. His wid. m. John Fox; and Ann m. Benjamin Lester. In our Reg. of Suffk. is a deed to him, of 23 Nov. 1671, from Wampas, an Ind. seaman of Boston, of 110 acres lying betw. Marlborough and Mendon ; but I think the considerat. does not appear. Five of this name at Harv. and two at Yale had been gr. in 1801.

STEDWELL, STUDWELL, or STEADWELL, JOSEPH, Rye 1683, Greenwich 1697, resolv. therefore to hold to jurisdict. of Conn. THOMAS, Stamford 1667, d. 1670. THOMAS, Greenwich, perhaps s. of the preced. in 1656 adm. the jurisdict. of New Haven, was of Rye 1662–72, but in the disput. claims betw. N. Y. and Conn. came back to G. 1692–97.

STEELE, EBENEZER, Farmington, youngest ch. of Samuel of the same, m. 15 Feb. 1705, Sarah Hart, prob. d. of the sec. Stephen of the same, had Mary, b. 15 June 1706 ; and Sarah, 15 May 1708 ; and d. 6

Oct. 1722. His wid. d. 26 Feb. 1751. *GEORGE, Cambridge 1632 or 3, freem. 14 May 1634, rem. with Hooker to Hartford, had Richard, wh. d. bef. his. f. unm. and he d. 1664. He was of gr. serv. one of the commiss. from Mass. to gov. the first colonists at Conn. and rep. almost every yr. fr. 1637 to 59 inclus. By first w. Rachel, wh. d. 1653, he had John, and Samuel, b. prob. in Eng. But this w. and childr. are by Cothren, it is thot. borrow. from John, his br. His will of 24 May 1663, ment. s. James, to wh. most of his est. was giv. and Eliz. w. of Thomas Watts. Perhaps he had ano. d. b. 1640, wh. m. and had d. Martha; but the fam. geneal. is very obscure. HENRY, Cambridge, nam. in Holmes's Hist. as of that town 1632, 1 Mass. Hist. Coll. VII. p. 10; but as the name never appears again, I think he d. soon, or perhaps went home. JAMES, Hartford 1657, s. of George, but prob. b. in Eng. m. late in life, perhaps as sec. w. Bethia, d. of John Hopkins, wid. of Samuel Stocking; but by former w. had s. James, b. a. 1658; and John, a. 1660, wh. d. bef. his f. beside ds. Sarah, a. 1656; Mary; Eliz.; and Rachel; their mo. perhaps was Ann, d. of John Bishop. He was commissa. for all Conn. forces in Philip's war. JAMES, Wethersfield, s. of Samuel of the same, was a capt. m. 19 July 1687, Ann d. of the first Samuel Welles, had Samuel, b. 1 Oct. 1688; Joseph, 27 Sept. 1690; Prudence, 17 Jan. 1693; Hannah, 18 Mar. 1697; Ann, 28 Oct. 1702; and David, 8 June 1706; and d. 15 May 1713. His wid. m. 20 Nov. 1718, James Judson of Stratford, whose first w. was her cous. JAMES, Hartford, s. of James of the same, m. Sarah Barnard, d. of Bartholomew, had a ch. bapt. 1691; James; Jonathan, b. 1693; Stephen, 1696, Y. C. 1718; Sarah; Eliz.; and Mary; and d. 1712. *JOHN, Cambridge 1632 or 3, by Farmer call. of Dorchester 1630, but without any high authority, was br. of George, freem. 14 May 1634, rep. in Mar. foll. and two next Cts. and in 1636, appoint. with Ludlow, Pynchon and others to admin. governm. over the gr. Exodus to Conn. (wh. was contin. 2 or 3 yrs. in that state of pupilage) rep. very oft. from the first assemb. 1639 to 57; was town clk. of H. until he rem. to Farmington 1645; by w. Rachel, wh. d. 1653, had John, wh. d. bef. his. f. and Samuel, b. in Eng. and ds. Lydia, wh. m. 31 Mar. 1657, James Bird; and Mary, m. (not b. as fam. geneal. pr. p. 7, gives it) the same day, William Judd; beside Daniel, b. 29 Apr. 1645, wh. d. next yr.; and Hannah, wh. d. 1655, prob. unm.; beside Sarah, wh. m. Thomas Judd. He took sec. w. 23 Nov. 1655, Mary, perhaps wid. of Richard Seymour; and d. not (as the vol. of fam. geneal. says) two days aft. the m. but 1664 or 5. His will of 30 Jan. 1664 names w. Mary, s. Samuel, two s.-in-law, William and Thomas Judd, and the three ch. of his dec. s. and Rachel, d. of Samuel. By fam. tradit. he is deriv. from Co. Essex, and this seems prob. eno.

JOHN, Farmington, s. of the preced. b. in Eng. m. 22 Jan. 1646, Mary, or Mercy, d. of Andrew Warner, had Mary, b. 20 Nov. foll.; John, 1650; Samuel, 15 Mar. 1652; and Benoni; and was ens. of the milit. 1651, but d. 1653. His wid. m. William Hills. JOHN, Farmington, s. of the preced. freem. 1677, m. Ruth, d. of deac. Thomas Judd, had Mary, Eliz. bapt. 28 Mar. 1680, not 1678, as print. in Geneal. Reg. XII. 38, wh. was Thursday; Sarah, 25 Nov. 1683; John, 6 Mar. 1687, not 7 Mar. 1686, as print. in fam. geneal.; Rachel, not 2, as print. in fam. geneal. p. 11, wh. was Monday, but prob. 22 June 1689; Ruth; and Ebenezer, 1697, wh. d. young; and d. 26 Aug. 1737 or 8. NICHOLAS, Taunton 1654, then witness to a will, but perhaps not an inhab. as Baylies does not name him. * SAMUEL, Farmington, s. of John the first, m. Mary, d. of James Boosey, had Mary, b. 5 Dec. 1652; Rachel, 30 Oct. 1654; Sarah, bapt. 28 Dec. 1656, but both these have wrong dates of bapt. in fam. geneal.; Samuel, b. 1659, prob. d. young; John, bapt. perhaps 1, certain. not (as print. in Geneal. Reg. XI. 327) 10 Dec. 1661, wh. was Tuesday; James, 1662, or 4, not as pr. in fam. geneal. 31 Aug. 1644, when his mo. was less than nine yrs. old; Hannah, 1668; and Ebenezer, 13 Aug. 1671 (in fam. geneal. mispr. 1701, wh. was 56 yrs. later than his f.'s m. and many aft. his d.), and d. at Wethersfield, 14 Aug. 1685. His will was of 10 June preced.; serv. as rep. 1669–73, ens. 1668, and lieut. 1674. SAMUEL, Hartford, s. of the sec. John, m. 16 Sept. 1680, Mercy, or Mary, d. of Lieut. Gov. William Bradford, had Thomas, b. 9 Sept. 1681; Samuel, and Jerusha, tw. 15 Feb. 1685; William, 20 Feb. 1687; Abiel, 8 Oct. 1693; Daniel, 3 Apr. 1697; and Eliphalet, 23 June 1700; and d. 1710. His wid. d. 1720. Ten of this name, half without final e, had, in 1847, been gr. at Yale, sev. at other N. E. coll. if Farmer be right, wh. I doubt, and two at Harv. of wh. one has double l.

STEERE, JOHN, Providence 1645, took engag. of alleg. in June 1668, m. Hannah, d. of William Wickenden, had John, William, and Thomas, but no dates are found. Descend. are now very num. RICHARD, New London 1690, fined for libel 1695, m. a. 1692, Eliz. wid. of John Wheeler.

STENT, or STINT, ELEAZER, New Haven, had Eleazer, b. mid. Jan. 1645, bapt. 16 Aug. 1646. The wid. m. Thomas Beamont. A d. Eliz. m. 29 Mar. 1666, Thomas Harrison. ELEAZER, Branford 1667, s. prob. of the preced. unit. then in ch. cov. freem. 1672, in Dec. 1682 came to Cambridge to procure Edward Oakes for their min. m. Sarah, d. of John Butler of the same, had Thomas, b. 10 Sept. 1671, d. soon; Dorothy, 13 Sept. 1672; Mary, 28 Nov. 1674, d. young; Eliz. 25 Sept. 1676; Samuel, 5 Mar. 1678; Eleazer, 26 Apr. 1680; Mehitable, 17

Jan. 1682 ; Elnathan, d. very soon; Joseph, 27 Sept. 1691 ; Mehitable, again, 14 Sept. 1699 ; and Hannah, wh. may have been bef. or aft. Elnathan. He was sev. yrs. Clk. of the Ho. of Reps. of the Col. and d. Feb. 1706. His will of 9 Apr. preced. with codic. of 4 Feb. names w. Eliz. Samuel, Eleazer, and Joseph, ds. Dorothy Barnes, Eliz. Tyler, and s. Hannah Tyler.

STEPHENS. See Stevens.

STEPHENSON, ANDREW, Cambridge, brot. from Eng. w. Jane, and d. Deborah, a. six yrs. old, wh. m. Robert Wilson of Sudbury ; and had here Sarah; Rebecca; John, b. 29 Dec. 1644; Mary; Lydia, 2 Aug. 1648; Andrew; and Hannah. BARTHOLOMEW, Dover, s. of Thomas of the same, m. 10 Oct. 1680 Mary Clark, had Mary, b. 21 Sept. 1681 ; Bartholomew, 30 June 1683 ; Joseph, 13 Sept. 1686 ; Eliz. 8 Dec. 1688; Thomas, 28 Dec. 1691 ; Sarah, 21 May 1695 ; Abraham, 8 Nov. 1700 ; and Deborah, 11 Apr. 1709; and he was k. by the Ind. 8 May aft. JOHN, Boston, shoemaker, by w. Sarah had Onesimus, b. 26 Dec. 1643, bapt. 24 Mar. foll. this ch. Farmer had giv. to Henry Stephens, prob. by the error of his transcriber, but from F. Dearborn had tak. the mistake into the valuab. list of inhabs. of B. for first 26 yrs. that is found in his Boston Notions, 42–65 ; John, bapt. 28 Sept. 1645, a. 5 days old; Joseph, wh. d. 10 Sept. 1652; James, 1 Oct. 1653 ; and Sarah, 6 Feb. 1656. His wid. m. 4 July 1659, Rev. William Blaxton, and his s. JOHN went with his mo. to the farm of her h. on Blackstone riv. there had pt. of Blaxton's domain assign. to him by the Plymouth Ct. and d. 16 Sept. 1695. Daggett. MARMADUKE, Boston 1659, a quaker, call. to prophesy, he said, in 1656, from Yorksh. compan. with William Robinson in suffering, wh. as well as S. was little above 20 yrs. old, when convict. of the offence, sentenc. to d. 20 Oct. of that yr. and execut. 27 ; on wh. sad delus. of our judges wh. thot. they "were doing God serv." John Hull, in his Diary, remarks : "most of the godly have cause to rejoice, and bless the Lord, that strengthens our magistrates and deputies to bear witness against such blasphemies." See, also, Hutch. I. 199. THOMAS, Dover bef. 1641, had Margaret, wh. m. bef. 1663, William Williams ; Thomas, 1654 ; Joseph ; and Bartholomew, bef. ment. perhaps first b. Mary, m. 5 Apr. 1667, Enoch Hutchins ; d. 7 Dec. 1663, his w. Margaret hav. d. eleven days bef. THOMAS, Newtown, L. I. 1655, sec. nam. in the patent 1686, in wh. yr. appear Edward and Jonathan, also freeholders, perhaps his s. as may have been John, of the same place in 1666. His d. Abigail m. Daniel Whitehead. Easily this name appears as Stevenson.

STEPNEY, FRANCIS, Boston 1685, a dancing-master, forbid. to exercise his skill, of wh. Judge Sewall had pleasure in writ. that " he ran away for debt," 28 July 1686.

STERRY, ROGER, Stonington 1670, m. that yr. Hannah, wid. of Thomas Huet, of the same.

STERTT, perhaps STERITT, WILLIAM, Boston, wh. d. prob. 1645, had w. Jane, as the rec. of her adm. 4 Oct. in that yr. titles her, or Sarah, as when next day, the d. Sarah was bapt. a. one yr. and 46 wks. old, she is call. " our sis. wid. of one William Stertt."

STETSON, STITSON, STUDSON, STEDSON, or STUTSON, * BENJAMIN, Scituate, s. of Robert of the same, by w. Bethia had Benjamin, b. 16 Feb. bapt. 19 May 1668 ; Matthew, 12 June 1669, wh. d. Nov. 1690 in the wretched exped. of Phips ; James, 1 May 1670 ; Samuel, Oct. 1673 ; Bethia, 14 May 1675 ; Mary, 21 Apr. 1678 ; Hannah, 1 June 1679 ; Deborah, 3 Dec. 1681 ; Eunice, Mar. 1683 ; and Margaret, Sept. 1684, d. soon ; was rep. 1691, at Plymouth, and aft. the union with Mass. at Boston 1693, 4, and 1700, and d. 4 May 1711. JOHN, York, d. 1673, his inv. bearing date 1 July. No w. or ch. is ment. JOHN, Scituate, br. of Benjamin, by w. Abigail had Abigail, b. May 1677 ; John, bapt. 4 May 1679 ; Barnabas, 16 July 1682 ; Honour, b. Mar. 1684 ; and Ann, Dec. 1690, prob. posthum. for he d. in that sad yr. of the Canada crusade, with his neph. Joseph. JOSEPH, Scituate, eldest br. of the preced. by w. Prudence had Joseph, bapt. June 1667 ; Robert, b. 9 Dec. 1670 ; Lois, Mar. 1672 ; William, Dec. 1673 ; Desire, Sept. 1676 ; Prudence, Sept. 1678 ; Samuel, Dec. 1679 ; and Hannah, June 1682. His will was of 4 Apr. 1722, and he d. bef. 8 May 1724. * ROBERT, Scituate 1634, came, as reasonab. tradit. says from Co. Kent, perhaps in the yr. preced. aged a. 20, by first w. of whose name is no report, he had Joseph, b. June 1639 ; Benjamin, Aug. 1641 ; and Thomas, 11 Dec. 1643 ; all bapt. 6 Oct. 1645 ; Samuel, June, bapt. 12 July 1647 ; John, Apr. 1648 ; Eunice, 28 Apr. bapt. 19 May 1650 ; Lois, Feb. 1652, prob. d. young ; Robert, 29 Jan. bapt. 26 Feb. 1654 ; and Timothy, bapt. 11 Oct. 1657, prob. d. young. He was a man of gr. public spirit, cornet of the first body of horse in Plymouth Col. was rep. 1654–62, and oft. aft. in 1664 a commissnr. for sett. bounds betw. the Cols. of Mass. and Plymouth ; in perilous time, of the counc. of war, bef. and aft. the gr. dangers of Philip's hostil. dur. wh. his serv. was active ; made his will 4 Sept. 1702, pro. 1 Mar. foll. in wh. his w. is call. Mary, presum. to have been tak. aft. 1682, and wid. of John Bryant. In it he provides for d. Eunice Rogers, and Abigail, wid. of s. John, and d. 1 Feb. 1703, aged 90. ROBERT, Scituate, s. of the preced. liv. in that pt. wh. bec. Pembroke, m. 1676, Joanna Brooks, says Barry, the later and higher authty. tho. Deane says Deborah, d. of William, had Isaac, Timothy, Resolved, Sarah, and Nathaniel, but no dates can be found for either by Barry. Yet descend. are very num. SAMUEL, Scituate, br. of the preced. had

perhaps w. Mercy or Mary, wh. d. 1687, but Barry says, that the ch. on
rec. of the town are nam. of Samuel and Lydia (and possib. the entry
was not made bef. the time of sec. w.) ; Samuel, June 1679 ; Eliz. 1 Apr.
1682, and with her, as Barry supposes, a tw. br. Judah, bec. he finds one
of that name on ch. rec. of bapt. 14 May 1682; Lydia, July 1683 ;
Patience, Dec. 1687, ; Jonah, Apr. 1691 ; Mary, June 1692 ; John, Mar.
1694; Silas, June 1696; Seth, June 1698; Nathaniel, June 1700;
Deborah, Oct. 1704; and Rachel. He was liv. 1722. THOMAS, Scituate, br. of the preced. m. 1671, Sarah, d. of Anthony Dodson, had
Hannah, b. Nov. 1671; Thomas, Sept. 1673, bapt. 31 May foll.; Gershom, Jan. 1676; Sarah, Jan. 1678; Joshua, Jan. 1680; Caleb, Mar.
1682; Elisha, Mar. 1684; Elijah, Mar. 1686; Mary, 3 Mar. 1691 ;
Ebenezer, 22 July 1693 ; Ruth, 11 Dec. 1695; and Margaret, 4 Aug.
1698 ; and prob. his. w. d. bef. him, as she is not nam. in his will of 2
July 1729. VINCENT, Milford 1646, was of Marblehead 1674, as I
judge, but ret. to Milford, where a d. m. George Barlow. * ‖ WILLIAM,
Charlestown 1632, with w. Eliz. wh. had been wid. Harris, prob. m. in.
Eng. adm. of the ch. 22 Mar. 1633, freem. 11 June foll. but no ch. is
ment. in the list of bapt. wh. is very defic. from 1642 for 17 yrs. yet he
had kindness for the ch. John, Thomas, William, and Daniel Harris, s.
of his w. Eliz. and her d. Ann, wid. of Elias Maverick, provid. for
them in his will ; was of ar. co. 1648, and rep. 1667–71; was deac.
Oct. 1659, and Eliz. his wid. d. 16 Feb. 1670. He made his will 12
Apr. 1688, and d. 11 Apr. 1691, aged 90, hav. m. 27 Aug. 1670, Mary,
wid. of Capt. Francis Norton.

STEVENS, BENJAMIN, Salisbury, s. of John of the same, m. 28 Oct.
1673, Hannah, d. of Thomas Barnard of the same, had Elinor, and
Catharine, tw. b. 2 Jan. 1675; Benjamin, 7 Oct. 1677 ; Mary, 7 Nov.
1679 ; Hannah, 30 Apr. 1682 ; Ebenezer, 29 June 1684; and John, 29
Jan. 1689 ; and d. 13 Mar. 1691. BENJAMIN, Andover, youngest s. of
the first John of the same, was a capt. and magistr. d. 1730, without
male issue. CYPRIAN, Lancaster, had come, a. 1660 from London, in
his youth under 14 yrs. where his f. Thomas liv. wh. was, perhaps, that
armorer of Buttolph lane, wh. contract. with our Gov. and Comp. there
in Mar. 1629 for supply of arms, was a mem. of the comp. and beside
giv. £50 to the com. stock, sent us three s. and d. Mary, as his adven-
ture in our cause ; and one of the signers of the instruct. to Capt. Endicott bef. his com. for wh. see Hutch. I. 9 in note, tho. the fam. was of
Devonsh. in earlier days. He perhaps was first at Rumney marsh, now
Chelsea, m. 22 Jan. 1672, Mary, d. of Simon Willard, the major, had
Cyprian, b. 22 Nov. foll. ; Mary; Dorothy, wh. d. young; Simon; Eliz.;
and Joseph. Some of these ch. were, perhaps, not b. at L. for in the gr.

war of 1675–6 he had been driv. by the Ind. to make his resid. nearer Boston, prob. in some of the interval, at Sudbury, and had authty. to receive an Ind. ch. of six yrs. prob. of a friendly tribe whose f. might be serv. in our ranks; but he went back, aft. the peace, to L. Mary m. Samuel Wright of Rutland. EDWARD, Boston, by w. Mary had Thomas, b. 15 Apr. 1669. EDWARD, Marshfield, is by Miss Thomas seen there, prob. some time betw. 1665 and 1691, but no date is supplied exc. by infer. and tho. she gives him ch. Edward, William, Eliz. and Patience, she could not tell his f. EDWARD, Boston, wh. m. 8 Oct. 1700, Rebecca, wid. of Thomas Harris, first, however, wid. of John Croakham, d. of Abraham Josselyn, had mov. in from ano. town, for he was not householder in 1695. EPHRAIM, Andover, s. of John of the same, m. 11 Oct. 1680, Sarah, d. of the first George Abbot, had Sarah, b. 8 Nov. 1681; Eliz. 18 Aug. 1683; Hannah, 29 Nov. 1685; Mehitable, 10 Oct. 1691, d. young; Mary, 21 Feb. 1694; Ephraim, 24 July 1698; and Mehitable, again, 10 Sept. 1700. His w. d. 28 June, 1711; and he d. 26 June 1718, a. 69 yrs. old. ERASMUS, Boston, by w. Eliz. had John, b. 16 Aug. 1671; and Mary, 1673, but the mo. and day are lost by the leaf of rec. being torn. He prob. kept an inn, for, 1686, a poor Carolina overseer of a planta. hav. been made prison. by pirates, and escap. from them at Casco, was by Ed. Randolph, collector of our port, referr. to him for food and clothing. See 3 Mass. Hist. Coll. VII. 157. FRANCIS, Rehoboth 1658, had div. of lds. there in that yr. and ten yrs. later. His inv. of 1 Jan. 1670 shows that he was then d. and being call. sen. makes it prob. that he had s. FRANCIS, Rehoboth, wh. had Gilbert, b. 26 Feb. 1675; and his w. Eliz. was bur. six days aft. GEORGE, Boston, cooper, d. Oct. 1655, by will giv. all his little prop. to Isaac Collimore, so that he may well be thot. unm. and prob. only trans. HENRY, Boston, stone mason, as the ch. rec. calls him, came in the Defence 1635, from London, aged 24, liv. in the pt. call. Muddy riv. now Brookline, by w. Alice, on London custom ho. emb. 2 July in the Abigail on the same day with her h. (no doubt by error of the clk.) aged 22, had John, b. 10 Sept. 1637; James, 10 Apr. 1640; Joseph, 1 Sept. 1642; all bapt. 18 June 1643, on the same day, that she join. our ch. and Deborah, 25, bapt. 27 Apr. 1645; and by sec. w. Mary had Joanna, 28 May 1652; Henry, 20 July 1656, d. young; Joshua, 15 May 1659; Henry, again, 25 May 1663; and Samuel, 24 Sept. 1665; was there in 1674. Ano. HENRY was of Lynn 1634, serv. to John Humfrey, Esqr. and for burn. his master's ho. was 1640, sentenc. to 21 yrs. serv. as in Col. Rec. I. 311, wh. may be compar. with the detail in Winth. II. 13. By a letter from ano. HENRY, 29 June 1675, wh. I suppose was of Stonington, 1670, but the preced. day, an inhab. of Swanzey, perhaps s. of

16 *

Francis of Rehoboth is giv. the first acco. of the outbreak of Philip's war. See 3 Mass. Hist. Coll. X. 117. He may have rem. to Stonington aft. this destruct. and there m. Eliz. d. of that brave Capt. John Gallop, wh. fell in the gr. swamp fight. Still ano. HENRY, was a propr. of New Haven 1685, hav. m. 6 Feb. 1678, Joanna, d. of Philip Leeke, had Eliz. b. 10 Dec. 1678 ; Philip, 16 Jan. 1684 ; and prob. others, and d. 1689. *JAMES, Gloucester, s. of William of the same, prob. b. in Eng. m. 31 Dec. 1656, Susanna, d. of Sylvester Eveleth, had William, b. 10 Mar. 1658 ; John, 23 Jan. 1661, d. at one wk. ; James, 4 Jan. 1662, d. bef. his f. ; Isaac, 15 Aug. 1664, d. at 4 mos. ; Samuel, 5 Dec. 1665 ; Isaac, again, 11 Nov. 1668, d. in few days ; Ebenezer, 20 Sept. 1670 ; Mary, 13 June 1672 ; Hannah, 9 Apr. 1675 ; David, 5 Nov. 1677 ; and Jonathan, 7 Mar. 1680. He was freem. 1671, oft. one of the selectmen, deac. and rep. 1689 and 90 beside other yrs. bef. and aft. and d. 25 Mar. 1697. His d. Mary m. 24 Jan. 1693, the sec. Francis Norwood. JAMES, Boston, s. of Henry of the same, had w. Sarah at Muddy riv. for wh. dur. his absence in 1674, the f. of her h. engag. to furnish a ho. JEREMIAH, Boston, a young man, d. early in Oct. 1663, perhaps sent by his f. to deal out books, for of his inv. amt. to £72 4s. 11½d. they made up £68 17s. 5d. JOHN, Hingham, had div. of ld. 1638, may have rem. JOHN, Newbury, perhaps came in the Confidence from Southampton 1638, aged 31, hav. liv. at Caversham in Co. Oxford, but Drake in Geneal. Reg. XIV. 335 reads the name of the parish Gonsham. This is the more strange, from his explanat. in note, and especial. since the error in G. R. II. 109 had been point. out in G. R. IV. list of Errata aft. p. 385. In old chirogr. as first vol. of Boston Rec. the capital C. much resembles G. Caversham is the most S. part of Oxfordsh. close to Reading in Berks. He had John, b. 20 June 1639 ; Timothy, 23 Sept. 1641 ; was freem. 18 May 1642 ; rem. to Andover and had Nathan, the first b. of A. says tradit. ; Ephraim ; Joseph, 15 May 1654 ; and Benjamin, 24 June 1656 ; and d. 11 Apr. 1662, aged 56, leav. wid. Eliz. wh. prob. he brot. from Eng. and she d. 1 May 1694, aged 80. JOHN, Salisbury, perhaps the freem. of 2 June 1641, by w. Catharine had John, b. 2 Nov. 1639 ; Eliz. 7 Mar. 1641, d. soon ; Eliz. again, 4 Feb. 1642 ; Nathaniel, 11 Nov. 1645 ; Mary, 1647 ; and Benjamin, 2 Feb. 1650. His w. d. July 1682, and he d. Feb. foll. Eliz. m. 14 Oct. 1661, Morris Tucker, and d. Oct. foll. JOHN, Guilford 1650, is on the list of freem. there 1669, d. 2 Oct. of next yr. In his will nam. the four ch. s. John in old Eng. Thomas, and William here, and d. Mary, w. of John Collins, wh. had first h. Henry Kingsnoth, that d. in 1668, and had m. the other, 2 June 1669. JOHN, New London 1664, Caulkins thinks came from Guilford, s. of the preced. shipwright,

m. Mary, d. of John Coit, was propound. for freem. 1669, had John, and
Mary, both bapt. 12 Mar. 1671; James, 17 Sept. foll.; Samuel, 20
Sept. 1674; beside Joseph and Thomas; and he rem. 1676 to New
Haven. JOHN, Dover, of wh. no more is kn. but that he was on the
list, 1662. He may have liv. 1668, at Marblehead to petitn. against
imposts. JOHN, Andover, s. of John of the same, m. 13 June 1662,
Hannah, d. of Robert Barnard of the same, had, it may be, several ch.
beside Jonathan, wh. d. 15 June 1674; and Nathan; but we have from
that town only rec. of m. and d. His w. d. 13 Mar. 1675; and he m.
10 Aug. 1676, Esther, d. of Richard Barker, and may have had more
ch. JOHN, Salisbury, eldest s. of John of the same, b. on our side of
the ocean, m. 17 Feb. 1670, Joanna Thorn, had John, b. 26 Dec. foll.;
Eliz. 8 Apr. 1673, d. next yr.; Jeremiah, 6 Oct. 1675; Eliz. again, 4
Feb. 1678; and Judith, 18 Jan. 1687, perhaps by sec. w. Hannah; and
d. 26 Nov. 1691. JOHN, Newbury, prob. s. of William of the same, m.
9 Mar. 1670, Mary, d. of the first Aquila Chase, had Mary, b. 6 Feb.
1671; Thomas, 3 July 1676, and perhaps rem. aft. being adm. freem.
1669, to Chelmsford, for one of the name there d. June 1691. JONA-
THAN, a soldier in Philip's war, of the Conn. forces, severely wound.
was prob. of Guilford, or Killingworth, then call. Kenilworth. JOSEPH,
Salisbury, perhaps eldest s. of the first John of Newbury, m. Mary, d.
of Ralph Blaisdale in 1667. JOSEPH, Mendon, freem. 1673. JOSEPH,
Braintree, by w. Sarah had a d. Trial, b. 16 Dec. 1677. JOSEPH,
Andover, s. prob. of John of the same, m. 28 May 1679, Mary Ingalls,
prob. d. of Henry of the same, wh. d. 21 Sept. 1699, had perhaps sev.
other ch. beside Joseph, b. 20 June 1682, H. C. 1703, min. of Charlestown (ord. 13 Oct. 1713, and d. of smallpox, 16 Nov. 1721, with w.
sole d. Sarah, w.'s sis. his s. Joseph, and a serv. all in few days, wh. was
f. of Benjamin, H. C. 1740, the disting. min. of Kittery); was a deac.
and d. 1743, aged 88. JOSEPH, Sudbury, s. of Cyprian, wh. d. 1769, by
w. Prudence had Phineas, b. 20 Feb. 1707; Abzubah, 21 Oct. 1708;
and Samuel, Sept. 1711; rem. to Framingham, and had Mindwell, 24
Feb. 1714; Isaac; and Mary; rem. to Rutland, there had Dorothy,
1721; Joseph, 1723; Lucy, 1725; Joseph, again; was town treasr.
selectman, and deac. On 14 Aug. 1723 he lost all his s. viz. Samuel,
and the new b. Joseph, k. by the Ind. with Rev. Joseph Willard, Yale
1714, min. of the town; when the others, Phineas, and Isaac, were by
them carr. capt. to Canada. Phineas was much disting. for milit. serv.
JOSIAH, Braintree, perhaps br. of the preced. d. 19 June 1677.
NATHAN, the first b. of Andover, d. there, Feb. 1719, says the rec. wh.
calls him cornet; but I find not evid. of any w. or ch. NATHANIEL,
Dover, perhaps s. of John of the same, tho. Mr. Quint marks him as first

of the stock, by w. Mary had Mary, b. 4 Oct. 1672 ; and he m. 20 Dec.
1677, Mehitable, d. of Edward Colcord, had Samuel, Edward, and perhaps others. NATHANIEL, Guilford 1685–95, was s. of William. NICH-
OLAS, Charlestown, d. 17 May 1646, as Farmer says ; but I doubt he was
not long a resid. OBADIAH, Stamford, eldest s. of Thomas of the same,
had Thomas, b. 1679 ; Ephraim, 1681 ; and some others, of wh. or the
mo. I hear not the names. RICHARD, Concord, perhaps that s. of Thomas,
the London armorer, d. 1683. If my conject. be right, his wid. and only
d. says Willard, in note to Barry, went home. RICHARD, Taunton, had
Richard, b. 23 Feb. 1670 ; Mary, 8 July 1672 ; Thomas, 3 Feb. 1675 ;
Thomasin, 3 July 1677 ; Nathaniel, 30 July 1680 ; nam. 1689 as one of
the inhab. to wh. William Bradford made confirmat. gr. ROBERT,
Braintree, had Sarah, b. 31 Oct. 1641 ; and his wid. Mary d. 22 Jan.
1692, near 90 yrs. old. SAMUEL, Newbury, s. of William, was prob.
that soldier serj. k. by the Ind. at Bloody brook, 18 Sept. 1675, with his
townsmen, serg. Thomas Smith and others, tho. Felt, II. 505, claims him
for Salem, and he was s.-in-law of Joshua Rea of S. His wid. Rebecca
had admin. and d. Sarah is ment. SAMUEL, Marlborough, s. of Richard,
perhaps brot. by his f. was a deac. early in eighteenth centu. THOMAS,
Sudbury, may be the youth in the Abigail, from London, 1635, aged 12,
perhaps s. of Thomas of London, the armorer, may have gone home
and come again, with Cyprian, and was freem. 1665, by w. Mary had
Ann, b. 20 Mar. 1664 ; Thomas, 14 Apr. 1665 ; John, 23 Apr. 1667 ;
Cyprian, 19 Apr. 1670 ; and Jacob, 1 Mar. 1674 ; was freem. 1665 ;
and town clk. 15 yrs. Barry thinks he was first at Charlestown, a
blacksmith, and late in life liv. at Stow, but at Sudbury had been offer.
ld. to keep a sch. THOMAS, Stamford 1641, had Thomas, Benjamin,
Joseph, Ephraim, and Obadiah the eldest ; but d. 19 Aug. 1658, when
all were so young, that without nam. one, he gave est. to w. to bring
them up. THOMAS, Boston 1670, a baker, was an early inhab. by w.
Sarah had John, b. 15 May 1648 ; Thomas, 28 Dec. 1651, d. young ;
Jonas, 27 Oct. 1653 ; Aaron, 28 Feb. 1655 ; Sarah, 31 Aug. 1657, d.
soon ; Thomas, again, 20 May 1658 ; Moses, 22 Apr. 1659 ; Joseph, 17
Apr. 1661 ; and Sarah, 8 Dec. 1663. *THOMAS, Guilford 1650, s. of
John of the same, prob. b. in Eng. rem. to Killingworth, or as by its first
sett. call. from their native place in O. E. in 1665, Kenilworth, but why
the name was degrad. to its mod. form, is beyond the knowl. of any in
the last three or four generat. yet easily conject. He was among the
freem. 1669, rep. 1671 of K. but bef. that planta. was sett. he had, by w.
Mary, sev. ch. b. at G. tho. larger pt. may be claim. possib. by K.
They were Mary ; James, b. 21 Feb. 1651 ; Rebecca, wh. m. Edward
Rutty ; Sarah, 25 Jan. 1657, wh. m. 18 Apr. or May 1678, Stephen

Dod; John, 10 Mar. 1660; Thomas, 21 Feb. 1662; Timothy, 1664; Joseph, and Abigail, tw. 23 Apr. 1666 (she m. Edward Lee); Eliz. 14 July 1668, m. Nathaniel Chittenden; Ebenezer, 26 Jan. 1671; Phebe, 21 Feb. 1673; and Jonathan, 2 Feb. 1676; and d. 18 Nov. 1685. THOMAS, Boston, mariner, d. at Roanoke, and admin. was giv. to his br.-in-law, George Kelly, 15 Oct. 1672. THOMAS, Newbury, m. 15 Apr. 1672, Martha, d. prob. of the first Christopher Bartlet, and perhaps the same man took sec. w. 13 Oct. 1681, Mary, d. of Thomas Mighill of Rowley. THOMAS, Casco, sw. alleg. to Charles II. 8 Sept. 1665, bot. of Ind. Westgustago riv. a. 1673, but sold his right next yr. THOMAS, Amesbury, sw. alleg. 20 Dec. 1677. One THOMAS was of Westerly 1680; and one d. at Middletown, call. sen. 9 Sept. 1714. THOMAS, Plainfield 1689, s. of Thomas of Sudbury. TIMOTHY, Roxbury, s. of the first John of Newbury, m. 12 Mar. 1665, Sarah, prob. eldest d. of Tobias Davis, had Timothy, b. 28 Jan. 1666, H. C. 1687, the first of this name at the Coll.; Sarah, 6 Mar. 1668; John, 24 July 1670; Joseph, 7 Apr. 1673; Eliz. 21 Aug. 1675; Maria, 6 Apr. 1678; Hannah, 27 Aug. 1680; Samuel, 30 Mar. 1682; Abigail, 25 Nov. 1685; and Nathaniel, 6 June 1688; was deac. and d. 31 Jan. 1708. TIMOTHY, Glastonbury, s. of the preced. ord. 1693, m. 17 May 1694, Eunice, d. of John Chester of Wethersfield, had Timothy, b. 23 Mar. 1695, d. next mo.; Sarah, 19 Mar. 1696, d. at 21 yrs.; and John, 4 June 1698, d. soon; and his w. d. 16 of the same mo. He m. sec. w. 19 May 1701, Alice, wid. of Rev. John Whiting, d. of Joseph Cook, had John, again, 13 Sept. 1702, d. young; Eunice, 14 Sept. 1704, d. soon; Martha, 6 Sept. 1705, d. young; tw. s. 8 Sept. 1707, d. very soon; Timothy, again, 9 July 1709; Joseph, 15 Aug. 1711; and Benjamin, Mar. 1714, and d. 14 Apr. 1726. *WILLIAM, Gloucester, a man of eminent skill as shipbuild. prob. first at Salem, and join. the ch. 29 Dec. 1639, freem. 13 May 1640, with prefix of resp. had desir. early in 1634, to build a float. battery for protect. of Boston as in Col. Rec. I. 113 and 120, selectman 1642, and aft.; rep. 1644. He had built many large sh. at London, bef. he came hither, I suppose in 1632, for in Jan. aft. Emanuel Downing, writ. in London to the Rt. Hon. Sir John Coke, princ. Secr. of State, that from high author. he hears, that he is "so able a man, as they believe there is hardly such an other to be found in this kingdom." See the letter in 3 Mass. Hist. Coll. VIII. 324. He had bapt. at Salem, Isaac, and Mary, not perhaps tw. 26 Jan. 1640; Ruth, 7 Mar. 1641, wh. m. 7 Oct. 1663, Stephen Glover; beside James, bef. ment. prob. the oldest, and William, certain the youngest, but whether all were by w. Philippa, or when he or she d. is unkn. WILLIAM, Newbury, may be that passeng. in the Confidence from Southampton 1638, aged 21, prob. br. of John, a fellow-passeng. both from Caversham in Oxfordsh. and was not, I think, as Farmer said, first sett. at Salem, freem. with John, 18 May 1642, by w. Eliz. d. of Samuel Bidfield, m. 19 May 1645, had, says Coffin, Bidfield, b. 16 Mar. 1649, d. young; John, 19 Nov. 1650; and Samuel, 18 Nov. 1652; and d. 19 May 1653, prob. sudden. as his will has that date. It was pro. 30 June foll. names only ch. John and Samuel, made w. Eliz. extrix. WILLIAM, Killingworth 1665, whither he rem. from Guilford, br. of Thomas of the same, b. in Eng. freem. 1669, m. 3 Mar. 1653, Mary, d. of John Meigs, had John, b. 3 Mar. 1654; Samuel, 1 Mar. 1656; Nathaniel, 10 May 1659, d. soon; Nathaniel, again, 29 Oct. 1661; Judith, 1 Oct. 1668; Josiah, 8 Dec. 1670; and Mary, 2 Nov. 1677. When he d. is not mark. but it was prob. bef. 1685, when among proprs. of G. no other of the name, beside Nathaniel is found. Yet he may have been of K. at that time, and giv. his G. est. to Nathaniel. Others of his ch. however did settle at G. His w. or wid. d. 30 Apr. 1703. WILLIAM, Charlestown, m. 1 July 1673, Abigail Green, so comm. a name that it is perilous to conject. wh. was her f. WILLIAM, Gloucester, eldest s. of James of the same, m. 15 June 1682, Abigail, prob. d. of William Sargent; and Mr. Babson says he d. 24 Sept. 1701. A wid. Ann S. perhaps the mo. of John and William of the same, d. at Newbury, July 1650; and a wid. S. at Newtown, L. I. 1656. Farmer omit. to ment. as he was wont, the numb. of gr. found by Harv. Catal. fourteen, and at Yale ten, up to 1852.

STEVENSON, JAMES, Reading, m. 18 Apr. 1661, his w. Naomi. It is easily made Stephenson.

STEWART, or STEWARD, oft. STUART, ALEXANDER, Charlestown, shipwright, by w. Hannah, nam. with ch. James, and John in the will, Jan. 1669, of her gr.f. Richard Prichard of C. of wh. I suppose James d. young, but both prob. b. in ano. town; had at C. Hannah, Samuel, and Margaret, all, with John, bapt. 9 May 1675, the mo. hav. d. on 21 Aug. preced. To C. he had come from ano. town, not kn. as I conject. from that bapt. when he was not a ch. mem. and rem. to Marlborough, there m. 22 May 1688, Deborah, wid. of Daniel Farrabas, or Farrowbush, d. of John Bediat, the first, of Sudbury. But a very dilig. inquir. A. H. Ward, Esquire, calls her his third w. yet I kn. not the sec. He had by Deborah a d. and d. 6 Apr. 1731, his w. hav. d. ten or more prob. eleven yrs. preced. DANIEL, Barnstable, was there bef. 1666, as Mr. Hamblin says, and prob. had ch. for I find many in a third generat. but kn. nothing of sec. DUNCAN, Newbury, shipwright, perhaps br. of Alexander, had Martha, b. 4 Apr. 1659; Charles, 5 June 1661; James, 8 Oct. 1664; Henry, 1 May 1669; rem. to Rowley, had three more, and d. 1717, aged, as Coffin says, prob. from exagger. tradit. 100. JAMES, Plymouth, came in the Fortune 1621, prob. without w. or ch. as he has, in the div. of lds. 1624, only a single sh. and we may well suppose he had soon d. or rem. as in the div. of cattle, 1627, his name is not found among the 156, compos. the total populat. JAMES, Middlebury, L. I. 1656. JAMES, Weymouth, by w. Ann had Susanna, b. 23 May 1669 ; JAMES, 26 June 1672 ; and Ann, 22 Jan. 1675 ; possib. others earlier. JAMES, Norwalk 1687, eldest s. of Robert, was ens. in 1713. JAMES, Newbury, s. of Duncan, by w. Eliz. had James, b. 29 July 1688 ; and Charles, 10 Jan. 1690. JOHN, Springfield, perhaps as early as 1650, m. Sarah, d. of the first John Stiles ; sw. alleg. 1678, and d. 21 Apr. 1690. His wid. m. next yr. John Sacket of Northampton. JOHN, Newbury, perhaps s. of Alexander, by w. Eliz. had Eliz. b. 11 Dec. 1680, and his w. d. in few days ; aft. wh. perhaps he rem. to Rowley. JOHN, Norwalk 1708, s. of Robert. JOSEPH, Salisbury, by w. Mary had Joseph, b. 19 Dec. 1667. RICHARD, by Farmer is ment. as of ar. co. 1652, but to me the exist. seems shadowy. ROBERT, Norwalk, mov. in from Milford, where he had not been long, buying est. in N. 1660, m. 12 June 1661, Bethia, d. of Thomas Rumball of Stratford, had James, b. 19 Mar. 1662 ; Abigail, Aug. 1666 ; John, 18 Mar. 1668 ; Deborah, May 1669 ; Eliz. Sept. 1671 ; and Phebe, Feb. 1673, or 4 ; and was liv. 1687. From him descend. the late learned theolog. profess. Moses Stuart, tho. the degr. are less sure. WILLIAM, Lynn, d. 18 Mar. 1664, and his wid. Sarah ret. inv. 29 June foll. A capt. S. is nam. by Sewall, in his Diary, as d. early in Aug. 1693. Of the gr. historic name, the clan of Stuart, were Austin, Charles, Neil, and Robert, prisoners of war from the sad field of 3 Sept. 1651, at Worcester, Cromwell's crowning mercy, sent to Boston, where they arr. 13 May 1652, to be sold, but not to perpet. servit. as John Cotton gently suggests to Oliver. I can feel no doubt, that the gr. majority, betw. three quarters and nine tenths, d. of scurvy or broken heart ; and not one in fifty of these young men left progeny.

STICKNEY, or STICKNEE, AMOS, Newbury, was from Hull Co. York, s. of William, perhaps b. in Eng. is said to have been first at Boston, next at Rowley, of course, with his f. but at N. m. 24 June 1663, Sarah Morse, prob. d. of Anthony the first, had John, b. 23 June 1666; Andrew, Dec. 1667 ; Amos, 3 Aug. 1669 ; Joseph, 14 Apr. 1671 ; Benjamin, 4 Apr. 1673 ; Sarah, 19 Oct. 1674, d. next yr. ; Hannah, 31 Mar. 1676 ; Moses, 26 Nov. 1677 ; and perhaps Sarah, again, posthum. sw. alleg. 25 May 1669, and he d. 29 Aug. 1678. His wid. m. 17 Dec. 1684, Stephen Acreman. ANDREW, Newbury, s. of the preced. by w. Rebecca had Rebecca, b. 16 Jan. 1693, and his w. d. a few days later ;

but of him I find no more, exc. his tak. sec. w. Eliz. eldest d. of sec.
James Chute, and d. at Rowley 29 Apr. 1727. BENJAMIN, Rowley, br.
of the preced. m. Mary Palmer, had six s. and one d. and d. 5 Mar.
1756. JOHN, Rowley, s. of William, m. Hannah, d. of that capt.
Samuel Brocklebank, which was k. in Philip's war, had John, Samuel,
and five ds. JOHN, Newbury, s. of Amos, m. 10 Dec. 1689, Mary Poor,
d. prob. of sec. John of the same, had Mary, b. 1 July 1691 ; John, 30
July 1693; Sarah, 10 May 1696 ; Prudence, 15 Sept. 1699 ; and
Joseph, 19 Dec. 1700. * SAMUEL, Bradford, eldest s. of William, b. in
Eng. rep. 1689 and 90, m. 18 Feb. 1654, Julian, or Susan, d. of Richard
Swan of Rowley, had four ch. of wh. I see the name of Samuel only,
b. 5 Apr. 1663, at R. and aft. rem. to B. by sec. w. m. 6 Apr. 1674,
Prudence Gage, wid. of Benjamin, and d. of Thomas Leaver, town clk.
of R. by which he had three more ch. of wh. no names are kn. He
was freem. 1682, and d. 1716, leav. wid. Prudence. SAMUEL, Bradford,
eldest s. of the preced. was a man of good serv. as selectman, had w.
Mary, and it is said, twelve ch. of wh. I see not the names, exc. that the
first s. was Thomas, bapt. 1695 ; and that Sarah and Mary were also
bapt. that yr.; Richard, 5 June 1709 ; Abraham and Jonathan, perhaps
tw. 21 Jan. 1711; and Dorothy, 6 Apr. 1712. THOMAS, Newbury, s.
of William, sw. alleg. 25 May 1669, was of Bradford, when freem.
1685. WILLIAM, Rowley, was adm. of Boston ch. 6 Jan. 1639, hav.
come prob. the yr. preced. from Hull in Yorksh. and on 24 Nov. aft.
was with others dism. to found the new ch. at R. was freem. 7 Oct.
1640, but prob. he brot. w. and one or more ch. from Eng. His w. was
Eliz. and of the ch. are kn. Samuel; John, b. 1640; Andrew, 1644 ;
Thomas, 1646; Mary; Faith; and Mercy; beside the first ment.
Amos; and he d. 25 Jan. 1665. But the order of success. is uncert.
and perhaps he had other ch. than Farmer could tell. Faith m. 10
June 1674, at Bradford, Samuel Gage, and an Eliz. S. m. 21 July 1680,
also at B. Daniel Tenny.

STILEMAN, or STYLEMAN, ELIAS, Salem, an early sett. even, as Felt
suggests, may have come in the fleet with Higginson, 1629, prob. brot.
s. Elias, but of his w. Judith we hear no more; freem. 3 July 1632,
licens. to keep an ordinary in 1635, when he was constable, gave up
prob. that employm. in 1653, and was made clk. of the Court for the
Co. and d. 1662. His inv. was tak. 7 Nov. of that yr. ‡ * || ELIAS,
Salem, perhaps s. of the preced. b. a. 1617, adm. of the ch. 18 Aug.
1639, and freem. 18 May 1642, had Elias, bapt. 15 Mar. 1640; and
Eliz. wh. m. a. 1687, John Jordan; was of ar. co. 1645, rem. perhaps
not bef. 1663 to Portsmouth ; m. sec. w. 10 Apr. 1667, Ruth Maynard,
had Ruth, wh. m. 5 Sept. 1687, William Buswell or Bussell. In the list of

early sett. of N. E. pr. Geneal. Reg. I. 139, E. S. is by mistake call.
constable of Boston 1673. The names of seven chos. that yr. to that
office have only Skarlet and Shrimpton of that initial fam. letter, and
not one Elias. He was almost always in office; was rep. 1667 and five
yrs. more, a counsel. under Presid. Cutt, or Gov. Cranfield, 1681 or 2 a
capt. and major, rep. again 1690, and d. 19 Dec. 1695, aged 78. RICH-
ARD, Cambridge, by w. Hannah had Samuel, b. 23 May 1644, bapt. at
Salem, 20 July 1651, he hav. rem. thither, and soon aft. to Portsmouth,
where by w. Mary were b. Mary, 6 Jan. 1658; Eliz. 8 May 1663;
Sarah, 30 June 1665; and Richard, 20 Mar. 1668; and d. 11 Oct.
1678. Prob. he was br. of the preced. tho. sometimes the name is print.
Stillman.

STILES, or STYLES, BENJAMIN, Woodbury, s. of Francis, m. Eliz.
Rogers of Milford, perhaps d. of Eleazer, had Sarah, bapt. May 1683;
Thomas, Nov. 1685, prob. d. bef. his f.; Ruth; Abigail, Apr. 1689; and
Francis; rem. to Stratford, there d. 13 Apr. 1711, and his wid. d. 13 June
1719. EPHRAIM, Stratford, eldest s. of Francis, freem. 1668, m. 8 July
1669, Ruth, wid. of Obadiah Wheeler, and afterwards m. Bathsheba
Tomlinson, d. of Henry, by wh. he had, and left, at his d. 21 June
1714, three ds.: Eliz. b. 18 Feb. 1687; Sarah, 4 Nov. 1693; and
Phebe, 25 Mar. 1696; wh. all m. His est. was large. EPHRAIM,
Springfield, s. of John the sec. m. 1694, Abigail Neal, d. of Edward
of Westfield, had Rachel, b. 21 May 1695; Isaac, 6 Oct. 1696;
Ephraim, 5 Dec. 1699; Abigail, 15 Mar. 1704, d. young; and Hannah 31 July 1708. FRANCIS, Windsor 1636, one of the first freem.
of Conn. 1640, had come from London, where he was a carpenter,
early in the yr. preced. aged 35, in the Christian, and sat down short
time at Dorchester. Prob. he was s. of Thomas of Milbrook, near
Ampthill in Co. Bedford, bapt. 1 Aug. 1602, wh. makes us presume,
that the age of the London rec. should be 33, as the reg. of the parish,
certif. to me by the min. in 1842, deserves much higher credit than that
of the custom ho. I presume he brot. w. Rachel, unless she was sis. aged
28, but two ws. and two ch. beside the four brs. in the same sh. are
diffic. to be appropr. Cothren, p. 694, makes him, from fam. tradit. to be
engag. in prepar. of a park for Richard Saltonstall, not Sir Richard, wh.
is a mistake, for Suffk. reg. of deeds, Vol. I. 98, has the release of all
demands by him up to date of Sept. 1647, as well against Sir Richard,
as s. Robert. He work. I suppose under direct. of Robert, wh. was less
judicious than his elder br. He made over to Robert Saltonstall, by
deed dat. 22 Sept. 1647 all his lds. at W. includ. 1500 acr. in one parcel
on the E. side of the riv. but the debt exceed the val. He then calls
hims. of Saybrook, yet bec. three of his four s. were aft. at Stratford.

Cothren tells, that he rem. a. 1640 to Stratford, wh. must be sev. yrs. too early (as tradit. oft. is), for Ephraim was b. at W. 3 Aug. 1645, and his is the only b. found in the old rec. He was never of S. and he prob. at W. d. 1653, or earlier. Of childr. he had Ephraim, Samuel, Benjamin, Thomas, Hannah, and Mary, wh. m. Hope Washburn of Derby; Hannah m. Edward Hinman. Her mo. was Sarah, as Hinman, 141, tells. She m. Robert Clark of Stratford, and by her will of 5 June 1677 left little prop. to disp. among her ch. The inv. of 2 Feb. 1682, showing only £85. HENRY, Windsor, eldest br. of the preced. bapt. 27 Nov. 1593, at Milbrook, near Ampthill in Co. Bedford, a carpenter, adm. to be citizen of London on 2d Tuesday of Apr. 1632, emb. in the Christian, at London, Mar. 1635, aged 40, says the London custom ho. rec. with John, Thomas, and Francis, his brs. also, and went with the earliest migrat. from Dorchester, where he could have liv. but few mos. was never m. is nam. on the first page of Conn. rec. as hav. trad. a musket with an Ind. in Apr. 1636, which he was direct. to regain. He was k. by casual shot of a gun in a milita. train, Cothren from the fam. mem. says, 3 Oct. 1651. HENRY, Windsor, s. of John, brot. by his f. in the Christian 1635, at the age of 3 yrs. freem. 1669; had ch. wh. d. with the mo. whose name in the Stiles MS. is call. Ketch, of Stratford; and for sec. w. he m. 16 Apr. 1663, Eliz. Wilcockson, prob. d. of William, had Eliz. b. 30 Nov. 1664; Margaret, 6 Feb. 1667; Mary, 28 Sept. 1669; Mindwell, 19 Dec. 1671, wh. d. bef. 13 yrs.; and Samuel, 16 May 1674. To these Cothren adds Henry, wh. was the first b. Joseph, Benjamin, John, and Jonathan, but without desirab. dates of b. tho. of some he gives day of d. and approxim. of age, and says the f. d. 22 Aug. 1724, aged 95, wh. is perhaps less exagger. than usual, not more than three yrs. too large. ISAAC, Stratford, s. of John the first, of Windsor, liv. first at Wethersfield 1665, and when freem. 1670, had, says Cothren, from Presdt. Stiles's MSS. Isaac, b. 1663; John; Joseph; Jonathan, 10 Mar. 1688; Sarah; Lydia or Deborah; and Hannah; but he is not able to inform us of the name of the mo. or dates of sev. ch. JOHN, Windsor, s. of Thomas, bapt. at Milbrook, Co. Bedford, 25 Dec. 1595, came with his brs. Francis, Henry, and Thomas, in the Christian from London, Mar. 1635, tho. his age in the custom ho. rec. is call. 35, wh. I judge to be liable to correct. by exchang. the yrs. of Henry and John; he also brot. w. prob. Jane, aged 35; and s. Henry, 3 yrs. and John, 9 mos. Of course he first liv. at Dorchester or Boston, and prob. rem. with others of D. by ld. to Conn. Beside the ch. he brot. from Eng. he had Isaac, and Sarah, and d. 4 June 1662. His wid. whose name is not kn. d. 3 Sept. 1674. Cothren says his will was of 30 May 1662. Sarah m. first, John Stewart of Springfield; and next, 1691, John Sackett of Westfield. Fam. tradit.

claims for the w. of John, that she was the first Eng. woman that ever
stept ashore at Conn. wh. is as reasonab. as the similar stories for Mary
Chilton at Plymouth, and Ann Pollard at Boston. JOHN, Windsor, s. of
the preced. b. in Eng. m. 28 Oct. 1658, Dorcas, d. perhaps youngest, of
Henry Burt of Springfield, had Sarah, b. 12 Sept. 1661 ; Hannah, 23
Mar. 1664 ; John, 10 Dec. 1665 ; beside Ephraim and Thomas, not rec.
was freem. 1668, and d. 8 Dec. 1683. Hannah m. 21 Jan. 1687, Samuel
Bliss of Springfield; and Sarah m. 1 or 5 May 1681, Ephraim Bancroft, and next, Thomas Phillips. JOHN, Windsor, eldest s. of the preced. m. Ruth Bancroft, had Ruth, b. 5 Feb. 1691 ; John, 17 Dec. 1692 ;
Margaret, 23 Feb. 1695 ; Isaac, 30 July 1697 ; Ebenezer, 7 Apr.
1701 ; Noah, 31 Jan. 1703 ; Abel, d. soon ; Hannah, and ano. tw. both d.
soon, as had a pair tw. some yrs. bef. ; Abel, again, 5 or 10 Mar. 1709 ;
Hannah, again, 9 Oct. 1711 ; and Benoni, 1714, d. soon. He was gr.f.
of Rev. Ezra, disting. equal. for his extensive erudit. and amiable credulity, wh. was b. 29 Dec. 1727, eldest ch. of Isaac, and only one by w.
Kezia, d. of Rev. Edward Taylor of Westfield, wh. d. five days aft.
The chronology of too many of the fourteen ch. belong. to John, is so
strangely confus. in Cothren, 697, that it defies restorat. JOHN, Boxford, freem. 1690, may have been s. of Robert of the same. JOHN,
Dorchester 1692, perhaps was s. of Robert of the same ; but certain.
is beyond reach, and all that can be kn. is, that his w. was Mary, that he
had John, Joseph, Eliz. Mary, Nathaniel, and Nehemiah, of wh. Joseph,
Mary, and Nathaniel d. of smallpox in the fatal season of Jan. 1721–2.
ROBERT, Boxford, m. 4 Oct. 1660, Eliz. d. of John Frye of Andover ;
was of Rowley 1661, but perhaps rem. to Dorchester, where I find one
of this name 1663, yet in my opin. this Dorchester man was older than
him of B. possib. but not prob. was s. of John the first ; and inscript. on
gr. stone is of his d. 2 Nov. 1710, and age, a. 91, that may seem something too high. SAMUEL, Stratford, br. of Benjamin, in the freem.'s list
of 1669, m. 31 Dec. 1664, says Cothren, Eliz. Sherwood, but d. childless, prob. bef. 1682, as in 1673 he had agreed with others to begin the
sett. of Woodbury, and was not in the list of 1682. THOMAS, youngest
br. of Francis, Henry, and John, came in the same ship with them, aged
20, says the custom ho. rec. but that of his bapt. 7 Feb. 1613, in the
native parish, would give him two yrs. more. Yet it would be of higher
interest, to kn. where he liv. on our side of the water, and what could
be told of him, beyond the single fact, that, at the assault on the Pequods
in their last shelter of the swamp, 1637, he was shot, but not hurt, by an
arrow strik. in his neckerchief. See Mason's Hist. of that war. He
may have been of Windsor, but it is at least equal. prob. that he was of
Dorchester, neither town hav. proof or presumpt. in its favor. Had he

left descend. one might hope to hear of the birth-place of the ch. Some slight note is seen in Stiles's MSS. indeed that he went to Flushing, L. I. had two ds. no s. THOMAS, Stratford, s. of Francis, had w. wh. d. bef. him, but no ch. and he d. early in 1683. THOMAS, Windsor, youngest s. of John the sec. m. Bethia Hanmer, d. perhaps of John of Scituate, as the fam. tradit. may indicate, had no ch. and d. 1745. Eleven of this name had been gr. at Yale in 1851, and one at Harv.

STILLMAN, * GEORGE, Hadley, m. 1686, Rebecca, d. of the first Philip Smith, had George, b. 1686 ; Rebecca, 14 Jan. 1688; Mary, 12 July 1689 ; Nathaniel, 1 July 1691 ; John, 19 Feb. 1693 ; Sarah, 28 Dec. 1694 ; Martha, 28 Nov. 1696 ; Ann, 6 Apr. 1699 ; Eliz. 19 Oct. 1700 ; Hannah, and Lydia, tw. 7 Nov. 1702; and Benjamin, 29 July 1705 ; all at H. of wh. town he was rep. 1698; rem. to Wethersfield, where he was a promin. merch. and d. 17 Nov. 1728, in his 74th yr. His wid. d. 7 Oct. 1750, in 83d yr. Descend. have been num. in Conn.

STILLWELL, or STILWELL, JASPER, Guilford 1650, one of the first planters 1640, d. Nov. 1656. Dr. Stiles was able to add nothing. But my dilig. friend Judd gives him w. Eliz. and d. Eliz. wh. m. 26 Nov. 1657, John Graves.

STILSON, VINCENT, Milford 1646, d. 1690, but more than half that interval, liv. away from M. and at Marblehead is seen 1668–74. In his will names w. Mary, 5 s. Vincent, James, Hugh, Charles, Moses, and ds. Agnes Hawkins, and the w. of George Barley, wh. may be the same as Barlow. VINCENT, Marblehead, call. junr. in the sign. of petitn. of inhabs. of M. 1668, may have been s. of the preced.

STIMPSON, or STIMSON, ANDREW, Cambridge, by w. Jane had Rebecca, b. 20 Jan. 1643 ; and Mary, 17 Jan. 1647. ANDREW, Charlestown, s. of the preced. with w. Abigail join. the ch. 28 Jan. 1683, when she, and d. Abigail were bapt. had also Andrew, bapt. 18 Feb. foll. d. young; Mary, 26 Oct. 1684; Andrew, b. 9 Jan. 1686, d. very soon; John, bapt. 16 Jan. 1687 ; Bethia, 23 Mar. 1690; Benjamin, 18 Sept. 1692, d. under 30 yrs.; Joseph, 22 Dec. 1695 ; Lydia, 22 Aug. 1697 ; and Joseph, 18 Feb. 1700 ; and d. says Bond, 14 Dec. 1721, aged 72. GEORGE, Ipswich 1668, m. 22 July 1676, Alice Phillips, had George, b. 17 Aug. 1677, d. within one yr.; Richard, 10 Mar. 1679 ; Eliz. 11 Jan. 1681; Mercy, 11 Mar. 1683; Alice, 18 Feb. 1685 ; Sarah, 14 June 1691 ; John, 27 Aug. 1694; and Mary, 4 Mar. 1696. JOHN, the freem. of 1645 I can assign to no resid. JOHN, Charlestown, with w. Abigail join. the ch. 22 Feb. 1685, and had John, Joseph, Benjamin, Jonathan, Abigail, Susanna, and Deborah, all bapt. the Sunday foll. JONATHAN, Watertown, m. a. 1673, Eliz. d. of Joshua Stubbs of the same, had

James, his eldest ; Jonathan, b. 8 Aug. 1675 ; Abigail; Mary ; Eliz. 31
Jan. 1681 ; Samuel, 15 Feb. 1683 ; Rebecca, bapt. 7 Nov. 1686 ;
Joseph, 24 May 1688 ; and Benjamin, 24 Apr. 1690 ; by sec. w. Abi-
gail he had John ; was freem. 1690, and d. 22 Dec. 1692.   Bond thinks
he was br. of sec. Andrew.   JONATHAN, Charlestown, with w. Wait,
join. the ch. 22 Feb. 1685, had Jonathan, bapt. on Sunday foll. JOSEPH,
Dover 1665–75, by Mr. Quint, a good judge of the case, is thot. to be
Stevenson.
   STINT. See Stent.
   STIRK, GEORGE, the gr. of Harv. 1646, is all unkn. to us by f. and
mo. br. sis. or friend, but W. Winthrop on his Catal. had quot. from MS.
of Rev. Andrew Eliot, "that Mr. S. was an emin. chemist, and wrote
sev. Latin treatis."   As he did not have his A. M. we may presume he
went to Eng. early ; and that he was d. 1698 is almost our whole rec.
of his life.   But it is highly prob. that the true name was Starkey,
wh. see.
   STOCKBRIDGE, BENJAMIN, Scituate, s. of Charles the first, m. 1701,
Mary Tilden, had Benjamin, b. 1704, a physician of emin. and perhaps
other ch.   CHARLES, Scituate, s. of John, brot. from Eng. by his f. in
the Blessing at the age of 1 yr. liv. first at Boston, a wheelwright, and
by w. Abigail had Charles, b. 9 Dec. 1659, d. with the wrong name of
John by rec. in 2 mos. and at Charlestown had Abigail, 24 Feb. 1662 ;
at Scituate, Charles, again, 4 Feb. 1664 ; Sarah, 30 May 1665 ; Thomas,
6 Apr. 1667 ; Eliz. 13 Aug. 1670 ; Joseph, 28 June 1672 ; Benjamin,
9 Oct. 1676 ; and Samuel, 9 July 1679 ; and d. 1683, and his wid. m.
Amos Turner.   Abigail m. 4 Nov. 1676, Henry Josselyn ; Sarah m.
Israel Turner ; and Eliz. m. David Turner.   CHARLES, Scituate, eldest
s. of the preced. had Rachel, b. 9 Apr. 1690 ; Mary, 11 Aug. 1692 ;
Abigail, 22 Mar. 1695 ; Hannah, 30 Jan. 1698 ; Ruth, 30 July 1700 ;
Experience, 1 Jan. 1704 ; Judith, 19 July 1706 ; and Charles, 13 Oct.
1709, d. prob. in few mos. as may, perhaps, one or more other s.   He
was one of the first selectmen of the new town of Hanover, sett. off
from S. 1727, and d. it is thot. 7 Apr. 1731.   JOHN, Scituate, wheelwright, came in the Blessing from London 1635, aged 27, with w. Ann,
21, and s. Charles, 1 ; there his w. join. the ch. 16 July 1637, and had
Hannah, bapt. 24 Sept. foll. ; and Eliz. bapt. at Boston, 10 July 1642 ;
m. a sec. w. 1643, wid. Eliz. Soane, had Eliz. 1644 ; Sarah, 1645 ; and
Esther, 1647 ; and by third w. Mary, nam. in his will, had Abigail,
1655 ; and John, 19, bapt. 26 July 1657, wh. prob. d. young ; this last
at Boston, whither he had rem. and there made his will 4 Sept. 1657,
and d. 13 Oct. foll.   His wid. m. 8 Apr. 1660, Daniel Henrick. Hannah m. 29 Oct. 1656 at B. William Ticknor of S. ; Eliz. m. 1 Jan .
                         17 *

1661, Thomas Hyland; and Sarah m. 6 Jan. 1669, Joseph Woodworth.
JOHN, Haverhill, sw. fidel. Dec. 1677. JOSEPH, Scituate, br. of Benjamin, m. Margaret, d. of Joseph Turner, had Joseph, b. 1 Oct.
1698; Grace, 1700; John, bapt. 2 July 1704; Barshua, 1 Dec.
1706; Margaret, 31 Oct. 1708; Susanna, 25 Nov. 1711; and
David; was selectman some yrs. at Hanover, and deac. longer, d.
11 Mar. 1773, therefore more than 100 yrs. old by 7 mos. and 3
days. SAMUEL, Scituate, br. of the preced. m. 1703, Lydia, d. of
William Barrell, had Samuel, and perhaps more. THOMAS, Scituate,
br. of the preced. m. 28 July 1697, Sarah, d. of Thomas Reed of Weymouth, had Sarah, b. 25 Apr. 1699; Mary, 31 Mar. 1701; Thomas, 13
Feb. 1703; Deborah, 21 June 1705; Ann, 31 May 1710; Micah, 22
Nov. 1714; and Sarah, 26 Oct. 1718. His wid. d. 7 Sept. 1758; but
the date of his own d. is not told.

STOCKER, DANIEL, perhaps of Lynn, took w. Margery Salmon in
1672. EBENEZER, Lynn, m. 15 July 1674, Sarah, prob. d. of Capt.
Thomas Marshall of the same, had Thomas, b. 24 Apr. 1675; Ebenezer,
July 1677; Sarah, 11 Dec. 1679, d. soon; Sarah, again, 27 Feb. 1681;
and Samuel, 29 Nov. 1684; was freem. 1691. SAMUEL, Lynn, m. 6
June 1666, Mary Witt. THOMAS, Chelsea and Lynn 1651–72, by w.
Martha, had, perhaps, other ch. beside Thomas and Eliz. both bapt. at
Boston 6 May 1655.

STOCKIN, STOCKEN, or STOCKING, DANIEL, Middletown, youngest s.
of Samuel of the same, m. 27 Aug. 1700, Jane Mould, perhaps d. of
Hugh of New London, had Daniel, Joseph, Ebenezer, John, Jonathan,
Elisha, Jane, all b. Mr. Parsons says, bef. 1712. GEORGE, Cambridge,
freem. 6 May 1635, rem. to Hartford, prob. with earliest sett. and his
name is in the list of freem. 1669, tho. excus. prob. by reason of age, in
1660, from the com. duty of train. watch. and ward. He d. May 1683,
at gr. age, leav. Samuel, and had three ds. Hannah, w. of Andrew Benton; Sarah, w. of Samuel Olcott; and the w. of John Richards; but
Benton's w. was d. leav. childr. GEORGE, Middletown, s. of Samuel, by
w. Eliz. had Stephen, b. 1694; Eliz. 1697; Samuel, 1700; Bethia,
1703; George, 1705; Nathaniel; but the rec. is defic. in mos. and
days; and he d. 17 Feb. 1714. *SAMUEL, Hartford, s. of the first
George, b. prob. in Eng. m. 27 May 1652, Bethia, d. of John Hopkins
of H., had Hannah, b. 30 Oct. 1654, wh. d. bef. her f.; Samuel, 19 or
29 Oct. 1656; Bethia, 10 Oct. 1658, wh. m. 16 Oct. 1675, Thomas
Stowe; John, 24 Sept. 1660; Lydia, 20 Jan. 1663; George, 20 Feb.
1665; Ebenezer, 23 Feb. 1667; Stephen, 28 Mar. 1673; and Daniel,
14 Apr. 1677; liv. at Middletown, when freem. 1654, and was rep.
1665, 9, and 74, was deac. and perhaps serv. in Philip's war, for in

1677 he was made serg. and he d. 31 Dec. 1683. His wid. m. James
Steele.

STOCKMAN, JOHN, Salisbury, m. 10 May 1671, Sarah, eldest d. of
maj. Robert Pike, wid. of Wymond Bradbury, took o. of alleg. 22 Dec.
1677, had Joseph, b. 29 Feb. 1672 ; William, 2 Nov. 1675 ; Dorothy,
20 Apr. 1678, d. under 18 yrs.; John, 5 Feb. 1681 ; and Robert, 8
Aug. 1683 ; and d. 10 Dec. 1686. JOSEPH, Salisbury, eldest s. of the
preced. m. 14 Jan. 1702, Hannah, d. of Jacob Morrell, had Dorothy, b.
14 Sept. foll.

STOCKTON, THOMAS, came in the Truelove, from London, 1635, aged
21, but no more is heard.

STOCKWELL, QUINTIN, Hatfield, by w. Abigail had John, b. 1676, at
Deerfield, was tak. by the Ind. 19 Sept. 1677, with sev. more, and carr.
to Canada and got back next yr. of whose suffer. story at gr. length is
giv. by Increase Mather in his Remarka. Providences. He took o. of
alleg. 8 Feb. 1679, and went to Branford, where he had Eleazer, b. 25
Apr. of that yr. in 1692 liv. at Suffield until 1709, when he, w. Abigail,
and s. Eleazer were there.

STODDARD, ANTHONY, Boston, 1639, call. a linen draper, was rec.
into our ch. 28 Sept. of that yr. freem. 13 May foll. by first w. Mary, d.
of Emanuel Downing of Salem, niece of Gov. Winthrop, sis. of Sir
George, absurdly call. Lord George in the fam. geneal. had Benjamin,
bapt. 23 Aug. 1640, not nam. in the pr. geneal. that supplies but ill the
deficiency of accuracy by its beauty ; Solomon, H. C. 1662, bapt. 1 Oct.
1643, a. 4 days old, tho. most of the print. books say he was b. 4 Oct.
and this error has been indecently *interpol.* into the town's copy of rec.
of b. perhaps by the hand that made the geneal. perhaps by ano. confid.
in the print. vol. and lightly regard. the sanctity of a public rec.; and
Samson, b. 3, bapt. 7 Dec. 1645. His w. d. 16 June 1647, and he prob.
m. the same yr. Barbara, wid. of Capt. Joseph Weld, of Roxbury, niece
prob. of Edward Clap, of Dorchester, hav. made the contr. for m. so
early as 24 Aug. and she being, in Dec. as his w. rec. on dism. from the
ch. of R. by that of B. had Samuel, bapt. 20 Jan. 1650, a. 6 days old,
but in the careless fam. gen. not nam.; Simeon, not ment. in the rec. of
b. but bapt. 25 May 1651 ; tho. the fam. geneal. gives him to the first w.
wh. had been d. more than 3 yrs.; Sarah, b. 21, bapt. 24 Oct. 1652 ;
and Stephen, 6, bapt. 8 Jan. 1654; and this w. d. 15 Apr. 1655. By
third w. Christian, tak. as was the custom, within a yr. of whose name,
b. or d. we are ign. he had Anthony, b. 16, bapt. 22 June 1656 ; Christian, 22, bapt. 28 Mar. 1658 ; Lydia, 27 Mar. bapt. 1 Apr. 1660, tho.
the fam. geneal. says b. 27 May ; Joseph, 1, bapt. 8 Dec. 1661, d. at 5
mos.; John, 22, bapt. 26 Apr. 1663 ; Ebenezer, 1, bapt. 17 July 1664 ;

Dorothy, 24, bapt. 26 Nov. 1665, by name Deborah, says ch. rec. wh. no doubt is erron.; Mary, 25 Mar. 1668, not found in the ch. rec. where is a vacation for 16 or 17 mos. a. this date; and Jane, 29 July bapt. 6 Aug. 1669; to wh. the geneal. presumptuously adds to make ten by this w. a Grace, b. tw. with Jane, of wh. as neither town nor ch. rec. has notice, and the other was bapt. 8 days aft. b. I doubt the exist. but many of these ch. d. young.   Grace, call. d. in his will of 29 Dec. 1684, pro. 19 May 1687, to wh. he remits whatever she is indebt. was not otherwise entit. than as wid. of a dec. s. of wh. we kn. no more.   He was a man of gr. influence, constable as early as 1641, of his scruple in that office to obey the Govr.'s warrant for tak. Francis Hutchinson into custody, and freedom of remark, call. insolence by the author, the story is giv. by Winth. II. 39.   In 1650 he was chos. recorder of B. and a rep. also in 59 and 60, and nineteen yrs. successiv. from 1665, no man hav. ever been so oft. chos. for Boston to our days.   For a fourth w. he had Mary, wid. of Major Thomas Savage, d. of Rev. Zechariah Symmes, and he d. 16 Mar. 1687, "the ancientest shop-keeper in town," says Sewall in his Diary.   JOHN, Wethersfield, m. 1642, Mary, sec. d. of Nathaniel Foote of the same, had Mary, b. 12 May 1643; John, 12 Apr. 1646; Caleb, and Joshua, tw. 12 Sept. 1648, of wh. the former d. young; Mercy, Nov. 1652; Eliz. July 1656; and Nathaniel, 1661; and d. Dec. 1664, and his wid. m. John Goodrich Apr. 1674.   His d. Mary m. 10 Dec. 1663; and Mercy m. 10 Mar. 1685, as sec. w. the same man, Joseph Wright; Eliz. also m. a Wright.   JOHN, Wethersfield, s. of the preced. m. 26 May 1674, Eliz. d. of Thomas Curtis of the same, had eight ch. and d. 4 Dec. 1703.   Six ch. John, Jonathan, David, Samuel, Eliz. and Mary with w. Eliz. are nam. in the will of 30 Nov. 1703, so that two, prob. d. young.   He left good est.   See Foote Geneal. by Goodwin.   JOSHUA, Wethersfield, br. of the preced. m. 15 Aug. 1684, Bethia, d. of Richard Smith of the same, and d. a. 1725, leav. no issue. NATHANIEL, Wethersfield, br. of the preced. by w. Mary wh. d. 17 Jan. 1693, had one ch. and he m. 7 Dec. foll. Eunice, d. of Thomas Standish of the same, had three ch. and d. 9 Feb. 1714; and his wid. d. 5 Aug. 1716, aged 52, as Goodwin shows without nam. the ch. or giv. dates of b.   But the Wethersfield fam. had first writ. their names Stodder. SAMSON, s. of Anthony, in the geneal. hardly to be disting. as neither the name of w. nor date of m. nor place of resid. nor number of ch. nor time of d. is giv.   All that it tells, is that he had s. Samson, H. C. 1701. On turn. to our rec. we find, that he was of Boston, by w. Susanna had Anthony, 24 May 1672; Martha, 13 June 1678; and Christian, 11 May 1680; but prob. he rem. yet the b. of one of these ch. of Samson is found on the same page of one of Simeon, wh. found more favor in the

eyes of the compiler of the geneal. ‡ SIMEON, Boston, br. of the preced. by w. Mary had Mary, b. 15 Apr. 1677, d. young; Anthony,
24 Sept. 1678, H. C. 1697; Eliz. 10 Feb. 1680; Simeon, 20 Oct.
1682, wh. was, says the geneal. murd. in Eng. and in our Prob. office
admin. is giv. to the f. 26 Sept. 1706, on his s. d. near London; Mary,
again, 19 Sept. 1684; David, 5 Dec. 1685; Jonathan, 5 Feb. 1688;
Martha, 14 Dec. 1689; all wh. so nearly concur. with the fam. geneal.
that I adopt for the residue, without scrutiny, from that work; William,
8 Nov. 1693; Jonathan, again, 4 May 1695; and John, June 1697.
Only two of these ch. I think, outliv. the f. whose first w. d. 13 Aug.
1708; his sec. w. was, m. 31 May 1709, Eliz. wid. of Col. Samuel
Shrimpton, wh. d. 13 Apr. 1713. His third w. m. 12 May 1715, was
Mehitable, wid. of Peter Sargent, wh. had been wid. of Thomas
Cooper, d. of James Minot. He was freem. 1670, a mem. of Prov.
Counc. and d. 15 Oct. 1730; and his will of 15 Mar. 1728, pro. 31 Oct.
1730, provides for her, and gives resid. of large est. to s. Anthony, and
William, and one fourth to childr. of David, and one fourth to childr. of
his d. Legg. SOLOMON, Northampton, br. of the preced. at school to
famous master Corlet bef. Coll. and after his gr. went to Barbados, as
chapl. to the Gov. wh. had been here, was one of the chief divines of
N. E. in his days; m. 8 Mar. 1670, Esther Mather, wid. of Eleazer, d.
of Rev. John Warham, had thirteen ch. Mary, b. 9 Jan. 1671; Esther,
2 June 1672; Solomon, wh. d. 22 Mar. 1673, prob. not many hours old,
but omit. in the geneal. tho. town rec. ment. the d.; Samuel, 5 Feb.
1674, d. soon; Anthony, 6 June 1675, d. next day; Aaron, 23 Aug.
1676, d. in few hours, but the town rec. omits the name; wh. perhaps
was never solemnly giv. while his tw. br. Christian liv. to good old age;
Anthony, again, 9 Aug. 1678, H. C. 1697, the same yr. with his cous.
Anthony, wh. bec. the libr.; Sarah, 1 Apr. 1680; John, 17 Feb. 1682,
H. C. 1701, a gent. of uncom. sagacity and merit; Israel, 10 Apr.
1684, wh. d. a prison. in France; Rebecca, 1686; and Hannah, 21 Apr.
1688. He was ord. success. to the first h. of his w. 11 Sept. 1672, and
made freem. the same yr. yet sw. alleg. 1679, d. 11 Feb. 1729, aged 85;
and his wid. d. 10 Feb. 1736, aged 91. Of this name nine had been gr.
at Harv. and eleven at Yale in 1838. See Stodder.

STODDER, BENJAMIN, Scituate, s. of the sec. John of Hingham, m.
1705, Mary, d. of Israel Sylvester of S. had Benjamin, b. 1708; Mary,
1711; Elisha, 1715; Elijah, 1719; and Isaiah, 1723. DAVID, Hingham, s. of John the first, b. in Eng. m. 27 Dec. 1665, Abigail Law, perhaps wid. of John, certain. d. of the first Andrew Lane, had David, b.
12 July 1668; Abigail, 18 Sept. 1670; Sarah, 1 Dec. 1672; Deborah,
15 Apr. 1674, d. at 9 mos.; Josiah, 6 July 1678; Joseph; and Jael, 5

May 1683; Ruth, 27 July 1685 ; and Lydia, 10 Apr. 1694, d. in few hours. He d. 9 Mar. 1737, aged 104 yrs. the oldest that ever d. in that town. DAVID, Hingham, s. of the preced. m. 26 May 1690, Margaret Macvarlo, had Abigail, Sarah, Josiah, Joseph, and Samuel. HEZEKIAH, Hingham, br. of Benjamin, m. Lois, d. of Israel Silvester, 19 Nov. 1706, had Lois, b. 2 Mar. 1708, d. same mo. rem. to Scituate, there had Bathsheba, 1711 ; Joshua, 1713; Eunice, 1715 ; and Hezekiah, 1722. His w. d. 28 Oct. 1738, aged 60. JACOB, Hingham, br. of the preced. m. 17 Aug. 1704, Sarah Howard, had Nathaniel, b. 14 May 1705 ; and Sarah, 28 Dec. 1711; and he d. 25 Oct. 1734. JAMES, Hingham, br. of the preced. by w. Hannah had James. JOHN, Hingham 1638, but not one wh. came that yr. in the Diligent, had gr. of a house lot the same yr. freem. 18 May 1642, in that yr. liv. at Hull, brot. from Eng. s. John and here had Daniel; Samuel, bapt. 14 June 1640. He had ds. Eliz. wh. m. Feb. 1658, John Low ; and Hannah, wh. m. Gershom Wheelock, beside s. John, the eldest, Daniel, and Samuel, as we learn from his will of 20 Nov. 1661. It was pro. 31 Jan. foll. by John the Excor. and as it provid. for John and Eliz. Law the gr.ch. and made d. Hannah's sh. if she had not ch. at her d. devis. to her h. and his own three s. we may infer, that most of them were b. in Eng. Fam. tradit. makes his d. 18, prob. 28 Nov. 1661; and adds that Ann perhaps his wid. d. 8 Oct. 1675. JOHN, New London 1650, gave depon. in Feb. 1672, call. hims. 60 yrs. old, and d. prob. 1676, leav. wid. wh. m. John Sampson, beside two s. Robert, and Thomas, whose descend. are num. in that vicinage; beside one, John, the wonderful murderer (by his own confess. aged 16), of the w. of Thomas Bolles, and two of her ch. and his own half br. John Sampson. See that article. Ano. s. of Sampson six or seven yrs. old, at that time, constit. the whole fam. as far as is kn. JOHN, Hingham, s. of John of the same, b. in Eng. m. 13 Dec. 1665, at Scituate, Hannah, d. of John Bryant of S. had Hannah, b. 15 Nov. 1666 ; John, 7 June 1668 ; James, 16 July 1670 ; Tabitha, 1 Feb. 1672 ; Jacob, 17 Feb. 1674; Martha, 1 Nov. 1676; Hezekiah, 11 Feb. 1679 ; Nathaniel, 18 Mar. 1681, d. at 21 yrs. ; Benjamin, 23 Oct. 1683; Bathsheba, 1 Apr. 1686, d. next mo. His w. d. 17 Sept. 1702; and he d. 20 Dec. 1708. JOHN, Hingham, s. of the preced. by w. Mary had Mary, b. 6 May 1700 ; and Tabitha, 12 Sept. 1704. JOSEPH, Hingham, s. of David the first, by w. Mercy had Samuel, b. 22 Sept. 1728. RALPH, New London, on Groton side, in 1696, ment. by Caulkins, 159, may not have been the younger br. of the wretched homicide; and as the same author, 354, finds a ROBERT, also, at Groton, a. 1712, it serves to increase the doubt. SAMUEL, Hingham, s. of John the first, freem. 1677, m. 6 Feb. 1667, Eliz. d. of Thomas Gill, had Eliz. and Tabitha, tw. b. 1 Dec. 1667, of wh. Tabitha d. in few days; Samuel, 11 Aug. 1670, wh. d. at Scituate 25 July 1762; Mary, 30 Aug. 1672; Stephen, 18 Sept. 1674; Thomas, 19 Dec. 1676; Simon, 17 Feb. 1679; Rachel, 9 Mar. 1681; Jeremiah, 3 Nov. 1683; Jonathan, 1 May 1686; David, 9 July 1688, d. soon; and David, again, 19 Mar. 1693. His w. d. 8 May foll. and he m. 10 Jan. 1699, Martha, wid. of John Chubbuck, d. of Nathaniel Beal, and he d. 16 Sept. 1731, aged 92. Oft. the name was writ. Stoddard by strangers, as that name is freq. seen Stodder.

STOKES, HENRY, Pemaquid, took o. of fidel. to Mass. July 1674. Dr. Harris, the elder, in his Hist. of first ch. of Dorchester, misappro. this name to Fowkes. See that art. ISAAC, Dover 1660. Deborah, perhaps his d. m. 15 Aug. 1687, Richard Kenney. One Grace S. emb. at London, Sept. 1635 in the Hopewell, to come to Boston, of wh. I can tell no more.

STONARD, STONNARD, or STONHARD, JOHN, Roxbury 1645, in Aug. of that yr. mortgag. his est. to Gov. Dudley and the same was disch. Jan. 1647, was of the ch. but took not the freem.'s o. and was bur. 13 Aug. 1649, a middle-aged man, says Eliot. Perhaps he brot. w. and ch. from Eng. JOSEPH, Haddam, propos. for freem. 1669, may have been s. of the preced.

STONE, BENAJAH, Guilford, s. of the first William of the same, m. Esther, d. of John Kirby of Middletown, had Benajah; Esther, b. 3 Nov. 1676; Mary, 9 Oct. 1681; and Abraham, wh. d. young; and d. 1738. DANIEL, Cambridge, s. of Gregory, b. in Eng. freem. 10 May 1643; by w. Mary had Mary, b. 22 Mar. 1644; Sarah, 22 Sept. 1645; David, d. 1646, prob. very young; Daniel, 2 Jan. 1647; Eliz. 1 Jan. 1649; Abigail, 28 Apr. 1653; was a surgeon, rem. to Boston, where he had Mehitable, 1 Aug. and his w. d. 8 Aug. 1658, and was, tho. youngest s. excor. Nov. 1672, with the eldest. His d. Mary prob. m. 14 May 1667, Isaac Hart of Concord. DANIEL, Sudbury, s. of John the first, m. 2 Nov. 1667, Mary Ward, wid. of Richard, had Daniel, b. 22 Nov. 1668; Ann, 15 Jan. 1670; Tabitha, 4 May 1672; Sarah, 14 Feb. 1675; Mary, 10 Aug. 1677; Eliz. 9 Nov. 1678; Abigail, 13 Feb. 1680; and John; was deac. in S. rem. to Framingham, there was selectman two yrs. and his w. d. 10 June 1703. He m. 8 Feb. foll. Abigail Wheeler, wh. d. 28 Oct. 1711, and he m. 18 Nov. 1712, Ruth Haynes, and he d. 1719. DANIEL, Dover 1671. DANIEL, Watertown (whose f. Dr. Bond did not venture to conject. but), in my opin. was s. of the first Daniel, or of the first David, and so gr.s. of Gregory; but Bond informs us, that his w. Joanna, and three ch. Daniel, David, and Dorcas were bapt. 19 June 1687, at W. DAVID, Cambridge, s. of Gregory, b. in Eng. freem. 1647, by w. Eliz. had David, b. 6 Apr. 1649, but mo. and ch. d. soon; by w. Dorcas

had David, b. 6 Apr. 1650 ; Daniel; Dorcas, 18 Dec. 1652 ; John, a.
1654; Samuel, 19 June 1656; and Nathaniel, all these six bapt. says
Mitchell's Reg. in his ch. Lexington rec. ment. that David d. 16 Jan.
1704, and Dorcas, 13 July foll. prob. this h. and w. DAVID, Sudbury,
s. of John of the same, by w. Susanna had Susanna, b. 29 Jan. 1677 ;
Mary, 19 Feb. 1682 ; Samuel, 23 May 1685 ; Thomas, 11 Mar. 1688 ;
and d. 1737. DAVID, Cambridge, s. of the first David, m. 31 Dec.
1674, Sarah, d. prob. of Richard Hildreth, and d. 21 Aug. 1679.
DAVID, Cambridge, s. of Simon the sec. m. 12 Dec. 1710, Mary Rice,
perhaps d. of Richard of the same, had only d. Mary, or Mercy, and he
d. 7 Oct. 1750, had been blind 56 yrs.   ‡ * EBENEZER, Newton, s. of
Simon the sec. freem. 1690, m. 18 Mar. 1686, Margaret, d. of James
Trowbridge of the same, had Ebenezer, b. 21 Dec. foll.; Margaret, 1
Aug. 1688 ; Samuel, 1 July 1690; John, 18 Sept. 1692 ; Nathaniel, 6
Sept. 1694, d. young ; Mindwell, 26 June 1696 ; David, 15 May, 1698;
Mary, 19 Apr. 1700 ; Simon, 14 Sept. 1702 ; James, 8 June 1704,
H. C. 1724, min. of Holliston ; Experience, 1 July 1707.   His w. d. 4
May 1710, and he had sec. w. 12 June 1711, Abigail Wilson, wh. d.
1720, and he took 3d w. 8 Apr. 1722, Sarah, wid. of Samuel Liver-
more, wh. had been his third w. and wid. of Nathaniel Stearns, d. of
John Nevinson.   He was selectman oft. rep. 9 yrs. and a mem. of the
Provinc. Counc. d. 4 Oct. 1754.   ELIAS, Charlestown, by w. Abigail
had Elias, bapt. 24 July 1687 ; John, 16 Dec. 1688; William, 16 Feb.
1691, d. soon ; Abigail, 1 Nov. 1691, d. soon ; Abigail, again, 16 July
1693 ; Mary, 4 Nov. 1694 ; Thomas, 6 Dec. 1696 ; Eliz. 11 Dec. 1698 ;
Sarah, 22 Dec. 1700 ; Robert, 1 Nov. 1702; Hannah, 4 Feb. 1704 ;
Rebecca, 23 Mar. 1707 ; Richard, 12 Mar. 1709 ; and William, again,
4 Jan. 1713.   I presume, from find. neither f. nor mo. among the mem.
of ch. that they rem. to C. from some other town.   But the name Elias
was perpet. at C. thro. 3 or 4 generat.   * GREGORY, Cambridge, br. of
Simon, did not, I conject. come in the same sh. yet prob. in the same yr.
with him, tho. for a yr. or two he dwelt at Watertown, and had gr. there
of ld. freem. 25 May 1636, yet more import. is it, that he brot. w.
Lydia, formerly wid. Cooper, wh. d. 24 June 1674, with the ch. John
and Lydia of her first h. and his own ch. John, Daniel, David, Eliz.
Samuel, and Sarah, prob. all b. in Eng.   He was deac. rep. 1638, and
d. 30 Nov. 1672, aged 80.   His will, made 8 ds. bef. print. in Geneal.
Reg. VIII. 69, provides for w. his four s. beside John Cooper, and
Lydia Fiske's d. Lydia, wh. he calls the mo. gr.ch.   His wid. d. 24
June 1674.   Lydia Cooper m. David Fiske ; Eliz. S. m. prob. Anthony
Potter of Ipswich ; and Sarah m. 12 July 1653, Joseph Meriam of Con-
cord.   HUGH, Andover, m. 15 Oct. 1667, Hannah Foster, perhaps d. of

Andrew, had John, b. 1668, and others, says Barry, from wh. I would gladly have copied their names and dates, but the informat. is not giv. From the rec. we find the d. of his w. 20 Apr. 1689 "murd. by her h." whence it is safer to conclude, that he was insane. HUGH, Warwick, m. Abigail, a d. of Peter Bassaker, or Busicot, as the R. I. rec. gives the name, had Peter, b. 14 Mar. 1672 or 3 ; and Abigail, 10 Feb. 1678 or 9. He was in 1666 styl. "late serv. to John Paine of Boston." ISAAC, Salem, had a brick kiln 1692. JOHN, the capt. of violent temper, wh. in Sept. 1633, was forbid. by our Court to come again within this jurisdict. on pain of d. and soon aft. was k. by the Pequods. He belong. to Virg. yet our people made this one of the provoca. to the war, in wh. that tribe was destroy. tho. much stronger was the incitem. caus. by later acts of those Ind. JOHN, Salem 1636, kept the ferry across Bass riv. at the earliest day, had gr. of ld. 1637, was one of the found. of the Beverly ch. 23 June 1667, then call. sen. wherefore it may be that he had s. of the same name, and perhaps other ch. Possib. he was passeng. in the Elizabeth 1635, from London, when custom ho. marks the age of the person, 40. JOHN, with his w. admonish. (by our Court) to "make bigger bread" in 1639, may have, soon aft. such hint, rem. from Mass. *JOHN, Cambridge, s. of deac. Gregory, b. in Eng. came with his f. m. Ann, d. of Elder Edward Howe of Watertown, had Hannah, b. 6 June 1640 ; John, date of whose b. or d. is unkn. but he is thot. to be the eldest s. yet, infirm of mind, was subj. to the care of his younger brs. ; Daniel, 31 Aug. 1644 ; David, 31 Oct. 1646 ; Mary ; Eliz. ; Margaret, 22 Oct. 1653 ; Tabitha, 20 or 29 May 1655 ; Sarah 22 Sept. 1657 ; and Nathaniel, 11 May 1660 ; was freem. 1665, then call. of Watertown, and yet one of the earliest sett. of Sudbury 1640, where most of these ch. were b. and there he was Elder of the ch. but prob. in the gr. Ind. war rem. to Cambridge, again, and was its rep. 1682, and 3, and d. 5 May in this latter yr. His will of 16 Apr. preced. calls him aged a. 64 yrs. abstr. in Geneal. Reg. VIII. 145, provides for wid. and the ten ch. Hannah m. 1 July 1658 the sec. John Bent of Marlborough ; Mary m. 1665, Isaac Hunt, and next, 30 Sept. 1681, as his sec. w. Eliphalet Fox ; Eliz. m. Samuel Stow ; Margaret m. 11 Jan. 1676, William Brown ; Tabitha m. 2 or 27 (both dates giv. by Barry) Nov. 1674, John Rice ; and Sarah m. Jacob Hill. JOHN, Hartford, an orig. propr. perhaps is he to wh. the Conn. governm. in 1668, gr. 100 acres. But he had rem. early to found in 1639 the orig. compact at Guilford, there by w. Mary had John, b. 14 Aug. 1644 ; Samuel, 6 Dec. 1646 ; Nathaniel, 5 Feb. 1648 ; Thomas, 5 June 1650 ; and Noah, 1652, wh. d. unm. 3 or 4 yrs. bef. his f. wh. d. a. 1687. He, with

William S., is among the freem. of Guilford 1669. JOHN, Sudbury, by
w. Ann had Hannah, b. 6 June 1640. JOHN, Boston, by w. Mary had
Sarah, b. 16 Sept. 1659 ; and he d. soon, as may seem, for wid. Mary S.
at B. m. 23 Nov. foll. Roger Wheeler. JOHN, Hull, in his will of 5
May 1659, pro. 27 Jan. 1664, leav. to w. Joan all his real and pers. est.
she to pay £60 to the three ch. of his br. Simon wh. had liv. at Cothel-
stone in Co. Somerset, a. 6 miles N. of Taunton, so that it would be
infer. that he had no ch. and had come from that pt. of Eng. JOHN,
Hull, call. sen. in May 1666, when he sold a house lot, so that perhaps
he had s. of the same name. JOHN, Watertown, s. of Simon the first,
b. in Eng. prob. brot. in his mo.'s arms in the Increase from London
1635, being 5 wks. old, when emb. 15 Apr. yet Bond says the W. rec.
marks him b. 15 Aug. perhaps by blunder. By w. Sarah he had
Sarah; Joanna, b. 11 Jan. 1665 ; John, 15 Dec. 1666; Ann, 8 Aug.
1668; Mary, 14 Sept. 1670; Eliz. 5 May 1672; Samuel, 14 Feb.
1675 ; Hepzibah, 5 May 1677 ; Deborah, 25 Feb. 1680 ; and Rebecca,
22 Aug. 1682 ; was a deac. and d. 26 Mar. 1691. Sarah m. 15 or 18
Dec. for Bond ment. both dates, 1681, Manning Sawin ; Joanna m. 9
May 1693, Simon Tainter ; Eliz. m. 17 Nov. 1692, John Barnard, as his
sec. w.; Hepzibah m. 7 Jan. 1702, as his sec. w. John Morse ; and
Deborah m. 9 June 1703, Ephraim Cutter. JOHN, wh. had his A. B. at
our H. C. 1653, went to Eng. there was A. M. at Camb. Univ. but
the time of his d. is uncert. tho. by the Mather Catal. it was bef. 1698.
Farmer wh. was prob. mistak. thot. he was s. of Rev. Samuel of Hartford. JOHN, Milford, s. of John of Guilford, m. Susanna, d. of Rev.
Roger Newton, and d. 1686, leav. ch. Samuel, John, and Ezekiel.
JOHN, Beverly, s. of John of the same, d. a. 1691, leav. wid. Abigail,
wh. brot. inv. to pro. 25 Sept. of that yr. JOHN, Groton, was among
the early sett. on the sec. build. of the town aft. Philip's war, or certain.
was in Mar. 1692 assign. to partic. garrison in one pt. and by w. Sarah
had John, b. 23 Sept. 1699 ; and James, 23 Jan. 1701. JOHN, Watertown, s. of John of the same, by w. Mary, perhaps d. of John Barsham,
had John, b. 10 Apr. 1697; Nathaniel, 23 May 1699; Isaac, 8 Feb.
1703; Mary, 22 Feb. 1705 ; and Barsham, 15 Sept. 1710. JONA-
THAN, Watertown, youngest s. of the sec. Simon, m. 15 Nov. 1699,
Ruth, d. of Samuel Eddy, had Jonathan, b. 1702. His w. d. 7 or 13
Oct. of that yr. Bond gives both dates, and by sec. w. Mary, wh. d. 24
June 1720, he had no ch. but by third w. m. 15 Nov. 1720, Hepzibah,
d. of Nathaniel Coolidge, he had tw. Hepzibah, 9 Oct. 1722, d. in few
mos. and Ann ; and Moses, 16 Dec. 1723 ; and d. 7 Jan. 1754, and his
wid. d. 25 Mar. 1763, aged 83. MATTHEW, Lancaster and Sudbury, s.
of Simon the sec. by w. Mary had Joseph, Mary, Adams, and Rachel.

The dates of neither are giv. by Barry or Bond, yet they interchange priority betw. 2d and 3d. He d. at S. of wh. ch. he was deac. and his will was pro. 9 Aug. 1743. NATHANIEL, Beverly, perhaps s. of John of the same, may have been of Ipswich 1648, and was freem. 1668. He may have been the same, wh. by w. Mary, had, at Boston, Nathaniel, b. 25 Mar. 1664. NATHANIEL, Guilford, s. of John of the same, was made freem. 1677, m. 10 July 1673, Mary, d. of George Bartlett of the same, had Joseph, b. 11 June 1674; Ebenezer, 21 Aug. 1676; Nathaniel, 7 Oct. 1678; Ann, 29 Jan. 1681, d. at 3 yrs.; Caleb, 26 Mar. 1683, d. next yr.; Caleb, again, 10 Nov. 1685; Noah, 9 Nov. 1687, d. under 16 yrs.; John, 7 Oct. 1689, d. bef. 10 yrs.; Ann, again, 17 June 1692; and Timothy, 16 Mar. 1696; and d. 11 Aug. 1709. His wid. d. 1724. NATHANIEL, Cambridge, s. of John of the same, m. 25 Apr. 1684, Sarah Wait of Malden, perhaps d. of Hon. John, had Nathaniel, b. 15 Oct. 1685; Ebenezer, 16 Apr. 1688; Jonathan, 24 Mar. 1690; Isaac; John, 13 Apr. 1702; Mary, 19 Dec. 1705; Sarah, 12 Oct. 1708; Hezekiah, 5 Mar. 1711; and Barry says his will, of 23 June 1732, was pro. 2 Nov. foll. *NATHANIEL*, Harwich, s. of Simon the sec. m. 15 Dec. 1698, Reliance, youngest ch. of Gov. Hinckley, and this union prob. led him to be first min. of that town, where a ch. was gath. 1700; ord. 16 Nov. 1700, bef. wh. Mather's Hecatompolis would persuade us he had three sev. flocks at once. He had Hannah; Nathan, b. 18 Feb. 1708, H. C. 1726; Nathaniel; Mary; Reliance; Thankful; and four other ds. but of the last eight ch. no dates are found; and he d. 8 Feb. 1755, aged 88. His wid. d. 24 May 1759. NICHOLAS, Boston, by w. Hannah had Hannah, b. 8 Jan. 1652; Josiah, 4 Feb. 1654; Hopestill, 7 Jan. 1656; Abigail, 20 Nov. 1658; Eliz. 25 Sept. 1661; and Benjamin, 17 Feb. 1664; was a shipwright, and perhaps rem. Barry says that his d. Mary m. 1671 Isaac Johnson of Charlestown; but such d. is not kn. by me. PETER, Warwick, s. of Hugh of the same, m. 25 June 1696, Eliz. d. of John Shaw, had Eliz. b. 25 Mar. 1697; Peter, 22 Oct. 1698; Sarah, 17 Feb. 1700; Abigail, 15 Sept. 1701; Priscilla, 2 Feb. 1703; and John, 29 Sept. 1704. RICHARD, Hatfield, k. by the Ind. 19 Oct. 1675. ROBERT, Salem 1652, perhaps br. perhaps s. of John of the same, by w. Sarah had Samuel, b. 1657; Robert; Benjamin; and others, says Barry, but names them not. In Nov. 1660, as Felt, II. 583, tells, his w. was prosecut. as a Quaker, but the sentence in her case was not, we may hope, that she should be hang. or sold for a slave to the W. I. as in sev. other instances. Prob. both d. in their beds in advanced age. ROBERT, Salem, s. prob. of the preced. had w. Hannah, and d. 1688, and his w. d. 17 Apr. 1691, aged 29, as by the gr. stones we learn. *SAMUEL*, Hartford, was, it is said, b. at

Hertford in Co. Herts (a. 20 ms. from London), usually sound. Hartford, and tradit. tells that the city in Conn. out of regard to him was thus nam.; perhaps younger br. of Gregory, and of Simon, certain. bred at Emanuel, where he was matric. 1620, and took his degrees 1623 and 7, came in 1633, with Cotton, Hooker, and other men of note, passeng. embark. at the Downs, in the Griffin, arr. 4 Sept. at Boston, went with Hooker to Cambridge, where 11 Oct. next he was made teacher and H. pastor of the ch. and adm. freem. 14 May foll. in 1636 rem. with Hooker, and they found. the ch. of H. there with univers. accept. they fulfill. the same duties as bef. at C. and in the Pequot war, 1637, he was chapl. to the troops under Capt. Mason. Aft. the d. of our judicious Hooker, he had a sad controversy with some of his people, equally bitter and unintelligib. of wh. Mather thot. the origin undiscov. But aft. many yrs. of fruitless attempts at reconcil. Gov. Webster and many friends of influence rem. up the riv. beyond the rancor, and S. d. 20 July 1663. He had sec. w. m. 1641, Eliz. Allen at Boston, by her had Samuel and Eliz. and three ch. were of a former one, Rebecca, Mary, and Sarah. The whole five are ment. in his will. More than one fifth of his inv. was in books. It ought to be told, that the town rec. has other ch. Joseph, bapt. 18 Oct. 1646; Lydia, 22 Jan. or Feb. 1648; a s. bapt. 29 Apr. 1649, wh. may be the Samuel of the will; and Abigail, b. 9 Sept. 1650; but prob. all exc. Samuel, and Eliz. wh. must be the same as Lydia, or Abigail of the town rec. d. early. His wid. m. Mr. George Gardner, of Salem, outliv. him, and d. late in 1681. Her will of 6 June pro. 4 Jan. foll. names her own two ch. Samuel, and Eliz. wh. had been w. of William Sedgwick, was aft. many yrs. of neglect, divorc. from him, m. John Roberts, had s. John, wh. in this will was provid. for by his gr.mo. She names her ds.-in-law, the ch. of his first w. Rebecca, w. of Timothy Nash of Hadley; Mary, w. of Joseph Fitch of Windsor; and Sarah, w. of Thomas Butler of Hartford. SAMUEL, Hartford, only s. of the preced. was much respect. in Conn. and qualif. to assist Gershom Bulkley, in 1676, at Wethersfield, in his work of the ministry, while giv. his devot. to the other work of Surgeon to the forces in the Ind. war. He also preach. at Wethersfield, Middletown, and other places, was never m. nor sett. but he had liberal gr. of ld. by the legisl. of Conn. for his f.'s services, bec. very intemper. in 1678 and 80 was punish. by fines for drunk. "given over to the power" of that evil habit; and d. 8 Oct. 1683, by falling down the bank of the riv. on the rocks. SAMUEL, Cambridge, fourth s. of Gregory, prob. b. in Eng. freem. 1657, was m. 7 June 1655 to Sarah, d. of the first Isaac Stearns, had Samuel, b. 1 Oct. 1656; Isaac; both bapt. says the Reg. of matchless Mitchell, tho. it gives not their dates; and Isaac prob. d. young; Sarah, 5 Feb. bapt.

10 Mar. 1661, was adopt. by Richard Webb of Hartford, as a d. and
he brot. her up until m. to Thomas Butler, and she had half of his est.;
John, 12 May bapt. June 1663; Lydia, 25 Nov. bapt. 31 Dec. 1665;
Mary, 22 Feb. bapt. 22 Mar. 1668, d. soon; Ann, 30 June 1673; and
Joseph; he was deac. and d. 27 Sept. 1715 in his 80th yr. SAMUEL,
Guilford 1676, propound. for freem. Oct. of that yr. was s. of John of
the same, m. 1 Nov. 1683, Sarah Tainter, d. prob. of the first Michael of
Branford, had Sarah, b. 1684, d. soon; Samuel, 1685; Abigail, 1687;
Sarah, again, 1689; Deborah, 1690; Mary, 1693; Bathshua, 1695;
and Eliz. 1697; and he d. 5 Apr. 1708. SAMUEL, Concord, freem.
1682. SAMUEL, Beverly, perhaps s. of John of the same, m. Eliz. d. of
Zechariah Herrick, but the date of her b. is giv. by Barry, as that of m.
SIMON, Watertown, elder br. of Gregory, and perhaps of Rev. Samuel,
came in the Increase, from London 1635, aged 50, call. husbandman,
with w. Joan, or Jane, 38, d. of William Clark, and ch. Frances, 16;
Ann, 11; Simon, 4; Mary, 3; and John, 5 wks.; bec. freem. 25 May
1636, deac. had b. here, Eliz. 5 Apr. 1639; took sec. w. a. 1654, Sarah,
wid. of Richard Lumpkin of Ipswich, from wh. it may be presum. that
he had acquaintance with her bef. they came from Eng. and as her h.
had come from Boxted in Essex, perhaps S. was of that Co. Ano.
infer. may be, that his w. Jane had not long been d. This w. by her
contract of m. was permit. to make a will to dispose of her prop. of wh.
a full abstr. is in Geneal. Reg. VIII. She d. in 1663, and he d. 22
Sept. 1665, aged 80. Frances m. Rev. Henry Green; Ann, perhaps,
m. Lewis Jones; and in his will of 7 Sept. preced. pro. next mo. only
ch. nam. are Simon, John, Frances, and Mary. Abstr. is in Geneal.
Reg. III. 182. * SIMON, Watertown, s. of the preced. b. in Eng. freem.
1653, m. says Barry, Mary Whipple, d. I find, of John of Ipswich, had
John, b. 23 July 1658; Matthew, 6 Feb. 1660; Nathaniel, 22 Feb.
1662, d. in two days; Ebenezer, 27 Feb. 1663; Mary, 6 Jan. 1665;
Nathaniel, again, a. 1667, H. C. 1690, bef. ment.; Eliz. 9 Oct. 1670;
David, 19 Oct. 1672; one, Aug. 1674, d. very soon; Susanna, 6 Nov.
1675; and Jonathan, 26 Dec. 1677; beside that Simon, as I think,
earlier than the last four or even five, or perhaps the first b. His surname is misprint. in Geneal. Reg. XI. 76, as Stowe. He was town clk.
selectman, and rep. 1679–86, and again, aft. the overthrow of Sir E.
Andros, in 1689 and 90, and d. 27 Feb. 1708; and his wid. d. 2 June
1720, aged 86. Mary m. Comfort Starr of Dedham; Eliz. m. deac.
Isaac Stearns; and Susanna m. June 1697, Edward Goddard. SIMON,
Groton, s. of the preced. one of the orig. proprs. yet perhaps not actu.
sett. bef. Philip's war, but in Mar. 1692 had long eno. been there to be
assign. as also, John, wh. I judge to be his br. in the distrib. of garri-

sons against Ind. hostil. by w. Sarah had, prob. Simon, not rec.;
Susanna, b. 23 Oct. 1694; Isaac, 4 May 1697; and Benjamin, 12 Aug.
1706; beside Hannah, wh. d. 27 Sept. 1723; and Lydia, wh. d. three
days aft. of wh. the b. of neither is found by Butler. THOMAS, Guilford, freem. 1677, was s. of John of the same, m. 13 Dec. 1676, Mary,
d. of William Johnson, had Benjamin, b. 11 Mar. 1678; Mary, 6 Apr.
1680, wh. perhaps d. young; and Dorothy, the first and last being nam.
in the will of their gr.f. 1695. WILLIAM, Guilford 1639, sign. the
coven. of 1 June, perhaps br. of John of the same, by w. Hannah had
William, b. a. 1642; Hannah a. 1644; Benajah, a. 1647; beside
Samuel, wh. d. 1675; but this may have been by his sec. w. m. 1659,
Mary, wid. of Richard Hughes of G. He d. Nov. 1683. Hannah m.
bef. 1666, John Norton, and perhaps d. bef. her f. WILLIAM, Guilford,
s. of the preced. m. 20 Feb. 1673, Hannah Wolfe, tho. the surname is
uncert. had Samuel, b. 16 Mar. 1675, d. soon; William, 22 Mar. 1676;
Hannah, 27 July 1678; Daniel, 27 July 1680; Eliz. 28 Nov. 1682;
Josiah, 22 May 1685; Stephen, 1 Mar. 1689; Joshua, 3 May 1692;
and Abigail, 1 Dec. 1697. He was propound. 1669, for freem. and d.
28 Sept. 1730. Of a sec. w. Mary we kn. not the date. Of this name,
in 1834, Farmer marks thirteen had been gr. at Harv. six at Yale, and
seventeen at the rest of the N. E. coll.

STONHILL, HENRY, Milford 1639–46, soon aft. went home, tak. dism.
from the ch. of M. which he had join. with, 1641, to Thomas Goodwin's
ch. in London.

STORER, BENJAMIN, Wells, perhaps s. of William, was k. by the Ind.
Apr. 1677. *JOSEPH, Wells, br. of the preced. sw. alleg. and was ensign
1680, rep. 1681, and 5, a man of distinct. and energy in the Ind. wars; by
w. Hannah, d. prob. of Roger Hill, had Hannah, b. 6 May 1680; Sarah,
9 Dec. 1682; Mary, 12 May 1685; Abigail, 29 Oct. 1687; Joseph, 29
Aug. 1690; John, 5 Sept. 1694; Joseph, prob. at Charlestown, whither
the Ind. war may have compel. the mo. to flee, and certain. bapt. there 8
Nov. 1696; Keziah, 2 May 1697; Ebenezer, in Saco fort, 4 June 1699;
and Seth, 26 May 1702, H. C. 1720, min. of Watertown. RICHARD,
Boston, came in the George from Bristol, prob. 1635, with his mo. Eliz.
w. of Robert Hull, f. of Capt. John, but no more is told of him.
SAMUEL, Wells, br. of Joseph, was disting. in the defence against
French and Ind. of their position, common. call. Storer's garrison,
1692; but his resid. for sev. yrs. was Charlestown, where he had Wil-
liam, bapt. 28 June 1691; the f. call. of the ch. of York; Lydia, 4
Mar. 1694; Mehitable, 10 May 1696; Jemima, 30 Oct. 1698; and
David, 27 Oct. 1700. But prob. aft. peace he went again to Maine.
WILLIAM, an early sett. in Maine, had Joseph, Jeremiah, Samuel, and

Benjamin. Farmer in his MS. had mark. that six of this name had been gr. at Harv. and five at Bowd. in 1834.

STORES, in mod. times STORRS, CORDIAL, Mansfield, youngest ch. of the first Samuel, m. 15 Dec. 1724, Hannah, d. of Thomas Wood of Rowley, had Jabez, b. 26 July 1725, d. next yr.; Cordial, 3 Jan. 1728; Hannah, 15 Apr. 1732; and Mehitable, 15 Apr. 1737; and he had sec. w. m. 10 Oct. 1765, Catharine, wid. of Zechariah Bicknell of Ashford. SAMUEL, Barnstable, is said to have come from Sutton in Nottinghamsh. but as there are four parishes of that name in the Co. we may be uncert. wh. is meant. He m. 6 Dec. 1666, Mary, d. of Thomas Huckins, had Mary, b. 31 Dec. 1667; Sarah, 26 June 1670; Hannah, 28 Mar. 1672; Eliz. 31 May 1675; Samuel, 17 May 1677; and Lydia, June 1679; beside Mehitable, bapt. 16 Sept. 1683. His. w. d. eight days aft. and he m. 14 Dec. 1685, Esther Egard, had Thomas, 27 Oct. 1686; Esther, Oct. bapt. 16 Dec. 1688; and Cordial, 14 Oct. 1692. He rem. to Mansfield, Conn. and there d. 30 Apr. 1719, and his wid d. 13 Apr. 1730, aged 88. SAMUEL, Mansfield, s. of the preced. by w. Martha had Samuel, b. 22 Aug. 1701; John, 7 Oct. 1702; Martha, Feb. 1704; Huckins, 10 Dec. 1705; Eliz. Aug. 1708; Mary, May 1710; and Joseph, 8 Mar. 1712; and d. 9 Aug. 1727. THOMAS, Mansfield, br. of the preced. by w. Mehitable, m. 14 Mar. 1708, had Mehitable, b. 30 Mar. 1709; Rebecca, 29 Aug. 1710; Zeruiah, 27 Aug. 1712; Cornelius, 30 Dec. 1714; Thomas, 16 Jan. 1717; Prince, 12 Mar. 1719; Josiah, 25 Mar. 1721; Judah, 26 Sept. 1723; Lemuel, 13 Mar. 1726; Amariah, 11 June 1728; and Ann, 18 Jan. 1732; and d. Apr. 1755; and his wid. liv. to 10 Mar. 1776. Farmer's MS. show that, in 1834, there had, of this name, been gr. nine at Yale, eight at Dart. and six at other N. E. coll. of wh. none at Harv.

STORKE, JOHN, Rowley, m. prob. betw. 1660 and 70 Mercy, d. of the first Thomas Nelson of the same. SAMUEL, Lynn 1677.

STORY, ANDREW, Ipswich 1639, may be the youth sentenc. to be whip. Sept. Court, 1635, for run. from his master, and aft. had serv. in the expedit. against the Pequots two yrs. later. AUGUSTUS, or AUGUSTINE, Exeter 1639, had the yr. bef. been of Boston, and join. with John Wheelwright of Exeter (wh. was banish. 1637, from Mass.), in purchase, 3 Apr. 1638, from the sagamore of Piscataqua, of a large tract, thirty miles square, of wh. authentic copy may be seen in N. H. Hist. Coll. I. He is call. of Boston, as well as Samuel Hutchinson, ano. grantee, br.-in-law of Wheelwright, therein nam. of Piscataqua. But how this person spell. his name is very uncert. varying from Star, thro. Storr, to Storre and Story; yet with no fortuitous combina. of letters can I found prob. ground for placing him at Boston for any long resid. He was not a mem. of the ch. he was not a landholder, nor indeed is any thing more certain. kn. of him aft. the gr. authentic purchase. If he were m. and cont. in our country, he may have been ancest. of that Charles, wh. bec. Secr. of the Prov. of N. H. 1696, and was acting in the same place 1714, beside being judge of the admiralty, and indeed may have been counsel in the gr. cause, 1707, to support the forged deed of the whole province of N. H. to Wheelwright, Story, and others, print. as Appendix in the first vol. of Belkn. orig. Ed. with date of 17 May 1629, seven yrs. bef. Wheelwright was on this side of the ocean. Wrestling Brewster (the mythical) m. his d. Emila, says Ashbel Steele in his fictitious portion of that interesting work. See Brewster. GEORGE, Boston 1642, a young merch. wh. by tak. up the cause (trover for a pig) brot. against Capt. Keayne by the w. of one Richard Sherman, with wh. he liv. perhaps in a suspicious way, during the abs. of her h. brot. on the gr. quarrel betw. rep. and Assist. that shook the colony that yr. and the next to its foundat. but no more is kn. of him, unless he were, in 1643, of Maine. ISAAC, Watertown 1635, only come in by mistake of surname for Stearns in Geneal. Reg. VII. 159. ROWLAND, Boston, shipwright, bot. est. 1673, by w. Bethia had Bethia, b. 15 July 1677; Abigail, 3 Apr. 1679; and by sec. w. Ann d. of the first Joseph Belcher, had Rowland, 3 Sept. 1683; Joseph, 31 Mar. 1685; Ann, 28 Oct. 1686; John, 20 Mar. 1689; Ann, 14 Mar. 1691; Abigail, again, 11 Mar. 1693; Samuel, 20 Aug. 1694; Rebecca, 2 May 1696, d. soon; William, 30 Mar. 1698; Rebecca, again, 1 Feb. 1700, d. soon; Rebecca, again, 28 Aug. 1701; Jeremiah, 2 July 1702; Zechariah, 27 June 1706; and Benjamin, 15 Nov. 1707; yet in the rec. of one of these (I think it is John), the name of the f. is giv. Richard, wh. whoso will may believe. He d. prob. July 1709, for his inv. dat. 9 of that mo. was by the admor. wid. Ann, produc. 14 Sept. foll. SAMUEL, Ipswich, by w. Eliz. had Ann, b. 31 Mar. 1691; Ephraim, 22 Oct. 1692; John, 19 June 1694; Solomon, 13 Mar. 1696; and Stephen, 7 Oct. 1697. SETH, d. 1669, leav. w. Sarah, and ch. Seth, aged 21, William, 19; and Abigail, 15; may be gather. from Mr. Coffin in Geneal. Reg. VIII. 53; but of what town we are left to ask, and my informat. yields no ans. SETH, Ipswich, s. of William of the same, had. w. Eliz. and ch. Zechariah, b. 14 Mar. 1685; Martha, 28 Sept. 1691; Seth, 4 Apr. 1694; and Damaris, 24 Jan. 1697; and he d. 9 Oct. 1732. WILLIAM, Ipswich, came 1637, from Norwich, Co. Norf'k. as serv. of Samuel Dix, emb. 8 Apr. and call. then 23 yrs. old, as seen in 4 Mass. Hist. Coll. I. 97. He was a carpenter of I. 1648, and beside d. Hannah, b. 19 Aug. 1662, and others perhaps, had Seth and William, to wh. in 1693 he gave his prop. WILLIAM, Dover 1656, was there tax. 1657, had four ch.

by a former w. and m. a. 1658, Sarah, d. of Edward, and sis. of Nathaniel Starbuck, and d. not long aft. for his wid. m. a. 1659 or 60,
Joseph Austin, wh. was appoint. admor. 27 June 1661, d. early in 1663,
and her third h. was Humphrey Varney. WILLIAM, Ipswich, s. prob.
of first William, freem. 1671, m. 25 Oct. of that yr. Susanna Fuller,
had Eliz. b. 14 Oct. 1672. Six of this name had in 1845 been gr. at
Harv. But of the disting. jurisconsult, late of the Supreme Ct. of the
U. S. Joseph Story, hardly more celebr. for his uprightness and learn.
as a judge, than for his amenity as a man of letters, I have not been able
to find progenit. bef. Elisha in the third generat. preced. wh. prob. came
from Eng. in the last yr. of King William III.

STOTT, EDWARD, Wethersfield, by Hinman, 165, rank. among early
sett. aft. 1640; tho. in my opin. the name was mistak. by him for Scott,
as *c* and *t* are in old handwriting frequently read for ea. other.

STOUGHTON, ‡ * ‖ ISRAEL, Dorchester, a man of prop. and distinct.
came, I presume, in 1632, when is found the earliest ment. of him, was
adm. freem. 5 Nov. of the yr. foll. rep. at the first and sec. Gen. Court
1634 and 5, when he was ens. but at this latter was disabl. from hold.
any office in three yrs. for writ. a book, that gave offence, wh. against
the natural yearn. of authors, he desir. "might forthwith be burnt;"
was restor. in 1636 to his former capacity, was rep. again in Dec. 1636,
and Apr. foll. and when the antinomian excitem. against Wheelwright,
Cotton, and Mrs. Hutchinson was high, in May 1637, had command
of the Mass. force sent against the Pequots, ar. co. 1638, and its
capt. 1642; and bec. an Assist. in wh. place, by ann. elect. he contin.
until he went home, and in 1644 aft. he had gone. He had been
in Eng. 1642, bef. the civil war; but when no doubt could remain of
its speedy begin. and on his sec. going, was made lieut. col. of Rains-
burrow's regim. soon fell sick, and d. at Lincoln 1644. His will made
at London, 17 July 1644, of wh. abstr. may be read in Geneal. Reg. IV.
51, w. Eliz. Extr. provides well for his w. s. Israel, the eldest; William,
to be brot. up to study, as he was, H. C. 1650; and John; beside the
possib. of ano. and sev. ds. whose names are not ment. nor their number. One, Hannah, b. in Eng. a. 1628, m. 9 Dec. 1653, James Minot,
and d. 27 Mar. 1670. John is never heard of aft. The wid. liv. long.
‖ ISRAEL, Dorchester, eldest s. of the preced. was, perhaps, of ar. co.
1645, and is not more ment. He was d. bef. May 1665. ISRAEL, s. of
the sec. Thomas, was liv. in 1700, when his sis. Eliz. Eliot, gave him
£200. Stiles, 807, gives him many ch. bef. 1732, but aft. 1713 I see
reason to fear, from comparison with his p. 539, that he was 21 yrs.
older than his w. JOHN, Windsor, br. of the preced. m. 11 Aug. 1682,
Eliz. d. of Thomas Bissell of the same, had John, b. 16 Oct. 1683, and

William, 10 Mar. 1686. His w. d. 17 July 1688, and he m. 23 Jan.
1690 Sarah Fitch, had Eliz. b. 19 Feb. 1693, wh. three ch. are nam. in
the will of their aunt Eliz. Eliot, 1700. Aft. wh. he had Nathaniel, 23
June 1702, and d. 24 May 1712. NICHOLAS, of New Eng. in the
Geneal. of Sir Nicholas S. Geneal. Reg. V. 350 is, I doubt, a misnomer,
perhaps for the first Israel. Yet a Nicholas of later date there certain.
was, wh. liv. at Taunton, at least there m. 17 Feb. 1674, Eliz. Knapp,
wh. may have been d. of Aaron, and there had Hannah, b. 4 July 1679.
He took sec. w. 25 Feb. 1692, Sarah, d. of Hezekiah Hoar. SAMUEL,
Windsor, s. of the sec. Thomas, tax. in 1691, had Samuel, b. 1702, perhaps others. *THOMAS, Dorchester 1630, br. of Israel, the first, came,
no doubt, in the Mary and John, or next mo. in the fleet with Winth.
desir. adm. as freem. 19 Oct. 1630, and was sw. 18 May foll. constable
by appointm. of Court, Sept. 1630, in the exercise of wh. office, Mar.
foll. he commit. the indiscret. of solemnis. a mar. betw. Clement Briggs
and Joan Allen, for wh. he was fin. £5, tho. some yrs. after it was
remit. I hope the contr. of m. held good. Early in 1635 (after he had
tak. for sec. w. Margaret, wid. of Simon Huntington, wh. says the Roxbury ch. rec. had d. on the voyage, of smallpox, bef. reach. Boston in
1633), the planta. of Conn. was project. by many people of Watertown,
Newtown (since nam. Cambridge), and Dorchester, and from the two
latter the majority of ch. mem. rem. to found new sett. on the gr. river,
as it was call. but they were requir. to contin. under the jurisdict. of
Mass. He was one of those, oft. rep. betw. 1639 and 48, not ment.
later in my opin. (exc. that Windsor town and ch. rec. mark his d.
mean. some other person, 25 Mar. 1661) and liv. the resid. of his days
at Windsor, wh. was the nam. giv. to the Dorchester planta. How long
this time was, is unkn. or what ch. he had, but as he was ens. 1636, and
in 1640 made lieut. the freem. on the list of 1669, may well seem to be
a s. Hinman, 243, says he d. Sept. 1684, leav. good est. to ch. six by
name; but as the names all agree with those of the ch. of sec. Thomas,
I doubt not the other circumstances belong to him. The same conclusion is drawn as to John, wh. follows on the same page. For this first
Thomas, from the Conn. rec. Trumbull, I. 83, as to distrib. of the sev.
portions of Mr. Stoughton's childr. and his w.'s 27 Mar. 1643, I infer,
that he d. late in 1642, and 42 yrs. earlier than Hinman's date. Yet it
is remarka. that Stiles in Hist. of W. has utterly sunk this first Thomas,
one of the founders of his town, follow. Hinman inst. of the careful
Hist. of Dorchester, wh. however he innocent. refers to. THOMAS,
Windsor, s. of the preced. b. in Eng. an orig. propr. of Hartford, m.
Mary, d. of William Wadsworth, had John, b. 20 June 1657; Mary, 1
Jan. 1659; Eliz. 18 Nov. 1660; Thomas, 21 Nov. 1663; Samuel, 8

Sept. 1665; Israel, 21 Aug. 1667; and Rebecca, 19 June 1673. He
was, prob. that freem. on the list of 1669, and had been many yrs. d.
Sept. 1684, leav. fair est. we may believe, as also that his line was prolong. for in 1755, John S. was gr. at Yale. Mary m. 3 June 1677,
Samuel Farnsworth; Eliz. m. first, 1680, James Mackman, a rich
merch. and sec. in 1699, John Eliot, Esquire; and Rebecca m. 1694,
Atherton Mather. THOMAS, Windsor, s. of the preced. m. 31 Dec.
1691, Dorothy, d. of the sec. John Talcott, had Mary, b. 4 Jan. 1693,
and his w. d. 28 May 1696. He m. 1697, Abigail Lothrop, perhaps
wid. of Samuel the sec. of New London, certain. not, as Stiles, in Hist.
807, calls her, d. of Rev. Timothy Edwards, for she was his sis. had
Thomas, 9 Apr. 1698; Daniel, 13 Aug. 1699; Benjamin, 28 Apr.
1701; Timothy, 27 June 1703; Abigail, 21 Dec. 1704; David, 9 Sept.
1706; Mabel, 19 Aug. 1708; Jonathan, 7 Oct. 1710; Eliz. 20 Dec.
1712; Isaac, 2 Nov. 1714; and John, 11 Dec. 1719; was a capt. and
d. 14 Jan. 1749. His wid. d. 23 Jan. 1754. †‡WILLIAM, Dorchester, s.
of the first Israel, perhaps b. in Eng. where, aft. gr. at Harv. he resort.
and stud. at Oxford Univ. being by order of Parliam. creat. a fellow of
New Coll. and preach. at a parish in Co. Sussex, says Farmer, but
with unkn. authority, and by Calamy is put with min. eject. for losing
his fellowship soon aft. the restor. Aft. coming back, he was disting.
for preach. the Election serm. 1668, but would not confine his powers
to the pulpit; and was one of the selectmen 1671–4, an Assist. 1671–86,
some yrs. commissnr. for the Unit. Col. and in the end of Oct. 1677
went, with Bulkley, as agent to defend our cause at London. In the
gr. contest with the crown he lost support of many friends, and stood
the very lowest in the nominat. of the eighteen Assist. in 1686, being
justly suspect. as guilty of moderat. He was appoint. by k. James
one of the Counc. to Sir E. Andros, but partook of the N. E. spirit,
when the Gov. was depos. and so gain. the favor of Mather, that he
nominat. him for lieut. gov. in the new charter, in wh. office, as also
ch. just. in 1695, he contin. till his d. 7 July 1701. Unhap. for his
reputa. he was made chief in 1692 of the unlawful special court of oyer
and terminer for trials of witches with the more amiable Sewall and
Saltonstall, of wh. the one left the bench in disgust at the outrages on
justice, and the other most bitterly repent. in public sackcloth; but
Stoughton, a bach. was made of sterner stuff. From the unerring tribunal in the gr. day of retrib. justice, he may receive the mercy that
he knew not how to show; and some tenderness might be felt even by
fellow mortals for his murderous proceeding in the case of Rebecca
Nurse, did not such conduct in a judge, aft. verdict of acquittal, neces-
sarily stimulate execration. In the dark rec. of criminal adjudicat. no

instance can be found to parallel his blindness; yet if pity for delus. in the man must be express. what excuse may be fram. for ignorance in a magistrate presid. in such unlawful tribunal. See Quincy in Hist. of the Univ. I. 178–9. He join. in most unseemly union the various functions of legislat., judicial, and executive authority; and in execut. of his sad duty he was so virulent. *possessed* against the accused, when he heard of reprieve of some under sentence of d. at a former term, as to complain of obstruction of justice, and withdrew from the Court. The recall of Sir William Phips left him in chief command in the prov. until arr. of Lord Bellomont in 1699, and he had the gratifica. of laying the corner stone of a coll. at Cambridge, built at his cost, and honor. with his name. Again he bec. ch. magistr. on d. of his superior. His monum. in the grave-yard at D. bears a long inscript. very closely imitat. from that of the learned Pascal, and has no reference to the judicial murders at Salem. See scrupul. Eliot's Biog. Dict. and Quincy's Hist. Harv. Coll. In his will, execut. one day bef. his d. pro. 23 of same mo. many good gifts out of his large est. are made, as beside others, £50 to the ch. beside two pieces of plate, £50 to the poor of the town, and £150 to the sch. to the wid. and childr. of Rev. John Collins £100, to Rev. John Danforth, wh. m. his niece, £50, beside a negro slave, and an orchard to his w. and £300 to Theophilus Minot, besides less sums to other relat. and made William Tailer, his neph. afterwards lieut. Gov. and nieces Eliz. Danforth, Eliz. Nelson, and Mehitable Cooper Excors. Of Theophilus Minot I find no other ment. and am led to conject. that he was a gr.ch. of the testator's elder sis. Hannah, wh. had m. James Minot.

STOVER, or STOVARD, JOHN, Pemaquid, perhaps s. of Silvester, sw. fidel. to Mass. 1674. He liv. in later yrs. at York or Wells, and his was the fam. that suffer. from the Ind. in Oct. 1705, as Niles tells, when two of the ch. were k. and two more carr. away. SILVESTER, York, submit. to Mass. 1652, and sw. alleg. to Charles II. Mar. 1681.

STOW, EDWARD, Watertown 1643, may have been only trans. visitor, for his name is not found in Bond; nor have I seen it in any other pt. of N. E. ICHABOD, Middletown, s. of the Rev. Samuel, m. 22 Oct. 1688, Mary, d. of the first David Atwater, of New Haven, had Abigail, b. 25 Jan. 1693, d. at 7 yrs.; and Hope, 31 Oct. 1694. He d. 25 Jan. 1695. *JOHN, Roxbury, came 1634, arr. says the ch. rec. 17 May, in one of those six sh. that came in, as Winth. tells, in the wk. of the Gen. Ct.'s meeting, brot. w. Eliz. and six ch. Thomas, Eliz., John, Nathaniel, Samuel, H. C. 1645, and Thankful; was freem. 3 Sept. foll. and his w. d. or was bur. 21 Aug. 1638; was rep. at two Courts in

1639, and d. 26 Oct. 1643, by Eliot's rec. descr. as "an old Kentish man." His d. Eliz. m. 4 Dec. 1639, Henry Archer; on the same day her br. Thomas m. and Thankful m. John Pierpont. I suppose, aft. the d. of f. the residue of the fam. rem. to sev. towns, but princip. to Concord and Middletown. JOHN, Concord, Farmer says, had s. Nathaniel, wh. I think a mistake. He was, prob. s. of the preced. and may have not rem. to Middletown, yet perhaps serv. in Philip's war, when one John S. of Capt. Newberry's comp. was wound. near the end of May, and cured last of Jan. foll. tho. this soldier may have been a younger man, and I have some ground for presum. that John, s. of Roxbury John, was d. bef. Sept. 1653, and perhaps never m. bec. his brs. Thomas, Nathaniel, and Samuel then unit. with Hopestill Foster, all legatees under the will of Rachel Bigg of Dorchester, in a composition as to their respect. shares in est. of Smallhope Bigg, and John Bigg, their uncles in Co. Kent, old Eng. and it is almost certain, that the other brs. of those three must have had equal int. beside that John had m. a d. of Rachell Bigg, and was made excor. of her will. JOHN, Middletown, s. of Thomas, of the same, m. 13 Nov. 1668, Mary Wetmore, had John, b. 10 Oct. 1669, drown. at 2 yrs.; John, again, 3 Mar. 1672; Thomas, 10 Apr. 1674; Nathaniel, 22 Feb. 1676; Mary, June 1678; Hannah, 25 Aug. 1680; Sarah, 25 Mar. 1683; Samuel, 30 Apr. 1684; Thankful, 15 July 1686; and Experience, 30 Sept. 1688; of wh. Samuel, Sarah, and Thankful d. young; and the f. d. 18 Oct. 1688. JOHN, Middletown, s. of the Rev. Samuel, m. a. 1678, Esther, wid. of John Wilcox, d. of William Cornwell, had Hope, b. 10 Sept. 1679; Samuel, 1684, d. at 22 yrs.; and Thankful, wh. d. young in 1700; and he d. 30 June 1732; and his wid. d. 2 May foll. ea. 82 yrs. old. He was, perhaps, that John, of Capt. Newberry's comp. wound. in Philip's war. NATHANIEL, Concord, s. of John the first, b. in Eng. by w. Eliz. had John, b. 29 or 30 June 1657, both dates being in the rec. d. in few mos. Hannah, wh. d. 14 May 1658, perhaps few hours old; and Thankful, 4 Jan. 1660; beside Samuel, nam. in the will of his uncle the Rev. Samuel. His w. d. 8 June 1661, he was freem. 1690. NATHANIEL, Middletown, s. of Thomas of the same, m. 4 Apr. 1677, Hannah Wetmore, had no ch. His w. d. Oct. 1704, and he d. 16 Feb. foll. His est. went in six equal pts. to brs. Thomas, Samuel, and the rep. of John, sis. Mary, Thankful, and the heirs of Eliz. RICHARD, call. by Farmer of Mass. as early as 1630, I fear to count any thing but a misnomer. SAMUEL, Middletown, s. of John the first, b. in Eng. tho. Dr. Field in his valua. acco. of Middlesex Co. Conn. makes him native of Concord, wh. error he was led into by Shattuck, but it wd. have been impossib. had he recollect. the yr. of his gr. at Harv. 1645; and in his invalua.

Memor. of Grad. Farmer, misled by the same high vouchers, erron. calls him s. of Thomas, instead of his br. He was freem. 1645, while undergr. but had his degr. few wks. aft.; went to preach at Middletown a. 1653, where no ch. was gather. for many yrs. and seems never to have been ord. but was the first and only min. there bef. 1668, by the gen. assem. as early as 1660, the town had been liberat. from contrib. to his support, on condit. of giv. him a recommend. to others. He, however, was well content with civil duties, tho. during Philip's war, as sev. yrs. bef. he preach. in various near towns, instead of more popular persons, wh. were sometimes invalid, or call. from their pulpits to accomp. the soldiers. By w. Hope, d. of William Fletcher he had John, b. at Charlestown, 16 June 1650; Ichabod, at M. 20 Feb. 1653; Hope, 4 Feb. 1657; Dorothy, 1 Aug. 1659, wh. m. Jonathan Gilbert sec. and d. 14 July 1698; Eliz. 1 Aug. 1662; Thankful, 5 May 1664; Rachel, 13 Mar. 1667; and Margaret (nam. in the will of her f.) whose date of b. is not kn.; and he d. 8 May 1704, aged 82, says Judge Sewall. His will, of 13 Aug. 1702 is very minute, and enlarges our geneal. details by ment. of his br. Nathaniel's s. Samuel, of his dec. br. Thomas's s. Nathaniel, Thomas, and John, of wh. the latter being d. his heirs are ment. as also Samuel, s. of that neph. Thomas; beside his cous. Rev. James Pierpont, whose mo. was sis. of the testat. His w. was d. as was the younger of his two s. leav. only ch. Hope, and his oldest d. Hope, wh. m. 13 Feb. 1678, Abraham Smith, and d. 17 Nov. foll. only 5 days aft. the d. of her newborn inf. Aft. s. John, and the only ch. of Ichabod, therefore, of his own ch. only the five surv. ds. are to be looked for; Dorothy, wid. of Jonathan Gilbert; Eliz. wh. had m. 1691, Maybee Barnes; Thankful, w. of William Trowbridge; Rachel, w. of Israhiah Wetmore, m. 13 May 1692; and Margaret, w. of Beriah Wetmore. SAMUEL, Marlborough 1676, yet as he was then station. at the garris. ho. of Joseph Rice, as a soldier, he may have liv. at Concord, or other neighb. town. I guess he was s. of Nathaniel of Concord. ‖ THOMAS, Braintree, eldest s. of the first John, b. in Eng. ar. co. 1638, m. 4 Dec. 1639, at Roxbury, Mary Gragg, or Griggs, had John, b. 3 Feb. 1641; and Mary, 6 Feb. 1643; by 1648, or earlier, rem. to Concord, there freem. 1653, thence a. 1654, to Middletown, had, also, Thankful, Eliz. Nathaniel, Samuel, and Thomas. His w. d. 21 Aug. 1680, and he d. prob. early in 1684, as his inv. is of 23 Feb. in his will names only John, Nathaniel, and Thomas as his s. and Samuel Bidwell, h. of his dec. d. Eliz. Perhaps his est. was too small to give any pt. to two other m. ds. or they may have had full shares on m. A d. says Hinman, 243, m. Samuel Bidwell; Mary m. a Spaulding; and Thankful m. a Hill, perhaps John, the sec. of Guilford. THOMAS, Middletown, s. of the preced. m. 16 Oct. 1675, Bethia, d. of Samuel Stocking of the same, had Bethia, b. 6 or 16 Apr. 1678, d. soon ; Samuel, Oct. 1681 or 2 ; Bethia, again, 22 Feb. 1685 ; Mary, Aug. 1688 ; Thomas, 7 May 1691 ; Hannah, 11 Feb. 1696 ; and Joseph, 5 Aug. 1703. He d. 19 Mar. 1730, and his wid. .d. 6 Nov. 1732.

STOWELL, JOHN, Hingham, was not s. prob. of Samuel, m. Sept. 1683, Mary Beal, to wh. admin. on his est. was giv. 28 Apr. 1691. SAMUEL, Hingham, m. 25 Oct. 1649, Mary, d. of John Farrow of the same, had Samuel, b. 18 July 1655, and prob. others bef. or aft. or both, as David, Mary, 15 Oct. 1653, wh. m. 25 Feb. 1681, John Gardner the sec. of the same ; and Remember, wh. m. Mar. 1688, Thomas Remington. His will of 27 Oct. 1683, pro. 30 Jan. foll. provides for w. Mary to bring up the childr. aft. giv. to eldest s. Samuel, and makes her and two s. Samuel and David excors. SAMUEL, Hingham, s. prob. of the preced. m. Jan. 1685, Rachel, youngest ch. of the first Thomas Gill.

STOWERS, or STOWER, JOHN, Watertown 1634, came from Parham in Co. Suffk. says Bond, as highly prob. for John sen. and jr. liv. there, was freem. 25 May 1636, by w. Jane had Eliz. b. 10 Apr. 1635, bur. in Dec. foll. ; Eliz. again, 14 Apr. 1637 ; and Sarah, 8 Mar. 1642 ; had sec. w. Phebe ; rem. in latter days to Newport, and in Dec. 1685, being aged, and a town charge, sold his est. JOSEPH, Charlestown, s. of Nicholas, a householder 1658, had Mary, bapt. 1 July 1677 ; but no other, bef. or aft. is found in the ch. rec. and we learn, that she on same day renew. the covenant, bec. her f. d. in her infancy, perhaps she was the only ch. He d. 29 Dec. 1672. Perhaps Mary m. 4 Aug. 1687, Matthew Castle. JOSEPH, Salisbury 1667, m. Mary, d. of Ralph Blaisdell, unless it were John S. for both are nam. in Gen. Reg. VIII. 53–4 as the h. I think the fam. spread to N. Hampsh. NICHOLAS, Charlestown 1629, one of the eleven earliest sett. in that penins. came prob. in the fleet with Higginson to Salem, and went with the Spragues, as the compilat. of the rec. of C. made in 1664 calls the date 1628, but clearly meaning 1629 ; in 1630 he was on the inq. 28 Sept. on the body of Austen Bratcher, that charg. Walter Palmer with the manslaught. of wh. he was acquit. by the jury ; freem. 18 May next, stands No. 70 on the list of Boston ch. and with w. was among found. of that in C. 35 in all, 2 Nov. 1632 ; and had, by w. Amy, Joseph, b. 21, bapt. 23 Feb. 1633 ; Abigail, 27, bapt. 28 June 1636 ; and John, wh. d. 15 Aug. 1638, perhaps few hours old. But he had other ch. Richard, Jane, and a d. m. Starr, as Frothingham reads the will, but Farr, acc. Geneal. Reg. III. 180, perhaps all three, certain. the first and last b. in Eng. Unless the orig. will can be seen, that is not likely, we must decide by our con-

temp. rec. in wh. Farr is plain; but I have gr. delight in find. that
George F. of Lynn was a passeng. from Eng. at the same time with S.
and it is quite prob. they were in the same ship, and their ch. wd. thus
bec. acquaint. besides that the fathers, six yrs. aft. arr. were made freem.
on the same day; was appoint. constable 1639, and d. 17 May 1646.
His will was made the day bef. His wid. d. soon, at least her inv. was
of 1 July aft. Yet in the list of inhabs. wh. drew sh. in wood and
commons on Mystick side, 1658, her name is ent. but prob. this was
only as the mo. of heirs entitled. RICHARD, Charlestown, s. of the
preced. b. in Eng. join. the ch. 12 Apr. 1650, and was made freem. next
mo. and Mar. foll. Joanna, perhaps his w. join. had Samuel, b. 12 July
1647; Mary, 9 Feb. 1654; and Sarah, 21 Mar. 1656, and perhaps others b. bef. or aft. or both, certain. Hannah, wh. m. Oct. 1666, Abraham
Hills. He d. 8 July 1693, says Frothingham; and his w. Hannah d. 3
Feb. 1698–9 aged 81, says the gr. stone. His d. Mary, unless it was
the d. of Joseph, bef. ment. m. 4 Aug. 1687, Matthew Castle. SAMUEL,
Malden, s. of the preced. d. 26 Dec. 1721.

STRAIGHT, or STRAITE, THOMAS, Watertown 1644, took o. of alleg.
1652, m. Eliz. d. of Henry Kimball of the same, wh. was b. in Eng.
says Bond, had Susanna, b. 1657; Thomas, 19 Feb. 1660; and Eliz.
was a capt. and d. 22 Nov. 1681, in his nuncup. will, 4 Oct. preced.
gave portions to the ds. and good provis. for life to his w. wh. d. 1 Jan.
1719, aged 89. Susanna m. John Wellington, and Eliz. m. 6 June 1684,
as his sec. w. Joseph Wellington. *THOMAS, Watertown, s. of the
preced. by w. Mary, wh. d. May 1727, aged 75, had no ch. was freem.
1690, and rep. 1716.

STRAINE, or STRAINER, RICHARD, Boston 1647, a brewer, went
home bef. 1659, in Apr. of wh. yr. call. hims. of Westminster, he sold
his est.

STRANGE, GEORGE, Dorchester 1634, freem. 6 May 1635, rem. to
Hingham, says Farmer, there our rec. shows he sold his tenement 1639.
JOHN, Boston 1651, by w. Sarah had Sarah, b. 18 Oct. 1651, d. bef.
Dec. 1657, when his admor. sold his est. JOHN, Boston, perhaps s. of
the preced. was in business 1681. LOT, Portsmouth, R. I. by w. Mary
had Comfort, b. 4 June 1689; Alice, 15 Oct. 1694; James, 18 Sept.
1696; and Lot, 4 Mar. 1699.

STRANGUAGE, or STRANGEWAYS, WILLIAM, Boston 1651, a mariner.

STRATTON, CALEB, Boston 1661, a mariner. ELEAZER, Andover, d.
at the E. on milit. serv. 15 Mar. 1689. JOHN, Scarborough 1633, or
earlier, aft. rem. to Salem, Felt says, had gr. of ld. 1637, but prob. rem.
soon aft. 1643 perhaps join. with the Lynn people to Easthampton,
L. I. where was a John early. JOHN, Watertown, s. of Samuel the first

of the same, prob. b. in Eng. m. 10 Mar. 1659, Eliz. d. of John Train of the same, had Eliz. b. 23 Feb. 1660, d. soon; John, 24 Aug. 1661; Eliz. again, 2 July 1664; Joseph, 13 Jan. 1667; Samuel, 18 Sept. 1669; Rebecca, 16 May 1672; Ebenezer, 2 Nov. 1677, d. soon; Ebenezer, again, 2 Oct. 1678; and Jonathan, 6 Mar. 1680, was freem. 1663, and d. 7 Apr. 1691. His wid. d. 7 May 1708. JOHN, Watertown, not s. of the preced. and Bond thinks he may have been s. of Salem John, m. 26 Nov. 1667, Mary, d. of Thomas Smith of the same, had John, b. 3 Mar. 1669; Thomas, 26 Oct. 1670; James, 18 Jan. 1673; Mary; Judy, 13 Aug. 1680; Jonathan, 22 Aug. 1684, d. young; Mercy, bapt. 3 July 1687; John, 28 July 1689, unless Bond gives wrong name; and Samuel, 10 May 1691, posthum. He d. 7 Apr. 1691, and in June foll. admin. was giv. to wid. and s. John, when the sec. s. of that name was not two yrs. old. JOHN, Watertown, s. of John, first of the same, by w. Abigail had John, b. 4 May 1689; Ebenezer, 12 Dec. 1692, bapt. by right of mo. 7 May foll. at Charlestown; Jonathan, b. 1695; Abigail, and Mary, tw. 14 Sept. 1698; and Jabez, 28 Mar. 1701; and d. 20 Feb. 1718. His wid. d. 25 Oct. 1732, aged 66. JOSEPH, Marlborough, br. of the preced. m. 14 Nov. 1695, Sarah, d. of Abraham How, had Joseph, b. 1696; Sarah, 1700; Eliz. 1710; Jonathan, 1714; and perhaps more. RICHARD, Watertown, s. of Samuel the first, b. in Eng. may be he wh. hav. been left at home by his f. perhaps at sch. came in the Speedwell, 1656, from London to Boston, by w. Susanna had Samuel, b. 8 Apr. 1658; and d. 25 July foll. aged a. 30 yrs. SAMUEL, Watertown, came bef. 1648, with s. Samuel, and John, but the precise time is unkn. all three took the o. of fidel. 1652, and he was freem. 1653. Perhaps he brot. a w. that d. early, and 27 Aug. 1657, he m. in Boston, wid. Margaret Parker, whose h. Bond suppos. might have been William of W. but no reason is giv. He d. 20 Dec. 1672, in his will of wh. s. John was excor. made the day preced. pro. 31 Mar. foll. aft. provid. for his w. names only ch. Samuel, and John, and gr.ch. Samuel, s. of Richard. SAMUEL, Watertown, s. of the preced. b. in Eng. m. 25 Mar. 1651, Mary Frye, possib. d. of William of Weymouth, had Ann, or Hannah, b. 4 Apr. 1652, rem. to Concord, where in July 1648 he had bot. ho. and ld. there had Mary, b. 19 Jan. 1657; Samuel, 5 Mar. 1661; Eliz.; and John; he m. Shattuck says, 1675, Hannah, d. of Moses Wheat. But no more is kn. Bond thinks he was freem. 1655, but I am satisf. that list is only repet. of the one of 1653. Mary m. 19 July 1677, Daniel Hoar; and Eliz. d. 19 Apr. 1762, aged 100, says tradit. slightly exagger. SAMUEL, Concord, s. of Richard, sold the est. giv. by his gr.f. to Palsgrave Wellington, in 1682; is perhaps the man wh. m. at Watertown, 15 Feb. 1692, Mary Butters. SAMUEL, Watertown, s.

of John, the first of the same, m. 20 Dec. 1699, Mary Perry, had Sarah, b. 6 Aug. 1701; Samuel, 23 Apr. 1703; Nathaniel, 23 Nov. 1705; Sarah, 24 Nov. 1710; Eliz. 20 June 1713; and Jonathan, 4 Apr. 1716. His w. d. perhaps, 27 Nov. 1719; and he d. 28 Sept. 1723.

STREAME, STREME, or STERTE, JOHN, Milford 1646, is perhaps he wh. came in the Truelove, with his uncle Zechariah Whitman, from London, to Boston 1635, aged 14, with Thomas, prob. his br. aged 15; m. 20 Dec. 1649, Martha Beard of the same, had Abigail; Mary, b. 12 Oct. 1653; John, Dec. 1657; Thomas, 1 Apr. 1661, d. young; Martha, 1664; and Sarah, 1667, and he was freem. of Conn. 1665, ens. 1669, and d. 1685. Abigail m. Thomas Tibbals, of Milford; Mary m. 11 Nov. 1674, David Baldwin of the same; Martha m. Thomas Cooley; and Sarah was in 1690 unm. I had tak. the spell. of this surname in June or July 1842, as here it stands first, but 17 yrs. later, Mr. Drake's copy of the same rec. gives it STERTE, and his eyesight may have been better than mine, or that of the keeper of her majesty's public office, wh. confirm. mine. Diversity in reading old MS. must be expected. See 3 Mass. Hist. Coll. VIII. 272, and Geneal. Reg. XIV. 323. But the probabil. of the true version may be infer. from look. at the name of the Weymouth man in Geneal. Reg. XI. 173, or under Otis in my preced. vol. JOHN, Milford, s. of the preced. m. wid. Mary Simpson, d. of Samuel Coley, and d. without ch. 1689, leav. good est. to his wid. and four sis. With him ceas. the male line. THOMAS, Weymouth, said to be brot. from Eng. prob. with br. Benjamin by his mo. Eliz. wh. bec. sec. w. of John Otis of W. He was d. in June leav. decent est. on wh. his mo. Eliz. O. had admin.

STREET, FRANCIS, Taunton, a purch. in 1637, prob. liv. bef. 1644 in ano. town, and not in the Plymouth jurisdict. for his name is not ret. in the list of those able to bear arms in the Col. nor does it seem, that he was near relat. of Rev. Nicholas. Yet Emery, I. 20, thinks he was there bef. 1640, and perhaps a passeng. in the Susan and Ellen, from London to Boston, Alice, aged 28, may have been his w. He d. early in 1665, or, at least his inv. was tak. 3 June of that yr. and his wid Eliz. (wh. name, in old times, was convertib. with Alice), m. 10 Dec. foll. Thomas Lincoln. He left no ch. but Mary. NICHOLAS, Taunton, ord. teacher, on the same day that Hooke was made pastor, but what day that was, is ask. in vain, and only prob. conject. fixes the yr. 1637. He had, no doubt, adequate educ. but none of the inquisit. scholars of New Haven have ascert. in what place he was b. or taught. Emery says, his first w. was a sis. of the maiden found. of the town, and his sec. was the wid. of Gov. Newman, but of neither do we hear the name. All his ch. Samuel, H. C. 1664; Susanna; Sarah; Abiah; and Hannah; were, I doubt not, by the first. Hooke being drawn to Eng. from New Haven, where he had been teacher conjunct. with famous Davenport, our Taunton min. was call. 1659 to take his place, and was induct. 26 Nov. there d. 22 Apr. 1674. Dodd, in East Haven reg. tells, that Susanna m. a Mason, whose name is not found; Sarah m. 1662, James Heaton; Abiah m. 28 Sept. 1663, Daniel Sherman; and Hannah m. an Andrews. *SAMUEL*, Wallingford, only s. of the preced. m. 3 Nov. of the same yr. in wh. he had his A. B. Ann, d. of Richard Miles, had Ann, b. Aug. 1665; Samuel, July 1667; Mary, Sept. 1670; Nicholas, 14 July 1677; and Sarah, 13 Jan. 1681; of wh. the first three d. young. He began to preach at W. 1672, and was ord. in 1674, took sec. w. 1 Nov. 1684, Maudlin Daniels, had Samuel, again, 8 Nov. 1685; James, 28 Dec. 1686; Ann, again, 26 Aug. 1688; and he took third w. 14 July 1690, Hannah Glover, had Eleanor, 3 Dec. 1691; Nathaniel, 19 Jan. 1693; Elnathan, 2 Sept. 1695; Mary, 16 Apr. 1698; and John, 25 Oct. 1703; and d. 16 Jan. 1717, being, as his successor wrote in 1770 with some exagger. eighty-two yrs. old, but Dodd says above 75. STEPHEN, freem. of Mass. 1644, may have been of Concord or Sudbury; but the sagacity of Farmer suggest. better habitat. as in the next artic. WILLIAM, came in the Jonathan, 1639, and exc. that Peter Noyes of Sudbury paid for his pass. whereby it might be judg. that he brot. him as a serv. no more is kn.

STREETER, SAMUEL, Concord, s. prob. of Stephen the first, by w. Mary had Judah, b. 1666; Eleazer, 1668; beside a John, wh. d. 1667; and ano. John 1671. SAMUEL, Edgartown 1663, was drown. there 19 Nov. 1669. STEPHEN, Gloucester 1642, perhaps was owner of a ho. earlier, rem. to Charlestown, there by w. Ursula had Hannah, b. 10 Nov. 1644; was freem. prob. as Farmer happily conject. that yr. in May, but not adm. in right of the Charlestown ch. to wh. he unit. with his w. 21 Mar. not Oct. as Barry made it, 1652. He prob. had other ch. bef. or aft. or both, Stephen, Samuel, and John, and, I think, d. bef. 1657, in wh. yr. the wid. m. 13 Oct. Samuel Hosier; and she had third h. and 15 July 1673 took for her fourth Griffin Crafts. STEPHEN, Watertown, s. prob. of the preced. by w. Deborah had Stephen, b. 20 June 1667; Sarah, 2 Oct. 1669; and Barry gives them, at Cambridge, Rebecca, 1683; Deborah, 1685; Joseph, 1687; and Benjamin, 1689; d. next yr. and the mo. d. 7 Apr. 1689. Barry finds ano. STEPHEN, with w. Rebecca, at Muddy riv. (Brookline) 1679.

STRETCHER, HENRY, Watertown 1687, appears to have been unm.

STRETTON, BARTHOLOMEW, Boston, by w. Eliz. had William, b. 30 Jan. 1659; but I hear no more of him. Perhaps this surname may be the same as Stratton.

STRICKLAND, or STICKLAND, EDMUND, Middleburg, L. I. prob. s. of John, was there in 1656–86. See Riker, Ann. of Newtown. JOHN, Mass. 1630, came, prob. in the fleet with Winth. but no rec. shows of what town he was inhab. and neither Bond, exc. as Stickland, p. 950, Felt, Frothingham, Ellis, Holmes, Lewis, nor Snow claim him for their towns, as citizen, yet he desir. adm. as freem. 19 Oct. and was sw. on 18 May foll. then call. serj. Perhaps he was not a mem. of either of the chs. but a man of good consider. evidently, as he serv. on that sp. jury at the Ct. of Assist. May 1631, wh. gave the exempl. damages in the action of battery by Dexter against Capt. Endicott. At the Ct. in Sept. 1632 he was fin. £3 for refus. to watch, but at the Gen. Ct. Sept. 1638, it was remit. to him, as were those of Sir Richard Salton-stall, Gov. Dudley, Edward Gibbons, and so many others, that it per-haps gave more satisfact. than any session has ever done since, and may be call. the gr. remission term. With certainty no more is kn. of him, but, I suppose, he was one of the patentees of Hempstead, L. I. 1644, and one of the first sett. at Huntington 1650. He had, we can hardly doubt, a fam. JOHN, Wethersfield, perhaps s. of the preced. m. Esther, d. of Richard Smith, the gr. landholder of that town, on the E. side of the gr. riv. wh. bec. Glastenbury in 1690. In his will of 1680 Smith ment. him; but I can find no more, exc. that Chapin, in the Centen. Disc. 193, names his ch. John, Samuel, and Benjamin. JONATHAN, Wethersfield, perhaps br. of the preced. of wh. no more is heard, than that he was a witness, 23 Jan. 1680, brot. to prove against John Hale, that he curs. k. Charles. See Kilbourne, 15, note. PETER, New Lon-don 1670 (Miss Caulkins informs me), by w. Eliz. had Eliz. bapt. 1 Aug. 1675; Peter, 11 Aug. 1678; Priscilla, 5 Mar. 1682; Thomas; Samuel; Sarah; and Mary; and d. 1723. Eliz. m. Richard Dart, s. of Richard, I suppose; and Priscilla m. William Mynard. PETER, s. of the preced. d. 1710, leav. only ch. Ann, inf. THWAITES, or THWAIT, Dedham 1643, perhaps s. or br. of John, his w. join. the ch. 3 May 1650, and had her ch. Eliz. and John bapt. on Sunday aft. ; and Re-becca 19 Jan. foll. He rem. to the Narraganset country, on serv. of Gen. Gookin, wh. built a ho. for him at Misquamicut, now Westerly. See Trumbull, Col. Rec. II. 546. His d. Eliz. m. Samuel Andrews of Hartford. Farmer MS. notes, that of this name was one of the celebr. Westminster Assemb. and that the fam. was of Co. Westmoreland.

STRIKER, JOSEPH, Salem, m. 10 Apr. 1673, Hannah, d. of Richard Waters of the same, had Hannah, b. 10 Jan. 1674; Dorcas, 2 Mar. 1676, d. at 2 mos.; Deborah, 17 June 1677; Dorcas, again, 4 Apr. 1680; Joseph, 14 Nov. 1681; and Abigail, 4 Mar. 1684.

STRONG, EBENEZER, Northampton, fifth s. of Elder John, m. 14

Oct. 1668, Hannah, d. of Nicholas Clap of Dorchester, had Hannah, b. 7 Oct. 1669; Ebenezer, 2 Aug. 1671; Nathaniel, 25 Sept. 1673; Sarah, 29 Sept. wh. d. 19 Dec. 1675; Preserved, Sept. 1679, d. next Aug.; Sarah, again, 29 Sept. 1681; Jonathan, 1 May 1683; Noah, 18 Oct. 1684, d. under 15 yrs.; and tw. without names, wh. d. prob. in few hours, 3 Oct. 1689. He took the o. of alleg. 8 Feb. 1679, with his f. and three brs. and was freem. 1683, ch. elder oft. call. deac.; and d. 11 Feb. 1729, aged 86. Thro. his s. Jonathan is the line of Caleb, Gov. of Mass. deriv. JACOB, Windsor, s. of the sec. John, m. 10 Nov. 1698, Abigail, d. of Nathaniel Bissell of the same, and d. 25 Mar. 1749, nearly 76 yrs. old. It is prob. he had ch. but their names are unkn. JEDEDIAH, Northampton, third s. of Elder John, m. 18 Nov. 1662, Freedom, d. of Henry Woodward, of the same, had Eliz. b. 9 June 1664; Abigail, 9 July 1666, d. prob. 15 July 1689; Jedediah, 7 Aug. 1667; Ford, 2 Sept. d. 1 Nov. 1668; one, without name, 11 Oct. 1669, d. very soon; Hannah, 3 Feb. 1671; Thankful, 15 Apr. 1672; John, 15 Nov. 1673, d. same mo.; Lydia, 9 Nov. 1675; Mary, May 1677; Experience, 19 Aug. 1678, d. 16 Sept. foll.; Preserved, 29 Mar. 1680; and John, 10 May 1681; his w. d. 17 of the same mo. He m. 28 Dec. foll. Abigail, wid. of John Stebbins of N. d. of Robert Bartlett, had Mary, 1683; and his w. d. 15 July 1689. He m. 5 Jan. 1692, Mary, wid. of John Lee of Farmington, for third w. and took the o. of alleg. 8 Feb. 1679, and was adm. freem. 1690, but his w. Mary being k. 9 Oct. 1710, by fall of her horse, he late in life rem. to Coventry; and there d. 22 May 1733, not in his 96th yr. prob. as said. JERIJAH, Northampton, youngest of the sixteen ch. of Elder John, m. 18 July 1700, Thankful, youngest d. of John Stebbins of the same, had Jerijah, b. 8 Sept. 1701, d. soon; Thankful, 26 Aug. 1702; Jerijah, again, 14 May 1705; Eunice, 10 Sept. 1707; Ithamar, 24 June 1710, d. next yr.; and Ithamar, again, 8 Aug. 1713, d. next yr.; Seth, 4 Apr. 1716; and Bela, 4 Oct. 1719; and his w. d. 24 May 1744, aged 66; and Cothren says, he d. 24 Apr. 1754. *JOHN, Hingham 1635, among first proprs. wh. drew ho. lots Sept. of that yr. freem. 9 Mar. 1637, next yr. was of Taunton, and count. there as one of the first proprs. made freem. of that jurisdict. 4 Dec. chos. rep. 1641, 2, 3, and 4, as Baylies shows II. 2 and 3, and a juror 1645; three or four yrs. aft. is found at Windsor, and made freem. of Conn. May 1651, unless this were his s. wh. seems very improb. and soon aft. 1661 was inhab. of Northampton. With very gr. doubts as to most of the items, and utter reject. of part most import. in tradit. report. of his com. in the Mary and John to Dorchester with Warham in May 1630, and of the d. of his first w. on the pass. and tak. a sec. w. in 1630, I think it prob. that he brot. John in 1635, and at

Hingham had Thomas, possib. also ano. ch. wh. d. inf. and that his w. d. there, and that he m. perhaps in 1638, Abigail, d. of Thomas Ford of Dorchester, for in that single yr. is the only ment. of his name as resid. at D. had prob. at Taunton Jedediah, bapt. 14 Apr. 1639, at D. tho. the ch. rec. implies, that the parents liv. at H. Return ; Ebenezer ; and Abigail; at Windsor, certain. had Eliz. b. 24 Aug. 1647, or 24 Feb. 1648; Experience, 4 Aug. 1650 ; Samuel, and Joseph, perhaps sometimes call. Josiah, tw. 5 Aug. 1652 ; Mary, 26 Oct. 1654. At W. he m. 26 Nov. 1656, Mary, only d. of Joseph Clark, had Sarah not on rec. perhaps 1657 ; Hannah, 30 May 1659 ; and Esther, 7 June 1661 ; at Northampton had Thankful, 25 July 1663 ; and Jerijah, 12 Dec. 1665. Cothren favors him with three more ch. one wh. d. inf. two mos. aft. arr. of f. in 1630 ; Josiah, wh. d. young, unm. but I distrust the exist. of both ; and Sarah, wh. m. 19 Dec. 1675, or 13 Jan. foll. (either of wh. may be thot. more prob. date, than that of fam. tradit. 13 July 1675) Joseph Barnard of Hadley, and next, 1698, Capt. Jonathan Wells of Deerfield. She may have come betw. Mary and Hannah. On the high authority of Dr. Allen I can find but sixteen ch. beside the inf. wh. d. He was, very likely, b. at Taunton in Co. Somerset, and his f. may have been Richard, and his sis. Elinor may have been w. of Walter Dean ; but that he ever liv. at Dorchester is highly improb. for Harris, or any more search. inquirer has not found his name there, bef. or aft. 1638, exc. once as witness to a deed, wh. may have been writ. at Hingham ; and it is hardly to be believ. that the same w. wh. bore the two ch. at N. had been taken at D. in 1630. That he was indeed ever resid. at D. aft. 1638, can be surmis. from the trifling incident only, that John Hill was m. at Boston 16 Jan. 1657 to Eliz. Strong by Humphrey Atherton, the Assist. wh. was a Dorchester man. Nor is it more prob. as the tradit. ornaments the story, that he came from Eng. with Warham or accomp. him in 1636 to W. Hitchcock, Parsons, Cothren, Geneal. Reg. VIII. 180, and Emery too easily adm. such relat. in my opin. that relies on the powerful contempo. silence of his br.-in-law, Roger Clap, wh. did come in that sh. and m. a d. of his fellow passeng. Thomas Ford. For the modern origin of these improb. tradit. I presume that, as the ancest. was at Windsor, within twelve yrs. of its settlem. and a s. of his m. a Warham, and as Ford rem. with W. to Windsor the story spread grad. that he had come from Eng. to Dorchester, with W. and accomp. him to his next home in Conn. but the reporters did not consider two points, that many people were of Dorchester, wh. did not come with Warham, and many of Windsor, wh. did not come from Dorchester. In McClure's acco. of sett. of Windsor, writ. in 1797, pr. 1 Mass. Hist. Coll. V. 167, is seen the list of the sixteen male mem. of the ch. of Dorchester that went with Warham thither, among wh. is NO Strong. As Roger Clap had m. a d. of Ford two or three yrs. *bef.* the exodus, the d. wh. bec. the sec. w. of Strong, as it seems to me *after* it, may have contin. at D. to comfort her sis. and avoid the perils of ano. first planting. He was a tanner, one of the pillars at foundat. of ch. Elder 1663, and his w. d. 6 July 1688, and he d. 14 Apr. 1699, aged 91, says his s. Jerijah, wh. in mod. tradit. is easily corrupt. to 94. Beside Sarah, above ment. Abigail m. 12 Nov. 1673, Rev. Nathaniel Chauncy, and 8 Sept. 1686, deac. Medad Pomeroy; Eliz. m. 17 Mar. or 11 May 1669, Joseph Parsons; Experience m. 27 May 1669, Zerobabel Filer; Mary m. 20 Mar. 1679, John Clark; Hannah m. 15 July 1680, William Clark jr.; Esther m. 15 Oct. 1678, Thomas Bissell, the younger, of Windsor; and Thankful m. a Baldwin of the countless tribes of Milford, as Cothren reports, no doubt from the fam. acco. So there were eight ds. and seven s. of the prosperous tanner, wh. liv. to m. and thirteen of this number were b. to him by the sec. w. Abigail Ford. JOHN, Windsor, eldest s. of the preced. b. perhaps, in Eng. m. 26 Nov. 1656, Mary Clark, d. of that wid. Frances C. wh. had m. Thomas Dewey, had Mary, b. 22 Apr. 1658; Hannah, 11 Aug. 1660; and his w. d. 28 Apr. 1663, aged 25. He m. sec. w. 1664, Eliz. Warriner, perhaps d. but (unless the name should be Warner) more prob. sis. of William of Springfield, had John, 25 Dec. 1665; Jacob, 8 Apr. 1673; and Josiah, 11 Jan. 1679, bapt. next day; was freem. 1667; his w. d. 7 June 1684, and he d. 20 Feb. 1698. The five ch. were liv. at the d. of f. Mary m. Timothy Stanley of Farmington; and Hannah m. Stephen Hopkins. JOHN, Windsor, s. of the preced. m. 26 Nov. 1686, Hannah, d. of Joseph Trumbull, it is suppos. had Mary, b. 1688; Eliz. 1689; Hannah, 1692; Jonathan, 1694; Abigail; Esther, 1699; Sarah; David, 1704; and John, 1707; and his w. Mary prob. 2d d. 4 July 1747. He d. 29 May 1749. JOSIAH, Windsor, br. of the preced. m. 5 Jan. 1699, Joanna Gillet, d. of Cornelius of the same, had Joanna, 1699; John, 1701; Damaris, 1703; and prob. others. RETURN, Windsor, younger br. of the preced. a tanner, freem. 1666, m. 11 May 1664, Sarah Warham, d. of Rev. John, had Sarah, b. 14 Mar. 1665; Abigail, 8 Mar. 1667; Return, 10 Feb. 1669; Eliz. 20 Feb. 1671; Samuel, 20 May 1673, d. soon; Damaris, 3 July 1674; Samuel, again, 27 Dec. 1675; and his w. d. 26 Dec. 1678, aged 36. He m. 23 May 1689, Margaret Newbury, d. of Maj. Benjamin, had Joseph, b. 1694, d. young; Hannah; Margaret, 1700; and Benjamin, 1703. He had large est. and d. 9 Apr. 1726; in his will, of 1719, he names the liv. s. Samuel and Benjamin, six ds. and also the childr. of s. Return wh. had dec. 1708. Both John and Return are in the list of freem. 1669, and the latter was one of the returning officers. SAMUEL,

Northampton, br. of the preced. took o. of alleg. with his f. three brs. and a neph. 8 Feb. 1679, m. 19 June 1684, Esther, d. of deac. Edward Clap, had Esther, b. at Dorchester 30 Apr. 1685; Samuel, 21 Jan. 1687, wh. was k. by the Ind. 10 Aug. 1711, when his f. was tak. by them, and carr. to Canada; Susanna, 26 Feb. 1688; Abigail, 1 Jan. 1689, d. very soon; Abigail, again, 23 Nov. 1690; Christian, 1 Mar. 1693, d. soon; Nehemiah, a. 1694, f. of the Hon. Simeon, one of the S. J. C. Judges; Ezra, 14 Oct. 1697. His w. d. 26 Jan. 1698, and he m. 28 Oct. foll. Ruth, wid. of Joseph Wright, d. of Isaac Sheldon, and had Mary, 19 May 1701; Joseph, 9 May 1703, d. at two yrs.; Josiah, 17 Aug. 1705; and Samuel, again, 11 Feb. 1712; prob. bef. his ret. from captiv. He d. 29 Oct. 1732, in his will of 1728 names only Nehemiah, Ezra, Josiah and Samuel, beside four ds. Esther White, Susanna Lane, Abigail Church, and Mary Edwards. THOMAS, Northampton, an elder br. of the preced. was a trooper in 1658 at Windsor, under com. of Maj. Mason, m. 5 Dec. 1660, Mary, d. of Rev. Ephraim Hewett, had Thomas, b. 16 Nov. 1661; Maria, 31 Aug. 1663; John, 9 Mar. 1665, wh. d. 21 May 1699, unm.; Hewett, 2 Dec. 1666, wh. d. under 23 yrs.; Asahel, 14 Nov. 1668; Joseph, 2 Dec. 1672; Benjamin, 1674; Adino, 12 or more prob. 25 Jan. 1676; Waitstill, 1677 or 8; Rachel, 15 July 1679; Selah, 22 Dec. 1680; Benajah, 24 Sept. 1682; Ephraim, 4 Jan. 1685; Elnathan, 20 Aug. 1686; Ruth, 4 Feb. 1688; and Submit, posthum. 23 Feb. 1690; but the last eleven were by sec. w. His first d. 20 Feb. 1671, and he m. 10 Oct. foll. Rachel, d. of deac. William Holton. He with his s. Thomas took the o. of alleg. 8 Feb. 1679, and he d. 3 Oct. 1689; his wid. m. 16 May 1698, Nathan Bradley. From this branch, thro. the eleventh s. Elnathan are deriv. in Conn. famous Doctors in Divinity; and in that state the fam. is wide distrib. Ano. Hewitt d. 25 Mar. 1694; and Azariah, and Esther are found among the early deaths, if the rec. is correct, whose f. is uncert. Of this fam. name Farmer notes, in MS. thirty-nine had been gr. in 1834, at Yale, three at Harv. and twenty-three at other N. E. coll.

STUART. See Stewart.

STUBBS, JOSHUA, Watertown, m. a. 1641, Abigail, d. of John Benjamin, had Samuel, b. 3 Aug. 1642; Mary; and Eliz. was freem. 2 May 1649, and d. a. 1654. His wid. in Mar. 1656, join. the ch. in Charlestown, and soon m. John Woodward. Mary m. 24 Mar. 1675, John Train; and Eliz. m. earlier Jonathan Stimpson. RICHARD, Hull, m. 3 Mar. 1659, Margaret Reed, at Boston. His will of 22 May 1677, pro. 21 June foll. gives all to his wid. but if she m. then only one third to her, and resid. to four ch. whose names are not kn.

STUCKEY, once only writ. STOCKEY, GEORGE, Windsor, 1640, aft.

some yrs. rem. to Stamford, where his w. Eliz. d. 1656 ; and he m. 1657, Ann Quimby, and d. 28 Nov. 1660. By his will he div. est. equal. betw. his only ch. Eliz. and w. Ann.

STUDLEY, BENJAMIN, Scituate, prob. s. of John of Boston, m. 1683, Mary, d. of John Merritt, had John, b. 11 Dec. 1684; Benjamin, 7 Dec. 1687 ; James, 15 July 1690 ; Jonathan, 19 June 1693 ; David, 19 Jan. 1697 ; Mary, 23 Sept. 1698; Eliz. 8 June 1701, d. young; Deborah, 19 Dec. 1703; and Eliab, 10 Sept. 1706. Ano. Studley branch came into Scituate from Sandwich, as Barry tells in Hist. of Hanover, and perhaps was deriv. from John, s. of John. JOHN, Boston, by w. Eliz. had John, b. 8 Dec. 1659; and Benjamin, 23 May 1661. Perhaps he rem.

STUKELEY, JOHN, a soldier under Capt. William Turner in 1676, perhaps s. of Thomas. THOMAS, Suffield, freem. 1681.

STURGIS, or STURGES, EDWARD, Charlestown 1634, but tho. he was resid. there at least two yrs. he was not of the ch. rem. in few yrs. to Yarmouth, where he was count. 1643, able to bear arms, and had address. with others in Apr. 1639 to the Gov. had Mary, bapt. at Barnstable, 1 June 1646; Eliz. b. at Y. 20 Apr. 1648; Joseph, bur. 16 Apr. 1650, few days old. Prob. he had other ch. and one of his s. may have m. Mary, d. of Capt. William Hedge, nam. in his will. JOHN, Fairfield 1660, adm. freem. 1668, was next yr. a selectman, in 1679 gave ld. to his s. Jonathan; and wide has been, prob. the circulat. of his progeny. No exact account, however, is accessib. David, Eleazer, John jr. and Peter are found in 1691, of wh. some, but not perhaps all, were gr. ch. JOHN, Rhode Isl. 1672. JoSEPH, Yarmouth 1650, perhaps s. of Edward. JOSEPH, Fairfield, prob. s. of John first of the same, is nam. 1679. PETER, Fairfield, br. of the preced. SAMUEL, Barnstable, m. 14 Oct. 1697, wid. Mary Orris, had Nathaniel, b. 8 Jan. bapt. 19 Feb. 1699, d. at 12 yrs.; John, 6 June, bapt. 6 July 1701; Solomon, b. 25 Sept. 1703; Mary, 14 Feb. 1706; Moses, 18 June 1708; Jonathan, 1 Nov. 1711; and Nathaniel, again, 2 Feb. 1715. THOMAS, Yarmouth, by w. Abigail had a d. b. 1681; and Judy, 1683; Edward, 10 Dec. 1684; Thomas, 4 Apr. 1686; Hannah, 18 Sept. 1687 ; John, 2 Dec. 1690; Eliz. 25 Dec. 1692; Abigail, 28 Oct. 1694; Thankful, 18 Mar. 1697; Jacob, 14 Jan. 1700; and a s. 1702; beside tw. intermed. that d. as did, in early life, two other ch. Perhaps he was s. of Edward. It is vexatious to be unable to supply better acco. of a name so disting. in N. E. Always in Conn. the spelling is Sturges ; and eight are gr. at Yale, five at Harv.

STURTEVANT, or STURDEVANT, JOHN, Plymouth, perhaps br. of Samuel, more prob. his s. m. Hannah, wid. of William Crow, d. of Josiah Winslow the first. SAMUEL, Plymouth 1643, had Ann, b. 4 June 1647 ;

John, 17 Oct. 1650, d. soon; Samuel, 19 Apr. 1654; Hannah, 4 Sept. 1656; John, again, 6 Sept. 1658; James, 11 Feb. 1660 : and Joseph, 16 July 1666; beside Mary, 7 Dec. 1651; and Lydia, 13 Dec. 1660; of wh. Ann m. 7 Dec. 1665, John Waterman. He d. 1669, prob. in Oct. in his will of 1 Aug. preced. provid. for the four s. and a ch. unb. beside s.-in-law John Waterman. Descend. have been very num. but no acco. is obtain. of the respective ch. James, it is said, d. 1756, leav. s. Caleb. See Geneal. Reg. VI. 211. WILLIAM, Norwalk, had John, b. 20 July 1676; and Sarah, 9 Apr. 1678. No more is found in Hall's Hist.

STUTCH, JOHN, if the rec. may be suffic. authty. for such a name, by w. Sarah had Sarah, b. 21 Oct. 1662. My refer. is lost.

STYCHE, HENRY, Lynn, was an efficient workman at the iron foundry in 1653, and was then 103 yrs. of age, as Lewis in Hist. of Lynn, Ed. 2, p. 143 asserts; and he adds : " How many yrs. longer he liv. history has not inform. us." That remark may raise a doubt in the mind of any reader, even if the writer be not thot. to distrust the marvel. Yet in the first Ed. I think the age was call. 102. Lamenta. that the line was not perpet. wd. be unavailing and perhaps unwise.

SUCKLING, or SUCKLIN, THOMAS, Hingham, came with Francis James, as one of his serv. in the Diligent, 1638. Lincoln, Centen. Addr. 44. He was of Providence 1646, and on freem's. list 1655, tho. not adm. bef. May 1658, engag. his alleg. to Charles II. June 1668.

SUMMERS, HENRY, Woburn, m. 21 Nov. 1660, Rachel Reed. His wid. d. 15 June 1690, and in Apr. of that yr. Henry, perhaps his s. of W. was adm. freem. JOHN, perhaps of Duxbury, m. Mary Sampson, d. of Henry, prob. bef. 1680.

SUMNER, BENJAMIN, Milton, s. of George, m. 3 May 1706, Eliz. Badcock, had Zebiah, b. 19 Nov. 1707 ; Benjamin, 26 Nov. 1709, d. young; Joseph, 13 Feb. 1712, d. at 20 yrs.; Abijah, 6 Mar. 1714; David, 6 Jan. 1717 ; Daniel, 3 May 1719 ; Samuel, 4 May 1722 ; and Benjamin, again, 21 Feb. 1725; and d. 1727. CLEMENT, Boston, s. of the sec. William, m. 18 May 1698, Margaret Harris, had William, b. 18 Mar. 1699 ; Ebenezer, 1 Sept. 1701; Margaret, 7 Dec. 1702, d. very soon ; Margaret, again, 18 July 1705 ; Eliz. 18 Oct. 1707 ; Samuel, 31 Aug. 1709 ; and Benjamin, 28 May 1711 ; of wh. all, but Ebenezer, were bapt. at sec. ch. 15 July 1711, and Ebenezer was bapt. 9 Nov. 1712. EBENEZER, Mendon, s. of George of Milton, had, perhaps by w. Silence, Daniel, b. a. 1710 ; Abigail, a. 1711 ; and Silence, a. 1715, wh. were liv. at his d. 1721. EBENEZER, Dorchester, s. of Roger of the same, m. 14 Mar. 1700, Eliz. d. of Nathaniel Clap, had Eliz. b. 20 Dec. 1700 ; Rebecca, 11 Apr. 1703 ; Nathaniel, 18 July 1705 ; Ebenezer, 1 Apr. 1708 ; Mehitable, 15 Feb. 1710 ; Jaazaniah, 19 July 1713 ; and Thankful, 19 Feb. 1716. EDWARD, Roxbury, s. of the first George, m. 25 Sept. 1701, Eliz. d. of Elder Samuel Clap of Dorchester, had Edward, b. 16 July 1702; Eliz. 30 Apr. 1704, d. in few wks.; John, 1 Aug. 1705, H. C. 1723; Eliz. again, 7 Apr. 1708; Samuel, 21 Oct. 1710; Increase, 9 June 1713, f. of Increase, b. 27 Nov. 1746, Gov. of Mass.; Hannah, 8 May 1715; Mary, 9 Oct. 1717; Nathaniel, H. C. 1739; Ebenezer, 10 June 1722; and Benjamin, 29 Dec. 1724; and d. 1763. GEORGE, Milton, s. of William the first, b. in Eng. 14 Feb. 1635, m. at Northampton (where he had resid. some yrs. aft. being freem. at Dorchester 1657, at the same time with his br. Roger, tho. his name is writ. Sumer in the rec.), m. 7 Nov. 1662, Mary, d. of Edward Baker, had Mary, b. 11 Feb. 1664; George, 9 Feb. 1666; Samuel, 19 Oct. 1669; William, 7 Apr. 1671; both, the elder, an ens. the jun. a serj. beside four privates of the fam. perish. in the wild expedit. of Phips against Quebec, 1690; Ebenezer, 9 Dec. 1673; Edward, 29 Aug. 1675; Joseph, 26 Aug. 1677; and Benjamin, 15 Dec. 1683; was a deac. and d. 11 Dec. 1715; and his wid. d. 1 Apr. 1719, as the sev. gr. stones say, she aged 77. His d. Mary m. a Swinerton. GEORGE, Milton, s. of the preced. m. a. 1694, Ann Tucker, prob. d. of Benjamin of Roxbury, had Samuel, b. 13 Nov. 1695; George, 4 or 14 Sept. 1697; Ann, 13 Sept. 1699; Mary, 2 Nov. 1702; William, 20 Oct. 1704; Susanna, 13 Apr. 1707; Eliz. 30 June 1709; Josiah, 13 Mar. 1712; and Abigail, 3 Nov. 1718; and he d. 1733. HENRY, aged 15, with Eliz. 18, emb. at London, 4 July 1635, in the Abigail, as may be read in 3 Mass. Hist. Coll. VIII. 266, or Geneal. Reg. XIV.; but nothing more is kn. INCREASE, Dorchester, s. of William the first of the same, m. 26 Mar. 1667, Sarah Staples, had Increase, b. 15 Jan. 1668, d. at 15 yrs.; Sarah, 12 May 1669; William, 9 July 1670; Sarah, 15 July 1672, d. young; Benjamin, 29 Aug. 1676; Thankful, 20 June 1678; Roger, 24 Apr. 1680; Samuel, 27 July 1684; and Mehitable, 18 June 1686; was freem. 1678, selectman 1693, one of the constables, 1694, and rem. 1696, with Rev. Joseph Lord and others, to found the settlem. in Berkley Co. S. C. aft. nam. Dorchester. JOSEPH, s. of George the first, was perhaps of Milton, and is thot. to have had w. Sarah, both liv. 1730. ROGER, Dorchester, s. of William the first, b. in Eng. freem. 1657, m. Mary, d. of Thomas Josselyn of Lancaster, formerly of Hingham, had perhaps Waitstill, as eldest ch. Abigail, b. 16 Nov. 1657, d. in few mos.; Samuel, 6 Feb. 1659; rem. to Lancaster, had there Mary; William, 1673; Rebecca; and Ebenezer, bef. ment. b. 28 May 1678 aft. his ret. to D. from the destruct. by the Ind. of his resid. at L. He bec. deac. of the ch. at Milton, and d. 26 May 1698, aged 66, so b. 1632. Waitstill is said to have m. bef. 1679, Manassah Tucker; Mary m. 10 June 1688, Israel Nichols; and Rebecca m. 27

Jan. 1697, Aaron Hobart; both of Hingham. SAMUEL, Dorchester, br. of the preced. by w. Rebecca, m. 7 Mar. 1659, had Preserved, b. 14 May 1660, d. at 15 yrs.; Rebecca, 3 Jan. 1662; Mary, 29 Mar. 1664; Samuel, 5 Mar. 1666, d. in few wks.; Mehitable, 21 June 1668; John, 1 Apr. 1670, d. young; Thankful, 9 Dec. 1671; Samuel, again, 8 Mar. 1674; Eliz. 19 Mar. 1676; Ann, 8 Aug. 1678; Nathaniel, 9 Nov. 1680; and Increase, 21 Aug. 1684, d. in few days; was freem. 1690, but of him or his w. no more is told. THOMAS, Rowley 1643. * WIL-LIAM, Dorchester 1636, came prob. with w. Mary, and ch. William, Roger, George, Joan, and perhaps Abigail, wh. d. 19 Feb. 1658, was made freem. 17 May 1637, had Samuel, b. 18 May 1638; and Increase, 23 Feb. 1643; very oft. selectman, and rep. many yrs. His w. d. 7 June 1676, it is report. and he perhaps d. Mar. 1692, aged a. 86. He is thot. to have been only ch. of Roger of Bicester in Co. Oxford, 12 ms. from the city of O. and could only be two yrs. old when his f. made nuncup. will 3 Dec. 1608, pro. 22 Mar. foll. as set out in Geneal. Reg. IX. 300. WILLIAM, Dorchester, mariner, s. of the preced. b. in Eng. m. Eliz. d. of Augustine Clement, had Eliz. bapt. 27 June 1652; Mary, 6 May 1654; rem. to Boston and had William, b. 9 Feb. 1656; Hannah, 10 June 1659; Sarah, 14 Feb. 1662; Experience, 22 Sept. 1664; Ebenezer, 30 Oct. 1666; Deliverance, 18 Mar. 1669; Clement, 6 Sept. 1671; two of wh. prob. were d. in Jan. foll. when gr. f. Clement, in his will, refers to seven; and Mercy, Jan. 1675; but the last eight were, no doubt, b. in B. where his business drew him, and he d. soon aft. the latest b. Eliz. m. Joshua Henshaw; Mary m. 19 Jan. 1672, Nicholas Howe. On 4 May 1687, divis. of his prop. among the ch. shows, that one d. had m. Thomas Gould, prob. ano. perhaps Hannah, m. John Goffe; and ano. Thomas Pratt. Yet in Geneal. Reg. VIII. 128 f. where this suppos. appears, the dilig. inq. says, that Eliz. m. Joshua Henshaw; Mary m. 19 Jan. 1672, Nicholas Howe, and next, John Trew, prob. of Newport; Sarah m. a Turell, and aft. a Weeks; Experience m. Eleazer Carver of Taunton; and Deliverance m. May 1689, Ebenezer Weeks. * WIL-LIAM, Middletown, blacksmith, s. of the preced. by w. Hannah had, b. at Boston, William, 22 Nov. 1675; Hezekiah, 21 Feb. 1683; but perhaps Hannah, wh. d. at Middletown 18 Mar. 1689, was also b. at B. aft. William, and bef. Hezekiah; and Sarah, 29 Dec. 1685; rem. a. 1687 from Boston to M. there had Daniel, 26 Sept. 1688; and Ebenezer, 28 Sept. 1691, d. at seven yrs. was deac. 1695, rep. 1701, 2, and d. 20 July 1703, when only Hezekiah, Daniel, and Sarah were liv. Descend. in Conn. perpet. the stock. Of this name Farmer found eleven gr. at Harv. four at Yale, and two at other N. E. coll.

SUNDERLAND, SUNDERLINE, or SYNDERLAND, ‖ JOHN, Boston, parchment maker, as in deeds he styl. hims. adm. of our ch. 9 Apr. 1643, as was Dorothy, his w. 4 Apr. 1646; was sw. freem. 10 May foll. his adm. (tho. on Col. rec. spelt Sanderbant) had John, b. says the rec. Dec. 1640, bapt. 16 Apr. 1643, a. 2 and a half yrs. old; and Mary, the rec. says, 12 Mar. 1642, bapt. at same time, a. one yr. and six wks.; Hannah, 29 Sept. 1644, tho. rec. of her b. Oct. aft. is found; James b. 18, bapt. 21 Mar. 1647, d. soon; James, again, bapt. 6 Aug. 1648; Benjamin, 26 July 1652; and his w. d. 29 Jan. 1664. By w. Thomasine, d. of William Lumpkin, wid. of Samuel Mayo, he had Mary, b. 15 July 1665; and Samuel, 14 Apr. 1668. He was of ar. co. 1658, but had fallen into pov. and in 1672 made convey. of his goods to John Vial in tr. for Mary w. of his s. and d. of Vial, and her childr. His d. Mary the first m. 29 Nov. 1656, Jonathan Rainsford. He rem. to Eastham, there d. in his 85th yr. 26 Dec. 1703. His wid. d. at E. 16 June 1709 in 84th yr. His will of 27 Sept. 1700, pro. 4 Apr. 1704, provides for wid. and her ds. Mary Bangs; Sarah Freeman; and Mercy Sears; but I do not discov. the hs. of either, tho. perhaps the last was w. of Silas. JOHN, Boston, s. of the preced. m. 26 Jan. 1659, Mary, d. of John Vial, had John, b. 22 Jan. 1661; Dorothy, 7 Apr. 1664; and Nathaniel, 17 Nov. 1667.

SUSSELL, RICHARD, rec. as freem. 1653, at Portsmouth, R. I. as by the print. Vol. I. 263, and repeat. 300, of R. I. Col. Rec. appears, is by me conject. to be the same man, whose controv. relat. to a m. with Abigail Davis, in 1656, may be seen in Ib. 349, 59, 60, and 5. Yet Ussell may seem as wilful a pervers. as the other.

SUTHERLAND, MATTHEW, R. I. 1639.

SUTLIFFE, ABRAHAM, Scituate 1640, by w. Sarah had Abraham and perhaps others, was liv. 1661, and the s. Abraham had a ho. in 1670. NATHANIEL, Medfield 1678. THOMAS, Branford, one of the found. in 1668 of civ. and eccles. order.

SUTTON, BARTHOLOMEW, Boston, by w. Hannah had William, b. 3 Mar. 1667; Hannah, 12 Apr. 1669; and by sec. w. Eliphael had Catharine, 15 Apr. 1670. DANIEL, Boston, by w. Martha had Daniel, b. 19 Feb. 1667. GEORGE, Scituate 1638, m. 1641, Sarah, d. of Elder Nathaniel Tilden of the same, had John, b. 1642; Lydia, 1646; Sarah, 1648, d. soon; Sarah, again, 1650; and Eliz. 1653; but Deane tells not of his d. JOHN, Hingham, came in the Diligent, 1638, with w. and four ch. as the rec. of blessed Daniel Cushing assures us, from Attleburg in Co. Norfolk, a town a. 15 ms. from Norwich, but less than half that dist. from Hingham; encourag. the sett. of Rehoboth, where ld. was assign. him 1644, but forfeit. by non. rem. As he is call. sen. perhaps one of his ch. may have been s. John; but of the stock I gather no more. JOHN, Scituate, s. of George, m. 1661, Eliz. d. of Samuel House, had Eliz. b.

1662; John, 1664; Mary, 1666; Sarah, 1668; Hannah, 1670; Esther, 1673; Benjamin, 1675; Nathaniel, 1677; and Nathan, 1679; was an ens. in Philip's war, and d. in 1691, by his will ment. w. and all the ch. exc. Eliz. and Benjamin, wh. perhaps were d. Ano. JOHN, wh. d. at Rehoboth 1670, is by Deane thot. to be s. of Simon, and by me of the first John. JOSEPH, freem. of Conn. sw. 1658, was of unkn. town. JOSEPH, Boston, by w. Sarah had Sarah, b. 31 July 1659. JULIAN, Rehoboth, was bur. 4 June 1678; but no more is kn. of him. LAMBERT, Charlestown, was adm. of the ch. 4 Apr. 1641, liv. in Woburn, freem. 1644, d. 27 Nov. 1649. RICHARD, Charlestown, a householder 1677, may have been of Roxbury 1650, where his w. Rachel d. 10 Nov. 1672, and a propr. of Lancaster 1653. RICHARD, Andover 1664, may aft. have liv. at Reading. SIMON, Scituate 1647, perhaps br. of George, of wh. we kn. no more, but that he was witn. of Nathaniel Tilden's will, and was there 1643. WILLIAM, Eastham, m. 11 July 1666, Damaris Bishop, had Alice, b. 13 May 1668; Thomas, 11 Nov. 1669; Mary, 4 Oct. 1671; may be the man of Newbury, wh. m. 27 Oct. 1679, Mary Gassell, or Gaffell, as Coffin has the name, and d. 7 May 1690. Of ano. William the inv. was giv. 20 June 1680 by his wid. Sarah. One William was a soldier in the Phips expedit. of 1690 under Gallup.

SWADDON, PHILIP, Watertown, serv. of Robert Seely, 1630, set free next yr. on condit. of pay £10 to his master, was of Kittery 1640.

SWADOCK, JOHN, Haverhill 1685, took o. of alleg. Nov. 1677.

SWAIN, SWAYNE, or SWAINE, sometimes SWEYEN, * DANIEL, Branford, s. of William, b. in Eng. one of the found. of the ch. and town 1664, in freem's. list 1669, was rep. 1673–7, his signat. in fac-simile, Geneal. Reg. III. 153, is pervert. by change of the two final letters, ne for er. He did not partake of the excitem. that carr. many of his town with their min. to N. J. but was engag. build. up fam. and town, m. 1651, Dorcas, d. of Robert Rose of Stratford, had Daniel, b. 26 July 1652; Deborah, 24 Apr. 1654; Samuel, 23 Dec. 1655; Dorcas, 2 Dec. 1657; John, 20 Dec. 1660; Joshua, 12 Jan. 1663; Rachel; David; and Hannah; and he d. 1690 or 1. Samuel, Joshua, and Hannah, as well as eldest ch. Daniel, all d. without ch. bef. their f. so that two s. and three ds. had his est. with the wid. wh. d. early in 1708, and in her will of 1707 names, David hav. d. without ch. only d. Deborah's childr. d. Dorcas Wheeler, formerly Taintor, s. John's childr. and d. Rachel unm. Deborah m. 20 Nov. 1671, Peter Tyler; and Dorcas m. John Taintor, and next a Wheeler. FRANCIS, Exeter 1645, rem. to Middleburg, L. I. 1657, was s. of Richard of Hampton, b. in Eng. brot. by his f. at the age of 14, with his elder br. William from London, 1635, in the Rebecca, while he came later in the same yr. had w. Martha, d. under mid. age,

and his wid. m. Caleb Leverich. HENRY, Charlestown, s. perhaps of
Jeremy the first, was one of the comp. of Capt. Moseley in Philip's war,
a householder in 1678, m. 21 Aug. 1679, Hannah, d. of Benjamin Lothrop of the same. Frothingham, 88, counts Henry an inhab. of 1638 ;
but that seems, as he was not in 1658, prob. a mist. for Jeremy. JER-
EMY, Charlestown 1638, by w. Mary, or Mercy, had Jeremy, b. 1 Mar.
1643 ; John, 30 Jan. 1645 ; and perhaps others, certain. at Reading, Sarah, 29 Jan. 1655 ; and he d. at R. 2 Apr. 1658. ‡ * JEREMY, Reading,
s. prob. of the preced. rep. 1689, and the same yr. chos. Assist. but had
a very small vote at the pop. elect. 1692, and was not nam. in new
Chart. may have been f. of Jeremy, freem. 1691, was certain. much engag. in the Ind. war, as head of a regim. Aug. 1691. See Magn. VII.
67, and Niles. JOHN, Nantucket, prob. s. of Richard the first, had John,
b. 1 Sept. 1664, by tradit. the first male, b. there ; Stephen, 21 Nov.
1666 ; Sarah, 13 July 1670 ; Joseph, 17 July 1673 ; Eliz. 17 May
1676 ; Benjamin, 5 July 1679 ; and Hannah ; all perhaps by Mary, d.
of Nathaniel Wyer, but we are not sure of more than that he d. 1717 ;
and is said to have been b. 1633, but I doubt the report. JOHN, Branford, s. of Daniel of the same, and the only one, wh. had ch. yet d. 1694,
bef. mid. age, leav. Eunice, and John. NICHOLAS, Hampton 1643.
RICHARD, Rowley 1639, came in the Truelove, 1635, aged 34, or rather
more, emb. at London, 17 Sept. hav. in Apr. sent, perhaps his w. Eliz.
in the Planter, s. William, and Francis, in the Rebecca ; and d. Eliz. in
the Susan and Ellen, under care of various friends, freem. 13 Mar.
1639, had liberty the yr. bef. to plant, with others, at Hampton, where
in 1639 he had authty. to sett. small causes, but had Eliz. bapt. at Newbury 9 Oct. 1638 ; m. 1658, or 9, Jane, wid. of George Bunker, perhaps
by her had Richard ; and in 1663 had sett. at Nantucket, and d. 14
Apr. 1682. He had, also, d. Dorothy, wh. m. Thomas Abbot, and
next Edward Chapman ; and Eliz. m. Nathaniel Weare. RICHARD,
Nantucket, perhaps s. of the preced. had Abigail, b. 7 Feb. 1684 ;
and Jonathan, 23 Dec. 1685 ; and may have had more. * SAM-
UEL, Branford, elder br. of Daniel, b. in Eng. was lieut. and rep. 1663 ;
as friend of Rev. Mr. Pierson, went with first sett. to Newark, N. J. and
was rep. in the first assemb. of that province, but Whitehead, in " E Jersey under the Proprs." 52, calls him Swarne. Who his w. was, is not
kn. but he had some ch. as Eliz. wh. m. Josiah Ward, and next David
Ogden ; and Mary, b. 1 May 1649, both bapt. at New Haven, 1 June
1651, of wh. Mary d. at 6 yrs. ; Phebe, b. 24 May 1654 ; Mary, again,
12 June 1656 ; Christian, 25 Apr. 1659, wh. m. Nathaniel Ward ; Sarah, 7 Oct. 1661 ; and perhaps more bef. or aft. rem. ‡ * WILLIAM,
Watertown, came in the Elizabeth and Ann, from London, 1635, aged

50, was adm. freem. at the Gen. Ct. 3 Mar. foll. when he was appoint.
with Ludlow, and others, commissnrs. to rule the new settlem. at Conn.
serv. as rep. 1636, May in Mass. and in Sept. held Court in the young
Col. next yr. he contin. to act as Assist. perhaps under the Mass. delegat. but not in 1638, when the inhab. of Conn. took the whole admin. of
their own affairs, tho. their formal constitut. was not adopt. bef. Jan.
1639. He sat down at Wethersfield, of wh. he was rep. 1641–3; soon
aft. being chos. again Assist. 1644, he rem. with s. Samuel and Daniel to
the W. and lighted on or near Branford 1644, there prob. d. His d.
Mary, early a mem. of Roxbury ch. m. and went to New Haven says the
rec.   WILLIAM, Hampton, s. of Richard the first, b. in Eng. by w. Prudence had William, Prudence, Hannah, Bethia, and Hezekiah, of wh.
the order of success. is not kn. and he and his w. d. a. 1657 or 8.   WIL-
LIAM, Hampton, s. of the preced. took the o. of alleg. 1678. Very oft.
this name is mistak. for Swan, and that for this.   In Winth. II. 29, is
the story of one S. of York, wh. fell into despair, and hang. hims. in Mar.
1641.

SWALLOW, AMBROSE, Chelmsford 1692, perhaps, says Farmer in MS.
was previous. of Dunstable.

SWAN, or SWANN, EBENEZER, Cambridge, s. of John of the same, d.
27 July 1740, by w. Eliz. had Eliz. b. 29 Mar. 1699; Sarah, 26 Feb.
1701; Ebenezer, 23 Mar. 1704; Mary, 4 Mar. 1707; Samuel, 5 Apr.
1711; and William, 31 Jan. 1714.   GERSHOM, Cambridge, s. of John
of the same, m. 20 Dec. 1677, Sarah, d. of Richard Holden, had
Sarah, b. a. 1679; Rebecca, 24 Aug. 1681, d. young; John, 3 Oct.
1683; Ruth, 25 Dec. 1685; Abigail, 12 Feb. 1687; Lydia, 10 Nov.
1689; Rebecca, bapt. 14 Aug. 1698; and perhaps more; and he d. 2
July 1708.   HENRY, Salem, adm. of the ch. 19 May, and freem. 22 May
1639, had Thomas, bapt. 26 Feb. 1643; and Eliz. 8 Feb. 1646.   HEN-
RY, Boston, and no more is kn. of him, but that by w. Joan he had
Sarah, and d. bef. her, whose d. is rec. at B. 23 Dec. 1651.   JOHN,
Cambridge, serv. to Thomas Bittlestone, nam. in his will, 1640, m. 1
Jan. or as ano. acco. says, Feb. 1651, Rebecca Palfrey, d. prob. of a wid.
wh. came from Eng. had Ruth, b. 10 Mar. 1652, and Gershom, 30 June
1654.   She d. 12 July 1654, and he m. 1 Mar. 1656, Mary Pratt, had
Samuel, b. 3 Apr. or 1 May 1657, d. 19 June 1678, says the gr. stone;
Mary, 2 May 1659; Eliz. 14 July 1661; Lydia, 28 July 1663; John,
1 May 1665; Hannah, 27 Feb. 1668; and Ebenezer, 14 Nov. 1672.
The f. was freem. 29 Apr. 1668, and d. 5 June 1708, aged 87, and his
w. d. 11 Feb. 1703 in her 70th yr. as Harris tells.   Eliz. m. Ezekiel
Richardson of Woburn.   JOHN, Westfield, is an alias name of SEVAN, as
the Rev. Mr. Davis read the orig. rec. wh. is hardly to be call. a possib.

one; but a more practis. eye gave me the assurance that the name was
SCORE. Nobody will dispute the prob. that Mr. Judd got hold of the
right letters. * RICHARD, Boston, join. our ch. 6 Jan. 1639, had John,
bapt. next Sunday, and was dism. 24 Nov. foll. with others to form a ch.
at Rowley, freem. 13 May aft. was rep. 1666 and many yrs. more, and
d. 1678. His w. was Ann, ch. Richard, Frances, Robert, Jonathan, Susan, or Julian, and perhaps more ch. certain. ds. Frances, m. Mark
Quilter, and Sarah m. Joseph Boynton. Julian had m. 18 Feb. 1654,
Samuel Stickney, bore him four ch. and d. bef. her f. But his will, of
1678, beside these, name ds. Abigail Bailey, Mary Kilborn, and s. Caleb
Hopkinson, John Hopkinson, and John Trumbull. I conject. that John
Trumbull rem. from Roxbury to Rowley soon aft. Swan, m. his d. Ann,
and d. 1657, leav. sev. ch. prob. Joseph and Judah among them. RICH-
ARD, Rowley, prob. s. of the preced. freem. 1684. ROBERT, Haverhill
1646, by w. Eliz. had prob. Robert, and perhaps Timothy and others.
* ROBERT, Haverhill, prob. s. of the preced. took o. of alleg. 28 Nov.
1677, and was rep. 1684. TIMOTHY, Andover, s. of Robert the first, d.
1 Feb. 1693, aft. long afflict. suppos. by witchcraft, as Rev. Mr. Hale in
his Hist. p. 38, tells, of wh. Eliz. Johnson, perhaps w. of Stephen, acknowl. bef. Justice Dudley Bradstreet, 10 Aug. 1692, that she had a
hand in it, but she was so liberal in confess. many other torments bestow.
by her upon other neighbors, that I believe she saved her life by her
falsehoods. See 3 Mass. Hist. Coll. I. 124. But the magistr. was slow
to believe the horrible confess. of his neighb. against themselves, and so
the baffled bloodhounds wh. rejoic. in the diabolical delus. were let loose
upon him, as a Sadducee. THOMAS, Roxbury, m. Mary, d. of Thomas
Lamb, had Henry, b. in Boston (where prob. he first pursu. his profess.),
16 May 1665, wh. d. young; and Thomas, wh. d. 1668; but at R. had
Thomas, again, b. 15 Sept. 1669, H. C. 1689; Dorothy, 29 Dec. 1672;
Peter, and Dorothy, prob. tw. 1674, d. very soon; Henry, 29 Mar.
1678, d. soon; Henry, again, 24 Mar. foll.; Mary, 4 June 1681; Peter,
17 June 1684, d. soon; and Ebenezer, 12 May 1686; was a physician
and d. perhaps in Feb. 1688. His ho. was burn. in the night of 11 July
1681, for wh. Maria, a negro serv. of Joshua Lamb, being convict. by
her confess. at the Court in Sept. foll. the Gov. benignant Bradstreet,
pronounc. the sentence of d. by the form. of burn. and the horrid solemnity was public. THOMAS, Roxbury, s. of the preced. m. 27 Dec. 1692,
Prudence Wade of Medford. Twelve of this name at Harv. and two at
Yale had been gr. in 1846.

SWARTON, JOHN, Beverly 1672.

SWASEY, SWAZEY, or SWAYSY, JOSEPH, Salem 1668, had a fam. prob.
for the name was perpet. to our day; and in 1680, Eliz. perhaps his d.
m. John Lightfoot at that town.

SWATMAN, JOHN, Cambridge, is no doubt error in Genealog. Reg. IX. 168 (but truly tak. from the old book in Boston), for Thomas Sweetman; and the date of b. of the first ch. is one yr. too early.

SWELUS, an unfortun. name in Geneal. Reg. II. 264, belongs, I am confident, to Robert Twelves of Braintree. See, also, an equal mistake in Quelves.

SWEET, SWAITE, or SWEETE, BENONI, Warwick, or Kingstown, s. of the first James, had James, b. 1688; Margaret, 1690; Benoni, 1692; Mary, 1696; Eliz. 1700; and Thomas, 1703; perhaps all, perhaps only the last two, by w. Eliz.   DANIEL, Warwick, s. of the first John of Warwick, made his will in 1728.   HENRY, Swanzey, m. 29 Jan. 1687, Eliz. d. of Philip Walker, and was aft. of Attleborough, had five ch.   JAMES, had been of Salem 1631, call. s. of Isaac, wh. prob. d. in Eng. and a wid. S. perhaps his mo. had gr. of ld. there 1637, on the list of freem. 1655, of Warwick, there m. Mary, d. of the first John Greene of the same, had Philip, b. 15 July 1655; James, 8 May 1657; Mary, 2 Feb. 1660; Benoni, 28 Mar. 1663; Valentine, 14 Feb. 1665; Samuel, 1 Nov. 1667, b. at Prudence isl.; Jeremiah, 6 Jan. 1669; Renewed, 16 July 1671; and Sylvester, 1 Mar. 1674, at Potowomut.   JOHN, Boston 1640, shipwright, or caulker, join. our ch. 30 Jan. and was freem. 2 June 1641, by w. Temperance, wh. d. Jan. 1645 (strange. misprint. Temperance Jewett in ment. of her ch. censure by Drake, Hist. of Boston, 252), had Temperance, wh. d. 28 Nov. 1661; and by w. Susanna, wh. join. our ch. 23 May 1647, he had Susanna, b. 3, bapt. 11 Apr. 1647; John, 8, bapt. 21 Sept. 1651, d. young; Mary, 28 Jan. bapt. 5 Feb. 1653; Abigail, 4 May 1656, d. in few days; Mehitable, b. 8, bapt. 11 Oct. 1657, d. soon; Mehitable, again, b. 8 Dec. 1659.   JOHN, Charlestown, shoemaker, d. 18 May 1695, near 80, says the gr. stone. His w. d. 16 July 1666, aged 44, and he d. 25 Apr. 1685, aged 82, as the gr. stones in Copp's hill show. and Sewall's diary says, he was bur. 20 Apr.   JOHN, Warwick, br. of James, prob. elder, perhaps brot. from Eng. by his mo. Mary, wid. of Isaac Sweet, wh. there m. Ezekiel Holliman, hav. two s. this John, and br. James, beside a d. Meribah, whose name by Holliman was alter. to Renewed, bef. she m. John Geraerd; is on freem's. list 1655, had a grist mill, and other works on the Potowomut, in the Naraganset country, burnt by the Ind. in Philip's, war, 1675, in his will of 1677, then of Newport, names w. Eliz. and ch. John, Daniel, James, Henry, Richard, Benjamin, William, and Jeremiah, beside a d.   JOHN, Wickford, had w. Eliz. and ch. John, Eliz. James, and Sarah, as from his will, in 1716, on rec. of Wickford, appears.   Ano. JOHN, of Wickford, was f. of the preced. but d. the yr. aft. him, had beside him, Deborah, James, and Mary, as also sec. w. Rachel.   RICHARD, Westerly, s. prob. of John, m. 15 Dec.

1673, perhaps Mehitable, d. of Edward Larkin the first of the same; and prob. for sec. w. had Priscilla, d. of the sec. William Carpenter of Rehoboth. THOMAS, passeng. in the Mary and John, 1634, wh. took the o. of suprem. and alleg. 24 Mar. to pass. for N. E. where in May the sh. arr. but of this person I hear no more. WILLIAM, Roxbury 1654.

SWEETMAN, SWETMAN, or SWETNAM, THOMAS, Cambridge, freem. 2 May 1638, by w. Isabel had Eliz. b. 6 Jan. 1647; Rebecca, 7 Apr. 1649; Mehitable, a. 1650; Sarah, b. 2 May 1554; Thomas, 18 Jan. 1656, d. in few days unbapt.; Ruhamah, 28 Mar. 1657; the others all bapt. says Mitchell's Reg. wh. adds to them Samuel, b. 19 Apr. bapt. 22 May 1659, H. C. 1677, whose d. is unkn. to the Catal.; Bethia, 7 July 1661; and Hepzibah, b. 19, bapt. 24 June 1666; and he d. 8 Jan. 1683, aged 73. His wid. had alms from the ch. up to 12 Dec. 1709. Eliz. m. 7 Dec. 1671, Benjamin Wellington; Rebecca m. Michael Spencer; Sarah m. 9 Jan. 1674, Josiah Treadway, and d. 5 Mar. 1697; and Bethia m. James Hewes of Boston.

SWEETSER, or SWITZER, BENJAMIN, Charlestown 1658, s. of Seth of the same, b. in Eng. then a householder, was next yr. fined £50 and imprison. as a Bapt. Prob. he had s. Seth, and perhaps other ch. and certain. d. 22 July 1718. SAMUEL, Malden, by w. Eliz. had Samuel, b. 3 Apr. 1701; John, 12 Feb. 1703; Jacob, 6 Apr. 1705; and Michael, 19 May 1707. SETH, Charlestown 1637, aged a. 31, came from Tring in Hertfordsh. a. 30 ms. from London, with s. Benjamin, join. the ch. Jan. 1639, as did his w. Bethia in Sept. aft. had Hannah, bapt. 12 Jan. 1639; Eliz. b. 27 Jan. 1643, prob. bapt. as may have been other childr. when for some yrs. the rec. is defic. was freem. 14 Mar. 1639, a moderate Bapt. in latter days, and d. 21 or 24 May 1662, aged 56, leav. wid. Eliz. m. Apr. 1661, wh. had been wid. of Thomas Oakes of Cambridge, and ch. Benjamin, Sarah, Mary, w. of Samuel Blanchard, and Hannah Fitch. His wid. m. Samuel Hayward of Malden and outliv. him. See Frothingham, 67. SETH, Charlestown, perhaps s. of Benjamin, m. 12 Jan. 1692, at Malden, Sarah Clark of C. wid. of Thomas, d. of Joseph Lynde of the same. Large. is the name diffus. in this neighborhood.

SWETT, BENJAMIN, Newbury, s. of John the first, b. in Eng. 1626, m. as said in Geneal. Reg. VI. 50, Esther, d. of Peter Weare, had Esther, b. 7 June 1648, perhaps mean. Jan. 1649; Sarah, 7 Nov. 1650; Mary, 7 Jan. 1652, prob. d. young; Mary, again, 2 May 1654; Benjamin, 5 Aug. 1656; Joseph, 21 Jan. 1659; and Moses, 16 Sept. 1661; wh. is all tak. from Coffin, wh. adds, that he rem. to Hampton; and the fam. acco. proceeds to give Hannah, 16 May 1664; Eliz. 2 July 1667; John, 17 May 1670; Stephen, 13 Sept. 1672; and ano. ch. whose name is not

told; was ens. 1650, lieut. 1675, and fell in the Ind. war at the E. with
60 of his men, 29 June 1677, in Scarborough. His wid. m. Capt. Stephen Greenleaf, 31 Mar. 1678, as fam. rep. says, but Coffin, with better
regard, calls it 1679, as the first w. of this sec. h. d. Nov. 1678. Of his
ds. Esther m. 1668, Abia Green, acc. fam. acco. but wh. he was is unkn.
Sarah m. 1678, in same rep. Maurice Hobbs; but Coffin makes him m.
Sarah Eastow. BENJAMIN, Hampton, s. of the preced. took o. of fidel.
Apr. 1678. JOHN, Newbury, among the early sett. freem. 18 May 1642,
brot. from Eng. prob. Stephen, Benjamin and Joseph; beside Sarah,
perhaps, wh. d. 11 Dec. 1650; and possib. others. A wid. Phebe d.
May 1665 wh. prob. was his. JOHN, Newbury, s. of Stephen, m. 6
Dec. 1670, Mary, d. of Samuel Plummer, had Mary, b. 10 Apr. 1672;
Hannah, 15 June 1674; John, 20 Feb. 1677; Samuel, 10 Sept. 1680;
prob. rem. to Charlestown for some yrs. as in Dec. 1680 he was adm. of
that ch. by dism. from the ch. of N. as the rec. tells; yet perhaps went
back to N. and had the other ch. Stephen, 27 Jan. 1684; Joseph, 2
Feb. 1687; and Benjamin, 11 Apr. 1688. JOHN, Narraganset 1687.
JOHN, Hampton, s. of Benjamin the first, m. 3 Oct. 1696, Bethia, d. of
Thomas Page, had Huldah, b. 16 July 1699; Sarah, 23 Dec. 1700;
John, 4 Dec. 1702; Elisha, 30 Sept. 1705; Benjamin, 17 Oct. 1707;
and Joseph; and rem. to Kingston, N. H. there d. early in 1753, leav.
wid. Sarah. JOSEPH, Newbury, perhaps s. of the first John, m. 1650,
says Coffin, but tells no more; was of Haverhill 1653, and I judge, that
he rem. to Boston, there by w. Eliz. had Joseph, b. 26 Oct. 1658; and
Benjamin, 22, bapt. 29 Jan. 1660. Yet nothing more is found. Jo-
SEPH, Hampton, s. of Benjamin the first, took o. of fidel. Apr. 1678.
MOSES, Hampton, br. of the preced. took o. of fidel. Dec. 1678, m. 12
May 1687, Mary Hussey, had Mary, b. 2 Feb. 1689; and Esther, 10
June 1690, beside four or five others, of wh. one was Deliverance. His
will of 15 Apr. 1719, perhaps wd. allow us to suppose all the ch. dec.
STEPHEN, Newbury, s. prob. of the first John, b. a. 1620 in Eng. m. 24
May 1647, Hannah, d. of the first John Merrill, had John, b. 20 Oct.
1648, d. at 4 yrs.; Stephen, 20 Aug. 1650, d. in few days; Hannah, 7
Oct. 1651; Stephen, again, 28 Jan. 1654; Eliz. 16 Jan. 1656; Joseph,
28 Nov. 1657; and Mary, 17 Mar. 1662. His w. d. 4 Apr. foll. and he
m. 4 Aug. 1663, Rebecca, d. of Thomas Smith, had Benjamin, 20 May
1664; Rebecca, 4 Dec. 1665, d. within 6 mos.; and Rebecca, again, 27
Feb. 1670; and his w. d. 2 days aft. In old rec. the name is oft. Sweet.
Six had in 1828 been gr. at Harv. as Farmer MS. notes. So oft. is
the interchange of Sweet and Swett in old rec. that we must not depend
on spell.

SWIFT, EPHRAIM, Sandwich, s. of William sec. perhaps by w. Sarah, wh. surv. him, had Eliz. b. 29 Dec. 1679 ; Joanna, 7 July 1683 ; Samuel, 9 Apr. 1686 ; Ephraim, 9 Dec. 1688 ; Sarah, 12 Apr. 1692 ; Hannah, 19 May 1695 ; and Moses, 15 Sept. 1699. His will of 10 Apr. 1735, was pro. 17 Feb. 1742. JIRAH, Sandwich, br. of the preced. m. 26 Nov. 1697, Abigail Gibbs, and had sec. w. Mary, nam. in his will of 29 Mar. 1744, pro. 1 May 1749. Of this br. are the Swifts of New Bedford. JOSIAH, Sandwich, br. of the preced. m. 16 Apr. 1706, Mary Bodfish, prob. d. of Joseph, and next m. Experience Nye, perhaps d. of Ebenezer. OBADIAH, Dorchester, s. of Thomas of the same, m. 15 Mar. 1661, Rest, d. of Humphrey Atherton, had Remember, b. 5 Feb. 1662, d. very soon ; Rest, 13 Dec. 1662 ; Obadiah, 28 Jan. 1671 ; Hopestill, 11 Mar. 1674 ; Eliz. 7 Sept. 1675, d. in few days ; Abigail, 4 Jan. 1676 ; Eliz. again, 4 Jan. 1679, d. young. He had sec. w. Abigail, was freem. 1673, and d. 27 Dec. 1690 ; but his wid. liv. to 19 Mar. 1737. SAMUEL, Sandwich, br. of Ephraim, had w. Mary, nam. in his will of 5 Oct. 1730, pro. 6 June 1733. THOMAS, Dorchester, one of the early sett. was s. of Robert of Rotherham in Co. York, freem. 6 May 1635, by w. Eliz. wh. prob. was d. of the first Bernard Capen, had Joan, perhaps b. in Eng. ; Thomas, b. 17 June 1635 ; Obadiah, 16 July 1638 ; Eliz. 26 Feb. 1641 ; Ruth, 24 Aug. 1643 ; Mary, 21 Sept. 1645 ; Ann, 14 Nov. 1647 ; and Susanna, 11 Feb. 1652 ; but in these dates I foll. Barry only, wherever rec. fails, tho. he may have foll. higher authority than our rec. with wh. for the first four he does not concur. He d. 30 May, says gr.stone, but other acco. 4 May 1675, aged 75, and his wid. d. 26 Jan. 1678, aged 67. Joan m. 5 Nov. 1657, John Baker of Boston, says a false certificate in the copy of rec. prob. mean. ten yrs. earlier (see Vol. I. 97 of this Dict. and Geneal. Reg. XI. 202) ; Ruth m. 10 Oct. 1660, William Greenough of Boston ; Mary m. 11 Jan. 1664, John White ; Ann m. 19 Aug. 1664, Obadiah Read ; and Susanna m. 18 Apr. 1672, Hopestill Clap. THOMAS, Milton, eldest s. of the preced. m. 9 Dec. 1657, Eliz. d. of Robert Vose, had Thomas, b. 30 July 1659 ; Eliz. ; William, 5 May 1670, wh. perish. in the expedit. of Phips against Quebec ; John, 14 Mar. 1679, H. C. 1697, first min. at Framingham ; and Samuel, 1683 ; was deac. and d. 31 Jan. 1718. WILLIAM, Watertown 1634, had been here some time prob. com. from Bocking, Co. Suffk. or its neighb. sold his est. 1637, and rem. prob. to Sandwich, there d. Jan. 1644. His wid. Joan, perhaps a sec. w. made her will 12 Oct. 1662, nam. s. William, and his ch. and sev. others, whose relat. is not discov. but we may inf. that Daniel Wing, to whose two s. she makes gifts, had m. Hannah, d. of her h. as also that other gr.ch. were Experience and Zebediah Allin, and Mary Darley. *WILLIAM, Sandwich, s. of the preced. b. in Eng. had

d. Hannah, b. 11 Mar. 1651, among other ch. as in the will of his mo.
designat. but not nam. His own will of 15 Dec. 1705, pro. 29 of next
mo. names w. Ruth, and s. William, 28 Aug. 1654; and Ephraim, 6
June 1656. He is by Baylies mark. as rep. 1673, 4, 7 and 8. Other ch.
were Mary, 7 Apr. 1659; Samuel, 10 Aug. 1662; Josiah; Jirah; Temperance; Esther; and Dinah. WILLIAM, Sandwich, s. of the preced.
had w. Eliz. nam. in his will, of 17 June 1700, pro. 12 May foll. as he
d. near five yrs. bef. his f. His ch. were William, Joseph, Benjamin,
Thomas, Josiah, and Ebenezer. Farmer notes, of this name nine had
been gr. at Yale, six at Harv. and eight at other N. E. coll.

SWILLAWAY, or SWILLOWAY, HENRY, Malden, had Hannah, b. Feb.
1666. Margaret m. 15 Aug. 1687, Robert Smith of Charlestown.

SWINERTON, or SWANNERTON, JOB, Salem 1637, when he had gr. of
ld. join. the ch. 1639, as did Eliz. prob. his w. or mo. was made freem. 6
Sept. of that yr. m. 19 July 1658, Ruth, d. of John Symonds, had two s.
and two ds. and his w. d. 22 May 1670. He liv. in Danvers, and d. 11
Apr. 1689. His d. Ruth d. 27 Oct. 1694, and was bur. next day, being
Sunday, when "more attend. the funer. than the sermon." JOB, a serg.
of Salem vill. now Danvers, was prob. s. of the preced. and freem. 1690;
in 1686 was 55 yrs. old; and d. 7 Apr. 1700. JOHN, Salem, perhaps
br. of the younger Job, a physician, d. 6 Jan. 1691, aged 57, leav. wid.
Hannah, wh. d. 23 Dec. 1713, aged 71. Felt.

SWYNDEN, or SWINDEN, WILLIAM, Ipswich, came in the Elizabeth
and Ann, 1635, aged 20.

SYDLIE, THOMAS, a passeng. aged 22, emb. at London in the Susan
and Ellen, for N. E. May 1635, as found by Mr. Drake, Geneal. Reg.
XIV. 309, and had been ment. in 3 Mass. Hist. Coll. VIII. 259; but
notice is never seen of him aft. and perhaps the name is mistak.

SYKES, RICHARD, Dorchester 1639, freem. 13 May 1640. See Sikes.

SYLVESTER. See Silvester.

SYMMES, JOHN, Scarborough, sw. alleg. to Mass. July 1658. TIMO-
THY, Charlestown, s. of Rev. Zechariah, m. 10 Dec. 1668, Mary Nichols, whose f. is not kn. had one ch. b. 6 Sept. 1669, and d. on same day,
and the mo. d. twelve days aft. He m. 21 Sept. 1671, Eliz. d. of Capt.
Francis Norton, had Timothy, b. 18 Nov. 1672; Eliz. 24, bapt. 26 July
1674; and Sarah, 6, bapt. 20 Aug. 1676, but why the first was not bapt.
and why the other two were, when neither f. nor mo. appear in the list
of ch. mem. is hard to explain. He d. of smallpox, 4 July 1678, and his
wid. m. 12 Apr. 1688, as his third w. Capt. Ephraim Savage, and d. 13
Apr. 1710. WILLIAM, Charlestown, eldest s. of the Rev. Zechariah,
b. at Dunstable, Co. Bedford, brot. by his f. had by first w. d. Sarah, wh.
m. bef. he got his sec. w. by wh. he had William, b. 7 Jan. 1679; Zech-

ariah; Timothy; and Nathaniel; beside two others, perhaps ds. whose
names are unkn. was householder bef. 1678, when he was chos. tythingman, but wh. was his first or sec. w. or when he was m. to either, and the
dates of b. of six ch. are unkn. He was not made freem. and finds not
place among Budington's ch. mem. d. 22 Sept. 1691, leav. seven ch.
His wid. m Rev. Samuel Torrey. Sarah m. 7 Nov. 1671, Rev. Moses
Fiske of Braintree. WILLIAM, Medford or Charlestown, s. of the preced. m. Ruth, perhaps d. of Josiah Convers of Woburn, had William, b.
10 Oct. 1705, wh. d. young; Zechariah, 1 Sept. 1707; Josiah, 7 Apr.
1710, d. young; Eliz.; Timothy; John; and William, H. C. 1750, min.
of Andover; and d. 24 May 1764. ZECHARIAH, Charlestown, came in
1634, with Rev. John Lothrop, William Hutchinson and his w. the gr.
prophetess, arr. 18 Sept. brot. w. Sarah and ch. Sarah; William, bapt.
10 Jan. 1627; Mary, 16 Apr. 1628; Eliz. 1 Jan. 1630; Huldah, 18 Mar.
1631; Hannah, 22 Aug. 1632; and Rebecca, 12 Feb. 1634; had here
Ruth, b. 18, bapt. 25 Oct. 1635; Zechariah, 9, bapt. 14 Jan. not 9, as
Geneal. Reg. XIII. p. 5, says, 1638, H. C. 1657; Timothy, 7, bapt. 10
May 1640, d. soon; Deborah, 28 Aug. bapt. 4 Sept. 1642; but the dates
of bapt. of the last three are wrong, in the copy by Budington scrupu-
lously foll. and the orig. being lost, we are always doubtful, whether the
transcript is correct. In ea. of the three cases, the Geneal. Reg. XIII.
135, has used the day of birth, but without turn. to the almanac, call. it
the day of bapt. Worse error than this readers may be led into by tak.
the order of the ch. where Sarah is rank. under 12, as the youngest d.
when she was the eldest of the eight ds. if not of the thirteen ch. Timothy, again, whose date is not found; and one more s. if Mather, III. 132,
has correct. quot. his epit. wh. is doubted. His neighb. Johnson, so
many yrs. his parishioner, speaks of ch. "their numb. being ten, both s.
and ds. a certain sign of the Lord's intent to people this vast wilderness,"
he adds, with juster application of the doings of Providence, than he
usual. exhibits. He was b. at Canterbury, in Co. Kent, 5 Apr. 1599, s.
of Rev. William, matric. 1617 at Emanuel, and took at the Univ. of
Cambridge his A. B. 1620–1, preach. as a lecturer at the ch. of St. Ath-
olines, London, m. July 1621, and there had eldest d. Sarah, but in 1625
bec. rector of Dunstable, in wh. office he had large serv. dur. the plague
that extend. wide. that yr. Mather, wh. confess. his informat. is not
large, says, he was always worried by the prelatists for insuffic. conform.
His liv. was not a very good one, as his success. in 1842 wrote me, and
his fam. being num. he saw prospects of more enlarg. usefulness on our
side of the water, join. the ch. of Boston, with his w. 5 Oct. 1634, and
that of C. 5 Dec. next, was freem. 6 May foll. was held in high regard, and d. 28 Jan. and was bur. I suppose 4 Feb. 1672, tho. various

yrs. are nam.   His wid. d. 1676.   Of his thirteen ch. ten were liv. to be nam. in his will of 20 Jan. 1664.   Sarah m. 1650, Rev. Samuel Hough of Reading, wh. d. Mar. 1662, and she m. Nov. foll. his successor in the pulpit, John Brock; Mary m. 15 Sept. 1652, as sec. w. Thomas Savage of Boston, and next Anthony Stoddard; Eliz. m. 2 Nov. 1652, Hezekiah Usher, as his sec. w.; Huldah m. as sec. or third w. William Davis; Rebecca m. Humphrey Booth; Deborah m. 13 Dec. 1664, Timothy Prout; Ruth m. 15 June 1668, Edward Willis; and Hannah had d. unm. bef. the confirmat. of the will, who bore a codic. 19 Dec. 1667, and spake of Ruth as still unm.   It was pro. 31 Mar. 1672, and names the s. William, Zechariah, and Timothy.   In his will br. William is ment. but he was prob. in Eng. and never came to our country.   ZECHARIAH, Bradford, s. of the preced. m. 18 Nov. 1669, Susanna, d. of Thomas Graves of Charlestown, had Sarah, b. 20 May 1672; Zechariah, 13 Mar. 1674; both at B. and at Charlestown had Catharine, b. 29 Mar. bapt. 2 Apr. 1676; and b. at B.   Thomas, 31 Jan. 1678, H. C. 1698; William, 7 Jan. 1680; and Rebecca, 20 July 1681.   His w. d. three days aft. and he m. 26 Nov. 1683, Mehitable, wid. of Samuel Dalton of Hampton.   Some confus. is seen a. this fam. in Geneal. Reg. XIII. 135, 6.   He had first preach. a short time at Rehoboth, but at B. preach. 14 yrs. Budington says, bef. he was ord. 27 Dec. 1682, and d. 22 Mar. 1708.   His s. Thomas was a man of distinct. and succeed. his f. Eliot's Biogr. Dict. gives agreeab. details.   Of one of this name, prob. a maiden, wh. d. at Cambridge 10 June 1653, no diligence of inquiry can be expect. to enlarge the report of Mr. Paige, " Mrs. Sarah Symmes had a gr. of ld. 1639.   She appears to have been a lady of wealth, and a mem. of the ch."

SYMONDS, BENJAMIN, Woburn, s. of William, freem. 1690, by w. Rebecca had William, b. 14 Feb. 1679; Benjamin, 14 Jan. 1681; Joseph, 1 Mar. 1683; John, 23 Mar. 1685; Rebecca, 6 June 1687; Daniel, 21 Feb. 1690; Jacob, 26 May 1692; Judith, 5 Oct. 1695; and Huldah, 25 Oct. 1700.   CALEB, Woburn, br. of the preced. freem. 1690, m. 25 Sept. 1677, Sarah Bacon, had Samuel, b. 30 June 1678; James, 15 Jan. 1684; and Sarah, 11 Nov. 1687, wh. d. in few days.   HARLAKENDEN, Gloucester, s. of Samuel the first, b. in Eng. a. 1628, brot. by his f. in 1637, freem. 1665, had w. Eliz. call. in the will of 3 May 1670, made by Sarah, wid. of Richard Mather (wh. had been wid. of great John Cotton, and in Eng. by him m. as the wid. Story), her gr.ch. and may well be judg. the same in Cotton's will, 1652, nam. as his gr.ch. Betty Day.   We know, Cotton then had no gr.ch. and this ch. must have been b. of some d. of the wid. Story, wh. in Eng. or here had m. a Day.   That name is found early both at Ipswich and Gloucester; but, tho. Mr. Felt has large

acquaint. with the early inhab. of both those towns, he can discov. no f.
for this w. of Symonds. By her he had, at G. Sarah, b. 2 July 1668, wh.
by the will of her gr. gr.mo. Mather, had gift of one of her cows. But I
kn. no more of him, exc. that he went home and was liv. at Wethersfield
in Eng. 1672; nor is it kn. that he ever came back. Mr. Babson informs us, that the wid. ret. to G. where the d. m. a. 1692 Thomas Low ;
and her mo. d. 31 Jan. 1728, aged 90. HENRY, Boston 1643, perhaps
the freem. of 10 May, a man of enterprise, undertook the work of mak.
the mill creek for a mill power, under a vote of July, with George Burden, John Button, John Hill and assoc. as is fully stat. in Snow's Hist. of
Boston, 124, 5. But he d. in Sept. foll. and was bur. 14th. He had been
recommend. by pastor of a ch. at Southampton, and in that right his
posthum. ch. was bapt. here 21 Apr. 1644, a. 3 days old by the name,
Richgrace, giv. by the wid. mo. no doubt. So it might be infer. that he
had gone from Lynn with Rev. Abraham Pierson ; and Lechford's Plain
Dealing, 43, makes it certain, that he was one of the found. of Pierson's
ch. gather. at Lynn, 1641, as Winth. tells, II. 6, for the object of going to
the E. end of Long Island, tho. it is implied from Lechford's language,
that he never went. His wid. m. Isaac Walker, and her name was Susan, as appears in the act of our Gen. Ct. Rec. II. 104, confirm. to Christopher Lawson est. in Boston that S. had engag. to sell him. JAMES,
Salem, s. of John of the same, suppos. to be b. in 1633, perhaps in Eng.
m. 20 Nov. 1661, Eliz. Browning, perhaps d. of Thomas, had Mary, b.
1 Nov. 1662 ; Ruth, 19 Feb. 1664 ; John, 8 July 1666 ; James, 14 Oct.
1670, d. young ; Eliz. Mar. 1673, d. soon ; James, again, 14 Apr. 1674 ;
Benjamin ; Thomas ; Eliz. again, d. young ; Joseph ; Sarah ; and Eliz.
again, wh. d. young. As I find not his d. I presume he rem. His eldest d. m. I suppose, 3 Dec. 1685, the third Edward Norris. JAMES, Woburn, m. 29 Dec. 1685, Susanna Blodget, perhaps d. of the first Samuel,
had James, b. 1 Nov. 1686 ; Susanna, 2 May 1689 ; Abigail, 17 Jan.
1692 ; Sarah, 13 Dec. 1694 ; Nathan, 12 June 1697 ; and Ruth, 12 Dec.
1699. Prob. he rem. JOHN, Salem 1637, freem. Mar. 1638, had w. Eliz.
and ch. beside James bef. ment. ; Samuel, whose bapt. was 4 Nov. 1638 ;
Catharine ; and Ruth ; and d. a. 1671. His will of 16 Aug. was pro. 19
Sept. of that yr. Catharine, m. 26 June 1657, Jacob Towne of Topsfield ; and Ruth m. 19 July 1658, Job Swinnerton of Salem, and d. 22
May 1670. JOHN, Braintree, had d. Ann wh. d. June 1640. JOHN,
Portsmouth 1631, one of the men sent by Mason the gr. propr. was aft.
of Kittery, in 1650 was " sw. constable for the riv. of Pascataquack," as
my copy of York rec. says ; and it is prob. that he kept his precinct in
good order, for he submit. in 1652 to Mass. and in 1655 and 8 he was of
the gr. jury. JOSEPH, Hartford, m. Abigail, d. of Samuel Spencer.

MARK, Ipswich, in 1634 was call. 50 yrs. old, freem. 2 May 1638, d. 28 Apr. 1659. By Joanna, wh. d. 29 Apr. 1660, he left Susanna, w. of John Ayres, or Ayers; Abigail, w. of Robert Pierce, or Pearce; Priscilla, w. of John Warner; and gr.childr. by d. Mary, first w. of Edward Chapman, wh. d. bef. her f. † ‡ * SAMUEL, Ipswich, a gent. of ancient fam. at Yeldham in Co. Essex, where, Morant tells us, he was a Cursitor in the Chancery, and he m. a. 1620, Deborah Harlakenden, of the old gentry of Earl's Colne, prob. sis. of Roger, and had ten ch. bef. com. over to us in 1637. He owned an est. in the adjac. parish of Toppesfield, and prob. left some ch. certain. John, at home; but we may not exact. discern the names of all he brot. tho. of William, Harlakenden, and Samuel, perhaps Dorothy, and Eliz. only of the ds. can we be justif. in guess. that they accomp. the f. Being adm. freem. Mar. 1638, he was rep. at the first succeed. Gen. Ct. and very oft. aft. m. Martha Epes, a wid. from Co. Kent, prob. had by her Martha, Ruth, and Priscilla, perhaps 2d Samuel; but by some rec. it appears, that ano. w. Dorothy was liv. 1645; yet she may have been w. of his first s. Samuel, for, strange as it seems, he had two Samuels then liv. Farmer gives him other ds. Susanna, and Dorothy, wh. m. he says, Joseph Jacobs; and Mary, wh. m. Peter Duncan. But of the last we find that she was nam. Epes bef. m. so d. of his w.'s former h. and the two others were ch. of his s. William, prob. tho. it is said a d. Dorothy had early m. Rev. Thomas Harrison, wh. came from Virg. 1648. In 1643 he was chos. an Assist. and so serv. until 1673, when Leverett being rais. to be Gov. he was made success. as Dept. Gov. in wh. place he d. 12 Oct. 1678, during the sess. of the Gen. Ct. His wid. Rebecca d. 21 July 1695, in her 79th yr. She was third, possib. fourth w. had been wid. of Rev. William Worcester, and, bef. him, of John Hall, and bef. him, of Henry Byley. She was so happy in find. hs. that wh. was her f. has not been told. But one of his ws. was not (as frequent. has been boasted), a d. of the first Gov. Winthrop, wh. had only one of four ds. that outliv. two yrs. and she m. Samuel Dudley. The mistake arose from the use of the word sis. S. in the letter 30 Sept. 1648, of first Winthrop to his s. John wh. had been a mem. of the ch. at Ipswich, and may refer only to Christian relat. Under Truesdale will be found correct. of an error of Farmer aris. in the same way. Yet possib. the sec. w. of S. was a d. of Col. Edward Reed of Essex Eng. and so sis. of the sec. w. of the younger John Winth. Of his ds. Eliz. m. 20 May 1644, Daniel Epes, and d. 7 May 1685, aged 60; Dorothy m. as above; Martha m. first John Denison, and next Richard Martyn of Portsmouth; Ruth m. 1659, Rev. John Emerson of Gloucester; and Priscilla m. Capt. Thomas Baker of Topsfield. SAMUEL, Ipswich, s. of the preced. b. in Eng. d. prob. unm. in his will of 22 Nov.

TABOR. 247

1653, nam. four brs. and three unm. sis. beside neph. Samuel Epes.
SAMUEL, Salem, s. of John, m. 14 Apr. 1662, Eliz. Andrews, d. of Robert of Topsfield, had Eliz. b. 12 July 1663. SAMUEL, Ipswich, s. of
Hon. Samuel, b. on this side of the water, prob. yet many yrs. bef. the
d. of his br. Samuel, was of H. C. 1656, and the sole gr. of this name, d.
prob. unm. for in his will, 18 Dec. 1668, he ment. no w. or ch. but names
four m. sis. viz. Eliz. Martha, Ruth, and Mary, w. of Peter Duncan,
wh. was not ch. of his f. but of mo. by a former h. beside Priscilla then
unm. Perhaps this last nam. sustains my conject. that he was b. of the
same mo. with her. SAMUEL, Boxford 1680, may have been gr.s. of
Hon. Samuel. THOMAS, Braintree, had Joan, b. 8 Nov. 1638; and Abigail, 8 Nov. 1640, wh. d. 30 May 1642. THOMAS, Cambridge 1639.
WILLIAM, Ipswich 1635, is perhaps the same wh. was the first ferryman
betw. Haverhill and Bradford, of Haverhill 1659, and had w. Eliz.
WILLIAM, Concord 1636, had, by w. Sarah, wh. was bur. 3 Apr. 1641,
Judith, wh. m. John Barker; and Sarah, wh. m. John Haywood; was
constable 1645, and rem. perhaps, says Farmer, to Easthampton, L. I.
bef. 1650. WILLIAM, Woburn, m. 18 Jan. 1644, Judith, wid. of James
Hayward, had Sarah, b. 28 July 1644; Judith, 3 Mar. 1646; Mary, 9
Dec. 1647; Caleb, 11 Oct. 1649; William, 15 Apr. 1651; Joseph, 18
Oct. 1652; Benjamin, 18 Mar. 1654; Tabitha, 20 Aug. 1655, d. next
day; Joshua, d. soon; James, 1 Nov. 1658, d. soon; Bethia, 9 May
1659; and Huldah, 20 Nov. 1660; was freem. 1670. His wid. Judith
d. 3 Jan. 1690; but he had d. 7 June 1672. * WILLIAM, Wells, s. of
Hon. Samuel, b. in Eng. m. Mary, d. of Jonathan Wade of Ipswich, had
Susanna, b. 3 Jan. 1669; Dorothy, 21 Oct. 1670; Mary, 6 Jan. 1674;
and Eliz. 20 July 1678; and d. next yr. was bur. 27 May. He was of
the gr. jury 1659, and again 1662, freem. 1670, as Felt suppos. but it is
prob. that man was of Woburn; then prob. overseeing the prop. of his f.
in that region, and was rep. 1676 for Wells, but no doubt soon aft. if not
long bef. had come back to Ipswich, and went not more to the E. exc. as
an assoc. with Danforth and others to hold a county Ct. 1678. Susanna
m. Joseph Jacobs; and Eliz. m. an Allen.

TABOR, or TABER, * PHILIP, Watertown, in 1634 subscr. towards
build. the galley for secur. of the harbour, and was made freem. 14 May
of that yr. yet was one of the first sett. at Yarmouth, and mem. of the
earliest assemb. of Plym. Col. in 1639 and 40 for Y. as Baylies I. 305
and 7, shows. But he was aft. at the Vineyard, and thence went 1651
to New London and in 1656 I find him among the freem. of Portsmouth,
R. I. and not long aft. at Providence, of wh. he was rep. 1661. He liv.
later at Tiverton. Prob. he was progenit. of a num. race; tho. I find
not how; but he had John, bapt. at Barnstable, 8 Nov. 1640; Philip;

Thomas, Feb. 1646; and Job, or Joseph. In the will of John Masters, of Cambridge, 1639, he names his d. Lydia T. wh. may well be thot. w. of Philip, and he prob. was f. of Lydia, wh. bec. sec. w. 16 Feb. 1665, of the first Pardon Tillinghast. PHILIP, Dartmouth, s. of the preced. had Mary, b. 28 Jan. 1670; Sarah, 26 Mar. 1671; Lydia, 28 Sept. 1673; Philip, 29 Feb. 1676; Abigail, 27 Oct. 1678; Esther, 23 Feb. 1681; John, 18 July 1684; and Bethia, 18 Apr. 1689. *THOMAS, Dartmouth, s. of the first Philip, by first w. a d. of Rev. John Cooke of D. the latest male surv. of passeng. in the blessed Mayflower, had Thomas, b. 22 Oct. 1668; Esther, 17 Apr. 1671; and by sec. w. Mary, m. June 1672, wh. d. 3 May 1734, had Lydia, 8 Aug. 1673; Sarah, 28 Jan. 1675; Mary, 18 Mar. 1677; Joseph, 7 Mar. 1679; John, 22 Feb. 1681; Jacob, 26 July 1683; Jonathan, 22 Sept. 1685; Bethia, 3 Sept. 1687; Philip, 7 Feb. 1689; and Abigail, 3 May 1693. He was rep. 1679 and 93, and d. 11 Nov. 1730.

TAFFE, ROBERT, Mendon 1682, complain. of as trad. with Ind.

TAINER, or TAINNER, JOSIAH (perhaps had differ. bapt. name), Marblehead 1674, with ELIAS, and THOMAS, beside Eliz. and Ann, and Joanna (of wh. however Eliz. may be w. of one of the men, and the other fem. names of her ch.) are all nam. in the will, 9 Oct. 1678, of the wid. Ann Condy, wh. was, no doubt. mo. of Eliz. and may have been gr.mo. of sev. of the others; and prob. Josiah was f. of ano. JOSIAH, wh. m. a. 1706, Rebecca, d. of Richard Dike, as Babson, 256, tells. Among conject. I venture one, that this is the true surname, giv. TRINER in an extraord. paper, sign. by many of the inhab. of M. Geneal. Reg. VIII. 288.

TAINTOR, TAYNTOR, or TAINTER, BENJAMIN, Sudbury, s. of Joseph, perhaps serv. in Philip's war 1675, and no more is heard of him, but that, in 1691, he had w. Mary. CHARLES, Wethersfield 1643, rem. to Fairfield, said by tradit. to have come from Wales, with ch. Michael, Charles, Joseph, and Mary, and the same doubtf. autho. wh. takes care only of Michael, sends Charles the s. to Virg. a. 1656, and makes the f. lost at sea 1654. Perhaps he had no s. Charles, but was a merch. and may have been lost on coast. voyage, or in the sh. of Capt. Garrett, founder. 1657. His d. Mary m. 27 Nov. 1662, it is said, Thomas Pierson. JOHN, Branford, s. of Michael the first, m. Dorcas, d. of Daniel Swain, had no ch. and d. Sept. 1699; his wid. m. a Wheeler. JONATHAN, Watertown, s. of Joseph of the same, m. 6 Dec. 1681, Eliz. d. of Daniel Warren, says Bond, had Jonathan, b. 12 July 1682; Benjamin, 20 June 1685; Joseph, 25 May 1688; and Eliz. whose date of b. is not seen. His w. d. 14 June 1692, and he had sec. w. 5 Mar. 1703, Mary Randall, perhaps d. of John, and by her had Randall, b. 21 Jan. 1704, d. next yr.; and Susanna, 30 May 1705 or 6. He d. 1712; and his wid. m. John Tucker. JOSEPH, Watertown, came at the age of 25, emb. in the Confidence, at Southampton 24 Apr. 1638, as serv. of Nicholas Guy, wh. was of Upton, Co. Hants; m. Mary, d. of Guy, his fellow passeng. had Mary; Ann, b. 2 Sept. 1644, d. prob. bef. her f.; Joseph, 2 Sept. 1645, d. unm. 7 Aug. 1728; Rebecca, 18 Aug. 1647, d. prob. bef. her f.; Benjamin, 22 Jan. 1651; Jonathan, 10 Sept. 1654; Sarah, 20 Nov. 1657; Simon, 30 Sept. 1660; and Dorothy, 13 Aug. 1663. These were all liv. when their gr.mo. Guy made her will Aug. 1666; and the f. d. 20 Feb. 1690. His will, made two days bef. refers to ea. ch. The wid. d. 1705, it is said, aged 86. Mary m. a Pollard; Sarah m. Elnathan Beers; and Dorothy m. John Taylor. *MICHAEL, Branford, an early sett. perhaps s. more prob. younger br. of Charles, for no single circumstance is kn. to prove there were two call. Charles, was a trader, as capt. of Mr. Allerton's ketch, bound to Virg. Nov. 1653, took from Evan Thomas an advent. on half profits; by w. Eliz. had John, b. May 1650; Michael, Oct. 1652; Eliz. June 1655; Joanna, Apr. 1657; and Sarah, Oct. 1658; was town clk. and prob. draft. certain. record. the liberal planta. and ch. covenant, 1667, freem. 1668, rep. 1670 and 2, as in Geneal. Reg. III. 153 is print. His w. d. July 1659. Eliz. m. Noah Rogers; Joanna m. 30 June 1676, Josiah Gillet; and Sarah m. I presume, 1 Nov. 1683, Samuel Stone of Guilford. *MICHAEL, Branford, s. of the preced. rem. to Windsor, m. 3 Apr. 1679, Mary, d. of Thomas Loomis, had Michael, b. Sept. 1680; John, Oct. 1682; Mary, Sept. 1685; Joseph, Nov. 1687; and by w. Mabel, wid. of Daniel Butler, d. of Nicholas Olmstead, had Sarah, Nov. 1698. He bec. one of the first sett. at Colchester, and was oft. its rep. and d. Feb. 1730. SIMON, Watertown, youngest s. of Joseph, m. 9 May, acc. Bond, but Tainter Geneal. 17, says, with less prob. 9 Aug. 1693, Joanna, d. of deac. John Stone, had Simon, b. 28 Feb. 1694; Mary, 24 Jan. 1696, d. young; John, 13 Mar. 1699; Rebecca, 26 May 1701, d. young; Mary, 27 Nov. 1703; and Dorothy, 20 May 1706; his w. d. 3 Dec. 1731, and he d. 19 Jan. 1739. THOMAS, of unkn. resid. by w. Catherine, had Thomas, b. 4 May 1639; and d. 30 Sept. foll. as did his br. William; and sis. Eliz. d. 24 Apr. foll.

TALBOT, CHRISTOPHER, Boston 1686, a turner. JAMES, Boston, by w. Martha d. prob. of Michael Barstow of Charlestown, m. 14 Oct. 1663, had James, b. 23 Aug. 1664; Joseph, 21 Sept. 1666; and William, 26 Dec. 1668. JARED, or GARRETT, Taunton, m. 1 Apr. 1664, Sarah Andrews, prob. d. of Henry, had Jared, b. 20 Mar. 1667; Mary, 14 Dec. 1671; Samuel, 29 Feb. 1676; Josiah, 12 Oct. 1678; and Nathaniel, 21 Feb. 1681. JARED, Taunton, perhaps s. of the preced. m. 4 May 1687, Rebecca Hathaway. Baylies IV. includes him there 1703. JOSHUA,

Dorchester 1635. In support of this name, Farmer MS. had cited Harris, 64, but there is no such person found in the town list. LANCELOT, Boston 1675, merch. MOSES, Plymouth, was at Kennebeck trad. ho. under com. of John Howland, in Apr. 1634, k. by an interlop. trader from Portsmouth for attempt to cut his cable. The Portsmouth man was shot forthwith. Long agitat. of the matter ensued, as may be seen in Winth. I. 131; and very fully in Bradford's Hist. 316–22. WILLIAM, Boston 1651, sailmaker, by w. Cicely, had Judith, b. 24 July 1652, d. young; Mary, 21 June 1655; and Joseph, 13 Oct. 1657.

TALBY, or TOLBY, JOHN, Salem 1635, had sev. ch. by w. Dorothy, wh. was hang. 6 Dec. 1638, acc. to her sentence, two days bef. for murder of her d. Difficulty, that had been bapt. 25 Dec. 1636. See Col. Rec. I. 246 and Winth. I. 279. She had been pun. for beat. and attempt. to k. her h. and other ch. as well as hers. and Felt, II. 456, is satisf. that she was insane, and her h. was excommun. for unnaturalness to her. Hutch. I. 420. He d. Jan. 1645. STEPHEN, Boston 1662, a mariner, by w. Hannah had Stephen, b. 9 Aug. 1663; Samuel, 9 Jan. 1665; and John, 4 May 1671.

TALCOTT, TAILECOAT, TAYLCOAT, or other var. ‡* JOHN, Cambridge 1632, came that yr. in the Lion, emb. at London in June, arr. 16 Sept. is said to have been s. of John of Braintree in Co. Essex (and the only s. wh. surv. that f. in 1604, and a minor at that time, tho. he had five ds. then liv.), and to have m. Dorothy, d. of Benjamin Smith, brot. ch. John, Mary, and at C. had Samuel, b. a. 1635, H. C. 1658; was freem. 6 Nov. 1632, rep. at the first assemb. in May 1634, and five foll. cts. includ. May 1636, soon aft. wh. he rem. with Hooker and the gr. emigr. to Hartford, where a petty tradit. says his ho. was built in 1635; was rep. at the first Court in 1637, as also in every foll. yr. until 1654, when he was rais. to be Assist. and one of the two Commissnrs. of the N. E. cols. also made treas. of the Col. until aft. the elect. in May 1659, and soon d. His wid. liv. 10 yrs. more, and in her will of 22 Sept. 1669, names ch. John, and Samuel only; Mary, wh. m. 28 June 1649, Rev. John Russell of Wethersfield, being d. ‡* JOHN, Hartford, s. of the preced. b. in Eng. was ens. 1650, and m. 29 Oct. of that yr. Helena, or Ellen, Wakeman, prob. d. of John of New Haven, had John, b. 24 Nov. 1651, d. soon; John, again, 14 Dec. 1653, wh. d. 30 July 1683, or 1684, without issue; Eliz. 21 Feb. 1656; Samuel, 21 Aug. 1658, d. at 22 yrs.; Mary, 26 Apr. 1661; Hannah, 8 Dec. 1663; Dorothy, 20 Feb. 1667; Joseph, 16 Nov. 1669; and Helena, 17 June 1674; his w. d. 4 days aft. and he m. 9 Nov. 1676, Mary Cook, had Ruth, 12 Sept. 1677; Sarah, 16 Nov. 1679, d. in 3 wks.; Rachel, 23 Feb. 1682; Jonathan, 15 Feb. 1684; and Hezekiah, 24, bapt. 28 Feb. 1686; and this youngest ch. sett. at Durham.

The f. was freem. 1652, rep. 1660, and bec. a capt. in 1661 was chos. treas. of the Col. and an Assist. in wh. place he was cont. under the new ch. for un. of Conn. and N. H. chos. Commissnr. at the Congr. of the N. E. Cols. 1669, 70, 1, 3 and 6; in Philip's war was much in serv. a Col. sometimes hav. com. of all the Col. forces, and d. 23 July 1688. Eliz. m. prob. Joseph Wadsworth, wh. in his will speaks of br. Talcott's land; Mary m. Richard Edwards, as his sec. w.; Hannah m. Nathan Gould; Dorothy m. 31 Dec. 1691, the third Thomas Stoughton of Windsor; Helena m. Cyprian Nichols of Hartford; Ruth m. John Read, the gr. lawyer of Boston; Rachel m. 21 Mar. 1700, perhaps Peter, more prob. Gershom Bulkley. Gr. confus. among fam. reports arises from the identity of names, as herein is shown. Two Rachel Ts. m. in adj. towns two Bulkleys, one of wh. was Peter, s. of Gershom; but wh. Rachel m. this Peter, or wh. Bulkley m. the elder of the cousins, Rachel T. wh. was ch. of the younger br. T. must be very careful. weigh. In my opin. geography is to be regard. as influential in some degr. §JOSEPH, Hartford, s. of the sec. John, m. Abigail Clarke of Milford, says Chapin's Glastonbury, 168, wh. may be doubt. tho. no other partner is assign. He had John, b. 27 Feb. 1699; Joseph, 17 Feb. 1701; Nathan, 26 Nov. 1702; Abigail, 13 Apr. 1707; Eunice, 26 Jan. 1709; Matthew; Samuel; Jerusha, 1717; and Helena, 1720; and his w. d. 24 Mar. 1724. He was chos. Gov. of the Prov. in sixteen success. yrs. begin. 1725. *SAMUEL, Wethersfield, younger s. of the first John, freem. 1662, m. 7 Nov. 1661, Hannah, d. of Elizur Holyoke of Springfield, had Samuel, b. 1663; John, d. young, but prob. aft. his f.; Hannah, 1665; Elizur, 31 July 1669; Joseph, 20 Feb. 1672; Benjamin, 1 Mar. 1674; Rachel, 2 Apr. 1676; and Nathaniel, 28 Jan. 1679; of wh. the first three were b. at Hartford, but not rec. yet all nam. in his will; was rep. 1669–77. His w. d. 2 Feb. 1679, and he took 2d w. 6 Aug. foll. Mary, but had no more ch. and d. 10 Nov. 1691, leav. large est. Hannah m. 25 Nov. 1686, John Chester the sec. and Chapin says Rachel m. 1700, Peter Bulkley, wh. may provoke inq. That her h. was a gr.s. of the Rev. Peter, may well be; and that his bapt. name must make him s. of Gershom is almost certain, for Peter, of Fairfield, s. of the first Peter, was d. leav. s. of the same name too young to be m. in 1700; and Peter s. of Edward was d. without leav. s. of this name. But greater doubt in my mind is of the yr. to wh. this Rachel's m. is postpon. by him, tho. undoubted. the Wethersfield rec. says "Mr. Peter B. and Rachel T. were m. 21 Mar. 1699," i. e. 1700, N. S. My conject. is that Samuel's Rachel had been m. some yrs. bef. to Gershom, s. of the third Peter; and that John's Rachel, aft. her f's. d. and cous. Rachel's m. had liv. at her uncle Samuel's ho. and there was m. Confus. of this with his br. and of him with his f. is seen in the Index to the admir. Col. Rec. of Trumbull. Eight of this name have been gr. at Yale.

TALLEY, TOLLEY, or TAULLEY, RICHARD, Dorchester, m. Sarah, d. of Edward Blake of Milton, and was one of the excors. of his will. His w. d. 5 Aug. 1697, and he m. 27 Jan. foll. Eliz. Grosse, and he d. 8 Dec. 1717, aged 66. But he had first been of Boston, and by w. Sarah had Sarah, b. 16 Apr. 1684, bapt. 1 Nov. 1685 ; Richard, 21 Dec. 1685, whose bapt. is not seen ; and Abigail, 18, bapt. 22 Jan. 1688 ; beside Mary, bapt. says the Old South Rec. 5 May 1689 ; but these two are there call. of Richard and Mary. THOMAS, Boston, prob. br. of the preced. by w. Mary had John, b. 7 Apr. 1678, perhaps d. soon ; Hannah, 16, bapt. 18 Apr. 1680 ; Jane 2, bapt. 4 Mar. 1682 ; and John, again, 21 June 1685, whose bapt. is not seen at O. S. ch.

TALMADGE, or TALMAGE, ENOS, New Haven, m. 9 May 1682, Hannah, d. of Thomas Yale, was a propr. 1685. JOHN, New Haven, a propr. 1685. ROBERT, New Haven, by w. Sarah, d. of Thomas Nash, had Abigail, bapt. 13 May 1649 ; Thomas, b. 17, bapt. 20 Oct. 1650 ; Sarah, bapt. 19 Sept. 1652 ; John, b. 11, bapt. 17 Sept. 1654 ; Enoch, 4, bapt. prob. 5 Oct. 1656 ; and Mary, 2 Sept. bapt. prob. 27 Nov. 1659 ; as two or three of the days of bapt. in Geneal. Reg. IX. 362, are wrong, from the carelessness of the deac. or other rec. officer. He d. bef. 1685. Sarah m. 18 Mar. 1679, Samuel Hotchkiss. THOMAS, Boston, freem. 14 May 1634, rem. to Lynn 1637, and there prob. had Thomas, beside other ch. and, Lewis thinks, went to Easthampton, L. I. THOMAS, Lynn, s. of the preced. perhaps b. in Eng. rem. 1650 to L. I. was prob. at Milford 1656, and may be that lieut. at New Haven 1685, wh. was k. at the surprise of Schenectady 8 Feb. 1690 by the French and Ind. WILLIAM, Boston, perhaps br. of Thomas of the same, prob. came in the fleet with Winth. stands in the list of our ch. No. 59, was made freem. 14 May 1643, tho. the clk. spelt the name with a var. may have been dr. early to Roxbury ch. by acquaint. with Eliot, but on their ch. list it is mark. that he went to Lynn with his w. An Eliz. T. d. at Lynn 20 Dec. 1660. WILLIAM, Boston, in that part call. Muddy riv. carpenter, m. a d. of John Peirce, and on the engagem. of P. to support him and his two ds. T. made conveyce. of his est.

TALMAN, or TALLMAN, JAMES, Portsmouth, R. I. perhaps s. of Peter, m. 18 Mar. 1689, Mary, d. of John Devoll, of the Niantick country, as the rec. at P. reads, had John, b. 19 Sept. 1692 ; Joseph, 13 July 1694 ; and Eliz. 13 June 1699. He next m. 14 Sept. 1701, Hannah, d. of John Swain of Nantucket, had Stephen, 30 June foll. ; Mary, 26 June 1704 ; Peter, 17 June 1706 ; Jemima, 11 Sept. 1708 ; James, 10 Apr. 1710 ; Jeremiah, 25 Sept. 1712 ; Silas, 10 Sept. 1717 ; Joseph, 1 June 1720 ;

and Hannah, 14 Sept. 1723. PETER, is in the list of freem. at Newport 1655, prob. had childr. certain. Peter by w. Ann b. 22 Mar. 1658; among proprs. of Guilford 1685. PETER, was s. of the preced. and with the title of Dr. m. 7 Nov. 1683, Ann Walstone, wid. of John, tho. more likely it may seem to be his sis. and had Eliz. b. 22 June 1687; Ebenezer, 1 Sept. 1692; and Peter, 13 Nov. 1694, wh. d. at 22 yrs.; and d. 28 July 1728. His wid. d. 1731.

TANKERSLY, GEORGE, Boston, by w. Tabitha had Sylvanus, b. 24 Sept. 1673, d. soon; and Sylvanus, again, 17 Sept. 1674.

TANNER, NICHOLAS, Swanzey 1663, in 1666 of Rehoboth, was fin. in 1667, as a Bapt. and in 69 had quiet as supporter in his form of worship. He was town clk. afterwards.

TAPLEY, CLEMENT, Dorchester, freem. 13 May 1640. See Topliff. GILBERT, Salem 1689, innholder, had w. Thomasine, and d. 17 Apr. 1714, aged 79, says Felt, first Ed. 546; but he meant perhaps 80; and his wid. d. 4 Nov. 1715. By her he had Gilbert, b. 26 Aug. 1665; Joseph, 10 Mar. 1668; and Mary, 4 Apr. 1678. Joseph had, prob. renewal of license in his f's. place. JOHN, Salem, prob. br. of Gilbert, m. 6 Dec. 1663, Eliz. Pride, d. perhaps of John, had Eliz. b. 20 Jan. 1665; Mary, 10 Feb. 1667, d. next yr.; John, 7 Apr. 1669; William, 30 Aug. 1670; Hannah, 21 Apr. 1672; Robert, 17 Feb. 1674; Mary, again, June 1678; Samuel, Feb. 1683; and Benjamin, 3 Feb. 1688. WILLIAM, Salem, perhaps s. of John, m. 7 Mar. 1697 or 9, Eliz. d. of William Cash, had Eliz. b. 15 May 1701; John, 4 Feb. 1705; Mary, 1 Mar. 1708; and William, 5 Feb. 1711.

TAPP, ‡ EDMUND, Milford 1639, one of the seven pillars at found. of the ch. 22 Aug. in New Haven, that yr. may have been an Assist. of that Col. tho. Mather certain. gives a false date to all the earliest. He d. says Lambert, 1653. His will, wh. is lost, bore date 1 Apr. 1653, and his inv. was tak. 26 of the same mo. Of his fam. we kn. little. His d. Jane, wh. d. 8 Apr. 1703 (and had prob. 35 yrs. bef. less than the ch. assign. by tradit.), was w. of Gov. Robert Treat; but from the will of his wid. 17 Aug. 1673, shortly bef. her d. we find two other ds. ment. Ann, d. of William Andrews, wh. had first been w. of William Gibbard, and Eliz. w. of John Nash. Beside this, she calls in that docum. William Fowler, her s.-in-law, gives something to him and three ds. of his, term. by testat. her cous.

TAPPAN, TAPIN, TAPPIN, TOPPING, TOPAN, or TAPPING, ABRAHAM, Newbury 1637, freem. 2 May 1638, had m. in Eng. Susanna Goodale of Yarmouth in Co. Norfk. had Peter, b. 1634; perhaps Eliz. 16 Oct. 1635, tho. Coffin erron. gives it 30 yrs. later, and on this side of the ocean had, perhaps first, Isaac; Abraham, 1644; Jacob, 1645; Susanna, 13

June 1649; and John, 23 Apr. 1651; and d. 5 Nov. 1672, aged 64.
His wid. d. 20 Mar. 1689. I presume only part of Coffin's acco. was deriv. from authentic rec. Eliz. m. 21 Nov. 1657, Samuel Mighill of Rowley. ABRAHAM, Newbury, s. of the preced. m. at Woodbridge, N. J. Nov.
1670, Ruth, d. of John Pike, had perhaps one or more ch. b. there, and
at N. had Mary, b. 25 Oct. 1674; Hannah, 14 Apr. 1677; and Joseph,
1681. BARTHOLOMEW, Boston, freem. 1671. *CHRISTOPHER*, Newbury, youngest s. of Peter, ord. 9 Sept. 1696, wh. in his Hecatompolis,
Mather denies a Christian name, tho. he gives it in his Coll. Catal. m. 13
Dec. 1698, Sarah Angier, d. of Edmund of Cambridge, had Christopher, b.
24 Feb. 1700 ; Edmund, 7 Dec. 1701, H. C. 1720 ; and Bezaleel, 7 Mar.
1705, H. C. 1722 ; his w. d. 20 Feb. 1739, aged 63 ; and he d. 23 July
1747, hav. for above four yrs. suffer. much in his mind by reason of the gr.
div. in religious sentiments then prevail. ISAAC, Newbury, s. of Abraham,
m. 19 Sept. 1669, Hannah, d. of Stephen Kent, had Isaac, b. 20 Sept. 1673;
Eliz. 25 Jan. 1676 ; Jacob, 12 June 1678 ; David, 2 Nov. 1680 ; John, 16
Mar. 1683 ; Hannah, 23 Dec. 1686. His w. d. 10 Dec. 1688 ; and he m.
27 Mar. 1691, Mary March, d. possib. of Hugh the first, had Mary, 17
Nov. 1693 ; and Benjamin, 18 May 1695. JACOB, Newbury, s. of the
first Abraham, took the o. of alleg. 1669, was freem. 1677, ens. 1683, m.
24 Aug. 1670, Hannah, eldest ch. of the sec. Henry Sewall, had Jacob,
b. 20 May 1671 ; Samuel, 30 Sept. 1672, wh. d. of smallpox, 25 Aug.
1691; Jane, 28 Sept. 1674; John, 29 Jan. 1677 ; Hannah, 4 Mar.
1679 ; Eliz. 20 Dec. 1680 ; Abraham, 29 June 1684 ; and Ann, 16 May
1686. His w. d. 11 Nov. 1699, and he m. ano. Hannah Sewall, wid. of
John, br. of his former w. and d. 30 Dec. 1717. His wid. d. 4 Apr. 1723.
JAMES, Milford, by w. Ann had Ann, b. 18 or 29 Sept. 1662 ; James, 19
Aug. 1665 ; Mary, 15 or 18 Aug. 1668; Eliz. 3 Aug. 1673, d. 18 Feb.
foll.; and he d. 6 Aug. 1712 ; and his wid. d. 7 Feb. 1732. Ann m. 6
Dec. 1683, Thomas Ward of Middletown, where all the ch. exc. the first
were b. He was in May 1661 one of the three men appoint. by the
magistr. to make search for the regicides Whalley and Goffe; and their
ret. on the precept, aft. three days, was that they had made dilig. search,
and so easi. satisf. the author. He was in 1667 propound. to be freem.
but Middletown ret. is lost in the list of 1669. JOHN, Boston, feltmaker,
or hatter, m. 20 Aug. 1654, Mary, d. prob. of Robert Woodmansey, had
(if one must believe the rec. wh. I do not) John b. 31 May 1654; Joseph; and James, 4 July 1664, all bapt. 17 July foll. was freem. 1665;
was snub. by our Gen. Ct. in 1672, with others of his craft. solicit.
favor. He d. 14 Sept. 1678. JOHN, Newbury, s. of the first Abraham,
serv. in Philip's war, and was wound. at the hard battle of Bloody Brook,
18 Sept. 1676; by w. Martha had James, b. 15 Mar. 1702 ; and d. in

Salisbury, 26 Dec. 1723. JONATHAN, Southampton, L. I. 1673, perhaps s. of Thomas of Milford. JOSEPH, Boston, shopkeeper, possib. s. of Richard, by w. Marian had John, b. 12 Aug. 1678; and d. 20 Dec. 1678, aged 23. NATHANIEL, New London, had gr. of ld. 1652, but forfeit. and no more is kn. PETER, Newbury, eldest s. of Abraham the first, b. in Eng. m. 3 Apr. 1661, Jane, d. of Christopher Batt, said to be his first cous. had Peter, b. Dec. 1662, prob. d. young; Eliz. 13 Oct. 1665; Peter, again, 22 Dec. 1667; Samuel, 5 June 1670; Christopher, 15 Dec. 1671, H. C. 1691; and Jane, 4 Jan. 1674; was a physician, and d. 3 Nov. 1707. PETER, Newbury, s. of the preced. m. 28 Apr. 1696, Sarah Greenleaf, had Peter, and Timothy, perhaps tw. b. 2 Feb. 1698; Jane, 24 Jan. 1700; and Eliz. 25 Apr. 1702. RICHARD, Boston 1632, with w. Judith, join. our ch. Nov. 1633, and bec. freem. 4 Mar. aft. had Timothy, bapt. 15 Dec. foll. d. soon. His w. d. 1635; and by w. Alice he had Joseph, b. 30 Sept. if the town rec. be foll. but the ch. rec. says, bapt. 28 Sept. 1645, a. 4 days old, wh. d. next mo.; and Joseph, again, bapt. 11 June 1648. Alice join. the ch. 17 Apr. 1647, and no more is learn. of her or h. but that he was liv. 1654. SAMUEL, Newbury, s. of the first Peter, m. 1702, Abigail, d. of Rev. Michael Wigglesworth of Malden, and had Samuel, b. 24 Nov. that yr. but Coffin tells no more. ‡*THOMAS, Milford 1639, but earlier was of Wethersfield and rep. 1639, join. the ch. of M. with his w. Emma in 1640, had Elnathan, bapt. 2 Aug. of that yr. and James, 12 Feb. 1643. In 1651, he was a capt. and chos. Assist. and in that rank by an. elect. most of the next twelve yrs. kept on acco. evid. of resid. at Southampton, on L. I. On 20 Oct. 1666 a contr. made at Milford for his m. with Mary, wid. of Timothy Baldwin is by her refer. to ten yrs. later, when she was dispos. of her prop. in conform. with said contr. to her childr. He had, bef. June 1678, made Lydia, the wid. of John Wilford, his w. and for the resid. of his days liv. at Branford, where 5 Oct. 1686 he gave by deed to his s. Elnathan and James at Southampton all his lds. at S. to d. Mary Quinny (or some such name) ten cows; to d. Martha Herrick £10 in add. to what she had rec. to be paid by the s. wh. then had the keep. of the cows also. His wid. in Oct. 1688, transact. with those s. and d. Nov. 1694. Thirteen of this name had been gr. at Harv. and two at Yale, 1845.

TAPPER, JOHN, Boston, by w. Hannah had John, b. 11 July 1688, d. young; Michael, 6 Dec. 1692; Lydia, 26 Jan. 1695; and John, again, 1 Nov. 1697.

TARBELL, TARBOLE, or TARBALL, JOHN, Salem, freem. 1690, liv. at the vill. now Danvers, where he made much trouble to his min. poor Samuel Parris, for his witchcraft delus. THOMAS, Watertown 1644, then bot. ld. in that town, but liv. in ano. where he had Thomas, Abigail, and perhaps John; and at W. had Eliz. b. 5 Jan. 1657; William, 26 Feb. 1659; and rem. to Groton, a. 1663. When G. was destr. by the Ind. he rem. to Charlestown, there m. 15 Aug. 1676, Susanna, wid. of John Lawrence, and d. early in 1681. His wid. join. the ch. 6 Mar. of that yr. and d. says gr.-stone 5 Jan. 1691. THOMAS, Groton, s. of the preced. m. 30 June 1666, Ann Longley, d. of the first William, had Thomas, b. 6 July 1667; Ann, 10 June 1670; William, 1 Oct. 1672; and Mary, 2 Apr. 1675; rem. to Charlestown, on destruct. of G. by the Ind. and there his w. join. the ch. 28 Oct. 1677, and he d. 1678, of smallpox.

TARBOX, JOHN, Lynn, may well seem an early sett. without giv. full faith to Farmer, wh. rel. on Lewis, that he was there 1630; had Jonathan, wh. d. 16 June 1654; Samuel, b. a. 1647; and John; but the dates of b. are not found; was engag. in the iron works, as a propr. in small way, 1656, and d. 26 May 1674. His will of 25 Nov. preced. ment. two s. JOHN, Lynn, s. perhaps of the preced. may have had by first w. that John wh. d. 27 Sept. 1661; and he m. 4 July 1667, Mary, d. of Richard Haven of the same, wh. d. 17 Nov. 1690, had John, again, b. 3 Apr. 1668; Joseph, 4 Mar. 1669, d. at six mos.; Mary, 11 Aug. 1670, d. at 1 yr.; Sarah, 1 June 1672; John, 29 July 1674; Jonathan, 18 Feb. 1676; Samuel, 5 Feb. 1678, d. in few days; Ebenezer, 4 Jan. 1679; and Hannah, Mary, and Susanna, 14 Oct. 1681; of wh. Susanna d. in two wks. and how long the other two liv. is not told. Nor is it told with suffic. distinctness, that ano. John had Joseph, wh. d. Nov. 1674. SAMUEL, Lynn, br. of the preced. m. 14 Nov. 1665, Rebecca, d. of Joseph Amitage, had Samuel, b. 20 June 1666; Jonathan, 3 July 1668; Godfrey, 16 Aug. 1670; Rebecca, 8 Aug. 1672; Sarah, 15 Oct. 1674; and Mary, 21 Feb. 1677, wh. d. as did her mo. next mo. and by sec. w. had Experience, 10 Sept. 1679; Joanna, 12 Mar. 1681; and Thomas, 8 June 1684; possib. more. WILLIAM, Ipswich, of date not exact. kn.

TARE, RICHARD, Boston, m. Jane, wid. of John Parker, as in the deed of hers. and s. Thomas P. to Stephen Greenleaf of Newbury, Oct. 1656, convey. the Boston est. she calls hers. w. of T. but of him this is all that I have gain. THOMAS, Portsmouth 1655.

TARLTON, ELIAS, Portsmouth, s. of Richard, had Elias, b. 1720, wh. Farmer says, liv. to the age of 91. HENRY, Boston, a passeng. 1671, in the Arabella from London, of wh. no more is kn. but that by w. Mary he had Robert, b. 6 Oct. 1678, and that his w. d. 11 Oct. foll. aged 22; and he m. 25 Sept. foll. Deborah, d. of Daniel Cushing of Hingham, and d. 12 Sept. 1680, aged 31. His wid. m. 31 Aug. 1686, Rev. Benjamin Woodbridge of Bristol. The name on Hingham rec. is pervert. to Tolton; and Mitchell's Bridgewater, 367, makes the Woodbridge min. 1679. RICHARD, Portsmouth, by w. Ruth had Elias, b. 13 Aug. 1693, beside

William, Richard, and Ruth, of wh. one or more may have been b. earlier.

TARNE, TERNEY, or TARNEY, MILES, Boston 1638, leather-dresser, had w. Sarah, wh. join. our ch. 14 Apr. 1639 ; but he was not mem. bef. 8 Oct. 1642, and freem. 10 May foll. Of ch. I kn. only Hannah, b. Oct. 1638, bapt. 21 Apr. foll. nam. in the will of Thomas Oliver, Mar. 1652, with beq. of £5 ; and Deliverance, bapt. 19 Sept. 1641, eight days old, when the town rec. says she was b. 30 of that mo. but that Sarah wh. m. 7 Sept. 1654, Edward Bobbet of Taunton, must have been older, perhaps brot. from Eng. He had 2d w. in Oct. 1668, Eliz. wh. had been wid. Rice, as I infer from deed of mortg. to trust. of the first ch. by Michael (wh. is the same as Miles) T. and Eliz. his w. and Joshua Rice, their s.

TARR, BENJAMIN, Gloucester, s. of Richard, m. 4 Feb. 1724, Rebecca Card, wid. of William the sec. had Benjamin, b. a. 1727, perhaps more. CALEB, Gloucester, br. of the preced. had w. Martha, and twelve ch. of wh. Caleb only is nam. by Babson ; and d. a. 1752. FERDINANDO, Braintree 1655. GEORGE, Lynn, prob. brot. w. and ch. when he came, for in his will of 1 July 1662, pro. Nov. foll. he names s. John, Lazarus, and Benjamin, as men, beside Joseph, as under age, and ds. Mary, Martha, Eliz. and Sarah ; yet, as nothing had bef. been kn. of him, I presume that he had not many yrs. been an inhab. JAMES, Portsmouth, R. I. 1638, is not aft. heard of. JOHN, Dover 1648, tax. there that yr. as Geneal. Reg. VIII. 130 gives it, tho. in Geneal. Reg. IV. 31, the name is Tart. He was of Maine, gr. jury 1649. JOSEPH, Gloucester, s. of Richard the first, m. 28 July 1719, Sarah Sargent, had Abigail, Joseph, Benjamin, and Nathaniel, and rem. to Maine. RICHARD, Gloucester, had been, 1680, at Marblehead, there m. and had William and John, but was attract. a. 1690, by the commodi. situat. of that part of the cape, call. Sandy bay, now Rockport, and was one of its earliest sett. had Eliz. b. 1691 ; Honour, 1693 ; Richard, 1695 ; Joseph, 1698 ; Benjamin, 1700 ; Caleb, 1703 ; Samuel, 1706 ; and Sarah, 1716. He was, of course, a fisherman, and is thought to have been k. by the Ind. off Penobscot 1724. RICHARD, Gloucester, s. of the preced. m. 20 Feb. 1722, Grace Hodgkins, as Babson says, had Hazelelponi, b. that yr. ; and William, 1724. SAMUEL, Gloucester, youngest s. of Richard of the same, m. 12 Oct. 1726, Eliz. Williams, had four s. but was drown. at Sheepscot riv. 1739. WILLIAM, Gloucester, eldest br. of the preced. m. 1708, Eliz. Felt, had sev. ch. of wh. Babson does not give names.

TART, EDWARD, Scituate, nam. as his serv. in the will of Nathaniel Tilden, and in 1643, serv. of Joseph Tilden, s. of N. THOMAS, Scituate 1640, had, as Deane thot. d. Eliz. wh. m. 1638, Thomas Williams of

*22

Boston; at B. had Jonathan, and Eunice, bapt. 11 Apr. 1641; but he rem. to Barbados.

TASKER, or TASKET, WILLIAM, Dover, 1675–89. SAMUEL, Dover, was prob. s. of the preced. and in June 1704 mort. wound. by the Ind.

TATENHAM, ELIAS, Boston, by w. Mary had Elias, b. 2 Dec. 1683.

TATMAN, or TOTMAN, JABEZ, Roxbury, s. of John, m. 18 Nov. 1668, Deborah Turner, perhaps d. of John, wh. d. 31 May or 1 June 1689, the town rec. giv. both days, had Eliz. b. 9 Dec. 1675, d. at 3 yrs.; Sarah, 9 Nov. 1683, d. June foll.; John, 13 Oct. 1685; and he d. 16 Apr. 1705. JOHN, Roxbury, came in the Lion, emb. June, arr. 16 Sept. 1632, with w. was freem. 2 May 1638, had Jabez, b. 19 Nov. 1641, of whose bapt. we kn. not, bec. the rec. bef. 26 Dec. of that yr. is lost; and d. 28 Oct. 1670. He had indulg. in 1639, from the Gen. Ct. for liv. more than half a mile from the ch. His will of 30 Sept. 1670 takes notice of nobody but s. Jabez, to wh. he gives all his prop. The name is Totman, in the London rec.

TAUNTON, MATTHEW, Boston, by w. Susanna had Eliz. b. 2 May 1688.

TAWLEY, THOMAS, Boston, by w. Mary had John, b. 7 Apr. 1678; Hannah, 16 Apr. 1680; and Jane, 2 Mar. 1682. At Salem, in 1686, the name occurs, and thither, I think, the Boston man rem.

TAY, or TOY, HENRY, Ipswich, d. a. 1655; and no more is kn. to Felt. *ISAIAH, Boston, s. of William of the same, serv. in Philip's war, was rep. in 1700, and oft. aft. JEREMIAH, Boston, br. of the preced. by w. Mercy had Jeremiah, b. 19 Jan. 1685, d. young; Woodward, 12 Feb. 1687; William, 16 June 1689; Jeremiah, again, 30 Oct. 1693; Isaiah, 5 Sept. 1696; and Mercy, 5 July 1703. JOHN, Boston, had been here but short time when he made his will, wh. is one of the first three in our Vol. I. pro. 7 Dec. 1641, refer. to s. Allen in Eng. wh. prob. never came. He was, I judge, a trader, as he speaks of goods remain. beside beq. of money and especial. of trees, no doubt fruit trees, as in Geneal. Reg. II. 104, may be read. NATHANIEL, Billerica 1679, br. of the preced. m. 30 May 1677, Bathsheba, d. of John Wyman. WILLIAM, Boston, in July 1643, gave Leonard Buttels two acres on Long Isl. and rec. from him 20 acres at Muddy riv. and in mid. life was a distiller, m. 14 Sept. 1644, Grace, d. of Abraham Newell, at Roxbury, had Grace, b. 23 Aug. 1645; John, bapt. at B. 21 Nov. 1647, being 5 days old; Isaiah, 4, bapt. 10 Mar. 1650; Abiel, 21, bapt. 23 Jan. 1653; Nathaniel, 23, bapt. Peter, on 25 (if the ch. rec. is good) Feb. 1655; Jeremiah, 18, bapt. 19 July 1657; and Eliz. 25 June, bapt. 1 July 1660; had est. in Billerica 1659, liv. there few yrs. and one yr. was town clk. was freem. 1663, not as Farmer made it 1650, with a supposit. s. of the same name. His will, of

28 Apr. 1680, pro. 12 Apr. 1683, calls hims. 72 yrs. old, makes w. Grace
sole excor. gives Jeremiah and Eliz. the ground "that the house was
burnt on," in the fire of 1679, I suppose; but they are charg. to pay £10
to his gr.d. Eliz. T. at age of 18, or m. " that is my eldest son's d." and of
est. at Billerica devises housing to Nathaniel, some to d. Grace Meade of
Billerica, whose h. is not of my acquaint. and some to s. Isaiah, beside
some in Boston. The wid. d. at Roxbury 11 Apr. 1712, aged 91 yrs.
His eldest s. f. of Eliz. whose mo.'s name is not within my guess, was
dec. as may be infer.

TAYLOR, TAYLOUR, or TAILER, ABRAHAM, Haverhill, in his will of
1673 names w. Hannah. ABRAHAM, Concord, freem. 1690. ANTHONY,
Hampton 1644, feltmaker, rem. to Dover, there was 1671; and is said
to have d. 4 Nov. 1687, aged 80; but in 1678 one Anthony perhaps his s.
sw. alleg. and certain. had s. John, and tradit. gives him Lydia, wh. m.
23 Mar. 1666, John Moulton, beside Martha, wh. m. 25 Sept. 1667,
Hezron Leavitt. CLEMENT, Dorchester, owes his being to Farmer under
introduct. of Harris, the creat. being due in the highest prob. to the same
bad writ. or ill read. as made Tapley out of Topliff. DANIEL, Saybrook
1689. EDWARD, Lynn 1639, freem. 1648, rem. to Reading and d. 1694.
EDWARD, Providence, by w. Hannah had Edward, b. 8 Oct. 1655.
EDWARD, Barnstable, m. 19 Feb. 1664, Mary Merks, had Ann, b. 11
Dec. 1664; Judith, 12 Dec. 1666, d. soon; Isaac, 3 Jan. 1669; Jacob,
19 Apr. 1670; Experience, June 1672; Mary, 15 Sept. 1674; Sarah, 6
Oct. 1678; John, 6 Sept. 1680; Abraham, 7 Feb. 1684; and Mehitable, 3 Oct. 1688. His w. d. Nov. 1701, and he d. 15 Feb. 1705.
EDWARD, Westfield, b. 1642, at Sketchley Co. Leicester, near Hinckley,
(not Sketelby, as Farmer prob. from some descend. had giv. and as rev-
erent. repeat. in Geneal. Reg. II. 395) came 1668, arr. at Boston 5 July,
and was gr. at H. C. 1671, and late in that yr. went by invit. to W. a
new planta. m. 5 Sept. 1674, Eliz. d. of Rev. James Fitch of Norwich,
had Samuel, b. 1675; Eliz. 1676, d. soon; James, 1678; Abigail, 1681,
d. young; Bathsheba, 1683; Eliz. àgain, 1684, d. soon; Mary, 1686, d.
young; and Hezekiah, 1687, d. young. His w. d. 1689, and he m. 2
June 1692, Ruth, d. of Hon. Samuel Wyllys, had Ruth, b. 1693; Naomi,
1695; Ann, 1696; Mehitable, 1699; Keziah, 1702; and Eldad, 1708.
He had preach. some yrs. there bef. he was ord. 27 Aug. 1679, was
freem. 1678, or 1680, for his name is in both lists, and d. 29 June 1729.
His wid. d. Jan. foll. Bathshua or Bathsheba m. 18 Feb. 1702, John
Pynchon; Ruth m. 1713, Rev. Benjamin Cotton; Naomi m. 1720, Rev.
Ebenezer Devotion; Ann m. 1720, Rev. Benjamin Lord; Mehitable m.
Rev. William Gager; and Keziah m. Rev. Isaac Stiles, and was mo. of
Presdt. Stiles. *ELDAD, Westfield, youngest s. of the preced. m. 1732,

Rhoda Dewey, had Eldad, b. 1733; Rhoda, 1735, d. young; Mehitable, 1736; and Rachel, 1740, when her mo. d. and she d. soon. In 1742 he m. Thankful Day, had Edward, b. 1743; Samuel, 1745; Thankful, 1747; James, 1750; Jedediah, 1752; John, 1755, d. young; Ann, 1757; Eliz. 1760; and John, again, 1762; and d. 1777, attend. the Gen. Ct. at Boston. ELISHA, Yarmouth, s. of Richard sec. of the same, had Shubael, Elisha, Rebecca, and Hezekiah. FRANCIS, Dedham 1671, a surveyor. GEORGE, Lynn, came in the Truelove, late in 1635, aged 31, freem. 2 May 1638, may be the man wh. bec. insane, there, 1640, as Winth. II. 21 tells; yet he prob. was in short time restor. for in Nov. 1663, his neighb. Rootens made him one of the overseers of his will; and d. 28 Dec. 1667. GEORGE, Scarborough, submit. to Mass. jurisdict. July 1658, had been there from 1636, and was liv. 1681. GREGORY, Watertown, an orig. propr. freem. 14 May 1634, constable 1642, by w. Achsa, says Bond, had Samuel, b. Apr. 1632, d. soon; and ano. s. 11 Mar. 1643, to wh. Bond, 601, gives a name, Seabred, that must be read wrong, in my opin. at least it is wrong as s. of Gregory, if right of Thomas. He soon aft. sold his lds. and is found at Stamford to d. 24 Sept. 1657. His w. d. 18 Aug. 1667, and no heir appear. to take the little prop. the Court allow. it to John Waterbury and his w. HENRY, Portsmouth 1640, was in 1648 brot. to prison at Boston, d. 1649. HENRY, Barnstable, m. 19 Dec. 1650, Lydia Hatch, prob. d. of William, or Thomas, of the same, had Lydia, b. 21 June 1655; and Jonathan, 20 Apr. 1658. HENRY, Boston, a surgeon, freem. 1665, by w. Mary had Hannah, b. 7 July 1665; John, 4 Aug. 1666; Mary, 6 June 1668; and Henry, 12 Oct. 1670; was one of the gr. body of petnrs. in 1666 to prevent quarrel with the governm. in Eng. [See 2 Mass. Hist. Coll. VIII. 103.] ISAAC, Boston, by w. Sarah had John, b. 16 Jan. 1692. ISAAC, Scituate, as Deane thot. came from Concord a. 1686, had Isaac, bapt. 1693; Mary, 1696; Jonathan, 1698; and David, 1700. JAMES, Concord, m. 1641, Isabel, or Eliz. Tompkins, had, says Shattuck, sev. ch. of wh. by my inq. I kn. only Samuel, b. 21 June 1656; Thomas, 12 July 1659, d. in few mos. and he perhaps rem. to Marlborough bef. 1675, and may have been by the Ind. hostil. driv. in to Cambridge, there by w. Sarah had William, b. 21 Aug. 1676; perhaps went again to Concord, there d. 22 Jan. 1690. JAMES, Springfield, m. 17 Jan. 1668, Mary, d. of Jonathan Taylor, had Rebecca, b. 18 Nov. 1668, d. in few wks.; James, 26 Nov. 1669; Mary, 28 Dec. 1671; John, 14 Mar. 1673, d. soon; Samuel, 26 Sept. 1674, d. young; Eliz. 5 Jan. 1678; Jonathan, 30 Oct. 1679; Ebenezer, 26 Aug. 1681, d. young; Thomas, b. at Suffield, 16 Jan. 1684, and d. at S. aged 19 yrs.; Samuel, 6 Apr. 1686; and Rebecca, 12 July 1689. Whence he came, wh. was his f. or when he d. is unkn. but he had been a serv. of John

Pynchon. JAMES, New Haven, a propr. 1685, of wh. no more is heard.
JAMES, Reading, may have been that surveyor, much employ. in 1671
and 2, d. at R. 1703. *JAMES, Boston, by w. Eliz. had Eliz. b. 24 Oct.
1674; perhaps is the same wh. by w. Rebecca had Samuel, 5 Dec. 1687;
Abigail, 2 Aug. 1690; Ann, 13 Nov. 1692; Sarah, 19 May 1695; William, 19 June 1696; Mercy, 13 Nov. 1700; and Mary, 15 July 1702;
and prob. also, was rep. 1689, 93 and 4.   JASPER, Barnstable, m. 6 Nov.
1668, Hannah, d. of Edward Fitzrandle of the same, had John, b. 29
Jan. 1670, d. soon; Mercy, 6 Nov. 1671; Hope, 24 Oct. 1674; Seth, 5
Sept. 1677; John, 24 Mar. 1680; Elinor, 6 Apr. 1682, d. in few days;
and Jasper, 29 Apr. 1684.   JOHN, Lynn, came prob. in the fleet with
Winth. desir. adm. as freem. 19 Oct. 1630, and was sw. 18 May foll.
Lewis tells, that he was from Haverhill, Co. Suff'k. and that his w. and
ch. d. on the passage.   JOHN, Windsor 1640, but is not kn. to have ever
been at Dorchester, was in esteem 1644, and no later is any ment. found,
so that he may have had w. and ch. and rem. to some uncert. place.   A
Rhoda T. at W. 1659, had seat in the meeting ho. and may be thot. his wid.
or ch.   An Amos T. d. at Windsor, 1644; and Hannah d. there 1650, wh.
may have been his ch. or possib. of Stephen.   JOHN, Weymouth, in his
will of 6 Jan. pro. 22 May 1668, names w. Rebecca, d. Rebecca, w. I suppose, of Richard Gurney, and s. John wh. is made excor.   JOHN, Cambridge
1644, freem. 1651, by w. Catharine had Joseph, bapt. at C. H. C. 1669;
d. 6 Sept. 1683, fill. the office of butler and was a faithf. serv. of H. C.
a. 40 yrs. says the gr.-stone.   JOHN, Damariscove 1651, by Sullivan, 287,
is found there in 1665.   JOHN, Weymouth, prob. s. of John of the same,
by w. Phebe, I presume d. of the wid. Ann Rockwood, had Mary, b. 18
May 1660; John, 10 Apr. 1666; and perhaps rem. to Braintree.   JOHN,
Ipswich, a soldier, k. in the gr. battle with Philip, 19 Dec. 1675.   JOHN,
Salem 1671, a joiner, may have been s. of Richard of Boston, and rem. to
Boston, there by w. Rebecca had John, b. 22 Nov. 1674; William, 21 May
1676; and Eliz. 1680; but I discov. nothing more.   JOHN, Hampton, took
the o. of alleg. 25 Apr. 1678; and later in the same yr. ano. JOHN of Hampton was equal. patriot.   One of the two, I suppose, by w. Deborah had Mary,
b. 3 May 1687.   JOHN, Hadley, m. 12 Dec. 1666, Mary, d. of the first
Thomas Selden, sw. alleg. 8 Feb. 1679, as did JOHN of Northampton on
the same day and this latter better kept his word in becom. freem. 1683.
He may have been s. of John of Windsor, and certain. m. 18 Dec. 1662,
Thankful, d. of Henry Woodward, had Thankful, b. 29 Oct. 1663; Joanna, 27 Sept. 1665; John, 10 Oct. 1667; Rhoda, 26 Sept. 1669; Eliz.
13 Jan. 1672, d. at 9 yrs.; Mary, 13 Oct. 1673; Jonathan, 19 Sept.
1675; Mindwell, 19 Aug. 1677; Lydia, 18 Mar. 1679; Thomas, 4 Nov.
1680; Eliz. again, 17 Sept. 1682; Experience, Oct. 1684; and Samuel,

30 Aug. 1688; was a very val. citiz. capt. of the troop of Hampsh. k. by the Ind. 13 May 1704, then in pursuit of them aft. their destruct. of Pascomuck. The wid. liv. with s. John at Norwalk 1724. But of the Hadley John my acco. is equal. good; as that he had Esther, b. 9 Dec. 1667; John, 6 Jan. 1670; Thomas, 5 June 1672; Stephen, 1674; Mary, 12 Oct. 1676, d. young; Thankful, 1680; Jacob, 1685; Samuel, 3 Dec. 1688; and Ebenezer, 1 Mar. 1697. JOHN, Yarmouth, s. of Richard first of the same, m. 15 Dec. 1674, Sarah Matthews, had Samuel, b. 14 Dec. 1675; and John, 15 June 1678. JOHN, Suffield, s. of Stephen the first, m. 25 Sept. 1682, Sarah Younglove, d. of John, had Benoni, b. 15 June 1683, d. in few days, as had the mo. in four days. He m. again, 24 Mar. 1686, Eliz. Spencer, d. of Thomas of S. and had John, 17 Jan. 1687; Nathaniel, 20 May 1688; rem. to Windsor, and had Samuel, 11 Apr. 1691; Eliz. 11 Nov. 1694; and Ebenezer, 11 Sept. 1697; as Stiles, in Hist. of W. 812, gives the last three suspicious days. The time of his dec. is unkn. JOHN, Charlestown, by w. Catharine had Richard, aged 3, and John, 1, when both were bapt. 6 Oct. 1689; Thomas, 24 July 1692; Catharine, 18 Nov. 1694; and Sarah, 31 Jan. 1697. JONATHAN, Springfield 1649, by w. Mary had Mary, b. 1 Aug. of that yr. wh. m. 17 Jan. 1668, James Taylor; Ann, 6 Apr. 1651, d. in few days; Samuel, 8 Sept. 1652; Jonathan, 11 Mar. 1655; Rebecca, 4 July 1657, d. at 11 yrs. and Thomas 9 Aug. 1660. His w. d. 9 Sept. 1683; and he d. in few wks. aft. at Suffield, prob. on visit to his s. He took o. of alleg. 31 Dec. 1678, or the next day, as did, also, Jonathan his s. wh. m. 11 July preced. Sarah, d. of William Brooks of Springfield, had b. at Suffield, Sarah, 23 Jan. 1682; Mary, 3 May 1684; and Mercy, 6 Sept. 1686; and perhaps more. He was deac. at Suffield. JOSEPH, Fairfield, sold ld. there 1667. *JOSEPH*, Southampton, L. I. s. of John of Cambridge, was sometime fellow of the Coll. ord. Mar. 1680, as success. to Rev. Robert Fordham, had liv. at New Haven, where was b. his s. John, 5 Oct. 1678; may have had w. of that place; and d. 4 Apr. 1682, leav. John, and Joseph, wh. sold in 1702 the est. at Cambridge of their gr.f. JOSEPH, Exeter, sw. alleg. Nov. 1677. JOSEPH, Marshfield, m. 25 Apr. 1684, Experience Williamson. JOSEPH, Boston, by w. Thomasin had Mary, b. 30 Oct. 1686. NATHANIEL, Windsor, m. 17 Oct. 1678, Abigail, d. of Thomas Bissell, had Hezekiah, b. 23 Aug. 1679. PHILIP, freem. of Mass. 18 May 1642 may have been br. of Richard, wh. in the list stands next bef. him, but I am not able to say more, than that he was of ano. ch. than that of Boston. RICHARD, Boston, br. perhaps of the preced. join. our ch. 1 Jan. 1642, then "a single man and a tailor," was adm. freem. 18 May foll. by w. Mary had John, b. 2, bapt. 6 Feb. 1647; d. 1673. His will of 30 July, pro. 2 Aug. of that yr.

names no ch. but John, sis. Joan in Eng. and w. Eliz. RICHARD, Charlestown, but a mem. of some other ch. when adm. freem. 18 May 1642, the same day with Boston Richard, d. 10 July 1659, of wh. I learn nothing but from his will, made 6 May bef. that his w. was Ann, and he had d. Frances Adams. RICHARD, Yarmouth 1643, m. says the fam. tradit. a Burgess, perhaps d. of Thomas, whose d. Ruth, also, m. ano. Richard T. His w. was drown. 4 Dec. 1673, and he d. next yr. leav. two s. six ds. John; Joseph; Mary; Martha, b. 18 Dec. 1650; Eliz.; Ann, bur. 29 Mar. 1650 aged a yr. and a half; Hannah, and Sarah, of wh. this last d. unm. 3 July 1695; Mary m. a Merchant; Martha m. 3 Dec. 1675, Joseph Bearse; Ann m. 25 June 1679, Josiah Davis; Hannah m. 19 July 1680, Job Crocker; and Eliz. m. 20 Dec. 1680, Samuel Cobb. RICHARD, Yarmouth, farmer, call. says tradit. rock Richard, from his first build. his cottage against a rock, m. a. 1646, Ruth Burgess, perhaps d. of Thomas, had Ruth, b. 29 July 1647, bur. next yr.; Ann, 2 Dec. 1648; Ruth, again, 11 Apr. 1650; Richard, 9 Jan. 1652; Mehitable, 23 July 1654; Keziah, 18 Feb. 1656; Joshua, 9 May 1659; Hannah, 17 Sept. 1661; Elisha, 10 Feb. 1664; and Mary, 12 June 1667; his w. d. 22 June 1693, and he d. 1 Aug. 1703. RICHARD, Charlestown, by w. Ann wh. join. the ch. 17 Sept. 1665, had Sarah, bapt. on Sunday foll.; Ann, 12 Jan. 1667; perhaps Thomas, 16 Apr. 1670; Richard, 16 Nov. 1673; and Alice, 2 Apr. 1676, was one of the tything men 1679. RICHARD, Yarmouth, s. of the sec. Richard of the same, serv. in the war against Philip, had Isaac, Joshua, Nathan, Ebenezer, and two ds. ROBERT, Newport, found by Dr. Stiles in the list of freem. 1655, m. Nov. 1646, Mary Hodges, whose f. is not found by me, had Mary, b. Nov. 1647; Ann, 10 Feb. 1650; Margaret, 30 Jan. 1652; Robert, Oct. 1653; John, June 1657; and Peter, July 1661. ROBERT, Boston, by w. Sarah had James, b. 17 Jan. 1661. SAMUEL, Ipswich 1648, had been ment. 1638, but never with indicat. of a fam. No w. or ch. is heard of, when at the age of 81 his will was pro. 29 June 1695, in wh. his ho. and ld. are devis. to Samuel Treadwell, perhaps a cous. as he calls Thomas, and Nathaniel Treadwell, Thomas, and Seaborn Wilson, Mary Gaines, Esther Hovey, and Martha Cross. SAMUEL, Windsor, had, as Parsons in Geneal. Reg. V. 365, quotes rec. d. Martha, wh. at the age of 20, m. 30 Oct. 1679, Josiah Ellsworth. But this is a sad mistake of Taylor for Gaylord. SAMUEL, Springfield, wh. sw. alleg. there 31 Dec. 1678, or next day, may be s. of Stephen of Windsor, was a blacksmith at Westfield, by w. Mary had a ch. b. 3 May 1672, d. in few days; Mary, 14 Dec. 1673, d. young; Mary, again, 1675, d. young; Samuel, 1677, d. young; a s. 30 Sept. 1679, d. in few wks.; Joseph, 1 May 1681, d. young; Eliz. 10 Mar. 1683, d. soon; Eliz. again, 27 July 1684;

Mary, again, 3 Mar. 1687; Sarah, 8 Oct. 1689; Hannah, 25 Aug. 1692; and Joseph, again, 4 Mar. 1694; beside a d. Mercy, in his will of 1723, nam. as dec. leav. ch. Mercy and Mabel Buck. This list varies slightly from that in Geneal. Reg. VI. 266, but seems to me of authori. His will names only s. Joseph, ds. Mary Bush, Eliz. Phelps, and Hannah Loomis, beside that Mercy, and Sarah, wh. had m. one of the innumer. tribe of Williams, was dec. leav. only ch. Sarah. SAMUEL, Wethersfield, s. of William of the same, by w. Sarah, m. 1679, had Sarah, b. 1680; William, 1683; Mary, 1685; John, 1688; Margaret, 1693; and Mabel, 1695. SAMUEL, Springfield, s. of Jonathan of the same, m. 24 June 1675, Ruth Cogan, had Rebecca, b. 4 July 1676; Ruth, 18 Aug. 1678, d. at six yrs.; Ann, 17 Aug. 1680; Mary, 1682; rem. to Suffield, there had Martha, 12 Feb. 1684; Ruth, 8 Apr. 1686; and Thankful, 19 May 1688; and he d. 7 Sept. 1689, leav. wid. Ruth and the six ch. SAMUEL, Westfield, s. of Rev. Edward, m. 1704, Margaret Mosely, had Eliz. b. 1705; and Margaret, 1707, d. the same yr. His w. d. 1708, and he d. next yr. SEABRED, Reading, s. of Thomas of Watertown, m. 22 Nov. 1671, Mary, d. of Richard Harrington, was freem. 1677, against wh. I hardly suppose that Farmer design. any imput. when he calls him Sinbred. STEPHEN, Windsor, perhaps br. of the first John of the same, m. 1 Nov. 1642, Sarah Hosford, d. of Rev. William, had Stephen, b. 11 Mar. 1644; Samuel, 8 Oct. 1647; and by sec. w. m. 25 Oct. 1649, Eliz. Newell, had John, 22 Mar. 1652; Thomas, 5 Oct. 1655; Abigail, 19 Mar. 1657; Mary, 18 June 1661; Mindwell, 5 Nov. 1663; and Nathaniel, 24 May 1668, d. at 14 yrs.; was in the list of freem. Oct. 1669. He d. 1 Sept. 1668, and his wid. d. 5 Aug. foll. acc. one rep. but Stiles says, 14 Dec. 1717. He call. hims. 66 yrs. old in 1684. STEPHEN, Hadley, m. at Hartford, Sarah, d. of John White, had only ch. Stephen, and d. 7 Sept. 1665. His wid. m. 15 Oct. 1666, Barnabas Hinsdale, wh. was k. by the Ind. 18 Sept. 1675; and she had third h. Feb. 1679, Walter Hickson. He may have been s. of John of Hartford, but whence he came, is uncert. STEPHEN, Boston, by w. Hannah had Hannah, b. 2 July 1668. STEPHEN, Suffield, s. of the first Stephen, m. 8 Nov. 1676, Joanna Porter of Farmington, prob. d. of Thomas, had Sarah, b. 16 July 1679; Joanna, 28 Mar. 1682; rem. to Windsor, had there Stephen, 9 May 1685; Stephen, again, 8 May 1688; William, 14 Mar. 1689; and perhaps others, and d. 3 Aug. 1707. THOMAS, Watertown 1642, by w. Eliz. had Seabred, b. 11 Mar. 1643; rem. to Reading, and d. 1690. THOMAS, Norwalk 1666, m. 14 Feb. 1668, Rebecca, d. of Edward Ketchum, had Thomas, b. 26 Nov. 1668; Deborah, June 1671; and prob. others, for the name was long cont. in that town, where he was freem. 1670, but he rem. to Danbury, as one of the early sett. THOMAS,

Suffield, perhaps s. of the first Stephen, m. 15 June 1678, Abigail, d. of Hugh Roe, had Eliz. b. 24 July 1679 ; Abigail, 6 Sept. 1681 ; Nathaniel, 24 Aug. 1684, d. next yr. ; Mabel, 1 Dec. 1685. His. w. d. a. 13 Oct. 1691, and he m. Hannah, d. of Lancelot Granger, had Jerusha, 1697; Hannah, 1699; Keziah, 1704; and Dorothy, 1710. His w. d. 1729, and he d. 1740. The f. of his first w. in leav. her a legacy by his will, declar. that "Thomas Taylor shall have nothing to do with it," and that was caus. by his ill conduct. THOMAS, Springfield, s. of Jonathan of the same, m. 29 Dec. 1687, Mary, d. of John Petty, had Hannah, b. 18 Aug. 1690; and d. at Springfield Apr. 1691. WILLIAM, Lynn 1642. WILLIAM, Wethersfield, by w. Mary had Samuel, b. 1647, perhaps d. soon ; John, 1649 ; Sarah ; ano. Samuel; Mary, 1654; William, 1659; Margaret, 1663; Jonathan, 1666; and the seven ch. were liv. 1720. WILLIAM, New London, kn. there, says Caulkins, only 1650 to 3, perhaps was not the freem. 1669 of Wethersfield. WILLIAM, Concord, m. Mary Meriam, perhaps d. of Joseph, had John, b. 19 Oct. 1653 ; Samuel, 3 July 1655, d. in few ds.; Abraham, 14 Nov. 1656; Isaac, 1659; Jacob, 8 May, 1662 ; Joseph, 1665; and Mary ; and Shattuck says, he d. 6 Dec. 1696. WILLIAM, Boston, merch. by w. Rebecca had Eliz. b. 17 May 1667 ; and Thomas, 18 Feb. 1674; was much disting. for active enterpr. but fell into melancholy, and d. by his own hd. 12 July 1682. See Russell's Diary in Geneal. Reg. VII. 53 and Bradstreet's in Ib. VIII. 332 or IX. 50. WILLIAM, Scituate, br. of Isaac of the same, and elder, as Deane thot. had Lydia, b. 1688 ; Eliz. 1692 ; and Mary, 1696. Of this name I see 20 gr. at Yale, and 15 at Harv.

TEAD, TEED, or TED, JOHN, Charlestown 1637, emb. 12 May of that yr. at Yarmouth, aged 19, as serv. of Samuel Greenfield of Norwich, but perhaps was not desir. by his master to accomp. him, aft. reach. this side of the ocean, if, as seems prob. he be the person call. Todd, in Frothingham, p. 88, may have rem. aft. 1640 to Woburn, there was one of the true-spirited petnrs. to the Gen. Ct. 30 Aug. 1653 in fav. of liberty of proph. had w. Margaret, wh. d. 1651, and he d. 24 Apr. 1657. By his will made 15 days bef. we find he had sec. w. Alice, and ds. Mary, and Eliz. beside gr.ch. Benjamin, Hannah, and ano. d. of one Savil; and John and Samuel Savil, of ano. Thomas Fuller, and John Kendall, also a s. of his own name. See Tidd. Yet one of this name was propound. for freem. in 1664, tho. no more heard of. See 4 Mass. Hist. Coll. I. 101, and Geneal. Reg. XIV. 328. JOSHUA, Charlestown 1637, perhaps br. of the preced. was adm. of the ch. 10 Mar. 1639, and freem. 22 May foll. and his w. Sarah join. the ch. 9 Sept. aft. By the town rec. they had John, b. 15 June 1641 ; and Joseph, 15 Dec. 1643. In the ch. bapt. wh. suffer. a sad blank for many yrs. aft. 20 Sept. 1642, the name of no

ch. but the first would be look. for, and that is not seen, so that it may
be the ch. d. soon. He was, in 1648, agent for Richard Young, wh. had
in London, contrib. to our com. stock, and obt. for him his share of 100
acres of ld. selectman 1660 and 8, lieut. in 1678, on 15 Sept. of wh. yr.
he d. aged 71. Oft. it was writ. Tydd, and in mod. days is altogether
Tidd.

TEAKE, HENRY, is the misprint in Geneal. Reg. VII. 226, for Feake,
Henry, of Lynn.

TEFFE. See Tiffe.

TELL, WILLIAM, Malden, freem. 1690, tho. in my opin. the name is
design. for Teal, wh. by w. Mary had Abigail, b. 1 Jan. 1686; Benjamin, 2 Nov. 1689; Eliz. 22 June 1696; Oliver, 19 July 1699; and Rachel, 1 Aug. 1703.

TEMPLAR, TEMPLE or TEMPLER, ABRAHAM, Salem 1637, had Abraham. ABRAHAM, Concord, s. perhaps of the preced. m. 1673, Deborah
Hadlock, had Richard, Abigail, Mary, and Joseph; had perhaps rem. to
Charlestown, there had a d. b. 1686; but certain. was at Concord freem.
1690. ISAAC, Concord, s. of Richard, freem. 1690. JOHN, Boston,
freem. 1671, was liv. 1695. RICHARD, Yarmouth, there in the list of
those able to bear arms, 1643, by w. Hannah, d. of Richard Pritchard,
had Hannah, b. 5 Jan. 1643; Samuel, 22 Jan. 1648; Esther, bur. 13
Sept. 1649; perhaps James; Deborah, d. 5 Aug. 1657; Deborah, again,
bapt. 4 Oct. 1657; beside Richard, 15 Oct. 1656, bapt. 5 July 1663;
but rem. with f. and mo. of his w. to Charlestown, 1660 From ascert.
that his wid. m. 10 Apr. 1674, Nathaniel Morton, Secr. of Plymouth
Col. I was led to correct the erroneous inference, authorized by Charlestown rec. that he was recent. d. in Mar. 1678, as his ho. is ment. but not
the person. She outliv. the dignitary, and d. 26 Dec. 1690, aged 66.
In the will of Pritchard, 22 Jan. 1669 are ment. Hannah, w. of R. T.
made extrix. and the three ch. By this docum. alone could the confusion
of Templar and Temple into wh. Farmer fell, be explained. Deborah
m. John Chamberlain of Charlestown, and aft. a Miller. RICHARD, Salem 1644, Charlestown, 1646, there by w. Joanna had Abigail, b. 15 July
1647; Richard, 1654; rem. to Concord, had Isaac, 19 June 1657, was
freem. 1672. RICHARD, Concord, s. of the preced. freem. 1690, by w.
Sarah had Richard, b. 1692; and Joseph, 1694; and d. 16 Feb. 1698
or 9. RICHARD, Reading, s. of Robert, m. Deborah, d. of the sec.
Thomas Parker of the same, had Josiah, b. 16 Mar. 1695; Thomas, 1
Nov. 1696, d. young; Jonathan, 19 Feb. 1699; Phebe; John, 19 Oct.
1704; Eliz. 17 Dec. 1706; Jabez, 2 July 1709; Ruth, 1712; Thomas,
again, 2 May, 1714; and Ebenezer, 7 May 1716; and d. 28 Nov. 1737,
in 70th yr. as gr.stone tells. ROBERT, Saco bef. 1670, perhaps, sev. yrs.

had Richard, b. a. 1668, and prob. other ch. wh. with their mo. it is thot.
on destruct. of the town in 1676, when he was k. by the Ind. were forced
to go to Boston for refuge. THOMAS, an Eng. knight and baronet, came
to Boston, with favor of appoint. by Cromwell to be Gov. of Acadia, in
1657, assoc. with Col. Crowne, as grantee of Nova Scotia, spent many
yrs. this side of the water, speculat. in lds. far and near, join the ch. of
Increase Mather in June 1670, yet was careful to hold good terms with
Charles II. (wh. renew. his office of Gov.) with wh. in former yrs. he
interpos. his kind offices to befriend N. E. One mark of this I copied in
the State Paper office at London, July 1842, being his letter to Secr.
Morrice from Boston, Aug. 1661, about the regicides, Whalley and Goffe,
with a very curious one from Rev. John Davenport, on the same subject,
addressed to Temple. The clerg. beats the courtier on that topic ; but
allowance is to be made for the cause, inasmuch as Temple was sincere,
we may well suppose, and be more sure that Davenport was not. He
thought a little equivocation justifiable for the glory of God, and safety
of the proscribed. A pleasant anecdote is relat. by Hutchinson of T.'s
persuad. the king, that the pine tree on the coin struck in Boston, was
the royal oak that saved his majesty. I doubt not, this is as near the
truth as tradit. oft. reaches ; perhaps it was uttered by the traveller to
our friend the Earl of Manchester, or even to the Earl of Clarendon,
whose well-tried loyalty quarrelled not with discretion ; and in the way
of trifling not uncommon in that court, may possib. tho. I think not, have
got up to the throne. If the merry monarch had been ill-natured eno.
to ask what the date, 1652, meant. Sir Thomas must have had awkward sensations. He d. in London, 27 Mar. 1674, had left at B. a will
of 14 Oct. 1671, pro. 28 July 1674, but all the excors. Gov. Leverett
capt. Lake, capt. Hull, and John Richards, immediat. renounced the
office, prob. thro. fear that the debts would much exceed the means.
Ano. will had been pro. the very day bef. at the Prerog. Ct. Doctor's
Commons, made 27 Mar. of that yr. so that the first, wh. may be found
in our Prob. Vol. VI. 59, is supersed. by this of Ib. 327.

TENCH, EDWARD, New Haven 1643. WILLIAM, Plymouth, came in
the Fortune 1621, alone, as count. in the allot. of lds. and, as is said, d.
bef. 1638. As his name does not appear in the div. of cattle, 1627, he
may as well be suppos. to have d. so much earlier, unless a rem. to ano.
place, can be plausib. assert. See Morton's Mem. and Young's Chron.

TENNEY or TENNY, DANIEL, Bradford, m. 21 July, 1680, Eliz. Stickney, perhaps d. of William. DANIEL, Rowley, youngest s. of Thomas,
by w. Mary had Thomas, b. 1681 ; Daniel 1694; John 1696 ; William
1698 ; Richard 1701 ; and Ebenezer 1703; beside two ds. JAMES,
Boston, m. 8 Sept. 1654, Eliz. d. of Abraham Hagborn. * JOHN, Scar-

borough, m. a d. of Henry Warwick, of Saco, and with her mo. fled from
Ind. hostil. to Gloucester, bef. 1690, may have been of Rowley 1673,
prob. eldest br. of the preced. rep. in 1692. MILES, Watertown, by w.
Martha had Ruhamah, wh. d. 22 Nov. 1665, says Bond, but he names
no more. SAMUEL, Bradford, m. 18 Dec. 1690, Sarah Boynton ; but by
former w. Abigail, d. of Joseph Bailey, wh. d. 28 Nov. 1689, had Abigail, b. 6 days bef. THOMAS, Rowley, 1640, by w. Ann, wh. d. 25 Sept.
1657, had John, b. 1640 ; Thomas, 1648 ; James, 1650; and Daniel,
1653 ; beside two ds. He or his s. of the same name, prob. the latter,
was made ens. by the Gen. Ct. 1677. *WILLIAM, Rowley 1643, perhaps
br. of the preced. prob. had William, b. 1640 ; was rep. 1681. Of this
name there had been, as Farmer in Ms. noted, four gr. at Harv. two at
Yale, and ten at other N. E. coll. in 1834.

TEREBERRY, HENRY, is a nickname, to be found on the Boston rec. of
births for Tewksbury. See that.

TERHAN or TURHAN, THOMAS, Guilford 1685, m. Mary, wid. of
Henry Wise, and d. 1696, leav. wid. Mary, and three ch. Henry, Samuel,
and Abigail.

TERRILL or TURRALL, JOHN, New London, d. 27 Feb. 1712, and his
w. Sarah, d. of Isaac Willey, d. next week. ROGER, Milford 1639, if
Barber, Coll. 231, be correct; is count. there among freem. 1669 ; and
at the same time John, perhaps his br. was propound. for freem. He m.
the d. of the first Thomas Ufford. His d. Abigail m. William Tyler.
Ano. Roger must be seen in Cothren's Ancient Woodbury, if he is correct. He was first of Stratford, but a signer of the fundam. articles for
settlem. of W. 14 Feb. 1673, and d. 17 Apr. 1722, and his wid. Sarah,
d. 13 Apr. 1728. The ch. were Abigail, bapt. Jan. 1682 ; Sarah, Mar.
1684 ; Stephen, Aug. 1686 ; Roger, July 1691 ; Ezra, Apr. 1693 ; and
Timothy and Martha, tw. b. 19 Nov. 1697. It may seem that he was
s. of the first Roger.

TERRY, EPHRAIM, Springfield, s. of the first Samuel, m. 25 July 1695,
Hannah, d. of James Eggleston of Windsor. JOHN, Windsor, may be
that one wh. came in the Abigail, 1635, aged 32, from London, fellow
passeng. with John Winth. perhaps was first of Dorchester, and may
have been br. of Stephen, is found among the freem. and prob. had been
for some yrs. in 1669, unless this freem. may rather seem to be JOHN,
Windsor, s. of Stephen, wh. m. 27 Nov. 1662, Eliz. d. of William Wadsworth, had Eliz. b. 16 Dec. 1663 ; or as ano. says 1664; Stephen, 6
Oct. 1666 ; Sarah, 16 Nov. 1668 ; John 22 Mar. 1670 ; Rebecca, 7 Jan.
1672, d. young; Mary, 19 July 1673 ; Solomon, 29 Mar. 1675 ; and
Rebecca, again, 27 Feb. 1677, d. young. RICHARD, Southold, L. I. 1662,
came at the age of 17, in the James, 1635, from London, with Thomas

and Robert, prob. his elder brs. and was accept. as freem. of Conn. in
1662. ROBERT, was aged 25, when he emb. at London, 1635, in the
James, with Thomas, prob. elder, and Richard, younger, brs. but no more
is found of this name. SAMUEL, Springfield, said to be brought in 1650,
by Pynchon, from Barnet 11 ms. from London, where he was b. Apr.
1632, was resid. as Dr. Sprague thinks a. 1654, m. 3 Jan. 1660, Ann
Lobdell, perhaps sis. of Simon, had Samuel, b. 18 July 1661; Ephraim,
26 Aug. 1663, d. young; Thomas, 6 Mar. 1665; Mary, July 1667; Rebecca, 25 July 1669, d. soon; Ephraim, again, 3 Feb. 1672; Rebecca,
again, 5 Dec. 1673; Eliz. 25 Mar. 1677, d. very soon; and Ann; and
on the last day of 1678 or first of 1679, he, and Samuel, jr. his s. took o.
of alleg. m. 19 Nov. 1690, sec. w. Sarah Scott, and after 1700 rem. to
Enfield and d. 1731. SAMUEL, Enfield, s. of the preced. m. 17 May
1682, Hannah, sis. of Isaac Morgan, I think, and said to have been the
first m. in that sett. bef. it was made a town by separat. from Springfield, had Hannah, b. 18 Nov. 1684; Samuel, 26 Mar. 1690; Rebecca,
15 Nov. 1692; Ebenezer, 31 Mar. 1696; and Benjamin, 13 Oct. 1698;
and his w. d. 17 Jan. 1697. By sec. w. m. 4 Jan. 1699, Martha, wid. of
Benjamin Crane, whose surname, as Goodwin has it, Credan, looks very
strange, he had Ephraim, b. 24 Oct. 1701; Jacob, 20 Feb. 1704; Martha, perhaps 18 Feb. 1706, d. next mo. Jonathan, 17 Nov. 1707; and
Isaac, 17 Apr. 1713; and d. 1730. His wid. d. 29 May 1743. STE-
PHEN, Dorchester, came 1630, prob. in the Mary and John, on 19 Oct.
req. adm. and 18 May 1631, was allow. freem. held in good repute, appoint. constable as in Coll. Rec. I. 151 appears evid. of his being sw. 7
July 1635, next yr. partook of the spirit of migrat. and prob. rem. with
the major pt. of the ch. and Rev. John Warham their min. at least we
kn. he was in Windsor 1637, and twenty yrs. aft. was one of those engag.
in the first troop of cavalry estab. in the country. Who his w. was, or
whether he brot. her from Eng. is not ascert. but of ch. Mary was b. at
D. 31 Dec. 1635; John, 6 Mar. 1638 at W. Eliz. 4, bapt. 9 Jan. 1642;
and Abigail, 21, bapt. 27 Sept. 1646. Mary m. 8 Dec. 1659, Richard
Goodman; and Eliz. m. 10 Jan. 1666, Philip Russell of Hadley as his
sec. w. and with two of her four ch. was k. by the Ind. Sept. 1677; Abigail m. 9 May 1667, as his sec. w. lieut. Joseph Kellogg, and was liv. in
1715. THOMAS, Southold, came 1635, aged 28, with Richard, and Robert, prob. his younger brs. in the James from London; they all, perhaps,
contin. in Mass. some yrs. tho. the town is not kn. at least we see, in
Dec. 1638, that this elder of the three was, by the Gen. Ct. order. to
appear at next Ct. See Rec. I. 248. To Long Isl. they went prob. by
1646, and Thomas was accept. as freem. of Conn. 1662. THOMAS,

Springfield, s. of the first Samuel, m. 21 Apr. 1687, Mary Cooley. One
of this name at Harv. and seven at Yale, had been gr. in 1852.

TETHERLY, GABRIEL, and WILLIAM are seen in Maine a. 1680, perhaps trans. But of William we kn. that he was of Biddeford in Co.
Devon, and at Boston, 1664, 5, 6, and 8.

TEW, ‡* RICHARD, styled s. and heir of Henry, Portsmouth, R. I.
1640; Newport 1654, on the list of freem. 1655, was rep. and assist.
is one of the grantees in the royal chart. 1663, had m. bef. com. from
Eng. Mary, d. of William Clark, of Hardwick Priors, Co. Warwick, and
had a d. b. 4 June 1640, on his voyage, and therefore nam. Seaborn; and
Elnathan, 15 Oct. 1644; perhaps others; Seaborn m. 5 Jan. 1658,
Samuel Billings; Elnathan m. 3 Nov. 1664, Thomas Harris; and Mary,
prob. ano. d. m. 30 Dec. 1670, Andrew Harris.

TEWKSBURY, TEWXBERRY, TUKSBERY, or TUXBURY, HENRY, Newbury, rem. to Boston, m. 10 Nov. 1659, Martha, wid. of William Harvey
of B. had Eliz. b. 22 Aug. foll.; Hannah, 1 Sept. 1662; Henry, 15
Dec. 1664; Naomi, 18 Jan. 1667; and Ruth, 10 Mar. 1669; took o. of
alleg. 13 May 1669, and again hav. rem. to Amesbury, was call. to the
same, 20 Dec. 1677; grew to be freem. 1680. * THOMAS, Manchester
1686, was rep. 1692.

THACHER, or THATCHER, * ANTHONY, Marblehead, came from Salisbury in Co. Wilts, where he had serv. occasion. as curate for Peter
Thacher 1631 and 4, the rector of St. Edmunds in that city, wh. prob.
was his br. He had been a non-conformist, liv. in Holland more than
20 yrs. bef. and emb. on 6 Apr. 1635 at Southampton in the James
(tho. we might by Hubbard, 200, be misled to think he came in the
Angel Gabriel, cast away, 15 Aug.), and arr. at Boston 3 June, in the
ship's clearance call. a tayler for decept. *not* of the inferiors at the
custom ho. wh. certif. that the total num. of men, youths, and boys, was
53, when we are sure there were many more perhaps, a hundred and
fifty per cent. He brot. a sec. w. and four ch. William, b. of first w. as
may have been some of the rest, Mary, Edith, and Peter, a babe, and
prob. was accomp. by his cous. Rev. Joseph Avery, with w. and six ch.
and his neph. Thomas, afterwards first min. of the third or O. S. ch. in
Boston, beside a serv. Peter Higden; but of all these, only the names of
Higden and of Anthony P. appear in that list of 53. Such was the
mode of evasion of the petty tyranny of the Lords of the Council. The
ship was of 300 tons, and might well have brot. 150 passeng. when so
many were eager to come, yet the names of 53 alone are giv. Most of
these went to Ipswich, and a large part of them sett. the same and foll.
yr. at Newbury; but Thacher with his friend Avery, wh. was invit. to

preach at Marblehead, with all their respect. ch. and fam. exc. his neph.
Thomas, then 15 yrs. old, wh. prefer. ld. travel, emb. in a pinnace of
Isaac Allerton to return from I. to M. on 15 Aug. 1635, and next day
were wreck. on a rock, or rather ledge off Cape Ann. Of 23 persons in
that little bark, all but Thacher and his w. were drown. He and she
were cast on the barren islet, ever since call Thacher's woe, as the outer
rock, gain. the name of Avery's fall. Slight acco. of this sad occur. is in
Magn. II. cap. 2, but fuller in Winth. I. 165, and the personal relat. of
the whole by the suffer. is in Young's Chron. of Mass. 483, and I can
recommend no more strik. narrative in our early hist. Hé was by the Ct.
made admor. of Joseph Avery, as Col. Rec. I. 154, shows. Our Gen. Ct.
bestow a good sum in money on the surv. suffer. as in Rec. I. 157 appears, and afterwards, Ib. 191, made a gr. of that disastrous isl. for an
inherit. wh. was not, I imagine, worth tak. into possess. He preach. perhaps, short time at Marblehead, where he had prob. Judah; John, b. 17
Mar. 1639; but went for perman. settlem. bef. 1643, to Yarmouth, and
had Bethia, wh. m. Jabez Howland; and Rodolphus in my conject.
For a season he was of Marshfield, rep. for Y. 1643–7. He had at
Salisbury in O. E. Benjamin, b. 13, bapt. 27 Apr. 1634, but this ch.
perhaps d. soon; as did his mo. Mary if a fam. mem. be correct, wh. says
that his sec. w. tak. a few wks. bef. sail. was Eliz. Jones; and he d. at
Y. where his inv. is dat. 22 Aug. 1667, if Alden's Epit. I. 120 may be
correct. aged 80. ‡* John, Yarmouth, youngest s. of the preced. m. 6
Nov. 1664, Rebecca, d. of the first Josiah Winslow, and niece of the
first Gov. W. had Peter, b. 26 Apr. as one report is, or by ano. 20 May
1665; Josiah, 26 Apr. 1667, both bapt. 26 Apr. 1668; Rebecca, 1, bapt.
6 June 1669; Bethia, 10, bapt. 16 July 1671; John, 28 Jan. bapt. 14
Feb. 1675; Eliz. 19 June, bapt. 22 July 1677; Hannah, 19, bapt. 24
Aug. 1679, d. at ten yrs.; and Mary, 3 Aug. bapt. 24 Sept. 1682, d.
young. His w. d. 15 July foll. and many lamentable verses he wrote on
her. By sec. w. m. 11 Jan. 1684, Lydia, d. of John Gorham, he had
Lydia, 11, bapt. 22 Feb. 1685; Mary, again, 5 Feb. bapt. 6 Mar. 1687;
Desire, 24 Dec. 1688, bapt. 27 Jan. foll.; Hannah, 9, bapt. 12 Oct.
1690; Mercy, 23 July 1692, d. next mo.; Judah, 20, bapt. 27 Aug.
1693; Mercy, again, 28 Dec. 1695, bapt. next day, d. at 8 mos.; Ann,
7 May, bapt. 27 June 1697; Joseph, 11, bapt. 16 July 1699; Benjamin,
25 June, bapt. 3 Aug. 1701; Mercy, again, 7 Feb. bapt. same day 1703;
and Thomas, 2 Apr. bapt. 20 May 1705, as the town rec. has it, tho. I
have seen a fam. MS. that makes the yr. 1711, wh. is prob. erron.
Forty-one yrs. would seem a suffic. period for hav. ch. He was rep.
1668 and twelve yrs. foll. Assist. many yrs. aft. and a counsel. under
new chart, d. 8 May 1713. Fourteen of his twenty ch. m. for the

blessing of the cape. JUDAH, Yarmouth, s. prob. eldest, of Anthony, on
our side of the water, m. Mary, d. of Rev. Thomas Thornton, and of
descend. this report is giv. Eliz. b. Oct. 1667, wh. was sec. w. of first
Joshua Gee; Thomas, 18 May 1669; Mary, 17 Mar. 1671, wh. was
sec. w. of Moses Draper, and next of Joseph Grant; Judah, d. soon;
Ann, 31 Oct. 1674; and Judah, again, 7 Dec. 1676. PETER, Yarmouth
1678, may have been s. of that John, b. aft. his f.'s shipwreck, and so
call. in mem. of that babe lost in the disaster of 1635. Yet I marvel,
that some earlier writer was not enabled to foll. up the geneal. PETER,
Milton, youngest s. of Rev. Thomas, freem. 1678, at the same time with
his friend, the first Ch. just. Sewall, accomp. ano. classmate, Samuel
Danforth, to Europe, and on his d. near the end of 1676, came back
soon; m. 21 Nov. 1677, Theodora, d. of Rev. John Oxenbridge of the
first ch. wh. had eight yrs. bef. been in fierce enmity with the third
ch. founded for his f. and so, I hope, some help was giv. to the quiet that
began, soon aft. the d. of Gov. Bellingham, to reign thro. the colony so
long disturb. He was ord. first min. of M. 1681, had Theodora; Bathsheba; Oxenbridge, b. 17 May 1681, H. C. 1698; Eliz.; Mary; Peter,
6 Oct. 1688, H. C. 1706, min. of Middleborough; John, d. young;
Thomas, 1693, d. at 28 yrs. and John, again. His ord. at M. was, if we
obey the auth. of Farmer, in Sept. 1681. There his w. d. 18 Nov.
1697, and he m. next Susanna, wid. of Rev. John Bailey, wh. d. 4 Sept.
1724 in her 59th yr. and he m. Eliz. wid. of the first Joshua Gee, and d.
Eliot says 17, but Farmer incorrect. 27 Dec. 1727. Strange. does
Farmer give him the wid. of Rev. Joshua Gee as 3d w. when Gee was
the surv. by many yrs. and his mo.-in-law Eliz. d. of Judah Thacher bec.
third w. of Peter T. He preach. a serm. that Eliot calls beautif. on the
d. of G's. w. but that was only a single yr. bef. his own. RODOLPHUS,
or RALPH, Duxbury, s. of Thomas, m. 1 Jan. 1670, Ruth, d. of George
Partridge of the same, had Thomas, b. 9 Oct. foll. Eliz. 1 Mar. 1672;
Ann, 26 Nov. 1673, d. young; Ruth, 1 Nov. 1675; Rodolphus, 9 Jan.
1678; Lydia, 24 Jan. 1680; Mary 8 Mar. 1682; Ann, again, 30 Mar.
1684; and Peter, 17 Aug. 1686; was constable 1678, and sev. yrs. from
1685, clk. of the town. But his benevo. carr. him to Chilmark on
Martha's vineyard, where he preach. many yrs. and in June 1711 gave
to his s. "Rodolphus, alias Ralph" est. of 60 acres. See Mather's
Hecatompolis, in Magn. I. 27, and Geneal. Reg. XI. 242. Winsor,
325, misleads. * SAMUEL, Watertown, freem. 18 May 1642, was deac.
oft. selectman, rep. 1665–9, on 30 Nov. of wh. last he d. by w. Hannah
adm. of the ch. at Cambridge, 31 May 1667, had Hannah, b. 9 Oct.
1645; and Samuel, 20 Oct. 1648. The wid. Hannah, in her will of 16
Apr. 1682, with codic. of 20 Dec. foll. pro. 3 Apr. next, ment. gr.-ch.

John, and Hannah, who were ch. of John Holmes and her d. Hannah, m. 13 Sept. 1664, wh. d. 24 May 1670; s. Samuel and his first ch. with sev. other persons, wh. I judge to be not relat. but only friends. SAMUEL, Watertown, s. of the preced. at Lynn m. 11 Apr. 1676, Mary Farnsworth, prob. d. of Matthias, had Mary, b. 1 Aug. 1681, d. at 9 mos. Samuel, 8 Apr. 1683; John, 22 Jan. 1686; Hannah, 30 Apr. 1688, d. young; Mary, again, 17 Sept. 1690; Hannah, again, 10 Dec. 1692; Abigail, 6 June, 1694; Mercy, 2 Jan. 1698; Sarah, 30 Nov. 1699; and Ebenezer, 17 Mar. 1704; freem. 1690, was a lieut. and d. 21 Oct. 1726. Of the Watertown fam. descend. all retain the old spell. as if deriving their name from the early occupat. of a thatcher, wh. seems very prob. THOMAS, Weymouth, s. of Rev. Peter, rector of St. Edmunds, Salisbury, in Co. Wilts, b. 1 May 1620, bef. his f. was induct. (but the fam. origin was prob. Co. Somerset) came with his uncle Anthony in the James from Southampton, arr. at Boston 4 June 1635, went to Ipswich with his uncle and other friends, but avoid the peril of their return in Aug. of the same yr. in wh. all but Anthony and his w. were lost, was put under the direct. of Rev. Charles Chauncey of Scituate, wh. prepared him for his profess. with great dilig. He m. 11 May 1643, Eliz. youngest d. of Rev. Ralph Partridge of Duxbury, and was ord. min. at W. (as success. of Samuel Newman, wh. rem. with many of his flock to Rehoboth) 2 Jan. 1645, not 1664, as in Gen. Reg. VIII. 183 the figures read, was freem. 1645, when the prefix of Mr. is strange. omit. His good sense unit. with a general acquaint. in science of that day acquir. for him great reput. as a physician, and to complete his honors, Mather wh. always loves an exaggera. makes him compose a Hebrew Lexicon, so compress. " that within one sheet of paper, he had every considerable word of the language." The ch. were Thomas, Ralph ; alias Rodolphus ; Peter, b. at Salem (we kn. not by wh. accid. the mo. was there) 18, bapt. 20 July 1651, H. C. 1671; Patience ; and Eliz. wh. m. Nathaniel Davenport, the brave capt. k. in the gr. Narraganset battle, 19 Dec. 1675, and next. m. 1677, Samuel Davis. His w. d. 2 June 1664, soon aft. wh. he m. Margaret, wid. of Jacob Sheaffe, d. of Henry Webb, and rem. to Boston, join. the first ch. 4 Aug. 1667, and was desir. to be min. of a new society there, since call. the O. S. ch. growing out of the dissatisf. at the decept. artifices for bring. of Davenport from New Haven to succeed Wilson. In Oct. 1669, to save the feelings of his fellow-worship. he took dismiss. to the ch. at Charlestown, and on 16 Feb. foll. was install. over the new ch. of B. and was held in high esteem. In 1674, he with Increase Mather, was add. to former licensers of the press ; and he d. 15 Oct. 1678, as on p. 152 of the Magn. III. is told, tho. on the next p. where he gives as a curiosity some elegiac strains in Latin and Greek by an Ind. youth nam. Eleazer, then student in the senior class at Harv. the Eccles. Histor. with his aptitude for error, makes it 18 Oct. Still his life is one of the best in the vol. tho. Eliot has judiciously curtail. it by four fifths. His wid. d. 23 or 4 Feb. 1694, as town rec. and Sewall's Diary tell. Patience m. William Kemp. THOMAS, Boston, merch. eldest s. of the preced. m. Mary, d. of Thomas Savage, had Eliz. b. 26, bapt. 31 Dec. 1671 ; Thomas 25, bapt. 28 Sept. 1673 ; John, 22, bapt. 24 Jan. 1675 ; Peter, bapt. 26 Aug. 1677, H. C. 1696 ; and Mary, 28 Jan. bapt. 1 Feb. 1680. He d. 2 Apr. 1686, and his wid. d. 22 July 1730, giv. all her prop. to s. Peter wh. was min. of Weymouth, m. 14 Oct. 1708, Hannah Curwin, but had no ch. His name is oft. repeat. on acco. of the extraord. circumst. of his being brot. from the pulpit at W. to the new North ch. in Boston, as collea. with Rev. John Webb, wh. had been gr. at Harv. 12 yrs. later. How long aft. 1696 he was ord. at W. or what were the concomitants of his lot there are unkn. That he must have been highly regard. at W. and not thro. the partiality of a few hearers, wh. rememb. the powers of his uncle half a century bef. is a reasonab. presumpt. and why many should have desir. him is easier to conject. than the reason for the bitter and most indecent repugnance to his installat. that any of the petty squabbles a. the introd. of a min. in any parish of N. E. have produced. Four, five, or six publicat. on the two sides, may be preserv. by the curious for this eventful yr. 1720, on 28 Jan. in wh. an ordain. council was oblig. to go secret. to the house of worship in Boston ; where the disord. vulgarity, as tradit. relates, was too bad to be entrusted even to printing. He d. 26 Feb. 1739. Of this name 19 had in 1854, been gr. at Harv. and 4 at Yale.

THARPE, NATHANIEL, New Haven, perhaps s. of William, was punish. 1664, for steal. from an Ind. contin. a propr. 1685. WILLIAM, New Haven 1647, had perhaps by first w. Nathaniel, bapt. 24 May 1640, Eliz. Apr. 1643 ; John, July 1643 ; Samuel, 14 June 1646 ; and Eleazer, 5 Nov. 1648 ; m. prob. for sec. or third w. 1662, Margaret, wid. of Robert Pigg, and is in the list of freem. 1669, but if, as I can hardly doubt was the case, the name be the one in other rec. spelled Thorpe, then d. bef. 1685.

THASK. See Trask.

THAXTER, * JOHN, Hingham, s. of Thomas, brot. by his f. from Eng. 1638, m. 14 Dec. 1648, d. of Nicholas Jacob, had John, b. 1651, d. soon ; Thomas, 4 June 1654 ; Joseph, 1 June 1656 ; Samuel, b. 17 Nov. 1658, d. young ; Eliz. 19 Feb. 1661 ; Benjamin, 4 Feb. 1663 ; Samuel, again, 1 Aug. 1665 ; Mary, 19 Aug. 1667 ; Deborah, 5 Sept. 1669 ; Sarah, 26 Sept. 1671 ; Daniel, 29 Aug. 1675, d. in few mos. ; and Jonathan, 18 Apr. 1677 ; was made lieut. 1664, when serv. against

the Dutch at N. Y. was prepared for, under orders from Cromwell; rep.
1666; in 1680, was in com. of the troop of cav. and d. 14 Mar. 1687.
Eliz. m. 8 Dec. 1680 the sec. Daniel Cushing; Mary m. 1688, Theophilus Cushing; Deborah m. 17 Oct. 1687 Thomas Cushing; and Sarah
m. 25 Mar. 1691, Peter Dunbar; and the mo. of all these ch. m. 9 Mar.
1691 Daniel Cushing, the venerable town clk. JOSEPH, Boston, s. of
the preced. had w. Mary, but no ch. and d. in early manhood, 1687, div.
his prop. by will, equally to w. Mary and his br. Samuel. SAMUEL,
Hingham, youngest br. of John, m. 19 Dec. 1666, Abigail, d. of Richard Church, had Abigail, b. 29 Sept. 1667, d. next mo.; Sarah, 16
Nov. 1668; Abigail, again, 18 Nov. 1670, d. at six mos.; David, 6 Apr.
1672; Mary, 16 May 1674, d. in few wks.; John, 27 July 1675, d. in
few days; and Samuel, 23 Apr. 1677, d. in few mos. His w. d. 25
Dec. foll. and he m. 13 June 1678, Deborah, d. of Thomas Lincoln, the
cooper, had Deborah, 24 July 1679; Samuel, again, 19 Feb. 1682, d. at
12 yrs. and Abigail, again, 4 Feb. 1685. His w. d. 7 Dec. 1694, and
he d. May 1725. ‡* SAMUEL, Hingham, s. of John, freem. 1678, m. 29
Dec. 1691, Hannah Gridley, had Eliz. bapt. 25 Sept. 1692; John, b. 1
Jan. 1694; and Samuel, 8 Oct. 1695, H. C. 1714; and d. 13 Nov. 1740.
He was a very serviceable man, col. rep. and counsel. of the prov.
THOMAS, Hingham, came 1638, with eldest s. John, and d. Eliz. had
here w. Eliz. and ch. Sarah; Samuel, b. 19 May 1641; and Thomas,
wh. d. 6 Jan. 1647, young; was freem. 18 May 1642, and d. 14 Feb.
1654. His wid. m. 29 Sept. foll. William Ripley of H. and next, 20
Jan. 1658, John Dwight of Dedham; and d. Sarah m. I presume, 13
Dec. 1655, Thomas Thurston of Medfield. THOMAS, Hingham, sec. s. of
John of the same, m. 31 Dec. 1696, Lydia Logan of Boston, but had no
ch. and d. 3 Sept. 1704. It is believ. that all the twelve gr. of this name
at Harv. are his descend. but there is none in the Yale Catal.

THAYER, BENJAMIN, Mendon, youngest s. of Ferdinando, m. 15 Sept.
1699, Sarah Hayward, perhaps d. of Jonathan, had Ruth, b. 1 Mar.
1700; Margaret, 17 Dec. 1701; Grace, 6 May 1704; Sarah, 23 Mar.
1706; Benjamin, 23 Sept. 1707, d. soon; and Lydia 24 Apr. 1709.
His w. d. 1711, and he m. 20 Dec. 1712, Hannah Hayward, possib. sis.
of the former w. had Benjamin, again, 13 July 1713; and Aaron, 11
Nov. 1715. CORNELIUS, Braintree, s. prob. of the first Richard, d. prob.
unm. at Weymouth early in 1663. CORNELIUS, Braintree, youngest s.
of the sec. Richard, by w. Abigail, d. of the sec. John Hayden, had Cornelius, b. a. 1696; Moses, 1698; Gideon, 1 Mar. 1700; David, 1702;
Ezekiel, 1704; Eliakim, 1706; Hezekiah, 1708; Jeremiah, wh. d. 9
Nov. 1711; Abigail, d. 11 Jan. 1712, both prob. very young; and Jeremiah, again, 20 Aug. 1716. His w. d. 1 Jan. 1731. EBENEZER, Brain-

tree, youngest s. of the sec. Thomas, m. 2 Aug. 1688, at Taunton, Ruth, d. of Henry Neale, had Ruth, b. 25 July 1690, d. at 14 yrs. Ebenezer, 3 May 1692; Hannah, 16 Oct. 1693; Thomas, 19 Feb. 1698, d. soon; Rachel, 3 Apr. 1699; Eleazer, 17 Jan. 1701, d. at 3 yrs. Deborah, 16 Mar. 1702; Eleazer, again, 28 Jan. 1704; Ruth, again, bapt. 26 Aug. 1705, d. young; Ruth, again, b. 26 June 1707; and Eliz. 12 Oct. 1709; and he d. 11 June 1720. EBENEZER, Mendon, br. of Benjamin of the same, by w. Martha, had Deborah, b. 13 Oct. 1696; Ebenezer, 12 Apr. 1699; Abigail, 3 Sept. 1701; Hannah, 15 Sept. 1704; Uriah, 10 Sept. 1706; and David, 5 May 1715. EPHRAIM, Braintree, s. of Shadrach, m. 7 Jan. 1692, Sarah, youngest d. of John Bass, had Sarah, b. 5 Feb. 1693; Ephraim, 8 July 1694; Philip, 14 Apr. 1696; Hannah, 13 Jan. 1698; Joseph, 28 July 1699; Shadrach, 18 Apr. 1701; Christopher, 4 Mar. 1703; Ruth, 1 Apr. 1704; Esther, 24 July 1705; Naphtali, 30 Jan. 1707; Peter, 12 July 1708; Priscilla, 7 Mar. 1710; James, 16 Mar. 1712; and Abigail, 15 Nov. 1713. His w. d. 19 Aug. 1751, and he d. 15 June 1757, hav. m. sec. w. after he was 84 yrs. old. His descend. are very num. all the 14 ch. hav. m. and had fams. FERDI-NANDO, Braintree, s. of Thomas the first, b. in Eng. m. 14 Jan. 1652, Huldah Hayward, had Sarah, b. 12 May 1654, or 3 Feb. 1655, as the numerals for mo. and day are respectiv. accept. Huldah, 16 June 1657; Jonathan, 18 Mar. 1659; David, 20 June 1660, d. at 14 yrs.; and Naomi, 28 Jan. 1662. In few yrs. he rem. to Mendon, there, unless some of these were (as is prob.) b. at B. had Thomas, Samuel, Isaac, Josiah, Ebenezer, Benjamin, and last, David, again, Apr. 1672. His w. d. 1 Sept. 1690, and he d. 28 Mar. 1713. ISAAC, Braintree, s. of the sec. Thomas, d. unm. 9 Aug. 1690, of smallpox, bef. Sir William Phips, in whose sad expedit. he was emb. had with his fleet, got out of our Bay. ISAAC, Mendon, br. of Benjamin of the same, by w. Mercy, had Mercy, b. 2 Nov. 1693; Isaac, 24 Sept. 1695; Ebenezer, 6 Sept. 1697; and Comfort, 19 Feb. 1700; and by ano. w. Mary, he had Mary, 22 Dec. 1704; John, 9 May 1706; Nathaniel, 20 Apr. 1708; and Moses, May 1710. JOHN, Braintree, s. of the sec. Thomas, by w. Mary, d. of Henry Neale, had John, b. 30 June 1686; and Henry, 4 Aug. 1688, d. at 7 mos. His w. d. aft. more than 35 yrs. insan. July 1724, and he d. 19 Dec. 1746, after much longer suffer. by paralys. JONATHAN, Mendon, br. of Ferdinando, by w. Eliz. had Huldah, b. 11 May 1682; Grace, 20 Dec. 1684; Deborah, 4 Nov. 1687; and Jonathan, 8 Sept. 1690. JOSIAH, Mendon, br. of the preced. by w. Sarah, had Sarah, b. 25 May 1691; Josiah, 4 June 1694; Susanna, 13 Sept. 1696; Miriam, 3 June 1699; Jonathan, 28 Feb. 1702; Rebecca, 29 July 1704; Bath-sheba, 10 Sept. 1706; and David, 6 Mar. 1710. NATHANIEL, Taunton, of wh. with confid. no more is kn. but that he had Joanna, b. 13 Dec. 1665, wh. m. 7 Jan. 1690, John Crossman, was a propr. 1668. But other ch. prob. he had, for in the list of ms. only few yrs. bef. and aft. appear the names of Mary, twice, Abigail, Eliz. and William, all of wh. may not be deriv. from Braintree. NATHANIEL, Boston, s. prob. of Richard the first, was freem. 1690, and d. 28 Mar. 1728; by w. Deborah, had Nathaniel, b. 28 Aug. 1671, prob. d. young; Nathaniel, again, 11 July 1681; Zechariah, 29 May 1683; Cornelius, 14 Nov. 1684; John, 2 Apr. 1687, d. soon; John, again, 2 July 1688; Ebenezer, 1 Feb. 1690, H. C. 1708; and Deborah, 14 Oct. 1691. From his s. Cornelius, through a gr.-gr.s. Ebenezer, H. C. 1753, min. of Hampton, came the late Rev. Nathaniel of Lancaster, H. C. 1789, f. of promin. men of this generat. NATHANIEL, Braintree, s. of Richard the sec. m. 27 May 1679, Hannah, eldest d. of the sec. John Hayden of the same, had Nathaniel; Richard; Hannah, b. 17 Feb. 1686; Zechariah, 16 Mar. 1687; Ruth, 17 July 1689; Dorothy; Lydia; and Daniel; was a housewright, of great esteem, and d. 28 Mar. 1726. He was progenit. of Col. Sylvanus, the disting. engineer of our day, former command. of the national milit. sch. at West Point. RICHARD, Boston, 1640, brot. from Eng. ch. Richard, Deborah, Sarah, and perhaps more, as prob. Cornelius, Nathaniel and Zechariah. Sarah m. 20 July 1651, Samuel Davis, rem. to Braintree, and had d. 27 Aug. 1695. In 36 Pages of Thayer's fam. Geneal. are compris. many of the progeny of this Richard alone. RICHARD, Braintree, s. of the preced. brot. from Eng. by his f. m. 24 Dec. 1651, Dorothy Pray, had Dorothy, b. 30 Aug. 1653; Richard, 31 Aug. 1655; Nathaniel, 1 Jan. 1658; and perhaps had Zechariah, and prob. ds. Jael, and Abigail, and Cornelius, 18 Sept. 1670; went home on business, and came back 1679, as is told, and d. 4 Dec. 1705. His wid. d. the next week aft. RICHARD, Braintree, s. of the preced. prob. serv. in Philip's war, of Johnson's comp. 1675, m. 16 July 1679, Rebecca Mycall, d. of James, had Rebecca, b. 16 Aug. 1680; Benjamin, 6 Oct. 1683; Richard, 26 Jan. 1685; John, 12 Jan. 1688; Mary, Feb. 1689; James, 16 Nov. 1691; Deborah, bapt. 11 Apr. 1697; Ann, 14 Nov. 1697; Gideon, b. 26 July 1700; and Obadiah, 1 May 1703; and d. 11 Sept. 1729. SAMUEL, Braintree, s. of Shadrach, m. 18 Jan. 1694, Susanna, d. of William Scant of the same, had Samuel, b. 8 Mar. 1695; Susanna, 23 May 1697; Lydia, 25 Dec. 1699; Timothy, 31 Dec. 1701; and Hannah, 27 Jan. 1704. SAMUEL, Mendon, s. of Ferdinando, by w. Mary had Samuel, b. 1 Dec. 1691; Sarah, 11 Feb. 1695; Huldah, 30 Nov. 1698; Mary, 11 Feb. 1701; Joseph, July 1707; and Benjamin, 11 Sept. 1709; was lieut. and d. 19 Dec. 1721. SHADRACH, SYDRACK, or SIDRICK, Braintree, youngest s. of the first Thomas, b. in Eng. m. 1

Jan. 1655, Mary Barrett, had Rachel, b. 9 Oct. 1655 (Geneal. Reg.
XII. 108, says 9 Nov.), d. next yr.; and Trial, 7 Feb. 1658. His w. d.
2 Apr. foll. and he m. Deliverance Priest, had Freelove, 30 June 1662,
d. in few wks.; Mary, 1 Apr. 1663; Timothy, 3 Sept. 1666; Samuel, 7
Sept. 1667; Ephraim, 17 Jan. 1669; Hannah, 8 Apr. 1672, d. bef. 6
yrs.; and William, 1 Aug. 1675. He d. 19 Oct. 1678, and his wid. d.
17 Jan. 1723. Of the descend. of Shadrach the numerat. is by thousands, and part of them fill 87 pages in Thayer's Geneal. THOMAS,
Braintree, shoemaker, perhaps elder br. of Richard the first, brot. from
Eng. perhaps as late as 1645, w. Margery, and three prolific s. Thomas,
Ferdinando, and Shadrach, or Sydrach, as in his will of 21 June 1664,
he calls him; was freem. 1647, when it is writ. Tayer; d. 2 June 1665,
well advanc. in yrs.; and his will was pro. 13 Sept. foll. His wid. d.
11 Feb. 1673. THOMAS, Braintree, s. of the preced. perhaps brot. from
Eng. w. Ann, and s. Thomas, here had Eliz. b. 23 Mar. 1647; Isaac, 7
Sept. 1654, d. young; John, 25 Dec. 1656; Experience, 15 Feb. or
Mar. 1659; Isaac, again, 30 May 1661; Ebenezer, 7 July 1665; and
Deborah, d. young. He d. 9 Aug. 1693, aged 69; and his wid. d. 7
Feb. 1698. THOMAS, Braintree, s. of the preced. perhaps, but not prob.
b. in Eng. m. 25 Mar. 1680, Abigail d. of William Veazie, had Thomas,
b. 14 Jan. 1681; William, 15 Aug. 1682; and Abigail, 13 July 1685;
and d. 7 Dec. 1705. His wid. d. 11 Jan. 1712. THOMAS, Mendon, s.
of Ferdinando, by w. Mary had Mary, b. 19 Jan. 1689; Thomas, 14
Jan. 1694; Samuel, 28 Mar. 1696; Temperance, 7 July 1698; David,
8 Feb. 1701; Eliz. 2 Mar. 1703; John, 17 Sept. 1706; William, 22
Jan. 1708; Margaret, 12 Dec. 1710; and Jemima, 13 Feb. 1712. WIL-
LIAM, Braintree, youngest s. of Shadrach, m. 22 Sept. 1699, wid. Hannah
Hayward, had Bethia, bapt. 18 Aug. 1700; Jonathan, 2 May 1703; and
William, 11 May 1705. ZECHARIAH, Braintree, s. prob. of Richard
the first, d. prob. unm. 29 July 1693. Remarkable may appear the fact,
that so few of these men took the o. of freemen, but it is kn. that fewer
from Braintree than any other town appear. In 1678, five were sw.
and hardly as many more can be seen in the long period preced. from
1630. So little, comparative. was the migrat. of these fams. of Thayer,
that in the catalog. of gr. at Harv. are seen nineteen, and not one at
Yale.

THEALE, THELE, THEELE, or THALE, * JOSEPH, Stamford, prob. s. of
Nicholas of Watertown, freem. 1662, is by me presum. to be that man
made freem. 1662, whose name in Conn. Col. Rec. I. 391, is giv. Theed;
but he was of too much value to be thus obscur. rep. 1671, 3, 5, 6, and
7; aft. 1687 had good est. rem. to Bedford, just beyond the Col. bound.
in jurisdict. of N. Y. and I regret that no genealog. details are attain.

NICHOLAS, Watertown 1638, by w. Eliz. had Joseph, b. 24 Oct. 1640; and Eliz. 5 June 1643; prob. in the autumn of 1645 rem. to Stamford, there d. 19 Aug. 1658. His will dispos. his prop. to w. and the two ch. Eliz. m. 27 Oct. 1659, William Ratcliffe. The wid. m. Thomas Ufford, and d. 27 Dec. 1660, soon aft. her sec. h.

THING, JOHN, Boston, freem. 1680. JONATHAN, Ipswich 1641, may have soon aft. been of Hampton, next at Wells, submit. 1653, to the governm. of Mass. and was appoint. constable. JONATHAN, Exeter, prob. s. of the preced. m. Mary, eldest d. of John Gilman, had Jonathan, b. 21 Sept. 1678; John, 16 June 1680; Bartholomew, 25 Feb. 1682; Joseph, Nov. 1684; Eliz.; Benjamin, 12 Nov. 1688; and Josiah, 1690; was of the gr. jury 1684, and constable next yr. and d. 31 Oct. 1694, in his 40th yr. his w. hav. d. in Aug. 1691, under 33 yrs. as the inscript. on the gr.stones prove. A jury of inq. on the body of capt. Jonathan, the same day, gave verdict, "shot by his own gun." SAMUEL, wh. m. Abigail, d. of John Gilman, in 1690, pray. for contin. protect. of Mass. over them, with the preced. was perhaps his br.

THISTLE, or THISSELL, JEFFREY, Marblehead 1668, petitnr. against imposts, own. ld. at Beverly. He was from Abbotsbury, a. 8 ms. S. W. from Dorchester, Co. Dorset, and near the coast, as from his will of 29 Oct. 1675, pro. June foll. abstr. in Essex Inst. Coll. II. 231, appears; and he d. at sea, on voyage from Sal Tortudas to N. E. It names d. Jane, then at Abbotsbury, s. Richard and his ch. Jeffrey and Mary. RICHARD, Beverly 1664, s. of the preced. had William, b. 1684, and perhaps others, certain. elder s. Jeffrey and d. Mary; and he was 42 yrs. old, when William was b.

THOM, JOHN, Exeter 1677, Nov. 30, sw. alleg. WILLIAM, Lynn 1638, rem. says Lewis to L. I. 1640.

THOMAS, BENJAMIN, Springfield, s. of Rowland, m. 1688, Ann Belding of Hatfield, had Sarah, b. 2 Sept. 1690; Mary, 26 Dec. 1692; a s. 20 Dec. 1694; Ann, 21 Nov. 1696; and Samuel, 7 Jan. 1699; rem. soon aft. and the name bec. ext. at S. DANIEL, New Haven, eldest s. of John of the same, was propound. for freem. 1670, m. 3 Feb. 1670, Rebecca Thompson, perhaps d. of John, of the same, had Dorothy; John, b. 1674; Daniel, 14 Feb. 1677; Dinah, 26 Dec. 1678; Samuel, 13 Jan. 1681, d. young; Recompense, 27 Mar. 1683; and Israel, 1689. He d. Feb. 1694; and his wid. m. a Perkins. His d. Dorothy m. 13 Apr. 1693, Henry Toll or Towle. DAVID, Marblehead 1648–68. EDWARD, Boston 1685, agent of Joseph Thompson, of London, merch. ‖ EVAN, Boston, 1640, came from Wales, bring. w. Jane and four ch. for wh. 1 Sept. the Court direct. assist. adm. of our ch. 4 Apr. 1641, and freem. 2 June foll. had Jane, bapt. 16 May 1641, wh. being Sunday, may be as well relied on as the town rec. that she was b. that day; Dorcas, bapt. 5 Feb. 1643, a. 11 days old, by the ch. rec. when the town rec. gives the same day for b.; but this may be better deserv. of credit, when add. that she d. 28 of the same mo. The w. join. our ch. 7 Mar. 1646, and d. 12 Jan. 1659. He was a vintner, had ano. w. Alice, wid. of Philip Kirtland, or Catlin, of Lynn, wh. he m. 1659 or 60, was of ar. co. 1653, had good est. and d. 25 Aug. 1661. His d. Jane m. 14 Nov. 1657, John Jackson. The wid. seems to have been less acceptab. in her control of the business at the King's Arms public ho. for she was warned to leave town as late as 1672, and not restor. bef. 1676. But she had a stout heart, reliev. the tavern in May 1680 from mortge. of £300, and liv. on till 1697, in her will of 26 Jan. pro. 21 Oct. of that yr. names plenty of ch. and gr.ch. of the latter class one, Abigail, was then w. of Rev. Joseph Belcher. FRANCIS, Boston, m. Rebecca, d. of Matthew Iyans, had John, b. 1665, was liv. with w. 1674. GEORGE, Salem, 1668. GEORGE, Boston, by w. Rebecca, had Peter, b. 5 Feb. 1683; George, 16 Mar. 1685; and Maverick, 19 Mar. 1694. Henry is in Geneal. Reg. IX. 354 giv. as one of Gallup's comp. against Quebec 1690; but he is not seen in the more correct list. of XIII. 133, where is no surname Thomas, nor even any bapt. Henry. HUGH, Roxbury, of wh. I can find no more, but that he was adm. freem. 1651, prob. had no ch. as he gave his est. to strangers in blood for the good of Roxbury sch. in order to insure support of hims. and w. Clement for residue of life in 1677, with decent interm. after respective dec. and d. 6 May 1683, aged 76 yrs. by town rec. and his wid. d. 24 Sept. foll. JAMES, Salem, 1646–49. JEREMIAH, Marshfield, s. I suppose of the first Nathaniel, had Nathaniel, b. 2 Jan. 1686; Sarah, 25 Dec. 1687; Jeremiah, 14 Feb. 1689; Eliz. 19 Nov. 1690; Mary, 5 June 1692; Lydia, 26 Mar. 1694; Thankful, 30 June 1695; Jedediah, 19 Aug. 1698; Bethia, 27 Mar. 1701; Ebenezer, 1 Nov. 1703; and Priscilla, 13 Oct. 1705. JOHN, Marshfield 1643, possib. is the adventur. wh. emb. at London, in the Hopewell, Sept. 1635, aged 14, may have been at Salem 1646, but m. 21 Dec. 1648, Sarah, d. of James Pitney of M. prob. had John, as in the will of P. 1663, he is titled sen. JOHN, New Haven, had Eliz. b. 15 Mar. 1649; Samuel, 5 Sept. 1651; Tabitha, 18 Dec. 1653; all prob. bapt. 12 Feb. 1654; and Joseph, 10 Nov. 1661; all bapt. in right of his w. Tabitha, but *all* the dates of these bapt. in Geneal. Reg. IX. 362, are wrong. He was freem. 1669, a propr. 1685, and f. also of Daniel, John, and Sarah, all nam. with the other four, prob. the younger brood, in his will of 1670. He d. 15 Dec. 1671. Sarah m. 14 Oct. 1658, William Wilmot; and Eliz. m. Jan. 1674, John Holt. JOHN, New Haven, s. of the preced. m. 1671, Lydia, d. of Edward Parker of the same, had Sarah, b. 13 Dec.

1672; Abigail, 21 Nov. 1674; John, 4 Mar. 1676; Hannah, 26 Apr.
1678; Josiah, 15 Jan. 1680; Rebecca, 20 Sept. 1681 or 2; Jeremiah,
16 Feb. 1685; and perhaps others. JOHN, Stratford, of wh. I kn. only
the curious caution, deriv. in part from the will of Rev. Adam Blakeman,
16 Mar. 1665, in which he gave £5 to his d. Dorothy (the wid. of his s.
John, wh. d. so long bef. as 1662) "if she m. not J. T. and shall take her
friends' consent in the matter; or contin. a wid." and in part from the
decision of a court, 10 Oct. 1665, relat. to a reference of the claim of T.
to the person of the wid. wh. prob. had giv. encouragem. to ano. suitor.
Poor Thomas lost by the award, we may presume, for on 31 Oct. 1665,
the wid. m. Francis Hall. See Goodwin's Genealog. Notes. JOHN,
Woodbury 1690 perhaps, but not prob. s. of the preced. had John, bapt.
30 Aug. 1695; Samuel, 10 Sept. 1699; and Thomas, 5 Mar. 1701. Of
one JOHN, wh. d. at Framingham 1730, Farmer in MS. relates that his
f. was one of the first sett. of Boston, to wh. tradit. his judgm. would
have yield. little credit, had it not been assail. on its weak side; for the
story went on, that he, the Framingham man, was upwards of 100 yrs.
old. Now only one man ever reach. his century at F. and that was
Isaac Clark, while the names of sixty-eight persons in F. wh. d. at the
age of 85 and upwards, furnish. us by Barry, do not include any Thomas.
The first part of the myth, then, may not be more than ten yrs. beyond
the truth, but this example of longevity is sixteen yrs. at least, short of
the pretence. JOSEPH, Springfield, s. of Rowland, by w. Mary had
Mary, b. 1674; a ch. 1675; ano. 1676, wh. all d. soon; Samuel, 1677;
the preced. all b. at Hatfield whence he rem. prob. to Springfield, and
lastly to Lebanon; but at S. may have been b. most of the other ch.
Mary, 29 Dec. 1679; Joseph, 14 June 1682; Rowland, 26 Mar. 1685;
Sarah, 5 Feb. 1687; Ebenezer, 24 Nov. 1688; Josiah, 7 Oct. 1690;
and Mercy, 12 Dec. 1692; sw. alleg. 8 Feb. 1679, and was adm. freem.
1690. ‡NATHANIEL, Marshfield, 1643, s. of William, b. in Eng. a.
1606, prob. came with his f. 1640, may have brot w. and ch. William;
had Nathaniel, b. 1643, and ds. certain. Mary; Eliz. b. 1646; and Dorothy; perhaps one or more b. in Eng. nam. in the will of their gr.f. and
d. 13 Feb. 1675. He was lieut. and soon made capt. Mary m. Simon
Ray of Block Island, as Miss Thomas tells. ‡* NATHANIEL, Marshfield, s. of the preced. m. 19 Jan. 1664, Deborah, youngest d. of Nicholas Jacobs of Hingham, had Nathaniel, Joseph, Deborah, Dorothy, William, Elisha, Joshua, Caleb, Isaac, and Mary; of wh. Dorothy b. 6 Nov.
1670, m. 20 Nov. 1688, Joseph Otis. His w. d. 17 June 1696, and he
took 3 Nov. foll. sec. w. at. Boston, Eliz. wid. of Capt. William Condy
(but the m. certif. by Cotton Mather is of Eliz. Dolberry) wh. d. 11 Oct.
1713, if we believe the inscr. on the gr.st.; was rep. 1672, and seven yrs.

more, also at Boston, under the new chart. 1692, had serv. in Philip's war as a capt. on the first outbreak, and was of the Mass. Counc. d. 2 by town rec. but 22 Oct. 1718, in his 76th yr. by the gr.st. His d. Deborah m. 1 Dec. 1692, John Croad. PETER, Boston, s. of George, m. Eliz. d. of the Rev. George Burrows (wh. had on 19 Aug. 1692 suffer. by judicial murder under Stoughton, at wh. Cotton Mather assist.) had George, Elias, Peter, William, and Moses. This last is head of a numerous and disting. progeny. RICE, or RISE, Kittery, 1647 submit. to Mass. Nov. 1652, was of Boston 1654, then 38 yrs. old. ROWLAND, Springfield, 1646, m. 14 Apr. 1647, Sarah, d. of Samuel Chapin, had Joseph, b. 6 Jan. 1648, d. next yr.; Samuel, 2 Mar. 1649, d. in few days; Mary, 25 Mar. 1650, d. in few days; Joseph, again, 25 Mar. 1651; Benjamin, 23 May 1653; Josiah, 4 Apr. 1655, d. soon; Josiah, again, 28 Oct. 1657, d. in few days; Samuel, again, 6 May 1662, d. at 39 yrs. unm.; a d. 14 Sept. 1666, wh. m. 1692, James Warriner the sec. Mary, 9 Jan. 1669, d. next yr.; and Mercy 15 May 1671, wh. m. 30 Mar. 1689 John Bagg; beside two others of wh. neither liv. long eno. to find a name, so that of 13 only 5 ch. liv. to adult age. He took o. of alleg. 31 Dec. 1678, or next day, had been at Hadley 1669, and perhaps at Westfield 1670; his w. d. 5 Aug. 1684; and he d. at S. 21 Feb. 1698. SAMUEL, Marshfield, s. perhaps of William the sec. m. 27 May 1680, Mercy, d. of the sec. William Ford, but I kn. no more exc. his d. 2 Sept. 1720. THOMAS, the first name in the list of passeng. in the William and Francis, wh. arr. at Boston, 5 June 1632, hav. sail. from London, 9 Mar. bef. was only placed there, as I am wholly satisf. to befool the officers wh. might make disagreea. inquir. See 4 Mass. Hist. Coll. I. 92. WILLIAM, Newbury, came in the Mary Ann of Yarmouth 1637, emb. in May, aged 26, unm. husbandman of Great Comberton in Co. Worcester [See 4 Mass. Hist. Coll. I. 99], m. 8 Mar. 1666, Susanna, wid. of Robert Rogers, wh. by this m. had no ch. and d. 29 Mar. 1677. He d. 30 Sept. 1690. ‡ WILLIAM, Marshfield, a. 1640, made freem. of the Col. 17 Mar. 1642, had come, I think, with Rev. Richard Blinman, Hugh Caulkins, and other pious persons from the princip. of Wales, or the W. of Eng. not in 1630, as Farmer had it, and Miss Thomas repeats, merely, I suppose, out of reverence for the inscr. on the gr.st. call. him "one of the founders of New Plymouth Col." as if a man of his reputa. and import. would not many yrs. earlier be made freem. or mortuary legends applied in a subseq. age were not proverbial for lack of precision. He was chos. Assist. 1642, and so contin. exc. in 1645 and 6 to his last yr. d. Aug. 1651, aged 78 nearly. His will of 9 July preced. is abstr. in Geneal. Reg. IV. 319. WILLIAM, Marshfield, s. perhaps of the preced. but more prob. of the first Nathaniel, and Miss Thomas says, in 1638, b. in Eng.

of wh. we kn. only that he d. unm. 21 by rec. but by gr.st. 30 Mar. 1718 in 80th yr. WILLIAM, Newton, by w. Eliz. had William b. 31 Aug. 1687; and by sec. w. Ann, wid. of Thomas Lovering of Watertown, wh. bore him no ch. m. 29 Aug. 1695, had Joanna, b. 28 Oct. foll. if Jackson be correct, wh. adds that he d. 1697. Seventeen of this name at Harv. three at Yale, and seventeen at all the other N. E. coll. are found by Farmer as gr. in 1834.

THOMPSON, TOMSON, THOMSON, or TOMPSON, AMBROSE, Woodbury, s. of the first John of Stratford, by w. Sarah, had John, Ambrose, and other ch. bef. 1701, but had a sec. w. bef. 1706. Grievous was the error of Goodwin, 254, in mak. his w. Sarah to be wid. of Benjamin Beach. ANTHONY, New Haven, 1639, br. of the sec. John and first William of the same, prob. came with Gov. Eaton, with w. and two ch. John, and Anthony, had Bridget b. here, and by sec. w. Catharine had three more ch. Hannah, bapt. 8 June 1645; Lydia, 25 (not 24, as the careless ch. rec. has it) July 1647; and prob. posthum.; Ebenezer, 15 Oct. 1648; and he had some mos. bef. made his will 1648. His d. Bridget m. John Bowers wh. bec. first min. at Derby; Hannah m. a Staunton; Lydia m. 20 Sept. 1665, Isaac Crittenden; and the wid. m. 14 July 1652, Nicholas Camp of Milford. ANTHONY, Milford, s. of the preced. had no w. or ch. and d. bef. mid. age, in his will of 26 Dec. 1654, giv. his prop. to br. John, own sis. Bridget, and three half sis. ch. of goodwife Camp, wh. had been sec. w. of his f. ARCHIBALD, Marblehead 1637, was drown. Nov. 1641, as Winthrop tells, II. 43. BENJAMIN, Braintree, s. of Rev. William, of some distinct. as a physician, schoolmr. town clk. 1696, and even poet, monoculus inter coecos; yet more claim our regard as leav. at his d. 13 Apr. 1714, eight ch. and 28 gr.ch. His w. was Susanna, d. prob. of Philip Kirtland the first of Lynn; their ch. were Abigail, b. at Boston, 25 Nov. 1670; Susanna, 10 June 1673; Ann, 2 Dec. 1677; both at Charlestown; Elinor, 29 Nov. 1679, at Braintree, as were the others; Benjamin, 8 Nov. 1682; Eliz. 14 Jan. 1685; Philip, 26 July 1687; Sarah, 23 Sept. 1689; and Mary, 29 Oct. 1692; and the sch. master adds to the rec. quos omnes Deus omnipotens, sui filii unigeniti ac servatoris nostri meritis vita eterna dignetur. His w. d. he says, 27 July 1693. I judge he was keep. the sch. at Roxbury, where his d. Mary d. 28 Mar. 1700. Having been gr. at Harv. bef. Cotton Mather was b. he gain. the advant. as master of the Boston gram. sch. of helping forward that precoc. youth, wh. in burdensome gratitude, enlivens the Magn. III. 160, with the strains that his cousin Whiting's d. drew from T. DANIEL, Newbury, said to be 40 yrs. old in 1678, if the list in Gen. Reg. VII. 350 be not wrong, as by the silence of Coffin may be feared. DAVID, Piscataqua, sent out by Gorges in 1623, rem. a. 1626, to that isl.

in Boston harbor, ever since call. by his name, of wh. it is said his agent, William Trevore, had tak. possn. 1619, as is suppos. to be prov. by evience of an Ind. sagam. of Trevore hims. and of capt. Standish; but the value of such testimony is small. See the note of Deane, on Bradford's Hist. 209. It belongs to the town of Dorchester, but gr. by our governm. to T. and there he d. a. 1628, leav. inf. ch. John. EBENEZER, Guilford, s. of the first Anthony of New Haven, m. June 1671, Deborah, d. of William Dudley of G. had s. Jabesh, b. 16 Oct. 1672, d. young; and John, 1674, wh. d. early; was propound. for freem. in 1669; but prob. d. bef. mid. age, his will of 16 Aug. 1676, recit. that he was "a. 28 yrs. old." It gave his prop. $\frac{1}{3}$ to w. $\frac{2}{3}$ to s. John; and his inv. was brot. in 6 Nov. foll. He is call. a Scotchman, but this must have regard to his f. and as the number of the name of John was unusually great, among the Thompsons, most of wh. would be Eng. yet one prob. was from the Northern kingdom. EDMUND, Salem 1637, from the neighb. of Framlingham in Co. Suff'lk, where he had m. Martha, d. of John Fiske, had Martha; Edmund; Thomas, bapt. 12 Feb. 1643; and Hannah, bapt. 4 July 1647; all b. in N. E. adm. of the ch. at S. 29 Dec. 1639; went home and liv. at Yarmouth, there had three more ch. wh. d. inf. John, Esther, and John, again; was a sea capt. and in the fine tract of Suffolk emigrants, by Mr. Hunter, 3 Mass. Hist. Coll. X. 159, he quotes Candler's MS. as saying, that aft. the d. of Charles I. he serv. the States of Holland. He was s. of John of Holkham, Co. Norf'k. EDWARD came in the Mayflower 1620, d. 4 Dec. bef. the sh. reach. Plymouth from Cape Cod. He was a serv. of William White. EDWARD, Newbury, s. of deac. Samuel of Braintree, says Farmer in MS. taught the sch. sev. yrs. bef. and aft. leav. coll. began to preach at Simsbury, June 1687, by w. Sarah had Samuel, b. 1 Sept. 1691, H. C. 1710 (the min. of Gloucester wh. d. 8 Dec. 1724); and Edward, 14 May 1695; was ord. at Marshfield, 14 Oct. 1696, and had William, 26 Apr. 1697, H. C. 1718 (min. at Scarborough, f. of Rev. John of Berwick, H. C. 1765, wh. d. 21 Dec. 1828, aged 88); John, 1699; and Joseph, 1704; beside ds. Sarah; Ann; and Abigail. He d. sudden. 16 Mar. 1705; acc. the ch. rec. in Gen. Reg. VIII. 229, tho. the inscript. on his gr.st. Gen. Reg. IV. 316, reads 10 Mar. and the dilig. Edit. had (Geneal. Reg. VII. 278) correct. Farmer on that author. as if the gr.st. had suffer. less by exposure to the weather, than the rec. of the ch. in a century and a half. GEORGE, Lynn, by w. Sarah, had Sarah, b. 25 Oct. 1659; rem. to Reading, there had John, b. 24 Mar. 1661; and d. 7 Sept. 1674. In his will of 4 Dec. 1669, of wh. he made w. Sarah extrix. he names ch. John, Mary, George, and Sarah; and by the codic. of 1 July 1674, s. Jonathan, all minors. HENRY, Cambridge, but of Boston perhaps short time aft. freem. 1670, m. 27 Apr. 1669, Eliz. d. of John Stedman, wid. of Nathaniel Upham, after being his w. only 15 days, had Eliz. b. 29 Jan. 1670; and Henry, 1673, wh. d. Sept. 1690. He was call. 1669, merch. JAMES, Charlestown, with w. Eliz. adm. of the ch. in the autumn of 1633, freem. 14 May 1634, was, says Frothingham, 82, one of the first selectmen of Woburn. His w. by wh. he had Jonathan, per- haps b. on this side of the ocean, as sure. was Simon, on the other side, d. 8 Nov. 1643; and he m. 15 Feb. foll. Susanna, wid. of Thomas Blodget of Cambridge, had James, b. 24 Jan. 1646, or 7, d. soon; James, again, a. 1649; and perhaps others. His w. d. 10 Feb. 1661; and he d. 1682. JAMES, Woburn, s. of the preced. freem. 1674, m. 27 Jan. 1675, Hannah Walker, had Hannah, b. 31 Dec. foll.; Joshua, 15 Sept. 1677; James, May 1680; Ebenezer, 26 July 1683; and his w. d. 4 Feb. 1686; and by sec. w. Abigail he had Richard, 21 Mar. 1688; Abigail, 30 Dec. 1689; Simon, 19 Oct. 1691; was a lieut. and d. 4 Sept. 1693. JOHN, Watertown 1634, or earlier, freem. 6 May 1635, by w. Margaret had John, bur. at 4 mos. 10 Apr. 1636; and Samuel, wh. d. young, bur. 28 Mar. 1642; but the f. had d. bef. aged 38 yrs. and was bur. 28 Feb. 1639. JOHN, New Haven, first of many of the name there, call. sen. brot. sev. ch. prob. with w. from Eng. here, perhaps, by ano. w. had Rebecca, and Abigail, tw. 26 Jan. 1652; and Sarah, 30 Apr. 1654, was one of the contract sett. in 1639, and d. a. 1656. His wid. m. that yr. Thomas Harrison; but the est. was not sett. for sev. yrs. aft. her d. Of seven ch. entit. to shares, John, Joseph, Hannah, Mary, Rebecca, Abigail, and Sarah, the first, as eldest, hav. double sh. only the three last are ment. in the rec. of b. JOHN, Fairfield, d. 1657, leav. wid. Eliz. with ch. Eliz. aged 13; Mary, 8; John, 6; and Esther 3. His wid. 25 Dec. of that yr. it is said, made contr. of m. with Daniel Finch. JOHN, Concord, may be he wh. came from London, in the Elizabeth and Ann 1635, aged 22, had John, b. 1642. JOHN, Stratford, had very good est. and good num. to div. among, as by his will of 17 July 1678, pro. next mo. we find w. Mirable ment. beside s. John, b. Sept. 1641; and Ambrose, 1 Jan. 1652; ds. Sarah, 1642, wh. m. 10 Dec. 1662, John Hurd; Abigail, 1 May 1646, wh. m. 1670, Jonathan Curtis; Esther, Jan. 1650, wh. m. 22 Mar. 1677, Samuel Galpin, and d. next yr. soon aft. f.; and Mary, the youngest, 20 July 1655, wh. m. Matthew Mitchell, and d. 18 Jan. 1711. JOHN, New Haven, br. of Anthony, m. 25 Feb. 1651, Ellen Harrison, had Mary, b. 24 Apr. 1652; Ann, 22 Sept. 1654; both bapt. (by rec. of ch.) 17 Sept. 1654; Eliz. b. 3 June 1657; Lydia, 13 Mar. 1664, d. young; prob. Sarah, 1667, d. at two yrs. and he d. 14 Dec. 1674. How inconsist. the b. of Ann found from town rec. is with the rec. of bapt. will be observ. by some, wh. may desire to kn. wh. date to reject, and from Mr. White, wh. furnish to Geneal. Reg. IX. that very valu. list of baptisms, I am instruct. that the town rec. is usual. the true one, and the ch. rec. frequent. false, or wonderful. careless rather. Prob. this was kept by Rev. John Davenport, less precise in facts than in doctrine. But the writer of that rec. little consider. to what vexations he would subject those who came in a future age to consult his ambiguous oracle. Often by omiss. as well as commiss. the teacher is blameworthy; and the scrupulous Mr. White was misled to ascribe, p. 362, three ch. to this John Thompson, by w. Ellen, scil. Hannah, Lydia, and Ebenezer, bapt. 1645, 7 and 8, respectiv. not one of wh. was hers, as her m. was some yrs. later than their bapt. These three belong to his br. Anthony, whose w. perhaps was the sis. Thompson ment. in the book by Mr. White mistaken for Ellen. She long liv. a wid. dispos. of three ds. in m. scil. Mary, Nov. 1674, to Samuel Lines; Ann or Hannah, 25 Dec. 1673, to Abraham Bradley; and Eliz. 29 Oct. 1677, to Benjamin Bradlee; and made her will Oct. 1689, giv. her prop. to them. * JOHN, Plymouth 1643, had John, b. 24 Nov. 1649, d. soon; was prob. rep. for Middleborough, 1674 and eight yrs. foll. JOHN, Dorchester, s. of that David the first sett. kn. in Boston harbor, had confirmat. of his right to the isl. giv. by our Gen. Ct. 1648; in Apr. 1650, pledg. to two Bristol merch. the isl. for a large sum, payable in codfish at Marblehead or Isle of Shoals; but the creditors had it in 1658, by appraise. of Robert Sedgwick and Richard Sprague, for less than amo. of the excon. He or ano. John was of Weymouth, the freem. of 1653. JOHN, Fairfield, eldest s. of John of Stratford, was a man of so great consequence, as in 1663, to have the Gen. Ct. of Conn. interpose to attempt adjustm. of his diffic. with the ch. there, is in the freemen's list of 1669. JOHN, Barnstable, had Esther, b. 28 July 1652; Eliz. 28 Jan. 1654; Sarah, 4 Apr. 1657; Lydia, 5 Oct. 1659; Jacob, 24 Apr. 1662; and Thomas, 19 Oct. 1664. JOHN, New Haven, 1659, call. for distinct. the farmer, m. at Branford, perhaps 29 Mar. or 22 May 1666, Priscilla, d. of Thomas Powell, had John, b. 6 Aug. 1667; Priscilla, 7 Aug. 1671; Samuel, 29 Jan. 1674, d. soon; Samuel, again, 1 May 1677; Abigail, 24 Feb. 1680; and Ann, 20 Mar. 1683, wh. prob. d. young; and he d. 13 Feb. 1694. This John is prob. s. of the first John of the same, liv. at East Haven, and made his will the same day he d. nam. four ch. only, the two s. and two ds. Priscilla Chidsy, or Chedsey, w. of Ebenezer, and Abigail, then unm. JOHN, Wethersfield, bef. 1640, rem. in few yrs. JOHN, Farmington, eldest s. of Thomas of the same, propound. for freem. 1670, m. 24 Oct. of that yr. Mary Steele, d. of the sec. John of the same, had John, b. 29 Dec. 1671; Thomas, 30 June 1674, but ano. acco. says, 13 Jan. 1675; Samuel, 29 Dec. 1676; Joseph, 25 Mar. 1679, d. in few wks.; James, 30 May, 1680; Mary, bapt. 1

Oct. 1682, wh. liv. over 100 yrs.; Ebenezer, 23 Nov. or by ano. rept. 21 Dec. 1684; and Nathaniel, 16 Jan. 1687. JOHN, Portsmouth, adm. freem. of Mass. 1672. JOHN, New Haven, the mariner, so call. for distinct. propound. for freem. 1671, and was propr. 1685. Mr. Judd thinks he was not relat. of the other Johns, but had a child, perhaps Mary, in Sept. 1667; Samuel, b. 12 May 1669; and Sarah, 16 Jan. 1672. JOHN, Stratford, s. of John of the same, call. jun. was propound. for freem. 1671, d. 1681, had no w. or ch. and by his will helps us to certainty in the field where doubt was most diffus. the affin. of memb. of so common a name. Thus to his mo. to John, s. of br. Ambrose, to childr. of John Hurd, wh. m. his sis. Sarah, to childr. of Jonathan Curtis and sis. Abigail, to a cousin, ch. of Matthew Mitchell, wh. was, we kn. the first of sev. we find gifts, and the silence as to Esther, would almost serve to show, without the rec. that she was d. JOHN, Reading, by Eaton marked as one of the early sett. JOHN, Rehoboth, m. 19 Sept. 1682, Sarah Smith, but to tell whose d. she was, or whose s. he was, I utterly despair. JOHN, New Haven, mariner, was a propr. 1685, as was also ano. JOHN, of the same call. jun. wh. may have been s. of one of the preced. or of William. JOHN, Salisbury 1690, that yr. m. a Brewer. JONATHAN, Woburn, s. of James of the same, m. 28 Nov. 1655, Susanna, d. of Thomas Blodget, had Susanna, b. 4 July 1661; Jonathan, 28 Sept. 1663; James, 1666, d. soon; James, again, 27 June 1667; Sarah, 1 June 1670; Simon, 15 June 1673; and Ebenezer, 18 Aug. 1676; and d. 20 Oct. 1691. Jonathan his s. was gr.-gr.f. of Sir Benjamin, knight. by Geo. III. the disting. philosoph. better kn. as Count Rumford, with wh. title he was hon. by the k. of Bavaria, wh. was b. at W. 26 Mar. 1753. Farmer had once suppos. that the Count was descend. of Rev. William, to wh. mistake he was led by the first Presdt. Adams; and the correct. is due to the investigat. of Francis Jackson of Boston. JOSEPH, Wallingford, perhaps s. of the first John of New Haven, had m. prob. as sec. w. the wid. of Isaac Royce of the same, and was d. in 1712, when his heirs are ment. * JOSEPH, Billerica, s. of Rev. William, m. 24 July 1662, Mary, d. of Richard Bracket of Braintree, at B. was sch.master, town clk. ens. 1678, and lieut. 1683, selectman, capt. deac. many yrs. and rep. 1692 under the new chart. also 99, 1700, and 1, and d. 13 Oct. 1732. His wid. Mary, a sec. w. d. 9 Oct. 1743, aged 91, Farmer says. MAURICE, Gloucester, a London merch. engag. in trade to Canada, as early as 1631, was much desir. by our governm. to sett. with us, hav. in 1639, begun a fishing trade at Cape Ann, but was only a trans. visit. if he ever came, wh. is improb. Winth. I. 307. MILES, Kittery 1659. ROBERT, Boston, a man of distinct. in London, where he m. I conject. a sis. of Gov. Hopkins of Conn. by wh. col. he was much confid. in, was a

trans. resid. here 1639, bought the old ch. edifice and ground on wh. it
stood in State Str. for £160 in 1639. See note in Winth. I. 318. Yet
he was satisf. I fear, with the outward benefit, for he did not join the
worship. assemb. But he was a powerful friend of Mass. and for serv.
our Ct. made gr. to him of 500 acres. In Hutch. Coll. some letters from
him show good disposition and judgment. SAMUEL, Braintree, s. of
Rev. William, b. in Eng. m. 25 Apr. 1656, Sarah, d. of Edward Shepard,
had Sarah, b. 27 Apr. 1657, d. soon; Deborah, 25 Mar. 1660; Samuel,
6 Nov. 1662; Edward, 20 Apr. 1665, H. C. 1684; Abigail, 10 Nov.
1667; Sarah, again, 28 Apr. 1670, d. young; Hannah, 5 Aug. 1672;
William, bapt. 11 Apr. 1675, d. soon; William, again, 3 June 1676;
and Sarah, b. 1 Jan. 1679; deac. 1679 tho. not found in the list of
freem. was rep. 1676–86 exc. 81 and 2, and again 1691. His w. d. 15
Jan. 1680, aged 43, and in 1680. he had sec. w. Eliz. Billings, perhaps
d. of Roger of Dorchester, wh. d. 5 Nov. 1706, aged 69; and he d. 18
June 1695. SAMUEL, New Haven, m. 14 Nov. 1695, Rebecca, youngest
d. of Hon. James Bishop. SIMON, Ipswich 1636, b. a. 1610, had Mercy,
wh. m. 26 Jan. 1653, Isaiah Wood; and Sarah, wh. m. 16 May 1655,
Abraham Fitts; and he took sec. w. 21 Aug. 1656, Rachel Glover, was
freem. 2 June 1641, and d. 1676. His will, 25 Mar. of that yr. provid.
for wid. names no s. and seven of W's. ch. made Wood and Fitts, excors. SIMON, Woburn, eldest s. of James the first, m. 19 Dec. 1643,
Mary, d. of Edward Converse, had John, b. 4 Apr. 1645, d. week foll.;
Sarah, 20 Feb. 1647; James, 29 Mar. 1649; a d. 25 Jan. 1652, whose
name, not then giv. we find to be Mary, when she d. 2 Feb. 1662; Ann,
30 July 1655; Rebecca, May 1658; was freem. 1648, and bec. a purch.
of Chelmsford, but d. in early manhood, making his will 15 May 1658,
in wh. he provides for the s. and three ds. names his f. and w. and her f.
and her two brs. Josiah and James. THOMAS, Farmington, may be that
youth of 18 yrs. wh. emb. in the Abigail at London, 1 July 1635, m. 14
Apr. 1646, at Hartford, Ann, d. of Gov. Thomas Welles, had there,
Beatrice, bapt. 17 Jan. 1647; John, b. 1649; Thomas, 1651; Mary, 7
June 1653; and Esther, posthum. bapt. 17 June 1655; the last four b. at
F. where he d. 25 Apr. of that yr. His wid. m. Anthony Hawkins; and
Beatrice m. a Parker; Mary m. a Hawley; and Esther m. Samuel Gridley. THOMAS, Easthampton L. I. 1650. THOMAS, Farmington, s. of
Thomas of the same, was adm. freem. 1677, m. Eliz. d. of William, as Por-
ter thinks, but in my opin. of Arthur Smith, the first, had Eliz.; Thomas,
b. 25 Mar. 1679; Arthur, 17 Oct. 1680; Philoleutheros, bapt. 12 Nov.
1682; John, 14 Dec. 1684; Margaret, 20 Feb. 1687; Ann, 10 Feb.
1689; Samuel, 18 Oct. 1691; and Daniel. But he had by a sec. w.
Abigail (wh. murder. him); and ano. ch. strange. nam. Mercy, b. 15

Oct. 1706, by his wid. in prison. On 14 Dec. 1705, the w. threw a pair
of shears at her h. of wh. the point penetrat. the brain, caus. his d. in
few days. She was convict. but after one or two reprieves, the sentence
was execut. His est. was div. in 1708 to only five liv. ch. Thomas,
Samuel, Ann, Daniel, and Mary, beside two ch. of d. Eliz. Woodruff,
dec. prob. w. of a s. of sec. Matthew W. *WILLIAM*, Braintree, had been
matric. at Brazen Nose Coll. Oxford, 28 Jan. 1620, at the age of 21,
but his degree is not found in the Fasti ; had been a preach. in Win-
wick, a parish of his native Lancash. bef. he came to our side of the sea,
in 1637, and was engag. first at Kittery or York, but after the ch. instit.
at B. 17 Sept. 1639, was ord. in co. with Rev. Henry Flint 19 Nov. of
that yr. if Winth. I. 324 be foll. tho. Hancock in his Centenn. prefers
24 Sept. Dr. Lunt, ano. success. in the same pulpit, in his fine celebr.
of the sec. Centenn. decides for Nov. He brought w. Abigail and s.
Samuel, William, H. C. 1653, perhaps d. Mary, and Elinor, wh. was b.
1626 ; was freem. 13 May 1640 ; had here, Joseph, b. 1 May 1640 ;
Benjamin, 14 July 1642, H. C. 1662 ; and his w. d. 1 Jan. 1643, while
he was abs. on a mission with Rev. John Knowles, and Thomas James,
to Virg. begun in Oct. preced. Our governm. had in 1640 gr. him 120
acres. By sec. w. Ann, wid. of Simon Crosby of Cambridge he had
Ann, b. 3 Mar. or 1 May, as the numeral for the day and month may
respective. be read, in 1648. He was made freem. 1656, but "fell into
the Devil's bath," as the Magn. III. cap. XVII. calls his state of melan-
cho. and gave up his pub. min. seven yrs. and d. 10 Dec. 1666 in 68th
yr. The wid. d. 11 Oct. 1675, aged 68. Mary m. 3 Dec. 1641, Joseph
Wise of Roxbury ; and Elinor m. 1644, William Veazey, and next John
French, and d. 23 Apr. 1711. Of this fam. it is obs. that they always
discard the sec. letter of the name, tho. Mather, whose biog. is exceed.
meagre, prints it as here. WILLIAM, New Haven 1647, br. of Anthony,
had perhaps accomp. Gov. Eaton, had neither w. nor ch. but d. 24 Apr.
1683, and to his will of 6 Oct. preced. we owe very much of our kn. of
ws. and ch. of others. He gave prop. to John, s. of his br. Anthony ; to
John and William, s. of his br. John ; to Bridget Bowers, Ann Staunton,
and Lydia Cruttenden, ds. of br. Anthony ; and to ds. of br. John, viz.
Mary Lines, Ann Bradley and her h. Abraham, and Eliz. Bradley and
her h. Benjamin. WILLIAM, New London, s. prob. of Rev. William of
Braintree, b. in Eng. after his degree at Harv. was a preach. at Springfield 1654–6, and m. 19 Nov. 1655, Catharine, d. of the first Richard
Treat of Wethersfield, was employ. in 1658, by the Commissnrs. of the
Unit. Col. acting for the London Soc. Prop. Gospel, and some yrs. succeed. as missiona. to the Pequot Ind. freem. 1660 ; but in 1664, he gave
his w. all his prop. by deed " suppos. mys. near d. and a. to take a voy-

age to Virg." From there he wrote to his w's br. James, 29 June 1665, and this is the last that is kn. of him, tho. in the Coll. catal. the yr. of his d. has never been giv. so that, from the blank in Mather, Farmer suppos. him liv. in 1698, when prob. he had left the world 30 yrs. bef. Yet a suspicion reasonab. arises, from the Conn. Col. Rec. I. 432, direct. the constable to secure prop. to amount of a certain debt, that his object was to escape creditors, rather than to preach the gospel. WILLIAM, Dover 1656, rem. to Kittery, there a. 1676 d. leav. ch. John, aged 18; William, 16; Robert, 14; James, wh. was cripple, 11; Alexander, 6; and Judith, 2; and the sec. and third were then apprent. at Dover. WILLIAM, Dover, s. of the preced. m. at Portsmouth 4 Sept 1682, Mary Lovering, wh. may have been d. of John of Dover. WILLIAM, Stonington, blacksmith, d. 1705, leav. wid. Bridget. By the rec. of our Gen. Ct. he seems, in his youth to have been fined for propos. m. with Sarah Coggan, without leave of her friends at Stonington, in 1653. See Vols. III. and IV. WILLIAM, Lyme, s. of the preced. prob. m. 19 July 1678, Philadelphia Tileston, had Rachel, Joanna, wh. d. soon, and Philadelphia; but no more is kn. Fifteen at Yale, and fourteen at Harv. of this name, including those wh. reject the *h*, had been gr. 1853, and many at other N. E. coll.

THORNCOMB, ANDREW, Boston, a bookseller in 1685, from London, as Thomas, in Hist. Print. II. 414, ment. We can have no hesitat. in presum. that he went back discourag.

THORNDIKE, John, Beverly, perhaps s. of Rev. George, rector of Little Carleton, near Lowth, Co. Lincoln, bapt. 23 July 1603, came to Boston as early as 1632, if not in the fleet with Winth. for he was one of the twelve allow. by the governm. 1 Apr. 1633 to go to plant Ipswich, with the eldest s. of the Gov. We are ign. who was his w. but think her name was Eliz. and kn. that he had six ds. Sarah, Eliz. Ann, Mary, Alice, and Martha, only s. Paul. In 1668, he went to Eng. and made his will there, 29 July of that yr. in contemplat. of his ret. and by·that instr. it is found, that d. Ann was insane, Alice and Martha in Eng. with him. Yet he d. bef. come back, a 1670. Sarah m. 10 Dec. 1661, John Low of Ipswich; and Eliz. m. Dec. 1662, that John Proctor of Salem, wh. was hanged 19 Aug. 1692 for witcher. but happi. she d. bef. the fanaticism began. * PAUL, Beverly, only s. of the preced. m. 28 Apr. 1668, Mary or Margaret, d. of James Patch, had Mary, b. 8 Jan. 1669; Eliz. 14 Oct. 1670; Hannah, 14 May 1673; John, 22 Jan. 1675; Paul, 17 Apr. 1677; Herbert; and Martha; was lieut. 1677, freem. 1680, and rep. 1681. Prob. all the eleven gr. at H. C. are his descend.

THORNDON, JOHN, Newport, one of the founders, 1644, of the bapt. ch. there, says Callender, 63. It may well be thot. that the *d* was design. by the writer for *t*.

THORNE, THOMAS, Roxbury, is the false name in town rec. giv. to WILLIAM, of Boston, a laborer, liv. at Muddy riv. whose w. was of the ch. at B. The keeper of that rec. enhances his wrong, by mutilat. the name of the ch. bapt. 23 Mar. 1645, Desiretruth, from wh. he withdraws the last syl. but I am happy to assure the admirers of a good name, that the evidence of the Roxbury ch. volume vindicates the *whole* truth. He was prob. liv. at Lynn, when freem. 2 May 1638, and Lewis makes him rem. to L. I. 1642. If so, ano. WILLIAM wh. is the same that in the town rec. of R. is call. Thomas, whose love of truth was so happi. exemplif. in the name bestowed on his first ch. at Roxbury under his true prefix of William, had Hannah, bapt. 9 May 1646; on 17 Apr. of the next yr. was adm. of the Boston ch. and had Israel, bapt. 14 July 1650. So he might well snap his fingers in contempt of the town clk. of R. especial. after John Acres of B. had m. his eldest d. wh. join. the ch. at R. 8 July 1666, and on the next Sunday triumph. brot. to bapt. her ds. Eliz. and Desiretruth by the Acres. WILLIAM, New London, was from Co. Dorset, m. 1676, Lydia, d. of James Redfield, wid. of Thomas Bailey.

THORNELL, THOMAS, Boston, call. capt. d. 11 Mar. 1660; and I supp. was only trans. resid.

THORNICOAST, THOMAS, Warwick, in the list of freem. there in 1655.

THORNTON, EBENEZER, Boston, s. of Timothy of the same, m. 15 May 1721, Eliz. d. of capt. Thomas Gilbert, had Eliz. b. 4, bapt. 10 Mar. 1722; Experience, 6, bapt. 7 Feb. 1725; Timothy, 2, bapt. 5 Feb. 1727, whose s. Thomas Gilbert T. of Saco was sole perpetua. of this fam. in the male line; Lydia, bapt. 8 Sept. 1728, d. soon; Ebenezer, 27 Oct. bapt. 2 Nov. 1729; Gilbert, 23, bapt. 28 May 1732; and Lydia, again, bapt. 19 Mar. 1738; all at Mather's ch. He rem. to Watertown 1731, there his w. d. 10 June 1740; and he m. Mary, wid. of Matthias Coussens, d. perhaps of Richard Boylston, and d. 12 June 1750. JOHN, Newport 1651, in the list of freem. 1655. PETER, Boston, came in the Elizabeth 1635, aged 20, by w. Mary had Joseph, b. 5 Apr. 1647; and one or two more. His wid. brot. inv. 9 Feb. 1652, and evid. of a nuncup. will, by wh. all his prop. was giv. to her, to bring up the childr. See Geneal. Reg. VIII. 57. ROBERT, wh. came in the Elizabeth 1635, from London, at the age of 11 yrs. was of Taunton, a carpenter; sold his est. there to the lady patroness Eliz. Poole, and rem. to Boston, m. 13 Nov. 1657, Mary, wid. of Walter Merry, but went back to Taunton, there liv. 1677, and 8. THEOPHILUS, Yarmouth, s. of Rev. Thomas, b. in Eng. was of Malden 1674, where he took o. of fidel. was the yr. preced. assoc. with a party of pioneers for sett. at Worcester, but no

more is heard of him. *THOMAS, Dorchester, freem. 3 Sept. 1634, Dr.
Harris thot. came in 1630, but no ment. of him is found bef. 1634, and
in very few yrs. he is heard of at Windsor, there was in good esteem,
and had five ch. but only Samuel is found by rec. to be b. there, and
that was 13 July 1645; and in 1647 alone, three ds. Thomas, Priscilla,
and Ann. He was a tanner, or at least sold a tanyard to Elder John
Strong. THOMAS, Stratford, of wh. very little is kn. exc. that he had
Theophilus, b. there, 10 June 1651; and aft. 1653 no more is heard of
him at Stratford, but he was rep. 1651. THOMAS, Hartford, a tanner,
perhaps s. of Thomas of Windsor, had liv. at Milford, there m. 1674,
Hannah d. of Nathaniel Farrand, had only ch. Samuel, wh. with w.
Hannah are nam. in his will made 1694, tho. he liv. to 22 Sept. 1703.
THOMAS, Yarmouth, came soon aft. the Bartholomew act of 1662, bring.
w. and ch. not prob. all he ever had, but the name of his w. is not ment.
Nor do I find the Univ. at wh. he was bred, or the liv. from wh. he was
eject. At Y. he was as early as 18 June 1663, and in 1677 rem. to Boston,
join. with Mather's ch. and d. 13 Feb. 1700, aged over 90 yrs. Sewall
calls him very near. 93. He was perhaps something advanc. towards
sec. childhood, when call. by Cotton Mather, Jan. 1694, to testify how
Margaret Rule was raised from her bed by an invisible force, to touch
the garret floor, "lifted up from all that was under her," as may be read
on p. 23 of the London ed. 1700 of "More Wonders of the Invisible
World" by Robert Calef of Boston. Of his ch. we guess at the success.
for the date of b. is unkn. and foll. Dr. Bond count. these seven: Ann, wh.
m. Nathaniel Hall of Yarmouth; Mary, m. Judah Thacher, and d. 30
Nov. 1708, aged 68; Eliz. m. Joshua Gee, of Boston, and next Rev.
Peter Thacher of Milton; Thomas; Theophilus; Priscilla, wh. d. at 11
yrs. whether at B. or at Y. is not indic. by Mather, wh. (tho. he tells of
the f. that he was "aged and faithful" adds not ano. syl. but) favors the
youthful maid near the end of his book VI. with more than a half of one
of his large fol. pages; and Timothy b. 1647. THOMAS, Watertown,
adm. into the ch. 19 Aug. 1688, is by Bond, reput. s. perhaps of the
preced. and one of the undertak. 1673, for sett. of Worcester. I find
him at Malden in 1674, taking o. of fidel. and apparent. younger than
Theophilus; yet no more can we gather. *TIMOTHY, Boston, merch. s.
of Rev. Thomas, b. in Eng. and Bond strange. thot. he may have been
eldest, tho. his earliest impress. was that he was youngest, freem. 1672,
by w. Experience, perhaps sis. of the first John Brooking, wh. d. 23 Mar.
1694, had Mary, b. 2 Apr. 1674; Thomas d. young; Eliz. 16 Nov.
1677; Timothy, 6 May 1681; Catharine, 16 Apr. 1683; Experience,
23 Feb. 1687; and Ebenezer, bapt. 12 Jan. 1690. He was rep. 1693,
4, and 5; had ano. w. Sarah, wh. d. 3 Dec. 1725, and he d. 19 Sept.

1726. Eliz. was in 1735, w. of Thomas Wade of Ipswich; Catharine m. 4 Oct. 1700, John Cannon; and next, 23 Nov. 1705, Samuel Edwards, wh. d. 17 June 1710; and for third h. 6 Dec. 1716, Isaac Russell; and Experience m. 24 Sept. 1713, Ebenezer Wakefield, and next m. a Coolidge. When one of the reps. for Boston, he was of the Comtee. charged with the service of issuing the first paper currency aft. the disastr. expedit. of Phips against Quebec. TIMOTHY, Boston, prob. not s. of the preced. m. 1716, Eliz. Danforth of Billerica, perhaps d. of the sec. Jonathan of the same, had Timothy, b. 5, bapt. 7 Apr. 1717; Danforth, 25 Feb. bapt. 1 Mar. 1719; Samuel, 25, bapt. 26 Mar. 1721, d. soon; Eliz. 1 Oct. 1722, bapt. 10 Mar. foll.; Samuel, again, 6 Dec. 1724, d. young; Hannah, 7 Nov. 1726; Thomas, 13 June 1729; Samuel, again, 25 Oct. 1731; and Mary, 2 Sept. 1736. But of the last 5 or 6, I feel less confidence, inasmuch as the rec. of bapt. in Mather's ch. does not concur with this acco. of the bs. WALTER, came in the Susan and Ellen 1635, aged 36; but no more is kn. of him, unless we suppose the next name on the custom-ho. list at London, Joanna Thornton, aged 44, to be relat.

THORPE, HENRY, Watertown, 1642, freem. 1646, d. 21 May 1672. He had a d. m. to Benjamin Bullard, wh. claim. the est. JAMES, Dedham, had James, bapt. 27 July 1652; and Hannah, 24 Sept. 1665, was freem. 1690. JOHN, Duxbury 1633, a carpenter, to wh. Winsor gives w. Alice, d. in Nov. that yr. JOHN, Scarborough, undertook to preach 1661, without good qualificat. and was silenc. by our Gen. Ct. NATHANIEL, New Haven, propound. for freem. 1669, is prob. the same as Tharpe. See that. ROBERT, York, 1660, was perhaps, in 1638, the man wh. in Dec. of that yr. our Gen. Ct. advised not to overload a boat. SAMUEL, New Haven, propound. for freem. 1670, was perhaps s. of William, and br. of Nathaniel, had Eliz. wh. bec. third w. of Abraham Doolittle. THOMAS, Ipswich, m. at Boston, 27 May 1656, Rebecca, d. of Thomas Milward of Gloucester, and he d. a. 1677. WILLIAM, New Haven. See Tharpe.

THRALL, TIMOTHY, Windsor, only s. of William of the same, m. 5 or 10 Nov. 1659, Deborah, d. of Thomas Gunn of the same, had Deborah, b. 9 Aug. 1660; Timothy, 7 Dec. 1662; Mehitable, Mar. 1665; Eliz. 1 May 1667; John, 8 June 1669, d. soon; John, again, 5 June 1671; Martha, 31 May 1673; Thomas, 5 May 1675, d. at 3 mos.; Thomas, again, 10 July 1676; Samuel, and Abigail 1681; and his w. d. 7 Jan. 1695. He d. June 1697, leav. good est. WILLIAM, Windsor, among the first sett. yet it does not seem certain that he was ever of Dorchester, but he serv. in the Pequot war, had only two ch. b. at W. Timothy, July 1641; and Philippa, prob. earlier, for she m. 5 Nov. 1657, John Hosford. "Old goody Thrall d. 30 July 1676," says the rec.

and he was a. 72 yrs old when he made his will, Dec. 1678, and d. 3 Aug. foll.

THRASHER, or THRESHER, ARTHUR, Newbury, m. 21 Apr. 1684, Mary Goodridge, perhaps d. of Jeremiah, had Dorothy, b. 4 Feb. 1692. CHRISTOPHER, Taunton 1643, had Israel, b. 15 Sept. 1648; and perhaps Hannah, wh. m. 29 Dec. 1672, Stephen Thrasher; and Sarah, wh. m. 15 Jan. 1679, Benjamin Leonard; and others. FRANCIS, Milford 1686, a clothier, sold his ho. and ld. in 1690, and rem. ISRAEL, Taunton, s. of Christopher, m. 15 Aug. 1676, Mary, d. of Thomas Caswell of the same, had Mary, b. 7 Aug. foll. SAMUEL, Taunton, perhaps br. of the preced. m. 4 Dec. perhaps 1683, Bethia Brooks of Rehoboth.

THREENEEDLES, BARTHOLOMEW, Boston, m. Damaris, d. of James Hawkins, had Eliz. b. 16 June 1660; Benjamin, 5 June 1666; Damaris, 26 Oct. 1670; James, 17 Apr. 1673; Ruth, 27 Feb. 1678; Sarah, 9 Nov. 1679; and Susanna, 8 Aug. 1688; as the copy of lost rec. in the City Clk's. office shows; but there may have been others, for my confidence is something abated by his giv. the name as Thredneedle. His will of 2 Apr. 1700, pro. 7 Apr 1702, of wh. w. Damaris was extrix. makes it prob. that the two eldest were not liv. but the other s. and four ds. Damaris Broffe, Mary Millings, Ruth, and Susanna being nam. render it certain that ano. d. was b. to him, and the testator's regard reach. to gr. ds. Eliz. Broffe, Mary Millings, and gr.s. Thomas M.

THROCKMORTON, or THROGMORTON, GEORGE, rather JOHN, came with famous Roger Williams, in the Lion, emb. Dec. 1 1630, at London, and arr. 5 Feb. foll. at Nantascut, adm. freem. 18 May of the same yr. He prob. brot. w. and was, in my judgm. properly nam. JOHN. Geo. is easily read thus from Jo. the common abbrev. At least one with this surname seems eno. for nothing more is ever heard of the freem. George, tho. on adm. he has the prefix of resp. JOHN, sen. at Providence owned alleg. 31 May 1666 to Charles II. and, it is said, rem. to Monmouth, N. J. there d. bef. 1687. His d. Patience m. Dec. 1655, John Coggeshall, the sec. and d. 7 Sept. 1676. Both he and his w. were excomm. by the ch. at Salem, under rule of Hugh Peter, at the same time, and for the same offences as Williams, his w. and other friends. They went to R. I. and were in good repute, he contin. on freemen's list, 1655, at Providence. JOHN, Providence, call. jun. when in June 1668, he engag. alleg.

THROOP, * WILLIAM, Bristol, was rep. 1691, then had five ch. beside s.-in-law.

THROPP, JOHN, is the name of a serg. in the comp. of capt. William Turner, on serv. 1676.

THROW, DAVID, Springfield, took o. of alleg. 31 Dec. 1678 or the next day.

THURBER, JAMES, Rehoboth 1690. He was b. in Eng. 1660, and perhaps came over bef. m. or at least with not more than one of the ch. here nam. Eliz. prob. d. soon, or young; James, b. 1685, wh. d. at 26 yrs.; John, 31 Oct. 1687, d. at 22 yrs.; Rachel; Eliz. again, 31 Dec. 1691, d. at 27 yrs.; Bethia; Jonathan; Priscilla; Samuel, 26 Aug. 1700; and Edward. JOHN, Swanzey 1669, by w. Mary had Mary, 10 July 1674; Thomas, 24 Nov. 1676; Eliz. 24 Aug. 1678; Rachel, 5 Mar. 1683. Baylies II. 241. SAMUEL, Rehoboth, s. of James of the same, m. Rachel Wheeler, had Samuel, b. 27 Oct. 1724; James, 28 June 1726; John, 26 Aug. 1730; Mary, 15 Sept. 1732, d. at 3 yrs.; Bryan, 14 July 1734; Mary, again, 25 June 1736; Daniel, 30 June 1739; and Hezekiah, 11 Aug. 1741. He liv. until 20 Dec. 1785, and had sec. w. Welthean Tourtellot, perhaps wid. of one of the Huguenot offspring. THOMAS, Swanzey, by w. Ruth, had Ruth, b. 16 July 1682; Abigail, 31 Oct. 1683.

THURLO, THURLA, THURRELL, or THORLEY, FRANCIS, Newbury, eldest s. of Richard, b. in Eng. a. 1630, m. 5 Feb. 1655, Ann Morse, perhaps d. of Anthony, had Eliz. b. 3 June 1656; Mary, 14 May 1658, d. next yr.; John, 25 Mar. 1660; Jonathan, 14 Mar. 1662; s. and d. tw. 20 July 1664, both prob. d. very soon; Richard, 25 Nov. 1665; Thomas and Francis, tw. 20 Apr. 1669. He came prob. with his f. was freem. 1670, and d. 26 Nov. 1703. GEORGE, Newbury, eldest ch. of Thomas, by w. Mary had Judith, b. 6 Sept. 1696; and Mary, 11 Apr. 1699. JOHN, Newbury, s. of Francis, m. 2 Mar. 1685, Sarah Howe, had Mary, b. 10 Feb. 1687; Sarah, 3 Oct. 1689; Ann, 29 Feb. 1692, d. young; Lydia, 20 Aug. 1695; Bethia, 3 Mar. 1698; and Hannah, 9 Sept. 1701. JONATHAN, Newbury, br. of the preced. m. 22 Dec. 1685, Mary, d. prob. of Abraham Merrill, had Eliz. b. 20 Nov. 1686; Abraham, 20 Oct. 1688; Francis, 20 Apr. 1692; Richard, 20 June 1694; Abigail, 10 Feb. 1696; Mary, 1 July 1698; Jonathan, 29 Aug. 1699; Prudence, 4 Sept. 1701; and John, 4 Mar. 1703. He d. 22 Sept. foll. and his wid. d. 19 days aft. RICHARD, Rowley 1643, among early sett. but it is not kn. if he were with the first, nor whether he came, as most of the others, from Yorksh. nor whether he brot. w. or other ch. than Francis, b. 1630; and Thomas, 1632; but his w. Jane, wh. d. 19 Mar. 1684, may have accomp. him. In 1651 he rem. to Newbury; in 1653 he had a gr. of ld. by the Col. and next yr. a toll for his bridge built over Newbury (i. e. Parker) riv. and d. 10 Nov. 1685. THOMAS Newbury, younger s. of the preced. m. 1670, Judith, d. prob. of Hugh March, had George, b. 12 Mar. 1671; Simon, 20 Feb. 1673, d. at 17 yrs. a d. 13 Dec. 1675, wh. perhaps d. soon; Judith, 29 July 1677, d. soon; Judith, again, 12 Nov. 1679, prob. d. young; Mary, 1 May 1682; and

Judith, again, 14 Apr. 1685. His w. d. 11 July 1689; and he d. 23 June 1713. He was, says the Diary of Sewall, one of two troopers impress. on the first outbreak of Philip's war late in June 1675.

THURSTON, or THIRSTON, BENJAMIN, Boston, weaver, perhaps s. of the first John, m. 12 Dec. 1660, Eliz. d. of Robert Walker, had Mary, and Eleazer, tw. b. 24 Apr. 1662; was freem. 1665, one of the founders of the 3d or O. S. ch. ar. co. 1675, in wh. yr. bef. Philip's war, the Gen. Ct. made him ens. and he d. 10 Nov. 1678, of smallpox, says his spec. frd. Ch. Just. Sewall. CHARLES, Plymouth 1643. DANIEL, Newbury, an early sett. hav. gr. of ld. Nov. 1638, whose first w. d. 25 May 1648, and he m. 29 Aug. foll. Ann Lightfoot, perhaps wid. of Francis of Lynn, d. 16 Feb. 1666, without ch. giv. his est. to Daniel T. a kinsman, wh. bef. was call. Daniel jr. DANIEL, Newbury, may have been short time at Ipswich in 1675, was perhaps the legatee of the preced. and may have come with him from Eng. m. 20 Oct. 1655, Ann Pell, perhaps d. of Joseph of Lynn, had Daniel, b. 2 July 1659, unless the yr. be too late by two, d. at 4 mos.; Hannah, 20 Jan. 1659, says Coffin; Daniel, again, 18 Jan. 1661; Sarah, 8 Jan. 1664; Stephen, 25 Oct. 1665; Joseph, 14 Sept. 1667; Ann, 6 Sept. 1669; James, 24 Sept. 1670; Stephen, again, 25 Oct. 1672, d. soon; Stephen, again, 5 Sept. 1674; and Abigail, 17 Mar. 1678; and he d. 19 Feb. 1693. DANIEL, Medfield, freem. 1678, may have been s. of John the first of Dedham. DANIEL, Rehoboth, m. 16 Dec. 1681, Hannah Miller, had Sarah, b. 2 Jan. 1683, posthum. tho. we kn. not the exact time of his d. DANIEL, Newbury, s. of the sec. Daniel, by w. Mary had Daniel, b. 26 June 1690; John, 12 June 1692; Mary, 7 Jan. 1694; Benjamin, 4 May 1695; Hannah, 26 Jan. 1698; Martha, 27 Nov. 1699; and Jonathan, 16 Mar. 1701. His will was pro. 27 Feb. 1637. * EDWARD, Newport, m. June 1647, Eliz. d. of the first Adam Mott, had Sarah, b. 10 Mar. 1648; Eliz. Feb. 1650; Edward, 1 Apr. 1652; Ellen, Apr. 1655; Mary, Feb. 1657; Jonathan, 4 Jan. 1659; Daniel, Apr. 1661; Rebecca, Apr. 1662; John, Dec. 1664; Content, June 1667; Thomas, 8 Oct. 1671. Perhaps his d. Rebecca bec. sec. w. of Weston Clark. He is on the list of freem. 1655, was rep. of Providence 1663, but ret. to N. His d. Elinor m. 1674, George Havens of Portsmouth, R. I. JAMES, Newbury, s. of Daniel the sec. by w. Mary, had Hannah, b. 15 Nov. 1694, d. at 7 yrs.; Dorcas, 20 Oct. 1696; Abner, 28 Feb. 1699; and Phebe, 20 June 1702. JOHN, Salem 1638, had gr. of ld. 1640, possib. but not prob. the same as JOHN, Dedham, wh. was of Wrentham in Co. Suffk. a carpenter, came in the Mary Ann of Yarmouth, 1637, aged, says my transcript of a rec. in Westminster Hall, 30, wh. should be 36, for by the parish reg. of Wrentham I find he was bapt. 13 Jan. 1601, and that would better agree with the age of

his w. Margaret, 32, wh. he brot. with two ch. Thomas, wh. was bapt. 4
Aug. 1633; and John, bapt. 13 Sept. 1635 in Eng.; had here Joseph;
Benjamin, b. 8 July 1640, bapt. with Joseph, 13 Sept. foll.; Mary, b.
8 Mar. 1643; and Judith, 29 May 1648. He was freem. 10 May 1643;
and his est. was part in Medfield, set off from D. 1651. His w. d. 9
May 1662. * JOHN, Medfield, s. prob. of the preced. brot. from Eng.
by his f. 1637, was freem. 1663, and rep. 1683, of wh. we should gladly
kn. more, than that he m. Mary, d. of Nicholas Wood. JOHN, Newport,
was on the list of freem. 1655. JOSEPH, Newbury, s. of Daniel the sec.
m. 1695, Mehitable Kimball. RICHARD, Salem 1637, rem. to Boston,
was a mariner, by w. Martha, d. of Christopher Stanley, as we may
infer from the will of Susanna Phillips, wh. had been w. of S. had Samuel, b. 11 July 1652, and perhaps others. We may obs. the want of
precise use of words, when T. in convey. of part of ship to William
Phillips, Sept. 1650, calls him f.-in-law, only bec. he (Phillips) had m.
the wid. mo. of vendor's w. * THOMAS, prob. s. of the first John, bapt.
in Eng. was of Medfield, m. 13 Dec. 1655, Sarah Thaxter, d. prob. of
Thomas of Hingham, had John, b. 4 Mar. 1657; Thomas, 11 Feb. 1659;
Nathaniel, 24 Jan. 1661; and others, whose names are not kn. He was
a man of much usefuln. serg. in 1675, bef. the war, made lieut. in 1678,
and rep. 1686, in the last Ct. bef. the abolit. of the good old Chart.
Farmer, MS. thinks he must have been the person, wh. had in Apr. of
that yr. some votes for Assist. as in Hutch. Coll. 544. THOMAS, a
quaker, aged 34, wh. came from London in the Speedwell, 1656, and
was sent away in the same sh. THOMAS, Hampton, sw. alleg. 1678,
and mark. by Dr. Belkn. 1681, as hav. been b. 1649, wh. was slight
ground for fear that he might be the Quaker, wh. emb. 30 May 1656,
aged 34, at London, in the Speedwell, and arr. at Boston, 27 July. But
this passeng. was prob. ret. by the same vessel; and Belkn. and Farmer,
and Geneal. Reg. VII. 203, 4, all spell without s the name of this Hampton man, wh. authority united does not prevail with me. He was Provost marshall in 1684, employ. by the Ct. THOMAS, Wrentham, perhaps
s. of the first Thomas, by w. Mehitable, had Mehitable, b. 1 Aug. 1686;
Mary, 16 Mar. 1688, d. soon; Thomas, 2 Nov. 1689; Ichabod, 9 Aug.
1692, d. soon; as his mo. had 2 days aft. bring. him into the world; and
by w. Esther had David, 20 Nov. 1693; and Daniel, 25 Sept. 1695,
perhaps more; and d. 15 Dec. 1704. Five of this name at Harv. and
two at Yale had been gr. in 1851.

THURTON. See Thurston.

THWAITS, ALEXANDER, Concord, came in the Hopewell from London, 1635, aged 20, perhaps d. or rem. early, or the giv. of his corn to
Rev. P. Bulkley, by our Gen. Ct. in May 1640, is dark. At the East
he may be seen sw. alleg. to Charles II. 8 Sept. 1665.

THWING, BENJAMIN, Boston, came as one of the serv. or apprent. of Ralph Hudson, in the Susan and Ellen, 1635, aged 16, by w. Deborah, wh. join. our ch. 9 Oct. 1642, had Deborah, b. 17 May and d. 23 Aug. bef.; John, 21 Nov. bapt. 1 Dec. 1644, the f. hav. join. the ch. Feb. preced. had also Edward, b. 14 Nov. 1652; Deborah, again, 13 Jan. 1660; and Benjamin, earlier, no doubt, than the last two; was freem. 1645. Farmer thot. he was a propr. at Concord. His master, by will, 1638, left him £10, when his time should be out, and his master's wid. left him ano. sum in 1651. BENJAMIN, Boston, s. of the preced. carpenter, by w. Abigail, had Benjamin, b. 24 July 1670, d. young; Lydia, 25 Jan. 1673, d. young; Benjamin, again, 20 July 1678; and Lydia, again, 20 July 1679; was freem. 1680. EDWARD, Boston, s. of the first Benjamin, freem. 1675, by w. Eliz. had Robert, b. 9 Jan. 1680; Eliz. 7 Feb. 1681, d. soon; Eliz. again, 19 Feb. 1685; Benjamin, 14 Apr. 1686; and John, 29 July 1688. JOHN, Boston, eldest br. of the preced. by w. Mary had Deborah, b. 29 Mar. 1673; Hannah, 4 Mar. 1675; Mary, 12 Apr. 1677; Rachel, 31 Jan. 1681; Sarah, 22 Feb. 1686; and Benjamin, 6 June 1688. He d. 6 Sept. 1690, when the gr.st. makes the age 47 yrs. 9 mos. and 13 days, so exactly wrong almost two yrs. Lucki. all regard to the truth of the inscript. is tak. away by the preposter. fals. caus. by change of the Arabic 9 to 2. WILLIAM, Boston, by w. Mary had Mary, b. 7 Apr. 1686; William, 8 July 1690; and John, 18 June 1692.

TIBBALS, JOHN, Milford, s. of Thomas of the same, was propound. for freem. 1671, liv. in Derby 1679–1703, had w. and childr. but names are unkn. JOSIAH, Milford, br. of the preced. propound. for freem. 1669, m. 13 July 1670, Mary Sherwood, prob. d. of Thomas. THOMAS, Milford 1646, was perhaps one of the first sett. 1639, had emb. in the Truelove 1635, the last sh. in that yr. from London, aged 20, and was, no doubt, soon aft. in some pt. of the riv. towns of Conn. happy eno. for serv. in the Pequot war 1637, and was among the freem. of 1669. In 1671 when he was serg. had a gr. of 50 acres for the serv. By w. Mary, wh. d. June 1644, had Mary, bapt. Feb. 1644, perhaps a yr. old; Samuel, 14 Apr. 1644; and both prob. d. young. By a sec. w. of wh. the name is unkn. he had John, bapt. late in 1645; Thomas, Mar. 1651; Mary, and Sarah, b. 29 Nov. 1654; Hannah, Mar. 1657; and Josiah; and d. 1703. In his will of 1699, pro. 1 June 1703, are nam. the three last nam. s. Sarah, wh. was w. of Joseph Warriner, and had first been of Daniel Collins; Mercy, wh. m. 12 July 1664, Nicholas Smith; and Hannah, w. of Eliakim Cooley. THOMAS, Milford, s. of the preced. m. 12 Dec. 1672, Abigail, d. of John Stream, had Thomas, Samuel, Joseph, and perhaps others, and d. 17 Oct. 1703.

TIBBETS, TYBBOT or TEBBETS, with sev. var. spell. EPHRAIM, Dover, s. of Jeremy, m. Rose, d. of Thomas Austin, had Ephraim, b. 31 Dec. 1694; Ann, 8 July 1698; Henry, 29 July 1700; Abigail, 12 Aug. 1701; Joseph, 14 Oct. 1702; Elisha, 16 Feb. 1705; Aaron, 26 Feb. 1706; Mary, 16 Nov. 1709; Elijah, 23 Mar. 1711; Rose, 4 Feb. 1713; and Eliz. 30 Oct. 1716. HENRY, Dover 1643, came in the James from London, 1635, aged 39, with Eliz. 39; Remembrance 28; one of wh. may perhaps have been his w. and one sis.; Jeremy 4; and Samuel, 2. In the ship's clearance he is call. shoemaker. Where he first sat down is unkn. He support. jurisdict. of Mass. in 1665; by w. Mary had Rebecca wh. m. Thomas Nock; also Thomas; and perhaps others; d. prob. 1678. HENRY, Wickford or Westerly, in 1670 was made a constable by auth. of Conn. but in the obscure controv. a. bounds between the Cols. of Conn. and R. I. he was claim. by both parties. HENRY, Dover, prob. youngest s. of Jeremy, by w. Joyce had Benjamin, b. 31 Oct. 1700; Edward, 2 Feb. 1703; Paul, 26 June 1705; and Susanna, 31 Oct. 1707. JEREMY, eldest s. of Henry the first, b. 1631 in Eng. stood up in 1665 for jurisdict. of Mass. m. Mary, d. by the first w. of Thomas Canney, had Jeremiah, b. 5 June 1656; Mary, 15 Apr. 1658; Thomas, 24 Feb. 1660; Hannah, 25 Feb. 1662; Joseph, 7 Aug. 1663; Samuel; Benjamin; Ephraim; Martha; Eliz. wh. m. John Bickford; Nathaniel; and Henry; was keeper of the gaol 1670. He made his will 5 May 1677, in wh. he names w. and all these ch. exc. Thomas. JOSEPH, Dover, br. of Ephraim, by w. Eliz. had Eliz. b. 10 Mar. 1697; Margery, 18 Jan. 1701; Judith, 3 Feb. 1703; Lydia, 4 Aug. 1704; Joseph, 2 Feb. 1707; and his w. d. three wks. aft. In 1711 he m. 2d w. Catharine Mason, had Catharine, 24 Aug. 1713; Mary, 11 Oct. 1716; and Hannah, 23 June 1721. NATHANIEL, Dover, s. of Henry the first, by w. Eliz. had Bridget, b. 26 Sept. 1700, and perhaps more; was tak. by the Ind. 2 Aug. 1706. SAMUEL, Dover, br. of the preced. m. 1 Sept. 1686, Dorothy Tuttle, prob. d. of the first John of the same, had Samuel, and perhaps others. THOMAS, Dover, br. of the preced. m. 6 July 1684, Judith, d. of John Dam, had John, b. 29 Aug. 1685; Thomas, 4 Nov. 1687; Ephraim, 4 Mar. 1690; Eliz. 8 Sept. 1692, d. next mo.; Samuel, 8 Oct. 1693; Eliz. again, 25 July 1696; Moses, 27 Jan. 1701; and Abigail, 2 Sept. 1705. WALTER, Gloucester, the freem. of 19 May 1642, was selectman that and three foll. yrs. d. 14 Aug. 1651. His d. Mary, the only ch. whose name is kn. m. 6 Nov. 1643, William Haskell, tho. it may be presum. that he had ano. d. Agnes, for he was, at his d. call. f.-in-law of Edward Clark, her h. and his will of 5 June 1651, mak. w. extrix. names gr.ch. Richard Dike, Joseph and William Haskell, John and

Joseph Clark, beside Eliz. Dike, perhaps mo. prob. sis. of Richard, Elinor Luscombe and Salome Trill. I am ign. of the last two.

TICKENOR, MARTIN, New Haven, took o. of fidel. 5 Aug. 1644, m. 16 May 1651, Mary Charles, perhaps d. of John, had John, b. 14 Apr. 1653; Abigail, 1 Feb. 1655; Daniel, 9 Oct. 1656; all bapt. 8 Feb. 1657; Hannah, bapt. 13 Mar. 1659; Samuel, 14 Oct. 1660; and a d. in 1663, all in his wife's right, beside a first b. Nathaniel, 25 Feb. 1652, wh. d. in 2 days, and a s. b. 1665.

TICKNALL, HENRY, is the name of a passeng. emb. at London in the Hopewell, in the autumn of 1635, aged only 15; but whether he ever reached Boston, or where he sat down, is untold.

TICKNOR, or anciently, TICKNER, WILLIAM, Scituate 1646, or earlier, m. at Boston, 29 Oct. 1656, Hannah, d. of John Stockbridge, had John, b. 1659, d. young; and William, 1664; perhaps others. His w. d. 1665; and he m. 1666, Deborah, d. of Thomas Hyland. He was from Co. Kent; but when he came, or when he d. is uncert. WILLIAM, Scituate, s. of the preced. m. Lydia, d. of deac. Joseph Tilden, had John, b. 1699; William, 1700; Lydia, 1702; and perhaps more. He rem. to Lebanon in 1710. John was gr.f. of the late Elisha Ticknor, Esq. of Boston, Dart. Coll. 1783, whose only s. George, is the widely kn. histor. of Spanish Literat.

TIDD, JOHN, Woburn, prob. s. of that John, spelled Tead, b. in Eng. m. 14 Apr. 1650, Rebecca Wood, had Hannah, b. 21 Sept. 1652, John, 26 Feb. 1655; Mary, 13 Nov. 1656; Samuel, 16 Jan. 1659; Joseph, 18 Jan. 1661, d. in 2 wks.; Joseph, again, perhaps, but not cert. JOHN, Woburn, s. prob. of the preced. by w. Eliz. had Eliz. b. 19 Sept. 1679; John, 2 Nov. 1681; Joseph, 8 Mar. 1684; Rebecca, 4 Aug. 1687; Mary, 8 Aug. 1690; and Ebenezer, 31 Aug. 1693. SAMUEL, Woburn, wh. d. 1651, may have been s. of the first John, writ. Tead, and b. in Eng. See Tead.

.TIFF, TIFT, or TEFFE, WILLIAM, Boston 1638, the freem. of 2 June 1641, with his w. Ann, had join. the ch. 2 Aug. 1640, when the spelling is Teffe, and he is call. tailor. His will of 1 May 1646, pro. 2 Nov. 1648, ment. w. Ann, d. Lydia, and br. John. The name is rare, and no doubt various. spell. at differ. times and places. Stephen Tift was one of the prisoners taken in Montgomery's attack on Quebec, 31 Dec. 1775. J. K. Tefft, Esq. an estim. mem. of the Georgia Hist. Soc. at Savannah, was prob. an emigrant from R. I.

TIFFANY, HUMPHREY, Rehoboth 1663, by w. Eliz. had Sarah, b. 6 July 1683; was, I think, inhab. of Dover for some time, but k. 15 July 1685, on the journey betw. Swanzey and Boston, by a stroke of lightn.

TIFFT, ELIAS, a soldier of our ranks in Philip's war. JOHN, Portsmouth, R. I. 1655, on the freemen's list that yr. In 1674 he was of Kingstown, made his will, then, in wh. he names s. Samuel, Joshua, and d. Tabitha, w. of Samuel Wilson. He was prob. br. of William Teffe or Tift of Boston. JOSHUA, Providence, at Wickford, 1674, a renegado, wh. hav. m. a Wampanoag, was true to the Ind. side, k. or wound. many Eng. it was said, especial. at the gr. swamp fight, 19 Dec. 1675, taken 14 Jan. foll. by some Providence men, was soon execut. with a stigma " that he had never heard a sermon but once for 14 yrs." See all the contempo. reports of the war. He was s. of John, and so I presume was SAMUEL, of Wickford 1674.

TILDEN, JOHN, Scituate 1643, is sometimes perhaps giv. Tilten. JOSEPH, Scituate, eldest s. of Nathaniel, b. in Eng. came in the Hercules 1635, from Sandwich, with his f. wh. was of Tenterden in Co. Kent, m. 20 Nov. 1649, Alice or Eliz. d. of John Twisden, had Nathaniel, b. Sept. 1650; John, Dec. 1652; Rebecca, Feb. 1655; Joseph, 12 Feb. 1657, prob. d. young, as he is not ment. in the will of his f.; Stephen, 14 May 1659; Samuel, 1660; Eliz. 1665; Lydia, 1666; and Benjamin 1668, wh. d. unm. at 25 yrs. He was deac. and d. in May 1670, leav. good est. by will of 12 of that mo. to wid. Eliz. and the eight ch. by name, and br. Stephen, and sis. Eliz. Garrett. But of this last some doubt is felt, whether it mean more than Christian relationship, or perhaps the sec. w. of Richard G. wh. for his first, had Lydia, sis. of this testat. NATHANIEL, Scituate, came in the Hercules 1635 from Sandwich, in Co. Kent, being one of an old fam. at Tenterden, near Cranbrook, in that shire, bring. w. Lydia, seven ch. and seven serv. He may have visit. our country bef. and went home to bring his household; but it does not appear by any facts. In May 1637, with his friend Hatherly, he was appoint. by Plymouth Col. to sett. the bounds betw. it and Mass. He was rul. elder in the ch. and d. 1641, the inv. being of 31 July, and his will of 25 May preced. in that yr. It names his w. Lydia, perhaps d. of Thomas Bourne of Marshfield, yet m. in Eng. to wh. he gives his ho. at Tenterden, all the seven ch. Joseph; Thomas, b. a. 1621; Mary, the w. of Thomas Lapham, m. 13 Mar. 1637; Sarah, the w. of George Sutton; Judith; Lydia; and Stephen; also two serv. wh. should serve his eldest s. Judith m. Abraham Preble, and Lydia m. Richard Garrett. NATHANIEL, Scituate, eldest s. of Joseph, d. 17 Dec. 1731. STEPHEN, Marshfield, youngest s. of Nathaniel first, m. 15 Jan. 1662, Hannah, d. of Thomas Little, had Hannah, b. 14 Oct. 1662; Stephen, 1664; Abigail, 1666; Mary, 1668; Judith, 1670; Joseph, 1672; Mercy, 1 May 1674; Ruth, 1676; Isaac, 1678; Ephraim, 1680; Ebenezer, 1681; and David, 1685. Thro. this br. descend. the late Hon. Joseph, of Boston. THOMAS, Plymouth, one of the first comers, arr. 1623, by the Ann, bring. prob. w. and ch. at least he had lds. for three rights assign. that yr. but as none of this name had sh. in div. of cattle 1627, and no d. is suppos. to have occur. in the Col. for some yrs. after 1621, my infer. is that he went home. Perhaps he was br. of the first Nathaniel; but most surely not, as Farmer thot. him, his s. THOMAS, Marshfield, prob. s. of the elder Nathaniel, b. at Tenterden, Co. Kent, was old eno. in 1643 to bear arms, when he liv. at Scituate; at M. his w. Eliz. whose f. is not ascert. d. or was bur. 12 Dec. 1663; and his d. Susanna was bur. 9 Sept. 1684; and s. John d. 20 Apr. 1685; but one or both may have been ch. of that Mary Holmes, maid or wid. is unkn. m. 24 Jan. 1665.

TILESTONE, or TILLSTON, THOMAS, Dorchester, had gr. of ld. 1634, freem. 9 Mar. 1637, had w. Eliz. s. Thomas, b. a. 1633; Timothy, a. 1637; Eliz. 1639; Ruth; Naomi, d. young; prob. Cornelius, wh. d. 20 July 1659; Bathsheba, b. 1649; Onesiphorus, 1651; and perhaps others; was fined in Sept. 1640 for abs. from a jury; but we can tell no more of him exc. his d. 24 June 1694, aged 83, says Blake. Ruth m. 11 Dec. 1657, Richard Denton; and next Timothy Foster; and Bathsheba m. John Payson. THOMAS, Dorchester, s. of the preced. perhaps (I dare not say prob.) b. in Eng. but the rec. allows us to kn. only that he d. 11 Sept. 1718, aged a. 85 yrs. Whether he had w. and ch. is uncert. Perhaps he was the author wh. compos. verses on the d. of John Foster, 1681, as Thomas in his Hist. of Print. I. 277, tells. * TIMOTHY, Dorchester, s. of the first Thomas, freem. 1666, m. 28 Apr. or 3 May 1659, Sarah, d. of James Bridgeman of Hartford, had Timothy, b. a. 1664; Eliz. 29 Mar. bapt. 1 Apr. 1666; Cornelius, 4 Sept. bapt. 4 Oct. 1668; Sarah, b. 7 Sept. 1671; Thomas, 19 Oct. 1675; James, 2 July 1678; Ann, 7 Dec. 1681. He was rep. 1689, 92, a cooper by trade, and d. 10 Aug. 1697, leav. large est. of wh. the mills have contin. in the fam. until this time; and the wid. d. 26 June 1712, aged 69.

TILL, or TYLLS, JAMES, Scituate 1643. PETER, Boston, a fisherman, in whose youthful days the Ct. 1639 order, that he shall be taught seamanship by his master, John Cloise or Cloyes; m. 26 Feb. 1652, Eliz. Nick; and was liv. 1671, a carpenter.

TILLEY, EDWARD, Plymouth 1620, came with w. in the Mayflower, and two ch. "their cousins," Henry Sampson, and Humility Cooper. He and his w. d. the first winter. Humility went home and d. HUGH, Salem, perhaps in 1629, as in Haz. I. 280, when he was serv. to Sir Richard Saltonstall, certain. at Yarmouth 1638 and 43, being a witness there to a will early in 1639, and enrol. to bear arms in the latter yr. Clearly this man's name is by some read Hillier, and he d. 28 Jan. 1648; and his wid. m. 3 Nov. foll. Thomas Hucking. JOHN, Plymouth, perhaps br. of Edward, came with w. and one ch. Eliz. in the Mayflower, 1620, and all (it was believ. by Shurtleff in Geneal. Reg. I. 52) d. next winter. But his d. Eliz. wh. m. John Howland outliv. all her fellow passeng. exc. three wh. were younger. JOHN, Dorchester 1630, is prob. the same, wh. was in 1624, engag. at Cape Ann, with Thomas Gardner, in the oversight of that planta. freem. 4 Mar. 1635, and perhaps the master of the coast. vessel, k. by the Ind. at Conn. riv. next yr. in Oct. with circumst. of horrid cruelty, as in Winth. I. 200 is told. His wid. cont. at D. NATHANIEL, emb. in the Abigail 1635, from London, aged 32, but I kn. no more of him. THOMAS, Plymouth 1643. WILLIAM, Boston, is perhaps the passeng. in the Abigail from London 1635, aged 28, with Nathaniel, and may have been his br. perhaps was the Barnstable man 1643. In 1649, he had w. Alice, and was inhab. 1658; but in 1665 was subject of complaint by w. Of Eliz. T. wh. in 1653 at Springfield, m. Thomas Merrick, tho. from that union, the Tilley has grown into a common baptism. prefix, it is, I fear, impossib. to find any trace of parentage.

TILLINGHAST, BENJAMIN, Providence, s. prob. youngest of the first Pardon, had three ds. of whose dates I hear nothing, nor names; but it is said that they m. Solomon Drown, Edward Kinnicutt, and Christopher Arnold, respective. JOHN, Providence, of whose descent I am ign. had perhaps other ch. beside Mary, b. a. 1689, wh. m. 2 Nov. 1709, Richard Ward. JOSEPH, Providence, br. of Benjamin, by first w. had Paris; and by sec. w. Lydia, had Eliz.; Samuel; Nicholas, b. 26 May 1726; and Daniel; to ea. of wh. I would gladly give dates. PARDON, Providence, b. a. 1622, it is said, near Beachy Head on the coast of Sussex, was sett. as Bapt. min. 1645. See Benedict, Hist. I. 478. He built at his own exp. the first meeting-ho. and gave it to the soc. in 1711, with the lot it stood on; and d. 29 Jan. 1718. By his sec. w. Lydia, prob. d. of Philip Tabor of Tiverton, he had Pardon; Philip; Joseph, b. 1677; Benjamin; Mary; Abigail; Mercy, b. a. 1679; Hannah; and Eliz. He d. 29 Jan. 1718; but he had three ch. by a former w. whose names are unkn. Mary m. one of the numerous Carpenters at Pautuxet, prob. a s. of William; Abigail m. Nicholas Sheldon; Mercy m. the third Nicholas Power, as his sec. w. had nine ch. and d. 13 Nov. 1769, aged 91; Hannah m. a Hale of Swanzey; and Eliz. m. a Tabor of New London. He is, I believe, founder of a long line, eight of wh. had, says Farmer, been gr. at Brown Univ. in 1834. PARDON, Providence, s. of the preced. rem. to East Greenwich, and had John, Joseph, and Philip, beside one d. Mercy, w. of Peter Mawney, as from his will is learn. That docum. names a great many gr.ch. PHILIP, Providence, br. of the preced. m. 3 May 1692, Martha Holmes, prob. a gr.d. of persecut. Obadiah, had Charles, b. 5 Mar. 1693; Philip, 9 Aug. 1694; John, 4 Apr. 1696; Jonathan, 18 Sept. 1698; Martha, 20 Dec. 1699; Pardon, 15 Dec. 1701; Obadiah, 2 Dec. 1703, d. young; Joseph, 18 Mar. 1706, d. at 18 yrs.; Lydia, 16 Oct. 1708; Sarah, 5 Mar. 1710; perhaps Samuel, 1711; Ann, 13 Apr. 1713; William, 22 Jan. 1715; Elisha, 29 Aug. 1716; and Mary, 16 Feb. 1718.

TILLOTSON, JOHN, Rowley, rem. to Newbury, m. 14 July 1648, Dorcas, sis. of Thomas Coleman, wh. perhaps brot. her in the James from Southampton 1635, arr. at Boston 3 June, had Mary, b. 13 Feb. 1650; John, 21 Feb. 1651; and James, 19 Dec. 1652. His w. d. 1 Jan. 1655, and he m. 24 May foll. Jane Evans, had Philadelphia, 28 Sept. 1656; Joseph, 11 Jan. 1658; and Jonathan, 6 July 1659. As Coffin tells no more of him, I judge that he rem. prob. to Conn. JOHN, Saybrook 1671, prob. s. of the preced. liv. on the E. or Lyme side of the gr. riv. and was involv. with many of his townsmen in the quarrel with New London people a. mowing the meadow intermed. wh. led to mut. indictms. as in Trumbull's Col. Rec. II. 558 appears. He m. 25 Nov. 1680, Mary Morris, d. of John of Hartford, had Mary, b. 30 Nov. 1681; John, 25 Oct. 1683; Joshua, 26 Mar. 1687; Joseph, 29 Mar. 1689; Martha, 1 Nov. 1691; and Thomas, 24 Mar. 1694; and d. 5 June 1719. JONATHAN, Lyme, perhaps br. of the preced. m. 10 Jan. 1683, Mary Jones, had Jonathan, b. 26 Oct. 1684.

TILLMAN, JOHN, in Maine, among those on W. side of Kennebec riv. wh. sw. alleg. to Charles II. Sept. 1665.

TILSON, EDWARD, Scituate, d. 1660; may be the same call. EDMUND, at Plymouth 1643; and 25 Oct. 1660, Eliz. wh. may have been his d. m. Benajah Dunham, of Eastham; and on the same day Mary T. m. Benjamin Dunham; but wh. was the Mary, that m. 23 Dec. 1652, James Cole jr. is quite beyond my conject. as is the Jane, wh. m. 20 May 1662, Giles Richard the elder. EPHRAIM, Plymouth, perhaps br. of the preced. m. 7 July 1666, Eliz. Hoskins, d. perhaps of William. JOHN, Rowley 1643.

TILTON, ABRAHAM, Ipswich, the freem. of 1681, was perhaps s. of William of Lynn, apprent. in 1653, to John Hood, wh. then being in Eng. discharg. him, and he m. the same yr. or earlier, a d. (prob. Deliverance) of Roger Shaw of Hampton; in 1669 was of Kittery, and at I. with w. made deeds of gift 1702, to s. Samuel and Isaac. His wid. Deliverance, in her will of 9 Nov. 1730, pro. 2 July 1733, names s. Abraham, Samuel, and Isaac, ds. Sarah Martin, Mary, w. of Tristram Brown, Rebecca, w. of Thomas Durges, whose former h. was John Lamb, and Abigail Bell, dec. late w. of Robert Bell, formerly of John Filmore. DANIEL, of Hampton or Exeter in 1689, was perhaps br. of

the preced. I conject. and m. 23 Dec. 1669, Mehitable Weare. Of one
Daniel, perhaps a s. more prob. gr.s. of William of Ipswich, with his br.
lieut. Jacob, striking proof of triumph. over Ind. captors in June 1722, is
told in Penhallow's Hist. with admirab. brevity; but much dilated in
verse, untutored as its subject, the heroic narrat. is contain. in Geneal.
Reg. II. 271. ISAAC, Pemaquid, a serg. at the fort, drown. there, 28
Mar. 1695, was br. of Abraham, as by his nuncup. will declar. JOHN,
Lynn, had John, b. 1642. ‡* PETER, Windsor, perhaps s. of William of
Lynn, may never have been of Dorchester, yet early at W. and possib.
came with Rev. Ephraim Huit, there m. 10 May 1641, Eliz. whose surname is lost, had Eliz. bapt. 19 June 1642, wh. d. at 13 yrs; Mary, 18
Feb. 1644; and Peter, 5 Dec. 1647, rem. a. 1659 up the riv. and was one
of the first sett. at Hadley, took the freeman's o. 26 Mar. 1661, and o. of
alleg. 8 Feb. 1679; was deac. rep. for H. 1665, and most yrs. foll. exc.
1667, when he was ret. mem. for Chelmsford, chos. Assist. in 1680, and
so contin. exc. dur. the usurp. of Andros, and on the last elect. under the
old chart. ten days bef. coming of the new, among the whole eighteen
only Phips, Sewall, Russell, and Cooke had more votes than him. See
3 Mass. Hist. Coll. X. 120. He d. 11 July 1696. His sec. w. Mary, d.
16 Apr. 1689; and he m. 3 Nov. 1690, Sarah, wid. of deac. Benjamin
Parsons, wh. had been wid. of John Leonard, both of Springfield; and
she outliv. him and d. at S. 23 Nov. 1711. Of the two surv. ch. Peter
was infirm in body and mind, kept under guardians, and did not perpet. the
name. Mary m. Joseph Eastman of Suffield, and next James Guernsey,
17 Feb. 1693. Aft. the d. of Peter jr. in 1707, all the Tilton est. vested
in Joseph Eastman gr.s. of the first Peter. WILLIAM, Lynn, had eldest
s. Samuel, others Peter, Daniel, and Abraham; perhaps William; d. a.
1653. His wid. Susanna, m. Roger Shaw of Hampton.

TIMBERLAKE, * HENRY, Newport 1644, then chos. corporal, rep. 1663 ;
had fam. of wh. I kn. only Eliz. that m. 24 Dec. 1670, the third John
Coggeshall. Perhaps it was his s. wh. was a soldier with the rank of
ensign, under capt. William Turner at the Falls fight in Philip's war,
by the scrupulous keeper of the muster roll call. Timberleggs.

TIMMINS, JOHN, Scarborough, unit. with many others in declar. 4 July
1663, unwilling to resist claim of jurisdict. by Mass. or by Patentees, but
wish the k. to settle whom they belong to.

TINGLEY, or TINGLE, PALMER, Ipswich 1639, is by Farmer nam.
as a soldier in the Pequot war. SAMUEL, Malden, d. 28 Dec. 1666,
leav. wid. Eliz. by wh. he had Samuel, b. Feb. 1666; and Thomas July
1667. His w. was d. of Thomas Call, and she next m. Daniel Shepardson the sec.

TINKER, AMOS, Lyme 1688, s. of John of New London, had there m.

26*

1 June 1682; but I kn. no issue. *John, Windsor, 1643, rem. in few yrs. to Boston, by w. Alice had Sarah, b. 2 Jan. 1652; Mary, 2 July 1653; freem. 1654; was one of the princ. sett. at Lancaster, there selectman 1655, and town clk. had John, 4 Aug. 1655; Amos, 28 Oct. 1657; rem. again to New London, where he was in good esteem, rep. 1660 and 1, had Samuel, 1 Apr. 1659; and Rhoda, 23 Feb. 1662; and he d. in Oct. foll. and the Gen. Ct. in Mar. 1664, order. the charges of his sickness and fun. to be disburs. from the public treas. His wid. m. 1664, William Measure, and d. 20 Nov. 1714, aged 85. THOMAS, Plymouth 1620, came in the Mayflower, with w. and a s. wh. all d. in the first winter. One Sarah T. join. the ch. at Scituate, 14 May 1637, but no more is heard of her.

TINKHAM, EBENEZER, Middleborough, s. of the first Ephraim, m. bef. 1679, Eliz. Liscom, was one of the first memb. of the ch. and deac. had Jeremiah, and prob. others, and d. 8 Apr. 1718, and his w. it is said, d. the same day, aged 64. EPHRAIM, Plymouth 1643, had Ephraim, b. 5 Aug. 1649; Ebenezer, 30 Sept. 1651; Peter, 25 Dec. 1653; Hezekiah, 8 Feb. 1656; John, 7 June 1658; Mary, 5 Aug. 1661; John, again, 15 Nov. 1663; and Isaac, 11 Apr. 1666. EPHRAIM, Middleborough, s. of the preced. by w. Esther had Ephraim, and Isaac, perhaps more.

TINNEY, JOHN, Scarborough, in 1658, own alleg. to Mass. as in Col. Rec. IV. part I. It may be Tenney.

TIPPETT, HENRY, Wickford, in the disput. territ. of Rhode Island, claim. by Conn. made a constable 1670, by the latter power, tho. the right belong. to R. I. See Trumbull, Col. Rec. II. 138, 540, and 553. Humbly I would inq. if Mr. Trumbull, in the Index, making the name Tibbots or Tibbets, had high authority for the spelling, or had followed the similarity of Henry Tibbets in N. H. adher. to the Mass. jurisdict. I submit the conject. that the true spell. was Lippet; yet with so much less confidence, as the Wickford man's name is found by Judd to be Tipler.

TIPPING, or TIPPEN, * BARTHOLOMEW, Exeter 1675, had commiss. from Mass. in Oct. 1676, to com. the forces in reëstab. the sett. at Scarborough, in 1677 k. the famous Ind. ch. Mugg; in 1680 was rep. See Mass. Col. Rec. V. 130.

TIRRELL, TURRELL, TYRRELL, TERRALL, or THURRILL, GIDEON, Weymouth, s. of William of the same, by w. Hannah had Gideon, b. 18 June 1689, prob. d. soon; Mary, 4 Oct. 1690; Gideon, again, 10 Apr. 1693; Miriam, 29 Sept. 1696; and perhaps more. JOHN, Milford, perhaps s. of Roger, was propound. for freem. 1669, and then a seaman, prob. liv. at New London, perhaps br. of William of the same, m. Sarah, d. of Isaac Willey, perhaps for sec. w. He had William and Mary, bapt. 7 May 1671; and d. 27 Feb. 1712; and his wid. d. 7 Mar. foll. ROGER, Milford 1639, one of the orig. sett. had, no doubt, a fam. is in list of freem. 1669, and Lambert says, d. 1682. ROGER, Stratford, perhaps s. of the preced. had Abigail, bapt. Jan. 1682; Sarah, Mar. 1684; Stephen, Aug. 1686; Roger, July 1691; Ezra, Apr. 1693; Timothy and Martha, tw. 19 Nov. 1697; as we learn from Cothren, wh. also inf. that he d. 17 Apr. 1722; and his wid. d. 13 Apr. 1728. WILLIAM, Boston, m. 29 Jan. 1655, Rebecca, d. of capt. Nicholas Simpkins, had Rebecca, b. 16 Dec. foll.; William, 16 Mar. 1657; Mary, 6 Apr. 1661; and Gideon, 16 July 1664; rem. to Weymouth, and may there have had more ch. but failure for a long series of yrs. of town rec. denies us certainty. WILLIAM, a tailor of New London, 1662, as Caulkins says only trans. inhab. WILLIAM, Weymouth, s. of William of the same, by w. Abigail, had William, b. 4 Aug. 1683; Samuel, 17 Nov. 1686; Abigail, 22 Aug. 1689; and Gideon, 14 June 1694.

TISDALE, JAMES, Taunton, perhaps s. of the first John, m. 5 Nov. 1666, Mary, d. of William Avery of Dedham, liv. in Middleborough, the part now Lakeville, when his w. d. 9 Sept. 1713, aged 66; and he d. 15 Jan. 1715, aged 71. * JOHN, Duxbury 1637, but in what yr. he came, or from what part of Eng. is uncert. tho. we kn. his end, k. by the Ind. 27 June 1675. Prob. he had John and James, both of wh. may have been b. here. JOHN, call. jr. Taunton, m. 23 Nov. 1664, Hannah Rogers, of Duxbury, had Abigail, b. 15 July 1667; John, 10 Aug. 1669; Ann, 27 Jan. 1673; and Remember, 8 July 1675; was rep. 1674, says Baylies II. 71, k. by the Ind. 27 June next yr. as Winsor tells, but this was the f. and the mo. Sarah d. Dec. 1676.

TITCOMB, or TITCOME, BENAIAH, Newbury, s. of William of the same, sw. alleg. 1678, as by the k. req. hav. in 1669, sw. fidel. to Mass. m. 24 Dec. in the latter yr. Sarah Brown, prob. d. of the first Richard, had Benaiah, b. 24 Oct. 1679; Joseph, 25 Jan. 1681, prob. d. soon; Edmund, 9 Dec. 1682; Eliz.; Sarah, 2 Mar. 1688; Joseph, again, 2 Apr. 1691; Enoch, 1 Apr. 1695; and Mary, 17 Feb. 1698. PENIEL, Newbury, br. of the preced. and the eldest wh. grew up to manhood, m. 8 Jan. 1684, Lydia, d. of Samuel Poor of the same, had Sarah, b. 22 Dec. 1684, d. soon; Sarah, again, 14 Dec. 1685; William, 8 Apr. 1687; and John, 24 Dec. 1689. THOMAS, Newbury, br. of the preced. m. 30 Nov. 1693, Mary Dam, had Hannah, b. 5 Sept. 1695; Judith, 30 July 1698; Mary, 17 Aug. 1700; and Ann, 27 Jan. 1703. * WILLIAM, Newbury, was of Newbury in Co. Berks, had taken pass. in the Mary and John, from London, 24 Mar. 1634, but was casual. depriv. of the opportun. and came next mo. in the Hercules, m. Joanna, d. of the elder Richard Bartlett, wh. d. 28 June 1653, had Sarah, b. 22 June 1640; Hannah, 8 Jan.

1642 ; Mary, 17 Feb. 1644 ; Millicent, 7 June 1646, wh. d. at 17 yrs.;
William, 18 Mar. 1648, d. at 11 yrs.; Peniel, 16 Dec. 1650 ; and Benaiah, 28 June 1653, the day of his mo's. d. He m. 3 Mar. 1654, Eliz.
Stevens, perhaps wid. of William, and had Eliz. 12 Dec. 1654 ; Rebecca,
1 Apr. 1656 ; Tirzah, 21 Feb. 1658 ; William, 14 Aug. 1659 ; Thomas,
11 Oct. 1661 ; Lydia, 13 June 1663 ; John, 17 Sept. 1664 ; and Ann, 7
June 1666 ; was freem. 22 June 1642, rep. 1655 ; and yet was not either
of his s. made freem. He d. 24 Sept. 1676. His will, made six days
bef. ment. only eleven ch. Sarah m. 16 Mar. 1665, the sec. Thomas
Treadwell of Ipswich ; Rebecca m. 25 Mar. 1678, Nathaniel Treadwell,
as his sec. w. WILLIAM, Newbury, s. of the preced. m. 15 May 1683,
Ann, d. of William Cottle, had Jedediah, b. 17 Jan. 1684 ; Joanna, 15
July 1686 ; Daniel, 22 Apr. 1691 ; Sarah, 17 Dec. 1693 ; Elias, 27 Feb.
1696 ; Joseph and Benjamin, tw. 30 Mar. 1698 ; Moses, 19 June 1700 ;
and Joanna, 3 Sept. 1702.

TITE, HENRY, Boston 1655, m. 11 Feb. 1658, Sarah Walton, but I
kn. no more of either.

TITERTON, TITTERTON, or TYTTERTON, *‖ DANIEL, was perhaps of
Boston 1643, when the ar. co. list includes such a name, with Samuel
instead of Daniel ; but I suppose he rem. to Stratford bef. 1647 ; was
rep. 1647, 49, 52 and 54 ; and d. 1661. His will pro. 6 July of that
yr. names three s. Daniel, Timothy, and Samuel, of wh. Timothy is the
only ch. whose b. is on rec. at S. and that was 25 Mar. 1651. To these
he gives his est. and lds. in Eng. beside some in N. E. Three ds. also
are ment. one, Wilcockson, perhaps the first w. of Timothy, and Mary,
and Eliz. unm. To these two £30 ea. beside £10 ea. for mar. dress.
His w. Jane outliv. him. Perhaps two of the s. went home to enjoy est.
there. DANIEL, Stratford, s. perhaps eldest, of the preced. b. in Eng.
had Mary, b. 11 June 1676, and perhaps others bef. He was one of
the sec. society of S. most of wh. rem. to Woodbury, but he did not;
freem. 1669.

TITUS, ABIEL, Newtown, L. I. was s. of Robert. JOHN, Rehoboth, s. of
Robert, b. in Eng. came with his f. perhaps m. a d. of William Carpenter of the same, wh. in his will of Dec. 1659, makes bequest to his s.
But JOHN, Rehoboth, wh. m. 17 July 1673, Lydia Redway, had Lydia,
b. 1674, may be s. of preced. and his w. was bur. at R. 25 Nov. 1676.
He m. sec. w. 3 July foll. Sarah Miller, had John, b. 12 Mar. 1678 ;
Hannah, 10 Nov. 1682. JONATHAN, Rehoboth, had Samuel, b. 29 July
1680. * ROBERT, Weymouth, came in the Hopewell, capt. Bundock, in
the spr. of 1635, from London, aged 35, with w. Hannah, 31 ; ch. John,
8 ; and Edmund, 5 ; freem. 13 May 1640 ; at W. had s. Abiel, b. 17
Mar. 1641 ; and d. Content, 28 Mar. 1643 ; rem. to Rehoboth next yr.

may have had other ch. aft. or bef. was rep. 1648, 9, and 50. SAMUEL, Newtown, L. I. 1664, favor. Conn. jurisdict. and the name is much diffus. SILAS, Rehoboth, had Silas, b. 12 Aug. perhaps 1679; Mary, 30 Mar. 1681. Sometimes it is writ. Tytus.

TOBEY, FRANCIS, in Mass. was fin. 1635, for something slight, £10, but three yrs. aft. it was remit. JAMES, k. by the Ind. at Kittery 1705. STEPHEN, perhaps of Portsmouth, N. H. m. 29 Nov. 1688, Hannah Nelson. THOMAS, Sandwich 1650, m. 18 Nov. of that yr. Martha Knott.

TODD, CHRISTOPHER, New Haven, was one of the orig. sett. 1639, a propr. 1685, and d. next yr. had John, bapt. Dec. 1642; Samuel, 29 Apr. 1645; Mary, prob. 19 Sept. 1647; Grace, b. 15 Dec. 1650; Michael, 18 June 1653; and Mercy, 18 Feb. 1656; the bapt. were in right of his w. Grace. I wish the ch. rec. had been as accurate as that of the town. His will of 25 Mar. 1686, names all the ch. but Mary, w. of Isaac Turner was dec. Grace had m. Richard Mattock, wh. desert. her; and Mercy m. a Bassett, prob. John. * JOHN, Charlestown 1637, was, I think, one of the early sett. at Rowley, of which he was rep. 1664, and 86; by w. Susanna, had John, b. 1655; Catharine, 1658; Thomas, 1665; Timothy, 1668; Samuel, 1670; James, 1672; prob. sev. others. JOHN, New Haven, s. of Christopher, m. 1668, Sarah, d. of Hon. Matthew Gilbert, had Sarah, b. 27 Aug. 1670, d. soon; and his w. d. 1672. He m. 1677, Sarah Blackman, had Sarah, 13 May 1678, d. soon; John, 11 May 1679; Jonathan, 20 Feb. 1681; Sarah, again, 17 Mar. 1682, d. soon; Mary, 26 Sept. 1683; and perhaps more. He was propound. for freem. 1670; and propr. 1685; JOHN, Rowley, s. of John of the same, m. Eliz. Broclebank, perhaps d. of capt. Samuel, had John, b. 1688; Samuel, 1693; Thomas, 1701; and Joseph, 1704; beside three ds. SAMUEL, New Haven, s. of Christopher of the same, m. 1668, Mary, d. of William Bradley, had Samuel, b. 1 July 1672; Joseph, 4 Feb. 1674, d. soon; Mary, 12 Feb. 1675; Sarah, 3 Feb. 1677, d. young; Joseph, again, 29 Jan. 1679, d. soon; Hannah, 7 Feb. 1680; Jonah, 16 Feb. 1684; and perhaps others. He was propound. for freem. 1670, and propr. 1685. SAMUEL, Rowley, s. of John of the same, by w. Priscilla, had Samuel, b. 1696; Abner, 1700; Daniel, 1706; and one d. WALTER, Warwick, is among the freem. there 1655; and liv. 1673. He had m. Margaret, wid. of Rufus Barton, but he left no ch. Of this name fourteen had in 1840 been gr. at Yale, and one at Harv.

TOE, SAMUEL, Newtown, L. I. 1656, is by me suspected to be the same as Coe, in the old writing the cap. T. and C. were so much alike.

TOKER, or TOKERS, SAMUEL, Southampton 1673.

TOLL. See Towle.

TOLMAN, JOHN, Dorchester, s. of Thomas the first, freem. 1678, at Lynn m. 30 Nov. 1666, Eliz. d. of John Collins, mo. of all his ch. wh. d. 7 Oct. 1690; and 15 June 1692, he took sec. w. Mary, wid. of Samuel Paul, d. of Edward Breck, wh. d. 25 Aug. 1720; d. 1 Jan. 1725, in 83d yr. He had Eliz. b. 14 Dec. 1667; John 8 Apr. 1671; Joseph, 6 Sept. 1674; Benjamin, 6 Dec. 1676; Henry, 13 Mar. 1679; Ann, 2 Mar. 1681; Ebenezer, 27 Mar. 1683; Ruth, 1 July 1685; and William, 2 Sept. 1687. THOMAS, Dorchester 1636, freem. 13 May 1640, by w. Sarah had Hannah, b. 27 July 1642; but prob. Thomas, bef. and perhaps also Sarah and Mary; beside John, perhaps, and Ruth and Rebecca, certain. after. He had also sec. w. Sarah; and d. 8 June 1690. His will of 29 Oct. 1688, names Thomas, his oldest s. and no other s. but John; d. Sarah. wh. had m. 18 Mar. 1669, Henry Leadbetter, Rebecca, w. of James Tucker, Ruth, w. dec. of Isaac Royal, Hannah, w. of George Lyon, and d. Mary Collins, whose h. is not kn. to me. His inv. was of 23 July 1690. THOMAS, Dorchester, s. of the preced. freem. 1678, by w. Eliz. d. of Richard Johnson of Lynn, m. 4 Nov. 1664, had Thomas; Mary, b. 26 Nov. 1671; Samuel, 11 June 1676; and Daniel, 1 May 1679. See his will in Geneal. Reg. XIV. 259.

TOMLINSON, AGUR, Stratford, s. of Henry of the same, m. 13 Dec. 1681, Eliz. d. of Jeremiah Judson. HENRY, Milford, 1652, rem. to Stratford prob. 1665, certain bef. 1669, when he is found in the freemen's list; had w. Alice, and ch. Jonas, Margaret, Mary, and Tabitha, not rec. at Stratford; Phebe, b. 14 Aug. 1656; Agur, 1 Nov. 1658; Bathshua, 3 Jan. 1661; and Abraham, perhaps b. earlier, d. 1662; and d. 16 Mar. 1681. His will of the day bef. ment. that Margaret had m. Jabez Hardier; Mary was w. of a Pierson; Tabitha, w. of Edward Wooster; Phebe, w. of ano. Wooster; and Bathshua, w. of Ephraim Stiles; and Jonas; all of wh. had been portion. and aft. good provis. for wid. Alice, gives resid. of est. to Agur. The wid. m. John Birdseye, sen. under a contr. of 8 Oct. 1688. JONAS, Stratford, s. of the preced. was adm. freem. 1669. Both f. and s. were active in project. var. settlem. the s. was one of the first sett. at Derby, as early as 1678, made his will in 1692, naming w. Hannah. He had copious progeny, prob. for the catal. of Yale names twelve gr. of this name, wh. is seen in the early rec. sometimes without the last sylla.

TOMLYNS, THOMLINS, or TOMLINS, BENJAMIN, prob. at Lynn, came in the Susan and Ellen, 1635, aged 18, from London, with ano. Edward, 30, from wh. I infer that they were brs. and likely to be s. of either the first Edward or his br. *‖ EDWARD, Lynn 1630, came, no doubt, in the fleet with Winth. and was adm. freem. 18 May 1631, was rep. at the first Gen. Ct. of deput. 1634, and next yr. ar. co. 1638, clk. of the writs 1643, hav. gone to L. I. to instr. a. the migrat. from L. but came back, rep. again 1644. He was prob. well advanc. in yrs. but I kn. no more of him; no ch. are ment. EDWARD, Lynn, perhaps s. perhaps neph. of the preced. came in the Susan and Ellen, but went home again, 1644, liv. in London, was prob. a merch. bot. of Joseph Redknap, 31 Jan. 1649, his est. call. Blackbush right, near Hampton Court, was of Dublin, 1679, says Lewis. JOHN, Boston, m. 26 Dec. 1660, Sarah, d. of Matthew Barnes. RALPH, Mass. 1636, of wh. no more is heard, but that some larceny of his goods had been detect. at that date. *TIMOTHY, Lynn, freem. 4 Mar. 1633, rep. in almost every Ct. from 1635 to 1640.

TOMPKINS, JOHN, Salem 1637, freem. 18 May 1642, by w. wh. I guess to be named Margaret, had Hannah, bapt. 10 Feb. 1639, b. some mos. bef. and d. soon aft.; Eliz. 9 May 1639, d. young; Hannah, again, 21 Feb. 1641; Sarah, 1 Jan. 1643; John, 16 Feb. 1645; Eliz. again, b. 29 Nov. 1646, bapt. 17 Jan. 1647; Mary, bapt. 29 Apr. 1649; and Deborah, 8 June 1651. Hannah m. 26 June 1660, Hugh Jones; Sarah m. 1 Aug. 1663, John Waters; and Mary m. 29 Nov. 1670, John Felton, all of Salem. But his inv. of 30 June 1681, ment. oldest s. Nathaniel, prob. b. in Eng. and Priscilla, prob. the youngest, wh. m. 14 Aug. 1679, Samuel Marsh. JOHN, Concord, had Ruth, b. 1 June 1640; and John, 25 Sept. 1642; rem. in less than two yrs. to Fairfield, there in 1669 was propound. for freem. sold land in 1673, and prob. liv. at East Chester. MICAH, or MICHAEL, Wethersfield, rem. to Milford 1639, and Lambert says he d. 1649; but of that I find cause to doubt, for in Trumbull's Col. Rec. II. 513, may be seen verificat. in 1661 and 5 by Michael T. of Milford, wh. must be thot. the same person, as only one with this prefix is ment. for a long course of yrs. He rem. with a great comp. of friends to New Jersey, 1666, and July 1667 bot. large tract from Ind. on the Passaic riv. where now is the city of Newark. See Whitehead, 42, 3. By w. Mary he had at M. Jonathan, and Mary, both bapt. 17 Dec. 1643, soon aft. he and his w. had join the ch.; Eliz. Feb. 1645; David, 1647, d. at 2 yrs. by casual.; Seth, 1649; Rebecca, b. 24 Nov. 1653; Abigail, 1655; Micah, bapt. at New Haven, 27 Nov. 1659. NATHANIEL, Newport 1675, tempor. resid. at Boston, a merch. in 1681; may be the same wh. was of East Chester sev. yrs. bef. but for perman. liv. at N. where by w. Eliz. he had Nathaniel, b. 31 Dec. 1676, perhaps d. very soon; Mary, 16 Sept. 1677, d. young; Priscilla, 24 May 1679; Samuel, 11 May 1681; and Mary, again, 20 Oct. 1685. RALPH, Dorchester, freem. 2 May 1638, rem. a. 1647 to Salem, there d. prob. in 1666, as his inv. is of 12 Nov. of that yr. SAMUEL, Duxbury 1640, had m. 1639, Lettice Foster, prob. sis. of Edward of Scituate, one of the grantees of Bridgewater 1645, was perhaps s. of Ralph.

TOMPSON. See Thompson.

TONGUE, GEORGE, New London, by w. Margery had Eliz. b. 20 Oct.
1652; Hannah, 20 July 1654; Mary, 17 Sept. 1656; and George, 8
May 1658; kept the inn, had good est. and d. 1674. His d. Eliz. m.
Fitz John Winthrop, wh. bec. Gov. of the Col. Hannah m. Joshua
Baker; and Mary m. 6 Nov. 1676, John Wickwire. STEPHEN, Salis-
bury, by w. Mary, wh. d. 24 Apr. 1700, had Deborah, b. 8 July 1687;
Mary, 24 July 1689; Joanna, 28 Dec. 1691, d. soon; Sarah, 11 Feb.
1694; and Stephen, 9 Dec. 1696.

TONY, JOHN, one of the early sett. at Reading, d. says Eaton, 1691.

TOOGOOD, TOWGOOD, or TWOGOOD, JOHN, a serv. of Thomas Marshfield, wh. had a. 1640, run away from his master at Springfield. NA-
THANIEL, Swanzey, 1669, rem. to Boston, by w. Eliz. had John, there b.
20 Apr. 1679; and Eliz. 25 July 1682. THOMAS, of wh. good story is
relat. by Niles in his Hist. of Indian Wars in 3 Mass. Hist. Coll. VI.

TOOKEY, or TUKEY, JOB, Beverly, charg. in 1692 with witchcraft.
JOHN, Charlestown, d. aft. 1665, his will of 16 Aug. in that yr. pro. 2
Mar. 1668, leaves us to inf. that he had neither w. nor ch. as he names
only his master William Batchelder, and his dame wid. Bridget Wines.

TOOLLY, TOLLY, or TOOLEY, CHRISTOPHER, Killingworth, by w.
Eliz. had Agnes, b. 1684; Judith, 1687; Andrew, 1690; Christopher
and Eliz. tw. 1692; William, 1694; John, 1697; Mary, 1700; Joanna,
1702; and Esther, 1705. The name may have passed into Tully.
EDMUND, New Haven, 1644, d. 19 Apr. 1685, without w. or ch. prob.
unm. certain. poor. THOMAS, Newport 1651, in the list of freem. 1655,
may be the man wh. at Lynn had Thomas, b. 3 Aug. 1665.

TOOTHACKER, TOOTHACRE, or TOOTHAKER, ROGER, came in the
Hopewell, capt. Babb, from London 1635, aged 23, with his w. Margaret,
and s. Roger, 1 yr. d. early, and it is not kn. where he sat down, but in
1638, his wid. m. Ralph Hill of Woburn, wh. soon aft. 1653 rem. to
Billerica, and d. 1663, in his will of 10 Nov. 1662, nam. his w. Margaret, and her son Roger Toothaker. She liv. to 22 Dec. 1683.
ROGER, Billerica, s. of the preced. had Roger, wh. also had Roger, and
all were, says Farmer, physicians.

TOPLIFFE, CLEMENT, Dorchester 1636, by w. Sarah had Jonathan, b.
Apr. 1637; Sarah, May 1639; Obedience, Oct. 1642; Samuel, 7 May
1646; and Patience. He was b. it is said 17 Nov. 1603, freem. 13
May 1640, when the name is writ. Tapley, and d. 24 Dec. 1672, says
the valu. acco. in Geneal. Reg. V. 466, but it strangely contradicts
itself in counting that date as his 69th instead of 70th yr. His wid. d.
29 July 1693, aged 88, or as that acco. has it in her 88th yr. Sarah
m. 11 May 1659 David Jones; Obedience m. 20 Feb. 1660, David

Copp; and Patience m. 27 Mar. 1667, Nathaniel Homes. Sometimes it was writ. Tapliff by wh. prob. came the error of Tapley. SAMUEL, Dorchester, s. of the preced. freem. 1673, by w. Patience had Mehitable, b. 19 Aug. 1673, d. soon; Samuel, 19 Aug. 1675, d. at 19 yrs.; Patience, 24 Jan. 1677; Thankful, 22 Feb. 1679; Jonathan, 23 Sept. 1682, d. at 18 yrs.; Waitstill, 6 Nov. 1684; Joseph, 24 Apr. 1687; Ebenezer, 14 Feb. 1689, d. at 32 yrs.; Nathaniel, 7 Sept. 1692; Samuel, 30 May 1695; and Sarah, 4 Nov. 1698; was deac. 9 yrs. and rul. elder 21 yrs. aft. d. 10 or 12 Oct. 1722, and his wid. d. 8 Sept. 1728, in her 76th yr. and one acco. says aged 76.

TOPPAN, or TOPPING. See Tappan.

TORREY or TORIE, JAMES, Scituate, lieut. in 1640, m. 2 Nov. 1643, Ann, d. of Elder William Hatch, had James, b. 3 Sept. 1644; William, 15 Mar. 1647, prob. d. young; Joseph, 18 Mar. 1649; Damaris, 26 Oct. 1651; Jonathan, 20 Sept. 1654; Mary, 14 Feb. 1657; Josiah, 1658; Sarah, 9 Feb. 1661; Joanna, 4 May 1663; and Bethia, posthum. 1665. What was the day of his d. is unkn. JAMES, Scituate, eldest ch. of the preced. m. 1666, Lydia, only d. of William Wills or Willis, as Deane shows, but of issue says nothing, and had sec. w. m. 1679, Eliz. d. of Nathaniel Rawlins; and he had ano. w. or perhaps it was the same, wh. in Dorchester gr.yard by the name of Eunice, wid. of deac. James, d. there 15 Oct. 1732, in her 72d yr. wh. agrees with the age of the d. of Rawlins. JONATHAN, Weymouth, prob. s. of William the first, by w. Ruth, d. of George Fry of the same, had Mary, b. 25 Sept. 1675; Ruth, 17 Aug. 1679; Ann, 3 Mar. 1682; Jonathan, 24 May 1684; Joshua, 11 Nov. 1690; and perhaps others, where the rec. is defect. JOSEPH, Rehoboth 1643, went to Newport in 1654 or earlier, was on the freemen's list 1655; with an assoc. met Dennison and Danforth, Mass. Comsnrs. in 1664 at Rehoboth, a. some quest. of jurisdict. was a lieut. and in 1670 sent with John Greene and others as comsnrs. to adjust bounds with Conn. rul. elder of the ch. of John Clark, at the time of his d. 1676. Perhaps he m. a d. wh. may have been the eldest, of that John Greene, as by the Geneal. I have seen. JOSIAH, Medfield, freem. 1683, was, perhaps, s. of James the first of Scituate. MICAJAH, Weymouth, s. of the first William of the same, freem. 1672, by w. Susanna had Micajah, b. 27 July 1673; Mary, 22 Mar. 1681; Susanna, wh. d. 29 Oct. 1687; Samuel, 15 Jan. 1688; and perhaps others, not found on imperf. rec. PHILIP, Roxbury, from Combe St. Nicholas, Co. Somerset, near Chard, in the edge of Devon, was freem. 1644, m. 1 Oct. 1647, Mary, wid. of John Scarborough, had Joseph, b. 2, bapt. 15 July 1649; Jonathan, 16, bapt. 22 June 1651; and Mary, 2, bapt. 9 Apr. 1654; and d. a. 12 May 1686. In Mar. 1674, aged 59, he testif. that he came

with William and his s. Samuel to N. E. from Combe St. Nicholas in
Somersetsh. that he kn. them bef. and ever since; and George Fry unit.
in the fame. testim. *SAMUEL*, Weymouth, eldest s. of William of the
same, was brot. in early youth, 1640, by his f. with Philip, perhaps his
uncle, perhaps a cousin, and tho. pass. thro. the first prescrib. course of
study for three yrs. would have tak. his A. B. in 1650, yet bec. the term
was lengthen. to 4 yrs. he and others, as Dr. Eliot in Biog. Dict. tells, left
the Coll. His f. had giv. him the first classic. preparat. and he had so
improv. his opportun. that he had great reput. as a min. and was ord. 14
Feb. 1665, to succeed Thomas Thatcher, hav. preach. some yrs. at Hull.
He preach. the elect. serm. 1674, again in 1683, again 1695, an honor in
no other instance confer. in Mass. and was so highly esteem. for his
discret. as to be chos. Presid. of the Coll. in 1681, aft. the d. of Oakes,
and again, aft. d. of Rogers; but in his Hist. of H. C. notice of these
things by Mather is not found. However, it seems that the Gen. Ct.
Rec. V. 345, gave him the same encouragem. to accept, as they had offer.
to Increase Mather. Both applicat. were in vain. He m. 15 May
1657, Mary, d. of Edward Rawson, when he liv. at Hull, and for sec. w.
30 July 1695, Mary, wid. of William Symmes, tho. what was her
maiden name is undiscov. Nor is my kn. any better as to childr. or
whether he had any. He was freem. 1669, and hav. preach. above 50
yrs. d. 21 Apr. 1707, aged 75. I suppose in 1703 he rec. a collea. in
Rev. James Bailey. See 1 Mass. Hist. Coll. IX. 195. * WILLIAM,
Weymouth 1640, came that yr. from Combe St. Nicholas, close to Chard,
in Co. Somerset, bring. s. Samuel, and accomp. by George Fry and
Philip T. wh. may have been his br. or near relat. here soon found a
sec. w. if as to me seems prob. the mo. of Samuel were d. had Naomi, b. 3
Dec. 1641; Mary, 3 Dec. 1642; Micajah, 12 Oct. 1643, unless as is very
prob. there be error in the rec. print. in Geneal. Reg. VIII. 349. By
the fail. of rec. in a long interval, we lose perhaps half a dozen other ch.
certain. William and Jonathan. He was adm. freem. 18 May 1642,
rep. 1642, and very oft. aft. even 1679–83, and aft. overthrow of Andros
in 1690, was early lieut. and later capt. chos. clk. of the house of reps.
1650, and usual. aft. hav. as Johnson says, special qualificat. in that office.
His will of 15 May 1686, nam. eldest s. Samuel, and the others, William, Micajah, Josiah, and Angel, was pro. July 1691. WILLIAM, Weymouth, sec. s. of the preced. freem. 1672, by w. Deborah had William,
b. 14 Sept. 1670; John, 23 June 1673; Philip, 2 May 1681; Josiah, 19
Sept. 1686, and perhaps others omit. from the rec. Farmer marks nineteen of this name as gr. in 1834, at N. E. coll. of wh. ten are seen at
Harv. includ. one *Torry* and one at Yale.

TOTENHAM, ELIJAH, Woburn, s. of Henry of the same, by w. Mary had Ann, b. 24 Sept. 1685; Mary, 18 Apr. 1688; Sarah, 13 July 1690; Elisha, 22 July 1696; Eliz. 8 Feb. 1699; Alice, 10 June 1701; Arminell, 30 July 1707; and by w. Rebecca, had Rebecca, 4 Aug. 1710. HENRY, Woburn, had Nehemiah, b. 23 Aug. 1646; Elijah, 28 Feb. 1652; and his w. Ann d. 23 Feb. 1654; and he m. 13 July foll. w. Alice, but had no ch. by her. He was one of the bold petitnrs. for liberty of prophecy, 30 Aug. 1653. See 3 Mass. Hist. Coll. I. 44.

TOTMAN, STEPHEN, Scituate, s. of Thomas, had Stephen, and Samuel; but from Deane I learn no more. THOMAS, Plymouth, rem. to Scituate bef. 1660, and had Stephen.

TOUCHWILL, JOSEPH, is the name of a soldier in capt. Mosely's comp. on march in Dec. 1675, to the great Narraganset fight; but how much it may be distort. on the roster is uncert.

TOUNG, or TONG, GEORGE, New London, 1656–72, kept the ordinary. JAMES, Boston, master-mariner, m. 8 Sept. 1654, Eliz. d. of Abraham Hagborne, and d. at Jamaica next yr. in his will giv. all his prop. to w. wh. took admin. 17 July 1656.

TOURTELLOT, or TOURTELOT, ABRAHAM, Boston, a Huguenot merch. was partner with his br. BENJAMIN, wh. d. 25 Sept. 1687,·on a voyage from London to B. in the Friendship; and he act. as Admor. on the est. by the inv. of wh. consist. in part of merchandise, it is inf. that they had carr. on trade extensive. He liv. at Roxbury, some yrs. aft. there by w. Mary had Gabriel, b. 24 Sept. 1694; and Esther, 12 June 1696. GABRIEL, Boston, perhaps br. of the preced. was b. at Bordeaux in France, as is relat. but came from Rochelle in comp. with Gabriel Bernon, whose d. Mary he m. and it is said he d. at sea. But that he had ch. is kn. by many descend. Prob. the fam. rem. to Oxford, as in that vicin. the name is still perpet.

TOUSLAND, TOUSLEY, TOWSE, or TOUSEY, RICHARD, Saybrook, perhaps had a w. and fam. bef. 1666, but in this yr. made contr. of m. with Dorothy, wid. of John Edwards, wh. had been wid. of Abraham Finch, of Wethersfield, d. early in Feb. 1674, giv. back to his w. the prop. she brot. him. THOMAS, Wethersfield, perhaps s. of the preced. by a first w. did not live at W. bef. 1674, was a weaver, an enterpris. man, had in comp. with William Pitkin, a fulling-mill in Hartford; d. 1712, aged 62; had Thomas, Y. C. 1707, ancest. of the late Secr. of the Navy, beside Eliz.

TOUTE, RICHARD, Scituate 1643, then able to bear arms, but no more is heard of him, exc. that in 1663, he was of Boston, a lighterman.

TOUTON, JOHN, a Huguenot physician of Rochelle in France, with others petition. our Gen. Ct. as early as 1662, for permiss. to rem. hither; and their prayer was gr. but whether any other then came is not appar. He liv. at Rehoboth, July 1675.

TOWER, or TOWERS, DAVID, Hingham, perhaps s. of John, more prop. his gr.s. perish. in the doleful exped. of Phips against Quebec, 1690, but as he d. of smallpox, I conclude it occurr. as did many others, bef. the squadron left our harbor. JEREMIAH, Salisbury, perhaps s. of John of Hingham, m. Eliz. d. of Richard Goodale. JOHN, Hingham 1637, came from Hingham in Co. Norf. it is said, freem. 13 Mar. 1639, m. Feb. preced. or foll. Margaret Ibrook, d. prob. of Richard, had Ambrose, Benjamin, Jonathan, Hannah, and Jeremiah; but perhaps he had s. John, at least we kn. that he was describ. as John sen. He was engag. in early plant. at Lancaster, 1654, and descend. are very num. WILLIAM, Boston 1668, a butcher.

TOWLE, TOWEL, TOALE, TOLE, TOLL, TOULE, or TOWELL, HENRY, Wethersfield, rem. to Saybrook soon aft. 1668, had w. Sarah, and one ch. prob. Henry, desert. his w. wh. in 1676 was divorc. for his desert. above six yrs. as in Trumbull's Col. Rec. II. 293, with liberty if shall "have opportun. to join hers. in m. with ano. man." HENRY, New Haven, s. prob. of the preced. m. 13 Apr. 1693, Dorothy, d. of Daniel Thomas. JOHN, Sudbury, by w. Catharine, had John, b. 20 Nov. 1641, wh. d. 31 Jan. 1643; Mary, b. 8 Dec. 1643; and, again, John, wh. d. 8 Jan. 1657. JOSHUA, whose m. 2 Dec. 1686, with Sarah Reed, is rec. was perhaps of Hampton. PHILIP, Hampton 1670, had prob. been an early sett. for PHILIP jr. took the o. of alleg. 1678, some mos. bef. his f. wh. d. 1696. ROGER, Boston 1640, in Col. Rec. is call. serv. to Mr. Henry Webb, wh. means, I suppose, appr. was freem. 1644, hav. been adm. of the ch. with the same designat. 20 Apr. preced. WILLIAM, Malden, by w. Mary, had Benjamin, b. 2 Nov. 1689, or Jan. 1690; for the person wh. made the copy of the rec. chang. the dates for Geneal. Reg. VI. 335, in most cases by mistaking the numeral for the mo.

TOWNE, EDMUND, Topsfield, was eldest s. of William, wh. prob. was s. of Richard of Braceby in Co. Lincoln, where Ann, wid. of said Richard, made her will 10 Dec. 1629, of wh. copy is in Geneal. Reg. X. 36. Braceby is 6 ms. from Grantham and 5 from Folkenham. He came, 1637, prob. in the Rose of Yarmouth, aged 18, as apprent. to Henry Skerry of Salem, m. Mary, d. of Thomas Browning, had Thomas; William, b. 1658; Joseph, 1661; Abigail; Benjamin, 1666; Rebecca; Samuel, 1673; Mary; Sarah; Eliz.; and ano. d. and he d. early in 1678. Abigail m. 12 Jan. 1686, Jacob Peabody; and next, 14 Jan. 1696, Thomas Perley. Abstr. of his will, of wh. wid. Mary had admin. is in Essex Inst. II. 277. JACOB, Salem 1637, had Joseph, and Sarah, perhaps not tw. bapt. there, 3 Sept. 1648. JACOB, Topsfield, b. in Eng. br. of Edmund of the same, m. 26 June 1657, Catharine, d. of John Symonds of Salem, had John, b. 2 Apr. 1658; Jacob, 13 Feb. 1660; Catharine,

25 Feb. 1662; Deliverance, 5 Aug. 1664; Edmund, 21 July 1666; and
Ruth; freem. 1686, d. 22 Nov. 1704, and his will was pro. 1 Jan. 1705.
JACOB, Topsfield, s. of the preced. may have been, instead of his f. freem.
1686, m. 24 June 1684, Phebe Smith, had Joshua, b. 1684; John, 1685;
and Abigail, 1689, acc. Barry. JOHN, Topsfield, s. of Jacob first of the
same, by w. Mary had Mary, b. 23 June 1681; John, 25 Nov. 1682, d.
young; Israel, 18 Nov. 1684; Esther, 1686; Ephraim; David, a. 1694;
Samuel; Edmund, 7 May 1699; rem. to Framingham, and had John,
31 May 1702; Zerviah; and Jonathan; was a selectman, 1700–1712
most of the time, and a propr. in new planta. of Oxford. His will was
pro. 1740. JOSEPH, Topsfield, youngest s. of William of the same, m.
Phebe, d. of deac. Thomas Perkins, had Phebe, b. 1666; Joanna; Mary;
Susanna; Joseph, 22 Mar. 1673; Sarah; Martha; John, 20 Feb. 1678;
and ano. d. was freem. 1690; and d. 1713. JOSEPH, Topsfield, s. of
Edmund, had two ws. of wh. Emma, m. 1687, was perhaps sec. Whether
by the former, Phebe, he had any, is not ascert. but ch. were Benjamin,
Daniel, Nathan, Jesse, Nathaniel, Amos, and Emma; and he d. 1717.
PETER, Cambridge, s. of William of the same, bapt. in Eng. had w.
Joanna, and I kn. no more, but that he was freem. 1690, and d. 2 Nov.
1705, aged 72 yrs. 10 mos. as Harris gives the inscript. THOMAS, Lynn,
m. at Reading 30 Oct. 1662, Hannah, of unkn. surname; gave evid. in
1681, then aged 50, a. lds. d. at R. 1684. Perhaps it is Tower. THOMAS,
Topsfield, s. of Edmund of the same, in early youth was in the flower of
Essex under capt. Lothrop, on Conn. riv. in 1675, but perhaps not present at Bloody Brook, m. 1685, Sarah French, perhaps d. of John of
Ipswich, had Edmund, Thomas, Richard, Experience, Sarah, Ednah, and
Mercy; and d. a. 1720. WILLIAM, Salem, had m. at Yarmouth, Co.
Norfolk, 25 March 1620 or 1, Joanna Blessing, and prob. came over the
water, 1635, tho. in what ship is not seen; in Dec. 1640, he had gr. of
ld. at S. but Felt spells the name Townde. He rem. to Topsfield a.
1651; and his ch. bapt. at Y. were Rebecca, Feb. 1622; John, Feb.
1624; Susanna, Oct. 1625; Edmund, June 1628; Jacob, Mar. 1633;
Mary, 24 Aug. 1634; and at Salem, Sarah; and Joseph, b. 1639; and d.
1672, leav. all these ch. exc. John and Susanna. Farmer in MS. makes
him the freem. of 1637, in wh. I do not concur. His wid. liv. a. ten yrs.
Rebecca m. Francis Nurse, had eight ch. and was execut. for a witch,
19 July 1692, to wh. her deafness was the chief inducem. Mary m.
Isaac Esty, had two ds. and was tr. on 9th execut. 22 Sept. 1692, under
the same sad infatuat. She was the heroic woman, that in our day gives
dignity to the cause, as set forth in Chandler's Crim. Trials. Sarah m.
11 Jan. 1660, Edmund Bridge or Bridges, had five ch. and next m.
Peter Cloyes, had two or three more, and was a gr. sufferer in the

27 *

witchr. proceed. barely escap. with life. WILLIAM, Cambridge 1635, freem. 18 Apr. 1637, had w. Martha, wh. d. 20 Jan. 1674, s. Peter, bapt. in Eng. d. Mary, b. 6 Sept. 1637, bapt. at C. was town clk. 1639, bot. in 1653, a ho. of David Stone, was tythingman 1680, and d. aged 80, 30 Apr. 1685, tho. Harris gives the rec. Mar. wh. I disregard, as Sewall, in two places, notes his bur. 1 May.

TOWNSEND, ANDREW, Lynn, perhaps s. or gr.s. of Thomas of the same, a soldier in Gardner's comp. at the gr. battle, 19 Dec. 1675, of the Narraganset campaign, when he was wound. for wh. in 1730, he ask. pension; m. 18 July 1678, Abigail, prob. d. of John Collins, of the same, had Thomas, b. 12 June 1679; Abigail, 23 Feb. 1681; and Mary, 7 July 1685; was freem. 1691. GEORGE, Reading, by Eaton nam. among early sett. may have been br. of John of the same. GEORGE, Warwick, s. of John of the same, m. Meribah, d. of Richard Harcutt. HENRY, Warwick, on the list of freem. 1655, of wh. I kn. no more, exc. that he m. Ann, a d. of Robert Cole. He may have been s. of Thomas of Lynn, and sett. at Oyster Bay on L. I. ‖ JAMES, Boston, s. of William, a carpenter, by w. Eliz. had James, bapt. 2 July 1671, H. C. 1692; John, 14 Dec. 1672; Mary, 10 Jan. 1675, d. young; Joseph, b. 24 Jan. 1678; Eliz. 18 July 1684; Mary, again, 27 Oct. 1687; and Ann, 26 Feb. 1690, posthum. was freem. 1672. He was a housewright, ar. co. 1679, and bef. 17 Dec. 1689, d. intest. when admin. was refus. by his wid. ‖ John, Lynn, perhaps s. of Thomas, and b. in Eng. was of ar. co. 1641, and of the early sett. on L. I. JOHN, Warwick, among the freem. there of 1655, may have been br. of Henry, or the same as the preced. had Rose wh. m. John Wicks the sec. His eldest ch. was John; and others were Thomas, Eliz. James, Sarah, Ann, George, and Daniel. His w. was Eliz. d. of Robert Cole. He d. at Oyster Bay 1669. JOHN, Reading, freem. 1678, may have been br. of George. JOHN, Lynn, m. 27 Jan. 1669, Sarah Pearson, d. of John of the same, had Sarah, b. 14 Sept. 1672; John, 17 Mar. 1675; Mary 2 Sept. 1677; Hannah, 11 Feb. 1680; and Eliz. 9 Nov. 1683. Perhaps he was a gr.s. of Thomas. JOSEPH, Boston, by w. Mary had Joseph, b. 23 Dec. 1665; had sec. w. Dorothy, perhaps was of Falmouth 1682. MARTIN, Watertown, a weaver, m. 16 Apr. 1668, Abigail, d. of John Train, had Abigail, b. 18 Sept. 1669; Martin; Hannah, 6 Oct. 1673, d. at 2 yrs.; John, 26 May 1679, d. at 4 yrs.; Jonathan, Apr. 1688, d. at 3 mos.; Jonathan, again; and his w. d. 16 Jan. 1691; and he m. 30 Aug. 1693, Esther Perry of Woburn; but no more ch. is kn. He was a witness 7 Apr. 1691, when he call. his age 47, and d. in few yrs. ‡*‖ PENN, Boston, s. of William of the same, wine merch. m. Sarah, youngest d. of the first Isaac Addington, had Penn, b. 31 July 1674, H. C. 1693; Sarah, 3 Apr. 1677, d.

soon; Sarah, again, 14 Sept. 1680; Rebecca, 15 Aug. 1685; Isaac, 14
Aug. 1687, d. at 15 yrs.; Ann, 1689, d. soon; and Ann, again, 10 Nov.
1690. His w. d. 11 Mar. 1692, and he m. Mary, wid. of Paul Dudley,
d. of Gov. Leverett, wh. was bur. 5 July 1699; and for third w. wh.
outliv. him, he took Hannah, wid. of George Jaffrey, Esq. of N. H. He
was of ar. co. 1674, freem. 1674, very much confid. in for public concerns, rep. 1686, being the last Court under the old Chart. and on the
overthrow of Andros, was rechosen almost every time for some yrs.
went as commissnr. with Hutchinson 1691, to make peace with Ind.
speaker of the house and counsellor many yrs. serv. thro. all the ranks in
the milit. from ens. to col. and d. 21 Aug. 1727. PETER, Boston, carpenter, s. of William of the same, by w. Lydia had William, b. 13 Sept.
1666; Susanna, 22 Feb. 1668, wh. d. soon; Susanna, again, 20 Feb.
1670; Peter, 9 Oct. 1671; Lydia, 5 Aug. 1673; and Thomas; by w.
Margaret had Margaret, b. 13 June 1677; by w. Ann had Hannah, 27
Oct. 1687; and d. 14 May 1696. RALPH, New Haven, rem.
to New London. RICHARD, Warwick, of the freem. 1655, was prob.
br. of Henry, and m. Deliverance, d. of Robert Cole, had John, Richard,
Dinah, Leah, and Hannah, of wh. Dinah m. Thomas Willet, and Leah
m. John Williams, both perhaps of Newtown, L. I. and for sec. w. he
took Eliz. d. of John Wicks. His wid. m. John Smith of Hempstead,
L. I. where prob. Townsend d. ROBERT, Portsmouth, in 1665 support.
the jurisdict. of Mass. SAMUEL, Boston, liv. at Rumney Marsh, Chelsea,
by w. Abigail had David, b. 29 Sept. 1666; Jonathan, 10 Sept. 1668;
perhaps, also, Samuel, and more ch. was freem. 1683, hav. join. the 2d
ch. 18 Sept. 1681. SAMUEL, Boston, prob. s. of the preced. was freem.
1690. THOMAS, Lynn, the freem. of 14 Mar. 1639, wh. d. 22 Dec.
1677 is thot. to have had Thomas, Henry, and John, b. prob. in Eng. all
early engag. in settlem. on L. I. THOMAS, Boston, perhaps br. of Samuel the first, with w. Mary adm. into the 2d ch. 30 Oct. 1681, was freem.
1683, but of him I kn. no more. WILLIAM, Boston, adm. of the ch. 3
Aug. 1634, the same day with Gov. Bellingham and his w. with John
Newgate and the w. of our br. Nicholas Wyllys, of wh. W. T. is then
call. serv. so that we may well infer, that he came early that yr. from
London. The simplicity of charact. was exhibit. in the puritan's household, and this stile of serv. did not imply inferior condit. so much as
obligat. to learn, otherwise, in case of males, term apprent. His w.
Hannah Penn, wh. had join the ch. 15 Mar. 1635, is call. "our br.
James Everill's maid serv." was sis. of the rul. Elder, James P. and if
she came with her master, and her h. with his, as the principles were rec.
in July preced. we may believe they all came in one sh. He was freem.
25 May 1636, had Eliezur, 12 June 1635; Patience, bapt. 28 May

1637 ; Hannah, b. 4, bapt. 11 Apr. 1641 ; Peter 26, bapt. 30 Oct. 1642 ; Mary, 24 Nov. 1644; James, b. 15 Jan. 1647; Penn, 20 Dec. 1651; John, 3 Sept. 1653, d. next yr. ; and Mary, wh. d. 29 Nov. 1658. With the maj. part of the Boston ch. he was adher. of Wheelwright's opin. and subject. in Nov. 1637, to the indign. of being disarm. as a danger. heretic, but was not of suffic. age or import. to be driv. away. He d. bef. Dec. 1689, and his wid. d. bef. 6 Feb. 1700, when admin. de bonis non on est. of her h. was giv. to s. Penn. Hannah, m. 3 Apr. 1657, Thomas Hull, and next, as Whitman says, lieut. Richard Way. Farmer found, in 1834, sixteen of this name among gr. at Harv. six at Yale, and five at other N. E. coll.

Towsly, Michael, Salisbury, had been in Philip's war, 1676, a soldier of Hampton, m. 4 June 1678, Mary Hussey, perhaps d. of Christopher, had Mary, b. 17 Mar. 1679, d. soon ; rem. to Suffield, next yr. had Mary, again, 12 Jan. 1681 ; Matthew, 18 Nov. 1690 ; and perhaps others. Mary m. 1699, Benjamin Allen.

Towson, Nicholas, New London, was on the tax list 1667.

Toy. See Tay.

Tozer, Tosier, or Tozier, Leonard, Salem 1668. Richard, Dover, liv. first at Boston, m. a d. of Robert Blott, wh. d. soon, and he m. at Boston, 3 July 1656, Judith Smith, had Thomas, b. 5 May 1657 ; Richard, bef. 1660 ; and prob. others ; was mort. wound. 16 Oct. 1675, at the Ind. assault of Salmon Falls, and d. soon at Kittery. Richard, Berwick, s. of the preced. m. Eliz. only d. of Elder William Wentworth, had Martha, Abigail, Sarah, Judith, and perhaps more ; liv. 22 Sept. 1734. His w. and hims. were prison. in Canada more than once ; but both were liv. Jan. 1733, when he sw. he was 73 yrs. old. Simon, Watertown, perhaps s. of Richard the first, flying from Ind. hostil. by w. Mary, had Mary, b. 16 Aug. 1693 ; John, 8 Oct. 1695 ; Richard and Abigail, tw. 26 July 1701 ; Susanna, 27 Jan. 1703 ; and Judith, 4 Jan. 1705.

Tracy, Daniel, Norwich, s. of Thomas of the same, m. 1682, Abigail, d. of Thomas Adgate of Saybrook, and was k. 1728, with others, by fall of a bridge, says Miss Caulkins, wh. does not ment. any ch. tho. we may believe, that he, as well as his bros. had fam. * John, Duxbury, s. of Stephen, wh. was one of the first comers, m. Mary, d. of Gov. Prence, had Sarah ; Stephen, 1673 ; perhaps others ; rem. to Windham, there d. 30 May 1718 ; was rep. 1683 and 6. John, Norwich, eldest s. of Thomas, m. at Marshfield, 10 June 1670, Mary, d. of the first Josiah Winslow, had Eliz. b. 6 Apr. 1690 ; d. 16 Aug. 1702. Stephen, Plymouth, came in the Ann, 1623, with w. Tryphosa (wh. he m. at Leyden, 2 Jan. 1621, when the Dutch rec. has the name Trifasa, and surname illegib.) and one ch. prob. Sarah, counted in the div. of lds. in the ensuing spr. for three heads, and in the div. of cattle 1627, ano. ch. Rebecca is count. had Ruth, Mary, and John, b. 1633; in 1645 was of Duxbury, and in 1650, or near that, went home in the early part of 1655 call. hims. of Great Yarmouth, by his will, made in London, of wh. John Winslow was made excor. names the five ch. to wh. he gives all his prop. so that we must presume the w. was d. Sarah m. George Partridge. *THOMAS, Salem 1637, carpenter, rem. soon to Saybrook, thence in few yrs. to Wethersfield, or Hartford, perhaps both, but at last took up perman. resid. at Norwich, of wh. he was one of the patent. rep. 1662, and almost always aft. ensign long, and lieut. His eldest ch. was John; other ch. he had, as Caulkins, p. 112 shows; Jonathan; Thomas; Solomon; Daniel, b. a. 1653; Samuel; and Miriam, wh. m. 1668, Thomas Waterman. He was Commissary in Philip's war. WILLIAM, is the first name on the list of passeng. in the Mary and John, wh. took o. of alleg. 24 Mar. 1634, and as so many of his compan. over the ocean sat down at Newbury aft. tempor. resid. at Ipswich, we may be justif. in think. that he did so; and possib. he is ancestor of those wh. gave high distinct. to this name near a century ago in that place. Farmer marks in 1834, that nine of this name had been gr. at Yale, three at Harv. and eight at other N. E. coll. most at Dart.

TRAFTON, THOMAS, York, sw. alleg. to Charles II. 22 Mar. 1681.

TRAIN, JOHN, Watertown, came in the Susan and Ellen 1635, aged 25, from London, perhaps as serv. of Percival Greene, with Abigail Dix, aged 18, also call. serv. by w. Margaret, wh. prob. was their fellow passeng. had Eliz. b. 30 Sept. 1640; Mary, 10 Oct. 1642; Sarah, 31 Jan. 1647; Abigail, 31 Jan. 1649; John, 25 May or Sept. 1651; Thomas, 1653; Rebecca; and Hannah, 7 or 8 Sept. 1657; his w. d. 18 Dec. 1660. He m. 12 Oct. 1675, Abigail Bent, sw. fidelity 1652, and d. 29 Jan. 1681; Eliz. m. 10 Mar. 1658, John Stratton; Sarah m. 12 Oct. 1679, as Bond has it, tho. certain. sev. yrs. I guess ten, too late, Jacob Cole; Abigail m. 16 Apr. 1668, Martin Townsend; Rebecca, m. 12 Jan. 1677, Michael Barstow; and Hannah m. 16 Jan. 1678, Richard Child. JOHN, Watertown, s. of the preced. m. 24 Mar. 1675, Mary, d. of Joshua Stubbs, had John, b. Dec. foll. d. very soon; Abigail, 5 June 1677; Eliz. 6 Jan. 1680; John, again, 31 Oct. 1682; Margaret, 18 Aug. 1685; Thomas, 20 May 1688; and perhaps Rebecca. He d. 1718. THOMAS, Watertown, br. of the preced. m. 25 Jan. 1693, Rebecca, d. of Charles Stearns, had Benoni, b. and d. that yr.; Rebecca, Apr. 1696, d. next mo.; Deborah, 16 Dec. 1698, d. at 20 yrs.; Rebecca, again, 1 Dec. 1701; and he d. 23 Jan. 1739. His wid. d. 23 Sept. 1746.

TRAPP, THOMAS, honor. by tradit. as one of the first sett. on Martha's Vineyard, some time betw. 1632 and 1642, but authentic hist. kn. nothing of him. Yet one of the same name, wh. may have been his s. d. at Edgartown, 15 Oct. 1719, in his 85th yr. testif. in Boston, July 1659, that he was a mariner, aged 20.

TRARICE, TRERICE, TRERISE, TREYRICE, TREREISE, or TREROICE, JOHN, Charlestown, s. of Nicholas of the same, by w. Hannah, d. of Thomas Lynde, m. 1663, had Nicholas; John; Hannah, perhaps the eldest, all bapt. 18 June 1671; and Rebecca, 14 Sept. 1673. NICHOLAS, Charlestown, adm. says Frothingham, a townsman in 1636, had been the two yrs. bef. capt. of the Planter, wh. brot. many persons from London, by w. Rebecca had Rebecca; John, b. 26 May, bapt. 3 June 1639; was fin. for contempt of Ct. 1641, rem. early to Woburn, there had Samuel, 7 May 1643. His d. Rebecca m. 22 May 1655, Thomas Jenner. His wid. Rebecca m. 6 Dec. 1665, Thomas Lynde. Barry, Framingham, 422, mistook the name Travis.

TRASK, BENJAMIN, Beverly, s. of Osmond, m. Mary Shattuck, d. of Samuel of Salem. EDWARD, Beverly s. of Osmond of the same, a soldier in Lothrop's comp. call. flower of Essex, k. at Bloody brook, 18 Sept. 1675. HENRY, Salem, came in the Mary and John 1634, m. Mary, d. of Lawrence Southwick, had Mary, b. 14 Aug. 1652; Ann, 14 Apr. 1654; Sarah, 27 July 1656; and Henry, Apr. 1669; and perhaps rem. with his injur. f.-in-law to enjoy the protection of the Sylvesters in their manorial est. at Shelter isl. at the E. end of L. I. If so, he came back, and his w. was imprison. many mos. for her perverse relig. but prob. it was bef. rem. He d. a. 1689, and his wid. m. William Nichols of Topsfield. His name is pervert. to Thask in the valua. Essex Inst. Coll. II. 277. JOHN, Salem, s. of capt. William, m. 19 Feb. 1663, Abigail Parkman, perhaps d. of the first Elias, and late in life took Christian, d. of Humphrey Woodbury, was liv. in 1695 at Beverly and had a fam. as is believ. no doubt by the first w. wh. were Abigail, b. 19 Nov. 1664; John, 7 June 1667; Mary, 14 July 1669; Samuel, 14 Aug. 1671; Rebecca, 23 Apr. 1674; Nicholas, 26 Mar. 1677; Elias, 13 July 1679; Christian was sad. disturb. in mind and k. herself. OSMOND, Beverly 1660, when he was 35 yrs. old, may have been br. of the preced. by first w. Mary, m. 1 Jan. 1650, wh. d. 2 Jan. 1663, had Sarah, b. Sept. 1650; Edward, 6 June 1652; John, 15 Aug. 1653; Mary, May 1657; William, 5 July 1660, d. next mo. and prob. Sarah, wh. d. young. Next he m. 22 May 1663, Eliz. d. of John Gally, had Mary, wh. m. but d. young; Samuel; Benjamin; Joseph; Eliz. wh. d. young; William; Jonathan; and Edward, prob. posthum. He d. early in 1676, his inv. being tak. 5 Mar. His wid. m. John Giles of Salem. * WILLIAM, Salem, one of the first sett. bef. Endicott, perhaps in 1626. He req. adm. as freem. 19

Oct. 1630, but was never sw. in (that we can find) yet was capt. in 1632, rep. in 1635, 6, 7, and 9, had com. in the exped. under Endicott, 1637, against the Pequots. For that serv. his modest petitn. of 1661, is print. in Geneal. Reg. VI. 370, and the gr. of 400 acres then made was in add. to one of 250, bestow. soon aft. the war of 1637. Of his ch. Sarah was prob. eldest; Mary, bapt. 1 Jan. 1637; Susanna, 10 June 1638; William, 19 Sept. 1640; John, 18 Sept. 1642; Eliz. 21 Sept. 1645; Mary, again, b. 14 Aug. bapt. 2 Oct. 1652; Ann, 14 Apr. bapt. 18 June 1654; we are ign. if one mo. bore all, but infer that the w. Sarah, perhaps bapt. 14 Sept. 1656, nam. in the will of 15 May 1666, was a sec. w. and had brot. him the last three; and that the first Mary, with Eliz. and Ann were d. bef. that. He d. at the age of 77 yrs. very soon aft. the will bears date, prob. next day. Of the ds. we kn. that Sarah m. 13 Oct. 1656, the sec. Elias Parkman; Susanna, m. 19 Feb. 1664, Samuel Ebborne, as sec. w. and Mary m. a Batter, prob. Daniel. WILLIAM, Salem, s. of the preced. m. 18 Jan. 1667, Ann, eldest d. of Thomas Putnam, had Ann, b. 7 June 1668; Eliz. Mar. 1670, d. young; Sarah, 14 June 1672; William, 7 Sept. 1674; and Susanna, 3 Nov. 1676; and was an innkeeper twenty yrs. aft. His w. d. 14 Nov. 1676; and he took to w. sec. Ann, wh. surv. him, and had John; Eliz.; Mary, b. Mar. 1683; and George, Jan. 1690. His will of 5 Sept. 1690, was pro. 30 June 1691.

TRAUL, THRALL, or TRALL, DAVID, Windsor, s. prob. of William of the same, had perhaps a fam. and d. 7 Dec. 1722, aged 72. TIMOTHY, Windsor, s. of William, freem. 1658, m. 10 Nov. 1659, Deborah, d. of Thomas Gunn, had Deborah, b. 19 Aug. 1660; Timothy, 7 Dec. 1662; Mehitable, Mar. 1664; Eliz. 1 May 1667; John, 8 June 1669, d. soon; John, again, 5 June 1671; Martha, 31 May 1673; and Thomas, 5 May 1675, d. soon; Thomas, again, 10 July 1676; Samuel, and Abigail, tw. 22 Feb. 1682. His w. d. 7 Jan. 1694, and he d. June 1697. WILLIAM, Windsor, serv. in the Pequot war 1637, for wh. in 1671 he obt. gr. of 50 acres, was early a freem. and so found in the list of 1669, had prob. a fam. tho. his w. is not nam. ch. David; Timothy, b. 25 July 1641; and Phillis, I suppose, wh. m. 5 Nov. 1657, John Hosford. His aged wid. d. 30 July 1676.

TRAVELL, NATHANIEL, perhaps only a trans. resid. in Mass. by our Gen. Ct. 1640, admonish. for slander.

TRAVERS, or TRAVIS, DANIEL, Boston 1652, carpenter, by w. Esther, had Daniel, b. 3 Oct. 1652; Ephraim, 13 Sept. 1659; to wh. Farmer adds Jeremiah, wh. d. 1 Nov. 1656; and Timothy; was freem. 1673, had long been chief gunner, and from 1 May 1680, was allow. £25, as in our rec. of the Col. V. 306; d. 19 Jan. 1683. HENRY, Newbury, came in the Mary and John 1634, from London, had Sarah, b. 1636, by wh. is uncert. but by w. Bridget had James, 28 Apr. 1645. His wid. m. 30 Mar. 1659, Richard Window of Gloucester; and Sarah m. 30 Aug. 1654, Nicholas Wallington, or Wallingford. A d. Eliz. I suppose m. Anthony Berry, for she is call. d.-in-law of Richard Window, after his d. in 1665, when disputes arose a. the est. of the wid. and childr. JAMES, Gloucester, s. of the preced. m. 18 Apr. 1667, Mercy, d. of John Pierce, had Eliz. b. 8 Feb. foll. rem. soon aft. and was of Brookfield 1672–5. RICHARD, Boston, m. 22 Dec. 1657, Grace Clements, d. of Francis of Glastonbury in Somersetsh. says the rec. ROBERT, is only heard of, as one of four ferrymen betw. Boston, and Charlestown, freed from impress. in Philip's war. SAMUEL, Boston, was a memb. of Mather's ch. 1670 or 1.

TREADWAY, TREDWAY, or TREADAWAY, JONATHAN, Watertown, eldest ch. of Nathaniel of the same, m. 1 Mar. 1666, at Medfield, Judith, d. of John Thurston, had b. there, Lydia, 8 Sept. 1667; and b. at Sudbury, where he liv. the resid. of his days, Nathaniel, 2 Dec. 1668, d. in few days; Jonathan, 4 June 1670; James, 6 Oct. 1671; Hannah, 14 June 1680; Ephraim, 14 Nov. 1681; Huldah, 1 Nov. 1687; and Benjamin; was insane from 1695, and d. 28 May 1710. His wid. d. 12 Oct. 1726, at Framingham. JOSIAH, Sudbury, m. Sufferance, d. of Walter Haynes of the same, had three ds. at least bef. 1664, as their uncle Thomas Noyes in his will of 20 May in that yr. gives to the two eldest ds. JOSIAH, Watertown, youngest br. of Jonathan, a weaver, m. 9 Jan. 1674, Sarah, d. of Thomas Sweetman of Cambridge, had Josiah, b. 28 Feb. 1675, d. under 9 yrs.; James, 17 Oct. 1676; Sarah, 18 Dec. 1679; Bethia, 2 Dec. 1681; Abigail, 24 Sept. 1683; Josiah, again, 16 Nov. 1686; Susanna, 6 Jan. 1689; and Tabitha, 15 Dec. 1690; was freem. 1690. His w. d. 5 Mar. 1697, and he rem. to Charlestown, m. 3 Feb. foll. Dorothy, wid. of Samuel Cutler, d. of Abraham Bell, had Catharine, bapt. 5 Dec. 1703; and he d. 15 Jan. 1733 in 81st yr. by gr.st. NATHANIEL, Watertown, prob. br. of the first Josiah, a weaver, first liv. at Sudbury, there m. Sufferance, d. of Edward Howe of Watertown, had Jonathan, b. 11 Nov. 1640; Mary, 1 Aug. 1642; and James; rem. to Watertown, where his f.-in-law gave him est. had Eliz. 3 Aug. 1646; Lydia; Josiah; and Deborah, 2 Aug. 1657; was oft. selectman betw. 1653 and 72. His w. d. 22 July 1682, and he made his will, 25 July 1687, in wh. all the ch. are refer. to, but as Mary was d. leav. d. Mary, this ch. was provid. for; and d. Eliz.'s childr. by first h. and he d. 20 July 1689. Mary m. first 12 Sept. 1665, John Fisher, prob. of Medfield, as his sec. w. and next 21 July 1675, Timothy Hawkins, as his third w. and d. in childbed 17 May 1677; Eliz. m. 21 Oct. 1664, Shadrach Hapgood of Sudbury, and next a Hayward; Lydia m. 2 Oct.

1667, Josiah Jones, and d. 18 Sept. 1743, aged 94 ; and Deborah m. 25 May 1680, Joseph Goddard.

TREADWELL, EDWARD, Ipswich 1637, was of Branford in 1646 and 8, of Southold, L. I. 1659. JOHN, Ipswich, s. of Thomas the sec. by w. Mary had Eliz. b. 16 July 1699. JOHN, Ipswich 1638. NATHANIEL, Ipswich, s. of Thomas the first of the same, m. 19 June 1661, Abigail, d. of Thomas Wells of the same, had Abigail, b. 2 Feb. 1663 ; Mary, 22 Oct. 1665 ; Nathaniel, 1668, d. at 4 yrs ; Hannah, 7 Feb. 1670 ; Thomas, 11 July 1672 ; Sarah, 15 Aug. 1674 ; Nathaniel, again, 13 June 1677 ; and his w. d. 3 days aft. He m. 25 Mar. foll.; Rebecca, d. of William Titcomb, of Newbury, had Eliz. 18 Jan. 1679 ; and Rebecca, 8 Apr. 1686 ; was freem. 1682. SAMUEL, Fairfield, propound. for freem. 1670, perhaps s. of Edward, was quite aged at his d. 1718, leav. s. Edward, had, also, Samuel, and Ephraim, both d. of wh. the latter's inv. was giv. in Feb. 1709. THOMAS, Ipswich 1636, had come in the Hopewell, capt. Babb, from London, in the autumn of 1635, hav. engag. his pass. 28 July, then call. his age 30, with w. Mary, 30, and s. Thomas, 1 yr. and first sat down at Dorchester, but at I. had Mary, b. 26 or 29 Sept. 1636 ; Nathaniel, 15 Mar. 1640 ; Esther, 21 Mar. 1641 ; and Martha, 16 Mar. 1644 ; was sw. freem. 7 Sept. 1638, and d. 8 June 1671, leav. wid. Mary, and ch. Thomas, Nathaniel, and Mary. His wid. d. Dec. 1685. Esther m. 8 Oct. 1665, the sec. Daniel Hovey. THOMAS, Ipswich, s. of the preced. brot. by his f. from Eng. m. 16 Mar. 1665, Sarah, eldest d. of William Titcomb of Newbury, had Thomas, b. 3 Mar. 1666 ; John, 28 Nov. 1670 ; Sarah, 10 Jan. 1673 ; Mary, 9 Aug. 1675 ; and Ann, 16 Aug. 1679, d. young. He was freem. 1682. THOMAS, Ipswich. s. of the preced. shoemaker, by w. Mary had Mary b. 8 June 1691. Farmer notes that, of this name, four had in 1825 been gr. at Harv. and two at Yale.

TREAT, HENRY, Marblehead 1673, may be thot. only casual. visit. and to be the eldest s. of Matthew, wh. m. at Hartford, a. 1673, Sarah, d. of Edward Andrews, had Sarah, b. a. 1674 ; and Matthias, a. 1676 ; and d. 1681. His wid. m. David Forbes, unless it may seem more prob. that it was the d. Sarah, wh. m. Forbes. * JAMES, Wethersfield, youngest s. of Richard the first of the same, yet perhaps b. in Eng. freem. 1657, m. 26 Jan. 1665, Rebecca, d. of John Latimer of W. had James, b. 1 Apr. 1666 ; Jemima, 15 May 1668 ; Samuel, 1669 ; Salmon, 1673, H. C. 1694 ; Richard ; Jerusha, 1678 ; Joseph, 1680 ; Mabel ; and Rebecca, 1685 ; was rep. 1672, 3, and 4, and d. 12 Feb. 1709. His wid. d. 2 Apr. 1734, aged 84. Jemima m. 17 Dec. 1691, Stephen Chester jr. Jerusha m. 17 May 1705, capt. Thomas Welles, and next, 25 Dec. 1712, Ephraim Goodrich, and d. 25 May 1727, tho. in Chapin, 185, by

error of type, d. instead of a. it would seem that she d. in few days
aft. m. Rebecca m. 27 Dec. 1704, Ebenezer Deming jr. JAMES, Wethersfield, s. of the preced. m. 17 Dec. 1691, Prudence, d. of John Chester of the same, had Abigail, b. 6 Dec. 1692; Charles, 29 Jan. 1695,
d. perhaps in few mos.; Prudence, 13 Apr. 1697; Eunice, 26 Jan.
1699; James, 22 Sept. 1701; Oliver, 31 May 1705; and Jerusha, 14
Mar. 1707; his w. d. 23 May 1727, and he m. Hannah, wid. of Daniel Boardman, d. of Samuel Wright, wh. outliv. him. He d. 18 Feb.
1742, and his wid. d. 25 Feb. 1746. JOSEPH, Wethersfield youngest
br. of the preced. m. 16 July 1713, Mary, d. of Joshua Robbins of W.
had Mary, b. 17 Mar. 1715; Elisha, 3 Apr. 1720; John, 23 Aug.
1733; perhaps others; and d. 15 Sept. 1756. His wid. d. 17 Sept.
1760, in 68th yr. MATTHEW, or MATTHIAS, Middletown, the freem. of
1657, may have been br. of James, certain. call. serv. of Richard of
Wethersfield, 1645, or soon aft. m. at W. 1648, Mary, d. of the first
Richard Smith of the same, had Henry, b. 1649; Susanna, 1651; Richard, 1655; Eliz. 1657; Abigail, 1659, wh. m. 1683, Stephen Hollister;
and Dorcas, 1661; and he d. 1662. His wid. m. Anthony Wright.
‡* RICHARD, Wethersfield, is one of the very few early sett. whom we
can find no trace of in Mass. where he may have been a serv. or apprent.
yet it is said that he was a rep. in the first Gen. Ct. 1637, tho. that is
not prob. for in Trumbull's Col. rec. I find not his name in that relat.
was chos. an Assist. 1658 to 65, but not after the union with New Haven
in that yr. He was nam. in the Royal Chart. of 23 Apr. 1662, for
junct. of the two Cols. and rem. to Milford, only, I suppose, to estab.
his s. Robert at that settlem. for he is counted on the list of freem. at W.
1669. In this yr. he d. hav. made his will of 13 Feb. of the same,
names without suffic. particular. of the ds. his w. Alice and ch. perhaps
all b. in Eng. Richard; Robert, b. a. 1622; James, a. 1634; Honor,
m. a. 1637, John Deming the first; Joanna, w. of John Hollister; Sarah,
m. a. 1644, Matthew Campfield; Susanna, m. a. 1652, Robert Webster
of Middletown; and one, Catharine, wh. m. 19 Nov. 1655, William
Thompson of New Haven, tho. by Chapin, Glastonbury, 185, the name
is giv. Johnson, wh. may have been sec. h. beside cous. Samuel Wells;
and gr.s. call. cous. Daniel Deming. His wid. was not the mo. of the
childr. it is suppos. bec. he is said to have brot. from Eng. w. Joanna.
RICHARD, Wethersfield, eldest s. of the preced. b. in Eng. is in the list
of freem. of W. 1669, as well as his f. but we may judge that each had
been so twenty yrs. or more; by w. Sarah, d. of Thomas Coleman, had
Richard, b. 14 Feb. 1663; Sarah, 8 June 1664; Mary, 8 Oct. 1666;
and Thomas, 12 Dec. 1668; was one of the three corporals of the first
troop of horse, 1658. His wid. d. 23 Aug. 1734. Sarah m. 20 May

1684, Ephraim Goodrich; and Mary m. 10 Dec. 1684, Thomas Chester, both of W. RICHARD, Wethersfield, s. of James, first of the same, m. 23 Nov. 1704, Catharine, d. of Rev. Gershom Bulkley, had only Catharine, b. 26 Aug. 1706; and d. 7 May 1713. §†‡* ROBERT, Milford, s. of the first Richard, b. in Eng. had liv. with his f. at Wethersfield, and was not, as oft. said, an early sett. at M. certain. not bef. 1647, was an Assist. of the New Haven Col. 1659, wh. rank of course, was not contin. aft. the union with Conn. where, tho. on withdraw. of his f. from that office in the older Col. 1665, he was put in nominat. but did not gain the honor until 1673, yet had the compliments of being a capt. and rep. under the new admin. in Philip's war, was command.-in-chief, and in 1676, when Leete was chos. Gov. aft. d. of Winthrop, he was made Dept. Gov. was oft. a commissnr. of the Unit. Col. of N. E. and aft. d. of Leete 1683, succeed. him as Gov. By the royal constitution of Sir Edmund Andros, to be head of all the Northern provinces, T. was nam. one of his council, and tho. he did not resist, but acquiesced, he was hailed Gov. on the overthr. In that place he serv. 15 yrs. retir. from old age, and d. 12 July 1710, aged 88. Lambert marks his d. 1712. He had two ws. Jane, only d. of Edmund Tapp, wh. d. 8 Apr. 1703; and he m. 22 Oct. 1705, a wid. Eliz. Bryan, wh. d. 10 Jan. 1706. It is said he had 21 ch. (and very glad should I be to prove above half of the tradit. num.) but ten only have been heard of by me; viz. Samuel, bapt. 3 Sept. 1648, H. C. 1669; John, 20 Oct. 1650; Mary, 23 May, not 28 (as my correspond. writes), 1652, bec. this was Friday, and ch. in our country, without except. in that age, were bapt. on Sunday only; Robert, b. 14 Aug. 1654; Sarah, 9 Oct. 1656; Hannah, 1 Jan. 1660, wh. m. Rev. Samuel Mather of Windsor; Joseph, a. 1662; Abigail, wh. m. Rev. Samuel Andrew of Milford; beside Jane, and Ann, wh. d. bef. their f. If any respect for tradit. would solicit explana. of its giv. twenty-one ch. to the Gov. it may be guessed to have sprung from the fact, that his ch. add. to the ten of the first w. of s. Samuel made up the desired number. Being above 83 yrs. old, when he took his sec. w. none by her was expect. Very observa. is it that in Goodwin's Geneal. Notes, 229, after the heading, " Descend. in the line of Robert," not one is giv. wh. must be regard. as a misfortune attending Goodwin's d. bef. one eighth of the vol. was print. for he was not the man to be frightened by such a mythical host. On p. 328 the list that was intend. to be insert. and may perhaps now seem imperfect, is found, and some error is seen, if the Milford rec. be correct. The Gov. in his will of 5 Jan. 1708, names only these seven ch. Samuel, John, Mary, Robert, Hannah, Joseph, and Abigail. No doubt the other three were d. and prob. the date of Abigail's b. in Goodwin is wrong. SALMON, Preston, s. of the first James, ord. the first min. at that place, 16 Nov. 1698, had m. 28 Apr. preced. Dorothy, d. of Rev. James Noyes of Stonington; had Ann, b. 26 Aug. 1699; James, 29 Nov. 1700; Dorothy, 9 Feb. 1702; Jerusha, 21 Nov. 1704; Prudence, 23 Nov. 1706; Sarah, 19 Sept. 1708; and Rebecca, 29 June 1710; resign. his charge, Mar. 1744, and d. 1746. This name in Mather's Hecatompolis is print. Tread. SAMUEL, Eastham, eldest s. of Gov. Robert, ord. 1672, m. 16 Mar. 1674, Eliz. d. of Samuel Mayo, had Jane, b. 6 Dec. 1674; Eliz. 24 July 1676; Sarah, 20 June 1678; Samuel, July 1680; Mary, 16 Mar. 1682; Robert, 24 Feb. 1684; Abigail, 13 June 1686; Joseph, 19 Nov. 1690; Joshua, 17 Mar. 1692; John, 17 May 1693; and Nathaniel, 15 Apr. 1694; and his w. d. 4 Dec. 1696. He m. 29 Aug. 1700, Abigail, wid. of Rev. Benjamin Estabrook, d. of Rev. Samuel Willard of Boston, wh. d. 27 Dec. 1746, had Eunice, 27 Sept. 1704; and Robert, 21 Jan. 1707; and d. 18 Mar. 1717, aged 69. THOMAS, Glastenbury, s. of the sec. Richard, wh. gave him all his lds. on the east side of the great riv. m. 5 July 1693, Dorothy, d. of Rev. Gershom Bulkley, had Richard, b. 14 May 1694; Charles, 28 Feb. 1696; Thomas, 3 May 1699; Isaac, 15 Aug. 1701; Dorotheus, and Dorothy, tw. 25, but in ano. place of his book Chapin writes it 28, prob. wrong, Aug. 1704; Sarah, 21 Jan. in ano. place, July 1707; and Mary, 9 Jan. 1710. He was a lieut. and engag. in promot. separat. from Wethersfield of the new town. He d. 17 Feb. 1713; and his wid. d. 1757. In 1837 the gr. at Yale counted eight, at Harv. four.

TREBY, TREBIE, or TRIBBY, JOHN, Marblehead 1668–74, had w. Mary, wh. took admin. of his est. Nov. 1675. PETER, New London, 1667, of wh. Caulkins tells no more.

TREE, RICHARD, Lynn, m. 21 Sept. 1669, Joanna Rogers.

TREFETHEN, HENRY, New Hampsh. serv. on gr. jury 1687.

TREFRY, TREFREY, TURFREY or TURFREE, * GEORGE, York, must have been a high patriot, for he was chos. rep. 1692. John, Boston, was assoc. somehow with the unpopular. of Gov. Andros, for he was seized by the people wh. imprison. Sir Edmund 1689. THOMAS, Marblehead 1674. This name, I think, in Geneal. Reg. VIII. 288, belongs to the same man ment. in Gen. Reg. VII. 70 then spell. Tenenys, but prob. not copy of his own writ. as it is sign. with a cross +. Both docum. are verified by the same clerk the same yr.

TRELAWNEY, JOHN, Kittery 1645, prob. s. of Robert of Cornwall, Eng. propr. of Richmond's isl. is nam. in Sullivan, 309, as cit. in Farmer MS.

TRENTHAM, or TRENTUM, THOMAS, a youth of 14, emb. at London, July 1635, in the Blessing.

TRERICE. See Trarice.

TRESCOTT, JOHN, Dorchester, s. of William of the same, freem. 1683, was a carpenter, d. 22 Jan. 1741; and his w. Rebecca d. 1 Aug. foll. aged 88. The newspaper of that yr. ment. that the h. and w. liv. together near sixty-six and a half yrs. No offspring is told of. Of the tendency to exagger. age, his gr.st. is an example, mak. him in 91st yr. when he was nine mos. short of 90. SAMUEL, Dorchester, eldest ch. of William, had Dyer; Samuel, b. 27 Apr. 1675; Jeremiah, 6 Oct. 1676; Abiah, or Ebenezer, 31 Oct. 1678; Thankful, 22 Feb. 1680, prob. d. soon; Eliz. 19 Jan. bapt. 27 Aug. 1682; as were, at the same time, her bros. Dyer, Samuel, Jeremiah, and Ebenezer; and Sarah, b. 5 Mar. 1684. On 7 Aug. 1687 he was dism. to the ch. at Milton, and d. 30 July 1730. THOMAS, Dorchester, mariner, d. early in 1654, leav. w. Ann, wh. d. 10 May of that yr. WILLIAM, Dorchester, br. of the preced. freem. 10 May 1643, m. Eliz. d. of George Dyer, had Samuel, b. 4 Nov. 1646; Mary, 23 Apr. 1649; John, 21 Oct. 1651; Patience, 7 May 1653; Abigail, 5 Nov. 1656; Martha, 8 Jan. 1661; and Eliz. 24 June, bapt. 2 July 1665. His w. d. 30 July 1699, aged 74; and he d. 11 Sept. foll. aged near 85. His will of 9 Aug. that yr. names only two ds. Martha Adams, and Sarah Mosely or Maudesly, but when she was b. or wh. was her h. is altogether unkn. three ch. Mercy, Mary, and Martha Hewins, ds. of Jacob, wh. had taken for his sec. w. 24 Oct. 1680, or 24 Feb. 1681, the d. Martha, Mary, m. 6 Oct. 1665, John Hemenway; Abigail, m. 21 Nov. 1682, Ammiel Weeks, and their ch. Ammiel and George, are rememb. in the will of gr.f.

TRESLER, or TRUSLER, NICHOLAS, Salem, s. of Thomas, had w. and two ch. as by the will of his mo. appears; but names are unkn. THOMAS, Salem, was adm. of the ch. 15 Dec. 1639, freem. 27 Dec. 1642, d. 5 Mar. 1654. His w. was Elinor, and he had a d. wh. m. Henry Phelps, for John P. gr.s. of Elinor T. is nam. in the Probate Ct. connect. with Phelps est. He was clk. in 1650 of the market. From the will of his wid. Elinor 15 Feb. 1655, abst. in Essex Inst. I. 48 we learn that she had s. Henry, Nicholas, and Edward, two ds. and gr.ch. John Phelps and Eliz. Samuel, and Edward, ch. of Nicholas; and that her late h. had a d. in Eng.

TRESWELL, HENRY, Salisbury, by w. Martha, had Sarah, b. 26 July 1686.

TREVETT, TREVY, or TRIVITT, HENRY, Marblehead 1646–74. THOMAS, Marblehead 1674, may have been s. of the preced.

TREVORE, or TREVOUR, WILLIAM, Plymouth, came in the Mayflower 1620, not as a perman. sett. but a hired mariner, not for the ship, but for the serv. of the comp. aft. her ret. to Eng. and for a single yr. He went home next yr. in the Fortune; and may have been a navigator in command of a sh. to our shore in 1632. He was here in Apr. 1650 [see Geneal. Reg. IX. 248], and gave depon. as to the taking possessn. by hims. for David Thompson of London, of Thompson's isl. mistak. the yr. 1619 for 1620.

TREWORGYE, TRUEWORGIE, or TREWORTHY, JAMES, Kittery 1636, merch. from Cornwall, m. Catharine, d. of Alexander Shapleigh, sis. of Nicholas, wh. surv. him, bef. com. from Eng. had d. Joanna, wh. m. John Ameridith, Meridith, or Merryday of Kittery; Eliz. wh. m. John Gilman of Exeter; and Lucy, wh. m. young Humphrey Chadbourne, and, next, Thomas Wells of K. from wh. part of K. got. its name Wells. He went to Newfoundland, perhaps for trade only, but d. bef. he was 35 yrs. old. His wid. m. Edward Hilton. JOHN and NICHOLAS are ment. slightly, in N. E. bef. 1649, and prob. were brs. of the preced. Nicholas is not nam. again; but John had m. at Newbury, 15 Jan. 1646, a Spencer, perhaps d. of Thomas of Piscataqua, had John, b. 12 Aug. 1649; and Coffin says, he rem. to Saco. Yet a writer of so great dilig. as Mr. Thornton, in Geneal. Reg. V. 349, doubts the exist. of any John. SAMUEL, Boston, by w. Mary had Samuel, and d. 1698.

TRIANS, ANANIAS, Saybrook, m. 6 Aug. 1667, Abigail, d. of Thomas Norton. JOHN, Saybrook.

TRICK, ELIAS, Pemaquid, or Damerill's Cove, at a Ct. held by Mass. commissnrs. July 1674, took o. of alleg. and with others was sw. on the gr. jury.

TRICKEY, or TRICKETT EPHRAIM, Dover, perhaps s. of Thomas of the same, had Joseph, wh. obtain. a lot of ld. 1701. FRANCIS, by Farmer in MS. mark. of Portsmouth 1655, means, I think, Thomas. ISAAC, Dover 1670, was perhaps s. of Thomas. JOSEPH, Dover, s. of Thomas, had w. Rebecca, to wh. as his brs. wid. Zechary gave some ld. 2 Feb. 1709. THOMAS, Dover 1648, by Farmer in MS call. of Exeter 1644, d. 1675; leav. s. Zechary, and Joseph, perhaps, also, Isaac and Ephraim. ZECHARY, Dover, s. of Thomas, was call. sen. 1709, so that he may have had s. Zechary. This name is frequent in that neighborhood.

TRILL, THOMAS, Hartford 1664, then a serv. a soldier in Conn. forces, 1675, of wh. I kn. only that he was fined for unseason. firing of his gun, had w. Ann, prob. s. Thomas, and d. 1700.

TRIMMINGS, OLIVER, Exeter 1644, had w. Susanna.

TRINER, THOMAS, Marblehead 1674; but I doubt the spell. may mean Tainer, wh. see.

TRIPP, ABIEL, Portsmouth, R. I. perhaps s. of John of the same, m. 30 Jan. 1679, Deliverance Hall, perhaps d. of William of the same, had Abiel, b. 22 June 1684; and the f. d. 10 Sept. foll. *JOHN, Portsmouth,

R. I. 1638, and on the list of freem. there 1655, had w. Mary, to wh. in his will of 1650, Anthony Paine had giv. a legacy, for wh. her h. gave discharge to testator's relict by name of Rose Weeden, and for sec. w. he m. 7 Sept. 1665, Susanna, d. of John Anthony the first of the same, had Susanna, b. 31 Oct. 1667; Mary, 9 Dec. 1670; John, 19 July 1673; Othniel, 5 June 1676; Benjamin, 21 Feb. 1678; and Lot, 26 Dec. 1684; was rep. 1656 and 1672, Alice m. 26 Jan. 1671, William Hall; Isbell m. 4 Mar. 1675, Samson Shearman; Martha m. 3 Feb. 1681, Samuel Shearman; and Susanna m. 20 Jan. 1687, Thomas Potter.

* JOSEPH, Dartmouth, perhaps s. of the preced. was rep. 1685.

TRISTRAM, or TRUSTRUM, BENJAMIN, Saco, s. of Ralph, was d. in Apr. 1679, when Francis Hooke took admin. RALPH, Saco 1647, adm. freem. of Mass. 1655, had been constable 1653, appoint. by our authority, was much respect. and d. 1678. Dominicus Jordan, his s.-in-law, had admin. on the f. and s. Nathaniel, both in Apr. 1679. His ch. b. betw. 1644 and 64 were Samuel, Nathaniel, Benjamin, Richard, Rachel, Ruth, Freegrace, Hannah, wh. m. Dominicus Jordan, and David. But Folsom, 180, was not so happy as to be able to give particulars.

TROOP, WILLIAM, Barnstable, m. 14 May 1666, Mary, d. of Ralph Chapman, had Mary b. 6 Apr. 1667; and prob. others, certain. Thomas, bapt. 16 Sept. 1683.

TROTMAN, JOHN, Boston 1643, went home next yr. and in Feb. 1645, by letter fr. London, gave his w. Catharine power to sell his est. here.

TROTT, BERNARD, Boston 1665, merch. for ten yrs. here. ELIAS, Wethersfield 1645, may have been s. of Richard. JAMES, Dorchester, s. of the first Thomas, d. 27 Sept. 1719, by the inscript. on the gr.st. JOHN, perhaps of Wethersfield, serv. on jury 1642. JOHN, Nantucket, by the rec. had Tabitha, b. 2 Mar. 1679; Joseph, 10 Mar. but in ano. place said to be Apr. 1681; Rachel, 23 Aug. 1683; but in ano. place it is said John was b. 28 of that same mo.; Benjamin, 8 Nov. 1685; James, 20 Jan. 1688; Mary, 31 Oct. 1690; Abigail, 8 June 1693; and Priscilla, 11 Mar. 1697. JOHN, Dorchester, s. of Thomas of the same, liv. at Milton, m. 20 Dec. 1703, Deliverance, wid. of Joseph Withington. MATTHIAS, defdt. in a suit 1646, but in my opinion is just as likely to mean Treat. * RICHARD, Wethersfield 1642, and thenceforward this surname occurs so oft. especial. on the gr. jury 1643, and as rep. every single yr. fr. 1644 to 1658, but without the baptismal prefix, in Trumbull's Col. Rec. perhaps in 50 or 60 places, when Richard Treat is found so seldom, that I doubt not this may be freq. substitut. SAMUEL, Dorchester, s. of the first Thomas, d. 3 Aug. 1724. SIMON, Wells, was sw. freem. of Mass. 1653. THOMAS, Dorchester, freem. 1644, had Thomas; Preserved; Sarah, b. 10 or 16 Jan. 1654; Mary, 26 Jan. 1657; Samuel, 27 Aug. 1660; John, 24 Nov. bapt. 4 Dec. 1664; Thankful, 5 Dec.

1667; James, 2 June 1671; all prob. by w. Sarah, wh. d. 27 May 1712; and he d. 28 Aug. 1696, aged a. 82 yrs. Preserved m. 11 July 1667, John Baker; Sarah m. 2 June 1675, Bernard Capen; and Thankful m. 1 May 1691, John Hinckley. THOMAS, Dorchester, s. of the preced. freem. 1690, was k. by a fall, 13 Jan. 1694.

TROTTER, WILLIAM, Newbury, m. 9 Dec. 1652, Cutbury Gibbs (herein I follow Coffin, with resolute protest of incredul. against the unchristian name), had Mary, b. 22 Jan. 1654; Rebecca, 5 July 1655; Samuel, 5 June 1657; Abigail, 1 Feb. 1664; Sarah, 3 May 1665.

TROUT, WILLIAM, sw. fidel. to Mass. at Pemaquid, 1674.

TROW, HENRY, Ipswich, or more prob. Salisbury, freem. 1676. I think this name may have bec. True, and was, perhaps at first, Trew.

TROWBRIDGE, CALEB, New Haven, s. of the sec. Thomas, had w. Mary, but no ch. d. 1704. CALEB, Groton, youngest s. of James the first, ord. Mar. 1715, soon aft. m. Sarah, d. of Hon. Thomas Oliver, had Oliver, b. 16 May 1716, wh. d. young. His w. d. 16 Jan. foll. and he m. 18 Sept. 1718, Hannah, d. of Rev. Nehemiah Walter of Roxbury, had Caleb, b. 6 Aug. 1719; Nehemiah, 14 Oct. 1722; Sarah, 3 Dec. 1724; Hannah, 16 Mar. 1729; Maria, 23 Dec. 1731; Thomas, 12 Nov. 1734; and Abigail, 30 Nov. 1740; and he d. 19 Sept. 1760. *JAMES, Dorchester, s. prob. youngest, of Thomas, perhaps brot. by his f. from Eng. where he may have been b. 1636, but bapt. 1638 at D. and soon carr. to New Haven, there left with brs. Thomas and William, when his f. went home to Taunton, Co. Somerset. From New Haven he rem. to D. and m. 30 Dec. 1659, Margaret, d. of Humphrey Atherton, had Eliz. b. 12 Oct. 1660; Mindwell, 20 June 1662; John, 22 May 1664; rem. to Cambridge, and had Margaret, 30 Apr. 1666; Thankful, 6 Mar. 1668; Mary, 11 June 1670; and Hannah, 15 June 1672. His w. d. two days aft. and he m. 30 Jan. 1674, Margaret, d. of deac. John Jackson, had Experience, 1 Nov. 1675; Thomas, 9 Dec. 1677; Deliverance, 31 Dec. 1679; James, 20 Sept. 1682; William, 19 Nov. 1684; Abigail, 11 Apr. 1687; and Caleb, 7 Nov. 1692, H. C. 1710; was freem. 1665; selectman, clk. of the writs, lieut. deac. and rep. 1700 and 3. He liv. in that part of C. wh. bec. Newton, d. 22 May 1717, and his wid. d. 16 Sept. 1727. Eliz. m. 1682, John Mirick; Mindwell m. 1684, Jonathan Fuller; Margaret m. 18 Mar. 1686, Ebenezer Stone; Thankful m. 15 Dec. 1690, Richard Ward; Mary m. a Stedman; Hannah m. John Greenwood; Deliverance m. Eleazer Ward; and Experience m. Samuel Wilson. JAMES, New Haven, third s. of William the first, a propr. 1685, m. 8 Nov. 1688, Lydia, d. of the first Joseph Alsop, had James b. 13 Sept. 1689; and he m. a sec. w. 29 Sept. 1692, Esther How, youngest d. of Ephraim. JAMES, Newton, s. of James of the same, m. 6 Jan.

1709, Hannah Bacon, had Margaret, b. 29 Oct. foll.; Daniel, 6 Apr.
1711; and by sec. w. Hannah, d. of Abraham Jackson, had Hannah,
1713; and Jemima; and he d. 21 July 1714. JOHN, New Haven, eldest s. of the sec. Thomas, m. 9 Nov. 1683, Ann Leete, d. of Gov. William, had John b. 2 Mar. 1684; and Ann, 20 July 1688; was a propr.
1685; and d. June 1689. His wid. m. 1696, Ebenezer Collins. JOHN,
Newton, eldest s. of James the first, m. for his sec. w. the first being not
kn. 27 Feb. 1708, Sarah, d. of Joseph Wilson, had Jonathan, b. 23 July
1711, was selectman, and d. 1737. SAMUEL, New Haven, fourth s. of
William the first, by w. Sarah had Samuel, Hannah, Eliz. and Sarah.
THOMAS, New Haven 1640, had, says tradit. first sat down at Dorchester, coming from Taunton, in Co. Somerset, a. 1637, but was prosecut.
voyages to and from Barbadoes. I think he was of Combe St. Nicholas, only a. 10 or 12 ms. S. E. from Taunton, near the borders of Devon.
More reasona. import. is ano. pt. of the tradit. that he brot. three s.
Thomas, assumed to have been b. 1632; William, a. 1634; and James,
bef. ment. Whether he was ever resid. in Dorchester is uncert. but a.
1644, he went home, leav. his boys to the care of serg. Thomas Jeffreys,
and his prop. to be manag. by Henry Gibbons, from wh. aft. 20 yrs. it
was not easy to obt. acco. He never came back, and d. at or near, Taunton 7 Feb. 1672. THOMAS, New Haven, eldest s. of the preced. b. in Eng.
was propound. for freem. 1668, and is found in the list next yr. made
commissary for the expedit. 1673 against the Dutch, and much esteem.
in 1675 and 6; m. 24 June 1657, Sarah, d. of Henry Rutherford; had
Sarah, b. 7 Nov. 1658, d. at 17 yrs.; John, 23 Nov. 1661; Thomas, 14
Feb. 1664; Lydia, 7 June, 1666; Caleb, 28 Oct. 1670; Daniel, 5 Jan.
1673; Eliz. 30 June 1676; and Sarah, 24 Sept. 1680, d. at 10 yrs.
His w. d. 22 Aug. 1687, and he m. 2 Apr. 1689, Hannah, wid. of Eliphalet Ball, d. of John Nash, had Hannah, 30 Mar. 1690; and he d. 22
Aug. 1702. His wid. d. 3 Feb. 1708. Lydia m. 22 Dec. 1681, Richard Roswell; Eliz. m. 1 Apr. 1691, John Hodgson; and Hannah m. 30
Jan. 1710, Joseph Whiting. THOMAS, New Haven, s. of the first Wil-
liam, m. 26 May 1684, Abigail Beardsley, had Abigail, b. 8 Apr. 1695;
Lydia, 16 Dec. 1697; William, 14 Apr. 1700; Ebenezer, 25 July
1702; and Eliz. 23 Apr. 1705. THOMAS, New Haven, s. of Thomas
the sec. m. 16 Oct. 1685, Mary, d. of John Winston, had Sarah, b. 26
Nov. 1686; Stephen, 7 Sept. 1688; Mary, 9 Apr. 1691; Eliz. 29 Mar.
1693; Thomas, 20 Dec. 1695; Joseph, 1 Apr. 1699; and Daniel, 25
Oct. 1703; and d. 15 Sept. 1711. His wid. d. 15 Sept. 1742. THOMAS,
Newton, s. of James the first, had John by a first w. as only ch. and he
next m. 3 Mar. 1709, Mary Goffe of Cambridge, perhaps d. of Samuel,
had Edmund, b. 1709, H. C. 1728, the learned Judge; Lydia, 1710;

and Mary, 1712; and he took third w. Susanna, 7 Jan. 1715, rem. to New London, there d. 1724. Lydia m. 31 Jan. 1737, Richard Dana, f. of the late Francis, H. C. 1762, Ch. J. of Mass. so that his s. and gr.s. were in two generat. one in the last preced. the war of Independ. and the other at the beginning of the nineteenth century, our luminaries of the common law. WILLIAM, New Haven, s. of Thomas the first, b. in Eng. m. 9 Mar. 1657, Eliz. Selivant, wid. of Daniel, d. of Capt. George Lamberton, had William, b. 12 Nov. foll.; Thomas, 2 Oct. 1659; Eliz. 5 Jan. 1662; James, 26 Mar. 1664; Margaret, 1 June 1666; Hannah, 6 July 1668; Abigail, and Samuel, tw. 7 Oct. 1670; Mary, 12 Oct. 1672; and Joseph, 1676; was propound. for freem. 1669, and d. Nov. 1690. The ten ch. were liv. in 1691. Eliz. m. 28 May 1678, Peter Mallory; Margaret m. a Goodwin; and Hannah m. a Jackson. WILLIAM, New Haven, eldest s. of the preced. m. Thankful, d. of Rev. Samuel Stow of Middletown, had Thankful, b. 25 Sept. 1687; Experience, 25 May 1690; and Abigail, 4 Nov. 1693, d. soon. WILLIAM, Newton, s. of James the first, m. 14 Dec. 1708, Sarah, d. of John Ward, had Mary, b. 18 Sept. 1709; William, 2 Feb. 1711, d. soon; Huldah, 13 Feb. 1712, d. soon; William, again, 13 Oct. 1713, d. soon; Huldah, 23 Mar. 1615, d. soon; James, 21 Apr. 1717; tw. ds. 1720, d. bef. b. prob. with their mo. By sec. w. m. 30 May 1721, Sarah, d. of Francis Fullam, he had Sarah, 9 Mar. 1722; Margaret, 16 Apr. 1724; Bethia, 29 Aug. 1726; Thaddeus, 28 Nov. 1728; and Abigail, 12 Oct. 1732, d. young; was selectman, lieut. and d. 19 Nov. 1744. Farmer, MS. notes that in 1834, two of this name had been gr. at Harv. two at Yale; but very curious is the fact, that rec. of town and ch. at Haddam, where one branch of the surname spread, both give it Strawbridge.

TRUANT or TROUANT, JOSEPH, perhaps s. of Maurice, Marshfield, m. 6 Jan. 1675, was drown. on enter. Plymouth harbor, a. 23 Feb. 1684. MAURICE, Duxbury 1643, had possib. first been at Watertown, and in 1631, was fin. for stealing pig's meat of Ralph Glover; perhaps only a youthful peccadillo; in few yrs. rem. to Marshfield. there had fam. of wh. I think, were Joseph; perhaps Hannah, wh. m. 11 Jan. 1682, Jonathan Eames; and also Mehitable, wh. m. 3 Sept. 1691, John Daggett; and he d. 21 Apr. 1685.

TRUE, HENRY, Salem 1644, had John, bapt. 13 July 1645; Mary, 14 Mar. 1647; Lydia, 4 Feb. 1649; Joseph, 8 Feb. 1652; Benjamin, 19 Feb. 1654; Jemima, 26 Apr. 1657. His w. was Israel, d. of John Pike, unless the books have mistak. her name; and he rem. prob. to Salisbury; was the freem. of 1676, spell. Trew, and read Trow. * HENRY, Salisbury, s. of the preced. m. 15, or 16 by ano. rec. Mar. 1668, Jane, d. of Thomas Bradbury, had Mary, b. 30 May 1668, if the Gen. Reg. VIII.

233, be correct. wh. is not prob. ; William, June 1670; Henry, 6 Jan.
1674; Jane, 5 Dec. 1676; John, 23 Feb. 1679; Jemima, 16 Mar. 1681;
and Jabez, 19 Feb. 1683. He was rep. 1689. JOSEPH, Salisbury, br.
of the preced. m. 20 Apr. 1675, Ruth Whittier, perhaps d. of Thomas,
had Joseph, b. 9 Jan. 1676, prob. d. young; John, 18 Aug. 1677, d. in 4
mos.; Joseph, again, 4 Mar. 1679; Ruth, 5 Oct. 1683; Israel, whether
male or fem. I kn. not, 14 Dec. 1687; and Benjamin, 5 Mar. 1691. He
took o. of alleg. 15 Dec. 1677, and was freem. 1690.

TRUESDALE, TRUSDELL, TREWSDALE TREUSDALE, or TRUESDALL,
RICHARD, Boston, call. on join. the ch. 27 July 1634, serv. to our teacher
John Cotton, freem. 4 Mar. foll. serv. in 1639 on the coroner's inq. on dead
body of Peter Fitchew, wilful. drown. and next yr. on the more import.
jury for trial of Hugh Bewett for heresy. He had no ch. prob. but his w.
is, I suppose, meant in two letters of our first Gov. Winth. to his s. John,
Nov. 1646, mention that his s. Wait was with sis. T. That phrase led
Farmer to write of Richard T. "perhaps br.-in-law of Gov. Winthrop."
By similar misunderstand. of the word sis. the descend. of Samuel
Symonds suppos. they were of the same blood of John Winth. of Conn.
whose only sis. that passed infancy was first w. of Samuel Dudley,
not Symonds. He was a butcher, and deac. of the first ch. but revolted
at the disingen. managem. by wh. Davenport was brot. from New Haven,
to be the min. and bec. one of the founders of the third or O. S. ch. in
1669, and d. 1671, leav. wid. Mary. SAMUEL, Cambridge, neph. of the
preced. from wh. by his will he rec. £50, m. 1671, Mary, d. of John
Jackson, first, of the same, had Richard, b. 16 July 1672 ; Mary, 3 Nov.
1673; Samuel, 13 Oct. 1675; Mindwell, 31 Aug. 1676; Rebecca, 25
Mar. 1678 ; Experience ; Thomas, 27 Apr. 1682; and Ebenezer, 1685.
He was freem. 1685, liv. on S. side of the riv. in what was call. Cambridge vil. now Newton, for separat. of wh. he was active; had sec. w.
Eliz. wid. of George Woodward, d. of Thomas Hammond of Watertown;
and a third w. Mary is nam. in his will. He d. says Jackson, 2 Mar.
1695, in 49th yr. wh. makes me concur with the diligent and judicious
author of the Hist. of N. in suppos. tho. ign. of the name of his f. that he
was b. in our country. Under this name, Farmer had includ. John and
John jr. of Kittery 1652 ; but I follow the rec. in spell. them Twisdale.

TRULL, JOHN, Billerica, m. 11 Dec. 1657, Sarah, d. of William
French, had John, b. 13 Jan. 1659, d. in few days; Sarah, 27 May
1660 ; was freem. 1690, then call. sen. so that perhaps he had John,
again, and other ch. He d. 15 June 1704, aged 70. SAMUEL, Billerica,
perhaps br. of the preced. is on the tax list of 1679, when the name of
John is not seen.

TRUMAN, JOSEPH, New London 1666, constable 1667, d. in 1697, made his will in Sept. 1696, ment. ch. Joseph, Thomas, Eliz. Mary, and Ann, all perhaps b. bef. he went thither. JOSEPH, New London, s. of the preced. m. 5 Dec. 1701, Mary Shapley, d. of Benjamin.

TRUMBULL, TRUMBALL, TRUMBOLL, TRUMBLE, TRUMBELL, or TRUMMELL, DANIEL, Lynn, 1647, as Lewis marks, but adds not a word more. JOHN, Cambridge 1636, said to have come from Newcastle on Tyne, was fin. £20 at the court, Mar. 1637, but for some cause so slight that it might have found lighter censure, as in June foll. three quarters of the penalty were taken off, and, at the general show of similar favor in 1638, £4 more were remit. Perhaps he is the sec. freem. of this name 13 May 1640, but in rec. giv. Thrumball. By w. Eliz. had Eliz. 6 June 1638; John, 4 Aug. 1641; Hannah, 10 Dec. 1642 ; rem. to Charlestown, there had Mary, 3, but ano. rec. says 9 Feb. 1645 ; besides that on Cambridge rec. comes, also, James, 7 Dec. 1647. He was capt. of a trading vessel, and may have been the man in the Col. Rec. of Conn. I. 162, willing to accept Matthew Griswold's oath to his demand in 1648, and prob. the one meant by Davenport in Epist. to Gov. Winth. 1655, as bring. him letters from Eng. See 3 Mass. Hist. Coll. X. 7. He was a shopkeep. in Charlestown 1673, a householder in 1678, and d. leav. wid. Eliz. early in July 1687, in his 80th yr. the inv. being tak. on 6 of that mo. and ret. by his s. John 19 Aug. foll. The wid. d. 15 Aug. 1696 in 86th yr. His d. Hannah m. 2 Mar. 1659 John Baxter. JOHN, Roxbury 1639, when in ch. rec. the spell. is Trumell, wh. caused a very experienced reader of early writ. to make it Trumtell, freem. 13 May 1640, is no more heard of at R. and, I think, was very soon at Rowley, there m. Ann, perhaps d. of the first Richard Swan, d. 1657, bur. 18 July. His inv. was by w. Ann brot. 29 Sept. and he left John, Joseph, Judah, and perhaps more. The s. John is made the progenit. of the great Conn. fam. and the common error found support in the Appx. to the Centen. Addr. by Bradford. The older s. stuck by the paternal mansion. JOHN, Rowley, s. prob. of the preced. freem. 1665, m. prob. a d. of William Jackson, of R. and made deac. 24 Dec. 1686, was appoint. ens. there by the Gen. Ct. 1685. JOHN, Charlestown, s. of the first John, m. 26 Sept. 1665, Mary, d. of Edward Jones, had Samuel, wh. was bapt. 25 July 1697 a. 14 yrs. old. He serv. in Mosely's comp. Dec. 1675. JOSEPH, Suffield 1677, s. prob. of the first John of Rowley, freem. 1681, as early as July 1675, liv. in Suffield, from wh. the Ind. hostil. soon drove him, there had Joseph, b. 16 Jan. 1679; Ammi, 1 Aug. 1681 ; Benoni, 10 Aug. 1684; beside some bef. he rem. to S. of wh. prob. Hannah, wh. m. 26 Nov. 1686, John Strong, the third, was one, as also John. His s. Joseph m. Hannah, d. of John Higley of Simsbury ; rem. to Lebanon, and was f. of the first Gov. Jonathan, b. 1710, H. C. 1727, a disting. patriot. JUDAH, Rowley, perhaps s. of the first John of the same, rem. to Suffield a. 1676, had a w. Mary, and ch. John, b. 5 Mar. 1674; Ebenezer, 1 Aug. 1675, d. soon; Joseph, 3 Jan. 1677; Judah, 2 Jan. 1679; Mary, 20 Mar. 1681; William, 9 July 1683; Samuel, 1 June 1685; and Ephraim, 6 July 1688; and d. 1 Apr. 1692. His wid. Mary 22 Dec. 1692, bec. third w. of Vicary Sikes. RALPH, Marshfield 1643, may possib. be a miswrit. surname, Trumle. Of this name, ten have been gr. at Yale, and five at Harv.

TRUSTRUM. See Tristram.

TRY, or TRAY, MICHAEL, Windsor, freem. 1640, freed in 1660 from watch and ward, had sev. yrs. bef. rem. to Fairfield, had only ch. Sarah, wh. m. John Gruman. To her and her childr. he gave most of his est. wh. was very considerab. when he d. 1676 or 7. He had above 20 yrs. earlier m. for sec. w. Margaret, wid. of Richard Roots of F.

TUBBS, SAMUEL, New London a. 1663, m. Mary, d. of Isaac Willey, but Miss Caulkins in letter of July 1860 tells me, that he had Mary and Bethia, bapt. on same day in May 1671; Samuel, July 1672; William, May 1674 (and I regret that the days of the several mos. are uncert.); Dorcas, b. 2 Mar. 1689; Joseph, 3 Sept. 1692; perhaps other ch. and d. 1696. His wid. was liv. 1725, then aged 77. WILLIAM, Plymouth and Duxbury, m. 9 Nov. 1637, Mercy d. of Francis Sprague, and was one of the proprs. of Bridgewater.

TUCKE, or TEWK, EDWARD, Hampton, s. of Robert, perhaps b. in Eng. had John, if the acco. of Congr. min. in Rockingham Co. by Rev. William Cogswell, Geneal. Reg. I. 247, be correct (wh. disagrees with Farmer MS.), d. a. 1653. *JOHN, Hampton, s. of Robert, says Farmer, by w. Bethia had John, b. 19 Apr. 1687, prob. d. young; Jonathan, Aug. 1697; John, again, 23 Aug. 1702, H. C. 1723, min. at Isle of Shoals, wh. d. 12 Aug. 1773, leav. John, H. C. 1758. He was rep. 1717, and d. 4 Jan. 1742. ROBERT, Watertown, came prob. in 1636, from Gorleston, Co. Suffolk, two ms. S. of Yarmouth, was freem. 7 Sept. 1639, but then was of Hampton, perhaps, where was his perman. resid. in latter days, though he may have been entit. a tailor of Salem at one time, was fin. for sell. beer, soon aft. had license for the first inn at H. 1643, and d. 4 Oct. 1664, leav. wid. Joanna, wh. d. 14 Feb. 1673, by wh. perhaps, he had Mary, wh. m. lieut. John Sanborn, and d. 30 Dec. 1668; Edward, bef. ment.; Robert; William, b. a. 1646; and John, 1652. Robert and William prefer. to live in Eng. THOMAS, Salem 1637, was then a. 25 yrs. old, if his memo. thirty yrs. later be true. THOMAS, Charlestown, by w. Eliz. d. of lieut. Randall Nichols, had Mary, bapt. 29 Jan. 1671; Catharine, 23 July 1676, d. soon; Catharine, again,

18 Nov. 1677; and Mary, 7 Oct. 1683; and he d. 12 Sept. 1687.
WILLIAM, Milford, a propr. bef. 1675, rem. a few yrs. aft.

TUCKER, ABRAHAM, and JOHN, early proprs. of Dartmouth, may have
been s. of Henry of Sandwich. ANDREW, Marblehead 1663, was perhaps
s. of Nicholas, and may be the man, whose name in the petitn. of Marblehead 1668, is giv. Stocker in Geneal. Reg. IX. 82. BENJAMIN, Roxbury, s. of Robert, had Benjamin, b. 8 Mar. 1671; Jonathan, 14 May
1675; Ephraim, 16 Aug. 1677; Ebenezer, 10 Oct. 1679; Mary, 7 Aug.
1682; Edward, 8 Aug. 1684; and by w. Amy, says the rec. tho. she
may have been mo. of all the preced. had Joseph, 2 Nov. 1686; and by
w. Ann, wh. I think the same, as the rec. is very careless, had Eliz. 20
Dec. 1688. He d. 27 Feb. 1714, aged a. 60, as the gr.stone tells. BE-
NONI, Salisbury, eldest s. of Maurice, m. June 1686, Ebenezer, d. of
Thomas Nichols, strange as the rec. reads, had Ebenezer, b. 31 Mar.
1687; Benjamin, 12 Jan. 1690; Nathaniel, 12 Nov. 1692; Eliz. 24 Mar.
1695; and Mary, 4 May 1697. EPHRAIM, Milton, s. prob. of Robert of
the same, was freem. 1678, and perhaps had w. and ch. GEORGE, Marblehead 1653, a fisherman. HENRY, Sandwich, by w. Martha, had, as the
Friend's rec. at Newport tells, Abraham, b. 30 Oct. 1653; John, 18 Aug.
1656; Martha, 14 July 1659; Hannah, 25 July 1662; James, 16 Mar.
1666; Mary, 16 Aug. 1668; and Sarah, 20 Sept. 1674. Mary m. 9 May
1690, Samuel Perry of Kingstown. But the Perry geneal. calls Tucker
of Dartmouth; and certain. Abraham and John, prob. his s. were proprs.
of D. JAMES, Milton, perhaps br. of Ephraim, m. Rebecca, d. of Thomas
Tolman, had, in 1678, a suit with the town of Dorchester, wh. gather. from
him and others taxes, wh. the Gen. Ct. req. the town to repay. Prob. he
had James, and perhaps others. JAMES, of some part of New Hampsh.
perhaps Portsmouth or Dover, in each were fams. of the name, in 1689,
when he join. other friends of liberty, in addr. the governm. of Mass. to
protect them. JOHN, Watertown 1636, a propr. and perhaps the same
man was next yr. at Hingham, propr. in ea. town, m. June 1649 wid.
Norton, it may be as his sec. w. and d. 5 Aug. 1661, making nuncup.
will in favor of John, and Mary, his ch. with injunct. to deal righteous.
by the mother, meaning, I suppose, the stepmother, Ann, his wid. His
d. Mary (by the former w.) to wh. Thomas Johnson and his w. Margaret gave all their prop. had bef. 30 Oct. 1662, m. Joseph Church.
JOHN, Boston, by w. Sarah had Eliz. b. 5 Feb. 1652; John, 8 Oct.
1655. JOHN, Isle of Shoals, fisherman, by his will of 31 Oct. 1670, gave
small sum to his min. Thomas Wells of Kittery, and bestow. the rest on
John Amerideth and Joanna his w. and as the inv. of Apr. foll. was of
so considera. amt. as £74, we may infer that he had no w. nor ch.

JOHN, Portsmouth, perhaps s. of Richard, was one of the founders of the ch. 1671, freem. 1673; and call. sen. may have join. with the great body of people to solicit protect. in 1689, from Mass. and d. 2 May 1706. JOHN, Boston, mem. of 3d. ch. freem. 1676. JOHN, Hingham, s. of John of the same, m. Mar. 1658, Eliz. Hobart, wh. may have been d. of Edmund the sec. of the same, was freem. 1677. JOHN, Newbury, m. 11 July 1670, Mary Richardson, had Mary, b. 13 May 1677, prob. d. soon; Mary, again, 25 Jan. 1679; Richard, 9 Mar. 1681; and John, 29 July 1683. JOHN, Gloucester, perhaps, but not prob. s. of Robert of the same, m. 9 May 1681, Sarah, d. of Thomas Riggs, had Mary, b. 1682; Sarah, 1685; John, 1686; William, 1690; Thomas, 1692; Richard, 1695; Abigail, 1697; Joseph, 1701; and Grace 1706; may have liv. at Casco, betw. 1680 and 90, some short time, but where or when he d. is unkn. JOHN, Dover, capt. by the Ind. 26 July 1696, may have been adult or minor. JOSEPH, Milton, was one of the comp. of the brave capt. Isaac Johnson, wh. was k. at their head in the great battle of 19 Dec. 1675, and T. may have fallen also, for I kn. no more of him. JOSEPH, Salisbury, s. of Maurice of the same, by w. Phebe Page had James, b. 25 Apr. 1697; Samuel, 16 Apr. 1699; and Joseph, 29 Aug. 1702. LEWIS, Casco 1680–90, was perhaps s. of Richard, b. 1643, certain. br. of John, had Hugh of Kittery, Lewis of Newcastle N. H. Eliz. wh. m. a Bragdon of York or Kittery, and Grace, wh. m. Isaac Pierce of Boston. Willis I. 213. MANASSEH, Milton, perhaps s. of Robert of the same, freem. 1678, m. bef. 1679, Waitstill, eldest d. of Roger Sumner, had Manasseh, b. a. 1681, and prob. others; was deac. MAURICE, or MORRIS, Salisbury, m. 14 Oct. 1661, Eliz. d. prob. of John Stevens of the same, had Benoni, b. 16 Oct. 1662, and she d. the same day. By sec. w. Eliz. he had John, 16 Aug. 1664; Mary, 21 May 1666; James, 28 Dec. 1667; Sarah, 19 May 1670; Joseph, 20 Feb. 1672; Jabez, 5 Feb. 1675; Eliz. 7 Apr. 1677; and Morris or Maurice, 6 Sept. 1679; was sw. to his alleg. 1677, and freem. 1690, when the name is giv. Meros, lucki. for him the last letter was not z. NICHOLAS, Salem or Marblehead, d. a. 1664. RICHARD, Casco, one of the earliest sett. in 1634, conjoint. with George Cleaves in maint. right of Laconia Pat. and agent for Sir Ferdinando Gorges, and next for Alexander Rigby [Winth. II. 256]; of the gr. jury 1640, in 1653 had rem. to vicin. of Portsmouth, in 1665 stood strong for jurisdict. of Mass. against the royal commissnrs. and d. 1679, as Willis I. 29 tells, wh. ment. that his w. Margaret outliv. him. Perhaps she was passeng. aged 23, embark. 1 July 1635, in the Abigail from London. * ROBERT, Weymouth 1638, had Sarah, b. 17 Mar. 1639, and I think, Ephraim, Benjamin, and Manasseh, beside possib. others, bef. or aft. rem. He was fin. in 1640, for upbraid.

James Britain, as a witness, call. him a liar, and said he could prove it, of wh. the charact. of Britain may lead us to think he might be right; rem. to Dorchester, that part wh. bec. in 1662, Milton, for wh. he was rep. 1669, 80 and 1. Sarah, m. 1 Aug. 1660, Peter Warren of Boston. * ROBERT, Gloucester, 1651, was rep. 1652, town clk. to 1656; and had w. Eliz. and Babson, 172, gives ch. Ebenezer, wh. d. 1653, Ephraim, b. in 1653, and one with an impossib. name, 1652. I regret to say, that I find little more of him. That he was the same as the Weymouth man was opin. of Babson, to wh. I have strong object. ROGER, Salem, d. a. 1661. WILLIAM, prob. of York, d. May 1666, and Nathaniel Fryer was admor. The inv. 22 June was £73. 19s. 6d. and he left a wid. Of this name, in 1834, Farmer notes thirteen had been gr. at Harv. three at Yale, and three at other N. E. coll.

TUCKERMAN, ABRAHAM, Boston, s. of the first John, m. 15 July 1692, Constance, d. of William Worcester, had no ch. but d. soon, and his wid. m. John Noiles jr. if such be a true name, of Newfoundland. JOHN, Boston, by w. Sarah had Eliz. b. 5 Feb. 1652; John, 8 Oct. 1655; Sarah, 20 Nov. 1657, d. in two wks.; Richard, 27 Nov. 1658; Christian, 8 July 1661; Priscilla, 5 Aug. 1666; Martha, 28 Aug. 1668; Abraham, 3 Dec. 1670; and Isaac, 6 Feb. 1673. JOHN, Boston, eldest s. of the preced. by first w. had John, and by sec. w. m. 14 Nov. 1693, Susanna, d. of Edmund Chamberlain of Malden, had Sarah, Abraham, Jacob, and Edward. He is ancest. of most of this surname in N. E. NATHANIEL, Ipswich, s. of Otho, by w. Martha, had Nathaniel, b. 9 Sept. 1684; Martha, 27 June 1686; John; and Eliz. He rem. 1712 to Portsmouth. OTHO, Portsmouth, by w. Emma, had Nathaniel, b. a. 1660; and other ch.; was drown. 24 May 1664.

TUCKEY, GEORGE, Windsor 1645, fin. for some idle words to old Mr. Eggleston's w. JOHN, Charlestown, join. the ch. 12 Apr. 1650, was a householder in 1658, but I kn. no more.

TUDOR, JOHN, Boston, by w. Eliz. had John, b. 12 Feb. 1673; and Thomas, 11 Nov. 1674. The f. of William of Boston, H. C. 1769, a disting. citizen, was also nam. John, but he prob. was not any relat. of the preced. or succeed. but brot. by his m. from Devonsh. as tradit. tells, a. 1715. OWEN, or OWYN, Windsor 1645, may have been at Dorchester, but no such tradit. exists, nor does any rec. show it; m. 13 Nov. 1651, wid. Mary Skinner, d. prob. of Joseph Loomis of the same, had Samuel, and Sarah, tw. b. 26 Nov. 1652; Owen, 12 Mar. 1655; Jane, 16 Oct. 1657; and Mary, 6 Mar. 1661; all bapt. 12 May foll. and all liv. at his d. 30 Oct. 1690. His w. d. 19 Aug. 1680. He is report. in the freemen's list 1669, had been prob. sev. yrs. was common. thot. to come from Wales, but that may be tradit. as to a progen. or childish claim of relationsh. to the possess. of the throne of Gr. Britain. All the ds. we kn. m. viz. Sarah, 1679, to James Porter; Jane, 28 Oct. 1680, to Samuel Smith of Wethersfield; and Mary m. a Judson bef. 1717, perhaps his sec. w. OWEN, Windsor, s. of the preced. d. 1717, without w. or ch. and by the court his prop. was distrib. to his br. Samuel, sis. Sarah, heirs of sis. Jane, and to sis. Mary. SAMUEL, Windsor, br. of the first Owen, m. 1685, Abigail, d. I suppose of Samuel Bissell of Windsor, had Abigail, b. 1686; Mary, 1689; Sarah, 1692, prob. d. young; Sarah, again, 1695; Margaret, 1697; and Eliz. 1700; perhaps ano. ch. bef. Samuel, Y. C. 1728, but the date of his b. I find not. He is absurdly said to have begun the settlem. on E. side of the gr. riv. 1677, when there were dwellers there, 20 yrs. bef. and so much had it gr. that in 1680, petitn. was offered for its incorpo. as separ. town. He d. 6 July 1727. Farmer notes, that in 1834, five of this name had been gr. at Harv. and three at Yale.

TUELLS, RICHARD, and THOMAS, were of Gallop's company 1690, but perhaps were truly Twelves, s. of Robert.

TUFTS, JAMES, k. by the Ind. at Bloody brook, 18 Sept. 1675, may have been a soldier of the flower of Essex. JOHN, Hingham, was from Old Hingham, came in the Diligent, 1638, as one of the serv. or apprent. of Thomas Cooper, but no more is kn. of him. JOHN, Malden, freem. 1690, was s. of Peter first of the same, m. Mary Putnam, had Mary, b. 11 Apr. 1688; John, 28 May 1690; Nathaniel, 23 Feb. 1693; Peter, 1696; Benjamin, 1699; Thomas; and Stephen; and d. 1728. JOHN, Malden, s. of Peter the sec. was ord. at Newbury, 30 June 1714, m. 9 Nov. foll. Sarah Bradstreet, perhaps d. of John of Topsfield, youngest s. of Gov. Simon, had Mary, b. 4 Sept. 1715; Joshua, 4 Oct. 1716, H. C. 1736; and for sec. w. m. 28 Mar. 1723, Eliz. Sargent, had John, b. 13 Dec. foll. wh. d. at 20 mos.; Sarah, 21 Apr. 1725; and John, again, 9 Jan. 1727; and I kn. no more. JONATHAN, Malden, s. of the first Peter, freem. 1690, by w. Rebecca had Jonathan, b. 1 July 1685, d. at 3 yrs.; John, 11 Apr. 1688; Jonathan, again, 6 Feb. 1691; Rebecca, 16 Oct. 1694; Samuel, 29 Apr. 1697; Persis, 2 May 1700; Joseph, 29 June 1704; and Abigail, 7 Jan. 1707; and he d. 18 Aug. 1722. His w. was d. of capt. John Waite, and his will was of 4 Aug. 1718. * PETER, Charlestown, liv. on Malden side, came a. 1650, with w. Mary, d. of Eliz. Pierce and prob. one or two ch. was freem. 1665, at M. had John, b. 7 May 1653; Mary, 19 June 1655; Jonathan, 19 June 1657, d. at one yr.; Jonathan, again, 3 Mar. 1660; John, a. 1665; Mercy; Sarah; Eliz. 22 Nov. 1672; and perhaps others, besides Peter, wh. I judge was the eldest. He was tythingman of C. 1679, rep. for Medford 1689, and d. 13 May 1700, aged 83, and his wid. d. Jan. 1703. He made a will 1693, with

codic. 1698, naming as left w. Mary, s. Peter, Jonathan, John, and four
m. or wid. ds. Mary m. 15 Oct. 1674 John Edes; Eliz. m. Joseph
Lynde; Mercy m. 24 Dec. 1688, Joseph Wait, and next a Jenkins; and
Sarah m. 22 July 1689 Thomas Oakes. The first and third were wid.
* Peter, Medford, eldest s. of the preced. b. in Eng. 1648, m. 26 Aug.
1670, Eliz. d. of the sec. Thomas Lynde, and sis. of the h. of his sis.
Eliz. had Ann, b. 25 Feb. 1677; Peter, 27 Jan. 1679; Mary, 30 Jan.
1682; and Thomas, 31 Mar. 1683, H. C. 1701. His w. d. 15 July
1684, and he m. 11 or 16 Dec. 1684, Mary, d. of Rev. Seaborn Cotton,
had Cotton, 11 June 1686, d. next mo.; Mary, 4 July 1687, d. at 10
mos.; John, 5 May 1689, H. C.' 1708; Samuel, 22 Aug. 1691, d. next
yr.; Dorothy, 5 May 1693, d. at 4 mos.; Mercy, 20 June 1695, d. at 2
yrs.; Dorothy, again, 27 Mar. 1697, d. at 8 mos.; Mercy, again, 7 Oct.
1698; Simon, 31 Jan. 1700, H. C. 1724; Sarah, 13 May 1702; Dorothy, again, 14 Dec. 1704; and Lydia, 30 Jan. 1707. His w. d. 18 June
1715, and he had 3d w. Prudence; was freem. 1679, a capt. and rep.
1689, 90, and 1, d. 20 Sept. 1721. SIMON, Medford, youngest s. of the
sec. Peter, was the earliest physician at M. m. Abigail Smith, had Simon,
b. 16 June 1727, H. C. 1744; Abigail, 23 Sept. 1730; William, 28
Aug. 1732; Cotton, 30 May 1734, H. C. 1749, a man of emin.; Samuel, 7 Jan. 1736; Mercy, 19 Oct. 1742; and Ann, 8 Nov. 1744; and
he d. 31 Jan. 1747. THOMAS, Medford, s. of Peter the sec. m. Emma,
d. of Samuel Phips of Charlestown, had Catharine, Samuel, Simon, Solomon, David, and Frederic; and d. a. 1737. Farmer says fifteen of
this name had been gr. at Harv. 1834, leav. implicat. that none had been
at any of the other coll.

TULLER, JACOB, Simsbury, youngest s. of John of the same, m. Mary
Moses, and I kn. no more. JOHN, Simsbury, m. 1684, Eliz. wid. of
Joseph Lewis, d. of John Case of the same, had Sarah, b. 4 Aug. 1685;
William, 10 June 1687; Mary, 27 Nov. 1692; Jacob, 22 May 1694;
and Mabel, 22 Feb. 1699; and his w. d. 9 Oct. 1718. He d. 1742.
The first two ch. were bapt. at Hartford. At Simsbury he was one of
the founders of the ch. 10 Nov. 1697. Sarah m. John Moses jr. Mary
m. Samuel Humphrey; and Mabel m. Samuel Chidester of Wallingford,
as is shown by the patient investigat. of Goodwin. WILLIAM, Simsbury,
elder s. of John of the same, m. Damaris Cornish; but no more is told of
him exc. that he d. 22 Sept. 1749.

TULLY, JOHN, Saybrook, was bapt. at Horley, Co. Surrey, 27 ms. from
London, 9 Sept. 1638, and the fam. tradit. proceeds to relate how his
mo. brot. him here two or three yrs. aft. the d. of his f. in 1644; was
propound. for freem. 1671, and m. 3 Jan. 1672, Mary, d. of William
Beamond, or Beaman, had John, b. 3 Dec. 1672; Sarah, 9 Apr. 1674,

d. at 18 yrs.; William, 5 Jan. 1677; Lydia, 15 Mar. 1679; Mary, 10 Aug. 1681; Deborah, 24 Feb. 1684; Lucy, 22 Mar. 1687, d. at 5 yrs.; and Hepzibah, 22 Dec. 1689. He had some fame as almanac mak. for 20 yrs. and d. 5 Oct. 1701. See Field, Hist. of Middlesex Co. 104; and Geneal. Reg. III. 167, where is much wild legend. The s. John d. at sea; Sarah m. John Smith; and Mary m. Daniel Clark, both of Haddam. WILLIAM, Saybrook, s. of the preced. a shoemaker, m. it is said, Abigail Maverick of Boston, call. with equal prob. and precis. d. of a min. wh. left Eng. in the time of persecut. had John, b. 18 Mar. 1702; Margaret, 28 May 1704; Abigail, 5 July 1707; William, 13 June 1709; Lydia, 24 July 1711; Elias, 17 Jan. 1714; Sarah, 6 Jan. 1716; Mary, 30 Mar. 1718, d. at 21 yrs.; Samuel, 29 Apr. 1721, d. at 28 yrs.; and Daniel, 24 July 1723, d. young; and the f. d. 5 July 1744. The wid. d. 9 Dec. 1750, in her 76th yr.

TUPPER, ELISHA, a soldier, 1690, in Gallop's abortive serv. against Quebec to please Sir William Phips, may have been s. of sec. Thomas. *THOMAS, Lynn, rem. with many others of that town to Sandwich 1637, was rep. 1646, and 16 yrs. aft. d. 28 Mar. 1676, aged 97 yrs. and 2 mos. and his w. d. 4 June aft. in her 90th yr. says Col. Rec. *THOMAS, Sandwich, s. of the preced. the town clk. wh. certif. the rec. of his parents' age, had Eldad b. 31 May 1675; was rep. 1679, and the first from that place under the new chart. 1692. He had been much engag. in preach. to the Ind. and in the Magnalia, VI. 61, we find he had 180 hearers.

TURBAT, or TURBUTT, PETER, in the list of those, sw. to alleg. at Wells, 5 July 1653, constable 1661, had w. Sarah, ch. John, Peter, and Eliz. His inv. was of £61, present. 14 Oct. 1669. But this name means Talbot, I think.

TURBEFIELD, HENRY, Weymouth, had Ann, b. 8 Sept. 1673. I have some doubt of the name.

TURELL, COLBURN, Boston, s. of capt. Daniel, was one of the volunteers wh. set forth, in Oct. 1689, on the successful expedit. under Colon. author. to capt. a pirate vessel in Vineyard Sound. See Geneal. Reg. II. 393. ‖ DANIEL, Boston, blacksmith, ar. co. 1656, came from Instow on the N. coast of Devonsh. midway from Barnstable to Bideford, and by his first w. Lydia, perhaps d. of Robert Blott, wh. join. our ch. 29 Aug. 1647, he had Daniel, b. 16 Aug. 1646; John, bapt. 4 Mar. 1649, a. 6 days old; Joseph, 27 Dec. 1653, d. in few mos.; Joseph, again, 25 Mar. 1655; prob. Ann, 20 Aug. 1657, wh. in the substit. rec. is assign. to Samuel, as in Geneal. Reg. X. 70; and Samuel, 14 June 1659. She d. 23 June 1659, and he m. at Roxbury, 10 Nov. 1659, Mary Barrell, wid. of John, and d. of Elder William Colbron, had Lydia, 30 Nov.

1660; Colburn, 4 Dec. 1662; Sarah and Eliz. tw. 14 Oct. 1663; and Benjamin, 24 June 1665; was a freem. 1669, capt. 1683 aft. fill. the lower ranks, and d. July 1693, was bur. says Sewall's Diary on 24. ‖ DANIEL, Boston, s. of the preced. blacksmith, ar. co. 1674, was adm. of 2d or Mather's ch. 7 Sept. 1672, but why neither he nor any other of the name exc. his f. took the freemen's oath at any time is uncert. He by w. Ann had, beside Mary, b. 4 Apr. 1672; Ann, 31 Mar. 1674; and Lydia, 17 Jan. 1678; Daniel, certain. and perhaps Joseph, and John, wh. by town rec. seems to have been b. 18 Apr. all bapt. 30 Apr. 1693; and certain. Humphrey, b. 22, bapt. 28 Sept. 1696. Prob. he d. 23 Jan. 1699, as Farmer erron. assigns that date to his f. JOHN, Boston 1663, a mariner, was prob. br. of the preced. JOSEPH, Boston, br. of the preced. by w. Sarah, had Sarah, b. 31 Oct. 1679; and Humphrey, 21 May 1681. SAMUEL, Boston, by w. Lydia had Ann, b. 20 Aug. 1657, says Geneal. Reg. X. 70, when Daniel the first was the true f. SAMUEL, Boston, br. of Joseph, m. Lydia, d. of Anthony Stoddard, had John, b. 3 July 1687; and Christian or Christopher, the rec. being uncert. 17 Dec. 1688, wh. do not seem to have been bapt. tho. he join. Mather's ch. 18 Jan. 1685; had Samuel, bapt. 5 Nov. 1693, prob. d. soon; Mary, 26 Jan. 1696; Samuel, again, 9 Apr. 1699; and Ebenezer, b. 5 bapt. 8 Feb. 1702, H. C. 1721, min. of Medford to wh. we owe the Memoir on famous Dr. Colman, whose d. he m. WILLIAM, Boston, by w. Rebecca, had Rebecca, b. 26 Dec. 1655; and William, 16 Mar. 1657. This name in some careless rec. is Turin.

TURFRY or TURFREE, * GEORGE, Saco 1685, a man of distinct. a capt. and rep. that yr. says Folsom, 147, wh. was in the assemb. in wh. Thomas Danforth, one of the Mass. Assist. was sent to be Presid. rem. to Boston bef. 1695, when he was taxed at B. had w. Mary and s. Edward, wh. d. of full age to make will a dozen yrs. bef. his f. By his will of 15 Oct. 1712, pro. 17 Nov. 1714, the old man bestows all his est. on w. exc. to " Susanna Milborne or Watson, and her offspring one shill."

TURNER, ANANIAS, Kenilworth 1668, present. for freem. by the name of Turriner, wh. in my conject. is error of spell. by false pronounc. May 1669. CHARLES, Salem 1643. DANIEL, Duxbury 1643, of wh. I would gladly kn. more. He may be the person wh. took o. of fidel. 1647, at New Haven, but did not cont. there, and perhaps the same wh. was punish. at Hartford 1649, for libel on Mrs. Chester. See Conn. Col. Rec. I. 194. DANIEL, Scituate, s. of Humphrey, m. 20 Jan. 1665, Hannah, d. of William Randall, was liv. 1699. DAVID, Rehoboth. DAVID, Scituate, s. of the sec. John, m. Eliz. d. of Charles Stockbridge the first. EDWARD, Milford 1651, sw. as freem. 1667, but not found in the town's list, having rem. to Middletown 1665, and d. 4 Apr. 1717.

He had bapt. at Milford, Mercy in 1662; a s. prob. Edward, 1664; and Mary 1666, tho. b. at Middletown, 5 Nov. 1665; Eliz. b. 14 Dec. 1667, prob. tho. rec. says 14 Dec. 1668, wh. must be wrong; John, 5 or 8 Aug. 1669; Stephen, 27 Nov. 1671; Abigail, 10 Sept. 1673; Hannah, 20 June 1675 or 6, the last fig. being indist. and Richard, 4 Mar. 1679. His w. was Mary. The s. Edward had ch. at Middletown 1694 and aft. EDWARD, Boston, wh. may be the same as the preced. m. 25 Oct. 1656, Mary, d. of Richard Sanford. ELISHA, Hingham, m. June 1687, Eliz. Jacob; but I am not sure that he did not belong to Scituate or Weymouth, and to H. only resort for w. ‖ EPHRAIM, Boston, eldest s. of Robert, the innholder, ar. co. 1663, freem. 1666, ens. in the comp. of capt. James Oliver, 1675, and held the colors until 1680; was a brazier. EPHRAIM, Hartford, apprent. to Phineas Wilson, wh. left him some est. by his will of 1691, had w. Mary, and d. late in 1705, or early next yr. EZEKIEL, New London, s. of John of Scituate, m. 26 Dec. 1678, Susanna, d. of John Keeny, d. 16 Jan. 1704, leav. Ezekiel and ten ds. HABACUCK, Salem, mariner, s. of the sec. Robert of Boston. * HUMPHREY, Scituate, had come with w. and eldest s. John, perhaps also a sec. John and tradit. would have him bring two more from a part of Eng. hitherto undeterm. where he had been a tanner, and a. 1628 sat down at Plymouth, some yrs. aft. rem. to S. where he was one of the found. of the ch. Jan. 1635, and earliest promin. men. There his w. join. the ch. 10 Jan. 1636. At P. he was taxed, we kn. by the rec. 1633 and 4, and there prob. were b. Lydia, and Thomas. But to S. we kn. he rem. 1634, and assign to this resid. Mary, bapt. 25 Jan. 1635; Joseph, 1 Jan. 1637; Nathaniel, 10 Mar. 1639; and Daniel. Certain. in 1643, two Johns are in the list of those able to bear arms for Scituate. There he was constable, rep. in 1640, 52 and 3; d. 1673. His w. Lydia had d. bef. that d. Lydia m. 15 Aug. 1649, James Doughty; and Mary m. 13 Nov. 1651, William Parker, as his sec. w. INCREASE, Boston, s. of Jeffrey, m. at Charlestown, 3 Oct. 1673, Mehitable, d. of the first Thomas Hett; sometime he was of Cambridge, liv. in that part that bec. Newton, d. 1689. ISAAC, New Haven, s. of capt. Nathaniel, among the freem. of 1669, was a propr. 1685. His w. Mary, d. of Christopher Todd, m. 19 Aug. 1668, brot. him Isaac, and Nathaniel, 3 July 1669; Joseph, 13 Nov. 1672; Mary, 9 Dec. 1674, d. young; and his w. d. 3 May 1676. He made his will 1 Jan. 1699, and d. 27 Mar. foll. leav. good est. to the three ch. ISRAEL, Scituate, s. of the sec. or young John, m. Sarah, d. of the first Charles Stockbridge. JACOB, Scituate, br. of the preced. m. 1692, Jane Vining, prob. d. of John of Weymouth, and there afterwards liv. and had Jacob, 4 Apr. 1693; Seth, 7 Apr. 1695; Jane, 13 Apr. 1698; Benjamin, 29 Jan. 1706, d. at 7 yrs.; Elisha, 5 Mar. 1708, d.

young; Micah, 8 July 1710; and Mary, 12 Apr. 1713; he d. 29 Nov.
1723, and his wid. m. Samuel Allen. JAMES, New Haven 1649, a
squint-eyed runagate from the Dutch. See New Haven Col. Rec. I.
422, 528. JAPHET, Scituate, eldest br. of Jacob, m. at Duxbury, Hannah, d. of John Hudson, had Ann, b. 18 Aug. 1679; Joshua, 9 Apr.
'1681; Japhet, 4 Jan. 1683; and Ruth, 19 Mar. 1685; and d. 1690,
leav. wid. Hannah. JEFFREY, Dorchester, by w. Isabel Gill had
Praisever, b. 22 Aug. 1640 (but in Hist. of D. is giv. Jeffrey, 22 May
1640); and Increase, 16 Oct. 1642; was freem. 1643, and d. 1654.
His will of 12 Apr. pro. 25 May of that yr. made w. excor. and provides for the two ch. His wid. d. prob. Dec. 1660, as the inv. was tak.
that mo. JOHN, Plymouth, came in the Mayflower 1620, with two in
fam. wh. Bradford calls his s. but all d. within three or four mos. He
left a d. in Eng. wh. came over, was m. at Salem, liv. in 1650 "well
appro." But I kn. not wh. was her h. JOHN, Scituate, eldest s. of
Humphrey, b. in Eng. m. 12 Nov. 1645, Mary, d. of Jonathan Brewster, had Jonathan, b. 20 Sept. 1646; Joseph, 12 Jan. 1648, d. in 3
days; Joseph, again, 12 Jan. 1650; Ezekiel, 7 Jan. 1651; Lydia, 24
Jan. 1653; John, 30 Oct. 1654; Elisha, 8 Mar. 1657. His d. Mary m.
a. 1683, Isaac Prince; and Lydia m. 1675, John James, and in 1680,
William Barrell. JOHN, Scituate, sec. s. of Humphrey, by his f. call.
young John, perhaps b. in Eng. tradit. says the name at bapt. was giv.
by godfather, but such folly should not have been allow. m. 25 Apr.
1649, Ann James, but her parents are not kn. had Japhet, b. 9 Feb.
1650; Ann, 23 Feb. 1652; Israel, 14 Feb. 1654; Miriam, 8 Apr.
1658; Sarah, 25 July 1665; Jacob, 10 Mar. 1667; David, 5 Nov.
1670; Philip, 18 Aug. 1673; and Ichabod, 9 Apr. 1676; and d. 1687.
Ann m. 1695, Joseph Green; Miriam m. 1687, Nathan Pickles; and
Sarah m. Ichabod Holbrook. JOHN, Salem, with w. Eliz. join the ch.
19 Nov. 1637, had John, and Eliz. wh. m. 9 June 1665, Eleazer Ged-
ney; was perhaps the freem. of 2 May 1649, a merch. and d. at Barbadoes 1668. JOHN, Roxbury, mem. of the ch. bef. 1650, had Eliz. b. 27
Sept. 1647; Deborah, bapt. 14 Jan. 1649; but no more is found in rec.
of town, so that he may be the freem. of 2 May 1649, and well judged
to have rem. and not unlikely to the new settlem. at Medfield, by w.
Deborah there had John, b. 3 Mar. bapt. 8 June at R. 1651; Isaac;
Mary, 18 Nov. 1658; Samuel; Sarah; Abigail; and Hannah; prob.
bapt. at M. aft. Wilson bec. min. Deborah m. 18 Nov. 1668, Jabez
Tatman of R. JOHN, Lynn 1647. JOHN, Weymouth 1653, had, perhaps, been there a dozen yrs. JOHN, Boston 1660, sec. s. of Robert the
first, foll. the business of his f. as a vintner, freem. 1666, m. Lucy, d. of
Thomas Gardner of Boston (Muddy riv.) had in 1673, secur. gr. of 150

acres, perhaps on acco. of the serv. of his f. was d. bef. Oct. 1681, when his wid. extrix. applied for confirmat. of the ld. to grantee of her h. She next m. George Monk. Ano. JOHN, Boston, descr. as s. of John of Walton, Co. Suffolk, binds hims. by indent. of apprent. 22 Apr. 1649, to Edward Bendall for 12 yrs. wh. seems a very long term. JOHN, Salem, s. of John of the same, m. 20 Apr. 1669, Eliz. Roberts, had John, b. 12 Sept. 1671; Eliz. 15 Dec. 1673; Eunice, 1 Jan. 1676; Freestone, 25 Oct. 1677; and Abiah, posthum. 14 Oct. 1680; the last two being ds. in spite of their names. In this last yr. he d. 9 Oct. leav. very large est. JOHN, Medfield, s. of John of the same, may have been a soldier in capt. Mosely's comp. Dec. 1675; had w. Sarah, and left John, Stephen, Edward, and Ebenezer, of wh. the last was b. a. 1694. JOHN, Guilford, d. 1696, leav. wid. Eliz. and two ch. JONATHAN, Scituate, eldest s. of John the first of the same, m. Martha, d. of Elisha Besbedge, had Jesse, and prob. other ch. JOSEPH, Scituate, s. of Humphrey of the same, m. Bathsheba, d. of Rev. Peter Hobart of Hingham, but I kn. no more. JOSEPH, Boston, s. of Robert the first, d. unm. in his will of 2 Nov. 1674, pro. 3 June foll. names mo. Penelope, sis. Penelope, w. of John Fairweather, and neph. John F. giv. to them his little prop. Prob. he was infirm from youth, and his inv. shows only £20, tho. a careless reader might think it was far larger in amount. JOSIAH, Scituate, is nam. as one of the witnesses to will of Joseph Wermall in 1662, but I do not see whose s. he was, or any thing further of him. LAWRENCE, perhaps of Exeter 1650, there had w. Sarah, certain. was of Newport, among the freem. of 1657, and rem. to Greenwich, and submit. the same yr. to the jurisdict. of New Haven. MICHAEL, Lynn 1637, rem. says Lewis, to Sandwich, bef. 1643, we kn. for there in this yr. his name is enrol. among those able to bear arms, and was constable the yr. bef. there had w. and gr. of ld. * NATHANIEL, Lynn, came 1630, in the fleet with Winth. req. adm. as freem. 19 Oct. of that yr. and was sw. in 3 July 1632, and was constable the same yr. was rep. 1634, at the first Court, when dep. came 1635 and 6, went against the Pequots 1637, had a w. whose name, fam. or bapt. we have not seen, and rem. next yr. to the new settlem. at New Haven, with his ch. Mary, prob. the name of eldest d. wh. m. Thomas Yale; Nathaniel; Rebecca; Abigail; Hannah, wh. was bapt. 17 Nov. 1639, being the earliest in the ch. rec. and Isaac, 7 June 1640. In 1640, he was one of the purch. of Stamford, always a man of enterpr. and public spirit, and sailed for London, in the ill-fated bark, with capt. Lamberton, Mr. Gregson and others, Jan. 1646, whose arr. was never heard of. The wid. m. Samuel Vangoodenhausen, and of the ds. beside the w. of Thomas Yale bef. ment. Rebecca m. a. 1649, Thomas Mix; Abigail m. 2 Sept. 1651, John Hudson; and Hannah m.

Samuel Hopkins, 5 Dec. 1667. Nathaniel d. unm. and in Jan. 1662, his share, £75, of the est. was distrib. NATHANIEL, Scituate, s. of Humphrey of the same, m. 29 Mar. 1665, Mehitable Rigby, and d. 31 Jan. 1715. PHILIP, Scituate, s. of Humphrey's s. young John, m. Eliz. Nash. PRAISEVER, Dorchester, eldest s. of Jeffrey, a soldier k. at Northampton, where he was some yrs. resid. 28 Sept. 1675, but whether he was m. or had fam. is unkn. RALPH, Scarborough or Falmouth, one of those inhabs. wh. unit. in addr. 4 July 1663, in wh. the loyalty is well exhibit. was constable in 1670. RICHARD, Boston, mem. of the ch. bef. Cotton came; but some yrs. aft. his resid. is unkn. nor much to be sought for, as of him nothing is found but his excommun. in Nov. 1638, for excessive drink of strong waters, being drunk more than once, and, as the Col. Rec. I. shows, mulct. for it in 1639. ‖ ROBERT, Boston 1633, or earlier, as he is call. our br. Edward Bendall's man serv. on adm. to the ch. 8 Sept. next to Rev. John Cotton and his w. tho. he may have come in the ship with them; freem. 4 Mar. foll. by w. Penelope had Ephraim, b. 13, bapt. 22 Dec. 1639; Sarah, 11, bapt. 14 Mar. 1641; John, 1, bapt. 4 Dec. 1642; Joseph, 7, bapt. 15 Sept. 1644; Benjamin, 6 Mar. 1647, wh. prob. d. bef. his f. at least is not nam. in his will; Daniel, 26 Nov. 1650, d. at 4 mos.; was ar. co. 1640, and lieut. 1662, a thrifty innholder, wh. at the sign of the anchor, furnish. lodgings and refreshm. to the mem. of the governm. frequent. to Commsnrs. of the Unit. Cols. of N. E. to juries, and to the clergy, when summon. into synod by our Gen. Ct. His will of 9 July 1664, pro. 24 Aug. foll. *as he spoke it* in Vol. I. 433, is to be read in Geneal. Reg. XIII. 11. Sarah m. 15 Nov. 1660, John Fairweather. ROBERT, Boston, shoemaker, came prob. in the Blessing from London, 1635, aged 24, was rec. into our ch. 17 Feb. 1644, and next day had bapt. his s. John, b. 28 Apr. preced. by w. Eliz. wh. join. 7 Mar. 1646. In three mos. from bapt. that ch. d. and John, again, b. 8 was bapt. 15 Sept. 1644; Habacuck, 18 Apr. 1647; and Eliz.; and d. Sept. 1651. With sev. others in 1648, he appl. to our Gen. Ct. for incorp. as a guild of shoemakers. His will of 14 Aug. preced. his d. gives half of est. to his w. provid. for the three ch. and ano. if it come. The sum of prop. was decent; wid. was extrix. and her posthum. s. Robert was b. 17 May foll. but d. at 3 mos. THOMAS, Exeter 1652, may be the person emb. at London, Sept. 1635 aged 42, in the Hopewell. THOMAS, Hingham 1639, s. of Humphrey of Scituate, perhaps b. in Eng. m. 6 Jan. 1652, Sarah, d. of Thomas Hyland, had Nathaniel, b. 1 Mar. 1655; Eliz. July 1656; and d. Nov. 1688. THOMAS, Marblehead 1668, is by me regard. as the same, wh. in Dana, p. 8 is giv. as inhab. of M. 1674. See Geneal. Reg. IX. 83. WILLIAM, Dorchester 1642, freem. 10 May 1643,

rem. to Boston, and was one of the founders of the first Bapt. ch. 1665;
would, early in Philip's war, have formed a comp. of volunteers for serv.
against the com. enemy, but, as most of the assoc. were of his relig. per-
suasion, his and their offers were slighted.   As the war grew more
danger. in the foll. spring, he was encourag. by the governm. and had
command on the upper waters of Conn. riv. on 18 May surpris. the Ind.
at the place where the falls have since borne his name, and gave them a
signal defeat, but on the return he was surround. at Green riv. and the
next day after the Falls fight was k. with fourteen of his men.   See
Niles strange. indistinct, in 3 Mass. Hist. Coll. VI. 184.   His w. was
Mary, wid. of Key Alsop, and ch. were, prob. by ano. perhaps Frances,
not all b. in Boston, at least only Prudence, 12 Oct. 1665, is to be found
in the rec. yet his will made 10 Feb. 1676, as he was sudden. call. to the
war, pro. 21 July foll. provid. for w. Mary and childr. without nam.
any, tho. he refers to his eldest d.   Farmer notes that eight of this
name had, in 1834, been gr. at Harv. eight at Yale, and six at other
N. E. coll.

    TURNEY, BENJAMIN, Concord, had Rebecca, b. 16 Feb. 1640; Sarah,
11 Dec. 1641; and Ruth, 28 Jan. 1644; was freem. 2 June 1641; rem.
to Fairfield, there had Benjamin, and d. 1648.   His inv. is of 6 June in
that yr. and ch. were Mary, 17 yrs. old; Robert, 15; Judith, 13; Ann,
11; all prob. b. in Eng.; Rebecca, 8; Sarah, 6; Ruth, 4; and Benjamin,
3.   His wid. Mary, perhaps mo. of all the ch. m. Joseph Middlebrook,
wh. had also, rem. from Concord to F.   Mary the d. m. in 1649, Nathaniel Seely; Rebecca m. Stephen Sherwood of Greenwich; and the other
ds. were m.   BENJAMIN, Fairfield, s. of the preced. d. 1694, prob. for
his inv. was present. in Nov. of that yr. leav. wid. Rebecca, and ch. Benjamin, 22; Robert, 20; Rebecca, 18; Thomas, and Sarah, 15; Jemima,
8; and Jonathan, 4.   JOSEPH, Stamford 1687–1701, of wh. no more is
told, hardly seems to be any connex. of the Fairfield fam.   ROBERT,
Fairfield, eldest s. of Benjamin the first, of wh. by his will of 31 Dec.
1689, and inv. 17 Jan. foll. we learn that he had w. Eliz. s. Benjamin
and Robert, and seven ds. Eliz. Mary, Ruth, Martha, Rebecca, and the
ws. of Joseph Jennings and of Ephraim Wheeler, call. s.-in-law, while
the ws. are not nam. and perhaps were d.   He was capt. some yrs. later
than freem. 1664.

    TURPIN, THOMAS, Isle of Shoals, fisherman, bot. in Dec. 1645, with
Richard Cummings, all the planta. of Francis Williams of Portsmouth.
WILLIAM, Providence, was the first sch.-master 1684.

    TURVILL, THOMAS, Newbury 1668, a tanner, was engag. in the con-
trov. next yr. betw. Mr. Parker and mem. of his ch. taking the side of
the min. d. 22 May 1677, leav. no ch.   His wid. Judith d. 11 July 1689.

TUTTLE, TUTTEL, or TUTHILL, DAVID, New Haven, s. of William, a propr. 1685, in 1687 put under the care of his br. Thomas, and d. 1693, without ch. EDWARD, Boston, freem. 1690. ELISHA, Boston, freem. 1690. HENRY, Hingham 1637, came with w. from some place in Co. Norfolk, freem. Mar. 1638, was made constable 1640. * JOHN, Ipswich, came in the Planter from London 1635, aged 39, with w. Joan, 42; and ch. Abigail, 6; Simon, 4; Sarah, 2; and John, 1; besides Jane Giddings, 20, and her h. George, 25, wh. are kn. to be call. ch. of T. They had prob. liv. at St. Albans, in Hertfordsh. and had emb. 2 Apr. to be join. four days aft. by sev. others of the same names in two fams. He was freem. 13 Mar. 1639, rep. 1644; and prob. had more ch. on our side of the ocean, as Simon (perhaps in place of him wh. d.) and Mary. After few yrs. he went home, was estab. to advantage in Ireland, whither in 1654 his w. foll. He d. 30 Dec. 1656 at Carrickfergus, whence his wid. in 1689 writes to George Giddings as her s. and so call. also John and Simon, and John Lawrence. His d. Sarah m. 1 Feb. 1654, Richard Martin. JOHN, New Haven 1640, appoint. constable 1642, had, says the careful town rec. Samuel, b. 9 Jan. 1660; Sarah, 22 Jan. 1662; Daniel and Mary, tw. 13 Apr. 1664; and Eliz. 21 Nov. 1666, wh. all were bapt. the yr. foll. but the blunder. ch. rec. has all with false dates, 23 inst. of 24 Mar. for the four first, wh. is a slight affair; but abominable for the youngest, said to be bapt. two days bef. she was b. JOHN, Southold, L. I. went prob. from New Haven with Rev. John Youngs, a. 1641. He was liv. 1681, had John, b. 16 July 1635; Joshua; and James. It is suppos. he was from Saxlingham, Co. Norf'k. JOHN, Dover 1642 or earlier, d. late in 1662, leav. wid. Dorothy, one d. m. s. John, ano. d. and s. Thomas, all perhaps minors. The last was k. 1664 by the fall of a tree. The younger d. was perhaps Dorothy, wh. m. 1 Sept. 1686, Samuel Tibbets of D. JOHN, Boston, s. prob. of Richard, m. 10 Feb. 1647, Mary, d. of Edward Holyoke, had Mary, b. 18 Apr. 1653; Rebecca, 17 June 1660; and Sarah; liv. at Rumney Marsh, perhaps rem. to Lynn, and may be the freem. there of 1671, possib. that lieut. of the corps of cavalry, wh. was disch. 1673. Mary m. 4 Dec. 1678, Caleb Carter; and Sarah m. Joseph Newell, both of Charlestown. JOHN, New Haven, perhaps eldest s. of William, brot. by his f. under 4 yrs. of age in the Planter, m. 8 Nov. 1653, Catharine Lane, had Hannah, b. 2 Nov. 1655; John, 15 Sept. 1657; Samuel, 9 Jan. 1660; Sarah, 22 Jan. 1662; Daniel and Mary, tw. 13 Apr. 1664; all bapt. Mar. 1666, but the day in Geneal. Reg. IX. 363, is wrong; and `Eliz. b. 21 bapt. 25 Nov. foll. and all in right of their mo. besides ano. later, David, 15 Nov. 1668. His inv. is of 12 Nov. 1683. JOHN, Southold, L. I. s. of John of the same, m. 17 Feb. 1658, Deliverance King, had John, b. 14 Feb.

1659; Eliz.; Henry, 1 May 1665; Hannah; Abigail; Dorothy; Deliverance; Daniel, 23 Jan. 1680; and Nathaniel, 10 Nov. 1683. He had sec. w. m. 28 May 1690, Sarah Young; and d. 12 Oct. 1717. *JOHN, Dover, s. of John first of the same, fill. many offices, town clk. 30 yrs. selectman, rep. and judge of C. C. P. had John, b. a. 1671; Thomas, 4 Apr. 1674; James, 7 Apr. 1683; and Ebenezer; beside two ds. and leav. large est. d. 1720. In his will calls w. Mary, ch. Ebenezer, and Mary; gr.ch. Thomas and John, s. prob. of John, wh. had been k. by the Ind. 17 May 1712; John, and Nicholas, s. perhaps of Thomas, wh. had d. 26 Apr. 1699, in the Bay of Campeachy, and Elijah and Phebe, ch. of James, wh. d. 1709; beside John and Peter Hayes, wh. must, I think, have been ch. of John. Mary was w. of John Wallingford, m. 6 Dec. 1687; and I find reason to differ from Mr. Quint, wh. supposes that she was the same wh. m. Hayes. JOHN, Ipswich, s. perhaps of the first Simon, m. 3 Dec. 1689, Martha Ward, perhaps sis. of Samuel, had Martha, b. 1690; and Mary, 7 July 1696; and he d. 26 Feb. 1716. JOHN, Boston, freem. 1690. JONATHAN, New Haven, s. of William, was in the freemen's list 1669, by w. Rebecca, d. of Francis Bell of Stamford, had Rebecca, b. 10 Sept. 1664; Mary, 7 Feb. 1666; David, 14 Nov. 1668; tho. this is manifest. wrong, for next comes, in less than five mos. Jonathan, 6 Apr. 1669; and David on the same 14 Nov. 1668, is, by the same author, giv. to John; Simon, 11 Mar. 1671; William, 25 May 1673; and Nathaniel, 25 Feb. 1676. His w. d. 2 May 1676. He was propr. 1685. JONATHAN, Boston, freem. 1690. JOSEPH, New Haven, s. of William, propound. for freem. 1669, m. 2 May 1667, Hannah, d. of Thomas Munson, had Joseph, b. 18 Mar. 1668; Samuel, 15 July 1670; Stephen, 20 May 1673; Joanna, 13 Dec. 1675; Timothy, 30 Sept. 1678, d. soon; Susanna, 20 Feb. 1680, d. young; Eliz. 12 July 1683; and Hannah, May 1685, wh. may have d. soon; and ano. Hannah came in her place. He d. 1690, aged, says Dodd, 62, when he could be only 50, if the s. of William. His wid. m. 1694, Nathan Bradley, and d. next yr. He was propr. 1685. JOSHUA, Southold, L. I. s. of the first John of the same, had Joshua. NATHANIEL, New Haven, s. of William, propr. 1685, may then have been some yrs. at Woodbury, there had Mary, bapt. May 1683; Ephraim; Hezekiah; Isaac, b. 3 Feb. 1698; Temperance and Ann; d. 20 Aug. 1721, leav. w. Sarah, and nam. in his will all those ch. exc. the first, wh. was, perhaps d. At New Haven the rec. names Ephraim, b. 20 July 1683; and Temperance, 24 Nov. 1684; and first rec. the m. 10 Apr. as one reads or ano. Aug. 1682, with Sarah Howe, eldest d. of Ephraim. So that the order of childr. taken above from Cothren must be incorrect, and possib. one of the names. RICHARD, Boston, came in the Planter, from London 1635, aged 42, call. husbandman;

with Isabel, 70, perhaps his mo.; w. Ann, 41; ch. Ann, 12; John, 10; and Rebecca, 6; he with his w. join. our ch. 27 Dec. aft. arr. was adm. freem. 3 Mar. foll. and d. 8 May 1640. Perhaps his d. Ann m. John Pantry of Hartford, and next, 23 June 1654, Thomas Welles of H. SAMUEL, New Haven, a propr. 1685, was s. of John, and gr.s. of William, but no more is kn. to me. SIMON, Ipswich, s. of John of the same, b. in Eng. m. Sarah, d. of John Cogswell, had Joanna, b. 24 Sept. 1664; Simon, 17 Sept. 1667; Eliz. 24 Nov. 1670; Sarah, 3 Sept. 1672; Abigail, 7 Oct. 1673; Susanna, 7 May 1675; William, 7 May 1677; Charles, 31 Mar. 1679; Mary, 12 June 1680; Jonathan, 11 June 1682; and Ruth, 16 Aug. 1685; and he d. Jan. 1692. Of the ch. nam. John and eight others were liv. at the d. of f. Two other ch. were b. of wh. one was John, but prob. the other liv. not many hours. His wid. Sarah, after these thirteen ch. liv. to 24 Jan. 1732. The eldest d. m. a Packard; Eliz. m. Samuel Ayres of Haverhill; Abigail m. Philemon Warner; Mary m. Thomas Burnham; and one m. Samuel Ward. SIMON, New Haven, had Daniel, b. 11 Nov. 1680; had in 1670 engag. to rem. to Wallingford, certain. did not long contin. there. SIMON, Ipswich, s. of Simon of the same, m. 16 Jan. or one acco. says June 1696, Mary, d. of Samuel Rogers, had Sarah, b. 11 Oct. 1697; Margaret, 24 Aug. 1699; and Eliz. 26 Sept. 1700. THOMAS, New Haven, s. of William, not the babe he brot. in 1635, with him, unless we reject (as I am very ready to do) the numeration of yrs. at his d. giv. by Dodd; was freem. bef. 1669, propr. 1685, m. 21 May 1661, Hannah, eldest d. of Thomas Powell, had Hannah, b. 24 Feb. 1662; Abigail, 17 Jan. 1664; Mary, 14 Jan. 1666; Thomas, 27 Oct. 1667; John, 5 Dec. 1669; Esther, 9 Apr. 1672; Caleb, 29 Aug. 1674; Joshua, 19 Dec. 1676; and Martha, 23 May 1679. His w. d. 15 Oct. 1710; and he d. four days aft. aged 68, says Dodd, prob. foll. the gr.st. inscript. too little by seven yrs. WILLIAM, Boston, came in the Planter 1635, aged 26, with w. Eliz. 23; ch. John 3½; Ann, 2¼; and Thomas, 3 mos. He is, by tradit. said to have come from Co. Northampton. His w. join. our ch. 24 July 1636, and brot. to be bapt. Jonathan, 2 July 1637; David, 7 Apr. 1639. Soon aft. he rem. to New Haven, there became a man of conseq. had Joseph, bapt. 22 Nov. 1640; Sarah, Apr. 1642; Eliz. 9 Nov. 1645; Simon, 28 Mar. 1647; Benjamin, 29 Oct. 1648; Mercy, b. 27 Apr. bapt. 19 May 1650; and Nathaniel, 24, bapt. 29 Feb. 1652. His est. was giv. to be admin. June 1673, all the ch. liv. and the w. d. 30 Dec. 1684. Of the ds. Sarah m. 12 Nov. 1663, John Slawson; Mercy m. 2 May 1667, Samuel Brown; Eliz. m. 19 Nov. foll. Richard Edwards. Farmer numbers the gr. in 1834, as six at Yale, four at Harv. and two at other N. E. coll.

TWELVES, TUELLS, or TWELLS, ROBERT, Braintree, was one of the petitnrs. for gr. of what did not belong to our governm. honestly to give (the region possess. by Gorton and his fellow misbelievers) in Oct. 1645, ra. 22 or 23 Nov. 1655, Martha, d. of Peter Brackett, had Mary, b. 8 July 1656; Martha, 17 Dec. 1657, or 19 Dec. 1658, as in Geneal. Reg. XII. 350, d. soon; Richard, 16 May 1660, by the rec. in Boston, but by ano. rec. Martha, again, 16 June 1660; Rachel, 8 May 1662; Peter, 10 Oct. 1666; Sarah, bapt. 29 May 1670; John, 14 July 1672; but these two were at the third ch. in Boston; Hannah, 21 Sept. 1673; Abigail, 27 or 28, bapt. 29 July 1677; was freem. 1663, and caught from his f.-in-law the milit. distinct. ens. 1671, lieut. in 1684, d. 2 Mar. 1691, aged (tho. gr.st. says eighty yrs.) a. 77 yrs. old. Mary m. 4 Nov. 1676, Ebenezer Tyng; Rachel m. 25 Sept. 1689, William French, and d. soon; and Abigail m. 12 June 1704, Shubael Seaver of Roxbury. His will of 18 Mar. 1697, pro. 6 May foll. shows that Mary had ano. h. one Clarke, and that three then unm. ds. were Hannah, Sarah, and Abigail. Of this name Mr. Secr. Increase Nowell, in the Col. rec. Vol. II. 128, made the ingenious, or ridiculous, perversion Quelves.

TWIDE, WILLIAM, is the name giv. to a passeng. in the Arabella, 1671, from London, for N. E. but he was not long liv. here unless he changed it.

TWINING, STEPHEN, Eastham, s. of William the sec. m. 3 Jan. 1683, Abigail, d. of John Young of the same, had Stephen, b. 30 Dec. 1684; Eleazer, 26 Nov. 1686; Nathaniel, 27 Mar. 1689; Mercy, 8 Sept. 1690; and John, 5 Mar. 1693. WILLIAM, Yarmouth 1643, rem. early to Eastham, had perhaps, by w. Ann, William, prob. b. in Eng. and Eliz. and Ann, prob. b. here. He d. 15 Apr. 1659, and Ann, w. of William sen. d. 27 Feb. 1681, but possib. this may not have been the w. wh. bore the sec. William, but his sec. w. Eliz. m. 19 Aug. 1669, John Rogers; and Ann m. 3 Oct. 1672, Thomas Bills. WILLIAM, Eastham, s. of the preced. prob. b. in Eng. m. Eliz. d. of Stephen Deane, had Susanna, b. 25 Jan. 1655; Joanna, 30 May 1657; Stephen, 6 Feb. 1660; and William. He was liv. in 1695. WILLIAM, Eastham, s. of the preced. m. 26 Mar. 1689, Ruth, d. of John Cole of the same, had Eliz. b. 25 Aug. 1690; Thankful, 11 Jan. 1697; Ruth, 27 Aug. 1699; Hannah, 2 Apr. 1702; William, 2 Sept. 1704; Barnabas, 29 Sept. 1705; and Mercy, 20 Feb. 1708.

TWISDEN, TWISDALE, or TWISDALL, JOHN, York 1648, had been of Scituate in 1639, and came from Co. Kent, was of gr. jury 1649, prob. had John, for in Nov. 1652, John sen. and jr. submit. to Mass. and SAMUEL is found in 1656. His d. Alice or Eliz. m. 20 Nov. 1649, Joseph

Tilden of Scituate. Both John and Samuel, wh. were prob. s. of the first John, sw. alleg. to Charles II. Mar. 1681.

TWITCHELL, TUCHILL, or TWITCHWELL, BENJAMIN, Dorchester, was prob. of Medfield 1663, with w. Mary and sev. ch. of wh. Joseph, and Benjamin, to wh. we can affix no dates of b. may have been, beside Mary, b. 8 Mar. 1659; Hannah; Bethia; Abiel, 1 Nov. 1663; were part; but no more is with precis. relat. exc. he was among grantees of Lancaster 1654. ⁕ BENJAMIN, Medfield, s. of the preced. m. 5 Apr. 1685, Mary White, perhaps as sec. w. had some yrs. dwelt at Sherborn, and there had Benjamin, b. 15 Sept. 1684; John, 4 Jan. 1688; Ebenezer, 10 Dec. 1691; Mary, 28 Aug. 1694; and Abigail, 5 June 1699. FRANCIS, Dorchester 1633, is by Dr. Harris call. Tuthill, in the easy mistake of a single letter, the c in engrossing hand frequent. (as scores of errors result. demonstr.) resembles t. JOSEPH, Dorchester 1633, perhaps br. of the preced. freem. 14 May 1643, was there liv. 1656, had Joseph, wh. d. 13 Sept. 1651. The last form of spell. prevails in the Col. rec. the first is now common, and the Dorchester rec. obey. the sound.

TWOMBLY, or TWAMBLY, JOHN, Dover, eldest s. of Ralph of the same, m. 18 Apr. 1687, Mary Kenney, and in his will of 18 July 1724, names sec. w. Rachel; but our informat. does not extend to tell of wh. the ch. were b. tho. there were nam. by the will eno. for both, five s. and five ds. the priority or order of b. being inscrut. John, Joseph, Samuel, wh. alone, enjoys a date, b. 10 Mar. 1699, Benjamin, William, Sarah, Mary, Rachel, Esther, and Hannah. NATHANIEL, Dover 1658, is only nam. as bound. his land. RALPH, Dover 1656, had w. Eliz. and ch. as by will of 28 Feb. 1685, pro. 7 Oct. 1686, we learn, John, Ralph, Joseph, wh. was b. 1661, Mary, Eliz. Hope, Sarah, Esther, and William. RALPH, Dover, s. of the preced. had Ralph, perhaps more.

TYBBOT, WALTER, Gloucester. See Tibbets.

TYDD. See Tead.

TYLEY, or TYLEE, THOMAS, Boston, a waterman in 1664, sold est. to Henry Kemble.

TYLER, ABRAHAM, Haverhill 1640, m. 26 Dec. 1650, Hannah Freeman, had Abraham, b. 4 June of unkn. yr. d. at 2 yrs.; Hannah, 16 Dec. 1655, d. at 6 yrs.; Abraham, again, 21 May 1659, d. at 9 yrs.; and the f. d. 6 May 1673. FRANCIS, Branford 1667, drew a lot there in 1679, and had Abigail, b. 1681, but no more is kn. of him. GEORGE, Branford 1674, by w. Hannah, had Isaac, b. 1680; Ann, 20 June 1682; Samuel, 25 Feb. 1685; Eliz. 6 Nov. 1687; Hannah, 1692; and by sec. w. Mary had Eliz. 1694; John, 1696; Roger, 1698; Deborah, 1700; and Ebenezer, 1703. HOPE, Mendon 1662, prob. eldest s. of Job, freem.

1673, driv. by the Ind. from M. had at Roxbury, Matthew, bapt. 9 Apr. 1676; John, b. 19 Feb. 1678; rem. to Andover (where Hopestill perhaps his s. was adm. to be freem. 1691), and there had Joanna, 21 Nov. 1681; and James, 28 Dec. 1683; and, as is said, sev. more. His w. Mary and two ds. were charg. with witchcraft, and imprison. at Salem, but happi. not being tr. bef. the smoke of the bottomless pit that affect. a jury much, and judges more, had begun to disperse (even aft. confess, by the w. and one of her ds. overcome by urgent appeals of friends), were acquit. 6 and 7 Jan. 1693. In 1697 he sold his est. at A. and prób. rem. JOB, Andover, may have had ch. bef. that town was sett. as Hope or Moses, and Dr. Stiles found his name, tho. I doubt a mistake in his vision, on the roll of adm. at Aquedneck, or Portsmouth, R. I. 1639. Certain. at Providence was early a wid. Joan T. wh. had sh. in div. of lots in 1638, at that point call. Tockwotton, and she is nam. again in 1640. Possib. she was mo. of Job, who was b. a. 1619. By w. Mary, those may have been b. to him, as certain. were Mary, a. 1643; John, wh. d. 28 Sept. 1652; John, again, b. 6 Apr. 1653; and Samuel, 24 May 1655; in 1665 he was at Roxbury, and his w. join. the ch. 28 May of that yr. and next Sunday had John and Samuel bapt. there. In 1669 he rem. to Mendon, thence driv. by the Ind. he ret. to R. but bef. 1681, was in Rowley, the part now Boxford, and next at A. where after d. of his w. prob. in 1700, he divid. his est. to s. JOHN, Bristol, m. Sarah, d. of William Havens, long bef. 1680, when her f. names her in his will. His d. Tamar m. 5 Dec. 1678, Robert Cook of Portsmouth, R. I. JOHN, Andover, s. of Job, m. 14 Sept. 1682, Hannah Parker, perhaps d. of Nathan, had Nathan, and perhaps others; was freem. 1691; rem. to Mendon, there was deac. and d. 4 May 1742. JOHN, Wallingford, s. of William of Milford. MOSES, Rowley, s. of Job, m. at Andover, 6 July 1666, Prudence, d. of George Blake, liv. in that pt. now Boxford, had John, b. 14 Sept. 1667, wh. was a sh.master, and d. 13 Jan. 1756; Moses; Joseph; Ebenezer; Job; Jonathan; Joshua; James, 7 Dec. 1685; and two other s. 10 in all by this w. wh. d. 19 Mar. 1689; and by a sec. w. Sarah, had ano. s. Jacob, and five ds. Joanna, Abigail, Martha, Catharine, and Sarah. Of these sixteen ch. all but Joseph, and two other s. without names, liv. to mature yrs. He was quarter-master by com. title, rem. to Andover a. 1700, and there d. 2 Oct. 1727, aged 85 or 6. His will is in Geneal. Reg. XII. 319. Eight s. three ds. and childr. of two ds. dec. had shares in his est. either by advancem. or testam. NATHANIEL, Lynn 1640, by w. Jane had Joseph, and in Oct. 1652, mak. his will, as he purpos. going on a voyage on the sh. "N. E. merch." he would that his s. wh. liv. at Shrewsbury in Co. Salop, should have £50. PETER, Branford 1668, perhaps br. of Francis, or George, or of both, propound. for freem. 1672, m. 20 Nov. 1671, Deborah, d. of Daniel Swain, had Peter, b. 20 Jan. 1673; John, 20 Nov. 1674; Deborah, 15 Mar. 1677; Dorcas, 3 May 1678; Hannah, 10 Feb. 1682; Ebenezer, 9 May 1684; and by sec. w. Hannah Whitehead, had Patience, 25 Sept. 1689; Joseph, 25 Apr. 1691; and Hannah, 8 May 169 ; but the last fig. is uncert. as is the date of his d. ROGER, New Haven, had been prob. in Mass. 1650, and d. at N. H. where his inv. was giv. 7 Feb. 1674. Perhaps he had liv. at Wallingford, where was ano. Roger, prob. his s. SAMUEL, Mendon, br. of Moses, by w. Hannah had two s. Ebenezer and Samuel, three ds. and d. 17 Dec. 1695. His wid. admin. 9 Apr. foll. THOMAS, Boston, by w. Hannah had Samuel, b. 1 May 1657; Mary, 10 Apr. 1660. THOMAS, Boston, came from Budleigh in Co. Devon, m. Miriam, d. of Pilgrim Simpkins, had Thomas, b. 15 Aug. 1685; William, 15 Mar. 1687; Andrew, 1692; John, 1695; and Miriam, 22 Feb. 1698, but this last at Weymouth, where, being a sea-capt. he may have been engag. in build. a vessel. His last voyage was in 1703, when he was tak. by a Barbary corsair, and no more heard of. Perhaps he was k. at the capt. but a fam. tradit. is ment. tha$ he d. at sea. His w. took admin. 12 May 1704. THOMAS, Derby, s. of William of Milford, d. 1704, without fam. and his est. went to his brs. William and John, sis. Mary Palmer, Eliz. Palmer, Abigail Rundell, and Hannah Tyler. There is a tradit. prob. of no value, that this Thomas was lost in the same way, 1695, as his f. of course when he was 10 yrs. old. WILLIAM, New Haven, took o. of fidel. 7 Apr. 1657, rem. to Milford, m. Abigail, d. of Roger Terrill, had Eliz. b. 1663; Abigail, 1664; William, 1665; John, 1667; all bapt. Sept. 1669; Mary and Thomas, tw. bapt. Feb. 1670, of wh. Thomas d. soon; Hannah, bapt. 1670; Tirzah, 1671, d. soon; Ephraim, 1676; and Ruth, 1678. But on the prob. rec. some discrepancy of names is seen, when the inv. is brot. in, as the oldest ch. appears, Mary, 32 yrs.; Eliz. Palmer, 29 ; Abigail Rundle, 28; William, 27; John, 25; Sarah (perhaps the tw. call. Mary), 21; Hannah, 20; and Thomas (wh. perhaps was first call. Ephraim), 18. His s. William liv. some time at Derby, but rem. to Wallingford. WILLIAM, Boston, s. of Thomas of the same, m. Sarah, d. of Joseph Royal of the same, had four s. Thomas, H. C. 1730; William, H. C. 1733; Royal, H. C. 1743; and Joseph; beside d. Sarah. For this name, of wh. Farmer found the gr. in 1834, to be ten at Harv. eight at Yale, and eight at the other N. E. coll. oft. is found mistake of Tyley, or even Tilley.

TYNG, ‡*‖ EDWARD, Boston, merch. but early wrote hims. brewer, came prob. with w. Mary, whose fam. name was Sears, as tradit. tells; if so, he had been, I think, here bef. m. her, a. 1636, and went home to find a w. She join. our ch. 5 Sept. 1640, and he join. 30 Jan. foll. was freem. 2 June foll. ar. co. 1642, and constable the same yr. rep. 1661 and 2, assist. 1668 to 80 inclus. and d. at Dunstable, 28 Dec. 1681, one acco. says aged· 81, but the credit is less, inasmuch as the same marks the day 28 Sept. as in Geneal. Reg. VIII. 19, and I concur with Farmer MS. wh. thinks more prob. the age 71. By w. Mary, by some thot. his sec. wh. may be doubt. he had Hannah, b. 7 Mar. 1640, bapt. 6 Sept. foll.; Mary, 17 Apr. bapt. 2 May 1641, perhaps d. young; Jonathan 15, bapt. 18 Dec. 1642; Deliverance, 6 Aug. says the town rec. wh. is falsif. by the ch. rec. bapt. 13 July 1645; Rebecca, 23 Mar. tho. the trustworthy ch. rec. gives bapt. 21, 1647, d. young; Edward; Rebecca, again, 13 July 1651; William, 3 Mar. 1653, prob. d. young; Eunice, 8 Mar. 1655; and Joseph, 12 July 1657, wh. d. young; Hannah, m. 8 May 1661, Habijah Savage; and next maj.-gen. Gookin; Deliverance m. Daniel Searle; Rebecca m. 1669, Joseph Dudley, afterwards Gov. of the Prov. and Eunice bec. 1679, sec. w. of Samuel Willard, Vice-Pres. of Harv. Coll. His will of 25 Aug. 1677 with codic. 7 Jan. 1681, tak. notice of Eunice as now w. of S. W. names gr.ch. Thomas, Mary, and Hannah Savage, whose f. was d.; Thomas, Edward, Joseph, and Paul Dudley; Samuel Searle; and John, s. of Jonathan T. It was pro. 19 Jan. 1682. ‡ ‖ EDWARD, Boston, s. of the preced. ar. co. 1668, m. Eliz. d. of capt. Thaddeus Clark of Falmouth, wh. was bur. as Sewall's Diary notes 4 July 1690. This gave him great interest in the question of jurisdict. and land titles in Maine. He had Edward, b. 1683; Jonathan, d. young; Mary; and Eliz.; was one of the council 1686, 7, not much in favor with Andros; after conq. of Nova Scotia, he was made Gov. of Annapolis, and on the voyage to his colony was tak. by the French, and d. in France. Admin. was had by his br. Jonathan, Apr. 1701. ‡* JONATHAN, Dunstable, eldest s. of Edward the first, m. Sarah, d. of Hezekiah Usher, had Francis, b. 11 Dec. 1669; Eliz. 28 Dec. 1670; Jonathan, 29 Jan. 1672, prob. d. young; John, 11 Sept. 1673, H. C. 1691; Mary, 16 Jan. 1677; but all these, prob. b. at Boston; and at D. William, 22 Apr. 1679; Jonathan, again, 29 Sept. 1686; Eleazer, 30 Apr. 1690, H. C. 1712; and Barsheba, 5 Feb. 1695. He rem. to Woburn, m. next, 30 May 1706, Sarah, wid. of Humphrey Davie, wh. had been wid. of James Richards of Hartford, and d. of William Gibbons of H.; she d. 8 Feb. 1714; and for third w. he had Judith, wid. of Rev. Jabez Fox, d. of John Rayner, wh. outliv. him, and d. 5 June 1756 in her 99th yr. He was of the Royal Council 1686, and 7, but did not partake in the princip. of Andros, was rep. 1692 under the new chart. and d. 19 Jan. 1724. * ‖ WILLIAM, Boston, elder br. of Edward the first, a merch. of distinct. came prob. in the Nicholas, of 300 tons, charter. by hims. at

London, arr. at Boston, 3 July 1638, as Josselyn, wh. was a passeng. tells in his curious vol. of Voyages. He join. our ch. 3 Mar. foll. and was adm. freem. 10 days aft. was of ar. co. 1638, rep. 1639, 40, 1, 2, 3, 4 and 7, treasr. of the Col. 1640–4; capt. of the Braintree milit. comp. and in latter days liv. in that town, was its rep. 1649, 50, and 1; his w. Jane, being his third, wh. may have been wid. of the first Enoch Hunt, d. 3 Oct. 1652, and he d. 18 Jan. foll. leav. larger est. than any in the country of that day. It is by his descend. Rev. William Brattle, said, that "his first w. was Ann Brown, by wh. he had two ch. wh. d. bef. he m. our gr.mo. Eliz. d. of Rowland Coytemore, whose maiden name was Myles, and had a former h. named Gray, by wh. she had my aunts Nowell and Graves." By Eliz. he had Eliz. b. I doubt not in Eng. 6 Feb. 1638, bapt. here, 10 Mar. 1639; Ann, 6, bapt. 12 Jan. 1640; Bethia, 17, bapt. 23 May 1641; and Mercy, 13 Jan. bapt. 5 Feb. 1643. Eliz. m. a. 1656, Thomas Brattle; Ann, m. 3 Nov. 1656, Thomas Shepard, afterwards min. of Charlestown; Bethia m. Richard Wharton; and Mercy, m. 1662, Samuel Bradstreet. Six of this name had been gr. in 1832 at Harv.

TYRRELL.   See Terrill.

TYSON, JOHN, Boston, a Quaker, brot. in a sh. for wh. he says in his letter to Gov. Bellingham, the master was fined £100 "if he send me not away the first opportun." He wrote from prison, 15 June 1667, a very forcible address to the Gov. and magistr. and hav. thro. their fears obt. his liberat. wrote again from London, 28 July 1670. Both epist. are append. to Groom's Glass for the people of N. E. a very rare tract in the libr. of my friend Charles Deane.

UFFORD, UFFOOTE, or UFFIT.   See Offit.   Prob. the first spell. here is the best.

UMPHERVILE, UMBERFIELD, HUMPHREVILLE or UMFREVILLE, JOHN, New Haven 1674, a propr. 1685, was perhaps f. of Samuel, and Mary, and may have had other ch. One Mary, perhaps his sis. m. 26 Mar. 1684, Thomas Mallery, and ano. m. 28 Nov. 1694, Ebenezer Downes, wh. may justify a conject. that two fam. of the name liv. there. SAMUEL, New Haven, perhaps s. of the preced. had by w. not nam. Sarah, b. 2 Apr. 1695; Ann, 28 Apr. 1700; John, 15 Mar. 1702; Thomas, 8 Feb. 1705; Eliz. 27 Oct. 1708; Esther, 12 Sept. 1710; Mary, 28 Aug. 1714; and David, 16 Aug. 1716.

UNDERHILL, GILES, was complain. of in New Hampsh. 1668, for not liv. with his w.   * JOHN, Boston, came in the fleet with Winth. as capt. of any milit. force that might be employ. or instruct. as he had serv. under the great Dutch prince in the war of the Netherlands, speedily join. the ch. being counted No. 57 in the list, and was sw. freem. 18

May 1630. His w. Helena join. 15 Dec. 1633, and their d. Eliz. was bapt. 14 Feb. 1636; and s. John, 24 Apr. 1642, a. 13 days old; but he was less fortun. in the ch. than in the town serv. rep. at the first Court that deputies came to, and in the earliest and the last hours of the Pequot war. He wrote a short story of his serv. wh. is the first Art. in 3 Mass. Hist. Coll. VI. Soon aft. ret. from the triumph at the total extirpat. of that tribe, our victor capt. was in Nov. 1637, the first nam. among the disarm. for the antinom. heresy, and driv. away to New Hampsh. where his rest lasted not long, tho. he was chos. gov. at Dover, in place of Burdett, 1638, the same infirmity render. his rem. unavoid. and he went to the Dutch. With them he succeed. obt. good est. on L. I. and to that jurisdict. transfer. his alleg. yet gladly resum. it on the conq. by the Eng. and d. bef. the reconq. late in 1671 or early in 2. His heirs enjoy. the lds. without the martial toils of their ancest. by the will of 18 Sept. 1671, of wh. his s. John was made admor. 4 Nov. 1675, no unusual provis. are made exc. that his youngest s. Nathaniel remain. with his mo. Eliz. until he be 21. In it he calls hims. of Killingworth, Oyster Bay. Bolton's Hist. of West Chester, II. 229, repeats the absurd tradit. about his serv. in Holland, eighty-five yrs. bef. under patronage of the Earl of Leicester, the favorite of Queen Eliz. Such ornaments belong to the work of fiction, under the name of Updike Underhill, by Reyal Tyler; and thence prob. they were deriv. by pop. credulity.

UNDERWOOD, HENRY, Newport, by w. Jane, had Jane, b. 17 Mar. 1670; William, 24 May 1671; and John, 3 Aug. 1673 at Canonicut. JAMES, Salem 1654, a baker. JOSEPH, Hingham 1637, rem. to Water-town, freem. 1645, had Joseph, b. 1650; Sarah; Mary; Martha; Han-nah; Eliz.; and Thomas, 11 Oct. 1658; and his w. d. 13 Feb. foll. Barry thinks he m. 1662, but Morse writes 29 Apr. 1665, Mary How of Dorchester, wh. d. 1667, and the d. 16 Feb. 1677. Mary m. 18 May 1670, Isaac Onge; Hannah, m. 14 Oct. 1680, John Gibson; and Eliz. m. 13 Sept. 1683, William Bull. JOSEPH, Watertown, s. of the preced. by w. Eliz. had John, b. 6 Mar. 1677; Eliz. 8 May 1679; Joseph, 28 May 1681; Joshua, 31 Jan. 1683; and by w. Mary had Sarah 9 May 1687; and Hannah, bapt. 13 Apr. 1690, was freem. 1690, and d. 1691, his wid. Eliz. Bond says, tho. he had not ment. 3d w. having admin. His will of 16 Feb. pro. 7 Apr. foll. names all these six ch. and Jonathan, beside, whose date is not seen in rec. MARTIN, Watertown, came with w. Martha, he aged 38, she 31, in the Elizabeth from Ipswich, Co. Suffolk, Apr. 1634. She was sis. of the first Nathan Fiske, had no ch. He was a cloth manuf. or weaver, freem. 3 Sept. 1634, and d. 7 Nov. 1672, giv. by his will more than 9 yrs. bef. all his prop. to w. for her life, next to one Fisk, neph. for his life, and remain. to ano. neph. His wid. d. 6

May 1684. PETER, came in the Rebecca 1635, from London, a husbandman, aged 22; but I hear no more of him. * THOMAS, Hingham, br. of Joseph, freem. 9 Mar. 1637, was rep. 1637 and 48; rem. to Watertown, there was selectman 1656, d. 1668, his will of 15 Feb. pro. 7 Apr. of that yr. gave to w. Magdalen for life, and remain. to Thomas, s. of his br. Joseph, so that we infer, that he had no ch. The wid. d. 10 Apr. 1687, aged 80. THOMAS, Watertown, s. of Joseph the first, had w. Magdalen, but she seems to have been his sec. w. and to her, by his will of 19 July 1679, he gave most of his prop. and resid. to his only s. Thomas, prob. by the first w. See Bond, 610. Very observ. is it that both uncle and neph. had ws. with this unusual Christian name, wh. is of very rare occurr. WILLIAM, Concord, m. wid. Pellet, mo. of Thomas, had Remembrance, b. 25 Feb. 1640; freem. 1650; rem. to Chelmsford as one of the first sett. there, had Deborah, 1653; Samuel, 14 Feb. 1656, bapt. 20 Apr. foll. but he may have had more bef. rem. as Sarah, 1642; Priscilla, 1647; and Aquila, wh. d. 17 June 1657, eight yrs. old.

UNTHANK, CHRISTOPHER, Warwick, among the freem. there in 1655, had first been of Providence. Susanna was his w. and the only ch. of wh. we hear was Mary, wh. m. Job Almy.

UPDIKE, GILBERT, Newport, came, it is said, in 1664, from New York, m. a d. of Richard Smith of Narraganset, had Lodowick, a. 1666, wh. was f. of Daniel, a man of distinct. in R. I. a century ago. JAMES, a soldier, perhaps from Dorchester or Milton, serv. in Mosely's comp. Dec. 1675, bef. the great Narraganset fight.

UPHAM, JOHN, Weymouth, came, as is thot. with Rev. Joseph Hull, certain. was freem. on the same day with him, 2 Sept. 1635, was rep. 1636, 7, 8, and 9, had John, wh. was bur. 5 June 1640, and perhaps others, certain. Priscilla, b. 1642. But he had prob. brot. from Eng. Mary, b. perhaps 1628; Eliz. 1630; Nathaniel, 1632; Hannah; and may have had soon aft. arr. Phineas, 1635. These were by w. Eliz. but bef. 1650 he rem. to Malden, favor. the cause of Marmaduke Matthews in 1652, and his w. d. late in 1670, or early next yr. took, in Aug. 1671, sec. w. Catharine, wid. of Angel Hollard of Boston, as we learn by his deed of relinquish. all her prop. was deac. 24 yrs. and d. 25 Feb. 1682, aged 84, says the gr.st. Mary m. John Whittemore; Eliz. m. Thomas Welsh; Hannah m. a Long, whose bapt. name is not seen; but Bond, 959, makes her first m. I think, erron. William Ballentine; and Priscilla m. Thomas Crosswell. JOHN, Malden, "a poor, friendless child" coming from Barbadoes, a. 4 yrs. old, with John Upham of B. (wh. d. on the voyage, Oct. 1652), had been adopt. by him, d. at Charlestown, 25 Nov. 1677, was engag. to m. Eliz. d. of John Mousal, and gave her all his prop. exc. a musket to young Phineas U. JOHN, Malden, s. prob. of

Phineas, m. 31 Oct. 1688, Abigail Hayward, d. prob. the youngest, of
Samuel of Malden. NATHANIEL, Malden, s. of the first John, b. in Eng.
preach. sometime at M. was freem. 1653, m. at Cambridge, 5 Mar. 1662,
Eliz. d. of John Stedman, and he d. 15 days after. His wid. m. 27 Apr.
1669, Henry Thompson. NATHANIEL, Malden, s. of the first John, as
the careful fam. hist. conject. mak. his name only of the first two syllab.
but my scruple is strong. Examina. of the Col. Rec. will satisfy instant.
that the freem. of 1653, and the freem. of 1655, was the same. By one
of the scandal. blunders of Mr. Secr. Rawson the list in the latter yr. is
(in large pt. on both sides, next above and below, of this Natha. U.) a
uniform copy of that for the former yr. PHINEAS, Malden, s. of the first
John, m. 14 Apr. 1658, Ruth Wood, perhaps d. of Edward of Charlestown,
had Phineas, b. 22 May 1659 ; Nathaniel, 1661 ; Ruth, 1664, d. at 12 yrs. ;
John, 9 Dec. 1666 ; Eliz. ; Richard ; and Thomas ; was lieut. of the
comp. headed by the brave Isaac Johnson of Roxbury, in the memo.
battle of 19 Dec. 1675, and after the capt. was k. rec. his mortal wounds
of wh. he languish. until Oct. foll. The Col. Rec. V. 122, shows how
the governm. provid. for relief of wid. and her seven minor ch. His
wid. d. 18 Jan. 1697, aged 60. What mean. to give the Malden rec. of
m. of Phineas Upham with Hannah Ensign, 19 Sept. or Nov. 1658, as
giv. in Geneal. Reg. VI. 337, when only one Phineas at that time is
heard of, I kn. not. But this is one of many errors in that transcr. wh.
cost me very large research. The true h. of Hannah Ensign, 19 Nov.
1658, was Thomas Shepard of M. The freem. of Woburn, 1684, I presume to be the s. of the lieut. Farmer notes that in 1834, nine of this
name had been gr. at Harv. and three at Dartm. Of one br. of this
fam. disting. for its proportion of lawyers, clerg. judges, politicians and
scholars, a good collect. of Notices by Albert G. Upham, M. D. one of
the later progeny, was publ. at Concord N. H. 1845.

UPSHALL, or UPSALL, NICHOLAS, Dorchester 1630, came, prob. in
the Mary and John, was first heard of as mem. of the inquest on the
body of Bratcher, k. by Walter Palmer, 30 Sept. req. adm. as freem. 19
Oct. of that yr. and was rec. 18 May foll. by w. Dorothy, wh. was prob.
d. of the first Bernard Capen, had Ann, b. Feb. 1636, d. young ; Eliz.
Feb. 1638 ; Susanna, 7 Feb. 1640, wh. m. 10 Nov. 1659, as Hist. of
Dorchester, 88, says, Joseph *Cock;* and Experience, 19 Mar. 1641, a s.
wh. d. under 19 yrs. ; was of ar. co. 1637, and the same yr. took license
for an ordinary, and serv. as selectman, 1638. After some yrs. he rem.
to Boston, and on the last Sunday of July 1644, he and his w. were
adm. of our ch. on recommend. from that of D. in 1656 he had so distinct. spok. against the intoler. of the governm. towards Quakers, as to
subject him to fine of £20, but the Ct. had so much tenderness in their

bigotry as, finding his w. innocent, they order that she should have part of the money. But he was cruelly imprison. for yrs. aft. and d. 20 Aug. 1666; and his wid. d. 18 Sept. 1675, aged 73. His will, that is very honora. to his charact. may be read in Vol. I. 490. Her will of 30 Aug. 1673, may be seen in Vol. VI. 108. Eliz. m. 4 July 1652, William Greenough, and after. capt. Timothy Prout.

UPSON, by vulgar spell. UPSUM, conform. to sound, STEPHEN, came to Boston, in the Increase from London, 1635, call. a sawyer, aged 23, was liv. 20 yrs. aft. and I presume that he had a fam. but am ign. of details. See 3 Mass. Hist. Coll. VIII. 261. Many yrs. aft. that publicat. Mr. Drake, in Geneal. Reg. XIV. 312, marks this Stephen, *a Lawyer*, yet gives him the same number of yrs. with my read. Perhaps his eyes were delud. by the handwriting, for my own experience proves how easy it is to be wrong in such puzzles. * STEPHEN, Hartford, s. of the first Thomas, liv. chief. at Waterbury, m. 29 Dec. 1682, Mary, d. of the first John Lee of Farmington, had Mary b. 5 Nov. foll.; Stephen, 30 Sept. 1686; Eliz. 14 Feb. 1690; Thomas, 1 Mar. 1693; Hannah, a. 16 Mar. 1695; Tabitha, 11 Mar. 1698; John, 13 Dec. 1702; and Thankful, 14 Mar. 1707; and all these eight were m. His w. d. 15 Feb. 1716; and he, aft. being rep. 1710, 12, and so late as 29, d. 1735, aged 80, or more. THOMAS, Hartford, of wh. we kn. not from what part of Eng. or when he came, may have been at Cambridge, or other town in Mass. bef. going to H. He prob. was br. of the first Stephen, and sett. very early at Farmington, m. for sec. w. 23 Jan. 1646, Eliz. Fuller, d. 19 July 1655, leav. w. Eliz. and ch. Thomas, Stephen, Mary, Hannah, and Eliz. all prob. some certain. b. in Eng. but the d. Eliz. d. the very day after her f. The wid. m. Edmund Scott. The name has been well perpet. but I kn. not whether by both of the s. or wh. of them. THOMAS, Saybrook, possib. s. of the preced. was k. casual. 9 Dec. 1672.

UPTON, JOHN, Salem 1658, a blacksmith, rem. perhaps to Reading, freem. 1691, there d. 1699. Prob. he had fam. and Samuel, with William, at Salem vill. 1686, and Ezekiel, with Joseph, Reading, may have been his s. Ann, perhaps his d. m. 4 Apr. 1684, Samuel Fraye, as his sec. w. acc. Essex Inst. II. 95, but the man was never heard of by me.

URANN, URAN, or URIN, JOHN, N. H. m. 12 Nov. 1686, Rebecca Cate, may have been of Newbury 1669. WILLIAM, of N. H. says Farmer MS. d. a. 1664.

URING, or YOURING, Boston 1674, fisherman.

USHER, * ‖ HEZEKIAH, Cambridge, freem. 14 Mar. 1639, by w. Frances had Hezekiah, b. June 1639; Rebecca; John, 11 Sept. 1643, wh. d. Dec. 1645 in Boston, whither the f. had rem.; Eliz. 1, bapt. 8 Feb. 1646,

a. 7 days old; John, b. 17 Apr. 1648; and Sarah, whose date is not
found. His w. d. 25 Apr. 1652, and he m. 2 Nov. foll. Eliz. d. of Rev.
Zechariah Symmes, had Hannah, b. 29 Dec. 1653; Zechariah, 26 Dec.
1654; and perhaps more. A third w. Mary, wid. of Peter Butler, d. of
William Alford, surv. him, m. Samuel Nowell, outliv. him, and d. 14
Aug. 1693. He was early mem. of the ar. co. rep. for Billerica 1671,
2, and 3, d. 14 May 1676. His d. Rebecca m. 1 May 1660, Abraham
Brown; and Sarah m. Jonathan Tyng. HEZEKIAH, Boston, s. of the
preced. m. 1686, Bridget, wid. of Leonard Hoar, wh. had been Presid.
of Harv. Coll. and d. of that lady Alicia, wid. of John Lisle, the regicide, wh. had most cruelly been execut. 2 Sept. preced. thro. infamous
abuse of the Stat. against treasons, after the suppress. of Monmouth's
rebell. This explains the mean. of Sewall's Diary, where he writes
"Mr. Hezekiah Usher's mother behead." This was not a happy m. and
she went home 1687, and came not to Boston again during his life. He
was of ar. co. 1665, d. at Lynn, 11 July 1697, but Sewall says was bur.
14th in his own tomb at Boston. †‡‖ JOHN, Boston, br. of the preced.
m. Eliz. d. of Peter Lidgett, had only ch. Eliz. b. 18 June 1669, and by
sec. w. Eliz. d. of Samuel Allen, the royal lieut.-gov. of N. H. had
John, b. a. 1699, H. C. 1719; Hezekiah; Eliz. and Frances. He was,
at first, a stationer, and encourag. by the Gen. Ct. prohibit. to all others
for 7 yrs. in 1672, publish. the valua. edit. of the laws of the Col. ar. co.
1673, freem. the same yr. col. of the Boston regim. under Andros' admin.
was one of the most trusted counsel. and treasr. of his noble province of
all N. E. yet manag. to be on the strong side, rem. to Portsmouth, was
in 1692, made lieut.-gov. of N. H. serv. five yrs. and in a later yr. had
the same honor for ano. term; rem. back to Mass. and d. at Medford, 5
Sept. 1726. His d. Eliz. by first w. m. 15 Sept. 1686, David Jeffries,
and d. 27 June 1698, leav. 8 ch. The compiler of the Parsons Geneal.
in Geneal. Reg. I. 268, mistakes in call. him s. of Hezekiah, by the sec.
w. * ROBERT, New Haven, sw. fidel. 1644, in few yrs. rem. to Stamford, was br. of Hezekiah the first, m. 12 May 1659, Eliz. wid. of Jeremy Jagger, was constable 1662, rep. 1665 and 7, d. in Sept. or Oct.
1669, leav. good est. to wid. and two ch. Eliz. b. 1660, and perhaps by a
former w. Robert. His inv. was made 26 Oct. 1669, and his will of 21
Sept. preced. dispos. of good est. to ch. in it desiring care of Hezekiah
to bring them up. ROBERT, Dunstable, s. of the preced. had John, b.
31 May 1696, and Robert, June 1700, k. in famous Lovewell's fight.

USSELL, RICHARD, Portsmouth or Newport R. I. 1653–6, tho. an odd
sounding name, is regard. by me as truer than SUSSELL; but the reader
may take his choice, if he agree with me, that only one man is intend.
where either appears in R. I. Col. Rec. Vol. I. 263, 300, 49, 59, 60,
and 5.

USSELTON, FRANCIS, Wenham, m. Sarah Barnes, a. 1657.

UTTING, ———, Dedham, whose w. Ann d. Jan. 1642.

UTTLEY, SAMUEL, Scituate, m. 6 Dec. 1648, Hannah Hatch, d. of the first William, had Lydia, b. 28 Dec. 1659, wh. m. Feb. 1684, Thomas Hewitt.

UXLEY, HENRY, Taunton, a. 1637, at the head of the list of first sett. 1639, Baylies I. 289. He assures us, Ib. 283, "none can tell, who he was, whence he came, or whither he went, or at what period he" arr. at T.

VALE, VAIL, or VAYLE, JAMES, Dedham, by w. Ann had James, bapt. 6 July 1656; John, 17 Oct. 1658. JEREMIAH, Salem 1644, had Abigail, bapt. 18 May 1645; Sarah, 21 Mar. 1647; Jeremiah, 30 Dec. 1649; and prob. rem. to L. I. for in 1662 one of this name, at that place was among a large party propos. to be rec. as freem. of the jurisdict. of Conn.

VALENTINE, JOHN, Boston, freem. 1675.

VALLACK, NICHOLAS, is the name of one wh. at Pemaquid, 1674, sw. fidel. to Mass.

VANDENBOSK, LAWRENCE, Boston 1685, a Huguenot clerg. wh. prob. in virtue of his function, had undertaken to solemnize m. perhaps the first ever perform. in Mass. except by a civil officer. He had been brot. bef. a tribunal for this enormity, and had promis. "to do no more such things," yet, says Judge Sewall, in Sept. he join. together Giles Sylvester and Hannah, wid. of Benjamin Gillam. These were in high life, and Sylvester may have indemnif. the poor min. perhaps by carrying him to his principality at Shelter Island. At least the rev. offender went to N. Y. the same week.

VANE, §*HENRY, Boston, s. of Sir Henry, came to N. E. 1635, in the Defence, says the writer of an elaborate eulogy on him, Geneal. Reg. II. 127, in wh. he sail. 10 Aug. and arr. 3 Oct. but if he emb. at London, it was prob. 30 days earlier, and Winth. marks the arr. 6 Oct. at the same time with the Abigail, in wh. his s. the Gov. of Conn. was passeng. in ten weeks voyage. On the first Sunday of Nov. foll. he join. our ch. bec. freem. 3 Mar. foll. and was the same mo. made a commissnr. for milit. affairs, and at the Gen. Ct. in May next, was chos. Gov. then aged 24 yrs. the youngest man ever raised to that station in Mass. In little more than six mos. he express. a strong wish to go home, as the agitat. of the antinom. controversy had begun with great warmth, and tho. the ch. of Boston and that of Braintree would sustain his side, all the others in the Col. were very strong against him. Being overrul. in his desire, he was a candid. next May, but fail. in the elect. and was chos. rep. for B. So extreme was the virulence of this theolog.

quarrel, that in July, when he was invit. by the Gov. to dinner, in co. with Lord Ley, heir of the E. of Marlborough, wh. had arr. a few days bef. he refused, "bec. his conscience withheld him," but add. to the incivility by carr. Lord Ley with him over to dine with Samuel Maverick at Noddle's Isl. However, early next mo. he went home, and ever after stood the friend of our people. He was among the chief men in the great civil war, and too conscientious or too ambitious to comply with Cromwell, wh. secur. him in prison as he did so many others of the republican party ; yet one of the few after the death of the protector, wh. did not feel the necessity of the restorat. of the monarchy, for wh. he was turned out of the ho. as one wh. had not been constant to parliament privileges. Maidstone, a sincere commonwealth's man, in his letter to Winth. writ. but a few weeks bef. the universal outbreak of enthusiasm for Charles II. explains the pleasure of the people at this dishonor to Vane, by add. that he was "unhappy in lying under the most *catholick* prejudice of any man I know." See 3 Mass. Hist. Coll. I. 196. Being exempt from the gen. pardon in the Act of indemnity, that may well seem bad policy, he was execut. 14 June 1662, after a conviction wh. did not benefit the royal cause, so much as it exalt. the suffer. Nothing in life became him like the losing of it. How faithful adher. to principle tho. esteem. erron. will surely be val. is shown in the history of his descend. The only s. was ennob. by William III. and the rank in the peerage was, for his lineal offspr. 3d Lord Barnard, raised to an Earldom, and he by m. with a Fitzroy (offspr. of that king wh. took off the ancestor's head) had s. created a Duke, with right to quarter the arms of Vane with those of Charles II. HENRY, had in Nov. 1644, the fine that at some unkn. time was impos. abated one half by the Court of Mass. on condit. that he should pay the other half in 2 mos. I find not his resid. JOHN, Portsmouth, R. I. 1639, had gr. of lot of ld. if he would build within a yr. but he may have forfeit.

VANGOODENHAUSEN, SAMUEL, New Haven, where sometimes the first syllab. of the surname was lost, a Dutch trader, m. a 1648, the wid. whose bapt. name is unkn. of the capt. Nathaniel Turner, embark. in that unhappy sh. built at New Haven, and sailing thence Jan. 1646, of wh. Lamberton was master, whose return near two and a half yrs. later in the clouds of heaven, adorns the Magnalia I. 25. Whether he had ch. by her is not told ; but sec. w. he took 11 Nov. 1662, Eliz. Parris, brot. him Eliz. b. 22 Feb. 1664 ; Samuel, 21 Feb. 1666 ; and John, 4 Mar. 1668. Soon aft. he sold his ho. and ld. that had been Turner's, for wh. he had paid the portions to the heirs, and rem. to New York.

VARLEET, VARLETH or VARLETT, CASPER or JASPER, Hartford 1656, a Dutchman of some conseq. wh. may have liv. there near 30 yrs.

31*

and d. there, Sept. 1662. He had w. Judith, but she had d. bef. him. We hear little of him, but that he had ch. Nicholas, Mary, Judith, and Jane; was engag. in lawsuit a. some question, had hard work to gain justice. NICHOLAS, Hartford, s. of the preced. connect. as his br.-in-law with Gov. Stuyvesant of N. Y. went into the Dutch serv. See Trumbull, Col. Rec. I. 387. Mary, sis. of Nicholas m. Johannes Ambeck, and next, 1658, m. Paulus Schrick; but Judith, ano. sis. was imprison. on the preposter. charge of witchery, and the interference of Gov. Stuyvesant of New York was invok. and found effectual. No doubt the precious case report. in the Magnalia VI. cap. 7, as the first instance or example of suffer. by Ann Cole, and her obtain. relief by the flight of some, and the execut. of one poor woman, so torment. by the charges and proofs against her, that she confess. as Mather exults to tell, "that the Devil had frequently carnal knowledge of her," naturally led to freq. recur. of such accusat. Her power of fascination was in happier hour suffic. to ensnare her m. with Nicholas Bayard, one of the patrician fam. of the neighbor. province.

VARNEY, EBENEZER, Dover, s. of Humphrey of the same, m. that Mary, d. of Stephen Otis, wh. had been tak. by the Ind. 1689, had Mary, b. 6 June 1693; Sarah, 10 Nov. 1695; Stephen, 7 Nov. 1697; Abigail, 11 Apr. 1699; John, 15 Jan. 1702; Ebenezer, 21 May 1704; Nathaniel, 17 Mar. 1706; Thomas, 7 Apr. 1708; Judith, 11 Apr. 1710; Samuel, 2 Apr. 1712; Martha, 18 Mar. 1714; and Ann, 6 July 1718. HUMPHREY, Dover, 1659, had first liv. at Gloucester, perhaps s. of William of Ipswich, b. in Eng. m. 2 Jan. or Mar. 1664, Sarah, wid. of Joseph Austin; wh. had been wid. of William Story; and was d. of Elder Edward Starbuck, had John, b. at Nantucket, 5 Sept. 1664, d. at 2 yrs.; Peter, 29 Mar. 1666; Joseph, 8 Oct. 1667; and Abigail, 10 July 1669; beside ano. John and Ebenezer, wh. Mr. Quint thinks may have been of former m. A Bridget V. d. at Gloucester 26 Oct. 1672. JOHN, Dover, s. of the preced. m. 1707, Susanna Otis, but had no ch. PETER, Dover, s. of Humphrey, by w. Eliz. had Joseph, Mary, Eliz. Hannah, and Peter. THOMAS, Boston 1664, join. Mather's ch. 8 Jan. 1665; by w. Mary, had Lydia, b. 6 Oct. 1672; and John, 1 Dec. 1676, of whose bapt. no acco. is gain. bec. all rec. of them for near 50 yrs. is lost; d. 4 Dec. 1692, leav. wid. Abigail, ch. Martha Smith, Abigail Burnham, with three ch. beside Mercy, perhaps w. of Thomas Choate; Rachel Fellows, Hannah, and Thomas. The wid. d. 1 Mar. 1732, aged 92. THOMAS, Ipswich, perhaps s. of William. WILLIAM, Ipswich, d. 1654 at Salem, leav. wid. Bridget, and ch. all perhaps b. in Eng. Thomas, Humphrey, Sarah, wh. m. 11 Nov. 1657, Jeffrey Parsons, and Rachel, w. of William Vincent, or Vinson. The wid. d. Nov. 1672. Oft. the name is Verney.

VARNUM, GEORGE, Ipswich, d. 1649, ment. w. in his will of 21 Apr.
names only ch. Samuel, and Hannah. SAMUEL, Ipswich 1648 s. of
George, by w. Hannah had Abraham, b. 28 Oct. 1659, d. at 5 mos.;
Hannah, 22 May 1661; Thomas, 19 Nov. 1662. In 1683 he was 64
yrs. old.

VASSALL, JOHN, Scituate, s. of William, brot. by his f. at the age of
10 in the Blessing 1635, from London, was a lieut. 1652, afterwards a
capt. in 1661 sold his est. and went to Jamaica, but in few yrs. was
engag. in the settlem. at Cape Fear in N. C. and in 1667 applied for
relief here to be sent to hims. and followers. ‡ WILLIAM, one of the
Assist. of the Gov. and Comp. of the Mass. Bay, nam. in the first
Charter by K. Charles, Mar. 1629, of wh. Cradock was first Gov. came
next yr. in the fleet with the next Gov. Winth. but went home in the
Lion, the first mo. aft. reach. this shore; came again 1635, in the Blessing, then aged 42, with w. Ann, 42, and ch. Judith, 16; Frances,
12; John, 10; Ann, 6; Margaret, 2; and Mary, 1. He sat down only
short time at Roxbury, and soon fixed at Scituate, in ano. jurisdict. and
join. the ch. of John Lothrop, 28 Nov. 1636. He seems to have differ.
from Mass. policy, especially after the triumph of the latitudinarians at
home, wh. desired freedom of worship; but as he could not bring many
to his opinions, went home again in the sh. with Child, Fowle, and perhaps others discontent. as hims. rem. to Barbadoes, there d. bef. 1655.
He was s. of John, alderman of London, wh. had gain. high reput. for exertions in organiz. resist. to the Spanish Armada, 1588. Mortifying is
the ignorance that represents this fam. as coming in the reign of James
and Charles I; and that Miss Thomas copied such authority is to be refer.
to the opposite of a common error, that unduly magnifies ancient renown.
Judith had m. 8 Apr. 1640, Resolved White; Frances m. 16 July 1646,
James Adams; and one of the other ds. it is said m. Nicholas Ware in
Virginia, wh. was Excor. of his will at Barbadoes. To the w. of Adams,
as d. of William Vassall, one of the patentees wh. prob. had rec. nothing
for his money advanc. in the first coloniz. our Gen. Ct. 1672, made gr. of
150 acres. His br. Samuel, ano. patentee of Mass. and Assist. nam. by
the king in the Charter, was too rich, and much absorb. in the line of his
traffic at London, to come to the ld. of the Pilgrims. Seven of this
name had been gr. at Harv. 1771. We owe much to Harris's Cambridge Epit. 180, for acco. of the memb. of this honor. fam. in the mid. of
last century; Lewis, H. C. 1728; John, H. C, 1732; and William, H.
C. 1733; all s. he says, of Leonard; to all of wh. the Catal. of the
Univ. gives dates of d. but much more glad. would I hear of Samuel, H.
C. 1695, of wh. there can be no doubt, from his position at the head of
the class, that he was of the same stock.

VAUGHAN, VAHAN or VAHEN, DANIEL, Newport, s. of John, m. 27
Mar. 1678, Susanna, d. of Samuel Grimes of Plymouth, had John, b. 14
Sept. 1679; Ann, 6 Apr. 1683; Daniel, 17 Mar. 1685; David, 13 Feb.
1687; and Samuel, 17 June 1690. GEORGE, Portsmouth 1631, sent
by Mason the patentee, arr. prob. in Sept. of that yr. and left the country
Aug. 1634, for home, whence it is not thot. he ever ret. again. GEORGE,
Scituate, m. 1652, Eliz. Henchman or Hincksman, perhaps d. of Edmund
of Marshfield, had Eliz.; Daniel; John, b. 1658, drown. at 18 yrs.; Mary;
and Joseph; and d. 1694, at Middleborough. Mary m. a. 1683, Jonathan
Washburn, of Bridgewater. GEORGE, Greenwich 1687, in the Narraganset cavalry, was s. of John, m. 26 July 1680, Margaret Spink, d. perhaps
of Robert, had George, b. 19 Apr. 1682; David, 29 Apr. 1683; Mary,
28 Feb. 1685; Christopher, 29 Apr. 1686; Abigail, 24 Feb. 1689; and
Robert, 7 Mar. 1691. † GEORGE, Portsmouth, s. of William of the
same, m. Mary, d. of Andrew Belcher, wh. d. 3 Feb. 1700, 3 days aft.
b. of a d. wh. soon d. and next 9 Jan. he m. Eliz. d. of Robert Eliot of
Newcastle, had Sarah, b. 8 Feb. 1702; William, 12 Sept. 1703, H. C.
1722; Margaret, 21 Aug. 1705, d. soon; George, 2 July 1706; Eliz. 8
Oct. 1707; Abigail, 11 Mar. 1709; Eliot, 12 Apr. 1711; Mary, 26 Apr.
1713; and Jane, 27 Dec. 1714; was lieut.-gov. betw. 2 and 3 yrs. and
d. 20 Nov. 1725. JOHN, Watertown 1633, may be consid. the same wh.
was in 1634, fin. 20s. but discharg. of it in 1638, and in 1640 again
subject to animadvers. when the Ct. order. him to m. a girl, and take care
of his ch. by her; and he is no more heard of at W. JOHN of Newport
1638, was among the freem. in 1655, and by w. Gillian had John, b. 19
Apr. 1644; Davy, 19 July 1646; George 20 Oct. 1650; Daniel, 27
Apr. 1653; and Mary, 3 July 1658. JOSEPH, Middleborough, s. of
George of the same, by the title ens. Joseph, had John, b. 8 Sept. 1692;
Mary, 6 Oct. 1694; Josiah, 2 Feb. 1699; and Joanna, 26 Jan. 1702.
WILLIAM, Newport, one of the founders of the Bapt. ch. there 1644,
says Calender 63; but bef. or aft. was of Providence, yet is on the list of
freem. 1655, of N. m. Frances, wid. of Jeremiah Clarke, and Backus II.
160 informs, that on format. of a 2nd ch. there, he was made min. 1677.
‡ WILLIAM, Portsmouth, b. prob. in Wales, came from London, m. 8
Dec. 1668, Margaret, d. of Richard Cutt, had Eleanor, b. 5 Mar. 1670;
Mary, 6 Mar. 1672; Cutt, 9 Mar. 1674; George 13 Apr. 1676, H. C.
1696; Bridget, 2 July 1678; Margaret, 20 or 30 Dec. 1680; Abigail, 5
May 1683; and Eliz. 26 Apr. 1686. His w. d. 22 Jan. 1692. He was
freem. 1669, under the jurisdict. of Mass. made 1672, lieut. of the cavalry under capt. Robert Pike, a counsel. of the Prov. of N. H. aft. the
separat. from Mass. and Ch. J. of the Sup. Ct. d. 1719. Of his ds. Eleanor
m. 6 Feb. 1693, Richard Waldron; Mary m. perhaps ——— Thing;

Bridget m. Nathaniel Gerrish; Margaret m. ——— Chambers of Charlestown; Abigail m. Richard Shannon; and Eliz. m. ——— Moulton.

VAULSTONE or VALSTON, THOMAS, Providence 1645, was of Newport among freem. 1655.

VEAZEY, VESEY, VEESIE or VEAZIE, GEORGE, Dover 1659. ROBERT, Watertown 1636, had Mary, or more prob. left that wid. whose name is once spell. Fewzie and one Pheza, wh. m. 24 Sept. 1650, George Packhurst the younger, as his sec. w. SOLOMON, Braintree, s. of William of the same, m. 23 Nov. 1680, Eliz. d. of Martin Saunders. WILLIAM, Braintree, freem. 10 May 1643, call. Phese, was one of the petitnrs. injuriously encourag. in 1645, by our governm. to settle on Gorten's ld. m. 1644, Elinor d. of Rev. William Tompson, had Hannah, b. 18 Mar. 1645; William, 6 Oct. 1647; Solomon, 11 May 1650; Eliz. 13 Oct. 1653; Samuel, 24 Aug. 1656; Ellen, 4 May 1659; Abigail; Mehitable, 17 Feb. 1666; and Mercy 20 Jan. 1670. He d. 16 June 1681; and his wid. m. John French as his sec. w. (under a contract witness. by her bros. Samuel and Benjamin, 8 July 1683, of wh. the details will repay the trouble of turn. to Geneal. Reg. XII. 353) and d. 23 Apr. 1711, aged 84. Hannah, m. 26 Feb. 1666, John Greenleaf; Ellen m. 20 Feb. 1682, Stephen Paine; Abigail m. 25 Mar. 1680, Thomas Thayer; Mehitable m. Josiah Fisher of Dedham, outliv. him and d. 18 May 1741; and Mercy, m. 24 Apr. 1690, John Ruggles. His will of 3 June, pro. 27 July foll. names w. and seven ch. I suppose Rev. William, H. C. 1693, wh. took an A. M. at Oxford, and was Episcop. ord. min. for New York; as also, John, H. C. 1700, whose d. 3 July 1707, is lament. by Sewall in his Diary, as of "a young hopeful min." were gr.ch. of this William. WILLIAM, Braintree 1673, s. of the preced.

VENN, THOMAS, was s. of John, one of the orig. patentees, and nam. Assist. in the royal chart. and came over in 1644, to claim the sh. of ld. for money put into the com. stock. by his f. but he was req. to show his authority from him.

VENNER, || THOMAS, Salem, a wine-cooper, adm. of the ch. 25 Feb. 1638, and freem. next mo. had Thomas, bapt. 16 May 1641; rem. to Boston there, had Ann, bapt. in Wilson's ch. 2 Feb. 1645, a. 18 days old, was of ar. co. that yr. and in 1648 was one of sev. wh. ask. of the governm. to make a corporat. of coopers, went home to London, bef. 1656, and was a great fifth monarchy man, aft. the restorat. in 1660, attempt. to renew the anarchy, and bring in k. Jesus to drive out Charles Stuart, and with a small number as wild as hims. rais. insurrect. in the streets of London with very trifling effect, was execut. Jan. 1661, tho. assert. to be invulnerab.

VENTRIS, VENTERUS or VENTROOS, MOSES, Farmington, freem.
1651, m. 14 Jan. 1647, Mary Graves, d. perhaps of Thomas, perhaps of
George, had Sarah, b. a. 1649; and Grace, a. 1652, both bapt. July
1653; Moses, bapt. 18 Feb. 1655; and Mary, 21 Feb. 1657; and he d.
a. 1697, his inv. being of 12 Apr. in that yr. tho. his will is of 1693.
Sarah m. John Brownson; Grace m. Samuel Blakesley; and Moses and
Mary d. unm. WILLIAM, Farmington, may have been br. of the preced.
freem. 1654, or 1657, liv. at Haddam 1669, was serg. in 1675, had
Mary, b. 20 Oct. 1654; William, 28 Jan. 1656; John, 8 Dec. 1657;
Moses, bapt. 17 Nov. 1661; and Susanna, of wh. perhaps the first two
d. young. He d. 2 July 1701, aged 78, in his will of Mar. 1700, names
w. Eliz. wh. was not his first w. and ch. John, Moses, and Susanna
Brainard, perhaps w. of sec. Daniel.

VERE, VEARE, or VEIR, EDWARD, Wethersfield 1640, d. 1645, in his
will of 19 July of that yr. names no relat. had little to give.

VERGOOSE, ISAAC, Boston 1662, s. of Peter, by w. Mary, d. of Jonathan Balstone, had Isaac, b. 5 May 1669, d. soon; Jonathan 25 July 1670;
Mary, 22 May 1672; Susanna, 3 May 1674, d. young; Peter, 17 Feb.
1678; John, 26 July 1682; Prudence, 21 Apr. 1684; Susanna, again,
5 May 1686, d. soon; Hannah, 8 Mar. 1688; Lydia, 19 May 1690.
His w. d. that yr. aged 42, and he m. 5 July 1692, Eliz. Foster, perhaps
d. of William of Charlestown, had Eliz. b. 5 May 1693, d. in few ds.
Eliz. again, 27 May 1694; Ann, 1 July 1696, d. soon; Isaac; Ann, a.
1703; and Peter, 7 July 1708; and d. 29 Nov. 1710, aged 73. His
will of 9 May preced. takes notice of 3 ch. by his former w. viz. John,
Prudence, and Hannah, and gr.ch. Mary Boyce, and the 4 ch. by the
present w. made Extrix. This is the same name with Goose, and sometimes is Vertigoose. PETER, Boston 1659, is the same as Fergoose, had
Isaac, the preced. b. prob. in some other place, perhaps at or near Norwich in Co. Norf'k, and very likely to be younger than Peter (left at
home, wh. never came that is kn. or at least was there resid. when his
mo. made her will) and Susanna; and he d. a. Dec. 1667. His wid.
Susanna was admx. and liv. many yrs.; in her will of 23 Dec. 1681, pro.
29 Jan. 1685, names her s. Peter in Eng. d. Susanna Rainsford, w. of
John, and then recently dec. give to her eldest ch. Eliz. £20, and to
John, Mary Shute, Susanna, Edward, Hannah, and Nathan, ea. £5;
and the same sum to Jonathan, Mary, Isaac, and unb. ch. of Mary, her s.
Isaac's w.

VERIN, VEREN, or VERING, HILLIARD or HILLYER, Salem, s. of
Philip, bapt. at Salisbury, Eng. 3 Mar. 1622, came prob. with his f. 1635,
m. 12 Apr. 1641, Mary Conant, niece of Roger, but whose d. is unkn.
had Mary, b. 15 Feb. 1642, and Deliverance, 23 Feb. 1645, both bapt.

28 Mar. 1647 ; Hilliard, Apr. bapt. 27 May 1649 ; Dorcas, bapt. 1 Mar. 1652 ; Sarah, 23 Apr. 1654 ; Abigail, 21 Oct. 1655 ; but sev. of these (how many may be hard to ascert.) were prob. ch. of his w. Dorcas. He was ens. 1664, and clk. or reg. of probate, collector of the port, 1679, d. 20 Dec. 1683. Dorcas m. 21 Feb. 1672, Timothy Hicks, and d. Jan. foll. ; Abigail m. 25 Nov. 1678, Benjamin Marston. HILLIARD, Salem, s. of the preced. m. 4 May 1670, Hannah, d. of Walter Price of the same, perhaps had ch. was a merch. and d. at Barbadoes a. 1680. JOHN, Boston, m. 12 June 1660, Mary, d. of James Wiseman, had John, b. 11 July 1661 ; Thomas, 15 Oct. 1663 ; James, 14 Mar. 1665 ; Mercy, 8 Jan. 1668 ; Joseph, 12 Mar. 1669 ; Benjamin, 19 Aug. 1673 ; and Mary, 20 May 1683 ; and by w. Penelope, as it seems to me, the same man had Mehitable, 25 Feb. 1687. Yet a hesitat. arises, bec. the rec. of Maine shows, that one John Vering is among those wh. on the W. side of Kennebec riv. sw. alleg. to Charles II. 8 Sept. 1665. JOSHUA, Salem, came in the James from Southampton, call. in the clearance, a roper of Salisbury, Co. Wilts, was a favorer of Roger Williams, went to Providence 1637, and his w. made some trouble there, came back, and in few yrs. he foll. her. JOSHUA, Salem, s. of Philip, m. and prob. had a fam. Yet no ch. is ment. in his will of 15 May 1695, pro. Dec. foll. wh. however gives pt. of his prop. to childr. of his cous. Lindall, and pt. to childr. of cous. Mary Williams, wid. of Samuel. He d. at Barbadoes. NATHANIEL, Salem, b. in Eng. br. of the preced. bapt. 6 Apr. 1623, by w. Mary had Mary, b. 1648, and prob. others, bef. or aft. or both. Mary m. 7 or 27 Feb. 1673, Timothy Lindall. PHILIP, Salem, br. prob. of the first Joshua, came 1635, arr. at Boston, in the James from South- ampton, in the ship's clearance call. "a roper," late of New Sarum, or the city of Salisbury, as in mod. times we designate it, bring. w. Dorcas, and ch. perhaps all b. in Eng. Philip, Nathaniel, Hilliard, and Joshua, yet possib. one or more were b. here, for he had sec. w. Jane, wh. join. the ch. 1640 ; was freem. 2 Sept. 1635, but twenty yrs. later was imprison. as a Quaker. PHILIP, Salem, eldest s. of the preced. b. in Eng. bapt. Mar. 1619, here adm. of the ch. 3 Jan. 1641 ; was freem. 2 June foll. ; by w. Joanna, wh. d. 30 Aug. 1664, had Bethia, bapt. 14 Nov. 1641 ; Dorcas, 16 Apr. 1643 ; Philip, 23 Mar. 1645 ; Hannah ; Adoniram ; Mary, b. 20 Aug. 1659, d. under 3 yrs. ; and Deliverance 1661, d. same yr. He was a wheelwright.

VERMAES, or VERMAYES, BENJAMIN, Boston, s. prob. of the wid. Alice V. of Salem, freem. 18 May 1642, but he belong. to Salem ch. m. by Yarmouth rec. 15 June, but by other rec. 21 Dec. 1648, Mercy, eldest d. of Gov. William Bradford, and rem. to Plymouth. MARK, Salem 1638, adm. of the ch. 22 Sept. 1639, freem. 13 May foll. when the name appears Formais, and in my opin. is the same as that call. Hermayes in Essex Inst. II. 15. He was, I guess, s. of that wid. Alice V. of Salem, whose d. Abigail was adm. of the ch. there 1640, and m. Edward Hutchinson, aft. being wid. of Robert Button of Boston. See the will of Alice V. 8 Feb. 1656 in Geneal. Reg. VIII. 277, in wh. Hutchinson is nam. Excor. but neither Benjamin nor Mark is found. She d. the next day.

VERNON, DANIEL, Kingstown, R. I. m. Ann, wid. of a Dyer, prob. William or Henry, and d. of the sec. Edward Hutchinson. In 1686 he was appoint. marshall of the Narraganset region that had been injuriously claim. by Conn. and was now call. the King's Province, but subject to R. I. but he had been bef. town clk. and constable. FRANCIS, Medfield, had gr. of 200 acres in 1658, was of Boston 1663, and sold in 1673 his est. at M.

VERY, BENJAMIN, Salem, s. of Samuel the first of the same, m. Jemima, d. of Joseph Newhall of Lynn, had Samuel, b. 1699 ; Ruth ; Joseph ; Benjamin ; all bapt. 1704 ; Jemima ; Keziah ; Ephraim ; Isaac ; and Daniel. ISAAC, Salem, br. of the preced. of wh. nothing is kn. but that he m. 1717, and his w. was Mary. JOHN, Salem, br. of the preced. by w. Hannah had John, Hannah, Abigail, and Desire. JONATHAN, Salem, br. of the preced. m. 1718, Mary, d. of James Symonds, had Mary, Abigail, Eliz. Martha, Bethia, and Jonathan. JOSEPH, Salem, br. of the preced. d. bef. mid. age. Inv. of his prop. bears date 23 May 1694. SAMUEL, Salem, s. of Bridget, a wid. wh. came from Eng. where he was b. a. 1619, by w. Alice, d. of John Woodis, Woodhouse, or Woodice, had Samuel ; Eliz.; Sarah ; Thomas; John, b. 1 May 1659 ; all rememb. in the will of gr.f. W. in that yr.; Joseph, 25 June 1661, d. at 2 yrs.; Isaac, 14 June 1663 ; Joseph, again, 13 Nov. 1664 ; Hannah, 22 Jan. 1666 ; Mary, 21 Mar. 1668 ; Benjamin ; and Jonathan. All the eleven liv. ch. are ment. with w. Hannah m. 1695, William Beans; Mary, m. 1697, Jonathan Marsh; and Eliz. and Sarah call. by names of h. John Nurse and James Cook respective. His mo. the bapt. name of whose first h. is unkn. m. Edward Giles, a. 1636, and in her will after his d. made 14 Jan. 1669, pro. 30 Nov. 1680, gives her prop. to two s. Samuel, and Thomas, to d. Mary, w. of Thomas Cutler, and to her s. Eleazer Giles, bapt. 1640, and his br. John 1645. SAMUEL, Salem, s. perhaps eldest of the preced. left two s. Samuel, b. 1683 ; and John ; with wid. Abigail, perhaps d. of John Woodin of Ipswich, to ret. inv. of his est. 20 Sept. 1697. THOMAS, Gloucester, younger br. of the first Samuel, b. in Eng. a. 1626, m. 6 July 1650, Hannah, d. of Thomas Giles, had Ephraim, b. 1651 ; Hannah, 1653 ; Bridget, 1654 ; Thomas, 1656 ; Samuel, 16 June 1659 ; Abigail, 1661 ; Edward, 16 Jan. 1663 ; Eliz. 15 Feb. 1666 ; and Francis, 8 Feb. 1668 ; and d. 1694. Hannah

m. 9 Nov. 1669, Bartholomew Foster ; and Abigail m. 12 Dec. 1682.
Ralph Andrews. The name was not perpet. at G. THOMAS, Marblehead, s. prob. of the first Samuel, serv. in Philip's war, and rec. a wound.
not cŭred in Feb. 1680, when the Ct. made him gr. of £6. m. 1681, Eliz.
Procter, had Thomas, Eliz. Jonathan, Joseph, and Alice.

VICARS, VICKERS or VICARY, EDWARD, New Haven 1670, d. 1684.
had w. Hannah and perhaps ch. GEORGE, Hull 1650, had been of
Marblehead, as early as 1637, m. Rebecca, d. of David Phippeny, and
perpet. the name, was in capt. Johnson's comp. in Philip's war. ISAAC,
Hull, perhaps s. of the preced. was freem. 1680. ISRAEL, Hull 1675,
perhaps br. of the preced. JONATHAN, Hull, perhaps br. of the preced.
freem. 1678. ROGER, Scarborough, wh. with others sign. the declarat.
4 July 1663, of loyalty to the k. yet wish. not to quarrel with Mass.
SETH, by Farmer made freem. at Hull 1680, is a mistake.

VIGERS, or VIGARS, THOMAS, Hartford, limeburner, call. 35 yrs. old
in 1685. Perhaps he was Dutch, and the name may be the same as
Vicars.

VINAL, JOHN and STEPHEN, Scituate 1640–1668, were perhaps ch.
of Ann, wh. d. 6 Oct. 1664. Mary, prob. her d. m. Apr. 1646, Isaac
Chittenden of Scituate. Of John, the gr.st. tells, that he d. 21 Aug.
1698, aged 62 ; but no more is heard of him, exc. that he m. 1664, Eliz.
d. of Rev. Nicholas Baker. STEPHEN, Scituate, m. 26 Feb. 1662, Mary
Baker, d. of Rev. Nicholas, had Mary, b. 29 Nov. foll.

VINCENT, ADRIAN, a passeng. in the Mary and John from London
1634, but we hear no more of him. HUMPHREY, Cambridge 1634, rem.
to Ipswich bef. 1638, when he had gr. of ld. d. 3 Dec. 1664, seems, by
his will, to have left no fam. nor much est. * JOHN, Lynn, rem. to
Sandwich at its early settlem. was liv. there 1663, rep. in 1639 and six
yrs. aft. JOHN, New Haven 1639, had Hannah, bapt. 28 Mar. 1647 :
and John, 8 Oct. 1648 ; d. 1659, leav. w. Rebecca wh. d. 1679, in her
will of 23 Jan. 1677, gives to childr. of d. Hannah, w. of Ebenezer Brown,
all her est. so that we may conclude that John d. young. NICHOLAS,
Manchester 1679, was b. a. 1612. PHILIP, a gent. of anc. fam. b. at
Frisby, near Coningsborough in the S. of Yorksh. bred at Peterhouse,
Cambridge Univ. was s. of Richard by Eliz. d. of Thomas Rokeby, a
fam. of distinct. in that Co. bapt. 23 Nov. 1600. His f. mo. and sis.
Jane, all d. June 1617. Aft. ordin. he was present. to a living in
Surrey, wh. he resign. Aug. 1629, and aft. the d. of his w. next yr.
went upon travels in various and distant countries, visit. Guiana, but
came to N. E. when the Pequot war had begun, seems to have partaken
in active serv. and aft. its terminat. went home, and publ. at London
1638, " The true relat. of the late battle fought in N. E. betw. the Eng.

and the Pequot salvages" of wh. reprint. may he seen in 3 Mass. Hist. Coll. VI. 29. Biogr. notice of him, writ. with admir. felicity of research, by Rev. Joseph Hunter, is giv. in 4 Mass. Hist. Coll. I. 86. WILLIAM, Salem, with w. whose name is not found, join. the ch. 1650, but as Felt I. 176 makes him to be a freem. aft. 1635, I cannot doubt that the sound and spelling Vincen, justify my calling him Vinson, as below. But the adm. as freem. was on 10 May 1643. WILLIAM, New London, had prob. liv. at Gloucester, there m. Rachel, d. of William Varney; did not improve the grant made him at N. L. in 1651, but was of Providence in May 1666, when he engag. his alleg. to Charles II. and m. 31 May 1670, Priscilla, d. of William Carpenter, perhaps as sec. w. and by a former one may have had Joanna wh. m. John Sheldon. It hardly seems possib. however, with every readiness to acknowl. the migrat. habits of our people, even in the earliest days, to admit this man to be the same as preced.

VINE, WILLIAM, Charlestown, by w. Eliz. d. of Richard Harrington, m. 15 Oct. 1674, wh. join. the ch. 10 June 1677, had Eliz. bapt. that day; and William, 19 June 1681.

VINES, RICHARD, Saco, had, in explorat. for Sir Ferdinando Gorges, very early visit. our coast. Belkn. thinks bef. 1615, but prob. made no perman. settlem. bef. 1636, tho. his name is forged as a witness to the deed of 17 May 1629, pretend. to be made by sev. Ind. chiefs to Rev. John Wheelwright, when he was in Eng. and Vines may well be thot. to be there too. He was much esteem. in the Col. and dept.-gov. in 1644; one of the very earliest travel. to the White mountains, wh. he visit. in the last week of Aug. 1642, was by the people chos. dept.-gov. "for our peace and safety" in Oct. 1645, and rem. to Barbadoes in 1646. WILLIAM, Charlestown 1677.

VINING, BENJAMIN, Salem, s. of William of Portsmouth, was collector of the port, but rem. to Salem, N. J. there d. 5 Sept. 1735, leav. s. John, wh. in Delaware, was speaker of the ho. ch. just. and chancellor, f. of John, a disting. mem. of Cong. early under the new Constitut. JOHN, Weymouth, by w. Mary, d. of Philip Read, had John, b. 15 Apr. 1662; Mary, 18 June 1664; Thomas, 30 Oct. 1667; Samuel, 2 Feb. 1670; Jane, 7 July 1672; Margaret, 19 Mar. 1682; and Benjamin, 22 July 1684; perhaps others; was freem. 1666. Jane m. 1694, Jacob Turner; and next 1729, Samuel Allen. JOHN, Weymouth, s. prob. of the preced. by w. Naomi, had John, b. 17 Jan. 1688; and Mary, 25 Mar. 1690. WILLIAM, Portsmouth, had Benjamin, b. a. 1683.

VINSON, JOHN, Weymouth, by w. Sarah, had John, b. 28 July 1675; Ebenezer, 26 Mar. 1684; John, 8 Nov. 1697; and Thomas, 20 Aug. 1699, perhaps more. Nicholas, in Farmer's MS. is call. of Mass. but no more is ment. except that he was b. 1624. THOMAS, Martha's Vineyard, acc. incoher. tradit. was one of the first four sett. there, but I doubt the whole story. WILLIAM, Gloucester, freem. 10 May 1643, by w. Sarah, wh. d. 4 Feb. 1660, had Sarah; and Hannah, both bef. he was at G.; Eliz. b. 16 May 1644; John, 15 May 1648; William, 1651, wh. d. 9 Dec. 1675; and Richard 1658, wh. d. young; was selectman 1646; but rem. some yrs. later to New London. He m. sec. w. 10 June 1661, Rachel Cooke, had Thomas, b. 1 Apr. 1662, wh. d. at 14 yrs.; and Abigail, 1668; d. 17 Sept. 1690, and his wid. d. 15 Feb. 1707. Sarah m. 11 Nov. 1657, Jeffery Parsons; and Hannah m. 8 Oct. 1664, William Ellery. Perhaps this name is often Vincent.

VINTON, BLAISE, Lynn, or Malden, youngest s. of John the first, was on serv. in Philip's war 1675 and 6, but aft. very diligent search, the scrupul. author of the Vinton Memo. could say no more of him; yet he makes Lydia, d. of the sec. John Hayden m. a Vinton, and as the only elder brs. John and William he supplied with wives of other names, my conject. may be indulg. that this Blaise got that Lydia, tho. no ch. is kn. EDWARD, Marblehead, d. 1678. JOHN, Lynn, by w. Ann had Eleanor, b. May 1648; John, 2 Mar. 1651; William, 30 Apr. 1652; Blaise, 22 Apr. 1654; Ann, 4 Apr. 1656; Eliz. Jan. 1658; and Sarah 16 Sept. 1662. He d. at New Haven 1663, and his w. also was d. in 1664, when the Ct. direct. the ch. to be sent to L. Eleanor m. 12 July 1666, Isaac Ramsdell. Ano. JOHN was of Boxford 1680. JOHN, Malden, s. of first John, m. 26 Aug. 1677, Hannah, d. of the sec. Thomas Green of M. had John, b. a. 1680; Hannah, 26 Jan. 1682; Rebecca, 26 Mar. 1683; Thomas, 31 Jan. 1687; Mary, 20 Aug. 1689, d. soon; Mary, again, 2 Jan. 1693; Samuel, a. 1695; and Abiathar, b. at Woburn, 10 May 1700. He was a blacksmith, rem. to Woburn, and d. 13 Nov. 1727. His wid. Hannah d. 1741, aged 82. WILLIAM, Malden, s. of John the first, m. a d. of Joseph Hills, perhaps Hannah, had Hannah, nam. in the will of her gr.f. 1687. This fam. is reasonab. thot. to have come from France, perhaps as Huguenots, in early days, and sett. in Eng.

VIXEN, ROBERT, Eastham, had Jemineth, a d. b. 30 Aug. 1655; Titus, 2 Dec. 1657; Eliz. 29 May 1660.

VOBEZ. See Fobes.

VODEN, VOEDEN, VORDEN or VOUDEN, JOHN, Salem, came from the Isle of Jersey, m. 2 Dec. 1669, a Waters, perhaps d. of Richard (but so perversely spell. is the bapt. name in the rec. Mr. Felt transcrib. for me, that I dare not present it, and venture only to suggest, that it is impossib.) had Mary, b. 14 Nov. 1672, wh. d. young; John, 5 Feb. 1674; and Eliz. 10 July 1675, wh. m. Benjamin Jones of Swanzey. MOSES, Salem, br. of the preced. b. in Jersey in the Eng. chan. m. 1 Mar. 1674,

Mary Ormes, eldest d. of John, had Mary, b. 6 Apr. 1677, wh. m. Richard Palmer; and Eliz. 9 July 1679, wh. m. John Preston or Presson, as was sw. 24 Oct. 1716, by three witness. at S. his neighbors and d. 28 Mar. 1681, leav. wid. Mary.

VORE, or VOAR, RICHARD, Windsor, bef. 1640, had been at Dorchester 1635, where he came, perhaps with Warham, in 1630, brot. from Eng. a fam. tho. neither their number, nor the ship, nor yr. in wh. they came, is kn. but of four ds. m. at W. two and prob. three at W. must have been b. bef. he arr. Mary m. 29 Oct. 1646, Alexander Alford; Lydia m. 29 June 1649, Nathaniel Cook; Sarah m. 1653, Benjamin Parsons; and Abigail, wh. was prob. b. at W. m. 27 Mar. 1662, Timothy Buckland. He d. 22 Nov. 1683, hav. been in 1660, excus. from watch and ward, was in the freemen's list 1669; and his wid. d. 15 days aft. him. This name was mistak. by Dr. Harris as Vose.

VOSE, EBENEZER, Dorchester, d. 1716, aged 80, says Milton rec. but a doubt arises, whether the name be not mistak. for Edward. EDWARD, Milton, s. of Robert, by w. Abigail, had James; Abigail; Nathaniel, b. 17 Nov. 1672; William; John; and Eliz. all bapt. 28 Sept. 1679, in right of their mo. but this was bef. he rem. to M. there d. 1716, aged 80. HENRY, Dorchester, s. of Robert, had Eliz. b. 8 Aug. 1661. ROBERT, Dorchester 1635, a gent. as he is call. in the deed of large est. July 1654, late of Hon. John Glover, by his wid. and childr. ROBERT, Dorchester, by fam. tradit. said to have come from Co. Lancaster, purchas. est. in that part of D. wh. bec. Milton, still enjoy. by descend. of whose line I am ign. in part. He was freem. 1666, had Thomas; Edward, b. a. 1637; Eliz.; Henry; and Martha, wh. was a wid. Buckminster when her f. d. His d. Eliz. m. 9 Dec. 1657, Thomas Swift. THOMAS, Milton, s. of the preced. was a capt. by w. Waitstill Wyatt, had Eliz. b. 8 Aug. 1661; Thomas; and Henry; and d. 23 Apr. 1708, aged 67. His wid. Waitstill, d. 8 Jan. 1727, aged 84.

VOWLES, VOULS, or VOWELLS, * RICHARD, Fairfield 1650–6, Greenwich or Rye, was made freem. 1662, and appoint. constable there, and the Conn. governm. (of wh. he was a rep. 1665, 8, and 9, when his name is by the secr. once spell. Fowels) creat. the town of Hastings for him, but I do not think the name lasted long.

VYALL, VIOL, or VIALL, JOHN, Boston, vintner, but bred a weaver, by w. Mary had Hopestill, b. 14 Aug. 1639, bapt. 9 May 1641, he hav. join. the ch. the Sunday preced. then call. a laborer; Mary, 30 Nov. bapt. Sunday foll. 1641, prob. d. young; John, bapt. 2 June 1644, a. 5 days old; Mary, again, 18 Mar. 1649, a. 7 days old; Sarah, b. 14 Mar. 1652; Joseph, 4 June 1654; others by first w. were Abigail and Nathaniel; was freem. 2 June 1641, had license for the ship tavern, near the N.

battery, wh. he own. I think, 1662, rem. in old age to Swanzey, and d. 1686. His will of 3 Jan. 1682 provides handsomely for the wid. Eliz. would have his corpse inter. at Rehoboth, and gives part of his est. to six ch. of the first w. of wh. he ment. that Nathaniel was blind. Mary m. 26 Jan. 1659, John Sunderland; and Hopestill m. 1 July 1659, William Shute. JOHN, Boston, s. of the preced. m. Mary, d. of Nathaniel Williams, had Eliz. b. 12 Nov. 1682; and no other ch. on rec. join. Mather's ch. 9 Apr. 1682, and was freem. Feb. foll.

WACOMBE, or WACKHAM, THOMAS, Portsmouth 1684, d. or his will was pro. 1709. He left wid. Mary.

WADDELL or WODEL, GERSHOM, Portsmouth R. I. only s. of William of the same, m. a d. of John Tripp of the same, had William, Richard, Return and Gershom, beside ds. Sarah, Mary and Innocent; but no date of the b. of either or of his d. can be found. * WILLIAM, Warwick, one of the comp. of Gorton, tak. Nov. 1643, and imprison. at Watertown, by the governm. of Mass. After liberat. he went to Portsmo. R. I. and there most of the residue of his days resid. and fill. import. offices, down to 1690. By w. Mary, he had Mary, b. Nov. 1640; Gershom, 14 July 1642; Sarah, Oct. 1644; Alice, 10 Feb. 1650; and Frances, 6 July 1652; and his w. d. 23 Mar. 1676. His will of 7 Oct. 1692, pro. 2 May foll. makes date of his d. nearly to be estimat. Mary m. Daniel Grinnel; Sarah m. 1667, John Sanford; Alice, m. 26 Dec. 1671, Abraham Anthony; and Frances m. 23 Nov. 1669, John Anthony. * WILLIAM, Portsmouth R. I. s. prob. of Gershom, yet perhaps of the preced. m. 10 Feb. 1681, Ruth, d. of George Lawton the first, and d. 6 Jan. 1699, aged 36 as says the Portsmouth rec. wh. gives no ch.

WADDOCK, HENRY, Saco, wh. was of the gr. jury 1645, own. alleg. to Mass. 1653, as in Col. Rec. IV. part I. is the same person nam. Maddocks or Mattocks, and wh. is better spelling, I dare not undertake to decide, without personal inspect. of the initial letter in the orig. When Paige and Shurtleff agree in read. ancient record, it may be safe eno. to follow. The strangeness of such a name might decide it adversely to the W. but the diligence of Folsom, in his admir. hist. of Saco, 124, shows that the exact truth of the patronymic is Warwick. See that.

WADE, HENRY, Hingham 1652. * JONATHAN, Ipswich, had come in 1632, in the Lion, arr. 16 Sept. perhaps with w. Susanna, and sat down at Charlestown, was a merch. and with his w. rec. into the ch. 25 May 1633, freem. 14 May 1634, aft. 1636 rem. to Ipswich, was of gr. jury 1637, had 200 acres gr. in 1639, and 400 more in 1649, but for a claim on acc. of £60. put into the common stock by his br. Thomas of Northampton in Eng. could not gain part of Plum isl. as he desir. was rep. 1669, 81 and 2, had Mary, bapt. at C. Oct. 1633; Jonathan; Sarah;

Nathaniel, b. a 1648; Prudence; Thomas, b. a. 1651; and perhaps more. His w. d. 29 Nov. 1678, and he d. 1684, was bur. says Sewall's almanac, 8 Nov. His will pro. 8 July 1686, by Presid. Dudley in Boston, had been made in London so long bef. as 17 June 1657, and was witness. by Sir William Peake, and Samuel Sedgwick, whose hands were sw. to by John Richards, correspond. of Sir William, and by a correspond. of Sedgwick, and also his wid. It provides for w. Susanna, and the childr. but names only the eldest Jonathan, to wh. he gives all his ld. in parish of Denver, Co. Norfolk, on W. side, one mile from Downham market. We may then infer, that was his native place. The d. Mary m. William Symonds; Sarah m. 13 Nov. 1661, Samuel Rogers, and Prudence m. 29 Dec. 1659 or 1666, Dr. Anthony Crosby, and next 9 July 1673, Rev. Seaborn Cotton of Hampton. JONATHAN, Ipswich, s. of the preced. rem. to Medford, m. Deborah, youngest d. of Gov. Thomas Dudley, had Deborah, bapt. at Charestown, 24 Mar. 1667; Prudence, 6 June 1669; Catharine, 27 Aug. 1671, d. soon; Catharine, again, 22 June 1673; Susanna, 10 June 1677; Dorothy, 10 July 1681; Dudley, 18 Oct. 1683; and by sec. w. Eliz. had Eliz. 1687; and Dorothy, 17 Feb. 1689; was capt. of the three county troop of horse, freem. 1669, and d. 24 Nov. 1689. *NATHANIEL, Medford or Malden, br. of the preced. m. 31 Oct. 1672, Mercy, youngest d. of Gov. Simon Bradstreet (but in Geneal. Reg. I. 77, wrong date is giv. 11 Nov. of that yr. and the Gov's. d. is nam. Mary) had at Charlestown, Nathaniel, b. 13, bapt. 20 July 1673; so that the date of b. in Geneal. Reg. IX. 121 is easy mistake, very frequent. obs. in read. old rec. 5 for 3; Simon and Susanna, tw. bapt. 9 Apr. 1676, wh. both prob. d. soon; beside Mercy, b. 19 Sept. 1678; Jonathan, 5 Mar. 1681; Samuel, 31 Dec. 1683; Ann, 7 Oct. 1685; and Dorothy 12 Mar. 1687; was freem. 1685, major in milit. rep. 1692, and d. 28 Nov. 1707. His wid. d. 5 Oct. 1714, prob. tho. gr.st. says 1715. NICHOLAS, Scituate 1638, m. Eliz. d. of Thomas Ensign of the same, had Joseph, wh. was k. by the Ind. in the bloody fight at Rehoboth 26 Mar. 1676, under capt. Michael Pierce; Nicholas, b. 1660; Jacob, 1661; John; Thomas; Nathaniel; and perhaps others. RICHARD, Lynn, freem. 9 Mar. 1637, but then he may have liv. at Dorchester, certain. had, that yr. a div. in the lds. of the Neck, now South Boston; rem. says Lewis, to Sandwich, but he is not in the list of 1643, there. ROBERT, Dorchester 1635, rem. soon to Hartford, there was adm. freem. 1640, afterwards liv. at Seabrook, and by the Gen. Ct. was divorc. from his w. Joane then in Eng. 1657, aft. 15 yrs. of separat. mov. last to Norwich, there liv. 1669. SAMUEL, is ment. in Col. Rec. sub anno 1639, as hav. been robb. by his serv. but we hear no more of him, exc. in 1641 his resid. was at Lynn. SIMON, Andover, k.

by the Ind. 22 Feb. 1698, if we trust the town rec. or 24th if we take
Sewall's Diary, yet perhaps the latter was the date of the news coming
to him. THOMAS, Ipswich, s. prob. youngest, of Jonathan the first, m.
22 Feb. 1670, Eliz. Cogswell, d. perhaps of William, had Jonathan;
Thomas; John, H. C. 1693, min. of Berwick; Nathaniel; and William,
wh. was k. at sea, 3 Apr. 1697; beside four others; was freem. 1682,
capt. and an active citizen, and d. 4 Oct. 1696, leav. wid. and nine ch.
WILLIAM, Middletown, m. 1658, Sarah, d. of William Phelps, the magistrate of Windsor. She d. 10 July 1659, and no more is heard of him.

WADFIELD, JOHN, Scituate 1643.

WADILOVE, NICHOLAS, Yarmouth 1643.

WADLAND, or WADLEN, CRISPIN, Charlestown, shipwright, had w.
Eliz. and d. 1671, in his will of 6 Aug. pro. 19 Dec. of that yr. gave all
his prop. to the w. made excor. and in her wid. state she enjoy. it
Mar. 1678.

WADLEIGH, WADLEY, WADELY, WADLAW, WADLEE, or WADLOW,
JOHN, Saco 1636, of gr. jury 1645, rem. to Wells, there kept an inn
1648, was a selectman, had Robert, subm. to Mass. 1653, and d. 1671.
His inv. 20 Sept. shows good prop. JOHN, Exeter, s. of Robert of the
same, sw. alleg. 30 Nov. 1677, was one of the excited declaim. against
the governm. of Cranfield, with his brs. JOSEPH and ROBERT, in concur.
with Edward Gove, wh. in 1683 were by the gr. jury charg. with high
treason. ROBERT, Wells, br. of John, own. alleg. to Mass. 1653, town clk.
1659, there was liv. 1668, and 9, yet this yr. was inhab. at Dover, and I
judge not to be the same wh. sett. at Exeter, and was in 1684, a counsel.
He must have disagr. with the royal Gov.

WADOM, WADAMS, or WADOMS, JOHN, Wethersfield, had John, b.
1655. His will of 19 Jan. 1677, names w. Susanna, and s. John. His
wid. m. a Bushnell of Saybrook, d. 18 Aug. 1683. JOHN, Wethersfield,
s. of the preced. had w. Hannah and d. Susanna, b. 1678, d. soon. He
was liv. 1693, with good est.

WADSWORTH, * CHRISTOPHER, Duxbury, was inhab. as early as
1632, and rep. 1666 and 7, had by w. Grace, Joseph; John, b. 1638;
Samuel; and Mary. His will is of 31 July 1677; and hers of 13 Jan.
1688. CHRISTOPHER, Milton, s. of Samuel, d. 4 Dec. 1687, aged a. 24
yrs. prob. unm. EBENEZER, Milton, prob. br. of the preced. had, I suppose, Benjamin to succeed him in the office of deac. His w. Mary d. 8
Mar. 1737, in her 77th yr. ‡* JAMES, Farmington, s. of John of the
same, was an important citizen of Durham, a col. rep. 1700–17, in wh.
last yr. he was speaker, an assistant 1718 to 52, and d. 1756. ‡* JOHN,
Farmington, eldest s. of William, b. in Eng. m. Sarah, d. of Thomas
Stanley, had Sarah, b. 1 Nov. 1657; Samuel, 3 Jan. 1660; John, 14

Apr. 1662; Mary, 13 Nov. 1665, d. young; William, 1671; Nathaniel, 1674; James, 1677; Thomas, 1680; and Hezekiah, bapt. 24 Dec. 1682. His inv. is of 6 Nov. 1689; the will of two mos. bef. ment. the seven s. and d. Sarah w. of Stephen Root. He was rep. 1672–7, and was nominat. in the last yr. for Assist. but not chos. until 1679, had distinct. in the milit. and with the Gov. and others was of the standing council for affairs in Philip's war. * JOHN, Farmington, s. of the preced. m. 20 Aug. 1696, Eliz. d. of John Stanley, had Sarah, b. 3 July 1697; Eliz. 3 May 1700; John, 9 Oct. 1702; Daniel, 14 Nov. 1704, Y. C. 1726; Lydia, 6 Oct. 1706; Ruth, 14 Apr. 1711; and Mercy, 11 Sept. 1713; was rep. for 9 sess. betw. 1703 and 16, and d. 1718. His w. had d. 25 Oct. 1713, and he took sec. w. Mary Gridley, wh. had been sec. w. of Samuel. * JOSEPH, Hartford, s. of William, was propound. for freem. 1676, with his brs. Samuel, and Thomas, and all adm. the same yr. was a lieut. and serv. in Philip's war; m. Eliz. d. of Bartholomew Barnard, wh. d. 26 Oct. 1710, had Joseph, b. 1682; Eliz.; Jonathan, bapt. 20 Feb. 1687, d. young; and we kn. other ch. (from Hinman 323) to have been Ichabod; Hannah; and Jonathan, again. His sec. w. was perhaps Eliz. d. of the sec. John Talcott. But he is most rememb. with gratitude in our times, as the preserver of the charter, in opposit. to the demand of the royal Gov. by the perilous expedient of extinct. of the lights in the Council chamber, 31 Oct. 1687, and hiding the parchment in the great oak. He m. late in life, Mary, d. of John Blackleach, the younger, wh. had been first w. of Thomas Welles, next of John Olcutt, and she surv. Wadsworth. He was capt. d. 1730. * NATHANIEL, Farmington, s. of John, m. 21 Mar. 1705, Dorothy, d. of John Ball of New Haven, had Eunice, b. 10 June 1706; Timothy, bapt. 5 June 1709; Esther, prob. 3 May 1713; Sarah, 20 Jan. 1717; Nathaniel, perhaps 14 Sept. 1718; Mary, 14 Aug. 1720; Hezekiah, 16 Sept. 1722; and Timothy, again, perhaps 26 Nov. 1727; was rep. 1727, and d. 20 Dec. 1761. SAMUEL, Milton, s. of Christopher, freem. 1668, m. Abigail d. of James Lindall of Marshfield, had perhaps Recompense, wh. d. 12 July 1679, only a few days bef. he would have been gr. at Harv. in 21st yr.; Ebenezer, b. a. 1661; Christopher, a. 1663; prob. others, and certain. Benjamin 1669, H. C. 1690, min. of the first ch. in Boston, ord. 8 Sept. 1696, and Presid. of Harv. Coll. He was disting. as a capt. in Philip's war, and in Apr. 1676, going to relief of Sudbury on a sudden assault by the enemy, was overpower. by numbers, and with his lieut. Sharpe of Brookline, and half his comp. cut off 21 Apr. Yet many authorities gave the date 18. The matter seems stated with much plausibility and with suffic. caution as to weight of evid. in Geneal. Reg. VII. 221. SAMUEL, Hartford, s. of William, d. 1682, his will of 16 Aug. in that yr. gave est. above

£1100. to brs. sis. a neph. and niece, so that we infer, he had no w. nor
ch. then liv. * SAMUEL, Farmington, s. of John, m. 12 June 1689,
Hannah, d. of Joseph Judson, had Hannah, bapt. 11 Feb. 1693; Sarah,
20 Oct. 1695; and Samuel, perhaps 23 Jan. 1698; was rep. 1699, and
1711, and d. 19 May 1731. His wid. d. 22 Aug. 1732. SAMUEL,
Milton, prob. s. of the first Samuel, was deac. and d. 31 Jan. 1734 in his
60th yr. THOMAS, Hartford, s. of William of the same, had w. Eliz. in
1677, and childr. John; Sarah, b. 1681; Eliz.; Rebecca, bapt. 16 May
1686; Thomas, 29 Jan. 1688; Hannah, 24 Aug. 1690; and William,
13 Nov. 1692; and d. 1725. TIMOTHY, Boston, freem. 1690, by w.
Susanna, had Susanna, b. 29 Oct. 1687; and Recompense, 19 Mar.
1690, H. C. 1708. * WILLIAM, Cambridge 1632 came, prob. with fam.
of four ch. Sarah, William, wh. d. young, Mary, and John, in the Lion
from London, arr. 16 Sept. See Winth. Hist. I. 90. This date over-
throws the slight presumpt. of some mem. of the mod. fam. that their
progenit. had been first of Braintree, inasmuch as the court had in the
preced. mo. order. the few friends of Hooker, wh. had sat down at B. to
rem. to a safer spot. He was freem. 6 Nov. 1632, and in the great
exodus, June 1636, rem. to Hartford, and there seems to have liv. in the
highest esteem, no man ever more oft. chos. rep. for betw. Oct. 1656 and
May 1675 (his last appear.), hardly a single yr. miss. his serv. Prob. he
d. soon aft. He m. 2 July 1644, Eliz. Stone, but this, of course, not his
first w. outliv. him. His ch. by this w. were Eliz. b. 17 May 1645;
Samuel, 20 Oct. 1646, wh. d. at mid. age; Joseph, a. 1648; Sarah, the
sec. 17 Mar. 1650; Thomas, a. 1651; and Rebecca, a. 1656; but of the
first w. we kn. nothing, nor the order of dates for her ch. nor indeed
date of a single one. The first Sarah m. 17 Sept. 1646, John Wilcox;
Mary m. a. 1656, Thomas Stoughton of Windsor, so that we can be sure
these two as well as John were of the first w. Eliz. m. 27 Nov. 1662,
John Terry of Windsor; and Sarah of the sec. w. m. 10 Nov. 1669,
Jonathan Ashley of Springfield. He d. 1675, his will of 16 May 1675,
with his inv. of 18 Oct. foll. and his wid. d. 1682, when Rebecca was unm.
* WILLIAM, Farmington, s. of John, m. 10 Dec. 1696, Abigail, youngest
d. of Capt. William Lewis, wh. d. 1707; and he m. 2 Jan. 1709, Sarah,
d. of Thomas Bunce, wh. d. 1748. By this w. he had only William, b.
2 Dec. foll. the m.; but by first w. were William, b. 7 Dec. 1697, wh. d.
young; Mary, 1700; Hannah, 27 July 1701; Abigail, 27 Jan. 1703;
and Ezekiel, 19 Oct. 1704. He was rep. 1718–40, and d. 26 Oct. 1751.
Of this name Farmer notes in 1829, that seven had been gr. at Harv.
five at Yale, and three at Brown.

WAINWRIGHT, FRANCIS, Ipswich 1637, serv. in the Pequot war, for
kn. of wh. fact we are indebted to the " True Relation " of the battle by

Rev. Philip Vincent, as may be seen in 3 Mass. Hist. Coll. VI. 40 and 1 ; was perhaps from Chelmsford in Co. Essex. FRANCIS, Ipswich, perhaps s. of the preced. b. in Eng. freem. 1671, was a merch. of distinct. a corporal 1664, by w. Phillippa wh. d. 9 Oct. 1669, had John, b. a. 1648 ; Sarah ; Mary ; Martha ; Simon ; Mehitable ; Eliz. ; and Francis, 25 Aug. 1664, H. C. 1686 ; and d. at Salem, 19 May 1692. His will, wh. is found in Suffk. rec. XIII. 17, provides for wid. Hannah, and ds. Mary w. of Rev. Jeremiah Shepard ; Martha, w. of Joseph Proctor ; Mehitable, w. of John Atwater ; Eliz. w. of Jonathan Cogswell ; gr.s. Francis s. of Jacob Perkins by his d. Sarah ; and Francis and John, s. of his s. John. His wid. m. Daniel Epes of Salem. Some presumpt. may arise that he is the same with the Pequot soldier. * FRANCIS, Ipswich, s. of the preced. m. Sarah Whipple, had only three ds. liv. at d. of his w. 16 Mar. 1709, but his s. John had d. 25 Sept. preced. in 18th yr. a senior at H. C. was maj. rep. and d. 3 Aug. 1711. JACOB, a soldier under capt. Lathrop, k. with the "flower of Essex" at Bloodybrook, 18 Sept. 1675, was perhaps s. of the sec. Francis. JOHN, Ipswich, br. of the last Francis, m. Eliz. d. of William Norton, had Eliz. wh. m. Nov. 1698, Addington Davenport ; Ann, m. Adam Winthrop ; Lucy m. 15 Sept. 1703, Paul Dudley ; Francis, H. C. 1707 ; and John, 19 June 1691, H. C. 1711 ; was col. of the regim. and tho. he d. so early as 30 July 1708, left very large est. His wid. m. 19 Nov. 1713, Hon. Isaac Addington. SIMON, Haverhill, br. of the preced. m. Sarah Gilbert, d. of unkn. f. had Sarah, b. 17 July 1682 ; was capt. and for sec. w. m. Mary wid. of Thomas Silver, had three more ds. and s. John, H. C. 1709, bef. he was k. by the Ind. in their surpr. of H. 29 Aug. 1708 ; still whether by the sec. w. were b. any, or wh. of the ch. is uncert. Sarah, m. 7 Feb. 1699, Charles Frost, and d. 5 June 1714, yet leav. the number of nine ch. as is shown in the Memoir, Geneal. Reg. V. 165, tho. the writer was so greatly excited by his relative's happiness, that he gives ten, of wh. two d. bef. her. THOMAS, Wethersfield 1643, serv. of Mr. Henry Smith, failed in suit against him, may have tak. disgust, and gone back to Dorchester 1659. Seven of this name have been gr. at Harv. but the only one for a hundred and forty yrs. is Jonathan Mayhew, 1812, the late excellent Bp. of New York.

WAITE, WAIT, or WAIGHT, ALEXANDER, in 1637 was whip. for sell. powder to Ind. BENJAMIN, Hatfield 1663, sw. alleg. 8 Feb. 1679, was serg. k. by the Ind. and Fr. in surpr. of Deerfield, to whose relief he hasted, 29 Feb. 1704. He m. 8 June 1670, Martha, d. of John Leonard of Springfield, had Mary, b. 25 Feb. 1672 ; Martha, 1673 ; Sarah, 1675 ; on 19 Sept. 1677 the mo. and the three ch. were tak. by the Ind. (when his ho. with those of others was burn.) to Canada, where she had Canada,

a d. 22 Jan. 1678 ; and next yr. all came back. She next had John, 17
Jan. 1680 ; Joseph, 17 July 1682, d. young ; Jeremiah, 24 Sept. 1684 ;
and Joseph, again, 11 Nov. 1688. His good est. was div. soon aft. his
d. when the d. Martha is not ment. Mary, the eldest d. m. 4 Dec. 1690,
Ebenezer Wells ; Sarah m. John Belding ; and Canada m. 15 Dec. 1696,
Joseph Smith. GAMALIEL, Boston, call. serv. to our br. Edward Hutchinson, on join. the ch. 15 Dec. 1633, was freem. 4 Mar. 1635, but, for
too easy recept. of Mrs. Hutchinson's errors, disarm. 1637 ; by w. Grace
had Moses, bapt. 3 Sept. 1637, d. at 6 mos. ; Grace, b. 10, bapt. 20 Jan.
1639 ; Moses, again, bapt. 23 Aug. 1640, as the ch. rec. tells, tho. that
of the town pretends he was not b. bef. Sept. yet it may be more trustworthy in ment. of his d. Sept. of next yr. ; Samuel, bapt. 7 Nov. 1641 ;
Deborah, bapt. 21 Jan. 1644, a. 4 days old ; and Barry adds John, wh.
would otherwise be unkn. to me. He had, also, Gamaliel, bapt. 17 Nov.
1650, was a fisherman, and on that score prayed, in 1657, exempt. from
train. in the milit. gave in 1674 ld. on Long isl. in our harbor to s. John ;
and d. 9 Dec. 1685 in 87th yr. says his neighbor Judge Sewall in his
Diary where he delights to add, "lately had sev. new teeth." GEORGE,
Providence, bef. 1646. JEREMIAH, Hatfield, s. of Benjamin of the same,
m. 1706, Mary Graves, had Benjamin, b. 1707 ; Mary, 1708 ; Nathan,
1711 ; Gad ; Reuben ; Simeon ; and Miriam ; all liv. when the f. d.
* JOHN, Charlestown, of the ch. 15 Jan. 1647, liv. in Malden, freem.
1647, was a strenuous support. in 1651 of Rev. Marmaduke Matthews,
and was fin. for his contumac. opposition to authority, m. perhaps a d. of
Joseph Hills, had Samuel, b. 11 Oct. 1650 ; Mary, 31 Aug. 1652, d. at 15
yrs. ; Hannah, 9 Sept. 1656 ; Mehitable, 15 Sept. 1658 ; Thomas, 1
Sept. 1660 ; and Rebecca, 22 Nov. 1662 ; John, perhaps, and Joseph,
may have been elder ; was town clk. 1662 ; rep. 1666–84 every yr. and
this last was speaker ; but next yr. by reason of age and blindness excus.
on his petitn. from further serv. as capt. in wh. place he had many yrs.
serv. d. 26 Sept. 1693, aged 75. He left wid. Sarah, wh. d. 13 Jan. 1708,
aged 81 ; but his first w. prob. mo. of his ch. was Mary. Hannah, m.
11 Oct. 1676, William Bucknam ; Mehitable m. John Portman ; and
Rebecca m. Jonathan Tufts. JOHN, Ipswich 1646, d. Dec. 1665. JOHN,
Watertown, s. of Richard of the same, m. 13 Jan. 1664, Mary, eldest d.
of George Woodward of the same, had John, b. May 1665, d. in few
mos. ; Mary, 9 Oct. 1666 ; Rachel ; John, again, 27 Dec. 1669 ; Sarah,
26 Oct. 1672 ; Amos, 4 Jan. 1680 ; and Rebecca ; and he d. prob. 1691,
for in Oct. of that yr. admin. of his est. was giv. to wid. Mary and s.
John. His wid. d. 23 Aug. 1718. JOHN, Malden, s. prob. of John of the
same, was call. to sw. alleg. Dec. 1674, had m. 4 or 12 June preced. Sarah
Mussey, perhaps d. of Benjamin of the same ; and ano. JOHN of Malden,

384 W A I T E.

perhaps, m. 4 June 1675, Sarah Parker, as is thot. JOHN, Boston, perhaps s. of Richard of the same, was one of the witness. to the will of Gov. Leverett. JOHN, Hatfield, eldest s. of Benjamin the brave soldier, m. 1702, Mary, perhaps d. of Daniel Belding of the same, had John, b. 1703 ; Martha, 1706 ; Mary, 1708 ; Lydia, 1710, d. soon ; Lydia, again, 1712 ; Sarah ; Benjamin, 1718 ; Eunice ; Eleanor, 1722 ; and Elisha, 1725. JONATHAN, Northampton, d. June 1696. JOSEPH, Malden, s. of capt. John, prob. call. to sw. alleg. at the same time with him, m. 12 July 1678, Hannah, d. of Thomas Oakes of Cambridge, as his wid. on m. with Samuel Hayward of M. had tak. her d. with her, had Joseph, and Thomas. For sec. w. he m. 24 Oct. or Dec. 1688, Mercy, d. of the first Peter Tufts, had Peter, b. 20 Jan. 1690 ; and Jonathan, 24 Feb. 1692 ; was freem. 1690. His wid. m. a Jenkins. JOSEPH, Watertown, s. of Richard of the same, m. Ruhamah, d. of William Hagar of the same, had Ruhamah, wh. d. 1714, aged 38, it is said ; William, b. 1679 ; John, 1692, d. soon ; and Joseph, 1695. He rem. to Marlborough ; but whether bef. during or aft. Philip's war may be quite diffic. to determine, tho. in Oct. 1675, he was there in garrison. JOSEPH, Hatfield, youngest s. of the brave soldier Benjamin of the same, m. 1713, Hannah Billings, had Moses, b. 1714 ; and Hannah, 1716. His w. d. that yr. and he m. 1720, Mary Warner, had Rhoda, 1721 ; David, 1722 ; Martha, 1724 ; Lucy, 1727 ; Mary, 1730 ; and ano. whose name is not kn. ‖ RETURN, Boston, s. of Richard of the same, ar. co. 1662, was an officer of governm. a serg. in regular pay 1674–81, had import. part of the show at Gov. Leverett's funer. Mar. 1679. RICHARD, Boston, tailor, br. of Gamaliel, adm. of the ch. 28 Aug. 1634, freem. 9 Mar. 1637, by w. Eliz. had Joseph, wh. d. 20 Nov. 1651, aged 14 yrs. ; Isaac, b. 9 Aug. 1638, d. soon, of wh. I find neither brot. to bapt. perhaps bec. he was serv. as serg. in the Pequot war ; for wh. in later days he obt. gr. of 300 acres, yet held fast by the deadly heresies of Mrs. Hutchinson, and was therefore in Nov. 1637 compel. to surrender his arms to better believer, and was in Jan. 1639, subject. to maledict. by the ch. for tak. a portion of buckskin leather to make gloves, so that his next ch. Return, 8 July foll. was next Sunday bapt. in right of its mo. wh. had come from the ch. of Newbury, says our rec. The next ch. was Hannah, b. 14 Sept. 1641, Barry tells from the town rec. wh. to me seems wrong, bec. the ch. to the good will of wh. he was restor. shows rec. of the bapt. 12th of that mo. declares she was 6 days old ; next, Nathaniel, bapt. 5 Nov. 1643, a. 11 days old ; Mary, b. 15, bapt. 22 Feb. 1646, a. 6 days old ; Samuel, bapt. 9 July 1648, a. 20 days old ; and Eliz. 17 Nov. 1650. Barry supplies a sec. w. Rebecca, wh. brought John 1 Nov. 1653, prob. d. soon ; Richard, 1658 ; John, again, 9 Feb. 1660 ; and Abigail. He was marshall or sheriff of the Col. 1653, and was entrust. next yr. as messeng. to the Ind. His will was pro. 1680, by his br. Gamaliel, Excor. RICHARD, Watertown, by w. Mary had Stephen, b. 27 Feb. 1638, d. in few days; John, 6 May 1639; Thomas, 3 Mar. 1642; and Joseph; and d. 16 Jan. 1669, aged 60; and the two elder s. gave their mo. all the est. to bring up Joseph. His wid. d. 1678, aged a. 72. RICHARD, Springfield, took o. of alleg. 31 Dec. 1678, or next day, was on serv. in Philip's war, and when lieut. Thomas Cooper was slain by the Ind. was badly wound. for wh. in 1680 the governm. reliev. him from poll tax. SAMUEL, Wickford 1674, may, by w. Alice, have had Joseph, b. 1697; George, 1699; Samuel, 1701; Benjamin, 1702; Martha; and John, 1708; unless a later SAMUEL, perhaps s. at North Kingstown had these ch. SAMUEL, Malden, s. of capt. John had w. Mehitable, d. of the first William Bucknam, was freem. 1690, and d. 17 Sept. 1720. THOMAS, Ipswich, perhaps s. of John of the same, was serg. 1664, had John, b. 11 Dec. 1658; and was liv. 1678. THOMAS, Portsmouth, R. I. 1639, was among the freem. 1655, and of him I learn no more but that he had d. Mary wh. m. 5 Apr. 1676, Joseph Anthony of the same. THOMAS, Watertown, s. of Richard of the same, by w. Sarah, had Richard, b. 29 Jan. 1675, d. at 15 yrs.; Phebe, 26 July 1676; Thomas, 7 Mar. 1678; John, 16 Feb. 1681, d. at 10 yrs.; Joseph, 4 Feb. 1683; Sarah, 13 Jan. 1688; Mary, 20 Jan. 1690; Richard, again, 25 June 1691; and Abigail, 3 Dec. 1697; and he d. 3 Jan. 1723, and his wid. d. 17 Jan. 1744, aged 91, or by ch. rec. only 89. WILLIAM, Northampton, sw. alleg. 8 Feb. 1679, m. 1681, Sarah, d. of Enos Kingsley, had William, b. Aug. 1682; Sarah, 18 Apr. 1687; John, Aug. 1689. His w. d. 22 Jan. 1691, and he m. 29 July 1691 or 2, Ann, d. of John Webb jr. had Joseph, b. a. 1693; Ann, Jan. 1695; Jonathan, 1696, d. very soon; Mary, 17 Feb. 1698; Abigail; Jonathan, again, 18 Mar. 1703; Thankful, 27 Jan. 1706; Samuel, 19 Jan. 1708; Jemima, 13 Dec. 1709; Noah, 20 Feb. 1712; and Experience, 3 Mar. 1715; and d. 6 Feb. 1732. His wid. d. 7 Oct. 1748. Who was his f. or whence he came to N. is unkn.

WAKE, WILLIAM, Salem, was by our Court, in 1640, advis. to go home to his w. but seems not to have complied, and was frequent. fined for his disregard until he d. 1654; but from his will of 17 Apr. in that yr. seems to have left no ch. exc. Catharine, and beside ment. only br. John, both in Eng.

WAKEFIELD, JOHN, Salem 1638, may have been next yr. of Plymouth, and aft. at Wells, where he was of gr. jury 1656. He m. prob. Eliz. wid. of Edmund Littlefield. JOHN, Watertown 1646, may bef. and aft. have been of New Haven, there by w. Ann had Hannah, bapt. 29 Dec.

1644; Mary, 24 Aug. 1645; and Martha, b. 19 Apr. bapt. 19 May
1650, prob. for the date in Geneal. Reg. IX. 363, is, manifestly, wrong
for Sunday. So is, perhaps, ano. ch. Mary, as if he had two of that
name, bapt. three days apart, when only one of them could be Sunday.
He d. 1660, leav. wid. and three ds. The wid. m. 17 Oct. 1661, James
Clark of New Haven, and d. 1695. Hannah m. 1662, as his sec. w.
Edward Grannis; Mary m. 27 Oct. 1663, Ebenezer Dibble, and next,
15 June 1677, James Hillier; and Martha m. 21 Oct. 1668, Nicholas
Buckland. JOHN, Boston, had Eliz. wh. m. 20 Aug. 1660 Joseph Frost,
and perhaps rem. the same yr. to Edgartown, but he may have been the
one, wh. at Wells 1653, submit. to the jurisdict. of Mass. JOHN, Boston,
perhaps s. of the preced. by w. Deliverance, had Deliverance, b. 8 Sept.
1664; Ann, 2 Sept. 1666; John, 27 Jan. 1669; Samuel, 1 May 1674,
prob. d. soon; and Samuel, again, 15 Jan. 1678; was, I suppose, that
householder in 1695, wh. d. 1703. His will of 18 Oct. 1698, pro. 14
Mar. 1704, gave all to w. Deliverance for her life with power, on few
occasions bestowed, to div. among his ch. at her pleasure. OBADIAH,
Boston, join. Mather's ch. June 1682, and was adm. freem. Feb. foll. had
w. Susanna, and ch. Obadiah, b. 4 May 1674, d. soon; Obadiah, again,
11 Nov. 1677; John, 4 July 1682; and Samuel, 15 May 1686; not
any more on town rec. but on ch. rec. are found, Ann, bapt. 8 Dec.
1689, perhaps d. soon; Ann, again, 29 May 1692; Deborah, 21 Apr.
1695; Ann, again, 27 Feb. 1698. ‖ SAMUEL, Boston, by w. Eliz. had
Eliz. b. 2 Mar. 1675; Ebenezer, 12 Sept. 1684; Joshua, 19 Aug. 1686;
and Dorcas, 5 Feb. 1689; was the mem. of ar. co. 1676, to wh. the Gen.
Ct. in 1684, did not grant his req. to set up a wooden frame. WIL-
LIAM, Hampton, the freem. of 13 Mar. 1639, town clk. in 1641, is prob.
he wh. came in the Bevis, the yr. bef. from Southampton, aged 22, with
w. or sis. Ann, 20, as serv. of Stephen Dummer of Newbury; and, Coffin
says, came again to Newbury 1646.

WAKEHAM, or WAKCOME, EDWARD, perhaps of Dover, wh. may have
been s. of John, m. 16 Mar. 1692, Sarah, d. of John Meader. JOHN,
Dover, or that neighborhood, in 1689, prayed for governm. of Mass. to
be extend over their country.

WAKELY, WAKLEE, or WAKELIN, HENRY, Hartford, but not orig.
propr. own. two lots there, yet rem. to Stratford, perhaps yr. bef. the
enumerat. as freem. 1669. His will of 11 July 1689, names three s.
Deliverance, James, and Jacob, ds. Patience, Abigail, and Mary Stevens. It gave also to Thomas Lettin, and Eliz. Squier; and names his
w. Sarah. ISAAC, Gloucester, s. of Thomas, was lost by shipwreck with
Muddle a. 1662; but ano. Isaac, also s. of Thomas, was k. by the Ind.
JAMES, Hartford 1649, may have been earlier inhab. there, and rem. to

Wethersfield, where he m. Alice, wid. of James Boosy. Some controv. was rais. a. this m. as it seems, for the Gen. Ct. of Conn. in Feb. 1653, judg. the act of Dept. Gov. Haynes in m. them to be legal. However he was not long content. to live with old neighbors. and rem. to Newport, 1665. At Providence he sent, 1680, to Conn. petitn. for divorce, and his w. desir. divorce also. Neither prevail. JOHN, Falmouth, s. of Thomas, had been of Gloucester 1656, m. 10 May of unkn. yr. but perhaps 1657, Eliz. Sowers, says Geneal. Reg. IV. 366, had Hannah, of whose b. we have the day 12, but not the mo. nor yr.; Thomas, b. 3 Sept. 1659, d. in 3 days; and Eliz. 31 Jan. 1662; was k. with w. and ch. by the Ind. Sept. 1675. His d. Eliz. however, was tak. by the Ind. at that time, and in June 1676 restor. and m. Richard Scammon of Dover, and had plenty of ch. He is the man, whose name in the inestimable Coll. of Hutchinson, 398, is print. Marklie. RICHARD, Haddam, had been made freem. 1657, bef. H. was incorp. d. 6 Aug. 1681. His est. was distrib. to the wid. two s. and one d. all nameless. THOMAS, Hingham 1635, freem. 3 Mar. 1636, had perhaps that Thomas, wh. d. 23 June, 1644, rem. to Falmouth 1661, was there in 1675, with w. s. and his w. and four ch. k. by the Ind. Willis I. 137.

WAKELING, LUKE, Rowley 1662, is prob. the same fam. name as the preced.

WAKEMAN or WAKMAN, EZBON, ISBUN or ISBON, Stratford, among the freem. 1669, s. of Samuel of Hartford, had liv. at New Haven 1653, m. 1 Apr. 1669, at Guilford, Hannah Jordan, but bef. 1671, had purch. est. at Fairfield, where he d. 1683, leav. only d. Abigail, wh. m. Thomas Hill. His wid. Hannah, m. 1685, Joseph Bastard. JOHN, New Haven 1639, was treasr. of that Col. 1656, d. 1661; had a w. for the Hist. Disc. of Dr. Bacon, in his seating of the meeting-ho. 10 Mar. 1646, gives the name of sis. W. s. Samuel, and Eliz. m. 11 Mar. 1657, Samuel Kitchell, one of the early sett. at Newark, N. J.; and Ellen, ano. d. m. 29 Oct. 1650, the sec. John Talcott. Goodwin calls him Rev. but the reason for this distinct. is not seen. The f. made his will at Hartford and d. there. *SAMUEL, Roxbury 1631, br. of John, came in the Lion, arr. in Nov. freem. 7 Aug. foll. prob. rem. to Cambridge, was rep. at the May sess. 1635, and rem. with Gov. Haynes, or rather as his forerun. to Hartford, where in Apr. 1636, he was made constable, and engag. in adjust. the bounds of the first settlem. of Windsor and Wethersfield, was k. in the summer of 1641, with capt. Pierce at Providence in the Bahamas, as told by Winthrop, II. 33. His est. was in Dec. 1645, sett. on Nathaniel Willett, wh. had m. his wid. Eliz. but he was to pay £40. to the s. when 21 yrs. old, and £20. to ea. of 3 ds. on their coming to 18. They were all young, for the ch. rec. of Roxbury informs us, that he bur. his only ch. at sea, and his first b. here by w. Eliz. was Eliz. wh. m. Joseph Arnold ; Joanna m. Francis Hacleton ; and the other m. John Kelly. SAMUEL, Fairfield, s. of John, was bred at Harv. but left coll. in 1655, "Upon a dissatisfact. a. an hardship, wh. they [seventeen of the schol.] thot. put upon them, in mak. them lose a good part of a yr. of the time, whereupon they claim. their degr." says Magn. IV. 135. But Mather is too indefinite, and, with refer. to Brimsmead and Torrey, prob. mistak. so that we feel little confid. in his narrat. He m. 29 Oct. 1656, Hannah, d. of Stephen Goodyear, at New Haven, there had Samuel, b. 12 Oct. foll. rem. to F. was ord. 30 Sept. 1665, much esteem. and d. 8 Mar. 1692. His will bears the same date, and his inv. is of 8 Apr. foll. He names w. Hannah, ch. Samuel, wh. was d. 1691 ; John ; Joseph ; and Jabez. The est. was div. by John, Joseph, Jabez. He had also Ebenezer ; whose est. was div. among the three brs. and three brs.-in-law : Albert Denny, Abraham Howell, Nicholas Clegstone, prob. hs. of three ds.

WALCOT, WALLCOT, WALCUT, or WALCOTT, ABRAHAM, Salem vill. now Danvers, husbandman, first heard of 1678, freem. 1690, m. 22 Nov. 1682, Ruth Hooper, perhaps d. of the first William, and by sec. w. m. 30 Apr. 1689, Abigail Briggs, had Nathaniel, b. 11 Feb. 1694. JOHN, Danvers, s. perhaps eldest of Jonathan, by w. Mary had Eliz. b. 20 June 1693 ; Jerusha, 20 Dec. 1696 ; Mary, 11 Apr. 1699 ; and Jonathan, 9 May, 1700. JONATHAN, Salem, in that part wh. bec. Danvers, m. 26 Jan. 1665, Mary, d. of John Sibley, had beside ds. Hannah and Mary, John ; Jonathan, b. 1 Sept. 1670 ; and Samuel, 12 Oct. 1678, H. C. 1698. His w. d. 28 Dec. 1683 ; and he m. 23 Apr. 1685, Deliverance, d. of Thomas Putnam, and had Thomas ; William ; Ebenezer ; Benjamin, 23 Apr. 1695 ; and Ann. He was perhaps br. of Abraham, capt. and freem. 1690, and d. 16 Dec. 1699. JOSIAH, Salem, by w. Penelope, m. 19 Feb. 1685, wh. d. 28 Dec. 1690, had Eliz. b. 30 Mar. 1688 ; and Josiah, 21 Dec. 1690, d. in two wks. He took sec. w. 1 or 6 May 1694, Mary, d. of John Freke of Boston. WILLIAM, Salem 1637, was excommun. by Hugh Peter's influence with his ch. at the same time, and for the same cause, as famous Roger Williams, with whose opinions on some points of ecclesiast. customs he sympathiz. rem. Farmer thinks, to Providence, but I kn. no more.

WALDEN, EDWARD, Wenham, d. June 1679, in his will of 22 Mar. preced. ment. s. Nathaniel, appoint. excor. other ch. all under age, John, Hannah, Ruth, Naomi, and Eliz. beside omit. Mary and Thomasin, for wh. as Rev. Joseph Gerrish sw. he told him, "he had done eno. already." So we may conclude, that these were elder. See Essex Inst. Coll. III. 48, 9.

WALDO, CORNELIUS, Ipswich 1654, m. a d. of John Cogswell, had John and Cornelius, perhaps others, prob. Eliz. wh. m. 4 Feb. 1673, Josiah Bracket of Billerica, rem. to Chelmsford, was deac. and d. 3 June, 1701. *CORNELIUS, Dunstable, s. of the preced. one of the founders of the ch. 16 Dec. 1685, was rep. 1689, had perhaps Cornelius and others. *JOHN, Chelmsford 1675, s. of the first Cornelius, was rep. a short sess. 1689, for Dunstable. He rem. in the Ind. war to Windham, Conn. there d. a. 1700. His will of 14 Apr. in that yr. names w. Rebecca, wh. was d. of Samuel Adams of C. s. John, and refers to other childr. not nam. His inv. was £292. beside the est. at Chelmsford. ROBERT, Charlestown, d. 2 Aug. 1677, says Farmer MS. but I doubt he was only trans. Five of this name had, in 1818, been gr. at Harv. and one at Yale, and others at other N. E. coll.

WALDRON, WALDREN, WALDERNE, or WALROND, ALEXANDER, Dover 1664, kinsman, perhaps, but not younger br. of the first Richard, had not, that we kn. any fam. but d. at Newcastle, or great isl. 7 June 1676, naming five brs. to take his prop. with a sis. Mary, namely, Isaac, William, George, Samuel, and Edward, as Farmer, MS. shows. EDWARD, Ipswich 1648, perhaps br. of the preced. prob. went home soon. GEORGE, Dover 1661, of wh. we hear no more, but his being br. of Alexander, exc. that he rem. to Boston, there by w. Rachel had John, b. 25 Aug. 1676; and Benjamin, 22 May, 1679; unless, indeed, he were that other GEORGE, of Boston, wh. by w. Constant, had Benjamin, b. 24 Apr. 1678, and no more on the rec. ISAAC, Portsmouth, br. of the preced. a physician, was of York, 1670; in 1676 rem. to Boston, had w. Priscilla, and ch. Isaac, b. 23 June 1677; Priscilla, 6 Dec. 1678, prob. d. soon; Priscilla, again, 23 June 1680; and Priscilla, again, 12 July 1681; and he d. 1683. JOHN, Dover, s. of William of the same, had w. Dorothy, was, in 1665, 40 yrs. old; and perhaps late in life m. Eliz. wid. of the William Horne, k. by the Ind. at the assault on that town, 27 June 1689. JOHN, Marblehead, 1673, m. 25 Sept. 1679, Dorcas Rice, had been perhaps of Ipswich, the yr. bef. The childr. were Mary, b. 30 Jan. 1681; John, 8 Dec. 1682; Edward, 23 Nov. 1687; Tabitha, 22 Sept. 1689; Naomi, 10 Aug. 1691; Tamisin, 9 May 1693; Joseph, 15 Feb. 1695; Sarah, 9 Jan. 1699; and Nathaniel, 27 Aug. 1700. Of ano. JOHN at Dover, apprent. to John Heard, at the time of his will, 21 Apr. 1687, confus. tradit. of his m. with William Horn's wid. and hav. eight ch. aft. 1689, when the poor woman had brot. plenty from 1661 to 1676, as well as the strange manner of his being kidnap. and brot. from Eng. it is hardly worth the trouble of unwinding the narrat. possib. of two very blind narratives. Very detail. acco. of the k. by the Ind. of two of the ch. of the ages of 7 and 5 yrs. and large partic. of the resid. of the fam. was giv. in the Dover Enquirer; but so much is of a mythic and fabulous charact. as not to deserve attent. PAUL, Dover, eldest s. of the first Richard, was charg. for unlicens. sale of liquor 1668, as by our Col. Rec. is shown, soon aft. went abroad, and, it is said was tak. by Algerines, and d. a. 1669. RALPH, Boston, d. at Barbadoes, says Farmer, 29 Nov. 1653. ‡* RICHARD, Dover 1645, b. at Alcester, Co. Warwick, bapt. 6 Jan. 1616, m. prob. in Eng. whither he ret. aft. first coming, says tradit. in 1635, had, perhaps, after sec. coming, Paul; Timothy, wh. is said to have d. at Harv. Coll. bef. gr.; Richard, b. 1650; Ann; Elnathan, 6 July 1659, d. at 5 mos.; Esther, 1 Dec. 1660; and Mary, 14 Sept. 1663, perhaps d. soon, and so may have also, her mo. (these three last rec. at Boston); and by sec. w. Ann, perhaps sis. of the first Richard Scammon, had Eleazer, 1 May 1665; Eliz. 18 Oct. 1666; Mary, again, 17 July 1668, d. a. 14 yrs. old; was a man of great influence, rep. 1654, 7, 61, and very oft. aft. speaker 1666 to 9, 73, part of 74 to 76, and last in 1679, was a capt. early and maj. in the great Ind. war 1675 and 6; one of the counsel. under new form of governm. of N. H. 1680, and on the d. of Presid. Cutt, 1681, was head of the Prov. until the arr. of royal gov. His w. d. 7 Feb. 1680, and he was k. by the Ind. 27 June 1689, with circumst. of unusual cruelty, aged 74, not, as Farmer says, 80. His d. Ann, m. a. 1670, Rev. Joseph Gerrish of Wenham; Esther m. Henry Elkins wh. d. early, and she next m. 21 June 1686, Abraham Lee, wh. was k. at the same time with her f. and she next m. Richard Jose, sheriff of the prov. outliv. him, m. once more, and went across the ocean to d. in the isl. of Jersey; and Eliz. m. John Gerrish of Dover. ‡* RICHARD, Dover, s. of the preced. rem. to Portsmouth, and m. 16 Feb. 1681, Hannah, d. of Hon. John Cutt, the presid. of the prov. had Samuel, b. 1682, d. in few mos. as did his mo. 14 Feb. 1683, tho. by ano. report. it was 7 Feb. 1686. He m. 6 Feb. 1693, Eleanor, d. of William Vaughan, had Richard, b. 21 Feb. 1694; Margaret, 16 Nov. 1695; William, 4 Aug. 1697, H. C. 1717, first min. of the New Brick ch. Boston, set up by seceders from the New North, on acco. of install. of Peter Thacher, ord. 23 May 1722, wh. d. 20 Sept. 1727; Ann, 27 Aug. 1698; Abigail, 28 July perhaps, 1702, but ano. auth. says 1704; and Eleanor, Apr. 1704 or 6, d. at 20 yrs. was rep. at Boston, aft. overthr. of Andros, 1691 and 2, aft. being in 1681 of the royal council in N. H. milit. offic. and was long a judge. His w. d. Sept. 1727, and he d. 30 Nov. 1730. WILLIAM, Dover, prob. elder br. of the first Richard, bapt. 18 Oct. 1601, s. of William of Alcester, Co. Warwick, wh. was the s. of George, wh. was the s. of Edward of the same, perhaps brot. w. and ch. from Eng. took side early for Mass. and was freem. 19 May 1642, rep. for that sess. one

day, and again in 1646 was made not only recorder for the Prov. of
Maine, as Geneal. Reg. V. 182, has it, under Sir Ferdinando Gorges,
but Recorder for Dover, by power of our Col. See Col. Rec. II. 153.
He was drown. at Kennebunk in Sept. of that yr. not, as Farmer and
most others report, 1647. See Winth. II. 278. His d. Prudence m.
1661, Richard Scammon. WILLIAM, Dover 1664–83, but at Boston
1672, a gunsmith, may have been the br. of Alexander, or, as Farmer
conject. s. of the preced. Oft. in old rec. the name is Walden.

WALES, JOHN, Dorchester, s. of Nathaniel, b. in Eng. prob. as he
was bailiff 1653, by w. Eliz. had Content, b. 14 May 1659 ; Eliz. 1 July
1662 ; Elkanah, 16 June 1665, d. at 24 yrs.; and John, the freem.
1677, wh. d. 16 June 1683, aged 29, so was prob. the first b.; was
freem. 1677, same yr. with his s. of the same name. Content m. John
Mason. Content and Elkanah were bapt. 29 July 1677. NATHANIEL,
Dorchester, a shipwright, one of the passeng. with Rev. Richard
Mather, in the James of Bristol, 1635, of whose voyage the interest.
details are giv. in Mather's Journal, publ. in Young's Chron. was freem.
2 Nov. 1637, had w. Isabel, wh. outliv. him but two wks. and ch. Timothy, John, and Nathaniel ; yet if these were all, or whether any were b.
here, is unkn. One acco. calls his w. Susan, with wh. he rem. to Boston
a. 1654, and he d. at Boston, 4 Dec. 1661, hav. made his will 20 June
bef. NATHANIEL, Dorchester, s. of the preced. b. in Eng. d. at Boston, 20 May aft. his f. leav. four young ch. Nathaniel, Samuel, Mary,
and Jonathan, k. in Philips' war. NATHANIEL, Braintree, s. of the
preced. by w. Joanna, youngest d. of Thomas Faxon the sec. of the
same, had Eliz. b. 10 Feb. 1676, if Vinton or Thayer is right in mak.
the mo. less than fourteen and a half yrs. old ; Joanna, 18 Apr. 1679, d.
in few days ; Sarah, 11 Mar. 1680 ; Nathaniel, 29 Dec. 1681 ; Joanna,
again, 19 Dec. 1683 ; Elkanah, 1 Dec. 1685 ; Deborah, 16 Oct. 1687 ;
Thomas, 6 Oct. 1689, d. soon ; Mary, 1 Apr. 1691 ; Samuel, 23 June
1693 ; Thomas, again, 19 Apr. 1695 ; Joseph, 29 Apr. 1697 ; John, 25
May 1699, H. C. 1728 ; Rachel, 15 Oct. 1701 ; Atherton, 8 Mar. 1704,
H. C. 1726, being 15 ch. in all ; was made Rul. Elder, 27 Feb. 1701.
His w. d. 11 May 1704, and he d. 23 Mar. 1718. Of this br. descend.
have been num. SAMUEL, Dorchester, s. of the sec. Nathaniel, freem.
1690. His wid. Hannah, d. 1 June 1731, aged 68. TIMOTHY, Dorchester, s. of Nathaniel the first, prob. b. in Eng. had Eleazer, b. 25 Dec.
1657 ; and others. He may have been f. of that TIMOTHY of Hadley,
wh. sw. alleg. 8 Feb. 1679. By Farmer, Ms. we kn. that in 1834, six
of this name had been gr. at Yale, four at Harv. and two at other
N. E. coll.

WALFORD, JEREMIAH, Portsmouth 1631, s. of Thomas, d. 21 Apr.

1660, leav. wid. Mary, ch. Jeremiah, Thomas, and two ds. Mary wh. m. John Thomas, and Martha, wh. prob. m. a Westbrook. JEREMIAH, Portsmouth, s. prob. of the preced. was liv. it is said, in 1688, and prob. many yrs. later. JOHN, Portsmouth, not perhaps of this fam. unless he were s. of the sec. Thomas, was one of the royal counc. 1692. THOMAS, Charlestown 1628, found there by the first comers of the Mass. comp. in 1629, and call. a smith, but rem. a. 1631, to Portsmouth, where he was better treat. than in Mass. serv. on the gr. jury 1654, and d. 1660. In Gen. Reg. IX. 220, one says his will was made 15 and pro. 21 Nov. of that yr. His w. Jane was b. perhaps 1597, at least was old eno. to be call. a witch in 1657, but we may rejoice that the epithet was not deadly. He left s. Thomas and Jeremiah, beside ds. of wh. one m. successiv. Thomas Hinckson and John Westbrook; one m. a Jones; Jane m. a Peverly, perhaps Thomas; Hannah m. a Pease; Mary, b. 1635, m. William Brookin, and next William Walker; and Eliz. m. Henry Savage.

WALKELY. See Wakeley.

WALKER, ARCHIBALD, Providence, m. 18 July 1690, Mary Gardner, had Charles, b. 6 May 1691; Susanna, 28 Sept. 1695; Abigail, 13 Jan. 1699; Hezekiah, 14 Mar. 1701; Nathaniel, 26 June 1704; and Ann, 14 Feb. 1709. AUGUSTINE, or AUSTIN, Charlestown 1638, a sea capt. and merch. join. the ch. 20 Sept. 1640, and was adm. freem. 2 June foll. by w. Hannah, had Hannah, b. 12, bapt. 27 Sept. 1640; Samuel, 1 Oct. 1642; Augustine, 14 Dec. 1646; James, 25 July 1648; and perhaps more, but the blank in bapt. occurs early in the rec. He d. 1 Jan. 1653 at Bilboa in Spain, and his descend. were early at Woburn. By fam. tradit. he came from the vicinity of Berwick on Tweed. BENJAMIN, Boston, one of the found. of Brattle st. ch. DANIEL, Sudbury, s. of Thomas of the same, by w. Dorothy had Daniel, b. 27 Oct. 1710; Eliphalet, 11 Feb. 1712; Jabez, 18 July 1714; Dorothy, 12 Mar. 1717; Mary, 11 Oct. 1718; Josiah, 13 Sept. 1721; and Bezaleel, 7 May 1724; and d. 1755. EBENEZER, Rehoboth, youngest s. of Philip of the same, m. 19 Nov. 1700, had two ch. wh. d. soon, and his w. d. 1702. He next m. Oct. 1703, Dorothy Abell, and had nine ch. of wh. five surv. him, and d. 13 Mar. 1718. EDWARD, Charlestown, may have been s. of Augustine, was a soldier in Philip's war, freem. 1684, then liv. at Woburn, and d. 6 July 1690. ELEAZER, Taunton, s. of James, d. 15 Dec. 1724, aged 62. FRANCIS, Middleborough 1668, rem. to Duxbury 1672, and m. Eliz. d. of George Soule, bef. the former date. GEORGE, Reading, by Eaton call. one of the early sett. but was, I think, s. of an earlier one, and may be mistake for Walkup, or if Walker, possib. that man of Portsmouth in 1689, wh. d. 7 Dec. 1748, aged 86. Farmer,

MS. Henry, Gloucester 1647, perhaps of Ipswich 1651, m. as her third
h. at G. 26 Sept. 1662, Mary, wid. of William Brown, wh. had been wid.
of Abraham Robinson, was freem. 1672, and d. 1693. Yet ano. Henry
may have been the resid. of Ipswich. ‖ Isaac, Boston, merch. by w.
Susanna, wid. of Henry Symonds, m. 1644, had Isaac, bapt. 12 Oct. 1645,
a. 15 days old, in the right of his w. recom. says our ch. rec. from the
ch. of Salem, wh. d. in few days; and 2 May foll. he join. our ch. of B.
and was made freem. a few days aft. had Leah, bapt. 6 Dec. aft. His
w. d. 30 Sept. 1646. He was active propr. of Lancaster, but did not
rem. thither, had second or third w. Susanna, if the rec. is right, and by
her had Experience, bapt. 20 Oct. 1650; Nicholas, b. 1 Dec. 1651;
Stephen, 13, bapt. 17 Aug. 1656; and possib. more; and w. Hannah in
1682; was lieut. ar. co. 1676, and d. 19 Oct. 1688. Yet that he had w.
bef. m. with that wid. of Symonds, seems clear eno. for in Sept. 1662
is rec. of a deed from him to Susannah Walker, his d. of "that little
shop wh. now she keeps." This opinion I still retain, tho. in Mar. 1666
is found ano. deed of hims. and Susanna, his (third) w. to their d.
Susanna. Israel, Woburn, had Israel, b. 29 Sept. 1672, d. at 11 yrs.;
Susanna, 1 Mar. 1674; Phebe, 11 May 1676; Eliz. wh. d. 21 Jan.
1682; Henry, 1 Feb. 1679; Hannah, 26 Apr. 1681, d. very soon;
Nathaniel, 15 Apr. 1682; Israel, again, 26 July 1684; Hannah, again,
24 Sept. 1686; Abigail, 26 Sept. 1688; and Edward, 6 Nov. 1690.
He was freem. 1674, may have been br. of Edward, but perhaps both
came from Eng. Susanna m. 18 Oct. 1697, Ebenezer Locke, and d. 13
June 1699. Jabez, Eastham, youngest s. of William of the same, by
w. Eliz. had Richard, b. 1 June, 1695; Rejoice, 13 May 1697; Mary,
14 Sept. 1699; Jeremiah, 17 May 1702; and Mercy, 7 Nov. 1704;
Jabez; Sarah; and Patience. Jacob, Killingworth, perhaps s. of
Robert of Boston, propound. for freem. 1672; as admor. of est. of
Samuel, one of the s. of Rev. Adam Blakeman, whose wid. Eliz. he m.
6 Dec. 1670, he had great trouble with the wid. and other ch. of Adam,
as in the Col. Rec. of Trumbull, II. in many places appears. He had
Samuel, b. 7 Nov. 1671; Moses, bapt. Dec. 1673; John, 9 Oct. 1674;
Eliz. July 1676; Mary, 1 Jan. 1679; and Mercy, 11 Mar. 1681.
*James, Taunton 1643, prob. is that youth of 15 yrs. wh. came from
London 1635, with Sarah W. his sis. 17, in the Elizabeth, as found.
in 3 Mass. Hist. Coll. VIII. 260; may have been 1644 at Rehoboth,
but was perman. inhab. of T. m. Eliz. d. of William Phillips, and bec.
a man of gr. esteem, in 1652 constable, frequent. selectman, rep. 1654,
and oft. aft. had James, b. a. 1646; Peter, 1649; Eleazer, 1662; wh.
d. prob. unm. yet at mature age, in his will giv. prop. to cousins, the
ch. of brs. and sis. and Esther. His w. d. 30 July, or 14 Aug. 1678,

aged 59; and he m. sec. w. 4 Nov. foll. Sarah, wid. of Edward Rew, d. of John Richmond; and d. 18 Feb. 1692, aged 73. Esther m. 1 Jan. 1680, Joseph Wood or Atwood, and d. 8 Apr. 1696. In Col. Rec. we read that JAMES, jun. of T. m. 23 Dec. 1647, Barsheba, whose surname is lost, and I conject. that the order of numerals of the yr. is wrong, and should be 1673, and points to the foll. JAMES, Taunton, s. prob. of the preced. m. 23 Dec. 1673, Bathsheba Brooks, d. of Gilbert of Rehoboth, had James, b. 24 Dec. 1674; Eliz. 1676; Nathan, 1678; David, a. 1681; Bathsheba; Nehemiah, 1689; Mercy; Mehitable; Josiah; Rebecca; and Mary; but dates are not supplied; was constable 1682; and d. 22 June 1718, aged 72, and his wid. d. 24 Feb. 1739, in her 85th yr. JOHN, Boston, freem. 14 May 1634, had been of the ch. of Roxbury, when adm. but rem. to B. to find, perhaps, wider sympathy for his heresy, was of the number disarm. with the major pt. of fellow worship. Nov. 1637, rem. to R. I. very soon, and is one of the earliest subscr. to the coven. of civ. governm. JOHN, New Haven 1639, of wh. I learn that he had Mary, bapt. Mar. 1641; and Hannah, prob. 27 Sept. 1646. He d. early, for his inv. is tak. 22 Apr. 1652. The wid. Grace m. 1 July 1652, Edward Watson; Mary m. 1 Jan. 1661, John Brown; Hannah m. May 1668, Samuel Hall. JOHN, Marshfield, 1643, m. 20 Oct. 1654, Lydia Read, had Lydia, b. 1656; John, 1657; Isaac; Martha; and Mary; and he d. 11 Dec. 1663. His wid. had admin. His d. Lydia m. 17 Mar. 1684, William Fisher. JOHN, Woburn, m. 14 Oct. 1672, Mary Pierce, perhaps d. of Robert of the same, had Benjamin, b. 25 Jan. 1674, d. next yr.; Mary, 27 Dec. 1675, d. next mo.; and John, 27 Dec. 1677. JOHN, a soldier under capt. William Turner at the Falls fight, 18 May 1676, was k. by the Ind. next day. JOHN, Charlestown, m. Ann or Hannah, d. of John Mirick, unless she were d. of Jacob Leager of Boston, had not long life, for his wid. was praying adv. of the Gen. Ct. in June 1680; nor do I kn. of the ch. exc. by ch. rec. of bapt. Joseph, 17 Oct. 1675; Ann, 16 Apr. 1676; Lydia, 6 June 1680; and Benjamin, 7 Aug. 1681; of course here is little to indicate the dates of b. especially of the first and last. His w. had gain. the benefit for the ch. by join. the ch. 3 Oct. 1675. JOHN, Beverly, m. Eliz. d. of Humphrey Woodbury, had Sarah and Eunice, rememb. in the will of their gr.f. Mar. 1686. JOSEPH, Portsmouth, stood up for Mass. jurisdict. 1665, m. Hannah, d. of Thomas Philbrick of Hampton, wh. aft. his d. m. 29 July 1686, John Seavey. JOSEPH, Stratford, s. of Robert of Boston, m. 14 Nov. 1667, Abigail, d. of Rev. Peter Prudden, had b. at Milford, 5 Aug. 1668, Robert, and at Stratford, Sarah, 23 Jan. 1670; both bapt. 22 May of this last yr.; Abigail, 18 Feb. 1672; Mary, 18 Dec. 1680; and he d. 1687, his inv. being of 19 Nov.

*JOSEPH, Billerica, m. 15 Dec. 1669, Sarah, d. of John Wyman, was freem. 1678, rep. 1689. NATHANIEL, Boston, by our Col. Rec. IV. seems to have obt. gr. of 240 acres in the right of Isaac Morrill of Roxbury, dec. long bef. OBADIAH, Reading, by Eaton nam. as one of the early sett. but of him I kn. no more. PETER, Taunton, s. of James the first of the same, m. Hannah, d. of the sec. Edward Hutchinson, had Hannah; Peter, b. a. 1689; James; Edward, a. 1692; Abigail; and Catharine; and d. 4 Apr. 1711, aged 60; his w. had d. 15 Jan. 1705, in her 47th yr. *PHILIP, Rehoboth 1653, d. 21 Aug. 1679. He was br. of James, and constable 1658; selectman, oft. deac. and rep. 1669. His w. was Jane Butterworth, and ch. Samuel, b. Feb. 1655; Sarah, Feb. 1657; Philip, Mar. 1661; Eliz. 1662, d. soon; Mary, May 1663; Experience, wh. d. 10 Nov. 1674; Eliz. again, 1 Apr. 1666; Michael, Mar. 1668, d. young; Martha; and Ebenezer, 15 Nov. 1676. He was a weaver, bec. the most thrifty man in the town, and his contribution to carry on the war against Philip, the gr. Ind. prince, was £26. being the largest of any in the municipality. Sarah m. 27 Dec. 1677, Abraham Perrin; Eliz. m. 29 Mar. 1687, Henry Sweet of Swanzey. PHILIP, Rehoboth, s. of the preced. m. 31 Dec. 1687, Mary Bowen, had Ebenezer, b. 21 Oct. 1688; James, 3 Sept. 1690; Philip, 13 Aug. 1693; and his w. d. the next yr. By sec. w. Sarah, had Sarah, b. 8 Jan. 1696; Esther; Mary; Ann; Nathaniel, Jan. 1704; Daniel, 10 Oct. 1706; and Stephen, 7 Aug. 1709. *RICHARD, Lynn 1630, as Lewis claims for him, was freem. 14 Mar. 1634, a milit. offic. serg. ens. rep. 1640 and 1, 8, and 9, made a capt. 1653, had Richard, prob. b. in Eng. and Samuel, Tabitha, and Eliz. prob. b. at Lynn, was some yrs. of Reading, wh. town he rep. 1650, 60, unless his eldest s. may have thus serv. in the latter yr. but he went back to L. there d. very aged, says Sewall, and was bur. 16 May 1687, by Lewis, wh. may have authority in rec. aged 95. Tabitha m. 11 Mar. 1663, Daniel King, Jr. and Eliz. m. 2 Mar. 1664, Ralph King. RICHARD, Boston, may have been that shoemaker, wh. emb. at Southampton Apr. 1635, in the James, or perhaps he wh. came from London, the same mo. in the Elizabeth, aged 24, m. 1637, Ann, wid. of Robert Houlton; perhaps had ch. for his unlucky w. being cast out of the ch. 29 Apr. 1639, for intemp. in drink. and other misbehav. was next day, by the civil power, sentenc. to the whipping-post, but the punishm. postpon. bec. she was with ch. of wh. no rec. of b. is found. See Winth. II. 349. RICHARD, Salem, wh. had gr. of ld. 1637, may have been h. of that Persis, wh. join. the ch. 1639; and perhaps was aft. of Manchester, and f. of Richard of Ipswich 1700, for great uncert. prevails. He, or one of the same name, was call. as witness in witchcr. case 1692. *RICHARD, Reading, s. of Richard the first, perhaps left by his f. in Eng. was, I think, rep. 1660 and 73 for that town, may possib. have been of Ipswich, freem. 1671, wh. m. 29 Oct. 1661, Sarah Story, had Hannah, b. 10 Sept. 1662; Sarah, 29 Nov. 1666; Richard, 6 Feb. 1675; and Joseph, 29 Dec. 1679; rem. to Lynn, was made capt. of the troop 1679, and rep. that and the foll. yr. RICHARD, Newton, L. I. 1686. ROBERT, Boston, join. the ch. 1632, was a weaver, freem. 14 May 1634, had Elishua, a s. by the town rec. b. 14, but a d. by the ch. rec. of bapt. 28 Feb. 1636; and she was happy eno. to obt. a more Christian name bef. m.; Zechary, 15 Sept. bapt. 1 Oct. 1637; John, 22, bapt. 29 Sept. 1639, d. young; Sarah, 15, bapt. 28 Nov. 1641, d. at 2 yrs.; Jacob, 21, bapt. 24 Mar. 1644; Joseph, bapt. 19 July 1646; Thomas and Mary, tw. bapt. 22 Apr. 1649, a. 10 days old; Timothy, 1 Sept. 1650; Eliakim, 3, bapt. 4 July 1652; Mary, 1, bapt. 5 Nov. 1654; and John, again, 14, bapt. 20 July 1656, prob. all by w. Sarah, tho. of the first five the name of mo. is not put upon the rec. In a deed of 30 Apr. 1646 from him to Bryan Pendleton, of est. in Watertown, he is styled, I think carelessly, of that town, wherein he never liv. He testif. 10 Apr. 1679, calling hims. linen webster, that he was a. 72 yrs. old, had liv. with f. at Manchester in Lancash. a. 56 yrs. bef. and then kn. Henry Sewall, f. of Henry of Newbury. He was one of the founders of Old So. ch. 1669, and d. 29 May 1687, a "very good man," says Sewall, when noting his bur. 31; and 21 Dec. 1695 d. of his wid. is mark. by the same hand; his d. Eliz. m. 12 Dec. 1660, Benjamin Thurston. SAMUEL, Exeter or Hampton 1644. SAMUEL, Rehoboth, m. Joan, d. of the first Michael Metcalf, wh. names her in his will of Apr. 1654. SAMUEL, Reading, s. of the first Richard, of wh. no more is ascertain. *SAMUEL, Woburn, s. of Augustine, m. 10 Sept. 1662, Sarah Read, had Edward, b. 12 Oct. 1663; John, 2 July 1665; Samuel, 25 Jan. 1667; Sarah, 6 Mar. 1670; Timothy, 16 June 1672; Isaac, 1 Nov. 1677; and Ezekiel, 5 Mar. 1679. His w. d. 1 Nov. 1681. He was freem. 1674, rep. 1689; deac. had sec. w. Judith, wid. of Andrew Alger (wh. had been k. by the Ind. at Scarborough 1675), and was driv. to the W. by the war, and d. 18 Jan. 1704. His wid. d. 14 Nov. 1724, aged 57. SAMUEL, Boston 1654, merch. m. Sarah, d. of Joshua Scottow, wh. gave him in 1672, an est. in B. *SAMUEL, Rehoboth, eldest s. of Philip of the same, m. 11 Nov. 1681, Martha Ide, d. prob. of Nicholas the first, had Samuel, b. 11 Nov. 1682; Patience, 30 Mar. 1685; Timothy, 14 Sept. 1687; Peter, 18 Sept. 1689; Ephraim, 4 Sept. 1692; and Martha, 8 Sept. 1696; and his w. d. Aug. 1700. By sec. w. Eliz. he had Eliz. b. 10 Aug. 1702; and Benjamin, 12 Aug. 1703; and d. 12 Aug. 1712. He serv. in Philip's war, was constable in 1682, afterwards lieut. and rep. 1705; his wid. m. John Smith of Roxbury.

SHUBAEL, Rowley, early the town clk. m. at Lynn, 29 May 1666, Patience Jewett, prob. d. of Joseph of Rowley, was some time at Reading, sw. alleg. at Haverhill, being then capt. 28 Nov. 1677, liv. at Bradford, d. Jan. 1689, and his wid. m. Richard Dole. THOMAS, Boston, brickburner, by w. Ann had Eliz. b. 18 Aug. 1650; John, 15 Mar. 1652; Ann, 27 Feb. 1654; and Samuel, 26 June 1656.; beside Thomas, perhaps eldest; and d. 11 Aug. 1659. THOMAS, Sudbury, by w. Mary had Mary, b. at Boston, as Barry presumes, 9 Aug. 1661; Thomas, 22 May 1664; William, 22 July 1666; Hannah, 26 Nov. 1668, d. soon; Hannah, again, 1669; Daniel, 10 Feb. 1674; Sarah, 25 July 1677; Abigail, 29 Oct. 1679; John; and Eliz. wh. both prob. d. young. He had encouragem. to keep the sch. at Sudbury in 1664, but in 1672, renew. his license for an ordinary. His will was pro. 1697. THOMAS, Boston, brickmaker, perhaps eldest s. of Thomas of the same, m. 25 Mar. 1662, Susanna, d. of John Collins, was freem. 1690. THOMAS, Bristol 1687, one of the founders of the town with famous capt. Church. THOMAS, Framingham, eldest s. of Thomas of the same, m. 1687, Martha, d. of Samuel How, had Thomas, b. Sept. 1688, d. soon; Samuel, 24 Sept. 1689; Obadiah; Martha; Mary; Thomas, again; Asa, 7 June 1702; Hannah, 17 June 1705; Jason, 28 Oct. 1708; and John, 1 Feb. 1714; and d. 25 Oct. 1717. WILLIAM, Salem, gave trouble to the ch. in 1637. WILLIAM, Hingham 1636, perhaps that youth, wh. came 1635, aged 15, in the Elizabeth from London, and possib. br. of Richard wh. was a fellow passeng. and may have been one of the first sett. at Eastham, where he m. 25 Feb. 1655, Sarah Snow, perhaps d. of Nicholas, had John, b. 24 Nov. foll. wh. was k. by the Ind. in 1676; William, 12 Oct. 1657, d. soon; William, again, 2 Aug. 1659; Sarah, 30 July 1662; Eliz. 28 Sept. 1664; and Jabez, 8 July 1668. WILLIAM, Sudbury, s. of Thomas of the same, m. 1686, Sarah Goodnow, perhaps d. of the sec. John of the same, had William, b. 1687; Sarah, d. soon; Thomas, 15 Aug. 1689; John, Sept. 1693; Abigail, 15 Aug. 1702; Mary, 30 Oct. 1706; and Hezekiah, 8 Oct. 1711; and d. 1732. WILLIAM, Eastham, s. of William of the same, had William, b. 1693, and perhaps John, earlier, and Mehitable, later. ZECHARY, Stratford, s. of Robert, was educ. at Harv. says Mather's Magn. IV. 135, but left without degree on acco. of the term of study prolong. preach. first at Jamaica, L. I. 1663 to 8, when he rem. and was made min. of a portion yet no sec. parish at S. not without much disquiet, as the Col. Rec. of Trumbull II. 111, 124, shows; was among the freem. 1669; ord. 5 May 1670; but when Woodbury was sett. that yr. the new town's folk was content. with Walker, tho. he did not rem. his fam. bef. 1678; and so good Israel Chauncy contin. to serve the people of S. reunited. W. liv..

until 20 Jan. 1700, and to Cothren's Hist. of the town, we owe most of
the particulars. He left wid. Susanna by wh. he had Eliz. b. 1 Mar.
1675; but other ch. Zechariah, beside Abigail, wh. d. young, both bapt.
22 May 1670. An agreem. in Mar. 1700 betw. the wid. and Zechariah
and Eliz. W. for the partition of the est. renders this certain. One
Sarah W. aged 17, came in the Elizabeth, 1635, from London, m. not
many yrs. aft. John Tisdale, not Brown, as plausib. is said in Geneal.
Reg. IX. 219. Roxbury town rec. tells, that Dorcas W. was bur. 14
Apr. 1640, but it is beyond my means to conject. wh. she was, unless
mo. of that John, the only man of the name found in that town bef.
and she were too wise to partake his heresy, or too old to rem. with her
s. Farmer marks, that, in 1834, of this name, fourteen had been gr. at
Harv. seven at Yale, and fourteen at the other N. E. coll.

WALKLEY, HENRY, Hartford, one of the first sett. but not orig. propr.
1637.

WALKUP, GEORGE, Reading, m. 4 Nov. 1688, Naomi Stephenson of
the same, says Barry, wh. ment. tradit. that he was a Scotchman, had
Thomas, b. 16 Mar. 1689; George, 6 Jan. 1691; Naomi, 28 Mar.
1692, d. young; Rachel, 29 Jan. 1704; Naomi, again, Apr. 1709; and
Thankful; and d. 1748.

WALL, JAMES, Portsmouth 1631, carpenter, sent over by Mason the
patentee, was a witness to the true deed to Wheelwright, Farmer says,
from the Ind. in Apr. 1838, rem. to Hampton 1643, when his d. Eliz.
m. Thomas Harvey, at Exeter 1646, as our Col. Rec. II. shows, tax. at
Dover 1649, but in Oct. of that yr. is call. of Exeter, carpenter, when
he rec. from Waldron, his right to erect a sawmill with sixty acres, stock
of cattle, &c. at D. went back to H. and in 1654 his w. was d. and prob.
he d. soon. His d. Sarah m. 1663, Thomas Dow. One Joan W. emb.
at London, June 1635, aged 19, in the Abigail. A JOHN, said to have
come in 1630, was of Exeter 1639, and Portsmouth 1640.

WALLACE, is not found in Farmer, nor, I believe, in N. E. bef. 18th
cent. By the Index in sev. vols. of the Geneal. Reg. it was introd. when
Wallis was not seen there, tho. in the passages referred to, if relat. to
men of the first, sec. or third generat. this name appears to be the
true one.

WALLEN, WALLING, or WALLINE, JAMES, and JOHN, Providence,
perhaps brs. and may be s. of Thomas of the same, gave engagem. of
alleg. to the k. May 1682. RALPH, Plymouth, came in the Ann, 1623,
prob. with w. Joyce, wh. surv. him. RICHARD, Providence, engag.
alleg. to Charles II. June 1667, may have had perhaps John, James,
and Thomas, or may have been br. of the last. THOMAS, whose name
is once giv. Walwin, Providence 1645, and there on the freemen's list

1655, may have been br. of the preced. had w. Mary wh. d. 1669, and
prob. by her, s. Thomas, and other ch. d. 19 July 1674. THOMAS,
Providence, perhaps s. of the preced. liv. at P. when he took the o. of
alleg. in May 1682, and thro. the war with Philip. He m. 19 June
1669, Margaret, wid. perhaps of Robert Caldwell.

WALLER, CHRISTOPHER, Salem 1637, tray-maker, had gr. of ld.
1649, rem. to Ipswich, there d. 1676. His will of 17 Oct. pro. 30 Nov.
names w. Margaret, no ch. JOHN, Damariscove, and Monhegin, d.
1670, says our Col. Rec. V. 18, when the Gen. Ct. gave admin. of his
est. JOHN, Lyme, br. of Samuel, m. 28 Dec. 1678, Mary Durin, had
John, b. 10 Nov. 1679. JOSEPH, Boston, by w. Lydia, had Joseph, b. 3
Feb. 1670; rem. to Fairfield, prob. there d. 1672, his inv. 25 Dec. of
that yr. shows very small est. to support wid. and two ch. Joseph and
Lydia. The wid. m. John Davis, wh. rem. to Woodbury. MATTHEW,
Salem 1637, rem. to Providence, there was liv. in 1655 in the list of
freem. and had before been at New London, and liv. there 1667–74.
He had ds. Rebecca, wh. m. Thomas Bolles, as his sec. w. and d. Feb.
1712; and Sarah, wh. in 1699, was unm. SAMUEL, New London, s. of
William of Lyme, d. 1742, very aged, says Caulkins. THOMAS, Boston
1670, a shoemaker, s. of wid. Joan W. wh. m. Francis Croakham, may
have been the same, wh. by w. Martha had Thomas, b. 26 July 1667;
and by w. Mary had Mehitable, 18 Feb. 1675; Sarah, 5 Nov. 1676;
and Jane, 23 June 1678. Ano. THOMAS, was of Providence, 1676.
* WILLIAM, Salem 1637, may have had w. Sarah, wh. join. the ch. 1648,
was of Saybrook 1649, br. of Matthew of the same, rep. 1665, the first
Court after union with New Haven, and oft. aft. a lieut. 1671, m. Mary,
only d. of Reynold Marvin, and had John, Samuel, William, propound.
for freem. 1677, and Matthew. He was of Lyme side.

WALLEY, CHRISTOPHER, Concord, freem. 1682, whose name by Paige
is read Walley from the Col. Rec. and by Shurtleff, Walers; so unusual
a patronymic that I doubt the skilfulness of the clk. JOHN, Boston,
mariner, freem. May 1673, adm. the same day with John W. the merch.
and what is peculiar. vexatious, for a series of yrs. ea. had w. Eliz. and
one or two ch. with same bapt. names; so that the confus. seems inex-
tricab. Prob. he had sec. w. Sarah, and by her Hannah, b. 23 July
1680, and by third w. Eliz. had possib. some ch. certain. Sarah, 27 Apr.
1695. But the first w. m. 3 Apr. 1661, was Eliz. d. of Robert Wing,
wh. brot. him John, 27 Aug. 1662; Eliz. 8 May 1665; Eliz. again, 28
July 1667; Samuel, 1 Feb. 1671; Thomas, 26 Feb. 1673; and after
many hours devot. at var. times to this name, I acknowledge little confidence and less satisfact. ‡ ‖ JOHN, Boston, s. of Rev. Thomas of London, b. in Eng. and came bef. his f. by w. prob. nam. Sarah had Sarah,

25 Aug. 1684; Abiel, 30 Aug. 1686; William, 23 Dec. 1687; John, 19 July 1689; but Bridgman makes him b. at Bristol, 11 Sept. 1691. Strong suspicion is felt that some of these may be ch. of the other John. But indeed the whole is uncert. exc. John. He was of ar. co. 1671, freem. 1673, capt. in the milit. 1679, in 1683 rem. to Barnstable, or other town in Plymouth jurisdict. was engag. much in settlem. of Bristol, and assist. of that Col. 1684, and one of the council nam. in the royal commissn. to Andros 1686. The yr. foll. the overthrow of A. Walley had the disadvantage of being chief milit. officer in the expedit. of 1690 against Quebec, wh. Sir William Phips had project. and of wh. he took all the command; and thus was Walley reliev. of real responsibility, tho. expos. to pop. censure by the errors of Phips. Sir W. on board ship summoned the city, and directed all the land operations of the campaign, for wh. he had no adequate skill, and in the ill success of wh. his eminent. incautious panegyrist natural. saw more of "the hand of heaven" than of the ignorance and rashness of his hero. See Magn. II. 51, the most curious biogr. of Sir William Phips, afterwards made Gov. of Mass. by the f. of Mather dictat. to King William III. Hutch. Hist. of Mass. I. gives Walley's acco. in Appx. In the same charter W. was nam. of the Council, and by the Gov. and Council appoint. one of the Sup. Ct. judges 1700–11. He d. 11 Jan. 1712, aged 68, wh. might be suspect. for 58, if as Bridgman, 34, says he was b. at our Barnstable. Nothing can be more certain, than that he was b. at least 8 or 10 yrs. bef. the com. of Rev. Thomas, for he was an Assist. of Plym. Col. as early as 1684, beside being sw. as freem. 1673. His d. Sarah m. first Charles Chauncy of Boston, merch. and bore him 1 Jan. 1705, a s. of the same name, one of the most disting. divines on our side of the ocean, and prob. she aft. m. a Willoughby, and Eliz. m. 29 Oct. 1713, Rev. Joseph Sewall, and with much study good fam. connex. can be learn. from his will of 4 Feb. preced. pro. 25 foll. It makes s. John Excor. gives him beside ho. ld. and whf. £3,000. two unm. ds. Eliz. and Lydia £1,500. ea. and refers to no other ch. beside Sarah, wid. of Charles Chauncy, nam. her four ch. Charles, Mary, Isaac, and Walley; but neph. and niece had favor, as Hannah, w. of James Leonard, d. of Thomas W. the br. of testat. with her two ch. by first h. William Stone, and also Eliz. Adams, ano. d. of said br. Thomas. JOHN, Boston, s. of the preced. m. it is prob. Eliz. d. of the sec. John Alden, perhaps d. in distant ld. and his wid. m. 30 Apr. 1702, Simon Willard, s. of Rev. Samuel. THOMAS, Barnstable, one of the eight min. wh. came from London (where he had been rect. of St. Mary's Whitechapel) in the Society, capt. Peirce, arr. at Boston 24 May 1663, bring. not as too oft. said s. John, but ds. Hannah, wh. m. 10 May 1664, Samuel Allyn or

Allen, acc. Bridgman, 34, but I prefer the old Col. record, that makes George Shove (tho. so much reverenc. as to be call. Mr. *without* a bapt. name) to m. 18 Feb. 1674, 5, Mistris Walley, wh. in her maidenly glory as d. of Rev. Thomas, need. not other designat. and Mary, wh. m. Nov. 1668, Job Crocker. He perhaps had other ch. wh. d. in London; was call. a man of great esteem, d. on Sunday, 24 Mar. 1678, aged 61, as in Farmer, wh. mistook the yr. by foll. the law, when custom had begun to change the enumera. of the first month in the yr. for the forward not the backward yr. as well from the *first* day, as from the 25th. Bradstreet's Journal of May 1678 ment. of the d. in Feb. or Mar. preced. settles the question. See Geneal. Reg. IX. 49. His wid. Hannah m. THOMAS, Barnstable, s. of the preced. prob. some yrs. older than John, the milit. com. had fam. we kn. as two m. ds. are ment. in the will of their uncle. Perhaps he had one or more sons; but no certain kn. has reach. me. THOMAS, Boston, m. 22 Sept. 1692, Christian Johnson; but I kn. nothing more of either. WILLIAM, Charlestown, m. 18 Feb. 1684, Sarah Marshal, perhaps d. of William.

WALLINGFORD, or WALLINSFORD, JOHN, Dover, m. 16 Dec. 1687, Mary, d. of John Tuttle the sec. of the same, had Thomas, b. a. 1697, and prob. others, bef. or aft. or both. NICHOLAS, Bradford, m. 4 Dec. 1678, Eliz. Palmer. It is strange that we kn. nothing of this fam. for wid. Sarah hav. ten ch. wish. admin. of her h. (one of the ch. may have been that Nicholas) applied to the Gen. Ct. 1683 for some purpose, on wh. the Ct. resolv. that the County Ct. in Essex was authoriz. to do all that was proper. I conject. that her h. was Nicholas of Rowley 1663.

WALLINGTON, NICHOLAS, Newbury, " a poor boy " says the customho. rec. of the passeng. in the Confidence from Southampton 1638, when by the place in wh. his name is insert. I judge that he was, with others, serv. of Stephen Kent; a short time was of Rowley, a. 1663; m. 30 Aug. 1654, says Coffin, Sarah, d. of Henry Travers of N. had John, b. 16 Sept. 1655, d. soon; Nicholas, 2 Jan. 1657; John, again, 7 Apr. 1659; Sarah, 20 May 1661; Mary, 20 Aug. 1663; James, 6 Oct. 1665; Hannah, 27 Nov. 1667; William, 7 Feb. 1670; and perhaps others aft. was freem. 1670; and Coffin says was tak. at sea, perhaps sev. yrs. aft. by some Barbary corsair, no doubt, and never came back. My suggest. is that he is the h. of that wid. wh. is ment. in the article preced. for sometimes the name is Wallingford.

WALLIS, or WALLACE, GEORGE, a youth of 15 yrs. came in the Abigail, from London 1635, perhaps s. of Ralph, wh. came at the same time; in Dec. 1656 was of Rumney Marsh, part of Boston now Chelsea, there had good est. may have been f. of the foll. GEORGE, Ports-

mouth, m. 18 Nov. 1686, Ann, perhaps d. of Richard Shortridge, was of
the gr. jury that yr. JOHN, Woburn, d. 8 Aug. 1670. JOHN, Scarborough 1658, perhaps in the Ind. war was driv. to Gloucester, there was
liv. 1678, d. 1690. NATHANIEL, Scarborough, perhaps br. of John, was
from Cornwall, constable for Falmouth, and sw. alleg. to Mass. 1658 ;
but in July 1660 had three ch. bapt. by Robert Jordan, wh. adher. to
the ch. of Eng. in that her lowest hour of distress, and was censur. for
it, by our Gen. Ct. as the Col. Rec. IV. shows. I kn. he had w. Margaret, and s. John, wh. may have been one of those bapt. acc. the
rubric ; and the fam. was driv. to the W. by the Ind. war, and he sat
down at Beverly, call. hims. 58 yrs. in 1692, and d. 18 Oct. 1709, and
his wid. d. 14 May 1711, aged more than 80. Shurtleff has print. the
name as represent. on the rec. by the wild hand of the clk. but in Hutch.
Coll. 398, and Paige's list of Freemen, I imagine we have the true one.
* NICHOLAS, Ipswich, s. of Robert, m. a d. of Humphrey Bradstreet,
had Samuel, prob. others bef. or aft. or both, was freem. 1674, and rep.
1691. RALPH, came in the Abigail from London 1635, aged 40, perhaps bring. s. George, at least, we kn. that a youth with that name was
fell. passeng. RICHARD, Saybrook 1659, rem. next yr. to Norwich.
ROBERT, Ipswich 1638, had Nicholas, perhaps more. THOMAS, freem.
of Mass. 1643, with prefix of respect, yet my inq. for his resid. is not
successf. WILLIAM, Charlestown, adm. of the ch. 30 Nov. 1642, of wh.
no more than Budington's copy of the copy of that rec. (the orig. being
lost) is kn. to me ; yet I see that somebody of this surname at C. had a
ch. b. a. 1659, tho. the clk. omits name and date.

WALSALL, or WALSHALL, WILLIAM, Boston, with his w. were recommend. by the ch. to that of Lynn, 10 July 1647 ; but of h. or w. I find
not, how or when either was recd. of our ch.

WALSBY, or WALSBEE, DAVID, Braintree, freem. 1651, by w. Hannah, wh. d. 2 Feb. 1656, had Samuel, b. 9 Apr. 1651 ; and David,
1655 ; and 24 Sept. next yr. m. sec. w. Ruth Ball. DAVID, Boston, s.
prob. of the preced.

WALSINGHAM, is a fictitious name, I presume, for Francis Johnson of
Marblehead, by Farmer adopt. from Dana's Hist. Disc. p. 7. See Johnson.

WALSTON, or WALSTONE, JOHN, Killingworth, perhaps s. of Thomas
of Hartford, m. 1677, Ann, d. of Benjamin Wright of Guilford, had
Thomas, b. 1678 ; and d. 1680. His wid. m. 7 Nov. 1683, Dr. Peter
Tallman of Guilford. THOMAS, Hartford 1644, was fin. 20s. for in-
veighl. the affections of Mr. Olcott's maid. That prohibit. of law was
borrowed by Conn. from Mass. The name seems an unusual one ; yet
in the Truelove, at London, 1635, the latest ship in that yr. for this

country, emb. Jane W. aged 19, wh. may have been sis. of the Hartford youth.

WALTER, or WALTERS, *NATHANIEL*, Roxbury, s. of Rev. Nehemiah, ord. 10 July 1734, min. of 2d ch. m. 24 Apr. 1735, Rebecca, d. of William Abbot of Brookline, had Sarah, b. 29 Mar. 1736; William, 7 Oct. 1737, H. C. 1756, the rector of Trinity ch. and aft. of Christ ch. in Boston; Rebecca, 19 Apr. 1739; Nehemiah, 13 June 1741; and Maria, 10 Mar. 1743; and he d. 11 Mar. 1776; and his wid. d. 30 Apr. 1790. *NEHEMIAH*, Roxbury, br. of Thomas, b. at Youghall in Ireland, and tradit. says he was sent by his f. to be apprent. to an upholsterer in Boston in 1674, but H. C. 1684, ord. 17 Oct. 1688, collea. with blessed John Eliot at first ch. freem. 1690, m. 1691, Sarah, third d. of Rev. Increase Mather, had Increase, b. 8 Oct. 1692, H. C. 1711, d. at 26 yrs.; Sarah, 4 Mar. 1695; Thomas, 13 Dec. 1696, H. C. 1713; Hannah, 8 July 1699; Nehemiah, 22 Apr. 1701, d. within a yr.; Maria, 4 Aug. 1703; Nehemiah, again, 17 Sept. 1705, d. young; Samuel, 24 July 1710; and Nathaniel, 15 Aug. 1711, H. C. 1729; was an able man, d. 17 Sept. 1750, and his wid. d. 1758. Sarah m. 25 Sept. 1723, John Walley; Hannah m. 18 Sept. 1718, Rev. Caleb Trowbridge of Groton as his sec. w. THOMAS, Boston, a lawyer, said to have sprung from Lancashire, but sett. at Youghall in Ireland, where his s. Nehemiah was b. 1663, wh. he brot. a. 1678, and 2 Nov. 1680 join. Mather's ch. He had sec. w. Abigail, wid. of David East, formerly wid. of Jonathan Woodbury, d. of Henry Phillips, as the pedigree in Gen. Reg. VIII. 209 shows, and by her had Nathaniel, b. 30 Jan. 1688; and Abigail, wh. it is said, m. 18 May 1721, Benjamin Wolcott; and d. bef. Dec. 1698. THOMAS, Falmouth, is by Willis I. 215, said to have come with w. Hannah, a. 1682, from Salem, where he was a mariner, and sett. at Perpooduck, wh. is now the town of Cape Elizabeth lying across the riv. from Portland, and he adds that his w. was 25 yrs. old at that date; and further, that his s. William in 1732 liv. in Boston, in a deed convey. his f.'s prop. at Falmouth, call. hims. "s. and only heir." But he errs in mak. the late Bp. W. of this stock. *THOMAS*, Roxbury, s. of Rev. Nehemiah, ord. 29 Oct. 1718, collea. with his f. m. 25 Dec. foll. Rebecca, d. of Rev. Joseph Belcher of Dedham, had Rebecca, b. 1722; and he d. of consumpt. 10 Jan. 1725 hav. much disting. hims. in his short serv. WILLIAM, Boston 1674. Sometimes this name, of wh. six, Farmer says, had been gr. in 1834 at Harv. one at Yale, and two at other N. E. coll. has final *s*.

WALTERS, JACOB, and STEPHEN, whose ws. Sarah and Sarah join. the Charlestown ch. 1681 and 2, acc. Budington, 250, seem to me, more truly, as Frothingham, 183, call. Waters, wh. see.

WALTHAM, * HENRY, Weymouth merch. by his business relat. I judge he was from Weymouth, in Co. Dorset, engag. 1635, with Dudley and others, to promote fishing trade, rep. 1636, had Henry, Thomas, William, Ann, and Phillis, prob. all b. in Eng. d. 29 Jan. 1659, unless this were his s. of the same name. HENRY, Weymouth, s. of the preced. may have had Jonathan, and other ch. * THOMAS, Weymouth, s. of Henry the first, was rep. 1636. WILLIAM, Weymouth, br. of the preced. fin. by Gen. Ct. for drunk. 1639, and d. next yr. unm. it is presum. for his will of 3 Nov. 1640, the day of d. mak. f. his Excor. pro. 30 Dec. next, names no w. nor ch. tho. we are indebt. to it for kn. of the f. and brs. and sis. Oft. it is Walton in the rec. but that in Geneal. Reg. VIII. 349, call. him s. of William, may be a mistake of the bapt. name as well as spell. of surname.

WALTON, GEORGE, Exeter 1639, had been fin. for swear. 1638, as our Col. Rec. I. shows; was of Dover 1648, was a vintner, 1662, at Portsmouth, had George, b. 1649; Shadrach, 1658; Dorcas; Mary; and perhaps other ch. by w. Alice; and d. 1686, at the neighbo. town of Newcastle, or Great isl. aged more than 70. His relig. was not suffic. in his old age, to protect him from diabolic. disturb. in 1682, of wh. in Mather's Magn. VI. 69, some trifling report may be seen, but it is slightly shorten. from his f.'s Remarkab. Providences. Similar occur. in the same yr. at the same neighbor. are relat. in the next. artic. in both works. Much of the same wretched stuff in the Magnalia, was by the s. borrowed from the same storehouse. HENRY, Boston, by w. Mary, had Job, b. 29 Sept. 1639; Adam, 8 May 1643; William, 29 Sept. 1645. JOHN, Portsmouth 1640, had come, a. 1638, from Plymouth, in Eng. and aft. liv. here above 20 yrs. was sent by our Gen. Ct. home for his w. in the voyage was tak. by the Dutch, and d. soon aft. JOSIAH, Marblehead, youngest s. of Rev. William, a. petitnr. in 1668, was prob. unm. a mariner, struck by lightning 23 June 1673, at sea, made nuncup. will, as Essex Inst. II. 126 gives. NATHANIEL, Marblehead 1658, s. of Rev. William, was there much esteem. freem. 1680. SAMUEL, Marblehead 1668–74, s. of Rev. William, is by Eaton, nam. among the early sett. at Reading. * SHADRACH, Newcastle, N. H. s. of George, was, in 1689, aft. overthrow of Andros, desir. of union betw. Mass. and N. H. a capt. and major, in Ind. war; engag. in the campaign of 1707 for conq. of Nova Scotia; made a royal counsellor 1716, d. 3 Oct. 1741, aged 83. He was f. of George; Benjamin, H. C. 1729; Eliz.; Abigail; Sarah; and Mary. * THOMAS, Weymouth, s. I suppose, of the first Henry, rep. 1636. WILLIAM, Marblehead 1639, had been bred at Emanuel Coll. Cambridge, where he took his degr. 1621 and 1625, and was, no doubt, ord. and serv. at Seaton, Co. Devon, where it is kn. that sev. of his ch. were b. came in some sh. earlier than has common. been thot. at least drew for houselot at Hingham, 18 Sept. 1635, and was freem. 3 Mar. foll. was but few yrs. at H. prob. longer at M. certain. in 1648, perhaps at Lynn a short time a. 1642, and may have taught for most of his latter yrs. part of ea. season, perhaps at Manchester, to wh. he was activ. as a propr. of Jeffery's cove, in bring. the governm. to gr. incorp. 1645, and d. in autum 1668; inv. of his est. was tak. 23 Nov. of this yr. and he had allowance for his min. serv. up to that time at Marblehead. His w. was Eliz. ch. b. in Eng. were, as is said, John, 6 Apr. 1627; Eliz. 27 Oct. 1629; Martha, 26 Apr. 1632; and at H. was Nathaniel, 3 Mar. 1636; and at M. were Samuel, 5, bapt. 20 June 1639; Josiah, 20 Dec. 1640, bapt. 2 Jan. foll.; and Mary, 14, bapt. 26 May 1644. Eliz. m. a Conant; Martha m. a Munjoy, perhaps Walter; and Mary m. Robert Bartlett. Mather spelt this, in his list of min. of the first classis, Magn. III. 3, Waltham, and his authority (suppos. he must *sometimes* be right) I preferred to Johnson's in my note to Winth. I. 169, for wh. Dr. Farmer admin. gentle rebuke. Increase Mather relat. in Remark. Providenc. the d. of Josiah by lightning, spells the name correctly, as I now have.

WALVER, *ABRAHAM*, H. C. 1647, is all that can be told of this man on our side of the Atlantic. He went home, and was a min. in the shire where his fam. friends liv. as Hutch. I. tells.

WALWIN, THOMAS. See Wallen.

WALWORTH, WILLIAM, New London 1691, with w. Abigail, came from Eng. on invit. of Gov. Fitzjohn Winthrop, to manage his farm on Fisher Isl. had Martha, bapt. 24 Jan. 1692; Mary; John; Joanna; and tw. ch. Thomas and James. He d. 1703, and his wid. surv. until 14 Jan. 1752.

WAMPAS, JOHN, Boston, an Ind. wh. has sev. conveyances of ld. in Boston 1657–68.

WANDELL, THOMAS, Newtown, L. I. 1648, by idle tradit. said to have been a maj. in the army of Oliver Cromwell, and hav. a dispute with the unfledg. Protector, to have fled for safety to Holland, thence to our country, m. the wid. of William Herrick, had no ch. but fine est. wh. he gave to his neph. Richard Alsop, wh. he brot. from Eng. when he visit. home many yrs. aft. and d. 1691. See Riker, Ann. 335.

WANNERTON, THOMAS, Portsmouth, Kittery, and anywhere along shore, where drink was easily got, a milit. offic. in serv. of Mason, sent prob. in 1633, when his Gov. Neal was req. to go home; but he was also one of the patentees in the Laconia gr. perhaps had no w. or ch. yet honor. with agencies of Mass. 1641 and 2; and was k. 1644 in a wild

affray growing out of the rivalry of La Tour and D'Aulney, the French
govs. See Winth. II. 178.

WANTON, EDWARD, Boston, ship-carpenter, had Edward, b. 1658;
and Margaret, 1661, d. young; in this yr. rem. to Scituate, there had,
by sec. w. Joseph, 1663; George, 1666; Eliz. 1668; William, 1670;
John, 1672; Sarah and Margaret, tw. 1674; Hannah, 1677; Michael,
1679; Stephen, 1682; and Philip, 1686; and d. 1716. §JOHN, Newport, s. of the preced. m. 4 Mar. or 1 June 1689 (as the day or mo. be
first read in num.) a d. of Gideon Freeborn, had Eliz. b. 5 Jan. 1691;
Edward, 20 Apr. 1692; Gideon, 20 Oct. 1693; Sarah, 27 Apr. 1696;
Joseph, 9 June 1698; and Mary, 10 June 1700; was chos. gov. of R. I.
seven yrs. from 1734, and d. 5 May 1740. JOSEPH, Tiverton, br. of
the preced. m. 4 Mar. 1689, Sarah, d. of Gideon Freeborn, had Sarah
and Mary, rememb. in the will of their maiden aunt Susanna; d. 1754.
§WILLIAM, Newport, br. of the preced. Gov. 1732 to his d. next yr. m.
1 Jan. 1691, as is shown by the rec. of Portsmouth, R. I. Ruth Bryant,
perhaps d. of John of Scituate, had Margaret, b. 24 Oct. 1692, d. young;
George, 24 Aug. 1694; William, 22 Oct. 1696; Peter, 22 Mar. 1698,
d. young; Ruth, 12 July 1701, d. soon; Edward, 11 Apr. 1702; Joseph, 15 Aug. 1705; Benjamin, 9 June 1707; and Eliz. 4 Oct. 1709, d.
young.

WAPLES, WHAPPLES, or WHAPLES, THOMAS, Hartford 1643, was
still there in the list of freem. 1669, but nothing more is to be found of
him, exc. that he d. 10 Dec. 1671, leav. wid. and seven ch. whose ages
and names appear next mo. at the Prob. Ct. Rebecca, aged 18; Hannah,
16; Thomas, 15; Joseph, 11; Jane, 7; Ephraim, 6; and John, 4. Of
the s. some had fams. but the details are not to be obt. The name is not
kn. to be borne by any now.

WARD, *ANDREW, Watertown, freem. 14 May 1634, rem. to Wethersfield next yr. and with Ludlow, and others, had commissn. from Mass.
to gov. the people at Conn. 1635, for one yr. yet in the docum. in our
Col. Rec. I. 171, his name, on the repetit. is Warner; was rep. 1636
and 7, rem. to Stamford 1641, and Trumbull, Hist. thinks he was of
Hempstead, L. I. 1643, yet in 1653, I find him again rep. no doubt, for
Fairfield; but went at last to the Dutch, and is ment. in Bolton's West
Chester I. 161, as founder of gr. reput. Yet Goodwin gives no coun-
tenance to such a rem. but says he d. at F. 1659, and by w. Esther, wh.
d. not, as he says, in 1667, but early in 1665, he supplies him these ch.
Edmund, William, Mary, Andrew, Samuel, Abigail, Ann, John, and
Sarah, of not one of wh. is the date of b. kn. exc. Andrew's, 1647.
Mary m. the sec. John Burr; Ann m. prob. Caleb Nichols; and Sarah

m. Nathaniel Burr. ANDREW, Kenilworth, or Killingworth, as it was soon barbarously made, s. of the preced. adm. freem. 1668, m. Trial, d. of John Meigs of Guilford, had Andrew, b. 1669; John, 16 Mar. 1671; Abigail, 15 Sept. 1672; Sarah, 15 Nov. 1674; Peter, 14 Oct. 1676; William, 18 Oct. 1678; Samuel, 24 Sept. 1680, d. next yr.; Esther, 2 May 1684, d. next mo.; Mary; and Ann; and he d. a. 1691. ANTHONY, Wethersfield, s. of the wid. Joyce, wh. d. Feb. 1641, was prob. brot. by her, from Co. Rutland; but of him we see no more than the ment. in the will of his mo. 15 Nov. 1640, giv. in Trumbull, Col. Rec. I. 451. BENJAMIN, Boston 1639, with w. Mary, join. our ch. 6 June 1640, was freem. 2 June foll. a ship carpenter, had no ch. was liv. in 1651, to serve on a jury, but d. bef. 1679, as well as his w. when William Holloway appears heir. EDMUND, Westchester, s. of the first Andrew, in 1693, calls hims. of the manor of Fordham in that Co. but no more is kn. of him. EDWARD, Newton, s. of John of the same, m. Grace Lovering, but whose d. she was is unkn. had Abigail, b. 22 Jan. 1699; Esther, 1 Mar. 1702; Mary, 1 Apr. 1703; Sarah, 26 July 1708; Hannah, 26 Jan. 1712; Timothy, 17 Mar. 1714; and Samuel, 27 Oct. 1720; rem. to Needham, and d. Jan. 1749. His wid. d. 30 Nov. 1754. ELEAZER, Marlborough, youngest s. of William first of the same, m. 10 July, as one has it, but more prob. 5 Aug. 1675, Hannah, d. of Henry Rice; had Hannah, whose birthday is not found, but is nam. in the will of her maternal gr.f. when giv. legacies to mo. and ch. She was prob. posthum. and was k. by the Ind. in Apr. foll. His wid. m. 17 Oct. 1677, Richard Taylor of Sudbury. ELEAZER, Newton, br. of Edward, m. bef. 20 Mar. 1707, Deliverance, d. of deac. James Trowbridge, of the same, had Jonas, b. 17 Sept. 1708; Abigail; Ruth, 19 May 1710; Tabitha, 24 Mar. 1712; Phineas, 22 Dec. 1713; Rebecca, 30 Dec. 1715; and Samuel, 16 Apr. 1718; rem. aft. being selectman of N. 1734 to Oxford, and d. bef. 1751. GEORGE, New Haven, is one wh. sign. the covenant 1639; rem. to Branford 1646, and d. 7 Apr. 1653, leav. w. and childr. but no names are ment. HENRY, Hingham, perhaps s. of Samuel, was engag. in the early settlem. of Lancaster, m. at H. Feb. 1660, Remember, d. of John Farrow of the same, had Eliz. but no more is kn. of him. INCREASE, Marlborough, s. of William of the same, by w. Record, had Tabitha, b. 16 May 1675; Record, 28 Jan. 1677; Rebecca, 1678, d. under 20 yrs.; Increase; Eleazer, 12 Sept. 1681; Thomas, 1684; and Oliver, 1686; was freem. 18 Apr. 1690; and d. 4 Aug. as the Ward geneal. says, but ano. acc. 25 Aug. foll. His wid. d. 26 July 1726. JAMES, Ipswich, s. of Rev. Nathaniel, b. in Eng. prob. at Stondon, Co. Essex, of wh. his f. was incumb. bred at Harv. Coll. where he was unfortun. in receiv. punishm. by whipp. at the hds. of the

Presid. in June 1644, and more unfortun. in deserv. the disgrace, yet thot. worthy to have his degr. of A. B. next yr. This strange event is told by Winth. II. 166, without giv. names, wh. are found in the very valua. Hist. of Newbury, by Coffin, 41. His assoc. in the infamy of the juvenile offence, was a s. of Rev. Thomas Welde. He went home, soon aft. prob. with his f. wh. procur. favor for him at Oxford, where he was in 1648, made a fellow of Magdalen, and had a master's degr. and in 1649, an M. D. JOHN, Ipswich, physician, had perhaps liv. in Boston, for a mortg. to him of est. rec. here Vol. X. 233, titles him now of Ipswich, chirurg. and the date is 9 Oct. 1652. His Excor. Robert Paine sold, Dec. 1677, the Boston est. to William Hudson. He perhaps resid. at Hampton 1640, some time at Salem, was cous. of Rev. John, and that benefact. of Harv. Coll. ment. by Pierce, 35 ; also, I presume, the freem. of 1643 ; in his will of 28 Dec. 1652, pro. on new. yrs. day,'25 Mar. 1656, speaks of no. w. or ch. [See abstr. in Essex Inst. I. 50.] His benefaction to Harv. Coll. was realiz. in 1658, as the invaluab. History, by Quincy, shows us : "obtained in horses £72." See I. 513 of that work. JOHN, Haverhill, elder br. of James, b. at Haverhill in Co. Suff k. 5 Nov. 1606, as Mather tells, III. cap. 31, or p. 167 in the London ed. of Magn. Yet "where his educ. was, I have not been inform." he says, "the first notice of him that occurs to me, being in the yr. 1639, when he came over into these parts." In Eng. I found that he was matric. at Emanuel, 1622, and had his A. B. 1626, and A. M. 1630. He had begun his serv. in Eng. "at a very small place" wh. was Hadleigh in Co. Suff k. and in this country, preach. first at Kittery or York in 1641, as Winth. II. 29 relates, but Mather, wh. loves always to be indefinite, and sometimes hides his ignorance under periphrasis, would magnify his watch over the flock at H. to "as many yrs. as there are sabbaths in the yr." We kn. that he was chos. and ord. in Oct. 1645, when the ch. was gather. Winth. II. 252 ; and that flock he could, of course, serve but 48 yrs. He d. 27 Dec. 1693 ; and could the truth ever be sufficient for the author of the Magnalia, he might have call. it a very honor. and protract. course of duty. On 19 Nov. preced. he preach. an excell. sermon, enter. the 88th yr. of his age, "the only sermon that ever was, or perhaps ever will be preach. in this country, at such an age," adds the ecclesiast. historian, tho. since that day sev. more aged pastors have in like kind, obey. their call. He was prob. the freem. of 3 May 1649. By his w. Alice Edmunds, brot. from Eng. wh. d. bef. him, he had Eliz. b. 7 Apr. 1647, wh. m. 1665 Nathaniel Saltonstall, and d. 29 Apr. 1714 ; and Mary, 24 June 1649, m. 3 June 1672, Rev. Benjamin Woodbridge, and d. 11 Oct. 1680. *JOHN, Newton, s. prob. eldest, of William of Sudbury, b. in Eng. a. 1626, m. a. 1650, Hannah, d. of the first Edward Jackson of the same, had Hannah; John, b. 26 Jan. 1654, d. in few mos.; Rebecca, 15 June 1655; John, again, 8 Mar. 1658; Eliz. 18 June 1660; Deborah, 19 July 1662; William, 19 Nov. 1664; Richard, 15 Nov. 1666; Mercy, 27 Jan. 1669; Edward, 13 Mar. 1671; Eleazer, 26 Feb. 1673; Jonathan, 22 Apr. 1674; and Joseph, 15 Nov. 1677. He was of the first selectmen when the town was set off from Cambridge, freem. 1685, rep. 1689 and sev. yrs. aft. and d. 2 July 1708. His w. had d. 21 Apr. 1704, aged 73. Hannah m. 8 June 1670, Thomas Greenwood; Eliz. m. 7 June 1679, Joshua Fuller; and Deborah m. 2 Feb. 1682, John Wythe. JOHN, Newport, came late in life, aft. hear. of d. of his s. Thomas, as inconsist. tradit. tells, prob. a. 1690, took charge of his gr.childr. and d. says the gr.-st. in Apr. 1698, aged 79. Possib. he had serv. fifty-five yrs. bef. in the Parliam. army in the gr. civil war, and that was the origin of the fable as to Thomas. But Thomas d. at mid. age, and as the sacred tradit. of serv. in Cromwell's army belongs to him, and not his f. it will be seen that he was not old eno. to be a powder monkey to the gr. Protector. *JOHN, Branford, a serg. s. of the wid. Joyce W. was rep. 1666, may have been there many yrs. and one of the signers of the new planta. and ch. covenant, Jan. 1668; by w. Sarah, had John, b. 10 Apr. 1650; Sarah; Phebe, 11 June 1655; Nathaniel, 30 Nov. 1656; Abigail, 4 June 1658; and Josiah, 16 Nov. 1661. He rem. soon aft. to N. J. JOHN, Wethersfield, s. of the wid. Joyce, of wh. nothing more is kn. than by her will of 15 Nov. 1640. JOHN, Middletown, perhaps s. of Andrew of Wethersfield, prob. the man sw. freem. May 1667 at Hartford, certain. had recommend. from the ch. of Rowley to that of Wethersfield for hims. and w. m. 18 Apr. 1664, Mary, d. of William Harris of R. had John, b. 15 Nov. 1665; Andrew, 1 Dec. 1667; Esther, 15 Dec. 1669; Mary, Aug. 1672; William, 30 June 1674; Samuel, 1679; and ano. prob. posthum. wh. d. inf. says the careful scrutiniz. of fam. hist. Dr. T. W. Harris. Prob. he d. early in 1684, for his inv. is of the date of 22 Feb. in that yr. and his wid. m. Josiah Gilbert of Wethersfield. JOHN, Branford 1663, drew lot that yr. in 1665, unit. with the other John and many others in project. rem. to N. J. *JOHN, Newton, eldest s. of John of the same, m. 30 Nov. 1681, Mary, d. of John Spring, had Mary, b. 10 Apr. 1683, d. soon; Sarah, 25 Mar. 1685; was freem. 1690, selectman sev. yrs. rep. many; and d. 5 June 1727, leav. will to be execut. by wid. Mary, wh. d. 30 Apr. 1731, and deac. William Trowbridge, wh. had m. 14 Dec. 1708, his only ch. and liv. under his roof. JONATHAN, Newton, br. of the preced. m. 1700, Abigail Hall of Cambridge, had Ebenezer, b. 2 Nov. 1701, d. soon; Thankful, 14 Oct. 1702; Nehemiah,

20 July 1704 ; Remember, 1705 ; Ebenezer, again, 17 Apr. 1709 ; Ichabod, 14 Sept. 1712 ; Mary, 3 Feb. 1714 ; and d. 1723, and his wid. m.
1732, John Woodward. JOSEPH, Newton, youngest br. of the preced.
m. Esther, d. of John Kenrick of the same, had Esther, b. 1 Mar. 1702 ;
Mary, 6 Nov. 1704, d. young ; Joseph, 21 Sept. 1706 ; John, 7 July 1710 ;
Mary, again, 3 Feb. 1714 ; Enoch, 3 Feb. 1717, H. C. 1736 ; Margaret ;
and Esther, again, 11 Oct. 1722 ; and he d. 1742. His wid. d. 1761.
JOSHUA, Salem, s. of Miles, suppos. to be brot. by his f. Miles, m. 18
Jan. 1669, Hannah, d. of William Flint, had, beside three ds. one nam.
Hannah, wh. respective. m. a Pitman, perhaps Thomas, of Marblehead ;
a Collins, of Salem ; and a Moses ; two s. Joshua or John wh. was k. in
youth by a cartwheel, and Miles, b. 11 Mar. 1672, the progenit. of the
num. fam. of that name in that city ; and was lost a. 1678, in a fishing
shallop. His wid. m. a Keyzer, perhaps George. JOSIAH, Branford
1660, drew a lot that yr. and perhaps was s. of George of the same.
JOSIAH, Branford, s. of John, car. by his f. to Norwich, there d. 1713.
*LAWRENCE, New Haven 1639, or soon aft. rem. to Branford 1646, was
br. of George of the same, in 1661 was employ. by the governm. of New
Haven to search for the Regicides, Whalley and Goffe, at Milford, where
it was prob. kn. they were not to be seen ; rep. 1665 and 6, aft. wh. he rem.
to N. J. and d. 1671, at Newark. Seven ch. b. at B. belong. either to him,
or to John Ward, viz. Sarah, 22 May 1650; John, 29 May 1654 ; Samuel,
22 Sept. 1656 ; Hannah, 20 Nov. 1658 ; Eliz. 24 Jan. 1660 ; Dorcas, 10
May 1662 ; and Abigail, 20 Apr. 1665. MARMADUKE, Newport, there
in 1638, adm. freem. 1640, and among them 1655. MILES, Salem 1639,
from Erith in Kent, few miles below London, on the Thames, and only two
from Crayford, came with w. Margaret, had there bapt. a ch. whose name
is not giv. in the rec. perhaps Joshua, b. 25 Apr. 1641 ; John, 26 Dec.
1641; Lydia, 1647 ; and Martha, 11 Mar. 1649; and he d. 1650. His inv.
was tak. in Sept. but he d. in Virginia, 3 Mar. Lydia m. 12 July 1665,
Robert Glanfield ; and Martha m. 2 Dec. 1668, the sec. Pasca Foote.
MILES, Salem, s. of Joshua of the same, m. 1694, Sarah, d. of John Massey, sometimes call. but falsely, the first b. male of that city, had, beside
others, Joshua, b. 15 Aug. 1699 ; John, 27 Nov. 1701, d. under 2 yrs. ;
Miles, 18 Apr. 1704 ; John, 7 July 1707 ; and Ebenezer, 10 Apr. 1710
(this last had ten ch. and from him descend. the late Thomas W. Ward) ;
and nineteen grew up to be m. as he boasted, and ch. and gr.ch. were
91 ; and his w. d. 20 Nov. 1728. He had for sec. w. Sarah, d. of William Ropes, and d. 20 Aug. 1764, aged 92 yrs. His wid. d. 7 Feb. 1768,
aged 85. NATHANIEL, Ipswich, came in 1634, was b. 1570 at Haverhill in Suffk. where his f. John was a min. in high esteem by the Puritans of Elizabeth's day, bred at the Univ. of Cambridge, where he was

matric. of Emanuel Coll. 1596, and proceed. A. M. 1603, serv. as curate at St. James, Duke's place, London, first, and soon aft. had the living of Stondon Massey in Co. Essex, where he was resid. when recommend. for the serv. of the Gov. and Comp. of Mass. Bay in 1629, by the Rev. John White of Dorchester, our effic. friend. But he was not at liberty to leave his flock, until he was driv. from his place, where a new rector was induct. Aug. 1633. Greatly was he honored here, in 1639 unit. with Cotton to frame a body of laws, to wh. prob. he was in some degree equal, as Mather tells us, in a few lines with wh. he begins his life of the s. John, he had first been a student of the law. Yet he was more extensive. kn. by his wit, in the overflow of wh. he produc. the Simple Cobler of Agawam, wh. by its humor almost compensates for his asper-ity. He preach. the sermon for the gen. election, 1641, and was very judicious in dissuad. our governm. from taking side in the strange con-test betw. La Tour and D'Aulney 2 yrs. later ; went home bef. 1647, and preach. to the Ho. of Commons, on the month. fast, 30 June in that yr. obtain. the living of Shenfield in Essex, where he d. 1653. Most clear. did his independ. shine at that day of trouble, for he publish. that ser-mon, when Parliament was afraid to. Against the arrogant claim of the army, that early in the mo. usurp. control of the person of the k. then conduct. a treaty with Parliam. in whose custody he was, Ward support. with abundant spirit the legal power of that body to make a thoro. paci-ficat. Such a bold vindicat. the Commons of Eng. dared not print. Of his fam. our acco. is imperf. but of his s. John and James eno. is bef. ment. and his d. Susan m. famous Giles Firmin. NATHANIEL, Hartford 1638, an orig. propr. was held in respect, m. prob. for sec. w. Jane, wid. of John Hopkins, but aft. some yrs. disgusted with the ch. quarrels, rem. to Had-ley 1660, there, by special delegat. of author. to Pynchon and Holyoke from our Gen. Ct. he and the other Conn. emigr. were adm. freem. 26 Mar. 1661, and he d. May 1664, leav. no ch. His will of 27 May in that yr. gives of his good est. above one half to William Markham, a kinsman, residue to Hadley sch. and sev. friends and relatives. *OBA-DIAH, Sudbury 1654, b. in Eng. s. of the first William, rem. to Marlbo-rough 1662, by w. Mary, m. a. 1667, had Alice, b. 14 Nov. 1668 ; William, 7 Jan. 1670 ; Obadiah, 18 Sept. 1672 ; Bethia, 1674, d. soon ; Mary, 4 May 1676 ; Jane, 1677 ; Edmund, 21 Jan. 1679 ; Sarah, 29 Jan. 1681 ; Richard, 26 Apr. 1683 ; Eliz. 4 Dec. 1685 ; Hannah, 3 Jan. 1688 ; Eleazer, 2 Nov. 1689 ; and Prudence, 1691 ; was rep. 1689, and d. 5 Jan. leaving sec. w. Joanna, m. 20 Dec. 1693, as the fam. report is, d. of Isaac Mixer, and wid. of Joseph Harrington, wh. outliv. him. But I am convinc. that the Ward Family, p. 12, has here fallen into error, for on p. 23 it makes Obadiah, s. of Richard, m. on the same day, the same Joanna, that, on the former page, was giv. to his uncle of the same name. OBADIAH, Sudbury, s. of Richard of the same, m. 20 Dec. 1693, Joanna, the young wid. of Joseph Harrington, d. of Isaac Mixer, had Richard, b. 1694; Obadiah, 1695; Hannah, 1696; Daniel, 1700; Sarah, 1701; Dorinada or Dorinda (if either be not too absurd a name), 26 Nov. 1702; Uriah, 23 Dec. 1704, k. by the Ind. at Rutland, in garrison, 3 Aug. 1724; Isaac, Mar. 1707; and Thankful, 15 Feb. 1712; rem. 1716 to Worcester, there d. 17 Dec. 1717, in his will of the preced. day, prov. Joanna to be his wife, not his uncle's, giv. only to his two oldest ch. portions of his prop. and residue to his w. at her discret. for the other childr. The wid. liv. with s. Isaac in Framingham 1725. OBADIAH, Marlborough, s. of the first Obadiah, by w. Eliz. had Hannah, b. 1704; Jedediah, 14 Apr. 1706; and Jabez, 1707. By sec. w. Eliz. Flood, m. 12 Dec. 1711, he had Thankful, b. Mar. 1713; Mary, 26 Apr. 1714; Sarah, 6 Mar. 1716; Silence, 28 Sept. 1717, d. at 2 mos.; Eliz. 16 May 1721, d. in few weeks; and Beriah, 23 Jan. 1726; and d. 14 Mar. 1752, having made his will, 8 Aug. 1749. RICHARD, Sudbury, s. of William the first, b. in Eng. m. 8 Sept. 1661, Mary Moore, had Obadiah, b. 10 Dec. 1663; and Lydia, 16 Mar. 1665; was drown. 31 Mar. 1666. His wid. m. 22 Nov. 1667, Daniel Stone. * RICHARD, Newton, s. of the first John of the same, m. 15 Dec. 1690, Thankful, d. of James Trowbridge, the first of the same, had Lydia, b. 13 Aug. 1692; Thomas, 8 Jan. 1694; James, 6 Jan. 1696, d. soon; Hannah, 13 May 1697; William, 12 Sept. 1699; James, 14 Aug. 1701; Ephraim, 1703; and Margaret, 28 Feb. 1706; was selectman and rep. sev. yrs. d. 27 Mar. 1739, and his wid. d. 1742. § RICHARD, Newport, s. of Thomas of the same, m. 2 Nov. 1709, Mary, d. of John Tillinghast, had Amy, b. 4 Sept. 1710, d. next mo.; Thomas, 24 Oct. 1711; Mary, 16 Dec. 1713; Eliz. 19 Feb. 1715, d. young; Amy, again, 21 Feb. or July 1717; Isabel, 19 Sept. 1719; Hannah, 4 Sept. 1721; John, 4 Aug. 1723, d. next yr.; Samuel, 27 May 1725; Mercy, 3 June 1727; Margaret, 14 Apr. 1729; Richard, 22 Jan. 1731, d. at 2 yrs.; Henry, 27 Dec. 1732; and Eliz. again, 6 June 1635. He was Gov. of the Col. 1741 and 2, d. 21 Aug. 1763; and his wid. d. 1767. ROBERT, s. of the wid. Joyce of Wethersfield, nam. in her will Nov. 1640, but of wh. no more is kn. by me, unless he be the Robert of Boston wh. by w. Sarah had Hannah, b. 6 May 1660. ROGER, by the diligent Farmer adm. freem. of Mass. 1637, must be a supernum. for no such person is found in the rec. of that yr. nor indeed does a single baptismal Roger turn up. * SAMUEL, Hingham 1636, cooper, freem. 9 Mar. 1637, was rep. that yr. in Nov. and the next in Mar. made town clk. 1646; may have been f. of Henry, and perhaps had more ch. I presume he is the benefactor wh. gave to Harv. Coll. the island lying off the harbor of Hingham, call. Bunkin's or Ward's island, and he may be the same that liv. 1658–77 at Charlestown, and d. there, 31 Aug. 1682, aged 89, wh. as Noadiah Russell in his Diary tells, gave £4. to the Coll.   See Geneal. Reg. VII. 57. His wid. Frances, wh. was not his first w. d. 10 June 1690, aged 83. * SAMUEL, Marlborough, s. of William of the same, b. prob. in Eng. took o. of fidel. 1652 ; was capt. and rep. 1679 and 80 ; m. 6 June 1667, Sarah, d. of John Howe of the same, had Sarah, b. 22 Apr. 1668 ; Joseph, 1670 ; Eliz. 1672 ; Mary, 1676 ; Samuel, Mar. 1678 ; Bethia, 25 May 1681 ; and Daniel, 1687, d. at 13 yrs. and his w. d. 11 Aug. 1707. His will of 22 May 1727, near 2 yrs. bef. his d. was disput. by the heirs on acco. of most of the est. being giv. to s. Samuel.   He had sec. w. Eliz. wh. outliv. him.   Conject. is wholly unable to explain, wh. she was. SAMUEL, Fairfield, among the freem. in the list of 1669, s. of the first Andrew, and d. bef. 1693, leav. wid. Hannah, and ch. Edmund, Samuel, and ds. Hannah, and Sarah, if not more.   His wid. had been w. of Jonathan Nichols of Stratford, and was not mo. of any of these ch. SAMUEL, Branford, freem. 1668, m. 1658, Mary Carter, was not of the number wh. rem. to N. J. as he is found at B. 1679. * SAMUEL, Marblehead, freem. 1665, serg. next yr. lieut. 1670, capt. 1679, m. prob. for sec. w. Sarah, wid. of Mr. Richard Hubbard of Ipswich, d. of Gov. Bradstreet, and he d. a maj. in the expensive and fruitless crusade of Phips against Quebec, in 1690.   SAMUEL, Boston, a cooper whose orig. is unkn. to me, m. 10 Dec. 1691, Mary, wid. of Ephraim Sale, had Joanna, b. 31 Oct. 1692 ; Mary, 27 Nov. 1694, prob. d. soon; Samuel, 22 June 1696 ; and Mary, again, 19 Nov. 1699.   His will of 4 Oct. 1701, pro. 17 Sept. 1702, gives £3. to ea. of his brs. John and Thomas, a silver spoon to ea. of the ch. of his w. by her former h. two thirds of his est. and residue to Joanna, so that we may be sure she was the only surv. of his own four.   SAMUEL, Marlborough, s. of Samuel of the same, was perhaps the freem. 1691, when it was desirable to make a show of names ; by w. Mary had Ephraim, b. 26 June 1705 ; Absalom, 20 Sept. 1706 ; Tamar, 11 Feb. 1708 ; Samuel, 11 Jan. 1710 ; Ursula, 23 Aug. 1711 ; Uriah, 2 Aug. 1716 ; and Benjamin, 10 Nov. 1719 ; and d. 27 Feb. 1738.   His wid. d. 17 Jan. 1758.   THOMAS, Hampton 1639, had prob. come in 1630, and serv. that yr. on the inquest relat. to d. of Bratcher, caused by blows from Walter Palmer, freem. 18 May 1642, when the name is spell. Worde, not as Farmer says 1635, had perhaps other ch. beside Mary, b. a. 1652, wh. m. John Dearborn, and d. 14 Dec. 1725.   THOMAS, Milford 1657.   ‡ THOMAS, Newport, s. of John, came aft. 1690, from Gloucestersh. as is said, had serv. as the most ridiculous tradit. tells, in Cromwell's army, for its crowning serv. was render. on 3 Sept. 1651, in the dreadful field of Worcester, bef. he was eleven yrs. of age; was a Bapt. freem. 1671, chos. an Assist. 1679, when he was only 38 yrs. old, and the progenit. of the disting. family of W. in that State. He d. 25 Sept. 1689, hav. made his will, 9 June 1683, wh. was pro. 2 June 1690. In it he names ch. Thomas, Margaret, and Mary. By his first w. he had two ds. only, Mary, wh. m. Josiah, s. of Gov. Benedict Arnold, Margaret, wh. m. Robert Weightman, and d. 26 Sept. 1728, aged 57, neither of wh. left issue that liv. to be m. and by sec. w. he had two s. only, Thomas, b. a. 1683, and Richard, 15 Apr. 1689, wh. bec. the Gov. of the Col. That he was freem. of Portsmouth 1655, might be seen on p. 300 of R. I. Col. Rec. but *that* surname is a mistake for Waite, as Stiles copied it nearly a century bef. His wid. Amy or Ammi m. Arnold Collins, and d. 11 Jan. 1732. Thomas the s. d. 22 Dec. 1695, aged 12 yrs. and the fam. name was perpet. by the s. not nam. in the testament. THOMAS, Middletown, eldest s. of William by his sec. w. m. 6 Dec. 1683, Hannah, d. of James Tappan. He had sec. w. Eliz. m. in 1714, and d. 2 June 1728. WILLIAM, Sudbury, came in 1639, with five ch. prob. John, b. a. 1626; Joanna, a. 1628; Obadiah, a. 1632; Richard, a. 1635; and Deborah, a. 1637; and sec. w. Eliz. had b. here, Hannah, a. 1639; William, 22 Jan. 1640; Samuel, 24 Sept. 1641; Eliz. 14 Apr. 1643; Increase, 22 Feb. 1645; Hopestill, 24 Feb. 1646; Eleazer, a. 1649; and Bethia, a. 1658; was freem. 1643, rep. 1644; rem. 1660 to Marlborough, and was rep. 1666; was deac. at the first organiz. of the ch. and d. 10 Aug. 1687. He made his will, 6 Apr. the yr. bef. and his wid. d. 9 Dec. 1700, aged 86. WILLIAM, Wethersfield, s. of the wid. Joyce W. of wh. no more is kn. than the ment. in the will of his mo. Nov. 1640, unless, wh. is not very prob. he be the freem. of Fairfield 1657–1669, wh. perhaps was s. of the first Andrew. WILLIAM, Fairfield, s. of the first Andrew, had good est. and his only heir was his wid. Esther, wh. m. 1678, Ebenezer Hawley, was an ens. and the inv. bears date 4 Mar. 1676. WILLIAM, Middletown, perhaps s. of the wid. Joyce, by w. Sarah had William, b. 24 June 1659, d. young; as did the mo. soon; and he m. 28 Mar. 1660, sec. w. Phebe, by wh. he had Thomas, 7 Feb. 1661; Phebe, 17 Apr. 1663; William, again, 2 Aug. 1665; Sarah, 18 Dec. 1667; Ann, 20 Mar. 1670; Dorothy, 5 Mar. 1672; Susanna, 6 June 1674; and John, 12 May 1678; and d. 28 Mar. 1690. His wid. d. 1 Sept. 1691. At the date of his will, 25 Dec. 1688, all the eight last b. ch. were liv. Sarah m. 14 June 1688, Benjamin Hands. WILLIAM, Marlborough, s. of the first William, m. 4 or 6 Sept. 1679, Hannah, d. of Solomon Johnson, wid. of Gershom Eames, not d. as the Memoir in Geneal. Reg. V. 271, gives it, had William, b. 27 May or Mar. as the valuab. Ward Family,

p. 14, says, 1680 ; Bethia, 1682 ; Nahum, 18 Dec. 1684 ; Elisha, 12 Jan. 1687, k. by the Ind. in his 23d yr.; Bathsheba, 16 May 1689, d. young; and Gershom, 3 Jan. 1694; and d. 25 Nov. 1697. His wid. d. 8 Dec. 1720. WILLIAM, Newton, s. of John of the same, and gr.s. of the preced. m. 31 Dec. 1689, Abigail, d. of lieut. John Spring, had John, b. 23 Feb. 1691, was freem. 1690, and selectman sev. yrs. but rem. as Jackson thinks, late in life. WILLIAM, Marlborough, eldest s. of the first Obadiah, by w. Judith had William, b. 9 June 1691 ; Jemima, 5 July 1693 ; Gamaliel, 2 Oct. 1694; Jacob, 9 Mar. 1697 ; Judith, 6 Mar. 1700 ; Keziah, 4 June 1703; and Dinah, 2 Oct. 1704; rem. in few yrs. aft. to Conn. there d. 8 Jan. 1731, and his wid. d. 21 Jan. 1746. Of this name Farmer in MS. finds fourteen among gr. at Harv. five at Yale, and nine at other N. E. coll. 1834.

WARDALL, WARDHALL, WERDALL, WARDLE, WOODELL or WAR-DELL, sometimes WARDWELL (and Farmer thinks the last form may be the most correct), ELIAKIM, Hampton, s. of Thomas, m. Lydia Perkins, was a favorer of Quakers, so far as to show his hospitality, for wh. he was abused, as is seen in the Hist. of Sewel, Lond. 4to ed. p. 330. Of his w. is told in the County Ct. rec. May 1663, the surpris. extravag. behav. in going naked into the meeting ho. at Newbury, for wh. she was whipt, and this seems to have led Bishop, in his New Eng. Judged, to more surpris. vindicat. of her. See in Coffin's Hist. 66. ELIHU, Hampton, s. of William of Boston, m. 26 May 1665, Eliz. Wade, per-haps d. of Jonathan, had Eliz. b. 15 Dec. 1666 ; Elihu, 2 Jan. 1669 ; Prudence, 6 Oct. 1670 ; Jonathan, 26 July 1672 ; and Susanna, 9 Aug. 1684. Part of his life was, I think, spent at Ipswich. JOSEPH, Lynn 1669. SAMUEL, Andover, s. prob. of William, m. 9 Jan. 1673, Sarah Hawkes, prob. as sec. w. by the former or the latter may have had Mercy, wh. m. 31 Aug. 1697, John Wright; and Eliz. wh. d. 9 Sept. 1675. He was execut. 1692, for the damnable or preposterous crime of witchcraft. Farmer says he had Samuel, William, and Eliakim. THOMAS, Boston 1634, perhaps br. of William, a shoemaker, adm. of the ch. 9 Nov. of that yr. and freem. 4 Mar. foll. by w. Eliz. had Eliakim, bapt. 23 Nov. 1634; Martha, b. Aug. bapt. 3 Sept. 1637 ; Benjamin, b. Feb. 1640 ; and Samuel, 16 May 1643; but the last two were not bapt. at Boston, on acco. of the heresy or rem. of f. and d. 10 Dec. 1646. He was disarm. Nov. 1637, as a supporter of Wheelwright, yet in Jan. 1639, as they had long bef. rem. to Exeter, was recommend. from our ch. with eight others to " the ch. of Christ at the falls of Piscataqua, if they be rightly gathered," and in 1643 had commiss. from Mass. Ct. to try small causes there. Perhaps he was of Ipswich 1648. UZELL, Ipswich 1673, carpenter, s. of William of Boston, m. 3 May 1664, Mary

Ring, had Abigail, b. 27 Oct. 1665; Alice, 27 Dec. 1670; Hannah; and Mary, Sept. 1677. He sold est. in Boston 1673. WILLIAM, Boston, on adm. to the ch. 9 Feb. 1634, call. "one of our br. Edmund Quincy's serv." with wh. he came prob. the yr. bef. by w. Alice had Meribah, b. 14 May, bapt. 25 June 1637; Usal, Usual, Uzal, Usewell, Uzell, or other outlandish name, 7 Apr. 1639, not bapt. at B. bec. the f. had gone to Exeter, in disgust for being disarm. Nov. 1637, as being one of the friends of Rev. John Wheelwright, yet was, by our ch. recommend. to the ch. there; came back bef. long time, and had Elihu, bapt. 5 Dec. 1641, tho. the poor copy of town rec. makes him b. Nov. 1642; Mary, bapt. 14 Apr. 1644, a. 9 days old; and Leah, b. 7 Dec. 1646; in each instance the name in town rec. being Werdall. He m. for sec. w. 5 Dec. 1657, Eliz. wid. of John Gillet, or Jillett, and had Abigail, b. 24 Apr. 1660. His wid. Eliz. was liv. 1673. Of the contr. of m. betw. h. and w. and construct. of same by the Ct. during the life of the parties, see Geneal. Reg. XII. 275. WILLIAM, Wells 1649, then sold wine, sw. alleg. to Mass. 5 July 1653.

WARE, HENRY, Dorchester, rec. as townsman, Dec. 1668, on a certific. from the Gov. of being allow. to settle in Mass. *JOHN, Dedham, s. of Robert of the same, m. 10 Dec. 1668, Mary, d. of Michael Metcalf, had John, b. 17 June 1670; Eleazer, 13 July 1672, d. soon; Eleazer, again, perhaps d. soon; perhaps Eleazer, again, so rec. at Wrentham, 28 Sept. 1676; but his w. d. prob. bef. he rem. from D. and by a sec. w. Joanna he had m. at D. Jan. 1680, had Joseph, 2 June 1681; but the town rec. disagr. with fam. geneal. for that latter makes the last named d. b. 1681, and the s. 1682; and the town rec. proceeds with Mary, 15 Nov. 1684; and Zechariah, next day, wh. d. soon; and Benjamin, 8 July 1688; while the fam. geneal. throws in d. Hannah 1686, yet the town rec. of her is 24 Sept. 1687. He went to Wrentham aft. he was freem. 1677, and was rep. for W. 1689. JOSEPH, Salem 1682. *PETER, York, a rep. 1665 and 9, is by me thot. to have wrong spell. of his name in our Rec. and to belong to the fam. of Weare. ‖ ROBERT, Dedham 1643, m. Margaret, d. of John Hunting of D. had John, bapt. 11 Oct. 1646, but Geneal. Reg. VI. 146, says b. 6 Oct. 1648; Nathaniel, bapt. 1 Oct. 1648, tho. in that geneal. said to be b. 7 Oct. 1650; Robert, b. 1 Aug. 1653; Esther, 28 Sept. 1655; Samuel, 30 Sept. 1657; Ephraim, 5 Nov. 1659; and Ebenezer, 28 Oct. bapt. 3 Nov. 1667; was of ar. co. 1644, freem. 1647, and d. 1699. His will of 25 Feb. pro. 11 May, provid. for w. Hannah, and equal portions to ea. ch. exc. larger to John, is abstr. in Geneal. Reg. VI. 146; but the laborious collector must be in error in assum. that this was the Robert impress. for serv. in Philip's war. We can have no doubt, that it was his s. of the same name. Each of the ch. liv. to gr. age. The wid. d. at Dorchester (or, at least was bur. there), 20 Apr. 1721, aged 84. Esther m. 13 May 1673, Rev. Samuel Mann of Wrentham, where, also, others of the fam. liv. ROBERT, Wrentham, s. of the preced. serv. in Dec. 1675, under Mosely in Philip's war, m. 4 June 1677, Sarah, d. of Michael Metcalf, had Robert, b. 6 Dec. 1680; Michael, 11 June 1683; Margaret, 6 June 1685; Jonathan, 28 Feb. 1687; Sarah, Mar. 1689; and Esther, 7 May 1693; and was freem. 1681. Prob. the w. and nine ch. giv. to him in Geneal. Reg. VI. 147, may belong to his s. of the same name. SAMUEL, Boston, adm. of the first ch. 28 Feb. was freem. in May 1675, of wh. no more is kn. and that may seem strange to cursory readers of N. E. affairs. Perhaps he perish. in Philip's war that yr. perhaps he rem. soon. ‖ WILLIAM, Dorchester 1643, ar. co. freem. 10 May of the same yr. but when he came, or how, is not told. Yet that he brot. fam. is sure; rem. within ten yrs. to Boston, was a shoemaker, and d. 11 Feb. 1658, leav. wid. Eliz. and ds. Eliz. w. of John Gill, mariner, and Sarah, w. of Edward Grant, shipcarpent. Abstr. of his will of 26 Mar. 1656, pro. 1 Apr. 1658, may be seen in Geneal. Reg. VIII. 353.

WARFIELD, JOHN, Medfield, freem. 1682, of wh. I find no more, but that he had been of Dedham more than 40 yrs. bef. and had m. Hannah, d. of Robert Randall of Weymouth, wh. in his will of 27 Mar. 1691, remembers her, as then of Mendon.

WARHAM, *JOHN*, Dorchester, came in the Mary and John from Plymouth 1630, having been a min. at Exeter in Co. Devon, where capt. Roger Clap, wh. in his humble, but invalu. tract, gives the best acco. of him, had in his youth, heard his teaching; yet we kn. not, at wh. of the univ. he was bred, if at either, tho. so much may be presum. as he was episcop. ord. At Plymouth, bef. embarc. he with an elder br. in the gospel, Rev. John Maverick, and many of their fellow passeng. had formed a strictly congregatio. ch. He was sw. a freem. 18 May 1631, and the w. wh. he brot. d. 1634, without having any ch. as is believ. Ano. w. Abigail, m. a. Oct. 1662, wid. of John Branker, outliv. him, and d. 18 May 1684, but she was not the mo. of his four ds. for her former h. did not die bef. 1662. He was with the body of his ch. rem. 1635 to Windsor, and there officiat. till his d. 1 Apr. 1670, tho. for near six yrs. preced. a dissatisf. party of the worshippers had desired the serv. of a younger preach. From the whole page of Magn. III. 121, it is found that he was afflict. with melancholy in his latter days, and earlier had deliv. sermons from notes; but betw. these two distinguish. traits of his life, no connex. is pretended by the profound author. His d. Abigail, bapt. at W. 27 May 1638, m. Oct. 1658, Thomas Allyn;

Sarah, b. 28 Aug. 1642, m. 11 May 1664, Return Strong, and d. 26 Dec. 1678; and youngest d. Esther, bapt. 8 Dec. 1644, m. Rev. Eleazer Mather of Northampton, and next Solomon Stoddard, and bore ch. to ea. Of the sec. d. Hepzibah, bapt. 9 Aug. 1640, rept. of her d. 1647 is furnish. The mo. Jane, wh. he m. at W. no doubt, tho. date is not found, nor parent, d. at Norwalk, 23 Apr. 1645, says the Parson's transcr. of Windsor rec. in Geneal. Reg. V. 363, tho. we might be sure this is wrong, for the town of N. was not sett. for more than four yrs. later. She d. Apr. 1655. WILLIAM, Newbury, whose name, says Coffin, is sometimes Worm, and he adds that he m. 10 Feb. 1682, Hannah Adams, d. of the first Robert, had Paul, b. 2 Oct. 1683.

WARNER, ANDREW, Cambridge 1632, freem. 14 May 1634, rem. to Hartford with the body of orig. proprs. but whether Hutch. I. 99, be justif. in mak. him, with Ludlow and other Commissnrs. to gov. the people under Mass. as Farmer quotes him, is to me doubtful. See our Col. Rec. I. 171, where the last of the eight so honor. is Andrew Ward, but in the repetit. of the names in the same instr. becomes Warner. In 1659 he rem. with a new w. Esther, wid. of Thomas Selden, wh. brot. him no issue, to Hadley at its first settlem. was liv. to take the o. of alleg. at H. 8 Feb. 1679, and d. 18 Dec. 1684, or possib. the month foll. aged almost 90. Of his ch. nine in number, we kn. neither the mo. nor order of succession, nor dates, exc. of Isaac, by approxim. a. 1645. The others were Andrew; Mary, wh. prob. was b. in Eng. m. first, 1645, John Steele, jr. of Hartford, wh. d. 1653, and next William Hills; Ruth, ano. d. m. a Pratt; Daniel; Robert; John; and Jacob. Of his wid. Esther, the inv. was tak. Dec. 1693. ANDREW, Middletown, s. of the preced. left Abigail, b. 3 Sept. 1660; Andrew, Mar. 1662; Mary, Apr. 1664; Hannah, 14 Nov. 1668; John, 8 Apr. 1671; Joseph, 20 Feb. 1673; and Rebecca, 12 July 1675; and he d. early in 1682. He may have liv. first at Milford, where Lambert gives resid. to one of the same name 1653. His wid. wh. m. Jeremiah Adams, was Rebecca, d. of John Fletcher, m. 1653, had first Samuel, b. Aug. 1659, d. soon; also John, Sept. 1667, d. in few days. DANIEL, Ipswich 1639, s. of William of the same, and brot. prob. by him, freem. 2 June 1641, by w. Eliz. had Simon, b. 6 June 1658, d. in few days; but prob. sev. earlier; and his w. d. 1 Nov. 1659. He m. 1 July foll. Faith Brown, wh. d. 10 Nov. 1679; and had brot. him Daniel, b. 25 Aug. 1671; Sarah, 22 Oct. 1672; and Rebecca, wh. d. 10 June 1679; but perhaps others earlier. He m. third w. 1 June 1686, wid. Ellen Jewett of Rowley, and d. 9 Sept. 1688; leav. wid. Ellen, and ch. Daniel, John, William, perhaps Nathaniel, Eliz. Abigail, Susanna, beside Hannah, w. perhaps of John or Joshua Batchelder. DANIEL, Farmington, s. of the first John of the same, was engag. with sev. of the inhabs. of F. 1673 in project. settlem. of Mattatock, now Waterbury, but d. a. 1680, leaving Daniel, b. a. 1667; John, a. 1671; Abigail, a. 1673; Samuel, a. 1675; and Thomas, a. 1677. Wh. was his w. is unkn. but she was d. DANIEL, Hadley, in that part wh. bec. Hatfield, s. of the first Andrew, by first w. Mary, had Mary, b. 24 Feb. 1663, wh. prob. d. young; Daniel; Sarah, 24 June 1667; Andrew; Ann, 17 Nov. 1669; and Mary, again, 19 Sept. 1672. His w. d. the same day, and he next m. 1 Apr. 1674, Martha, d. of Robert Boltwood, and by her he had Hannah, b. 24 Jan. 1675; John, Apr. 1677; Abraham, 20 Dec. 1578; Samuel, 13 Apr. 1680; Ebenezer, 5 Nov. 1681; Mehitable, 1 Oct. 1683; Eliz.; Esther, 15 Dec. 1686; Martha, 3 Apr. 1688, d. young; and Nathaniel, 15 Oct. 1690. He d. 30 Apr. 1692; and his wid. d. 1710. DANIEL, Ipswich, freem. 1682, m. 23 Sept. 1668, Sarah, d. of John Dane the sec. had Sarah, b. 22 Oct. 1673; Philemon, 1 Aug. 1675; John, 30 July 1677; Rebecca, 16 Mar. 1679; Dane, and William, tw. 14 Apr. 1680, of wh. William d. at four mos.; William, again, 24 Mar. 1682, d. in three mos.; and Mercy, 5 Nov. 1686; and he d. 24 Nov. 1696, in his will nam. wid. Hannah, ch. Dane, Philemon, John, and Mercy, brs. John and Philemon Dane. DANIEL, Ipswich, s. of the first Daniel, by w. Dorcas had Dorcas, b. 7 Dec. 1700, d. next mo.; and he d. 20 Jan. 1754. ELEAZER, Hadley, s. of the first John, m. 27 May 1689, Esther Taylor, had Esther, b. 3 Aug. 1692; Eleazer, 29 July 1694; Stephen, 3 Nov. 1698; Mary, 30 Oct. 1699; Joanna, 22 Sept. 1706; and Ruth, a. 1712; and he d. 8 May 1729, aged 66. His wid. d. 28 Dec. 1748, aged 82. GABRIEL, Boston, by w. Mary, had Ann, b. 3 Dec. 1681; and Joseph, 22 Nov. 1685; perhaps rem. but whither, or whence he came, or of what descent, are all unkn. GEORGE, New Haven, d. in May 1681, by his will of 2 May in that yr. naming only Edward and George, his s. in O. E. By his inv. of June foll. amount to £36. 2s. 8d. it may seem, that he was only a transient inhab. ISAAC, Hadley, s. of the first Andrew, m. 31 May 1666, Sarah, d. of Robert Boltwood, had Sarah, b. 2 May 1668; Isaac, 13 Jan. 1670; Mary, 6 Jan. 1672; Andrew, 24 Feb. 1673; Hannah, 14 Nov. 1674; Ebenezer, 1676; Daniel, 25 Feb. 1678; Samuel, 14 Mar. 1681; Ruth, 18 Oct. 1682; Mercy, 25 Sept. 1685; Ichabod; Lydia; Thankful; and Mehitable. He d. a. 1691, and his wid. m. 1696, deac. John Loomis of Windsor. JACOB, Hadley, was s. of Andrew, old eno. to take o. of alleg. 8 Feb. 1679, and was sw. into the rank of freem. 1690. His first w. Rebecca, and only ch. Jacob d. 1687; and by w. Eliz. Goodman, d. of deac. Richard of the same, had Rebecca, b. 31 Mar. 1690; Jacob, 29 Sept. 1691; Mary, 22 July 1694; Eliz. 20 Mar. 1696, d. young; John, 10 June 1698, d. in few days; John, again, 10 Mar. 1700; Joseph, 30 Apr. 1707; and David, 4 June 1710; and d. 29 Nov. 1711. JOHN, Ipswich, s. of William, brot. by him prob. for it is said he was b. a. 1616, or he may as well seem to be that passeng. emb. at London in the Increase 1635, aged 20, wh. m. 1655, Priscilla, d. of Mark Symonds, was one of the first sett. a. 1670 of Brookfield, then hav. ch. Mark; John; Nathaniel; Mehitable, b. 16 Apr. 1659; prob. Daniel, 16 Apr. 1661; Eleazer, 13 Nov. 1662; but bef. rem. from I. had Joseph, 15 Aug. 1657, wh. d. at 10 mos.; and Daniel, 1660, wh. d. 8 June of that yr; beside Mark and John, some of wh. were perhaps by a former w. On the destr. of B. in Philip's war, he found refuge at Hadley, where Mark had sett. bef. and Mehitable d. 12 June 1678; and he prob. d. there. JOHN, Providence 1637, m. Priscilla, d. of Ezekiel Holliman, and perhaps his only ch. one of the orig. purch. from the Ind. of Shawomet, of whom Samuel Gorton was chief, and was involv. with him in the violent proceeding of Mass. against that humble col. brot. prisoner to Boston, in Oct. 1643, but was set at liberty in Mar. aft. and in 1652, hav. differ. with Gorton, Holden, Greene, and Potter, old friends, was indulg. with leave to ship hims. and fam. for Eng. from any of the ports of Mass. "provid. he take up his abode in the ship, and thence not to come forth until his depart. exc. upon urgent occasion for his voyage, by order from two magistr." Col. Rec. III. 274 and Winth. II. 147 and 8. Such tyran. acts did not prevent him from desir. to come back from Eng. but the fam. tradit. is, that the vessel in wh. he was emb. for his ret. perish. with all on board. He left here only Rachel, wh. was then a babe, m. 16 Nov. 1669, Abel Potter; and John, b. 1 Aug. 1645, with Susan and Mary, were carr. to Eng. whence John alone came back, being sent for by gr.f. Holliman, in 1658, to inherit his est. JOHN, Farmington, had been of the early sett. of Hartford, m. 1649, Ann Norton, d. of the first Thomas; freem. 1664, as was JOHN jr. of the same town soon aft. both names being in the list of 1669. The sen. went in 1673, to view Matatock, to ascert. if it were desirable to plant there. He was, Hinman says, p. 90, a soldier in the Pequot war, d. 1679, leav. wid. Margaret and s. Daniel; John; Thomas; and s.-in-law, h. of his d. Sarah, William Higginson, to wh. he gave the tr. of ld. grant. by the Col. of Conn. for his serv. The younger John foll. the recommend. of good ld. at Waterbury, former. Mattatock, but d. 1707, at F. hav. had John; Ephraim; Robert; Ebenezer; and Lydia, bapt. 13 Mar. 1680, wh. m. Samuel Brunson; and Thomas, 6 May 1683. JOHN, Middletown, prob. br. of Andrew of the same, m. 14 Dec. 1669, Ann Ward; but if that be true, nothing else can be, of the issue in Geneal. Reg. XIV. 135. JOHN, Warwick, s. of John of the same, was bd. apprentice to William Field for 7 yrs. from 1 Aug. 1659, m. 4

Aug. 1670, Ann, d. of the great heretic Samuel Gorton, had John, b. 5
June 1673; Ezekiel; Ann; and Priscilla; and d. 9 May 1712. JOHN,
Ipswich, m. 20 Apr. 1665, Hannah Batchellor, d. of Joshua of the same,
had Eliz. b. 30 June 1666; William, 22 Sept. 1672, d. soon; William,
again, 20 June 1673, d. next mo.; Hannah, 14 May 1674; Susanna, 3
Mar. 1677; William, again, 2 Mar. 1679, d. young; and Abigail, 18
Oct. 1681, d. at 2 mos. His w. was bur. 10 Mar. 1688, and perhaps he
had ano. w. JOHN, Hadley, s. of John the first, m. 2 Apr. 1674, Lydia,
d. of Robert Boltwood, rem. to Springfield bef. more than one of his ch.
was b. had Lydia; Priscilla, b. 11 Apr. 1677; John, 22 Feb. 1679;
Ebenezer, 16 Feb. 1681; and Mary, 15 Jan. 1683, d. in two weeks.
His w. d. bef. the babe; and he m. a sec. w. Sarah Warner, 31 Aug.
1683, and had Nathaniel, b. 19 Aug. 1684, beside two other ch. wh. d.
without name, and he m. 30 June 1687, Sarah Ferry wh. had no ch. but
d. 25 July 1689; and a fourth w. was Rebecca Cooley, the wid. of Obadiah, m. 26 Nov. 1691, wh. brot. no ch. and d. 18 Oct. 1715. He d. 21
Jan. 1724. His will of 1718, names a d. Sarah Dewey, whose mo. we
kn. not. JOHN, Cambridge, a soldier in Philip's war, for a wound was
grant. 1678, by our Gen. Ct. the sum of £3. JOHN, Woburn, had
John, b. 26 May 1684; Sarah, 18 Mar. 1686; and perhaps rem.
JOHN, Middletown, prob. s. of the first Andrew, d. 24 June 1700, leav.
John, Jonathan, and other ch. beside reps. of a d. Mary, wh. had m.
John North, and was dec. JOSEPH, Hadley, the freem. of 1673, is ot
unkn. lineage. MARK, Hadley, s. of the first John, m. 8 Dec. 1671,
Abigail, d. of Richard Montague, had Abigail, b. 18 Aug. 1675; and
Mark, 20 Feb. 1678; and was freem. 1683; rem. to Northampton a.
1684, thence to Westfield, after d. of his w. 1705, where he m. 1713,
wid. Mary Root of W. wh. d. 1732; but ret. on her d. to Northampton,
there d. 3 May 1738, aged 92, perhaps. NATHANIEL, Ipswich, perhaps
s. of the first Daniel, m. 24 Nov. 1673, Hannah Boynton, perhaps d. of
William, had Nathaniel, b. 20 Mar. 1677, wh. d. at 20 yrs.; Daniel, 11
Feb. 1678, d. at 8 yrs.; John, 12 Oct. 1679, d. next mo.; Hannah, 13
Feb. 1681, d. young; and Hannah, again, posthum. 28 Aug. 1684.
He was freem. 1675, d. bef. 29 Apr. 1684; and his wid. d. in less than
10 yrs. NATHANIEL, Hadley, br. of Mark, with him, and br. John, and
some cous. took o. of alleg. 8 Feb. 1679, m. 3 Feb. 1680, Joanna Gardner, d. of Samuel, had a ch. a. 12 Oct. 1680, whose name is not found;
Nathaniel, 28 Sept. 1681, wh. was k. at Deerfield, in the surpr. by the
Fr. and Ind. 29 Feb. 1704; John, 3 Sept. 1683; Samuel, 15 Jan. 1686,
by town rec. but 29 Jan. by ano. rec. yet prob. a differ. of a yr. renders
it likely there were two of the name; Daniel, 7 Aug. 1690; and Israel,
16 Apr. 1696. He was freem. 1683, and d. 15 Jan. 1713, aged 64;

and the wid. d. 18 Mar. 1729, aged 66. Both were bur. at H. PHILE-
MON, Ipswich, perhaps s. of Daniel the first, m. 27 Apr. 1690, Abigail
Tuttle, had Philemon, b. 7 Jan. 1698; and Daniel, 20 May 1699.
RALPH, Dorchester, adm. inhab. 11 July 1664; but no further ment. is
found of him, unless as to me seems prob. he were of Newtown, L. I. in
few yrs. *ROBERT, Middletown, s. of Andrew the first, was freem. 1657,
rep. 1663, 4, 5, by first w. Eliz. Grant, m. Feb. 1655, had Samuel, b.
Sept. 1656, d. young; Seth, 1 Mar. 1658; Eliz. Mar. 1660; John, 1
Feb. 1662; Mary, Sept. 1664; Sarah, 6 Mar. 1670; and Mehitable, 21
Nov. 1673; this w. d. 26 Dec. 1673; and by sec. w. Deliverance, wid.
of John Rockwell, had Ruth, Nov. 1675; Bethia, 8 Oct. 1680; and
Samuel, 9 or 19 May 1683. He d. 10 Apr. 1690; and his wid. m. a
Bissell, as from the indistinct express. of Geneal. Reg. XIV. 135, may
be hazardous. infer. and she d. 12 June 1718. SAMUEL, Ipswich, whose
f. is not kn. m. 21 Oct. 1662, Mercy Swan, perhaps d. of Richard of
Rowley, had Priscilla, b. 25 Sept. 1666; Samuel, 5 July 1668; John, 2
Aug. 1670, d. within a yr.; Dorothy, 2 June 1672; Sarah, 28 May
1674; and Richard, 13 Aug. 1676. He was freem. 1675. SAMUEL,
Springfield, or Hadley, by my conject. is the man assoc. with Thomas
Parsons, in votes for reimburs. to them by our Gen. Ct. Vol. V. 58 and
75, for cattle tak. by a commiss. for the use of troops in 1675, as I judge.
SETH, Middletown, s. of Robert, m. Mary Ward, whose f. is not seen,
had Mary, b. 1 Dec. 1687; Robert, 22 June 1692; Samuel; and Seth,
29 July 1705; and d. 28 Nov. 1713. His wid. d. 17 July 1729.
THOMAS, Wells, wh. took the o. of alleg. to Mass. 1653, may be the
same wh. in 1639, had been fined [Rec. I. 270] for a quarrel with
Richard Rodman; and perhaps was the fisherman wh. d. at Boston
1660. THOMAS, Norwalk, sold 1 Sept. 1665, his ho. and lds. says Hall,
wh. tells no more; and I conject. that he was k. by the Ind. at Hatfield,
19 Oct. 1675, prob. a soldier. THOMAS, Waterbury, s. of the first John
of Farmington, by w. Eliz. had John, b. 1680; Mary, 1682; Martha
and Thomas, tw. 1687 ; Samuel, 1690; and Margaret, 1693; and he d.
1714. WILLIAM, Ipswich, one of the earliest sett. 1637, had Daniel,
and John, beside a d. wh. m. Thomas Wells. WILLIAM, Wethersfield,
s. of Daniel of Ipswich, by w. Hannah, m. 1667, had William, b. 1672 ;
John, 1676; Daniel, 1680; Abigail, 1683, d. soon; Abigail, again,
1685 ; beside Hannah, perhaps the first b. was deac. and d. 28 Feb.
1714 ; and his wid. d. 3 Mar. aft. Twelve of this name had been gr. at
Yale, two at Harv. and eight at other N. E. coll. in 1834, as Farmer
notes.

WARR, ABRAHAM, Ipswich, as print. in Geneal. Reg. VIII. 165, must
be abbrev. of Warren.

WARREN, sometimes spelt WARIN, or WARINS, ABRAHAM, Salem
1637, was of Ipswich 1648, where he d. 1654, his will of 22 Apr. in
that yr. (Essex Inst. I. 10) ment. d. Sarah, and wid. not her mo.
ARTHUR, Weymouth, was in Mar. 1638, charg. with keep. comp. with
the w. of Clement Briggs, and in June foll. she was enjoin. not to come
into his comp. but this does not, of necessity, prove any guilt, and soon
after he m. and had Arthur, b. 17 Nov. 1639; Abigail, 27 Oct. 1640;
Jacob, 26 Oct. 1642; and Joseph, whose date of b. is not mark. nor is d.
of the f. ascert. He was one of the petitnrs. 1645, for gr. of the Narraganset ld. suppos. to be forfeit. by the heresy of Gorton, Holden, and
the others just proprs. Abigail m. a Wright. ARTHUR, Chelmsford,
perhaps s. of the preced. m. Abigail, d. of John Rogers of Billerica, and
d. 25 Apr. 1671. His will of 7 Mar. preced. speaks of w. and ch. and
the young wid. d. 15 June foll. Her will, casual. burnt in Oct. was pro.
13 Nov. next. BENJAMIN, Plymouth, s. of the first Joseph, m. 1697,
Hannah Morton, had Benjamin, b. 1698, d. young; Abigail, 1700;
Hannah, 1704; Nathaniel, 1706; Benjamin, again, 1709; and Priscilla,
1712. By sec. w. Esther Cushman, d. or wid. of unkn. Cushman, m.
1716, he had Joseph, and Mary, wh. prob. both d. young, and he d.
1745. DANIEL, Watertown, s. of the first John, b. in Eng. m. 10 Dec.
1650, Mary, eldest d. of Ellis Barron, had Mary, b. 29 Nov. 1651;
Daniel, 6 Oct. 1653; Hannah; Sarah, 4 July 1658; Eliz. 17 Sept.
1660; Susanna, 26 Dec. 1663, d. under 15 yrs.; John, 5 Mar. 1666;
Joshua, 4 July 1668; and Grace, 14 Mar. 1672. He sw. fidel. 1652,
was selectman betw. 1680 and 98, twelve yrs. Mary m. 29 May 1668,
John Child, and next, 13 Apr. 1677, Nathaniel Fiske; Hannah m. 24
Sept. 1675, David Mead; Eliz. m. 6 Dec. 1681, Jonathan Tainter; and
Grace m. 20 Jan. 1691, Joseph Morse. * DANIEL, Watertown, s. of the
preced. freem. 1690, m. 19 Dec. 1678, Eliz. d. of John Whitney of the
same, had Eliz. b. 16 Oct. 1679, d. at 16 yrs.; Ruth, 15 Oct. 1681;
Mary, 25 Jan. 1684, d. young; Daniel, 30 Apr. 1686; Hannah, 25 Jan.
1691; Sarah, wh. was bapt. 14 Dec. 1701; Jonas, or possib. Josiah, 25
July 1695; Jonas, 30 Apr. 1697; Deliverance, 10 Oct. 1699; and
Mary, bapt. 2 May 1703. He was oft. selectman, rep. 1701. EPHRAIM,
Boston, by w. Eliz. had Sarah, b. 10 Aug. 1685, but no more is kn. of
him. HUMPHREY, a man of wh. no more is heard, but that in 1678 he
was nam. by the crown with Edmund Randolph and some of the princ.
gentlemen, to take the Gov's. o. of alleg. as told by Hutch. I. 330, of wh.
the Gov. inform. the Gen. Ct. that in Aug. he perform the duty as in
Col. Rec. V. 191. Perhaps he was nothing but an official and soon
went home. JACOB, Chelmsford, freem. 1674, perhaps was one of the
first sett. at Plainfield a. 1700, or it may have been a s. of the same

name. JAMES, Kittery 1656 or earlier, then had gr. of ld. was of the gr. jury 1666, liv. in the upper part, wh. bec. Berwick, made his will 9 Dec. 1700, which was pro. 24 Dec. 1702, names w. Margaret, s. Gilbert, and James, ds. Margaret, and Grizzel, and gr.ch. Jane Grant, and James Stackpole. JAMES, Plymouth, s. perhaps youngest of Nathaniel of the same, m. 1687, Sarah, eldest d. of the sec. Edward Dotey, had John; Edward; both d. young; Sarah; Alice; Patience; James, b. 1700; Hope; Mercy; Mary; and Eliz. of wh. the last three d. unm. He was gr.f. of the emin. James, Presid. of Mass. Counc. 1779. JOHN, Watertown, came prob. 1630, in the fleet with Sir Richard Saltonstall, then aged a. 45, and hav. w. and ch. (four certain. are nam. in his will, and of them only Eliz. could be b. here). There may have been others, but no rec. of b. or d. is found. He was adm. freem. 18 May 1631, chos. selectman 1636–40. Late in life he fell under the censure of the laws, unwisely levelled at dissent. from the relig. course of the major part of the inhab. and Bond informs us of proceedings against him in 1651, 4, and 61; but he d. in peace, 13 Dec. 1667, aged 82. His w. Margaret d. 6 Nov. 1662. She was prob. the mo. of all his ch. John, b. 1622; Mary; and Daniel, b. 1628; beside Eliz. wh. m. a. 1654, James Knapp. Mary m. 30 Oct. 1642, John Bigelow. He had good est. in lds. in W. His will of 30 Nov. 1667, names the four ch. and Mary, w. of Daniel, gr.ch. Daniel W. and Mary Bigelow. JOHN, Watertown, s. of the preced. prob. the freem. of 1645, m. 11 July 1667, Michal, d. of Robert Jennison, wid. of Richard Bloise of the same, had Margaret, b. 6 May 1668; Sarah, 25 Jan. 1671; Eliz. 8 July 1673; Mary, 25 May 1675; John, 21 May 1678; Grace, 12 Mar. 1680; and Samuel, 23 Jan. 1683; was a capt. and d. 1703. His will of 12 Jan. of that yr. was pro. 22 Feb. foll. It names all the ch. exc. Sarah, wh. perhaps d. young. Eliz. m. 18 Oct. 1705, Daniel Harrington; and Mary m. 30 Dec. 1698, Joseph Pierce. JOHN, Ipswich 1654. JOHN, Boston, tobacconist, or cardmaker, as in the will he is call. by first w. had Joshua; Thomas; Mary, b. a. 1665; and perhaps Sarah; but the name of his w. is unkn. nor is any b. found on the rec. so that it seems prob. that he had these ch. in ano. town, where the mo. may have also d. I think he was early of Exeter, there m. 21 Oct. 1650, Deborah Wilson, wh. d. 26 June 1668. In 1669, he m. Eliz. wid. of John Combs, wh. had d. in May of the yr. preced. She had first been wid. of Thomas Barlow. By this w. he had Nathaniel, b. 27 May 1670, and this w. d. next yr. or early in 1672, for in Feb. of this yr. he exhibit. inv. of her goods, and engag. to fulfil her desire towards her three ds. and his s. by her, in their distrib. to one Barlow, two Combs, and Nathaniel. This s. and Mary Combs, in 1685, chose for their guardian, Joseph Ryall of Charlestown, wh. they call.

uncle. A third w. Eliz. brought him Abigail, 10 May 1676; and John, posthum. 10 Feb. 1678. He may have been the freem. of 1670, and d. in July 1677, mak. his will 10, wh. was pro. 31 of that mo. and his wid. 4 Oct. 1681, bec. sec. w. of Samuel Lendall, by contr. of that date, in wh. he provid. good portion for her, as did also her third h. John Hayward, the Not. Pub. to wh. 1685, she bec. sec. w. and for her fourth h. she had a rich man, Phineas Wilson of Hartford. Neither of the last three hs. had by her any ch. He seems to have had small est. and in his will is nothing of interest exc. the gift to his s. Joshua, "my engine with wh. I cut tobacco." JOHN, Ipswich 1670, may have been the man at Salem long aft. wh. was a spinner, and in 1685 had loan from the town treas. of £5. to pay his work people. See Felt, Ann. II. 159. JOHN, Watertown, s. of the first Daniel, m. 22 May 1683, Mary, d. of Jonathan Brown of the same, had John, b. 15 Mar. 1685; Jonathan, 26, bapt. 29 Apr. 1688; and Daniel, bapt. 1 Sept. 1689; was ens. freem. 1690, and d. 11 July 1703. His wid. m. 14 Mar. 1704, Samuel Harrington. JOHN, Watertown, s. of John sec. m. Abigail, d. of John Hastings, had John, b. 3 Apr. 1701; Sarah, 20 Sept. 1702; Samuel, 18 Mar. 1704; Thomas, 11 Mar. 1706; and David, 22 June 1708. His w. d. 19 July 1710, and he m. 14 May 1711, Lydia, d. of Nathaniel Fiske, had Benjamin, 4 Apr. 1715; David, 8 Jan. 1717; Abigail, 28 Oct. 1719; Lucy, 26 Oct. 1721; William, 21 Oct. 1723, d. at 15 yrs.; and John, bapt. 1725. He d. next yr. and his wid. m. 17 June 1730, Benjamin Harrington. *JOSEPH, Plymouth, s. of Richard, but not eldest in my judgm. tho. so call. in the Warren Geneal. that may have unconsciously been influenc. by the baptismal designat. was not brot. by his mo. from Eng. m. a. 1651, Priscilla, sis. of the famous rul. elder Thomas Faunce, whose f. had been fellow-passeng. with his mo. was held in gr. esteem 1677, rep. by ann. elect. 1681–6, and d. 1689. His wid. d. 1707. Of his ch. it will be very hard to find exact dates of b. but the order is confident. trusted; Mercy, b. 23 Sept. 1653; Abigail, 15 Mar. 1655, d. young; Joseph, 8 Jan. 1657; Patience, 15 Mar. 1660; Eliz. 15 Aug. 1662; and Benjamin, 8 Jan. 1670. Mercy m. Winsor says, 1674, or 5 Feb. 1675, as the Bradford Geneal. has it, John Bradford, liv. with him near 62 yrs. and d. Mar. 1747. Patience m. 1686, Samuel Lewis, as the name seems prob. to be read, and Eliz. m. 19 Jan. 1688, Josiah Phinney. It is observ. that his male descend. since the fourth generat. are confin. to those of his gr.-gr.ch. Benjamin. JOSEPH, Plymouth, eldest s. of the preced. m. 1692, Mehitable Wilder, had Joseph, b. 1694; and Priscilla, 1696; and he d. the same yr. JOSEPH, Roxbury, housewright, sec. s. of Peter of Boston, m. Deborah, d. of Samuel Williams of Roxbury, had Samuel, b. 13 Aug. 1694, d. in few days; Joseph, 2 Feb.

1696; Ebenezer, 26 Jan. 1699; Sarah, 27 July 1702; John, 18 Sept. 1704; and Hannah, 31 Mar. 1707; and he d. 13 July 1729. His wid. d. 6 Oct. 1743. In the Geneal. of Warren, print. 1854, p. 45, the most sumptuous vol. of genealogy ever issued from the press on our side of the water, they are said to have had eight ch. but the rec. contains no more than the above, nor does the pedigree at the opening of the book. In his will of 22 Jan. bef. d. he gives all his real and personal est. to s. Joseph, exc. the household goods giv. to w. orders him to pay her £8. per an. keep a cow for her, find. 2 bls. of cider, and one cord of wood per an. for her, beside the choice of one room in his dw.-ho. during her wid. But of the ch. Samuel and Sarah are not ment. so that I presume the first was d. and the other had got changed into Deborah, wh. is the name marked aft. Ebenezer and John, yet bef. Hannah, and to ea. of these four, Joseph was direct. to pay £65. He was gr.f. of the illustrious patriot, Maj.-Gen. Joseph Warren, k. at Bunker Hill. JOSHUA, Watertown, s. of Daniel the first, m. Rebecca, d. of Caleb Church of the same, had Lydia, b. 3 Nov. 1696; Joshua, 4 June 1698; Nathaniel, 25 May 1700; Rebecca; Eliz. 19 June 1704; Abigail, 20 Dec. 1705; Susanna, 2 Feb. 1707; Hannah, 2 June 1708; Prudence, 5 Dec. 1709; Daniel, 28 July 1712; and Phineas, 21 June 1718; and d. 30 Jan. 1760. *NATHANIEL, Plymouth, s. prob. elder of Richard, m. 1645, Sarah Walker, as the Geneal. says, and that work names ch. Richard; Jabez, wh. d. young; Sarah, b. 29 Aug. 1649; Hope, 7 Mar. 1651; Jane, 10 Jan. if Col. Rec. be true, or 31 Dec. 1652; Eliz. 5 Sept. 1654; Alice, 2 Aug. 1656; Mercy, 20 Feb. 1658; Mary, 9 Mar. 1660; Nathaniel, 19 Mar. 1662; John, 23 Oct. 1663, d. young; and James, 7 Nov. 1665; and d. 1667. Very short abstr. of his will is found in Geneal. Reg. VII. 177. His wid. d. 1700. Sarah m. somebody call. Blackwell, unkn. to me; Jane m. 19 Sept. 1672, Benjamin Lombard of Barnstable; Eliz. m. a Green, but the individ. is unkn.; Alice m. Thomas Gibbs; Mercy m. Jonathan Delano; and it is said that Mary m. but the h. is unkn. and the dates of all the ms. but one are defic. NATHANIEL, Plymouth, s. of the preced. m. Phebe Murdock, it is said, but left no issue, was a man of reput. and d. 1707. PETER, Boston 1659, mariner, purchas. 23 Mar. of that yr. from Theodore Atkinson, dwel.-ho. and ld. m. 1 Aug. 1660, Sarah, d. of Robert Tucker of that part of Dorchester, wh. soon aft. was incorp. as Milton, had John, b. 8 Sept. 1661, d. young; Joseph, 19 Feb. 1663; Benjamin, 25 July 1665; Eliz. 4 Jan. 1668; these three bapt. 29 May 1670; Robert, 14, bapt. 25 Dec. 1670; Ebenezer, 11 Feb. bapt. 2 Mar. 1673; and by sec. w. Hannah had Peter, bapt. 6 June 1675, d. soon; Peter, again, b. 20, bapt. 23 Apr. 1676; Hannah, b. 19 May 1680, whose bapt. is not found;

Mary, 21, bapt. 25 Nov. 1683; and Robert, 27 Dec. 1684, bapt. 4 Jan. foll. but the town rec. blunders the name of the mo. into Abigail. He had third w. Esther, whose name was, but whether as wid. or maid. is uncert. Woodward, rec. into the third ch. 11 Oct. 1687, as had been the first w. 22 May 1670, and the sec. 30 Apr. 1675. He d. 15 Nov. 1704, by his will of 20 June 1700, provid. for w. during wid. not otherwise, yet making her joint excor. with s. Joseph, and nam. other ch. only Ebenezer, Peter, Robert, and Hannah. I find no later acco. of any of them exc. Joseph, bef. ment. RALPH, Salem 1638, of wh. Felt could tell no more than that a gr. of ld. was that yr. confirm. to him. RICH-ARD, Plymouth 1620, came in the Mayflower, leav. w. Eliz. and five ds. to come in the third sh. 1623, d. 1628, hav. no other ch. but those b. in Eng. viz. Mary, wh. m. 1628, Robert Bartlett; Ann m. 19 Apr. 1633, Thomas Little; Sarah m. 28 Mar. 1634, John Cooke jr.; Eliz. m. 1636, Richard Church, d. at Hingham, 4 Mar. 1670; and Abigail m. 1639, Anthony Snow of Marshfield; beside the two s. Nathaniel, and Joseph, b. here, bef. ment. all liv. in 1650. His wid. wh. join. with the first purch. of Dartmouth, d. 2 Oct. 1673, aged a. 90, says the rec. but fond-ness for exagger. makes it 93. RICHARD, Plymouth, s. of Nathaniel of the same, perhaps eldest, m. it is said, and rem. to Middleborough, there d. a. 1696, leav. s. James, b. 13 Jan. 1680, at P. wh. had no ch. and Samuel, 7 Mar. 1683, whose progeny is in that neighb. SAMUEL, Wa-tertown, youngest s. of the sec. John of the same, m. 8 Jan. 1707, Lydia Cutting, had Sarah, and Lydia, tw. b. 19 Aug. 1714; Samuel, 19 July 1719; Eliz. 16 May 1721; Ephraim, 5 Apr. 1723; Nathan, 10 July 1725; John, bapt. 23 Aug. 1727; and Mary, 17 Aug. 1729. He d. 13 Nov. 1759; and his wid. d. 15 July 1766. THOMAS, Salem 1640, a witness to the will said to be the first brot. into Ct. for that shire. THOMAS, Boston, m. 14 Dec. 1694, Sarah Fitch; but as no more is heard of him, I doubt he was only trans. resid. But he may have been a soldier in Mosely's comp. Dec. 1675. WILLIAM, Hartford, freem. 1658, and perhaps was sw. again in 1665, ea. vol. of the Col. Rec. of Trumbull prov. the right, m. Eliz. d. of John Crow, had two ws. as in his will of 20 Oct. 1689, he tells, without nam. them, assign. to first w. three s. John, William, and Thomas, and to the liv. w. four ch. of wh. Abraham was one. He d. soon aft. for his inv. is of 1 Nov. in that yr. So we may see the wild work of tradit. that he had only Abigail, wh. m. 14 Jan. 1693, Richard Lord, and aft. Jan. 1713 m. Rev. Timothy Wood-bridge. His wid. m. Phineas Wilson, a rich merch. it was erron. said, but she was very infirm or insane, and certain. Wilson found a better w. Strangely out of place is the confusion a. the wid. of Phineas Wilson, in the address of Mr. Day, Presid. of the Conn. Hist. Soc. 26 Dec.

1843, at the foundat. of the beautiful edifice for the Wadsworth Athenæum, title to the realty being deduc. from her. But great uncertainty is found in the identity of the w. of Richard Lord; and aft. large investigat. it is clear, that no derivation from, or connection with, Hartford William can be traced. Certain. the wid. of Phineas Wilson did not m. Lord, but her d. Abigail did. WILLIAM, Boston, mariner, m. 1 Nov. 1690, Abiel Rogers, had Mary, b. 24 Sept. foll. but he had on 11 June preced. made his will in favor of the mo. and ch. unborn, nam. w. his excor. yet as it was not pro. bef. 10 July 1706, he prob. liv. to near this date, and had no other ch. or went on a voyage and d. abroad. So common. was this name in Eng. diffus. over the E. S. and W. shores, that I can find no proof of connex. betw. the Plymouth, Watertown, and Boston fams.

WARRINER, or WARRENER, JAMES, Springfield, eldest s. of William of the same, took o. of alleg. 31 Dec. 1678, or the day aft. m. 31 Mar. 1664, Eliz. d. of Joseph Baldwin the first of Milford, had Samuel, b. 21 Nov. 1666, d. at 2 yrs.; James, 19 July 1668; Eliz. 1 Aug. 1670; William, 6 Jan. 1673; Hannah, 15 Feb. 1675; Joseph, 6 Nov. 1677; Samuel, again, 26 Jan. 1680; Ebenezer, 4 Mar. 1682; and Mary, 1 Apr. 1685. His w. d. 24 Apr. 1687, and he m. 10 July 1689, Sarah, d. of Alexander Alvord, had Sarah, 1690; Jonathan, 1692; John, 29 Nov. 1694, d. in few mos.; John, again, 1696, d. young; Benjamin, 15 Apr. 1698; and David, 8 Oct. 1701. This w. d. 16 May 1704, and he m. 29 Dec. foll. Mary, wid. of Benjamin Stebbins, being her third h. but had no more ch. and d. 14 May 1727. His wid. d. seven days aft. Of these fifteen ch. twelve were m. and the lot of the youngest was to be blest with eight s. and four ds. JOSEPH, Hadley, younger br. of the preced. sw. alleg. 8 Feb. 1679, m. 25 Nov. 1668, Mary, d. of Richard Montague of the same, had Mary, b. 1669; Joseph, 6 Jan. 1672, d. soon; Joseph, again, 6 Jan. 1673, d. young; Hannah, 1674; Ebenezer, 1676; Dorcas, 1678; Abigail, 1680, d. young; Joanna, 1682; and Eliz. 1686; rem. 1687 to Enfield, where his w. d. 22 July 1689, aged a. 47. He m. 15 July 1691, Sarah, wid. of Daniel Collins, had Abigail and Mary, tw. 4 May 1692; d. 1697; and his wid. m. Obadiah Abbee. RALPH, Marblehead, wh. was fin. Sept. 1639 for being at excess. drink. at Thomas Gray's, may have been only a trans. person, not inhab. At least no more is heard of him. WILLIAM, Springfield, freem. 2 May 1638, m. 31 July 1639, Joanna Searl, as Mr. Boltwood reads the name, d. of John, as he thinks, but Mr. Judd is sure the name was Scant, had James, b. 21 Jan. 1641; Hannah, 17 Aug. 1643; Joseph, 6 Feb. 1645; and his w. d. 7 Feb. 1661. He m. 2 Oct. 1661, sec. w. Eliz. wid. of Luke Hitchcock of Wethersfield, and d. 2 June

1676. His wid. m. Joseph Baldwin of Hadley. Eliz. W. wh. m. John Strong jr. was perhaps his sis. or the name may be wrong. Hannah, his only d. m. 1 Nov. 1660, Thomas Noble.

WARWICK, or WARRICK, HENRY, Saco 1636, had s. John and two ds. and d. a. 1673. Folsom, 124, tells that commonly the name is writ. Waddock, but not by the owner; that one d. Joan m. 1658, John Helson; and the other d. m. John Tenney of Scarborough, thence driv. by Ind. hostil. with her mo. to Gloucester, by or bef. 1690; and the f. was an active and useful man. JOHN, Saco, s. of the preced. was one of the chief men of the place, but rem. to Scarborough.

WASHBURN, or WASHBORNE, BENJAMIN, Bridgewater, s. of the sec. John of the same, one of the many hundreds whose lives were lost, without renown or benefit, in the expedit. of Sir William Phips against Quebec. He made his will bef. embark. but left no ch. prob. was not m. HOPE, Stratford, is among the freem. in 1669, tho. Trumbull in Col. Rec. II. 522, gives the name without h. Perhaps he was s. of William, m. Mary, d. of Francis Stiles of Windsor, had Sarah, b. Dec. 1661; John, May 1666; William, Mar. 1668; Samuel, Mar. 1670; Ephraim, 1673; Mary; and Jane; perhaps the last two at Derby, where he d. 1696. In Nov. of that yr. an agreem. was made for div. the est. by the wid. and all the ch. exc. Sarah, John, and Ephraim. Mary m. 1694, John Johnson; William and Samuel were inhabs. at D. 1702–17. William m. 1696, Hannah Wooster. JAMES, Bridgewater, youngest s. of John the sec. m. 1693, Mary Bowden. Mitchell indic. the ch. thus: Mary, b. 1694; Ann, 1696; James, 1698; Edward, 1700; Moses, 1702; Gideon, 1704; Sarah, 1706; Martha, 1709; and Eliz. 1710. JOHN, Plymouth 1632, came, I suppose from Evesham, Co. Worcester, and in 1635, his w. Margaret, aged 49, with ch. John, 14; and Philip, 11, foll. him in the sh. Elizabeth and Ann from London, as by certif. of the mayor and the min. of E. He was of Duxbury side of the water, and bec. one of the orig. sett. of Bridgewater, and d. bef. 1670. JOHN, Bridgewater, s. of the preced. brot. by his mo. 1635, from Evesham in Co. Worcester, on Shakespeare's Avon, at the age of 14 yrs. m. 1645, Eliz. d. of Experience Mitchell, had John; Thomas; Joseph; Samuel, b. a. 1651; Jonathan; Benjamin; Mary, 1661; Eliz. Jane; James, 1672; and Sarah. He had prob. liv. at Duxbury some yrs. but rem. bef. 1670, and made his will 1686. Mary m. Samuel Kinsley; Eliz. m. James Howard, and next Edward Sealey; Jane m. William Orcutt jr.; and Sarah m. 1697, John Ames. JOHN, Stratford, s. of William, m. 7 June 1655, Mary, d. of Richard Butler, had John, b. 20 Nov. 1657. He prob. rem. to Hempstead, L. I. JOHN, Bridgewater, s. of the first John, m. 1679, Rebecca Lapham, prob. d. of Thomas, had Josiah, b.

1680; John, 1682; Joseph, 1683; William, 1686; Abigail, 1688; Rebecca; and perhaps other ch. says Mitchell. JONATHAN, Bridgewater,
br. of the preced. m. a. 1683, Mary, d. of George Vaughan of Scituate,
had Eliz. b. 1684; Josiah, 1686; Benjamin, 1688; Ebenezer, 1690;
Martha, 1692; Joanna, 1693; Nathan, 1699; Jonathan, 1700; and
Cornelius, 1702. JOSEPH, Bridgewater, br. of the preced. m. Hannah,
d. of Robert Latham, had Joseph, Jonathan, Ebenezer, Miles, Ephraim,
Edward, Benjamin, Hannah, and, Mitchell says, perhaps others. PHILIP,
Duxbury, s. of the first John, brought by his mo. 1635, aged 11; had no
ch. perhaps no w. and, in his latter days, was under the care of his neph.
John or Joseph, liv. in 1700. SAMUEL, Bridgewater, s. of John the sec.
m. Deborah, d. of Samuel Packard, had Samuel, b. 1678; Noah, 1682;
Israel, 1684; Nehemiah, 1686; Benjamin; and Hannah; and he d.
1720. THOMAS, Bridgewater, br. of the preced. had two ws. Deliverance, d. of Samuel Packard, and Abigail, d. of Jacob Leonard. Mitchell arranges these ws. in differ. order from me, but his informat. was not
exact, and even for the ch. he had no more happy source for gather.
their names, Nathaniel, Thomas, Timothy, Hepzibah, Patience, Deliverance, and Eliz. than the will of their f. 1729. WILLIAM, Stratford,
rem. prob. with s. John to Hempstead, L. I. Farmer notes, that in
1834, two had been gr. of this name at Harv. two at Yale, and twelve
at other N. E. coll.

WASS, or WASSE, JOHN, Charlestown, by w. Catharine had John, b.
22 Sept. 1645; and Thomas, 29 Nov. 1646. THOMAS, Haverhill, sw.
alleg. Nov. 1677, had taught a sch. there 1660, afterwards at Ipswich,
and Newbury, where he d. 18 May, says Coffin, other auth. says Aug.
1691.

WASSON, or WASON, BENJAMIN, Dover, m. 30 Jan. 1687, Martha
Kenney, perhaps d. of Richard.

WASTALL, WESTALL, or WASSTOLL, JOHN, Wethersfield, an early
sett. rem. to Saybrook, among the freem. of 1669, and liv. there 1675.
See Westall.

WATERBURY, DAVID, Stamford, s. of John, was a propr. 1701. JOHN,
Watertown, of wh. little more is kn. than that he sold ho. and ld. there,
15 Oct. 1646. He had rem. to Stamford, there d. 31 July 1658, leav.
John, Jonathan, David, Sarah, and Rachel. Rose, his wid. m. 11 May
1659, Joseph Garnsey; Rachel m. 11 May 1659, John Holmes; and
Sarah m. 10 May 1666, Zechariah Dibble, for his ill conduct obt.
divorce 1672, and m. Nicholas Webster. JOHN, Stamford, s. of the
preced. d. 28 Nov. and in his will prov. 11 Dec. 1688, names w. Mary,
s. John, David, Thomas, and d. Mary, mak. brs. Jonathan and David,
overseers. JONATHAN, Stamford, br. of the preced. had ch. betw. 1677

and 91 inclus. WILLIAM, Boston, prob. came in the fleet with Winth. with w. Alice, was adm. of our ch. the first yr. their names being Nos. 35 and 6. As no more is heard of either, I conclude they d. soon, or went home.

WATERHOUSE, oft. WATERUS, ABRAHAM, Saybrook, s. of Jacob of New London, by w. Rebecca, m. 1674, d. of capt. John Clarke of the same, had Abraham, b. 23 Dec. 1675; Rebecca, 20 Sept. 1677; Isaac, 17 Apr. 1680; John, 3 Nov. 1682; Joseph, 12 July 1690; and Benjamin, 17 Feb. 1693; and his w. d. 14 Oct. 1704. ‖ DAVID, Boston 1679, then of ar. co. was a warm patriot in the outbreak of 1689 against Andros, one of the signers of the energet. letter 18 Apr. requir. the Gov. to give up his authty. and forts, and serv. in the Comtee. of Safety; but aft. the restorat. of quiet, we hear no more of him. ISAAC, Lyme, eldest s. of Jacob the first, made freem. 1671, m. 20 Apr. 1670, Sarah, d. of William Pratt of Hartford, had Eliz. b. 22 Mar. 1672; Sarah, 24 Feb. 1675; Gideon, 20 Aug. 1678; Isaac, 29 Jan. 1681; Jabez, 16 Mar. 1683; Samuel, 21 July 1685; Ruth, 31 July 1687; Rebecca, 28 Aug. 1693; and Gershom, 30 Mar. 1696; and d. 7 Oct. 1713. His wid. d. 8 Dec. 1725. JACOB, New London 1645, had, bef. that town was sett. liv. in Wethersfield 1639, yet from what town in Mass. he went is unkn. by w. Hannah had Isaac, Jacob, Abraham, John, Joseph, Benjamin, wh. d. abroad in the hands of pirates, as tradit. says, and Eliz. wh. m. John Baker. JACOB, New London, s. of the preced. m. Ann, d. of Robert Douglas, and had John, William, Robert, Joseph, and Gideon. JOHN, New London, br. of the preced. a soldier in the gr. Narraganset fight, Dec. 1675, d. 1687, leav. Jacob, an inf. his only ch. Caulkins, Hist. of N. L. 295. Of this Conn. tribe the name has been abbrev. to Watrous, sometimes Waterus. RICHARD, Boston 1672, a tanner, may have rem. to Portsmouth, by w. Sarah, had Richard, b. 19 Apr. 1674; Samuel, 9 May 1676; and perhaps others; was of the gr. jury 1688. *THOMAS*, Dorchester 1639, a sch.-master, freem. 13 May 1640, by w. Ann Mayhew, d. of John, m. at Codenham, in Co. Suffk. had Ann b. here, bapt. 7 Mar. 1641. Mr. Hunter in his Suffk. emigr. 3 Mass. Hist. Coll. X. 169, shows him to have been a clerg. serv. as curate at C. and that on hear. of d. of br. of his w. by wh. est. came to her, he went home, had six more ch. was sch.-master some time, and min. at Ash Bocking, Co. Suffk. eject. by the Act of Uniform. 1662, and d. at the age of almost 80, in the yr. 1679 or the next.

WATERMAN, JOHN, a passeng. in the Jonathan, arr. at Boston 1639, of wh. I kn. no more but that his pass. was paid by Peter Noyes of Sudbury, and therefore we may suppose him a serv. JOHN, Marshfield, s. of Robert of the same, m. 7 Dec. 1665, Ann, d. of Samuel Sturtevant, had Samuel, b. 16 Oct. 1666; and Eliz. 15 Jan. 1669; Ann, 1671; Lydia, 1678; Robert, 1681; and John, 1685. JOSEPH, Marshfield, eldest br. of the preced. by w. Sarah Snow, had Sarah b. 1674; Joseph, a. 1677; Eliz. 1679; Abigail, 1681; Anthony, a. 1685; Bethia, 1687; Lydia, 1689; and d. 1 Jan. 1712, aged 69, and his wid. d. 11 Dec. 1741, aged 90. JOSEPH, Providence, perhaps s. of Richard of the same, m. 17 Dec. 1669, Lydia Olney of the same, prob. d. of the elder Thomas, possib. of the younger Thomas. NATHANIEL, Providence, eldest s. of Richard, own. alleg. to k. Charles, 31 May 1666, m. 14 Mar. 1663, Susanna Carder, prob. d. of Richard, had Richard; Benjamin; Nathaniel, wh. acknowledg. alleg. 29 May 1682; Daniel; and Bethia; liv. thro. Philip's war without leav. the town, and had his reward. RESOLVED, Providence, br. of the preced. own. alleg. to Charles II. on the same day; by w. Mercy, youngest d. of blessed Roger Williams, had Richard, John, Resolved, Waiting, and Mary or Mercy. His wid. m. Samuel Winsor, and next John Rhodes. RICHARD, Salem, came in the fleet with Higginson 1629, sent by the Gov. and Comp. as an expert hunter, and he k. a wolf in July 1632, had Nathaniel, bapt. 20 Aug. 1637, and two other ch. in July 1638, whose names do not appear, as the f. had bec. heretic, and in Mar. of that yr. had liberty to follow Roger Williams to Providence, and there was nam. the twelfth among the grantees of his settlem. Prob. Joseph, and certain. Resolved were also his s. and perhaps he had more; ds. were Mehitable and Waiting. Disagree. with some of Williams's friends, he join. Holden, Gorton, and others, tho. he did not rem. with them, wh. purch. from Miantonomo, planting place on the W. shore of Narraganset, now Warwick, and suffer. by monstrous injustice from Mass. in 1643. Yet, tho. some of his est. was confisc. at the Court in Oct. 1643, he got off better than most of his fellow misbelievers wh. narrow. escap. sentence of death, still he was bound to appear in May foll. See Winth. II. 146–8. At the Gen. Ct. in May next "being found erroneous, heretical, and obstinate, it was agreed that he should be detain. prisoner till the Quarter Ct. in the 7th mo. unless five of the magistr. do find cause to send him away; wh. if they do, it is order. that he shall not ret. within this jurisdict. upon pain of death," as the Col. Rec. II. 73 says; as also Felt's Ann. II. 579; but in his Eccles. Hist. I. 558, the tender heart of the writer prevail. over his judgm. to suppress the last words. Yet even an Ecclesiast. Hist. should not be afraid of the truth. He was ch. offic. of the milit. call. col. and d. 28 Oct. 1673. His wid. mo. of the ch. Bethia, d. 3 Dec. 1680. Mehitable m. a Fenner. Of the tradit. of his coming in the Lion with Roger Williams Feb. 1631, no respect is felt, but its origin may easily be referr. to the subordinate truth that he was one of the first sett. at Providence, with R. W. tho. he was earlier than him at Salem. *ROBERT, Plymouth 1638, had been at Salem 1636, m. at Marshfield, 9 or 11 Dec. 1638, Eliz. d. of Thomas Bourne, and rem. to M. had Joseph, b. 1639 ; John, 1642 ; Thomas, 1644 ; Robert, a. 1652 ; and Joseph; was rep. 1644–9, and d. Sept. 1652, tho. Deane says 1665. ROBERT, Hingham, prob. s. of the preced. m. 1 Oct. 1675, as Hobart says, but town rec. 30 Sept. Susanna, d. of Daniel Lincoln, had Susanna, b. 4 May 1677 ; a ch. b. and d. 4 Feb. 1681 ; Eliz. 18 Aug. 1682, d. at 13 yrs.; Robert, 14 Nov. 1684, d. at 19 yrs.; Josiah, 28 Nov. 1687 ; and a ch. wh. d. 24 Sept. 1694, too young to have a name ; and his w. d. 10 Feb. 1696. He m. 20 Feb. 1699, Sarah, wid. of Thomas Lincoln, d. of James Lewis of Barnstable, had Lydia, 13 May 1700 ; Thomas, 19 Jan. 1702 ; and Hannah, 22 May 1704 ; and his w. d. 30 Jan. 1732. He d. 18 May 1741, aged 88. THOMAS, Roxbury, br. of Robert of Plymouth, had w. Hannah, wh. d. 5 June 1641 ; unit. with petitnrs. in 1645 for right from Mass. to plant at the settlem. of Warwick, whence the heretic inhabs. of wh. his namesake Richard was one, had been forcib. eject. and he d. 22 Jan. 1676, unless the town rec. wh. contains the notices of d. of both, and no account of m. or b. may be design. for differ. persons. Farmer, MS. makes a Thomas of Hingham 1679, to be only s. of the preced. but I fear he mistook the name of the f. THOMAS, Newport, among the freem. adm. 1655, was of Wickford 1674. THOMAS, Saybrook, by Miss Caulkins conject. s. of the preced. bec. one of the first sett. of Norwich, there m. Nov. 1668, Miriam, d. of lieut. Thomas Tracy. He was ens. and propound. for freem. 1671, had ten ch. as in the valua. Hist. of N. p. 114 is told ; but the fair writer gives only the three s. Thomas, b. Sept. 1670 ; John, Mar. 1672 ; and Joseph, 15 Jan. 1685. Names are heard of five others, Eliz. b. Aug. 1675 ; Miriam, Apr. 1678 ; Martha, 6 Dec. 1680 ; Lydia, Aug. 1683 ; and Ann, Apr. 1689. Eliz. m. 10 July 1695, capt. John Fitch of Windham. Of this name, Farmer found in 1834, three had been gr. at Harv. four at Yale, and five at other N. E. coll.

WATERS, ANTHONY, Hempstead, L. I. was town clk. 1663, favor. the jurisdict. of Conn. and it may be, that he had gone from Conn. to promote annex. BEVIL, Hartford, found in the list of freem. 1669, had good est. d. 14 Feb. 1730, says the gr.-st. in 97th yr. Wh. was his first w. and mo. of his ch. is not kn. but when 92 yrs. old, he took ano. w. 13 Dec. 1722, Sarah, wid. of Joseph Mygott. His will of 1 Feb. 1721 ment. Thomas, d. bef. his f. and ds. Sarah, wh. m. 10 Feb. 1698, Joseph Benton ; Hannah m. 1708, Wilterton Merrills ; Mary m. 1711, Thomas Seymour. EDWARD, New Haven, took o. of fidel. 1647 ; and one of

the same name liv. at Westchester 1663. EZEKIEL, Salem, s. of Richard, had Samuel, b. 3 Sept. 1673; Mary, 19 Apr. 1676; Eliz. 4 Aug.
1678; Ezekiel, 1 Aug. 1680; Sarah, 9 Aug. 1682; Joyce, 9 Mar.
1684; Susanna, 1 Jan. 1686; Elias, 11 May 1688, wh. d. next mo.;
Ebenezer, 26 Oct. 1690; and Martha, Oct. 1692. JACOB, Charlestown,
had w. Sarah, wh. join. the ch. there 12 Nov. 1682, and of wh. I find no
more. JOHN, Boston, came with Winth. 1630, I suppose, for he and w.
Frances are among the very early mem. of our ch. Nos. 23 and 4, and
d. since is add. to the first copy of rec. He was from Neyland, in Co.
Suffk. was a serv. of the Gov. wh. in letters to his w. the first autumn
after arriv. ment. his loss. See Appx. A. to his Hist. Nos. 47 and 49.
JOHN, Milford 1658, if Lambert be correct; but no more is found of
him, not even his name among freem. of 1669. JOHN, Salem, perhaps
s. of Richard of the same, m. 1 Aug. 1663, Sarah, d. of John Tompkins of the same, had Richard and John, b. last of June foll. and both d.
in few days; John, 4 July 1665; Sarah, 30 Aug. 1667; Richard, again,
13 Nov. 1669; Nathaniel, 6 Feb. 1672; Samuel, 29 Mar. 1674, d. in
few wks.; Samuel, again, 6 May 1675; and Eliz. 10 Jan. 1678. He
was call. Aug. 1692, witness against George Jacobs. His will of 14
Feb. 1707, was pro. 1 Mar. 1708. JOSEPH, New Haven 1649, aft.
1653, prob. rem. to Milford, at least had gr. of ld. in that town 1656
and 9; but no more is heard of him. JOSEPH, Boston, m. 13 Sept.
1655, Martha, d. of Oliver Mellows, and no more is told of him. LAW-
RENCE, Watertown 1634 or earlier, by w. Ann, d. of Richard Linton,
had Lawrence, b. 14 Feb. 1635; Sarah, 7 Dec. 1636; Mary, 27 Jan.
1638; Rebecca, Feb. d. 1 Mar. 1640; Daniel, 6 Feb. 1642; in 1638,
he or his w. or both, were warned for hav. danced, and may have been
induc. to rem. early to Lancaster, where the high authty. of Willard
makes him build the first ho. in that settlem. See Centenn. Celebr. 75.
There prob. he had, Bond thinks, Joseph, Ephraim, Jacob, and Rachel;
was blind in 1676, but happily rem. bef. the Ind. whirlw. fell on L. and
resid. at Charlestown, there d. 9 Dec. 1687, aged near 85. Adam his s.
d. 15 Sept. 1670 at Charlestown. LAWRENCE, Boston, s. of the preced.
by w. Hannah, had Joseph, b. 14 Oct. 1663; Hannah, 26 Jan. 1666;
Jonathan, 2 May 1671, d. young; Jonathan, again, 3 Oct. 1674; and
Stephen, 3 Apr. 1677; was freem. 1663; and d. 1693. RICHARD,
Salem 1637, a gunsmith, had a ch. bapt. prob. John, 29 Nov. 1640;
Eliz. 26 Feb. 1643, d. unm. at 20 yrs.; Abigail, 18 May 1645; Ezekiel, 4 Apr. 1647; Susanna, 1 Apr. 1649; and Hannah, 30 Jan. 1653;
tho. in whose right the act was admin. does not so well appear, as the
adm. of Joyce, wh. may have been his w. is by Felt insert. under 1641.
That w. I presume to be the person made by Farmer a man (GEORGE),

and by him enrol. of the ch. 23 May 1641. Such error is not so ludicr. as that he commits in mak. our Walter Merry, the shipwright of Merry's point, now the North battery, Merry Waters, as if any Boston puritan two hundred and twenty yrs. since, could have been call. Merry, instead of Sad, Stern, or Severe. Dearborn, in Boston Notions, 63, foll. the blunder of so high authority. He is mark. by Felt as freem. tho. he omits his name among mem. of the ch. and in my opin. the person so entit. was the Ipswich man. He was one of the petitnrs. in 1665 for conciliat. betw. the Col. governm. and the crown, and was licensed to sell ale in 1668, and by his will of 16 July 1676, pro. 25 Nov. 1677, mak. w. Joyce extrix. we find other ch. beside the forenam. viz. James, William, Martha, and Mary. Then Abigail was w. of William Punchard ; Mary of Clement English ; Susanna of Benedict Pulsifer ; and Hannah of Joseph Striker. Martha was perhaps unm. and in that instrum. ment. as well as her mo. and infirm br. William. Perhaps Sarah, wh. m. 26 Feb. 1652, Joshua Ray, and Phebe, wh. m. 11 Oct. 1658, Thomas West, may have been his ds. RICHARD, Ipswich 1638, was prob. the freem. of 22 May 1639. SAMPSON, Boston 1666, mariner, by w. Rebecca, had Mary, b. 28 Aug. 1667 ; William, 3 Mar. 1669 ; John, 2 Jan. 1673 ; Rebecca, 28 May 1677 ; Eliz. 1 Feb. 1683 ; Sampson, 20 June 1685 ; and Robert, 5 May 1688 ; was in 1685, sent out with 40 men, in pursuit of Veale and Graham, pirates on the coast, off New London, says Farmer, in MS. SAMUEL, Woburn, freem. 1684, by w. Mary, had Mary, b. 19 Oct. 1675 ; Sarah, 15 Jan. 1678 ; Daniel, 30 Nov. 1679 ; Samuel, 6 Nov. 1681 ; Abigail, 29 Nov. 1683 ; John, 22 Sept. 1685, d. in 4 yrs. ; Ephraim, 12 Oct. 1687 ; John, again, 11 Dec. 1689 ; Nathaniel, and Daniel, tw. 10 Oct. 1691, both d. soon ; Josiah, 19 Sept. 1694 ; and Joanna, 28 Nov. 1696. STEPHEN, Charlestown 1678, perhaps br. of Jacob, had w. Sarah, wh. join. the ch. 26 June 1681 ; but of him I learn no more. THOMAS, Hartford, only s. of Bevil of the same, m. 19 May 1696, Sarah, d. of the sec. Benjamin Fenn, of Milford, had Mehitable, b. 1697, d. young ; Joseph, 1698 ; Sarah, 1699 ; Mehitable, again, 1701 ; Dorothy, 1704 ; Samuel, 1707 ; Benjamin, 1709, perhaps d. young ; and Abraham, 1712 ; neither of the last two are nam. in the will of gr.f. while the others liv. all are. WILLIAM, Pemaquid, sw. alleg. to Mass. 1674, and was appoint. constable. WILLIAM, Marblehead 1674, was prob. s. of Richard of Salem, and d. 1684, leav. ch. William, Thomas, Hannah, and Mary. WILLIAM, Boston 1653, of wh. I find no more but that when he made a deed June 1668, he is call. senr. so that it seems prob. there was a junr. WILLIAM, Marblehead, perhaps s. of William of the same, m. 1 Aug. 1686,

Eliz. Lattimore, perhaps d. of Christopher. Farmer's num. of gr. in 1834, is two at Harv. one at Yale, and four at other N. E. coll. WATHEN, or WATHIN, EZEKIEL, Amesbury, sw. alleg. Dec. 1677. It may be that he was s. of that John Watten, dec. on whose est. at the Gen. Ct. Oct. 1654, admin. was giv. to capt. Brian Pendleton, "that some course may be taken for relief of his wid." See Col. Rec. III. 366. Pendleton was a selectman of Portsmouth, and Watten was one of the mem. of ch. May 1640. See Geneal. Reg. IX. 180. GEORGE, Salem, reckon. by Felt among mem. of the ch. 1641. THOMAS, Gloucester, was s. of Edmund, d. 1652, had bef. serv. in the civil war under Prince Rupert. The est. of a wid. W. was, it is said, sett. in Essex Co. 1644.

WATKINS, DAVID, Stratford, with prefix of resp. upon his inv. 20 July 1688, tho. of no more than £50. left wid. Sarah and one d. only to partake. JOHN, Salem, came a. 1641, and d. in few wks. as Mr. Felt assures me. JOHN, Cambridge 1651. ‖ THOMAS, Boston, tobacco maker as he is call. in the deed to him, Oct. 1653 of his est. in B. by Robert Breck of Dorchester; by w. Eliz. had Eliz. b. 27 Nov. 1652; John, 21 Mar. 1654; Sarah, 1 Mar. 1657, prob. d. young; Thomas, 10 May 1659; Sarah, again, 7 Nov. 1661; Rowland, 5 Dec. 1663; Hannah, 9 Apr. 1665, d. soon; Hannah, again, 28 Oct. 1666; Mehitable, 14 Feb. 1668; and Joseph, 15 Jan. 1670. He was freem. 1660, of ar. co. 1666, had planta. at Kennebeck, wh. he sold 1669, to Thomas Gyles; and d. 16 Dec. 1689. THOMAS, Kennebeck 1665. See Sullivan, 237.

WATSON, ABRAHAM, Cambridge, s. of John of the same, by w. Mary Butterfield, had Isaac, b. 3 Mar. 1690; John; Abraham; both bapt. 21 Feb. 1697; William, 8 May 1698; Jonathan, 18 Oct. 1702; and Jacob, 7 May 1704; and d. 23 Mar. 1705, aged 44, says Harris's Epit. His wid. m. Samuel Whitmore of Lexington. CALEB, Roxbury, s. of John of the same, m. 15 Dec. 1665, Mary, d. of George Hyde, of Boston, freem. 1666, was of Hadley 1668, a sch.-master at Hadley bef. and aft. but soon rem. to Hartford, for many yrs. taught there, and d. says the Coll. Catal. 1725, rather aged. His case affords a perfect example of fondness for exaggera. Hinman, 246 of Ed. I. tells that "he is suppos. to have d. over one hundred yrs. of age," when we find fairly 84 only betw. b. and d. No ch. was liv. perhaps none ever b. to him, so that he gave est. to sis. Dorcas Adams of Ipswich, wh. was older than hims. but w. Mary was made excor. of his will. EDWARD, New Haven, m. 1 July 1653, Grace, wid. of John Walker, had Grace, bapt. some day, but not 31, in Mar. 1653; and John, b. 22, bapt. prob. 28 Sept. 1656. See Geneal. Reg. IX. 363. He d. 1660, leav. only these ch. ELKANAH,

Plymouth, s. of George, a blacksmith, by w. Mercy had John, b. 1678;
Phebe, 1681; Mercy, 1683; and Mary, 1688; was drown. in co. with
the sec. Edward Doty and his s. John, by shipwr. on the Gurnet's nose,
in a pass. from Boston home, 8 Feb. 1690. His wid. m. John Freeman
of Harwich, and tradit. exults in add. that her three ds. m. three of his
s. GEORGE, Plymouth, m. 1635, Phebe, d. of Robert Hicks, wh. d. 22
May 1663, had John; Phebe; Samuel and Eliz. tw. b. 18 Jan. 1648, of
wh. Samuel d. 20 Aug. 1649, but Eliz. liv. to be m.; Mary; Jonathan,
9 Mar. 1652; Elkanah, 25 Feb. 1656; Jonathan, again, 1659; and perhaps others; and d. 1689, aged 87. Phebe m. 22 Jan. 1657, Jonathan
Shaw; Mary m. 21 Aug. 1662, Thomas Leonard; and Eliz. m. 1667,
Joseph Williams of Taunton. JACOB, Cambridge, s. of John of the
same, by w. Mary, wh. d. 16 Sept. 1728, aged 60, had ch. prob. Jacob,
and d. 29 Mar. 1724. JOHN, Roxbury, arr. in the Lion, 16 Sept. 1632,
was adm. freem. 5 Nov. 1633, m. 3 Apr. 1634, Alice, wid. of Valentine
Prentice, had John, b. Jan. 1635; Edmund, 12 July 1636, d. bef. his f.:
Joshua, Aug. 1637, and d. 1639, as Ellis says (but by ch. as well as
town rec. 30 Apr. 1649); Dorcas, 20 Sept. 1639; Caleb, 29 July 1641,
H. C. 1661; Mary, 2, bapt. 5 May 1644, but Ellis puts it one yr. bef.;
and he d. Jan. 1672, tho. Ellis, confus. the f. with the s. makes it 1693.
By his will of 4 Mar. 1671, pro. 5 Feb. foll. we find to the four ch. then
liv. John, Caleb, Dorcas, w. of Timothy Dwight of Medfield, and Mary
w. of Thomas Stedman of Muddy riv. and to three gr.ch. bequests are
made, as also to his s. John Prentice, mean. the s. of his w. by her first h.
£5. JOHN, Cambridge, by Farmer confus. with the preced. freem. 1645;
m. Rebecca, d. of wid. Ann, and sis. of Abraham Errington, wh. d. 11
Nov. 1690, aged 65, was selectman 1680, and much empl. in town affairs.
His ch. named in Mitchell's Reg. as bapt. in his flock, Rebecca; John,
b. 14 Oct. 1653, d. of smallpox at 25 yrs.; Abraham, 26 June, bapt. 28
July 1661; Ann, 21 Aug. bapt. 16 Sept. 1666, d. young; beside Isaac,
24 Sept. 1669; and Jacob, 20 Dec. 1671. He d. 20 May 1711, aged
92, as Harris Epit. marks. JOHN, Hartford 1644, d. bef. 1656, leav.
wid. Margaret, and s. John; d. Sarah, m. John Merrills; and Mary m.
John Seymour. The wid. d. 1683, in her will of Mar. in that yr. names
the three ch. JOHN, Rowley 1658, freem. 1672, m. Eunice, I think d.
of James Barker of the same. JOHN, Hartford, only s. of John of the
same, by w. Ann, had John, b. 1680; Thomas, 1682; Zechariah, 1685;
Ann, 1688; Cyprian, 1690; Sarah, 1692; and Caleb, 1695. Perhaps
he had been of Wickford 1674. That Narraganset country was much
coveted by the Conn. governm. as belong. to their jurisdict. JOHN,
Roxbury, eldest ch. of John of the same, had w. Mary, but no ch. is
found on rec. or nam. in his will, made 27 July 1693, pro. 27 Sept. aft.

in wh. provid. for the w. as long as she contin. wid. to have all his est. and giv. some small sums to his br. Caleb, and cous. John Dwight, Dorcas Adams, and to cous. Thomas, Joshua, Joseph, and Mary Stedman, beside £20. to cous. Tabitha Brooks, he devis. all resid. to cous. Caleb Stedman. He d. 13 Aug. JOHN, Boston, binds hims. apprent. Feb. 1675. JOHN, New Haven, s. of Edward, m. 30 Mar. 1681, Eliz. Hudson, had Eliz. b. 16 Jan. 1682 ; Mary, 11 Dec. 1683 ; and prob. more ; was propr. 1685. JOHN, Salisbury, m. 1688, Ruth Griffin, had Abraham, b. 13 Dec. 1688 ; John, 11 Dec. 1690, d. soon ; Hannah, 5 Apr. 1695, d. at one wk. ; and Jonathan, 12 Oct. 1696. NATHANIEL, New London 1647, of wh. no more is seen in Caulkins. NATHANIEL, Windsor, s. of Robert of the same, m. 1685, Dorothy, d. of the sec. John Bissell, had Nathaniel, and Ann, the latter 4 yrs. old, the other 6 mos. when he d. 19 Aug. 1690. PHILIP, Rowley 1678, had liv. at Salisbury, where his s. William d. 19 Dec. 1657. ROBERT, Windsor, m. 10 Dec. 1646, Mary, d. of the first John Rockwell of the same, had Mary, b. 11 Jan. 1652 ; John, 7 Mar. 1653 ; Samuel, 14 Jan. 1655 ; Hannah, 8 Aug. 1658 ; Ebenezer, 25 Apr. 1661 ; Nathaniel, 28 Jan. 1664 ; and Jedediah, 30 Sept. 1666. He is in the list of freem. 1669, but freed from train. the yr. preced. His w. d. 21 Aug. 1684 ; and he d. 19 July 1689. All the s. were then liv. Hannah m. 28 Mar. 1679, John Birge of W. ROBERT, Dover 1665, of wh. no more is learned. THOMAS, Salem 1637, adm. of the ch. 1639, freem. 13 May 1640, was prob. h. of that Joan W. wh. is count. ch. memb. 1636, and d. Dec. 1674 ; but no ch. is ment. He was, perhaps, the tailor wh. d. 1 Mar. 1672. THOMAS, Boston, kept the prison 1674, may be the same, wh. at Ipswich, m. 15 Jan. 1672, Sarah Perley, had Sarah, b. 2 Nov. foll. was of Topsfield 1684. WILLIAM, Newbury, m. says Coffin, 6 Dec. 1670, Sarah Perley, had Mary, wh. m. Joseph Hale. In 1834, of this name by Farmer's reckon. eleven had been gr. at Harv. four at Yale, and six at other N. E. coll.

WATTLES, or WATTELLS, RICHARD, Ipswich 1648, was there 1663.

WATTS, HENRY, Saco, Scarborough 1636 and 1658, subm. to jurisdict. 1658, and sw. as freem. of Mass. 1659, same yr. constable, and next yr. as also 1661, commissnr. or rep. under the jurisdict. of Mass. yet in 1663, unit. with the major pt. of his neighb. in declar. their neutrality betw. k. and col. and his town was presented for disobey. the warrant to them direct. for choos. of officers, and when he appear. 1664, as commissnr. my transcr. of the rec. show that he was disallow. Aft. this no polit. distinct. is seen. He is point. at by Willis I. 55, as one of the Assist. in the governm. of Cleeves as early as 1648 ; and in 1685, he was aged 71, had w. and perhaps ch. but Southgate in his valu. hist.

could tell no more. JAMES, Marblehead 1668. JEREMIAH, Salem 1678–80. LAWRENCE, New Haven, d. in 1643, prob. without w. or ch. RICHARD, Hartford, one of the first sett. tho. not orig. purch. liv. on the S. side of the riv. bef. 1640; was f. of William and Thomas. He had also ds. Eliz. wh. m. George Hubbard of Middletown; and Eleanor, wh. m. 23 Dec. 1647, Nathaniel Brown. His wid. Eliz. d. in H. 1666, was sec. w. made her will in Feb. of that yr. and her h. had been d. some nine yrs. or more. SAMUEL, Haverhill, sw. alleg. 1677, was liv. 1690. SAMUEL, Boston, tr. as a pirate, Jan. 1690. THOMAS, Hartford, s. of Richard, call. serg. in the list of freem. 1669, grew to be ens. 1673, lieut. in 1675 bef. the war, and capt. in the same yr. aft. the hostil. and head. his comp. in the desperate Narraganset fight 19 Dec. 1675, as told in Niles's hist. and seventeen of his comp. were that day k. or wound. was in good repute, certain. 1677, when once more he was put at the head of forces to go up the riv. He m. 1 May 1645, Eliz. d. of George Steele, had no ch. made his will, 6 Aug. 1683, had very good est. of wh. the use of all to w. dur. life, and made judicious dispos. aft. The wid. d. 25 Feb. 1685, and gave her est. to her br. James Steele and his four ds. and other relat. WILLIAM, Hartford, is by Porter rank. among first sett. yet not orig. propr. bef. 1641, was s. of Richard, certain. not among freem. 1669; but he had gone home, and d. bef. 1668, in Eng.

WAUGH, DOROTHY, Boston, a quaker, came in the Speedwell from London 1656, aged 20, arr. 27 July, and prob. was soon rem. to a better place to diffuse her light in.

WAY, AARON, Dorchester, freem. 1651, may have been s. of Henry the first, m. prob. Joan, d. of William Sumner, had Susanna, bapt. 1 Apr. 1660, "being a. 2 or 3 mos. old at this time, but not bapt. till now, being b. at the farm," and no doubt sev. more, certain. Aaron and William, perhaps both aft. his rem. in that yr. to join the sec. ch. of Boston, with his w. AARON, Salem, perhaps s. of the preced. freem. 1690, was one of the body of worshippers wh. in Apr. 1693 began the three yrs. labor of compel. the withdraw. of their pastor, unhappy Samuel Paris, for his sad activ. in the delusion of witchcraft, that caused the death of so many of his flock. See Calef, Salem Ed. 123; and 3 Mass. Hist. Coll. III. 169, where is most valua. copy from the rec. of the ch. of the pastor hims. made by Mr. Felt, where we must regret what is not a common subj. of compl. that his extr. are too brief. EBENEZER, Hartford, s. prob. of Eliezer, had w. Irene, and I kn. no more of him. ELIEZER, Hartford 1666, had suit in Mass. as early as 1657, against Thomas Purchase of Kennebeck. See our Col. Rec. IV. p. 334. He was propound. for freem. May 1669, had good est. at H. for we learn from the very curious addr. of Mr. Day on the Wadsworth Athenæum, that the edifice was erect. on the ld. by Thomas Welles in Feb. 1667, convey. to Way, and by him held to his d. 12 July 1687, and in 1696, assign. to Ebenezer, his only ch. b. at H. 4 Nov. 1673, by w. Mary. The wid. Mary d. 1701. Of three ds. we kn. the m. Sarah, 4 Sept. 1684, to Ichabod Welles; and Eliz. to his br. Joseph; and Lydia m. 1705, Jabez Whittlesey. GEORGE, said to be a partak. with Thomas Purchase, in the early settlem. of the country near the junct. of the Androscoggin with the Kennebeck, bef. 1630. He was a contribut. in Eng. GEORGE, Dorchester, s. prob. of Henry the first, had div. in neck lds. now South Boston, 1637, aft. at Boston, by w. Eliz. had Eliz. b. 19 Mar. 1651; and as no more is heard of him at B. it seems to me prob. that he was of Providence soon aft. there bound hims. in alleg. to Charles II. 31 May 1666. GEORGE, Saybrook and Lyme, m. Eliz. only d. of John Smith of New London, whither he rem. had George and Thomas, wh. d. there. GEORGE, New London, s. of the preced. m. Susanna, d. of Joseph Nest, and d. a. 23 Feb. 1717. By reason of the marvellous deep snow, his corpse could not be brot. to bur. bef. 7 Mar. See Caulkins, 362. HENRY, Dorchester, prob. br. of the first Aaron, came in the Mary and John, 1630, says Roger Clap, a fellow passeng. well adv. in life, bring. w. Eliz. and ch. prob. Samuel, Henry, Richard, and Eliz. beside ano. of his s. wh. was lost in the winter pass. hither of the Lion, that had been charter. here soon aft. arr. of the Gov. and comp. to go to Bristol for food, and was coming back in Dec. and Jan. 1630–1. He had good est. but never desir. to be freem. liv. to 1667, aged 84, as Blake's Annals tell. His w. had d. 23 June 1665, at the same age. HENRY, Dorchester, s. or more prob. gr.s. of the preced. had in his will of 2 Dec. 1674, nam. sis. Eliz. and br. Richard, beside uncle Aaron, so that my infer. is, that he had no w. or ch. was a mariner, and s. of Richard. JAMES, Newtown, L. I. is first found there in 1656, and had large est. soon, was a Quaker, had ch. James, Francis, John, Hannah, Eliz. and Martha, and d. 2 Oct. 1665. Riker, 378, makes Hannah m. Jeremiah Burroughs; Eliz. m. Arthur Albertis; and Martha m. Thomas Taylor. Highly respect. are descend. ‖ RICHARD, Dorchester, s. of Henry the first, b. in Eng. a. 1624, adm. freem. 10 May 1643, rem. to Salem, there by w. Esther, d. of Thomas Jones, had Henry, bapt. 28 Dec. 1651; Eliz. 8 Sept. 1653; Richard, 1654; Jonathan, 29 Dec. 1657, d. young; with his w. join. the 2d ch. in Boston 17 Feb. 1661, yet had no more ch. bapt. here, tho. by town rec. it seems, that w. Esther brot. him Hannah, 23 May 1662; and w. Bethia brot. Hannah, 13 July 1677. I strongly suspect that in this last rec. by carelessness of the writer mo. and ch. changed names; but it is of very slight importance, for his will of 2 Jan. 1697, pro. 28 Oct. foll. gave all his est. to w. Hannah, "hav. no

reason to believe any of my own childr. are surv." This latter w. was
wid. of Thomas Hull, d. of William Townsend. He was a cooper, a
man of substance, of ar. co. 1671, was lieut. and serv. at castle island
under Roger Clap, was farmer gener. of the impost in 1674, and lost
money by his speculat. and some persons wished him to be made postmaster, in place of John Hayward the notary, perhaps out of compassion
for that ill success. RICHARD, "was of Scituate in 1651," says Farmer,
but no evid. is kn. to me. ROBERT, an apprent. in 1634, with Dept.-
Gov. Ludlow, yet in few wks. was under ens. Jennison, wh. soon lawfully assign. him to Edward Burton, and not long aft. was with Samuel
Hosier, wh. early in 1636 got rid of him to William Almy to take him
from Israel Stoughton, Jennison, Burton, and Hosier having to pay 20s.
each for the benefit of Almy. See pp. 119, 122, 123, and 163 of Col.
Rec. I. Such an inhab. was not object of regret if soon lost sight of.
SAMUEL, Dorchester 1664, perhaps s. of the first Henry, but nothing
more is heard. THOMAS, Isle of Shoals 1649, in few yrs. aft. was liv.
in some part of Essex Co. THOMAS, New London, s. of the first George
of the same, m. says Caulkins, Ann, d. of Andrew Lester, but if so,
she was the sec. d. of that name, prob. by his sec. w. of the same name
(for the first Ann by first w. had m. Nathaniel Millet), had Thomas,
wh. d. at 20 yrs.; David, James, John, and six others betw. 1688 and
1714, rem. a. 1720 to New Haven, and d. 1726. WILLIAM, Boston,
prob. s. of Richard, with w. join. Mather's ch. 9 Mar. 1677, was freem.
1678. WILLIAM, Salem, br. prob. of Aaron of the same, freem. 1690,
with him was active in protest. against the cruel hypochondria of Rev.
Samuel Paris. See Felt in 3 Mass. Hist. Coll. III. 169.

WAYMOUTH. See Weymouth.

WEADEN, EDWARD, a soldier in Mosely's comp. at the Narraganset
gr. fight, Dec. 1675. Perhaps this name may be Weeden, or Whee-
don.

WEARE, ‡* NATHANIEL, Newbury, s. perhaps of Peter of the same,
b. in Eng. a. 1631, or more prob. 1635, as in Oct. 1695, he was sw. to be
only 60, m. 3 Dec. 1656, Eliz. Swain, perhaps d. of Richard of Rowley,
had Nathaniel, b. 5 Jan. 1658; Peter, 5 Nov. 1660; rem. a. 1662 to
Hampton, there had six others, as Coffin says, and yet of not one is the
proof accessib. was freem. of Mass. 1666, a rep. and bec. counsel. of N.
H. aft. our new chart. 1692, and d. 13 May 1718, aged 83, wh. is in
more than one book swell. to 87. * PETER, Kittery, a man of large
acquaint. with the New Hampsh. and Maine early settlem. whose name
first appears on the gr. jury 1645, under the Gorges jurisdict. and in
1654 under that of Mass. of wh. he was adm. freem. 1652, as Farmer
counts the sw. of alleg. was rep. for York in 1659, in the subordin.

legislat. held by Wiggin and Danforth by virtue of commissn. from
Mass. but rep. at Boston in 1660 for Kittery ; in 1665, the great important sess. of controver. with the royal commissnrs. and 1669 for York,
again 1670 in Presid. Danforth's Court for the Province, in 1676 as
"the old Treasr. was direct. to square his accounts," and in 1680 sw.
alleg. to the k. Charles II. Aft. this I find his name no more in the
Maine rec. and he prob. d. soon. PETER, Newbury, wh. d. as Coffin
notes, 12 Oct. 1653, may have been br. or f. rather more prob. of Nathaniel. ‡PETER, Hampton, s. of Nathaniel, of wh. it is mortifying
confess. that I kn. no more exc. that he was made counsel. of the Prov.
1698. Neither Belkn. nor Farmer give m. progeny or d. It has been
asked if Peter Weare and Peter Wyer were the same man. ROBERT,
Hampton, the freem. of 1678, may have been br. of Nathaniel. In a
very valua. note to Belkn. Hist. by Farmer in his Ed. 364, 5, uncertainty rests even on the f. of Meshech, b. 1714, H. C. 1735, one of the
most serviceable men that State has ever produc. wh. was its first Presid.
under revolut. const. Yet F. thinks he was s. and the youngest of four
of Nathaniel, wh. was s. of the last Peter.

WEATHERHEAD, or WITHERHEAD, MARY, one of the Quakers, wh.
arr. at Boston 27 July 1656, from London, aged 26, in the Speedwell,
but was, I hope, discreet eno. to go quietly to prison until the evil
spirit in our governm. sent her home by the same ship. The silence
of Hutchinson I. 196, permits us to indulge such a suspicion of rare
tolerat.

WEATHERS, JOHN, Hadley, sw. alleg. Feb. 1679.

WEAVER, CLEMENT, fined for drunk. in Mass. 1640, may have not
been perman. resid. certain. not the Mr. Weaver, order. by court to be
sent home, 1 Mar. 1631, in the Lion, as one "unmeet to inhabit here."
Passing over the drunk. we may find him as Clement senr. a freem. at
Newport in the list of 1655. CLEMENT, Newport, in the list of freem.
1655 call. junr. may well seem s. of the preced. and he m. Mary, eldest
d. of William Freeborn, had perhaps the misfortune of being a capt.
1690 serv. with Walley in the expedit. of Phips against Quebec, if such
latitude of construct. may be applied to the exact statem. in Arnold's
Hist. of R. I. Vol. I. 520, 2. EDMUND, a husbandman, aged 28, with his
w. Margaret, 30, came in the Planter, 1635, from London. They are
call. in the London cocket for clearance, of Auckstrey in Herefordsh.
yet my search for their resid. in this country is unsuccess. JAMES, perhaps br. of the preced. came fellow-passeng. at least with him, and was
aged 23. THOMAS, Boston, by w. Eliz. had Sarah, b. 6 Nov. 1674,
but of him no more can be found here, tho. possib. it might be in ano.
town.

WEBB, ADEY, ADY, ADDEY, or ADDY, Plymouth 1631, was tax. in two foll. yrs. and on the list of those able to bear arms in 1643, his name appears with a star bef. it. He was not a severe puritan, but oft. prosecut. for work. on the Lord's day, bound as serv. to Gov. Prence, and prob. had no w. or ch. See Felt, Eccles. Hist. I. 347. BENJAMIN, Malden, m. 7 Dec. 1669, Mercy, d. of William Bucknam, and, were it in my power, I would gladly tell more than that he was freem. 1690. *CHRISTOPHER, Braintree, freem. 1645, had perhaps Peter, but the old town rec. is incomplete, not nam. the mo. nor date; and it cannot be that, as Farmer had it, he was b. 1657, and so more likely to be s. of sec. Christopher; was one of the petitnrs. that yr. for leave to go and possess the ld. from wh. our governm. had unrighteous. driv. Gorton, Holden, and other misbeliev. planters; but the right of the sufferers was vindicat. in Eng. *CHRISTOPHER, Billerica, prob. s. of the preced. b. in Eng. m. 18 Jan. 1656, Hannah Scott, perhaps d. of the first Benjamin, had John, b. 23 Oct. foll.; Samuel, Aug. 1660, as the town rec. certifies, tho. I have seen a statem. that it was 28 July 1660; Christopher, 25 Mar. 1663; Hannah, 5 Sept. 1665; Benjamin, 12 Apr. 1667; Mary, 6 Sept. 1669; Joseph, 15 Mar. 1672; Abigail, 13 Oct. 1675. He was town clk. 1678, early in life, and rep. in the difficult times of 1689 and 90, d. 30 May 1694, aged 64. DANIEL, Salem, licens. as innholder 1689, had m. 20 July 1675, Mary Beckett, d. of John, had John, b. 17 Apr. 1676; Margaret, 20 Feb. 1678, d. at 2 yrs.; Perez, 1 Apr. 1680; Mary, 14 Aug. 1682; Daniel, 5 Sept. 1688; and Eliz. 17 May 1692. FRANCIS, by Mr. Felt in Ann. I. 171, is represent. erron. as coming in the fleet with Higginson in June 1629 to Salem, and by him correct. as in II. 630 a doubt is express. however. He was a contrib. of £50. to encourage the planta. but never came over, I think; and was one of the most active promoters, no other mem. of the comp. being so sure to attend their meet. In Oct. 1629 he join. with Gov. Cradock, Dept.-Gov. Goffe, Winthrop, Saltonstall, treasr. Harwood, Johnson, Pynchon, and Vassall, in writ. from London to Higginson and Skelton, as to the " divers scandalous and intemp. speeches passed from one or both of you in your publ. sermons or pray." as report. by the two members John and Samuel Browne, wh. had accomp. those min. Of course he was not a fellow-passeng. but was (under direction of the Gov. and comp. in Eng. to Endicott) to have a mill privilege in the Col. and all this appears from the rec. I. 39, 401, and 408, in connex. with 128, showing that our Gen. Ct. in Boston, Sept. 1634, wrote to him, George Harwood, and other great friends in London, to intreat them to choose one of themselves treasr. for this planta. in lieu of Harwood. Tho. the Edit. of Transact. of Amer. Antiq. Soc. III. suppos. that he d. bef. sett. up his sawmill

here, to me it seems equal. prob. that he was engag. in business of too
much import. at London to come over, and intend. to carry forwards the
mill business by a serv. or factor.   GEORGE, Dover 1642, tax. 1648, d.
1650.   HENRY, Boston, merch. came from Salisbury, Co. Wilts, with w.
Dosabell, perhaps in 1637, when Felt marks a gr. of ld. to him, but
more prob. in 1638, adm. of our ch. 6 Feb. 1639, as was she on Sunday
foll. made freem. 13 Mar. next, constable 1641, brot. only ch. Margaret,
wh. had been bapt. at S. 25 Sept. 1625.   Prob. she was b. by a first w.
for in the parish rec. of St. Edmunds at S. may be seen, that Henry W.
m. 23 Apr. 1627, Jane Woolford, and so we may assume that Dosabell
was third w.   This w. d. 28 Feb. 1660, and he d. 7 Sept. foll. and prob.
his d. was sudden, as Eliz. the d. of his only ch. was m. on the same
day to Robert Gibbs.   Margaret had by spec. license of the Gen. Ct.
permiss. Sept. 1642, to m. first Jacob Sheaffe, and sev. yrs. aft. his d.
she m. Rev. Thomas Thacher.   His will of 5 Apr. 1660 is very full,
and may be read in Geneal. Reg. X. 177–80.   It was pro. 13 Sept. foll.
and perhaps his est. was the largest that had so early come into Ct. Inv.
was £7,819. 5s. 2d.   Six clerg. were favor. with small legacies, and
John and Samuel Sanford, s. of his sis. Eliz. had £80. ea. but perhaps
they were in Eng. as was a sis. of his w. also a legatee.   Webb was
largely engag. in the Lynn iron works and a great benefactor to
Harv. Coll. beside legacy of £50. gave that fine prop. betw. Washing-
ton and Devonshire streets in B. where the great publishers, Little,
Brown & Co. have long exhibit. their treasures.   JEREMIAH, Northampton, s. of the first John of the same, m. a. 1693, Priscilla McLathlin,
had Joanna, b. 16 Mar. 1694, d. in two wks. and in Geneal. Reg. III.
400, her name was mistaken for Jonathan ; Priscilla, Aug. 1695 ;
Esther, 23 Dec. 1697 ; Josiah, 28 Mar. 1700, d. at 23 yrs. ; Daniel,
1702 ; Sarah, Apr. 1704; Joseph, Mar. 1707, d. at 2 mos. ; Eliz. 6
May 1708 ; Experience, 12 Nov. 1710 ; and Moses, 20 Mar. 1713 ;
had sec. w. Sarah, but no ch. by her is kn. and he d. 5 Mar. 1734.
* ‖ JOHN, Boston, adm. of the ch. 9 Feb. 1634, then call. single man, and
of wh. I hear no more, unless he went home that yr. and came again
with Stephen in the James from Southampton, emb. in Apr. 1635, and
arr. 3 June.   Both are call. laborers or husbandmen, said to be of Marlborough in Wilts, but favored also with an alias Evered, and it may be
that both points of the description were to delude the tyrannic. formality.
He was adm. freem. 7 Dec. 1636, ar. co. 1643, one of the early sett. of
Chelmsford, there was ens. and rep. 1663, 4, and 5, but in the last yr.
was expell. fin. and for a season disfranch. but soon restor. had gr. of ld.
at Dracut 1667, d. 16 Oct. 1668, by the strange occur. of being drown.
by a whale, unless a false report was spread, wh. may be seen in Rev.

Samuel Danforth's writ. for Roxbury ch. where he insert. it the next day. See Rev. Simon Bradstreet's Journal in Geneal. Reg. IX. 44. JOHN, Saybrook 1648, may be s. of Richard of Hartford, for he is enum. the same yr. as of that place, and is perhaps the man wh. d. there 27 May 1684. JOHN, Boston, a brazier, adm. inhab. 24 Nov. 1651. JOHN, Northampton 1655, had by first w. Ann, at Hartford, Mary, b. 5 Feb. 1648, wh. m. 24 Mar. 1663, John Earle ; Sarah, wh. m. 17 Dec. 1668, Zechariah Field; Richard, 1654; and perhaps Lydia, wh. d. at N. 1667. His w. d. 26 Aug. of that yr. and he m. 16 Oct. next, Eliz. Swift, had Jeremiah, 12 July 1668 ; and Peter, 23 June 1670, posthum. for the f. d. 19 May preced. The wid. m. Robert Danks. JOHN, Northampton, s. of the preced. m. 12 Dec. 1665, Susanna, wid. of Matthew Cole, only ch. of Henry Cunliffe of the same, had John, b. 8 Jan. 1667 ; Henry, 27 Nov. 1668 ; Ann, 4 Feb. 1671 ; Ebenezer, 16 Jan. 1673 ; Sarah, 28 Dec. 1674 ; Mindwell, 31 May 1678 ; Mary, 20 Aug. 1681 ; and Thankful, 21 Apr. 1684 ; and he d. 3 Apr. 1720, in ripe old age. His wid. d. 30 Oct. 1735, aged 90. JOHN, Salem 1667, is prob. the same wh. m. Bridget Whitford of the same, and had Bridget, b. 17 Aug. 1678. JOHN, Braintree, m. May 1680, Bethia, d. of Joseph Adams of the same. JOHN, Northampton, perhaps not s. of John of the same bef. ment. sw. alleg. Feb. 1679. JONATHAN, Malden, d. Sept. 1658. JONATHAN, Northampton, d. 1694. JOSEPH, Boston, eldest s. of Richard of the same, freem. 1675, d. or was bur. 11 Oct. 1698. He by w. Grace had Joseph, b. 10 May 1666 ; Mary, 27 Aug. 1671 ; Sarah, 14 Oct. 1673 ; and Elisha, 13 Feb. 1676. JOSEPH, Stamford, d. 1684, leav. ch. Joseph, Mary, Hannah, Sarah, and Margery. JOSEPH, Fairfield, perhaps s. of the preced. nam. in Mather's Hecatompolis, bred at H. C. 1684, first of the name, where he was expel. as by the Diary of Noadiah Russell in Geneal. Reg. VII. 53 is relat. and he tells how soon he was restor. m. 1691, Eliz. youngest d. of Isaac Stratford, ord. 15 Aug. 1694, had prob. Joseph, Y. C. 1715, and d. 19 Sept. 1732. NEHEMIAH, Boston, youngest s. of Richard of the same, cordwainer, sold, 1670, his sh. of paternal est. RICHARD, Weymouth, had Joseph, b. 19 Aug. 1640 ; and Nehemiah, 19 Oct. 1641 ; rem. to Boston, prob. in 1644, there offer. those ch. to bapt. 12 Jan. 1645, the rec. of first ch. varying from certif. copy of W. town rec. only in call. 17 Oct. the day of b. of the younger, but shockingly proving its falsity as to the f. of the other. He was a shoemaker, had w. Mary, and in Oct. 1648 unit. with James Everill and others in ask. incorpo. for their handicraft ; made his will wh. names no w. 1 July 1659, and d. next day. RICHARD, Cambridge, freem. 6 Nov. 1632, is count. as one of those order. by Ct. to

rem. from Braintree, by Dr. Holmes in 1 Mass. Hist. Coll. VII. 10, certain. went in the great migrat. with Gov. Haynes, and other friends of
Hooker, and sat down at Hartford, was of the gr. jury 1643, in few yrs.
aft. rem. to Norwalk, and there, too, was one of the first sett. He had
w. Eliz. and d. July 1665, his wid. wh. d. 24 Jan. 1681, being then
charg. for est. larger than any exc. three in that town. He left no ch.
but took Sarah, d. of Rev. Samuel Stone, and brot. her up, until she m.
Thomas Butler of Hartford; and in Hall's Hist. we see that the wid.
empower. a friend, in 1677 to adj. with Butler and his w. for their claim
of the est. of her h. Butler's w. had half, and by the Court was distribut. other portions to Bartholomew Barnard, wh. was h. of Sarah, d.
of Thomas Birchard, to Richard Homes, Stephen Beckwith, Thomas
Barnum and others, of whose degrees of consanguin. it may not be easy
to determine. Still, in 1694, among the voters in that town is Ebenezer
W. RICHARD, Northampton, br. of the sec. John of the same, sw.
alleg. 8 Feb. 1679, by w. Patience had Ebenezer, b. 27 July 1684;
Ann, 2 June 1686, d. at 5 yrs.; Patience, 7 Sept. 1687; Jonathan;
John and Thankful, tw. 28 Feb. 1692, of wh. Thankful d. soon; Richard, wh. d. soon; and Ann, 11 Mar. 1698. He d. 23 Aug. 1700; and
13 May 1704, when the Ind. destroy. the hamlet of Pascomuck, near
the S. part of the town, Patience was k. She was prob. the wid. not
the d. SAMUEL, Braintree, perhaps younger br. of John of the same,
m. 16 Dec. 1686, Mary, d. of Joseph Adams of the same. STEPHEN,
perhaps br. of John, was fellow-passeng. in the James 1635, from
Southampton, both honor. with the alias Evered, and both from
Marlborough in Wilts; but no more is kn. of him on our side of the
ocean. THOMAS, Charlestown, by w. Mary, had Sarah, bapt. 17 June
1666; Thomas, 5 Mar. 1668; may be that mariner of Boston, taking
deed of ho. and ld. Mar. 1661, from Nathaniel Fryer, and perhaps went
home for short time, coming back in 1671. WILLIAM, Boston, had been
one of Roxbury ch. bef. adm. freem. 25 May 1636, and in the list of
mem. to his name is add. the informat. that his w. was excom. in 1642.
Of course she was restor. on express. of penitence, rem. not long aft.
and with recommend. tho. Ellis omits his name; was adm. of Boston ch.
with his w. Rebecca, 7 Apr. and d. Dec. 1644. His wid. in Apr. 1653,
sold the Roxbury est. That William wh. Farmer call. of Weymouth,
was Richard, as we may well believe, when the same Joseph, that the
copy of W. record says was his s. was brot. up by Richard to be bapt.
as his. Farmer counts in 1834, eighteen gr. of wh. nine at Harv. four
at Yale, and five at other N. E. coll.

WEBBER, JOHN, Boston, by w. Eliz. had Martha and Mary, tw. b. 18
Feb. 1675; John, 23 Mar. 1678; Eliz. 25 Jan. 1678, if the miserable

copy of the orig. town rec. can be believ.; and Barachiah, 4 Oct. 1686.
JOSEPH, Falmouth 1680, had gr. of ld. that yr. prob. from regard to the
propr. loss of his f. Thomas, driv. with his fam. to Charlestown in
Philip's war, when F. was destroy. See Willis I. 215. JOSIAS, Read-
ing, of wh. I find no ment. but in Eaton's hist. of early sett. RICHARD,
Portsmouth, N. H. 1688, one of the petitnrs. for jurisdict. of Mass.
when Andros was overthr. SAMUEL, Falmouth 1681, perhaps s. of
Thomas, rem. during the next Ind. war, to Salem, there was one of the
witnesses against Rev. George Burrows, prov. his witchcr. by unusual
bodily strength; and d. at York 1716, leav. wid. Deborah, and ch.
Samuel, John, Thomas, Benjamin, Waitstill, Joseph, Mary, w. of Joseph
Sayward, Deborah, and Dorcas. THOMAS, Boston, mariner, join our ch.
7 Apr. 1644, by w. Sarah, had Sarah, b. 1643, says the base copy of the
town rec. but the ch. rec. says bapt. 8 Dec. 1644, a. 3 days old; Bathsheba, bapt. 24 Sept. 1648, a. 3 days old; Thomas, 2 Feb. 1651; but
these two are not found on the town imperfect rec.; and Mehitable, b.
10, bapt. 13 June 1652, wh. is call. s. on town rec. of its d. at three mos.
was master of the ship Mayflower, and sold here 7-32 parts of that vessel of 200 tons, as our reg. of deeds in 1652 shows; perhaps rem. to
Kennebeck, there had other w. Mary, sis. of John Parker, the great
propr. and prob. more ch. Willis says his fam. rem. to Charlestown
during the sec. great Ind. war, but the time and place of his d. are not
seen. He also says, that in 1681, the town of C. had made her gr. of
ld. for wh. six yrs. aft. she appl. for a patent from the autocratic Gov.
Sir Edmund Andros. THOMAS, York, prob. s. of the preced. may not
have any thing discernib. a. him beyond what Willis tells I. 215. In
Apr. 1695, the wid. Mary W. was adm. of the ch. in Charlestown, but I
can only look on her as his mo.-in-law.

WEBSTER, BENJAMIN, Salem, wh. was wound. in the gr. Narraganset
fight, 19 Dec. 1675, when k. Philip's power was brok. was of Appleton's
comp. and may therefore have been of Ipswich, yet by Felt II. 505, call.
of S. EBENEZER, Hampton, sec. s. of Thomas of the same, m. 25 July
1709, Hannah Judkins, had Rachel, b. 17 May 1710; Susannah, 9 July
1712; Ebenezer, 10 Oct. 1714 (wh. m. 20 July 1738, Susanna Batchelder,
and by his first ch. of the same nam. was gr.f. of Ezekiel and Daniel, the
disting. advocates and statesmen); William, 26 Aug. 1716, d. in few yrs.;
John, 4 Aug. 1719, d. in few yrs.; Hannah, 1722; Mary and Joseph, tw.
15 Sept. 1724; and Edward, 9 Feb. 1728; and d. at Kingston, 1 Feb.
1736. HENRY, Boston, by w. Esther, had Ann, b. 9 Feb. 1683; and John,
28 Sept. 1688; yet no more can be told of him. ISAAC, Kingston, s. of
Thomas, m. 1 Apr. 1696, Mary Hutchins, had John, bapt. 27 June 1697;
Jonathan, 30 Apr. 1699; Hannah, 22 Feb. 1702; Eliz. Mar. 1704; Sarah,

d. young; Samuel, b. 26 Mar. 1714, d. soon; Samuel, again, 25 Aug. 1715; and Gideon, 20 Dec. 1716; and d. 1718. ISRAEL, Newbury, s. prob. not eldest of John of Ipswich, b. in Eng. a. 1624, perhaps in Co. Norfolk, m. says Coffin, 3 Jan. 1666, perhaps 1667, Eliz. Brown, had Eliz. b. 7 Oct. 1668; and his w. d. 3 days aft. His sec. w. m. 9 Nov. 1669, Eliz. Lunt, d. of the first Henry, brot. him Ann, July 1672; Joseph, 15 Mar. 1676, d. at 4 yrs.; Mary, 18 May 1679; and Lydia, 20 Dec. 1681; and he d. 7 Dec. 1683. The wid. d. 3 Aug. 1688. JAMES, Boston, a brewer, by w. Mary, had James, b. 16 July 1659; Thomas, 11 Jan. 1662; John, 5 Aug. 1664; William, 25 Mar. 1667; Eliz. 14 May 1670; Mary, 9 Dec. 1672; Mary, again, 15 July 1686; and James, again, 27 Aug. 1688. But may it not be prob. that the last two were by a sec. w. or prob. offspr. of the eldest s.? JOHN, Ipswich, came, says tradit. from Ipswich in Co. Suffk. 1634, freem. 4 Mar. 1635, had John, b. 1632, prob. in Eng. and here d. 1645, leav. 4 ds. Mary, Hannah, Eliz. and Abigail, and three other s. Stephen, Israel, and Nathan, as the Gen. Ct's. act on wid's. petitn. shows in Col. Rec. II. 184; beside wid. Mary, wh. m. John Emery, as Farmer says. Much diligence had been by him bestow. on this fam. yet more was giv. to ano. wh. he found, contra. to his first impress. was entitl. rather than this man to be regard. as the progenit. of the late illustrious statesman, Daniel Webster. I regret to obs. the slight error of Dr. Bond (if it be an error) in mak. Thomas, wh. is the true progenit. of Daniel, m. a d. of deac. William Godfrey, bec. Godfrey in his will truly calls him s.-in-law, as he was s. by a former h. of Godfrey's w. But more desir. is it to avoid the error of Miss Thomas, who would make John of our Ipswich, the ancestor, and Thomas his son, when it appears plainly that John had not son Thomas, and that Thomas's f. d. at Ormsby, in Co. Norfolk, prob. as there the s. was b. and the mo. had m. deac. Godfrey bef. leav. Eng. §†‡*JOHN, Hartford 1636, but from what place in Mass. he went is uncert. By fam. tradit. he was from Co. Warwick. He was rep. 1 May 1637, a magistr. from 1639 to 1655, when he was made dept.-gov. and next yr. gov. In the gr. contest a. ch. governm. he took sides with Rev. Mr. Russell of Wethersfield, and that caused his rem. up the riv. to found Hadley in 1659, by our Gen. Ct. was adm. freem. of Mass. and in May 1660 made a magistr. there, d. 5 Apr. 1661. Robert, William, and Thomas, his s. are said to have foll. their f. but tho. the respectab. ref. in Farmer's MS. for this tradit. is made to letter of the late Noah Webster, the grammarian, I doubt his studies had been too long turned in ano. direction to justify unlimit. confidence in all parts of his relat. and that Robert did not foll. but accomp. his f. to Mass. He brot. from Eng. w. Agnes, ch. Matthew, Robert, Ann, Eliz. and Mary; perhaps, also, Thomas and William, tho. one or both of the latter may have been b. on our side of the ocean; and fam. tradit. makes William b. 1617. No dates of b. of any of the seven are giv. by the most valua. work of Goodwin, pub. since the d. of the compiler. From the will of 25 June 1659, little is learn. but the names of four s. two ds. Ann Marsh, w. of John, and d. Markham, beside two gr.ch. Jonathan and Mary Hunt. The name of mo. was not ment. and prob. she was oldest d. if not even oldest ch. When or where she m. Hunt, or what even was his bapt. name is unkn. Tradit. in the fam. makes his name John, and hers, Mary; and it may be conject. that both were d. JOHN, Portsmouth 1648, a brewer, as constable was allow. charge for bring. Henry Taylor a prisoner to Boston, in Col. Rec. III. 140. He may be the man to wh. gr. of ld. was made by Salem 1638, in hope to draw him, and d. 1662. JOHN, Newbury, s. of the first John, b. in Eng. was in milit. trouble as Col. Rec. IV. 362, and, very briefly, Coffin, 62, sufficient. relate. He may have been the man by Farmer call. a blacksmith, early at Haverhill; but to N. went back, had with his mo. and the younger childr. says Coffin, rem. from Ipswich, m. 13 June 1653, Ann Batt, perhaps d. of Nicholas, had John, b. 11 Feb. 1656; Mary, 29 Mar. 1658, d. in few wks.; Sarah, 1 July 1659; Abigail, 16 Mar. 1662; Lucy, 19 Dec. 1664; Mary, again, 24 May 1667; Stephen, 8 May 1669; Ann, 7 Sept. 1671; Nicholas, 19 Oct. 1673; and Jonathan, 21 May 1676. JOHN, Newbury, s. of John of the same, took o. of alleg. 1678, and was freem. 1690, m. 9 Mar. 1681, Bridget Huggins, perhaps d. of John, had Ann, b. 9 June 1682; John, 2 Nov. 1683; Sarah, 28 Dec. 1685; Israel, 9 Apr. 1688; Hannah, 5 Oct. 1692; and Stephen, 11 Jan. 1698. JOHN, Hampton, s. of Thomas of the same, m. 21 Sept. 1703, Abiah Shaw, and had sec. w. Sarah. His ch. were Jeremiah, b. Dec. 1703; Charity and Josiah, tw. 2 Apr. 1706; John, 10 Feb. 1712; Thomas, 1 July 1715; Caleb, 19 Mar. 1719; Abiah, 20 Jan. 1722; and Eliz. 27 Sept. 1724. MATTHEW, Farmington, s. of Hon. John, freem. 1645, and contin. on the list 1669, had only s. John, and a d. NICHOLAS, Stamford, m. Sarah, d. of John Waterbury, wh. had been 1672 divorc. from Zechariah Dibble for his bad conduct, had John, David, and Rachel, made his will 4 May 1687, and d. soon, giv. est. to w. Sarah, and these three ch. The s. were proprs. there 1701, but no more is kn. * ROBERT, Middletown, s. of Hon. John, m. a. 1652, Susanna, d. of Richard Treat, the first of Wethersfield, had John, b. 10 Nov. 1653; Sarah, 30 June 1655; Jonathan, 9 Jan. 1657; Susanna, 26 Oct. 1658; aft. rem. to Hartford had Samuel, Robert, Joseph, William, Mary, and Eliz. to neither of wh. are affix. dates of b. was made a lieut. 1654, town clk. and rep. 1657, had gr. of 300 acres in 1672, was on serv. in the war of 1675, but d. bef. May 1677, when his wid. Susanna had leave to sell est. Trumbull, Col. Rec. II. 310. STEPHEN, Haverhill, m. 24 Mar. 1663, Hannah, d. of John Ayer of Salisbury. STEPHEN, Newbury, by Coffin, thot. s. of John of the same, m. 1 Nov. 1698, Sarah, d. of Nathaniel Clark, had Joanna, and Sarah, b. 10 Dec. 1701, prob. tw. but Coffin does not say so much. THOMAS, Boston, mariner, adm. of the ch. 7 Apr. 1644, and freem. next mo. THOMAS, Hampton, brot. to Watertown, by his mo. Margery, then w. of William Godfrey, perhaps 1638, from Ormsby in Co. Norfolk, where he had been bapt. 20 Nov. 1631, and from W. to Hampton carried in youth by Godfrey, m. 2 Nov. 1657, Sarah Brewer, perhaps d. of Thomas of Roxbury, had Mary, b. 19 Dec. 1658; Sarah, 22 Jan. 1661; Hannah, 27 Dec. 1663; Thomas, 20 Jan. 1665; Ebenezer, 1 Aug. 1667; Isaac, 2 Apr. 1670; John, 16 Feb. 1674; Joshua, 8 Nov. 1676; and Abigail, 1 Jan. 1679; sw. alleg. Feb. 1669, and d. 5 Jan. 1715, tho. Farmer in MS. says Feb. in 84th yr. This is the ancestor of the conspicuous lawyers wh. the research of Farmer ascert. THOMAS, Northampton, s. of Gov. John, m. 16 June 1663, Abigail, d. of George Alexander of the same, had Abigail, b. 9 Jan. 1668, d. soon; Abigail, again, 10 Jan. 1669; George, 7 Nov. 1670; John, 26 Nov. 1673; rem. next yr. to Northfield, thence driv. 1675 by the Ind. wh. destroy. his prop. he sat down at Hadley, sw. alleg. there 8 Feb. 1679, and had Eliz. 26 Nov. 1676; Thankful, 12 Jan. 1679; and Mary, 25 May 1681; again went to Northfield, there d. 1686, and his wid. d. bef. Mar. 1690. THOMAS, Hampton, s. of Thomas of the same, m. as is suggest. in Bond's Hist. of Watertown, his cous. d. of William Godfrey, but whether this be so, is doubt. By w. Sarah, wh. d. 15 Feb. 1718, he had Sarah, b. 15 Sept. 1690; Thomas, 1693; Mary, 19 May 1696; Alice, 5 Aug. 1698; Joshua, 2 Sept. 1703; Abigail, 15 Apr. 1706; Samuel, 3 Apr. 1708; and Eliz. 11 Jan. 1711; and he d. at Kingston, 7 Mar. 1733. WILLIAM, Hadley, s. of Gov. John, in his MS. by Farmer said (follow. tradit. prob. without reason) to be b. 1617; sw. alleg. 8 Feb. 1679; m. 17 Feb. 1670, Mary, d. of Thomas Reeve of Springfield, wh. brot. him no ch. but was accus. of familiarity with the devil, sent all the way to Boston for trial as witch in 1684, and yet was not found guilty. Had it been very few yrs. later, the result might have been differ. when the gr. adversary was foil. with his own weapons, as in the Goodwin case. He d. a. 1688, and his wid. was permit. to live till 1696. WILLIAM, Boston, m. Mary, d. of capt. Samuel Mosely or Maudsley, may have had s. of the same name, wh. d. 28 Dec. 1725, aged 28. Farmer says that in 1834, ten of this name had been gr. at Harv. six at Yale, and twelve at the other N. E. coll.

WEDGEWOOD, JOHN, Hampton 1639, had, in 1637, when he belong to Ipswich, serv. in the Pequot war, and was wound. but in Oct. of the later yr. was sentenc. to be set in the stocks for being in the comp. of drunk. See Col. Rec. I. 269. No doubt his conversat. improv. for his will of 24 Nov. 1654, pro. 10 Apr. foll. names w. Mary, and five ch. John, the eldest, Jonathan, David, Mary, and Abigail. JONATHAN, Hampton, s. of the preced. took the o. of alleg. 26 May 1669, and once more, 16 Dec. 1678.

WEEBON, STEPHEN, wh. d. at Boston, Sept. 1659, inv. of whose goods and clothing, 16 Nov. foll. is in Geneal. Reg. IX. 348, from Prob. Rec. III. 171, was, I judge, only casual visitor, perhaps from the West Ind. and the expense of his board was to be reimburs. by his host being made admin. He may have come only from New York, under the Dutch, and had very small stock.

WEED, DANIEL, Stamford, s. of Jonas, had been of Rye 20 yrs. bef. he d. 29 Nov. 1697, leav. four s. and a d. whose names are not found. GEORGE, Salisbury, s. of John of the same, took o. of alleg. 20 Dec. 1677, at the same time with his f. and brs. Samuel and John. JOHN, Salisbury, m. 14 Nov. 1650, Deborah, d. of Samuel Wensley, or Winsly, had Samuel, b. 15 Feb. 1652; Mary, 5 Sept. 1653; John, 1 Nov. 1655; Ann, 26 July 1657; Deborah, 15 June 1659; George, 25 May 1661; and Ephraim, 24 Feb. 1667. He was, it is said, b. a. 1627, and his d. Deborah m. 29 Nov. 1677, Christopher Barnard the sec. of Newbury. JOHN, Stamford, s. of Jonas of the same, m. Joanna Westcoat, d. of Richard, had Jonas, b. 1665; Daniel, 1667; John; Samuel; Joseph; Isaac; Mary; and Hannah, all nam. when the inv. was brot. in 15 Jan. 1690. JONAS, the freem. of 18 May 1631, of wh. nothing more is told, exc. by Bond wh. discov. from Trumbull, Col. Rec. I. 2, that he had been dism. from the ch. of Watertown to that of Wethersfield, but the date in Bond, p. 963, 29 May 1635, is by me confidently read 29 Mar. 1636. Of course he came in the fleet of 1630, and by Bond's reasonab. conject. in the ship with Sir Richard Saltonstall. I find a Jonas, perhaps his s. at Stamford 1669, then seek. to be made freem. of Conn. but he is accomp. in the same good purpose by JOHN wh. may be gr.s. of the first Jonas. Mr. Judd enlarges our acquaint. with him by tell. that he was of Stamford 1642, until he d. 1676, his inv. being of 5 June in that yr. He made his will Nov. 1672, nam. four s. John, Daniel, Jonas, and Samuel, four ds. Mary, w. of George Abbot; Dorcas Wright, w. of James; Hannah, m. 5 Jan. 1670, Benjamin Hoyt; and Sarah. His wid. Mary, d. early in 1690, at least her inv. was brot. in 10 Mar. of that yr. JONAS, Stamford, s. of the preced. m. 16 Nov. 1670, Bethia, d. of John Holley, had perhaps ch. not certain. kn.

Farmer notes that in 1834, seven of this name had been gr. at N. E. coll. of wh. I find four at Yale, two at Harv.

WEEDEN, EDWARD, Boston, came in the Susan and Ellen from London 1635, aged 22, by w. Eliz. d. of Samuel Cole, had Samuel, b. Aug. 1644; John; Edward; and Eliz. wh. m. a. 1673, Sampson Cole (perhaps her first cous.), Hannah, and Mary. In a deed of June 1672, these six ch. unit. with their f. wh. calls hims. of Rumney Marsh, carpenter, in convey. six acres of meadow on E. point of Hog island in B. EDWARD, Boston, s. of the preced. may have been that soldier in Mosely's comp. in Philip's war, whose name is writ. Weaden, wh. see; by w. Jane had Dorothy, b. 22 Apr. 1687; and Edward, 3 July 1688. JAMES, Portsmouth, R. I. came in the Martin, 1638, to Boston, there, with Chad Brown, 13 July, pro. the nuncup. will of Sylvester Baldwin, a fellowpasseng. is on the list of freem. at P. 1655, and call. senr. JAMES, Newport, in the list of freem. 1655, call. junr. may be thot. s. of the preced. by w. Mary, had James, b. 7 Jan. 1674. JOHN, Boston, s. of Edward the first, by w. Ruth had Sarah, b. 16 Nov. 1687. He may have been br. of the sec. Edward, as the ws. of both join. Mather's ch. in 1691. ROBERT, Salem 1638, then by Felt, spelt Wheaden. SAMUEL, Newport, by Benedict enumer. among the founders of the ch. 1644. WILLIAM, Newport, one of the founders of the Bapt. ch. 1644, may have been br. of the preced. and is found in Dr. Stiles's list of freem. there 1655, and a deac. d. 1676, early in that yr. nam. one of the trustees of a charity.

WEEDER, JAMES, Newport, among the freem. of 1655, unless the last letter should be *n*, as seems prob.

WEEKS, AMMIEL, Dorchester, perhaps s. of George of the same, brot. in early youth, freem. 1657, by w. Eliz. had Eliz. b. 18 Oct. 1657; Thankful, 24, bapt. 29 Apr. 1660; Ammiel, 15, bapt. 21 Sept. 1662; Ebenezer, b. 15 May 1665; Joseph, 3 Sept. 1667; Supply, 26 Aug. 1671; Thomas, 20 Nov. 1673; and Hannah, 14 May 1676; and he d. 20 Apr. 1679, aged 46. His wid. d. 10 Apr. 1723, aged 89. Eliz. m. 20 Mar. 1679, Richard Mather, s. of Timothy, as one auth. assures me, while old Dorchester, in Geneal. Reg. V. 467, asserts that her h. was Timothy. AMMIEL, Dorchester, s. of the preced. m. 21 Nov. 1682, Abigail, d. of William Trescott, had Ammiel, b. 26 Feb. 1683; Abigail, 29 Apr. 1687; and George, 20 Mar. 1689; both the s. being rememb. in the will of their gr.f. T. leads one to presume the other ch. d. young. CHRISTOPHER, Boston, by w. Mary, had Christopher, b. 24 Sept. 1695; and Mary, 29 Nov. 1697. EBENEZER, Dorchester, s. of Ammiel the first, m. May 1689, Deliverance, d. of William Sumner, rem. to Boston, there had William, b. 20 Feb. 1690; Jane, 29 Mar. 1692; Eliz. 25 Oct.

1694; Hannah, 5 Jan. 1696; and Ebenezer, 17 Sept. 1699. FRANCIS,
Providence 1637. But for insert. of this and the other R. I. numerous
hosts, whose name is more common. spelt Wickes, ano. place may seem
better. GEORGE, Dorchester, freem. 13 May 1640, brot. w. said to be
Jane, sis. of Roger Clap, and s. Ammiel, William, and Joseph, tho. the
last may have been b. at D. d. 27 Oct. 1659, says Farmer, foll. the town
rec. in wh. date Geneal. Reg. V. 467 follows him; but the inv. in
Geneal. Reg. VII. 334, unless the figures be wrong, proves that he d.
28 Dec. 1650, for it was taken 22 Jan. foll. and perhaps the d. of Oct.
1659 may have been of inf. s. of Ammiel the first. Plainly the numerals
a. the inv. in Geneal. Reg. are erron. for aft. that date, four ch. of his
are bapt. viz. John, 7 Mar. 1652; Eliz. 18 Sept. 1653, wh. prob. d. soon;
William, 20 Aug. 1654; and Eliz. again, 14 Sept. 1656. In the Hist.
of D. compiled, with unusual diligence, by Ebenezer Clapp, 137, is the
true date. JOHN, Dorchester, perhaps s. of William of the same, m. 4
Nov. 1674, Sarah Hammond, but no more is kn. of him. JOSEPH, Dorchester, s. of George, prob. b. in Eng. m. 9 Apr. 1667, Mary, d. of
maj. Humphrey Atherton, had Mary, b. 20 May 1668; Joseph, 26 Mar.
bapt. 3 Apr. 1670, d. at 20 yrs.; Repent, 22, bapt. 27 Feb. 1675; and
perhaps others. He was freem. 1673, and d. 31 Oct. 1690; and his
wid. d. 17 Sept. 1692, aged 56, if the inscript. in Geneal. Reg. IV. 169,
be not erron. as I suspect. It was a mistake of Dr. Harris, very easily
made, to read the names of this man and his f. as Wilkes. JOSEPH,
Dorchester, prob. s. of Ammiel the first, by w. Sarah, had Eliz. b. 31
Aug. 1691; Sarah, 3 Apr. 1693; Hannah, 6 Apr. 1695; Experience, 2
June 1697; and Thankful, 29 Apr. 1699. His w. d. 12 Feb. 1736,
aged 74, says the gr.-st. LEONARD, Portsmouth, one of the men wh.
stood rather for Mass. than for the crown, in 1665, as in our Col. Rec.
IV. pt. 2, 270; by w. Mary had John, b. 14 June 1668; Samuel, 14
Dec. 1670; Joseph, perhaps, 11 Mar. 1672; Joshua, 30 June 1674;
Mary, 19 July 1676; Margaret, 4 June 1679; and he had a sec. w.
Eliz. d. of Samuel Haynes the first. SUPPLY, Marlborough, s. of the
first Ammiel, m. 4 June 1699, Susanna Barnes, d. perhaps of Richard of
the same, had Thomas, b. 5 Sept. 1700; Jemima, 23 Feb. 1702; Abigail, 26 Jan. 1704; Ammiel, 13 Oct. 1705; John, 3 Mar. 1707; Elijah,
11 Feb. 1710; and Susanna, 11 Jan. 1712. His w. d. four days aft.
and he d. 22 Sept. 1755. THOMAS, Charlestown 1636, rec. as inhab. at
Salem 1639, there had Bethia, bapt. 27 Feb. 1642; and Hannah, 5 Jan.
1645; d. soon aft. mak. his will in 1656. Hannah m. 27 Aug. 1667,
John Pickman. THOMAS, Stamford, an orig. sett. 1641, sometimes
spell. Weekes, rem. to Oyster Bay, L. I. bef. 1654, there d. 1671, leav.
w. and ch. Thomas, John, Rebecca, Martha, Eliz. Mary, and Sarah,

seven in all. At Huntington, L. I. the spell. is Wicks. WILLIAM,
Dorchester, s. of George, freem. 1665, had Eliz. b. 16 Sept. 1653;
Mary, 10 Nov. 1656; William, 26 Nov. 1658; Renew, 12 Aug. 1660,
but Geneal. Reg. V. 467, has 1662; Jane, 30 Sept. bapt. 5 Oct. 1662;
George, bapt. 2 Oct. 1664; Sarah, 19 Aug. 1666; Samuel, b. 25 Jan.
1670, beside John, the eldest, 23 Feb. 1652, wh. is the only ch. nam. in
his will of 10 Dec. 1677, pro. Feb. foll. He is the bold innovator as
was perhaps thot. wh. being success. as clk. of the writs, after d. of William Poole, early in 1675, restor. the practice of call. months by their
names, instead of numbers in the Julian calendar; and d. 13 Dec. 1677.
Of his ds. Mary m. Henry White; Renew m. Benjamin Carpenter;
Jane, m. 26 Mar. 1685, John Blackman. WILLIAM, Falmouth, C. C. m.
16 Mar. 1669 or 70, Mercy, d. of Isaac Robinson by his first w. In
1834, Farmer says three of the name had been gr. at Harv. one at
Yale, and five at the other N. E. coll.

WEIGHT, RICHARD, Boston 1655, aged then 55 yrs. may have been
trans. inhab. THOMAS, the freem. of 8 Oct. 1640, may have enjoy. a
various spell. of his name, but with this form it is very difficult to follow him. For the same reason pursuit is unsatisfact. as to the next
surname.

WEIGHTMAN or WIGHTMAN, DANIEL, Newport, pastor of the Bapt.
ch. a. 50 yrs. d. 1750, aged 81, prob. leav. descend. JOHN, said to have
been adm. into the ch. of Charlestown, 31 July 1641. See Budington.
ROBERT, Newport, perhaps, br. of Daniel, m. Margaret, sec. d. of
Thomas Ward of the same, wh. d. as her gr.-st. says, 26 Sept. 1728,
aged 57. By her he had no issue that liv. to m. This name sometimes
is made Whitman.

WEILLUST, or WILLUST, JOST, or JOIST. See Willis.

WEIMOUTH, ROBERT, Kittery, in Nov. 1652 submit. to jurisdict. of
Mass.

WELLY, GEORGE, Lynn 1638, of wh. Lewis in his Hist. 64, or Ed.
sec. 104, tells no more.

WELCH, EDWARD, an Irish youth sent over by the rul. power in
Eng. in the Goodfellow, to be sold here, 1654. See Dalton, William.
JACOB, of wh. I kn. not the resid. came in the Rebecca, 1635, aged 32,
then call. husbandman. JAMES, Swansey, m. 9 Nov. perhaps 1683,
Mercy Sabin of Rehoboth. JOHN, Boston, perhaps s. of Thomas of
Charlestown, mariner, by w. Eliz. had Eliz. b. 3 June 1689. His will
in Pro. Rec. XVIII. 152, shows that he had sev. other ch. at the time
of mak. 14 July 1704, and bef. it was pro. 1 May 1714, prob. he had
two more, for his w. join. Mather's ch. 26 Jan. 1690, and then had three
ch. bapt. whose names are not seen; Rachel, 15 Jan. 1693; Susanna,

10 May 1696; William, 18 Sept. 1698; Benjamin, 8 June 1701;
Ebenezer, 28 Jan. 1705; and Jonathan, 20 July 1707. It nam. the w.
sole extrix. gave her all his prop. dur. wid. and provid. that on the m.
or com. of age of 21 yrs. of the youngest ch. equal div. be made among
all, then liv. NATHANIEL, Enfield, the gr. of Harv. 1687, wh. d. 10
July 1689, aged a. 23, was s. of Thomas of Charlestown, says the rec.
of Enfield, but not min. as Farmer calls him, tho. he may have preach.
for the Coll. Catal. prints him in Roman let. and adds that he d. 1689.
This last fact could not have been within the kn. of F. as the custom of
noting the yr. of d. has been wisely introd. since his time, but he would
have been more precise in his latitude of dying bef. 1699, had he turned
to the Hecatompolis, while consult. Mather, he would have seen, that in
1696, he marks Enfield vacant. PHILIP, Ipswich 1664, m. 1665, Hannah, d. of Henry Haggert of Wenham, had Philip, b. 27 Dec. 1668;
and Moses, 25 Nov. 1685; perhaps others; rem. to Kingston, N. H.
there his s. Samuel had Samuel, b. 1 Sept. 1710, wh. d. 5 Apr. 1823,
aged therefore 112 yrs. 6 mos. and 23 days, as Farmer, in 3 Mass. Hist.
Coll. I. 158 notes, prob. the oldest man kn. as native of any part of
our country. See also his Ed. of Belkn. N. H. I. 208. * THOMAS,
Milford 1639, one of the found. of the ch. that yr. as Dr. Trumbull
says; was freem. 1665, and rep. the same yr. He had m. Hannah, d.
of Thomas Buckingham, and his ch. were Mary, b. 14 Aug. 1655;
Thomas, 28 Jan. 1658; Sarah, bapt. 1660; Esther, 1664; and Lydia,
wh. d. 1685 at 16 yrs. He d. 12 Aug. 1681, and his wid. d. a. 1684.
It is shown in Trumbull, Col. Rec. II. 132, that in 1670 he was fin. £10.
for entrust. a subordin. with power to whip a negro slave, wh. caus. his
death. THOMAS, Milford, s. of the preced. d. early in 1704, in his will
names w. Eliz. and s. Thomas, John, and Paul; and gives legacies to
two ds. not nam. THOMAS, Charlestown, unit. with the ch. 12 Apr.
1650, and was adm. freem. next mo. by w. Eliz. d. of deac. John Upham
of Malden, had John, b. 8 July 1657, d. soon; John, again, 26 Nov.
1658; and d. 31 Dec. 1680. Ano. THOMAS, of Charlestown, as his
gr.-st. tells, d. 10 Apr. 1701, aged 79, and by the same testimo. we may
believe ano. Thomas there, d. 15 June 1703, a. 50 yrs. To discrimin.
the spell. of these fam. names by c, and s has been impossib. and
Farmer did not attempt it, tho. he div. the tribes as arbitrarily as was
necessary. He marks the gr. in 1834, under Welch as 7 at Yale, 3 at
Harv. but under Welsh gives Yale none; and I find at Harv. three
more with the s.

WELCOME, PETER, Boston, mariner, had, I suppose, mov. in from
some other place; possib. he was s. of William of Pemaquid, bec. nothing of him is found in town or ch. rec. but his will of 23 Feb. 1695,

pro. 28 Mar. foll. gives to his d.-in-law Mary Howard, half of his dw.-
ho. and shop, salt ho. wharf, &c. she paying his s. Joseph, on his com.
of age, £30. or if not so paid, he should have that moiety, and the other
half to s. Peter; all personal est. to d. Mary Townsend, exc. sea books
and instrum. with wear. apparel, that should all go to Joseph. WIL-
LIAM, Pemaquid, took o. of fidel. to Mass. 1674, as is seen in Col. Rec.
V. 18.

WELD, or WELDE, DANIEL, Braintree 1640, freem. 2 June 1641, by
w. Alice, wh. d. 18 Apr. 1647, had Dorcas, b. 6 Apr. 1643, d. in few
wks. By ano. w. Ann, wid. I think, of George Hyde of Boston, he had
at Roxbury, whither he rem. with recommend. of Braintree ch. 1651,
Benjamin and Mehitable, tw. b. 1655, bapt. 16 Mar. 1656, both of wh.
d. next yr.; Daniel, b. 14, bapt. 17 Oct. 1658; beside ano. Mehitable,
whose b. or bapt. we find not (yet she may be d. of ano. Daniel); but
the town rec. ment. d. 12 Jan. 1680. He was town clk. 1654, and much
interest. in sch. for wh. the Gen. Ct. in 1659 reward. him with 200
acres, a gr. equal to that of Corlet at the same time, Col. Rec. IV. pt.
I. 397; and d. 22 July 1666, aged 81, says the town rec. His will of 1
July preced. was pro. 3 Nov. foll. In it he gives all his prop. to his w.
Ann, dur. wid. ment. s. Daniel as hav. had his full portion of est. and
more than remain. yet liv. in Eng. and whether liv. or d. unkn. to the
testator, yet he leaves him 20s. and aft. provid. for w's. third, if she m. gives
all resid. to her s. Timothy Hyde, equally with his own ch. Joseph and
Bethia. He makes his cousins Edward Denison, Thomas Weld, and
John W. overseers of the will. Now great uncertainty arises hereon,
whether the yrs. of his age in the town rec. be not far too high, if he be
f. of those tw. in 1655, and also whether the Daniel b. Oct. 1658, were
s. or gr.s. DANIEL, Roxbury, s. of Joseph first of the same, was sch.-
master aft. leav. coll. perhaps at Cambridge, but soon rem. to Salem,
there was a physician, had early m. Bethia, sec. d. of Edward Mitchel-
son, serv. in Philip's war, at least in the Narraganset campaign, 1675, as
chief surg. and d. May 1690. At Salem were b. to him, as Felt says,
Barbara and Eliz. besides at Cambridge had Daniel, b. 20 Aug. 1663;
Edward, 7 June 1666, wh. was also a physician, but d. 3 Oct. 1702, at
36 yrs.; and Bethia, 24 Jan. 1668. His wid. d. 24 Oct. 1719, in her
70th yr. Perhaps the same man at Roxbury, of whose derivat. aft.
great search, I am unable to conject. otherwise, had Mary, b. 19 Feb.
1676, and may have been f. of that Mehitable, wh. d. 12 Jan. 1680.
EDMUND, Roxbury, youngest s. of Rev. Thomas, bapt. at his parish 3 or
8 July 1631, brot. by his f. in the William and Francis next yr. went to
Ireland soon aft. gr. at H. C. 1650, was min. at Inneskean, d. 2 Mar.
1668, says Alden; but he has unduly swell. the number of his yrs.

WELD. 457

EDMUND, Roxbury, s. of Thomas the sec. freem. 1690, m. 10 Nov. 1687, Eliz. White, but whose d. she was is not seen, had Joseph, whose b. is not giv. but he d. 21 Feb. 1695; Edmund, b. 23 June 1695; Samuel, whose b. is not found, but he d. 29 Mar. 1698; and Thomas, Nov. 1702. His w. d. 20 Dec. 1721, but his own d. is not on town rec. JOHN, Roxbury, eldest s. of capt. Joseph, b. in Eng. as Farmer cites a fam. MS. to prove, 28 Oct. 1623, and came over in 1638 wh. is not improb. m. 24 Dec. 1647, Margaret Bowen, perhaps sis. of Griffith, had Joseph, b. 6 June, bapt. 12 Aug. 1649, d. in few mos. not as Ellis says, "only 17 days old;" Joseph, again, 13, bapt. 15 Sept. 1650; John, 25 May, bapt. 26 June 1653; Eliz. 14, bapt. 18 Nov. 1655; Margaret, 29 Sept. bapt. 11 Oct. 1657, d. at 17 yrs.; Mary, 3, bapt. 8 Apr. 1660; Abigail, b. 27 Aug. 1663, d. young; Esther, 28 Dec. 1664, d. in few days; and Hannah, 5 Sept. 1666; was freem. 1650, and serv. in Philip's war few days, mak. his will 19 June 1676, bec. he was call. into an expedit. but did not die until 20 Sept. 1691. His wid. d. 15 Sept. 1692. Eliz. m. 28 Aug. 1672, Samuel Gore; Mary m. 1680, Joshua Gardner; and Hannah m. 11 Nov. 1685, William Heath. JOHN, Roxbury, eldest s. of Rev. Thomas, brot. by his f. from Eng. where the reg. of his f. certif. that he was bapt. 6 June 1625, did not go home with him in 1641, bec. he was the undergr. at Harv. Coll. wh. in 1644 was whip. by the Presid. for break. and rob. his uncle's ho. wh. was then in Eng. and this disastrous discipline would naturally induce the youth to hide there bef. his return. See Winth. II. 166. The fam. tradit. is that he was min. of a parish in Durham, whose name call. Riton is not to be easi. found, near his f. prob. and he may have been eject. instead of that Thomas, wh. Calamy names, by the Bartholomew Act, as the f. was in his grave bef. that day. JOHN, Roxbury, s. of the first John, m. 22 Jan. 1679, Hannah Portis, had John, b. 22 Apr. 1680, d. in few days; Hannah, 14 Dec. 1681, d. in few mos.; John, again, 7 Oct. 1683, d. in few wks.; Joanna, 15 Sept. 1685; Abigail, 19 Aug. 1687; Margaret, 6 Mar. 1690; Eliz. 20 July 1692; Sarah, 17 Nov. 1693, d. at 15 yrs.; Dorothy, 21 June 1695, d. in few days; Samuel, 18 May 1697, d. in few mos.; and John, 18 Nov. 1698. His w. d. 10 Dec. 1721, and he d. 21 Feb. 1739. *JOSEPH, Roxbury, br. of the first Daniel, prob. and of Rev. Thomas, certain. came, it is thot. 1635, bring. w. Eliz. and ch. Eliz. Mary, Hannah, and Thomas (wh. by his f. design. for a coll. educ. d. at 17 yrs.), a. the ages of 10, 8, 6, and 3 yrs. respectiv. and leav. at home the eldest John, here had Edmund, b. 14 July 1636; and his w. d. Oct. 1638. He m. 20 Apr. foll. Barbara, niece of Edward Clap of Dorchester, had Sarah, bapt. 21 Dec. 1640, says the copy of town rec. wh. we might kn. to be wrong, as that was not Sunday; but the other copy from the ret.

to the County recorder, as in Geneal. Reg. VI. 377, makes her to be b.
31 Dec. of that yr. Yet what was the day of bapt. is unkn. since the
earliest ch. rec. of Roxbury is also lost; Daniel, 18, bapt. 25 Sept.
1642; Joseph, 6, bapt. 9 Feb. 1645, d. at 10 mos.; and Marah, bapt. 2
Aug. 1646, tho. the town rec. makes her bapt. on the impossib. day 6
July, and the child's name Jeremiah. The apostle Eliot in his rec. assigns
the cause for the *bitter* name, that the f. "is now in gr. afflict. by a sore
on his tongue." He was freem. 3 Mar. 1636, rep. 1637 and sev. yrs.
more, was capt. of the milit. of good est. and high reput. and d. of a
cancer, or was bur. not as Ellis says, 8 Sept. but 7 Oct. foll. the b. of his
last ch. His will of 2 June, with codic. of 22 July preced. is well abst.
in Geneal. Reg. VII. 33. The wid. m. next yr. Anthony Stoddard of
Boston, whose mar. contr. in our register of Deeds I. 137, bound him to
pay portions to the three ch. she bore to W. on their com. of age, or m.
but if all d. then to div. among his ch. by former w. Eliz. had m. 20
Mar. 1641, Edward Denison; Mary m. a. 1648, Daniel Harris of
Middletown; Hannah seems by the lang. of her f.'s will, to have been
engaged to m. a s. of famous Hooker, but nothing is kn. further; Sarah
m. 23 July 1663, John Franks of Boston; and Marah m. Comfort Starr,
says Ellis. JOSEPH, Roxbury, s. of John the first, m. 2 Sept. 1674,
Eliz. d. of Edward Devotion, had Margaret, b. 5 Nov. 1675, d. young;
and Eliz. 1 Jan. 1678, d. 12 of next mo. and the mo. d. 3 days aft. He
m. next, 27 Nov. 1679, Sarah, d. of Thomas Faxon of Braintree, had
Margaret, 16 Feb. 1681; Joseph, 12 July 1683; Sarah, bapt. 25 Oct.
1685, d. at 2 mos.; Sarah, again, 16 June 1687; John, 19 Aug. 1689;
Thomas, 10 Jan. 1692, d. soon; Deborah, 22 Feb. 1694; Mary, 10
Apr. 1695 (but of these last four, I find not any entry on the town rec.
and am indebt. for them to an elegant memo. of the sev. descend. of
Rev. Thomas, and capt. Joseph, by William G. Weld, Esq.); Daniel,
14 Aug. 1697; Edward, June 1700, d. Feb. foll.; and Ebenezer, 19
Oct. 1702; and the f. d. 14 Feb. 1712. Yet he had made his will 6
Dec. 1692, in a season of illness. The wid. m. 29 Apr. 1719, Jacob
Chamberlain of Brookline, outliv. him, and d. 14 Oct. 1745. SAMUEL,
Roxbury, s. of Thomas the sec. m. 23 June 1683, Susanna, d. of John
Polley of the same, had Dorothy, b. 28 May 1684; Samuel, 31 July
1686, d. in few days; Samuel, again, 30 Oct. 1687, d. in few mos.;
Ebenezer, 24 Jan. 1690, d. young; was freem. 1690. His w. d. 20
Apr. 1729, and he d. 2 Sept. 1737. *THOMAS*, Roxbury, br. of Joseph
the first, and prob. younger than him, was bred at Trinity Coll. Cam-
bridge, where he had his degr. 1613 and 18, was min. 1624, at Terling,
Co. Essex, a. 38 ms. from London, by w. Margaret had John, bapt. 6
June 1625; Thomas, 1626; Samuel, 8 Oct. 1629; and Edmund, 8 July

1631, H. C. 1650; according to certif. from the present vicar of the parish to my young friend Weld, that the rec. is made and sign. by the f. and obs. his handwrit. was so obscure, that the day and mo. of the bapt. of sec. s. could not be made out. Perhaps the third s. did not live long, at least we hear nothing of any other ch. than the three brot. by him, with their mo. in the William and Francis, leav. London 9 Mar. and arr. at Boston 5 June 1632, he hav. enjoy. the benefit of being excommun. the yr. bef. by the driveling malevolence of archbp. Laud, then only bp. of London. Next mo. he was sett. at Roxbury, and 6 Nov. foll. made freem. but whether he had more ch. or when his w. Margaret d. and a sec. w. Judith was tak. as the Roxbury ch. rec. proves, and other details, are not found.

He was earnest in the synod of 30 Aug. 1637 against the antinom. doctrines of Mr. Wheelwright, in stat. the eighty-two errors, and their confutat. with some unsound axioms as decid. by that grave Assemb. with wh. the first twenty pages of the work, call. a Short Story of the Rise, Reign, and Ruin of the Antinominian's Familists, &c. publish. by him in London, 1644, are fill. and the authorship of that part would do no discredit to him or any other divine of the land. Of the next twenty-three pages, the proceedings of the Gen. Ct. 2 Oct. (should be Nov.) 1637, another hand may have been the reporter; but no more blame attaches to any other portion, than to the copy of the petition, writ. as Winth. tells, by William Aspinwall, in favor of Wheelwright, with wh. these proceedings are appropriat. introd. Whatever hand report. these proceed. it could not well have been Gov. Winth. at least in the full transcr. for on p. 27 it is alleg. that Wheelwright was requir. if he did not in 14 days depart from our jurisdict. "to render hims. at the ho. of Mr. Stanton, one of the magistr. there to abide as a prisoner, till the Ct. should dispose of him." Now this could not have fallen from the Gov. whose narrative in sev. items, p. 246 of Vol. I. varies from this report, and does not name the magistr. but uses the phrase, "one of the magistr." wh. were then only seven, beside hims. and the Dept. But Col. Rec. I. 207 has the name of Stoughton; and no Stanton was ever one of the magistr.

Next comes, strange interject. betw. that report of the judicial proceed-ing of the Nov. 1637 Court and the Apology for the proceedings of the Gen. Ct. 9 Mar. *preced.* i. e. Mar. 1636–7, the nauseous detail of the monstrous birth 17 Oct. 1637, by Mrs. Dyer, one of Wheelwright's ad-herents, as the same was popular. circulat. in Boston, and in almost the same language as Winth. I. 261–3, has giv. it. A briefer narrat. of her misery in that untimely birth, was print. at London 1642, with other similar cases of misfortune, as I saw in the British Museum. This acco.

varies only as one relat. of so disgust. a story must be expect. to differ
from ano. especial. as every admir. of horrors could then be easi. gratif.
when the Gov. had, as he tells us in his hist. by advice of the magistr.
and min. caused the decaying remains to be disinterr. Yet what thus
bec. fully kn. to prob. most of the men, women, and half gr. ch. within
four miles (and Weld liv. only two miles off), is by the Hist. of Boston
held for proof, that Winth. not Welde, was the author, as "two men
without close confer. could not have writ. things so exactly coinciding."
See Drake, 218. Ano. proof of the same nature is brot. forward by a
writer with the signature of Hutchinson in the recent. issued Historical
Magazine for Nov. 1857, fill. almost four pages at the begin. of the No.

After the apology (wh. covers thirteen pages) for the early proceedings
at the Gen. Ct. against Wheelwright's Fast sermon, near the top of 59th
page, begins prob. Weld's "additions to the conclusion of the book," written in a very different style from the apology, and evident. a continua.
from near the bottom of p. 43, and now reaching to the end of the little
vol. on p. 66. What gives the chief value to this humble 4to. however,
is the Preface, signed T. Welde, in small Rom. cap. for the earlier copies,
in small Italic, not cap. in the later. It fills sixteen pages of small type,
and is written with great spirit. Equal in pungency to the style of this
preface, is that of the conclusions in the last seven pages. Such pungency, using a mild term to express what in the writing of any but a
clergym. seems malignity, is not seen in any other writer on that subj.
But *bef. the Preface* is print. a remarkab. address "To the Reader." "I
meeting with this Book, newly come forth of the press, and being earnestly pressed by divers to perfect it, by laying down the order and sense
of this story (wh. in the Book is omit.) tho. for mine own part, I was
more slow unto it; not as if I think it contains any thing but truth, but
because the names of some parties that acted in our troubles, that have,
since that time (I hope) repented, and so God having pardon. their sins
in Heaven, I should have been loth to have reviv. them on earth. But
considering that their names are already in Print, without any act of
mine, and that the necessity of the times call for it, and its requisite that
God's great works should be made known, I therefore, in a straight of
time, not having had many hours, have drawn up this following Preface,
and prefixed hereunto with some additions to the conclusion of the Book.
I commend thyself and this to the blessing of God.   T. W."

If to disting. the tone and temper of the Apology, that may natural.
be presum. the composition of Gov. Winth. [see his Hist. I. 221]
from other parts of the tract, except the documenta. pieces proper [Ib.
248] resort be had to critic. comparis. of style, slight difficult. will
attend the separat. of what is betw. the two covers of the binding.

Against the errors of Wheelwright, and the fantastic revelations of Mrs. Hutchinson, Welde could not more sincerely show his zeal, than Winth. but his zeal is denunciatory, fierce, and virulent, while that of the Gov. seems cautious, calm, and moderate in terms, decisive in spirit. Even in type of the same forms, it may be followed, like that fabled river, in its nameless course under the sea, as told by Virgil, En. III. 686, bearing the true, unmixed proof of its fountain:

nunc
Ore, Arethusa, tuo Siculis confunditur undis.

Some slight regard to a charge, publish. 26 May 1853, in the Hist. of Boston by Mr. Drake, against my argum. as to the authorship of the " Rise, Reign, and Ruin," on p. 249 of Vol. I. of Winth. Hist. of N. E. may decent. now be shown. That my remarks therein involve an accusat. of Welde " as absurd as it is unjust," may pass without comment ; but as the Histor. of Boston proceeds to observe on my criticism that " it is criminal so to do," I appeal from his decision to the competent tribunal of gentlemen and scholars in this and all succeed. ages.

Weld had gone home, in comp. with Hugh Peter and Mr. Hibbins in Aug. 1641, they being jointly charg. with a commiss. from the governm. to represent our means and wants, in wh. they met extraord. good success, procuring benefact. to extent of £500. bef. Hibbins's ret. in Aug. foll.· I have seen among MSS. in the Col. Libr. copious acco. of Dr. and Cr. of Weld, wh. seems to have suffer. no little suspicion, and rec. some unkind treatm. from our Gen. Ct. wh. hardly ever fail. to be dissatisf. with their agents in Eng. and wh. in Oct. 1645, adopt. a vote, that Mr. Peters and Mr. Weld " having been long absent, may understand the Ct.'s mind, that they desire their presence here, and speedy return." On this ungracious invit. neither came, but ea. gain. distinct. in the mother land. Weld obt. a living at St. Mary Gateshead, Co. Durham, and d. says the rec. of Roxbury ch. (not likely in such a case to be wrong), 23 Mar. 1661 ; I think it is said, at London. This was soon aft. the Restorat. of the k. and bef. the great ejectm.

Perhaps I may be excus. for a long explanat. as to what is said in my sec. ed. of Winthrop in a note on I. 248, publish. 1853. Having never bef. 1842, heard any doubts of the agency of Weld in the publicat. of that interest. little volume of wh. everybody knew he acknowledg. the preface and conclusion, and my suspicion being excited, at the British Museum, by the unexpl. address to the Reader, that suspicion in 1843, was express. by me in a *single line* of my Gleanings in 3 Mass. Hist. Coll. VIII. 285. Attention was thus drawn to the matter, and it was supposed by some that in Baylie's " Dissuasive from the Errours of the Time," London 1645, and Cotton's " Way of Congrega. Chhs. cleared,"

London 1648, wh. had a reply to some of Baylie's aspersions, it might appear, that Gov. Winth. was as much engag. as Weld in the publicat. of Short Story of the Rise, Reign, and Ruin. A friend lent me these two works, and they did not produce on me the impress. some persons receiv. perhaps without close examinat. For instance, in Ecclesiast. Hist. of N. E. I. 329, Mr. Felt observes on my suppos. that Welde compos. and arrang. the greater part of the work so publish. and that Gov. W. was auth. of the rest, entit. a Brief Apology, &c. and adds, "But it is clear from Baylies and Cotton, that Winth. did write "The Book" as stated by Weld "to the Reader." Now each of the three parts of this affirmat. is wrong. Weld hims. does not state "that Winth. did write the Book," wh. is too bold and direct assert. for the crafty writer of that addr. wh. does nothing more than suggest that somebody beside T. W. was the writer or editor. Baylies, p. 57, in strong desire to censure Cotton for his familism and antinom. relies upon "the witness of Master Winth. the wisest of all the N. E. Governors hitherto, and of Master Wells, a gracious minister of that land in their printed Relations of the Schisms there;" and he proceeds to cite passages equally from the Preface or conclusion, as well as from the Proceedings or the Apology, a dozen or twenty from each, but a *diligent*, not a *superficial* scrutiny through his quotations will give a great preponderance to those acknowledg. to be Weld's. On p. 64 also, Mr. Felt refers to Winth.'s Narration, but in the very last line preced. refers to this work as the testimony also of Weld. In defence of hims. Cotton follows Baylie *very closely*, quoting the exact phrases of his antagon. and so, p. 56, refers to "the witness of Winth. and Wells," not even correct. the spell. of his name. On p. 57 citing from B. the "testimony from the Court, wh. (it is likely) was deliv. by Mr. Winth. being then Gov. [as in] p. 35 of the Short Story," &c. so that the weight of his evidence is, to the least scruple or even grain, of the same weight, and no more, with Baylie's, to prove in Mr. Felt's words "that Winth. did write the Book." Prob. Mr. Felt had not, when he compos. that passage, examin. those authors, or, at least, his survey was cursory, for in Ib. 534, speaking of the publicat. of this pamphlet in 1644, he uses similar words: "Its preface was by Mr. Weld, and the rest of it by Gov. W." overlook. the acknowledgm. of Weld, that the conclusion, wh. even slight observ. must make seven pages, was by him. Writing of the end of Weld's life, Mr. Felt uses more precision, p. 436. "He was engag. with Gov. W. sen. in prepar. the Rise, Reign, and Ruin," &c. in N. E. Yet what Gov. W. contrib. was in Mar. 1636-7, the Apology and perhaps part of the Proceedings in Nov. 1637, publ. in Boston as much as in London, but NOT PRINT. in either, while Weld was the publisher, by his own confess. overrul. the London press in 1644, so that my expression, as he fairly gives it on his p. 329, may stand unreprov. Beside, Mr. Felt candidly, p. 554, takes notice, that Wheelwright, s. of Rev. John "endeavors to show from the concessions of Weld, that his f. did not adopt the main principles of his sis.-in-law, Mrs. H." and he still more fairly quotes a let. of 1647, from Hooker of Hartford to Shepard of Cambridge, both of wh. must have kn. what the truth, and the whole truth was a. the publicat. "I cannot be persuad. but these men" [the Scotch Presbyterians, Rutherford and Baylie] HAD A SECRET HAND TO PROVOKE MR. WELD TO SET FORTH HIS SHORT STORY," &c.

Certain. Weld's desire was not to be thot. author of the "Short Story," &c. and he would gladly have the reader presume that Gov. Winth. whose name belongs to part of *the official documenta.* matter therein print. had issued the vol. tho. any careful student could detect the most of the pages due to ano. hand. The assist. librar. at Harv. Univ. drew my attention to the vol. of Rutherford, professor at St. Andrews, call. Survey of Spiritual Antichrist, London 1648, p. 171, where he says of our N. E. heretics, "They held these wicked tenets especially, that follow, as may be gathered out of the story of the Rise, Reign, and Ruin of the Antinomians and Libertines that infected the Chhs. of N. E. penned (as *I am informed*) by M. Winthrope, Gov. a faithful witness, and approv. by M. T. Weld in his preface to the book." This is in c. XV. yet in the next c. p. 180, he twice names Weld as author of that work, as in the first sentence of the same c. p. 176, of Mrs. Hutchinson, one of the authors of the "wicked opinions," he borrows the happy designat. of our Roxbury historian, saying "This woman is call. the American Jezabel." How R. was *informed* that Gov. W. penned the work, may easily be conceiv. for in his sev. journeys from St. Andrews to London, and back, his road lay straight thro. Gateshead, opposite Newcastle, wh. was Weld's resid. So high was his estimat. of the vol. that in the sec. pt. of R.'s work, it is cit. hardly less than three hundred times, always by the tit. of Rise, Reign, and Ruin. It must be kept. constant. in mind, that Rutherford and Bailie were of the four great Scotch magicians employ. as mem. of the famous Westminster Assembly, that sat above five and a half yrs. to regulate the true faith for all future time. Great opportunities for acquir. knowl. as to every thing, espec. of a relig. value, that had occur. in N. E. were, of course, enjoy. by them.

Being sharp. reprov. in the Geneal. Reg. VIII. 84, for what in my sec. ed. of Winth.'s Hist. of N. E. was utter. about the attempt of Weld to conceal his *first* connex. with this work, I may be permit. in explanat. if not justificat. to add not a little. By the change of words, "the authorship" of Short Story is made the matter of controversy, and that man of straw is put forward, wh. may be left to the critic; for my chief inq. was confin. to the publicat. or editorship; having only in a single instance named Weld as author of Rise, Reign, and Ruin, and then in note on Vol. I. 258, in the closest relation to a passage from the preface, signed by hims. and the very last words of the conclusion on p. 66. So that the differ. betw. the critic and myself is very slight, as to material passages by me ascrib. to Weld, "BEYOND WHAT HE HAS HIMS. ACKNOWLEDG." In the further opin. of the same writer "that whatever Mr. Weld did, he did under the direction or by the adv. of the dominant party here," all may readi. agree. A little outbreak of bitterness in the Preface, or in the "additions to the conclusion of the Book," may seem very natural in that age; and in the larger report of the case of Mrs. H. in Hutch. Hist. II. 482–520, wh. should be read by every one that desires to know the full extent of the tyranny, we easily discern, how eager in the prosecut. were Dudley, the Dept.-Gov. wh. was of Weld's ch. at Roxbury, Endicott, Bartholomew, and Nowell, of the laity, as, of the clerg. Symmes, fellow-passeng. with her, Shepard and Hugh Peter, the fellow-passeng. of W. on the homeward voyage. No one could be misled by my words, as if I asserted that Weld, more than Peters or anybody else, wrote the *petition in favor of Wheelwright,* or *the Apology,* or the *Proceedings of the Court* in the larger part, or *the popular report* of poor Mrs. Dyer's affliction. He is responsible, as Editor, for all but the strictly official docum. Now without intend. any invidious allegat. as to a single word in the vol. "beyond what he has hims. acknowl." I renew my remark, that he bears the responsib. for all exc. from p. 46 to the third line of p. 59 inclus. bec. it was print. under his direct. and most of it is evident. his own composit.

The friend, wh. the critic says pointed out my error, was, yrs. ago, satisfied that I had good grounds for my opinion. The diligent assist. librar. of Harv. Coll. in his MS. on the reverse of the title-page of "Antinomians and Familists condemned," had noted, that it was the same work with Weld's Short Story, and infer. that it was an *earlier* impression, because Short Story gain. the Note to the Reader and the Preface; and he then adds (without hesitat.) from that address, that it appears, Thomas Welde "was not the author of what is contained in the present vol." His caution was not excit. by the admiss. of Weld hims. as to the "additions to the conclusion of the book," and he believ. what the rev. casuist cunning *desir.* rather than what he *said.* My suggestion that this title-page was a sneaking device to give support to the false implicat. in the Note to the Reader, is by the Geneal. Reg. critic submerg. in the conject. that it "might have been, and no doubt was, a printer's error"!! Large inq. has been provok. by this bold assumption and unusual state of things. The first result is from collation by Mr. Livermore of the copy in College Libr. of "Antinomians and Familists," with the Athenæum copy of the "Short Story," and he assures me that it is apparent that from p. 1 to 66, where the Athenæum copy breaks off, the correspondence is perfect in every letter, typographical error or not, as l. 6 on p. 46 *spread* has the let. r pushed out of its place, so that the lower is as high as the upper part of the letters on either side ; — as p. 1 of Short Story, begins with signat. B. in the copy that has sixteen or eighteen pages of prefatory matter, so begins with signat. B. the copy devoid of those pages ; and so on p. 9 in each of these books is signature C — on 17 D — on 25 E, &c. with the trifling except. on p. 62, l. 8, the parag. ends in one with the words "slighted had so much," in the other, "had so much slighted," no letter being changed. An expert in printing, or *even* an apprentice, would judge of Antinomians and Familists, &c. from sig. B on p. 1, that sig. A had once preced. it, tho. page 1 follows next aft. title-page. Mr. Marvin, an accomplish. printer, on first sight observ. that the Preface had been suppressed, and that the title-page was print. from the same form as Short Story, substituting other words, for all *above* the imprint. Indeed, to suppose it possib. that the work, without the preface, was issued first, is very like the expectat. of seeing the second story of an edifice sustain itself in the air before the first is built for its support. The forms are identical, the ornaments unchanged, as on the title-pages of both a border of twenty-one types or beads runs by the sides, nineteen more at the top, and eighteen at the bot. ; and no letters were distrib. from the form to the case betw. the strikings off for one and the other through the whole. Yet so widely differ the title-pages, that one would judge instantly, that years might interven. betw. them, one showing only *forty-one words*, the other, *one hundred and fifty-six*, above the imprint ; while that imprint of three lines disproves the whole cunning of the change, for there exactly as in the body of the two books, all the letters, and figures, and imperfections, and punctuation, and errors, were immovable. The words above the imprint in one are removed from the other, and new ones inserted, except the very large letters of the single word NEW-ENGLAND running wholly across the wide page, some of wh. the keen eye of my young friend, W. H. Whitmore, detected as unmoved ; and a less practised vision would instantly perceive, when directed to it, how the first *E* in that word differs from the sec. *E*, and confidently assume that the enormity of the first *E* might prove it to be the only one of the kind in the print. office of Ralph Smith. The last letter but one of that word in a copy wh. to me seems clearly, by a hundred indicat. to have been among the earliest taken off from the standing form, is a well looking, perfect capital, but in two other copies appears to have its face battered, as if it had been in *irregular company*, and in the only other copy ever seen by me, the body appears to have a twist, wh. may account for the bruise on its face.

Which now, of these two, both print. early in 1644, was prior? Very short time, only few hours prob. elaps. betw. them; and further scrutiny of the note to the Reader may be useful to aid the decision of that question. The opening words are "meeting with this Book, newly come forth of the Press;" and it is very strange, that no other man than Thomas Weld is kn. to have ever seen such a supposed book, bef. or since. Industry was most active, in that day of civil war, to hunt up every thing as soon as *print*. The eager friend of King Charles I. in London, whose assiduous attent. to such serv. furnishes one of the most curious and complete assortment of treasures in the British Museum, contain. near. thirty thousand pieces and tracts, bound in over two thousand vols. in the order of success. dates betw. 1640 and 1660, must be inq. of whether this be one book or two. Now in that vast collect. this tract stands with only the tit. Short Story, &c. obtain. by the book collector 19 Feb. 1643, and no such work as "Antinomians and Familists condemn." &c. is nam. Next, in reference to the point of priority, should be weigh. what is told in that note to the Reader, as to the names of some that acted in our troubles, wh. the writer says "are already in print. without any act of mine." But we are left uncertain, whether that print without his act means (as seems fairly to follow) in the Book newly come forth. Unless it may be shown, that such print. of the names can be found elsewhere than in Short Story, bef. the issue of Antinomians and Familists condemn. it may well be thought this addr. to the reader is only a subterfuge. Such evidence it may be hard to find; yet no other man than Weld can be nam. wh. would in London be so deeply engag. in such cause. But what motive had Weld to make such a statement? To this question, a reasonable reply is, that he might fear prosecution for libels by one or another. Friends of the parties implicat. must have been numerous eno. in London; for tho. Gov. Cradock, Sir Richard Saltonstall, Sir Bryan Jansen, treas. Harwood, Alderm. Andrews, Col. Ven and others, may have been impartial, Sir H. Vane would, of course, sympathize with Cotton, Wheelwright, and the majority of his fellow-worship. in Boston ch. Mr. Hutchinson also had a br. there, wh. had liv. here, was of high esteem and large property, and beside others of the Antinom. party, Coggeshall was a man of influence in Boston, and Aspinwall a ready writer, both able to command friends in the great city; while Wheelwright, s. of one of the princip. suffer. was able to issue the very next yr. in "Mr. Weld's his Antitype" observat. on "a paper styled a Short Story of the Rise, Reign," &c. Even without suppos. any unworthy fear in him that prompt. what he wish. to have cohsid. as a sec. ed. of a Book bef. issued by ano. person, and that, as he says, "the necessity of the times call for it, and its requisite that God's great works should be made known," he might deceive himself into the hope, that "Antinomians and Familists condemn." tho. issued by the same publisher, the same yr. if publish. without preface, would be taken to be a different composure from Short Story, with a preface one quarter as large as the whole work. Well might he believe, that in those stirring times of extreme convulsion and civil war, nobody would have the leisure and take the trouble to ascertain, that his publicat. was indeed *two faces under one hood.* Next may our scrutiny be applied to his excuse of "being earnestly pressed by divers to perfect" the work, "by laying down the order and sense of this story." Perhaps any other man, with half as much literary skill as T. W. would have giv. a very differ. ORDER to his materials, at least so far as chronology is concerned. If he did not print the Apology for the Gen. Ct. of Mar. 1636–7, begin. p. 46 before the result of the Synod 30 Aug. — 22 Sept. foll. wh. begins on p. 1, he would naturally (unless blinded by a strong sensibility) have giv. it place prior to the proced. of not merely a later sess. of the same, but of ano. Gen. Ct. in Nov. 1637, wh. begins on p. 21. See our Col. Rec. I. 187 to 205. What *good* reason for breach of such natural sequence of time can be conjectur. I see not, nor is it necessary to think of a *bad* one; especial. as in putting all the matter bef. p. 46, Mr. Weld, the Editor, seems to have arrang. with high regard to this point, making a blunder of Oct. 2 for Nov. 2 as date of open. the session of the Ct. that the postponement of Mrs. Dyer's unhappiness, wh. had been at two *public lectures* of the first ch. largely spoken of by Mr. Cotton (as Winth. tells, in his Hist.) when prob. Mr. Weld and other min. from the neighb. towns (wh. usually attend. the Thursday lect. were present) 17 Oct. might seem to be in a fit place. A reasonable cause for this breach of natural order may be found in the circumstances that led Weld (but would lead no other person) to think more of Mrs. Hutchinson than any thing else in the long agony of the antinom. controv. In Nov. 1637 she was commit. to custody of Joseph Weld, own br. of the casuist, in the town of Roxbury, her banishm. being suspend. until the spring. While thus a prisoner for more than four mos. all access of husband, childr. friends denied, exc. with leave of the Ct. as in Col. Rec. I. 207–25 is seen, she was expos. to visitat. of any holy inquisitor; and the min. of R. must have used his sacred office with equal ardor for her conversion, and vexation at his ill success. This will explain to milder natures, the wondrous malediction with wh. he closes the Short Story. Still the suspicion arises, from the anxious reference to "laying down the order and sense of the story," that the ill arrangement is due to design rather than accident. How else could occur the interrupt. on p. 43, where the parag. ends with the words "issue whereof is set down in the next," when we are unable to find the next, and connect. thread for more than fifteen pages onward, or a chasm of near one quarter of the surface of the vol. Would not any ingenuous mind, on sec. reading, become suspicious at the apparent anxiety express. in that "addr. to the Reader" (whether spring. from fear or ill-will), lest the writer of the long preface, might be thot. to have had too intimate connex. with the production of the ensuing short story? Words are liable to misapprehens. we all know, from carelessness or ignor. of him who uses them; but especially when equivocat. is resolv. on; and in writing much more than in oral speech, we wish for precision, not ambiguity. Yet an author's idea may be mistaken when he intended to be punctiliously precise, tho. less frequent. than if he be habitual. careless. His words convey sometimes more, at others less than he intend. Of course two readers may obtain from the same words quite dissimilar impressions. A recent example will illustrate. In note 1, on p. 238 of Winth. I. my first ed. 1825, I had printed this remark. "The work has not, I presume, been often quoted within a century." Of course the same words stand in the next ed. 1853. Citing this passage, the writer, careless or over cautious, of the review in Geneal. Reg. 1854, adds, "and yet *we* know that it has been *very* often quoted within a *quarter of a century.*" On cursory perusal, this may, in one man's opin. seem a *contradiction ;* while a slower reader would perhaps give it a *very differ. name.* If the two readers call for solution of the oracular ambiguity of the writer, prob. a short minute's explanat. would make their judgments agree.

Now to conclude the point of priority of issue — the fictitious title-page "Antinom. and Fam. condemn. "assum. in Geneal. Reg. to be "no doubt a printer's error," as if by fortuitous concourse of atoms, it fell into that place, I had presum. to be unique, having only heard of the single copy in the Coll. Libr. I have gain. recent knowl. of ano. copy in the collection of Rev. Dr. Choules, since his d. together with his copy of Short Story, dispers. by auction. Whatever value, more or less, was then due to my infer. from the Coll. copy, as a device to cover Weld's connect. with the Book, is of course doubled, and proportional. weaken. is the assumpt. that it was "no doubt printer's error." Evidence positive, is, also, obtain. that the Choules copy of Short Story, with the note to Reader, Preface, and P. S. and ano. own. by Col. Aspinwall, which-

ever of the two were first struck off, came both from the press BEF. the
delusive publicat. of the same work under the title of "Antinomians,"
&c. WITHOUT the malignant preface. The testimony is indubita. it
appeals to the eye; and tho. the form of ea. of the 66 pages in all the
copies is unchanged, slight correct. of errors in the earlier ones are
traced clearly in' the later. For instance, the sig. of p. 1 of Short Story,
in the copies of Aspinwall and Choules, is C. 2; — of p. 3 is C. 3, and
so onward to p. 65 wh. is L. 2, whereas the two copies of Coll. and
Choules of the same work, under the NEW title without Preface, begin.
(as does the Athenæum copy with the Preface and old title) with B. for
sig. of p. 1, and so proced. to p. 65 wh. is K. Will any sagacious ob-
server doubt about priority? Each of the copies, of so great rarity, has
worth of its own; and that of our Athenæum, tho. wanting the four last
pages, derives high value from the notes in sev. places, writ. by Thomas
Prince above one hundred and twenty yrs. since, especially his testimon.
on the title-page, " Preface and conclusion by Thomas Welde." This is
the well-kn. handwrit. of the Annalist. My presumpt. is that this identical tract was once his, for in his own catal. he inserts, in its proper
place, " T. Welde's Short Story, &c. London 1644," ard it is *not* now
found in his N. E. library.

A very valua. copy of the unmutilat. work, own. by Charles Deane,
concurs with the Coll. copy depriv. of its Preface, and issued under the
new name, in every word and letter, monk or friar, or other irregularity,
like the imperfect copy of the Athenæum, exc. as bef. explain. in the
changed *place* of a single word, *slighted*, on p. 62, that requir. no edito-
rial cunning, but must have been done by a compositor. Will any one
doubt that Mr. Deane's copy (after the Preface, wh. is not seen in the
Coll. copy) was struck off from the same forms as that, when he com-
pares not pages merely, but words, and even letters in each, as on p. 12,
the remarkab. first letter of Error 65, unlike any other in the long enu-
meration, or p. 4, the strange initial of Confutation 19, or asks, without
expecting answer, why the letter C. should have different shapes,
proudly beginning Confutat. 1, 2, 3, 6, 7, 13, 15, 18, 20 to 40 inclus.
42–56 inclus. 61–65 inclus. 68–75 inclus. 81 and 82, in ITALIC TYPE *in
each of the books*, while it subsides into the modest Roman in 4, 5, 8, 9,
and all the others? Similar exact conformity as to the spelling of the
word, according to the then established usage, Errour, is found in both,
and similar, also, is the use or non-use of the double *e* in be, he, me, she.
For instance " *Antinomians and Familists* " of the Coll. Libr. has the
important word, for the first twenty times that it heads a parag. p.
1–4 spelled without *u;* but the next nineteen times the *u* creeps in; the

ensuing twenty-seven times it is ejected; fourteen times next follow. is bless. with *u;* and lastly No. 81 is written with five letters, and No. 82 with six; while in every one of them Mr. Deane's copy of *Short Story* agrees. More striking is this conformity, because apparently earlier copies vary much in such petty particulars. The *solitary*, abnormal *E.* in Mr. Dean's copy, Error 65, changes places with Col. Aspinwall's *E.* in Error 72, and so no complaint of partiality can arise.

Still, it may be said, the identity of Deane's "Short Story" with Coll. "Antinomians and Familists" being established, nothing is yet clearly shown to prove, wh. *first* came from the press, but only that, whichever was first, the other follow. very soon, perhaps in few hrs. or even minutes. Now by comparing with Deane's copy (that has the preface) that of Aspinwall (wh. is equally complete) it may easily be seen that A's. is several hours, or even days, earlier in its issue. But bef. taking up the *preface*, where the diversity is greater, let the curious student look at two or three small points in the *body* of the work, wh. is identical in substance, and seeming. in letter also, with the Coll. tract that wants the preface. On p. 1 in the Confutat. 4 and 5, the citation from the prophet Isaiah viii. 20, in A's. copy writ. *Esa*, in D's. and Coll. copies becomes *Esay;* p. 2, under Error 8, Corinth. in A's. copy, is properly shortened in the other two to Cor. — p. 3, line 5, *true* (in the brackets) is changed from Italic, as it is in A's. copy, into Roman letters to conform with other Roman letters in the same passage of the other copies; p. 21, in the blunder of date of the term of Court (wh. could not have been mistak. by Gov. Winth.) October in A's. copy is abbrev. in the others to Octob. Weld in London wrote the wrong mo. P. 33 in two places, A's. copy has Hutchinson, but in seventeen other places the name is Hutchison, without *n* in sec. syl. while the other copies give the name *every time* without that letter, so preserving uniformity betw. spell. and sound; p. 35, the rule "I permit not a Woman to teach," in A's. copy is print. in the Italic; in the other two, in Roman character, conformably to the rest of the page, and the cap. W. of A. is reduced in these to a small letter; and other examples abundantly serve to prove, that A's. was the *earlier* impression, correct. by the compositor in later ones. The texture of the paper in the different copies seems different, Aspinwall's being manifest. coarser. The top of Aspinwall's p. 7 is printed 9, and 10 is used for 8, 11 for 9, and so on, until, by giv. 15 and 16 twice, his copy agrees with others, in all the later pages; but the other copies throughout have a military accuracy of count. A correct. copy may certain. well seem later than one less correct, and instances enough may be seen in that of Col. A. having double *e*, where Mr. Deane's has single *e*, as in the passage on p. 62, so oft. refer. to, the latter reads "she had so much slighted " when the former adds an *e* to the first word, and crowds ano. *e* bef. *i* in the last word. May I not suggest, with becoming modesty, that the *better* copy is the *later* ?

Yet more direct is the evidence (to the same point) derived from what printers call overrunning or spacing out, to improve the appearance of a line or a page. Several such I pass by in the first fifteen pages, as also words chang. from Italic to Roman letters, but on 16th p. the top line of Aspinwall's copy contains at the end the citat. " Acts 15 : 9," wh. is made the whole of sec. line in the others. Then to equalize the number of lines in the respective pages, the last line of A's. copy becomes first of p. 17 in the others. Many more might be quoted, but beside that it would be tiresome to do it, the GREAT evidence of unlikeness of beginning and ending of lines, without changing word or letter, exc. in space, is found in the preface. Let the introduct. note to the Reader, sixteen lines in A's. seventeen in D's. copy, be compar. in the two books *by laying one alongside of the other*, and the same heavy mass of ornament at the top of the page is seen, — as well as the beautiful decoration around the big I. with wh. Weld opens in ea. — the types are the same in every letter, exc. that " *straite* of time " in A's. copy gains one letter in D's. by spell. " *straight.*" Yet, altho. the initials append. (T. W.) are identical in both, the technical sig. A. 2 in Aspinwall's is deficient in Deane's ; so also A. 3 on the p. next but one of A. in D's. appears * 3 ; and the page in A's. copy with sig. B. has two stars in D's. copy instead of a letter, and so onward, until the page last but one of the preface in A's. copy, with sig. C. becomes sig. A. and last but two in D's. copy. Of the earlier impress. every one of the lines is overrun, and spaced out in the later. The same cap. I. imbedd. in an ornam. wh. is seen in the opening of note to the reader for both copies of A. and D. appears the first letter on p. 1 of three copies of Aspinwall, Coll. and Deane ; but in the third the color of the decoration is very much darker than in those two. Very great variety is seen in the preface, especially in the ornament across the first page, and the types for title, while hardly a letter is changed, and the forms plainly are the same ; that is, the types were never distrib. A's. copy gives the first word " AFter," while D's. uses Italic caps. for the *whole* word ; and the first letter is twice as large in the latter copy, and fivefold more decorat. Nine lines of the first page run over from Aspinwall's to the sec. of Deane's ; and the last nine lines on the next of A. become ten lines in D. and twelve lines at the foot of next p. in A. swell into fourteen upon the top of the foll. in D. The accumulat. is seventeen on D's. next page, eighteen on next ; but with that number the addition ceases ; and the Col's. awkward squad is made to dress regularly in lines thus altered ;

that is the last eighteen lines, inclus. of the previous signat. T. Welde, closing the preface, run over from the foot of Aspinwall's page, and spread upon the upper middle of Deane's. Nothing else is seen to change betw. Aspinwall's and Deane's beyond the trifling amendm. that a compositor naturally introduces, such as substituting " and " for &, and reduc. the author's name from Roman caps. to Italic in conformity with the preced. type. Deane's is the more *correct* exemplar, but Aspinwall's for its very *incorrectness* ten times more *valuable* in petty history.

Will any one but Mr. Drake believe, that all this succession of appearances proves nothing to strengthen into certainty my conject. how Weld desired to supply a shield for his temerity, or a cover for his cowardice? — that the long title-page of " Short Story " was not print. bef. " Antinomians and Familists " was writ.? — that this *new* title for the *same* book instead of a *"printer's error"* sprang not from design and intent to mystify? — or that it is *wrong* in me, at this late day, to expose such a *typograph. curiosity?* Would any London printer in 1644, I dare to ask, after having a corrected copy of a work, as Antinomians and Familists (if printed *first*) is shown to be, immediately *after* issue, from the same forms, an impression of Rise, Reign, and Ruin, with a copious preface and address to the Reader, and postscript, containing many errors and obliquities of type (in the BODY of same work) as Aspinwall's and Choules's copies exhibit? Two questions natural. arise to embarrass those that would glad. seem believers of Weld's ingenuousness, — first, wh. was *corrector of the press* that obtain. aft. three or four trials, as pure a *text* for " Short Story," as was enjoy. by " Antinomians and Familists," if *this* tract were print. bef. *that*, when both tracts are tak. from the *same* types lock. up into the *same form* AT LAST, when " Antinomians and Familists " agree wholly with the *latest* impression of the Short Story? — sec. who gave Thomas Weld the right to put a preface equal to one fourth of the tractate, with an address to the Reader, beside " laying down the order and sense wh. in the book is [was] omit." " as also additions to the conclusion of the book?" He prob. utter. indirect suggestions, *ambiguas spargere voces*, that the orig. work was above six yrs. bef. concoct. in Boston, where Winth. was in the chair of Gov. when SHORT STORY was purch. in London by the King's purveyor, perhaps in few hours from its issue, and where I doubt not the publisher of ANTINOMIANS AND FAMILISTS had act. as the Editor of what, on our side of the water, when forgotten on the other, was down to 1843, always called Weld's Rise, Reign, and Ruin.

As to any moral delinquency in my regard " to the memory of Mr. Welde," that may be left in silence, without fear, to *any* human tribunal; but in the Court of *criticism*, I can kiss the rod cheerfully, and desire only that my submiss. continue until competent opinion be obtained as to whose back it should fall upon. Yet the sentence pronounc. against my *criminality*, in exposing the attempt at decept. by Rev. T. Weld, may lessen the reverence due to the spotless judicial ermine, even on the shoulders of the historian of Boston. Some readers perhaps will rejoice that so many hours were giv. to this investigat. by sev. of my friends, tho. that the collation of both copies of Mr. Choules's vol. under the *true* and the *spurious* title, was confin. of necessity to few hours by a most cautious reader in the auction room, only few days bef. the sale, is much regret.; yet they may hereafter be on their guard against the artifice of a casuist, that for a season delud. the sagacity of the sub-librarian of Harv. and triumph. over the innocence of Felt.

*THOMAS, Roxbury, s. of the preced. b. in his f's. parish in Eng. where certif. of his bapt. may be seen, freem. 1654, m. 4 June 1650, Dorothy, d. of Rev. Samuel Whiting of Lynn, had Samuel, bapt. 20 July 1651, d. at 2 yrs.; Thomas, 12 June 1653, H. C. 1671; Samuel, again, b. 10, bapt. 19 Aug. 1655; John, 9, bapt. 11 Oct. 1657, wh. d. 25 July 1686, prob. unm.; Edmund, 29 Sept. bapt. 2 Oct. 1659; Daniel, bapt. 16 Mar. 1662, d. says town rec. that omit. his b. next yr.; Dorothy, 2 or 28 Apr. 1664; Joseph, 3 May 1666; and Margaret, 29 Nov. 1669; but of the three last, my list of bapt. extend. only half way thro. 1662, is defic. He was greatly esteem. as in Col. Rec. IV. pt. 2, pp. 434 and 55, was rep. 1676 and 7, and d. of fever, 17 Jan. 1683. His wid. d. 31 July 1694; and d. Dorothy m. 12 May 1686, William Dennison, and next Samuel Williams of Roxbury; Margaret m. 17 Mar. 1690, Nathaniel Brewer. * *THOMAS*, Dunstable, s. of the preced. may have liv. at Ipswich, and there when adm. freem. 1675, but preach. sev. yrs. bef. he was ord. when the ch. was found. 16 Dec. 1685, and had m. 9 Nov. 1681, Eliz. d. of Rev. John Wilson of Medfield, had Eliz. b. 13 Oct. 1682; and Thomas, 7 Feb. 1685, H. C. 1701, wh. d. at Roxbury, 21 July 1704. His w. d. 19 July 1687, and he m. next, Mary, d. of Habijah Savage of Boston, and so gr.gr.d. of that pestifer. Mrs. Hutchinson, wh. his gr.f. so painfully labored to convert from the errors of her imagina. and all in vain, whereby he was in spirit and in print compel. to leave her under the delusions of the gr. adversary; had Samuel, b. 4 Mar. 1701, d. at 13 yrs.; and Habijah, H. C. 1723, posthum. 2 Sept. 1702, unless 20 June, as Roxbury town rec. has it, be tak. as more prob. He serv. as rep. for Deerfield soon aft. overthr. of Andros, if Farmer's Collect. in 3 Mass. Hist. Coll. IV. 291 be not distrust. and d. 9 June 1702, and his wid. d. 2 June 1731. Of this name Farmer in MS. says nineteen had been gr. in 1834, of wh. I find fourteen at Harv. and three at Yale.

WELDEN, CHRISTOPHER, Charlestown, d. says Farmer, wh. gives him distinct. of sen. 29 Apr. 1668; yet I much doubt this must be mistake, unless he were only transient, not perman. resid. for he was not householder in 1658, nor do I see the name among ch. mem. nor find any jr. ROBERT, Charlestown, chos. a capt. d. 16 Feb. 1631, bur. with milit. honors two days aft. He is respectful. ment. both by Winth. I. 45, and Dudley. On the list of Boston ch. mem. No. 91 is Eliz. W. and append. is writ. " gone to Watertown," wh. furnish. Bond occasion for conject. doubly felicit. that she was wid. of the capt. and that she bec. w. of Rev. George Phillips, whose first w. had d. at Salem soon aft. arr. 1630, and wh. had sec. w. Eliz. in 1631.

WELLER, ELIEZER, Westfield, freem. 1681, was s. of Richard of Northampton, by w. Hannah Pritchard, perhaps d. of Nathaniel, m. 14 Sept. 1674, had Eliezer, b. 8 Oct. 1675; Hannah, 16 Feb. 1678; Eliz. 17 Apr. 1680; and ano. d. b. 19 May 1682, d. with the mo. in two days; and he d. 16 Aug. 1684. JOHN, Northampton, sw. alleg. 8 Feb. 1679, m. 24 Mar. 1670, Mary, d. of Alexander Alvord, had John, b. 14 Feb. 1671; Mary, 11 Sept. 1672; Hannah, 14 May 1674; Eliz. 12 Feb. 1676; Sarah, 15 Apr. 1678; Thomas, Aug. 1680; and Experience, 4 Dec. 1682; rem. soon aft. to Deerfield, there d. 1686. His s. both sett. at New Milford. NATHANIEL, Westfield, s. of Richard of Northampton, by w. Deliverance, d. of Thomas Hanchet, had Thankful, b. 15 Oct. 1674; Sarah, 6 June 1677; and Deliverance, 20 Aug. 1679, d. at 17 yrs. and his w. d. 22 Nov. 1711. He was deac. and d. nine days bef. his w. RICHARD, Windsor, m. 17 Sept. 1640, Ann Wilson, had Rebecca, b. 10 May 1641; Sarah, 10 Apr. 1643; John, bapt. 10 Apr. 1645; Nathaniel, 16 July 1648; Eliezer, 24 Nov. 1650; and Thomas, 10 Apr. 1653, wh. d. unm. at 22 yrs. rem. to Farmington, where his w. d. 10 July 1659; and he m. 22 June 1662, Eliz. wid. of Henry Curtis, wh. had drawn him to Northampton; took o. of alleg. 8 Feb. 1679; perhaps of Deerfield 1682, d. at Westfield prob. with his ch. 1690. Sarah m. 20 Nov. 1662, John Hannum of N.

WELLES, or WELLS, EBENEZER, Hatfield, s. of Thomas of Hadley, m. 4 Dec. 1690, Mary Waite, eldest d. of Benjamin, had Ebenezer, b. 1691; Thomas, 1693; Joshua, 1695; Martha, 1697; John, 1700; Jonathan, 1702; and his w. d. soon aft. He m. 1705, Sarah, wid. of John Lawrence of Brookfield, had Mary, 1707. EDWARD, Boston 1644, by w. Sarah had Hopestill, b. 13 Oct. 1645. EPHRAIM, Hatfield, s. of Thomas of Hadley, m. 1696, Abigail, d. of John Allis, and rem. to Colchester, there resid. 1714. GEORGE, Lynn, rem. to Southampton, L. I. in the gr. migrat. of 1640. HUGH, Wethersfield, m. at Hartford, 19 Aug. 1647, Mary, d. of William Rusco, had John, b. 24 May 1648;

Mary, 15 Aug. 1649, d. soon; Mary, again, 15 Oct. 1650; Rebecca, 10 Jan. 1652; and Sarah; and he d. 22 Dec. 1678. In his will of the mo. bef. he ment. w. Mary, s. John, and the ds. as Mary Robinson; Rebecca, mo. of Samuel and Sarah Latham; and Sarah Bishop. The Geneal. Reg. IV. 343, is elaborately wrong, in mak. him one of the founders of Hartford, and in much of the detail as to the residue. He is seen in the list of freem. 1669, and was made ens. 1677. ICHABOD, Hartford, s. of Thomas sec. of the same, m. 4 Sept. 1684, Sarah, d. of Eleazer Way of H. had Mary, b. 15 Apr. 1686; Jonathan, 17 Sept. 1689; Ebenezer, 5 Oct. 1694; Sarah, 1 Dec. 1701, d. soon; and Ann. ISAAC, Barnstable, join. the ch. there, as Lothrop's rec. shows, 27 May 1643; but had prob. been at Scituate five yrs. earlier. JAMES, Haddam, present. for freem. 1669, as Trumbull, Col. Rec. II. 106 proves. He came 1650, as serv. to William Pincheon, to Springfield, P. hav. paid for his pass. and his will of 9 June 1694, then a capt. on milit. serv. names w. Eliz.; s. James, b. 27 Nov. 1668; and Thomas; d. Eliz. m. and Mary and Susan unm. He d. bef. 5 Jan. 1698. JAMES, Haddam, s. of the preced. m. Rebecca, d. of Joseph Selden of Lyme, had Rebecca, b. 1699; Susanna, 1701; Mary, 1703, d. young; James, 7 Jan. 1706; Joseph, 24 Mar. 1708; and Martha, 1710; was lieut. and d. 21 Dec. 1744. JOHN, Wells, s. of Thomas of Ipswich, b. in Eng. d. a. 1677. His wid. Sarah, d. of Francis Littlefield, m. a. 1660, s. Nehemiah, and Thomas, min. of Amesbury, were made Admors. and there were other ch. as Nathaniel, from wh. is deriv. a long honor. line. The town is call. from the f. The wid. m. William Sawyer. ‡ * JOHN, Stratford, s. prob. eldest, of Gov. Thomas, by him brot. from Eng. was freem. 1645, rep. 1656 and 7; Assist. 1658 and 9, prob. d. within two yrs. aft. by w. Eliz. m. a. 1647, had John, b. 1648; Thomas and Robert, tw. 1651; Temperance, 1654; Samuel, 1656; and Sarah, 28 Sept. 1659; and prob. posthum. Mary, 29 Aug. 1661. He d. a. one yr. aft. his f. His will of 19 Oct. 1659 provides for his w. "all that is due to her in Eng. and £40. to carry her to Eng. if she choose to go. If she do not go, she to pay d. Temperance £10. but to have one third of my est. of all kinds, the two thirds to my childr. to be equal. divid." This seems to render it very unlikely, that she was, as Goodwin, 251, makes her, d. of John Curtis; but rather an Eng. woman, nam. Eliz. Bourne, as from the adjudicat. of the Court, upon est. of Ellen Bostwick, a relative, we infer. His wid. m. 19 Mar. 1663, John Willcoxson; Sarah m. 1 Feb. 1678, Benjamin Beach of Stratford (and next Ambrose Thompson, was erron. said by Goodwin, 254, for B. bur. her, and had sec. w.); and Mary, the youngest d. was first w. of Joseph Booth. JOHN, Hatfield, br. of Thomas of Hadley, had first liv. at Stratford, had three

ch. Sarah, Mary, and Abigail, bef. rem. to H. at least not rec. at H. and
there had Hannah, b. 12 Nov. 1665, d. at 11 yrs.; Esther, 26 Apr.
1668; John, 15 Sept. 1670; Eliz. 1675, k. by the Ind. 19 or 20 Sept.
1677; Jonathan, 14 Dec. 1682; and Eliz. again, 10 Jan. 1686. He
sw. o. of alleg. 8 Feb. 1679, was freem. 1690, and d. 1692. His wid.
had been wound. by the Ind. at the same time her d. rec. the fatal blow.
JOHN, Newbury, took o. of alleg. May 1669, and was sw. freem. same
mo. was a carpenter, m. 5 Mar. 1669, Mary, prob. d. of Edmund Greenleaf, had Mary, b. 16 Dec. foll. d. next yr.; Mary, again, 16 Feb.
1673; and William, 15 Jan. 1675. JOHN, Stratford, eldest s. of John
of the same, m. Mary, d. of John Hollister of Wethersfield, had Mary,
b. 29 Nov. 1670; Thomas; Sarah 2 Jan. 1674; John; Comfort; Joseph, 21 June 1679; Eliz.; and Robert, Sept. 1688; was propound. for
freem. 1671, and d. 24 Mar. 1714. JOHN, Roxbury, of wh. I kn. no
more but that he was sw. freem. 10 Oct. 1677. JOHN, Wethersfield, s.
of Hugh, by w. Margaret had John, b. 31 Mar. 1680; Margaret, 19
May 1682; Ann, 28 Jan. 1684, d. soon; Ann, again, 30 Aug. 1685;
Mary, 11 Oct. 1687; Allyn, 27 Oct. 1689; and Silas, 8 Dec. 1691.
JOHN, call. jr. when he sw. alleg. at Hatfield, 8 Feb. 1679, was s. of
Thomas of Hadley, and drown. 20 Jan. 1680. JOHN, Hatfield, s. of
the first John of the same, m. Rachel Marsh, d. of Samuel of the same,
had John, 1700; Joseph, 1702; Samuel, 1704; Aaron, 1707; Sarah,
1710; Jonathan, 1713; Noah, 1719; and Abigail; all nam. in the yr.
of div. of his est. one yr. aft. his d. 1720. *JONATHAN, Deerfield, s. of
Thomas of Hadley, wh. had been wound. in Philip's war, m. 13 Dec.
1682, Hepzibah, d. of George Colton of Springfield, had Jonathan, only,
b. 1684; and his w. d. 27 Aug. 1697. He m. 1698, Sarah, wid. of
Joseph Barnard of Deerfield, d. of Elder John Strong, had David, 31
Jan. 1700, d. soon; and his w. Sarah d. 10 Feb. 1733. He was rep.
1692, and d. 3 Jan. 1739. JONATHAN, Hartford, br. of Ichabod, d.
1688. His inv. was sw. bef. Sir Edmund Andros, 12 Nov. in that yr.
and his prop. was div. betw. brs. and sis. Prob. he had no w. or ch.
JOSEPH, Hartford, youngest s. of the sec. Thomas of the same, m. Eliz.
d. of Eleazer Way, had John, Joseph, and Joshua, wh. all d. soon; and
Eliz. b. 1696; and he d. 1698. JOSEPH, Groton, s. prob. eldest, of the
first Thomas of Westerly, m. 28 Dec. 1681, Hannah Reynolds, d. 26
Oct. 1711, in his will ment. w. and ch. Joseph, John, Thomas, and Ann.
NATHANIEL, Ipswich 1678, eldest s. of Thomas of the same, d. prob. in
Mar. 1682, his inv. being dat. 18 of that mo. by w. Lydia, had Abigail,
b. a. 1662; Lydia, a. 1667; Nathaniel, 1669; Sarah, 1671; Thomas,
1673; Hannah; and Eliz. 1677. NOAH, Hatfield, s. of Thomas of
Hadley, m. Mary, prob. d. of Daniel White of the same, had Noah, b.

Aug. 1686; Mary, Dec. 1687; and Sarah, Oct. 1692; rem. to Colchester as one of the first sett. there had John, Jonathan, Samuel, and Hannah; and he d. 1712. RICHARD, Lynn 1638, freem. 14 Mar. 1639,
rem. to Salisbury, there was prominent town offic. 1650 and 2; had w.
Eliz. was a deac. and d. 12 July 1672. ROBERT, Wethersfield, s. of
John the first of Stratford, m. 9 June 1675, Eliz. d. of William Goodrich of W. had Thomas, b. May 1676; John, June 1678; Joseph, Sept.
1680; Prudence; Robert; and Gideon. By a sec. w. Mary he had no
ch. and d. 22 June 1714. SAMUEL, Wethersfield, s. prob. youngest of
Gov. Thomas, by him brot. from Eng. freem. 1657, ens. 1658, lieut.
1665, capt. 1670, rep. 1657–62, and 1675, m. 1659, Eliz. d. of John
Hollister, had Samuel, b. 13 Apr. 1660; Thomas, 29 July 1662; Sarah,
29 Sept. 1664; Mary, 23 Nov. 1666; Ann, 1668; and Eliz. 1670. By
sec. w. Hannah, d. of George Lamberton of New Haven, he had no ch.
and d. 15 July 1675. His wid. m. Hon. John Allyn of Hartford. Of
his ds. Sarah m. 4 Dec. 1683, Ephraim Hawley of Stratford, and next
Agur Tomlinson of the same; Mary, 1695, bec. sec. w. of Samuel
Hale, and d. 18 Feb. 1715; Ann m. 19 July 1687, capt. James Steele,
and next, 20 Nov. 1718, James Judson, whose first w. was her cousin;
and Eliz. m. 4 Apr. 1692, Daniel Shelton of Stratford. SAMUEL,
Stratford, s. of John first of the same, had three ws. but ch. prob. only
by first, Abigail, Samuel, b. 15 Oct. 1686; Abigail; Ann; and Eliz. 31
Jan. 1694; and he d. 1729. SAMUEL, Glastonbury, eldest ch. of Samuel
the first, m. 20 June 1683, Ruth Rice, had Mercy, b. 15 Oct. 1684, d. in
few days; Samuel, 9 July 1688, d. in few weeks; Samuel, 24 Dec.
1689, Y. C. 1707 (the min. of Lebanon, ord. 5 Dec. 1710, thence, at his
req. dism. 4 Dec. 1722, rem. to Boston, here had Samuel, b. 5 Mar.
1725, H. C. 1744, wh. d. Oct. 1799; and Arnold, 25 Dec. 1727, H. C.
1745, wh. d. Aug. 1802; and in the catal. of Yale, the yr. of his dism.
is mark. with star for that of his d. but he liv. long aft. was a most active
mem. of his majesty's counc. for Mass. and d. says the Glastonbury
book, 20 May 1770); Thomas, 14 Feb. 1693; Thaddeus, 27 Mar.
1695; and Silas, 4 Mar. 1700; and d. 28 Aug. 1731. His wid. d. 30
Mar. 1742, aged 82. Of this branch descend. most of the name in
Boston, the late Hon. John, H. C. 1782, long the last surv. of his class,
having been gr.s. of Rev. Samuel. SAMUEL, Hatfield, s. of Thomas of
Hadley, m. 11 Dec. 1684, Sarah, d. of Nathaniel Clark of Northampton, had Samuel, b. 1688; and d. 9 Aug. 1690. His wid. m. Thomas
Meakins of Hartford. SAMUEL, Hartford, s. of Thomas sec. of the
same, by w. Ruth had Hannah, b. 22 Nov. 1689; Samuel, 26 Dec.
1693; Ruth, 29 Jan. 1697; Sarah, 16 Dec. 1700; Rebecca, 3 Oct.
1704; and James, 1706; and d. 3 Oct. 1733. His wid. d. 2 May 1744,

aged 79. § † ‡ Thomas, Hartford, an orig. propr. as also at Wethersfield, appears first in the Rec. of that Col. Trumbull I. 9, as the sec.
magistr. at the Gen. Ct. 1 May 1637, when war was denounc. against
the Pequots, they hav. long been hostile, and the proportion of 90 men
fixed for the sev. planta. viz. Hartford, 42, Windsor, 30, and Wethersfield, 18. Yet it is quite uncert. when he came from Eng. tho. satisfactor. kn. that he brot. three s. John, Thomas, and Samuel, and three
ds. Mary, wh. d. bef. her f. prob. unm. Ann, and Sarah; equal. uncert.
is the name of his w. though we can hardly doubt whether he brot. one;
and stranger still is the uncertainty of his prior resid. in Mass. He had
good proportion of the patents for Swampscot and Dover, wh. he sold
Aug. 1648, to Christopher Lawson. We may then safely conclude, that
a person of his educ. and good est. had not come over the water bef.
1636, and that he staid so short a time at Boston or Cambridge as to
leave no trace of hims. at either, and he was estab. at Hartford bef.
Gov. Haynes left Cambridge. There is, indeed, a very precise tradit.
of his coming, with f. Nathaniel, in the fleet with Higginson, 1629, to
Salem; but that is merely ridiculous. He took, for sec. w. a. 1645,
Eliz. wid. of Nathaniel Foote of Wethersfield; on the d. of Gov. Haynes,
1 Mar. 1654, the Dept. Edward Hopkins being in Eng. on pub. business, he was made head of the Col. with title of Moderator, but on the
day of elect. in May, Hopkins was chos. Gov. and Welles Dept. tho. H.
never came back to Conn. being tak. by the great Protector into his
Parliam. so that in 1655, hav. had the duty to fulfil in the vacation of
the chair, he was chos. Gov. and Webster, Dept. and in 1656, accord. to
the constitut. of the Col. "that no person be chos. Gov. above once in
two yrs." Webster was made Gov. and in 1657, Winthrop Gov. while
Welles was Dept. both yrs. and in 1658 made Gov. again with Winth.
for Dept. Both chang. places in May 1659, and Welles d. 14 Jan. foll.
at Wethersfield. His wid. d. 28 July 1683; d. Ann m. 14 Apr. 1646,
Thomas Thompson of Farmington, and next, Anthony Hawkins; and
Sarah m. Feb. 1654, capt. John Chester, outliv. him less than ten yrs.
and d. 16 Dec. 1698. Thomas, Ipswich, perhaps a physician, came in
the Susan and Ellen from London, with young Richard Saltonstall,
aged 30, and perhaps w. Ann, 20; was made freem. 17 May 1637, had
three s. Nathaniel, John, and Thomas, this last b. 11 Jan. 1647; ds.
Sarah, w. of John Massey, by tradit. falsely call. first b. male of Salem;
Abigail, m. 19 June 1661, Nathaniel Treadwell of Ipswich; Eliz.;
Hannah; and Lydia. He had good est. gave his lds. in Wells, to s.
John, was deac. made his will 3 July, and d. 26 Oct. 1666. See a very
judic. memoir in Geneal. Reg. IV. 12. Ano. Ann W. came in the
Planter, 1635, aged 15. Thomas, New London 1648, aft. 1661 per-

haps rem. to Ipswich, was a ship-builder, and in 1677, bargain. with Amos Richardson to build a vessel for him at Stonington, wh. bred lawsuit in 1680, hav. then two s. Joseph, aged 22, and Thomas, 17, wh. were witnesses in the suit. He was aft. of Westerly, d. 12 Feb. 1700, had w. Naomi, made will 27 Dec. 1699, nam. Joseph, Thomas, Mary, Ruth, Sarah, John, and Nathaniel. Mary m. 15 Dec. or Jan. 1690, Ezekiel Maine the sec. ‡*THOMAS, Hartford, s. of Gov. Thomas of the same, m. 23 June 1654, Hannah, wid. of John Pantry of the same, d. of Richard Tuttle of Boston, as I think, had Rebecca, b. 1655; Thomas, 1657; Sarah, 1659; Ichabod, 1660; Samuel, 1662; Jonathan, 1664; and Joseph, 1667; was nam. in the royal chart. obt. by Gov. Winth. Apr. 1662, as a grantee, rep. May foll. Assist. 1668, and next mo. was k. by a fall, as the ch. rec. of Roxbury notes "from one of his cherry-trees." Those *cherry-trees* some unpractis. reader of old rec. has by conject. giv. *chariot*, in copy. Bradstreet's Journal, as if in 1668 in the streets of H. chariots were plenty as cucumbers. See Geneal. Reg. VIII. 326, and correct. in the ensu. vol. His wid. d. 9 Aug. 1683. Rebecca m. 18 Aug. 1680, James Judson of Stratford, and d. 3 Nov. 1717; and Sarah m. 6 Nov. 1678, John Bidwell, jun. THOMAS, Boston, by w. Naomi, had Joseph, b. 7 June 1656, wh. may have been the soldier under capt. Lothrop, k. 18 Sept. 1675 at Bloody Brook. *THOMAS*, Amesbury, s. of John of Wells, gr.s. of Thomas of Ipswich, wh. gave in his will, very lib. sh. of est. to his s. John, expect. this gr.s. to be educ. at coll. (from H. C. what circumst. prevent. his being gr. is now not within reach, but the very first honor. degree of A. M. ever confer. by the coll. was to him, 1703); was ord. first min. of A. 1672, m. at N. 3 Mar. 1673, Mary Parker, and had John, b. 4 Feb. 1696; d. 1734, 10 July, mark. contrary to his wont, by Farmer, in 86th yr. when he was more than 87. He had liv. at Newbury, in 1669 took o. of alleg. preach. next yr. at Kittery and Isle of Shoals. THOMAS, Stratford, s. of John of the same, had w. Eliz. was deac. and d. 7 Jan. 1721. THOMAS, Hadley, s. of that wid. Frances, wh. m. Thomas Colman, by w. Mary had Thomas, b. 10 Jan. 1652; Mary, 1 Oct. 1653; Sarah, 5 May 1655; John, 14 Jan. 1657; both d. young; Jonathan, a. 1658; all b. at Wethersfield; and at H. had John, again, 3 Apr. 1660; Samuel, a. 1662; Mary, again, 8 Sept. 1664; Noah, 26 July 1666; Hannah, 4 July 1668; Ebenezer, 20 July 1669; Daniel, 11 Dec. 1669, says the foolish rec. and d. 11 June 1670, by the same authority; Ephraim, a. 1672; and Joshua, 18 Feb. 1674; and d. 1676. His wid. m. Samuel Belden, 25 June 1678, and d. 1690. THOMAS, Hadley, eldest s. of the preced. m. 12 Jan. 1673, Hepzibah, d. of Peter Buel of Simsbury, had Mary, b. 12 Nov. foll.; Sarah, 1676; Thomas; Eleazer; John, k. 1709 by the Ind.; Daniel; David; and Hepzibah; and rem. to Deerfield, a. 1684, where one or two prob. were b. was a lieut. and d. 1691. His wid. and three ds. on 6 June 1693, were knock. on the head and escaped, but only two of the ds. were k. at that time. THOMAS, Hartford, s. of Thomas sec. of the same, m. 1689, Mary, d. of the sec. John Blackleach, had Thomas, b. 16 Oct. 1690; and John, 16 Dec. 1693; and d. 16 Mar. 1695. His wid. m. 1695, John Olcott, and next, capt. Joseph Wadsworth. THOMAS, Wethersfield, s. of the first Samuel of the same, m. 7 Jan. 1697, Thankful, d. of John Root of Deerfield, had Thomas, b. 10 Jan. 1698; and Hezekiah, 12 Aug. 1701, wh. d. at 10 yrs. His w. d. 1704, and he m. 17 May 1705, Jerusha, d. of lieut. James Treat of Wethersfield, had William, 12 Jan. 1706; Wait, 4 Jan. 1708; John, 10 Feb. 1710; and Ichabod, posthum. 26 Apr. 1712. He was a capt. d. 7 Dec. 1711, and his wid. m. 25 Dec. 1712, Ephraim Goodrich, and d. 15 Jan. 1754. THOMAS, Westerly, s. of Thomas of the same, had w. Sarah, ch. Edward, Thomas, and Sarah, all nam. in his will of 11 Apr. 1716. WILLIAM, Lynn, may have been bound over in £10. by our Ct. to answ. for oppress. 1641, as in Col. Rec. I. 335, appears; prob. went to Southold, L. I. Of this name, under its two forms of spell. the same sound, wh. are oft. for the same man, interchang. especial. in rec. of Conn. Farmer notes, in 1834, there had been gr. twenty-two at Yale, fourteen at Harv. and four at other N. E. coll.

WELLINGTON, or WILLINGTON, BENJAMIN, Watertown, s. of Roger of the same, m. 7 Dec. 1671, Eliz. eldest d. of Thomas Sweetman of Cambridge, had Eliz. b. 29 Dec. 1673; Benjamin, 21 June 1676; John, 26 July 1678; Ebenezer; Ruhamah; Mehitable, bapt. 4 Mar. 1688, wh. was mo. of famous Roger Sherman; Joseph, 4 Jan. 1691; and Roger, the youngest, rememb. in the will of his gr.f. He was made freem. the same day with his f. 1690, made his will 13 July 1709, and d. 8 Jan. foll. JOHN, Cambridge, eldest br. of the preced. m. Susanna, d. of capt. Thomas Straight, but prob. had no ch. was, Bond says, freem. 1677; but this means no more than that he took o. of alleg. for he was not adm. freem. made his will 4 Jan. 1715, and d. 23 Aug. 1726. His wid. d. 27 Jan. 1729. JOSEPH, Watertown, br. of the preced. by first w. Sarah, wh. d. 5 Feb. 1684, had prob. no ch. and he m. 6 June foll. Eliz. youngest d. of Thomas Straight, had Eliz. b. 27 Apr. 1685; Thomas, 10 Nov. 1686; Mary, 7 Oct. 1689; Susanna, 5 Feb. 1691, d. young. He sw. alleg. 1677, and d. 30 Oct. 1714. OLIVER, Watertown, br. of the preced. sw. alleg. 1677, m. late in life, Ann, wid. of Samuel Livermore, d. of Matthew Bridge, had no ch. but d. 30 Aug. 1727, his w. hav. d. two ds. bef. His will of 5 Nov. 1715, provides for childr. of his w. by her former h. and for Oliver Livermore, oldest gr.ch. of his w.

and gr.ch. of his sis. Mary. PALGRAVE, Watertown, youngest s of
Roger of the same, m. 29 Jan. 1690, Sarah, d. of William Bond, wh
bore him no ch. but d. young. He was a physician, made freem. 1690,
the same day with his f. and d. 22 Oct. 1715, by his will of 26 Apr.
preced. gave some personal prop. to Sarah Bond, a niece of his w. and
most of his est. to John Maddock, gr.ch. of his sis. Mary. ROGER,
Watertown, ancestor, as is usual. said, of all bear. this name, is first
heard of 1636 ; but in what ship he came, or from what pt. of Eng. is
unkn. m. a. 1637, Mary, eldest d. of Dr. Richard Palgrave of Charlestown, had John, b. 25 July 1638 ; Mary, 10 Feb. 1641 ; Joseph, 9 Oct.
1643 ; Benjamin ; Oliver, 23 Nov. 1648 ; Palgrave, 1653 ; was selectman 1678, and oft. aft. until 1691, yet not made freem. bef. 1690 ; had
good est. and in his will 17 Dec. 1697, names all the s. but not w. wh.
was, no doubt, dec. nor ds. whose ch. John Maddock, and Mary Livermore, are ment. He d. 11 Mar. foll. Mary, his only kn. d. m. 21
May 1662, Henry Maddock, and next, 16 Sept. 1679, John Coolidge,
and their d. Mary had m. Daniel Livermore few mos. bef. the will of
gr.f. Nine of this name are gr. at Harv. and one at Yale.

WELLMAN, ABRAHAM, Lynn, s. of Thomas of the same, m. Eliz. d.
of John Cogswell of Ipswich, wh. d. 10 May 1736, hav. sev. yrs. been
under guardian, had Thomas, b. 11 Oct. 1669 ; Eliz. 16 Feb. 1671,
d. at 2 yrs.; Abraham, 25 Nov. 1673 ; John, 3 May 1676 ; and Eliz.
again, 25 July 1678 ; Abigail ; Mary ; and Martha. His will of 15
Mar. 1716, provides for wid. Eliz. and the liv. ch. ISAAC, Lynn, br. of
the preced. m. 13 Mar. 1679, Hannah Adams, had Isaac, b. 7 Feb.
1680, d. young ; and Stephen, 6 Sept. 1681 ; Isaac, again ; and he was
liv. late in 1723, but his w. d. aft. 1711, and bef. her h. STEPHEN, a
soldier of "the flower of Essex," cut off by the Ind. 18 Sept. 1675, at
Deerfield, was perhaps br. of the preced. THOMAS, Lynn 1640, d. 10
Oct. 1672. His w. was Eliz. and in his will she is provid. for ; and the
childr. most of them under age, were Abraham, perhaps b. 1643 ; Isaac ;
Eliz. ; Sarah ; and Mary. WILLIAM, Gloucester 1649, m. that yr. Eliz.
d. of William Spencer, had Mary, b. 1650 ; Martha, 1652 ; Benjamin,
1654, d. young ; Eliz. 1657 ; William, 1661 ; at New London was
freem. of Conn. 1658, soon aft. 1663 rem. had Sarah, 16 Oct. 1665 ;
and Samuel, 19 Jan. 1668 ; wh. both d. young ; and perhaps Rachel,
aft. 1669, while liv. at Killingworth ; there d. 9 Aug. 1671. His will of
14 Mar. 1669 was reject. by the Ct. His wid. m. 23 May 1672, Jacob
Joy. By order of Ct. distrib. of est. was to wid. three s. and four ds.
May 1673. Mary m. Jan. 1667, Thomas Howard of Norwich, and
next, Aug. 1677, William Moore ; and aft. Jan. 1673 his d. Martha bec.

sec. w. of Clement Minor, and d. 5 July 1681; Eliz. m. 9 Jan. 1679, John Shethar, and d. 5 Feb. 1718. WILLIAM, Killingworth, s. of the preced. by w. Eliz. Joy, wh. d. 5 Jan. 1729, aged 68, had Mary, b. 26 Mar. 1692; William, 2 May 1694; Gideon, 8 Mar. 1696; and Benjamin, 26 Dec. 1697. He m. 25 June 1700, Eliz. wid. of Isaac Griswold, wh. d. 27 Oct. 1732, and he d. 23 Aug. 1736.

WELLOW, DANIEL, Cambridge, freem. 1666.

WELSH. See Welch.

WELSTEED, or WELSTEAD, WILLIAM, Charlestown 1665, first constable of four in 1690, m. Mehitable, d. of James Cary, had perhaps other ch. besides WILLIAM, wh. m. Eliz. d. of Henry Dering of Boston, and was, as Farmer in MS. notes, naval officer of the port. This sec. William had William, H. C. 1716, wh. m. a sis. of Gov. Hutchinson, was sec. min. of the New Brick ch. in Boston, ord. 1728, successor to Waldron.

WELTON, JOHN, Farmington, bef. 1673, by w. Mary, had John, Stephen, Mary, and perhaps more, b. there, but rem. to Waterbury, and there had Richard, b. 1680; Hannah, 1683; Thomas, 1685; George, 1687; and Else, 1690. His w. d. 1716; and he d. 1726.

WENBOURNE, WINBORN, or WENBANE, JOHN, Manchester, preach. bef. 1686, and left there 1689; whence he came, or whither he went, is quite unkn. WILLIAM, Boston, by w. Eliz. had John, b. 22 Nov. 1635. [See Geneal. Reg. IX. 166, where the name stands only with its first syllab.] But the rec. is made with a curious correct. 21 Sept. 1638 in ano. place Geneal. Reg. II. 191; rem. to Exeter, there on Friday, 4 Oct. 1639, with liberty-loving John Wheelwright, sign. the civil compact, and aft. says Farmer, from our Col. Rec. I. was clk. of the writs, freem. 1645; but he ret. to Boston, I think, bef. 1649, at least was so describ. 1662. See Winbourne.

WENDALL, THOMAS, Ipswich 1643, serv. of some one, wh. was order. to be whip. at Boston and Ipswich for the abuse of a girl, and the master to pay the expense of the inflict. in Col. Rec. II. 46.

WENSLEY, WINSLYE, or WINSLEY, DANIEL, perhaps was of Salisbury, and s. of Samuel senr. but d. unm. making will 17 Aug. 1665, in which he ment. brs. Nathaniel, and Elisha, sis. Weed, &c. *EDWARD, Salisbury, rep. at the Gen. Ct. 7 Mar. 1644, is insert. here, tho. in Col. Rec. II. giv. Winslowe. Perhaps he was br. of Samuel of the same. ELISHA, Salisbury, s. of Samuel the first, of wh. no more is kn. but that he is nam. in the will of br. Daniel. EPHRAIM, Salisbury, br. of the preced. m. 26 Mar. 1668, Mary Greely, had Mary, b. 1669; Samuel, 21 Dec. 1670; Eliz. 16 Feb. 1674; Martha, 21 Mar. 1677, d. soon; Martha, again, 6 Mar. 1685, d. at 12 yrs.; and Hannah, 23 Mar.

1689. His w. d. 11 Aug. 1697. JOHN, Boston, mariner, m. Eliz. eldest
d. of deac. William Paddy, had Richard, b. 18 Apr. 1664; Eliz. 14 Mar.
1666; and Mercy, 14 Feb. 1668; beside Sarah, 11 Aug. 1673, wh. m.
11 July 1700, Isaac, s. of the sec. Gov. Winslow. This union is worthy
of note, because in our rec. the two fam. names Winslow and Wensley,
interchangeab. may be seen confus. a thousand times, the same individ.
in one line call. different from ano. line on same page. Ano. ch. was
John, b. 8 Feb. 1675. From his will, 9 Dec. 1672, we find he was
bound on a voyage, divides est. into eight equal parts, of wh. two to his
w. two to s. Richard, left one ea. to the ds. of wh. the youngest was then
unb. but by codic. in our Vol. VI. made 26 Dec. 1675, is told that " God
hath giv. me two ch. more since the above." Very curious is it, that the
will of this Wensley, in the rec. immediately follows that of Samuel Winslow, also of Boston, mariner. His d. Mercy m. Joseph Bridgham, Esq.
and next, 8 Dec. 1712, Hon. Thomas Cushing. NATHANIEL, Salisbury,
s. of the first Samuel, b. prob. in Eng. old eno. to be tax. 1650, m. 14 Oct.
1661, Mary Jones, in the will of her f. Thomas, call. Winslow, as memb.
of the milit. force, took o. of alleg. 13 Dec. 1677, bot. of John Alcock,
in 1661 part 1-32 of Block Island. It had been sold to A. by John
Endicott, Daniel Dennison, and William Hathorne, to wh. it was giv. by
Mass. governm. for their serv. in the Pequot war, when the conquest
was made; and he seems to have been at Block Island 1685. *SAMUEL,
an early grantee, with Bradstreet, Dudley, and others, of Colchester
1638, but not orig. sett. of Salisbury, dignif. with prefix of respect in
1650, when he and s. Nathaniel, and Samuel, were tax. The s. I suppose, as well as d. Deborah, with w. Eliz. he brot. from Eng. but other
ch. b. here, were Ephraim, 15 Apr. 1641; Elisha, 30 May 1646; and
the w. d. 2 June 1649. He was freem. 22 May 1639, and invent. mode
of mak. salt, to wh. our Gen. Ct. gave encouragem. as in Rec. I. 331
and II. 5, or Felt II. 176. He was rep. 1642, 5, and 53; d. 2 June
1663; and his wid. Ann, a sec. w. m. 1657, wid. of Henry Boade of
Wells, d. 21 Mar. 1677. SAMUEL, Salisbury, s. of the preced. perhaps
eldest, b. prob. in Eng. made his will 1665, but whether he had w. or
ch. is not kn. to me. What wid. W. Sewall refers to, in his diary, sub.
Dec. 1686, Geneal. Reg. VI. 73, when he ment. d. of her s. Jenner in
Eng. is beyond my conject. but it may not prob. be Ann, the wid. of
Henry Boade of Wells or Saco, wh. in 1657 agreed to m. this Samuel;
nor should I refer to so unimport. a fact, were it not to save trouble to
some hunter of the Indexes of Geneal. Reg. that Wersley VI. 243,
means the same man. Sometimes this name is confound. with Winslow;
and almost as oft. the name in Col. Rec. is Winslow, as otherwise.

WENTOM, EDWARD, Kittery, submit. to jurisdict. of Mass. in Nov.
1652.   Col. Rec. IV. pt. I. 129.

WENTWORTH, BENJAMIN, Dover, s. prob. youngest of William, by w.
Sarah Allen, m. a. 1697, had William, b. 14 Aug. 1698; Sarah, 16
Apr. 1700; Tamasin, 4 Jan. 1702; Benjamin, 5 Dec. 1703; Ebenezer,
9 Sept. 1705; Susanna, 9 Dec. 1707; Joseph, 22 Dec. 1709; Eliz. 8
June 1712; Dorothy, 26 July 1714; Martha, 25 July 1716; Abra, 14
Feb. 1718; and Mark, 30 May 1720; and was drown. in the summer
of 1728.   EPHRAIM, Dover, br. perhaps youngest, of the preced. m.
Mary, d. of Ephraim Miller, had sev. ch. but the geneal. in the Reg.
IV. 327, owing to the lateness of bapt. in that ch. of sev. adults, so
that gr.childr. seem to be confus. with childr. was exceeding. difficult, and
elud. the persever. dilig. of Hon. John W. of our day, wh. suppos. him
to be the man, whose will of 16 Mar. 1738, was pro. 29 June 1748.
EZEKIEL, Dover, perhaps fourth s. of Elder William, by w. Eliz. thot.
confident. to be d. of Ezekiel Knight of Wells, was taxable at D. 1672,
had six s. and two ds. prob. the foll. Paul, Thomas, John, Gershom,
Eliz. Tamosine, William, and Benjamin, wh. is presum. to be the youngest, bapt. Sunday, 25 Nov. 1722, as capt. Benjamin W. and d. 1714.
GERSHOM, Dover, perhaps third s. of William, taxable 1670, m. 18
Mar. 1696, Hannah French of Salisbury, there had Mary, b. 14 May
1697; Samuel, 5 Dec. 1699; soon aft. went again to D. there had Ezekiel, 4 Feb. 1702; and Gershom, 4 Apr. 1705; and John, wh. was k.
by the Ind. at Rochester, with three others, 27 June 1746.   He was
deac. 1717, had good est. and d. 2 Mar. 1731, at Somersworth.   JOHN,
Dover, perhaps sec. s. of Elder William of the same, tax. 1668, sw.
fidel. next yr. with his elder br. rem. 1675, or earlier, to York, there m.
Martha, d. of Ephraim Miller of Kittery, had sev. ch. but where b. or
when, can hardly be made out with any satisfact.   From York he rem.
to Falmouth, and betw. the first and sec. destr. of that town, i. e. a.
1685, his s. Charles was b. but an elder one, John, had been b. perhaps
at Kittery or York, some time a. 1677.   From the doomed Falmouth, in
the gr. East. war, he had rem. to Dorchester, and spent the resid. of his
days in the part since call. Canton, and there Edward, Shubael, Eliz.
and Abigail, or most of the four may have been b.   He was d. bef. Jan.
1710, when his wid. Martha, gave receipt in full to Judge Sewall, for
all she had ever done for the Punkipaug Ind.   Compare the discord.
reports that the unwearied genealog. of the fam. (the Mayor of Chicago)
had to encounter in Reg. IV. 327, VI. 213, and VIII. 246.   PAUL,
Dover, s. of William of the same, tax. there 1682, sold his est. at D.
says the fam. acco. 15 Apr. 1696, then call. hims. of Newbury, but Mr.

Coffin omits him. He belong. to Rowley at that time, where eleven of his ch. by w. Catharine were bapt. 17 May 1696, said Farmer, but only ten had been b. at that time. However, he had thirteen, as he caused them to be put upon rec. at Norwich, whither he had rem. from New London, if Farmer be right, as he gives him recommend. from R. to that place, June 1707 ; but prob. Miss Caulkin's would not have been silent on so good a point, and we may presume his change was only from R. direct to Norwich. The ch. may have been b. at Dover, Newbury, or Rowley ; but more import. is the name and date of ea. William, 25 Dec. 1680 ; Sylvanus, 28 Feb. 1682 ; Paul, 10 May 1682 (wh. or the two preced. must be wrong) ; Ebenezer, 18 June 1683 ; Martha, 9 Feb. 1685 ; Mercy, 18 July 1686 ; Aaron, 13 July 1687 ; Moses, 17 Apr. 1689 ; Mary, 25 Dec. 1692 ; Catharine, 28 July 1694 ; Sarah, 8 Apr. 1697 ; Benjamin, 28 Dec. 1698 ; and Edward, 20 June 1700. He was liv. May 1746 (but his w. was then d.), and d. bef. Jan. 1751. See Reg. VII. 265. SAMUEL, Dover, eldest s. of William of the same, tax. 1659, sw. fidel. 1669, freem. 1676, by w. Mary, whose fam. name was prob. Benning, and perhaps she was d. of Ralph, had Samuel, b. 9 Apr. 1666 ; Daniel, 21 Oct. 1669, d. at 21 yrs. ; John, 16 Jan. 1672, wh. was made Lieut.-Gov. of the Prov. ; Mary, 5 Feb. 1674 ; Ebenezer, 9 Apr. 1677 ; Dorothy, 27 June 1680 ; and Benning, 28 June 1682, d. young ; and the f. d. at Portsmouth, 25 Mar. 1690, of smallpox. In 1681 the Treasr. of Mass. was direct. to pay him £30. but the serv. is not ment. Rec. V. 317. His wid. m. next yr. Richard Martin, as his third w. SYLVANUS, Dover, one of the younger s. of Elder William of the same, it is said, m. at Rowley, 7 Nov. 1685, Eliz. Stewart, possib. d. of Duncan, but why the est. on wh. he was liv. 1693, was then giv. by his f. to s. Benjamin, unless he took dislike to Sylvanus, may be hard to conject. nor is any thing more told of him in the fam. acco. See Geneal. Reg. IV. 327 and VI. 213. TIMOTHY, Dover, br. of the preced. m. Sarah Cromwell, perhaps d. of Philip of Dover, tho. by extrav. tradit. she has been by some equal. ignorant and credul. thot. d. of Richard, Lord Protector, for short time, of Eng. rem. aft. 1702 to Berwick, there d. 17 July 1719, aged 70, says Geneal. Reg. VI. 213, but on the same p. a little lower, the writer wild. says 1748, and at Dover. His will of 3 May, pro. 8 July in that yr. 1719 as my memo. reads, ment. w. and ch. Timothy, Samuel, Mary, and Sarah. But his w. d. near the same time with him, it is said, and was bur. in the same gr. WILLIAM, Dover, rul. Elder, had first been at Exeter, 1639, in the orig. combina. with thirty-four others, and it may be that he had accomp. his fr. John Wheelwright across the ocean in 1636. He had foll. him from E. to Wells, where he was made constable 1648, but in 1650 seems to have fix. his resid. at D.

where he was selectman 1665, as resolute for Mass. jurisdict. as he had been against it; preach. in 1666, had w. Eliz. and ch. Samuel, b. 1641, perhaps at E. perhaps at W.; John; Gershom; Ezekiel; Timothy; Paul; Sylvanus; Ephraim; and Benjamin; yet the order of success. is conject. d. 16 Mar. 1698, aged near 90, it is thot. His only d. Eliz. whose date of b. is uncert. but suppos. a. 1663, m. Richard Tozer the sec. A plausible case for ano. d. Sarah, was furnish. in Geneal. Reg. VII. 304, because Paul W. being guardian of those ch. by their own choice, as appears in Bond, 14, is call. uncle of Sarah and Benjamin Barnard, ch. of Benjamin and Sarah B. To this in the next vol. of Reg. p. 48 is repl. that perhaps the w. of Paul was a Barnard, sis. of their f. and again it may be equal. prob. that their mo. was sis. of the w. of Paul; so that the chance is two to one against the suppos. Six of this fam. as Farmer notes, had been gr. at Harv.

WERMALL, or WORMALL, JAMES, Duxbury, had, Deane says, been of Scituate 1638, but at D. had Josiah, b. 1670; and John, wh. Winsor adds, m. 9 June 1698, Mary Barrows, and d. 1711 at Bridgewater. JOSEPH, Scituate 1638, rem. soon to Duxbury, had w. Miriam, ch. Josiah, Sarah, and perhaps Esther, wh. m. 20 Aug. 1669 as his sec. w. Joseph Dunham. JOSEPH, Boston, 1650. JOSIAH, Duxbury, perhaps s. of Joseph of the same, m. 15 Jan. 1696, Patience, d. of William Sherman of Marshfield, had Josiah, Mehitable, Mercy, Samuel, and Ichabod.

WESCOTT, WASCOTT, WESTCOATT, or WESTCOTT, AMOS, Warwick, eldest s. of Stukely, on the freeman's list, 1655, m. 13 July 1667, Sarah, d. of Thomas Stafford, wh. d. 1669, and next m. 9 June 1670, her sis. Deborah S. had Amos, wh. d. 1692, without issue; and Solomon, wh. d. without issue; and three ds. Perhaps he was of Wickford 1674, and his name may have been by the Conn. Commissnrs. call. Aaron. DANIEL, New Hampsh. of wh. all that I kn. is, that he join. with most of the other inhabs. 20 Feb. 1690, in desir. the protect. of Mass. to be extend. over them. JEREMIAH, Warwick, s. perhaps youngest of Stukely, m. 27 July 1665, Ellen England, had Jeremiah, b. 7 Oct. 1666; Elenor, 20 Oct. 1669; Pevis? wh. d. Aug. 1673, near three yrs. old; Stukely, Oct. 1672; and d. 1686; but his will, then made, accord-ing to the strange custom of that jurisdict. ment. four other ch. Josiah; Samuel; William; and Benjamin, of wh. Josiah had abund. offspring. RICHARD, Wethersfield 1639-44, rem. to Fairfield, there d. a. 1651, leav. four ch. John; Daniel; Joanna; and Abigail. His wid. Joanna m. Nathaniel Baldwin; d. Joanna m. a. 1664, John Weed; and Abigail, m. a. 1669, Moses Knapp. Tho. both the s. liv. many yrs. at Stamford, nothing more can be told of either; but they were gone by d. or rem.

bef. 1700. ROBERT, Warwick, s. of Stukely of the same, is among the freem. of 1655 in Haz. II. 372, by w. Catharine had Catharine, b. 6 May 1664, at W.; Zorobabel, 13 Apr. 1666; rem. to Portsmouth or Newport, and had Dinah, Feb. 1670; Mary, 2 June 1672; Samuel, 18 Sept. 1672; and Robert, 2 Apr. 1678. He had connex. with the Wickford planta. 1674. STUKELY, Salem 1636, impress. with views of the Bapt. by Roger Williams, he was, with his w. excommun. 1639, with W. and others, and they had gone, 1637, to Providence. Aft. the establishm. of the rights of Gorton and assoc. Wescott rem. to Warwick 1648, was one of the freem. 1665, and there resid. I judge, until the end of his days, 12 Jan. 1678. His ch. were Damaris, Amos, Jeremiah, Robert, and Mercy or Sarah. He is the first nam. grantee in Roger Williams's deed to his assoc. Damaris m. Benedict Arnold; and Mercy or Sarah m. Samuel Stafford. WILLIAM, Wethersfield 1639.

WESSON. See Weston.

WEST, BENJAMIN, Enfield 1686, m. 14 Mar. 1692, Hannah, d. prob. of Elias Shaddock, had Hannah, b. 24 May 1693; rem. to Middletown, there had Benjamin, 1 June 1696; Mary, 1 Apr. 1699; beside Abigail, 23 July 1716; and perhaps others. The name of his w. is read Shattuck by one; but ano. calls it Haddock, and conject. of a skilful antiq. makes it to be Hadlock, perhaps d. of James. * EDWARD, Lynn 1637, of wh. all I can say is, that Farmer quotes Lewis 64. * EDWARD, Medfield, freem. 1672, was, I presume, of Sherborn few yrs. aft. a lieut. 1682, selectman 1684, and rep. 1689. EDWARD, Dorchester, freem. 1673, wh. may seem only a repetit. of the name of the freem. of the yr. bef. call. of Medfield, for none with this is heard of at D. The succeed. ages owe much to the heedlessness of Secr. Rawson. FRANCIS, Duxbury 1643, was one of the first proprs. of Bridgewater 1645. Baylies II. 254. HENRY, Salem, freem. 1668, was a saddler. His w. Eliz. d. of George Meriam of Concord, bore to him Eliz. 22 June 1665; Samuel, 25 Jan. 1667; Susanna, 16 Nov. 1668; Henry, 14 Jan. 1671; Eliz. again, 4 Mar. 1673; and Mary, 22 Feb. 1676; and d. 26 Aug. 1691, aged 50. In 1693, he was empower. to take acco. of strangers com. to the town. JOHN, Ipswich 1648. JOHN, Saybrook, or other place in its neighb. may be he wh. came in the Abigail, 1635, from London to Boston, aged 11 yrs. in 1649 was fin. £10. for sell. a gun to an Ind. but four other reputa. men were equal suffer. for the same misdemean. He was employ. 1663, by the Col. to survey the bounds betw. S. and Killingworth. * JOHN, Saco, was of gr. jury 1640, sw. alleg. to Mass. 1653, sold his est. in few yrs. to maj. Pendleton, and d. betw. 29 Sept. 1663, the date of his will, and 5 Oct. next, when it was pro. It

gave to gr.ch. Ann, Lydia, Thomas, and Samuel Haley, ch. of Thomas.
*JOHN, Beverly, there rep. 1677. JOHN, Newport, is seen on the list
of freem. 1655. JOHN, Swansey, by w. Mehitable had William, b. 11
Sept. 1683. JOHN, Boston, Secr. of the arbitra. governm. of Sir
Edmund Andros, was seiz. and sent home with him 1689. I presume
his only ch. d. Feb. 1688, as Sewall notes bur. 29 of the mo. in his
diary. JOHN, Ipswich, perhaps s. of John of the same, by w. Sarah had
Eliz. b. 31 July 1688; and John, 25 Feb. 1691. JOHN, Rowley, 1691.
MATTHEW, Lynn 1636, freem. 9 Mar. 1637, was aft. 1646 of Newport,
and is seen in the freemen's list 1655. NATHANIEL, Newport, by
Farmer is call. one of the founders of the first Bapt. ch. 1644. ROBERT,
Providence 1641, one of the friends of Williams, wh. denounc. Gorton
and his assoc. to the Mass. as seen in Geneal. Reg. IV. 216, or 3 Mass.
Hist. Coll. I. 4; and tho. there on the list of freem. 1655, yet the rec.
tells nothing of w. or ch. SAMUEL, Salem, d. a. 1685, for his inv. is of
4 Aug. in that yr. SAMUEL, Salem, m. 29 Jan. 1690, Mary Poor, had
Samuel, b. 21 Nov. 1691; Eliz. 11 Sept. 1693; Jonathan, 2 Sept.
1697; and Daniel, 22 Apr. 1699. THOMAS, Salem, came in the Mary
and John, 1634, had gr. of ld. 1640, m. 11 Oct. 1658, Phebe Waters,
perhaps d. of Richard, was freem. 1668, and there liv. 1686. His w.
Phebe, d. 16 Apr. 1674. THOMAS, Beverly, freem. 1670, a man of
conseq. petitions the Gen. Ct. Feb. 1682 with others, by command
of the town, for protect. in their est. against the claims of Mason.
THOMAS, Newbury, took o. of alleg. 1669, may have liv. at Haverhill
1675. THOMAS, Wethersfield, m. 1677, and by w. Eliz. had Christopher, b. 1678; and Mary, 1680; was poor. *THOMAS, Hadley, rep.
1686. TWYFORD, Marshfield 1643, had come from London to Boston
in the autumn of 1635, aged 19, by the Hopewell, capt. Babb, and was,
I think, of Rowley 1667; and liv. at Salem, perhaps 1677, and Ipswich
1678. WILLIAM, Salem, m. 30 Aug. 1672, Mary Hilliard, perhaps d.
of Edward of the same, had Joseph, b. 30 May 1673, d. 26 Aug. foll.
Of this, tho. Farmer had no census of the name, I find thirteen gr. at
Harv. and four at Yale.

WESTALL, WESTELL, or WESTOLL, DANIEL, New Hampsh. in
Farmer's MS. notes, must, I believe, be the man by me giv. from
Geneal. Reg. VIII. 235 as Wescott. JOHN, Saybrook 1653, allow. to
keep an inn 1663, and there d. 12 Feb. 1683. His wid. Susanna d. 18
Mar. 1684. By her he had Susanna, b. 1650, wh. d. bef. her f. She
was b. at Wethersfield, where he liv. some yrs. bef. rem. to S. He had
good est. and made John, s. of Nathaniel Kirtland, and neph. of the w.
of W. his sole heir, some time bef. his d. reserv. right to make some
legacies. His w. had br. John Kirtland, childless, to wh. she gave small

ho. and lot, she hav. aft. the d. of her h. that power. JOHN, Dover 1648.

WESTBROOK, JOB, and JOHN, were of Portsmouth early, perhaps from Co. Surrey in Eng. both petnrs. for Mass. protect. in Feb. 1690. John was there in 1665, a selectman in 1697, and prob. f. of that col. Thomas, wh. in the expedit. of 1720 to Kennebeck, hoped to have seized Father Rasles at his mission of Norridgewock.

WESTCAR, JOHN, Hadley, fin. for sell. liquor, 1665, was a trader, m. 17 Oct. 1667, Hannah, d. of Francis Barnard, petitions against imposts 1669. He had no ch. was in 1673 licens. to practise physic and surgery, but d. 1675, aged 30 yrs. His wid. m. Simon Beaman.

WESTEAD, or WESSTEAD, WILLIAM, Saybrook, there purch. ho. June 1679, then said to be from Charlestown, where was not in the yr. bef. any man of that name, as head of a fam. but he is call. mariner, and so prob. was unm. bef. rem. to S. had Samuel, b. 20 May 1683; and Eleanor, an elder ch. d. 20 May 1684.

WESTERHOUSEN, WILLIAM, New Haven 1648, a merch. from New Amsterdam, took o. of fidel. 18 Oct. 1648, had Willielmus, b. 13 June 1650; and rem. bef. 1656, prob. on acco. of the war betw. Eng. and his native country, for a final *n* in his name betray. his origin. He had good est.

WESTGATE, ADAM, Salem 1647–62, mariner, by w. Mary had Robert, b. 1 July 1647; a s. without name, 15 Apr. 1650; Thomas, 12 Feb. 1654; Joseph, 30 Apr. 1657, d. at 2 yrs.; Mary, 14 Feb. 1660, d. at 2 yrs.; and Benjamin, 26 July 1662, d. in few days. DANIEL, Stamford, propound. for freem. 1670. ‖ JOHN, Boston, was a single man when adm. of the ch. 12 Sept. 1640, ar. co. 1641, went home, I suppose, bef. tak. w. for in the rec. of the ch. 26 Sept. 1647 is his dism. "on desire of the ch. of Pulham Mary in Norfolk, Eng." and in May 1677 was of Harlestone in that Co. Thence he had writ. to capt. Lake, 5 Apr. 1653, to inq. if the report of the d. of his former teacher, John Cotton, was true.

WESTLEY, WILLIAM, Hartford 1638, an orig. sett. tho. not orig. purchas. was excus. from watch, in 1646, perhaps on acco. of age. No fam. is heard of, but he left a wid. wh. was assist. by the ch. at Hadley, bec. she had been of their party, bef. they rem. from Hartford.

WESTMORELAND, JAMES, Boston 1652, says Farmer, but no more is kn.

WESTON, EDMUND, Duxbury, came in the Elizabeth and Ann from London to Boston, 1635, aged 30; m. a d. of John Soule of the same, as Winsor suppos. and had, perhaps, Elnathan, Samuel, and John. The informat. is little. EDWARD, in Philip's war, was a corpo. in

Mosely's comp. Dec. 1675. *FRANCIS, Salem, freem. 5 Nov. 1633, a friend of Roger Williams; but whether he came with him, or when, or whence he came, is unkn. nor have we the date of his join. the ch. He was rep. at the first Gen. Ct. that was attend. by dep. but was unfortunate in his w. wh. was punish. by the bilboes, tho. her offence was, as Felt presum. Eccles. Ann. I. 341, "of a religious character," and he fell into the impractica. notions as to the duty of separat. of chhs. and went to Providence with Williams, there was one of the founders of his ch. but in few yrs. disagreed with him, and symboliz. with Gorton, Wicks, Holden, and others, rem. with them to ld. a little down the Bay, purchas. from the Ind. now Warwick, was denounc. by the authority of Mass. seiz. and brot. prison. to Boston, by Ct. sentenc. Nov. 1643, as in Rec. II. 52, to be kept at labor in Dorchester, with suffic. irons to prevent escape; and liberat. at last, thro. fear of his influence over his keeper's relig. sentiments, wh. under threat of death he was prohibit. from attempt. to pervert, d. bef. June 1645, leav. no issue. FRANCIS, Plymouth, stands in the tax list for Jan. 1633, but not in that of next yr. nor is more told of him in any place within my knowledge, unless he be the same as was call. at Duxbury, Francis West. JOHN, Salem, join. the ch. 1648, being then 17 yrs. old, if the fam. tradit. be correct, wh. seems very prob. that he came in 1644, aged 13, from Buckinghamsh. Still we must be careful to doubt in proper places, for the same valua. testim. notes on his gr.-st. "that he was one of the found. of the ch. in Reading." Now we kn. the falsity of this, for he could be only 14 yrs. old on that event. He had rem. to Reading, prob. bef. m. and his early ch. were carr. to Salem for bapt. they were Sarah, b. 15 July 1656, bapt. 10 May 1657; Mary, 25 May 1659, perhaps d. very soon, certain its bapt. is not found at Salem first ch.; John, 9 Mar. bapt. 29 Aug. 1661; and Eliz. bapt. Oct. 1663; Stephen, b. a. 1665; and perhaps Samuel, and Thomas, as Eaton in Geneal. Reg. II. 48, indicates. In 1691 he was adm. freem. and d. 1723. MATTHEW, Providence 1644, may be the same man call. Matthew West. STEPHEN, Reading, s. of John, had Stephen, and d. 1753, aged 88. See Geneal. Reg. I. 278. THOMAS, a London merch. had engag. in plant. a col. in 1622 at Weymouth, but his sett. were very incompet. persons, much disqualif. by former habits of life and charact. the next yr. on visit to the country, he was dishearten. and gave up his hopes, went home, and in the gr. civ. war, d. at Bristol. Of this name Farmer notes fifteen gr. in N. E. coll. up to 1834, of wh. I find only four at Harv. and one at Yale. Oft. it is writ. as the sound was Wesson.

WESTOVER, JONAS, Windsor, 1649, rem. to Killingworth, freem. 1658, is found in the list 1669. By w. Hannah, m. 1663, had Margaret, b. 19 Feb. 1666; Hannah, 8 Apr. 1668; Eliz. 3 May 1670; Jane, 26 Mar. 1672; and these are all appear. on the rec. but others he had, as by his will, in 1702, two other ds. and two s. are nam. Jonas, Jonathan, Mary, and Joanna. Perhaps one or more were not b. at K. but at Simsbury, where he d. Jan. 1709.

WESTWOOD, *WILLIAM, Cambridge, where he may have been as early as 1632, came in the Francis, from Ipswich 1634, had liv. in the adj. Co. of Essex, aged 28, with w. Bridget, 32, brot. two serv. John Lea, and Grace Newell, as, being a man of good est. he had made his explora. here bef. bring. his fam. wh. in the earliest days of the Col. was judicious; freem. 4 Mar. 1635, rem. with the earliest companions of Hooker, to Conn. as an orig. propr. of Hartford, and was rep. 1636 at the first Gen. Ct. in Hartford, Windsor, and Wethersfield, then call. by the names, carr. from Mass. Newtown, Dorchester, and Watertown, respectiv. had authty. as the first constable of the Col. from Mass. afterwards at Hartford 1642–4, 1646–8, and 1650–6, rem. to Hadley 1659, and there d. 9 Apr. 1669. His wid. d. 12 May 1676; but the name was not perpet. and his only ch. Sarah, m. 30 May 1661, the sec. Aaron Cook; and large prop. was giv. to her, and her mo.

WETHERBEE, JOHN, Marlborough 1675, rem. to Sudbury, by w. Mary had Thomas, b. 5 Jan. 1678.

WETHERELL, WETHERILL, WITHERELL, WETHEREL, and oft. in Conn. rec. WITHERLY, *DANIEL, New London, s. of Rev. William, b. at Maidstone, Co. Kent, where his f. kept the free sch. 29 Nov. 1630, m. 4 Aug. 1659, Grace, d. of Jonathan Brewster of the same, had Hannah, b. 21 Mar. says the rec. perhaps by mist. for May 1660; Mary, 7 Oct. 1668; Daniel, 26 Jan. 1671; and Samuel, bapt. 19 Oct. 1679; of wh. both s. d. young; Hannah m. 16 May 1680, Adam Picket; and Mary m. Thomas Harris, and next, 1694, George Denison. He was a man of the chief charact. in town for many yrs. says Miss Caulkins, recorder or clk. 1667, and oft. aft. selectman, rep. 1669, 70, 1, 3, 5–7, judge of prob. capt. and milit. commiss. and d. 14 Apr. 1719. Two letters from him to Gov. Winth. announc. apprehens. of instant war with Philip, may be seen in 3 Mass. Hist. Coll. X. 118. JOHN, Watertown, freem. 18 May 1642, by w. Grace, wh. d. 16 Dec. 1671, aged 75, he had only Mary, b. prob. in Eng. wh. d. Apr. 1655, aged 20; and he d. 23 June 1672, aged 78. His will of 9 Jan. preced. gives decent legacy to Rev. John Sherman, and prop. to kinsm. Ralph Day, and James Thorpe, of Dedham, with William Price of W. JOHN, Scituate, s. of Rev. William, had John, b. 1675; William, 1678; Thomas, 1681; and Joshua, 1683; but the name of w. and other parties are not seen in Deane. JOHN, Taunton, s. of William of the same, by w. Susanna, m.

a. 1687, had John, b. 8 Oct. 1688, and call. the first ch. b. in that pt. of
T. that bec. Norton, beside seven other ch. whose names are unkn.
SAMUEL, Scituate, not eldest s. of Rev. William, yet b. perhaps in Eng.
by w. Isabel had Samuel, b. 1678; Hannah, 1680; and Joshua, 1683;
in wh. yr. the f. d. SAMUEL, Scituate, s. of the preced. m. 26 May
1698, Ann Rogers, had ten ch. and descend. remain. THEOPHILUS,
Middleborough, third or fourth ch. of Rev. William, m. Mary, eldest d.
of William Parker of Scituate, had sev. ds. was a serg. severely wound.
in the gr. Narraganset swamp fight, 19 Dec. 1675; had sec. w. Lydia,
wh. I presume to be sis. of the former, and the inscript. on her gr.-st. is,
d. 7 Sept. 1719, aged 67. *WILLIAM*, Scituate, 1644, came with w.
Mary and three ch. and one serv. in the Hercules from Sandwich 1635,
under certif. of 14 Mar. in that yr. from the mayor of Maidstone, Co.
Kent, where he was sch.-master, hav. been bred at Bennet (now Corpus
Christi) coll. Cambridge, and there took his A. B. 1622, i. e. Jan. 1623,
and A. M. 1626, is by Frothingham, 85, claim. for resid. at Charlestown 1636, to wh. I have nothing to object, but that his name is not
found in Budington's list of ch. memb. Farmer had provid. him a
resid. in Cambridge also; but this, I presume, to be the same as
Charlestown. He seems to have preach. at Duxbury, but bec. min. of
the sec. ch. at S. in 1645, and had sev. ch. b. in this country, as prob.
John; Theophilus; Eliz.; Sarah; and Hannah, 20 Feb. 1647; but the
last, it is thot. d. young; and he d. 9 Apr. 1684, aged perhaps 84.
Mary, b. perhaps in Eng. m. 20 Nov. 1656; Eliz. m. 22 Dec. 1657,
John Bryant; and Sarah m. Jan. 1670, Israel Hobart of Hingham.
* WILLIAM, Taunton 1643, possib. neph. of the preced. came, tradit.
tells, as a cabin-boy, adm. freem. 1658, constable 1662, oft. selectman.
His w. was Dorothy, but surname is not heard; and ch. were William,
John, Ephraim, and Dorothy, nam. in his will of 15 Aug. 1691, pro. 18
Nov. foll. but E. was d. bef. the date of will. Dorothy had m. 26 Aug.
1674, Elias Irish, and next, 1 Apr. 1686, William Wood. He was rep.
1671 and 85, in this last yr. is call. serg. WILLIAM, Taunton, call. jun.
prob. s. of the preced. m. 14 Mar. 1681, Eliz. Newland, perhaps d. of
Jeremiah of the same, had William, b. prob. 1651; Jeremiah, 1664;
and two other ch. but their names are not seen, nor their dates. Yet
the name of William is perpet. in the eighth generat. unbrok.

WETHERIDGE, EDWARD, prob. of Boston, freem. 1644, obtain.
abatemt. of excise on his wines, as in Col. Rec. II. 152. But he
was, perhaps, not many yrs. here.

WETMORE. See Whitmore.

WEYBORNE. See Wyborne.

WEYMOUTH, EDWARD, Dover 1662, perhaps s. of Robert, was b.

1639, and aft. at Kittery, m. 25 Dec. 1663, Esther Hodsden, perhaps d. of Jeremiah. His ho. was burnt by the Ind. 1677. JAMES, perhaps of Dover, d. 1678, leav. says Farmer MS. w. Mary, and ch. William, George, James, and Eliz. NICHOLAS, Dorchester, a soldier in Johnson's comp. in Philip's war, Dec. 1675. ROBERT, Kittery, came from Dartmouth, Co. Devon, as early, says Farmer, as 1652. One Titus W. from Virg. was found d. at Plymouth 1656. WILLIAM, N. H. br. of Robert, says Farmer, MS. d. 1654. WILLIAM, Dover, perhaps s. of James, had Reuben, b. 14 June 1686; William, 10 Sept. 1689; Robert, 15 Feb. 1692; Joshua, 11 June 1695; Tabitha, 14 Oct. 1698; and Samuel, 13 Oct. 1701.

WHALE, PHILEMON, Sudbury 1646, freem. 10 May 1648, m. 7 Nov. 1649, Sarah Cakebread, d. of Thomas, wh. d. 28 Dec. 1656; and he m. 9 Nov. foll. Eliz. Griffin, perhaps d. of Hugh; but whether he had issue by either w. is unkn. and he d. 21 Feb. 1676. SAMUEL, Kingston, R. I. only s. of Theophilus of the same, had two ws. first a Hopkins, next, a Harrington, as Potter reports; and that his ch. were seven, Thomas, Samuel, Theophilus, James, or Jeremy, John, and two ds. and that he d. a. 1782. THEOPHILUS, Kingstown, R. I. came from Virg. with w. Eliz. a. 1676, had Joan, Ann, Theodosia, Eliz. Martha, Lydia, and Samuel; but it is thot. that if not more, the eldest two were b. in Virg. Great uncertainty attaches to almost every thing he said or did, as is found oft. in regard to those wh. emig. from a dist. country, and liv. to gr. age. Potter says he knew Hebrew, Greek, &c. and d. a. 1719 or 20, aged a. 104. It would have been strange, if more than one myth had not sprung out of his grave. My first exercise of caution would be to examine the means of reducing his yrs. by 20 or near, for his only s. it is said, d. a. 1782, and it is quite improb. that when he was b. the f. was much beyond 70. Beside that his w. d. 8 or 10 yrs. bef. her h. Dr. Stiles in the exuberance of conject. that was requisite to sustain his credulity, supposes he may have been one of the regicides. But we kn. the names of all wh. acted in that tragedy, as well as of those wh. were nominat. and declin. to act, or withdrew, as did sev. aft. participat. some hours in the mockery of trial, bef. its end, among all of wh. is not that of Theophilus Whale. One of those misguid. men would have resort. to any other part of the world, sooner than to Virg.

WHALEY, GEORGE, Cambridge, by w. Catharine, had George, b. 19 Apr. 1653.

WHALLEY, EDWARD, Hadley, one of the gr. officers wh. had fought in the civil war, and serv. Cromwell more aft. it, first in the pretended

Court for trial of Charles I. and next as one of the major-gen. to
wh. the country in milit. districts, twelve in numb. like the tribes of
Israel, was made subject, as if martial law could forever be contin. Of
that power, aft. short trial, tho. he was a relative of the great Protector,
Cromwell's iron will was compel. to strip him, so odious had the tyranny
grown. He fled from Eng. on the restorat. and with his s.-in-law, William Goffe, reach. Boston July 1660. In the foll. spring they resort. to
New Haven, and thro. various suffer. found hiding at last in the shelter
of Rev. John Russell's ho. at H. where he d. in few yrs. and there was
bur. The stone wh. was fondly suppos. from the initial letters E. W. to
have been erected over his remains at New Haven, belong. no doubt, to
the resting-place of Edward Wigglesworth, and bore date 1653, wh.
was clumsi. attempt. to be alter. to 1673, or 8, as this might have been
the yr. of Whalley's death. See Goffe.

WHARFF, NATHANIEL, Casco, 1658, m. Rebecca, d. of Arthur Mac-
worth, and d. 1673, says Willis, in Maine Hist. Coll. I. 65, 135. Inv.
of £193. 18s. 6d. was render. 23 June. NATHANIEL, Gloucester 1683,
perhaps s. of the preced. d. 1701.

WHARTON, EDWARD, Salem 1655, call. a glazier, began to suffer
1658 as a Quaker, and in 1661 assist. in bur. the corpse of William
Leddra, one of their martyrs, execut. at Boston, 14 Mar. as he had
been whip. a year and a half bef. for his expression a. the hanging of
the youths, Robinson and Stephenson, and in an intermed. time, a. 1660
whip. for pilot. some from Lynn to Salem. Similar treatm. for some
yrs. later fail. to enlighten him, yet he did not rem. from S. there d. 3
Mar. 1678. PHILIP, Boston 1656, by w. Mary had Rebecca, b. 5 May
1660, was displeas. with his w. for wh. he found no redress, and went
away eight yrs. later, yet by order of Ct. his w. should have food and
clothing. See Rec. IV. pt. II. 382 ; and in our Reg. of deeds it will be
seen, Vol. VI. 134, that his lds. were charg. for the supply. ‡RICHARD,
Boston 1661, a very active gent. largely concern. in purch. of lds. as
in 1683, the Pegypscot, of 500,000 acres, at the E. and engag. in public
good, m. a. 1659, Bethia, d. of William Tyng, and next, 1672, Sarah, d.
of Rev. John Higginson of Salem, and had two ds. Sarah and Bethia.
Felt, in Geneal. Reg. IX. 339, calls him a lawyer, but perhaps he was
only atty. for partic. individ. not a mem. of the profess. Under appointm.
as one of the Counc. of Sir Edmund Andros, he thwart. some of his
oppress. designs, and went home with others in July 1687 to complain
against his measures, and d. in London a. 1690. He left much embarrass. est. and his ds. kept a small shop in Boston. Sarah m. John
Cotta, in B. See Higginson Letters in 3 Mass. Hist. Coll. VII. 198–
205. RICHARD, Boston, m. Martha, d. of the sec. Gov. John Winth. had

Richard, bapt. 28 Nov. 1675; Ann, 29 June 1679; Winthrop, 17 Apr. 1681; Martha, 29 Oct. 1682; John, 5 Oct. 1684; and Dorothy, 31 Oct. 1686.

WHATELY. See Wakely.

WHEATE, JOHN, Boston, a trader, wh. obtain. relief in 1686 for one half of the impost on wine, may have rem. in few yrs. JOSHUA, Concord, emb. in Apr. 1635, aged 17, in the Elizabeth, at London, but Shattuck says he went home in 1640, giv. his br. Moses his lds. here, for the share of f's. est. in Eng. JOSHUA, Groton, prob. s. of Moses of Concord, by w. Eliz. had Moses, b. Sept. 1686, and Butler tells no more. MOSES, Concord, br. of the first Joshua, came with him, says Shattuck, 1636, but prob. not in the same sh. as none such is found in the custom-ho. docket, where Joshua has place, and eno. may be thot. to justify a suppos. that they were found together at C. in its sec. yr. He was made freem. 18 May 1642, had Moses, wh. d. June 1641; Samuel, b. 25 Oct. 1641; Hannah, 12 or 19 (town rec. says both, but prob. the latter refers to bapt.) Feb. 1643; Joshua; Remembrance; John; Sarah; and Aaron, of wh. the rec. gives the name of mo. Thomasine, when it tells his d. 13 June 1658, prob. quite young. He was tythingman 1679, then call. sen. wh. renders it prob. that he had also s. Moses again. His w. Tamsen d. 9 July 1689, and he d. 6 May 1700. SAMUEL, Concord, s. of the preced. freem. 1690, well perpet. the name; but s. Benjamin, wh. d. 1758, aged 49, at Norwich, a physician, is the only one heard of. It is said, he was of Cambridge, a physician, 1717.

WHEATELY, or WHEATLEY, GABRIEL, Watertown, d. July 1637, by nuncup. will provides for a d. but names not w. or other ch. JOHN, Braintree, of wh. we kn. only that he was made freem. 1643, and his name then writ. Whetley, and unit. with many others of the same town for gr. of Showamet, that Gorton and others had bought. His d. Rachel m. 22 Sept. 1679, John Loring of Hingham, being then wid. of Benjamin Buckland of B. to wh. she had b. two ch. at least. LIONEL, Boston, by w. Elinor had Samuel, b. 29 Apr. 1654, d. next mo.; and Jane, 28 May 1655; was freem. 1673.

WHEATON, CHRISTOPHER, Hull 1675, fisherman, serv. in Johnson's comp. Dec. 1675. JEREMIAH, Rehoboth 1676, had Sarah, b. 29 Sept. 1673; Ebenezer, 7 Mar. 1677; Nathaniel, 6 Mar. 1679; and Mehitable, 2 Apr. 1681. OBADIAH, Milton, a soldier in Philip's war 1675, of Johnson's comp. ROBERT, Rehoboth 1643–6. Baylies II. 217. SAMUEL, Swanzey 1669, by w. Eliz. had Samuel, b. 21 July 1683; and the f. d. 2 Feb. foll. A tradit. that the first of this name in our country was of Rehoboth, and came from Swansea in Wales, Geneal. Reg. V. 476, may

have nearer resemblance to truth than is always found in such elements
of history. Farmer notes, that fourteen of this name had, in 1829, been
gr. at N. E. coll. of wh. five are at Harv. two at Yale, and more at
Brown.

WHEDON, THOMAS, New Haven, had been bound appr. in Eng. to
John Meigs, just bef. com. to learn his art of tanner, took o. of fidel.
1657, m. 24 May 1661, Ann Harvey, had Thomas, b. 31 May 1663;
Sarah, 23 Apr. 1666; Esther, 26 Jan. 1668; rem. to Branford where
he had been propr. bef. 1667, there had John, a. 1671; and Hannah, a.
1675; join. the new compact of settlem. in lieu of that wh. by those wh.
went to N. J. had govern. until then; and d. 1691, leav. wid. and five
ch. Sarah m. Samuel Elwell; and Esther m. Edward Johnson.
THOMAS, Branford, s. of the preced. by w. Hannah, as we learn at the
return of the inv. had Hannah and Abigail, of full age, in 1707;
Thomas, aged 16; John, 13; Nathaniel, 10; Rebecca, 6; Jonathan, 3;
and Martha, posthum. He left good est. See Weaden and Weeden.

WHEELER, DAVID, Newbury, s. of John, b. 1625, at Salisbury, Co.
Wilts, came in the Confidence of London, Apr. 1638, from Southampton, prob. betrust. to some friend wh. should pass him as a serv. of 11
yrs. old, m. 11 May 1650, Sarah Wise, perhaps d. of Humphrey, had
first, I conject. Sarah, wh. m. 9 Mar. 1675, John Spofford; John, b.
5 Dec. 1653; Abigail, 2 Feb. 1656; Jonathan, 6 Jan. 1658; Nathan,
27 Dec. 1659; Lydia, 7 May 1662; and Jethro, 26 Mar. 1664; rem.
to Rowley, there had Joseph, 1669. He had liv. at Hampton bef. m.
EPHRAIM, Concord, freem. 13 Mar. 1639, had, says Farmer, Isaac, b.
1638, but prob. d. soon; Isaac, 13 Dec. 1642; rem. to Fairfield with
Jones, one of the Concord min. in 1644, among the first sett. there was
bless. with plenty of est. and ch. and d. 1670. The inv. 28 Oct. was
£1,026. and his will of 22 Sept. 1669, names w. Ann, wh. may not have
been mo. of all the four s. Isaac, Samuel, Timothy, Ephraim, and six
ds. Mary, Ruth, Hannah, Rebecca, Judith, and Abigail. EPHRAIM,
Milford, s. of Thomas of the same, was propound. for freem. Oct. 1669;
m. 8 Sept. 1675, Mary, d. of Richard Holbrook, had two s. and two ds.
and d. early in 1685. The inv. in Feb. was £534. Both the s. were
d. in 1696, but ds. Mary and Abigail alive. He left wid. Mary.
EPHRAIM, Newton, had first w. Abigail, wh. d. 1687; and by sec. w.
Sarah, had Sarah, b. 28 Oct. 1689; Mary, 6 Jan. 1692; Josiah, 13
Dec. 1693; Eliz. 6 Jan. 1695; and Samuel, 11 May 1699; was select-
man 1706. FRANCIS, Charlestown, join. the ch. 1 July 1645. FRANCIS,
Salem 1646. GEORGE, Concord, freem. 2 June 1641, had Sarah, b. 30
Mar. 1640; John, 19 Mar. 1643; and by w. Catharine, wh. perhaps
was mo. of the two former, Mary, 6 Sept. 1645; and possib. more.

Mary m. 26 Oct. 1665, Ebenezer Fox. GEORGE, Newbury, s. of John
of the same, m. 30 Apr. 1660, Susanna Stowers, had Samuel, b. 15
June 1661, d. at 2 yrs.; Ephraim, 21 Oct. 1662; and Samuel, again, 15
Sept. 1664; d. bef. 28 May 1668, when his inv. was tak. The will of
his f. in that yr. names his d.-in-law Susanna, and her two s. HENRY,
Salisbury, by w. Abigail had Henry, b. 13 Apr. 1659; Abigail, 9 Mar.
1661; William, 6 Sept. 1663; Moses, 24 June 1665; Ann, and James,
tw. 27 May 1667; Josiah, 23 Apr. 1669; Ruth, 15 July 1671; Nathaniel, 28 Mar. 1675; Jeremiah, 17 July 1677; Benjamin, 15 Jan.
1682; and Mary, 5 June 1685. HENRY, Salisbury, eldest s. of the
preced. by w. Rachel, had Rachel, b. 19 May 1684; and he d. I presume, soon aft. At least his wid. m. 3 Apr. 1686, Benjamin Allen.
ISAAC, Charlestown 1639, by w. Frances had Eliz. b. 8 July 1641; and
Sarah, 13 Mar. 1643; beside Isaac, wh. d. I think 1712, aged 66; and
Thomas. He join. the ch. 30 Nov. 1642, was freem. 10 May 1643;
and as Farmer thot. with wh. I do not concur, rem. 1644 to Fairfield.
His wid. Frances m. Richard Cook by wh. they are nam. in his will.
His d. Eliz. m. at Malden, 13 Sept. 1659, William Greene; and Sarah
m. 18 Dec. 1660, John Green of Malden. ISAAC, Stonington 1649,
perhaps, but not prob. b. in Eng. propound. for freem. 1669; was s. of
Thomas of the same, m. 10 Jan. 1668, Martha, d. of Thomas Park of
the same, had Mary, b. 22 Nov. foll.; Martha, 6 Feb. 1670; Thomas,
1 Dec. 1671, wh. was k. at 20 yrs. by an Indian at Quinebaug; Isaac, 6
Aug. 1673; Ann, 20 Aug. 1675; Richard, 19 Mar. 1677; Dorothy, 6
Dec. 1679; William, 9 Sept. 1681; Eliz. 22 May 1683; and Experience, 21 May 1685. ISAAC, Fairfield, perhaps s. of the first Isaac, or
of John of the same, propound. for freem. 1670. JETHRO, Rowley, s.
of David of the same, m. Hannah French, d. of Edward of Salisbury,
had Jethro, b. 1692; Benjamin, 1695; Moses, 1700; Abijah, 1702;
John, 1710; beside two ds. JOHN, Newbury, came, I think, in the
Mary and John, 1634, tho. the name, print. *in the copy of the copy of
the copy*, Geneal. Reg. IX. 267, is Whelyer, from Southampton, the
nearest port of embarcat. from his native city, Salisbury, leav. four s. at
home, but perhaps brot. Roger, and George, with ds. Ann, wh. m.
Aquila Chase, and Eliz. perhaps w. of Matthias Button, besides Mercy,
wh. may have been b. on our side of the water, was one of the orig.
proprs. of Salisbury. His w. Ann, d. 15 Aug. 1662, and he d. 1670,
hav. made his will, 28 Mar. 1668, from wh. some of the detail is learn.
It names childr. and gr.childr. here, and s. Adam, Edward, and William, in Salisbury, Eng. *JOHN, Fairfield, s. of Thomas of the same,
brot. from Concord by his f. wh. rem. with Rev. Mr. Jones and others a.
1644 to Fairfield, there is on the freemen's list, 1669, was had in respect,

42*

rec. gr. of 100 acres from the Assemb. was rep. 1671, 2, 4, and 7, d. early in 1690, leav. large est. to wid. Eliz. and thirteen ch. whose names, with the inv. tak. 8 Mar. of £1,566. were, with their ages, Judah, or Judith, 29 ; John, 26 ; Eliz. 23 ; Thomas, 21 ; Mary, 19 ; Rebecca, 18 ; Joseph, 16 ; Hannah, 14 ; Abigail, 10 ; Obadiah, 8 ; Ann, 6 ; Jonathan, 3 ; and David or Daniel, 1. Perhaps the wid. was a sec. w. and liv. sev. yrs. aft. his d. for distrib. of the est. was made so late as 3 Apr. 1700 to ten ch. being all the bef. ment. exc. first, third, and tenth, wh. no doubt, had dec. It is observa. that no d. had then been m. JOHN, Stratford, freem. 1669, s. of Thomas the first of Milford, m. 5 Nov. 1662, Sarah, prob. d. of the first Thomas Sherwood, had Sarah, b. 24 Feb. 1664 ; Mary, 26 Aug. 1666 ; Eliz. Feb. 1669 ; Mary, bapt. 19 Jan. 1671 ; Thomas, 25 May 1673 ; Ruth, b. 30 June 1679 ; Dinah, bapt. 1681 ; and John, May 1684 ; and he d. at Woodbury, 12 May 1704 ; Cothren calls his w. Ruth, and that may have been a sec. at Woodbury, mo. of the last three ch. Four of the ch. are on rec. at S. JOHN, New London 1667, merch. was very enterpris. in foreign trade, by w. Eliz. had Zaccheus, b. a. 1675 ; Joshua, 1680 ; and William, 1683 ; besides prob. one or more ds. and d. 16 Dec. 1691. His wid. m. a. 1692, Richard Steere. JOHN, Concord, made freem. 21 Mar. 1690, and ano. JOHN, of Concord, made free the next day, may have been s. of George, or of Obadiah, or of either of the other fams. of this name in that town, where liv. betw. 1650 and 1680, thirty distinct ones, as Farmer quotes Shattuck to verify. JONATHAN, Newbury, s. of David of the same, took o. of alleg. 1678, rem. to Rowley, there own. good est. 1691. JOSEPH, Concord, freem. 13 May 1640, by w. Eliz. had Ephraim, b. 14 Apr. 1640, d. at 2 yrs. ; Joseph, 1 Dec. 1641, d. in few mos. ; and Mary, 20 Sept. 1643 ; yet the rec. says her mo. was bur. two mos. bef. and by w. Sarah he had Rebecca, 6 Sept. 1645. Farmer thinks he may be the man wh. d. at Newbury, 13 Oct. 1659, that seems less prob. to me than an alternat. propos. by him in MS. that he was k. by the Ind. 22 Aug. 1675 or 6, at Lancaster. JOSEPH, Boston, a tailor, freem. 1672, was prob. s. of Thomas of the same, and a householder 1695. JOSEPH, Newbury, s. of Roger of the same, m. 24 Sept. 1685, Sarah, d. of John Badger of the same, had Mary, b. 22 Sept. 1686 ; and perhaps more, may have rem. JOSEPH, Milford, s. of Thomas first of the same, was there liv. 1687–1700 ; but of his fam. no acco. is obtain. There was a Joseph, a physician at Salem 1704. JOSHUA, Concord 1636, says Farmer, but I fear the date demands 20 or 30 yrs. addit. for by w. Eliz. it is seen that he had Joshua, b. 1663, d. at 3 yrs. ; Eliz. and Timothy, tw. 28 Mar. 1665. JOSHUA, Concord, freem. 1690. JOSHUA, New London, s. of John of the same, liv. to old age, and left descend. says Miss Caulkins, but she has neither indic. them nor their mo. JOSIAH, Salisbury, s. of Henry the first, by w. Eliz. had Henry, b. 25 Feb. 1693; Eliz. 12 July 1695; Jeremiah, 9 Aug. 1697; Benjamin, 13 July 1699; and Moses, 16 Aug. 1702. MOSES, Stratford 1648, is found in the list of freem. 1669, was a shipwright and thriving man, had Eliz. b. 1 Aug. 1642; Miriam, 28 Mar. 1647; Samuel, 28 Apr. 1649; Moses, 5 July 1651; Mary, 13 Sept. 1655; and Joanna, 1659. His inv. bears date 1 Mar. 1698, but his will of 1690. Perhaps wrong date is giv. to Miriam, for she m. 1667, James Blackman. He may have liv. at New Haven 1643. MOSES, Stratford, s. of the preced. m. 28 Oct. 1674, Sarah, eldest d. of Caleb Nichols, but long it was thot. she was w. of Daniel Brimsmead; had Moses, b. 8 July 1675; Caleb, 29 Jan. 1677; Sarah, 21 June 1678; and other ch. whose names I have not seen. NATHAN, Newbury, s. of David of the same, took o. of alleg. 1678, by w. Rebecca, had Sarah, b. 4 July 1692; Rebecca, 11 Sept. 1694; Mercy, 30 Aug. 1696; and Abigail, 16 Dec. 1698. NATHANIEL, Milford, s. of the first Thomas of the same, m. 27 June 1665, Esther, d. I presume, of Henry Botsford, and he rem. to Newark, N. J. as did her younger sis. Ruth, wh. m. John Baldwin. OBADIAH, Concord 1638, freem. 2 June 1641, had John, b. 27 Jan. 1641; Ruth, 1642, prob. d. young; a s. as the rec. blindly states, b. 25 Dec. 1643, d. 29 Nov. preced.; Samuel, 22 Feb. 1645; beside Obadiah, Josiah, and Susanna, nam. in his will made three wks. bef. he d. 27 Oct. 1671, in his 63d yr. OBADIAH, Stratford, s. of Thomas of Milford, d. 1668 (his will was made in May), without ch. leav. wid. Ruth, wh. m. 8 July 1669, Ephraim Stiles. OBADIAH, Concord, perhaps s. of the first Obadiah, freem. 1690. RICHARD, Medfield 1649, the freem. of Mass. 1669, prob. was of Lancaster, m. 2 Aug. 1658, Sarah, d. of John Prescott of the same, had Jacob, b. 25 Nov. 1662, d. next yr.; Deborah, 2 Jan. 1664; and Sarah, 1 Feb. 1667. He at his garrison ho. was k. by the Ind. 10 Feb. 1676. Willard, 38. His wid. m. —— Rice. ROGER, Newbury, s. of John, m. 7 Dec. 1653, Mary Wilson, had Mary, b. 12 Feb. 1655; and Joseph, 29 Aug. 1656. His w. d. 27 Dec. 1658, and he d. 13 Oct. foll. ROGER, Boston, m. 23 Nov. 1659, Mary, wid. of John Stone, and d. 7 Dec. 1661. SAMUEL, sw. freem. of Conn. 1667, s. of Moses of Stratford, m. 29 May 1678, Eliz. Harris, but I kn. not of any ch. He made his will Nov. 1698, and inv. was ret. 29 Mar. foll. was of Newtown, L. I. 1686. THOMAS, Boston, a tailor, join. the ch. 11 Sept. 1636, by w. Rebecca, had Jonathan, b. 20 Oct. bapt. 12 Nov. 1637; Joseph, 15 May, but rec. of bapt. is 10 May 1640; Rebecca, 17, bapt. 25 June 1643; was freem. 17 Apr. 1637, but involv. with the gr. majority of the town, as friends of Mrs. Hutchinson and favorers of

Wheelwright, for wh. he was disarm. 20 Nov. 1637; yet he did not
rem. d. 16 May 1654, in his will a few days bef. naming ch. only Joseph
and Rebecca. His wid. m. 10 Aug. 1654, John Pierce; and d. Rebecca
m. 26 Dec. 1661, John Curtis of Roxbury. THOMAS, Concord, s. I
judge, of Thomas of Fairfield, b. in Eng. freem. 18 May 1642, m. Ruth,
d. of William Wood, had Alice, wh. d. 17 Mar. 1641; and by w. Sarah
had Sarah, b. 10 July 1649; Joseph, 18 Aug. 1651; Ann, 20 Dec.
1653; John, 18 Feb. 1656; Mary, 20 Dec. 1658; and Thomas, 29
Mar. 1662; in Philip's war was a capt. wh. saw hard serv. espec. on
the Quaboag ambuscade, 1 Aug. 1675, when hims. was wound. with the
s. of little above 13 yrs. old; and his sup. officer, Edward Hutchinson,
was mortal. wound. Wheeler wrote a modest narrat. wh. is repub. by
the N. H. Hist. Soc. in Vol. II.; and he d. 16 Dec. 1686. Admin. was
giv. to his wid. Hannah and s. Thomas upon his small est. 21 Sept. foll.
by Gov. Andros. How old he was, or in what part of Eng. b. cannot
be ascertain. tho. tradit. with her customary tale, makes three brs. come
from Wales. His d. Ruth, m. 7 May 1673, Ephraim Jones of Concord.
* THOMAS, Milford 1639, by w. Joan, wh. join. the ch. 1640, had John;
Samuel, both bapt. 16 Aug. of that yr.; Nathaniel; Obadiah, bapt. 10
Mar. 1644; Ephraim, 1646; Eliezer, 1648, d. next yr.; Thomas, 1650;
Josiah, 5 June 1653, d. young; Joseph, b. 23 Nov. 1655, d. soon; and
Joseph, again, bapt. 1660; own. much est. in Derby then call. Paugus-
set or Pawgasuck, and liv. there short time in 1664, but usually resid.
at M. was lieut. rep. 1670 and 1, had large est. and d. 26 Nov. 1672;
and his wid. d. Jan. 1673. His will made eight days bef. his d. provides
for w. Joan, s. John, and his ds. Nathaniel and his d. Esther, wh. phrase
may mean no more than w. of N. and s. Ephraim, Thomas, and Joseph.
No d. could be nam. and the s. Samuel and Obadiah d. in early manhood. He ment. also, William, Thomas, and Sarah, childr. of his br.
William of Stratford. THOMAS, Lynn or Salem, may have been the
passeng. in the James, embark. Apr. 1635, call. serv. of Austin Clement;
or any other of the well-diffus. name. Perhaps he had s. Isaac.
THOMAS, New Haven 1644, took o. of fidel. 1 July, was accomp. by s. of
the same name, but one or both were not so well educat. as most of the
sett. for the signature is found with a mark only; yet no ment. of w. or
ch. appears on rec. wherein we read that "old Thomas Wheeler" d. 22
Jan. 1673. THOMAS, Stonington, perhaps br. of John of New London,
may have gone with s. Isaac, wh. was b. 1646, from Lynn or other town
of Mass. not a few yrs. bef. 1669, when he was propound. for freem. was
rep. 1673, and next yr. with his w. Mary, unit. in gather. a ch. for Rev.
Mr. Noyes, of wh. he was one of the seven pillars; had also Sarah and
Eliz. both m. the latter to sec. John Gallop of Stonington; and d. 1685,

says his gr.-st. in his 85th yr. THOMAS, Fairfield 1645, was a lieut. in 1653, came from Concord with first sett. bring. w. Ann, and ch. prob. all adult, or marriageable, exc. one or two, and perhaps his eldest s. Thomas may not have accomp. the f. At least from his will, pro. 23 Aug. 1654, wh. we read imperfect. as part of the rec. in this place is burn. it is clear that the est. in Concord, old homestead, was giv. to Thomas; Fairfield est. to John; with notice of wid. and three ds. of wh. Hannah, the eldest, m. a. 1639, James Bennett, had two ch. at Concord, and was now d. leav. four; ano. was Sarah Sherwood; and a third not m. without name. His wid. in her will of 21 Aug. 1659, pro. Oct. foll. names eldest s. Thomas, and ch. THOMAS, New Haven, s. it is presum. of the first Thomas of the same, since they are ment. as tak. o. of fidel. on the same day, had Thomas, b. 21 Apr. 1652; and certain. one other ch. if not more, bef. or aft. and d. Dec. 1656, as seems prob. bec. the inv. of £200. was dat. 2 Jan. foll. His wid. Alce or Alice m. 1657, Josiah Stanborough, or Stanbury of Southampton, L. I. THOMAS, Boston 1674, may be the same man as THOMAS, Charlestown, a householder 1677, prob. s. of the first Isaac. THOMAS, Concord, m. 10 Oct. 1657, Hannah Harrod, had Hannah, b. 25 Oct. 1658, d. within 10 mos.; Thomas, 1 Jan. 1660; and John, 2 Sept. 1661; perhaps others; was tythingman 1680, and freem. 1690. THOMAS, Milford, s. of Thomas of the same, was propound. for freem. 1671, and liv. there aft. 1687; but no details of his fam. are acquir. Of his cousin, THOMAS, Milford, s. of William of Stratford, the same deficience is felt. *TIMOTHY, Concord, freem. 13 May 1640, ens. in 1646, was a capt. late in his days, but more oft. call. lieut. on rec. rep. 1663, and very oft. aft. d. 10 July 1687, aged a. 86, as the gr.-st. tells; had Sarah, b. 22 June 1640; and his w. Jane d. 12 Feb. 1643; and by w. Mary, d. of capt. Thomas Brooks, had Mary, 3 Oct. 1657, d. at 3 yrs.; Eliz. 6 Oct. 1661, wh. m. 1678, Eleazer Prout; Rebecca, 1666, wh. m. 1684, James Minot; and prob. others, perhaps TIMOTHY of Concord, freem. 1677, for one, wh. m. 29 June 1670, Ruth Fuller, and d. 7 June 1678. TIMOTHY, Concord, the freem. of 1690, had, I suppose, f. of the same town, but my inabil. to point him out among the scores of Concord Wheelers may be excus. WILLIAM, Stratford, br. and I think, younger, of Thomas sen. of Milford, prob. rem. from Concord with him, had w. Sarah, ch. William, Thomas, and Sarah; rem. to New Jersey, soon fell ill, and the w. and ch. came back aft. his d. in 1666. His inv. was tak. in Nov. He had made his nuncup. will, pro. 9 Aug. 1667, in wh. he gave his prop. to the w. charg. to bring up the ch. and desir. his br. Thomas to adv. her. The wid. m. William Brooks; and Sarah m. 6 Nov. 1676, James Briscoe. WILLIAM, Concord, freem. 1660, m. 30 Oct. 1659, Hannah, d. of

William Buss or Bussey, had Hannah, b. 23 Oct. 1660; Rebecca, 25 Oct. 1661; and perhaps more. WILLIAM, Boston, m. 16 May 1686, Ann, d. of Gamaliel Phippen, had Ann, Hannah, William, and Jeremiah, bapt. at Mather's ch. betw. 1692 and 7. WILLIAM, New London 1700, s. of John of the same, liv. to old age, and left descend. but Miss Caulkins has not nam. either the w. or ch. Farmer notes, that of this name, eight had, in 1834, been gr. at Yale, six at Harv. and twelve at the other N. E. coll.

WHEELOCK, BENJAMIN, Medfield 1678, s. perhaps eldest, of first Ralph, sett. at Mendon, and m. (as I judge from note in Geneal. Reg. XII. 353, relat. to distribut. of est. of her f.) Eliz. d. of John French of Braintree; but no further acco. is obtain. ELEAZER, Medfield, s. of Ralph of the same, m. 1678, Eliz. Fuller, and d. 24 Mar. 1731, had Ralph, b. 1683, wh. d. at Windham, 15 Oct. 1748, was f. of Rev. Eleazer, b. 1711, first Presid. of Dartmouth Coll. and Ephraim, 1697, wh. resid. at M. GERSHOM, Medfield, s. of Ralph, by w. Hannah had Hannah, b. 25 June 1659, d. in few days; Samuel, 14 Jan. 1661, d. very soon; Hannah, again, 26 Jan. 1662; Samuel, again, 21 Jan. 1664, d. at 16 yrs.; and John, 8 Dec. 1670. His w. was d. of John Stodder of Hingham. RALPH, Dedham, b. it is said in Co. Salop, bred at Clare Hall, Cambridge Univ. where he took his degr. 1626 and 31, came in 1637, prob. with w. Rebecca and d. Rebecca, first sat down at Watertown, rem. 1638 to D. there was made freem. 13 Mar. 1639; had Benjamin, b. 8 bapt. 12 Jan. 1640; Samuel, b. 22 Sept. 1642; Record, 15, bapt. 22 Dec. 1644; Experience, bapt. 3 Sept. 1648; Gershom; and Eleazer, 3 May 1654; perhaps others; was rep. 1639 and 40, made 1642, clk. of the writs in place of Edward Alleyne, dec. was inhab. of that pt. wh. bec. Medfield, and its first rep. 1653, 63, 4, and 6. His w. d. 1 Jan. 1682; and he d. 11 Jan. 1684, in his 84th yr. SAMUEL, s. of the first Ralph, I have power to tell nothing of, exc. that he liv. at Shrewsbury; but his sis. Rebecca m. at Roxbury, 7 June 1654, John Crafts, the first b. of R. Of gr. of this name in 1834, Farmer notes none at Harv. two at Yale, and eight at other N. E. coll.

WHEELWRIGHT, JOHN, Braintree, bred at Sydney Coll. Cambr. where he had his degr. 1614 and 18, was min. at Belleau, near Alford in Co. Lincoln, whence with his w. Mary, sis. prob. of William Hutchinson, and of his ch. certain. Thomas, Catharine, and prob. Samuel, perhaps all exc. John, he came to Boston in the same ship with Rev. Samuel Whiting, arr. at Boston, 26 May 1636, and on 12 June foll. he, his w. and the wid. Susanna Hutchinson, her mo. as I judge, unit. with Boston ch. and on 25 June 1637, his d. Mary was bapt. But the long troubles of the antinom. controv. had begun, and being banish. with his princip. friends and adherents in 1638, he rem. to Exeter, of wh. he is justly call. the founder, being the first signer of the civil combinat. on Friday, 4 Oct. 1639; there prob. had Rebecca and Hannah, and at his next home, prob. Eliz. and Sarah. When the N. H. planta. came under rule of Mass. in 1642, he rem. to Wells, but aft. reconcil. with Winth. and the rest of the governm. went 1647 to be collea. in the serv. of the ch. with Dalton at Hampton, in 1657 was in Eng. and had favor with Oliver Cromwell, wh. had been intimate with him at the Univ. but he came back soon aft. the restorat. and was sett. min. 9 Dec. 1662 at Salisbury, there d. 15 Nov. 1679, aged above 80 yrs. Of his s. John it may be presum. that he was oldest ch. and never came to our side of the Atlantic, but was a scholar, perhaps a preach. in Eng. wh. publish. at London, a vindicat. of his f. in Nov. 1645, against the bitter aspersions of Thomas Welde, and very likely may have thot. it useful to display equal spirit. I can have no doubt that he was d. bef. the will of his f. His will of 25 May preced. pro. 26 Nov. foll. names s. Samuel, but not Thomas, wh. prob. was d. s.-in-law, Edward Rishworth, and gr. ch. Edward Lyde, wh. was to pay something to his mo. Mary, then w. of the first Theodore Atkinson, Mary White, d. of Edward Rishworth, Mary Maverick, and William, Thomas, and Jacob Bradbury. In Lincolnsh. and in Maine he had est. to bestow in beq. to heirs, but he thot. very little of any in N. H. Several of these seem here not to be represent. but prob. they had been provid. for at earlier days, or were d. without heirs. We must look for fuller acco. to the will (made twelve yrs. bef.) of his bach. br. Samuel Hutchinson. Of the six ds. with considerable confidence, I assign hs. to all: Sarah, the youngest, m. 1671, as his sec. w. Richard Crispe (to her, for her portion, the f. call. hims. late of Belleau, Co. Linc. gave, 22 Oct. 1677, his messuage, with appurtenanc. at Mawthorpe in the parish of Willoughby, Co. Linc. to be enj. aft. d. of donor); Eliz. m. George Parsons, Person, or Pearson; Rebecca m. 4 Dec. 1660, Samuel Maverick, and next, 12 Jan. or more prob. Mar. 1672, William Bradbury; Mary m. 4 Dec. 1660, Edward Lyde, and next, Oct. 1667, Theodore Atkinson; Hannah m. Anthony Checkley; and Catharine m. Robert Nanny, and next, Edward Naylor. *JOHN, Wells, s. of Samuel, prob. or of Thomas, perhaps; was a col. and one of the reps. 1692, bef. and aft. the new chart. a gent. of character above suspicion, wh. to McGregor and his noble assoc. the pure blood of Londonderry or Scotch Irish presbyterians, gave *quitclaim* deed, 20 Oct. 1719, at Boston, of the ld. "NOT TO EXCEED TEN MILES SQUARE," call. Nutfield. That sale he deriv. authty. for, as he said, in the deed of Ind. sachems to his gr.f. 17 May 1629, wh. most elaborately spurious, purported to convey many thousand sq. miles, and has been satisfactor. shown to be a forgery, used, to be sure, above a dozen yrs. bef. the Nutfield deed, and prob. unsuspect. by him, and never seen by his f. as we may confident. believe it never was by the gr.f. wh. had honest title only to *five* or *six hundred thousand* acres under Ind. deed of a portion of the same region, made near nine yrs. later. He d. 1745. *SAMUEL, Wells, s. of the first John, m. Esther, d. of Jeremy Houchin of Boston, was town clk. 30 yrs. in 1665 appoint. by the governm. of Mass. a commissnr. for the town, or justice of the peace, rep. for York and Wells 1671, for Wells in 1677, in 1681, nam. of the Council for the Province under Presid. Danforth, and d. 1700. THOMAS, York, s. perhaps eldest, of the first John, made freem. of Mass. with prefix of respect, Nov. 1652, and Col. Rec. III. 333, shows he then dwelt at Wells, a selectman 1653, and commissnr. the same or the next yr. prob. d. bef. his f. Among gr. at Harv. Coll. are nine of this name.

WHELDEN, WHELDING, or WHELDON, GABRIEL, Malden, had w. Margaret, nam. in his will 11 Feb. 1654, pro. 4 Apr. foll. HENRY, Yarmouth 1643, of wh. no other ment. is ever found, but that he m. 25 Jan. 1648, tho. the rec. is too much worn to be sure of his w. yet if he were f. or even br. of Catharine, wh. m. Oct. 1639, Giles Hopkins, it would be observa. Sarah W. b. 21 June 1650, may have been his d.

WHELPLEY, HENRY, Stratford 1645, in 1653 sold ld. and ho. in Fairfield. His wid. prob. nam. Sarah, m. Ralph Keeler. Perhaps he had Joseph and Nathan, and even more. JOSEPH, Fairfield, propound. for freem. 1670, perhaps s. of the preced. was d. in May 1682, leav. wid. Deborah, wh. d. 1690; but he had former w. Rebecca, d. of Thomas Bulkley, wh. prob. was mo. of his three ch. Sarah, Rebecca, and Joseph. NATHAN, New Haven, from 1678 was master of a vessel, and in 1687, on voyage from Barbadoes d. and by nuncup. will gave ho. at New Haven to Samuel Knifton, or some such name, s. of his sis.

WHELYER, JOHN, a passeng. from Southampton 1634, in the Mary and John, if we follow the copy of the copy of custom-ho. paper, but in my opin. it meant John Whittier, or more prob. Wheeler.

WHETCOMBE, JAMES, Boston, merch. freem. 1669, one of the commissn. nam. by the k. to admin. the o. 1679, to new Gov. of Mass. hav. borne a part in the funer. ceremonies of Leverett in Mar. of that yr. d. 23 Nov. 1686, says Sewall's diary.

WHETNELL, JEREMY, New Haven 1639, never heard of since, I think, but see Whitnell.

WHETSTONE, INCREASE, k. by the Ind. 14 Mar. 1676, at Northampton, was a soldier, I suppose, but am unable to conject. from what town,

unless Barnstable where Mercy W. was m. 30 June 1698 to Joseph
Parker. JOHN, a passeng. emb. 7 Mar. 1632, at London, prob. in the
William and Francis with Edward Winslow, but perhaps the real name
was Whiston, wh. see, and compare 4 Mass. Hist. Coll. I. 92, also
Geneal. Reg. XIV. 300.

WHICHALLS, EMANUEL, is the strange name of one, wh. it is said,
took o. of fidel. at Pemaquid 1674.

WHIDDEN, RICHARD, Fairfield, had d. bef. 3 Nov. 1690, when his
inv. was brot. in by his w. Sarah, by wh. we find he own. part of a
sloop, was a mariner, had ds. Eliz. and Sarah. SAMUEL, N. H. 1680.
Perhaps the name may be the same as Whedon, and that he had w. or
d. Jane, wh. m. 3 Dec. 1691, Thomas Edgerly.

WHIPPLE, BENJAMIN, Providence, s. of John of the same, own.
alleg. to Charles II. 29 May 1671, when under 17 yrs. of age, m. 1
Apr. 1686, Ruth Matthewson, prob. d. of James, had Benjamin, b. 11
Nov. 1688; Ruth, 12 May 1691; Mary, 8 May 1694; Jonah, 29 July
1697; John, 26 Feb. 1700; and Abigail, 12 June 1703. DAVID,
Providence, br. of the preced. m. at Hingham, 11 Nov. 1676, Hannah
Tower of H. had Israel, b. 16 Aug. 1678; Deborah, 12 Sept. 1681;
Jeremiah, 26 June 1683; William, 27 May 1685; Sarah, 18 Nov.
1687; Hannah, 9 Jan. 1691; and Abigail, 20 Oct. 1692. ELEAZER,
Providence, br. of the preced. own. alleg. to the k. 1 June 1667, as did
his elder br. Samuel, m. 26 Jan. 1670, Alice, d. of Thomas Angell of
the same, had Alice, b. 3 June 1675; and Margaret, perhaps more.
JAMES, Barnstable, m. Experience, d. of Gov. Hinckley, but I kn. no
more, exc. that he may be found in Boston under the name of Whippo,
and no doubt his w. d. early. *JOHN, Ipswich, an early sett. freem. 13
May 1640, was rep. that yr. and 41, 2, 6, 50–3, clk. of the writs 1642,
in place of Giles Firmin, was deac. or rul. Elder, perhaps both, had
John, prob. b. in Eng. and Sarah, beside other elder ds. Susanna, Mary,
and Eliz. His first w. Sarah d. 14 June 1658; but he left wid. Jennet,
and d. 30 June 1669, says respectab. authty. in Geneal. Reg. VI. 66, tho.
two pages aft. he makes it 1670. His d. Susanna m. Lionel Worth;
Mary m. a Stone; Eliz. m. perhaps, Anthony Potter; and Sarah m.
Joseph Goodhue of I. and her pious adv. to her childr. has been preserv. in print. JOHN, Providence, was first at Dorchester, as early as
1632, in the serv. of Israel Stoughton, was a carpenter, join. with the
ch. in 1641, had John, bapt. 7 Mar. 1641; Sarah, 6 Feb. 1642;
Samuel, 17 Mar. 1644; Eleazer, 8 Mar. 1646; Mary, 9 Apr. 1648;
William, 16 May 1652; Benjamin, 4 June 1654; and David, 28 Sept.
1656; sold his ho. and 40 or 50 acres to George Minot, 1658, and rem.

soon aft. to P. and in the summer of 1659 was adm. there as inhab. own. alleg. to the k. 31 May 1666, with his eldest s. had Joseph ; Jonathan ; and Abigail there ; prob. d. soon aft. 16 May 1685, the date of his will. Sarah m. a Smith ; Mary m. 9 Mar. 1666, Epenetus Olney ; and Abigail m. William Hopkins. *JOHN, Ipswich, s. of John of the same, b. in Eng. freem. 1668, was capt. rep. 1674, 9–83 on 10 Aug. in wh. yr. he d. His est. was ample, will of 2 Aug. pro. 25 Sept. next ; had for first w. Martha, d. of Humphrey Reyner ; and for sec. Eliz. Paine ; and ch. John, and Susanna, wh. m. 20 Mar. 1680, John Lane ; Joseph, b. a. 1666 ; Sarah ; and Matthew ; all outliv. him. Yet the childr. of two Johns seem inextric. confus. A large est. was inherit. by them. JOHN, Providence, eldest s. of John of the same, m. 4 Dec. 1663, Mary, d. of the first Thomas Olney, had John, b. 2 Oct. 1664 ; beside Mary, absurd. mark. as b. the same yr. ; and a d. strangely call. Elnathan, 2 Jan. 1676 ; and by sec. w. Rebecca Scott, d. perhaps of John of the same, m. 15 Apr. 1678, had Deliverance, 11 Feb. 1679, and Dorothy, and he d. 10 Dec. 1700. JOHN, Ipswich, s. of Matthew, b. in Eng. perhaps, m. 5 May 1677, Eliz. Woodman. JOHN, Ipswich, s. perhaps of the sec. John of the same, is call. cornet Apr. 1695, when he succeed. his f. capt. W. as trustee of the gram. sch. as the capt. had succeed. his f. or uncle. JONATHAN, Providence, s. of the first John of the same, own. alleg. to Charles II. in May 1682, with his br. Joseph ; by w. Margery, had Jonathan, b. 22 Feb. 1692 ; and Thomas, 26 Feb. 1695. JOSEPH, Ipswich, s. of the first Matthew, freem. 1674, had by w. Sarah, wh. d. 16 July 1676, Joseph, b. 1 Nov. 1665, d. in few days ; Joseph, again, 31 Oct. 1666 ; Margery, 28 Aug. 1668 ; Sarah, 29 Mar. 1670 ; Matthew, 25 Nov. 1672 ; and Mary, 25 Dec. 1674 ; and d. 11 May 1699. JOSEPH, Salem vill. s. of the sec. John of Ipswich, was deac. and d. 19 Sept. 1740. JOSEPH, Providence, br. of Benjamin, m. 20 May 1684, Alice Smith, had John, b. 18 May 1685 ; Jeremiah, 3 Sept. 1686 , Joseph, 30 Dec. 1687 ; Amphillis, 8 Oct. 1689, but my informat. does not disting. the sex ; Sarah, 29 Mar. 1691 ; Susanna, 14 Apr. 1693 ; Freelove, 18 Mar. 1695 ; Alice, 6 Feb. 1697 ; Ann, 16 June 1699 ; Christopher, 14 Apr. 1701, d. soon ; Mary, 9 Apr. 1704 ; and Christopher, again, 6 Mar. 1706. MATTHEW, Ipswich, br. of the first John of the same, had gr. of ld. 1638, and d. 1647, leav. eldest s. John, b. no doubt in Eng. wid. Rose, wh. was his sec. w. and ch. Mary, Matthew, Ann, Eliz. and Joseph, b. a. 1646, whose order of success. is not kn. MATTHEW, Ipswich, s. of the preced. b. in Eng. m. 24 Dec. 1657, Mary, d. of William Bartholomew, at Gloucester, had Matthew, posthum. 20 Dec. foll. and d. 20 Oct. MATTHEW, Ipswich, s. perhaps of the preced. or of the sec. John of the same, by w. Jemima, d. of Job

Lane of Malden, had Matthew, b. 20 Oct. 1685. SAMUEL, Providence, s. of the first John of the same, m. 26 Feb. 1691, Eliz. Eddy, only d. of Zechariah of Swanzey, had Alice, and Samuel, tw. b. 10 Apr. 1693; Samuel, again, 8 Nov. 1695; Daniel, 27 Oct. 1698; Hope, 12 Aug. 1701; Nathan, 5 Apr. 1704; and Zechariah, 2 Feb. 1707. WILLIAM, Providence, s. of the first John of the same, own. alleg. to the k. May 1671. Farmer notes, MS. that in 1834, there had been of this name, six gr. at Harv. and seven at other N. E. coll.

WHIPPO, JAMES, Barnstable, m. 25 Feb. 1692, at Boston, as his sec. w. Abigail Greenough, wid. of Luke, d. of Lawrence Hammond, had James, b. 27 Nov. foll.; Laurence, 16, bapt. 17 June 1694; Jane, 12 May 1696; George, 12 Apr. 1698, d. in few mos.; Margaret, 12 Aug. 1699; Eliz. 6 Feb. 1701; George, again, 22 Feb. 1703; Benjamin, 22 July 1705, d. in few wks.; and Martha, 10 Sept. 1706. Under Whipple will appear the first m. of this same man.

WHISTON, HENRY, Huntington, L. I. 1664, accept. to be freem. of Conn. JOHN, Scituate, came with Hatherly, in the William and Francis, 1632, and was there sev. yrs. after.

WHITACRE, WHITTACRE, or WHITAKER, ABRAHAM, Haverhill, had prob. Abraham, b. a. 1657; and William, a. 1659; and with s. Abraham took o. of alleg. Nov. 1677. JOHN, Watertown, had promis. m. to Mary Linfield, but while still under age, took w. Eliz. had Eliz. and John; and rem. to Billerica, perhaps was of Chelmsford 1691. RICHARD, Rehoboth 1668, had Mehitable, b. 27 Dec. 1674; Ephraim, 27 Jan. 1679; Noah, 31 Jan. 1683.

WHITCHER, NATHANIEL, Salisbury, freem. 1690.

WHITCOMB, or WHETCUMBE, JAMES, Boston, merch. by w. Rebecca, had James, b. 30 Nov. 1662; and Peter, 1 Mar. 1665. JOB, Lancaster, s. of John the first of the same, had w. Mary. He prob. went with Rev. Joseph Rowlandson, whose altar at L. had been overthr. to Wethersfield, where he d. 1683, made his will 27 Oct. of that yr. in it names his w. and ch. Job, John, Mary, and Jemima, and br. Jonathan and Josiah to be overseers. JOHN, Dorchester 1635, had fam. bef. com. from Eng. rem. bef. 1644 to Scituate, where his d. Catharine m. Rhodolphus Ellms that yr. was freem. of the Plymouth col. 3 June 1652, soon after rem. to Lancaster, had five s. besides ds. Catharine, Abigail, and Mary, wid. Frances, s. John, Jonathan, Job, and Josiah, made the youngest d. Mary extrix. As one s. Robert and d. Catharine do not find place in that instrum. they were prob. provid. for at earlier day. He d. at L. 24 Sept. 1662, and his wid. made her will 12 May 1671, and d. five days after. It names the three ds. and remembers five s. JOHN, Lancaster, eldest s. of the preced. b. no doubt in Eng. by w. Mary who surv. him, had perhaps other ch. certain. John; beside Ruth, b. a. 1671; and Sarah, a. 1673; and he was d. 1683. JONATHAN, Scituate, perhaps br. of the preced. by w. Hannah, who surv. him, had Jonathan, Hannah, Abigail, Eliz. and John, and d. a. 1690. JOSIAH, ——, by w. Rebecca had three s. Josiah, wh. m. and had fam. but d. bef. his f. David, and Hezekiah, beside five ds. Rebecca, Joanna, Mary, Damaris, and Abigail, who were all m. but neither of s. nor ds. is the b. or order of success. kn. He made his will 20 Mar. 1718, wh. was pro. 22 Apr. foll. and his wid. made her will 1720, pro. 1726. ROBERT, Scituate, s. of John of the same, m. 1660, Mary, d. of James Cudworth, had eldest s. Israel, perhaps other ch. beside Robert, James, Mary, and Eliz. rem. to Cohasset.

WHITE, ANTHONY, Watertown, came 1634, aged 27, from Ipswich, Co. Suffk. emb. in Apr. on the Francis of I. and hav. good pass. was first a propr. at Sudbury, but m. 8 Sept. 1645, Grace Hall, and at W. had Abigail, b. 21 June 1646; John, 25 Feb. 1649; and Mary, 1 Mar. 1651; and d. 28 Mar. 1686. His will of 16 Nov. preced. names no w. but made Rebecca, wid. of his s. John, extrix. Abigail m. a Buttrick; and Mary m. 23 Oct. 1677, Jacob Willard. BENJAMIN, Roxbury, m. perhaps at Ipswich, Susanna Cogswell, d. of Martha, possib. w. of William, at R. had Susanna, b. 25 or 29 Mar. 1683, d. young; Ann, 4 July 1685; Mary, 27 Aug. 1688; Susanna, 12 Dec. 1690; Edward, 10 July 1693; Eliz. 8 Jan. 1696; and Joanna, 4 Nov. 1701; and he d. at Brookline, 9 Jan. 1723. DANIEL, Hadley 1662, s. of John of Hartford, took o. of alleg. 8 Feb. 1669, liv. on Hatfield side, freem. 1690, m. 1 Nov. 1661, Sarah, d. of John Crow, she then much less than 15 yrs. old, had Sarah, b. 14 Oct. 1662; Mary, 1664, d. soon; Mary, again, 5 or 25 Aug. 1665; Eliz. 13 Nov. 1668; Daniel, 4 July 1671; Hannah, 4 July 1674, d. young; Esther, d. 1675; John, 16 Nov. 1676, d. soon; Esther, again; Hannah, again, Sept. 1679; Esther; and Mehitable, 14 Mar. 1683; was a lieut. He d. 27 July 1713. The wid. d. 1719. His will of two wks. bef. his d. names one s. and six ds. of wh. Mary m. first a Wells, and after 1713, a Barnard. DANIEL, Marshfield, eldest s. of Peregrine, m. 19 Aug. 1674, Hannah Hunt, and d. 6 May 1724, in his 70th yr. leav. seven s. but the names or dates cannot be seen in Miss Thomas's Memor. of M. 33, to wh. we owe so much, that gladly would we have had more. But Dr. Thatcher's Hist. of Plymouth, gives the names, tho. as dates are defic. we may doubt the order, John, Joseph, Thomas, Cornelius, Benjamin, Eleazer, and Ebenezer; beside feeling a vague suspicion that some d. may have been forgot. DANIEL, Middletown, s. of Nathaniel of the same, m. Mar. 1683, Susanna, d. of Hugh Mould of New London, had Daniel, b. 8 Dec. foll.; Nathaniel, 3 Sept.

1685; Joseph, b. and d. 1687; Joseph, again, 8 Oct. 1688; Hugh, 15 Feb. 1691; John, 27 Nov. 1692; Susanna, 16 Oct. 1694; Isaac, 9 Nov. 1696; Jonathan, b. and d. 1702; Ruth, 28 Sept. 1703; and Rachel, 3 Feb. 1705; and he d. 18 Dec. 1739. DOMINGO, Lynn, had John, b. 25 Oct. 1668; Sarah, 19 Aug. 1672; Mary, 31 Aug. 1675; Joseph, 25 May 1678, d. in 3 days; and Hannah, 5 Dec. 1679. EBEN-EZER, Weymouth, s. of Thomas of the same, freem. 1674, by w. Han-nah, d. of Nicholas Phillips, had Ebenezer, b. 1672, H. C. 1692; Thomas, 19 Aug. 1673; Samuel; Joseph; Hannah, 12 May 1681; Abigail, 3 Mar. 1683; Benjamin, 21 Feb. 1685; Experience, 1 July 1686; and Eliz. 9 Nov. 1688. EDWARD, the freem. 7 Dec. 1636, was of Dorchester, came, I presume from Cranbrook, Co. Kent, in the Abi-gail from London, June 1635, then aged 42, with w. Martha, 39; and two ch. Martha, 10; and Mary, 8; had James, bapt. at D. 1638; and John, 15 Dec. 1639; but when he or she d. or whether he rem. or not, is all unkn. EDWARD, Roxbury, the freem. prob. of 1647, had Zecha-riah, b. 5, bapt. 7 Aug. 1642; Samuel, bapt. 26 Jan. 1645; and Elie-zur, 12 Dec. 1646; and perhaps Henry and Peter, but my acco. is very indistinct. Barry in Hist. of Framingham, 450, calls the name of f. of the first two ch. Edward Wright. ELIAS, Marblehead 1669–74. EMANUEL, Watertown 1636, had w. Catharine, rem. bef. 1642 to Yar-mouth. FRANCIS, from London to Boston, had pass. in the Elizabeth, Apr. 1635, aged 24, but what next befell him is not kn. GAWIN, Scituate, m. 15 Oct. 1638, Eliz. who is call. a serv. of Mr. Hatherly, perhaps was f. of Eliz. wh. m. 18 Sept. 1662, Thomas Pinson, as well as of Timothy and Joseph, who return. inv. of his humble est. 8 Dec. 1664. GEORGE, Rowley, m. 5 Apr. 1671, Lydia Sampson, had Lydia, b. 5 Jan. 1673; and Nathaniel, 3 Feb. 1675; was liv. there 1691. HENRY, Hadley, took o. of alleg. 8 Feb. 1679. HENRY, Dorchester, s. perhaps of Edward of the same, by w. Mary, d. of William Weeks of the same, had Return, who d. Dec. 1680; Josiah, b. 14 June 1680; William, 7 Feb. 1684, bapt. 5 July 1685; Eliz. bapt. 22 Aug. 1686; Submit, b. 9 Dec. 1688; Jerusha, 19 Feb. 1690; Josiah, again, 30 Dec. 1692; Sarah, 11 Oct. 1693; Ann, 6 June 1695; Rebecca, 10 Dec. 1696; and Abigail, 25 Mar. 1698. HUMPHREY, Ipswich 1640. IGNATIUS, m. 4 June 1683, Ruth, youngest d. of John Burrage of Charlestown, but I kn. no more of him, not even the place of his resid. JACOB, Hartford, youngest s. of John, freem. 1668, m. Eliz. d. of Thomas Bunce, d. 1701, leav. good est. no ch. JACOB, Middletown, s. of Nathaniel of the same, m. 4 Feb. 1692, Deborah Shepard, d. of the first John of Hartford, who d. 8 Feb. 1721, had Eliz. b. 22 Nov. 1692, wh. d. unm.; Deborah, 26 Feb. 1694; Rebecca, 12 Aug. 1695, d. young; Jacob, 29 Jan.

1697; Hannah, 28 Mar. 1699; Thomas, 14 Aug. 1701; Samuel, 24
May 1703, d. young; Rebecca, again, 14 Sept. 1707, d. young; Samuel,
again, d. at 14 yrs.; and John, 19 Oct. 1712. He had sec. w. Rebecca,
wid. of Thomas Ranney, m. 16 Dec. 1729; and d. 1738. JAMES,
Salem 1633, may be the same who was that yr. fin. 30s. for drunk. and
behav. so well aft. that in 1638 the sent. was remit. as in our first
Vol. of the Rec. of the Gen. Ct. is seen. JAMES, Dorchester, perhaps
eldest s. of Edward of the same, took o. of fidel. 1678, m. 22 Feb.
1665, Sarah, d. of Richard Baker, had Sarah, b. 8, bapt. 10 Dec. 1665,
d. in few wks.; Thankful, 18, bapt. 25 Aug. 1667; Ichabod, b. 26 Apr.
1669, d. soon; John, 7, bapt. 12 June 1670; Experience, bapt. 2 Mar.
1673; Martha, 28 Aug. bapt. 3 Oct. 1675; Mary, bapt. 11 Nov. 1677;
James, 29 May, bapt. 13 July 1679; Richard, 2 Mar. 1681; Edward, 4
Aug. 1683; and Ebenezer, 3 July 1685, H. C. 1704. His w. d. 13
Oct. 1688 or 9, but he took not sec. w. Eliz. Withington, wid. of capt.
John, until 13 Feb. 1696, and d. 11 Nov. 1713, aged 76. His wid. d.
19 Nov. 1722, in her 70th yr. JAMES, Haverhill, s. of William of the
same, m. 16 Apr. 1678, Eunice Kingsbury of Amesbury, who may
have been wid. of Ephraim, but we have less informat. for that stock of
K. than would satisfy so dilig. an inquir. as J. W. Dean. See Geneal.
Reg. XIII. 157. *JOHN, the freem. of 4 Mar. 1633, came in the Lion,
arr. at Boston from London, 16 Sept. 1632, with so many of the gent.
wh. first sat down at Cambridge, then call. Newtown; and in four yrs.
went to Hartford; there he is found early in good repute, had brot. d.
Mary (wh. m. 29 Jan. 1646, Jonathan Gilbert); s. Nathaniel, and rem.
to Hadley 1659, and went back to Hartford bef. 1675, had been rep. for
Hadley 1664 and 9; was Elder, and d. Dec. 1683, or next mo. His
will of 17 Dec. 1683 is foll. by inv. of 23 Jan. His w. was Mary.
Other ch. were Daniel, Sarah, and Jacob, b. at Hartford 8 Oct. 1645,
prob. the youngest; but one or more may have been b. at Cambridge;
Sarah m. first, Stephen Taylor; next, 15 Oct. 1666, Barnabas Hinsdale;
and third, Feb. 1679, Walter Hickson, and had ch. by ea. JOHN, Lynn,
possib. as early as 1630, rem. to Southampton, L. I. had John, James,
Sarah, Hannah, Martha, Abigail, and two more ch. for wh. he made
good provis. in his will, and d. 1662. His wid. Ann m. Zorobabel
Phillips; Martha m. 12 June 1678, John Howell; and Abigail m. 19
Oct. 1682, Abraham Howell. JOHN, a merch. fin. £10. for drunk.
1636, as Winth. II. 346, tells, may not have been a perman. resid.
JOHN, Salem 1638, had gr. of ld. next yr. join. the ch. 1643, was one of
the first plant. with s. John at Lancaster; and from his will of 10 Mar.
1673, pr. in abstr. by Essex Inst. II. 125, other ch. are kn. as Josiah,
wh. was made excor.; Thomas, wh. was d. leav. s. Thomas, and wid.

Ruth for good provis. to be furnish. by testat. in one half of his Wenham farm to ea. — beside his own ds. that were m. and already portion. Joan, Eliz. Mary, and Sarah, as also youngest Hannah wh. liv.
with him. JOHN, Watertown 1642, mortgag. his est. at W. and at Cambridge that yr. to John Sherman as guard. of ch. of wid. Ong. JOHN,
Kittery 1640, took o. of fidel. to Mass. 1652, as did ano. John at Wells
next yr. and one or both may have been of Kennebeck 1665. JOHN,
Boston, liv. in that pt. now Brookline bef. 1654, had John, Joseph,
Mary, Martha, but the ds. both d. young. He d. betw. 30 Apr. 1691,
the date of his will, and Mar. 1692, where it was pro. and may have
resid. in Roxbury. His est. was good. JOHN, Charlestown 1658.
JOHN, Lancaster, s. of John who was first at Salem, had Thomas, and
prob. sev. other ch. of wh. Mary, w. of Rev. Joseph Rowlandson, has
been long rememb. for her gr. suffer. with her fam. on the destruct. of
the town by the Ind. Feb. 1676. He had d. the yr. bef. JOHN, Sudbury, by w. Eliz. had John, b. 8 Aug. 1653; Thomas, 9 Sept. 1655;
Eliz. 1658; and Hannah, to wh. Barry gives date of 1669. JOHN,
Boston 1669, a feltmaker. JOHN, Hatfield, s. of John of Hartford, m.
Sarah, d. of Thomas Bunce of Hartford, d. 14 Sept. 1665, leav. ch.
John and Sarah, both quite young; and his wid. m. a. 1668, Nicholas
Worthington, and she d. 20 June 1676. JOHN, Haverhill, s. of Wil-
liam of the same, freem. 1666, m. Hannah, d. of Edward French, and
d. early. Evidence remains that he had cultivat. in some reputa. degree
his mental powers, and a copious illustra. of shorthand writing by him is
still preserv. His will was pro. Apr. 1669. It names s. John, and f.
His wid. m. Thomas Philbrick, under a m. contract in very judicious
terms of 2 Aug. 1669. JOHN, Dorchester, had Thankful, b. 18, bapt. 20
Jan. 1678; in right of his w. a mem. of the N. ch. at Boston; and
Susanna who d. 18 Jan. 1679, prob. very young. JOHN, Taunton, m.
24 Feb. 1680, Hannah Smith, had John, b. 16 Aug. 1681; Hannah, 19
Apr. 1683. JOHN, Watertown, only s. of Anthony, m. 11 Apr. 1684,
Rebecca, d. of Joseph Bemis of the same, was k. in few wks. and his
wid. m. 1 Apr. 1686, Thomas Harrington. JOHN, Roxbury, the freem.
of 1677, liv. perhaps sev. yrs. bef. at Muddy riv. now Brookline, was a
lieut. and m. Eliz. eldest d. of Elder John Bowles. He d. 28 Mar.
1695, aged 53, and his wid. d. 7 Jan. 1700, aged 48, tho. gr.-stone makes
it something less. JOHN, Hartford, s. of Nathaniel of Middletown, by
w. Mary had John, b. 24 June 1687; Mary, 14 Aug. 1689, both d.
young; John, again, 8 Feb. 1691; a d. that d. soon; Nathaniel, 8 Apr.
1694; Mary, again, 4 May 1696, d. young; Eliz. 11 June 1698; Jacob,
22 Sept. 1700; Sarah; and Ann; and he d. July 1748. JOHN, Boston, made req. to the Gen. Ct. in 1683 and 4, for leave to erect wooden

build. wh. was refus. JOHN, Hatfield, s. of John of the same, freem. 1690, m. 7 July 1687, Hannah, d. of Thomas Wells of Hadley, had John; Mary, b. 1692, d. young; Hannah, 1695; Mary, again, 1697; Jonathan, 1700; Sarah; Eliz.; Martha, 1708; David, 1710, Y. C. 1730, first min. of Hardwick, d. 1784; and Eunice, 1713; and his w. d. 17 Dec. 1733. JONATHAN, Middleborough, s. of Peregrine the first, and this is all that Miss Thomas could tell; but he had first liv. at Yarmouth. JOSEPH, Boston 1646, by me suppos. to be an orphan. ship. from London, since our Gen. Ct. order. him in May of that yr. to be apprent. to Sampson Shore of B. a tailor, for seven yrs. JOSEPH, Weymouth, s. of Thomas of the same, m. 19 Sept. 1660, Lydia Rogers, had Joseph, b. 16 Dec. 1662; rem. next yr. I presume to Mendon, and had Samuel, 14 Feb. 1667; John; Ebenezer; Experience; Hannah; Thomas; Ann, who m. a Trask; ano. Joseph; Lydia, who m. a Cook; and Mary, who m. a Hill; eleven in all. Of course, some of these must have been b. in ano. town, tho. we kn. not certain. to wh. he rem. when the Ind. in Philip's war, destroy. Mendon. JOSEPH, Roxbury, perhaps br. of Benjamin, by w. Hannah, had Samuel, b. 13 Dec. 1684. He was f. of John, also, b. 1677, H. C. 1698, min. of Gloucester. JOSEPH, Middletown, youngest s. of Nathaniel of the same, m. 3 Apr. 1693, Mary, d. of Hugh Mould of New London, had Martha, b. 6 Dec. 1693; Sarah, 27 Feb. 1696; Mary, 2 Oct. 1698; Joseph, 17 Dec. 1700, d. young; Jerusha, 27 July 1703; Joseph, again, 17 Aug. 1705, d. in few mos.; and Ebenezer, 22 May 1707. He d. 28 Feb. 1725, leav. good est. JOSIAH, Hampton, took o. of alleg. 1678. LAWRENCE, Boston, call. a lighterman in taking deed of ld. 1670. *NATHANIEL*, the s. of H. C. 1646, whose yr. of d. is not found, nor do we kn. his f. went forth to preach, and first was at Bermuda a short time, soon aft. in one of the Bahamas, and Wonder-work. Providences sends him to Nevis, where Sir George Downing had bef. been the evangelist. See Felt. Eccles. Hist. I. 577. But I have had a letter from him of 12 Sept. 1664, at Somer's Islands, to Michael Wigglesworth, who had visit. for his health that early resort of invalids, and aft. return home, wrote to his christian br. there under date of 12 July preced. *NATHANIEL, Middletown, s. of John of Hartford, b. prob. in Eng. was of the gr. jury 1662, rep. 1665-77 every yr. and almost every sess. with title of ens. but aft. the gr. Ind. war it swell. to lieut. was capt. bef. he d. 27 Aug. 1711. His w. Eliz. brot. him Nathaniel, b. 7 July 1652; Eliz. 7 Mar. 1655; John, 9 Apr. 1657; Mary, 7 Apr. 1659; Daniel, 23 Feb. 1662; Sarah, 22 Jan. 1664; Jacob, 10 May 1665; Joseph, 20 Feb. 1667; and she d. 1690; he had sec. w. Martha, wid. of Hugh Mould, d. of John Coit, wh. d. 14 Apr. 1730, in her 77th yr. by town rec. and a. 86

by gr.-st. I am impartial betw. the two, but the prob. is strong against the town clk. NATHANIEL, Hadley, s. of Nathaniel of Middletown, m. 28 Mar. 1678, Eliz. d. of John Savage of Middletown, had Eliz. b. 13 Jan. foll. d. young; Nathaniel, 4 Nov. 1680; John, 28 Nov. 1682; Sarah, wh. prob. d. young; Joseph, 28 Feb. 1687; Daniel, 1 Mar. 1690; Jacob, 5 Dec. 1691, d. soon; Mary, 16 Oct. 1693; Eliz. 8 Nov. 1695; William, 15 Aug. 1698; and Ebenezer, 9 Apr. 1701; sw. alleg. 8 Feb. 1679, was freem. of Mass. 1690, a deac. and d. 15 Feb. 1742. One NATHANIEL was a prisoner wh. the Ind. in 1691, tortur. as Miles tells in 3 Mass. Hist. Coll. VI. 226. NICHOLAS, the freem. of 10 May 1643, happy to have his name repeat. in the list, in 1642 had resid. in Dorchester; but aft. m. Susanna, d. of Jonas Humphrey, sold his ld. and rem. to Taunton, and no more is kn. of him. NICHOLAS, Taunton, s. prob. of the preced. m. 9 Dec. 1673, Ursilla (Ursula?) Macomber of Marshfield, had Nicholas, b. 25 Oct. 1676; Ephraim, 8 Feb. 1679; and Dorcas, 24 Sept. 1680. NICHOLAS, Scarborough, submit. to Mass. jurisdict. July 1658. PAUL, Pemaquid, purch. half of patent 1651, from Thomas Elbridge, rem. with w. Bridget to Newbury, a. 1653, there his w. d. 11 Dec. 1664, and he m. 14 Mar. 1665, wid. Ann Jones, was freem. 1671, and d. 20 July 1679, aged 80. * PEREGRINE, Marshfield, s. of William, the first b. of New Eng. com. into life on board the Mayflower, Nov. 1620, in the harb. of Cape Cod, was brot. up by Edward Winslow, who m. his mo. Susanna, 12 May foll. his f. hav. d. 21 Feb. preced. m. 1648, Sarah, d. of William Bassett, had Daniel; Jonathan, b. 4 June 1658; Sylvanus (wh. it is said, d. bef. his f.); Peregrine; Sarah; and Mercy; of wh. we kn. not the order of success. exc. that Daniel is call. eldest s. and Mercy the youngest d. nor is the date of b. of either told, but Sarah's, Oct. 1663; (tho. of Peregrine we gain approxima. to certain. by the remarka. fact that he was bapt. 16 Feb. 1724, then aged 64, at the ch. in Brattle str. by Rev. William Cooper of Boston). He was ens. of Standish's milit. 1642 (tho. in the list of those able to bear arms in 1643, his name is unseen, exc. as "Mr. Winslow's man," wh. seems hardly so dignified a compellation as the first b. of the Mayflower might well challenge), but lieut. some yrs. later, and capt. 1673, rep. 1660 and 1673; and d. 20 July 1704, as the Boston Newsletter tells, add. "altho. he was in the former part of his life extrava. yet was much reform. in his last yrs." His wid. d. 22 Jan. 1711. Miss Thomas in her valua. Memorials, says, his homestead is own. by descend. of the sixth generat. Sarah m. Thomas Young, outliv. him, and d. at Scituate, says the Boston Newsletter, 9 Aug. 1755, in her 92d yr.; Mercy m. 1697, William Sherman, and d. 1739. PEREGRINE, Weymouth, s. I suppose of the preced. by

w. Susanna had Benoni, b. 26 Jan. 1686, rem. to Middleborough, and Miss Thomas in Memo. tells no more. But he may have liv. long at Boston bef. 1724 the yr. of his bapt. PETER, Milton, perhaps s. of Edward of Dorchester, if so, the youngest, by w. Rachel had John, b. 3 Sept. 1683; Peter, 20 Feb. 1685; George, 5 Oct. 1686; Sarah, 21 Dec. 1693; Paul, 20 Feb. 1695, d. in few mos. ; Paul, again, 24 July 1699; Benjamin, 6 Feb. 1701, d. young; and Philip, 26 July 1705. His w. d. 20 Oct. 1732, and he d. 7 May 1743, as my inform. read; but more prob. is the inscript. of his gr.-st. 23 Jan. 1737 in his 77th yr. RESOLVED, s. of William, brot. to Plymouth in the Mayflower 1620, by his f. wh. d. in few wks. aft. land. sat down first at Scituate, there m. 8 Apr. 1640, Judith, eldest d. of Mr. William Vassall, had William, b. 10 Apr. 1642; John, 11 Mar. 1644; Samuel, 13 Mar. 1646; Resolved, 12 Nov. 1647, d. at 22 yrs.; Ann, 4 June 1649; Eliz. 4 June 1652; Josiah, 29 Sept. 1654; and Susanna, 1656. His w. d. 3 Apr. 1670, but he had eight yrs. bef. rem. to Marshfield, and thence, soon aft. her d. prob. to Salem, m. 5 Oct. 1674, Abigail, wid. of William Lord of S. was made freem. 1680, and was the last surv. exc. John Cooke, of the male passeng. in the first sh. that brot. colonists to N. E. Various fam. bec. call. White, claim descent from the Mayflower, some with good reason, many without. RICHARD, Sudbury 1639, is prob. the same wh. came from London 1635, a carpenter, aged 30, as the custom-ho. docket makes it, in the Elizabeth and Ann, but I can tell of him only, from Barry, that he had sh. in three div. of ld. in that town; and Col. Rec. that he refus. to watch in 1642. ROBERT, Charlestown, had d. bef. 4 Aug. 1635, when admin. was given to William Stitson. See Col. Rec. I. 153. *SAMUEL, Weymouth, s. of Thomas of the same, freem. 1666, m. says Shattuck, Mary, d. of Joseph Dyer, but had no issue, was rep. 1679, and d. soon aft. date of his will, 2 Dec. 1698, of wh. w. Mary was made extrix. and the ten ch. of his br. Joseph legatees. SAMUEL, Rochester, s. of Resolved, is all that I can learn of him. SAMUEL, Braintree, by w. Ann had Susanna, b. 12 Mar. 1689; Mary, 12 Sept. 1690; Lydia, 4 Sept. 1693; Ann, 4 Oct. 1696; Thankful, 17 Apr. 1700; Rachel, 20 Mar. 1703; and Experience, 1 Jan. 1706; and I find not that the seven sis. had any br. *THOMAS, Weymouth, freem. 3 Mar. 1636, rep. same yr. and 1637 and 1657, in 1659 was aged 60, and rep. again 1670; d. Aug. 1679, leav. Joseph of Mendon; Samuel, both bef. ment. ; Thomas; Hannah, wh. m. 24 June 1660, John Baxter; and Ebenezer, bef. ment. Of Thayer's Genealogy, eight pages are occup. with this Weymouth stock and progeny. THOMAS, Sudbury, freem. 13 May 1640, selectman 1642, says Barry, had sh. in the first three div. of lds. THOMAS, Charlestown 1658, d. there, as Farmer

says, 30 May 1664, in his will made five days bef. names w. Susanna,
perhaps d. of Richard, and prob. sis. of Rev. John Miller, and s.
Thomas of Cambridge, and d. Sarah. THOMAS, Charlestown, wh. join.
the ch. 22 Mar. 1668, had m. 17 Nov. 1663, Mary, d. of William Froth-
ingham, was freem. 1670, and perhaps s. of the preced. had Thomas, b.
15 Oct. 1664; William, 12 Sept. 1667, both bapt. 29 Mar. 1668;
Samuel, bapt. 31 Oct. 1669; Eliz. b. 28 Feb. bapt. 10 Mar. 1672.
His w. wh. unit. with the ch. 3 Apr. 1670, d. and he m. 5 May 1673,
Eliz. Chamberlain, and he is in the list of householders 1678. THOMAS,
Wenham, s. of John, by w. Ruth had Thomas, b. 10 Mar. 1665; Mar-
tha, 26 Dec. 1668, d. soon; Martha, again, 5 Apr. 1670; and he d. 1
Oct. 1672. The s. Thomas, by will of his gr.f. had devise of one half of
the est. at W. and his mo. the other. Perhaps his wid. m. 12 June 1679,
John Dennis. THOMAS, Marblehead 1674. THOMAS, Weymouth, freem.
1681, was prob. s. of the first Thomas, and had w. Mary Pratt, and ch.
Mary, Samuel, Joseph, and Ebenezer, but no more is kn. WILLIAM,
Plymouth, woolcarder, as the rec. at Leyden calls him, when banns
of m. were pub. 27 Jan. 1612, and the m. 1 Feb. foll. with Anna Fuller, perhaps a relat. of Dr. Samuel wh. attend. at the ceremony, and
prob. the same wh. was call. Susanna, came with w. and s. Resolved,
and two serv. William Holbeck and Edward Thompson, in the Mayflower 1620, and had Peregrine, b. at Cape Cod, bef. the sh. reach. P.
Nov. of that yr. and he d. 21 Feb. two mos. aft. land. His serv.
Thompson had d. betw. Cape Cod and P. and the other serv. d. soon
aft. His wid. m. 12 May foll. Edward Winslow, whose w. had d. only
31 days aft. d. of W. WILLIAM, Newbury, freem. 22 June 1642, had
come from London in the Mary and John 1634, and first sat down at
Ipswich, thence rem. prob. in 1635 or 6, with many of his fellow-passeng. to N. had John and James, the latter b. says Coffin, a. 1649; rem.
to Haverhill, there d. 1690, aged 80. Prob. he had other ch. left very
good est. as the inv. shows real £346. with a proport. of personal, far
better than in those days was custom. with our yeomanry, and descend.
especially thro. John's s. John, are very num. and have been among the
most useful and honorable of the ld. WILLIAM, Ipswich, had w. Catharine, wh. d. 2 June 1671, and perhaps d. Ruth, aged 30 in 1663, and he
d. 25 Aug. 1684, aged 74. WILLIAM, Boston, a man of some skill in
natural science, from wh. a letter to the Gov. (aft. he had fail. to realize
what Dr. Child promis. a. search for mines, and July 1645 was resolv.
to withdr. from the country) may be seen in 2 Mass. Hist. Coll. IV.
198. It may amuse, if not enlighten. WILLIAM, Boston, by w. Eliz.
had Cornelius, b. 7 Jan. 1647; and, I presume, m. a sec. w. 4 Aug.
1653, Philippa Wood, wh. d. 5 July 1654, and had Dorcas, 19 Apr.

1654. Farmer, I think, was misinform. a. s. William. WILLIAM, Ipswich, the freem. 1671, may have been that youth, in 1635, aged 14, wh. came from London in the Increase, under protect. of Philemon Dalton, and perhaps his serv. His w. Mary, by wh. he had ch. unkn. to me by name, d. 22 Feb. 1682, and he m. 21 Sept. foll. Sarah Foster, wid. perhaps of Renold. WILLIAM, Boston, nam. with two others by Sir Edmund Andros in one of his few reasonable commiss. to obt. contribut. for build. an Episcop. ch. in Boston, Mar. 1688. See 3 Mass. Hist. Coll. I. 84. ZECHARIAH, Haverhill, call. serv. of Stephen Webster, 1665, was of Salem 1669, but sett. at H. took o. of alleg. 28 Nov. 1677, m. 23 Oct. 1678, Sarah Rumery, had Zechariah, b. 15 May 1680. Among the ch. mem. of Boston, No. 511 is Charity White, singlewoman, adm. 13 June 1641, wh. had ho. and ld. to dispose of at her d. 18 yrs. later, but prob. no near relat. as she gave most of her property to the deacons of the same. See Geneal. Reg. X. 265. Seventy-nine gr. of this name, in 1834, are noted by Farmer, of wh. thirty at Harv. seventeen at Yale, and thirty-two at the younger N. E. coll.

WHITEHAIRE, or WHITHEIRE, ABRAHAM, Salem, as Mr. Felt's Ann. I. 171 ment. under 1638, perhaps stands for Whittier, sometimes appears Whiteyear. He was 60 yrs. old in 1669.

WHITEHAND, GEORGE, Charlestown, join. the ch. 4 Aug. 1633, was made freem. 14 May 1634, and no more is heard of him by me.

WHITEHEAD, DANIEL, Huntington or Newtown, L. I. 1650, was one of the patentees in the gr. of Gov. Nichols 1666, left s. Daniel, Jonathan, David, and Adam. DANIEL, Newtown, L. I. s. prob. eldest of the preced. m. Abigail, d. of Thomas Stevenson, sett. at Jamaica on the isl. was major, and d. 1704 in his 58th yr. leav. s. Jonathan, Thomas, and sev. ds. ISAAC, New Haven 1648, had Susanna, b. 5 Aug. 1650; Isaac, 20 Nov. 1652; Mary, 20 Nov. 1654; Sarah, 3 Jan. 1656; Samuel, 15 June 1658; Joseph, 29 Apr. 1661; and Grace, 12 Nov. 1663; rem. soon aft. 1666, perhaps to N. J. JOHN, Branford 1660, m. 25 May of that yr. Martha, d. of Lesley Bradfield, had Mary, b. 6 May 1662; Hannah, 10 May 1664; John, 20 Feb. 1666; Martha or Mercy, 10 Jan. 1668; Damaris, 20 Jan. 1670; Samuel, 24 Nov. 1672; Eliphalet, 27 Sept. 1674; Eliz. Oct. 1677; and Thomas, 17 Feb. 1681; and he d. 1695. Seven ch. and wid. Martha attend. the inv. He was one of the party to new ch. covenant in 1667, and in 1669 nomin. for freem. RICHARD, Windsor, serv. on the jury at July Ct. 1640, m. Mary, wid. of William Hopkins, and no more is kn. of him; but his w. was liv. 1670 with her d. Lewis. SAMUEL, Cambridge 1635, Hartford, perhaps an orig. propr. serv. in the Pequot war 1637, and long aft. he had rem. to New Haven had gr. of 50 acres, in 1671, was made serg. of the N. H.

comp. 1665, where he sett. 1639, and is in the freemen's list 1669, m. 9 May 1676, Sarah, wid. of John Gilbert, d. of Thomas Gregson, had Samuel, b. 9 June 1678; and Stephen, 29 Jan. 1681; and d. Sept. 1690. His wid. d. a. 1698, leav. two Gilberts and two Whiteheads to enjoy her est. SAMUEL, New Haven, s. of the preced. prob. by w. Tabitha had s. Samuel. STEPHEN, New Haven, br. of the preced. had Stephen, prob. by w. Mary, wh. surv.

WHITEHOUSE, THOMAS, Dover 1658, m. a d. of William Pomfret, had Pomfret, to wh. his gr.f. gave est. 26 Mar. 1679; and Thomas; perhaps more. I suppose JOSEPH in Geneal. Reg. IV. 249 is error for Thomas. He prayed, 1689, for protect. of Mass. and was liv. says Quint, 1694. Pike's Journal tells of his d. 3 Dec. 1707.

WHITFIELD, EDWARD, Reading 1649, as I learn from Col. Rec. II. 283, but as Eaton does not name him, I judge he rem. soon. HENRY, Guilford, came to New Haven in July 1639, with Col. George Fenwick and his lady, and a ch. of famous John Davenport, who, in a letter of 27 Sept. aft. to lady Mary Vere, tells of the ship, that she was the first "that ever cast anchor in" that place. See Geneal. Reg. IX. 149. No doubt he was bred up for the pulpit, but of his place of educ. we are ign. The common acco. of him is, that he was s. of a lawyer, b. a. 1597, sett. as min. at Ockham, a. 20 ms. from London, in Co. Surry, but others say Ockley or Okely in that sh. a. three ms. from the metrop. was one of the founders of the ch. at G. yet the establishm. of the ch. seems to be postpon. to 1643, prob. from the slow growth of the town. He had propty. eno. and disregard. the fulminat. of Bp. Laud for not read. the royal proclam. for sports on Sunday, resign. his place without dispute, after serv. at the altar near twenty years in his native ld. Late in the autumn of 1650, he went home, publish. the two foll. yrs. relations of the spread of the gospel among our aborig. and d. in the city of Winchester, it is said, in the office of min. tho. of this I much doubt, if my construct. of the lang. of letters from his s.-in-law and neph. both nam. John Higginson, as to his long life, be correct. See 3 Mass. Hist. Coll. VII. 200, 1 and 4. Commonly it is said he had ten ch. but I kn. only of Abigail, the first w. of Rev. James Fitch, and Sarah, wh. m. Rev. John Higginson. JOHN, Dorchester 1634, rem. to Windsor, prob. next yr.

WHITFORD, JONAS, perhaps of Salem, may have been s. of Walter, d. 1690. WALTER, Salem, by w. Bridget had Samuel, b. 21 Oct. 1668; and perhaps John, wh. was his admor. return. inv. 19 Sept. 1692.

WHITHAM, HENRY, Gloucester, m. 15 June 1665, Sarah, d. of Morris Somes, had Thomas, b. 29 Sept. 1666; Henry, 27 Oct. 1668; John, 19

Feb. 1671, d. soon; Samuel, 26 Jan. 1673; and Joseph, 21 Dec. 1676. I have foll. the spelling of Mr. Felt, but may easily believe the name was Witham.

WHITING, GILES, Hartford, or the town above, or the town below, excus. from train. 1643, paying 1s. every train. day for support of drums and colors; but I kn. not that any thing beyond Trumbull, Col. Rec. I. 99, can be seen of him, exc. that he was a propr. of Norwalk 1654. JOHN, Salem, s. of William of Hartford, b. prob. in Eng. tho. Goodwin, 330, makes the date 1635, of wh. I much doubt, bec. 30 Sept. 1654, when he should have been of yrs. of legal discretion, agreem. relat. to distrib. of est. of his f. was sign. by him as well as his elder br. and Mr. Fitch who had m. his mo. and the gr. friends, Webster and Stone, in wh. the f. had confid. After receiv. his A. B. at Harv. 1653, and A. M. 1655, was a tutor at the coll. but soon call. to the pulpit at S. in aid of aged Rev. Edward Norris, and from 1657 to 1659, acc. Felt II. 626, preach. there, but he would not sett. and went to Hartford, where he was ord. 1660, as collea. with Stone, and was adm. freem. May 1665. Rev. Joseph Haynes succeed. S. a controv. soon sprang up betw. him and W. a. bapt. of infants, of wh. the import may, I suppose, be gather. from a letter of famous John Davenport, June 1666, to Gov. John Winthrop, in 3 Mass. Hist. Coll. X. 60-2; and Trumbull, Col. Rec. II. 120. The result is more intelligib. a new ch. was gather. and 1670, W. was made pastor, and serv. until his d. 8 Sept. 1689. He had m. at Cambridge, a. 1654, Sybil, d. of deac. Edward Collins of the same, had Sybil, b. 1655, prob. at C.; John, 1657, prob. at C. d. young; both bapt. at C.; William, 1659, bapt. at C. says Mitchell's Reg. 19 Feb. 1660; Martha, 1662; Sarah, 1664; Abigail, 1666; and Samuel, 22 Apr. 1670. In 1673 he m. sec. w. Phebe, d. of Thomas Gregson of New Haven, and had Thomas, b. 1674, d. soon; Mary, 1676, d. at 13 yrs.; Eliz. 1678; Joseph, 1680; Nathaniel, 1683, d. young; Thomas, again, 1686, d. young; and John, again, 1688, who was a merch. at Hartford, and d. unm. at 27 yrs. He had been appoint. chaplain, Aug. 1675, for the troops in Philip's war, and d. not as Trumbull says, in 1700, but as bef. said. His wid. m. 1692, Rev. John Russell of Hadley, but aft. his d. went to her s. Joseph, at New Haven; and d. 19 Sept. 1730. Sybil m. Alexander Bryan; Martha m. 25 Dec. 1683, Samuel Bryan; both of Milford; Sarah m. 19 Mar. 1685, Jonathan Bull of Hartford; and Abigail m. Rev. Samuel Russell of Deerfield, aft. of Branford. JOHN, Lynn, s. of Rev. Samuel of the same, may have gone, soon after his gr. at Harv. to Eng. and "was intend. for a physician, but bec. a preach." says Mather, "first at Butterwick, then at Leverton in Lincolnsh. where he d. a godly conformist." Magn. III.

cap. 28. It seems from Thompson's Hist. of Boston, 349, if Farmer, in
MS. be correct, that he was bur. 11 Oct. 1689, so that the Coll. catal.
wh. notes his d. 1723, is strangely at fault. JOHN, Lancaster, s. of Rev.
Samuel of Billerica, ord. 3 Dec. 1691, there was k. by the Ind. 11 Sept.
1697, leav. wid. Alice, d. of Joseph Cook of Cambridge, whose two ch.
(Alice, d. 19 Oct. 1697, aged 2 yrs. 10 mos. and Eunice, d. 4 Nov. foll.
aged 1 yr.) have gr.-st. inscript. preserv. in Harris, call. ch. of John and
Alice. His wid. m. 19 May 1701, Rev. Timothy Stevens of Glastenbury. JOHN, Wrentham, s. prob. of Nathaniel the first, m. 24 Dec.
1688, Mary Billings, had Nathaniel, b. 2 Feb. 1691; Mary, 14 Oct.
1692; and John, 16 Jan. 1695. JOSEPH, Lynn, s. of Rev. Samuel of
the same, assist. his f. sev. yrs. and succeed. him by ord. 1680, m. Sarah,
eldest d. of dep.-gov. Thomas Danforth, had Samuel, b. 3 July 1674;
Joseph, 22 Nov. 1675, d. in 3 days; Joseph, again, 8 May 1677, d.
soon; Thomas, 20 May 1678, d. in few days; Joseph, again, 14 Jan.
1681, d. in few wks.; John, 20 Jan. 1682, H. C. 1700, the min. of Concord, wh. d. 4 May 1752, from wh. descend. are very num. A. 1682,
he rem. to Southampton, L. I. where he was "a worthy and painful
min. of the gosp." when Mather wrote 1698, and liv. to 7 Apr. 1723.
JOSEPH, Westfield, s. of the first William, m. 5 Oct. 1669, as Goodwin
says, but town rec. 6 Aug. 1670, Mary, d. of John Pynchon of Springfield, had Mary, b. 19 Aug. 1672; Joseph, 5 Oct. 1674; and his w. d.
soon aft. He was made cornet of Hampsh. troops 1672, freem. of
Mass. 1671, being then of Westfield pulpit, as Farmer in MS. thought,
mistak. him. for the preced. but he was a merch. went back to Hartford,
m. Ann, d. of Col. John Allyn, had Ann, 28 Aug. 1677, d. at 6 yrs.;
John, 13 Nov. 1679, d. young; Susanna, 18 June 1682; William, 14
Mar. 1685, d. at 17 yrs.; Ann, again, 18 Aug. 1687; Margaret, 5 Jan.
1691; and John, again, 15 Dec. 1693. He was treasr. of the Col.
Goodwin says, from 1678 till his d. 39 yrs. and was succeed. 32 yrs. by
his s. John. Farmer makes him to be chos. an Assist. 1683, but I doubt.
His wid. d. 3 Mar. 1735. ‡*JOSEPH, New Haven, s. of Rev. John of
Hartford, m. 30 Jan. 1710, Hannah, d. of Thomas Trowbridge the sec.
of the same, had Hannah, b. 21 Feb. 1712; Mary, 5 Feb. 1714; Eliz.
8 June 1717; Phebe, 23 Oct. 1720; John, 1 Mar. 1722; Sarah, 15
Apr. 1725; Joseph, 28 Jan. 1727; and Elisha, 29 July 1729; chos.
rep. 1716, and sev. yrs. later, and assist. 1725–46; and d. 4 Apr. 1748,
as did his wid. 9 Aug. foll. NATHANIEL, Dedham, had a gr. of ld. in
Lynn, 1638, but was of D. 1641, freem, 18 May 1642, m. 4 Mar. 1643,
Hannah, eldest d. of John Dwight of the same, had Nathaniel, b. 7
bapt. 29 Sept. 1644; John, 29 Sept. bapt. 11 Oct. 1646, prob. d. soon;
ano. John, next yr. d. soon; ano. s. 30 Dec. 1649, whose name eludes

me, tho. Goodwin calls him Samuel, b. 20 Nov.; Hannah, 17, bapt. 22 Feb. 1652; Timothy, b. 5 Jan. 1653; Mary, 8 July 1656, d. soon; Mary, again, 12, bapt. 24 Oct. 1658; Sarah, 3 Dec. 1660; Abigail, 7 June 1663; John, again, 19, bapt. 23 July 1665; and Jonathan, 9, bapt. 20 Oct. 1667, and perhaps more. Goodwin adds Judah, b. 20 Mar. 1670; and Ann, 25 Feb. 1672. I suppose he liv. in that part wh. bec. Medfield. NATHANIEL, Medfield, s. of the preced. was freem. 1672, driv. by Ind. hostil. to Roxbury, by w. Hannah had Jonathan, b. 9 Oct. 1677; and prob. had other ch. at M. for the name spread much in that vicinage. OLIVER, Billerica, s. of Rev. Samuel of the same, m. 22 Jan. 1690, Ann, d. of capt. Jonathan Danforth of the same, had nine ch. of wh. only Samuel, b. 6 Sept. 1702, f. of a respecta. line, is kn. to me; d. 22 Dec. 1736. SAMUEL, Lynn, b. at Boston, Co. Linc. 20 Nov. 1597, s. of John Whiting, the mayor of the borough, was matric. 1613 at Emanuel, the Puritan Coll. of the Univ. of Cambridge, as it was then stigmatiz. had his degrees 1616, and 1620, preach. as chaplain three yrs. in private fams. if Mather be correct, after his master's degr. and then went to Lynn Regis, Co. Norfolk, spent ano. three yrs. as collea. or curate of the rector, and being disturb. by his diocesan, rem. to Skirbeck, close to his native place. Aft. bur. his first w. by wh. he had two s. who d. in Eng. and one d. brot. to our country, Mather says he m. a d. of Oliver St. John, a Bedfordsh. man. of fam. nearly relat. to the Lord St. John of Bletso, wh. may all be true, but the writer confuses the *time* very cruelly, when he should tell the date of her m. or d. by saying she "stayed with her worthy consort forty-seven yrs. went in the seventy-third yr. of his age unto him to whom her soul had been," &c. Taking the pains to extract meaning out of this gabble, by common arithmetic, we find reason to see that Mather need not be believed literally; as thus, W. was in his 73d yr. in 1669, and the union having existed 47 yrs. of course it began in 1622, wh. is rather early for him who had obt. his master's degree in 1620, m. one w. had three ch. and lost her. I have learn. to distrust the author of the Magnalia in *all* cases where he employs roundabout instead of direct phraseology, and even in this is *sometimes* careless. He came in the same ship with Wheelwright, who had been his neighbor in Co. Linc. arr. 26 May 1636, and sett. 8 Nov. next in the ch. of Lynn, freem. 7 Dec. foll. tho. the prefix of respect is not found with his name. With him came w. s. Samuel, b. at Skirbeck, 25 Mar. 1633, H. C. 1653, but not entit. to his A. M. until 1656, and two ds. of wh. one was Dorothy, b. by the first w. who m. 4 June 1650, Thomas Weld of Roxbury; and the other, Eliz. by sec. w. m. Rev. Jeremiah Hobart. At L. he prob. had John, H. C. 1657, bef. ment. and certain. Joseph, b. 1641, H. C. 1661, bef. ment. ano. s. and ano. d.

if Mather may be trust. whose names are not giv. His w. d. 3 Mar.
1677. The letter of 1 Oct. 1677 to Rev. Increase Mather, wh. he calls
cousin, in Geneal. Reg. II. 198, is valua. and the s. and d. with him to
wh. reference is made, were Samuel, jr. and prob. his w. But why
Increase M. was call. his cousin or neph. is uncert. unless from his m.
with d. of famous John Cotton, to wh. the Magn. asserts "some affinity"
of W. He d. not 11 Nov. as Lynn Rec. in Geneal. Reg. V. 342 has
it, but 11 Dec. 1679. In our Col. Rec. IV. 406, the liberality of governm. in giv. him 600 acres for the rights wh. his br. John, and
Richard Westland, aldermen of Boston in Eng. had assign. him, aris.
from the original stock taken in the comp. bef. settlem. wh. would have
given them claim to 200, is to be read. SAMUEL, Billerica, s. of the
preced. b. in Eng. freem. 1656, m. 12 Nov. of that yr. at Charlestown,
Dorcas, d. of Leonard Chester of Wethersfield, had Eliz. b. 6 Oct.
1660; Samuel, 19 Dec. 1662; John, 1 July 1664, H. C. 1685, bef.
ment.; Oliver, 8 Oct. 1665, bef. ment.; Mary, 28 Apr. 1667; Dorothy,
23 Aug. 1668; Joseph, 7 Jan. 1670, H. C. 1690, d. 6 Aug. 1701;
James, 20 July 1671; Eunice; Benjamin; and Benjamin, again; the
four last d. inf. He was ord. 11 Nov. 1663, the first min. of B. tho. he
had preach. there more than five yrs. bef. and he d. 28 Feb. 1713, his
w. hav. d. a fortnight earlier. One of this name, perhaps a trans.
stranger, d. at the ho. of capt. Thomas Lake, in Boston, 6 Sept. 1658.
SAMUEL, Dedham, perhaps s. of the first Nathaniel of the same, m. 23
Nov. 1676, Sarah, d. of Thomas Metcalf of the same. SAMUEL, Billerica, s. of Rev. Samuel of the same, Farmer says, had issue, tho.
he names neither w. nor ch. but adds that he d. 14 Mar. 1715.
SAMUEL, Windham, s. of John of Hartford, m. at Norwich, when he
was stud. in divin. 14 Sept. 1696, Eliz. d. of Rev. William Adams of
Dedham, was ord. 4 Dec. 1700, first min. of W. where he had first
preach. almost eight yrs. earlier, and d. 27 Sept. 1725, on a visit to Rev.
Nathaniel Collins, his br.-in-law, at Enfield. His ch. were Ann, b. 2
Jan. 1698; Samuel, 20 Feb. 1700, who was lost at sea, aged 18 yrs.;
Eliz. 11 Feb. 1702; William, 22 Jan. 1704; Joseph, 17 Feb. 1705;
John, 20 Feb. 1706; Sybil, 6 May 1708; Martha, 12 Mar. 1710, d.
young; Mary, 24 Nov. 1712; Eliphalet, 8 Apr. 1715; Elisha, 17 Jan.
1717; Samuel, again, 15 May 1720; and Nathan, 4 May 1724. His
wid. m. 1737 Rev. Samuel Niles of Braintree, and after his d. 1 May
1762, went to her youngest ch. at New Haven, col. Nathan, and there d.
21 Dec. 1766. TIMOTHY, Dedham, freem. 1690, was perhaps s. of the
first Nathaniel. ‡*WILLIAM, Hartford 1636, a wealthy merch. who
had been engag. in a patent for lds. at Swamscot with Lord Say and
Lord Brook, and had w. Susanna, s. William and perhaps John bef.

leav. Eng. but possib. came over in 1633 with their agent or gov. Thomas Wiggin, whose w. I think was his sis. as in his will he gives to her and ea. of her ch. decent legacies. Indeed we kn. not from what part of Mass. he went, but prob. from Cambridge, since other promin. persons rem. thence that yr. and he in 1637 was one of the first ho. of reps. in 1641 an Assist. and Treasr. of the Col. from 1643 to his d. in 1647, when he was call. major. Yet he was mak. voyages oft. certain. in anticipat. of one, made his will 20 Mar. 1643 (in wh. he calls his s. William less than 21 yrs. of age, and so, when draw. codic. 2 Apr. 1646), but it may have been only to the Delaware riv. where he maintain. trad.-ho. as also at Westfield, addit. to that will was declar. 24 July 1647, soon after wh. he d. for his wid. had admin. 2 Sept. foll. We kn. not dates of b. of any one of the five ch. nam. in that will, the two bef. ment. and Samuel, of wh. however we never hear more, Sarah, who m. first, Jacob Mygatt, near the end of 1654, and in 1683, John King, or Mary, who m. 3 Aug. 1664, Rev. Nathaniel Collins of Middletown; but of Joseph, ment. in the first codic. we learn from Goodwin, that he was b. 2 Oct. 1645; and ano. s. was b. posthum. as we learn from the order of Ct. in Trumbull, Col. Rec. I. 495, but of him no more is told. His wid. m. 1650, Samuel Fitch of H. and next m. Alexander Bryan of Milford, but d. bef. him, at the ho. of her d. Collins, and was bur. at Middletown, 8 July 1673. WILLIAM, Hartford, eldest s. of the preced. b. prob. in Eng. went home perhaps, bef. m. was a merch. in London, honor. by the Assembl. of Conn. in 1686, as their agent to present addr. to the throne a. their charter, and was thank. for his good serv. d. in 1699, leav. Joseph his s. to admin. his est. *WILLIAM, Hartford, s. of John of the same, was capt. major. col. of the troops in the *old* (or Queen Ann's) French war, sheriff of the Co. 1722; m. 6 Oct. 1686, Mary, d. of Col. John Allyn, had Mary, b. 1 Apr. 1688; Charles, 5 July 1692; and William, 15 Feb. 1694. His w. d. 14 Dec. 1724; and he rem. to Newport, there prob. d. In Suffk. Emigrants, a tract of great research, print. by Mr. Hunter in 3 Mass. Hist. Coll. X. 171, he thinks that the fam. sprung from Boxford in that Co. of wh. may be count. prob. the Hartford and Dedham stocks, should incl. even the Rev. Samuel, tho. he certain. was last from Co. Linc. Boston in that sh. had furnish. many of our planters bef. W. and for £50. contrib. by Richard Westland, an Alderman of Boston bef. our colony of Mass. was occup. gr. of six hundred, instead of two hundr. acres, was many yrs. after giv. to his friend Rev. Samuel Whiting, as in our Col. Rec. Farmer in MS. 1834 notes that fourteen of this name had been gr. at Yale, thirteen at Harv. and eight at the other N. E. coll.

WHITLOCK, JOHN, Fairfield, had d. in 1658, the inv. being in Oct.

leav. wid. and sev. ch. of wh. the name of only John is preserv. JOHN,
Fairfield, prob. s. of the preced. had d. bef. 7 Apr. 1698, the date of his
inv. but whether he had w. or ch. is not kn.

WHITMAN, in early days oft. spell. WHITEMAN, ABIAH or ABIJAH,
Weymouth, s. of John of the same, was freem. 1681, m. Mary Ford,
perhaps d. of Andrew, had Eliz. b. 1673; Lydia, 1678; John, 1681;
Mary, 14 Oct. 1683; Zechariah, 2 Jan. 1686; but the Fam. Mem.
exchanges the dates of the last two; Elinor, 3 Sept. 1688; and Abiah,
30 Nov. 1690. He liv. with his f. who devis. to him his homestead-
farm, wh. has contin. undiv. to posterity in sixth generat. But he had
also lds. at Easton, wh. he gave to some ch. ABRAHAM, Weymouth,
freem. 1680, may not have been br. of the preced. but nothing is kn. of
him. EBENEZER, Bridgewater, s. of Thomas of the same, m. Abigail
Burnham, had Abigail, b. 1702; Zechariah, 1704; Hannah, 1709; and
Ebenezer, 1713; and in that yr. d. His wid. m. a Hobart of Hingham.
EBENEZER, Weymouth, s. of John the sec. of the same, m. Deborah
Richards, prob. d. of Joseph of the same, had Daniel, b. 1706; Ann,
1711; David, 1713; beside Silence; Sarah; and Deborah; whose
dates are not told. GEORGE, Wickford 1674. JOHN, Weymouth, was
first of Dorchester, freem. 13 Mar. 1639, but soon aft. at W. had Hannah, b. 24 Aug. 1641; but other ch. he had, some b. no doubt, in Eng.
Thomas; John; Abiah or Abijah; Zechariah, b. 1644, H. C. 1668;
Sarah; Mary; Eliz.; Hannah; and Judith; these nine all liv. to be
nam. in the will of f. 1685. A fam. tradit. that the mo. with s. Thomas,
aged 12 yrs. and others of the ch. came in 1641, may deserve a partial
credence beyond what such evidence gains usually from the judicious.
Prob. conject. is that, beside Abijah and Zechariah, and Hannah, Judith,
also, and Eliz. were b. on this side of the water; but the order, in wh.
names of ch. occur in a will, is not always sufficient guide to determine
relative ages. He was ens. 1645, appoint. by the Gen. Court " to end
small causes," deac. and d. 13 Nov. 1692, little, if any, short of 90 yrs.
and may well seem to be the ancest. of the larger portion of the thousands bear. the name in our region. Sarah m. a Jones; Mary m. John
Pratt; Eliz. m. Joseph Green; Hannah m. Stephen French; and
Judith m. a King. JOHN, Charlestown, spell. on ch. rec. Weightman,
when adm. of the ch. 31 July 1641, and Withman, on Col. Rec. when
adm. freem. 18 May foll. JOHN, Weymouth, sec. s. of the preced.
freem. 1681, by w. Ruth Reed had no issue, as she d. soon; and by sec.
w. Abigail Hollis had Ruth, b. 1 Feb. 1664; Mary, 10 Mar. 1666;
John, 22 June 1668; Ebenezer, 4 Dec. 1670; Experience, 1 Apr.
1673; but this last is call. Samuel in the Fam. Mem. JOHN, Bridgewater, eldest s. of Thomas of the same, m. Mary Pratt of Weymouth,

was a stout soldier in Philip's war, and d. 1727, leav. no ch. JOHN, Weymouth, s. of the sec. John of the same, by w. Dorothy had Dorothy, b. 1704; Abigail, 1707; John, 1709; Matthew, 1712; Sarah, 1714; Mary, 1716, prob. d. young; and Mary, again, 1721. His w. d. 1733, and he m. 22 Aug. 1734, Christina Farrar. JOSEPH, Huntington, L. I. adm. to be freem. of Conn. 1664, as in Trumbull, Col. Rec. I. 428, was, I presume, s. of Rev. Zechariah of Milford, and prob. d. bef. his f. NICHOLAS, Bridgewater, s. of Thomas of the same, m. Sarah Vining, d. perhaps of John of Weymouth, had Thomas, b. 1702; John, 1704; David, 1709; Jonathan, 1710; and Seth, 1713. His sec. w. was Mary Cary, and by her he had Eleazer, 1716; and Benjamin, 1719. By third w. Mary Conant, he had Josiah, 1724; Sarah, 1726; Nicholas, 1731; and Ebenezer, 1736; beside five others who d. inf. chief. but not all by the last w. He was k. by accid. 6 Aug. 1746, but had many descend. wh. attain. gr. age, five ch. d. at 80, 86, 87, 90, and 94 yrs. ROBERT, Ipswich, came in the Abigail, 1635, aged 20, had w. Susanna, m. 1648, wh. d. 1664; and 9 Nov. of that yr. he m. Hannah Knight, and was liv. 1679, but I kn. no more of him. SAMUEL, Weymouth, s. of John the sec. m. Mary, prob. d. of Joseph Richards of the same, had Ruth, b. 1710; and Samuel, 1717; was deac. for half a hundr. yrs. and prob. d. fairly a century old. THOMAS, Weymouth, eldest s. of John the first, b. in Eng. a. 1629, perhaps not brot. by his f. but left at home to foll. with mo. and other ch. as fam. tradit. tells, freem. 1653, m. 22 Nov. 1656, Abigail, d. of Nicholas Byram, had s. John, b. 5 Sept. 1658; Ebenezer; and Nicholas, as, from his will of 1711, we find also ds. Susanna, w. of Benjamin Willis; Mary, w. of Seth Leach; Naomi, w. of William Snow; and Hannah, then unm.; but no date of b. for more than one of the seven is found; perhaps bec. he sold his est. at Weymouth, and rem. to Bridgewater bef. the b. of sec. ch. and he d. 1712. His wid. long surv. VALENTINE, Providence, by w. Mary had Mary, b. 16 Nov. 1652; Eliz. 3 July 1655; Susanna, 28 Feb. 1658; and Valentine, 28 Aug. 1668; perhaps others. He took engagem. of alleg. to Charles II. 31 May 1666; and was much employ. as interpret. with Ind. (See Hutch. Coll. 267) and d. 26 Jan. 1701. VALENTINE, Providence, s. of the preced. m. 12 Dec. 1694, Sarah Bartlett, had Sarah, b. 26 Jan. 1696; John, 1698; Henry, 16 Jan. 1700; and Abijah, 4 Jan. 1707. ZECHARIAH, Milford, br. of the first John, came in the autumn of 1635, aged 40, with w. Sarah, 25, and s. Zechariah, 2½, by the Truelove from London, was at M. 1639, perhaps, or at New Haven 1643, but nothing is told of him, exc. that he was a rul. elder. Felt, in Eccles. Hist. of N. E. I. 564, says he was ord. teacher of the ch. at M. and assist. in the installa. of Rev. Roger

Newton, may have had s. Joseph, bef. ment. He d. 25 Apr. 1666; outliv. if he had any ch. as, by his will of 24 Apr. 1666, he gave his est. at M. after life of his w. Sarah, to his neph. Zechariah, to George Clark and John Stream, ea. £20. His wid. d. 2 Jan. 1671. ZECHARIAH, Hull, youngest s. of John the first, was ord. 13 Sept. 1670, the only min. wh. ever contin. to reside at H. for life, soon after m. Sarah, d. of John Alcock, by the contr. of m. bind. to Richard Russell, and Samuel Alcock, physician, her uncle, the est. at Milford, left him by his uncle, and his own at H. had Zechariah; John; and Samuel, H. C. 1696, wh. three yrs. later kept the gr.sch. at Salem, and bec. min. at Farmington, beside Joanna, Sarah, and Mary; was freem. 1673; and d. 5 Nov. 1726. Farmer notes as gr. in 1834, twelve at Harv. five at Yale, and nine at other N. E. coll.

WHITMARSH, EBENEZER, Weymouth, s. of John of the same, by w. Christian had Ebenezer, b. 26 Dec. 1683, prob. d. soon; Richard, 10 July 1685; Ebenezer, again, 10 Mar. 1688; and Ruth, 18 Mar. 1691. EZRA, Weymouth, br. perhaps of the preced. by w. Bathsheba had Sarah, b. 9 Nov. 1689, d. soon; and Sarah, again, 19 Oct. 1694. JOHN, Weymouth, by w. Sarah had Increase, b. 1655, says Farmer, but that is earlier than our rec.; Ebenezer, 14 May 1658; Simon, 11 May 1661; a ch. whose name is lost on the rec. 14 Aug. 1663; Zechariah, 1 Sept. 1667; Judith, 2 Sept. 1669; Ezra, 13 Oct. 1670; and Jane, 8 Sept. 1675; was freem. 1691, unless this means his s. as seems more prob. His will of 1695 does not name Increase, nor Simon, nor Jane, but to the other ch. adds John, Sarah, Deborah, and Ruth, and gr.s. Richard. Prob. his w. was d. as she is not nam. The will was not pro. bef. 1709. Judith m. Joseph Shaw. JOHN, Weymouth, s. of the preced. prob. eldest, serv. in Philip's war in Johnson's comp. in the " direful swamp fight," 19 Dec. 1675. NICHOLAS, Weymouth, br. perhaps of the first John, by w. Hannah had Hannah, b. 25 Mar. 1661; Jane, 8 Apr. 1664; Samuel, 27 Oct. 1665; Susanna, 18 Jan. 1668; Sarah, 26 Nov. 1669; and Nicholas, 21 Aug. 1673; was freem. 1681. NICHOLAS, Weymouth, s. prob. of the preced. by w. Mary had Nicholas, b. 20 Mar. 1699. SAMUEL, Weymouth, br. of the preced. by w. Hannah had Hannah, b. 27 Dec. 1691; Susanna, 11 Feb. 1695; David, 13 Oct. 1696; and Mary, 20 Feb. 1698. SIMEON, Weymouth, perhaps br. of the first John and Nicholas, by w. Sarah had James, b. 8 Feb. 1669; Eliz. 15 Feb. 1671; Mary, 12 June 1674; and possib. by w. Eliz. had Alice, 14 Nov. 1695; at least the rec. gives such w. and ch. to one Simeon, but it may be mistake for the next. SIMON, Weymouth, s. of the first John, may, perhaps, legally claim the w. and ch. last ascrib. to Simeon, for, by his will of 1708, he names w. Eliz. and ch. Simon, Mary Jackson, s.-in-law Edward Darby (whose w. was Ruth when his ch. were born), Alice, and John.

WHITMORE, oft. WETMORE, BERIAH, Middletown, s. of the first Thomas, m. 1 Apr. 1691, Margaret, d. of Rev. Samuel Stow, had Sarah, b. 6 May 1693; Hope, 27 Oct. 1695; Thomas, 8 Feb. 1698, d. in few days; Margaret, 16 July 1700; Hannah, 2 May 1703; Bethia, 12 Nov. 1705, d. in few wks.; and Beriah, 23 Apr. 1707; and his w. d. 21 Feb. 1710. He m. 11 Nov. 1714, Mary, d. of Obadiah Allen, had Mary, 6 Oct. 1715, wh. d. in two mos. His w. d. 24 July 1737, aged 62, and he d. 11 Apr. 1756; and he and all other descend. of his f. adopt. the spell. Wetmore. FRANCIS, Cambridge, s. prob. of John of Wethersfield, b. in Eng. a. 1625, m. Isabel, d. of Richard Park of Cambridge, freem. 1654, had Eliz. b. 1 May 1649; Francis, 12 Oct. 1650; John, 1 Oct. 1654; Samuel, 1 May 1658; Abigail, bapt. 3 July 1659; Sarah, b. 7 bapt. 30 Mar. 1662; and Margery, bapt. 27 Mar. 1664, d. young; and the w. d. 31 Mar. 1665. He m. again, 10 Nov. 1666, Margaret Harty, and had Hannah, bapt. not perhaps as Mitchell's rec. says, 15 Feb. but Sept. 1667, d. soon; Margaret, b. 9 Sept. 1668; Francis, 3 Mar. 1671; Thomas, 1673; and Joseph, a. 1675; and d. says the gr.-st. in Harris, 11, on 12 Oct. 1683, tho. he notes that rec. of the town gives 1685; and this is better than the stone. His will of 8 Oct. in this yr. is abstr. in Geneal. Reg. IX. 134. The wid. d. 1 Mar. 1686. Eliz. m. 3 Nov. 1669, Daniel Markham; Abigail m. 9 May 1683, Samuel Wilcox of Middletown; Sarah m. William Locke; Margaret m. Thomas Carter of Woburn; and Frances m. Jonathan Thompson. FRANCIS, Middletown, eldest s. of the preced. m. 8 Feb. 1675, Hannah, d. of William Harris, had Francis, b. 25 Nov. 1675; Hannah, 23 Nov. 1677; Eliz. 1679; Abigail, 23 Jan. 1681; Martha, 1683; Joseph, 1 Aug. 1687; William, 18 Dec. 1689; Edith, 3 Mar. 1692; Isabel, Dec. 1694; and John, Apr. 1698; was a lieut. and d. 9 Sept. 1700. IZRAHIAH, Middletown, s. of Thomas, m. 13 May 1692, Rachel, d. of Rev. Samuel Stow, had Izrahiah, b. 28 June 1693; Stow, 31 Jan. 1695; James, 25 Dec. 1695; Ichabod, 18 Apr. 1698, d. young; Seth, 18 Nov. 1700; Jeremiah, 8 Nov. 1703; Caleb, July 1706; and Josiah, 1 Mar. 1709; and d. 1743. *JOHN, Wethersfield 1639, but in what part of Mass. he had first liv. is not found, but prob. he brot. from Eng. all the five ch. he ever had, Thomas, b. a. 1615; Francis, a. 1625; and John, a. 1627; beside two ds. Ann, said to be b. a. 1621; and Mary, a. 1623; rem. a. 1641 to Stamford, and was one of the first sett. At S. he was in good repute, m. a wid. Jessup, was chos. a rep. to New Haven assemb. 1647, and murd. by Ind. in Oct. 1648. The act was not a case of private hatred, but seems to have been the deed of the whole tribe,

and the Col. of Conn. was moved to unite with that of N. H. in a just
revenge. See Trumbull, Col. Rec. I. 197. JOHN, Hartford 1646, s.
perhaps of the preced. had Sarah, b. 16 Dec. 1647; rem. prob. to
Stamford bef. or soon after d. of his suppos. father. JOHN, Medford, s.
of Francis the first, m. Rachel, d. of Francis Eliot of Braintree, wid. of
John Poulter of Cambridge, had Francis and Abigail, tw. b. 8 May
1678, of wh. Francis d. young; and John, 27 Aug. 1683; was freem.
22 Mar. 1690, but the yr. bef. had been impress. into serv. against the
Ind. in the gr. war of 1689, and was on duty beyond Piscataqua. See
Magn. VII. 67. His w. d. 20 Mar. 1723, and he m. 3 June 1724,
Rebecca Cutler, and he d. 22 Feb. 1739. JOHN, Middletown, eldest s.
of the first Thomas, m. 30 Dec. 1680, Abigail, eldest d. of Andrew
Warner, had Thomas, b. Apr. 1682; and Abigail, 2 May 1685, both d.
young; and his w. d. 5 May 1685. He m. 1 Apr. foll. Mary, d. of
John Savage of the same, had Eliz. 20 Mar. 1687; Mary, 18 Jan.
1692, d. young; John, 21 May 1694; and Ebenezer, posthum. 17 Sept.
1696. He had made his will 6 Aug. 1689, and d. 31 Aug. 1696; and
his wid. m. Obadiah Allen. JOSEPH, Woburn, youngest s. of the first
Francis, m. 13 Feb. 1698, Mary, d. of Thomas Kendall of the same,
wh. d. 19 Nov. 1760, had Joseph, b. 17 Feb. 1699. JOSEPH, Middle-
town, seventh s. of Thomas the first, m. 6 or 26 June 1706, Lydia, d. of
Nathaniel Bacon, wh. d. 24 Jan. 1750, had Joseph, b. 19 Mar. 1707;
Lydia, 22 Sept. 1708; Ann, 11 Feb. 1711, d. soon; Ann, again, 14
Mar. 1713; and Nathaniel, 22 Feb. 1716; and d. 25 Mar. 1717.
NATHANIEL, Middletown, br. of the preced. perhaps had by first w.
Thomas and Moses, but for sec. w. m. 29 Dec. 1703, Dorcas, wid. of
Obadiah Allen, jr. had Deborah, b. 22 Sept. 1704; and Esther, 13 Feb.
1706, d. soon; and he d. 7 Mar. 1709. SAMUEL, Lexington, call. Cam-
bridge Farms, s. of Francis the first, m. 31 Mar. 1686, Rebecca Gard-
ner, had Francis, b. 9 Dec. foll.; Samuel, 1 Apr. 1688; Rebecca, 9
Feb. 1690; John, 1692, d. young; Benjamin; Abigail, 8 May 1698;
Sarah, 10 Apr. 1701; Nathaniel, 7 May 1702; and Mary, 4 May
1704. His w. d. 5 June 1709, and he m. Mary, wid. of Abraham
Watson, had John, again, 25 Jan. 1715; and d. 22 May 1724. His
wid. d. 14 Nov. 1730. SAMUEL, Middletown, third s. of Thomas the
first, m. 13 Dec. 1687, Mary, d. of Nathaniel Bacon, had Mehitable, b.
14 Nov. 1689; Samuel, 13 Mar. 1692; Mary, 29 June 1694; Benjamin, 17 May 1696; Thomas, 20 Aug. 1698; Daniel, 9 May 1703;
Bethia, 22 Jan. 1707; and Jabez, 14 May 1709. His w. d. ten days
aft. and he d. 12 Apr. 1746, aged 90 and a half yrs. but mistake of
Geneal. Reg. XV. 136, makes him 40 yrs. more. *THOMAS, Middletown, who spelt his name Wetmore, as have all the descend. s. of the

first John, m. 16 Dec. 1645, Sarah, d. of John Hall, had John, bapt. 6 Sept. 1646; Eliz. b. 1648; Mary, 1649; Sarah, bapt. 20 Apr. 1651, d. young; Thomas, 19 Oct. 1652; Hannah, 13 Feb. 1654; Samuel, 10 Sept. 1655; Izrahiah, 8 Mar. 1657; Beriah, 2 Nov. 1658; Nathaniel, 21 Apr. 1661; Joseph, 5 Mar. 1663; Sarah, again, 27 Nov. 1664. His w. d. 7 Dec. foll. and he m. 3 Jan. 1667, Mary Akinson, wid. of Luke, and d. of deac. Richard Platt, had Josiah, 29 Mar. 1668; and Mehitable, 17 June 1669, and his w. d. the same day. He m. 8 Oct. 1673, Catharine Roberts, had Benjamin, 27 Nov. 1674; Abigail, 6 Nov. 1678; and Hannah, 4 Jan. 1681. He d. 11 Dec. foll. and his wid. d. 13 Oct. 1693. THOMAS, Middletown, sec. s. of the preced. m. 20 Feb. 1685, Eliz. d. of George Hubbard of the same, had Eliz. b. 2 Sept. 1686; and Thomas, 8 June 1689, who d. at 22 yrs. He d. 1 Feb. 1690, and his wid. d. 6 Dec. 1725. THOMAS, Cambridge, s. of Francis of the same, perhaps was some time of Lexington, by w. Mary had Thomas, b. 4 Nov. 1694; Francis, 5 Sept. 1696; Samuel, 22 Sept. 1698; Mary, 4 Sept. 1700; Daniel, 22 Feb. 1702; Ephraim, bapt. 1709, with Hannah, Abigail, and Sarah at the same time. Aft. liv. many yrs. at Billerica, he rem. to Killingly, and d. 23 Jan. 1751.

WHITNELL, JEREMIAH, New Haven 1639, is found in the list of freem. 1669, print. in Trumbull, II. 524, but there is giv. Whitwell, as prob. in the constable's or selectmen's certific. He m. Eliz. wid. of Thomas Mitchell, after 1662, had no ch. and d. Mar. 1682. His will of 10 Mar. in that yr. gives all his prop. to wid. for life, and after to Philip Alcock, and his w. Eliz. d. of the wid.

WHITNEY, BENJAMIN, Watertown, youngest s. of John the first of the same, sat down first at York (but was, I think, tax. at Dover 1667 and 8), there got w. Jane, there went to sw. alleg. 1680, but at W. had Jane, b. 29 Sept. 1669; rem. prob. next yr. to Shirborn, there had Joshua, 21 Sept. 1687, but perhaps others bef. His w. d. at S. 14 Nov. 1690; and he took ano. as is thot. 11 Apr. 1695, Mary Poor, but Barry thinks her name Esther, and he is said to have liv. to 1723. By that sec. w. he had Benjamin, 22 May 1709. BENJAMIN, Watertown, youngest s. of John the sec. of the same, m. 30 Mar. 1687, Abigail, d. of William Hager, had Abigail, b. 3 May 1688; Ruth, 1689; Benjamin, both bapt. 10 July 1698; John, b. 15 June 1694; David, 16 June 1697; and Daniel, 17 July 1700. Barry, Hist. of Framingham, 436, gives him sec. w. Eliz. says, his will was pro. 1736, and that he left Benjamin, Samuel, Joseph, and Eliz. Yet the last name may be of w. not of ch. BENJAMIN, Shirborn, youngest s. of Jonathan of the same, m. 24 Oct. 1700, Mercy Trayis, had prob. no ch. and d. 1718, his will is pro. 25 Sept. of that yr. ELEAZER, Sudbury, s. of Thomas of Watertown, m. 11 Apr. 1687, Dorothy, d. of James Ross of S. had Sarah, b. 1688, at S. rem. soon to W. and there had James, wh. d. young; Thomas; James, again; Mary; these three bapt. 28 Jan. 1700; but sec. James d. young; Dorothy, bapt. 16 June 1700; Eleazer, 5 Apr. 1702; Elnathan, 6 May 1705; James, again, 6 June 1708; and Jonas, perhaps older than the latter nam. but some of these dates of bapt. do not concur with those in Bond, wh. perhaps had mark. the day of b. as that of bapt. His w. d. 22 June 1731. His will, pro. 1735, nam. two other s. Isaac and Timothy, as Dr. Bond many yrs. since wrote to me; but as in his Geneal. they are omit. I fear he had early mistak. their parentage. HENRY, Norwalk 1665, had the yr. bef. at Jamaica, L. I. favor. the jurisdict. of Conn. propound. for freem. 1667, and is found in the list of 1669, project. 1672 the settlem. of a new town, but made his will the same yr. and d. the next, giv. est. to his w. and only ch. John. ISAIAH, Cambridge, s. of Thomas of Watertown, by w. Sarah, wh. may have been d. of George Woodward, but could never have been wid. of that John Eddy, ment. by Bond, had John, Isaiah, John again, Nathaniel, Sarah, Elijah, and Jonas; but Barry furnish. no dates for any of them. He d. Jan. 1712, at least, his inv. is of 10 of that mo. and his wid. in 1715, says Bond, was of Lexington. JEREMIAH, Plymouth 1643. JOHN, Watertown, came from London 1635, aged 35, in the Elizabeth and Ann, with w. Elinor, 30, and five s. John, 11; Richard, 9; Nathaniel, 8; Thomas, 6; and Jonathan, 1; but a slight reason may be seen for think. one of these ages too low; as in the rec. of W. the f. is call. at his d. 1 June 1673, 84 yrs. old; and Richard was releas. from train. in 1691, "being 70 yrs. of age," when he could only be 65, if the custom-ho. rep. be accept. was a man of propty. and relig. charact. adm. freem. 3 Mar. 1636, was by the Gen. Ct. made constable 1641, a selectman sev. times betw. 1638 and 55, and in 1665 he was town clk. had b. at W. Joshua, 5, but the Register's vol. for W. (preserv. at Boston, giv. the name John) makes the date 15, July 1635, see Geneal. Reg. VII. 159; Caleb, bur. 12 July 1640, prob. very young; and Benjamin, b. 6 June 1643. His w. d. 11 May 1659, and he m. 29 Sept. foll. Judith Clement, wh. prob. d. bef. he made his will, 3 Apr. 1673, nam. all the s. exc. Nathaniel and Caleb, and d. 1 June foll. That Nathaniel prob. d. under 20 yrs. JOHN, Watertown, eldest s. of the preced. brot. from Eng. by his f. m. Ruth, d. of Robert Reynolds of Boston, had John, b. 16 Sept. 1643; Ruth, 15 Apr. 1645; Nathaniel, 1 Feb. 1647; Samuel, 28 July 1648; Mary, 29 Apr. 1650; Joseph, 15 Jan. 1652; Sarah, 17 Mar. 1654; Eliz. 9 June 1656; Hannah; and Benjamin, 28 June, says Bond, perhaps by town rec. but the reg. of Co.

Middlesex has 28 Nov. 1660. He was adm. freem. 26 May 1647, and made good his f's. place as selectman in his riper yrs. and d. 12 Oct. 1692. Ruth m. 20 June 1654, John Shattuck, and next, 6 Mar. 1677, Enoch Lawrence; Sarah m. 18 Oct. 1681, Daniel Harrington; and Eliz. m. 19 Dec. 1678, Daniel Warren. JOHN, Roxbury, prob. eldest s. of John the sec. of Watertown, by w. Eliz. eldest d. of Robert Harris, m. 1669, had Eliz. b. 9 Sept. 1670; John, 1 Apr. 1672; Ruth, 31 Aug. 1674; Timothy, 16 Apr. 1678; Daniel, 3 Dec. 1681; and Sarah, 2 or 7 Aug. 1684, d. under 5 yrs.; was freem. 1684, and d. 4 Mar. 1727. His will of Sept. 1718, was pro. nine days aft. his d. JOHN, Norwalk, only s. of Henry, m. 17 Mar. 1675, Eliz. d. of Richard Smith, prob. of L. I. had John, b. 12 Mar. 1677; Joseph, 1 Mar. 1679; Henry, 21 Feb. 1681; and Richard, 18 Apr. 1687; but no more is kn. of him, exc. that he was a miller, had good propty. and his ch. perpet. the name in that region. JOHN, Framingham, s. of Jonathan the first, m. 10 Apr. 1688, Mary, d. of Shadrach Hapgood of Shirborn, had Mary, b. at S. 27 Mar. 1689; at F. Eliz. 29 Jan. 1691; James, 28 Dec. 1692; and by sec. w. Sarah, d. of Richard Haven of Lynn, had Lydia, 18 Apr. 1695; and Hannah, 27 Sept. 1697; and this w. d. 23 Apr. 1718. His third w. Martha Walker, m. 10 Nov. 1718, d. 14 Nov. 1721, and he d. 1735. JONATHAN, Watertown, s. of the first John, b. in Eng. brot. at the age of 1 yr. freem. 1668, m. 30 Oct. 1656, Lydia, only d. of Lewis Jones of Watertown, had Lydia, b. 3 July, 1657; Jonathan, 20 Oct. 1658; Ann, 28 Apr. 1660; John, 4, by the Co. Register, but by Bond, prob. recent town rec. 27, June 1662; Josiah, 19 May 1664; Elinor, 12 Oct. 1666, d. at 12 yrs.; James, 25 Nov. 1668, d. at 22 yrs.; Isaac, 12 Jan. 1671, d. at 20 yrs.; Joseph, 10 Mar. 1673; Abigail, 18 Aug. 1675; and Benjamin, 6 Jan. 1679; in that yr. rem. to Shirborn, there d. 1702. Goodwin interposes ano. d. betw. the last two ch. but Bond prevails with me. Lydia m. 15 Apr. 1681, Moses Adams; Ann m. as Barry thinks, Cornelius Fisher; and the other ds. may not have m. JONATHAN, Watertown, s. of the preced. m. Sarah, wh. was, Barry judges, d. of Shadrach Hapgood, had Sarah, b. 2 Mar. 1693; Jonathan, 27 Sept. 1694, d. young; Tabitha, 22 Aug. 1696; Shadrach, 12 Oct. 1698; Jonathan, again, 25 Nov. 1700; Ann, 22 May 1702; Amos, 1 May 1705; rem. to Sudbury, and had Zaccheus, 16 Nov. 1707; rem. again, prob. to Concord, there had Timothy, 20 Feb. 1709; and perhaps Daniel; in his will, made 14, pro. 18 Mar. 1735, nam. other ch. Isaac, and his w. surv. him. JOSEPH, Watertown, s. of the sec. John, m. 24 Jan. 1675, Martha, d. of Richard Beach of the same, had Joseph, b. 15 Aug. foll.; Martha, 20 Dec. 1677; John, 29 July 1680; Isaac, 10 Mar. 1682, d. in few days; Isaac, again, 4 Feb. 1683, d. young; Benjamin,

31 Jan. 1685; Mary, 21 Apr. 1694; and Sarah, bapt. 20 June 1697;
and d. 4 Nov. 1702, leav. wid. wh. took admin. 30 Nov. foll. JOSEPH,
Shirborn, s. of the first Jonathan, Barry thinks, by w. Rebecca Burge,
had Jonas, b. 7 June 1708; Joseph, 1710; Sylvanus, 1712; James,
1714; and Ephraim, 1716. JOSHUA, Groton, s. of the first John, by w.
Lydia had Joshua, b. 14 June 1666; and Sarah, 10 Oct. 1668; by w.
Mary had no ch. and she d. 17 Mar. 1672; and he m. at Watertown, 30
Sept. foll. Abigail, prob. d. of Thomas Tarbell, had Mary, 1 July
1675, at Groton; thence driv. by the Ind. war, had at W. William, 28
Feb. 1678; and for the other ch. we must rely upon his will of 17 Apr.
1713, in wh. he calls them Cornelius, David, Martha, Eliz. and d.
Hutchins, by Bond thot. to be Abigail, w. of John H. and d. Woods,
wh. he thot. was Alice, w. of Nathaniel W. but the last is uncert.
JOSIAH, Wrentham, s. of the first Jonathan, by w. Abigail, who surv.
him, had Josiah, b. a. 1698; Jonathan, a. 1703; and Abigail, 1709;
and he prob. d. Jan. 1718, at least his inv. is of 15th of that mo.
MOSES, Sudbury, s. of the first Richard, m. 30 Sept. 1686, Sarah
Knight; but Bond was able to tell no more; and Barry is equal. silent.
From investigat. of T. B. Wyman, jr. it is kn. that he had Sarah, b. 2
July 1687; Moses, a. 1690; Abraham, 29 May 1692; Jonas; Jason, a.
1704; perhaps John; and certain. Lemuel, 1 Aug. 1714. His first ch.
was b. in Stow. NATHANIEL, Watertown, s. of the sec. John, m. 12
Mar. 1674, Sarah, d. of William Hagar of the same, had Nathaniel, b.
5 Mar. 1676; Sarah, 12 Feb. 1679; William, 6 May 1683; Samuel,
bapt. 17 July 1687; Hannah, Mar. 1689; Eliz. b. 15 Dec. 1692; and
Grace, bapt. 3 Dec. 1700; perhaps ano. d. Mercy should be add. He
rem. to Weston, there d. 7 Jan. 1733, "aged a. 90 yrs." says the
extravag. rec. and his wid. d. 7 May 1746, "aged a. 88 yrs." thus rob-
bing her of more than it had bestowed on him, as if the days of b. of
ea. were not well kn. RICHARD, Watertown, sec. s. of the first John,
brot. by his f. at nine yrs. old from Eng. m. 19 Mar. 1651, not, as Barry
says, Mary (foll. the Co. rec.), but Martha Coldham, d. of the first
Thomas of Lynn, had Sarah, b. 17 Mar. 1653; Moses, 1 Aug. 1655;
Joanna, 16 Jan. 1657; Deborah, 12 Oct. 1658; Rebecca, 15 Dec.
1659, d. in two mos.; Richard, 13 Jan. 1661; Elisha, 26 Aug. 1662;
and Ebenezer, 30 June 1672; was freem. 1651, rem. to that pt. of Concord call. Stow, bef. 1682, and there d. but the time is unkn. RICHARD,
Stow, s. of the preced. from his will only is kn. to us, as f. of Richard,
not eldest ch. perhaps, b. a. 1704; Jonathan; Joshua, a. 1707; Hannah Farr; Eliz. Wetherbee; Sarah, d. 1703; Ruhamah, a. 1705; and
Hepzibah, a. 1710; and the mo. Eliz. d. 24 Nov. 1723. He made his
will a few days aft. and d. 5 Dec. next, and Barry says the will was

pro. 23 of the same mo. The two first nam. s. were excors. SAMUEL, Watertown, s. of the sec. John, m. 16 Feb. 1684, Mary, d. of Joseph Bemis, had Mary, b. 30 Sept. 1689 ; but Bond tells no more, tho. by his putt. Arabic num. 1 bef. the name of the ch. we might expect addit. STEPHEN, one of the first sett. of Huntington, L. I. THOMAS, Plymouth, had w. Winifred, wh. d. 23 July 1660, but from Col. Rec. I learn no more. THOMAS, Watertown, fourth s. of John the first of the same, brot. from Eng. at six yrs. of age, m. 11 Jan. 1655, Mary, whose surname may never be satisfactorily shown, any more than that of the w. of Theophilus Phillips, wh. in my opin. was her sis. but in opin. of a judic. reader of old rec. seems Kedell, in one place, and Keedell in ano. had Thomas, b. 24 Aug. 1656 ; John, 19 May 1659, d. same day ; John, again, 22 Aug. 1660, d. soon ; Elnathan, and Eleazer, 7 Apr. 1662 ; Mary, 22 Dec. 1663, d. young ; Bezaleel, 16 Sept. 1665 ; Sarah, 23 Mar. 1667, wh. is said to have m. Charles Chadwick ; Mary, 6 Aug. 1668 ; Isaiah, 16 Sept. 1671 ; and Martha, 30 Jan. 1674. Date of his d. was 20 Sept. 1719, but Bond calls him the freem. of 1690, wh. title may as well, I think, fall to THOMAS, Watertown, s. of the preced. m. 29 Jan. 1679, but Bond says, 18 Oct. 1681, Eliz. d. of George Lawrence of the same, rem. to Stow and had Thomas, b. 17 Sept. 1681 ; Eliz. 16 Feb. 1683 ; John, 13 May 1684 ; Mary, 13 Jan. 1686 ; Benjamin, 7 Oct. 1687 ; Nathan ; Susanna ; and Abigail ; and he was liv. Feb. 1722. Farmer notes that of this name seventeen had in 1834 been gr. at Harv. three at Yale, and ten at other N. E. coll.

WHITON, WHITTON, WHITTUN, or WHITTEN, ENOCH, Hingham, s. of James of the same, m. 11 Jan. 1688, Mary, d. of Stephen Lincoln of the same, had Mary, b. 21 Sept. 1690, d. soon ; Mary, again, 5 Nov. 1692 ; Bethia, 30 Jan. 1695 ; Abigail, 8 Sept. 1697 ; Enoch, 25 Sept. 1699 ; and Margaret, 28 Jan. 1702 ; and d. 5 May 1714. His will was of 29 Sept. 1708, and his wid. d. 2 Oct. 1716. JAMES, Hingham 1648, by w. Mary, d. of John Beal the first, m. 30 Dec. 1647, had James, b. 10, bapt. 15 Apr. 1649, d. next yr. ; James, again, bapt. 13 July 1651 ; Matthew, 30 Oct. 1653 ; John, 16 Dec. 1655, d. young ; David and Jonathan, tw. b. 22 Feb. 1658, both d. in few wks. ; Enoch, 8 Mar. 1659 ; Thomas, bapt. June 1662 ; and Mary, 29 Apr. 1664. He was freem. 1660. His w. d. 12 Dec. 1696, and he d. 26 Apr. 1710. Mary m. 3 Jan. 1689, Isaac Wilder. JAMES, Hingham, s. of the preced. by w. Abigail, had Hannah, b. 4 July 1678 ; James, 17 Feb. 1680 ; John, 1 Apr. 1681 ; ano. ch. 5 Sept. 1683, d. at 12 yrs. ; Samuel, 12 Nov. 1685 ; Joseph, 27 Mar. 1687 ; Judith, 6 May 1689 ; Rebecca, 6 Dec. 1691 ; Benjamin 21 May 1693 ; and Solomon, 10 June 1695 ; and d. 20 Feb. 1725. His wid. d. 4 May 1740, aged 85. MATTHEW, Hingham, br. of the preced. m. 27 Dec. 1677, Deborah, wid. of Daniel Howard, had Mary, b. 25 Sept. 1678; John, 10 Jan. 1680; David, 5 June, 1681; Matthew, 28 Nov. 1682; Eliz. 31 Mar. 1685; Susanna, 14 Nov. 1686; Lydia, 2 Apr. 1693; and Isaac, 25 Mar. 1696; and d. 22 July 1725. His wid. d. 19 Sept. 1729, aged 76. THOMAS, came in the Elizabeth and Ann from London, 1635, aged 36, Audry, 45, perhaps his w. and Jeremy, 8; but where he sat down is not heard. THOMAS, Hingham, youngest s. of the first James of the same, m. 26 Jan. 1690, Joanna Gardner, writ. in rec. Garnett, wid. of Francis of the same, d. of Samuel May of Roxbury, had Joanna, b. 27 Jan. 1691; Jael, 12 Feb. 1693; Leah, 4 Apr. 1695; Thomas, 10 Feb. 1698; Rachel, 12 July 1700; Jonathan, 5 Mar. 1703; and Eleazer, 15 Nov. 1706, and d. 17 Sept. 1708. His wid. m. 23 Mar. 1711, Nathan Farrow. The sound of this name having its first syl. short or long, at the whim of some of the descend. who prefer. the long, easily slid into Whiting in the fourth or fifth generat. as they spread into various towns.

WHITRED, WHITTEREDD, WHITTRIDGE, or WHITRIG, JOHN, Salem 1668, is prob. the same who was k. under capt. Turner, by the Ind. at the Falls fight, 19 May 1676, and perhaps left posterity. NATHANIEL, Lynn 1637. SAMUEL, a soldier of Lothrop's comp. k. at Bloody Brook with the flower of Essex, 18 Sept. 1675. THOMAS, Ipswich 1648, s. of William, brot. by him. from Eng. had w. Florence, of whose d. 1672, a most doleful report may be seen in the diary of Rev. William Adams, pr. in 4 Mass. Hist. Coll. I. 17. He had a s. 13 yrs. old at that time. By sec. w. Charity, he had Rebecca, b. 27 May 1689, wh. m. 11 Jan. 1711, the sec. William Cleaves of Beverly. WILLIAM, Ipswich 1637, perhaps br. of Nathaniel, had come in the Elizabeth 1635, aged 36, with w. Eliz. 30, and s. Thomas, 10, and was of Beninden, Co. Kent. Late in life he m. a. 1663, Susanna, wid. of Anthony Colby, and d. 9 Dec. 1668, his inv. showing est. one third less than debts.

WHITTEMORE, WITAMORE or WHITAMORE, BENJAMIN, Malden, s. of Thomas, by w. Eliz. d. of William Buckman, had Benjamin, b. Jan. 1668, d. in few wks.; Eliz. Apr. 1669; Benjamin, again, 2 Nov. 1670, d. at 6 yrs. and prob. others, as Benjamin, again, the inscript. on whose gr.-st. says he d. 6 Oct. 1703, aged 23; and d. 16 July 1726, in 87th yr. and his wid. d. in two days in her 83d yr. BENJAMIN, Malden, s. of the first John, m. 17 Aug. 1692, Esther Brooks, had Mary, b. 12 July 1694; Benjamin, 9 Apr. 1696; Nathaniel, 23 Nov. 1698; Grace, 20 Mar. 1701; Hannah, 15 July 1703; Mehitable, 19 Apr. 1705; Esther, 3 May 1707, d. at 2 yrs.; Joel, 29 Apr. 1709; Aaron, 13 Dec. 1711; Susanna; and Esther, again, and he d. 8 Sept. 1734. DANIEL, Watertown, br. of the preced. b. perhaps in Eng. m. 7 Mar. 1662, Mary, d. of

Richard Mellen, as seems prob. had Daniel, b. 27 Apr. 1663 ; John, 12
Feb. 1665 ; Thomas, 5 Mar. 1667 ; Mary, 12 Feb. 1669 ; and Nathaniel, 7 Feb. 1670, beside others. His w. d. 11 May 1683, but the date
of his own d. is unkn. and he had bef. 1678, rem. to Malden. The will
names two oldest ch. and refers to seven others. DANIEL, Malden, s. of
the preced. m. Lydia Bassett of Bridgewater, had Daniel, b. 28 Feb.
1690 ; Lydia, 24 Jan. 1692 ; Joseph, 13 Mar. 1694 ; Mary, 26 Mar.
1696 ; Richard, 14 Mar. 1698 ; Eliz. 28 Jan. 1701 ; Jonathan, 11 Apr.
1705 ; Hannah, 18 Mar. 1707 ; William, Jan. 1709 ; and Sarah ; and
he d. 21 Sept. 1756. His will of 8 Feb. 1743 names all the ch. but
Joseph, prob. d. DANIEL, Malden, s. of the first John, had William, b.
1709, as is said. JOHN, Charlestown, s. of Thomas of the same, b.
prob. in Eng. one of the tythingm. 1678, m. Mary, d. of deac. John
Upham of Malden, had John ; Thomas, b. 1 Sept. 1664 ; Joseph, 29
Jan. 1666 ; Benjamin, 1 Sept. 1669 ; all bapt. 1671, in right of the mo.
wh. join. the ch. five wks. bef. ; Nathaniel, 9 Mar. bapt. 13 Apr. 1673 ;
Joel, b. and d. 27 Apr. 1676 ; and Joel, again, 15 June, bapt. 8 July
1677. His w. d. twelve days after, and he m. 8 Nov. foll. Mary, d. of
Rev. John Miller, had Mary, b. 24 Oct. 1678 ; Pelatiah, 7 May, bapt.
27 June 1680 ; Amos, 25 July, bapt. 2 Oct. 1681 ; Eliz. 26 Sept. bapt.
11 Nov. 1683 ; Daniel, 28 Dec. 1685, d. at 3 mos. ; Rebecca, 3 Mar.
bapt. 17 Apr. 1687 ; Hannah, 10 Feb. 1689 ; prob. rem. to Watertown,
and his 15th ch. was Daniel, again, 7, bapt. 17 May 1691. Of his own
d. the date 8 Dec. 1694 is told, but his wid. d. 28 Jan. 1732, aged 78.
JOHN, Charlestown, s. of the preced. perhaps, at least, is call junr. m.
26 May 1684, Eliz. Annable, and had John, b. next Feb. 23 ; Jonathan,
15 Mar. 1690, d. soon ; Richard, 20 Mar. 1692 ; Joseph, 13 Feb. 1694 ;
Sarah, 25 Mar. 1695 ; Experience, 12 Apr. 1696 ; Thomas, Apr.
1697 ; Experience, again, 20 May 1698 ; Jonathan, again, 23 May
1699 ; Abigail, 15 Aug. 1700 ; Ann, 21 July 1701 ; and Josiah, 28
Aug. 1702. Yet of these ch. few of wh. grew up to adult yrs. all but
one, I suppose, may be by w. Sarah, but he d. 6 Apr. 1702. JOSEPH,
Malden, br. of the preced. m. 30 Mar. 1687, Joanna Mousall, d. prob.
of John of Woburn, had Joseph, b. 22 Feb. 1689 ; Joanna, 27 Oct.
1691 ; Jabez, 20 Jan. 1695 ; Susanna, 11 Apr. 1697 ; Huldah, June
1699 ; and Abiel, 6 Aug. 1701. He had for sec. w. Susanna Frost, and
d. 1741. LAWRENCE, Roxbury, came 1635, emb. Apr. in the Hopewell,
capt. Bundock, at London, aged 63, with w. Eliz. 57, was adm. freem.
18 Apr. 1637. His w. d. 13 Feb. 1643, "of an apoplexy wh. she had
more than two yrs. bef." says the ch. rec. wh. next yr. on 18 Nov. ins.
him under the same descript. " an ancient Christian of 80 yrs. of age,"
and the town rec. borrows the statem. that will bear six or seven yrs.

subtract. They were of Stanstead Abbey in Co. Herts, had prop.
suffic. and no ch. só that he gave all his est. to the free sch. all generat.
foll. of R. bless his name therefor. NATHANIEL, Malden, s. of Thomas,
b. prob. in Eng. m. a d. it is said, of deac. John Upham, tho. I doubt, as
the name is giv. Mary, who was w. of his br. John; yet by w. Mary
had Mary, b. 26 Apr. 1668; Nathaniel, 26 Sept. 1670; and Rebecca;
d. at 33 yrs. and by his will of 22 Oct. 1671, pro. 19 Dec. foll. made w.
extrix. She m. 3 May 1673, John Mirable. NATHANIEL, Malden, s.
of the first John, had Eliz. b. 24 Aug. 1696. PELATIAH, Malden, s. of
the first John, m. 14 Nov. 1706, Margery, d. of William Pepperell of
Kittery, sis. of Sir William, had Pelatiah, b. 20 Jan. 1708; William,
10 Mar. 1710; Mary, 2 Nov. 1712; Margery, d. soon; and Joel, 15
Dec. 1716; and d. 21 Oct. 1724, lost near the Isle of Shoals. All the
four surv. ch. are nam. in the will of the conqueror of Louisburg.
SAMUEL, Charlestown, s. of Thomas the first, by w. Hannah had
Samuel, b. 24 Dec. 1672; Hannah, 16 Dec. 1676; Eliz. 17 June
1679; Sarah, 16 Jan. 1682; and Mary, 9 Sept. 1684; all bapt. 5 June
1687, with the mo. also, then aged 30 yrs.; Abigail, 31 Jan. bapt. 8
Apr. foll.; Susanna, 17 Oct. bapt. 10 Dec. 1693; and d. 15 Sept. 1726,
aged a. 75 yrs. and his wid. d. May 1728, aged a. 76, as Harris (Cambridge) Epit. teaches. THOMAS, Charlestown, d. 25 May 1661, hav.
made his will 8 Feb. preced. in wh. he names w. Hannah, eldest s.
Thomas, then in Eng. if alive; Daniel; Nathaniel, bapt. 1 May 1636;
John, 11 Feb. 1638; and Eliz. beside five other minor ch. Benjamin;
Thomas; Samuel; Pelatiah; and Abraham. Why he call. two s.
Thomas might, by conject. be explain. as if the last five were b. by the
sec. w. sure. and the first five were by w. Sarah, wh. d. in Eng. and for
the boys the opinion would answer better than for the d. Yet perhaps
few, if any, of the ten, were b. in this country; at least, he is not found
among inhabs. of C. in 1658; tho. he may have liv. in some other town
of Mass. at that day, as he did few yrs. bef. at Reading. The wid. m.
3 June 1663, Benjamin Butterfield of Chelmsford. THOMAS, Woburn,
perhaps s. of the preced. m. 9 Nov. 1666, Eliz. Pierce, d. prob. of
Thomas of the same, had Joseph, b. 14 Aug. 1667; and d. I think, in
Mar. 1670, for 5 Apr. of that yr. his w. Eliz. had admin. She m. 15
Oct. 1670, Hopestill Foster of Boston. THOMAS, Malden, s. of the
first John, m. wid. Mary Pease, had Thomas, b. 18 Mar. 1694; and
Martha, 17 Apr. 1709.

WHITTIER, or WHITYEARE, ABRAHAM, Manchester, had Edward
and John by first w. and others Isaac and Abraham by a sec. w. as in
his will of 6 Aug. 1674, nuncup. in his last sickn. is seen, Essex Inst.
II. 128. Edward had admin. but d. too soon aft. to permit him to act.

JOHN, Newbury, perhaps s. of Thomas of the same, d. says Coffin, 20 Feb. 1699. The Prob. rec. supplies us with inv. of ano. JOHN, perhaps of Beverly, s. of Abraham, wh. d. 29 Dec. 1681, leav. no w. or ch. but the admor. was order. to pay his minor brs. Isaac and Abraham. JOSEPH, Haverhill, perhaps s. of Thomas, m. Mary, d. of Joseph Pease- lee of the same. NATHANIEL, Salisbury, prob. s. of Thomas, took o. of alleg. 28 Nov. 1677, m. 26 Aug. 1685, Mary Osgood, perhaps d. of John of Salisbury, had Reuben, b. 17 Mar. 1686; Ruth, 14 Oct. 1688; and I presume he is the man who m. June 1710, wid. Mary Ring. THOMAS, Newbury, is, in my opin. that passeng. in the Confidence from Southampton, 1638, call. serv. of John Rolfe, and by Henry, br. of John R. in his will nam. as "kinsman," tho. in Geneal. Reg. V. 440, and XIV. 335, his name is giv. Whittle, was some time at Salisbury, there by w. Ruth had Mary, b. 9 Oct. 1647; John, 23 Dec. 1649; soon after rem. to Haverhill, had Ruth, 6 Nov. 1651; Thomas, 12 Jan. 1654; Richard, 27 June 1663; and Joseph, 8 May 1669; was freem. 1666, and d. 28 Nov. 1696. Thomas, Coffin says, d. at sea, 20 Feb. 1679. Mary m. 21 Sept. 1666, Benjamin Page; and Ruth m. 20 Apr. 1675, Joseph True. A descend. in our day, the poet of Haverhill, has "warbled his native woodnotes wild," with success equal. by very few of our bards. Sometimes it is seen Whitheire or Whitheare.

WHITTINGHAM, ‖ JOHN, Ipswich 1637, ar. co. 1638, posthum. s. of Baruch, and gr.s. of William, the disting. reform. in the Eng. ch. exil. for his faith in the days of Mary, and reward. in the foll. reign with deanery of Durham, was from Southerton, near Boston, Co. Linc. where he own. est. m. Martha, d. of William Hubbard of the same, sis. of the histor. of N. E. had John; Martha; Richard; William, H. C. 1660; Eliz.; and Judith; but dates for any one are not seen; was ens. 1644, lieut. 1645, and capt. in short time, and d. early in 1649. His will was pro. 27 Mar. of that yr. His wid. m. a. 1651, Simon Eyre of Boston. John d. at Boston 1653; Judith d. 1656; and Richard, it is said, d. unm. in Eng. where, perhaps, he went to look after fam. est. How Rev. Samuel Hough was his br. I do not kn. exc. in the bonds of the gospel, yet H. calls William W. s. of this John, his neph. Strange looseness in the fam. story, of the Boston Weekly Journal of Jan. 1730, is read in Geneal. Reg. XI. 26 (tho. unnotic. by the Ed.), would lead us to believe, that his mo. "came over, and was deliv. of a s. wh. she nam. John," whereas he must have been b. a dozen yrs. at least, prob. forty yrs. bef. N. E. was sett. Wretched blunder, too, is his m. with d. instead of sis. of Rev. William Hubbard, when, after. hav. six ch. here, he d. bef. the venerab. historiogr. had any d. to give him. WILLIAM, Boston, s. of the preced. m. Mary, d. of John Lawrence of Ipswich, who had rem. to New York, on the conq. in 1664, by the Eng. had Martha; Mary; Richard, H. C. 1689; Eliz.; and William. His w. d. at Boston, Nov. 1671; he d. in London, or on his way thither, to recov. the est. of his fam. as tradit. goes.

WHITTINGTON, EDWARD, Andover, had, says Abbot, gr. of ld. 1673.

WHITTLESEY, ELIPHALET, Wethersfield, s. of the first John of Saybrook, m. 1 Dec. 1702, Mary Pratt, had Mary, b. 1 Oct. 1703; Hannah, 13 May 1711; and Eliphalet, 10 May 1714; perhaps others. JOHN, Saybrook, where was gr. to him the right of a ferry over Conn. riv. still enjoy. by his descend. m. 20 June 1664, Ruth, d. of the first William Dudley of the same, had John, b. 11 Sept. 1665; Stephen, 3 Apr. 1667; Ebenezer, 11 Dec. 1669; Joseph, 15 June 1671; Josiah, 21 Aug. 1673, d. young; Jabez, 14 Mar. 1675; David, 28 June 1677; Eliphalet, 24 July 1679; Ruth, 23 Apr. 1681; and Sarah, 28 May 1683; but Cothren enlarg. our knowl. by Samuel, Y. C. 1705; and exchanges Sarah for Eliz. He d. 15 Apr. 1704. His wid. d. 29 Sept. 1714. Cothren, from whose large gather. is deriv. part of this detail, believes that he was first of the name on this side of the water, and that he came a. 1650, and bec. a tanner and shoemaker. Of course, he was then a ch. JOHN, Saybrook, eldest ch. of the preced. had John, Hezekiah, and David, but in Cothren, neither the name of their mo. nor any date of b. is found. JOSEPH, Saybrook, br. of the preced. had Joseph. *SAMUEL*, Wallingford, was s. prob. the youngest, of John the first, had Samuel, Y. C. 1729; and Chauncey, Y. C. 1738; but that the name of w. date of m. and of subseq. b. could not be ascert. to enrich Cothren's geneal. is hardly reputab. for the clerg. of Conn. STEPHEN, Saybrook, s. of the first John, m. 14 Oct. 1696, Rebecca, d. of Abraham Waterhouse, had Stephen, b. 25 Sept. 1697, d. young; Rebecca, 20 Nov. 1701; Sarah, 31 Aug. 1704; Samuel, 18 July 1710, perhaps or prob. Y. C. 1729; and Ambrose, 13 Jan. 1713. None of this name is found among the gr. of Harv. but at Yale twenty-six are count. of wh. seventeen have *e* bef. *l* in the sec. syl.

WHITTRIDGE. See Whitred.

WHITWAY, THOMAS, Wethersfield, rem. bef. 1646, to Branford, d. 12 Dec. 1651, had ho. and ld. but of fam. we are ign.

WHITWELL, BARTHOLOMEW, Boston 1665. WILLIAM, Boston, by w. Joanna had Samuel, b. 15 Mar. 1653; was an innholder 1659; but left wid. Mary to admin. his est. 1686.

WIBORN. See Wyburn.

WICKENDON or WICKINGTON, more common. WICKENDEN, WILLIAM, perhaps of Salem 1639, but was of Providence 1640, a strong friend of Roger Williams, and oppon. of Samuel Gorton, d. 3 Feb.

1670, had three ds. Plain, who m. Samuel Wilkinson; Ruth m. Thomas Smith; and Hannah m. John Steere. An extravag. tradit. assigns the name of his first ment. d. to her want of beauty, but as a descend. rejoices in our day in the same prefix, we may give less than the usual credit allowed to such tales.

WICKHAM, WIKEHAM, WICKUM, WICUM, or WICOM, *DANIEL, Rowley, had Daniel, b. 1641; and John; was a lawyer, rep. 1689 and 90, and d. 15 Apr. 1700, says Farmer, but I think in mark. his age 65, he, for a rarity, much underestim. Yet perhaps there were two Daniels, f. and s. His two s. were old eno. to be in the tax list of 1691, and he bore a large share that yr. RICHARD, Rowley 1661. SAMUEL, Warwick, m. Barbara, sixth d. of Randall Houlden the first of the same, and rem. to Newport. THOMAS, Wethersfield, freem. 1658, was liv. 1679; by w. Sarah had Thomas, b. 1648, d. soon; Thomas, again, 14 Oct. 1651, at New Haven, but the first was, as all the others, at W.; Sarah, 1653; William, 1657; beside Samuel, Joseph, and John, nam. in the will of their mo. 15 Dec. 1699, who d. 7 Jan. foll. The f. had d. 1689. Sarah m. a Hudson. THOMAS, Wethersfield, s. of the preced. by w. Mary, m. 1673, had Thomas, b. 1674; William, 1676, d. at 12 yrs.; Gideon, 1678, d. young; Sarah, 1682; Ann, 1684; and Mary, 1687; and no more is kn. of him, but that Ann m. 5 Sept. 1706, Charles Deming.

WICKS, oft. WEEKS, FRANCIS, Salem 1635, a supporter of R. Williams, rem. with him next yr. says Felt, Eccles. Hist. I. 248, and the name is found at Providence 1637, spell. Weeks. *JOHN, Warwick 1643, had first liv. at Portsmouth, on the isl. of Aquedneck, and bef. that at Plymouth 1637, where began his affect. for Gorton, is thot. to be the passeng. emb. at London, Sept. 1635, in the Hopewell, capt. Babb, aged 26, with w. Mary, 28, and d. Ann, 1. He was a tanner from Staines, Co. Middlesex, a. sixteen ms. S. W. from London, where his fam. enjoy some est. here had John, Mary, and Eliz. and unit. with Gorton, Holden, Greene, and others, all of a faith diverse from that of Mass. in purch. 12 Jan. 1643, from Miantinomo, of part of the W. side of Narraganset, the region after. call. by these just proprs. Warwick, in honor of the Earl, admiral of all Eng. their protector from the violence of their better believ. neighbors. He was brot. prisoner, with his assoc. to Boston, and escaping the full maledict. of the clerg. and the majority of Assist. who denounc. death for their erron. belief, or extravag. express. were mildly sentenc. by lenity of the reps. to be confin. to Charlestown at labor, in irons, "during the pleasure of the Ct." See the entire story in Winth. II. 140–149, or the result in Col. Rec. II. 52. His fellow-citizens on 8 Aug. 1647, made choice of him as one of the two town magistr. was after. a rep. and his name is on the freemen's list, 1655; and he was k. by the Ind. Nov. 1675. See the very valuab. note in Rh. I. Hist. Coll. II. 86. Ann m. William Burton; Mary m. 8 June 1671, Francis Gisborne; and Eliz. m. first, Richard Townsend, as his sec. w. and next John Smith of Hempstead, L. I. JOHN, s. of the preced. m. Rose, d. of John Townsend, had John, Thomas, Robert, and Sarah, who surv. him. RICHARD, Malden, m. 2 Dec. 1686, Mercy Lee, perhaps d. of Samuel. THOMAS, Salem, had w. Alice, ds. Bethia, and Hannah, as by his will, 9 Sept. 1655, pro. June foll. is seen in Essex Inst. I. 49. THOMAS, Huntington, L. I. adm. as freem. of Conn. 1662, is prob. he who m. Isabel, d. of Richard Harcut. ZACHARY, Mass. sw. fidel. 1652.

WICKWIRE, JOHN, New London, m. 6 Nov. 1676, Mary, d. of George Tongue, had George, b. 4 Oct. 1677; Christopher, 8 Jan. 1680; John, 2 Dec. 1685; Eliz. 23 Mar. 1688; Jonathan, 19 Feb. 1691; Peter, 2 Mar. 1694; and Ann, 25 Sept. 1697; and he d. in Mar. or Apr. 1712, says Caulkins, 357.

WIDGER, JAMES, Pemaquid, took o. of fidel. to Mass. 1674.

WIFFE or WIFE, HUMPHREY, is by Farmer, ins. in MS. on authty. of Mr. Felt, as one of Essex Co. d. bef. 1640. Against this surname our ears instinctiv. protest; yet to sustain the reading of Mr. Felt, might be cited Geneal. Reg. IV. 248, among the assessmts. of tax July 1657, of Dover, is one for Nathell wife, tho. it must be fear. that this is too indistinct to be valued much; and wh. a most sagacious reader of our old MSS. presumes to be Nicho. Wise, the freem. of 1645. Then comes in Geneal. Reg. VI. 377, from the pub. reg. purport. to transcribe rec. of Roxbury, Jane Wife, wid. bur. 1637; but my copy of the town rec. giv. it plain Wise, detracts from the weight of this item. She prob. was wid. bef. coming, and the rev. patriot Wise, min. of Ipswich, drew his orig. from Roxbury, where also were brs. and sis. Less reliance may be giv. to Geneal. Reg. VIII. 346, from the same public docum. purport. to copy Cambridge rec. John Wife d. 9 Sept. 1644, bec. Harris, 168, quot. the town rec. makes it Wise.

WIGGIN, ANDREW, Exeter, s. of Thomas of Dover, m. at Andover, 3 June, but other rept. is 14th, 1659, Hannah, d. of Hon. Simon Bradstreet, and easy is it to acco. for the diversity, as the same rec. that has 3 for her m. gives m. of her sis. Dorothy on 14. What reverence is due to the biogr. sketch of Gov. Bradstreet in Geneal. Reg. I. 77, is of little conseq. here, for this d. who m. Wiggin is count. twice. He had Thomas, b. 5 Mar. 1661; Simon, 17 Apr. 1664; Hannah, 10 Aug. 1666; Mary, 1668; Sarah; Jonathan; Andrew, 6 Jan. 1672; and Bradstreet; beside two other ds. it is said, whose names are thot. to have been Abigail, and Dorothy; and d. 9 Jan. 1710. JAMES, Dover or Hampton, perhaps younger br. of the preced. may have d. unm. at least nothing is told of him, nor is the story larger a. JOHN, a youth of 15 yrs. passeng. in the Speedwell from London to Boston 1656. ‡ * THOMAS, Dover, one of the earliest mem. of governm. there, 1631, went home next yr. and show. regard for Mass. in a letter of Aug. to Emanuel Downing, and Nov. to Sir John Cooke, wh. are print. in 3 Mass. Hist. Coll. VIII. came back in Oct. 1633, with agency of the puritan peers, Say and Brooke, prob. bring. w. Catharine, by wh. he had Andrew, b. 1635; Mary; and Thomas; all bapt. 20 Sept. 1641, and prob. others, as Henry Sherborne is said to have m. his d. Sarah. He favor. the union of the N. H. people with Mass. was rep. 1645 for Hampton, and in 1650 chos. an Assist. in wh. office he contin. serv. till three yrs. bef. his d. 1667. In the artifices for support of the spurious deed of the larger part of N. H. 17 May 1629, Wiggin's name is used with Walter Neale's in a forged letter of 13 Aug. 1633, print. in Belkn. N. H. Vol. I. of first Ed. in Appendix 6, with the valua. letter of Cotton Mather, in aid of the cause, whether with his eyes open, or only winking, may be disput. The docum. is self-destruct. inasmuch as Wiggin was agent of the party in Eng. oppos. in interest to Mason, whose agent was Neal, but far more open to object. by one inquir. only after the truth, as purport. to be writ. by them at Dover, call. Northam in the trickery, when Neale had one week bef. sail. for Eng. from Boston, and Wiggin was in Eng. embarking at Gravesend in the James for Salem, where he arr. 10 Oct. after eight weeks' pass. See Winth. Hist. I. 115. THOMAS, s. of the preced. may have liv. at Hampton or Exeter, was freem. of Mass. 1669, but very little is kn. of him exc. that his w. was Sarah, sis. of capt. Walter Barefoot, yet in 1690 he was one of the many petnrs. for the renewal of Mass. jurisdict. against wh. Barefoot had act. and ch. were Thomas, Sarah, and Susanna.

WIGGLESWORTH, EDWARD, New Haven 1638, had come in Aug. of that yr. to Mass. brot. w. Esther, perhaps sis. of Rev. John Rayner, and s. Michael, b. in Eng. 28 Oct. 1631, and taught his rudiments by famous Ezekiel Cheever, H. C. 1651, had there, Abigail, bapt. Dec. prob. 13, 1640, was a man of good repute, and comfortab. est. d. 1 Oct. 1653. Of his last sickness he gave acco. stat. his age 49, in a letter to John Winthrop, 18 July bef. his d. wh. may be read in 3 Mass. Hist. Coll. IX. 296, 7. In his will, made six days bef. that let. he names only ch. Michael, and Abigail, to wh. he gives £160. and £80. severally, but directs that her share be paya. at 20 yrs. of age, and all the resid. to w. Esther, wh. tho. constit. extrix. was, with her d. commit. to the s. then resid. at Cambridge, studying for his profess. and an officer of the coll. with this injunct. "that he do endeavor so far as he may with conven. have them near unto him, wherever it please God to cast him." By the inv. his est. appears £401. 14s. 2d. In his diary, the s. writes " news is brot. to me," Friday, 14 Oct. 1653, " of my f.'s d. My f. d. 1 Oct." From New Haven to Cambridge the news pass. in thirteen days, while in our time the traveller requires only half as many hrs. At New Haven the inscript. on his gr.-st. back of the first ch. was alter. from 1653 to 1678, as the *fac simile* in Stiles's Hist. of the Regicides shows, with the vain surmise, that it had been erect. over Edward Whalley, wh. prob. d. after 1670, but earlier than 1675. *EDWARD*, Cambridge, youngest ch. of Rev. Michael, had been perhaps min. of some town, whose importance was not such as to require the ment. of it in the common repts. and prob. never ord. in any place, but taught a sch. in Boston, call. to the chair of theolog. instr. estab. by Hollis only twelve yrs. after taking his first degree in arts, as its first incumb. when he was less than 30 yrs. old, inaug. 24 Oct. 1722, m. 15 June 1726, Sarah, d. of the Hon. and Rev. John Leverett, Presid. of the coll. who d. 9 Nov. of next yr. and by w. Rebecca, eldest d. of deac. Joseph Coolidge of the same, m. 10 Sept. 1729, who d. 5 June 1754, had Rebecca, b. 18 June 1730; Edward, 7 Feb. 1632, H. C. 1749, successor in off. to his f.; Mary, 26 Apr. 1733; and Sybil, 19 Sept. 1736, d. young; and he d. 19 Jan. 1765. *MICHAEL*, Malden, s. of the first Edward, b. in Eng. was ord. 1654, but aft. serv. at the altar eight or nine yrs. his wretched health, of wh. the melancholy influence runs sadly thro. his chief poem, was forced to forego his min. above twenty yrs. and by first w. Mary, whose surname is untold (but once erron. thot. to have been a d. of John Rayner of Plymouth, tho. others suppos. her to have been a Hobson of Rowley, and certain. was niece of that Rayner, and d. of Humphrey of Rowley, wh. calls him S. in his will) wh. d. 21 Dec. 1659, had Mercy, b. Feb. 1656. He partly regain. his strength and practis. medicine until wholly restor. resum. labor in the pulpit. I have seen a copious epistle to him from Rev. Nathaniel White, dat. " Overplus in Somer Island, the 12th of the 7th mo. 1664," acknowledg. rec. of his letter of 12th of 5 mo. inform. of safe ret. to our shore. By w. Martha he had Abigail, 20 Mar. 1681; Mary, 21 Sept. 1682; Martha, 21 Dec. 1683; Esther, 16 Apr. 1685; Dorothy, 22 Feb. 1687; and Samuel, 4 Feb. 1689, H. C. 1707, the min. of Ipswich hamlet or Hamilton. This w. wh. prob. was d. of Thomas Mudge of M. d. Sept. 4 or 11, as inscript. may be read, 1690, aged only 28 yrs. if the rec. be trust. and by third w. of the name of wh. I believe the acco. of Farmer in MS. may be rec. that she was Sybell, d. of the sec. Nathaniel Sparhawk, wid. of Jonathan Avery, he had Edward, b. 1693, as is said, H. C. 1710, the

first divin. prof. at the coll. tho. common report, on ment. of his d. early
in 1765, makes him 72 yrs. old.　Now the s. could not have been the
ch. of that third w. (wh. by Dr. Allen in his Biog. Dict. Ed. 1857,
was thot. to be his only w.) unless we reduce the number of his yrs. for
her former h. Jonathan Avery of Dedham, d. less than 72 yrs. bef. the
d. of her s. by the next h.　This youngest s. was prob. of the sec. w.
He was freem. 1690, of very considerab. reput. for talents, preach. elect.
sermon in the trying days of 1686, and later the Artil. elect. sermon ;
but is most spoken of as author of the Day of Doom, a poem of appropr.
sadness, wh. pass. thro. sev. ed. on our side of the water, last in 1829,
and was print. to instr. rather than amuse readers in Eng. and d. 10 June
1705.　His wid. d. 6 Aug. 1708, in her 54th yr. as Harris, Epit. 40, shows.
He had tak. his mo. and sis. to live with him. Of his ds. Mary is suppos.
to have m. a. 1673, Samuel Brackenbury, and next Rev. Samuel Belcher ; Abigail m. 23 Dec. 1700 or 1702, Samuel Tappan ; Martha m. a
Wheeler ; Esther m. 8 June 1708, John Sewall, wh. d. 1711, and next
21 Oct. 1713, Abraham Tappan ; and Dorothy m. 2 June 1709, James
Upham.　SAMUEL, Ipswich, eldest s. of Rev. Michael, was ord. over
the parish, call. the hamlet, 27 Oct. 1714, but he had stud. theory of
medicine soon aft. leav. coll. and for a few mos. began the practice, but
soon was forced to undertake a sch. at Malden.　He preach. 1712 at
Dracut, and next yr. at Groton.　On 30 June 1715, he m. Mary, d. of
John Brintnal, had Mary, Michael, Martha, and Phebe ; and his w. d.
6 June 1723.　He m. 12 Mar. 1730, Martha, d. of Rev. Richard
Brown of Reading, had Sarah ; Phebe, again ; Samuel, b. 25 Aug.
1734, H. C. 1752 ; Catharine ; Eliz. ; Edward, 3 Jan. 1742 ; John ;
Abigail ; and William ; and d. 13 Sept. 1768, and his wid. liv. to 1784.
Of the thirteen ch. wh. may not however, be an accur. number, four s.
and four ds. outliv. the f.　In his interleav. copy of the Reg. Farmer
notes that eleven of this name had, in 1834, been gr. at Harv. and at
other N. E. coll. none.

WIGHT, DANIEL, Dedham, s. of Henry of the same, m. 17 Feb.
1686, Hannah Dewing, d. of Andrew, had David, b. 19 Dec. foll. ;
Daniel, 25 Jan. 1690 ; and John, 22 Apr. 1699 ; was freem. 1690, and
d. 1 May 1719.　His wid. d. 10 May 1725.　EPHRAIM, Medfield,
youngest s. of Thomas of the same, freem. 1672, m. 2 Mar. 1668,
Lydia Morse, had Lydia, b. 14 Mar. 1669 ; Esther, 13 Jan. 1670 ;
Ephraim, 25 Jan. 1672 ; Miriam, 22 Aug. 1675 ; Nathaniel, 12 Sept.
1678 ; Daniel, 19 Nov. 1680 ; Bethia, 8 Mar. 1683 ; Deborah, 1 Dec.
1685 ; and Ruth, 20 July 1688 ; and he d. 26 Feb. 1722.　His wid. d.
14 July foll.　Of this branch descend. are very num.　HENRY, Dedham, s. of Thomas, prob. eldest, b. in Eng. freem. 1647, made constable

by the Gen. Ct. 1658, and was ten yrs. selectman, m. Jane, d. of the first John Goodenow of Sudbury, had John, b. 13 Dec. 1652, d. bef. his f.; Joseph, 11 May 1654; Daniel, 24 Nov. 1656; Benjamin, 18 June 1659; and Jonathan, 2 July 1662; and d. 27 Feb. 1681. His wid. d. 16 May 1684. ISRAEL, Boston 1664. JOHN, Medfield, s. of Thomas of the same, brot. from Eng. by his f. d. 28 Sept. 1653, having been adm. freem. in May bef. and by w. Ann had only ch. Abigail, b. 1 Jan. foll. His wid. m. 11 Apr. 1655, Isaac Bullard. JONATHAN, Wrentham, youngest s. of Henry, m. 19 Apr. 1687, Eliz. Hawes, had Jane, b. 6 Sept. 1688; Eliz. 28 June 1692; Mehitable, 6 Sept. 1694; Marah, 13 Oct. 1696; Jonathan, 6 Jan. 1700; and Sarah, 19 July 1703; and d. 20 Mar. 1718. JOSEPH, Dedham, s. of Henry of the same, freem. 1678, was 33 yrs. deac. and many yrs. town clk. m. 15 Jan. 1680, Deborah Colburn, had Joseph, b. 10 Dec. 1681; Deborah, 25 Aug. 1684; and his w. d. five days after. He m. 22 Apr. foll. Mary Stearns, had Nathaniel, 13 Sept. 1688; Ebenezer, 22 Jan. 1696; and Jabez, 12 July 1701, H. C. 1721; and d. 23 June 1729; and his wid. d. 25 Dec. 1733, aged 73. Descend. are among us, to enjoy est. of his f. in the eighth generat. SAMUEL, Medfield, s. of Thomas of the same, m. 25 Mar. 1663, Hannah, d. of Benjamin Albee, had Hannah, b. 25 Mar. 1664, d. soon; Samuel, 11 Nov. 1665; Hannah, again, 4 Feb. 1667; John, 22 May 1670; Nathaniel, 11 Oct. 1672; Benjamin, 30 Jan. 1675; Ahiel, 3 Nov. 1676; Joseph, 7 Sept. 1679; and Jonathan, 11 Sept. 1682; was freem. 1672. He suffer. great loss in Philip's war, as did his br. Thomas, and they appl. to the Gen. Ct. in 1678 for relief; d. 21 Dec. 1716, and his wid. d. 24 Apr. 1723. THOMAS, Dedham 1637, came from Isle of Wight, by reasonab. tradit. with w. Alice, s. Henry, John, and Thomas, here had Samuel, b. 5 Feb. bapt. 6 Sept. 1640; Mary; and Ephraim, 27 Jan. bapt. 8 Feb. 1646. His w. d. 15 July 1665; and he m. 7 Dec. next, Lydia, wid. of James Penniman, sis. of the apostle Eliot. He was of the Medfield incorpo. 1652, and selectman almost every yr. to his d. 17 Mar. 1674. His inv. of seven days aft. shows good propty. and the will of his wid. was pro. 27 July 1676. Mary m. 21 May 1659, Thomas Ellis. THOMAS, Exeter, in the first sett. means the same person call. Wright. THOMAS, Medfield, s. of Thomas of Dedham, b. in Eng. by w. Mehitable had Mehitable, b. 12 June 1663; Thomas, 27 Oct. 1665; Miriam, 20 Feb. 1668; Eleazer, 1 June 1671; and Joshua, 25 July 1679; and d. 1690. Seven of this name, in 1843, had been gr. at Harv. and eight at other N. E. coll. all. believ. to be descend. of Thomas. Of his fam. an exempla. Memoir was publish. by Danforth P. Wight, H. C. 1815, a descend. of the fifth generat.

WIGHTMAN. See Weightman.

WIGLEY, EDWARD, Concord 1666.

WIGNALL, ALEXANDER, is the name of one who ask. 19 Oct. 1630, to be adm. as freem. of Mass. and took the o. on 18 May foll. in both the lists hav. prefix of respect to show that he was either a scholar, or a man of property; yet so brief was his sojourn in our country, that we find not the place, where he sat down. Slight conject. may be rais. from the circumstance of his standing in ea. roll next above capt. William Jennison, that he was assoc. with that gent. but at Watertown he does not appear, and the safest opin. is, that he came in the fleet with Winthrop, and that he went home soon. Frothingham, 80, names John Wignall of Charlestown in 1630, and he may be the same person.

WIK, WILLIAM, is a name sign. with very many others of Marble-head to a petitn. Oct. 1668, against the duties on imported goods. Whether it be correct. spell. may be doubt. but not that it is extinct.

WILBORE, WILDBOARE, WILBUR, WILBOR, WILLBORE or WILD-BORE, JOHN, South Kingstown, s. of the sec. Samuel, d. 1685. JOSEPH, Taunton, s. of Samuel of the same, m. Mehitable, d. of John Deane of the same, and had Ann, certain. as nam. in the will of her uncle Samuel, and perhaps other ch. In Col. Rec. we read that his w. Eliz. d. 9 Nov. 1670, but he had by ano. w. a d. Ann, 7 May 1672. SAMUEL, Boston, with w. Ann, who was d. of Thomas Bradford of Doncaster in the S. part of Co. York, as in his will of 1 Mar. 1607 is shown, adm. of our ch. 1 Dec. 1633, had no doubt, brot. his ch. Samuel, Joseph, and Shadrach from Eng. and prob. had not any ch. b. on our side of the water, unless we might see cause to give him a William. When his w. d. is not seen, but a sec. w. Eliz. was rec. into the ch. 29 Nov. 1645. But long bef. he had fall. in sympathy with the major pt. of his fellow-worshipp. under the danger. doctrines of Cotton and Wheelwright, so that the body of the peop. at other places in the Col. deem. it necess. to disarm them in Nov. 1637, when his charact. stood high eno. to serve on the gr. jury two mos. earlier, and in Mar. foll. he was banish. With Coddington, and seventeen others, among the best men of Boston, then purchas. Aquedneck or Rhode Island, he form. corpo. by solemn compact, 7 Mar. 1638, and was held in high esteem there many yrs. so that tho. he had rem. to Taunton, his name as sen. and Samuel, jr. was ea. retain. on the list of freem. 1655. He had wisdom eno. to hold on by his est. at Portsmouth, on R. I. at Taunton, and at Boston, to wh. place he came again to live bef. mak. his will 30 Apr. 1656, pro. 6 Nov. foll. See Geneal. Reg. VI. 290. It made w. Eliz. and s. Shadrach, excors. A note on that p. says he d. 29 Sept. In that will is giv. to his youngest s. Shadrach the time of serv. of a Scotchman John Mock-liet, as there spell. perhaps John Maclude or McCloud, one of the wretched victims of the civil war, either that importa. of 1652, of wh. large acco. is seen in Geneal. Reg. I. 377–80, show. the names of most of a shipload, 272, sold from the shambles the yr. preced. being the yr. after the fatal field of Worcester; tho. it may have been his fortune to have experience of the tender mercies of Cromwell after his victory of Dunbar in the preced. yr. Whether the Dunbar invoice contain the names of as many young men as the Worcester, or more, or less, is unkn. but it is an object of high interest to find that one, out of a hundred, outliv. by four or five yrs. their cruel banishment and servitude. SAMUEL, Portsmouth, R. I. or Newport, eldest s. of the preced. m. a d. of John Porter, is nam. as one of the patentees of the royal charter of 1663; in his will of 1678, are nam. John, the only s.; Eliz. who m. Morris Freelove; Mary, wh. is thot. to have m. Samuel Forman; Rebecca, the youngest d. who had m. as Mr. Potter thinks, Samuel Browning; gr.s. Latham Clark, from wh. it is presum. that ano. d. had m. his f. of the same name; gr.s. Samuel Arnold, from wh. it may seem that ano. d. Hannah, had m. Caleb Arnold; Ann, d. of Joseph Wilbor; and Samuel, s. of Shadrach Wilbor, his brs. sis. Sarah Shearman, wh. is unkn. to me; cousin, i. e. neph. William Wilbor, sen. perhaps s. of his br. William, or of his br. Joseph; or of his br. Shadrach (for it is only certain by the addit. sen. that there was ano. William); and Francis Gisborne, to ea. of wh. he devis. lds. and the residue to his w. Hannah, perhaps d. of the first John Porter. SHADRACH, Taunton, younger br. of the preced. gain. all the lds. in T. that had been his f's. acc. his will, was more than 35 yrs. town clk. of T. oppos. the governm. of Sir Edmund Andros, for wh. tho. agent of the town, he was sent to prison in Boston, 30 Aug. 1687. See 3 Mass. Hist. Coll. VII. 190. We may suppose that he suffer. not long; and regret most the loss by fire, a few yrs. since, of most of the evid. of his long offic. serv. Baylies, IV. 81, commends the chirogra. Prob. he had other ch. beside Samuel, b. 1 Apr. 1663, rememb. in the will of his uncle Samuel; as Mary, 18 Mar. 1662, wh. d. under 13 yrs.; Rebecca, 13 Jan. 1665; Hannah, 24 Feb. 1668, d. at 7 yrs.; Joseph, 27 July 1670; Shadrach, 5 Dec. 1672; John, 2 Mar. 1675; Eliezer, 1 July 1677; Benjamin, 23 July 1683. WILLIAM, Portsmouth, R. I. br. prob. of Joseph, had Martha, wh. m. 12 May 1681, William Shearman of Marshfield; and perhaps other ch. and d. prob. bef. 1678. WILLIAM, Portsmouth, R. I. call. sen. in the will of his uncle Samuel, may have been s. of the preced. or of Joseph, or Shadrach, as the will calls him cous. had Thomas, and perhaps others. Farmer thot. this fam. name the orig. of Wilbur in our days.

WILBORNE, MICHAEL, Boston, m. 17 Oct. 1656, Mary, as in the

careless Boston town book of ms. call. d. of ens. William Beamsley, but the rec. should be Mercy, wh. is the designat. in her f's. will, 14 Sept. 1658, as in rec. of b. He liv. not long, and his wid. m. Andrew Peters.

WILBY, GEORGE, a youth of 16 yrs. came in the Susan and Ellen, 1635, from London, but no more is kn. of him.

WILCOCKS, or WILCOX, DANIEL, Portsmouth, R. I. chos. to serv. on gr. jury in Mar. 1644, first was perhaps of Narraganset, and f. of him who m. 28 Nov. 1661, at Plymouth, Eliz. d. of the first Jacob Cook. This bridegroom, perhaps d. young, and his wid. m. John Doten of P. * DANIEL, prob. s. of the preced. may have liv. at Little Compton, and been the rep. 1692 to Plymouth Gen. Ct. bef. the new chart. Yet at Portsmouth, R. I. I find a DANIEL, hav. by w. Hannah, Mary, b. 25 Feb. 1683; Hannah, 11 Apr. 1684; and Joseph, 28 Oct. 1687. ED-WARD, Newport, one of the first sett. form. the civil combinat. 20 May 1638, of wh. I would gladly kn. more. Perhaps he was br. of the first Daniel. EPHRAIM, Middletown, youngest s. of the sec. John, by w. Silence Hands, m. 23 Aug. 1698, had Esther, b. 31 Oct. 1699; James, 20 Sept. 1701; Thankful, 16 Sept. 1703; Mary, 10 Dec. 1705; Jane, 4 Jan. 1707; Ephraim, 4 June 1709; and John, 8 Aug. of yr. not mark. as also is the final numeral in ea. of the five preced. ch. and d. 4 Jan. of unkn. yr. ISRAEL, Middletown 1675, br. of the preced. m. 28 Mar. 1678, Sarah, d. of John Savage, had Israel, b. 16 Jan. 1680; John, 5 July 1682; Samuel, 26 Sept. 1685; Thomas, 5 July 1687; and Sarah, 30 Nov. 1689. He d. 20 Dec. foll. and his wid. d. 8 Feb. 1724. JOHN, Hartford, an orig. propr. 1639, had prob. s. John to accomp. him from Eng. and perhaps other ch. beside that Ann wh. m. John Hall, bef. his com. to our shores, or else she was his sec. w. John was of adult age in 1648, and may have tak. disgust at the act of the town in Nov. 1653 (Trumbull, Coll. Rec. I. 249), so as to cause rem. to Dorchester. In Oct. 1667, the s. was order. by the Ct. to pay £6. to his wid. per an. How long he had been d. is unkn. but he had made a will, of wh. the orig. and copy are lost. The wid.'s will was pro. Jan. 1669, in wh. she gave to cous. Sarah Long, d. Ann Hall, s.-in-law John Bid-dle, whose w. or mo. Mary present. the inv. All these circumst. tend to the infer. that the wid. was not mo. of John or Ann. JOHN, Dorches-ter, whose young wid. Mary m. 9 Jan. 1655, Jacob Eliot. JOHN, Hartford, s. of the first John, b. in Eng. m. 17 Sept. 1646, Sarah, eldest d. of William Wadsworth of the same, had Sarah, b. 3 Oct. 1648. His w. d. soon aft. and he m. 18 Jan. 1650, Catharine (Boltwood in Geneal. Reg. XIII. 141, read the name Retorn wh. perhaps was writ. Katern), d. prob. of the first Thomas Stoughton, had John, b. 29 Oct.

foll.; and Thomas; both prob. d. aft. 1660, but bef. the will of f. He had bef. 1654, liv. at Middletown, where were b. Mary, 13 Nov. 1654, d. bef. her f. Israel, 19 June 1656; Samuel, 9 Nov. 1658; and this sec. w. d. and he had new w. Mary wh. d. 1671; and by the fourth w. Esther Cornwell, d. of William, had Ephraim, 9 July 1672; Esther, 9 Dec. 1673; and Mary, 24 Mar. 1676; and he d. 24 May foll. Sarah had m. a Long, perhaps Thomas, as thus she is nam. in the will of her gr.f. Wadsworth. JOSEPH, Killingworth 1663. SAMUEL, Middletown, s. of the sec. John of the same, m. 9 May 1683, Abigail, d. of the first Francis Whitmore, had Samuel, b. 20 Feb. foll.; Francis and Abigail, tw. 5 July 1687, of wh. Abigail d. next yr. and the mo. d. in a fortnight aft. their b. and he d. 16 Mar. 1714. In the Col. Rec. of Trumbull, II. 175, a Samuel W. is propound. for freem. 1672, wh. could not have been this man; but prob. stands for Samuel, the s. of William Wilcockson. STEPHEN, Stonington, bef. 1670, but on the E. or R. I. side of the Pawcatuck, I presume, call. Misquamicuck, m. Hannah, d. of Thomas Hazard of Portsmouth, R. I. had Stephen, and perhaps other ch. ‖ WILLIAM, Cambridge, freem. 25 May 1636, ar. co. 1638, d. 28 Nov. 1653. His will of two days preced. speaks of w. as sick, but no ch. yet names cous. John Woods, sis. wid. Hall, and her s. William, and d. Susan, br. Richard Francis, and br. John Taylor; still, all these, exc. the cous. may only refer to Christian relationsh. Yet, in ano. part, ano. meaning may belong to the phrase, when he alludes to "sister's childr. in O. Eng. wh. were the ch. of sis. Christian Boyden." Farmer found gr. in 1834, three at Yale, and eight at other N. E. coll. but none at Harv.

WILCOCKSON, WILLCOXSON, or WILCOKSON, JOHN, Stratford, s. of William, brot. by his f. at the age of two yrs. in the spring of 1635, m. 19 Mar. 1663, Eliz. wid. of John Welles of the same, as his sec. w. had Patience, b. 1 Feb. 1664; Hannah, 14 Feb. 1665; Eliz. July 1666; and Mary, Apr. 1668; was freem. 1669, but what seems strange is, that the freemen's list of Kenelworth, bef. it was degrad. to Killingworth, contains the same name for the same time, and he d. 1690. Who was his first w. or whether by her he had any ch. beside John, b. Mar. 1657, is not ascert. Patience m. 4 Oct. 1681, Ebenezer Blakeman; and Eliz. m. 1688, Barnabas Beers. JOSEPH, Kenelworth, br. of the preced. by w. Ann had Joseph, b. 1659; Thomas, 1661; Samuel, 1663; Hannah, 19 Jan. 1666; Nathaniel, 29 Aug. 1668; William, 9 Jan. 1671; Margaret, 1673; and John, 1675; and d. bef. 1684. OBADIAH, Kenelworth, br. of the preced. present. for freem. May 1669, had three ws. Mary, wh. d. 8 Aug. 1670; Lydia; and Silence; and ch. Mary, b. 1676; Lydia, 1678, d. soon; Obadiah, 1679; Ebenezer, 1682;

Ephraim; Mindwell; Timothy, 1690; Silence; John, 1692; Joseph, 1694; Janna; Jemima, 1699; and Thankful, 1701; and he d. 1713; and all these ch. were prob. b. at Guilford, whither he rem. a. 1676. * SAMUEL, Windsor, br. of the preced. had Samuel, b. 1666; rem. to Simsbury, there had, perhaps, William and Joseph, and was rep. 1689. TIMOTHY, Concord, rem. to Stratford 1639, says Farmer MS. quot. Trumbull, I. 109, as authty. for his being one of the first sett. But I presume that is a mistake for William, whose s. Timothy, a very small ch. certain. even if not unb. at that time, wh. is on the list of freem. 1669, m. 28 Dec. 1664, Joanna, d. of John Birdseye, had Joanna, b. 1667; Phebe, 1669; Sarah, 1671; Eliz. 1673; and Rebecca, 1680. * WILLIAM, the freem. in Mass. of 7 Dec. 1636, came in the Planter from London, in the ship's clearance call. linen weaver, aged 34, with w. Margaret, 24, and s. John, 2, but at what town he first sat down, is not cert. We can be sure it was not Boston, nor Salem, nor Charlestown, nor Dorchester, nor Roxbury, nor Watertown, and of the few others Concord seems most likely. To what part of Conn. he first rem. is unkn. or at what time; but he is seen in 1647, as rep. at Hartford, and prob. in a high degree is it, that he had more s. and ds. Joseph, Samuel, Obadiah, Timothy, Eliz. wh. m. at Windsor 16 Apr. 1663, Henry Stiles; and Hannah, wh. m. also at W. 17 Mar. 1665, Daniel Hayden; Sarah, wh. m. 1665, John Meigs; and Phebe, m. 11 Dec. 1669, John Birdseye, jr. of Stratford, so that it is not improb. that he had chos. W. for his resid. Yet he may have early rem. to Stratford, where he d. 1652. Some of his descend. have sunk the last syl. of the ancestor's name.

WILCOME, or WELCOME, RICHARD, kept an aleho. 1683, at Isle of Shoals. WILLIAM, Scituate 1673, was k. at Rehoboth fight 26 Mar. 1676, under Pierce.

WILCOT, JOHN. See Woolcot.

WILD, WYLDE, WILDES, or WILDE, EPHRAIM, Topsfield, s. of John the first, was constable 1692, and unhappi. call. to serve a warrant of arrest of one charg. as a witch, wh. cunning. confess. the truth of all the diabolic. nonsense. By her, wh. thus sav. her own life, was the mo. of this min. of the law accused of the same crime; and the s. thot. she had her full revenge, when his mo. was hang. GEORGE, call. a husbandman, aged 37, came in the Elizabeth and Ann, 1635, but I kn. not where he sat down. JOHN, Topsfield 1660, then aged 40, perhaps s. of William, m. Priscilla, d. of the first Zacheus Gould; may be that youth of 17 yrs. coming from London, 1635, in the Elizabeth. From Coffin's gatherings in Geneal. Reg. VIII. 167, it may be infer. that he had s. JOHN, wh. in his will of Oct. 1676, after ment. of his gr.f. Gould, names brs. Jonathan, Ephraim, and sis. Sarah, Eliz. Phebe, Priscilla, and Martha. His sec. w. Sarah was old eno. in 1692 to be condemn. and execut. as a witch, but not young eno. to falsely accuse herself or others during the execra. delusion. RICHARD, Charlestown, adm. inhab. 1636. WILLIAM, Rowley 1643, is thot. to have come in the Elizabeth, 1635, aged 30, unless the number should rightly be larger, with Alice, 40, wh. may have been his w. and John, 17; was of Ipswich 1650 to 1663. He had d. Sarah, w. of the sec. Edward Bishop. Perhaps the wid. Eliz. ment. in the rec. at this latest day, when he was d. is the same as Alice, emb. 28 yrs. bef. Nine gr. at N. E. coll. name Wild, Wilde, and Wildes are noted by Farmer.

WILDER, EDWARD, Hingham, came, tradit. says, from Lancashire, 1638, with his mo. Martha, a wid. wh. d. 20 Apr. 1652, was freem. 1644, m. Eliz. Eames of Marshfield, had John, Ephraim, Isaac, and Jabez, with four ds. and d. 18 Oct. 1690. His wid. d. 9 June 1692. Eliz. m. 22 July 1673, Israel Fearing. EDWARD, Hingham, a soldier in the comp. of the brave Isaac Johnson of Roxbury, Dec. 1675. ISAAC, Hingham, s. of Edward of the same, m. 3 Jan. 1689, Mary, d. of the first James Whiton, had Thomas, b. 11 Oct. foll. and d. 6 Sept. aft. His wid. m. a Jordan. JOHN, Lancaster, s. of Thomas of Charlestown, to wh. again he was driv. in Philip's war, by w. Hannah had John, bapt. at C. 30 Apr. 1676; Thomas, b. 2 Mar. 1677; Hannah, bapt. 31 Oct. 1680; Ebenezer; and prob. other ch. From Ebenezer descends Hon. David of Leominster. NATHANIEL, Lancaster, prob. youngest s. of Thomas of Charlestown, was perhaps a soldier under sentence of d. in 1676, wh. had showed his hatred of some friend. Ind. in Philip's war, disch. by the Gen. Ct. with Daniel Hoar, his fellow offender, on paym. of cost, and some £10. ea. to the Ind. His youth might plead in extenuat. He had by the Ind. war in wh. L. was destroy. been driv. to Sudbury, and there by w. Mary had Ephraim, b. 16 Apr. 1677; Mary, 12 May 1679; Eliz. 14 Feb. 1681; and went back to L. and prob. had more; but was k. by the Ind. July 1704. ROGER, Plymouth, came in the Mayflower 1620, as serv. of Gov. Carver, d. in few days aft. land. THOMAS, Charlestown 1639, by tradit. call. br. of Edward, join. the ch. 30 Mar. 1640, and was adm. freem. 2 June 1641, by w. Hannah had Mary, b. 30 June, bapt. 3 July 1642; Thomas, b. 4 Sept. 1644; John; Eliz.; Nathaniel, 3 Nov. 1655; and Ebenezer, perhaps others wh. d. young, either at C. or at Lancaster, whither he rem. 1 July 1659, was a selectman in the new town, and d. 23 Oct. 1667. His will of 22 Jan. preced. names w. Ann, the four s. and two ds. and made the wid. and s. Thomas, excors. THOMAS, Charlestown, s. of the preced. in his will of 10 May 1716, pro. 25 Aug. foll. names James and Joseph his s. to be excors. and ds. Mary Fairbanks, Eliz. Hutchins, Ann Willard, and

Sarah Hartwell, w. of Edward. Of the passeng. in the Confidence from Southampton, emb. 1638, a "Martha W. of Shiplake, Oxfordsh. spinster, and Mary W. her d." print. in Geneal. Reg. II. 109, we can make no exact settlem. yet perhaps the *spinster* was a wid. and she may have first sat down at Hingham. Farmer notes gr. of this name, 1834, two at Harv. two at Yale, and four at other N. E. coll.

WILDGOOSE, JOHN, Pemaquid, took o. of fidel. 1674, to Mass.

WILEY, JOHN, Reading 1640, or at least an early sett. TIMOTHY, Reading, the freem. of 1690, may have been s. of the preced. Easy is it to mistake this name for Willey, either in index or rec.

WILFORD, GILBERT, Ipswich 1668, was of Bradford 1671. *JOHN, New Haven 1641, took o. of fidel. 1644, was a merch. rem. to Branford bef. 1663, rep. 1665, and most of the time to May 1677 incl. had w. Lydia, and d. early in 1678. His will of 23 Feb. in that yr. gave his est. to a neph. John Wilford, in London, aft. d. of his wid. She m. soon, capt. Thomas Tappan of Milford, and disput. the effect of the will, bec. the est. had been hers, bef. her m. with testat. JOHN, Boston, by w. Bridget, had John, b. 26 May 1656. RICHARD, Branford 1679, or later, agent of John W. some yrs. in the suit for est. giv. to him by will of his uncle.

WILKES, or WILKS, GEORGE, Dorchester 1639, of wh. no more can be kn. for the name is a mistak. of Dr. Harris. JOSEPH, Dorchester 1668, s. of the preced. as cop. erron. by Dr. Harris for Weekes. ROBERT, Salem, merch. d. 24 Sept. 1677, prob. unm. for in his will of that same day, pro. 27 Nov. foll. he made Isaac Woodbury excor. and gave his sis. Mary, w. of said Isaac, and their ch. Robert and Mary, all his prop. See Essex Inst. II. 274. THOMAS, Salem 1656, shipwright, was d. in 1662. WILLIAM, Boston 1633, had w. Joan, wh. join. our ch. 9 Feb. 1634. He rem. to New Haven, prob. with Gov. Eaton, and aft. few yrs. went home, a. 1644, as is kn. by the will of his w. 12 Jan. 1646, " call. to go to her h. but not knowing whether he be liv. or not," embark. that mo. for London, in the ill-fated sh. with Grigson, Lamberton and others. She left ho. ld. and goods to pay her legacies. Her inv. is of 11 Jan. 1647.

WILKEY, or WILKIE, JOHN, Boston, by w. Eliz. had Samuel, b. 3 Apr. 1653; and Mary, 17 Dec. 1655.

WILKINS, BENJAMIN, HENRY, and THOMAS, Salem vill. now Danvers, were adm. freem. together 1690, but I have no kn. of either, nor can conject. any thing, exc. that as the last (wh. was decid. against the hypochondr. Rev. Samuel Paris a. the witchcr. delus. that long torment. the ch.) is call. sen. he may have been f. of the other two. BRAY, Lynn 1630, if Lewis is right, freem. 14 May 1634, but in Dorchester

1633, kept the ferry over Neponset, 1638, and for certainty that he was inhab. of D. in 1641, we may see his signat. to donat. of right in Thompson's isl. with most, if not all, other proprs. to the town, for support of free sch. forever. In his latter yrs. was tenant of Gov. Bellingham's farm at Lynn, where his ho. was burn. 1664, near Salem. He d. 1 Jan. 1702, aged 91. In his name is sometimes seen the addit. *on* in the rec. JOHN, Salem, had w. Mary, and ch. Eliz. John, Mary, and Abigail, all under age, when his w. adminx. render inv. of his little prop. 24 June 1672. JOHN, Boston, the freem. of 1673, may be the person, wh. Babson, 84, says, came from Wilts, had Abigail, b. 1676, wh. m. 30 July 1696, Benjamin Ellery. RICHARD, Boston, freem. 1690. He is the man nominat. for postmaster, aft. the overthrow of Andros; but in 1685 was a bookseller, from Limerick. Of him we learn from the agreeable book of John Dunton, wh. in his visit to Mass. saw much of all that appertain. in any way to his trade. In Thomas's Hist. of Print. II. 412, he is noticed, and he d. at Milton, 10 Dec. 1704, aged 80. THOMAS, Topsfield, m. May 1667, Hannah, d. of William Nichols, but no issue is kn. WILLIAM, Gravesend, L. I. favor. the jurisdict. of Conn. 1664, with James Hubbard, appoint. in a commissn. Of this name Farmer counts gr. in 1834, four at Yale, three at Harv. and two at other N. E. coll.

WILKINSON, often WILKESON, EDWARD, Milford, m. 2 July 1672, Rebecca, d. of Henry Smith of Stamford, had Eliz. aged 24; Rebecca, 22; Edward, 19; Ruth, 16; Hannah, 13; Abigail, 11; Samuel, 8; John, 6; and Thankful, less than 2; at the giv. of his inv. 21 Mar. 1698. HENRY, Ipswich, is prob. the tallow chandler, emb. at London, early in May 1635, aged 25, in the Elizabeth and Ann, but all else is unkn. JOHN, Malden, by a wid. Prudence W. who was of Charlestown 1635, in her will of 1655, pro. July in that yr. call. her only s. and she names no other person but gr.ch. John Bucknam, wh. had been tak. by her from inf. as in the will of his f. is explain. and d. Eliz. w. prob. of George Felt. He d. 12 Dec. 1675, hav. fam. I judge from seeing the summons to John, prob. his s. in 1674, to come up to take o. of fidel. JOHN, constable of Scarborough 1640. JOHN, Providence, s. perhaps youngest, of Lawrence, by w. Deborah, m. 16 Apr. 1689, had John, b. Mar. 1690; Mercy, 30 June 1694; Sarah, 22 June 1696; Freelove, 25 July 1701; Daniel, 8 June 1703; and Jeremiah, 4 June 1707. This last was ancest. of the disting. prophetess Jemima Wilkinson. His eldest s. m. Rebecca, d. of the sec. Richard Scott. JOSEPH, propound. for freem. 1667, in Conn. as Trumbull, Col. Rec. II. 60, shows; yet the name is not seen on the list of 1669, and he may have gone to Providence to take engagem. of alleg. 1668 to Charles II. JOSIAH,

Providence, perhaps eldest s. of Lawrence, took engagem. of alleg. to Charles II. 29 May 1682, had no male offspring to surv. him, and only d. Ruth wh. m. a Dexter, of wh. are still descend. LAWRENCE, Providence, bef. 1646, m. Susanna, d. of Christopher Smith, had beside three s. Joseph, Samuel, and John, the first b. 2 Mar. 1654; ds. Susanna, b. 9 Mar. 1652; Joanna, 2 Mar. 1657; and Susanna, again, Feb. 1662; own. alleg. to the k. 31 May 1666, and d. 9 Aug. 1692. He was call. capt. and tradit. tells that he was a capt. under Cromwell, but it is rather inconsist. that he should have hurried to get out of that serv. and be so early at Providence, as to avoid much of the peril of the civil war, and forego all the benefits of the triumph of the holy brethren in his native ld. ROSIMUS, if the real name were not Erasmus, d. 22 Aug. 1669, by shipwreck in the W. I. and Henry Coggan claim. 5 Nov. 1670, his little prop. under the nuncup. will. SAMUEL, Providence, s. of Lawrence, engag. alleg. to the k. 29 May 1682; m. 1672, Plain, d. of William Wickenden, had Samuel, b. 18 Sept. 1674; John, 25 Jan. 1678; William, 1 Aug. 1680; Joseph, 22 Jan. 1683; Ruth, 31 Jan. 1685; and Susanna, 27 Apr. 1688. Ruth m. William Hopkins, and thus bec. mo. of Ezek. the first commodore of an Amer. fleet in 1776, and of the more disting. Gov. Stephen, whose chirography is so sacred. legib. on the Declarat. of Independence. THOMAS, "for disord. carriage in the meeting-ho." on Sunday, was commit. to pris. in Conn. Sept. 1649, " till the Ct. sees cause to free him;" but we find not in what town he was inhab. THOMAS, Billerica 1675, was complain. of next yr. for pract. of chirurg. and physick contra. to law, but he contin. an inhab. and is found in the tax list 1679; and at B. d. 8 Feb. 1692, Ann W. says Farmer, aged 94, wh. may have been his mo. A wid. Isabel W. d. at Cambridge, 23 Feb. 1656, whose d. Margaret was w. of Edward Goffe, and next of John Witchfield; and perhaps her d. Jane was the first w. of Edward Winship.

WILLARD, or WILLERD, BENJAMIN, Sudbury, eighth s. of major Simon, m. a. 1691, Sarah, d. of John Lakin of Groton, had Sarah; Joseph, b. 1693; Margaret; Esther; Simeon, b. 27 Apr. 1701; Hannah, 6 Dec. 1702, d. soon; and Hannah, 19 Jan. 1704; but Barry makes it 1707, wh. prob. is wrong, as certain. is Dorothy 1706, when some other man's ch. is meant; yet in naming ano. ch. Benjamin, 19 Jan. 1708, possib. the author is right; rem. to Grafton, was a capt. in serv. against the Ind. in King William's war, but declin. appointm. as Lt. Col. and d. 16 June 1732. DANIEL, Yarmouth, first s. of George, m. 10 June 1695, Esther Matthews, prob. d. of James, had no ch. and d. 20 Apr. 1712. His wid. d. 28 June 1726. DANIEL, Charlestown, sixth s. thirteenth ch. of Simon, m. 6 Dec. 1683, Hannah, d. of John

Cutler, as is said, tho. the name of mo. giv. by Willard in the valua. Geneal. seems doubtful, had Ann, b. 9 Nov. 1684, d. in few days, rem. to Sudbury, had Ann, again, 5 May 1686; and Eliz. 10 Mar. 1688. His w. d. 22 Feb. 1691, and he rem. to Boston, m. 4 Jan. 1693, Mary Mills, d. of Jonathan, says the Geneal. 377, tho. I prefer to call her of the sec. John of Braintree, had Daniel, b. 3, bapt. 8 Oct. foll.; George, 22 Oct. 1694; Mary, 16 Nov. 1695; at Braintree had Edward, 28 Feb. 1697; Benjamin, 10 July 1698; again at Boston had Susanna, 15 Nov. 1700; William, bapt. 1 Feb. 1702; Sarah, 12 June 1703, d. at 14 mos.; Sarah, again, a. 1704; and Mehitable, 12 Jan. 1706; and he d. 23 Aug. 1708. His wid. m. 29 Nov. 1723, David Melvill. GEORGE, Scituate 1638, younger br. of major Simon, and s. of Richard of Horsmonden, Co. Kent, where he was bapt. Dec. 1614, heavily fined in 1641, for erroneous opinions, had Deborah and Daniel, both bapt. 14 Sept. 1645; and Joshua, 2 Nov. foll. rem. soon aft. perhaps to Maryland. Deborah m. Paul Sears, and, it is said, descend. are num. HENRY, Groton, fourth s. of major Simon, m. 18 July 1674, Mary Lakin, d. of John of the same, had Henry, b. 11 Apr. 1675; Simon, 8 Oct. 1678; Mary, 3 Aug. 1680; John, 3 Sept. 1682; Hezekiah; Joseph, a. 1686; and Sarah; but it must not be thot. that all these exc. the first, were b. at G. or any one other town, in those yrs. of Ind. incurs. At Lancaster he liv. in the latter part of his life, but L. as well as G. was more than once destr. by the enemy. By sec. w. Dorcas Cutler, sis. perhaps, of the w. of his br. Daniel, he had Samuel, 31 May 1690, a man of distinct. wh. command. a regim. at the capt. of Louisburg, 1745; James; Josiah, a. 1693; Abigail; Jonathan, a. 1696; Susanna; and Tabitha, wh. d. soon; and he d. 1701. His wid. m. 1704, Benjamin Bellows. JOHN, Rehoboth 1658, of wh. no more is kn. unless he be that inhab. of Salem vill. charg. with witchcraft in 1692, commit. to pris. 18 May, from wh. he escap. but was soon retak. found guilty by delud. Ct. and jury, execut. 19 Aug. JOHN, Concord, fifth s. of major Simon, m. 31 Oct. 1698, Mary Hayward, d. of John of the same, had David, b. 9 Sept. foll.; Jonathan, 28 Apr. 1701; Mercy, 4 Jan. 1704; Simon, 7 Aug. 1706; and d. 27 Aug. 1726. His wid. d. bef. 9 Mar. 1729. JONATHAN, Roxbury, youngest br. of the preced. m. 8 Jan. 1691, Mary Brown, d. of major Thomas of Sudbury, had Jonathan, b. 27 June 1693; rem. soon, and had Mary, Hannah, and Hepzibah, but their dates are unkn. as also places of b. but he d. at Sudbury 1706. JOSEPH, seventh s. of major Simon, was prob. a shipmaster, and liv. at London; there m. and had his ch. of wh. we kn. only John and Joseph. He was liv. in 1714, but d. bef. June 1721, when his oldest s. styles hims. of L.

mariner, but, in 1723, mariner of Boston. JOSIAH, Wethersfield, oldest
s. of major Simon, m. at Concord, 20 Mar. 1657, Hannah, d. of Thomas
Hosmer of Hartford, had Samuel, b. 19 Sept. 1658; and Josiah, 13
Mar. 1660; both at Hartford, where he was then sch.-master, and so
was after empl. at W. where he prob. had Dorothy; Simon; Stephen;
Thomas; John; and Hannah; was freem. 1665, bec. a trader, and d.
1674, when his est. was insolv. NATHANIEL, Northampton 1668.
RICHARD, Northampton 1668, f. of the preced. but both belong. in ano.
place, the surname being Weller, not as giv. in Geneal. Reg. IX. 89.
SAMUEL, Groton, sec. s. of major Simon, began to preach there 1662,
was ord. 13 July, and m. 8 Aug. 1664, Abigail, d. of John Sherman, the
min. of Watertown, and of that Mary Launce of wh. is told in the
Magn. the preposterous myth, of her being gr.d. of Earl Rivers, as also
of the happiness of the two ws. of Sherman, the latter count. by the
score, in bring. him ch. He had Abigail, b. 5 July 1665; Samuel, 25
Jan. or 17 Mar. 1668, d. young; Mary, 10 Oct. 1669; John, 8 Sept.
1673, H. C. 1690, merch. at Kingston, Jamaica (wh. was f. of Rev.
Samuel, H. C. 1723, wh. was f. of the Rev. Joseph, H. C. 1765, and
presid. of the Univ. from 1781 to his d. 25 Sept. 1804); Eliz. 27 Feb.
1675; and Simon, the latter b. at Boston, aft. the Ind. destr. Groton, 6
Dec. 1676, H. C. 1695. But two more ch. of this first m. are report.
wh. d. too young to have names. His w. d. soon after, and he m. a.
1679, Eunice, d. of the first Edward Tyng, had Edward, 6 July 1680,
d. young; Josiah, 21 June 1681, H. C. 1698 (wh. was long Secr. of
our Prov. a counsel. and judge of pro. d. 6 Dec. 1756); Eunice, Jan.
1683, d. young; Richard, May 1684, drown. 28 June 1697, few hrs.
after ent. coll. in his 13th yr. says Sewall's diary; William, bapt. 14
Feb. 1686; Margaret, b. 3 Dec. 1687; Edward, again, Sept. 1689, d.
young; Hannah, Dec. 1690; Sarah, Feb. 1693, d. young; Eunice,
again, bapt. 16 June 1695; Sarah, again, b. 10 June 1697, d. young;
and Richard, again, Sept. 1699. Only six of these twelve by the sec.
w. outliv. their f. and only the sec. Eunice and Josiah liv. to mid. age.
Nor is there now remain. any male descend. of the progenit. exc. in the
line of John through Rev. Samuel. He was freem. 1670, instal. 31
Mar. 1678 at the O. S. ch. as success. to Thacher, the first min. and was
highly esteem. call. by the Gen. Ct. to preach their sermon on a fast, in
the anxious days of Feb. 1683, and doing gr. service, in recov. the public judgm. from the horrible delusion of the witchcraft cruelty, and on
the forced resignat. of Increase Mather, as Presid. of the coll. was made
his success. as vice-presid. 6 Sept. 1701, without the obligat. of resid. at
Cambridge, the fatal necessity that disgusted his predecess. He resign.
14 Aug. 1707, and d. 12 Sept. foll. ‡*SIMON, Cambridge, s. of

Richard of Horsemonden, Co. Kent, where he was bapt. 7 Apr. 1605, came 1634, arr. in May, with w. Mary, d. of Henry Sharpe of Horsemonden, bapt. 16 Oct. 1614; and d. Mary; rem. next yr. to the new settlem. of Concord, where prob. this d. soon d. aft. m. with Joshua Edmunds, and b. of her first ch. 16 Feb. 1650. At Cambridge or Concord, he had Eliz. whose date of b. is not found, wh. m. 8 Apr. 1653, Robert Blood; Josiah, whose date is also unkn.; Samuel, in recorder's rec. at Boston, call. Simon, b. 31 Jan. 1640; Sarah, 27 June or 24 July 1642, wh. m. 2 July 1666, Nathaniel Howard of Charlestown, and d. 22 Jan. 1678; Abovehope, 30 Oct. 1646, d. at 17 yrs. unm.; Simon, 23 Nov. 1649; Mary, again, 7 or 27 Sept. 1653, wh. m. 22 Jan. 1672, Cyprian Stevens; Henry, 4 June 1655; John, 12 Jan. or Feb. 1657; Daniel, 29 Dec. 1658; but of these the last four were b. of a sec. w. Eliz. Dunster, sis. of the presid. of the coll. or third w. Mary Dunster, a niece of the presid. for the dates of m. are not giv. But bef. the b. of his next ch. he rem. to Lancaster, there had Joseph, 4 Jan. 1661; Benjamin, 1665; Hannah, 6 Oct. 1666, wh. m. 23 May 1693, capt. Thomas Brintnall of Sudbury, and was the last surv. ch. of her f.; and Jonathan, 14 Dec. 1669; beside two others, Eliz. and Dorothy, wh. both d. young. I suppose he must have had some acquaint. in Eng. with milit. duty, for he was made lieut. here so early as 1637, capt. 1646, and maj. the highest rank at that time, in 1655; and was rep. 1636–49, chos. Assist. 1657 to his d. 24 Apr. 1676. Bef. the Ind. destr. Groton in 1676, to wh. he had rem. a few yrs. earlier, he had estab. his retreat at Salem, but d. at Charlestown, during the sess. of the Ct. of Assist. For his serv. the governm. had many yrs. bef. made him a gr. of 1,000 acres, wh. he had never taken up, but had giv. to his d. Eliz. on her m. but his wid. Mary was compel. to petition for it in the yr. of his d. SIMON, Salem, third s. of the preced. m. a. 1679, Martha, d. of Richard Jacob of Ipswich, where he liv. some time, had at I. Jacob, b. perhaps 17 Sept. 1680; but at S. Josiah, 24 May 1682; Martha, 27 Jan. 1684; Simon, 4 Nov. 1685, d. under 2 yrs.; and Richard, 26 or 29 Jan. 1687; was freem. 1680, capt. in the E. war with the Ind. 1689, and deac. (had sec. w. 30 Apr. 1702, Eliz. wid. of John Walley, perhaps, but the Geneal. 371, ignores this sec. w.) and late in July 1722 took ano. w. Priscilla Buttolph, and d. 21 June 1731. THOMAS, Northampton 1668, br. of Nathaniel of the same, and subject to the same maledict. See Weller. Farmer notes in 1834, that gr. of this name at Harv. were 23; at Yale, 2; at other N. E. coll. 11. In ea. of the seven generat. from maj. Simon are one or more s. of the coll. to our times.

WILLET, ANDREW, Boston, merch. twelfth ch. seventh s. of Thomas, m. 3 Mar. 1694, Susanna, d. of the sec. Thomas Holbrook of Braintree,

had Francis, b. that yr.; Thomas, a. 1696, d. unm. at 29 yrs.; Ann;
Mary; and Martha; and he d. at South Kingstown, R. I. then call. Boston neck, 1712, if the fam. report, in Geneal. Reg. II. 376 be cor. tho.
for m. of Ann 1707, at 8 or 9 yrs. of age, it must be doubt. DANIEL,
Windsor 1672, d. 1690, of wh. we kn. not the f. nor whether he had w.
or ch. FRANCIS, Newbury, b. a. 1634 or 5, m. 20 Dec. 1669, Martha,
d. of Thomas Silver, had Martha, b. says Coffin, 24 Feb. foll.; Francis,
22 Feb. 1671; Sarah, 19 Jan. 1673; Joseph, 11 May 1674; William,
12 Feb. 1681; Thomas, 24 Dec. 1682; Hannah, 5 Aug. 1685; and
John, 9 July 1687. FRANCIS, Newbury, s. of the preced. m. 29 Jan.
1696, Eliz. Lowell, d. prob. of John of Boston, had Mary, b. 20 Sept.
1698; Judith, 10 May 1702; and Ruth, 2 May 1704; perhaps others,
but Coffin is silent. HEZEKIAH, Swanzey, tenth ch. fifth s. of Thomas,
m. 7 Jan. 1676, his first cousin, Ann, d. of John Brown the sec. and
was k. by the Ind. 1 July foll. JAMES, Rehoboth, eighth ch. third s. of
Thomas, m. 17 Apr. 1673, Eliz. d. of Peter Hunt of the same, wh. d.
July 1676. Whether he had ch. by her, or had ano. w. is unkn. but it
is highly prob. that he had fam. in 1681, when adm. inhab. of New
London. JOHN, Cambridge, eldest br. of the preced. m. prob. in 1663,
Abigail, youngest d. of deac. Edward Collins of the same, and d. 2 Feb.
foll. suddenly, no doubt, for his will, pro. within a fortnight, by his br.
Thomas, and the w. of Gen. Gookin, was nuncup. He provid. for a
posthum. ch. made f. Willet and f. Collins overseers, direct. mourning
for his w. and his three br. at Cambridge sch. and brs. Samuel C. and
Edward C. His wid. m. 12 May 1665, Lawrence Hammond. Caulkins, 266, claims one John for inhab. at New London 1682; but I have
strong doubt that some misprint or misspell. occurs. NATHANIEL,
Hartford 1642, m. Eliz. wid. of that Samuel Wakeman, k. at New
Providence 1641, and I judge that it was in that yr. for in June of the
next, he is with w. defend. in one suit, and plt. in ano. and in 1645, the
Ct. gave all the prop. of Wakeman to him, charg. to pay the s. on
reach. 21 yrs. £40. and ea. of the three ds. £20. at 18 yrs. By a sec.
w. Eleanor, d. of Jeremy Adams, he had Rebecca who m. 1690,
Thomas Rumney of Middletown; Abigail, m. John Bishop of New
Haven; Sarah, m. Zachary Sandford of Hartford; and Hannah, m.
1697, Baysey Baker of Hartford; and he d. 4 Jan. 1698, by his will
giv. est. of good amt. to his w. and four ds. SAMUEL, L. I. youngest
ch. of Thomas, was sheriff of Queen's Co. had, it is said, s. Edward, b.
1701, wh. liv. to 93 yrs. as is said, and had as many ch. as his f. was f.
of Marinus Willet, a soldier of distinct. in the revolut. war, and after
mayor of N. Y. wh. by tradit. was blessed with the same number of ch.
Elbert of Albany, wh. liv. to great age; and Isaac, lost at sea, 1758.

‡THOMAS, Plymouth, was in his youth assoc. with the Leyden congregat. 1629, and came over, as I judge, in the Lion, 1632, emb. in June.
See 4 Mass. Hist. Coll. I. 94, where the official docum. makes his name
Tobie W. He m. 6 July 1636, Mary, d. of John Brown, one of the
Assist. that yr. wh. many yrs. aft. liv. at Swansey; had Mary, b. 10
Nov. 1637, wh. by the mem. of the Willet fam. in Geneal. Reg. II.
376, is said to have d. without issue, 11 Dec. 1678, but in my opin. m.
22 Sept. 1658, Rev. Samuel Hooker of Farmington, bore him eleven
ch. and after bec. sec. w. 10 Aug. 1703 of Rev. Thomas Buckingham;
Martha, 6 Aug. 1639, m. 2 Dec. 1658, John Saffin of Scituate; John,
21 Aug. 1641; Sarah, 4 May 1643, wh. m. Rev. John Eliot, s. of the
apostle, and d. 13 June 1665; Rebecca, 2 Dec. 1644, d. at 7 yrs.;
Thomas, 1 Oct. 1646; Esther, 10 July 1648, tho. Col. Rec. says 6 July
1647, m. 24 Jan. 1672, Rev. Josiah Flint of Dorchester, and d. 26 July
1737; James, 23 Nov. 1649; Hezekiah, d. inf. 26 July 1651; Hezekiah, again, 17 Nov. 1653; David, 1 Nov. 1654, prob. d. soon; Andrew,
5 Oct. 1655; and Samuel, 27 Oct. 1658. He was entrust. with command at the trad.-ho. of the Plymouth people at Kennebeck, 1639, and
Winth. in Hist. I. 322, tells a pleasant incident of his peaceful control of
the Ind. He had been forcibly dispossess. some three or four yrs. bef.
of the establishm. at Penobscot, by D'Aulney, the French lieut.-gov. of
Acadia. See, in 3 Mass. Hist. Coll. VII. 92 and 94, the relations of the
affair by the rival French officers, D'Aulney and La Tour. He was an
Assist. 1651 to 1664, and when the Eng. conq. N. Y. he accomp. them,
and was made mayor. Not long aft. however, he went back to his first
friends, took sec. w. 19 Sept. 1671, Joanna, wid. of Rev. Peter Prudden,
resid. at Rehoboth, and Swanzey, d. at the latter 3, the gr.-st. says 4
Aug. 1674. The inscript. on the gr.-st. of the wid. (HIS ONLY W.)
says she d. 8 Jan. 1699, a. the 65th yr. of her age, wh. proves how
errors may be found in such places, as she could only be 5 yrs. old
when her first ch. by Prudden was b. Prob. the yr. of d. was 18 yrs.
earlier. See Prudden. What could explain the error of her gr.-st. that
she was the only w. is difficult to conject. Commonly we look to such
muniments of history for a different sort of failures in truth. Perhaps
only was error for *sec.* The brief mem. in Geneal. Reg. II. 376, cor-
rects some current mistakes, but makes some others. THOMAS, Newtown, L. I. s. prob. of the preced. d. bef. his f.

WILLEY, ABRAHAM, New London, s. of Isaac the first, m. Eliz. d. of
Thomas Mortimer, d. at Haddam 1692, leav. wid. Eliz. and ch. Thomas,
then aged 7½ yrs.; Abraham, 5⅓ yrs.; and Jane, 2 yrs. ALLEN,
Boston, call. husbandman, when rec. into the ch. 2 Nov. 1634, as was
his w. Alice on the Sunday foll. but no more is kn. EDWARD, Boston,

in Mr. Drake's list of names, Geneal. Reg. I. 139, should, perhaps, be giv. to Willis. ISAAC, Boston, by w. Joanna had Isaac, bapt. in her right, 2 Aug. 1640; Hannah, 6 Mar. 1642; rem. to Charlestown, there had Sarah, b. 19 June 1644; rem. next yr. with John Winth. to New London, as one of its first sett. Caulkins suppos. that "he and his w. had pass. the bds. of mid. age, and that all their ch. were b. bef." But this may be too large; at least we presume that Mary or Abraham, or both, and perhaps John (tho. he is said to have work. 1651, in build. the milldam, where he seems to be mistak. for his f.) were b. after the rem. He was selectman 1647, is seen on the freemen's list 1669; m. a. 1671, Ann, wid. who had been, Caulkins thinks, third w. but in my opin. only sec. of Andrew Lester, as I much distrust the exist. of any d. Joanna, w. of Robert Hempstead, to be tak. aft. his dec. by Lester; and he d. a. 1685. The wid. d. 1692. Hannah m. Peter Blatchford, and, next, Samuel Spencer of Haddam; Sarah m. John Terrill or Tyrrell, perhaps as sec. w. d. 7 Mar. 1712; and Mary m. Samuel Tubbs. ISAAC, New London, s. of the preced. m. at Boston, 8 June 1660, Frances, d. of Edward Burcham of Lynn, d. 1662, leav. young wid. who m. the same yr. Clement Miner. JOHN, N. London, br. of the preced. prob. younger, m. says Caulkins, 1670, tho. it seems prob. it was in 1668, Miriam, only d. of Miles Moore, d. 2 May 1688; and the Prob. rec. soon aft. gives the ages and names of ch. Isaac, 18¾ yrs.; Isabel, 17; John, 14¾; Miriam, 12; Allyn, 9; Abel, 6; and Mary, 4. JOHN, Dover 1689, s. of Thomas of the same, was in that yr. one of the favorers of Mass. jurisdict. as in Feb. 1690, he unit. with the great majority in petition. for it, and liv. 1697. RICHARD, Boston, m. Eliz. d. of capt. Edward Willis, had Ruth, and liv. not long aft. as from the will of Willis may be infer. SAMUEL, Dover, elder br. of John, by w. Mary had Samuel, b. 25 Feb. 1702; and perhaps more, bef. or aft. STEPHEN, Dover, elder br. of the preced. m. Abigail Pitman, perhaps d. of William, and was liv. 1694. THOMAS, Dover 1648, by w. Margaret had Stephen, b. a. 1649; Samuel; and John, 1659; was liv. 1677. WILLIAM, N. H. join. in petitn. 20 Feb. 1690, for Mass. jurisdict. may have been s. or gr.s. of the preced.

WILLIAMS, *ABRAHAM, Watertown, s. of William of the same, sw. fidel. 1652, m. a. 1659, Joanna, d. of the first William Ward, had Eliz. and William; liv. some time at Cambridge vil. but rem. to Marlborough, was freem. 1666; had Lydia, b. 1669; and John; was rep. 1679–81, and d. 29 Dec. 1712, aged 84; and his wid. d. 8 Dec. 1718, aged 90. ALEXANDER, Marshfield, of those able to bear arms in 1643. AMOS, Wethersfield, s. of Matthew of the same, had Amos, b. 1670; Samuel, 1675; Eliz. 1677; and Susanna, 1680, wh. all surv. him, and

he may have had more; and d. 20 Aug. 1683. His wid. Eliz. m. a.
1690, Thomas Hollister of W. ARTHUR, Windsor, freem. 1640, m. 30
Nov. 1647, Catharine, wid. of Joshua Carter of W. had Zebediah only;
rem. to Northampton 1659; and d. late in 1673, or early next yr. his
inv. being of 27 Mar. 1674. His wid. m. William Branch. AUGUS-
TINE, Stonington, rem. early to Kenilworth, by w. Hannah had Thomas;
Hannah, b. 1680; Daniel, 1683; Bethia, 1686; and Matthew, 1688.
His wid. m. John Browne. BELSHAZZAR, Salisbury, Coffin says d.
1651. BENJAMIN, Boston, s. of Robert of the same, by w. Rachel had
Nathaniel, b. 13 Apr. 1670; and by w. Ruth, had Benjamin, 2 Jan.
1673; by w. Rebecca had Solomon, 4 July 1678; and if it be the same
man, by w. Rachel had Eliz. 7 May 1687; and Eliz. again, 7 Jan.
1689. BENJAMIN, Taunton, s. of Richard of the same, m. 18 Mar.
1690, Rebecca, perhaps d. of George Macy of the same, had Rebecca,
b. 27 Nov. foll.; Josiah, 7 Nov. 1692; Benjamin, 31 July 1695; and
John, 27 Mar. 1699. CHARLES, Preston, whose f. is not ascert. m.
Sarah, d. of George Geer of New London, had Mark, b. 12 Jan. 1689;
Hannah, 3 Feb. 1693; Isaac, 11 July 1694; Daniel, 2 Dec. 1696;
David, 4 Nov. 1698; Jeradiah, 26 Oct. 1702, prob. d. young; Boaz, 10
Jan. 1706; and Jeradiah, again, 12 Jan. 1710. DANIEL, Providence,
not, I think, one of the first proprs. as Coffin inform. Farmer, for he is
not found among the freem. of 1655, but he own. alleg. to Charles II. on
1 June 1668, m. 1 Dec. 1676, Rebecca, d. of Zachary Rhoades, wid. of
the sec. Nicholas Power, had Mary; Roger, b. May 1680; Providence;
Daniel; Peleg; Patience; and Joseph; but the order of b. is not certain. He was s. of famous Roger. DAVID, Windsor 1662, d. 7 Sept.
1684, was prob. not m. EBENEZER, Dorchester, s. of Roger of the
same, m. Sept. 1674, Martha, d. of Richard Hall, was freem. 1683, d. 8
Feb. 1718, aged 69, says the gr.-st. EBENEZER, Stonington, s. of
Samuel the first, m. 24 Jan. 1687, or 8, at S. Mary, d. of Isaac Wheeler
of the same, had Theoda, b. 29 Oct. foll. d. young; a ch. 17 Sept. 1691,
d. in few days; Mary, 7 Jan. 1694; Samuel, 3 Feb. 1696; Theoda,
again, 3 Jan. 1701; Selina, 18 Dec. 1703; Eliz. and Ebenezer, tw. 21
Oct. 1705; and Martha, 3 Apr. 1708. His w. d. 3 Jan. foll. and he m.
12 July 1711, Sarah Hammond, had two ch. that d. without names;
Nathan, 24 July 1715; and Elisha, 12 Jan. 1719; and d. 13 Feb. 1747.
His wid. d. 5 Sept. 1751. EDWARD, Scituate 1643. ELEAZER, Salem
1635, join the ch. 6 Aug. 1637; had w. Eliz. and d. Eliz. bapt. 6 Apr.
1663, perhaps aft. d. of f. FRANCIS, Portsmouth, sent over by Gorges
and Mason, the patentees, 1631, and when their Gov. Neal went home,
they made W. the successor. He seems to have act. with discret. and
when Mass. acquir. the rule of the country he had authty. with Brad-

street and others to hold judicial power at Dover, as in our first Vol. of
Rec. is seen. He was, however, attract. to Barbadoes a. 1645. FRAN-
CIS, Boston, by w. Mary had Francis, b. 12 Oct. 1686. FREEBORN,
Providence, eldest s. of famous Roger, m. a Hart of Newport, of whose
bapt. name or her f's. I kn. nothing, had Mary, b. a. 1663, wh. m. Gov.
Samuel Cranston. His wid. m. Gov. Walter Clark, as his third w.
GEORGE, Salem, freem. 14 May 1634, had Jonathan, bapt. 25 Dec.
1636; Samuel, 12 Aug. 1638; Joseph, 10 May 1640 ; Bethia, 13 Nov.
1642; and George, 1 Sept. 1644 ; beside elder ch. John ; Mary; and
Sarah ; was made an offic. of the custom-ho. in the Col. admin. 1654,
and d. in the same yr. From his will of 23 Sept. 1654, of wh. w. Mary
and s. John were excors. pro. Nov. foll. is seen, that Mary had double
portion " in respect of her infirmity." His wid. Mary d. the same yr.
her will of 1 Oct. was pro. next mo. Mary m. Richard Bishop, and she
and two ch. are rememb. in will of her f. GREGORY, Isle of Shoals,
was constable 1674, says Farmer's MS. GRIFFIN, Boston, by w. Sarah
had Sarah, b. 2 Jan. 1686. HENRY, Scarborough 1651, was one of the
three betrust. by Rigby, the patentee of a large province, as Assist. and
selectman 1652 and 69, was wound. 10 Oct. 1676 at Saco. Of HENRY,
wh. was in 1683, at Derby, and d. 1687, I find not that he had fam. and
for CHARLES of the same, I kn. nothing but as bef. said, and that in
1686, he was one of the petitnrs. for gr. of the town of Preston. HUGH,
Boston, hatter, call. also " a single man," when he join. our ch. 1 Jan.
1642; freem. 18 May foll. was prob. never m. at least his will of 21
Oct. 1674, ment. no w. or ch. but gives one third of his est. to ch. of br.
Hilton of Charlestown, and two thirds to his sis. Mary Hale and her
childr. On 12 Nov. foll. when the excors. friend John, and sis. Hale
renounce their trust, he is call. late of Block Isl. wh. leads me to
imagine him to be the one against wh. Caulkins, Hist. of New London
248, says action for defamat. of his w. was 1665, brot. by Thomas
Beeby. *ISAAC, Newton, s. of Robert of Roxbury, was lieut. freem.
1685, by w. Martha, d. of deac. William Parke of Roxbury, had Isaac,
wh. d. 7 Mar. 1661, very young ; Isaac, again, b. 11 Dec. 1661, bapt.
16 Mar. foll.; Martha, 27 Dec. 1663; William, 2 Feb. 1665, H. C.
1683, min. of Hatfield, ancest. of a long line of disting. clerg.; John,
31 Oct. 1667, in wh. date the error of Fam. Geneal. is correct. by Jackson ; Eleazer, 22 Oct. 1669 ; Hannah, 8 Oct. 1671 ; Eliz.; the two last
being lost from Fam. Geneal. ; and Thomas, 23 Dec. not as that book
tells, Oct. 1673. By sec. w. Judith Cooper, m. at Taunton, 13 Nov.
1677, had Peter, 31 Aug. 1680; Mary; Sarah, 2 Oct. 1688; Ephraim,
21 Oct. 1691 ; was rep. 1692, and aft. oft. but in favor of this last ch.
by influence of the mo. the f. wh. d. 11 Feb. 1707, had made in 1704,

an improp. convey. confirm. by his last will, wh. was set aside. His
wid. d. 1724. ISAAC, Salem, cordwain. by w. Margery had Eliz. b. 23
Aug. 1660; Isaac, 20 Dec. 1662; Benjamin, 18 Mar. 1664; and Sarah
and Ebenezer of date not kn. but all exc. Benjamin nam. in the will of
wid. 1702. Eliz. m. 1 Apr. 1678, Joseph Mansfield; and Sarah m. a
Lander. Ebenezer's w. is nam. in the will of his mo. but nothing of
him or her has reach. me. JAMES, a preacher at Plymouth, of wh.
resid. that must have been short, no acco. is found. JAMES, Hartford,
serv. of Nathaniel Sanford, at first, m. 1691, Sarah, d. of Thomas Richardson of Farmington, had James, bapt. 1693; Hepzibah, 1696; Sarah,
1699; Samuel, 1700; Abigail, 1707; and Daniel, 1710. He rem. to
Wallingford, but date of his d. is unkn. JENKIN, Scarborough 1673.
JOHN, Boston, ship carpenter, lately come to this country, was hang. for
murder, 28 Sept. 1637. JOHN, by Farmer seen at Piscataqua 1631, of
wh. is no more told. JOHN, Scituate 1643, had prob. been some yrs. in
the Col. as Deane thot. he came with Hatherly in 1632, brot. s. John,
Edward, and d. Ann, perhaps also, younger d. Mary, and w. Ann. By
his will of 10 Dec. 1667, he names these, and permits us to infer, in
connex. with collat. knowledge, that Anthony Dodson, wh. m. 1651,
Mary, was then d. that Ann had been 1632, w. of John Barker, was
then w. of John Pratt, and that she, by the former h. had Deborah,
then w. of William Burden, and John, Abraham, and Mary Barker.
JOHN, Newbury, had (perhaps by two ws.) Sarah; John; Mary, b. 20
Sept. 1641; and Lydia, 15 Mar. 1643; prob. rem. to Haverhill; had
there b. Joseph, 18 Apr. 1647; Sarah, m. 5 May 1646, John Ayer.
His sec. w. was Jane, and his will of 9 Dec. 1670, was pro. 18 Mar.
1674. JOHN, Windsor 1639, m. 29 June 1644, Mary Burkly, if we
follow Parsons in his spelling, Geneal. Reg. V. 364; but a more practised eye reads the name Brelly, Bralley, or Burlly, perhaps the same as
Burleigh in our times; and we gain no light from the early dwellers at
W. had John, b. 26 Mar. 1646; Nathaniel, 25 Oct. 1647; Rebecca, 20
Apr. 1649; Hannah, 13 Apr. 1651; Mary and Eliz. tw. 5 Jan. 1653;
Abiel, 2 Sept. 1655; and Abigail, 31 May 1658; and he d. 1665. Of
the five ds. we kn. that Rebecca m. 1670, Obadiah Cooley of Springfield; Hannah m. 1677, Nathaniel Bancroft of Westfield; Mary m.
1678, John Gunn; Eliz. d. in few wks.; and Abigail m. 1681, Edward
Griswold; Abiel may have d. unm. JOHN, Salem, by w. Eliz. had
John, b. 29 May 1664; Henry, 29 June 1666; George, 2 July 1668,
d. in few days; Mary, 25 Aug. 1669; George, again, 1 Mar. 1671;
and Ruth, 4 Aug. 1674. His will of 22 Oct. 1696, pro. 15 Feb. foll.
names w. Eliz. (perhaps not the mo. of the ch.); John; Eliz. w. of
Thomas Marston; Mary; Ruth, w. of Abraham Purchase; and Sarah,

d. of his s. Joseph. In 1690, he was aged 70, with w. ten yrs. older, says Felt. JOHN, Boston, butcher, may be the testator, of whose will, Dec. 1684, pro. 26 Mar. foll. speak. of two ds. Hannah (wh. was b. 27 Apr. 1661), and Sarah, wh. were m. to wh. only 5s. ea. is the beq. gives all est. to w. Mary to bring up two younger ch. Rachel and Martha. It may be read in Vol. VI. 492 ; but no other informat. is gain. of him, exc. that in 1673, he receives deeds of two est. in B. JOHN, Roxbury, s. of Robert of the same, b. prob. in Eng. and no doubt eldest, d. 6 Oct. 1658, as is seen at the Prob. off. when admin. was giv. to his f. nine days aft. It is observ. that neither ch. nor town rec. ment. him. nor did the Fam. Genealogist, nor Ellis, the histor. of the place, express any knowl. of ever hear. of such a man. By the ch. rec. I find his d. (unless, wh. is not wholly unreasonab. the name be mistak. by the abbrev. for that of his f. Robert) Eliz. in full commun. bef. the d. of her f. but wh. was her mo. is unkn. JOHN, Scituate 1643, fit to bear arms, prob. s. of John of the same, was a capt. d. 22 June 1694, aged 70. He serv. in Philip's war, and had command of a comp. when the great Ind. sachem was k. His est. was good, but his will of 1691, names no w. nor ch. and to his relatives, serv. and friends, gives freely. JOHN, Boston, s. of the first Nathaniel of the same, m. 1670, Ann, eldest d. of Dr. John Alcock of Roxbury, as in the m. contr. of rec. Vol. VI. 241, may be read ; rem. to Newport, but first had at B. Mary ; Ann ; Palsgrave ; Nathaniel ; and Arabella, as from his will of 18 Apr. 1687 is found, in wh. provis. is made for them, and ano. ch. expected. That instr. was pro. 22 June 1688, before Francis Brinley, Esq. wh. had by Andros, been constit. judge for that portion of his dominions ; but it was requir. to be rec. here in Boston, as in Vol. X. 329 appears. It refers to br. Nathaniel, br.-in-law, Zechariah Whitman, and made excors. w. with s. Nathaniel when he should come of age. JOHN, Windsor, s. of John of the same, was in the list of freem. 1669, m. 8 Aug. 1672, Bethia, d. of Thomas Parsons, wid. of Thomas Mascall of the same, had Francis, b. 25 May 1673 ; and John and Ebenezer, tw. 7 Jan. 1676. His w. d. 1681, and he m. 1686, wid. Esther Egglestone ; but it is unkn. whether he had more ch. JOHN, Boston 1670, styles hims. of Camberwell, Co. Surrey, late of London, merch. in B. but to appropr. to ea. John severally, the births for the first sixty or seventy yrs. on Boston rec. when the designat. of the parents, is barely, John and Ann, John and Eliz. John and Jane, John and Mary, thro. various generat. must be undertak. with high presumpt. and would be abandon. with utter despair. Oft. one John is blessed with a ch. b. in few wks. after ano. John has obtain. the similar favor. JOHN, Haverhill, s. prob. of John of the same, m. 9 Sept. 1661, Rebecca, d. of Anthony Colby of

Salisbury, had Sarah, b. 27 June 1662; Mary, 24 Nov. 1663; a d. prob. Rebecca, May 1666; a d. 1 Aug. 1668, d. in few days; Mercy, 4 Dec. 1669; Susanna, 11 Apr. 1672. His w. d. 10 June foll. and he m. 5 May 1675, Esther, wid. of John Bond of H. He took o. of fidel. 28 Nov. 1677, at the same time with his br. Joseph; and he d. 30 Apr. 1698, leav. wid. Esther. See Geneal. Reg. XII. 297. JOHN, Salem, s. perhaps of John of the same, m. 8 Dec. 1686, Sarah Manning, d. prob. of Richard of Ipswich, had Sarah, b. 18 Aug. 1689. Other ch. he had, perhaps by ano. w. to wit, Anstis, 25 Dec. 1700; John, 14 Nov. 1702; Henry, 2 Feb. 1705; Mary, 8 May 1706; George, 14 Mar. 1708; and Richard, 27 Aug. 1710. JOHN, New London, is seen, by Miss Caulkins, liv. on Groton side, and m. a. 1686, Jane, wid. of Hugh Hubbard, d. of Carey Latham; but even her diligence could learn no more exc. that he d. 3 Dec. 1741, at gr. age, as was his w. and left only s. Peter. JOHN, Deerfield, s. of deac. Samuel of Roxbury, began soon after leav. coll. to fit for the pulpit, and m. 21 July 1687, Eunice, d. of Rev. Eleazer Mather of Northampton, and had Eleazer, b. 1 July 1688, H. C. 1708, and if we follow the very doubtful Fam. Geneal. even an earlier s. Eliakim, who d. young; preach. first at D. 1686, but was not ord. bef. 18 Oct. 1688; had also, Samuel, 4 Jan. 1690, d. at 23 yrs.; Esther, 10 Apr. 1691; Stephen, 14 May 1693, H. C. 1713; Eunice, 16 Sept. 1696; Warham, 7, bapt. perhaps 16 Sept. 1699; Eliakim, again; John, 15 Jan. 1704, k. by the Ind. on 29 of next mo. as was his young br. Eliakim; and all the rest of the fam. exc. Eleazer, were tak. towards Canada, but his w. d. of suffering on the road. He m. aft. resettlem. of D. Abigail Allen of Windsor, had Abigail, 1708; John, 23 Nov. 1709, d. young; Eliakim, again, 6 Feb. 1711; Elijah, 13 Nov. 1712; and Sarah, Sept. 1716; and he d. 12 June 1729. The story of his Redeemed Captive has been very much read, in all succeed. times, and the ch. Stephen publ. also, a very agreeable narrat. JOSEPH, Taunton, s. of Richard of the same, m. 28 Nov. 1667, Eliz. d. of George Watson of Plymouth, had Eliz. b. 30 July 1669, drown. at 19 yrs.; Richard, 26 Nov. 1671, d. under 17 yrs.; Mehitable, 7 June 1676; Joseph, 13 Feb. 1679; Benjamin, 15 Oct. 1681; Ebenezer, 21 Apr. 1685; Phebe, 25 Sept. 1687; and Richard, 26 Mar. 1689; and d. 17 Aug. 1692. JOSEPH, Salem, s. perhaps youngest, of George of the same, m. 20 Nov. 1661, Sarah, d. of Thomas Browning; had Mary, b. 19 Aug. 1662, d. soon; Joseph, Aug. 1663, d. in few mos.; Joseph, again, 17 Mar. 1665; Sarah, 28 Oct. 1666; George, 22 Feb. 1670; Daniel, 3 Jan. 1672; Benjamin and Abigail, tw. 7 Dec. 1673; and David, 7 Sept. 1676. He d. 1682, at least his wid. returns inv. on 27 June of that yr. JOSEPH, Boston, by w. Lydia

had Joseph, b. 14 Feb. 1670; William, 13 Dec. 1671; Richard, 8 Feb.
1673, tho. rec. would make the mo. to be Eliz. wh. is, in my opin. a cleri-
cal blunder, as the foll. seven ch. are all count. for Lydia; that is to say,
Hannah, 20 May 1674; Daniel, 25 Dec. 1676; Hannah, again, 26 May
1679; Jeremiah, 22 Aug. 1683; Eliz. 22 Aug. 1686; Eliz. again, 9
Dec. 1688; and Mary, 6 Nov. 1689. ‡JOSEPH, Providence, youngest s.
of famous Roger, wh. gives, in let. of Feb. 1660 to his frd. Gov. Winth.
account of the youth's cure of epilepsy by taking tobacco, and the cure
did not shorten his days. [See 3 Mass. Hist. Coll. X. 28.] He m. 17
Dec. 1669, Lydia, youngest d. of Thomas Olney the first, had Joseph, b.
26 Sept. 1670, d. soon; Thomas, 16 Feb. 1672; Joseph, again, 10 Nov.
1673; Mary, June 1676; James, 24 Sept. 1680; and Lydia, 26 Apr.
1683; and d. 17 Aug. 1724 at Cranston, where the gr.-st. is encumb.
with more doleful verse than is often seen. His wid. d. three wks. aft.
He engag. alleg. to Charles II. 31 May 1666; was an Assist. 1704, and
on 28 Sept. of that yr. verif. the declarat. made by his f. in 1682.
JOSEPH, Haverhill, youngest s. of the first John of the same, took o. of
alleg. 1677, m. 18 Nov. 1674, Mary Fuller of Barnstable, d. of the first
Samuel, had Sarah, b. 17 Nov. 1675; Mary, 29 Nov. 1677; John, 17
Feb. 1680; Hannah, 30 Sept. 1683; but no more is told of him.
MATTHEW, Wethersfield, by w. Susannah had Amos, b. 1645; Matthew, 1647, d. soon; Matthew, again, 1651; and Samuel, 1653. Of
him the Col. Rec. of Trumbull tells no good, but that he seems to be d.
in 1664. MATTHEW, Dover, tax. there 1657–1668, was perhaps br. of
the first William of the same. NATHANIEL, Boston, glover, as he grew
to be, but call. laborer, on adm. to the ch. 26 May 1639, freem. 13 May
foll. by w. Mary had Ruth, bapt. 2 June 1639, a yr. old; Eliz. 18 Oct.
1640, tho. town rec. says b. 21; Nathaniel, 25 Sept. 1642, "a. six days
old;" John, 18 Aug. 1644, "a. three days old;" Mary, b. 30 Nov.
1646, and when bapt. 6 Dec. foll. is call. "a. a day old;" and Hannah,
bapt. 7 Jan. 1649, "a. nine days old." He was held in good esteem,
had fair est. and d. 1661. His will was of 22 Apr. and his inv. of 7
May in that yr. His wid. m. Peter Brackett of Braintree, d. Ruth m.
Joseph Belknap of Boston, and Mary m. John Viall, jr. of Braintree.
NATHANIEL, Taunton, s. of Richard of the same, m. 17 Nov. 1668,
Eliz. d. of John Rogers of Marshfield or Duxbury, had John, b. 27
Aug. 1675; Nathaniel, 9 Apr. 1679; and Eliz. 18 Apr. 1686. NA-
THANIEL, Boston, s. of Nathaniel of the same, was much engag. in
Philip's war, as a commissa. in 1676, by w. Mary, had Nathaniel, b.
Aug. 1675, H. C. 1693, by the careful Mr. Whitmore thot. to be suc-
cessor of famous Master Cheever in the Boston sch.; Eliz. 28 Feb.
1678, d. soon; Oliver, 21 Aug. 1679; Eliz. again, 22 Jan. 1682; James,

3 Mar. 1687; and Sarah, 30 Sept. 1692; freem. 1676; and had gr. of ld. in 1679. NATHANIEL, Windsor, s. of the first John of the same, m. 3 Oct. 1681, Mary, d. of John Owen of the same, had Mary, b. 1682; rem. to Westfield, there had Abiel, 23 Mar. 1684; Rebecca, 27 Sept. 1685; Eliz. 1687; John, 3 Nov. 1689, d. next yr.; Nathaniel, 25 Aug. 1691; Abigail, 1693; Hannah; Keziah, 1701; Naomi, 1703; Orpha, 1706; and John, again; and d. 1711. His wid. with two s. and nine ds. enjoy. his est. 1714, and she d. 1750. NICHOLAS, Roxbury, freem. 1652, but he is not nam. by Ellis, nor can I find any acco. of him, exc. that Robert in his will calls him br. and beq. to him 30s. a yr. charg. upon the est. therein giv. to his eldest s. Samuel. OWEN, Newport, among the freem. 1655, rem. in few yrs. to Norwich, there d. 1682; and, it is said, that descend. are in Preston, wh. was pt. of N. PARK, Lebanon, youngest s. of deac. Samuel of Roxbury, by w. Priscilla had Bathsheba, b. at Roxbury, 28 Aug. 1701 (unkn. to the compiler of the fam. geneal.), Samuel, John, Ebenezer, Eleazer, William, Theoda, Sarah, Eliz. and Martha; but the print. vol. gives no date to either s. or d. yet tells that his w. d. in 1742, aged 71, and he only ten yrs. older in 1751. Roxbury rec. gives John, b. 6 June 1706. RICHARD, Saco, d. in Oct. 1636, engag. with Gov. Cradock, as "a clapboard cleaver," may be the same who had been fined for drunk. in Mass. Mar. 1634, tho. the same Vol. I. of our Col. Rec. shows the fine was remit. perhaps bec. it could not be collect. four yrs. after. *RICHARD, Taunton 1637, went from Salem, whither Baylies I. 284, suppos. he came, bec. his w. Frances Dighton was sis. of the first w. of Capt. Endicott, wh. is a sad error, as it was Gov. Thomas Dudley's w. that was meant. Perhaps the historian of Plymouth was misled in his assumpt. of first resid. at S. by ano. suppos. that he was br. of Roger; but either of these seem to me very improb. tho. not so wild as the tradit. that he was a relat. of Oliver Cromwell. He was one of the first purch. of the territ. from the Ind. and was the chief male inhab. for many yrs. sprung from Glamorgansh. and m. it is said, by Emery I. 44, in Gloucestersh. had ch. John, prob. d. young; Samuel, Joseph, Nathaniel, bapt. 7 Feb. 1641, Thomas, Benjamin, Eliz. and Hannah; not one has date of b. nor is there approxima. for any of the eight, exc. Eliz. a. 1647, prob. therefore one of the oldest half, wh. m. John Bird of Dorchester; Hannah m. John Parmenter of Boston, as his sec. w. As it is very clear, that all these ch. were b. long after he sett. at T. I greatly distr. the tradit. of his very early coming to our country, and more the Gloucestersh. w. He was rep. 1646, 8, 50, and sev. later yrs. but the time of his d. is not found. Descend. have been num. and highly respect. RICHARD, Boston, had Phebe, b.

Aug. 1643; and Benjamin, Aug. 1645, if the substitute for Robert in the rec. marg. of the vol. of births be adjudg. reasonable, when the ch. rec. of the bapt. of Phebe, a. eight days old, on 3 Sept. 1643, assigns her to Robert; and the same Robert had s. Benjamin, tho. the ch. rec. has John, of Robert, bapt. 7 Sept. 1645. RICHARD, Branford 1646, had Samuel, b. 13 Sept. 1655; and Daniel, 15 Apr. 1657; rem. to Fairfield 1658, but soon rem. again, and it is not kn. to what place. One Richard was a town officer, says Mitchell, at Bridgewater, in 1665. RICHARD, Stonington, or the disput. Narraganset territ. 1670, in 1677 had long controv. with Isaac Hall, a. lds. at Misquamicut or Squama-cuck, or such Ind. name, now perhaps Westerly, in wh. W. beat H. at last. RICHARD, Boston, by w. Bathsheba, had Joseph, b. 3 Dec. 1672, d. very soon; John, 24 Oct. 1673; and Joseph, again, 7 Mar. 1677. RICHARD, New Haven, a physician in 1691, of wh. no more is heard. ROBERT, Roxbury 1637, freem. 2 May 1638, came, it is said, from Nor-wich, Co. Norfolk, with w. Eliz. by fam. tradit. nam. Stratton, and ch. Samuel, Mary, if not more, as that ch. was five yrs. old, and I think ano. s. John was a passeng. with his f. for clear is it, that he was not b. at R. where the only b. appear, Isaac, 1 Sept. 1638; Stephen, 8 Nov. 1640; and in the fam. geneal. is nam. also Thomas, by Ellis said to be b. after, and in the Hist. said to have d. young; but I doubt both the authorities, as neither b. nor d. after long search is found in the rec. of either town or ch. Still the deficiency of rec. is seen in other respects, as the will of 26 Nov. 1685, names gr.ch. Deborah Totman, and Eliz. Robinson, for wh. I find not the mos. so that we are uncertain, whether he had two ds. m. or three. His eldest d. Mary m. Nicholas Wood; w. Eliz. d. last of June, or 28 July 1674, by strange carelessness in the town rec. call. 80 yrs. old, when she prob. was a dozen yrs. younger. He m. 3 Nov. 1675, Margaret, wid. of John Fearing of Hingham, but whether he had a third w. is less certain, tho. in fam. geneal. he is sup-plied with one, Miss Martha Strong, said to have d. 1704, in her 92d yr. He d. 1 Sept. 1693, in the first art. of his will providing for the per-formance of the covenant with his w. ROBERT, Boston, in 1641 was, with Edward Goodwin, lessee of Winisemet ferry, wh. may render it prob. that he was s. of Thomas, adm. of the ch. 10 Apr. 1642, freem. 10 May 1643, had Joseph, b. July 1641, bapt. 17 Apr. 1642; Phebe, 3 Sept. 1643, a. 8 days old; John, 7 Sept. 1645, wh. d. young; and Ben-jamin. His will of 12 Oct. 1677, pro. 30 Jan. foll. gives lds. to his eldest s. Joseph and Benjamin, beq. to d. Phebe Eglin and her childr. to the eldest s. of Joseph and of Benjamin, and gr.d. Mary Eglin. ROBERT, Boston, of wh. I kn. no. more than is seen in the diary of Sewall, where he says, under 25 Aug. 1695, " R. W. the grave-digger, bell-ringer,

&c. &c. d." ROBERT, Providence, tho. among the freem. of 1655, and a br. of the noble founder of Providence, yet little more is kn. of him, but that he was, ten yrs. later, a sch.-master at Newport. ROBERT, Killingworth 1667, was propound. to be freem. 1669, had a d. b. 1671, but no more is kn. of him. Ano. ROBERT was of Oyster Bay, L. I. 1650; and Farmer MS. ment. one of N. H. as early as 1670, but he could not detain him there, certain. not long eno. for any story of him to reach us. ROBERT, Boston, by w. Margery, had Martha, b. 7 May 1672; Jonathan, 22 Sept. 1673; Mary, 2 Dec. 1675; James, 20 Feb. 1678; Jacob, 19 Dec. 1679; Eliz. 8 Nov. 1681; Robert, 13 Jan. 1686, prob. d. young; Hepzibah, 1 Nov. 1688; and Robert, again, 3 Apr. 1691. Dr. Thaddeus William Harris, the late learned libr. at our Univ. count. the b. of his ancest. deac. Jonathan Williams eight yrs. too early. See p. 319 of the Geneal. and Hist. of the Williams fam. ROGER, Dorchester 1630, came in the Mary and John, prob. with w. Frances. req. adm. as freem. 19 Oct. of that yr. and was sw. on 18 May foll. serv. on the jury 30 Sept. of the first yr. upon the k. of Bratcher by Palmer, rem. early, prob. 1636 or 7, to Windsor, there was in good repu. had comfort. est. serv. on the jury 1642, 3, and 4, lost his w. by d. 10 Dec. 1645. He soon aft. 1647, or in that yr. sold ho. and ld. and came back to D. m. 1649 or bef. Lydia Bates, d. of the first James, had Ebenezer, b. Jan. 1650, in that yr. call. hims. of Boston, when he sold ld. in D. to Thomas Thaxter; but no more is told of him. § ‡ * ROGER, Providence, the great assert. of relig. freedom, b. in Wales 1599, as uncert. tradit. says, and she would make him, partly, at least, educ. at Oxford, where ano. Roger, or Roderic, was adm. 30 Apr. 1624, wh. was s. of William, and by Felt in Eccles. Hist. I. 147, receiv. as our N. E. reformer, wh. to me, seems nearly impossib. But a strong prob. is, that he was not b. earlier than 1605; and the fact is, he was bred up at the Charter Ho. as in mod. days the sch. is call. but when W. was there, Sutton's Hospital. On that foundat. he was chos. a scholar 25 June 1621, and on 9 July 1624, gain. an exhibition under powerf. patronage. This we learn from Mrs. Anne Sadler, d. of the gr. lawyer, Sir Edward Coke, in a collection of letters, at the library of Trinity Coll. Cambridge, by Williams, writ. a. 1652, to her; she wrote on the back of one of them (wh. had shocked her devotion to ch. and king) that her f. "took such liking to him, that he put him to Sutton's Hospitall, and he was the sec. that was placed there," mean. perhaps by his gr. patron. From this favor of Coke arose, prob. the tradit. that our benign. founder of Providence had enjoy. the protection of the Lord Ch. Justice of the Common Pleas, had been support. at the Univ. of Oxford, and stud. the law for a profession under the great oracle of jurisprudence. But from

Winth.'s Hist. we kn. he had been a minister. The exhibition obtain. in the London Inst. 9 July 1624, seems to disprove his identi. with the stud. ent. at Jesus Coll. Oxford in Apr. preced. and my ignorance of the rules and customs of the Charter Ho. forbids me to speak with confidence. To write his life and illustrate his charact. has long been felt as a duty by the scholars of the beautiful city he found. and after sev. attempts more may be said. Professor Elton, wh. sev. yrs. since, publish. his biogr. has had means of discover. how he had been deceiv. as to the b. and educ. of the amiable hero; and we hope for ano. ed. of his vol. If at either of the Eng. Univ. he was educ. wh. seems very uncert. to me, Cambridge is entitl. to the honor, rather than Oxford. He came from Bristol, 1 Dec. 1630, in the Lion, and reach. Boston 9 Feb. foll. with w. Mary; and in few wks. during wh. he was desir. to settle in the ch. of Boston, by their *unanimous* choice, in the spring of 1631, as he tells, in a letter (most characteristic of the writer, equal in value to any one in a thousand of our New Eng. epistles) to Rev. John Cotton of Plymouth, print. in Mass. Hist. Transactions of the Soc. 1855 — 8 pp. 313–6, but his tender conscience did not dare to officiate to "an unseparated people." This statement of Williams I accept without hesitat. tho. in a note on p. 406 of Vol. I. of Hist. of N. E. by Prof. Palfrey, whose eye had been blessed with the orig. MS. a doubt might have pass. thro. his mind to extort the remark : "it is very extraordin. that the fact is not ment. in any record of the time." But no contempo. rec. exc. that of the Col. would possib. contain it, for no other is in exist. Our earliest rec. of Boston civil affairs begins abrupt. in the middle of a sentence, Sept. 1634, preced. pages being lost, yet that is four or five yrs. bef. we have an orig. ecclesiastic. rec. of any thing exc. bapt. Even the name of Williams, our gr. reformer, is FIRST read in Col. Rec. Sept. 1635, being that of his banishm. Vol. I. 160 ; as ea. of the sev. prior read. of Roger Williams manifest. refers to the Dorchester man. But quite concur. with the sense and even *phrase* of that let. to Cotton is the lang. of Winth. Hist. I. 53 in the order of Court, recit. that he "had refused to join with the congregat. [i. e. church] at Boston, because they would not make a pub. declarat. of their repent. for hav. commun. with the chhs. of Eng." &c. That order was in Apr. 1631, less than a fortnight after Boston ch. was left without a min. by Wilson's depart. for home, and two and a half yrs. bef. com. of Cotton's father. Assuredly he was not likely to *refuse* before he was *asked*. He next went to be assoc. with Skelton at Salem, in teach. that congreg. but was more wanted at Plymouth, in the autumn of that yr. and contin. good pt. of two yrs. to minister there; hardly had he got back to Salem, where the people wish. him as successor of Skelton, bef. his overscrupul. conscience made him and others trouble; and in two yrs. the affections of his people could not prevent the Gen. Ct. from banishm. of their teacher. He had been excommun. at S. for refus. to bring his ch. to bapt. &c. In the winter of 1635–6, he meekly obey. the cruel sentence, and next spring, or more prob. in June, laid the foundat. of the prosperous city by him, with pious emotion, call. Providence. See the opening chap. of Arnold's Hist. of R. I. There he was usually held in much honor, tho. occasional. overborne by antagon. against wh. his revenge was exhaust. in show. kindness. He always had the friendship of Gov. Winth. tho. circumstances, consist. with the honor of both, enforced their long and sad separat. As the Col. agent in London, or chief Magistr. here, he was equal. discreet and disinterest. to his d. in Apr. 1683. Of his w. Mary, the fam. name, or date of the m. is unkn. but she came with her h. and may have had ch. in Eng. for only six can be precisely kn. to be b. on our side of the water; Mary is said to have been b. at Plymouth, the first week in Aug. 1633; Freeborn, at Salem, late in Oct. 1635; Providence, late in Sept. 1638, wh. d. unm. Mar. 1686; Mercy, 15 July 1640; Daniel, a. 15 Feb. 1642; and Joseph, early in Dec. 1643. Mercy m. Resolved Waterman, and next, Samuel Winsor; for third h. having John Rhodes, and bear. ch. to all; Freeborn m. Thomas Hart of Newport, and next, Walter Clark, the Gov. of the Col. ROGER, Milford, d. 1656, leav. very little inv. SAMUEL, Yarmouth 1643, then of age to bear arms, but he may have been old, or liv. not long. SAMUEL, Roxbury, eldest s. of Robert of the same, b. in Eng. a. 1632, was a shoemaker, join. the ch. when under 16 yrs. freem. 1650, a deac. m. 2 Mar. 1654, Theoda, eldest d. of deac. William Park of the same, had Eliz. b. 1, bapt. 11 Feb. foll. and d. 10 of next mo.; Samuel, 15, bapt. 27 Apr. 1656; Martha, 29 Apr. 1657, unless the rec. be, as I doubt not it is, wrong, bapt. 28 Mar. 1658, d. or was bur. 6 Feb. 1661; Eliz. again, 11, bapt. 26 Feb. 1660; Theoda, 27 July, bapt. 3 Aug. 1662, d. at 16 yrs.; John, 10 Dec. 1664, H. C. 1683; Ebenezer, 6 Dec. 1666; Deborah, 20 Nov. 1668; Martha, again, 19 May 1671; Abigail, 12 July 1674; and Park, 11 Jan. 1677; and d. 28 Sept. 1698, aged 65. His wid.'m. Stephen Park, and d. 26 Aug. 1718. SAMUEL, Salem, a cooper, sec. s. of George of the same, m. 2 Apr. 1662, Mary, eldest d. of Hilliard Veren, I suppose, had Samuel, b. 26 Dec. foll. d. in few wks.; Samuel, again, 21 Nov. 1664; Mary, 7 Mar. 1667, d. soon; Hilliard, 26 Dec. 1668; George, 12 Feb. 1670, d. in few wks.; Sarah, 15 July 1672; Mary, again, 27 Nov. 1674, d. young; Richard, 3 Mar. 1679; Mary, again, 2 Mar. 1681; Joshua, May 1683; and Nathaniel, 25 Jan. 1687; and d. 1689, betw. the date of his will, 23 May, and its prob. 26 Nov. of that yr. SAMUEL, Taunton, sec. s. of Richard of the same, m. Jane, d. of Thomas Gilbert, had Mary; Sarah; Hannah, b. a. 1670; Seth, a. 1676; Samuel, a. 1680; and Daniel, a. 1682. SAMUEL, Roxbury, eldest s. of Samuel of the same, m. 24 Feb. 1680, Sarah May, d. prob. of the sec. John of the same, had Samuel, b. 6 Apr. 1681; Theoda, 8 Dec. 1682; John, 1 Dec. 1684; a ch. 1 Jan. 1687, d. same day; Sarah, 19 May 1688; Ebenezer, 12 Aug. 1690; Eliz. 12 Jan. 1693; Eleazer, 20 Feb. 1695; William, 24 Apr. 1698; and Martha, 10 Aug. 1701. His w. d. 29 Dec. 1712, and he m. 28 Apr. 1720, Dorothy, wid. of William Denison, d. of Thomas Weld; and d. 8 Aug. 1735. SIMON, Hatfield, took o. of alleg. 8 Feb. 1679. STEPHEN, Roxbury, fourth s. of Robert of the same, m. Sarah Wise, d. of Joseph of the same, had Sarah, b. 13 Aug. 1667; Mary, 20 Dec. 1669; Eliz. 1 Oct. 1672; Bethia, 26 Apr. 1676; Stephen, 27 Aug. 1678; Robert, 13 July 1680, d. at three mos.; Joseph, 24 Feb. 1682; John, 1 Dec. 1684; Henry, 9 Apr. 1686, d. at 4 mos.; Grace, 2 Apr. 1688; Catharine, 9 Nov. 1690, d. at 16 yrs.; and Thomas, 27 July 1694, d. in few wks.; and d. 15 Feb. 1720. His wid. in her will of 18 June 1723, pro. 30 Aug. 1728, names s. Stephen and John, ds. Mary, w. of Samuel Story; Eliz. Tucker; Grace, w. of John Metcalf; the childr. of her dec. d. Bethia Rice; Abigail, wid. of her s. Joseph; and the childr. Robert Sharp, and Sarah Hastings, of her d. Sarah. THOMAS, Plymouth 1620, passeng. in the Mayflower, one of the signers of the mem. compact at Cape Cod in Nov. had no fam. and d. soon after the land. as Gov. Bradford tells. Ano. THOMAS, Plymouth, not s. of the preced. was serv. of the wid. Warren, in 1635 charg. with profane speech. THOMAS, Boston 1630, was call. to serve on coroner's jury 18 Sept. of that yr. so that it may be presum. that he came in the fleet with Winth. req. adm. as freem. 19 Oct. with an alias as Harris, without such alias was sw. 18 May foll. and the same day allow. to set up a ferry betw. Winisemet and Charlestown, and Winisemet and the younger town of Boston. As nothing more is ever heard of him, exc. that in 1651, he bot. a ho. of Walter Merry, I suppose he must have brot. fam. from Eng. and his w. d. early. Perhaps he was f. or br. of Robert of the same, wh. by lease from a Comtee. of the Gen. Ct. Sept. 1641, was made partaker of the interest in that Winisemet ferry, as in Rec. I. 341. THOMAS, Saco 1636, own alleg. to Mass. July 1653, then the chief man in that planta. where he had liv. near 20 yrs. THOMAS, Plymouth 1643, then able to bear arms. Ano. THOMAS, Boston, made his will 25 Apr. 1646, pro. 5 Nov. foll. calls John Spoore his master. See Geneal. Reg. III. 180. Farmer mistook him for the earlier Thomas of Boston. But later by a whole generat. may be seen in the rec. of b. the same puzzle that confound. me about four, five, or six Johns, as Thomas and Ann have many ch. Thomas, b. 29 Mar. 1661 ; Charles, 20 Sept. 1662 ; Thomas, again, 9 Apr. 1664 ; Hannah, 22 Mar. 1666 ; Eliz. 6 Feb. 1668 ; and Susanna, wh. may all belong to a single couple ; yet, when Thomas and Eliz. bring in a contribut. 'to the registry, doubt arises whether the f. be the same of Thomas, b. 1 Jan. 1677. THOMAS, perhaps of Rehoboth, bef. 1647, at least Thomas Bliss of R. in his will, 1649, calls him. h. of his eldest d. THOMAS, Eastham, had Nathaniel, b. 24 Apr. 1655, as Col. Rec. tells. THOMAS, Wethersfield, had ten ch. of wh. we kn. the names, but of only seven the b. and that he had w. Rebecca is also kn. but whether she was the only one is less clear. He made his will 16 Dec. 1689, yet prob. d. not bef. Feb. 1693 ; left w. and eight ch. had Thomas, b. 9 Mar. 1657 ; Samuel, 11 June 1659, d. bef. his f. ; John, 15 Apr. 1662 ; Jacob, 7 Mar. 1665 ; Sarah, 1667, d. bef. her f. ; Rebecca, 1669 ; Mary, 1671 ; Abraham ; Hannah ; and Ruth. Four s. liv. at W. 1693. THOMAS, Groton, of whose f. the name or resid. is unkn. by w. Mary, m. says Butler, 11 July 1666, had Thomas, b. 17 Mar. foll. ; John, 3 Nov. 1668 ; Mary, 3 Feb. 1672 ; and Hannah, 1 Feb. 1674. THOMAS, New London 1670, d. 24 Sept. 1705, a. 61 yrs. old, leav. wid. Joanna, s. John, Thomas, Jonathan, William, Samuel, and Ebenezer, beside five ds. the childr. being betw. 12 and 33 yrs. of age, and a gr.ch. as heir of a d. says Caulkins, 349. THOMAS, Watertown, s. perhaps of William of the same, m. Mary, d. of Richard Holden, and may be the same as THOMAS, Taunton, s. of Richard of the same, by w. Mary had Mary, b. 1680 ; Jonathan, 1683 ; Sarah, 1685 ; Mercy, perhaps is the intend. name, print. Macy, 1687 ; Hannah, 1689 ; Bethia, 1692 ; Mehitable, 1695 ; and Damaris, 1698. His wid. m. 1707, Rev. James Keith of Bridgewater. THOMAS, Newbury, m. 16 Jan. 1696, Mary, d. of Benjamin Lowell, had Mary, b. 2 July 1697 ; and Henry, 27 Sept. 1699 ; but wh. was his f. or any more of him, we can learn nothing from the diligence of Coffin. TIMOTHY, Marshfield, of wh. we kn. that he was in the list of those able to bear arms 1643, and no more. WILLIAM, Salem 1637, if he may so claim in right of a gr. of ld. that yr. ment. by Felt, and I find he came that yr. from Great Yarmouth, Eng. aged 40, with w. Alice, 38, and two ch. whose names are not seen ; and Eliz. aged 31, wh. may have been his sis. came on the same day from Yarmouth. One Ann W. aged 15, came from Norwich, three days bef. with a differ. fam. He may have been of Watertown, for there was a propr. says Bond, of that name in that town, 1642 ; and the act of the Ct. in Apr. 1641 to be read in Rec. I. 316, refers to him. If not the same man, WILLIAM, Dover, had a gr. of ld. 1653, and was tax. there 1657–1668, says Quint, had William. WILLIAM, Hartford, cooper, early there, m. 25 Nov. 1647, Jane Westover, as Goodwin thot.

the name imports tho. it reads more like Westupor, perhaps d. of Jonas of Windsor; was freem. 1654; and he d. 17 Dec. 1689, and his wid. d. 25 of the same mo. His will of 1688 names five s. William, John, James, Gabriel, and Samuel (of wh. the first four had childr. bapt.), beside four ds. Eliz. Jane, Ruth, and Mary. He was aged 66 at his d. but dates of b. of s. and gr.ch. are not ascertain. Ano. WILLIAM of Huntington, L. I. was, by Conn. authority, order. to be made freem. of its jurisdict. 1664. WILLIAM, Dover, s. of William of the same, m. Margaret, d. of Thomas Stephenson of the same, had William, b. 22 Dec. 1662; John, 30 Mar. 1664; and Eliz. 25 Oct. 1665; perhaps other ch. WILLIAM, New London 1664, is by Miss Caulkins, placed on the E. or Groton side of the riv. and she adds that he d. 1704, leav. s. Richard, William, Henry, and Stephen, beside d. Mary, w. of Samuel Packer. WILLIAM, Boston, m. 19 July 1660, Joanna Lynn, had Sarah, b. 20 Apr. 1662; Mary, 15 Jan. 1664; John, as I judge, 20 Dec. 1666 (tho. the name of mo. is then call. Hannah); Eliz. 4 Jan. 1669; James, 18 Sept. 1670; Joanna, 18 Apr. 1673; William, 25 Jan. 1675; and was press. into serv. in Philip's war, as is told in Geneal. Reg. I. 139, and was k. at Medfield, I suppose, on 21 Feb. 1676. Ano. WILLIAM, Boston, by w. Sarah, had Joseph, 30 Nov. 1687. WILLIAM, Lynn, m. June 1681, Martha Tuf, had John, b. June 1682. ZEBEDIAH, Northampton, s. of Arthur of the same, m. 18 Dec. 1672, Mary, d. of William Miller of the same, had Mary, b. 24 Dec. 1673; and Zebediah, 1675, but bef. this last, had rem. to Deerfield, there was k. with capt. Lothrop, at Bloody Brook, 18 Sept. of that yr. His wid. m. 28 Nov. 1677, Godfrey Nims. His s. d. a capt. in Canada, 1706, but he left poster. of wh. in our age, are inhab. of Amherst. The grad. of this name at N. E. coll. had been in 1834, as Farmer reckon. them, 137, of wh. 50 at Harv. 48 at Yale, and others almost equal. distrib.

WILLIAMSON, CALEB, Barnstable, m. 3 May 1687, Mary Cobb, prob. d. of James of the same, had Mary, b. 25 June 1688; William; Timothy, 29 Sept. 1692; Sarah, 2 Jan. 1695; Ebenezer, 4 Apr. 1697; Mercy; all bapt. 13 Aug. 1699; and Martha, 13 Feb. bapt. 14 Apr. 1700. He was capt. of a comp. under col. Church in the E. expedit. 1704; as Hutchinson has compil. from Niles's Hist. of the Ind. and French wars. He was, perhaps, s. of Timothy, but no earlier deriv. can prob. be successful, tho. fondly Dr. Cogswell in Geneal. Reg. I. 90, adopt. the suggest. to honor the fam. by refer. to Mr. Williamson, wh. 22 Mar. 1621, walk. with Capt. Standish acting as escort for Edward Winslow to meet the friendly sachem Massasoit, on the other side of the brook, when he made his first visit to Plymouth. No Williamson was there, we know, as passeng. in the first voyage of the Mayflower, wh.

had not sail. on her return, nor had any other vessel arr. See Young's
Chron. 192. Prince ought to have detect. this error, wh. is the reverse
of a very common one in the old rec. or even print. books, of sinking
the final syllab. In the Memorials of Marshfield, the fancy of the
writer borrows for this fictitious pilgrim from two or three later generations, the Christian name of George to bestow on him. Winsor, 337,
may have seduced the fair author or hims. been misled by her. After
1700, he rem. to Hartford, was a trader with good est. and there his w.
d. 1737, in her 77th yr. Capt. W. d. 24 Dec. 1738, aged 87, had made
his will, 29 June 1734, nam. in it d. Martha, w. of Ozias Goodwin; d.
Mercy unm.; and ch. Samuel, Ebenezer, and Rebecca, of d. Sarah, prob.
dec. w. of Samuel Barnard of H. m. 1714; beside s. Ebenezer W. to
wh. much of his est. was giv. MICHAEL, Ipswich, came in the Planter,
early in 1635, aged 30, as one of the serv. of George Giddings; and I
would gladly learn more of him; for in three or four yrs. aft. he is
heard of at Rhode Island. PAUL, Ipswich 1635. TIMOTHY, Marshfield 1649, had two yrs. bef. been adm. freem. of the Col. prob. then liv.
at Plymouth, m. 6 June 1653, Mary, d. of the first Arthur Howland,
had Mary, b. 1654; Timothy, 1655, d. at 27 yrs.; Joanna, 1657; Experience; Martha; Abigail; George; and Nathan; and was bur. 6
Aug. 1676. His wid. m. 22 Jan. 1680, Robert Stanford, as Miss
Thomas in her agreeable Memorials of M. relates. WILLIAM, came in
the Defence, 1635, aged 25, with Mary, 23, prob. his w. but where he
sat down, is not seen. One Ann W. aged 18, came the same yr. but
later by two mos. in the Hopewell, and of her I kn. nothing.

WILLIS, BENJAMIN, Bridgewater, s. of the first John of the same, m.
Susanna, d. of Thomas Whitman of the same, had, beside two ds. perhaps one nam. Susanna, the other Eliz.; Thomas, b. 1694; and Benjamin, 1696, in wh. yr. the f. d. 12 May. COMFORT, Bridgewater, br. of
the preced. had serv. in the cavalry in part of Philip's war. EDWARD,
Boston, m. 15 June 1668, Ruth, d. of Rev. Zechariah Symmes, had
Edward, b. 5 July 1670, d. soon; Edward and John, tw. 5 Nov. 1672;
as the town rec. (or rather the copy, for the orig. may have been lost a
hundred yrs.) has it by mistake, possib. for the rec. of their bapt. at the
O. S. ch. might seem to indicate 27 Oct. yet I would not hastily give
preference to the eccles. over the civil rec. in this case; but take this
occasion to warn all inquirers to ask for orig. of old rec. where accessib.
Very little is the importance of accuracy, in the present instance, for
both of the ch. d. soon; ano. ch. was Eliz. He was freem. 1673, when
the name appears twice in the column for that Court, and again heads
the list of 1684; was capt. bore a part in the ceremonies at the funer. of
Gov. Leverett, Mar. 1679, ask. leave of Gen. Ct. to build a wooden ho.

in 1683, but was steadily refus. and d. 11 Dec. 1698, as mark. in the
Diary of his friend, Samuel Sewall, wh. he made one of the overseers
of his will of 25 Feb. 1696, pro. 22 Dec. 1698. That instr. div. his
prop. half to his w. R. and half to his d. Eliz. wh. had m. Richard
Willey, and her d. Ruth. ELKANAH, Bridgewater, s. of Nathaniel of
the same, by w. Mercy had Nathaniel, b. 1678 ; and Judith, 1682. His
w. d. 1709, and he d. 1711. EXPERIENCE, Boston, by w. Eliz. had
Mary, b. 9 Oct. 1672 ; John, 29 Aug. 1673 ; Michael, 9 July 1674 ;
Experience, 28 May 1676 ; Eliz. 8 Dec. 1677 ; Samuel, 31 Aug.
1682 ; Joseph, 2 Feb. 1684 ; John, 4 Sept. 1685 ; Obadiah, 5 Mar.
1687 ; Experience, again, 19 Aug. 1688 ; Ebenezer, 23 Dec. 1689 ; and
Temperance, 8 Apr. 1695. GEORGE, Cambridge 1637, freem. 2 May
1638, m. perhaps in Eng. wid. Jane Palfrey, wh. brot. her s. John P.
had Thomas, b. 28 Dec. 1638 ; and Stephen, 14 Oct. 1644 ; both bapt.
says Mitchell's reg. in that ch. when the name is writ. Willowes. Oft.
his name appears Willow ; and a very valu. petition from him thus call.
at the age of 86, and John Gibson, 87, to the king, complain. of disturb-
ance of title to ld. quiet. possess. for almost 60 yrs. is preserv. in Hutch.
Hist. I. 367. Hon. William W. the historian of Portland, not less
deserv. the gratitude of readers for diligence in research than their confidence for soundness of judgment, is descend. thro. the sec. son. One
wh. gain. enviable reput. as a poet, thirty yrs. or more since, is thot. to
be deriv. from the same line, but thro. a Charles of wh. the b. is not
ascertain. §†‡ GEORGE, Hartford, s. of Richard (or Timothy as ano.
report makes him), a gent. from Fenny Compton, Co. Warwick, came
in 1638, and is found one of the Assist. next yr. Dept.-Gov. in 1641,
and Gov. next yr. d. 9 Mar. 1645, hav. made his will 14 Dec. preced.
with codicil of 22 Feb. and 4 Mar. as may be seen in Trumbull, Col.
Rec. I. 468–72. In it we learn that his w. was Mary, eldest s. George,
wh. had not come from Eng. and should have the Fenny Compton est.
and if he came over was to have Wethersfield lds. ; s. Samuel, wh. was
here, to have est. aft. his mo. d. ; Hester, wh. m. 17 Oct. 1645, capt.
Robert Harding ; and Amy, wh. m. 30 of the same mo. (or 6 Nov.
by Hartford rec.) John Pynchon. Wyllys is oft. the spelling in rec.
HENRY, Boston, by w. Mary had John, wh. d. 8 Mar. 1653, prob. very
young; Mary, b. 26 July 1655; and Henry, 2 Aug. 1657. From Farmer
we learn, that one Henry, prob. not this man, was a volunteer in the
expedit. 1636, against the Pequots; and that would make his resid. to
have been in or near Salem, as Endicott was head of the force. Felt
does not give the name. HEZEKIAH, Hartford, s. of Samuel, m. 2 May
1704, Eliz. d. of Rev. Jeremiah Hobart, had Ruth, b. 1705 ; Eliz.
1708 ; George, 1709, d. soon ; George, again, 1710 ; Mabel, 1713 ;

Samuel, 1714, d. at 18 yrs.; was Secr. of the Col. 1712 to 1734, and d. 24 Dec. 1741. JEREMIAH, Lynn 1637, found at Newport in the free-men's list 1655. JOHN, Boston, so early a mem. with his w. Jane, in the ch. at Boston, that it was not only bef. the date of orig. rec. and numb. 135 and 6 in our ancient copy, but not a short time even prior to 6 Nov. 1632, when he was sw. freem. He perish. in the harbor, 21 Nov. 1634, as in Winth. Hist. I. 150 is told. His w. d. early, as we may infer from the fact being noted on the copy, that it was bef. the beginning of the subsist. first ch. rec. An error in the Index to my early Ed. of Winthrop's Hist. of N. E. had misled Farmer to the opin. that this Boston man was the rep. in the first Gen. Ct. from Lynn, or at least, to refer to my suppos. of identity. JOHN, Boston, m. 11 Jan. 1655, Hannah Else, as the rec. shows, but wh. was either h. or w. is unkn. *JOHN, Duxbury 1640, bec. one of the first sett. of Bridgewa-ter, where he was deac. m. Eliz. wid. of the sec. William Palmer, wh. was a Hodgkins, had five s. and three ds. John; Nathaniel; Jonathan; Comfort; Benjamin; Hannah; Eliz.; and Sarah; says Winsor; but Mitchell gives Joseph instead of Jonathan. In the absence of the means of informat. I would suggest the inquiry, if that wid. were not sec. w. of Mr. Willis, and some of his ch. b. by a former one. Mitchell says his will, of 1692, pro. 1693, refers to the eight ch. of wh. Hannah was w. of Nathaniel Hayward; Eliz. m. a Harvey; and Sarah was w. of John Ames; further he tells that he had four brs. Jonathan, Law-rence, Nathaniel, and Francis, and leaves us to regret that only two of them can be well discern. thro. the distance. He was the first rep. that town ever sent, in 1657, and very oft. later. JOHN, Bridgewater, s. of the preced. was a deac. m. Experience, d. of Nicholas Byram, had John; Samuel, b. 1688; Experience; and Mary; and d. a. 1712, the only date, and that uncert. that the historian of the town yields. JOSEPH, by Mitchell made s. of the first John, was of Taunton, a propr. 1668–84, m. there a d. of Thomas Lincoln, and rem. to Scituate, where he liv. 1689. JOSHUA, Windsor. See Wills. JOSIAH, Boston, mari-ner, m. Oct. 1675, Hannah, d. of Mahalaleel Munnings, as in the deed to him by her mo. wid. of Thomas Overman, who had first been wid. of said Munnings, appears by our Reg. IX. 318. JOST, or JOIST, employ. Mar. 1631, as surveyor of ordnance and cannonier, at £10. per. an. prob. was a Dutchman, whose surname is near. as outlandish as that of his bapt. being Weillust in one place, Willust in others of our Col. Rec. I. wh. teaches us that in July 1632, he had leave to go home, not with-out regret of Gov. Winth. and was paid £5. towards his pass. but as in Mar. 1635, Humphrey and Endicot were appoint. to admin. on his est. to be div. among claimants, it may be feared that his skill was lost by untimely d. on his way. LAWRENCE, Sandwich 1643, in the list of those able to bear arms, had Mary, b. 14 Apr. 1648, may have been br. of the first deac. John of Bridgewater, and liv. at B. when he m. 5 Sept. 1656, Mary, d. of Thomas Makepeace of Boston, but nothing is ascertain. with confidence, nor whether the freem. of Mass. 1669, were the same man, wh. is very prob. for the f. of his w. in the will made aft. his rem. to Boston, makes encourag. legacy to her in June 1666. MICHAEL, Dorchester, freem. 2 May 1638, by w. Joan had Joseph, bapt. 3 Feb. 1639, wh. prob. liv. not long; rem. with Powell to Boston, there was one of the found. of sec. ch. by w. Mildred had Michael, b. 11 Nov. 1652; whether he had any more bef. com. or any other than this one aft. I cannot learn, exc. by inf. from his will of 21 June 1669, pro. 7 Oct. foll. wh. makes it certain that he had s. Experience bef. and some ds. m. how many, or what their names is not kn. beside d. Temperance wh. was bapt. 13 Feb. 1648, unm. yet of inq. for sev. gr.ch. to wh. he gave legacies (of wh. none but Joseph Phillips is call. out), obscure diligence may fail of its reward. His w. to wh. he had giv. power to dispose of some of his prop. aft. her own d. in her will of 20 Sept. 1680, increases the confus. in part, and lends no clue to other part, only that one of his ds. Abigail was a. 1658, sec. w. of Thomas Bill. Other ds. are Lydia Nowell; Joanna Ellis; and beside the darkness that hangs upon gr.s. Michael and gr.d. Marah, tho. we may guess the former to be s. of Experience, suffic. trouble would remain in the search for " daur. Pollard's childr." yet the diffic. seems inextrica. when we find that beyond the thick clouds wherein we would hunt for the ds. of her h. she scatters all hope of success, by speaking of her " five *own* ds." So the only safe conclus. is that she was a young wid. with five ds. when Michael took her; but perhaps the ds. m. that he refers to in his will, may have been, some at least, not his offspr. but those of the sec. w. bef. their union. MICHAEL, Boston, s. of the preced. by w. Eliz. had Joseph, b. 4 Jan. 1680 ; Abigail, 12 Mar. 1682 ; Deliverance, 1 Nov. 1684; Hannah, 14 June 1688 ; and Michael, 4 July 1694 ; was a cooper, went to London, it is believ. and there d. 1712. NATHANIEL, Bridgewater, br. of the first John of the same, an orig. propr. and perhaps the earliest sch.-master of the town, had Elkanah, and Bethia, and d. bef. 1687, is all that Judge Mitchell teaches. NATHANIEL, Bridgewater, s. of the first deac. John of the same, by w. Lydia had Nathaniel, Jonathan, John, Ebenezer, Sarah, and Mary, and d. 1716. NICHOLAS, Boston, a mercer, as he is call. on join. the ch. 27 July 1634, as did his w. Ann the next Sunday, freem. 3 Sept. foll. was foreman of the jury on cap. trial of Marmaduke Pierce or Percy, Col. Rec. I. 283, of wh. details may be seen in Winth. I. 318. Prob. he had left s. (if he had one) at home, for no b. or bapt. is found here. He d. early in 1650, for in June of that yr. Peter Oliver, James Penn, and James Johnson were by our Gen. Ct. as rec. III. 199 shows, made admors. and his inv. of same mo. was good. Perhaps he was from Co. Suffk. for Henry W. in Feb. 1651 call. hims. of Bury St. Edmunds, gave power of atty. with others, to recover from the admors. and I presume he was either br. or s. NICHOLAS, Boston, mark. as of first ch. when adm. freem. 1680, may have been, but prob. was not, s. of the preced. RICHARD, Plymouth, whose f. is not kn. m. 28 Dec. 1670, Patience, d. of George Bonum. ROBERT, Boston, by w. Sarah had Sarah, b. 10 Jan. 1643; and Mary, 18 July 1653; and no more is seen in town rec. but in Col. rec. we see he was on serv. at the castle on 15 July 1665, when it was struck by lightning, and the capt. of the garris. k. while he rec. injury, from wh. he was not recov. in May foll. ROBERT, Rowley 1691. ROWLAND, Scituate 1670, had, says Deane, been sev. yrs. bef. brot. by John Williams. ‡ SAMUEL, Hartford, s. of George of the same, b. in Eng. 1632, H. C. 1653, next yr. chos. Assist. m. Mary, d. of Gov. John Haynes, says Farmer strangely, for her name was Ruth, had Mary, b. 1656, wh. a. 1684, bec. sec. w. of Rev. Joseph Eliot; Mehitable, a. 1658, wh. m. first, a. 1676, Daniel Russell, next, a. 1680, Rev. Isaac Foster, and last Rev. Timothy Woodbridge, as his first w.; Ruth, wh. m. 2 June 1692, Rev. Edward Taylor, as his sec. w.; and Hezekiah, 3 Apr. 1672. He is the first nam. Assist. in the royal chart. Apr. 1662, and d. 30 May 1709. SAMUEL, Scituate, s. of William of the same, had Lydia, b. 1676, wh. m. 1691, as Deane tells, William Clift of Marshfield. STEPHEN, Braintree, s. of George, m. 3 Aug. 1670, Hannah, d. of Francis Eliot, had Hannah, b. 1 Jan. 1672; Stephen; and Rebecca; as is said, bef. rem. to Medford, where he had Abigail, 3 Oct. 1677; Thomas, 19 Sept. 1679; John, 6 Aug. 1681; Jonathan, 23 Feb. 1684; Benjamin, 30 Oct. 1686; and Mary, 15 July 1690; and he d. 29 July 1718. His wid. d. 22 Mar. 1732. *THOMAS, Lynn 1630, a farmer of good est. and sense eno. to be one of the reps. in the first Gen. Ct. when delegates attend. instead of the body of the commons, 14 May 1634, yet in very many foll. Gen. Cts. he is never seen, perhaps bec. he was not a freem. until 14 Mar. 1639, aft. wh. he was commissn. to hold Ct. with others at Salem sev. yrs. He had gr. of ld. in 1638, in the town, 500 acres, none of the inhabs. hav. more, yet a. 1642 he was of Sandwich, prob. THOMAS, Billerica, s. of the patriot George of Cambridge, aft. some yrs. rem. with w. Grace to Medford, there had Jane, b. 1677, wh. m. Percival Hall, and was liv. in 1689, as Farmer's MS. tells. WILLIAM, Scituate, m. early in Sept.

1638, w. Lucy, had Samuel, b. May 1640; and Lydia, Apr. 1645; and d. 1688, aged 90, if Deane be correct. His wid. d. 1697. Lydia m. 1666, James Torrey the sec. His name is usually Wills, as often is that of one or ano. of the foregoing. Six of this name at Yale, and five at Harv. may be seen as gr. in the respect. Catal.

WILLISTON, or WILLINGSTONE, JOHN, Ipswich 1668, may be the same, wh. was, in Dec. 1675, march. under capt. Mosely. JOHN, Springfield, youngest s. of Joseph of the same, d. 6 Sept. 1750, leav. wid. Sarah, and ch. John, Sarah, Phebe, Ithamar, Beulah, Sylvester, and Mary Ann. JOSEPH, Springfield, brot. up by John Williams of Windsor, was in 1691, of Westfield, but then unm. and at S. m. 2 Mar. 1699, Mary, d. of the first Joseph Parsons, wid. of Joseph Ashley, had Joseph, b. 28 Dec. 1700; Margaret, 30 Mar. 1703, d. at 13 yrs.; and Nathaniel, 28 Jan. 1707. His w. d. 23 Aug. 1711, and he m. 1714, Sarah, wid. of Thomas Stebbins, had John, 6 Nov. 1715; and d. 10 Nov. 1747, aged 80. JOSEPH, Springfield, s. of the preced. m. 1727, Hannah Stebbins, and d. 21 Aug. 1747, leav. ch. Joseph; Noah, Y. C. 1757; Thomas S.; Consider; Gad; Margaret; and Hannah. NATHANIEL, Springfield, br. of the preced. m. Miriam Stebbins, and d. 18 July 1748, leav. Nathaniel, Elihu, Israel, Mary, and Miriam.

WILLIX, BELSHAZZAR, Salisbury, m. prob. in 1643, Mary, wid. of Thomas Hawksworth, was tax. 1650, and d. next yr. 23 Feb. as one reads the rec. or as ano. 23 (1) wh. I call. Mar. but in Geneal. Reg. VIII. 167, without the usual skill of Mr. Coffin, is mark. Jan. His wid. d. July 1675. From the unusual name, I can hardly think him an Englishman.

WILLMAN, ISAAC, Southampton, L. I. 1649. In my opin. this is the same name as Wellman, and this Isaac may have been br. of Thomas an early sett. at Lynn, where long predominat. the fam. with e instead of i.

WILLOUGHBY, † ‡ * FRANCIS, Charlestown 1638, s. of William, came from Portsmouth, Hampsh. with s. Jonathan and w. Mary, and join. the ch. with her, 10 Oct. of next yr. made freem. 13 May 1640, by sec. w. Sarah had Sarah, bapt. 13 June 1641; Hannah, b. 17 May 1643, d. at 4 mos.; Nehemiah, 8 or 18 June 1644; William, wh. d. 28 Aug. 1678, of smallpox; and d. Jerinnah, 29 July 1647, tho. the poor girl's name in Geneal. Reg. IX. 170, copied from Farmer, is made Jeri- miah; in 1647 he went to Eng. perhaps after d. of his w. took a third w. Margaret there, and had by her, after ret. hither, Francis, wh. d. 15 June 1678 of smallpox; Nathaniel, who d. 1663, says Frothingham; and Susanna, b. 19, bapt. 21 Aug. 1664. By the will of his mo. made in London, May 1662, call. hers. wid. of William, late of Portsmouth,

aft. ment. of her s. William dec. we gain informat. that her s. Francis
had six ch. of wh. Sarah is call. "only d." that her sis. Jane Hammond
of Virg. has s. Lawrence (wh. in my opin. was of Charlestown, and m.
the wid. of W.), that John Greene of C. had been serv. of her h. and
afterwards was serv. of her s. Francis. He had good est. was rep. 1642,
6, and 9, Assist. 1650, and chos. Dept.-Gov. 1665 to his d. in 1671,
when Leverett succeed. Of the exact date some uncert. arises, bec.
Sewall, in almanac, marks it 4 May, and Bradstreet in his Diary denotes
Apr. as the mo. while Budington, 208, ment. 4 Apr. and this is most to
be trust. In his will of 4 June preced. he uses great care, mak. w.
extrix. giv. eldest s. Jonathan "being a prodigal" only £10. yet provides for his ch. secures to his own w. the large prop. she brot. him,
orders his own est. to be div. into eight parts, of wh. three and a half
should go to his w. and the residue to be part. one sixth to s. Nehemiah,
same to s. William, one sixth and two thirds of ano. sixth to Francis,
the eldest ch. by my *now* w. one sixth and one third of ano. sixth to d.
Susanna, and one sixth to the unb. ch. expect. with remark, that his d.
Campfield had had her portion. His wid. m. 8 Feb. 1675, Lawrence
Hammond. JONATHAN, Charlestown, eldest s. of the preced. b. in
Eng. by w. Grizzel, had Mary, b. 1664, when he was preach. at Weth-
ersfield, or shortly bef. and betw. 1666 and 8, at Haddam, as Goodwin
decid. but aft. that is not heard of. Yet Chapin, p. 38, doubts of identi.
NEHEMIAH, Salem, br. of the preced. m. 2 Jan. 1672, Abigail, d. of
Henry Bartholomew, wh. unit. with the ch. 9 Feb. foll. d. 2 Sept. 1702 ;
was constable 1679, allow. to sell wine, &c. *out doors* in 1690, and he
d. 6 Nov. foll. leav. Francis, b. 28 Sept. 1672, bapt. 16 Feb. foll. ;
Eliz. 22, bapt. 28 June 1674 at Charlestown in right of their mo. ;
Nehemiah ; Abigail ; and Sarah. Perhaps the last three were b.
at S.

 WILLS, JOSHUA, Windsor, m. 5 May 1670, Azubah, d. of Thomas
Lamson of New Haven, had Jonathan, b. 24 Dec. foll. ; and Joshua, 10
Apr. 1672. His w. d. 12 Sept. 1676, and he m. next, 11 Aug. 1681,
Hannah, d. of Thomas Buckland of W. had Hannah, 24 Aug. 1682 ;
Susanna ; John, 14 June 1687 ; Henry, 14 Oct. 1690, Y. C. 1715 ; and
Jacob, 21 Oct. 1693 ; and this w. d. Nov. 1694. In 1696 he took third
w. Abigail, d. of John Ingersol, wid. of Thomas Rix ; and he d. 6 Jan.
1721, aged 74. We kn. not wh. was his f. but presume he was b. on
our side of the ocean. NATHANIEL, Ipswich 1670. THOMAS, Kittery,
m. prob. bef. 1670, Lucy, d. of James Treworgy, wid. of the sec. Humphrey Chadbourne, had Joanna wh. m. Richard Cutts, and perhaps
other ch. It is beyond my power to determine, how rarely, or how oft.
the name giv. as Willis may be reduc. lawfully to one syllab. but clearly

the name Wills may, in sev. old rec. be stretched as I have done it. Easily, too, the initial letter is mistaken for M.

WILMARTH. See Wilmot.

WILMORE, GEORGE, Portsmouth, R. I. 1638.

WILMOT, or WILMARTH, or WILMOUTH, ALEXANDER, New Haven, fourth s. of William, m. a d. of Francis Brown. BENJAMIN, New Haven, sw. fidel. 1647, had been prob. resid. sev. yrs. in his will of 7 Aug. 1669, "aged a. fourscore," names three ch. Benjamin, Ann, w. of William Bunnill, and William, the first two of wh. were d. three ch. of the first s. and four of the d. to stand in place of their parents; but the whole prop. was small. BENJAMIN, New Haven, s. of the preced. was b. in Eng. and one of the signers of the orig. compact of civ. governm. 1639, unless the signat. be his f's. (wh. is less prob.) m. Eliz. wid. of the f. of James Heaton, had Hannah, b. 25 Jan. 1645; Mary, as Mr. White reads the rec. or as ano. eye of equal experience made it Mercy, 16 Feb. 1647; both bapt. 21 May 1648; and Eliz. bapt. 23 Sept. 1649. He d. 8 Apr. 1651, and his wid. m. 8 Feb. 1660, William Judson; Hannah m. 9 Apr. 1667, Samuel Miles as his sec. w.; Mary or Mercy m. 15 July 1679, but the name of her h. is lost; and Eliz. m. John Mix. BENJAMIN, New Haven, perhaps s. of William, had Hannah, b. 9 Dec. 1701. JOHN, Rehoboth, had Ruth, b. 5 Oct. 1673; Mehitable, 19 June 1675, tho. Col. rec. has it 1665; Nathaniel, 20 Sept. 1677; Dorothy, 26 Aug. 1680; Sarah, 21 Dec. perhaps, 1682. JOHN, Boston 1662, prob. d. in 1670, for his inv. of 11 Feb. 1671, brot. in 4 May of that yr. by John and Sarah Smith, wh. had been his wid. amt. £171. 10s. of wh. apparel is £12. and ld. lying betw. Whitcomb's and Wharton's houselots, makes larger part, acquires explanat. from the Gen. Ct. rec. of 8 June foll. as seen in IV. pt. 2d, p. 500, when it seems that he had left a ch. under age to wh. said John and Sarah should on his or her maturity pay £50. tho. it demands more. Explanat. may be circuitously gain. from the deed of 19 Apr. 1670, in Reg. VI. 253, from Eliz. wid. of George Ruggles, to her d. Sarah, late w. of John Wilmot, mariner, dec. JONATHAN, Rehoboth, m. 29 Dec. 1680, Esther Peck, had Esther, b. 28 Nov. 1681; Rebecca, 30 Aug. perhaps 1683. Farmer MS. has NATHANIEL, who d. 12 Nov. 1676, but he could not mark his resid. exc. as Mass. however Rehoboth rec. shows he was bur. that day. NICHOLAS, Boston, by w. Mary had Mary, b. 5 Mar. 1650; Eliz. 26 Sept. 1657; if we believe the unhappy copy of rec. in the office of our Register, that gives next, Abigail, 2 Oct. 1657; and Hannah, 10 Feb. 1660; and leaves us to suppose these four were all. The orig. has prob. been lost a century and a half. Yet justly as we may, in some cases, distrust this copy of what was, perhaps, a true orig. it must sometimes be received, when an *earlier* copy, viz. that quarto vol. in parchment, wh. has also copies of the b. d. and m. in most of the neighb. towns of Middlesex and Norfolk, as well as Boston, prior to 1666, should be disregard. for from that we should find not one of these four, thus carelessly insert. in the *later ;* but he certain. had six if not seven ch. as from his will of 27 Sept. 1684, is to be partly learned, partly infer. It makes w. Mary extrix. and provides for distrib. to ch. John, Samuel, Eliz. w. of Caleb Rawlins, Abigail, w. of Abraham Adams, Hannah, w. of Nathaniel Adams, and the youngest, Ann, at home, beside gr.ch. John and Eliz. Alger, whereby it would be conclud. that ano. d. had been w. of that Andrew Alger, k. by the Ind. at Scarborough in Oct. 1675. RALPH, Charlestown 1640, by his master's consent had been set free, on his petition to the Gen. Ct. 7 Oct. 1640, as is seen in the rec. I. 306, and no more is kn. of him. THOMAS, Braintree, one of the petitnrs. for gr. of a planta. on lds. of Pumham, 1645, that the Ind. chief had sold to Gorton and his fellow believers, wh. our rulers for their misbelief, had confiscat. is prob. the same man, wh. at Rehoboth, m. 7 June 1674, Mary Robinson, liv. there 27 June 1678, a former w. hav. d. in Feb. 1677, m. Rachel Read, having his name ending with *h*, and, no doubt, in later days it has been expand. to Wilmarth, as Baylies II. 200 found this first sett. in 1645. He was then mark. sen. leav. it certain that a jun. was there, and such jun. was adm. 1673, as townsman, and there had Thomas, b. 7 July 1675; Eliz. 1 Sept. 1676; Mary, 29 Dec. 1678; Mehitable, 4 Mar. 1681; and Ann, 22 Aug. perhaps 1683. WILLIAM, New Haven, br. of the sec. Benjamin, b. prob. in Eng. sw. fidel. May 1654, m. 14 Oct. 1658, Sarah, d. of John Thomas of the same, had Benjamin, b. 7 Mar. 1661; Sarah, 8 Mar. 1663, wh. m. 27 Nov. 1677, Thomas Hotchkiss; William, 17 Oct. 1665; John, 20 Jan. 1668; Ann, 26 Feb. 1670; Alexander, 13 Dec. 1672; Tabitha, 12 Nov. 1675; Mary, 7 Jan. 1677; Thomas, 21 Sept. 1679; and Eliz. 24 Mar. 1682; and he d. 1689, aged 57. His inv. of 5 Nov. shows comfortab. est.

WILSHIRE, THOMAS, Boston 1652.

WILSON, ANDREW, Boston, by w. Bethia, wh. join. Mather's ch. 26 Jan. 1690, and same day had three ch. bapt. whose names are not seen in the rec. beside David, 27 Dec. 1691; and Mercy, 18 Feb. 1694; and perhaps more. ANDREW, Cambridge, youngest ch. of Robert of the same, by w. Hannah had Andrew, b. 12 May 1696; Hannah, 10 Aug. 1698; Deborah, 12 Oct. 1700; John, 28 Jan. 1703; Mary, 11 Mar. 1707; Damaris, 1 Nov. 1708, d. soon; Damaris, again, 25 Aug. 1710; and he d. 1722. ANTHONY, Fairfield 1643, m. Rachel, wid. of John Brandish, had Sarah; and next, m. Sarah, wid. of Thomas

Bulkley, d. of Rev. John Jones, and d. early in 1662, leav. good est. to his only ch. Sarah, beside £60. to his br. Samuel, and legacies to two other brs. Thomas, and John, to brs. William, and Ignatius Hill, and mo. Hill, and sis. Ann, but whether she was Wilson or Hill is uncert. and to four cousins, meaning nephews, Thomas Wilson, Peter Clapham, Edward Wilson, and Samuel, the last of wh. liv. with him. BENJAMIN, Taunton 1643, wh. was there among first sett. in 1638, as Baylies thinks, I. 289. BENJAMIN, Charlestown, by w. Ann had Ann, b. 1 July 1655; Benjamin, 6 Oct. 1657; soon aft. as we must suppose, both mo. and ch. d. for Benjamin and Eliz. are next seen on the rec. as hav. Benjamin, 4 June 1659, unless the name of w. is here perversely changed, as seems very prob. Some aid is furnish. by ch. rec. wh. certif. to us that Benjamin was bapt. 1 May 1664, but how old is not ment. and Jeremiah, 22 Oct. 1665. He was a mariner, d. "at sea lately," says the County rec. when admin. was giv. 17 Dec. 1667, to his wid. Ann. BENJAMIN, Roxbury, s. of Nathaniel of the same, had three ws. as Jackson tells. By first, Sarah, had Benjamin, b. 6 Oct. 1678; rem. to Newton, there had, says Barry, John, 17 Apr. 1688. His w. d. 15 Apr. 1689; and by sec. w. Grace, had, if Jackson be correct, John; Benjamin; Joseph; Sarah; Mary; and William, 14 Oct. 1697. His third w. Esther perhaps surv. him, and his est. was admin. 1705. * DANIEL, Northampton, rep. 1665. EDWARD of Boston or Roxbury, a miller, prob. unm. d. 1638, as one might be justified by the will to inf. See Geneal. Reg. VII. 30, where we may not be sure, that 19 Apr. was the date of mak. rather than of pro. It made his br. Thomas excor. gave him half his prop. and half to br. William, but if W. do not come over to N. E. then the whole to Thomas. By Col. Rec. I. 235, it seems that Thomas present. to the Gen. Ct. on 4 Sept. foll. inv. of £48. 2s. EDWARD, Charlestown, join. the ch. 29 July 1660, m. 6 Nov. 1656, Mary, d. of deac. Robert Hale, wh. join. 23 Feb. 1662, had William, bapt. 5 Aug. 1660; Mary, 20 July 1662; John, 6 Nov. 1664; Joanna, 21 Apr. 1667; Catharine, 14 Nov. 1669; Edward, 23 Apr. 1671; Eliz. 1 Feb. 1674, prob. d. soon; Samuel, 25 July 1675, prob. d. soon; Eliz. again, 2 Sept. 1677; Samuel, again, 23 May 1680; and Hale, 7 Aug. 1681. EDWARD, Salem 1646, had m. a d. of Michael Sallows, wh. in his will of Nov. in that yr. nam. W. as one of his excors. EDWARD, Fairfield, d. 1684, leav. Nathaniel, and Mary, w. of Jonathan Moorhouse, but not wid. His inv. is of 12 Nov. in that yr. EPHRAIM, Dedham, s. of Henry of the same, m. 10 May 1681, Rebecca, d. of Samuel Sumner, had Ephraim, b. 27 Feb. 1684; Samuel, 5 Apr. 1687; and Rebecca, 28 Jan. 1695. FRANCIS, Woburn, m. 6 Mar. 1683, Ruth Duntlen. GAWIN, Kittery, submit. to Mass. jurisdict. Nov. 1652.

GEORGE, Kittery, perhaps s. of the preced. or only by ill chirogr. may be pervert. to mean ano. was 36 yrs. old in 1654. HENRY, Dedham 1639, freem. 2 June 1641, m. 24 Nov. 1642, Mary, d. of Michael Metcalf the first, had Michael, b. 7 Aug. 1644; Mary, bapt. 21 Nov. 1652; Sarah, 22 Jan. 1654; Ephraim, June 1656. HUMPHREY, Exeter 1645, s. of Thomas, m. Dec. 1663, Judith, d. of William Hersey of Hingham. ISAAC, Newton, s. of the first Nathaniel, m. July 1685, Susanna Andrews, had Isaac, b. 14 May foll.; Samuel; Ebenezer; Susanna; Hannah; and Abigail. JACOB, Braintree, freem. 2 June 1641, had Isaac, b. 28 Jan. of that yr.; and Sarah, 28 Jan. 1642. JAMES, Woburn, by w. Deborah had a d. in 1688 whose name is not giv. prob. d. soon; Deborah, 27 Feb. 1690; and Abigail, 8 Feb. 1692. Perhaps he rem. JEREMIAH, New Shoreham, or Block Isl. s. of Samuel of Portsmouth, R. I. by w. Mary had Eliz.; Mary; Samuel; Jeremiah; John; Sarah; James; Mary; George; Alice; Ann; and Judith; and d. 1740. JOHN, Boston 1630, b. at Windsor where his f. Rev. William, of wh. he was third s. had a prebendal stall, in 1588, from Eton sch. went to the univ. of Cambridge in 1602, as Mather tells, much of whose story of his early days has apocryphal sound, there of Christ's Coll. had his A. B. 1605–6, and A. M. 1609, as by me in the registry of the Univ. seen, tho. Mather would have it Emanuel; and Farmer writes at King's, where, indeed, may, as the Magnalia tells, have been the adm. Aft. serv. as chaplain in sev. houses, he was induct. at Sudbury in the S. border of Co. Suffolk; there contin. ten or twelve yrs. but disgust. with the worship of forms and vestments growing in the ch. he encourag. the coloniz. of the Mass. Bay, and came 1630, with the Gov. and Comp. bring. the chart. in the Arbella. His w. Eliz. whose name is not distinct. read in Mather, tho. in his usual roundabout way he says, Magn. III. cap. 3, p. 42, that W. designed to m. a d. " of the lady Mansfield, wid. of Sir John," remain. in Eng. prob. with care of the ch. Edmund first b. (so nam. for his gr. uncle Edmund Grindall, the puritan archbishop of Canterbury 1575–83); John; and others, if there were more; but when he went back to Eng. and came again 1632, he brot. her and s. John, but the oldest s. perhaps never was on this side of the ocean. The w. was sis. of the w. of Robert Keayne, and her br. John with his fam. got over to Boston, two yrs. later, in poverty: and torment Keayne very much, if his will be good evid. as may, partly, be read in Geneal. Reg. VI. 156. He made sec. voyage to Eng. 1634, and came again in the summer of 1635, wh. led me to mistake, formerly, the time of his w.'s coming, as she did not join our ch. bef. 20 Mar. 1636; whereas we see, that his d. Mary was bapt. 8 Sept. 1633, unless the ch. rec. means a week later, the copy of town rec. certif. that she was b. 12 Sept. He had request. adm. as freem. 19 Oct. 1630, and was sw. 3 July 1632, and d. 7 Aug. 1667, and was bur. on the Sunday foll. Of the good desert of this first min. of Boston, abund. proof is found in the Magn. III. cap. 3, with some few lamentab. characteristics of the author, perhaps little to be regard. in derog. from the charact. of W. Yet of one trait in him, the zeal for the glory of God, as exhib. in "Ill Newes from New Eng." where the testimony of Obadiah Holmes, the Bapt. confessor, is fully giv. we must regret that it surpassed the limits of self-respect, as well as common decency. H. tells aft. his sentence to imprisonm. and cruel scourg. "as I went from the Bar, I exprest myself in these words: I bless God I am count. worthy to suffer for the name of Jesus; where-upon John Wilson (their Pastor as they call him) strook me bef. the judgm.-seat, and cursed me, saying, the curse of God or Jesus go with thee." For the imprecation upon the heretic lenity may be extend. as we hope, by the final Judge, when he cometh in the clouds of heaven; but at the tribunal of gentlemen the assault on a defenceless prisoner, even tho. convict. by his own confess. of the crime of preach. what he thot. truth, meets no indulgence. Gratitude has always been express. for this found. of Boston ch. no doubt in some degr. arising from the munific. contrib. of £1,000. by his br. William in Eng. and the most judicious invest. of part of that sum, as in Col. Rec. I. 128 alluded to, and may by any minute antiquary be seen in 2 Mass. Hist. Coll. VIII. 228, all assist. in keep. active the generous emotion. The eldest s. travel. in Holland and Italy, where he gain. the honor of M. D. but as I doubt whether he ever came across the sea, I do not inquire for much detail as to his m. or wh. was his w. nor can I tell more than that he liv. at London as a physician, d. a. 1658, leav. s. John, and d. Bridget, wh. m. Nicholas Prideaux, merch. of Barbadoes. His d. Mary m. 5 Nov. 1651, Rev. Samuel Danforth of Roxbury, and next a Buck of Boston (whose bapt. name eludes my search, for many hours, at var. times), and d. 13 Sept. 1713. Mather's life is, perhaps, the best of any in his catal. of min. yet the caution to be used in read. all other parts of the Magn. must not be neglect. here. In § 19 of that 3d chap. in proof of the "certain prophetic afflatus, wh. oft. directs the speeches of" men like Wilson, he refers to the success of John Hull, as foretold by W. bec. of his attention to his mother "weak in body and poor in est." Mather had no intent. of casting ridicule upon prophecy, for he was giv. to showing his ability in the same way, but his fancy, as usual, outran his judgment; and his memory, great as it was, forever calls on invention to come to the aid of truth. Hull's mo. Eliz. wh. d. above 16 yrs. bef. M. was b. is not to be specially mark. as "poor in est." and if the writer meant Judith the sec. w. of his f. and mo. of the young man's w. (as is

most prob.) the panegyric is even *less necessa.*; but indeed this sec. w.
d. nine yrs. bef. the b. of the historian. More or less accommodat. of fact
to theory is observ. in other authors than him whose Magnalia is the
monum. to delineate his character no less than his desire, tho. prob. to
few it is ascrib. in equal extent. *JOHN*, Medfield, s. of the preced. b. in
Eng. Sept. 1621, H. C. 1642, had the benefit of join. the ch. of his f. 3
Mar. 1644, but was not freem. until 1647, ord. as collea. with Rev.
Richard Mather at Dorchester in 1649, but contin. only two yrs. and
was then sett. at M. by w. Sarah had John, bapt. at Boston, 8 July
1648; Thomas, b. 12 Nov. 1652; Eliz. 1653; Increase, 1656; John,
again, 1660; and Thomas, again, 2 Mar. 1662, or, as Barry says, 18
Nov. of that yr.; beside Susanna, Dec. 1664, wh. m. 1683, Rev. Grin-
dal Rawson of Mendon; and d. 23 Aug. 1691. JOHN, Woburn, had
Samuel, b. 29 Dec. 1658; Abigail, 8 Aug. 1666; Eliz. 6 Aug. 1668;
Benjamin, 15 Oct. 1670; and Hannah, 31 May 1672, wh. d. soon;
John, 3 Jan. 1673; Hannah, again, 28 Dec. 1674, d. soon; Hannah,
again, 11 Mar. 1677; and Susanna, 11 Mar. 1679. He may be the
man wh. Barry says came 1651, in the John and Sarah from London.
In so common a name to discern whose s. was that JOHN, the soldier in
Beers's comp. k. by the Ind. with his capt. 4 Sept. 1675, must be very
diffic.; and he d. 2 July 1687. JOHN, Dover, there tax. 1666, as was
found by the dilig. of Rev. Mr. Quint. JOHN, Hartford, s. of Robert
of the same, propound. for freem. 1675, m. Lydia, d. of John Cole, had
John; Stebbing; Hannah; and Mary; and he d. 16 Jan. 1698. JOHN,
New Haven, prob. s. of Rev. John of Medfield, m. 4 July 1683, Sarah,
d. prob. of Rev. Roger Newton of Milford, had Sarah, b. 1 Apr. 1684;
and no more is there kn. of him. He was not a propr. 1685; but was
liv. at Medfield, there had John, b. May 1686; Eliz. Oct. 1689; and
Roger, 1691. JOHN, Billerica, freem. 1690, may have had fam. for in
the Court's list he is mark. sen. JOSEPH, Dorchester, freem. 2 May
1638, was perhaps, br. of Benjamin, as he is found with him among
earliest sett. at Taunton, in Baylies I. 286, and Mr. Clap has not included
either of the names at D. But whether either had fam. I see not.
JOSEPH, Lynn, m. 2 May 1670, Dorcas Randall, had Jacob, b. 3 Sept.
1671; and he may have rem. JOSEPH, Andover, s. of William of
Boston, m. 4 July 1670, Mary Lovejoy, prob. d. of John of the same,
had Mary, wh. d. 31 Mar. 1674, and his w. d. 18 June 1677. He next
m. 24 Apr. 1678, Sarah Lord, and d. 1718. His w. Sarah suffer. long
imprison. on charge of witchcr. 1692, and sav. her life by confession.
JOSEPH, Malden, had Joseph, b. 27 Sept. 1673, was freem. 1685, and
allow. to be ensign the same yr. but so early as Dec. 1674, had been
call. to take o. of fidel. as a soldier, bec. capt. and d. or was bur. 14 Jan.

1705, aged 58. JOSEPH, Newton, s. of Nathaniel of the same, by w. Deliverance had Hannah, b. 10 June 1685 ; Deliverance, 11 Oct. 1687 ; Margaret, 27 Feb. 1689; Sarah ; Thankful, 24 Mar. 1692; Mary, 24 Jan. 1694; Experience, 10 Nov. 1696; Abigail; Eliz. 30 May 1703; and Josiah, 31 Oct. 1704. JOSEPH, Andover, perhaps s. of Joseph of the same, m. 25 Jan. 1700, Mary Richardson. LAMBERT, Salem, the surg. sent over 1629, by the Gov. and Comp. in London. See their letter of instruct. to capt. Endicott, in Col. Rec. I. 396, by the hands of Higginson, wherein they inform. the people here that the bargain was for his service three yrs. but my doubt is strong, whether he contin. half the time. MATTHEW, New Haven 1642, of wh. no more is learn. MICHAEL, Wrentham, perhaps s. of Henry of Dedham, by w. Mary had Sarah, b. 18 Feb. 1676; Mary, 16 Feb. 1678; Michael, 6 Feb. 1682; Silence, 16 Feb. 1684 ; Noah, 4 Sept. 1686; and Henry, 9 Apr. 1690. NATHANIEL, Roxbury, whose f. is never ment. and perhaps he never came to our side of the ocean, m. 2 Apr. 1645, Hannah, d. of Griffin Crafts, had Hannah, bapt. 2 May 1647 ; Ellis gives, 135, Hannah and Mary, tw. 1647, yet perhaps this is mistake of the name of the month for that of a ch.; Susanna ; Nathaniel, b. 30 Apr. bapt. 8 May 1653; Joseph and Benjamin, tw. 31 Jan. bapt. 17 Feb. 1656 ;. Isaac, 24, bapt. 29 Aug. 1658 ; Mary, 22, bapt. 23 June 1661 ; Abigail, 1663; Samuel; and ano. d. perhaps Rebecca ; and d. 17 Sept. 1692, aged 70, says Jackson, wh. marks his rem. to Newton, then call. Cambridge vill. and was freem. 1690, unless his s. of the same name be there meant. His w. d. one mo. bef. him. Hannah m. 7 Feb. 1669, Shubael Seaver, as Roxbury rec. says ; Susanna m. 31 Dec. 1673, Thomas Gill ; Mary m. 19 Apr. 1682, Thomas Oliver as his sec. w. ; and Abigail m. 1687, deac. Edward Jackson, as his sec. w. ; and Jackson says Rebecca m. Shubael Seaver, and if that be correct, she was his sec. w. The d. of Hannah Wilson, 12 Nov. 1645, is ment. by Ellis ; but perhaps it was only a premat. b. NATHANIEL, Newton, s. of the preced. was a soldier in Johnson's comp. in the hard serv. of Dec. 1675, espec. when, in the swamp fight, his f.'s friend, the capt. was k. by the Ind. m. a. 1680 or bef. June 1681, Hannah, d. of Edward Jackson, sen. not (as the Hist. of Newton, 445, by the dilig. Francis Jackson, Esq. makes her) of Rev. John Oliver, a mistake easily fallen into, bec. Oliver had d. Hannah by the same w. who bec. w. of Jackson, who had also, by his first w. a Hannah who. m. John Ward ; but Oliver's d. Hannah d. young ; and his wid. mo. of that dec. Hannah, aft. m. with Jackson brot. him this sec. Hannah. He had Nathaniel, b. 4 Dec. 1682; Eliz. 9 Nov. 1684; Hannah, 18 Oct. 1686; Susanna, 6 Nov. 1688; and Edward, 3 Oct. 1689; and his w. d. 26 Sept. foll. He m. 11 Mar. 1693, Eliz. d. of Humphrey

Osland, had Mary; Relief; Thankful; and Abigail; all b. aft. his rem. to Framingham, where his w. d. 10 Mar. 1715, and he d. 26 Dec. 1721. NATHANIEL, Hartford, s. of Phineas of the same, m. Susanna, d. of Dep.-Gov. William Jones of New Haven, had Benjamin and Rebecca, but aft. much misconduct to her, and foll. the evil courses begun bef. m. he desert. her, went to parts unkn. and was regard. as d. insomuch that his est. was admin. 1703, when the inv. was only £606. 6s. and the w. d. 1705. Aft. est. was giv. to his sis. Rowlandson and Jesse, the repro-bate reappear. and long trouble in the law foll. until 1720, when the assembled wisdom of the Gen. Ct. was invoked for final adjustm. PAUL, Charlestown, a householder 1677, of wh. no more is learn. exc. that his w. Mary join. the ch. 10 Apr. 1687. PHINEAS, Hartford 1675, had come from Dublin, and was a prosper. merch. by first w. perhaps tak. in Eng. Mary, only d. of Nathaniel Sanford, had Nathaniel; Hannah; and Mary; and by sec. w. Eliz. m. a. 1690, whose fam. name is sought in vain, wid. of John Hayward the Notary of Boston, wh. had been wid. of Samuel Sendall, and earlier, the third w. of John Warren, had no ch. and d. 22 May 1692, aged 64. His inv. 6 June next, shows £4,102. By his will of 6 May 1691, he gave a small sum to ea. of three sis. of his, all liv. near Hull in E. riding of Yorksh. and an equal amount to Abigail Warren, d. of his w. wh. m. first, 14 Jan. 1693, Richard Lord, and next, Timothy Woodbridge; and the shares of his ds. were £955. ea. Hannah m. Joseph Rowlandson; and Mary m. David Jesse of Boston, and next Joseph King of Suffield. The son had, of course, a larger amo. quite eno. to ruin him. Aft. d. of this fourth h. the wid. transact. large business in money lending at H. until some yrs. bef. her d. 9 or 19 July 1727, aged 86, by her will gladdens many relatives, and the details may be agreeable: to her s. Rev. Timothy Woodbridge, who had m. her d. Abigail, £50.; to the five s. of said Abigail, Elisha, Richard, Epaphras, and Ichabod Lord, with Theodore Woodbridge, all her real est. and £200. to ea. and to the gr.ds. Jerusha Whiting, Mary Pitkin, and Eliz. Lord, £100. ea. and her furnit. and to d. Woodbridge all resid. of personal est. to ea. of Woodbridge's childr. a gold ring; Rev. Thomas Buckingham, £10.; Joanna Stone of Boston, £10.; to d. War-ren of Boston, and her s. Thomas, ea. £10.; to d. King, i. e. w. of Joseph, £10.; to Eliz. d. of John Hunlock of Boston, £3.; to d. Mary, w. of John Burr of Hingham, £10.; to d. Sarah Gardner, £10.; to d. Lydia Davis of L. I. £10.; and last to gr.d. Mary Jesse, £5.; beside £40. to poor wids. in Hartford; and the sum of inv. was £7,154. RICHARD, Boston 1639, a youth who stole money from his master, and was set to serv. for some yrs. to a new master, but abus. him, so as to be sentenc. to be whip. in 1641, may not reason. seem the same as the

foll. but may be he of Duxbury, able to bear arms 1643, of wh. no more
is heard. RICHARD, Boston, m. 7 Apr. 1654, Sarah Hurst, perhaps d.
of one wh. d. the yr. preced. made his will of 19 Aug. 1654, of wh.
William Kilcup was one of the overseers, and gave every thing to his
wid. and the amt. was worth having, tho. not large. See Geneal. Reg.
V. 305, and VIII. 277. ROBERT, Windsor, an early sett. tho. not
among the first, m. Eliz. d. of deac. Edward Stebbins, had John, rem. to
Farmington, and had Samuel, b. 1653; perhaps no other ch. and d. at
F. 21 July 1655. His wid. m. 1658, Thomas Cadwell. An Isabel W.
m. 4 June 1645 or 6, the sec. William Phelps of Windsor, was prob.
sis. of Robert. ROBERT, Salem 1662, in wh. yr. his w. was severely
punish. with her mo. Buffum, perhaps w. of Joseph or Robert, and sis.
Smith, perhaps w. of James or John, as Quakers. Yet six yrs. later, he
was join. with the majority in petition. against imposts. His wid. Ann
m. 21 Nov. 1683, Joseph Foster. ROBERT, Cambridge, of wh. we see
not when or whence he came, rem. to Sudbury, m. Deborah, d. of
Andrew Stephenson of C. had Deborah, b. 25, bapt. 30 Sept. 1666;
Sarah, 6 Oct. 1668; and Andrew, 17 Sept. 1670; and d. a. 1685.
ROBERT, one of the soldiers of capt. Lothrop's comp. call. " the flower
of Essex," cut off 18 Sept. 1675 at Deerfield. SAMUEL, New Haven,
sw. fidel. 1644, rem. a. 1649, and possib. may be the SAMUEL of Fairfield 1654, whose d. Mary, by w. Jane is ment. on Boston rec. of deaths
sub. an. 1654 for wh. various conject. may furnish explanat. The ch.
may have been sev. yrs. old, or but few days. Yet ano. SAMUEL of
Fairfield m. Phebe, d. of Joseph Middlebrook, under a contr. 1679, and
was liv. there 1686, when her f's. est. was to be distrib. Still we kn.
not eno. to authorize infer. that he was or was not the same as the
preced. SAMUEL, Portsmouth, R. I. is among freem. 1655, was in
1657 one of the gr. Petaquomscot purch. with John Hull and others,
and perhaps of Wickford 1674, m. Tabitha, d. of John Tift, had Samuel; James; and Jeremiah; beside Mary, wh. m. Robert Hannah; and
next, 1708, George Webb; and Sarah wh. m. John Potter; and he d.
a. 1682, aged 60. SAMUEL, Windsor, s. of Robert of the same, m. May
1672, Mary, d. of John Griffin, had Eliz. or Isabel, b. 24 Feb. 1674, to
wh. the damnable name of Jezabel is ascrib. by the queer blunder of
Geneal. Reg. V. 364; Mary, 5 Aug. 1675; Samuel, 21 Nov. 1678, d.
at 11 yrs.; Abigail, 1684; John, 1686; Samuel, again, 1692; and
Mindwell, early in 1696; and he d. 3 Aug. 1697, when all the ch. exc.
Samuel the first were liv. SAMUEL, Woburn, m. 24 Feb. 1682, Eliz.
Pierce, had Eliz. b. 28 Jan. foll.; Mary, 10 Apr. 1685; Samuel, 2 Feb.
1688, d. very soon; Hannah, 24 Dec. 1688; Rebecca, 5 Mar. 1693, d.
next yr.; Samuel, again, 21 Nov. 1695; and Rebecca, again, 5 July

1698. Ano. SAMUEL, perhaps that freem. of 1684, earlier by one yr. than Joseph of Malden, may have been his br. and prob. the lieut. of 1690. SAMUEL, Newton, s. of Nathaniel first, m. Experience, d. of the first James Trowbridge, had Experience, b. 21 Sept. 1697, d. young; Margaret, 28 Aug. 1699; Samuel, 18 Mar. 1701; Thomas, 8 May 1703; and Experience, again, 2 Aug. 1705. SHOREBORN, Ipswich, s. of William of the same, a cooper, m. 9 Sept. 1657, Abigail Osgood, d. perhaps of Christopher of the same, had Joseph, b. 1 June 1660; Mary, 24 Aug. 1662, d. very soon; Samuel, 4 Apr. 1664, d. in few wks.; John, 4 May 1665; Abigail, 10 Mar. 1667; William, 14 May 1672; Deborah, 22 Sept. 1673; Christopher, June 1677, d. soon; and Christopher, again, 13 Dec. 1679. THEOPHILUS, Ipswich 1636, had perhaps d. Seaborn, b. on his passage, freem. 13 Mar. 1639, was constable for long time, and prison-keep. had w. Eliz. in 1654, wh. d. 10 Jan. 1681; but she may not have been mo. of all, or even any of the ch. He d. 29 July 1689, aged 88, leav. s. Thomas, s.-in-law John Pindar, and David Fiske, and gr.ch. Eliz. Lovell, Eliz. Russell, and Thomas Pindar. THOMAS, Roxbury, came in June 1633, with w. Ann, and ch. Humphrey; Samuel; Joshua; there had Deborah, b. Aug. 1634; Lydia, Nov. 1636; was made freem. 14 May 1634; lost his ho. and goods by fire, as from the ch. rec. is seen, was delud. into the heresy of Wheelwright, with wh. on his banishm. he went to Exeter, came back and made peace with the ch. but contin. to reside at Exeter, there made his will, 9 Jan. 1643, in wh. w. and the five ch. are provid. for, as in Geneal. Reg. II. 384 is found. His wid. m. next yr. John Legat. See Col. Rec. II. 58. THOMAS, Ipswich, perhaps s. of Theophilus, had Mary, b. 27 Dec. 1657; and may also have had Hannah, wh. d. June 1682; but w.'s name is not heard. THOMAS, Fairfield, accept. to be made free 1664, was br. or neph. of Anthony of the same, had good est. and d. 1691, leav. wid. Hannah, no s. one d. whose name is not seen. THOMAS, Milford, had b. there Benjamin in 1673, and soon rem. THOMAS, Brookfield 1667–72, may not be the same as the preced. but no more is kn. of him. WILLIAM, Boston, a joiner, with w. Patience, was adm. of our ch. 6 Sept. 1635, had, as is seen in the rec. of Geneal. Reg. III. 40, Shoreborn, b. 6 Aug. preced. and brot. to bapt. 13 Sept. foll. but if this name imply that a ch. of the fam. had bef. been nam. Seaborn, as Bond suppos. I doubt, for the incident might as well be tak. for evid. that Theophilus was br. of William, since it is said that David Fiske, wh. is call. s.-in-law of Theophilus, had m. Seaborn Wilson. Also he had Mary, 11, bapt. 21 Jan. 1638; John, Jan. bapt. 9 Feb. 1640; Joseph, 10, bapt. 12 Nov. 1643, " a. five days old;" Newgrace, bapt. 23 Mar. 1645, "a. four days old," d. in Aug. foll. He was freem. 25 May 1636, dept.-marshall, and prison-keep. 1642, d. 1646, and the Gen. Ct. was hardly able to persuade his wid. that she must not always liv. at the pub. build. WILLIAM, Lynn, m. 26 Oct. 1663, Priscilla, perhaps d. of Oliver Purchase, had William, b. 28 Aug. 1664; Priscilla, 28 Mar. 1666; Oliver, 9 Feb. 1668; and Sarah, 5 June 1670 ; and his w. d. 21 Oct. 1671, unless the d. ment. on the rec. be of his ch. instead of his w. Of this name Farmer found forty-five had been gr. 1829 at N. J. and N. E. coll. of wh. I find ten at Harv. two at Dart. and one at Yale.

WILTERTON, WOLTERTON, or WINTERTON, GREGORY, Hartford, among orig. proprs. 1637, of wh. I can learn nothing but that he had good est. large tanworks, and no ch. m. perhaps as sec. w. a. 1663, Bennet, wid. of Thomas Stanley, wh. d. early in 1665, and he had ano. w. Jane, who outliv. him ; made his will 17 July 1674, and d. soon aft. Legacies to sev. distant relat. one of wh. was John Shepherd wh. call. him uncle, and ano. was James Wolterton, s. of Matthew, describ. as of Ipswich in Old E. perhaps a neph. are ment. but most of his est. was giv. to John Merrills, bec. he had adopt. him.

WILTON, * DAVID, Dorchester 1632, freem. 11 June 1633, rem. with the gr. migrat. to Windsor 1635 or 6, was rep. 1646, 7, 50–4, 6, rem. 1660 to Northampton, and was one of the pillars at the foundat. of the ch. 18 June next yr. and rep. to Boston 1665, ens. 1662, in 1663 was lieut. and serv. in Philip's war, d. at Windsor, on a visit, 5 Feb. 1678. His only ch. Mary m. 6 May 1652, that brave capt. Samuel Marshall, wh. fell in the gr. Narraganset fight, 19 Dec. 1675, and her f. in his will gave est. to her and her childr. with his wid. Catharine, wh. m. 6 May 1679, Thomas Hosmer. NICHOLAS, Windsor, br. of the preced. m. 20 Nov. 1656, Mary Staniford, had David, b. 13 Jan. 1661 ; and John, 8 Aug. 1664; of neither of wh. is any thing kn. He and his w. d. 4 Aug. 1683.

WINBOURNE, or WENBORN, JOHN, Manchester, a preacher 1686 and earlier, but was gone in 1689. He had m. 11 Apr. 1667, Eliz. Hart at Malden, but prob. did not reside there ; nor is it kn. where or whence he came, or whither he went. Possib. he was s. of William Wenbourne of Boston. See that.

WINCH, JOHN, Framingham, s. of Samuel, by w. Eliz. had Eliz. b. 21 Dec. 1706; John, 10 July 1710; David, 9 Dec. 1714 ; Jonathan, 3 July 1716; Deborah, 27 Dec. 1717; and d. 19 Jan. 1719. SAMUEL, Framingham, had been of Sudbury 1671, m. 11 Feb. 1674, Hannah, d. of Matthew Gibbs of Sudbury, had John, b. 1675, d. young; Samuel, 27 Mar. 1677 ; John, again, 8 Jan. 1680 ; David, 15 Mar. 1684; Hannah, 16 Jan. 1688 ; Silence, 10 Nov. 1690; and by sec. w. m. 12

Jan. 1699, Sarah, wid. of Benjamin Barnard of Watertown, had Mary, 23 Nov. 1700; and Daniel, 28 June 1702; and d. or was bur. 3 Aug. 1718. Of the orig. of this fam. no acco. is to be found. A maid of 15 yrs. nam. Mary W. had come 1634, in the Francis, with Rowland Stebbins, from Ipswich in Co. Suffolk.

WINCHCOMBE, JOHN, Boston 1670 or earlier, appoint. 1684 a sergeant to attend the Gov. with salary, by w. Mary had John, b. 22 July 1676, prob. d. young; Eliz. 8 Sept. 1678; Charles, 19 Sept. 1679; and John, again, 3 Jan. 1682.

WINCHELL, or WINSHALL, DAVID, Windsor, s. of Robert, m. 18 Nov. 1669, Eliz. d. of William Filley, had Joseph, b. 13 Sept. 1670; Christian, 9 Mar. 1673; Eliz. 9 Dec. 1675; and ano. d. perhaps two ch. rem. to Suffield, and had David, 19 Mar. 1682; Mary, 8 Feb. 1685; Jedediah, 13 Mar. 1688, d. at 2 yrs.; Jedediah, again, 29 Dec. 1690, d. young; and he d. 1723 or 4, leav. two s. and four ds. Perhaps the name of Eliz. W. aged 52, a passeng. in the Rebecca, from London, Apr. 1635, with John, 13, prob. her s. may rather be Wincol. JONATHAN, Windsor, br. of the preced. m. 16 May 1666, Abigail, perhaps d. of Richard Brownson of Farmington, had Jonathan, b. Feb. 1667, if the copy of rec. in Geneal. Reg. V. 363, be trusted; Jonathan, 14 Feb. 1669; Benjamin, 28 June 1674; rem. to Suffield, and had Abigail, 8 June 1679, and perhaps other ch. bef. or aft. for no acco. of him further is giv. but that he was on freemen's list, 1669. NATHANIEL, Windsor, eldest br. of the preced. freem. 1657, m. 4 Apr. 1664, Sarah Porter, eldest d. of Thomas of Hartford, had Nathaniel, b. 5 Aug. 1665; Thomas, 25 May 1669; Sarah, 26 Dec. 1674; Stephen, 18 Aug. 1677; John, 1680; and Mary, 1683; and he d. 8 Mar. 1700. ROBERT, Dorchester, but how early is not kn. nor how he came, but prob. with w. and perhaps one ch. was there 1635, and carr. two s. Nathaniel and Jonathan, to Windsor a. 1638, there had Phebe, bapt. 24 Mar. 1639, d. at 23 yrs.; Mary, 5 Sept. 1641; David, 22 Oct. 1643; Joseph, 5 Apr. 1646, wh. d. bef. his f.; Martha, 18 June 1648, d. in 7 yrs.; and Benjamin, 11 July 1652, d. at 4 yrs. His w. whose name is not heard, d. 10 July 1655, and he d. 21 Jan. 1668. In his will of that mo. s. Nathaniel, Jonathan, and David are nam. and Mary refer. to as hav. had her portion.

WINCHESTER, *ALEXANDER, Braintree, came over in the train of Henry Vane in the Defence, arr. 3 Oct. 1635, was rec. mem. of Boston ch. 8 Nov. foll. and made freem. 7 Dec. 1636; had Mary, bapt. 19 Nov. 1637; liv. at Braintree aft. that, was rep. 1641, and clk. of the writs, but rem. to Rehoboth, where he was one of the first combinat. 1644, as in Baylies II. 198, is seen, was selectman 1647, d. 16 July in that yr.

It appears id. 208, that he left childr. but their names are not found, exc. Eliz. b. 28 Mar. 1640; and Hannah, 10 Dec. 1642, both at Braintree; and Lydia at Rehoboth, beside the first ment. Boston ch. so that as his will names no s. we may believe that he never had one. JOHN, Hingham 1636, came in the Elizabeth the yr. bef. at the age of 19, with Clement Bates, and therefore may be suppos. from Co. Herts, was freem. 9 Mar. 1637, m. 15 Oct. 1638, Hannah, d. of deac. Richard Sealis of Scituate, had Mary, bapt. 1640; John; Josiah, b. 27 Mar. bapt. 20 May 1655; and Jonathan, says Farmer, wh. notes in MS. that this last d. of smallpox at Roxbury 1679, refer. to ch. rec. for his authority; and soon aft. 1650 rem. to the Muddy riv. part of Boston, d. 25 Apr. 1694, and in his will of 1691 gave his est. to the s. John and Josiah, wh. contin. to live upon the same. He had, in the great milit. quarrel of 1645, fallen under fine for the trouble, wh. he and his neighb. caused, wh. was next yr. remit. on acco. of his poverty as in Col. Rec. III. 80, is read. *JOHN, Brookline, s. of the preced. by two ws. Hannah, and Joanna, had six s. and four ds. of wh. Jackson gives the name of Stephen only, b. Feb. 1686, was the first rep. of the town, and d. 1718. In the copious Hist. of Newton may be read valuab. acco. of descend. of Stephen.

WINCOL, WINCALL, or WINKLE, HUMPHREY, Cambridge 1634, was perhaps, from little Waldingfield in Co. Sufflk. JOHN, Salem 1631. Felt. *JOHN, Watertown, s. of Thomas of the same, perhaps a passeng. aged 13, in the Rebecca from London, 1635, with Eliz. 52, wh. may have been his mo. tho. more prob. his aunt, is by Bond mark. as a propr. 1637, freem. 1646, rem. soon aft. to Kittery, where with many others he submit. 1652 to jurisdict. of Mass. and for wh. he was rep. at Boston 1653, 4, and 5, in the sec. yr. titled lieut. yet the yr. aft. call. at W. serg. and in 1658 rep. for W. in 1665 was of loyalty suffic. to be made a justice by the royal commissnrs. as of Newichawanock, that includ. perhaps both sides of the riv. tho. his resid. was in Berwick, and faithful to Mass. was rep. for K. again 1675, 7, and 8, and from 1676–85 in the commissn. under either or both Stoughton and Danforth, as Pres. to serve in the counc. clk. and reg. yet seeming most to rejoice in the style of capt. had w. Eliz. and d. 22 Oct. 1694, as we may be sure, by fall. from his horse, and also from the ment. in Sewall's Diary of the appoint. of Hammond to succeed him in Dec. of that yr. ROBERT, Mass. but of what town can hardly be judg. as all that is kn. of him is adm. as freem. 6 May 1635. THOMAS, by Farmer mark. of Salem 1631, may be the man fin. for drunk. 4 Mar. 1633. THOMAS, Watertown, a propr. in 1642, is therefore suppos. by Bond to have come over aft. his s. John, and to have brot. w. Beatrice, wh. d. 1 June 1655, and he d. 10 June

1657, well advanc. in yrs. Bond says he was allow. 1649 to keep an inn.

WINDALL, THOMAS, Ipswich 1643, Felt —— is the total of Farmer's MS. note; but little more worth having is to be seen under Wendall.

WINDIAT, JOHN, Dover, sen. and jun. are introd. on the authority of Farmer in MS. note, from rec. of Ct. of Quarter sess. in 1686; and without daring to propose a substitute, I suggest that the name may have been mistak. for aft. sev. hours' search, I am unable to discov. it in any quarter. But aft. a week's despair unexpected. I find solution of Farmer's puzzle. Such is the spelling in the Prob. Rec. X. 264, of the will of 12 Mar. 1684, with codic. 1 Dec. 1687, pro. 23 Mar. foll. bef. Walter Barefoot, whereof the excors. refus. admin. was giv. to the wid. 5 Apr. next, by Sir Edmund Andros, and I kn. from infallib. marks that the testator was WINGATE, first ancest. of a much disting. fam.

WINDOW, RICHARD, Gloucester 1648, selectman in 1654, had d. Ann by w. Elinor, wh. d. 16 May 1658, and he m. 30 Mar. 1659, Bridget, wid. of Henry Travers, made his will 2 May 1665, and d. 5 June foll. and in Col. Rec. IV. pt. 2, p. 304, the wid. and her s. obtain. relief, so far at least, as to be told by the Gen. Ct. that Essex Ct. might act. In his will are ment. d. Ann, Eliz. Bennet, call. d.-in-law, and Sarah Davis. His wid. wh. had childr. by former h. d. Oct. 1673; but the settlem. of her est. next mo. leaves me in doubt, as did his, as to some relationships of either.

WINDS, WENDES, WINES, or WYNES, * BARNABAS, or BARNABY, Watertown, freem. 6 May 1635, sold his lds. in 1642 and 4, and rem. to Southold, L. I. the Conn. jurisdict. adm. him as freem. 1662, and Barnabas, jun. prob. his s. in 1664 to the same privilege; but nothing more is kn. of his fam. In the mutations of this name from variety of sound prob. it will be seen to have the increm. into Winders; but my evid. can reach only to Barnabas the first, wh. was rep. 1664. FAINT-NOT, Charlestown 1635, was adm. of the ch. 4 Nov. 1643, as few mos. later was Bridget, prob. his w. freem. 29 May 1644, of wh. no ch. is ment. nor can any more be learn. but that he d. 25 Feb. 1665.

WING, ANANIAS, Sandwich, s. of the sec. John, by w. Hannah had nine ch. whose names I have not seen, and he d. 3 Aug. 1718. His wid. d. 9 Dec. 1730. DANIEL, Sandwich 1643, s. of John, b. in Eng. m. 5 Nov. 1642, Ann or Hannah, d. of the first William Swift, had eleven ch. Samuel and John, nam. in the will, 12 Oct. 1662, of Swift's wid. beside ds. of wh. was prob. Deborah, b. 10 Oct. 1648, and d. in 1659. See Geneal. Reg. V. 387 with VI. 96. Besides Deborah's exact date of b. I have gained those of the other ch. Hannah, 28 July 1642; Lydia, 23 May 1647; Ephraim or Daniel, 1649; Samuel, 20 or 28 Aug. 1652;

50*

Hepzibah, 7 Nov. 1654; John, 14 or 16 Nov. 1656; and Beulah, 16
Nov. 1658; beside Daniel, 28 Jan. 1664; and his w. d. 3 days aft.
He favor. the Quakers, and not a few of his descend. adhere to them.
DANIEL, Sandwich, s. of the preced. m. 1686, Deborah Dillingham,
had Samuel, b. 12 Oct. 1690, and prob. others. JOHN, Sandwich, had
m. in Eng. Deborah, d. of Rev. Stephen Bachiler, and had at least
three ch. Daniel, John, and Stephen, perhaps others, bef. cross. the
ocean, tho. in wh. yr. that was is uncert. but in 1643 the s. are all
enroll. among those able to bear arms, as in Geneal. Reg. IV. 257,
is seen; so that the youngest must have been b. bef. 1628. In rec.
of Yarmouth is read " Old goody Wing bur. 31 Jan. 1692," wh. by Otis
is refer. with prob. to w. of this first John. JOHN, Sandwich 1643,
may have been of Yarmouth 1648, when Col. Rec. says his s. as if he
then had but one, " was drown. in the snow a. 11 Dec." of that yr. and
it is seen that he had Ephraim, b. 30 May preced. may be he wh. perish.
in the snow; and again, Ephraim, 2 Apr. 1649, bur. 10 Dec. foll.
unless this were s. of Daniel; Joseph, 2 Sept. 1650; Ananias; Susanna; Osiah; and John. He was b. in Eng. br. of Daniel, and outliv.
him. He had been at Lynn 1638, there perhaps found first w. of unkn.
name, but he took later w. Miriam, d. of Stephen Dean, had no ch. by
her, and d. 1699. His wid. d. 1703. Susanna m. William P——, and
d. 2 Aug. 1717; and Osiah m. a Turner. JOHN, Sandwich, s. of the
preced. d. 1683, leav. one ch. whose name is unkn. as also that of his w.
and date of m. JOHN, Rochester, perhaps s. of Daniel, as he came
from Sandwich, had Stephen, b. 5 Sept. 1684; Joseph, 23 Dec. 1686;
Deborah, 15 Oct. 1688, d. soon; John, 1 Mar. 1690; Hannah, 10 Jan.
1692; Daniel, 8 Feb. 1694; Deborah, again, 23 Feb. 1696; Desire, 3
Feb. 1700; and Samuel, 12 Nov. 1704. ‖ JOHN, Boston, shopkeep. s.
of Robert of the same, ar. co. 1671, of wh. he was capt. 1693, m. Joshabeth, d. of James Davis of the same, had John, b. 14 Aug. 1660, d.
young; Joanna, 4 Sept. 1662, d. young; Sarah, 3 May 1664, d. soon;
Sarah, again, 9 Feb. 1666; Joshabeth, 15 Dec. 1667; Ebenezer, 15
Oct. 1669; Eliz. 19 Sept. 1671; Robert, 8 Sept. 1673; John, again, 7
Aug. 1678; and Joanna, again, 25 Nov. 1680. He was a very thrifty
man, so early as 1674 mak. bond to Samuel Shrimpton for £4,200.
secur. by Castle tavern near the midst of the town, and other est. of wh.
part was near the common, and this mortg. was disch. in three yrs. and
he d. 22 Feb. 1703. His will of 24 Feb. 1702, pro. 12 Mar. of next
yr. wh. may be seen in Vol. XV. 122, names w. s. Robert, John, and
ano. wh. is strange to me, Cord, beside the ds. Sarah Tomlin, and Eliz.
Dowell, and gr.ch. James Dowell, Sarah and Thomas Tomlin, of none
of wh. can I learn any thing. JOSEPH, Sandwich, s. of the sec. John,

m. 12 Apr. 1672, Jerusha Mayhew, but of wh. she was d. is not read, and my conject. calls her of the sec. Thomas; and he d. 3 May 1679. JOSEPH, Woburn, freem. 2 Oct. 1678, sw. again 15 Oct. 1679, unless two of the same name in that little town were then inhab. wh. I do not suppose; but the ghost of Secr. Rawson would refuse to appear, if summon. back from the other world to explain the suspicious condition of his rec. here or other parts. ROBERT, Boston, came in the Francis, 1634, from Ipswich, aged 60, with w. Judith, 43, wh. d. soon, and by w. Joan had John, the preced. b. 22 July 1637; Hannah, 14 Feb. 1640; Jacob, 31 July 1642; all bapt. 16 Oct. 1642; Eliz. b. July 1644; Joseph, 13 Oct. bapt. 1 Nov. 1646; and Benjamin, bapt. 18 Feb. 1649, a. 7 days old; in 1647 prays the Gen. Ct. for relief, being above 80 yrs. old, with nothing to live on, and four small ch. obtain favor of being releas. from fine, as in Col. Rec. II. 216 appears. How fast he had grown old, is quite observa. and may render us tender as to relators of similar mistakes; and d. leav. four ch. as by the rec. of Prob. Ct. appears in the autumn of 1651; but wh. one of the ch. had dec. is not seen; yet it was not that one, whose bapt. is unkn. His will was nuncup. Eliz. m. 3 Apr. 1661, John Walley. SAMUEL, Sandwich, s. of Daniel. STEPHEN, Sandwich 1643–59, br. of Daniel, b. in Eng. had, by w. Oziah Dillingham, Deborah, b. 10 Oct. 1648; and Mercy, 13 Nov. 1650. His w. d. 29 Apr. 1654, and he m. 7 Jan. foll. Sarah Briggs, but I do not ascert. the name of f. had Stephen, 2 Sept. 1656; Sarah, 5 Feb. 1658; John, 22 or 25 Sept. 1661; Abigail, 1 May 1664; Elisha, 2 Feb. 1669; Ebenezer, 11 July 1671; and Matthew, 1 Mar. 1674. His w. d. 26 Mar. 1689, and he d. 24 Apr. 1710.

WINGATE, or WINGET, JOHN, Dover 1660, had gr. of ld. there 1658, m. Mary, d. of Hatevil Nutter of the same, had Ann, b. 18 Feb. 1668; John, 13 July 1670; Caleb; Moses; Mary; Joshua, 2 Feb. 1680; and Abigail; but most of these latter five were by ano. w. for he had m. bef. May 1677, Sarah, wid. of the sec. Thomas Canney; was freem. 1672, and he d. 9 Dec. 1687. Ann m. Israel Hodgdon of Portsmouth. His will of 12 Mar. 1684, was pro. 23 Mar. 1688, under the Andros rule, wh. brot. it to Boston. Not the least of my causes of malediction against that usurp. Gov. and his subord. Walter Barefoote, is, that, under their admin. this name bec. pervert. into Windiat, to mislead honest, unskeptical Farmer. See Windiat. JOHN, Dover, s. of the preced. by w. Ann had Mary, b. 3 Oct. 1691; John, 10 Apr. 1693; Ann, 2 Feb. 1695; Sarah, 17 Feb. 1697; Moses, 27 Dec. 1698; Samuel, 27 Nov. 1700; Edmund, 27 Feb. 1703; Abigail, 2 Mar. 1705; Eliz. 3 Feb. 1707; Mehitable, 14 Nov. 1709; Joanna, 6 Jan. 1712; and Simon, 2 Sept. 1713; and d. 1715. *JOSHUA, Hampton, br. of the preced. m. 9

Nov. 1702, Mary, eldest d. of the sec. Henry Lunt, had Paine, b. 19 Sept. 1703, H. C. 1723 (wh. was f. of Hon. Paine, b. 14 May 1739, H. C. 1759, that long stood the oldest surv. in the Catal. and d. at Stratham, 7 Mar. 1838) ; Sarah, 8 Dec. 1705 ; Mary, 14 June 1708 ; Joshua, 7 Sept. 1710 ; Jane, 12 July 1712 ; Abigail and Ann, tw. June 1715 ; Martha, 30 Mar. 1718 ; Love, 4 Apr. 1720 ; Eliz. 21 Nov. 1722 ; and John, 24 Jan. 1725, H. C. 1744. He was rep. 1722 and aft. head of one of the comp. at the conquest of Cape Breton 1745, was aft. a col. and d. 9 Feb. 1769 ; and his wid. d. 27 May 1772, aged 90. OLIVER, from Bridgetown, Eng. Farmer says, was cast away at the Isle of Shoals in 1664, and gives such good authority as Coffin, for the relat. A mistake in geogr. of this sort, is not lightly to be imput. to the latter of these writers, and still less to the former ; but it can hardly be doubt. that he should have writ. Barbadoes instead of Eng. for Bridgetown is the chief mart of that island, and no place of the name is found in Britain. It is almost equal to that of the writer in Geneal. Reg. VIII. 86, wh. would correct the descript. of the bark Bachelor from London, of thirty-five tons, giv. by Winth. in his Hist. I. 173, to the bark in wh. Lion Gardiner came, 1635, when the Gov. as in his orig. MS. any one sees, calls her "a small Norsey bark," meaning a Norwegian built, as to me it seemed, while by the writer it is shown, that one of the patentees of Conn. wh. fitted out this bark dwelt at Nosely, Leicestershire, in the very centre of Eng. Whether the Bachelor could float in any of the rivulets of the est. of Nosely, that may be thot. not to be deeper than three or four inches, or in the head waters of the Avon, or the Welland, beside those of the Soar, and a dozen inferior, young tributaries of the Trent, springing in Leicestershire, that may be half as many feet in depth, was not perhaps seriously consid. by the author. No doubt they would serve for sailing to playthings of children. Farmer notes five of this name among gr. of Harv. and none at any other coll.

WINN, EDWARD, Woburn 1641, freem. 10 May 1643, by w. Joanna or Jane, wh. d. 8 Mar. 1649, had Increase, b. 5 Dec. 1641, the earliest on rec. of the town ; prob. earlier had Joseph ; beside ds. Ann and Eliz. yet whether these were all b. in Eng. as seems prob. or only a part of them brot. over by him, can be only conject. for no ment. of him at Charlestown is found bef. Dec. 1640. For sec. w. he m. 10 Aug. 1649, Sarah Beal, wh. prob. brot. him no ch. and d. 15 Mar. 1680. He took third w. Ann or Hannah, wid. of Nicholas Wood, wh. bef. was wid. of William Page ; and d. 5 Sept. 1682. His will of 6 May of that yr. pro. 6 Oct. foll. names s. Increase, s. Joseph's d. Sarah, three youngest ch. of s. Moses Cleaveland, wh. had m. his d. Ann, and youngest three ch. of s. George Polly, wh. had m. his d. Eliz. His wid. made her will,

9 Sept. 1685, pro. 1 Nov. 1686; but she does not enlarge our kn. of this fam. INCREASE, Woburn, s. of the preced. first b. aft. incorp. of the town, m. 13 July 1665, Hannah, d. of Richard Sawtell, had Hannah, b. 11 Apr. 1666; Edward, 15 June 1668; Mary, 1 May 1670; Sarah, 23 Dec. 1672; Abigail, 8 Jan. 1678; Rebecca, 5 Nov. 1679; Jacob, 4 Oct. 1681; Joanna, 24 June 1683; and Increase, 9 Feb. 1685. He was serj. and d. 14 Dec. 1690. JOSEPH, Woburn, s. prob. of Edward, b. in Eng. had Rebecca, b. 25 May 1665, prob. d. young; Sarah, 9 Nov. 1666; Abigail, 18 June 1670, d. next wk.; Joseph, 15 May 1671; Josiah, 15 Mar. 1674; Timothy, wh. d. 22 Mar. 1678; Rebecca and Hannah, tw. 14 Feb. 1679, of wh. Rebecca d. soon; Ann, 1 Nov. 1684, d. young; and Timothy, again, 27 Feb. 1687. TIMOTHY, Woburn, s. of the preced. had w. Eliz. wh. d. 14 May 1714, and he d. 5 Jan. 1753.

WINNOCK, JOSEPH, Scarborough 1665, then fin. by Ct. for call. Justice Hooke, a moon calf, and liv. 1675, when the gr. Ind. war began, as in the valua. Hist. of the town, 83.

WINSHIP, WINSHOPE, or WINDSHIP, * || EDWARD, Cambridge, freem. 4 Mar. 1635, ar. co. 1638, by w. Jane, prob. d. of Isabel Wilkinson, had Sarah, b. Apr. 1638; Mary, 2 July 1641; Ephraim, 29 June 1643; Joanna, 1 Aug. 1645; Edward, 8 June 1648, bur. the same day, if we believe the rec. and by sec. w. Eliz. wh. surv. him, had Eliz. 15 Apr. 1652; Edward, again, 3 Mar. 1654; Abigail, 13 Feb. 1656; Samuel, 24 Oct. 1658; Joseph, 21 June, bapt. 25 Aug. 1661; Margery, 11 Dec. 1665, bapt. 5 Feb. foll.; and Mehitable, 14, bapt. 17 Nov. 1667. He was selectman, Harris says, 1637, and many yrs. aft. to 1684, rep. 1663, 4, 81-6, the last Ct. under the good old chart. and he d. 2 Dec. 1688, in 76th yr. says the gr.-st. wh. adds the d. of his wid. 19 Sept. 1690, in her 58th yr. Joanna, long the maiden sch.mistress, d. 19 Nov. 1707. EDWARD, Cambridge, s. of the preced. m. 14 May 1683, Rebecca Barsham, d. of William of Watertown, had Edward, b. 9 Mar. 1684; Eliz. 19 June 1686; Ephraim, 4 Feb. 1688; Nathaniel, 16 Feb. 1690; William, a. 1691; John, a. 1697; Jason, bapt. 29 Oct. 1699; and perhaps more. His w. d. Aug. 1717; and he d. 10 June aft. EPHRAIM, Cambridge, freem. 1679, and 1681 (if the rec. may find credit, beyond what it deserves), was s. of the first Edward, m. 7 Apr. 1670, Hannah, d. of Samuel Rayner, wh. d. 10 Nov. 1674, had no ch. by her, nor by sec. w. Eliz. d. of Francis Kendall, m. 9 Nov. 1675; at least no ch. is heard of. He d. 19 Oct. 1696, and his wid. m. Joseph Pierce of Watertown. JOSEPH, Cambridge, br. of the preced. by w. Sarah wh. d. 28 Nov. 1710, aged 39 yrs. 6 mos. and 18 days, as the exact gr.-st. tells, had Joanna, b. 14 Jan. 1689, d. young; Sarah, a. 1691, perhaps d. young; Susanna, a. 1693; Joanna, again, a. 1695, the last two bapt. 14 Feb. 1697 ; Abigail, bapt. 16 Oct. 1698 ; Joseph, b. 28 Feb. 1701 ; Margery, 8 Oct. 1703 ; and he d. 18 Sept. 1725. He had sec. w. Sarah, wh. d. one yr. aft. him. SAMUEL, Cambridge, s. of Edward the first, m. 12 Apr. 1687, Mary, d. I suppose of John Poulter of Medford, had Samuel, b. 8 Jan. 1688 ; Mary, 12 Dec. 1689 ; Eliz. 26 Nov. 1691 ; John ; and Abigail ; all liv. 23 Feb. 1709, at partit. of the est. of the f. and he d. 18 June 1696. His wid. m. Isaac Powers.

WINSLEAD, WENSLAD, or WINSLEED, JACOB, Malden, s. of John the first, was freem. 1690, by w. Eliz. d. of Benjamin Whittemore, wh. he m. 26 May 1690, had Mary, b. 7 Jan. 1694 ; John, 29 Mar. 1699 ; and Jacob, 3 Apr. 1702. JOHN, Malden, m. 5 May 1652, Sarah Moulton, d. of Thomas of Charlestown, was f. of John, b. 1655 ; Jacob, 1657 ; and Mary, 27 Jan. 1660 ; beside Sarah, 1653 ; Jonathan, Oct. 1666 ; Thomas ; and Joseph. Sarah m. Jonathan Knower, Oct. 1676. Prob. he is the witness of execut. of a deed by Francis Small of Casco to Isaac Walker of Boston in Nov. 1658, and politic. reasons caus. the whole proceed. to be enter. on the rec. of our Gen. Ct. in Aug. 1683, as in Vol. V. 405. JOHN, Malden, s. of the preced. in Dec. 1674, took o. of fidel. tho. in Geneal. Reg. VII. 28, spell. Winglate, serv. in Dec. 1675, under capt. Moseley in the war against Philip, perhaps suffer. eno. to cause his d. 10 Jan. 1684, aged 28 as the gr.-st. tells in Geneal. Reg. IV. 65, tho. monstrous perversion gives the name Winshad, and wait. for correct. until IX. 328. But this name as well as that of Wensley is oft. misrepresent. by Winslow ; and the Malden rec. seem to me abundant in this mislead. Full as oft. may the wrong be prov. as the right, if the rec. faithful. copied (as I have the best testimony other than that of my own eyes), be turn. to in Geneal. Reg. X. 162, 4, 233, 4, 7, and 9, when seven times the occurrence is seen, where right of three and wrong of four is by me fully believed. In the transcript. made for Geneal. Reg. VI. 335–8, wherein the scribe fell into mistake as to the name of every month in the whole list nearly, he found, I suppose, the handwriting of this name where it was earliest insert. " Mary Winslade, of John Winslade — 27, 11, 59," utterly illegib. and therefore omit. it wholly.

WINSLEY. See Wensley.

WINSLOW, § ‡ EDWARD, Plymouth, eldest s. of Edward, b. at Droitwich, Co. Worcester, 18, bapt. 20 Oct. 1594, as Belknap, Am. Biogr. II. 281, gives the yr. but an ancient bible, erron. said to have been brot. by him, has a list of the ch. of his f. in wh. all the dates of bapt. purport to be insert. makes it 1595, yet my suspicion of a slight error was raised when observ. that 20 Oct. was Sunday in the earlier yr. and Monday in the foll. Baylies, II. 17, holds to the former yr. and the careful

authority of Dr. Young in his notes on Chron. of the Pilgr. 46, counts
the same, tho. 274 he adopts the later yr. on the faith of "extr. from the
rec. of St. Peter's ch. in that place" as foll. 1595, Oct. 20, bapt.
Edward, s. of Edward Winslow, b. the previous Friday, adding wh.
was the 19th. Whose blunder this was, is immater. Friday bef. 20
Oct. 1595 was the 17th. But for the yr. it might seem more desirab.
that should be mark. than the day, and perhaps, tho. not prob. it may be
as the informant of Dr. Young gave it, mak. the m. of his parents Nov.
1594. On the first sight of this bible, pasted to its left hand cover is
found the traditionary story of what is call. "Family Record," as in
Gen. Rec. IV. 298, the mind instantly rejects the right to such honor,
inasmuch as the whole rec. was evident. made at once, tho. entries for
eleven yrs. 1595–1606, purport to be expressed; and secondly, the
handwriting is manifestly of four generations later than the Govnr's.
father (who only ought to have made such rec.) could have written it;
and furthermore the age of the vol. (tho. early part of the old Test. is
lost, and the latter part of the new) is apparent. to a practised eye, at
least one hundred and forty yrs. later than the first child's b. No great
value attaches to such MS. and it has been, in more than three or four
places, correct. by erasures and interlin. prob. from presum. transcripts
of the Eng. parish rec. But modern tradit. gives a glorious myth to
this bible, that may be really of the time of George I. tho. to me it
seems more likely an imprint under George II. as if it were in the Mayflower, brot. by Edward in his first voyage, at least a century bef. the
paper was made. He had fallen into comp. on a tour in Holland, a.
1617, with the band of puritans at Leyden, and was led to join them,
there m. 16 May 1618, Eliz. Barker, when the Dutch rec. calls him
printer of London, came with her in the little vessel from Delfthaven
over to Eng. for embark. in the Mayflower from Southampton, and she
d. 24 Mar. aft. the land. at P. He had five in his fam. on reach. the
shore, George Soule, Elias Story, and Ellen More, count. with hims.
and w. but Story and More, as well as his w. d. in short season aft. the
end of that fatal voyage. On 12 May foll. he m. Susanna, wid. of William White, wh. had been his compan. in the ship, and wh. dec. only
thirty-one days earlier than Winslow's w. This was the first. m. in
N. E. as had in Dec. preced. been first the b. of her s. Peregrine, at
Cape Cod, bef. reach. P. By the sec. w. he had, bef. the div. of cattle
in 1627, Edward, and John, both d. young; Edward, again, b. 1629;
and Eliz. wh. m. Robert Brooks, and next, 22 July 1669, capt. George
Curwin of Salem. For his high public spirit, wh. took him, in the serv.
of his country, over to Eng. 1623, and four or five times more, besides
the freq. excurs. that were req. of him to Kennebeck, and all the adj.

colon. until 1646, he gain. great esteem for sagacity and faithfuln. and was most of his days inhab. of Marshfield, chos. as Assist. to the Gov. 1625, and every subseq. yr. while he cont. on our side of the water, exc. in 1633, 6, and 44, when he was made Gov. to change places with Bradford. Mass. made choice of him to manage her difficult controvers. at home in 1646, where powerful complaint might have prevail. against her in Parliam. and Gov. Bradford closes his Hist. with regret for his long abs. Seven yrs. later, Cromwell, the great projector of designs to overthrow the Spanish power in the West Indies, fitted out large naval and milit. forces under adm. Penn and gen. Venables, against Hispaniola; and (with his extraord. insight into human charact. almost equal to the skill with wh. he conceal. his own) as he had some grounds for suspect. the loyalty of both, nam. three commiss. with control. authority, of wh. our Gov. W. was the head. He d. of fever, exasperat. prob. by the ill success of the expedit. 8 May 1654; and his wid. d. 1 Oct. 1680, at the N. E. home in Marshfield, where he had left her. ED-WARD, Salisbury, the rep. at Gen. Ct. 7 Mar. 1644, as giv. in Col. Rec. II. 54, must have been Wensley. EDWARD, Boston, s. of the first John, by w. Sarah Hilton, perhaps d. of the first William, had John, b. 18 June 1661; Sarah, 10 Apr. 1663; and Mary, 30 Apr. 1665; and by w. Eliz. sec. d. of the sec. Edward Hutchinson, had Edward, 1 Nov. 1669; Catharine, 2 June 1672; Eliz. 22 Mar. 1674; and Ann, 7 Aug. bapt. 8 Dec. 1678; beside ano. d. whose name is not in the fam. tradit. found, 31 July 1675. He was a mariner, and d. early, for his will of 8 Nov. 1680, pro. 1 Feb. 1683, is in our Vol. VI. 418. It gives w. Eliz. if she cont. wid. use of all his est. for life, but if she m. then one third only, and the other two thirds in equal portions to his ch. exc. that ea. of the two s. should have double shares. GILBERT, Plymouth, third br. of Gov. Edward, with wh. he came in the Mayflower, 1620, had lot in the div. of lds. 1624, but none in the 1627 div. of cattle, so that perhaps he went home bef. that act; tho. Dr. Young, Chron. of Pilgr. 275, thinks he went to Portsmouth. But the indisputab. word of Bradford (in Hist. since discovered), 454, shows that he went to Eng. and there d. bef. 1650. ISAAC, Charlestown, s. of the first John, m. 14 Aug. 1666, Mary, youngest d. of secr. Increase Newell; and his w. was rec. of the ch. 23 Feb. 1668, had Parnel, b. 14 Nov. 1667, bapt. 1 Mar. foll.; and Isaac, 22, bapt. 24 July 1670, d. next mo. as did the f. wh. went in July to Jamaica. His will of 25 Aug. made there, pro. four days aft. provid. for w. ch. and the one unb. when he left home. *JOB, Freetown, s. of Kenelm, was rep. 1686, for the Col. of Plymouth, and in 1692, for Mass. under the chart. of William and Mary. At the break. out of the Ind. war, June 1675, his ho. at Swansey, wh. he had inhab. eight or nine

yrs. was burnt by the enemy.   Job had James, b. 9 May 1687, and
other childr. prob. bef. and aft.   *JOHN, Plymouth, br. of the first
Edward, said to have been b. Apr. 1597, on Saturday bef. his bapt.
18th, but I suspect an error of a day, came in the Fortune, 1623, m. a.
1627, Mary, d. of James Chilton.   She had come in the Mayflower,
and in her favor circulates the ridicul. tradit. that she was the first of
Eng. parentage that leapt on Plymouth rock, but the worthless glory is
equally well or ill claim. for John Alden, for neither of them is entitled
to that merit.   By her nine ch. at P. were count. of wh. the exact day
or mo. of b. is not found in any one case, but approxim. to date is prob.
as well as also to some line of succession; Susanna, wh. m. Robert
Latham; Mary, b. 1630, wh. m. 16 Jan. 1651, Edward Gray; Edward,
a. 1634; Sarah, wh. m. 15 Aug. 1660, Miles Standish, next, 1665,
Tobias Payne, and last, Richard Middlecot, and so happy as to bear ch.
to the two latter; John; Joseph; Samuel, 1641; Isaac, 1644; and
Benjamin, 12 Aug. 1653.   For this, I have partly foll. Russell's Guide
to P. 240; and from him we learn that the last ch. d. bef. m.   He was
rep. 1653 and two yrs. more.   In 1657 he rem. to Boston, was a thrifty
merch. was freem. 1672, and d. 1674.   In his will he names w. s. John,
William Payne, s. of his d. Sarah Middlecot, Parnel, d. of his s. Isaac,
Susan, d. of d. Latham, his s. Benjamin and Edward, childr. of Edward
Gray by his d. Mary, his s. Joseph's two ch. gr.ch. Mary Harris, wh.
was d. of Isaac of Bridgewater, his neph. Gov. Josiah, his br. Josiah's
s. and his niece Elinor Baker, d. of Kenelm W.   For this I have only
ref. to Dean's Hist. of Scituate; but perhaps he gives the name of.
Harris's d. wrong, and I am sure that he is mistak. in mak. the w. of
Miles Standish ano. d. of Kenelm.   His wid. d. 1679; and her will of
31 July 1676, pro. 24 July 1679, wh. may be seen in VI. 300, well
provides for s. John, d. Sarah Middlecot, with her ch. William Payne,
d. Susanna Latham, with her ch. Susanna L. and the gr.ch. Ann Gray.
JOHN, Boston, s. of the preced. merch. by w. Eliz. had John, b. 22 May
1669; and Ann, 7 Aug. 1670, wh. prob. d. young.   He had sec. w.
Judith, but d. early, mak. his will 3 Oct. 1683, pro. nine days aft. as in
Vol. VI. 435, in wh. he gives w. Judith half his dwel.-ho. and ld. in
Boston, while she cont. a wid. the other half to only s. John, his ld. at
Namasket, that is, Middleborough, to two s. of his sis. Latham, and £5.
to ea. of the s. of his three brs. Edward, Joseph, and Samuel.   His s.
John was the merch. wh. brot. to Boston in Feb. 1689, from the West
Ind. the declarat. of William, the Prince of Orange, on land. in Eng.
and was, by Gov. Andros, imprison. for publish. the libel.   JONATHAN,
Marshfield, only s. of the first Josiah, m. Ruth, d. of William Sargeant

of Barnstable, had John, b. 1664, as Miss Thomas in Memor. 29 tells; but we do not learn whether he had more ch. and the rec. of M. shows, that he was bur. 8 Sept. 1676, within a yr. and 9 mos. aft. his f. His wid. m. Richard Bourne, as his sec. w. JOSEPH, Boston, s. of John the first, by w. Sarah had Mary, b. 25 Sept. 1674; and Joseph, 16 June 1677, a legatee in the will of his uncle John; rem. to Long Island, prob. bec. his w. was d. of capt. Thomas Lawrence of Newtown; and he d. as Russell says, in 1679. His w's. f. took admin. 26 Jan. 1680, and the wid. m. Charles Le Bross, or Labros. See Riker, 284. *JOSIAH, Marshfield, youngest br. of Gov. Edward, b. 11, bapt. 16 Feb. 1606, at Droitwich, came with his br. Kenelm, a. 1630, as Miss Thomas teaches, but from Bradford's and Winthrop's contempo. Histories we know, that he came with Allerton in the White Angel, arr. at Saco, 27 June 1631; liv. some time at Scituate, m. Margaret, d. perhaps, of the sec. Thomas Bourne, had Eliz. b. 1637; Jonathan, 1638; Margaret, 16 July 1640; Rebecca, 1642; Susanna, 1644; and Mary; yet Miss Thomas miscalls Hannah, 1644, wh. m. 1 Apr. 1664, William Crow; and next, John Sturtevant. He was rep. 1643 (not as Farmer in MS. had confer. the honor on his neph. Josiah in the next line aft. tell. of his b. a. 1629), beside 1645, 7, and sev. later yrs. certain. 59 and 60. Also he serv. as town clk. from 1646 to his d. 1 Dec. 1674; and his wid. d. 1683. Margaret m. 24 Dec. 1659, John Miller; Rebecca m. 6 Nov. 1661, John Thacher; and Mary m. 10 June 1670, John Tracy. In his will of 12 Apr. 1673, pro. 4 June 1675, four of the five ds. are refer. to, without any being nam. so that one was prob. d. tho. wh. may be uncert. for of gr.ch. that he had plenty of, Hannah Miller alone is designat. and she, perhaps, on acco. of her liv. with him. §‡*JOSIAH, Marshfield, only s. of Gov. Edward that liv. to grow up, of admira. discret. yet brave, enterpris. constant in prosp. or adv. circumst. as early as 1657, was chos. an Assist. had been rep. a yr. or two bef. and was in milit. office at 23 yrs. of age, in 1658 became head of the forces of the Col. and one of the commiss. of Unit. Col. of N. E. when he did not subscr. their recommend. to put to d. the quakers, wh. should return aft. a former conviction and banishm. always reëlect. to this most import. duty until he was raised to the stat. of Gov. 1673, to his d. In the early part of the gr. Ind. war with Philip, that broke out in that Col. of Plymouth, June 1675, the Mass. seem. to have the chief direction of the body of troops, as later, in its Western sweep on Conn. riv. the Col. of Conn. was very forward with her supplies; but the advice of the Commiss. of the Unit. Col. in the autumn of the first yr. made him the Gen.-in-chief over the aggreg. soldiers of the larger communities for the gr. battle. He was a stud. at Harv. Coll. and with others left in disgust, says tradit. less entitled to any credit, than usual ; but truth is that he m. 1651, Penelope, d. of Herbert Pelham of Cambridge, had a d. b. 1658, d. very soon ; Eliz. 8 Apr. 1664, wh. m. 4 Sept. 1684, Stephen Burton ; Edward, 14 May 1667, d. young ; and Isaac, 1670, wh. well sustain. the ancestr. reput. He d. 18 Dec. 1680, and his wid. d. 7 Dec. 1703. Baylies, IV. 9, has giv. just character of this first native Gov. of any of the Col. * KENELM, Marshfield, br. of Gov. Edward, bapt. 3 May 1599, says the parish reg. hav. been b. the Monday bef. i. e. 30 Apr. came, perhaps, 1629, m. June 1634, Ellen or Elinor, not as Deane says d. but wid. of John Adams of Plymouth, the passeng. in the Ann, call. Elinor Newton, in the conject. of Judge Davis, had Kenelm, b. 1635 ; Ellen, 1637, wh. m. 29 Dec. 1656, Samuel Baker ; Nathaniel, 1639 ; Job, 1641 ; and was a man of good condition, rep. 1642, and oft. later, engag. in settlem. of Yarmouth and other towns, d. on a visit at Salem, 12 Sept. 1672. His wid. d. 5 Dec. 1681, aged, as Miss Thomas tells, 83. KENELM, Yarmouth, s. of the preced. had Kenelm, bapt. 9 Aug. 1668 ; Josiah, 3 July 1670 ; Thomas, 3 Mar. 1673 ; Samuel ; and Edward, b. 30 Jan. 1680 ; all at Scituate, as Deane, 389, shows. He liv. at Harwich, set off from Y. 1694, where he d. 4 Nov. 1715. His gr.-st. may be seen in the E. part of what is now Dennis, ano. offshoot from Y. His w. Mercy, whose fam. name is unkn. d. 23 Sept. 1688, aged 47. Of the ch. Kenelm, wh. left large posterity, d. 20 Mar. 1728 ; Josiah is not ment. ; and Thomas d. at 16 yrs. ; Samuel was of Roches-ter, and had six ch. whose dates are not heard ; and Edward, an import. magistr. and milit. officer, had Edward, five ds. and d. 25 June 1760. * NATHANIEL, Marshfield, s. of Kenelm the first, m. 3 Aug. 1664, Faith Miller, d. of Rev. John of Yarmouth, had Faith, b. 19 June 1665 ; Nathaniel, 29 July 1667 ; James, 16 Aug. 1669 ; Gilbert, 11 July 1673 ; Kenelm, 22 Sept. 1675 ; Elinor, 2 July 1677 ; Josiah, 21 July 1681, d. in ten mos. ; and Josiah, again, 13 Jan. 1684 ; was capt. and rep. in the yr. of liberty recover. 1689, and d. 1 Dec. 1709, in his 71st yr. His wid. d. 9 Nov. 1729, in her 85th yr. SAMUEL, Boston, s. of John of the same, mariner, by w. Hannah, d. of Walter Briggs, to wh. he convey. his est. 22 June 1675, as in our Vol. IX. of rec. is seen ; had Mary, b. 8 June 1678 ; and Richard, of wh. there is no rec. He d. early, as quite observ. is it, that so many of this fam. did ; and his will, in Vol. VI. 347, next preced. that of John Wensley, made 7 Oct. 1680, pro. 26 Jan. foll. names w. s. and d. makes brs.-in-law Richard Middlecot, and John Briggs, overseers. Of this name, in 1834, Farmer notes gr. nine at Harv. two at Yale, and four at other N. E. coll.

WINSOR, or WINDSOR, JOHN, Boston, of wh. no more is heard, but that by w. Mary he had Martha, b. 22 Aug. 1667, posthum. for his inv.

was tak. above six mos. bef. Prob. he had earlier Martha, as ment. in will of Thomas Emmons, 20 Jan. 1661, abstr. in Geneal. Reg. XII. 346, also in the will of Emmons's wid. 30 Mar. 1666, where is nam. ano. Winsor, Hannah, and the mo. of both, as is seen in Geneal. Reg. XV. 321. JOSEPH, Sandwich 1643, had come from Lynn 1637, where, perhaps, Lewis call. him John, and, in Hist. of Duxbury, it is said that he sw. alleg. 1657. JOSHUA, Providence 1637, said by tradit. to be s. of Samuel, and was by Roger Williams, rec. with a doz. others, as first purchas. in equal sh. and the indistinct mem. of his descend. renders it prob. that he brot. a w. whose name is not heard, had Samuel, Sarah, Susanna, and Mary; but no date of b. m. or d. of parents or ch. are found; but he was liv. 1655, on the list of freem. JOSHUA, Boston, s. of Robert of the same, had been a serv. of the first Gov. Winthrop, was mem. of Mather's or sec. ch. freem. 1678, by w. Sarah had William, b. 26 Nov. 1672, d. soon; Sarah, 3 Nov. 1673; William, again, 2 Sept. 1677; Joshua, 7 Nov. 1679, prob. d. young; Joshua, again, 16 Mar. 1684; and Eliz. 23 Dec. 1689; was constable 1686, and he d. Nov. 1717. His will of 9th pro. 25th of that mo. in Vol. XX. 53, names w. Sarah and ds. Sarah Sherand, and Rebecca Wilkinson, the latter nam. extrix. and both hav. childr. Yet when Rebecca was b. is not found in the rec. but she had first been w. of Thomas Leverett, wh. d. 1706, and next m. 4 Dec. 1712, Edward Wilkinson, as by the diligence of Winsor in Hist. of Duxbury set forth. Hutch. II. 223, ment. the epidemic by wh. so many people, over 70 yrs. of age, were this yr. 1717, tak. off, and among the cases were those of Henry Deering with his w. in one grave, and Robert Winsor and his w. in ano. all in one evening; wh. the writer of the Hist. of Duxbury, 340, has rec. without suspicion, as from Hutch. we usually may, tho. here, I doubt not, Joshua is intend. ROBERT, Boston 1644, a turner, by w. Rebecca had John, bapt. 16 Feb. 1645, a. 5 days old, perhaps d. young; Joshua, 13 June 1647, " upon 7 days old; " Mary, 30 Dec. 1649, a. 2 days; Thomas, b. 30 Sept. bapt. 3 Oct. 1652, d. young; Rebecca, 20, bapt. 31 Dec. 1654; Constance, 7, bapt. 10 May 1657; Thomas, again, 1, bapt. 9 Oct. 1659; Sarah, 7, bapt. 11 May 1662; Samuel, by town rec. 18, bapt. 25 Sept. 1664, by the name of William, if ch. rec. be good; Lydia, 1, bapt. 5 Aug. 1666; John, 22, bapt. 25 Apr. 1669 by the name of Eliz. unless we suppose confusion in the rec. of bapt. the same day of John, s. of William Read. He d. 1679, mak. his will 24 Apr. pro. 13 May of that yr. but no light is furnish. by it, exc. that wid. Rebecca was thot. worthy to have all his prop. for her life, and that equal div. not such as the law gave, should be made among the ch. aft. her d. but how many of the eleven were alive is unkn. for they have no names. SAMUEL, Providence, s. of Joshua of the same, m. Mercy, youngest d. of Roger Williams, wid. of Resolved Waterman, had Samuel, Joshua, and Hannah, but no dates are giv. exc. by infer. for Samuel, wh. preach. says the tradit. from 1733 to his d. in Nov. 1758, "aged 81 yrs. lacking one day," so that it may be guess. that he was b. 1677. The f. d. I suppose, in early life, for his wid. m. John Rhoades, and brot. him childr. THOMAS, Boston, s. of Robert of the same, by w. Rachel had Joshua, and Caleb, b. 29 Dec. 1692; Rebecca, 19 Mar. 1698; Robert, 16 Apr. 1699; and Mary, 24 Mar. 1701. WALTER, found by the mod. historian of Duxbury, a subject of animadv. by the Ct. 1671, for sell. liquor to Ind. but he can name no town in that Col. for resid. WILLIAM, is a traditional or mythical ancest. of the Duxbury fam. said to have come from Devonsh. to Boston, but too mod. for my pages.

WINSTON, or WENSTONE, JOHN, New Haven, had Eliz. b. 11 Dec. 1649, bapt. aft. a yr. old, prob. 15 Dec.; Esther, 25 Jan. bapt. 15 Feb. 1652, prob. d. young; Grace, 21 Apr. perhaps bapt. 30 of the same, certain. not as the wretched rec. says, 30 May of the same yr.; John, 21 Apr. 1657, as the careful town rec. has it, but whether the rec. of bapt. means any thing in calling the name Christian, and giving a false date, bec. an impossib. one, for bapt. is to be left in uncertainty; Esther, again, 11 Nov. 1662, and bapt. bef. 25 Mar. foll. is all that John Davenport's rec. supplies, but by scrupulous Mr. Herrick, libr. of Y. C. I am furnish. with one more ch. Mary, 24 June 1667. He was serg. and held in good esteem by fellow cit. d. prob. 1697. His will of 2 Mar. in that yr. names Samuel Alling, wh. had m. 24 Oct. 1667, his d. Eliz.; John Smith, wh. had m. 24 Oct. 1672, his d. Grace, whose ws. were d.: his d. Esther, wh. m. 2 June 1680, Joseph Morris; and Mary, wh. m. 16 Oct. 1685, Thomas Trowbridge. JOHN, New Haven, s. of the preced. m. 9 May 1682, Eliz. d. of Stephen Daniel of the same, had John, b. 13 Mar. 1683; John, 25 July 1685; Mary, 12 Mar. 1688; Stephen and Daniel, tw. 18 Aug. 1690; and Ann, 23 May 1697.

WINSWORTH, ROBERT, Boston, by w. Rebecca had John, b. 10 Feb. 1646; but nothing more is kn. of him.

WINTER, CHRISTOPHER, Scituate, m. Jane Cooper, perhaps d. of John of the same, with some irreg. in publish. the banns, for wh. he was fin. 10s. and aft. was excommunic. but with protest against such treatm. by Vassal and Hatherly, so that we may feel assured there could be no moral obliquity; had Martha, wh. m. 1668, John Hewett, and Mary, wh. m. the same yr. John Reed; but Deane tells not of his hist. further, than that he aft. liv. in that part of Plymouth wh. bec. Kingston, d. 22 Dec. 1683, at Marshfield. EDWARD, Marblehead 1668. JOHN, Watertown 1636, a tanner, brot. from Eng. s. John, prob. two yrs. old, but from his will of 4 Mar. pro. 16 June 1662, in wh. he ment. s. Richard, Thomas, and d. Alice Lachman, all of London, it may seem they were left behind, for neither is heard of on our side of the water. He d. 14 or 21 Apr. (as reports vary) at great age, and perhaps was f. of that Hannah wh. m. at Malden, Nov. 1653, Robert Burditt. JOHN, Scituate 1637, by Deane thot. br. of Christopher, but very little could he give us a. him, exc. that he was found d. suppos. by violence, in 1651, that his wid. m. James Turner, and that he left d. Catharine, s. John, bapt. 1 Apr. 1638, and Obadiah. JOHN, Scarborough 1638, "a grave and discreet man" liv. chiefly at Richman's Isl. was sent out 1632, by Trelawney and other fishermen of Cornwall to oversee their people, acquir. large est. had m. at Plymouth, Co. Devon, but in 1640 sued George Cleves for defam. of his w. Yet Cleves was foreman of the gr. jury that same yr. Such charges and the occasions for them were too common in the early days of that Province. He seems to exhibit some spirit of independ. 4 July 1663, against royal commiss. and republican usurpers, as in Geneal. Reg. V. 264 may be read. But some other person than the early sett. of this name, must there be intend. for Willis in his noble Hist. of Portland, I. 26, shows that Winter d. 1645. His d. prob. only ch. m. Rev. Robert Jordan. JOHN, Watertown, s. of John of the same, b. in Eng. prob. as he calls hims. 56 yrs. old at mak. his will, 12 Dec. 1690, pro. 1 May foll. It names no w. but three s. and three ds. John, Thomas, and Samuel, Sarah, Hannah, and Mary, but dates of b. are not found in Bond. Mary m. 17 Nov. 1681, John Harrington. JOHN, Watertown, s. of the preced. liv. as did his f. the larger part of their days at Cambridge Farms, now Lexington, had Sarah, bapt. 22 Apr. 1688; Hannah, 22 June 1690; John; Thomas; Abigail; and Patience, bapt. 12 Sept. 1698; of none of wh. does Bond discover the mo. or state whether he had more than one w. TIMOTHY, Braintree, of wh. nothing more definite was told by Farmer, or is heard by me, than that he was there early; still it may be worth insert. as affording me an opportun. for testif. that in his own copy F. had stricken out the name. WILLIAM, Lynn, perhaps the same as Witter.

WINTERTON, THOMAS, Providence 1657.

WINTHROP, ‖ ADAM, fifth s. of the first Gov. John, b. at Groton, Co. Sufflk. came in the Lion with his mo. arr. 2 Nov. 1631, m. prob. in Feb. 1642, Eliz. d. of that Rev. José Glover, wh. had d. on his passage hither, and whose wid. m. Presid. Dunster. Such may be the reasonab. construct. of an "Indenture between Gov. W. and his w. and s. Adam on one part, and Dunster and capt. Cook of Cambridge on the other, to stand seized of Governor's isl. in the harb. of Boston to the use of said

Adam and Eliz. and the heirs, &c. &c." bear. date 1 Feb. 1642, in considerat. of a m. intend. between them. By her, I suppose, was b. Adam, 15, bapt. 31 Oct. 1647, H. C. 1668, the first of the fam. in our Coll. Catal. and he was the only ch. unless a vague report of a d. Mary be accept. If there were one, she prob. d. near the same time with her mo. Sept. 1648, and the Col. Rec. III. 292, calls him the only ch. He was adm. of our ch. 4 July 1640, and freem. 2 June foll. and he had sec. w. Eliz. d. of Thomas Hawkins. He d. prob. suddenly, 24 Aug. 1652, little over three yrs. aft. his f. and only 32 yrs. 4 mos. and a few days old. His wid. m. 3 May 1654, John Richards, but prob. brot. no ch. to either h. ‡ *ADAM, Boston, only ch. of the preced. was freem. 1683, rep. in 1689–92, and as he was one of Mather's ch. memb. the king, by adv. of M. nam. him of the Govr's. Council in the new chart, but the first popular elect. May 1693 left him out, as, also, one or two others of Mather's men ; and he d. 3 Aug. 1700. Of the time of m. or b. of his ch. or bapt. of them, I have not heard, and this might seem strange, when the rec. shows that he and his w. Mary, d. of Col. Luttrell of Bristol, Eng. were rec. into the ch. 30 Apr. 1682. But the m. was in Eng. and there the childr. were b. From his will of 29 July 1700, pro. 5 Sept. foll. as in our Vol. XIV. 209, we find the w. Mary, s. Adam, H. C. 1694, and d. Mary, wh. m. 9 Mar. 1703, John Ballentine, ment. the w. s. and cousin John Appleton of Ipswich being made excors. ‖ DEANE, Boston, sixth s. of the first Gov. John, b. in Eng. and there by his f. left at sch. brot. by his br. John in the Abigail, 1635, at 12 yrs. of age, ar. co. 1644, by w. Sarah, d. of José Glover, had Deane, bapt. 15 June 1651, d. soon; Deane, again, b. 6 Sept. bapt. 23 Oct. 1653; John, prob. 1655; Sarah, 11 Feb. bapt. 24 May 1657; Margaret, 25 July, bapt. 2 Sept. 1660 ; Eliz. 9 July, bapt. 23 Aug. 1663; José, 3 May, bapt. 10 June 1666; Priscilla, 1, bapt. 16 May 1669 ; Mercy, 18 Jan. 1673, but no rec. of bapt. is seen; he was adm. freem. 1665, and d. 16 Mar. 1704. His name was deriv. from Sir John Deane, half br. of his mo. a d. of that Sir John Tindal wh. m. the wid. of William Deane, the f. of Sir John. Tho. he was early engag. with his uncle Downing in project of a new settlem. on the Nashua riv. below Lancaster, and lying on the Merrimack, that afterwards was nam. Groton out of complim. to his birthplace, his resid. was always at Pulling point in the harbor of Boston, and the place has been recent. erect. into a corpor. town by the name of Winthrop. Eliz. m. Samuel Kent. By d. of his s. José, 15 Nov. 1702, the hope of perpetuat. in male line, I presume, ceas. for his will of 29 of next mo. pro. 27 Apr. 1704, as may be seen in Vol. XV. 373, gives to w. Martha (but wh. she was, or whether she had ch. is unkn. to me) ; to gr.s. Deane, John and Jotham Grover, wh. were ch.

of his d. Margaret, whose h. was Jotham Grover; to gr.d. Priscilla Adams, but if she d. then £150. to her f. Eliab Adams, wh. is quite a stranger to me, and was h. of Priscilla; to gr.d. Priscilla Hough, d. of his d. Mercy, wh. had m. 11 Jan. 1700, Atherton Hough, with the same provision for her f. as in the case of Adams's ch. § ‡ * FITZ-JOHN, New London, eldest s. of John, disting. as first Gov. of the unit. Col. of Conn. no doubt was b. in Ipswich, went to Eng. early, and with commiss. from the s. of the gr. Protector, of 11 Sept. sign. Richard P. . . . . was a lieut. in Read's reg. of infantry 1658, with promot. as capt. 21 Dec. 1659, in Scotland; ano. commissn. 25 Feb. foll. and a third 23 June 1660, in the same regim. all sign. George Monck, just bef. and aft. the restor. of Charles II. to wh. no doubt he gladly contrib. with all the rest of the army and people; came back, perhaps, when his f. brot. the new chart. certain. was here in 1664, was rep. 1671, serv. in Philip's war, is usually titled major then, in 1686 was of Andros's council, taking his seat on the last day of Dec. and on recovery of liberty in 1689, an Assist. of the Col. command. 1690, the force destin. for Canada by land to coöperate with the naval of Sir William Phips, went to Eng. 1693, agent for the Col. and was chos. into the Royal Soc. and soon aft. his ret. in 1698, made Gov. and so by an. elect. to his d. wh. occur. 27 Nov. 1707, at Boston. In the same tomb are the remains of his f. Gov. of Conn. and of his gr.f. the first Gov. of Mass. His name in the town and Col. rec. usually appears John, without the prior syllab. as that of his br. in the same rec. is curtail. of the latter. Only one ch. is heard of, Mary, wh. m. Col. John Livingston, and d. 8 Jan. 1713, leav. no ch. and the name of the mo. was Eliz. d. of George Tongue, wh. outliv. the Gov. and d. 25 Apr. 1731, aged 78. HENRY, elder br. of Deane, and sec. s. of the first Gov. had m. in Eng. 25 Apr. 1629, his cous. Eliz. d. of Thomas Fones of London, apothecary, had Martha, bapt. 9 May 1630, at Groton, while he was on his voyage with the first Gov. and was drown. 2 July at Salem, soon aft. arr. The wid. came over with his br. John, prob. the next yr. early in Nov. for in Jan. foll. the Gov. in his Hist. takes notice of Robert Feake as her h. § † ‡ JOHN, Boston, the only s. of Adam, b. at Edwardstone adj. Groton, Co. Sufflk. at the home of the f. of his mo. 12 Jan. 1588, but of his educ. we have no details. Prob. he was at the sch. of high reput. at Bury St. Edmunds, or at Cambridge, where he was aft. 12 yrs. of age, but his early m. at the age of 17 yrs. hardly allows the univ. In the princip. of the common law, the solid foundat. of free governm. he was thorough. instruct. and pursued the practice in London and on circuits fifteen yrs. or more, holding chambers in the Temple, not giv. up the profess. until a few mos. bef. his resolut. to sett. in America. His f. d. early in 1623, and was bur.

28 Mar. but this s. was sev. yrs. bef. lord of the manor of G. as the f. had been, and patron of the ch. Educat. as he was in the moderate princip. of the puritans in ch. and state, he naturally felt the sympathy for the settlem. of this part of America, widely diffus. with their relig. sentim. in all the E. coast of the mother country, and was engag. at the meeting for the good cause, at Cambridge, 26 Aug. 1629, when Sir Richard Saltonstall, Dudley, Johnson, Pyncheon, Vassal, Humfrey, Colbron, Nowell, and others unit. with him to bind themselves, in the presence of God, to embark the foll. spring, " to pass the seas to contin. and inhab. in N. E. provided" that "THE WHOLE GOVERNM. TOGETHER WITH THE PATENT FOR THE SAID PLANTA. BE FIRST BY AN ORDER OF CT. LEGALLY TRANSFER. AND ESTABL. TO REMAIN WITH US AND OTHERS WH. SHALL INHAB. UPON THE SAID PLANTA." In pursuance of this design, wh. had first been project. by Gov. Cradock, and at the gen. meet. of the comp. in London, on 28 July preced. submit. " NOT TO CONTIN. THE GOVERNM. IN SUBORDIN. TO THE COMP. HERE, AS NOW IT IS," the vote of the whole body of the Corpo. on 29 Aug. aft. at London was adopt. On 20 Oct. Cradock and the other officers under the chart. resign. and " upon serious deliberat." in the nominat. of Winthrop, Saltonstall, Johnson, and Humfrey for Gov. " the said Mr. W. was, with a gen. vote and full cons. of this Ct. by erect. of hds. chos. to be Gov. for the ensuing yr. to begin on this present day ;" and the rec. goes on to finish the sentence, " wh. was pleas. to accept thereof, and thereupon took the o. to that place appertain." At the same time were chos. dep.-gov. and eighteen Assist. See Mass. Col. Rec. I. 49–60. On p. 70 is the rec. of the LAST meet. of Assist. in Eng. when, as at all intermed. ones, Winth. presid. and this was held on board the Arbella, 23 Mar. 1629–30, at Southampton ; but the same vol. in the very *next sentence* shows that the FIRST meet. or " Court of Assist. was holden 23 Aug. 1630 at Charlton," no doubt in the " great house ; " and it is equal. clear that the same man is there act. as Gov. So precisely, in the next foll. *forty* sessions of Assist. of Gen. Ct. Winth. sat, by annual choice, as Gov. until the elect. in 1634, of Thomas Dudley. He, of course, was the next Gov. of Mass. Col. aft. Cradock, wh. never came over ; and, therefore, W. was the earliest Charter Gov. here. Very strange might seem the error of the Hist. of Boston, by Mr. Drake, so valuab. for its many marks of industry, p. 94, in mak. the elect. of W. as Gov. on board the Arbella, at Charlestown, on Monday, 23 Aug. aft. arr. tho. Prince, the judic. annalist, had giv. caution to all readers ninety-eight yrs. bef. of the mistake of capt. Johnson in this very point. See Hale's ed. of Prince, 314. This error our Hist. of Boston would sanctify, without consider. first, that the Arbella was this day prob. half

way across the ocean on her return voyage; or, sec. that the election must, by chart. be made on the last *Wednesday* of *Easter* term, whereas this was almost the last *Monday* of *Trinity;* or, final. and especial. that this was not a *court of elections* at all, but a Court of Assist. the rec. being plain eno. It ought, however, in part, to excuse this blunder, to be noted, that this section of Mr. Drake's Hist. was issued in Jan. 1853, and the first vol. of Col. rec. (tho. accessib. bef. in MS. to everybody) came from the press in the latter part of the same yr. In 1630 there was no election, both people and governm. being upon the ocean, in the Arbella, and sev. other ships; the rec. call. Winth. Gov. at this first meet. in Mass. as at the last meet. in Eng. and capt. Endicott, wh. had been chos. one of the eighteen Assist. in Oct. 1629, was not qualified by tak. the o. bef. 7 Sept. of NEXT YR. By interchange of office with Dudley and others, W. sometimes was chos. dep.-gov. and sometimes an Assist. yet always by distant corresp. seems to have been regard. as chief in direct. of Colon. affairs. Of any details of his serv. since his life is in the annals of the country, no need is felt of transcript, for on both sides of the ocean he is commonly regard. as the f. of New Eng. He m. 17 Apr. 1605, Mary, d. of John Forth, Esq. of Great Stambridge, Co. Essex, had John, b. 12, bapt. 16 Feb. 1606; Henry, bapt. 19 Jan. 1608; Forth, prob. 1610 at London (wh. was adm. at the univ. of Cambridge, Apr. and matric. 4 July 1626 of Emanuel, in rank of pensioner, betroth. to a maiden, Ursula Sherman, when he d. and was bur. at Groton 23 Nov. 1630); Mary, prob. 1612, at London; Ann, bapt. 8 Aug. 1614, at Groton, bur. the same mo. Ann, again, bapt. 26 June 1615, the same day her mo. was bur. and she was bur. three days aft. He m. next, 6 Dec. of the same yr. Thomasine, d. of William Clopton, Esq. of Castleins, Groton, near five yrs. older than hims. had a ch. bapt. 2 Dec. foll. and bur. prob. bef. the mo. wh. was bur. 11 of the same. For third w. he took 29 Apr. 1618, Margaret, d. of Sir John Tindal of Great Maplestead, Co. Essex, a master in chancery, wh. had been assassina. by a suitor (against wh. he made report) 12 Nov. 1616. She was a. three yrs. younger than her h. and had Stephen, bapt. 31 Mar. 1619; Adam, b. 7, bapt. 9 Apr. 1620; unless we may assume (wh. I dare not) the error of a yr. in the ch. reg. of Grcton; Deane, 23 Mar. 1623; Nathaniel, 20 Feb. 1625, prob. d. young; Samuel, 26 Aug. 1627; Ann, 29 Apr. 1630, a few wks. aft. her f. left Eng. wh. he never saw, as she d. next autumn, on the voyage hither; William, at Boston, b. 14, bapt. 26 Aug. 1632; and Sarah, bapt. 29 June 1634; both prob. d. soon, as nothing is heard of them aft. This w. d. 14 June 1647, aft. very few hours' illness, and with brevity and elegance, he mark. her charact. in the Hist. II. 310. Martha, wid. of Thomas

Coytmore, sis. of Increase Nowell, of Charlestown, in Dec. foll. bec. his fourth w. and had Joshua, bapt. 17 Dec. 1648, wh. liv. little more than three yrs. The Gov. d. 26 Mar. 1649, and so totally had he giv. his est. as well as life to the public, that his inv. was only £103. 10s. 11d. His wid. m. 10 Mar. 1652, John Coggan of Boston, bef. six. mos. from wh. day all of the sixteen ch. exc. four, John, Stephen, Deane, and Samuel were d. Mary m. 1632 or 3, Samuel Dudley, and d. 12 Apr. 1643. She was the only d. wh. grew up to maturity. Samuel will not seem to be deserv. of a capital distinct. in this work, bec. he did not reside in N. E. but m. in Holland, had est. in Antigua, of wh. isl. he was dep.-gov. when he d. a. 1677, had three s. Joseph, Henry, and Samuel, as is said, and three ds. of wh. one m. Gov. Edward Byam, and there d. a. 1700. Ano. d. m. George Thomas, as is said in the Hist. of Antigua. To close this article without giv. extr. from a docum. found by me in a governm. office in London 1842, and print. in 3 Mass. Hist. Coll. VIII. 323, would be ungrateful. A letter of 19 Nov. 1632 to Sir John Cooke, princip. Secr. to his Maj. and one of the Privy Counc. from Thomas Wiggin, describes the condit. of Mass. wh. he had lately visit. and proceeds : " for the Gov. hims. I have obs. him to be a discreet and sober man, giv. good examp. to all the plant. wear. plain appar. such as may well beseem a mean man, drink. ordinar. water, and when he is not convers. a. matters of justice, putt. his hand to any ordina. labor with his serv. rul. with much mildness, and in this partic. I observ. him to be strict in execut. of justice upon such as have scandaliz. this state, either in civ. or eccles. governm. to the gr. contentm. of those that are best affect. and to the terror of offend." §†‡JOHN, Ipswich, eldest s. of the preced. b. at Groton in Co. Suff'k. bred. at Dublin Univ. 1622–5 (not, as Mather says, first at Cambridge), sail. in the great fleet, fitted out under the Duke of Buckingham, in June 1627, for relief of the Huguenots at Rochelle, serv. as Secr. of Capt. Best of the Due Repulse, but was not encourag. by the success of that expedit. to further serv. in ld. or naval force, in 1628 was an attaché of Sir Peter Wich, the ambass. from Charles I. to Turkey, and the next yr. assist. his f. in prepar. for the gr. work of coloniz. Mass. His f. left his w. and childr. exc. Henry, Samuel, and Stephen, Mar. 1630, under his care, and in Aug. of next yr. he brot. in the Lion all the rest of the fam. with his own w. Martha, his cous. (d. of Thomas Fones of London, dec.) wh. he m. at the age of 19, 8 Feb. 1631, at Groton. John Eliot, the gr. apostle of the Ind. was a fellow-passeng. and the ship arr. at Boston, 3 Nov. At the elect. in May 1632, being adm. freem. 30 Apr. bef. he was chos. one of the Assist. tho. "not above twenty-three yrs. of age," says heedless Mather, II. cap. XI. when his own figures in the same paragr. make him above twenty-six.

His num. as a mem. of Boston ch. is 121, and the wife's, 130. In
Mar. foll. he went to sett. with a small comp. at I. and there his w. d.
the next yr. Soon aft. he went home, took ano. w. Eliz. prob. d. of
col. Edward Read of Wickford, Co. Essex, and brot. her in Oct. 1635,
embark. at London, in the Abigail, for Boston, in July. On this side of
the water he had very import. serv. in direct. as Gov. a new planta. for
Lord Say and Seal, his puritan friend, and other gr. associates, at the
mouth of Conn. riv. By the first w. no ch. is heard of, but the sec. had
Eliz. bapt. at Boston, 3 July 1636, tho. the copy of town rec. (too oft.
suppos. orig.) says she was b. 24 of the same; Fitz-John, b. 14 Mar.
1638, perhaps bapt. at Ipswich; Lucy, 28 Jan. bapt. 2 Feb. 1640;
Waitstill, 27 Feb. bapt. 6 Mar. 1642; Mary, bapt. 15 Sept. 1644, a.
nine days old; all at Boston. He went to found New London, 1645,
and carr. his fam. next yr. had there Martha, b. 1646; Margaret; and
Ann. Yet the people of Mass. chos. him constant. one of the Assist.
thro. that yr. and three foll. and once or twice he took the o. for the
office; but in 1647 had been commiss. to execute justice under Conn.
jurisdict. tho. not adm. a freem. of that col. bef. 1650, and at the elect.
in 1651, was chos. first of the Assist. By annual choice of the people
he was made Gov. from May 1657 every yr. till his d. (for wh. purpose
their constitut. that permit. no man to be Gov. two yrs. in success. was
alter.) even tho. sent in May 1661, to present the congratul. address to
the k. wh. he had dr. up, together with petit. for chart. wh. by his judicious agency was obt. 23 Apr. 1662, and by him brot. in Sept. By this
very valua. instrum. of liberal privileges, the two Cols. of Conn. and
New Haven, were made one Col. At London he was assoc. in the
foundat. of the Royal Soc. Oft. he was one of the Congress of the
N. E. Colon. and his peculiar sagacity was need. there for gr. affairs, as
it had been much tried in the intrigues for so small matter as to draw
him from Hartford, aft. he had twice been made head of the Col. to the
humbler jurisdict. of New Haven; as is seen by Davenport's curious
letters in 3 Mass. Hist. Coll. X. 21–25. Ano. visit to Eng. in 1675, to
obtain from the crown some redress for the vexatious interfer. of Sir
Edmund Andros with the liberties of Conn. was in project by him, but
the gr. Ind. war prevent. and on 5 Apr. of the next yr. at the meeting
of the N. E. congress in Boston, he d. His w. had d. 24 Nov. 1672.
Of his will nothing special. deserves notice, but that it was made in his
illness, two days bef. his dec. that Rev. Thomas Thacher was one of the
two witnesses, that it was pro. 27 July foll. and made all the seven ch.
excors. giv. two ninths to ea. of the sons, and one to ea. of the ds.
abatem. to be made for the advances to Eliz. and Lucy, ea. in possessn.
of good farms. Eliz. m. 1658, Rev. Antipas Newman of Wenham, and

next Zerubabel Endicott, and d. 7 Dec. 1716; Lucy m. prob. 1660, Edward Palmes, wh. rem. that yr. from New Haven, and she d. 24 Nov. 1676; Margaret m. May 1665, John Curwin of Salem; Martha m. (I presume long aft. the dec. of her f.) Richard Wharton, for in Sept. 1677, she and her sis. Ann, as maidens, convey. to their two bros. all their right and claim in est. for £1,000. by deed, to be seen in our Reg. X. 167; Ann m. 1 Sept. 1692, as his sec. w. John Richards. * ‖ STEPHEN, Boston, fourth s. of first Gov. John, but first by his third w. came with his f. 1630, in the Arbella, adm. of our ch. 16 Mar. 1634, and freem. 7 Dec. 1636, when only 17 yrs. old, was appoint. in 1639 by the Ct. "to record things," in 1642 obtain. leave from the Gen. Ct. to go to Eng. but did not for three or four yrs. avail hims. of the gr. was ar. co. 1644, rep. in 1644 for Portsmouth. In Eng. he was quite successful in acquir. distinct. both milit. and politic. was made head of a regim. and so much trusted by Cromwell, that he design. it is said, to appoint. him successor to Major-Gen. Harrison, when he thot. good to send that fellow-laborer to prison, and direct. one of his subordinate places in Scotland to return Winth. as a mem. of one of his pretended parliam. those skilful architects of ruin that did nothing but build up anarchy. But he d. bef. the restorat. effect. by Monk, in whose army he was then serv. and might have gain. favor under the crown. He had early m. at Boston, Judith, sis. of Col. William Rainsborough, had Stephen, b. 7 Nov. bapt. 9 Dec. 1644, prob. d. 1647; and John, 24, bapt. 31 May 1646, wh. also prob. d. young; ano. Stephen was b. to him at Groton in Eng. 13 May 1651; but in his will he styles hims. of James Street, Westminster. He had three ds. Judith, w. of Richard Hancock; Margaret, m. Henry Ward, and next, Capt. Edmund Willey; and Joanna; but it may seem prob. that they were b. in Eng. ‡ WAIT-STILL, Boston, s. of Gov. John of Conn. with wh. he liv. long, and was one of the commiss. of the N. E. col. in 1672, and in the perilous days in 1675, 6, with his f. m. Mary, d. of William Browne, of Salem, had John, bapt. 12 Oct. 1679, d. soon; John, again, 28 Aug. 1681, H. C. 1700; Eliz. 11 May 1683, d. soon; William, 7 Dec. 1684; Ann, 28 Nov. 1686; and Joseph, 13 Sept. 1689. He was of the counc. nam. by the crown for Presid. Joseph Dudley in 1685, and for Sir Edmund Andros in 1686, and join. heartily in his overthrow; and by the self-form. counc. of safety he was put at the head of the milit. force, chos. an Assist. in 1692, under the old form of governm. ten days bef. the arr. of Sir William Phips with the new chart. In this he was made by the k. one of the counc. and thenceforward by popul. choice was contin. in that place, and also shortly aft. ch. justice of the Prov. appoint. by Gov. to his d. 7 Nov. 1717, not as Farmer says, 7 Sept. His first w. d. 14 June 1690, and William his s. d. 25 Sept. 1693, and Joseph d. two days aft. as Sewall's Diary shows. He took for sec. w. 13 Nov. 1707, Catharine, d. of Thomas Brattle, wid. of John Eyre, wh. d. 5 Aug. 1725. The s. John bec. disting. was a mem. of the Royal Soc. and left very disting. descend. Among gr. at the coll. Farmer ment. only five s. of a single branch; but it appears by the catal. that eight have been bred at Yale, and eighteen at Harv.

WINUS, JOHN, New Haven, m. 1664, Susanna Melyen, d. of a Dutchman, and was perhaps hims. a Dutchman, had John, b. 1 July 1665; and Susanna, 9 Feb. 1667.

WISE, HENRY, Guilford, perhaps s. of Joseph of Roxbury, had w. Mary, and two young ch. when he d. early in 1684. His inv. is of 1 Mar. and the names of ch. do not appear. HUMPHREY, Ipswich 1639, had w. Susanna, and ch. Benjamin, Joseph, Emma, Sarah, and Ann, when he d. His wid. m. Samuel Greenfield. * JOHN, Ipswich, s. of Joseph of Roxbury, aft. leav. coll. preach. at Branford (whence as chaplain to the soldiers in Jan. 1676, he march. with major Treat for Narraganset), there declin. invita. to sett. and preach. at Hatfield 1677 and 8, took the o. of fidel. in Feb. 1679, and was almost prevail. on to bec. the min. of that inf. town, but went to Ipswich, there was ord. 1682, or 1684, in a new parish, call. Chebacco, now Essex; at H. had m. 5 Dec. 1678, Abigail, d. of Thomas Gardner of Roxbury, had Jeremiah, H. C. 1700, min. of Berwick; Lucy; Joseph; Ammi Ruhami; Mary; Henry, H. C. 1717; and John; but no date is kn. nor whether these wh. outliv. him were the only ones. He was deeply engag. in the controv. raised by Andros's levy of a tax on all the towns of the col. and with his patriotic neighb. Col. Appleton was fin. and imprison. for words spok. in derogat. of the tyranny; and aft. overthrow of the usurp. he was one of the rep. 1689, next yr. one of the chaplains in the ill-concoct. expedit. of Sir William Phips against Quebec, and d. 8 Apr. 1725. JOSEPH, Roxbury, serv. of George Alcock, as nam. in his will of Dec. 1640, had perhaps been brot. by him, when he came the third time, 1636, from Eng. m. 3 Dec. 1641, Mary Thompson, as the town rec. tells, but whose d. she was is unheard, yet it may have been of William of Braintree, had Joseph, b. 1 Apr. 1643; Jeremiah, of whose b. the date is not seen (but the mo. hav. join. the ch.), both of her ch. were bapt. 24 May 1646; Sarah, 19, bapt. 26 Dec. 1647; Mary, bapt. 3 Feb. 1650; John, bef. ment. 15 Aug. 1652, H. C. 1673; Henry, 4 Mar. 1655; Bethia, 26 Apr. 1657; Benjamin, 7 Oct. 1660, wh. d. early in Dec. foll. says the ch. rec. but the rec. of the town, that omits the b. makes up for the deficiency by insert. the d. under 1664, on the principle of better late than never; and William, 9 Mar. 1662, whose b. is not found; Jeremiah, again, d. 1678; was a butcher late in his days, and d. 12 Sept. 1684; and his wid. d. 4 Aug. 1693. His d. Sarah m. a. 1666, Stephen Williams of R.; Mary m. 30 June 1669, Caleb Lamb. JOSEPH, Roxbury, s. of the preced. had Abigail, b. 20 June 1666; but wh. was his w. or when she d. are unkn. He d. 30 Jan. 1685. A wid. Jane Wise d. at Roxbury, Apr. 1637, perhaps mo. of Joseph the first; but wh. was that John, Cambridge, d. 9 Sept. 1644, is beyond the hope of certainty. NICHOLAS, freem. of Mass. 1645, is no more heard of. THOMAS, Saco 1636, is nam. in Folsom, 33.

WISEMAN, JAMES, Braintree 1639, had James, b. 8 Oct. 1640; and Mercy or Mary, 28 Mar. 1643; rem. to Boston, there by w. Dorothy had Joseph, 24 Dec. 1655; and Sarah, 18 Sept. 1657; perhaps these were by ano. w. than he had at Braintree. He was liv. 1677; and was a brazier. His d. Mary m. 12 June 1660, John Verin.

WISWALL, EBENEZER, Newton, youngest s. of Thomas of the same, m. 26 Mar. 1685, Sarah Foster, wid. of Elisha, and d. of Giles Payson, had no ch. was freem. 1675 or 80, as he sw. in both yrs. if we believe the rec. was lieut. and d. 21 June 1691, in his will giv. his est. (aft. the life of his w. wh. surv. to 22 Aug. 1714) to John, Oliver, and Samuel, s. of his br. Enoch, and made him, with his brs.-in-law, Samuel Payson and Nathaniel Holmes, excors. ENOCH, Dorchester, eldest br. of the preced. b. in Eng. a tanner, m. 25 Nov. 1657, Eliz. d. of John Oliver of Boston, the scholar, had John, b. 10 Dec. 1658, bapt. 20 Feb. foll.; Enoch, 10, bapt. 13 Jan. 1661, d. soon; Hannah, bapt. 6 Apr. 1662; Oliver, b. 25, bapt. 29 Jan. 1665; Eliz. bapt. 21 tho. rec. of b. is 28 Apr. 1667; Esther, b. 28 Dec. 1669, bapt. 2 Jan. 1670; Susanna, 2, bapt. 4 Aug. 1672; Enoch, again, 6, bapt. 11 Apr. 1675, d. young; Mary, 27 Aug. bapt. 2 Sept. 1677; Samuel, 2, bapt. 21 Sept. 1679, H. C. 1701, min. of Edgartown; and Enoch and Ebenezer, tw. b. and bapt. 25 Feb. 1683; and d. 28 Nov. 1706, aged 73. His wid. d. 31 May 1712, aged 75, says the gr.-st. of wh. we kn. the mistake, as she was under 72 yrs. and 3 mos. Susanna m. Edward Breck. ICHABOD, Duxbury, br. of the preced. had ent. H. C. 1654, but left in 1657 with the same cause of dissat. as carr. away Brinsmead and others, was some yrs. employ. perhaps at Pemaquid, there with a large part of the inhab. took o. of fidel. 1674, in 1676 was ord. at D. m. Priscilla, d. of William Peabody of that place, had Mary, b. 4 Oct. 1680; Hannah, 22 Feb. 1682; Peleg, 5 Feb. 1684, H. C. 1702; Perez, 22 Nov. 1686, prob. d. young; Mercy; Priscilla; and Deborah. He was sent 1689 to Eng. to procure new chart. for the Col. and stood stoutly for its independ. but was overpow. by the name and influence of Mass. yet he

ascrib. not the disappoint. of just expecta. as a train. politician might
have done, to any worse cause than the rashness and imprudence of
Mather, wh. had craftily alarm. the fear of Gov. Hinckley by suggest.
of the peril that Plymouth jurisdict. might be annex. to New York.
He d. 23 July 1700, and his wid. d. 3 June 1724, aged 71. Of his will,
very judic. in bestowing upon w. and five ch. the eldest d. w. of Elisha
Wadsworth having been provid. for at m. Francis Jackson, Esq. in
addit. to very many other favors, gave me a copy. * JOHN, Dorchester,
must have come in 1634 or earlier, as he was made deac. on the gather.
in Aug. 1636 of the new ch. at D. for Richard Mather, when the
larger part of the first mem. had gone to Conn. with Warham. He
brot. w. Margaret, d. prob. of Thomas Smith of London. He was
freem. 14 Mar. 1639, rep. 1646, and oft. aft. selectman in 1648 and bef.
and aft. went to Eng. (Mr. Clapp in Hist. of D. says) 1652, and in
few yrs. aft. his coming again, rem. to Boston, was an ironmonger, and
gen. trader, made rul. elder at the first ch. and d. 16 Aug. 1687, aged
85 or 6 yrs. From the numb. and dates of many of his ch. I feel confid.
that he had sec. w. as Benjamin, bapt. 15 Apr. 1649 ; Henry, 9 June
1650 ; Martha, b. 23 Feb. bapt. 14 Mar. 1652 ; Esther, 7, bapt. 11
June 1654, prob. d. young; Ruth, bapt. prob. 25 May 1656 ; but aft.
most patient investigat. Mr. Clapp is sure only of portion of these, as
ch. of John, and thinks the two first nam. may have belong. to his br.
Thomas.   No great value attaches to the decision, as neither liv. long.
But John, s. of John was also bapt. 15 Apr. 1649. By his will of 9
July preced. his dec. pro. 1 Sept. foll. are nam. only s. John ; ds. Han-
nah Overman, the eldest ch. w. of Thomas, wh. had first, in 1656, been
w. of Mahalaleel Munnings; Deborah, bapt. 23 May 1641, wh. m. a
Cutter, as Clapp in Hist. of Dorchester, 138, reads, but I doubt, bec. d.
Deborah seems ment. apart from d. Cutter ; d. Fisher, whose h. is call.
Daniel, tho. the reason is not seen, and perhaps the name is wrong ; d.
Johnson, wh. was Rebecca, perhaps the eldest, bapt. 2 Dec. 1638, sec.
w. in Oct. 1662, of Matthew ; d. Lydia Ballard, bapt. 13 Apr. 1645,
with whose h. I am unacq. ; d. Mary Edmunds, whose h. is unk. ; and
d. Mountfort, wh. prob. was Ruth, w. of Henry. JOHN, Boston, s. of
the preced. m. 5 May 1685, Hannah Baker, was freem. 1690, liv. perhaps some time at Dorchester, where his w. d. 18 Sept. of that yr. aged
28 yrs. NOAH, Newton, s. of Thomas of the same, m. 10 Dec. 1664,
Theodosia, d. perhaps eldest, of deac. John Jackson of the same, had
Thomas, b. 29 Apr. 1666, d. young ; Eliz. 30 Sept. 1668 ; Caleb; Margaret, 1 Mar. 1672; Hannah, 1 Apr. 1674; Mary; Esther, 1 Apr.
1678 ; Sarah, 5 Jan. 1681 ; and Thomas, again, 29 Apr. 1686 ; was
freem. 1685, capt. in 1690, when, march. to relieve Casco, in hard fight,

6 July, with Ind. he was slain, near Wheelwright's pond, in Lee, N. H. In the Magnalia, VII. 75, may be read an acco. of this action, embellish. as usual, in style, but as it is silent a. the d. of his s. John at the same battle, and we otherwise hear of no such s. I reject. the tradit. Forty-three yrs. later, a gr. of ld. in Lunenburg was extorted for these serv. from the tardy gratitude of the Province. OLIVER, Dorchester, s. of Enoch the first of the same, m. 1 June 1690, Sarah Baker, had Thomas; Enoch; Ebenezer; Oliver; Ichabod; John; and Samuel; and d. 28 Nov. 1706. His wid. d. 31 May 1712, aged 73. THOMAS, Cambridge, br. of John the first, long dwelt with him at Dorchester, where he sett. 1635, and was a very useful man, bring. w. Eliz. and s. Enoch, b. prob. in 1633, and perhaps Esther, bapt. here 1635; yet was not freem. bef. 1653; had also, at D. Ichabod, a. 1637, bef. ment.; Noah, bapt. 30 Dec. 1638, says Jackson; Mary; Sarah, bapt. prob. 19 Mar. 1643; Ebenezer, 1646; and Eliz. 15 Apr. 1649. Bef. July 1657 he had rem. to C. and gave his est. at D. to his s. Enoch. When John Eliot, s. of the apostle, was ord. 20 July 1664, the first min. of C. village, W. was made rul. Elder. He took sec. w. late in his days, Isabella Farmer, a wid. from Eng. mo. of Edward Farmer of Billerica, whose maiden name was Barbage, of Great Packington in Co. Warwick, from wh. by one more step of descent, than is giv. in the first art. of Geneal. Reg. I. came the diligent, judicious, and admired John Farmer, kn. thro. the length and breadth of N. E. as the author of the Geneal. Reg. of the first sett. print. at Lancaster 1829. W. d. at Newton, wh. had been incorp. from C. some yrs. bef. on 6 Dec. 1683; and his wid. d. at her son's in Billerica, 21 May 1686. Esther m. 16 May 1655, William Johnson of Woburn; Mary m. Samuel Payson of Dorchester, says Jackson, but she d. 25 May 1727 in 59th yr. if the gr.-st. tells truth, and ano. fate was that of this d. of Wiswall; and Sarah m. Nathaniel Holmes.

WITCHFIELD, JOHN, Dorchester, came in the Lion, arr. 16 Sept. 1632, freem. 11 June 1633, rem. with first sett. to Windsor, where his w. d. 26 Apr. 1659. He m. next, 1662, Margaret, wid. of Edward Goffe of Cambridge, but had no ch. by either. The sec. w. d. a. the end of June 1669 at Cambridge, where she had, 21 Apr. 1663, made her will, giving a piece of plate to W. her h. small legacies to the childr. of Samuel and Lydia, two ch. of her former h. by his first w. to her d.-in-law Eliz. Hayward, wh. is unkn. to me, to Rev. Jonathan Mitchell, Mr. Samuel Shepard, and Thomas Fanning ea. £5. to the childr. of her sis. Jane, first w. of Edward Winship, of wh. Joanna, the youngest, was to have double portion; but the larger part of her est. was for her own ds. Hannah and Abiah Goffe. This will was dr. by Thomas Danforth, witness. by him, Thomas Chisholme, and Caleb, that solitary aborig. gr. of H. C. 1665, wh. d. next yr. bef. he could be call. to verify his signat. wh. is very handsome. He was deac. and d. 16 Mar. 1678 at Windsor. The venerable Dr. T. M. Harris, mistook, in his Histor. Disc. 65, this name, and gave it Whitfield.

WITHAM, HENRY, Gloucester 1665, s. prob. of Thomas, d. 1702, had Thomas. THOMAS, Gloucester, wh. d. 1653, was, as Mr. Babson thinks, f. of Henry.

WITHERDEN, or WYTHERDEN, JOHN, Scituate 1643, rem. to Boston 1650, had a windmill 1654, on the common at Foxhill, by leave of the inhabs. and liv. 1661.

WITHEREDGE, or WYTHERIDGE, as the ch. rec. has it, EDWARD, Boston, mariner and merch. join. our ch. 24 Feb. 1644, and was made freem. in May foll.

WITHERS, *THOMAS, Kittery, came prob. with Neal, 1631, as one of his comp. for the patentee John Mason, and so may have liv. first on the W. side of the riv. in 1653 own. the jurisdict. of Mass. and was made a commissnr. the same yr. rep. 1656.

WITHIE, ROBERT, aged 20, with Susan, 18, and Mary, 16, prob. his sis. emb. at London, with a Mary With, 62, perhaps the mo. of them all, 11 Sept. 1635, in the Hopewell, Capt. Babb, but I can find no trace of them on our side of the water.

WITHINGTON, EBENEZER, Dorchester, s. of Richard of the same, freem. 1690, had w. Mary wh. d. 10 Jan. 1691; but I believe no ch. and d. 11 Feb. 1729, in 78th yr. and by his sec. w. Mary, d. of the church of Taunton, prob. m. 2 Feb. 1693, he had Ebenezer, b. 22 Dec. foll. wh. d. soon; and she d. 27 Dec. 1736, aged 76. HENRY, Dorchester, came prob. in 1636 or perhaps a yr. bef. was one of the six founders of the ch. 23 Aug. for Richard Mather instal. brot. w. Eliz. and ch. Richard; Faith, wh. m. Richard Baker; Mary, wh. m. 23 Feb. 1644, Thomas Danforth; and Ann, wh. m. James Bates the sec. His w. d. 16 Feb. 1661, and he m. 1662, Margaret, wid. of Richard Paul; was made a selectman, 1636, by the ch. rul. Elder, 1637, yet never a freem. and d. 2 Feb. 1667, aged 79. His wid. d. 20 May 1676. He had good est. and his will, of 8 Jan. 1665, div. it among the three ds. and his s. Richard's four s. HENRY, Dorchester, br. of Ebenezer, join. the ch. 2 Jan. 1677, as did his w. Sarah, 7 Nov. 1687. She was d. of Henry Leadbetter, m. 12 June 1684, had Sarah, b. 13 Apr. 1685; Henry, 7 Sept. 1686; and Silence, posthum. 19 Apr. 1688. He was freem. 1677, and d. 2 Feb. 1688. JOHN, Dorchester, s. of Richard of the same, freem. 1673, by w. Eliz. had Mary, b. 2, bapt. 7 Dec. 1673, d. young; Eliz. 5, bapt. 13 Aug. 1676; Mary, again, 10, bapt. 16 Mar.

1679, d. soon; Richard, 1, bapt. 8 Aug. 1680; Silence and Submit, tw.
15 Jan. 1682; Samuel, b. 4 May 1684; Hannah, 19 Dec. 1686; and
Susanna; was selectman 1688, and capt. of the comp. that went in the
mad expedit. of Sir William Phips against Quebec, 1690, from wh. he
came not back, tho. how he perish. is not told. His wid. m. 13 Feb.
1696, James White, outliv. him, and d. 19 Nov. 1722, aged 69. JO-
SEPH, Dorchester, youngest br. of the preced. by w. Deliverance had
Henry, b. 26 May 1696; and a d. Abia, posthum. 23 Nov. 1698, the
f. hav. d. 3 Aug. preced. His wid. m. 20 Dec. 1703, John Trott.
PHILIP, Dorchester, s. of Richard of the same, m. 17 Nov. 1682,
Thankful, d. of William Pond of the same, had John, b. 30 Dec. 1683;
Thankful, 15 Sept. 1685; Ebenezer, 21 Dec. 1687; William, 18 Feb.
1691; Henry, 5 Mar. 1693, d. young; Eliz. June 1696; Abigail, 28
Nov, 1698; and Sarah, bapt. 23 Aug. 1702. His w. d. 25 Dec.
1711, and he had sec. w. Sarah wh. outliv. him, and d. 18 Apr. 1746,
aged 75. He d. 27 Dec. 1736. ‖ RICHARD, Dorchester, s. of the first
Henry, b. in Eng. freem. 13 May 1640, ar. co. 1646, chos. rul. elder
1651, deac. 1669, m. Eliz. d. of Philip Eliot of Roxbury, had John,
bapt. 1 July 1649; Ebenezer, 7 Sept. 1651; Henry, 2 Oct. 1653; Eliz.
24 Aug. 1656, d. young; Philip, b. 26, bapt. 28 Mar. 1659; Constant,
16, bapt. 17 Nov. 1661; Eliz. again, 16, bapt. 22 Apr. 1666; and
Joseph, 15, bapt. 21 June 1668; and d. 22 Dec. 1701, aged perhaps 83
yrs. His wid. d. 18 Apr. 1714. WILLIAM, Newport 1638, on the list
of freem. 1655. Sometimes the name in old rec. is Withrington.

WITHMAN, JOHN, Charlestown 1641, whose name is Weightman on
the rec. of the ch. 31 July, when he join. as is also that of Susanna,
prob. his w. 30 Nov. 1642, freem. 18 May 1642, upon the list of house-
keep. 1658, was, by Farmer, suppos. the same as Whitman, tho. in a
later day he conject. Whitham.

WITT, JOHN, Lynn 1650, was, perhaps, one of the selectmen of
Groton 1655, to aid in organiz. town gov. but soon back at L. by w.
Sarah had Martha, b. 5 Mar. 1659; Thomas, 25 July 1661; Ebenezer,
6 Apr. 1665, d. in few wks.; and others. He d. 2 Dec. 1675, leav.
wid. Sarah, and ch. Ann Barney; Eliz.; Sarah; Mary; Martha; and
s. John; Thomas; and Jonathan. This John seems to have been of
Salem; but ano. JOHN, Lynn, m. 14 June 1676, Eliz. Baker, had Eliz.
9 Aug. 1677; John, 3 June 1679; and Mary, 14 Aug. 1681. JONA-
THAN, Lynn, perhaps br. of the preced. m. 23 Mar. 1663, Mary Diven
or Dinan, had Esther, b. 5 Feb. 1665, wh. m. 26 Dec. 1683, Ebenezer
Hathorne; and he d. 1665, his inv. being tak. 30 Jan. JOSHUA, Lynn,
perhaps br. of the preced. m. 10 June 1675, Eliz. Mansfield, had Moses,
b. perhaps 30 May foll. wh. d. in few days. WALTER, Andover, freem.
Apr. 1691.

WITTEN, MICHAEL, Scarborough, acknowledg. the jurisdict. of Mass. in Oct. 1658.

WITTER, JOSIAH, Lynn, s. of William of the same, m. 25 Feb. 1662, Eliz. Wheeler, had Eliz. b. 15 Mar. 1663; and Mary, 20 Feb. 1665; may have been at Stonington 1670, perhaps with f. of his w. WILLIAM, Lynn, an early sett. had w. Annis, and ch. Hannah, wh. m. a. 1650, Robert Burden; and Josiah, bef. ment. was troubled as a Bapt. early in 1646 by prosecut. of wh. the substance may be read in Col. Rec. III. 67, but d. 1659, aged 75. His will of 5 Aug. in that yr. mak. w. extrix. nam. s. d. and her h. was not pro. bef. June 1661. It is prob. that Burden stands for Burdett.

WITTOMS, PETER, Boston, m. 17 June 1652, Redigan Clark, had Mary, b. 15 Apr. 1653; Eliz. 26 May 1654, as the ancient copy of rec. says, but the modern copy has it 16, perhaps to conciliate favor for the rec. of her d. 25 May of the same yr.; and Peter, 15 May 1656.

WIXAM, or WICKSON, BARNABAS, Eastham, s. of Robert of the same, by w. Sarah had Barnabas, b. 15 Sept. 1693, d. soon, but not, perhaps, so early as Geneal. Reg. VII. 347, makes it; Joshua, 14 Mar. 1695; Lydia, 12 June 1697; Robert, 29 May 1698; and Prince, 2 Dec. 1700. ROBERT, Plymouth 1643, rem. to Eastham, by w. whose name is not seen clear. had Jeremiah, b. 30 Aug. 1655; Titus, 2 Dec. 1657; Eliz. 29 May 1660; and Barnabas, whose date is not found; and d. Oct. 1686. Eliz. m. 28 June 1678, Nathaniel Mayo the sec. of E.

WODELL. See Waddell.

WOLCOTT, WALCOTT, or WOOLCOT, GEORGE, Windsor 1640, s. of the first Henry, brot. by his f. rem. a. 1650 to Wethersfield, adm. freem. 1657, but d. at W. 1662, or, as is said, 12 Feb. 1664, having by w. Eliz. had Eliz. b. 1651; George, 1653; John, 1656; and Mercy, 1659. Very slight acco. is seen of any of this fam. Perhaps George and John may be discern. sometimes at Wethersfield. Mary was infirm, and under guardians; and Eliz. m. 1686, Gabriel Cornish. ‡ HENRY, Dorchester 1630, was b. a. 1578, in the S. part of Somerset sh. at or near Wellington, not far from the edge of Devonsh. and thus, prob. gain. sympathy with the puritans of the W. who project. the voyage of the Mary and John in Mar. of that yr. He was honor. with a commiss. from the crown, as a justice bef. leav. home, as tradit. tells, and had good landed est. as perhaps may be infer. from a very valua. letter of his br. John, 15 Apr. 1639, print. in Geneal. Reg. II. 373. He desir. adm. as freem. 19 Oct. 1630, and was sw. 1 Apr. 1634. His w. Eliz. Saunders, m. a. 1607, was his compan. in the traverse of the wilderness to plant the first town, nam. Dorchester, but soon aft. Windsor, on the

Conn. in Oct. 1635, and outliv. him but few wks. Their ch. Henry, b.
a. 1610; George; Christopher; Ann, b. a. 1620; Simon, 1625; and
Mary; were all brot. from Eng. He is the first officer nam. in the rec.
of Conn. p. 1, chos. 26 Apr. 1636, constable, and in Apr. 1643 Assist.
till his d. was largely engag. in business, and d. 30 May 1655. No will
is preserv. His wid. d. 7 or 17 July foll. aged 73. Ann m. Matthew
Griswold; and Mary m. 25 June 1646, Job Drake. Of Christopher
notice is never seen, but that he d. 7 Sept. 1662. ‡ * HENRY, Windsor,
eldest s. of the preced. b. in Eng. at Tolland near Wiveliscombe, Co.
Somerset, m. 8 Nov. 1640, Sarah, d. of that Thomas Newberry or
Newbury, wh. was engag. in the migrat. from Dorchester, but prevent.
by d. had Henry, b. 6, bapt. 8 Jan. 1643; John, b. 28 Feb. 1646;
Samuel, 8 Oct. 1647, prob. d. young; Sarah, 5 July 1649; Mary, 8
Dec. 1651; Hannah, 8 Mar. 1654; Samuel, 16 Apr. 1656; and Josiah,
22 July 1659; was rep. 1655, 6, and 61, Assist. 1662, bef. the com. of
the royal chart. of that yr. in wh. Gov. Winthrop had caus. the insert.
of his name, and was contin. in the office of Assist. as far as our publish.
rec. runs, was of the counc. of war in 1675-6, and d. 12 July 1680.
Sarah m. as fam. tradit. tells, Walter Price of Salem; but it should say
his s. John; Mary m. James Russell of Charlestown; and Hannah d.
at 29 yrs. for wh. tradit. found no h. His wid. d. 16 June 1684. The
will of Henry, 21 Sept. 1670, provides for w. and the seven ch. to the
ds. all then unm. £250. ea. to Henry, housing and ld. at Tolland Mill, to
John, other tenement in Tolland, and notices his est. at Wellington.
Other est. he had of large extent on our side of the water in Windsor
and Wethersfield; and he was very dilig. in the cultivation. Great
sales of fruit-trees thro. much of the region betw. Fairfield on the
Sound and Springfield on the bank of the Conn. are spoken of; and
Josselyn, wh. went home in the same ship when W. visit. his native ld.
in 1671, relates, that W. inform. him that he made 500 hogsheads of
cider from his orchard in a yr. What allowance for Josselyn's ciphers
should be made may be guessed from his enumera. of the dwelling-
houses in Boston, on his earlier visit, wh. Drake, in Hist. 244, fails to
explain. HENRY, Windsor, eldest s. of the preced. m. 12 Oct. 1664,
Abiah, youngest d. of Edward Goffe of Cambridge, whose wid. had two
yrs. bef. m. John Witchfield of W. had Eliz. b. 27 Aug. 1665; Henry,
13 Apr. 1667, d. soon; Abiah, 1 May 1669; Sarah, 27 Mar. 1671, d.
soon; Henry, again, 30 Jan. 1673, wh. d. at 24 yrs.; Sarah, again, 16
Apr. 1676; and Samuel, 26 Mar. 1679; was freem. 1667, and d. 15
Feb. 1710. His wid. whose name is so pervert. in Geneal. Reg. I. 252,
and again V. 463, d. 18 June 1717, in her 72d yr. Neither Henry, nor
Samuel, wh. d. 1712, had issue, and the male line of this branch ceased.

HENRY, Windsor, s. of Simon the first of the same, m. 1696, Jane Allen, wh. d. 1702, had, the fam. geneal. says, Henry, b. 1698; Thomas, 1702; Peter; Rachel; and Gideon; but it names no w. and gives no dates, exc. that of his d. Nov. 1746. JOHN, Salem, is by tradit. said to have own. the house that Roger Williams sold him, when driv. away in 1635, but no more can be told. *JOHN, Cambridge, or Watertown, freem. 4 Mar. 1635, rep. May foll. d. in July 1638, his inv. tak. 17th of that mo. by three of the ch. mem. Rev. George Phillips being one, and the prefix of respect, show that he was a man of esteem. JOHN, Newbury, a carpenter, b. a. 1632, perhaps s. of the first nam. John, m. 20 Nov. 1653, Mary Thorla, prob. d. of Richard of the same, had Mary, b. 1654; Sarah, 23 Aug. 1657; John, 25 Oct. 1660; Joseph, 2 Feb. 1664; Eliz. 24 Feb. 1667; Martha, 13 Sept. 1670; Lydia, 15 Jan. 1674; and Hannah, 18 Apr. 1679. Perhaps he rem. to Brookfield, and may have been by the Ind. driv. thence in 1689 to die 30 Sept. 1690 at Springfield. In his will he names w. the two. s. and three ds. the elder b. but neither of the younger three wh. were prob. d. He had ld. at Newbury, at Brookfield, and Watertown. JOHN, Windsor, s. of the sec. Henry of the same, propound. for freem. 1670, m. 14 Feb. 1677, Mary, d. of John Chester of Wethersfield, had John, b. 20 Nov. foll.; Henry, 7 Aug. 1679, d. soon; Charles, 3 Sept. 1681; George, 20 Oct. 1683, d. young; and Benjamin; and his w. d. 10 July 1689; by sec. w. m. 22 June 1692, Hannah Nichols of Stamford, had Mary, and he d. 3 Jan. 1713. When the wid. d. is not told, but she with the four ch. had good est. £1,300. Mary m. John Eliot of Windsor, gr.s. of the apostle. JOHN, New Haven 1680, a blacksmith, m. 8 Feb. 1684, Sarah Johnson, prob. d. of John of the same, but whether any issue foll. is unkn. When he sold ld. there in 1698 w. Abigail join. in the deed. JOHN, Newbury, s. of John of the same, m. 4 Jan. 1685, Mary Emerson, but Coffin tells no more. JOSEPH, Suffield, br. prob. of the preced. m. 4 Mar. 1686, Rebecca, d. of Launcelot Granger, had Joanna, b. 13 Sept. 1687; Joseph, 30 Aug. 1689; and Hannah, 8 Nov. 1691; the two latter b. at Springfield; rem. to Brookfield, there the ds. with their mo. were k. by the Ind. when they assault. the town in 1693. JOSIAH, Salem, in an early day m. it is said, Alice, d. of Richard Ingersol, but nothing more can I tell of h. or w. exc. that aft. the name is very oft. giv. with a, for o, in the first syl. JOSIAH, Salem, youngest s. of the sec. Henry, m. Penelope, d. of George Curwin of the same, had Eliz. b. 30 Mar. 1688, d. at 14 yrs. but her mo. had d. soon aft. b. of her ch. and he m. Mary Treat wh. brot. him nine ch. acc. the fam. rep. in Geneal. Reg. I. 252, tho. wh. she could be, unless one of the ds. of Gov. Robert's mythic. numb. of twenty-one by first w. is hard to find. The

Gov. had a Mary, but she was bapt. 23 May 1652, too many yrs. bef. the b. of Josiah to have such a platoon; yet it may be that he was happy eno. to have ano. younger of the same name. More important, however, is the file of the ch. Josiah, 21 Dec. 1690, d. in few ds.; Treat, 26 Mar. 1696, d. in few wks.; Thomas, 23 June 1697, d. in few wks.; Mehitable, 3 Aug. 1698, d. at 23 yrs.; Josiah, again, 11 July 1700, d. in few ds.; John, 12 Sept. 1702; Eliz. 1 Apr. 1705, d. at 11 yrs.; Mary, 13 July 1706, d. next wk.; and Treat, again, 9 Oct. 1712. §† ROGER, Windsor, youngest s. of Simon of the same, m. 3 Dec. 1702, Sarah, d. of the sec. Job Drake, had Roger, b. 14 Sept. 1704; Eliz. 10 Apr. 1706; Alexander, 20 Jan. 1708, d. young; Samuel, 9 Jan. 1710, d. young; Alexander, again, 7 Jan. 1712, Y. C. 1731; Sarah, 31 Jan. 1715, d. at 20 yrs.; Hepzibah, 23 June 1717; Josiah, 6 Feb. 1719; Erastus and Epaphras, tw. 8 Feb. 1721, of wh. both d. young; Erastus, again, 21 Sept. 1722; Ursula, 30 Oct. 1724; Oliver, 20 Nov. 1726, Y. C. 1747; and Mary Ann, 1 Jan. 1730. He gain. gr. distinct. was Lieut.-Gov. 1741 to 50, then Gov. for four yrs. and had milit. serv. at the conq. of Louisburg, 1745, in com. of the Col. force, and d. 17 May 1767. SAMUEL, Wethersfield, s. of the sec. Henry, m. 1678, Judith, d. of Samuel Appleton of Ipswich, had Samuel, b. 1679; Gershom, 1680, d. at 2 yrs.; Josiah, Feb. 1682; Hannah, 19 Mar. 1684; Sarah, 14 Aug. 1686; Lucy, 16 Oct. 1688; Abigail, 23 Sept. 1690, d. at 24 yrs.; Eliz. 31 May 1692; and Mary, 14 May 1694; and he d. 14 June 1695, leav. good est. *SIMON, Windsor, s. of the first Henry, prob. youngest, b. in Eng. 1625, freem. 1654, was rep. for Simsbury 1671 and 5, m. 1656, Joanna Cook, wh. d. Apr. 1657, and he m. next, 17 Oct. 1661, Martha, sis. of the first William Pitkin, had, says Parsons, in Geneal. Reg. V. 464, five s. and five ds. but the fam. geneal. I. 253, names only four ds. Eliz. b. 19 Aug. 1662, wh. m. 8 Dec. 1680, Daniel Cooley of Springfield, and d. 30 Jan. 1707; Martha, 17 May 1664, m. 1686, Thomas Allyn, and d. 7 Sept. 1687; Simon, 24 June 1666; Joanna, 30 June 1668, wh. m. 26 Sept. 1690, John Colton; Henry, 20 May 1670; Christopher, 4 July 1672, d. bef. 21 yrs. prob. unm.; Mary, 1674, d. at 2 yrs.; William, 6 Nov. 1676; and Roger, 4, if better authority be not for 28 Jan. 1679. He d. 11 Sept. 1687, and in Mar. foll. to elude the tyranny of Andros, wh. order. all admin. in N. E. on dec. persons' est. to be tak. at Boston, the eldest s. made partition betw. mo. and childr. How his minor four brs. and one sis. were bound by this arrangem. Sir Edmund had not time to inq. The wid. m. Hon. Daniel Clark, outliv. him, and d. 13 Oct. 1719. SIMON, Windsor, eldest s. of the preced. m. 5 Dec. 1689, Sarah, d. of John Chester of Wethersfield, had Sarah, b. 1690; Martha, 1692; Simon, 1694; Christopher, 1696; Eunice, 24

Sept. 1697; and James, 1700. His w. d. 3 Aug. 1723, and he d. 3 Aug. 1732. WILLIAM, Windsor, br. of the preced. m. Abia Hawley, perhaps d. of Ephraim of Stratford, had Abia; Lucia; William, b. 21 July 1711; Martha; and Ephraim; and d. 26 Jan. 1749. As in the Winth. fam. the choice of f. s. and gr.s. in early days to the office of Gov. by popular vote is observ. so in later generat. the Conn. steady habits made Roger and his s. Oliver and gr.s. Oliver their ch. rulers. Twelve of this name had been gr. at Yale, two at Harv. and two at other N. E. coll. in 1834, as is noted by Farmer in MS.

WOLFALL, or WOOLFALL, RICHARD, Boston 1677, of wh. I see nothing but that he is nam. in the will of the first Thomas Oliver, 1653, as hav. m. a d. of the testator, then liv. at Muddy riv. now Brookline.

WOLFE, or WOOLFE, EDWARD, Lyme 1671. PETER, Salem, freem. 14 May 1634, was so much of a milit. spirit, as hardly to fail of being chos. lieut. in 1646, yet in 3 Mass. Hist. Coll. VII. 256, with w. Martha, was one of the founders of ch. in Beverly 1667, and d. 6 Dec. 1675. One Susanna W. with sev. others, was order. to be releas. from prison in 1683, but on what grounds they had been arrest. I see not in Vol. V. of our Col. rec.

WOLLASTON, the capt. wh. form. a tempora. settlem. 1625, wh. aft. short time he abandon. and went to Virg. might hardly seem to deserve a place in this work, were it not for the possibil. that a passeng. of the Planter, from London, ten yrs. later, call. Mary Wolhouston, aged 30, may have been seek. the long abs. h. when she came to Boston; tho. more prob. is it that she was w. of a Mr. W. wh. is nam. in an act of the Ct. Sept. 1641, impos. fine of £13. 6s. 8d. perhaps the same as JOSIAH that I find a merch. of Boston in 1666. Very obscure, however, is the evid. for either suppos. Lewis claims one W. for Lynn 1637, but says he rem. to Sandwich.

WOLLEY, ROBERT, Southampton, L. I. one of those wh. in Aug. 1673, made representa. of their case to the inhabs. of the Unit. Colonies of N. E. as to the policy of their submit. to the Dutch, wh. had conquer. New York. See 3 Mass. Hist. Coll. X. 86–88. Perhaps the name might as well be read Walley.

WOLSEY, GEORGE, is, by Mr. Felt, seen with his w. 1653, in some part of the land; but I can trace them no later.

WOLTEN, JOHN, Piscataqua, said to have come from Plymouth, Eng. a. 1633, and resid. twenty-one yrs. when, strange as it reads, our Gen. Ct. in 1654, order. him to go home to his w. Farmer, MS. says he was tak. on his passage, by the Dutch, wh. kept all his prop. but set him on shore in Eng. where he soon aft. d.

WOOD, or WOODS, ABIEL, Middleborough, s. of Henry, m. 1683, Abiah Bowen, had Elnathan, b. 14 Apr. 1686 ; Abiah, 20 Feb. 1689 ; Abiel, 19 Mar. 1691 ; Timothy, 13 Oct. 1693 ; Jerusha, 11 Nov. 1695 ; Ebenezer, 4 Aug. 1697 ; Judah, 28 July 1700; and Thomas, 30 Jan. 1703. With his w. he was among the found. of the first ch. at M. 1694; and d. 10 Oct. 1719 ; and his wid. d. 21 May 1746, aged 83. ABRAHAM, Concord, s. perhaps eldest of Michael of the same, was freem. 1690. ANTHONY, Ipswich 1665, m. 1 June 1666, Mary Grover, perhaps d. of Edmund of Salem, had William, b. 20 Mar. 1667. CONSIDER, New London, by Miss Caulkins is mark. as hav. a gr. of ld. 1648, but forfeit. for non-resid. CONSTANT, a passeng. aged 12 yrs. in the Abigail from London, 1635, and there might seem some grounds for suspect. that he was the same as preced. DANIEL, Ipswich 1643, d. 1648. DANIEL, Rowley, rem. to Boxford, freem. sw. 22 Mar. 1690, and again in Oct. foll. if the Col. rec. be true, yet possib. the solemnity may have been for f. and s. by w. Sarah, wh. d. 27 Sept. 1714, had David, b. 1670 ; Daniel ; John ; and others, as Barry says. EDMUND, Springfield 1636, rem. to Wethersfield that yr. thence to Stamford 1641, and next, in few yrs. more to Hempstead, L. I. and may again have rem. EDWARD, Charlestown, was adm. to join the ch. 30 Mar. 1640, freem. 13 May foll. and his w. Ruth join. in few days. She perhaps had Ruth, and certain. Tabitha, bapt. 30 May 1641 ; d. 29 Aug. 1642, and he d. 27 Nov. foll. In Geneal. Reg. III. 81, the date of inv. would perhaps appear 4 Dec. aft. Farmer was led to mistake the name of the Springfield Edmund for Edward, and so to think he might be s. of this man. An EDWARD of Boston, mariner in 1659, had w. Eliz. and no more is kn. ELEAZER, Medfield, youngest ch. of Nicholas of the same, was struck down, when his br. Jonathan, 21 Feb. 1676, was k. by the Ind. wh. scalp. him, and suppos. he was d. yet he reviv. in a good degree, and some yrs. aft. m. Dorothy, perhaps d. of George Badcock of Milton, had Dorothy; Hannah, b. 11 Feb. 1689 ; and Abigail, 25 Nov. 1692 ; and he liv. to 20 May 1704, with occasional mental aberra. ELIAS, ELLICE, or ELLIS, Dedham, by w. Catharine had Mehitable, b. 17 June 1658; Abigail, 19 July 1660; and his w. d. 29 May 1663. He took for sec. w. Miriam, wid. of John Smith of D. wh. was the school-mistress many yrs. and d. 19 Oct. 1706, aged 73. The ludicrous solemnity of the gr.-st. inscript. is happily preserv. in Geneal. Reg. IV. 277. He rem. to Dorchester, where he was freem. 1673 and liv. 1692. GEORGE, Saybrook 1660, m. that yr. but the name of his w. is not seen; had George, b. 28 Sept. 1661, and prob. rem. HENRY, Plymouth 1643, m. a. 1645, Abigail, d. of John Jenny, rem. to Yarmouth, had Sarah ;

Samuel, b. 25 May 1647; went back to P. there had John, 1649;
Jonathan, 1 Jan. 1650; David, 17 Oct. 1651; Isaac, 1654; and Abiel;
and perhaps more ch. d. at Middleborough; but the time of his d. is not
seen, bec. the inv. ment. in Geneal. Reg. VII. 235 is defic. in date.
His d. Sarah m. 28 Nov. 1667, John Nelson. HENRY, Concord, by w.
Ellen had John, b. 17 Nov. 1651; Mary, 7 Sept. 1653; Hannah, 11
Mar. 1656; and Milicent, 4 Apr. 1660. Usually his name is Woods;
and I presume he rem. to Groton, was quarter-master of the troop of
W. Middlesex cavalry in 1671. HENRY, Newport, by w. Hannah had
Henry, b. 24 Nov. 1670; Abigail, 15 Aug. 1672; James, 9 Nov. 1674;
Hannah, 25 Sept. 1677; Richard, 28 Oct. 1679; and Eliz. 9 Jan. 1682.
It ought to be add. that the rec. spells this name as Whod, and possib.
that may mean Hood. ISAAC, Marlborough, s. of John of Sudbury, of
wh. from Barry I learn, that by two ws. he had Isaac, Joseph, Charles,
Solomon, Dinah, Mary, and Eliz. and that his will was pro. 17 Aug.
1720. Sewall's Diary, as giv. in Geneal. Reg. VI. 72, says under 1685,
July 4, " Isaac W. dies suddenly." Perhaps this was some young man,
fellow-worship. with S. but my knowledge is limit. by him. ISAIAH,
Ipswich 1668, then said to be 41 yrs. old, m. 26 Jan. 1653, Mercy, d. of
Simon Thompson of the same, had Mary, b. 31 Oct. 1653; Simon, 18
Feb. 1655; Thomas, Nov. 1656, d. in 5 mos.; Sarah, Jan. 1658, d.
next mo.; Samuel and Isaiah, tw. 20 July 1659, of wh. Isaiah d. soon;
Joanna, 14 Dec. 1661; William, 18 Feb. 1664; Sarah, again, 26 Dec.
1665; Thomas, again, 31 Jan. 1668; Thompson, 18 Feb. 1670; John,
Feb. 1672, d. soon; Joseph and Benjamin, tw. 22 May 1673, both d.
soon; and Ebenezer, 3 Dec. 1676, d. in 3 wks. He m. 23 Dec. 1684,
for sec. w. wid. Hannah Wheeler, but prob. had no more ch. JAMES,
on L. I. 1649. JAMES, Marlborough, s. of John of Sudbury, was in
garrison of serg. Wood, prob. his f. in 1675, freem. 1690, had w. Hopestill. JEREMIAH, Stamford 1641, went to Hempstead, L. I. perhaps
was br. of Edmund, or William, or of both. JOHN, Saybrook, employ.
by the younger John Winth. was k. by the Pequots, as appears in Conn.
Col. Rec. I. 29, prob. in 1637. JOHN, Sudbury, pinmaker, wh. seems
an odd trade for a wilderness pioneer; by w. Mary had John, b. 8 May
1641; perhaps Francis, 1645; James, 18 July 1647; Catharine; Isaac,
14 July 1655; beside Hannah, prob. the oldest ch. wh. m. 7 June 1665,
John Leavins of Roxbury, and d. early, leav. Hannah nam. in the will
of her gr.f. He d. 10 July 1678, and his wid. d. 1690, aged 80, says
Barry. In Oct. 1675 he was, I suppose, the serg. in one of the Marlborough garrison houses, as John, James, and Isaac, his s. were there also.
‖ JOHN, Lynn 1635, passeng. in the Hopewell, Capt. Babb, late in the
autumn of that yr. aged 26, br. possib. of William, the author of N. E.

Prospect, freem. 13 May 1640, ar. co. 1642, may have been at Salem 1646. JOHN, Dorchester, freem. 10 May 1643, perhaps rem. JOHN, Plymouth 1643, of wh. gladly would I learn more than that his s. John was b. 4 Mar. 1650 ; and Nathaniel, 25 Feb. 1652 ; and Isaac, 27 Feb. 1654 ; Sarah, Abigail, Mercy, Eliz. and Hannah ; beside that Mary wh. m. 11 Dec. 1661, Rev. John Holmes, wh. must have been b. long bef. either of the others, of wh. it is strange to find neither in Windsor, nor any other author, a precise report. His d. Sarah m. 13 Feb. 1668, John Fallowell; and his own name is sometimes mistak. for that of Atwood. JOHN, Newport, on the list of freem. 1655. JOHN, Taunton, sw. in 1662, as witness to a nuncup. will, that he was 42 yrs. old. JOHN, New London 1660, s. perhaps of the first John, as Miss Caulkins in her Hist. shows, 324, m. prob. Mary, d. of Walter Buddington. JOHN, Dorchester, m. Eliz. d. of Richard Hall. JOHN, Marlborough, prob. eldest s. of John of Sudbury, by w. Lydia had John, b. 1670; Lydia, 1672 ; Hannah, 1677 ; Joseph, d. soon ; Joseph, again, 1682 ; Sarah, 1685 ; Silence, 1689 ; Benjamin, 1691 ; and James, 1694 ; serv. under his f. in the garrison ho. Oct. 1675, was constable 1677, and deac. prob. that freem. of 26 Mar. 1691, exult. in the title of ens. JOHN, Ipswich, m. 1 May 1676, Mary Healey, had Margaret, b. Sept. 1679 ; Mary, 19 Dec. 1681 ; and he d. 14 Aug. 1684. JOHN, Concord, s. prob. of Michael of the same, freem. 1690. JONAS, Springfield 1636, rem. early to Wethersfield, sett. at Stamford 1641, unless this settlem. refer rather to Weed, and in few yrs. was of L. I. at Hempstead, prob. under patent of 1644, bef. 1654 was of Southampton, and in few yrs. was a commiss. under the jurisdict. of Conn. there. JONATHAN, Shirborn, as that part of Medfield has bec. elder s. of Nicholas of the same, had only posthum. d. appropri. call. Silence, as she was b. the day aft. the fall of her f. (and a few hrs. bef. d. of her mo.) He was k. in Philip's war, 21 Feb. 1676, tho. not prob. a soldier. JOSEPH, Taunton, m. 1 Jan. 1680, Esther Walker, d. of James of the same. JOSIAH, Charlestown, m. 28 Oct. 1657, Lydia Bacon, d. perhaps of Michael the sec. had Josiah, b. 10 Oct. 1658 ; Lydia, 23 Nov. 1659, d. next mo.; Lydia, again, prob. 1662, both bapt. 6 July 1662, the w. hav. join. the ch. on preced. Sunday; Samuel, 12 Nov. 1671 ; Joseph, 27 Dec. 1674 ; and Ruth, 4 June 1676. JOSIAH, Ipswich, br. of Obadiah of the same, m. 23 Dec. 1684, a wid. whose name I cannot make out, but kn. no more of him. JOSIAH, Woburn, s. of the first Josiah, by w. Abigail had Josiah, b. 31 Aug. 1687 ; Lydia, 1 May 1689 ; Abigail, 10 Sept. 1691 ; Samuel, 10 Dec. 1693 ; Joseph, 25 Apr. 1696, d. at 17 yrs. in Geneal. Reg. II. 387, mispr. 57 yrs.; Solomon, 23 Jan. 1699, d. at 9 mos.; and Ruth, 4 Jan. 1702. MARK, one of the soldiers in Turner's comp. 1676, was of Charlestown, prob. had m. 2 Feb. 1665, Eliz. d. of Nathaniel Hancock of Cambridge. MICHAEL, Concord, s. of William of the same, freem. 13 May 1640, had Abigail, b. 10 Apr. 1642; and Shattuck gives him other ch. Abraham, Isaac, Jacob, Thompson, or Thomas, and John, as left by him, at his d. 13 May 1674. Next mo. his wid. Mary brot. inv. Abigail m. Stephen Hosmer. NATHANIEL, a passeng. in the Increase from London, 1635, aged 12 yrs. of wh. no more is heard, nor can any indicat. be seen, exc. that in the same ship came Eliz. aged 38, wh. may have been his mo. NATHANIEL, Ipswich, took the o. of fidel. 1678. NATHANIEL, Groton, prob. s. of the first Samuel, by w. Alice had Nathaniel, b. 19 Oct. 1694; Daniel, 10 Aug. 1696; John, 4 Mar. 1698; Isaac, 20 Feb. 1700; Bathsheba, 5 Apr. 1702; Hannah, 16 Mar. 1704; Phebe, 13 Feb. 1706; Aaron, 26 May 1707; Moses, 6 July 1709; Reuben, 11 Apr. 1711; Phebe, again, 13 Mar. 1713; and Jonathan, 4 June 1716. NICHOLAS, Dorchester, had liv. at Braintree, when freem. 2 June 1641, and there m. Mary, d. of Robert Williams of Roxbury, as Mr. Clapp assures me, had Mary and Sarah, tw. b. 25 Dec. 1642 as the Roxbury rec. in Geneal. Reg. VI. 377, 8, affirms, tho. Clapp claims him as early as 1640 to be overseer of Glover's farm until 1654. He had also Hannah. In 1645, he was one of the petitnrs. for Pumham's ld. to be gr. to them. Farmer, relying on a passage in Hutch. I. supposes he was of Medfield 1656, and there he certain. was soon aft. and also earlier. Records at M. give to him and w. Mary, Jonathan, b. 3 Jan. 1652, wh. was k. by the Ind. 21 Feb. 1676; Mehitable, 22 July 1655, wh. m. 17 Oct. 1671, Joseph Morse; Abigail, 13 Sept. 1657; Bethia, 28 July 1660; and Eleazer, 14 Mar. 1662; and his w. d. 19 Feb. foll. and he d. 7 Feb. 1670. His d. Hannah m. 26 Nov. 1665, John Harding, but d. bef. her f. In his will of 16 Jan. 1670, all the six ds. are nam. of wh. Hannah was dec. and her s. Abraham, as well as the two s. are well provid. for, out of his ample est. Mary m. John Thurston; Sarah m. 4 Oct. 1660, deac. Thomas Bass of Braintree. Who was his sec. w. call. Ann in his will, or whether he had more ch. bef. or aft. is wholly unkn. Ano. NICHOLAS is nam. by Morse, as of Concord, but no more is told, than that he had Abigail, b. 10 Apr. 1642. OBADIAH, Ipswich 1649, a baker, by w. Margaret had a ch. b. 11 Apr. 1665; and Margaret, 28 June 1667, wh. d. the same yr. but the mo. d. next wk. By a sec. w. Hazabelponah, he had Obadiah, 5 June 1675; James, Nathaniel; Josiah; Samuel; Eliz.; Mary; Susanna; and Margaret; and he d. 3 Dec. 1694, leav. all these ch. and the wid. with the hard name. OBADIAH, a soldier wound. in Philip's war late in 1675; for whose cure the Conn. counc. made liberal paym. [see Col. Rec. II. 484], was of Hartford 1676, and perhaps s. of the

preced. had there bapt. Margaret, 1687 ; Abigail, 1699 ; and Margaret,
again, 1705 ; and prob. others ; but when he d. is not heard. ‖ RICH-
ARD, Boston, ar. co. 1642, was capt. of that comp. 1677, and d. 23 Apr.
1681, leav. good est. the amount of inv. giv. in by his wid. Frances
being £1,090. includ. 1,500 acres at Quinebaug at £30.   He wrote his
name Woodde, an unpleasant peculiarity, as it might be made into two
syllab. and so confound. with Woody, a distinct fam.   RICHARD, Hingham 1659, a witness with Thomas Lincoln the weaver, 10 Jan. 1660, to
the nuncup. will of wid. Margaret Johnson ; may have liv. at Marblehead, 1668, with s. of the same name.   RICHARD, Norwalk 1694, may
be the man, wh. d. at Wallingford, 1705, leav. wid. and d. Miriam.
ROBERT, Dedham, d. 30 Dec. 1638.   SAMUEL, Ipswich 1643.   SAMUEL,
Groton, one of the earliest, tho. not of the largest proprs. there, by w.
Alice had Thomas, b. 9 May 1663 ; Eliz. 17 Sept. 1665 ; Nathaniel, 27
Mar. 1668 ; Mary, 2 Aug. 1670 ; Abigail, 19 Aug. 1672 ; and Hannah,
18 Sept. 1674 ; and he d. 29 Sept. 1703.   SAMUEL, Danbury, a physician in the early days of that town, came from Eng.   SAMUEL, Groton,
by w. Hannah had Susanna ; Rachel ; Alice, b. 26 Sept. 1700 ; Abigail,
12 Sept. 1703 ; Esther, 13 Nov. 1705 ; Joseph, 21 June 1707 ; and
Martha, 15 Apr. 1709.   He was m. 1685 at Chelmsford.   SAMUEL,
Middleborough, s. of Henry of Plymouth, was one of the found. of the
ch. 1694, had m. bef. 1679 w. Rebecca, by wh. he had Ephraim,
Samuel, and perhaps others.   SAMUEL, Rowley, s. of Thomas the first
of the same, m. Margaret Elithorpe, prob. d. of the sec. Thomas of the
same, had Thomas, b. 1689, and prob. others.   SIMON, Ipswich, eldest
s. of Isaiah of the same, m. 8 Aug. 1674, Eliz. Foster, had Eliz. b. 16
Aug. 1675, d. next mo.; Mary, 27 Dec. 1676 ; Jonathan, 6 Mar. 1678 ;
Philemon, 4 Apr. 1679 ; Eliz. again, 15 Jan. 1683 ; Daniel, 12 June
1685 ; and William, 3 Jan. 1690.   He had sec. w. Abigail, wh. d. 1
Oct. 1732, aged 67.   STEPHEN, Plymouth 1643, had John, b. 1648 ;
and Hannah, 14 Oct. 1649 ; in the will of John Dunham, 25 Jan. 1669,
is call. his s.-in-law.   THOMAS, Rowley 1655, by w. Ann had John, b.
1656 ; Thomas, 1658 ; Josiah, 1664 ; Samuel, 1666 ; Solomon, 1670 ;
Ebenezer, 1671 ; James, 1674 ; and four ds. of wh. one m. the third
Joseph Jewett, and next John Lunt.   THOMAS, Rowley, s. of the preced.
of wh. I find no acco. of m. or fam.   THOMAS, Groton, prob. s. of
Samuel the first, by w. Hannah had Esther, b. 29 July 1697 ; Josiah,
15 Sept. 1701 ; Eliz. 9 Nov. 1702 ; and Thomas, 25 Nov. 1705.
TOMPSON, Ipswich, s. of Isaiah of the same, m. 8 Dec. 1691, Martha,
d. of Isaac Foster, had Jemima, b. 18 May 1693, d. within twenty days.
TRYALL, Salisbury, d. 11 June 1678, but we kn. not whether male or
fem. ch. or adult.   WALTER, Newport, perhaps br. of Henry, at least

the same perversity of spelling the name, Whod, leaves uncertain what to call it, by w. Amy had Martha, b. 2 May 1676. WILLIAM, the valu. author of New England's Prospect, London 1634, may well be thot. that freem. of 18 May 1631 ; but more prob. is it, that he was sett. at Lynn, as early as 1630, as claim. by Lewis. He prob. came to Salem, 1629, and 15 Aug. 1633 left our country, as his book relates. That was print. 1634, and it is conject. by Shattuck, wh. would magnify the honor of Concord by so respectab. a citizen, that he came again to our side of the water, and d. at C. aft. many yrs. resid. 14 May 1671, aged 86. For *a* William this is well vouch. Lewis has better appear. of proof in p. 84, of his sec. Ed. quot. Wood's words of *minute* descript. of Lynn river ; beside wh. the fact of one of this name being rep. at the Gen. Ct. Mar. 1636, when he was chos. either for Salem or Lynn, bef. any one came from C. with the resid. at Sandwich 1643, so large a proport. of the first inhab. of S. having gone from L. are no slight object. to the hopes of Shattuck. Still the fame of Bulkley may have drawn him from S. where we never hear of him more. One Miriam whose f. we kn. not, was b. 8 May 1648, bur. next day ; and Mary was b. 29 Mar. 1649, both at S. One WILLIAM came, 1635, in the Hopewell, Capt. Babb, a husbandman, aged 27, with Eliz. 24, wh. may have been his sis. or w. and John, 26, bef. ment. prob. his br. and it is clear, that if this be the author (wh. I neither affirm nor deny), two points decide against the Concord claim to him ; for at C. w. of William d. 1 Sept. 1659, was call. Margaret ; and the passeng. in the autumn of 1635 on the Hopewell, must have been b. 1608, while Shattuck's client could not have come into our world aft. 1585 ; or, if his faculties were not weaken. when he made his will, 15 Sept. 1670, reckon. hims. as 88 yrs. old, still earlier was his advent. At C. no ch. was b. to him ; but he had ch. perhaps all, certain most. b. in Eng. Michael ; Ruth, wh. m. Thomas Wheeler ; and Abigail, wh. m. 24 Mar. 1667, Stephen Hosmer. The will names, beside Michael, Ruth and her h. the gr.d. Abigail Hosmer. WILLIAM, Portsmouth, R. I. m. Martha, d. of the first Ralph Earle. WILLIAM, Marblehead 1668, had perhaps William, both old eno. to sign the petition to the Gen. Ct. that yr. and was liv. 1678. WILLIAM, Ipswich, took the o. of fidel. 1678. WILLIAM, Newtown, L. I. 1640–1686, may have come from Stamford, Conn. WILLIAM, Ipswich, s. of Isaiah, d. 27 Sept. 1689, prob. unm. as he nam. no ch. but did sev. brs. and sis. WILLIAM, Salem vil. now Danvers, freem. 1690. Gr. in 1834 were count. by Farmer, thirteen at Dartm. twelve at Harv. five at Yale, and ten at other N. E. coll. Woods are unit. as Wood.

WOODBRIDGE, *BENJAMIN*, Newbury or Cambridge, whichever may be prefer. by the reader as resid. of this first-b. of H. C. 1642, younger br. of our John, wh. prob. brot. him in the Mary and John, 1634, and s. of Rev. John of Stanton, near Highworth, Co. Wilts, where he was b. 1622. Strangely confus. is an acco. in Geneal. Reg. VI. 279, that he was brot. by his br. on his return from Eng. 1663, aft. wh. he " became one of the first gr. of Harv." He had, if we receive the acco. that Mather gives, Magnalia, III. 219, been tak. by that br. wh. had gone back to Eng. in 1637, on receiv. news of d. of his f. but I see no small reason to doubt the narrative in the Eccles. Hist. Yet it is more consistent with itself than the Geneal. Reg. story. He went home, soon aft. grad. and obtain. a living in his native Co. perhaps at Salisbury, into wh. he was induct. 16 Nov. 1648 ; and honor. at Oxford with degree of S. T. D. the same yr. He next succeed. famous Dr. Twiss at Newbury in the adjoin. shire of Berks, and in 1662 was eject. from office, and d. 1 Nov. 1684, at Englefield, in the same Co. His verses on our John Cotton, purport. to be inscript. on gr.-st. are in the Magnalia, III. 31. But in Allen's Biogr. Dict. the ingenious lines are ascrib. to his neph. and his opinion should have weight, yet it may be that either of us follow. no course of inquiry to ascertain, which Benjamin has the best claim. BENJAMIN, Medford, s. of Rev. John of Andover, b. in Eng. whither his f. had gone a. 1647, and was prob. brot. by him, when he came back in 1663, m. 3 June 1672, Mary, d. of Rev. John Ward of Haverhill, wh. d. 11 Oct. 1680. By her prob. was b. only ch. Benjamin, that had been heard of by Farmer, as in his MS. notes to his Reg. is told. But in the " Ancestry of the Jones Fam." of Geneal. Reg. VI. besides this s. he is enrich. with Dudley, of Barbadoes, and Rev. Samuel of E. Hartford, H. C. 1701. That article contains too many errors to entitle it to the confidence desirable, among others one suspic. point is, that this s. was b. 1683, some yrs. aft. the d. of his w. He preach. some yrs. at Bristol, and aft. at Kittery 1688, and was resid. 1694 at Newcastle, N. H. but at last sat down 17 June 1702 at M. says Farmer in MS. and there d. 15 Jan. 1710. I wish the fair author of that Jones Geneal. could teach us, wh. are the *two* Dudley Woodbridges, for only one should be ascrib. to Benjamin, in our Coll. Cat. 1694 and 1696. ‡ * *JOHN*, Newbury, s. of Rev. John of Stanton in the N. E. part of Wiltsh. b. 1613, had been bred at Oxford, Mather says, but on the requirem. of the o. of uniformity, he left the Univers. for " a course of more private studies," and was brot. by his uncle, Rev. Thomas Parker, whose living was at Newbury in the neighborhood, in comp. with his cous. Rev. James Noyes, 1634, in the Mary and John, was one of the first planters of our Newbury, but he seems to have little tendency to preach, as in 1637, the yr. when his f. d. in Eng. (for by the Registry of the Diocese I obs. that a successor was then appoint. to the vacancy) he was made "surveyor of the arms," and rep. to the Gen. Ct. He not long aft. taught a sch. in Boston, when Portmort had gone, in the religious schism, to Exeter, and he is even claim. as a mem. of ar. co. 1644, and m. a. 1639, Mercy, d. of Gov. Thomas Dudley, and was liv. at N. when his f.-in-law, in Nov. 1642, stir. him up to seek. advancem. as a min. and on 24 Oct. 1645 he was ord. not 16 Sept. 1644, wh. is Mather's date (more than a yr. bef. the ch. was gather.), as first min. at the new town of Andover. More trustworthy, however, is the tale, that he went, in 1647, "on the invitat. of his friends" to Eng. *once more*, exc. in this last circumstance; tho. why friends should withdraw him, in less than two yrs. from his first settlem. in the pulpit here, is not easi. explain. Sixteen yrs. he contin. in Eng. first having employ. in the serv. of the able men of that Parliam. commiss. for treating with the king in his prison at the Isle of Wight bef. the overthrow of Parliam. authority by the soldiers wh. adopt. the more summary mode of negotiat. for remodel. the old constitution of their country. Here, prob. he was fix. in the presbyter. views of ch. governm. in opposit. to the levellers and Cromwellians, and was employ. aft. as min. at Andover, in Hampsh. and a less import. parish in Wilts, finally at a sch. in Newbury, whence, Mather says, the Bartholomew Act exclud. him. In 1663, July 27, he reach. Boston in the ship Society, and in two yrs. was engag. as assist. in the min. of his uncle Parker. In this honorable duty, aft. two or three yrs. a sad controv. distract. the quiet of the ch. and he was dismiss. some time bef. 1670, tho. Parker remain. in the tempestuous sea to his d. in 1677. Of his ch. Coffin names Sarah, b. 7 June 1640; Lucy, 13 Mar. 1642, wh. m. 2 Oct. 1667, Rev. Simon Bradstreet of New London, her cous. and next, Capt. Daniel Epps; John, H. C. 1664; but this last and other eight or nine were b. aft. he left our Newbury, and most of them in Eng.; Thomas, 1649; Mary, 1652; Benjamin; Timothy, 1656, H. C. 1675; Dorothy; Ann; Joseph; Martha; but tradit. in Mather gives ano. without name, and he says eleven liv. to adult age. Aft. retiring from the ministry, the notice in Geneal. Reg. VI. 279, proceeds, "he was immediately chos. into the magistr." but it was not until 1683, and Mather left him out of the Counc. in his new chart. of 1691, as prob. too old. His w. d. 1 July 1691, and he d. 17 Mar. 1695. *JOHN*, Killingworth, s. of the preced. b. prob. at Andover, began to preach there 1666, but early in 1668 at Windsor, where in Oct. preced. had been gr. div. of the sentiment of the old parishion. of Warham, wh. was grown too infirm, a major part unit. in desire of one of the s. of Presid. Chauncey. Aft. long disquiet, the earlier and elder candidate went to Eng. and W. was ord. 7 Apr. 1669 for Kenilworth as the settlem. was first call. by the people and the rulers bef. modern

barbarity inflict. its present name; and the governm. of the Col. made
him a gr. of 250 acres of ld. next yr. for his good conduct, but in 1679
he was sett. at Wethersfield. He m. 26 Oct. 1671, Abigail, eldest d. of
Gov. William Leete, and Miss Jones in the Geneal. Reg. VI. gives him
s. John, b. at K. 1678, H. C. 1694, the min. of West Springfield; but
she makes the f. d. bef. 1682, while the Coll. catal. notes him 1690.
Ano. s. was Ephraim, H. C. 1701, ord. 8 Nov. 1704 at Groton, Conn.
For a gr.s. John, Y. C. 1726, min. at Windsor, and aft. at So. Hadley,
s. of the W. S. min. a weak tradit. that he was "ninth John W. in the
min. thro. as many successive generat." Farmer adopts. Sufficient
honor it may be esteem. if a begin. of this tale be true, as the judicious
author of the memoir indicates " Rev. John W. a follower of Wickliffe,
b. not far from 1492. His s. John braved the dangers of the same profession and faith, as also did John the third, John the fourth, and John
the fifth, in regular succession. The last named was the much esteemed
pastor of a puritan ch. in Stanton, Wilts." Now the same faith may
have been enjoy. in private by the first, sec. third, fourth, and fifth John;
but I shall doubt the profession was not public, until some account be
found of the benefices filled by them under the tyrannic. power of bluff
old Harry in his long reign, and during the power of his harder daur.
Queen Mary. On our side of the water, the fam. has been illustr. by a
long line of clerg. JOHN, Newbury, sch.-master 1719–31, was prob. s.
of Joseph of the same, d. 13 Dec. 1731. JOSEPH, Newbury, youngest
s. of John the first, b. in Eng. bef. 1634, and brot. that yr. by his f. m.
20 May 1680, Martha, eldest d. of Ezekiel Rogers of Ipswich, and gr.d.
of the historian, had Joseph, b. 7 May 1687; John, 13 Feb. 1690,
H. C. 1710; Nathaniel, 28 Jan. 1696; and Margaret, 1698; but when
he d. is not seen in Coffin's Hist. SAMUEL, Hartford, prob. s. of Timothy, was first min. of the parish on E. side of the riv. says Dr. Allen,
wh. could tell no more but that he d. 1746, acc. Coll. catal. THOMAS,
Newbury, sec. s. of the first John, b. in Eng. m. 12 June 1671, Mary
Jones, d. of Ann, sec. w. of Capt. Paul White by a former h. had Paul,
b. 12 Feb. 1673; Mary, 20 Feb. 1675; Thomas, 28 Jan. 1677; and
John and Benjamin, tw. 24 Feb. 1679. He was capt. and d. 30 Mar.
1681, of suffer. from burn. in his own ho. as Coffin, from Sewall's Diary
tells. His wid. m. Joseph Coker. TIMOTHY, fourth s. of the first John,
b. in Eng. was sixth min. of Hartford, but not ord. bef. 18 Nov. 1685,
m. Mehitable, d. of Samuel Wyllis, wid. of Rev. Isaac Foster, wh. was
predecess. of W. in the Hartford ch. but she had first been wid. of
Daniel Russell of Charlestown, by her had Samuel, H. C. 1701; Susanna; and prob. others, beside Ashbel, b. 1704, Y. C. 1724, wh. by
mistake in Geneal. Reg. VII. 75, I presume, is made s. by a sec. w. that

his f. did not have. The sec. w. of Rev. Timothy W. was Abigail, d. of the rich wid. of Phineas Wilson of Hartford, by her third h. John Warren of Boston ; and Goodwin, 349, wh. is wrong in call. her sec. w. of Warren when she was the third, must be right as to her d. Abigail, being wid. of Richard Lord, and giv. only to Woodbridge, Theodore, b. 23 June 1717. A third w. he had in Mary, d. of Hon. William Pitkin, wid. of some min. that Miss Jones has not nam. in her Memoir. Geneal. Reg. VI. 280, and to me it seems very strange, that such details cannot be gather. but she tells of his d. 30 Apr. 1732. Farmer counts, in 1834, gr. of this name, eighteen at Yale, twelve at Harv. two at Dartm. and four at other N. E. coll. add. that one half had been clerg. among wh. the first eight at Harv. and first four at Yale.

WOODBURY, sometimes WOODBERRY, ANDREW, Salem, 1668, s. of the elder William, wh. was br. of John and Nicholas, by w. Mary had Mary, b. 14 May 1657, d. next yr.; Susan, 9 June 1660 ; and Hannah, 1 Apr. 1664. His wid. Mary brot. inv. to Ct. 29 June 1685. HENRY, in Essex Inst. I. 12, nam. as overseer with two others in the will of George Williams, 23 Sept. 1654, seems to me a mistake, perhaps for Humphrey. HUGH, Salem 1650, s. of William the first, liv. prob. on Beverly side,.as he was one of the found. of ch. there, m. Dec. 1650, Mary Dixey, perhaps d. of Thomas of S. had Samuel, b. 6 Dec. 1651, bapt. 25 Jan. 1652, d. young ; Samuel, again, 2, bapt. 4 June 1654 ; Hugh, 12 Feb. bapt. 9 Mar. 1657 ; John, b. 5 Sept. 1658, bapt. 6 Mar. 1659 ; Priscilla, 8 Apr. 1666, but no more is kn. of him, unless he be the man of this name in 1686 at or near Taunton. HUMPHREY, Beverly, s. prob. eldest, of John, b. in Eng. a. 1609, had perhaps come with his f. 1626 to Cape Ann, rem. with Conant next yr. to Salem, and there he prob. contin. while his f. went home in 1627 to obt. assist. for the planta. and came back in June 1628, a. three mos. bef. Endicott. He unit. with the ch. July 1643, yet is not sw. freem. bef. 1678, even if this be not better evidence for his s. than hims. had w. Eliz. and ch. bapt. at S. ; Isaac, 4 Feb. 1644 ; Humphrey, 8 Mar. 1646 ; Susanna, 4. Feb. 1649 ; William, 4 May 1651 ; Peter, 17 Apr. 1653, yet said to be b. 28 Mar. 1652, and one or the other rec. may be wrong ; Richard, b. 28 Feb. 1655, bapt. prob. 11 Mar. foll. ; Eliz. b. 28 Apr. 1657, bapt. 30 May 1658, wh. m. John Walker ; Christian, b. 20 Apr. bapt. prob. 11 Aug. 1661, wh. m. John Trask, prob. as his sec. w.; and John, Thomas, and Joseph, all three nam. in his will, as also are Sarah and Eunice Walker, ds. of Eliz. He was one of the found. of the ch. at B. and its first deac. and d. Feb. 1681. By the change in process on wills and est. of dec. persons aft. overthr. of the old charter, under direct. of Presid. Dudley, his will, of 4 Mar. 1686, pro. 11 Oct. foll. is found in

Suffolk jurisdict. Vol. XI. His w. Eliz. was the extrix. His wid. by her will of 1 May 1689, with codic. of 8 Aug. foll. pro. 26 Nov. aft. at Salem, as giv. in Geneal. Reg. VII. 322, names the three ds. but only two s. William, wh. is made excor. and John, ea. hav. call. a s. Peter aft. her s. wh. was k. at Deerfield with Capt. Lothrop and the flower of Essex, 18 Sept. 1675. HUMPHREY, Beverly, s. of the preced. m. 8 Jan. 1671, Ann, perhaps d. of Richard Window of the same, had Bethia, b. 1672; Abigail, 1674; Humphrey, 1677, d. at 18 yrs.; Ann, 1680; Nehemiah, 1686; Abel, 1688; Nathan, 1691; and Israel, 1693; beside these at Gloucester, Nathaniel, 1684; Susanna, 1695; and Humphrey, 1698. He d. 9 Apr. 1727, and his wid. d. 28 Feb. foll. ISAAC, Beverly, s. prob. of William the first, m. Mary Wills, or Wilkes, sis. of Robert, wh. by his will of 24 Sept. 1677, in wh. he was made excor. gave est. to her and their ch. Robert and Mary, freem. 1678, was tak. 1689 in his fish. sch. by the French. *JOHN, Salem, had come from Somersetsh. perhaps some fish. village on the Bristol Channel, and sat down first at Cape Ann, soon form. with others, under direct. of Roger Conant, the settlem. at Salem in 1626, went home next yr. and came back early in 1628, prob. bring. w. Agnes and s. William, unless it be conclud. that they were brot. two yrs. bef. with s. Humphrey. In the notice of Roger Conant, one of the most valua. of Mr. Felt's illustra. of our early hist. Geneal. Reg. II. 235–8, is seen the degree of organiz. of governm. bef. the coming of Endicott, wh. did not, so far as we can learn, exercise any higher authority, and prob. bef. the arr. of Higginson, and the fleet of 1629, had not add. a greater num. of subjects than he found already in the planta. He was sw. constable, 28 Sept. as in our Col. Rec. I. 76, appears, and req. to be adm. freem. 19 Oct. 1630, aft. the governm. had been transfer. to this side of the water, and was sw. 18 May foll. was rep. 1635 and 1638, prob. took a sec. w. had Hannah, bapt. 25 Dec. 1636; Abigail, 12 Nov. 1637; and Peter, 20 Sept. or Nov. 1640; and d. 1641. His wid. Agnes did not produce the will until some mos. aft. being summon. and the inv. was not sw. bef. 20 Feb. 1644. JOHN, Beverly, s. of Humphrey, or of William, perhaps, freem. 1670, was next yr. at Rowley, and soon back to B. The s. of Humphrey nam. a ch. Peter in mem. of his own br. Peter, the soldier, wh. fell at Bloody Brook, 18 Sept. 1675, as in the will of the child's gr.mo. is seen, Geneal. Reg. VII. 322. But an elder JOHN of Salem, by w. Eliz. had Eliz. b. 15 Aug. 1654; John, 15 Mar. 1657, d. young; and Abigail, 8 June 1660. He may have been s. of William the first. JONATHAN, Boston, mariner, m. Abigail, d. of Henry Phillips, had Jonathan; and d. 1677, hav. made his will 22 Jan. of that yr. His wid. m. David East, and next, Thomas Walter. NICHOLAS, Beverly, came from Great Yarmouth, Co. Norfolk, was early of Salem, s. of the elder William, is call. br. in the will of James Patch 1658, perhaps from his m. a sis. had gr. of ld. 1638, tho. prob. he was then only a young man, m. Ann Palsgrave, d. perhaps of Richard of Charlestown, had Nicholas, bapt. 22 Nov. 1657 ; Joseph ; Isaac ; and Andrew, all 19 Nov. 1665 ; was freem. 1673, made his will, 1 Aug. 1685, and d. 19 May foll. aged 70. In it he ment. w. Ann, ch. Isaac, Andrew, Benjamin, Joan, w. of Samuel Plummer, and Abigail, w. of Richard Ober, and her ch. Ann and Hezekiah. To these he div. good est. here, but to his eldest s. Nicholas he devis. his ld. in the mother country at Great Yarmouth. But that w. had been d. some yrs. as I presume, for admin. 2 Dec. 1691, was giv. to his wid. Mary. * PETER, Beverly, s. of John the first, freem. 1668, was serg. 1685, by w. Sarah, d. of first Richard Dodge, had Peter, bapt. 21 July 1667 ; perhaps others beside Josiah, b. 15 June 1682, wh. was gr.gr.f. of Hon. Levi, late one of the Justices of the Sup. Ct. of the U. S. was deac. rep. 1689, and at the first Gen. Ct. under the new chart. 1692, d. 5 July 1704. RICHARD, Beverly, s. of Humphrey, d. 1690 on ret. from Phips's wild crusade against Quebec. Inv. was brot. in 20 Nov. 1690. His will of 1 Aug. preced. recit. "how being by God's providence call. out to the serv. of God and the country in the present expedit." nam. w. Sarah, eldest s. Richard, brs. Thomas and William, and br. Roger Haskell. THOMAS, Salem, when the petition of 1668 was present. but of Beverly when adm. freem. 1683, of wh. I find nothing more, but that he was s. of Humphrey, m. 2 Dec. 1661, Hannah Porter, perhaps d. of William Dodge, and wid. of Samuel Porter, had William, b. 17 Sept. foll. WILLIAM, Salem, br. of the first John, had gr. of ld. 1637, of wh. our ch. knowledge comes from his will and inv. In the will of 5 June 1663, pro. 26 June 1677, he names w. Eliz. s. Nicholas, William, Andrew, Hugh, and Isaac, and d. Hannah Haskell. The inv. says he was aged a. 88, and d. 29 Jan. 1677. WILLIAM, Salem, s. of the preced. unit. with the ch. 29 Dec. 1639, had Nathaniel, bapt. 12 Jan. 1640 ; and John, 24 Oct. 1641 ; freem. 2 June 1641 ; was one of the found. of the ch. at Beverly 1667, d. 1674. WILLIAM, Beverly, s. of Humphrey, had Peter, b. prob. aft. the fall of his uncle at Bloody Brook, for wh. he was nam. as rememb. in her will, by wid. gr.mo. 1689, wh. made this f. excor. I find six of this fam. gr. at Dartm. and two at Harv.

WOODCOCK, JOHN, Wrentham, is first heard of at Springfield 1638, where he was largely in trade, yet he may have gone thither from Roxbury, at least he was of R. so much as to own two houses there, for he mortgag. one, 25 Mar. 1651, to John Gore, and the other, 6 June aft. to Joseph Holmes. However, he had rem. from S. to Dedham 1642, and thence, perhaps, to Rehoboth, bef. 1673, but prob. liv. much at W. In Philip's war, his ho. in W. now perhaps within Attleborough bounds, was a famous garrison, and he says, in a letter of 26 Apr. 1676, that two of his fam. had been slain, and ano. s. was wound. Yet he prefer. the jurisdict. of Plymouth, and was rep. for R. 1691. See Baylies, II. 218, and III. 125. Of his fam. no full acco. is kn. but he was liv. 1694, had d. Sarah, wh. m. Alexander Balcom of Providence. JOHN, Rehoboth, prob. s. of the preced. call. jun. m. 26 Feb. 1674, Sarah Smith, had John, b. 18 Dec. 1674; Jeremiah, 6 Jan. 1676, and his w. was bur. 10 May foll. having prob. as the reports are inconsist. brot. forth Nathaniel but twelve days bef. NATHANIEL, Rehoboth, d. 28 Apr. 1676, may have been s. of John of Wrentham, and the same wh. was wound. in the war, and perhaps his d. was the conseq. ‖ RICHARD, Boston, ar. co. 1658, in Col. Rec. IV. pt. 2, is call. armorer, 1661, d. 12 Nov. 1662. WILLIAM, Salem, had d. Bridget, and d. 1648. WILLIAM, Salem 1662, perhaps s. of the preced. was a physician, d. 16 June 1669, leav. wid. Hannah, by wh. he had one ch. that d. soon. WILLIAM, Hingham, a soldier of Johnson's comp. Dec. 1675, liv. at Weymouth 1679.

WOODDAM, WOODAM, or WOODHAM, JOHN, Ipswich 1648, a bricklayer, had in 1664 w. Mary, and d. 29 May 1678. His wid. d. 12 Feb. 1682. Prob. he had Mary, wh. m. 26 Mar. 1663, John Ayer, jun.

WOODDY, WOODDEY, WOODIE, WODY, or WOODY, *HENRY, the freem. of 1656, may have been then of Concord, of wh. he was rep. 1685, and he seems to be the same, elsewhere call. Woodhouse, wh. see. ISAAC, Boston, m. 20 Mar. 1656, Dorcas Harper, perhaps d. of Joseph of Braintree, had Mary, b. 22 Mar. 1657 ; and John, 18 Sept. 1659. He was s. of Richard the first, prob. b. in Eng. but I kn. no more, exc. that in 1666, he was, with his br. Richard, engag. in mak. saltpetre as Col. Rec. shows. JOHN, Roxbury, s. of Richard the first, b. in Eng. m. Mary, d. of John Coggan of Boston, had John, bapt. 11 Mar. 1649, d. at 8 yrs. ; Isaac, 3 Feb. 1650 ; and d. 23 May 1650, of smallpox, "a christian and godly br." says the ch. rec. His wid. m. 10 Jan. 1653, Thomas Robinson of Scituate. RICHARD, Roxbury, came with w. Ann, wh. d. or was bur. 5 Apr. 1656, and prob. the s. Richard, John, and Isaac, was freem. 18 May 1642, and d. or was bur. 7 Dec. 1658. Abstr. of his will of 24 Sept. preced. is in Geneal. Reg. VII. 339. Its chief informat. is, that he had a new w. RICHARD, Roxbury, s. prob. eldest of the preced. b. in Eng. freem. 1644, m. 29 Dec. 1646, Frances, d. perhaps of Thomas Dexter, had Thomas, bapt. 12 Nov. 1648, d. under 2 yrs.; Mary, 21 July 1650 ; Martha, 24 Jan. 1652 ; rem. to Boston that yr. had there Eliz. b. 19 Sept. 1653 ; Ann, 12 July 1655 ;

Samuel, 11 Sept. 1656; and Sarah, 21 May 1661; was a soapboiler, in 1666 made saltpetre, was ens. 1674.

WOODEN, WOODING, WOODIN, or WOODDEN, JEREMIAH, New Haven, s. of William of the same, a propr. 1685 in his own right, beside being heir of his f. But no more is told of him. JOHN, Portsmouth perhaps in 1635, Hampton 1643, Haverhill 1646, had gr. of 150 acres from the governm. of Mass. 1667, on his petitn. stating that he had been 32 yrs. an inhab. in the ld. and had many ch. yet dates of birth and names of all are unkn. prob. by reason of his migrat. habits. JOHN, Ipswich, perhaps s. of the preced. took o. of fidel. 1678. NATHANIEL, New Haven, s. of William of the same, m. Dec. 1687, Martha, d. of John Sacket. WILLIAM, New Haven 1643, m. 25 Oct. 1650, Sarah Ollard, had William, b. 16 Nov. 1651; Jeremiah, 17 Feb. 1653; Sarah, 13 Sept. 1654; Susan, 5 Nov. 1655, d. young; Joseph, 16 Jan. 1657; Benjamin; Mary; Nathaniel; and Abigail; and d. Dec. 1684, when eight of the ch. were liv. His wid. d. 1693. Sarah m. 1682, Samuel Merwin; Mary m. a Sacket; and Abigail m. as his sec. w. Ebenezer Hill. Joseph was blind, and prob. infirm in mind, d. bef. 1701, as did Sarah. WILLIAM, New Haven, s. of the preced. d. Sept. 1711, leav. wid. and five ds. of none, however, can I see the names.

WOODFIELD, JOHN, Scituate 1646, had w. Esther, and d. June 1669; but neither from his will of 4th of that mo. nor hers of 27 May 1672, can be learn. that they had ch. tho. from her nam. sixteen legatees, we indeed may well judge, that none was alive.

WOODFORD, JOSEPH, Farmington, suppos. by some to be s. of Thomas of Hartford, without any evid. to sustain the conject. and against the presumpt. to be deriv. from the will of T. Perhaps he was b. in Eng. propound. for freem. 1663, and his name stands in the list; m. Rebecca, d. of Thomas Navell of the same, had Mary, wh. m. 1693, Thomas Bird; Rebecca, m. 2 Jan. 1696, John Porter; Esther, m. the same day, Samuel Bird; Sarah, m. Nathaniel Bird; Hannah m. 14 Dec. 1699, Thomas North; Joseph, b. 1676; Eliz. m. 11 June 1707, Nathaniel Cole; Susanna, bapt. 3 Dec. 1682, m. 26 June 1707, Anthony Judd; and Abigail, bapt. 27 Dec. 1685, m. 8 Aug. 1710, Caleb Cowles; and he d. 1701. JOSEPH, Farmington, only s. of the preced. m. 23 Jan. 1700, Lydia, d. of Joseph Smith, had Lydia, b. 22 Sept. 1702; Mary, 26 June 1704, d. soon; Joseph, 22 Aug. 1705; Eliz. 22 July 1707; Mary, 2 Mar. 1709; Rebecca, 22 Apr. 1711, d. soon; Samuel, 30 Mar. 1712; Sarah, 4 June 1714; Rebecca, again, 20 May 1716; John, 2 June 1718; Susanna; and William, 1722; and d. 7 Feb. 1760. But he had m. 1745, sec. w. wh. d. 1797, aged 100 yrs. THOMAS, Roxbury 1632, came from London in the William and Francis, emb. 7 Mar. arr. 5

June, with Edward Winslow; in wh. voyage, as from the Hist. of Winth.
is learn. were a. sixty passeng. when the custom-ho. rec. proves that
the names of only sixteen were made kn. to the governm. among wh.
was neither that of Rev. Stephen Bachiler, or of Rev. Thomas James,
or of Rev. Thomas Weld, tho. ea. was then on board to elude the malignant feebleness of Archbp. Laud. On adm. of our ch. he was call. serv.
was made freem. 4 Mar. 1635, had m. Mary, d. of Robert Blott, wh.
came in 1632, and may have been fellow-passeng. Early he rem. to
Hartford, and aft. d. of his w. that had brot. him ch. as in her f.'s will
refer. to, rem. a. 1656, to Northampton, there d. 6 Mar. 1667. To
three ds. he gave all his prop. nam. them in his will, Mary, wh. had m.
1653, Isaac Sheldon; Hannah, wh. m. 29 Nov. 1659, Samuel Allen;
and Sarah, b. 2 Sept. 1649, wh. m. 4 Sept. 1664, i. e. two days more
than 15 yrs. old, Nehemiah Allen; all of N. But from the will of
Blott, wh. d. less than two yrs. bef. W. I must infer, that two other ds.
wh. were d. had belong. to this s.-in-law, beside ano. that requires no
little study to form satisfact. opin. as to the liv.

WOODHOUSE, WOODIS, WOODICE, or WOODOWES, * HENRY, Concord 1650, is believ. to be the freem. of 1656, then spell. Wooddey; m.
Elinor Hopkinson, wh. had been a fellow-passeng. from London, had
Mary, wh. m. Joseph Lee of Ipswich; Elinor, wh. m. a Cheney of
Roxbury; Eliz. m. Dr. Simon Davis of Concord; John, wh. perish. in
the fire, 2 Feb. 1667; Sarah, b. 29 Feb. 1664, m. John Dakin of Concord; and Milicent, wh. m. 31 Dec. 1689, Joseph Estabrook of Cambridge, and his w. d. 4 Sept. 1693. His ho. was burn. says the Roxbury
ch. rec. in the winter of 1667, and his only s. perish. in it; and tradit.
tells that in the gr. fire of London, Sept. preced. he lost two houses.
He was rep. 1685, and aft. overthrow of Andros, 1690 and 92, m. 29
June 1694, Sarah, wid. of Samuel Rogers of Ipswich, wh. d. 19 Jan.
1718. He was an officer in 1690, of Henchman's regim. and d. 16 June
1700. JOHN, Salem, of wh. I kn. nothing but from his will of 24 May
1659, pro. 29 June foll. in wh. he names d. Alice, w. of Samuel Very,
and her ch. Samuel, Eliz. Sarah, Thomas, and John, beside ano. person,
of whose name I dare not be certain. See Essex Inst. I. 92. RICHARD,
Boston, fisherman, by w. Mary had Mary, b. Jan. 1638, bur. next mo.;
Mary, again, 14 Jan. 1639, bapt. 14 May 1643, a. 4 yrs. and 4 mos.
old; Joseph, bapt. at the same time, a. 2 yrs. and 5 wks. miscall. John
in the rec. of b. 9 Apr. 1641; and Hannah, if we take the town copy of
rec. b. 15, but by more trustworthy rec. of ch. bapt. 3 Mar. 1644, a. 5
days; and Jonathan, 25 Apr. 1647, a. 9 days old; all in right of the
mo. wh. had unit. with the ch. 7 May 1643. He was excus. from
train. in 1657, but this prob. on acco. of his employm. as by w. Sarah,

he, or more prob. ano. RICHARD had Francis and Hopestill, tw. b. 8 Mar. 1662. But the former, if there were two, was liv. in 1676, when he made convey. to his gr.s. George Pierce, whose f. had m. his d. Mary. Sometimes his name appears Woody, sometimes Wooddus. ROBERT, Boston, had Joseph, b. 1641, wh. may have been error of Farmer's informer for the s. of Richard, bef. ment. and Nathaniel, b. 1642.

WOODHULL, WOODHILL, or WODHULL, sometimes WOODHALL, * RICHARD, Brookhaven, says Wood's L. I. but the Conn. governm. in 1659 and foll. yrs. call. his resid. Setauket, wh. is nearly opposite to Milford on the continent. He was rep. 1664, and had a commissn. from the Col. under its new Charter Gov. Winth. that yr. WILLIAM, Portsmouth, R. I. is on the freemen's list 1655; but more common is the spelling Wodel, or Waddel, and under Waddell it is already giv.

WOODLAND, EDMUND, Salem 1673. JOHN, Braintree 1651, by w. Martha had John, b. 1653. Ten yrs. aft. he rem. to become one of the first sett. at Mendon, Sept. 1663.

WOODLEY, WILLIAM, Marblehead, d. June 1682, leav. wid. Eliz. young ch. Miriam.

WOODMAN, * ARCHELAUS, Newbury, nam. Hercules in the report to governm. of passeng. from Southampton in the James of London, embark. 6 Apr. arr. 3 June 1635, and call. mercer of Malford. Perhaps the custom-ho. officers knew more of Hercules than of the other name, tho. both are equal. heathenish, but prob. the sound was not unlike. He was b. 1618; but how entit. mercer, when only a minor, provokes inq. My conject. is, that his elder br. Edward, deserv. that descript. and came in that ship, but it was undesirable to give his name and excite suspic. that he was not authoriz. under the odious orders of the counc. to come to our country. Mr. Coffin wh. says his w. Eliz. d. 17 Dec. 1677, gives no ch. He was made freem. 17 May 1637, was lieut. 1670, rep. 1674 and 5, m. sec. w. 13 Nov. 1678, Dorothy Chapman, and d. 7 Oct. 1702. ARCHELAUS, Newbury, s. of Edward the sec. by w. Hannah had Mary, b. 26 Feb. 1696; Edward, 12 May 1698; and Archelaus, 15 May 1700; perhaps more. * EDWARD, Newbury, elder br. of Archelaus, came, says Coffin, with him, bring. w. and s. Edward, b. 1628, and John; had here Joshua, the first Eng. male ch. of the town, b. 1636 or 7; Sarah, 12 Jan. 1642; Jonathan, 5 Nov. 1643; Ruth, 28 Mar. 1646; and, Coffin adds, perhaps others; was freem. 25 May 1636, rep. Sept. foll. and 7, and sev. yrs. later. His wid. or w. Joanna is ment. 9 Nov. 1653 in the rec. but the time of his d. is not ment. EDWARD, Newbury, s. of the preced. b. in Eng. m. 20 Dec. 1653, Mary Goodridge, d. prob. of William of the same, had Mary, b. 29 Sept. 1654; Eliz. 11 July 1656, d. young; Edward, 1658, d. young;

Rebecca, 17 Sept. 1661, d. soon; Rebecca, again, 20 July 1663; Sarah, 18 July 1665; Judith, 18 Nov. 1667; Edward, again, 20 Mar. 1670; Archelaus, 9 June 1672; and Margaret, 31 Aug. 1676. He with his f. was long involv. in the gr. relig. quarrel of wh. large reports are giv. in the very valua. Hist. of N. by Coffin. EDWARD, Newbury, s. of the preced. m. 29 June 1702, Mary Sawyer, prob. d. of William of the same. *JOHN, Newbury, s. of Edward the first, had been perhaps at Ipswich 1648, but at N. m. 15 July 1656, Mary Field, and next yr. was establ. at Dover, freem. 1666, had John, Mary, and Sarah, wh. all outliv. him, and perhaps others; was capt. rep. 1684, and d. a. 1707. JOHN, Dover, s. of the preced. m. a d. of Francis Raynes of York, had only s. Jonathan, and d. 10 June 1705. JONATHAN, Newbury, s. of Edward the first, m. 2 July 1668, Hannah Hilton, perhaps d. of William of the same, had Hannah, b. 8 Mar. 1669; Sarah, 19 Oct. 1670; Ruth, 11 July 1672; Jonathan, 16 Apr. 1674; Ichabod, 26 Apr. 1676; Mary, 25 Apr. 1678; and William, 29 Mar. 1681. He took o. of alleg. 26 Feb. 1669, and in 1681 calls Stephen Greenleaf his uncle, for wh. I would glad. see the cause. JOSEPH, Salem, a youth, ment. in the will of Christopher Waller, Oct. 1676. JOSHUA, Newbury, elder br. of Jonathan, m. 22 Jan. 1666, Eliz. Stevens, perhaps d. of John of Andover, where the m. was, had Mehitable, b. 20 Sept. 1677; and Jonathan; but as Coffin gives not date of the last, nor any more ch. we may suppose that he rem. to Andover, where Farmer says he liv. yet Newbury can show his gr.-st. with inscript. that he d. 30 May 1703. RICHARD, Lynn 1644, d. Nov. 1647, as from prob. rec. Coffin tells, and that he had no ch. and he may have been that passeng. emb. at London in the Abigail, July 1635, aged 9. One Woodman whose bapt. name is not seen, m. Remember, d. of Moses Maverick of Marblehead. Six of this name are by Farmer found as gr. at N. E. coll. in 1834.

WOODMANSEY, JAMES, Boston, s. of John of the same, m. 17 May 1686, Abigail, d. of Jacob Melyen, had Eliz. bapt. 10 Apr. 1687, and a s. but d. Feb. 1694, and his wid. m. 1706, William Tilley, wh. had not, I think, been long resid. at B. and next she m. 29 Oct. 1719, Hon. Samuel Sewall, Ch. Just. of the Sup. Ct. and d. suddenly 26 May foll. He was, I presume, the last of the males bearing this name. JOHN, Boston 1659, merch. by w. Margaret had Margaret, b. 17 Oct. 1660. His w. d. 29 Dec. foll. and he m. 1 May 1662, Eliz. eldest ch. of George Carr of Salisbury, had John, 2 Feb. 1663, wh. d. young; James, 7 Dec. 1665; and again he m. 23 July 1672, Eliz. d. of Jonas Clark of Cambridge, had Eliz. 13 Aug. 1674, wh. d. next yr. and her gr.-st. inscript. is at Cambridge; Eliz. again, bapt. 16 Apr. 1676; Sarah, 8, bapt. 11 Jan. 1680; John, 28, bapt. 29 Jan. 1682; Mary, 21, bapt. 22

July 1683; and Ann, 20 July 1684, bapt. the same day. He was freem.
1673, belong. to 3d or Thacher's ch. and d. a. 1685, when, as Col. Rec.
V. shows, his wid. extrix. had to ask intervent. of the Gen. Ct. She m.
George Monk, the vintner, and outliv. him. ROBERT, Ipswich, with
prefix of respect, rem. early to Boston, with w. Margaret, and d. Ann,
wh. m. John Cutler of Charlestown; had at B. Seth, b. 26 Mar. 1644;
Joseph, bapt. 1 Apr. 1649, at four days old; Bethia, 15 Dec. 1650;
beside Sarah wh. may have been brot. from I. and d. 10 Nov. 1653.
He was sch.-master at £50. a yr. from 1650, and d. 13 Aug. 1667. His
wid. Margaret d. 1670.

WOODROP, WILLIAM, Lancaster, an eject. min. in Mather's Magn.
III. 4, of wh. he tells not a word. Farmer gave the name Woodroffe,
as if he had been progen. of the fam. not sparsely scatter. in our country; but I can hardly think so ill of the spell in the Magn. for Mather
must oft. have seen him, and prob. writ. letters to and rec. from him.
Hull, in his Diary, furnishes the desira. informat. that he arr. at Boston
from Jamaica, 29 Dec. 1674; and he must have found it no easy matter
to obt. employm. nor can I trace him again, exc. in the gr. ordina. of
Rev. Daniel Gookin at Sherburne, 26 Mar. 1685, when Woodrop assist.
Both Hull and Sewall give the spelling I have substitut. for Farmer's,
and my only further fact to be told is, that he sail. for Eng. 12 July
1687, no doubt to take advantage of King James's newborn or pretend.
favor to dissent. He left no descend. here, prob. had no w.

WOODROW, may be an independ. name, but as some of the Wood-
ruffs have this form of spell. I have chosen to combine the two.

WOODRUFF, WOODROW, WOODROFFE, or WOODROOFE, BENJAMIN,
Salem 1660–78, may have been br. of Joseph. JOHN, Southampton,
L. I. 1640 or 1, is by Wood's Hist. made one of the orig. compan. of
Pierson in settlem. JOHN, Farmington, s. of Matthew, d. 1692, his will
being of 18 Apr. and inv. so soon aft. as 16 May foll. when seven ch.
are nam. and their ages are giv. but wh. was the mo. or when she was
m. does not appear. The eldest was Mary, w. of John Root, 25; John,
23; Hannah, 21; Phebe, 16; Joseph, 13; Margaret, 10, wh. was bapt.
23 Apr. 1682; and Abigail, 8, bapt. 30 Mar. 1684. Lambert places him
at Milford 1685, but prob. without good reason. He was propound. for
freem. as early as 1663. JOSEPH, Salem, may have been the name of
him wh. m. Rebecca, d. of the wid. of William Canterbury, and had
Joseph and Mary, and the f. whether Joseph or other name, was d. as
also was his w. in July 1684. JOSEPH, Farmington, m. Hannah, d. of
John Clark, but of name of his f. or date of m. or any other incid. I am
ign. MATTHEW, Farmington, an orig. propr. by w. Hannah wh. join.
the ch. 2 Apr. 1654, had John, b. 1643; Matthew, 1646; Hannah,

1648; Eliz. 1651, all bapt. at once, 2 Apr.; and Mary, 5 Nov. 1654, wh. d. young; but of any more we kn. not, exc. Samuel, b. 26 Aug. 1661; was freem. prob. 1657, and d. 1682, his will being dat. 6 Sept. and pro. Dec. foll. In it he ment. w. three s. and d. Hannah Seymour, w. of the sec. Richard, only; but the Ct. supplied the deficience of his mem. in favor of Eliz. wh. had m. 1678, John Broughton of Northampton. MATTHEW, Farmington, s. of the preced. m. 16 June 1668, Mary Plum, d. of Robert of Milford, and there had Matthew, b. 1669; Mary, 1670; John, 1673; Sarah, 1674; Samuel, 1677; Eliz. 1679; Hannah, 1681; all liv. in 1704, to take share of their mo. in est. of gr.f. He was propound. for freem. 1671. Aft. d. of his first, he ret. to F. and took sec. w. Sarah, d. of John North, had Nathaniel, May 1687 (one of the first sett. at Litchfield, and there perpet. the name); and Joseph, bapt. 19 May 1689; and d. Nov. 1691. His wid. d. in the winter foll. NATHANIEL, in Trumbull's Col. Rec. I. 88, and 298, I doubt not, is misreading for the first Matthew. SAMUEL, Farmington, youngest s. of the first Matthew, m. 1686, Rebecca, d. of John Clark, had Samuel, b. 20 Jan. bapt. 6 Mar. 1687; Jonathan, 30 Nov. bapt. 2 Dec. 1688; Rebecca, 4, bapt. 8 Feb. 1691; Ruth, 15, bapt. 26 Feb. 1693; Ebenezer, 24 Dec. 1694, bapt. 3 Feb. foll.; and Daniel, 2, bapt. 8 Nov. 1696; rem. to Southington, there had David, b. 27 Feb. 1699; Hezekiah, 9 Aug. 1701; Rachel, 20 Nov. 1703; Abigail, 26 Feb. 1706; and John, 5 Apr. 1708; and d. 1742. Ten descend. of the first Matthew in the male line are in the Yale list of gr. betw. 1779 and 1836 inclus.

WOODWARD, AMOS, Cambridge, s. of George of the same, freem. 1677, d. 9 Oct. 1679, aged 38 yrs. as his gr.-st. tells, but from his nuncup. will, we do not learn that his w. Sarah, wh. had d. 24 Sept. 1677, left him any ch. He names brs. Thomas and Nathaniel Patten, wh. prob. were s. of William, and brs. of his w. Daniel and John W. and sis. Mary Waite, w. of John of Watertown; Sarah Gates, w. prob. of Stephen of Boston; and sis. Rebecca Fisher, wh. m. 11 Dec. 1666, Thomas Fisher of Dedham. DANIEL, Watertown, where he m. Eliz. d. of Richard Dana, and had Sarah, b. 5 Jan. 1689, at Medford; rem. to Woburn, had Hannah, b. 1 May 1691; and Amos, 5 June 1693. EDWARD, Ipswich 1665. EZEKIEL, Boston, by w. Ann, d. of William Beamsley, had Sarah, b. 21 Jan. 1654; Ann, 14 July 1653; Margaret, 24 Feb. 1656; and Eliz. 12 Oct. 1657; unless the date of the first ch. in Geneal. Reg. IX. 252, should be error for 1652; beside Prudence, 4 Apr. 1660. He was of Ipswich 1678, when he took the o. of alleg. and there had Martha, 3 May 1662; Mary, 8 Dec. 1664; Ezekiel, 9 Aug. 1666; and Rachel, 20 Jan. 1669. GEORGE, is the name of a fishmonger from St. Botolph's, Billingsgate, London, permit. to emb. in the

Hopewell, 1635, aged 35, or in the Rebecca, for I must suppose the same man to be intend. as the yrs. are the same, and the transact. in the same week, as told in the custom-ho. rec. by 3 Mass. Hist. Coll. VIII. 254, and 256. Of him, as nothing more is heard, we may presume he soon went home, and perhaps his visit was only for purpose of trade. GEORGE, Watertown 1641, s. of Richard of the same, with wh. he came from Ipswich, Co. Suffolk, in the Elizabeth, 1634, aged 13, by w. Mary had Mary, b. 12 Aug. 1641; Sarah, 3 or 6 Feb. 1643; Amos; Rebecca, 30 Dec. 1647; John, 20 or 28 Mar. 1649; Susanna, 30 Sept. 1651; Daniel, 2 Sept. 1653; and Mercy, perhaps, tho. town rec. says Mary, 3 June 1656. He was freem. 1646, took sec. w. 17 Aug. 1659, Eliz. d. of Thomas Hammond the first of Cambridge, had George, 11 Sept. 1660; and Thomas, 15 Sept. 1662; Eliz. 8 May 1664; Nathaniel, 28 May 1668; and Sarah, 3 Oct. 1675; and d. 31 May 1676. His wid. m. Samuel Truesdale, as his sec. w.; Mary m. 13 Jan. 1664, John Waite of W.; Sarah m. prob. Stephen Gates of Boston, and next, as Barry says, a Stow; Rebecca m. 11 Dec. 1666, Thomas Fisher of Dedham; Susanna d. unm.; Eliz. m. 7 Dec. 1693, Samuel Eddy; and the sec. Sarah m. an Eddy. GEORGE, Watertown, s. of the preced. m. 31 Dec. 1686, Lydia, d. of Abraham Brown, had Abraham, b. 1 Feb. 1688; George; Nathaniel; Lydia; and Ichabod; rem. aft. b. of his first ch. to that part of Boston, call. Muddy riv. now Brookline, and d. 1696. HENRY, Dorchester 1639, came, says Clapp, in his careful Hist. of Dorchester, p. 141, in the James, Capt. Taylor, in the summer of 1635, with Richard Mather, and he calls him a physician. He had there, Experience; Freedom, bapt. 1642; Thankful; and John; rem. 1659 to Northampton, with those ch. and the mo. Eliz. there was one of the founders of the first ch. and had been an early mem. at D. He was k. by accid. at the grist-mill, 7 Apr. 1685; and next mo. the wid. made her will, tho. she d. not bef. 13 Aug. 1690. Of her s. she says "has been a dutif. and well carriaged s. to me all my life." Experience m. 21 Nov. 1661, Medad Pomeroy; Freedom m. 18 Nov. 1662, Jedediah Strong; and Thankful m. 18 Dec. 1662, John Taylor; all of Northampton. ISRAEL, Taunton, m. 4 Aug. 1670, Jane Godfrey, perhaps d. of Richard the first, had Eliz. b. 15 June preced. if Col. Rec. be right, wh. I distr. and it adds that he d. 15 June 1674, had Israel, posthum. 4 Oct. 1674. JAMES, Dover 1646, may be the same wh. was of Watertown 1630, in serv. of Sir Richard Saltonstall, and then, by our Col. Rec. I. appears to have been not valua. citiz. JOHN, Watertown, s. of Richard of the same, brot. by his f. in the Eliz. 1634, aged 13, in Nov. 1639, partook of the paternal kindness of our governm. on a complaint "admonish. to take heed of drink. strong water again;" by w. Mary had

John, b. 20 Mar. 1650, prob. d. young; rem. to Sudbury, where his w. d. 8 July 1654; next he rem. to Charlestown, there m. Abigail, d. of John Benjamin, wid. of Joshua Stubbs, had Rose, 18 Aug. 1659, wh. m. 10 Aug. 1686, Richard Norcross the sec.; again, at Sudbury, had John, 12 Dec. 1661; and Abigail, m. 13 Jan. 1682, Jeremiah Morse, was freem. 1690, and d. at W. 17 Feb. 1696, his will being of 10 Jan. preced. JOHN, Cambridge, s. of George of Watertown, liv. in that part wh. bec. Newton, m. Rebecca, d. of Richard Robbins of the same, had John, b. 7 Sept. 1674, d. in few ds.; John, again, 18 July 1675; Richard, 26 Sept. or Dec. 1677; Rebecca, 29 Oct. 1679, d. young; Daniel, 24 Sept. 1681; Rebecca, again, 2 Feb. 1683; Mary, 6 Oct. 1684, d. young; Jonathan, 28 Sept. 1685; Joseph, 26 Nov. 1688; Ebenezer, 12 Mar. 1691; and Abigail, 25 May 1695. His w. d. next yr. and he m. Sarah Goodnow, wh. d. 22 Sept. 1723. He had rem. to Newton a. 1681, and d. 3 Nov. 1732, in his will of 1728 names five s. of wh. Joseph was not one, and ds. Rebecca Hunting and Abigail Greenwood; and made Ebenezer, excor. JOHN, Northampton, only s. of Henry of the same, freem. 1680, m. 18 May 1671, Ann, d. of Thomas Dewey of Windsor, had Eliz. b. 17 Mar. 1672; John, 2 Apr. 1674; Samuel, 20 Mar. 1676, d. at 7 mos.; Henry, 18 Mar. 1680; Thomas, 22 Apr. 1682; and Israel, 6 Feb. 1685; rem. to Westfield, and in few yrs. more to Lebanon, Conn. Much distinct. in the science of med. has been attain. by descend. JOHN, Taunton, m. 11 Nov. 1675, Sarah Crossman. Perhaps he had John, b. at Taunton, 2 Mar. 1678; and Israel, 30 July 1681. JOHN, Reading, by Eaton call. one of the early sett. was freem. 1691. *JOHN*, sec. min. of Norwich, s. of Peter of Dedham, succeed. Rev. James Fitch, the first min. of that city, aft. long agitat. ord. Oct. 1699, m. 1703, Sarah, d. I think, of Richard Rosewell of New Haven, but Caulkins, from wh. is learn. most of the little kn. of him, in her Hist. of N. ment. no issue. He had been Secr. to the Assembly of divines that formed the Saybrook platform, almost as powerful in moulding the machinery of eccles. discipline in Conn. as for a few yrs. was the Westminster Assembly in Eng. The majority of the people were dissat. with his rule, tho. the greater part of the ch. sustain. him, and aft. sev. yrs. of contention, he was dism. 13 Sept. 1716. Whether he obt. ano. parish, is not heard, and by the Coll. Catal. he liv. to 1746. JOHN, Sudbury, perhaps s. of John the first, in his will of 2 Oct. 1736, ment. s. John and Daniel, and gr.d. Susanna Haines. JOSEPH, Providence 1676, there had liv. thro. Philip's war. NATHANIEL, Boston, a mathematician and surveyor, employ. as our Col. Rec. I. 237, shows, to run the line, 1638, betw. Plymouth Col. and Mass. and Mass. and Conn. Afterwards he was sent to the Merrimac survey. See Winth. I. 284. It

is great mortificat. that we kn. not any thing of his fam. exc. that he had
s. John and Robert, of course b. in Eng. allow. to have lots in Boston
1637. NATHANIEL, Boston 1633, perhaps s. of the preced. but on join.
the ch. 1 Dec. of that yr. is call. serv. to our br. William Coddington,
and possib. brot. by him that yr. when he ret. from Eng. was freem. 17
Apr. 1637, by w. Mary had Elisha, bapt. 21 Apr. 1644, a. 6 days old;
Nathaniel, 12 Apr. 1646, a. 7 days old; and prob. other ch. but perhaps
he rem. for in 1648, he sold dwell.-ho. and garden to John Langdon.
* PETER, Dedham, freem. 18 May 1642, brot. a fam. of wh. the names
of four may be prob. found in the rec. Peter, William, Rebecca, wh. m.
1666, Thomas Fisher, and Ann, wh. d. in that yr. He was rep. 1665,
9, and 70, but strange. miscall. 1669, Woodwine. He d. 9 May 1685,
as the date of 11 May may be understood as that of the bur. from
Sewall's Diary in Geneal. Reg. VI. 72. But when he calls him f. of
the min. we must infer that he intends William. PETER, Dedham, prob.
s. of the preced. by w. Mehitable, had William, b. 1 Jan. 1669; Ann, 2
Feb. 1670; John, 10 Sept. 1671, H. C. 1693; Ebenezer, 15 Sept.
1675; Mehitable, 17 Nov. 1677; Peter, 29 Dec. 1679; Judith, Mar.
1683; and Samuel, 26 Dec. 1685. Possib. he was b. in Eng. and his
d. on 15 Feb. 1721, is noted as of the *aged* P. W. RALPH, Hingham,
was of Dublin 1635, came in 1637, was freem. Mar. 1638, deac. ord.
2 Feb. 1640, says Lincoln, was honor. by our governm. 1649, with a
commiss. to solemn. m. RICHARD, Watertown, came in the Elizabeth,
from Ipswich, 1634, aged 45, with w. Rose, 50, and two ch. George and
John, ea. 13, if we accept the custom.-ho. papers, was freem. 2 Sept.
1635. His w. d. 6 Oct. 1662, aged a. 80 yrs. says the rec. with the
usual tendency to exagger. and he d. 16 Feb. 1665; but first he m. 18
Apr. 1663, Ann, wid. of Stephen Gates of Cambridge, wh. d. 5 Feb.
1683. ROBERT, Boston, carpenter, s. of the first Nathaniel, by w.
Rachel, d. of John Smith of the same, tailor, wh. as his w. had join. the
ch. 6 Nov. 1641, had Joseph, b. 24 Oct. bapt. 7 Nov. 1641, d. prob.
soon; Nathaniel, bapt. 30 Oct. 1642, a. 4 days old; Smith, 4 Aug. 1644,
a. 5 days; Robert, b. 14 Nov. 1646; John, wh. d. 23 Aug. 1652; Jeremiah, wh. d. 26 Nov. 1653; the f. d. five days bef. His wid. m. 7 July
1654, Thomas Harwood. ROBERT, Boston, s. of the preced. was k. in
Philip's war at Pocasset, 1675. SMITH, Dorchester, perhaps s. of
Robert, had w. Thankful, d. 15 June 1738, aged 66, by her gr.-st. His
ch. were Sarah, bapt. 11 Sept. 1692; Thankful, 24 Dec. 1693; Mary,
15 Dec. 1695; Deliverance, 16 Jan. 1698; Ebenezer and Abigail, tw.
19 Nov. 1699; all in right of their mo. for he was adm. of the ch. not
bef. 1701, aft. wh. were bapt. John, prob. 29 Mar. 1702; Silence, 20
June 1703; Submit, 10 Dec. 1704; Samuel, 12 Jan. 1707; and Abigail,

WOODWORTH. 647

1 June 1712. THOMAS, Boston, carpenter, rem. to Roxbury, m. 7 Mar. 1660, Mary, d. of William Goose of Charlestown, had Thomas; Esther, both bapt. 1 May 1664, the f. hav. join. the ch. in the preced. mo.; Hannah, 14 May 1665; Eliz. 30 June 1667; Mary, 17 Jan. 1669; Rachel, 27 Nov. 1670; Robert, 19 Oct. 1673; and Mehitable, 29 Apr. 1675; and he d. Oct. 1685, says Farmer, trust. the town rec. wh. I distr. because it ment. not the day of d. contains not a single name of the childr. and the ch. rec. of bur. or d. is 10 Sept. evidently nearer to a contempo. authority. WILLIAM, Dedham, perhaps s. of Peter the first, was a "min. of the gosp." d. at D. 26 June 1669, as by the Roxbury ch. rec. is told, and the Diary of John Hull calls him "a young but powerful preach." Of this name Farmer notes, that in 1834, twenty-one had been gr. at N. E. coll. of wh. I count ten at Dartm. five at Yale, four at Harv.

WOODWELL, JOHN, Salem, wh. admin. 7 July 1701, on est. of his br. JOSHUA, was s. of MATTHEW, a seaman, in 1661, when ment. of him is first seen, but later is call. brickmaker, in 1671 had w. Mary, and names her in his will of 28 Dec. 1690, pro. 30 June foll. with ch. Samuel, John, Matthew, Joshua, Mary, Margaret, Eliz. and Dorcas. Eliz. was a witness allow. to sw. to ridicul. nonsense, or impertin. falsehood in the witcher. trials of 1692. MATTHEW, Salem, s. of the preced. left wid. Ann to admin. his est. 11 Apr. 1702. SAMUEL, Salem, prob. eldest br. of the preced. by w. Thomasine, had Jonathan, b. 5 Apr. 1693, who prob. d. soon, for, from his will of 25 Nov. 1697, pro. 10 Jan. foll. we find that he left wid. Thomasine, ch. Samuel, John, Gideon, Joseph, Benjamin, Eliz. and David. Mr. Felt confid. assures me that this is a differ. name from Wardwell or Wardell.

WOODWORTH, BENJAMIN, Scituate, s. of Walter of the same, had Eliz. Deborah, Abigail, and Robert, and d. in Philip's war. HENRY, the freem. of 10 May 1643, of wh. no diligence has discov. the resid. or any thing more. Farmer here introd. the name of Recompense Woodsworth, on Middlesex rec. call. A. B. wh. d. 12 July 1679; but this must be double error, prob. for Recompense Wadsworth, and certain. for the coll. honor. In the Catal. such a surname has never yet appear. and bef. 1680 the only instance of the bapt. name is, 1661, with Osborn; and in the foll. generat. is attach. to a Boston Wadsworth. JOHN, Taunton, had Nathaniel, b. 31 July 1679. JOSEPH, Scituate, s. of the first Walter of the same, prob. youngest, m. 1669, Sarah, d. of Charles Stockbridge of the same, had Joseph, b. 1670; Mary, 1673; Benjamin, 1676; Sarah, 1678; Eliz. 1680; Eunice, 1682; Abigail, 1685; and Ruth, 1688. THOMAS, Scituate, br. of the preced. m. 1666, Deborah Daman, prob. d. of John of the same, had Deborah, b. 1667; Hezekiah,

1671; and Catharine, 1673. WALTER, Scituate 1640, had Benjamin; Walter; Thomas; and Joseph; Mary, wh. m. 1677, Aaron Simons; Martha, wh. m. 1679, Zachary Daman; and Mehitable, wh. suffer. from witchcraft. WALTER, Scituate, s. of the preced. prob. eldest, left, says Deane, Mary, b. 1658; Mehitable, 1662; and Ebenezer, 1664.

WOOLCOT. See Wolcott.

WOOLLEN, or WOOLEN, JOHN, New Haven 1642, was imprison. next yr. by the Swedes at Delaware, as he was there trad. in the river, agent for Capt. Lamberton.

WOOLER, EDWARD, is the name of a man found by Coffin, among the rec. of Essex, or the tempora. Co. of Norfolk, of wh. all he tells is, that in 1658 he was 34 yrs old.

WOOLERY, or WOOLSWORTH, RICHARD, Newbury 1678, when he was 30 yrs. old, a weaver, whose name being copied in Geneal. Reg. VII. 349, as Woolpoorle, call. for indignant remonstr. in the ensuing No. of that periodic. from Mr. Coffin, m. 24 Dec. 1678, Hannah Huggins, had a d. b. 1 Feb. 1680, d. very soon; Hannah, 10 Feb. 1681; and Mary, 22 Feb. 1683. In 1685 he was of Suffield, there had Eliz. b. 29 Sept. of that yr. and ano. d. Abia, 16 Sept. 1691; and his w. d. 30 July of the same yr. a contradict. in the rec. that may seem easily reconcil. but it is of little conseq. whether the d. was b. 30 July, for she d. on 19 Oct. foll. and he d. 1696. His d. Hannah, tho. so young, was allow. to present. inv. wh. prob. was very small. Yet possib. an inf. s. was left, for in 1732, a Richard W. is at S.

WOOLEY, or WOOLLY, sometimes WOLLEY, CHRISTOPHER, Concord 1666. EMANUEL, Newport, on the freemen's list 1655, by w. Eliz. had Adam, b. Mar. 1654; Edward, Dec. 1655; Eliz. and Mary, tw. Nov. 1657; John, Oct. 1659; William, 15 Sept. 1662; Ruth, 12 Oct. 1664; Grace, Apr. 1666; and Joseph, May 1668; is nam. in Rh. Is. Hist. Coll. III. 251. ROBERT, Fairfield 1649 and 53, rem. soon aft. to parts unkn.

WOOLRIDGE, or WOOLRYCH, *JOHN, Dorchester 1630, perhaps came in the Mary and John, at least on 19 Oct. of that yr. desir. to be adm. freem. and as he did not appear in May foll. to take the requisite o. when ch. membership was not demand. as qualificat. I conject. that he had gone home, there found a w. Sarah, with wh. coming again, 1632, to our country, it seems they sat down at Charlestown, there join. the ch. 15 Mar. 1633, and he was made freem. 4 Mar. 1634, then by the Secr. on his rec. dignif. with prefix of Mr. was rep. 1635, and I regret to say, that no more of him is kn. so that it may be thot. that he went home. MICHAEL, Fairfield 1674, of wh. no more is told me, exc. that he was apparent. unm.

WOOLSON, JOSEPH, Watertown, s. of the first Thomas of the same, by w. Hannah had Joseph, b. 13 Dec. 1699; Mary, 13 Sept. 1701; Hannah, 8 Aug. 1704; Thankful, 3 June 1708; Isaac, 17 Feb. 1711; and Beulah, 1 Mar. 1714; made his will 27 Nov. 1751, and d. 16 May 1755. THOMAS, Watertown 1660, the freem. of 1690, had been of Cambridge 1653, m. 20 Nov. 1660, Sarah, d. of deac. Samuel Hyde of C. had Sarah, b. 1661, wh. m. 30 Sept. 1680, Thomas Bond; Thomas, 28 Feb. 1667; Eliz. 30 Apr. 1668, m. 3 Nov. 1686, John Howe; Mary, 28 Nov. 1673; Joseph, 16 Nov. 1677; perhaps Nathaniel; and d. 1713; had gr. of ld. 300 acres, in 1685, for mak. good a gr. bef. 1682, when the Ct. refus. to accept the survey, bec. it gave more ld. than was intend. This seems to throw discredit on the knowl. or honesty of the officer. Bond thinks the name may have been Wilson, as sometimes he found it. THOMAS, Watertown, s. of the preced. m. a. 1693, Eliz. d. of John Chadwick, had John, b. 8 July 1694; Eliz. 17 Aug. 1698; and Jonas.

WOORY, WOOREY, or WOORIE, RALPH, Charlestown, leather-dresser, came to dwell there 1640, by w. Margaret had John, b. 13 June 1641; and Abel, prob. a tw. if allowance for an easy error in Geneal. Reg. IV. 270, be made; and Hannah, 8 Mar. 1644. He join. the ch. 4 Nov. 1643, but was never sw. as freem. and the ment. of his ho. is found 1657. I can tell no more.

WOOSTER, WOSTER, or WORSTER, ABRAHAM, Stratford, s. of Edward, m. 22 Nov. 1697, Mary Walker, had Abraham; Ruth, b. 26 Sept. 1700; Joseph, 16 Jan. 1702; Sarah, 2 Apr. 1705; Mary, 3 Apr. 1707; Hannah, 23 Feb. 1709; and David, 2 Mar. 1710. DAVID, Derby, br. of the preced. left w. Mary to admin. upon his est. 29 May 1711, for three ch. Jerusha, then 9 yrs. old; Persis, 7; and Tamar, 1. EBENEZER, Stratford, s. of Edward, m. it is said, Margaret, d. of Zechariah Sawtell of Groton, had Henry, b. 27 May 1712; Zechariah, 17 Mar. 1714; and Ebenezer, 5 Jan. 1716. EDWARD, Milford 1652, had Mary, b. 2 Nov. 1654, d. young; perhaps Eliz. elder; Thomas; Abraham; Edward; David; the last two bapt. 1670; Henry, b. 18 Aug. 1666; wh. d. in the army of Queen Anne, serv. against Canada or Nova Scotia; and Ruth, 8 Apr. 1668; all thot. to be by first w. Prob. in 1669, he m. Tabitha, d. of Henry Tomlinson of Stratford, and had Timothy, 12 Nov. 1670; Hannah; Jonas; Tabitha; Sylvester; and Ebenezer. He had rem. to Derby bef. 1669, in wh. yr. he was made constable, and there the last six were prob. b. and he d. 8 July 1689, aged 67, hav. made his will that day. On settlem. of his est. twelve of the ch. took their shares. Ruth, wh. was d. had hers, when she m. Samuel Bowers, 1687. General David, wh. serv. with distinct. in the war of the Revo. mort. wound. 1777, was a descend. SYLVESTER, Derby, s. of the preced. d. 16 Nov. 1712, leav. w. Susanna, and ch. Moses, then aged 13 ; Tabitha, 11 ; Samuel, 8 ; Nathaniel, 5 ; Sylvester, 2 ; and Susanna, posthum. THOMAS, Derby, br. of the preced. d. 4 Jan. 1713, in his will names w. Phebe, s. Thomas, ds. Phebe Leavenworth, Eliz. Alice, and Zervia. TIMOTHY, Derby, br. of the preced. by w. Ann had Timothy, b. 29 Nov. 1699 ; Tabitha, 3 May 1701 ; Edward, 17 Sept. 1702 ; Ann, 7 Jan. 1704 ; Samuel, 17 Apr. 1706 ; Damaris, 20 Feb. 1708 ; Henry, 19 Feb. 1710 ; Elizur, 16 Oct. 1715 ; and Arthur, 26 Mar. 1718 ; as the print. geneal. tells.

WOOTERS, or WOUTERS, JOHN, Branford 1667–73, had a fam. it is thot. there ; was prob. of Dutch descent.

WORCESTER, or WORSTER, EBENEZER, Bradford, s. prob. youngest of Samuel, by w. Hannah, wh. d. 1705, had only Joseph ; and he m. 19 Nov. 1706, Deliverance, d. of Jonathan Looke of Rowley, and had Jonathan ; Mary, b. 26 Apr. 1711 ; Susanna, Feb. 1713 ; Hannah, 13 Dec. 1717 ; Eliz. 1721 ; and Ebenezer ; rem. to Littleton, and next to Harvard, there d. 5 Feb. 1764. FRANCIS, Bradford, br. of the preced. m. 20 Jan. 1691, Mary, d. of Peter Cheney of Newbury, had Hannah, b. 8 Feb. 1692 ; Timothy, 6 Dec. 1693 ; Jemima, 19 Jan. 1696 ; Francis, 7 June 1698 ; John, 5 Nov. 1700 ; Daniel, 19 Feb. 1703 ; William, 13 Nov. 1706 ; Benjamin, 25 Aug. 1709 ; James, 15 Sept. 1712 ; and Mary, 22 Dec. 1714 ; and he d. 17 Dec. 1717. Descend. of this branch have been emin. in letters and theolo. JOSEPH, Rowley, br. of the preced. by w. Sarah, wh. d. 27 July 1728, had Jane, b. 21 May 1703 ; and Eliz. 1 July, 1705 ; and he m. 29 Apr. 1730, Martha Palmer, but had no more ch. and d. June 1746. MOSES, Kittery, youngest s. of the Rev. William, by first w. of wh. the name is unkn. had Thomas, William, and Eliz. but dates of all are unkn. as also of the d. of his w. Yet it is said, that he took sec. w. 4 Apr. 1695, Sarah Soper ; had been famous as enemy of Ind. and was liv. in 88th yr. * SAMUEL, Bradford, was first at Rowley, eldest s. of Rev. William, b. perhaps in Eng. freem. 1670, constable and rep. 1679, d. at Lynn, in the road on his way from home to Boston, 20 Feb. 1681, to attend in his place at the Gen. Ct. leav. wid. Eliz. d. of Francis Parrott of Rowley, m. 29 Nov. 1659, by wh. he had William, b. 21 July 1661 ; Samuel, 31 Mar. 1663 ; Francis ; Joseph ; Timothy, 4 June 1669 ; Moses, 15 Jan. 1671, d. young ; Eliz. 16 Feb. 1673 ; Dorothy, 21 Jan. 1675 ; John, 31 Aug. 1677 ; Ebenezer, 29 Apr. 1679 ; and Susanna, 11 Feb. 1681. TIMOTHY, Salisbury, br. of the preced. was a mariner, had Sarah, b. 15 Aug. 1667 ; and Susanna, 29 Dec. 1671 ; d. early in 1672, and his wid. Susanna m.

the last week in Oct. of that yr. Henry Ambrose. TIMOTHY, Newbury, s. of Samuel of Bradford, but by Farmer easi. mistak. for the s. of William, by w. Huldah, d. of Peter Cheney, m. 29 Jan. 1691 (the same day on wh. two of his brs. m. two of her sis.), had Samuel, b. 23 Oct. 1691. Coffin tells no more of him; but the fam. geneal. gives d. Lydia, 21 May 1706, wh. d. in few mos. He d. 13 Aug. 1706, and his wid. m. 1718, Simon Dakin. WILLIAM, Salisbury, the first min. there, is suppos. to have come in 1639, and Mr. Coffin thot. he was from Salisbury, Co. Wilts, but the late historian of that city in 1842, aft. investigat. for me, found no trace of him, and add. " I think W. is not a Salisbury name." He had been min. in Eng. if the Magn. classif. be correct, yet nowhere have I seen the place of his educ. ment. but he brot. w. Sarah, and ch. Susanna, Samuel, and William ; had here, prob. Sarah, wh. d. 1 Apr. 1641 ; Sarah, again, b. 4 Apr. 1641, d. soon ; Timothy, 14 May 1642 ; Moses, 10 Nov. 1643 ; Sarah, again, 22 June 1646, d. young ; Eliz. 10 Mar. or 9 Apr. 1648, d. 9 Mar. foll.; and Eliz. again, 9 Jan. 1650. His w. d. 23 Apr. 1650, and he m. 20 or 23 July foll. Rebecca, wid. of John Hall, wh. had been wid. of Henry Byley. He was adm. freem. 13 May 1640, and d. 28 Oct. 1663, by town rec. and the wid. got fourth h. in dep.-gov. Symonds, outliv. him, and d. 21 Feb. or July 1695. WILLIAM, Rowley, s. of the preced. b. in Eng. a shoemaker, had w. Constant, by her, a s. Joseph, b. 20 June 1667, wh. prob. d. young; rem. to Boston, where he d. 1683 ; and his d. Constance was b. 10 Mar. 1668, wh. m. 15 July 1692, Abraham Tuckerman, and next John Noiles, jr. of Newfoundland. Other ch. were William, 7 May 1672 ; Timothy, 2 June 1674 ; Samuel, 23 Dec. 1679 ; and Joseph, again, 22 June 1681. But no descend. of any one of these six ch. is heard of. A passeng. in the Speedwell from London to Boston, 1657, was Rebecca W. aged 18, of wh. neither by accid. nor research have I learn. any thing more. Farmer in MS. noted, that in 1834 of this name were gr. seven at Harv. five at Dartm. two at Yale, and four at other N. E. coll. besides six with spell. of Wooster.

WORDEN, ISAAC, came in the Increase, emb. at London in Apr. 1635, aged 18, call. in the clear. from the custom-ho. serv. but to wh. or where he sat down is unkn. A Jane W. aged 30, came in the Christian, the first vessel in 1635 from London for our country. JAMES, Boston, by w. Mary had Joseph, b. 21 Mar. 1671 ; William, 9 July 1673 ; and Henry, 20 Jan. 1675. PETER, Yarmouth, m. 9 Feb. 1639, made his will, giv. all his est. to only s. Peter. PETER, Yarmouth 1643, s. of the preced. had a d. b. 10 Feb. 1649, perhaps that Mary, wh. m. 8 Sept. 1657, John Burge. SAMUEL, Boston, m. Mehitable, d. of Gov. Thomas Hinckley, had Samuel, bapt. at Barnstable, 24 Feb. 1684, not as the rec. has it, 25. He d. early, and his wid. m. 25 Aug. 1698, William Avery of Dedham.

WORKES, THOMAS, Huntington, L. I. adm. 1664, to be made free of the jurisdict. of Conn.

WORMALL, WORMAHILL, WORMELL, or WORMWELL, JOSEPH, Rowley 1640, had in 1642, the first ch. b. in that town, as one tradit. boasts, rem. in 1649 to Boston, and not long aft. to Scituate, there d. In his will of 4 Feb. 1662, pro. 24 June foll. as abstr. in Geneal. Reg. VI. 94, nothing is seen, but that his w. was Miriam, s. Josiah, and ds. Sarah, and Esther.

WORMLEY, or WORMELEY, RALPH, Dover 1684, ment. by Belknap, I. 484, Farmer's Ed. but the diligence of Quint has add. nothing to our knowledge of him.

WORMSTALL, ARTHUR, Wells, in Sept. 1653, acknowledg. submis. to Mass. jurisdict. See Col. Rec. III.

WORMSTED, came to Salem, being driv. by the Ind. from settlem. at the E. 1675.

WORMWOOD, HENRY, Lynn, had William, b. Apr. 1666; Eliz. 14 Mar. 1668, perhaps d. young; Daniel, Jan. 1676; Eliz. again, 1 May 1677; and Esther, 11 May 1683. WILLIAM, Kittery 1640, liv. on Isle of Shoals, I suppose, in 1647, when our Gen. Ct. order. his w. to be brot. as a prisoner. See Col. Rec. II. He took. o. of alleg. 22 Mar. 1681.

WORNUM, WILLIAM, Boston, had w. Christian, wh. join. the ch. 4 Apr. 1646.

WORRALL, JAMES, Scituate 1638, is by Farmer nam. on authority of Coffin.

WORSLEY, BENJAMIN, R. I. 1663, call. Dr. in the docum. relative to bounds with Conn.

WORTH, JOHN, Nantucket, s. of William of the same, m. 22 Sept. 1684, Miriam, d. of Richard Gardner, sen. wh. d. 1701, had Jonathan, b. 31 Oct. 1685; Nathaniel, 8 Sept. 1687; Judith, 22 Dec. 1689; John, wh. d. young; Richard, 27 May 1692; William, 27 Nov. 1694; Joseph; and Mary. A sec. w. he took, 5 Sept. 1704, Ann Sarson, and a third w. was Dorcas, d. of Benjamin Smith. By the former, wh. d. 14 June 1724, he had Sarah, 15 July 1708, wh. d. soon; and by the latter, wh. d. 4 Aug. 1730, had John, again, 14 Sept. 1725; Sarah, 5 Nov. 1727; and Dorcas, 6 July 1730. Most of his days he liv. at Edgartown, there d. 11 Feb. 1732. JOHN, Newbury, s. of Lionel of the same, m. 17 Mar. 1687, Eliz. d. of Israel Webster, had Eliz. b. 17 Aug. 1688; John, 7 Feb. 1690; Joseph, 7 Aug. 1693; and Edmund, 22 Oct. 1695. He was freem. 1690. LIONEL, Salisbury 1655, m. Susanna, d.

of John Whipple of Ipswich, had Sarah, b. Oct. 1656; Susanna; Mary; Judith; and John, 18 Sept. 1664; perhaps, adds Coffin, others, most of them, prob. at Newbury, where he d. 29 June 1667. His wid. m. next yr. Moses Pilsbury. RICHARD, Newbury, prob. br. of the preced. m. 11 Sept. 1667, Mary, d. of the sec. John Pike. WILLIAM, Nantucket, blacksmith and mariner, from Devonsh. was br. of the two preced. m. 11 Apr. 1665, Sarah, d. of Thomas Macy, had John, b. 19 May 1666, and prob. no other ch. was highly esteem. clk. of the Ct. July 1678, and Justice. His w. d. 1701, and he took, 3 Sept. 1703, sec. w. Damaris Sibley, d. Dec. 1724. His wid. d. 2 June 1745, if such be the true translat. of 2d of 4 mo.

WORTHEN, EZEKIEL, Salisbury, m. 4 Dec. 1661, Hannah, d. of George Martin of the same, had Hannah, b. 21 Apr. 1663; John, 12 Feb. 1665; and Thomas, 31 Oct. 1667; and possib. others, as Dorothy, wh. m. Ezekiel Wells.

WORTHINGTON, JOHN, Springfield, youngest s. of Nicholas, m. 22 May 1713, Mary, d. of John Pratt of Saybrook, had John, b. 26 Oct. 1714, d. by casual.; John, again, 24 Nov. 1719; Timothy, 1 July 1722, d. soon; Samuel, 11 July 1725; Mary, 8 Mar. 1728, d. young; and Sarah, 27 Jan. 1732; was lieut. and d. 30 Dec. 1744. The wid. d. 29 Oct. 1759, in the 72d yr. of her age, says Goodwin, p. 272; and there is very good reason to judge by rec. of her b. in Geneal. Reg. IV. 140, that she was past 82. JONATHAN, Springfield, br. of the preced. m. 19 Feb. 1708, Eliz. d. of John Scott of Suffield, wh. d. 8 or 18 Sept. 1743, had Eliz. b. 17 Feb. 1710; Margaret, 2 Feb. 1712; Jonathan, 17 June 1715; Nicholas, 26 July 1717, d. young; William, 16 Jan. 1720; and Amy, 3 Nov. 1725, d. under 18 yrs. NICHOLAS, Hartford, m. a. 1668, in wh. yr. he was made freem. Sarah, d. of Thomas Bunce, wid. of the sec. John White, had William, b. 1670; Eliz. wh. m. a Morton; and Mary, 24 Jan. 1674, d. young. His w. d. 20 June 1676, and by sec. w. Susanna he had Jonathan; and John, b. 17 Aug. 1679; and d. 6 Sept. 1683, at Hatfield, whither he rem. 1677; and his wid. m. a. 1685, Capt. Jonathan Ball, to wh. she bore twelve ch. and d. 9 Mar. 1727. Tradit. says he came from Liverpool, and sett. at Saybrook; and the latter half of her story may be true in some degree. WILLIAM, Hartford, eldest s. of Nicholas of the same, m. Mehitable, d. prob. youngest, of Isaac Graves of Hatfield, wid. of Richard Morton of the same, had William, b. 5 Dec. 1695, Y. C. 1716, min. of Saybrook; Daniel, 18 May 1698; Mary, 23 Sept. 1701; Mehitable, 18 July 1706; and Elijah, 16 June 1710; his w. d. 22 Mar. 1742, aged 70, and he d. at Colchester (whither he had rem. a. 1717), 22 May 1753.

WORTHLIKE, PETER, Scituate 1669, had, as Deane shows, Hannah and Alice, b. 1676, perhaps tw.; Mary, 1678; and Sarah, 1682.

WORWOOD, or WORWARD, RICHARD, Cambridge, d. 13 May 1644, of wh. no more can be found, but that he is call. s. of blank. Farmer, in Geneal. Reg. I. 195, makes him of Charlestown.

WOTTEN. See Wolten.

WRAY. See Ray.

WRIFORD, JOHN, Pemaquid 1674, sw. fidel. to Mass. and the same yr. was licens. to keep an inn.

WRIGHT, ABEL, Springfield 1655, m. 1 Dec. 1659, Martha, d. of Samuel Kitcherel of Hartford, had Joseph, b. 1 Sept. 1660; Martha, 29 Nov. 1662; Abel, 25 Sept. 1664; Benjamin, 14 Mar. 1667; Hannah, 28 July 1669; Henry, 23 May 1671, d. young; Sarah, 8 May 1673; Mary, 9 Mar. 1676; Henry, again, 6 Jan. 1677; Samuel, 17 June 1679; Eliz. 18 Aug. 1682, d. June foll.; John, 21 Apr. 1685, d. soon; and Eliz. again, 22 Aug. 1687, of wh. ten liv. to be m. His resid. was on the W. side of the river, at that part of what is now Westfield, then call. Skipmuck, much expos. to the invasion of border enemies, and his w. was scalp. by the Ind. 26 July 1708, but liv. until 19 Oct. foll. and he d. 29 Oct. 1725, when he is call. lieut. and said to be 94 yrs. old; but wh. brot. him over the sea is unkn. Martha m. 8 Dec. 1681, Thomas Morley; Hannah m. 1690, Joseph Saxton, both of Westfield; Sarah m. 1694, Thomas Chapin; Mary m. 1698, Nathaniel Bliss; and Eliz. m. 1709, Ebenezer Dewey of Lebanon. ABEL, Springfield, s. of the preced. m. 1691, Rebecca, d. of Samuel Terry of the same, had Rebecca, b. 1692; Samuel, 1694, d. soon; Abel, 1695; Samuel, again, 1698; and was freem. 1690, but no more is heard of this branch. ANTHONY, Sandwich 1643, rem. to Wethersfield bef. 1658, when he was one of the first troop of caval. in the Col. m. bef. 1670, Mary, d. of the first Richard Smith, and wid. of Matthew or Matthias Treat, had no ch. and d. 1679. BENJAMIN, Guilford 1649, rem. to Killingworth, and d. 29 Mar. 1677, leav. ch. Benjamin; Joseph; James; Eliz. b. 15 Oct. 1653, wh. m. Edward Lee or Lay; Jane, wh. m. Joseph Hand; and Ann, wh. m. John Walstone of K. His wid. Jane, d. 26 Oct. 1684. BENJAMIN, Killingworth, s. prob. eldest, of the preced. was propound. for freem. 1669. BENJAMIN, Northampton, s. of the sec. Samuel, in the imperf. notice of descend. of Samuel Wright, Geneal. Reg. IV. 357, is said to have m. Thankful Taylor, to have had Benjamin, three other s. and five ds. but many points of informat. beside dates, are omit. To make perfect the acco. of him, I add that his first w. Thankful m. 22 Mar. 1681, d. 4 Apr. 1701; and that the first ch. was b. 26 Feb. 1682; Thankful, 13 Nov. 1683, d. soon; a s. Remembrance, 26 Jan. 1685;

Thankful, again, 23 May 1687; Jacob; Mindwell, Oct. 1694; Daniel, 15 Apr. 1697; that he m. 19 July 1701, Mary Barker of Springfield, had William, 26 Nov. 1702; Mary, 7 Sept. 1704; and Experience, 9 Dec. 1706; all the ten at Northampton. He was famous for his readiness to fight Indians in every expedit. and soon after mid. life rem. to Northfield, there reach. mature age to d. 1743. BENJAMIN, Springfield, s. of the first Abel, m. 1694, Mary Chapin, perhaps d. of Henry, had Benjamin b. 22 May 1697; Henry, 19 May 1700; and Mary, posthum. 1 May 1705; he d. 25 Dec. preced.; and his wid. d. 13 Jan. 1708. BENONI, Hatfield, youngest ch. of Samuel the sec. b. ten days aft. the fall of his f. in Ind. war, m. Rebecca Barrett, prob. d. of Benjamin, had Rebecca, b. 1700; and Hannah, 1702. He d. in the same yr. quite young; and his wid. m. 1706, Samuel Dickinson. DAVID, Wethersfield, youngest s. of the first Samuel of the same, m. 28 Dec. 1699, Rebecca, d. of John Goodrich, sec. of the same, had Ann, b. 19 Dec. 1700; and David, 10 Apr. 1703; his w. d. same day, and he m. 8 June 1710, Mary, d. of Lieut. Jonathan Belden, and d. 6 Sept. 1752; and his wid. d. 9 Jan. 1769. EBENEZER, Northampton, s. of the sec. Samuel of Springfield, m. Hannah Hunt, d. of Jonathan, had Obadiah, b. 1695; Noah, 1699; Clemence, 1703; Elisha, 1705; and others, says the notice in Geneal. Reg. IV. 357. To supply the deficiencies as well as to correct the errors, of that notice, we may learn from the highest authority, that the m. refer. to, was on 19 Dec. 1691, and that the first issue of it was Experience, b. 20 Aug. foll. wh. d. next mo.; the next, Obadiah, 26 July 1693, not 1695; Experience, again, 1695; Noah, 29 Nov. of the yr. above; Clemence, 4 Nov. of the yr. above; Elisha, in May of the yr. above; Esther, 6 May 1708; and Mary, 8 May 1711. But the striking omiss. is of the first w. Eliz. d. of Jedediah Strong, m. 16 Sept. 1684, wh. d. 17 Feb. 1691, had only ch. Mary, wh. d. five days bef. her mo. The f. was a deac. and d. 1748. EDWARD, Concord, by w. Eliz. had Edward, b. 21 Jan. 1658; Matthew, 18 June 1659; perhaps others; Barry says Samuel; Peter; and three ds. and d. 1691. He was entit. says Barry, 451, to houses, lds. &c. in the manor of Castle Bromwich, in Co. Warwick. EDWARD, Boston, m. 27 May 1657, Mary Powell, had, says Barry, Mary, b. 19 Jan. foll. In a deed 1667, he is call. cordwinder. EDWARD, Sudbury, perhaps brot. by his wid. mo. Dorothy (wh. m. John Blanford), m. 18 June 1659, Hannah Axtell, prob. d. of Thomas of the same, had Hannah, b. 9 Jan. 1661; Dorothy, 20 Oct. 1662; Sarah, 17 Jan. 1665; Mary, 2 Jan. 1667; Eliz. 6 Mar. 1669; Samuel, 9 Apr. 1670; Abigail, 15 Sept. 1672; Edward, 16 Mar. 1677; and Martha, 25 Dec. 1681; was a capt. and d. 7 Aug. 1703. His wid. d. 18 May 1708. EDWARD, Scituate, m. 25 May 1664, Lydia, d. of

Richard Sylvester, wid. of Nathaniel Rawlins, had Mercy, b. 1666;
Hannah, 1668; Grace, 1669; David, 1670; Edward, 1671; and Joseph, 1673. One EDWARD was a soldier in Turner's comp. for Philip's
war, 1676. EDWARD, Sudbury, youngest s. of Edward of the same,
had Nehemiah, b. 23 May 1707, as Barry tells, and at Framingham,
Zerubabel, 14 Aug. 1708; Bezaleel, 22 July 1710; William, 21 Sept.
1711; Tabitha, 27 Mar. 1713; Eliz. 11 Mar. 1717; Hannah, 15 Apr.
1719; Edward, 10 Mar. 1721; Mehitable; and Lois, a. 1728. ELIZUR,
Northampton, s. of Samuel the sec. of Springfield, m. Mary Pardee, as
in Geneal. Reg. IV. 357, is said, and there are also giv. to him, ch.
Elizur, b. 1689; Azariah, 6 Mar. 1697; Nehemiah, Jan. 1699; Eldad,
2 Mar. 1701; Benoni, 26 Nov. 1702; Phineas, 20 July 1710; and five
ds. but no names of these are call. in that tract; and from ano. hand I
find them, Hepzibah, 14 Feb. 1691, d. at 2 yrs.; Mary, 12 Sept. 1695;
Martha, 8 Dec. 1704; Sarah, 10 Jan. 1707; and Miriam, 13 Feb. 1715.
I am also instruct. by the same, that he rem. to Northfield, and d. 12
May 1743. GEORGE, Salem 1637, of wh. we kn. no. more. Eliz. of
the ch. 1641, may have been his w. GEORGE, Braintree, freem. 18
May 1642, if we may add a W. to the Right of the rec. was a lieut.
there, may not, I hope, have been that capt. wh. in Jan. 1649, stab.
Walter Lettice at Newport, as Roger Williams writes to his friend John
Winth. jr. See 3 Mass. Hist. Coll. IX. 280. HENRY, Dorchester,
freem. 6 May 1635, by w. Eliz. had Mary, b. 1 Apr. 1635; and Samuel,
14 Feb. 1637. Of him, as no more is seen in the rec. it is safely conject. that he rem. but whither is uncert. One HENRY was a soldier of
Turner's comp. in 1676. HENRY, Springfield, s. of the first Abel of the
same, m. 1705, Hannah, youngest d. of John Bliss of the same, had
Hannah, b. 18 May 1706; Henry, 9 Jan. 1708, wh. was k. 26 July foll.
by the Ind. wh. at the same time, carr. away his w. and soon k. her.
He m. 1711, Sarah Root, prob. d. of Thomas of Westfield, had Moses;
Stephen, 1716; Caleb, 1718; Elisha, 1720; Sarah, 1723; and Deborah,
prob. earlier. His will of 1760, was pro. 1769. It names ch. Hannah,
Deborah, Sarah, Moses, Stephen, Caleb, and Elisha. ISAAC, Hingham
1637, came from Co. Norfolk, d. 1652; and of him we kn. nothing more.
ISAAC, Lancaster, of wh. that he d. in 1663, is all that is told. JAMES,
Wethersfield, s. prob. eldest of the first Thomas of the same, and b. in
Eng. freem. 1654, had w. Mary, wh. d. 6 Oct. 1659, and he m. 20 Nov.
1660, Dorcas, d. of Jonas Weed of Stamford, had James, b. 1661;
Thomas; Jonas; Daniel, 1674; and Hannah; to wh. Chapin, in p. 179
of Glastonbury celebrat. erron. adds Lydia. Middletown was later
resid. and his w. d. 24 Dec. 1692, and he d. 1705. JAMES, Northampton, s. of the first Samuel of Springfield, m. 18 Jan. 1665, Abigail, d.

prob. of William Jess of Springfield, had Abigail, b. 26 Dec. foll. d.
young; Helped, 2 July 1668, wh. liv. unm. to Jan. 1745; James, 9
Nov. 1670, d. at 18 yrs.; Lydia, 24 Mar. 1673, d. at 5 ds.; Samuel, 16
May 1675; Preserved, 6 Jan. 1679; Jonathan, 19 Dec. 1681; Esther,
20 Aug. 1684; and Hannah, 1688, wh. d. 1691; and his w. d. 24 May
1707. He d. 1723. Between this acco. and that of Geneal. Reg. IV.
358, some discrepance appears, but the correct vers. is here obey.
*JOHN, Woburn 1641, had been of Charlestown, and there was one of
the project. thirty-two in numb. for settlem. of the new ch. and town,
freem. 1643, had John; Ruth, b. 23 Apr. 1646; Deborah, 21 Jan.
1649; and Sarah, 16 Feb. 1653; rep. 1648. His w. Priscilla d. 10
Apr. 1687, and he d. 21 June 1688. *JOHN, Gloucester, rep. 1648,
with spell. of Write, of wh. I see no more, and think he may be the
preced. JOHN, Charlestown, had John, b. 27 Sept. 1646, if the rec. be
trustworthy, and I see no reas. to doubt it. JOHN, Newbury, by w.
prob. Alice, had Jonathan, b. 7 Dec. 1650; and Ruth, 31 May 1652;
rem. to Boston, bef. 1656, and d. 1658. Admin. was giv. 30 Dec. to
Edward Bragg. JOHN, Chelmsford, prob. s. of the first John, m. 10
May 1661, Abigail Warren, whose f. is not kn. but she, I suppose, d. at
Woburn, 6 Apr. 1726, aged 84; had Joseph, b. 14 Oct. 1663, was freem.
3 May 1665, liv. there in 1679, but, I think, rem. to Woburn, there d.
30 Apr. 1714, aged 83, if we agree to accept the gr.-st. inscript. JOHN,
Watertown, freem. 1690. An alderman of Boston, Co. Lincoln, in 1630,
was nam. John Wright, and may reasonab. be suppos. to have descend.
here. JOSEPH, Wethersfield, s. of the first Thomas of the same, freem.
1667, by fam. tradit. is said to have had two ws. By the first Mary, m.
10 Dec. 1663, wh. d. 23 Aug. 1683, aged 38, he had Mary, b. 15 Apr.
1665; Eliz. 18 Nov. 1667; Joseph, 14 Feb. 1670; Sarah, 16 May
1674; Thomas, 18 Jan. 1677; John, 19 May 1679; and Jonathan, 18
June 1681. His next w. Mercy, m. 10 Mar. 1685, brot. him Benjamin;
and Nathaniel, 16 Oct. 1688; and he is said to have d. early in 1715,
but to have made his will three yrs. bef. JOSEPH, Medfield, freem.
1674. JOSEPH, Northampton, sec. s. of the sec. Samuel of Springfield,
m. 6 Nov. 1679, Ruth, d. of the first Isaac Sheldon of the same, had
Joseph, b. 23 June 1681; Samuel, 13 Aug. 1683, d. young; Ruth, 14
Feb. 1685, d. in few wks.; Ruth, again, 26 Apr. 1687; James, 5 Dec.
1689, d. young; Mary, Jan. 1691; Samuel, 13 Aug. 1693; and Benoni,
4 Oct. 1697; supply. some failure in Geneal. Reg. IV. 357. He was
freem. 1690, and d. 16 Feb. 1697. His wid. m. 28 Oct. 1698, Samuel
Strong. JOSEPH, Springfield, s. of the first Abel, m. 1687, Sarah
Osborne, perhaps d. of John of Windsor, had Mindwell, b. 24 Sept.
1688, d. young; Joseph, 14 Oct. 1690; Sarah, 20 Nov. 1692; Ben-

jamin, 11 Nov. 1694, slain, 1712, by the Ind.; Mindwell, again, 4 Mar. 1697; Martha, 16 June 1699; Mary, 24 Sept. 1702; and Rachel, 4 Dec. 1706. JOSIAH, sometimes writ. Joseph, Woburn, m. 1 Nov. 1661, Eliz. Hassall, perhaps d. of Richard of Watertown, had Eliz. b. 2 July 1664; Joseph, 14 Mar. 1667; Sarah, 25 Feb. 1670; John, 2 Oct. 1672; Joanna, or Hannah, as ano. rec. has it, 18 Apr. 1675; James, 10 Nov. 1677; Timothy, 3 Apr. 1679; Stephen, 22 Feb. 1681; Jacob, 22 June 1683; Ruth, 10 Oct. 1685; and Bryan, 14 Mar. 1688. Of this w. I suppose, was b. 23 Feb. 1671, a creature, minutely describ. Farmer MS. says in p. 33 of Incr. Mather's Hist. Ind. Wars; and that explains the orig. of the love of the marvellous in his s. "greater than his f." For ano. w. he had Ruth, wid. of John Center, and she d. 18 Feb. 1717, aged 60, if the gr.-st. be true; but I have a memo. slightly inconsist. that he rem. to Charlestown, and m. 7 July 1692, Eliz. Bateman; wh. may seem very prob. bec. 2 Nov. 1686 his d. Eliz. m. Eleazer Bateman; and it may be that the wid. of Center bec. his third w. JOSIAH, Woburn, perhaps s. of the preced. was deac. d. 22 Jan. 1748, aged 73, by Mr. Wyman's inscr. of the gr.-st. JUDAH, Northampton, youngest s. of the first Samuel of the same, m. 7 Jan. 1667, Mercy, d. of Henry Burt, had Samuel, b. 6 Nov. foll. d. in 3 mos.; Mercy, 14 Mar. 1669; Esther, 18 Aug. 1671, d. soon; Judah, 14 Nov. 1673, d. in two ds.; Judah, again, May 1677; Ebenezer, Sept. 1679; Thomas, 8 Apr. 1682; Patience, 18 Apr. 1684; and Nathaniel, 5 May 1688. He was freem. 1676, m. sec. w. 11 July 1706, Sarah, wid. of Richard Burk, wh. d. 1712; and he d. 26 Nov. 1725. MORDECAI, Plymouth, of wh. I find only that he was b. 30 Oct. 1649 and bur. 20 Mar. 1650, but wh. was his f. must be left to conject. NATHANIEL, New Hampsh. in Feb. 1690, request. protect. of Mass. NICHOLAS, Sandwich 1643, had been of Lynn 1637. PETER, Sandwich 1643, had rem. to that place 1638. My conject. is that he was br. of Nicholas; and in his MS. collect. for new edit. Farmer had noted, that he had s. Adam, b. 20 Mar. 1650, wh. prob. sett. at Oyster Bay, L. I. RICHARD, Lynn, perhaps as early as 1630, certain. in 1632, one of the Comtee. of that town to confer with two others of ea. town in advis. the Gov. and Assist. a. rais. a public stock, freem. 14 May 1634, was of Boston 1636 or earlier, being No. 89 of the ch. so that it may well seem to be a differ. man. The Boston man had ld. at Mount Wollaston, and was call. capt. He there had a mill, wh. with forty acres, he gave, in 1640, to Thomas Dudley, as price of five cows. I hope he had a good bargain, but it seems a hard one. Prob. he liv. sometime at Dorchester, aft. 1636. RICHARD, Plymouth 1643, had Esther, b. 1649; and Isaac, 26 Aug. 1662. RICHARD, Rehoboth 1644. ROBERT, Boston, came as a runaway, 1630, from London, where he had been a draper in Newgate market, and a brewer in Thames street, was here arrest. as in his let. to the Countess of Lincoln, our Dept.-Gov. Dudley shows, and was to be sent home by the same ship that carr. the let. ROBERT, Boston, ar. co. 1643, by w. Mary had John, wh. was bur. Mar. 1645 ; John, again, wh. d. 22 June 1652; Robert, b. 16 June 1653; and Joseph, 14 Nov. 1655. SAMUEL, Springfield 1641, brot. w. and ch. some of wh. were b. in Eng. but in what town he had first liv. is unkn. freem. 13 Apr. 1648, was deac. and appoint. by the town (aft. ret. of Rev. Mr. Moxon, the first min. to his native ld. in 1653) "to dispense the word of God for the present;" but a. 1656, he rem. to Northampton. In his will of 1663, he names seven ch. Samuel; James; Judah, b. 10 May 1642; Mary; Margaret; Esther; and Lydia; beside wh. he had Helped, 15 Sept. 1644, wh. was d. Prob. most of the five elder ch. were b. in Eng. and all they, with Judah, were liv. in 1680; and he d. "in his chair," says the rec. 17 Oct. 1665. His wid. Margaret names, in her will of 1680, only the four ds. and she d. 24 July 1681. Of the ds. Esther m. 18 Feb. 1682, Samuel Marshfield ; Margaret m. 8 Dec. 1653, Thomas Bancroft; Lydia m. 25 Oct. 1654, Lawrence Bliss, and in 1678, John Norton, and in 1688, John Lamb, and in 1692, George Colton. The other d. Mary was m. but the date and name of the h. are unkn. SAMUEL, Springfield, s. prob. eldest of the preced. and b. in Eng. m. 24 Nov. 1653, Eliz. d. of Henry Burt of the same, had Samuel, b. 3 Oct. 1654; rem. to Northampton, there had Joseph, 2 June 1657 ; Benjamin, 13 July 1660 ; Ebenezer, 20 Mar. 1663; Eliz. 31 July 1666; Eliezur, 20 Oct. 1668; Hannah, 27 Feb. 1671; and Benoni, 12 Sept. 1675, posthum. He was a soldier on serv. at Northfield, there k. by the Ind. ten days bef. the b. of his youngest s. The wid. m. 16 Sept. 1684, Nathaniel Dickinson of Hatfield, and at the same time were m. her s. Ebenezer, and the eldest d. Eliz. m. Thomas Stebbins ; Hannah m. 18 Nov. 1686, she then less than 16 yrs. old, Samuel Billing of Hatfield. Of this Samuel descend. the late Silas, a Senator of the U. S. of no humble rank from New York. SAMUEL, Wethersfield, s. of Thomas of the same, b. prob. in Eng. freem. 1657, m. 29 Sept. 1659, Mary, d. of Deac. Richard Butler of Hartford, had Samuel, Mary, Hannah, Sarah, Mabel, and David, the last b. 12 Jan. 1678 ; had good est. and d. Feb. 1690, call. 56 yrs. old, hav. made his will the mo. bef. in wh. the ds. Sarah and Mabel are not nam. perhaps d. SAMUEL, Sudbury, m. 25 Mar. 1663, Hannah, d. of Benjamin Albee of Medfield, I think ; but 3 May 1664 m. Lydia Moore, and d. 21 Aug. foll. and his wid. m. 15 June next, James Cutter. SAMUEL, Northampton, eldest s. of the sec. Samuel of Springfield, freem. 1683, m. 3 Jan. 1678, Sarah, d. of John Lyman of the same, had nine ch. Sarah, b. 20 Dec. 1678;

Samuel, 17 May 1682 ; Dorcas, wh. d. 7 June 1686; John, 9 Aug.
1687 ; Hannah, 6 Feb. 1689 ; Stephen ; Hezekiah, 22 May, 1695 ;
Dorcas ; and Keziah, 21 Jan. 1702 ; as says the Notice in Geneal. Reg.
IV. 357, corrected and enlarged. He d. 29 Nov. 1734, at N. SAMUEL,
Westford, of wh. I see nothing exc. that he was f. of Abel, b. a. 1682,
over whose corpse, taken from Charles riv. in wh. he was drown. 28
June 1707, the monum. at Cambridge bears the inscript. of his date in
the UNIVERSITY, this term being thus early employ. SAMUEL, Wethersfield, s. of the first Samuel of the same, m. 12 May 1686, Rebecca,
d. of Moses Crafts ; she little older than 15 yrs. at that time, d. 14 Mar.
1711 ; and he m. Aug. 1723, Abigail, wid. of Samuel Walker, and d. 12
Oct. 1734. His wid. d. 1 Jan. 1740. SAMUEL, Sudbury, s. of Edward
of the same, m. Mary, d. of Cyprian Stevens, had Mary, b. 10 Feb.
1704 ; Dorothy, 7 Mar. 1706 ; Abigail, 19 Feb. 1708 ; Isabel, 3 Feb.
1710 ; William, 22 Dec. 1712 ; beside Cyprian, and Hannah, both
earlier ; and d. at Rutland, says Barry, 15 Jan. 1740, his w. hav. d. 18
May preced. SAMUEL, Springfield, youngest adult s. of the first Abel of
the same, m. 1710, Mary Case of Lebanon, and in 1724 liv. at Norwich.
THOMAS, Exeter 1639. THOMAS, Wethersfield 1639, may have been
earlier at Watertown, or other Mass. settlem. brot. from Eng. w. and ch.
sev. perhaps, had more on this side of the water. For sec. w. by wh.
he had no ch. he took Margaret, wid. of John Elson (wh. had been wid.
of Hilliard, perhaps Hugh, and had s. Benjamin, Job, and John H.)
He was much engag. 1658 in the controv. a. Rev. John Russell ; and
d. Apr. 1670. Of his ch. Samuel, James, Thomas, Joseph, Lydia, it is
very diffic. to make any arrangem. of dates. Chapin, p. 179, adds to
these a Mary. The wid. d. 1671 ; and the d. Lydia d. bef. he came to
W. m. Joseph Smith. THOMAS, Wethersfield, s. perhaps eldest, of the
preced. freem. 1654, d. 23 Aug. 1683, leav. good est. to ch. Thomas, b.
1 Mar. 1660 ; Mary, 4 Mar. 1664 ; Hannah, 10 Mar. 1670 ; and Lydia,
12 Mar. 1673. Eliz. b. 17 Feb. 1676 had d. bef. Wh. was his w. is
uncert. tho. Chapin gives him Eliz. d. of Lieut. William Chittenden, yet
this may more prob. belong to the succeed. THOMAS, Guilford, m. 16
Jan. 1658, prob. Eliz. d. of William Chittenden of the same, wh. d.
without issue. In 1673, he m. at G. Sarah Benton, had Mary, b. 1674,
wh. m. 1698, Gideon Allen ; Daniel, 1676, d. at 22 yrs. ; Mercy, 1680,
wh. m. Thomas Burges ; Mehitable, 1684 ; Abel, 1688, d. young ; but
aft. his f. wh. d. 6 Dec. 1692 ; and his wid. d. nineteen days aft. WAL-
TER, Andover, m. 26 Feb. 1668, Susanna Johnson, whose f. is unkn.
but prob. she was sis. of some of the many Johnsons in that town, had
Christopher, wh. d. 16 Jan. 1673 or 4, and perhaps others. His w. d. 3
June 1684, and he m. 9 Sept. foll. Eliz. with a surname to be reject. on

wh. the contribut. of that valua. rec. in Geneal. Reg. III. 67, wrote to me, shortly aft. its publicat. in 1849 : " Is not this name, Sadir, a strange one ? I could, however, make nothing else out of it, unless I call it Sadie." Resort to conject. would be unjustifiab. as the orig. may be turn. to, but I doubt the first letter more than the last. If some undiscip. eye assail the MS. he may scrutinize each letter, and if the initial seem an S, other letters may turn out adler, or any thing exc. Sadir. WIL-LIAM, Plymouth, came in the Fortune, 1621, had w. Priscilla, but by his will of 16 Sept. 1633, might seem to have no ch. at least to her he gives all. WILLIAM, Sandwich, whose rec. of bur. 2 May 1648 is all that is told of him. WILLIAM, Boston 1670. In 1834 Farmer count. ten gr. of this name at Yale, eight at Harv. four at Dartm. and thirteen at other N. E. coll.

WROTHAM, or WROTHOM, SIMON, Farmington 1653, freem. 1654, by w. Sarah had three ch. Eliz. wh. m. 5 Nov. 1679, Thomas Newell; Susanna, wh. m. 25 Nov. 1679, Samuel Hough; and Simon. His w. d. 16 Nov. 1684, and he made his will 1686, but liv. to Nov. 1689. The s. Simon d. unm. Jan. 1695, and the name is extinct.

WYARD, JOHN, Wethersfield, m. 1681, Sarah Standish, perhaps d. of Thomas, had Lois, b. 1682 ; John, 1684 ; Thomas, 1686 ; Eunice, 1688 ; Jonathan, 1690 ; and Sarah; was selectman, 1692. ROBERT, Boston 1662, Hartford 1666, may have been f. of the preced. d. 11 Sept. 1682, leav. wid. and prob. childr. Sometimes this name is Wiard, Wyer, or Wier.

WYATT, WIAT, or WYAT, EDWARD, Dorchester, freem. 1645, liv. in 1667, had w. Mary, wh. d. 6 Feb. 1706, aged 92, a wid. wh. had been instrumental for bring. into the world more than 1,100 ch. as told in Blake's Ann. 37. He was f. of Nathaniel, and of Waitstill, wh. m. Capt. Thomas Vose, and almost equal. her mo. in age. See Geneal. Reg. X. 294. ISRAEL, Hatfield, youngest s. of John of Haddam, m. 1690, Sarah Pratt, perhaps d. of the third John of Hartford, had Sarah, b. 1693 ; Israel, and Susanna, tw. 1696, of wh. Israel d. soon ; Israel, again, 1700 ; and Hannah, 1703 ; rem. to Colchester, and prob. had other ch. bef. or aft. *JAMES, Taunton 1643, was a lieut. rep. 1652–60, and d. July 1664. JOHN, Ipswich 1638, d. 1665, as Coffin inform. Farmer. JOHN, Windsor, sold his rights there 1649, and rem. to Farm-ington, where he had m. Mary, d. of John Bronson, had Mary, b. 1648 ; John, 1650 ; Hepzibah, 1652 ; all bapt. 23 Oct. 1653 ; Dorcas, bapt. 4 Feb. 1655 ; Sarah, 20 Mar. 1659 ; Joanna, or Hannah, 1663 ; Eliz. 1665 ; and Israel, Mar. 1668 ; and d. in Sept. of that yr. prob. as his inv. of 7 of that mo. is of rec. with ages of the ch. His wid. m. 1669,

John Graves of Hatfield, and next Lieut. William Allis, and last Samuel Gaylord. Sarah m. 1679, Isaac Graves; Joanna m. 28 June 1683, Joseph Field; Eliz. m. 1685, Samuel Gunn, all of Hatfield. JOHN, Woodbury, perhaps eldest s. of the preced. serv. in the Ind. wars 1676 and 7, as in sev. places of Trumbull's Conn. Rec. II. Cothren, p. 754, tells that he came from Stratford, and had Gershom, bapt. 16 Feb. 1680; Sarah, Feb. 1682; Eliz. Aug. 1685; and Mercy, Apr. 1688. NATHANIEL, Dorchester, s. of Edward, m. Eliz. d. of Robert Spurr of the same, had Nathaniel and Edward, both bapt. 13 Apr. 1684; and Jonathan and Rebecca, both bapt. 19 Oct. foll. perhaps none was tw. but all brot. to the ordin. in right of their mo. Farmer, MS. names THOMAS of New Hampsh. wh. d. 1670, but that is the whole of his story.

WYBORNE, WIBORNE, WEYBORNE, WIBURN, or WYBURN, JAMES, Boston, d. 7 Mar. 1659, says Farmer; but of him I kn. nothing, but that he was s. of the first Thomas, nam. in his will, and prob. unm. JOHN, Boston, younger br. of the preced. rem. to Scituate, there, as Deane shows, had John, b. 1670; but Deane, 384, borrows, from Thomas, Abigail, and other ch. On rem. from B. he gave, by deed of 1671, his prop. then in B. to his mo. Eliz. Fitch. THOMAS, Scituate, had come in the Castle, 1638, from Tenterden, Co. Kent, as from the will of Peter Branch in Geneal. Reg. II. 183, is presum. It seems to be that of a fellow-passeng. commit. only ch. under ten yrs. of age to the care of W. wh. had at S. Thomas, James, Eliz. wh. also was the name of his w. and John and Mary; rem. to Boston bef. 1653, there prob. had Jonathan, wh. d. 10 Dec. of that yr. and Nathaniel, b. 12 Mar. 1655; and d. 2 Oct. 1656. By his will of 12 Sept. preced. pro. 28 Oct. foll. we learn most of the particulars a. the ch. and that he own. half of the windmill in B. wh. he gave to his w. and names three elder s. and two ds. beside Deborah, the inf. d. of his d. Eliz. wh. had m. 3 Apr. 1655, John Merrick. Of the will, Thomas and James, the two eldest s. were made excors. and Edward Tyng, and John Hull, his friends, were made overseers. In a note of Geneal. Reg. VI. 289, where is giv. abstr. of this will, the Editor doubts, that the s. Nathaniel was s. of the jr. not sen. Thomas, but in the rec. the name of the mo. is Eliz. THOMAS, Boston, s. prob. of the preced. m. 16 Dec. 1657, Abigail, d. of the first Jacob Eliot, had Abigail, b. 6 Jan. 1659; and Thomas, 2 Apr. 1660. By w. Ruth, he had Thomas, 10 Aug. 1663; and John, 25 Sept. 1665; and soon aft. rem. to Scituate.

WYER, or WIER, EDWARD, Charlestown 1658, m. 5 Jan. 1659, Eliz. Johnson, d. of William of the same, had Eliz. b. 10 Nov. foll.; Edward; Robert; and Hannah, all bapt. 23 July 1665; Catharine, 9 Dec. 1666;

Nathaniel, 21 June 1668; Ruhamah, 25 Dec. 1670; Eleazer, 15 Dec. 1672; Zechariah, 26 Mar. 1676; Sarah, 4 July 1680; and William, 3 Oct. foll.; yet as we find neither f. nor mo. of these inf. to be adm. of Charlestown ch. in Buddington's list, we must choose to consider that good Mr. Symmes had poor rec. or ano. ch. must be presum. to wh. one or the other of the parents belong. NATHANIEL, Newbury 1637, rem. aft. not a few yrs. prob. to Nantucket, had w. Sarah, and d. Mary, wh. m. it is said, John Swain; and he d. 1 Mar. 1681. PETER, York 1640 or earlier, adm. freem. of Mass. 1652, made Clk. of the writs, 1665, and recorder of the Province, by the commiss. of our Gen. Ct. 1668; and he must be the same as Weare. ROBERT, Boston, by w. Mary had John, b. 1 Nov. 1646.

WYETH, WITHE, WYTH, or WIETH, BENJAMIN, Hampton 1644, says Farmer, MS. HUMPHREY, Ipswich 1638. JOHN, Cambridge, s. of Nicholas of the same, m. 2 Feb. 1682, Deborah, d. of John Ward of Newton, had Eliz. b. 6 Nov. 1684; Deborah, 20 Nov. 1686; John, 21 Dec. 1688; Jonathan, 3 Mar. 1690; and perhaps others; was freem. 1690. NICHOLAS, Cambridge 1647, brot. from Eng. d. Sarah, wh. m. 11 Dec. 1651, John Fiske of Watertown. Whether he brot. w. is uncert. but if he did, she d. early, and he m. a. 1648, Rebecca, wid. of Thomas Andrews of C. had Mary, b. 18 Jan. 1649; Nicholas, 10 Aug. 1651; Martha, 11 Jan. 1653; John, 15 July 1655; and William, 11 Jan. 1658; all bapt. at C. and d. 19 July 1680, aged 85. Martha, m. 1 Apr. 1672, Thomas Ives. NICHOLAS, Cambridge, s. of the preced. m. Lydia, d. of the sec. David Fiske, wh. d. 10 Mar. 1698, aft. he had rem. to Watertown, and he m. 30 June foll. Deborah Parker, had only ch. Mary, b. 5 July 1699, d. in few days. He and his w. wh. long surv. him, were paupers many yrs. WILLIAM, Cambridge, s. of the first Nicholas, freem. 1690.

WYLEY, WEYLEY, WILLEY, WYLIE, or WILEY, JOHN, Reading, may be the passeng. in the Elizabeth and Ann, aged 25, from London, in May 1635, of wh. I would gladly tell more than is seen in the rec. that he had Susanna, b. 16 July 1655; and Sarah, 4 May 1658. TIMOTHY, Reading, perhaps s. of the preced. was freem. 1691. THOMAS, Dover 1648-69.

WYLLIS. See Willis.

WYMAN, or WEYMAN, BENJAMIN, Woburn, s. of Francis of the same, m. 20 Jan. 1703, Eliz. d. of Nathaniel Hancock the sec. of Cambridge, had Eliz. b. 1 May 1705; Benjamin, 17 Dec. 1706, or a few wks. earlier; Lucy, 17 Apr. 1708; Zebediah, June 1709; Eunice, 16 Nov. 1710; Jerusha, 23 July 1712; Tabitha, 7 Apr. 1714; Abijah, 20 Sept. 1715; Catharine, 6 May 1717; Nathaniel, 26 Jan. 1719; Abigail, 26

Aug. 1720; Martha, 7 May 1722; Noah, 30 July 1724, d. young; Jonas, 21 July 1725, a soldier at capt. of Louisburg, d. soon aft.; and Reuben, 9 Nov. 1726; and d. 19 Dec. 1735. His wid. m. 22 Aug. 1739, Jonathan Bacon. DAVID, Woburn, a tanner, s. of John of the same, m. 27 Apr. 1675, Isabel, d. of John Farmer of Concord, had David, b. 29 Mar. 1676, d. in few ds.; Isabel, 5 July 1677; and d. of smallpox, 27 Dec. 1678, or very soon aft.; and his wid. m. 19 Nov. foll. James Blood of Concord. FRANCIS, Woburn, a tanner, one of the thirty-two inhabs. of Charlestown, wh. on 18 Dec. 1640, estab. the town of W. m. 30 Dec. 1644 or 30 Jan. 1645, Judith Pierce of W. b. at Norwich in O. E. d. of John, but of this union was no issue, nor is the time of her d. kn. yet he took sec. w. 2 Oct. 1650, Abigail, d. of William Read of W. had Judith, b. 29 Sept. 1652, d. in few wks.; Francis, a. 1654, d. at 22 yrs.; William, a. 1656; Abigail, wh. m. 2 Jan. 1675, Stephen Richardson; Timothy, 16 Sept. 1661; Joseph, 9 Nov. 1663, wh. d. unm. 24 July 1714; Nathaniel, 25 Nov. 1665; Samuel, 29 Nov. 1667; Thomas, 1 Apr. 1671; Benjamin, 25 Aug. 1674; Stephen, 2 June 1676, d. in few wks.; and Judith, again, 15 Jan. 1679, wh. m. Nathaniel Bacon. He was an early propr. at Billerica, freem. 1657, and d. 28 or 30 Nov. 1699, aged, perhaps, 82. JACOB, Woburn, a tanner, youngest s. of John of the same, freem. 1690, m. 23 Nov. 1687, Eliz. d. of Samuel Richardson of the same, had Jacob, b. 11 Sept. foll.; Samuel, 7 Feb. 1690; Eliz. 5 or 7 Jan. 1691; David, 14 Apr. 1693; Martha, 13 Oct. 1695; Mary, 8 July 1698; John, 11 Dec. 1700, H. C. 1721, d. very soon aft.; Solomon, 24 Apr. 1703, d. at 22 yrs.; Patience, 13 Apr. 1705; Ebenezer, 5 May 1707, H. C. 1731, min. of Union, Conn.; Isaiah, 28 Feb. 1709; Peter, 27 Sept. 1711; and Daniel, 27 May 1715. His w. d. 21 Nov. 1739, and he m. 4 Feb. foll. Eliz. Coggin of W. and d. 31 Mar. 1742. JOHN, Woburn, a tanner, was one of the inhabs. of Charlestown, that formed the town of W. m. 5 Nov. 1644, Sarah, d. of Miles Nutt of W. had Samuel, b. 20 Sept. 1646, d. in few ds.; John, 28 Mar. 1648; Sarah, 15 Apr. 1650, wh. m. 15 Dec. 1669, Joseph Walker of Billerica; Solomon, 26 Feb. 1652; David, 7 Apr. 1654; Eliz. 18 Jan. 1656, d. young; Bathsheba, 6 Oct. 1658, wh. m. 30 May 1677, Nathaniel Tay; Jonathan, 13 July 1661; Seth, 3 Aug. 1663; and Jacob; was a lieut. and d. 9 May 1684. His wid. m. 25 Aug. foll. Thomas Fuller of W. JOHN, Woburn, s. of the preced. m. 1671, Mary, eldest d. of Rev. Thomas Carter of the same, had John, b. 23 Apr. 1672; and Mary, 25 June 1674; was one of the troop under the brave Capt. Thomas Prentice, and was k. by the Ind. in Dec. 1675, in the Narraganset country, and his wid. m. 31 Oct. foll. Nathaniel Batchelder of Hampton. Ano. JOHN of Woburn, wheelwright, whose

f. is not seen, m. 14 Dec. 1685, Hannah, d. of John Farrar of the same, had John, b. 16 Nov. 1686; Thomas, 25 Mar. 1689; Jasper, 6 Jan. 1692; Nathan, 8 Jan. 1696; Hannah, Aug. 1703; Ann, 10 Apr. 1705; Rachel, 24 Oct. 1707; and he d. 19 Apr. 1728. JONATHAN, Woburn, s. of the first John, m. 29 July 1689, Abigail, d. of James Fowle of the same, wh. d. in few mos. and he m. 31 July foll. Hannah, d. of Peter Fowle of W. had Abigail, b. 1 June 1691; Hannah, 2 Nov. 1694; Mary, 26 Jan. 1697; Eliz. 15 Feb. 1701; Jonathan, 13 Sept. 1704; Sarah, 18 Aug. 1706; and Zechariah, 19 July 1709; was freem. 1690; and d. 15 Dec. 1736. NATHANIEL, Woburn, s. of Francis of the same, m. 28 June 1692, Mary Winn, perhaps d. of Increase of W. had Nathaniel, b. 23 May foll.; Mary, 28 May 1694; Abigail, 5 Oct. 1695; Ruth, 17 Apr. 1697; Hannah, 23 Apr. 1699; Eliz. 11 Nov. 1700; Phebe, 11 June 1702; Rebecca, 14 Apr. 1704; Joanna, 25 July 1705; Increase, 1 Mar. 1707; Sarah, 21 Aug. 1710; Kezia, 5 Apr. 1713; and he d. 8 Dec. 1717. His wid. m. 30 Nov. 1720, John Locke of W. SAMUEL, Woburn, br. of the preced. m. 1692, Rebecca, d. of Matthew Johnson of the same, had Rebecca, b. 11 Nov. 1693; Abigail, 5 Feb. 1695; Hannah, 10 Dec. 1696; Sarah, 2 Feb. 1698; Samuel, 18 Mar. 1700; Oliver, 5 Sept. 1701; Lydia, 1 Jan. 1703; Patience, 9 Jan. 1705; Matthew, 3 Aug. 1707; and Esther, 25 Feb. 1709, wh. liv. 100 yrs. less one month; and he d. 17 May 1725. SETH, Woburn, s. of the first John of the same, m. 17 Dec. 1685, Esther, d. of William Johnson of the same, had Seth, b. 13 Sept. 1686; Esther, 25 Oct. 1638; Sarah, 17 Jan. 1690; Jonathan, Nov. 1693, d. at two mos.; Susanna, 30 June 1695; Abigail, 6 Feb. 1698; and Love, 14 Feb. 1701; was freem. 1690; and d. 26 Oct. 1715. His wid. d. 31 Mar. 1742. STEPHEN, spell. Wayman, was in the Narraganset serv. Feb. 1676, but of what town, or in whose comp. I kn. not, nor any thing further of him. THOMAS, Boston, by the diligent inq. in the Geneal. Reg. III. 34, call. a tailor, said to have serv. in the Narraganset winter campaign 1675 and 6, and to have had Thomas, Daniel, Mary, Sarah, and Abigail, but dates of b. could not be found by him. At first, it is said, the name was Weymouth. THOMAS, Woburn, s. of Francis of the same, m. 5 May 1696, Mary, d. of Nathaniel Richardson of the same, had Thomas, b. 12 May 1697; Josiah, 18 Mar. 1700; Phineas, 1701; Timothy, 1 Mar. 1702; Benjamin, 12 June 1704; John, 6 July 1706; Mary, 10 Mar. 1708; Aaron, 6 Dec. 1709; Eleazer, 13 Apr. 1712; Nathaniel, 18 May 1716; Eliz. 19 Dec. 1718; and he d. 4 Sept. 1731. His wid. m. 17 Aug. 1733, Josiah Winn of W. TIMOTHY, Woburn, br. of the preced. by w. Hannah had Hannah, b. 7 July 1688; Timothy, 5 Apr. 1691; Solomon, 24 Oct. 1693; Joseph, 1 Nov. 1695; Eunice,

24 Feb. 1697; Ann, 26 Mar. 1700; Judith, 16 June 1702; Eliz. 11 Mar. 1704; Ebenezer, 21 Mar. 1706; Esther; Eliz.; and Prudence, 8 Mar. 1709; in wh. yr. he d. WILLIAM, Woburn, elder br. of the preced. m. Prudence, d. perhaps of Thomas Putnam of Salem, had William, b. 18, d. 20 Jan. 1683; Prudence, 26 Dec. foll.; William, again, 15 Jan. 1685; Thomas, 23 Aug. 1687; Eliz. 5 July 1689, d. next yr.; Francis, 10 July 1691; Joshua, 3 Jan. 1693; a d. 1694, d. very soon; Edward, 10 Jan. 1696; Eliz. again, 16 Feb. 1698; Deliverance, 28 Feb. 1700; and James, 16 Mar. 1702; was freem. 1690, and d. 1705. Farmer in 1834 counts the gr. of this name, seven at Harv. and two at other N. E. coll.

WYTHERDEN. See Witherden.

YALE, DAVID, Boston, came prob. with his f.-in-law, Gov. Eaton, in 1637, by w. Ursula (perhaps brot. from Wales, where was the home of his f. David, yet more prob. that he took her in Boston, tho. we kn. not her f.) had Eliz. b. May 1644, d. in few wks.; David, 18 Sept. 1645; Theophilus, 14 Jan. 1652, and soon aft. rem. perhaps home to Eng. He own. some ld. at New Haven, and may have liv. there two or three yrs. and even have had Joseph there, as on p. 24 of the "Yale fam." is presum. tho. to me it seems not prob. How Farmer was led to make him freem. 1640, is strange, for his name is not on the list, nor was he a mem. of the ch. of B. but he sympathiz. with the oppon. of our commun. wh. prob. induc. him to abandon our country. Gov. Hopkins wh. had m. his sis. Ann, in his will, made at London, 17 Mar. 1657, left him £200. ELIHU, New Haven, s. of the first Thomas, as Dr. Stiles positively says, tho. in more recent times, some at New Haven have doubted it, and offer very good presumpt. that he was s. of David, quot. the entry of the Merch. Taylor's sch. in London, where he was adm. 1 Sept. 1662, went home in his youth, and a. 1678, proceed. to the E. Indies, there resid. twenty yrs. and went home with large est. and three ds. two of wh. m. into noble fams. and he d. in London, 22 July 1721. His monum. is at Wrexham, in Co. Denbigh, bordering on Cheshire. The assid. antiquary, N. B. Shurtleff, in Geneal. Reg. IV. 245, in a brief, but comprehens. notice, slightly varying from Stiles, that is giv. in note to Winth. II. 217, shows how he was Gov. of the E. I. comp. and by his munificent legacy gain. the endur. credit, of founder of the flourish. instit. of Yale College in his native city. JOHN, New Haven, eldest s. of Thomas of the same, is in the list of proprs. 1685, and that was all that could be seen of him bef. the appear. of the Geneal. 1850, by a descend. of the same ancest. In that tract we learn, that, by w. Rebecca, whose surname is not told, he had John, b. 3 June 1694, when both parents had acquir. mature age (and of this s. it is carefully told, that he d. 11 Dec. 1711, aged 17 yrs. 6 mos. and 7 ds.) ; Elihu, 30 Mar. 1696 ; Abigail, 16 Nov. 1697 ; and David, 8 Oct. 1699 ; and d. 16 Dec. 1711, so few days aft. his s. of the same name, aged 65. His wid. d. 17 Oct. 1734, aged 78. NATHANIEL, New Haven, s. of Thomas of the same, was a propr. 1685, but little more was kn. of him, until in the fam. geneal. it is relat. that he m. 21 Oct. 1692, Ruth, d. of Hon. James Bishop, had David, b. 25 Sept. 1693 ; James, 31 July 1695, d. at 4 yrs.; Ann, 21 Aug. 1697 ; and Nathaniel, 31 Dec. 1702 ; and d. 29 Oct. 1730. His wid. d. June 1738 or 9, the Geneal. leav. the yr. uncert. THEOPHILUS, Boston, s. of David of the same, had very slight connex. I believe, at any time, with his native place, exc. that, in 1675, he advanc. passage-money for Edward Kidder, a shoemaker of Derbysh. to come over, wh. should serve therefor four yrs. THOMAS, New Haven, s. of David, b. in Wales, came prob. in 1637 to Boston, with Theophilus Eaton, wh. had m. for his sec. w. the wid. mo. of Thomas, and with his f.-in-law, went in 1638 to plant at New Haven ; there sign. the planta. covenant, 1639, m. Mary, eldest d. of Capt. Nathaniel Turner, had John, b. a. 1645 ; Thomas, a. 1646 ; Elihu, said by Dr. Stiles to have been b. 5 Apr. 1648, but some doubt, whether he was s. of Thomas, or even b. in New Haven, suggest. that he may have been s. of the br. David, or even br. but the town rec. contains not the b. of either of the three ; Mary, 16 Oct. 1650 ; Nathaniel, 3 Jan. 1653 ; Martha, 6 May 1655, bapt. 18 Mar. 1660, wh. d. under 16 yrs.; Abigail, 5 May 1660, bapt. perhaps, 22 July foll. ; Hannah, 6 July 1662 ; and Eliz. 29 Jan. 1667 ; was rep. 1672, and d. 27 Mar. 1683. His est. by inv. of 7 May foll. was £479. and in 1684 it was distrib. to the wid. three s. (Elihu not nam. but he may have declin. to partake) and four ds. of wh. Mary had m. Jan. 1673, Joseph Ives ; Hannah, m. 9 May 1682, Enos Talmadge ; and Eliz. m. 30 July 1688, Joseph Pardee. His wid. d. 15 Oct. 1704. THOMAS, New Haven, s. of the preced. was made freem. 1668, m. 11 Dec. 1667, Rebecca, d. of William Gibbard, had Hannah, b. 27 July 1669 ; and rem. to Wallingford, had there Rebecca, 2 Oct. 1671 ; Eliz. 25 July 1673 ; Theophilus, 13 Nov. 1675 ; Thomas, 20 Mar. 1679 ; Nathaniel, 12 July 1681 ; Mary, 27 Aug. 1684, d. under 19 yrs.; and John, 8 Dec. 1687 ; took sec. w. 8 Feb. 1689, Sarah, d. of John Nash, wh. d. 27 May 1716, and he took third w. 31 July foll. but had no ch. by either, and d. 26 Jan. 1736.

YARDLEY, JOHN, Braintree 1688, as found by Felt.

YATES, FRANCIS, Wethersfield, rem. 1641 to Stamford, says Hinman, but I judge him the same wh. was of Hempstead 1647, made a freem. of Conn. 1658, and perhaps at last a resid. at West Chester, in the prov. of New York, where he made his will, 1682, pro. and rec. in N. Y.

by wh. are nam. five ch. Mary, John, Dinah, Jonathan, and Dorothy.
GEORGE, made freem. of Conn. 1658, may have been br. of the preced.
HENRY, Guilford 1669, there d. Jan. 1705, in his will giv. all his prop.
to the ch. and to deac. John Meigs, and thus we may assume tho. the
amount was only £61. that he had no w. nor ch.   JOHN, Duxbury, by
w. Mary had John, b. 15 Aug. 1650; perhaps rem. to Eastham, and d.
soon, for his wid. m. Oct. 1651, Richard Higgins of E.   JOHN, Eastham,
perhaps s. of the preced. m. 11 Jan. 1700, Abigail Rogers, prob. d. of
Lieut. James.   One JOHN, perhaps the same, if the spell. of the name
on the roster, Yeates, may mean the same (as in the Boston rec. we call
Yeale, Yale), was a soldier in Moseley's comp. Dec. 1675.   WILLIAM
is the name of a passeng. aged 14, in the Abigail from London 1635, of
wh. no more is kn.

YEALES, TIMOTHY, Weymouth, m. at Boston, Naomi, d. of George
Frye of W. had Ann, b. 25 Apr. 1673, d. prob. young; Ann, again, 7
May 1679; and Nehemiah, 17 Sept. 1689; perhaps others.

YELINGS, ROGER, Boston, by w. Eliz. had John, b. 30 Aug. 1680;
and David, 12 Aug. 1682.

YELL, or YEAL, JOHN, Ipswich, m. says Mr. Felt, 27 July 1690,
Joanna Smith, had Eliz. b. 15 June 1691; and John, 20 June 1694;
and d. 20 Jan. 1701.

YEO, or YOW, SAMUEL, I find in the Essex rec. 1653, as is also
ALLEN; but the name is giv. Yew, and sometimes is spell. Yeow, and
in Drake's valua. Hist. of Boston, 800, is Yow.   THOMAS, Boston, m.
Sarah, d. of David Phippen or Phippeny of Hingham, bef. Nov. 1650,
as the will of P. calls him s.-in-law, had Eliz. b. 1 Oct. 1652; and
Thomas, 24 Apr. 1654; perhaps more.   Our Col. Rec. IV. shows that
in 1652 he was one of the projectors of the conduit in Ann street, long
a valua. supply of pure water, and discontin. in the present century.   I
think he had a br. Charles, at Bristol, Eng.

YEOMANS, EDMUND, Charlestown, by our Col. Rec. III. had w.
Susanna, and sold beer in 1650; but he is not seen as a householder
there in 1658.   He may be the man of Haverhill, 1666, by Coffin, in
Geneal. Reg. VIII. 168, call. Edward.   EDWARD, Boston, m. 21 June
1652, Eliz. d. of Thomas Joslin, Jocelin, or Josselin, had Edward, b. 6
May 1657; and perhaps other ch. but he d. not long aft. for his wid. m.
9 May 1662, Edward Kilby.   EDWARD and JOHN, early sett. of Plainfield, a. 1700, may have been s. of the preced.

YESCUTT, RICHARD, Ipswich, with w. Alice, giv. me by Mr. Felt,
prob. came to N. E. too late for adm. in this work.

YORK, or YORKE, BENJAMIN, Dover, s. of Richard, prob. of the
same, was first tax. there 1677.   JAMES, Stonington, had first liv. at

Braintree, where his s. James was b. 14 June 1648; was freem. of
Conn. 1666, but when he d. is not heard. JAMES, Stonington 1670, s.
of the preced. freem. 1673, sold the yr. preced. his est. in Boston, and d.
early, perhaps in 1678, for his wid. Deborah m. 12 Mar. 1679, Henry
Eliot. JOHN, Dover, prob. s. of Richard of the same, took o. of fidel.
1669, had w. Ruth, perhaps was of North Yarmouth 1684. RICHARD,
Dover 1648, was prob. f. of Benjamin, Edward, and John, and d. early
in 1674, his inv. being of 27 Mar. He left wid. Eliz. SAMUEL, Gloucester, by w. Hannah had John, b. 1695, but some yrs. bef. had liv. at
North Yarmouth. This s. and ano. (Thomas) d. says Babson, 1699,
and the f. d. 18 Mar. 1718, aged 73. But in his will he ment. other ch.
all prob. elder, Samuel, wh. had three s. Samuel; Benjamin; Richard;
beside three m. ds.

YOUDALL, PHILIP, Gloucester, of wh. nothing good is told by Babson, and no w. or ch. ment. nor any date giv. by him, 183, exc. that of
1648 in connex. with some offence.

YOUNG, CHRISTOPHER, Salem 1638, came from Yarmouth, Co. Norf.
by w. Priscilla had Sarah, bapt. 2 Dec. of that yr.; Ruth, Mar. 1641;
Judith, 1 Jan. 1643, d. soon; and Christopher, 18 Feb. 1644; and d. at
Wenham 1647, betw. 19 June, date of his will, and 8 July, when it was
pro. See Essex Inst. II. 6. By our Col. Rec. II. 272, it is seen that
discretion in our Ct. control the affection of the testator, by wh. he
directs his childr. to be sent to Eng. Coffin, in Geneal. Reg. VIII. 169,
has some slight variat. from the names and dates, but my bapt. are sure.
Sarah m. 20 Mar. 1662, I suppose, John Marsh. DAVID, Eastham, s.
of the first John of the same, m. 20 Jan. 1688, Ann, d. of John Doane
of the same, had Abigail, b. 28 Dec. foll.; Rebecca, 24 Oct. 1689;
Ann, 5 Oct. 1691; Hannah, 6 Sept. 1693; John, 20 Mar. 1695; Priscilla, 26 June 1697; Dorcas, 16 Dec. 1699; David, 25 Sept. 1701;
Lois, 2 Nov. 1704; Esther, 16 Nov. 1708; and Henry, 23 Mar. 1711.
EDWARD, Boston 1675, a fisherman, perhaps is the same, wh. by Coffin
is ment. at Newbury, having w. Hannah, and ch. Thomas, b. 17 Jan.
1691; and Richard, 7 Sept. 1693. GEORGE, Scituate 1660, m. 15 Jan.
1662, Hannah, d. of Thomas Pinson, had Thomas, b. 5 Nov. 1663;
Hannah, 1666; Margery, 1669; Eliz. 1671; and Patience, 1673; as
Deane, 393, tells. GILES, Boston, by w. Ruth had Susanna, b. 5 July
1672; and Naomi, 16 Dec. 1680. HENRY, Concord, was of Wheeler's
comp. and 2 Aug. 1675, at Brookfield, mort. wound. by the Ind. at the
same time with Capt. Edward Hutchinson. HENRY, Eastham, youngest
s. of the first John of the same, by w. Sarah had Martha, b. 28 July
1695; Eliz. 18 Jan. 1698; Reliance, 3 Mar. 1700; Moses, 15 Nov.
1702; Thomas, 24 Oct. 1705; and the f. d. 26 Apr. foll. JOHN,

Plymouth 1643, had perhaps the George bef. ment. and John, b. 9 Nov. 1649. JOHN, Salem 1638, rem. prob. to Charlestown, and d. 29 Dec. 1672. JOHN, Eastham, by w. Abigail, m. 13 Dec. 1648, had John, b. at Plymouth (where his w. had liv.), 16 Nov. 1649 ; Joseph, 12 Nov. 1651, d. soon ; Joseph, again, Dec. 1654 ; Nathaniel, Apr. 1656 ; Mary, 28 Apr. 1658 ; Abigail, Oct. 1660 ; David, 17 Apr. 1662 ; Lydia, 1664 ; Robert, Apr. 1667 ; Henry, July 1669, d. in few mos.; and Henry, again, 17 Mar. 1672 ; and d. 29 Jan. 1691. His wid. d. 7 Apr. 1692. Mary m. 3 Mar. 1677, Daniel Smith ; and Abigail m. 3 Jan. 1683, Stephen Twining. JOHN, Portsmouth, had John, b. 1649, perhaps others. JOHN, Southold, L. I. 1662, had, perhaps, been of Windsor 1641, whence he rem. bef. 1650, and in that yr. sold his est. at W. was by S. employ as agent to manage affairs with Conn. jurisdict. and Hammond has in his Index, mark. him as rep. but not so print. him in the body of the Vol. was a capt. and so much betrust. by the Gen. Ct. of Conn. that he was made a magistr. over that part of L. I. wh. the people of Conn. hoped to extort from the weakness of the Dutch ; and he was, in 1663, by act of the Ct. put in nominat. for an Assist. That he was never chos. was prob. the conseq. of the conquest of N. Y. from the Dutch, and royal gr. to the Duke of York. Oft. this man's name appears in Conn. Col. rec. without the *u*, and once an addit. *es* is seen ; and I am much inclined to believe that he was s. of the Rev. John Youngs. JOHN, Exeter, perhaps s. of John of Portsmouth, took o. of alleg. 1677, was k. by the Ind. 10 June 1697. JOHN, Eastham, eldest s. of John of the same, m. Ruth, d. of Daniel Cole of the same. JOSEPH, Salem 1638, of wh. I kn. only that he was one of a Comtee. in early days, to adjust the line of boundary betw. S. and Ipswich. See Col. Rec. II. JOSEPH, Eastham, br. of the preced. m. 23 Oct. 1679, Sarah Davis, prob. d. of Robert of Barnstable, had Samuel, b. 23 Sept. 1680 ; Joseph and Isaac, tw. 19 Dec. 1682 ; James, 4 Apr. 1685 ; and perhaps others. MATTHEW, Hartford, apprent. of William Williams to learn the trade of a cooper, in 1658 assent. to transfer to ano. master ; and that is all I hear of him. NATHANIEL, Eastham, s. of the first John of the same, left wid. Mercy, wh. m. 10 June 1708, Nathaniel Mayo of the same. PAUL, Boston, d. 1641, perhaps sudden. at least we see in Col. Rec. I. 318, that a commissn. to sett. his est. was giv. by the Gen. Ct. RICHARD, by Farmer giv. as the freem. of 1652 at Kittery, but was of Cape Porpus, when he d. left wid. Margery, wh. ret. inv. 18 Feb. 1673, for £124. ROBERT, York, perhaps br. of Rowland, took o. of alleg. 22 Mar. 1681. ROBERT, Eastham, s. of the first John of the same, m. 22 Mar. 1694, Joanna Hicks, whose f. is not told, had Robert, b. 11 Apr. 1695, d. at 2 mos. Robert, again, 11 Dec. 1696 ; Lydia, 29 May 1699 ; Joanna, 1

June 1703; and Jennet, 22 May 1708. ROWLAND, York, freem. 1652, sw. alleg. 22 Mar. 1681, may have been f. or rather gr.f. of that Rowland, a boy, prisoner in Canada, 1695, wh. is call. of Dover. THOMAS, perhaps of Warwick, m. Eliz. d. of Richard Harcutt of W. but he may have come from L. I. or at least went thither. THOMAS, Scituate, s. of George, m. Sarah, eldest d. of Peregrine White, wh. long outliv. him, and d. 9 Aug. 1755, aged almost 92 yrs. had George, b. 1689; Joseph, 1692, d. young; Sarah, 1695; Thomas, 1698, d. young; Thomas, again, 1700; Joseph, again, 1701; Ebenezer, 1703; Joshua, 1704; and Isaac, 1706; and d. 25 Dec. 1732. See Boston Newsletter of 29 Aug. 1755. One Thomas I find of New Hampsh. among the petnrs. in Feb. 1690, for protect. of Mass. Farmer counts the gr. of this name at Harv. five, Yale, four, and other N. E. coll. four up to 1834.

YOUNGLOVE, JAMES, Brookfield, d. without fam. and his br. John had admin. on his est. ret. inv. 13 Jan. 1667. JOHN, Hadley, perhaps s. of Samuel of Ipswich, was appoint. as appears by Col. Rec. IV. part 2d in 1667, with John Pynchon of Springfield, a Comtee. for Quaboag, aft. nam. Brookfield, freem. 1676, with prefix of respect, as he had preach. there a yr. or two, with no great satisfact. sch.-master at H. six or seven yrs. and was a preach. at the settlem. of Suffield 1681, in that Co. and there met no better accept. than at B. d. 1690, leav. wid. Sarah and ch. four s. and three ds. John; Samuel, b. 10 Feb. 1677, at H.; James; Joseph, 6 Nov. 1682, at S.; Mary, w. of Thomas Smith; Hannah, wh. bec. 1695, w. of George Norton; and Lydia, wh. m. 1693, George Granger. But he had also Sarah, wh. m. 1682, John Taylor, and d. next yr. with new b. ch. Prob. he was never ord. and when the Court advis. him to cease preach. it may derogate nothing from his moral worth, for as my correspond. says, "he may have had an unhappy temper, but it is not unlikely that the temp. of the people was worse than his." The wid. d. 17 Jan. 1711. SAMUEL, Ipswich, came in the Hopewell, Capt. Babb, in the autumn of 1635, aged 30; with w. Margaret, 28; and Samuel, 1 yr.; prob. had other ch. aft. arr. perhaps James; certain. Joseph; and d. in 1668, then call. 62 yrs. old, as Coffin gives it in Geneal. Reg. VIII. 169, with the name of Simon. SAMUEL, Ipswich, s. of the preced. b. in Eng. wheelwright, was adm. freem. 1671, m. 1 Aug. 1660, Sarah Kinsman, had Sarah, b. 5 Feb. 1663; Samuel, 30 Oct. 1665, d. soon; Mary, 17 Mar. 1668; Samuel, again, 27 July perhaps (for the yr. is indistinct) 1671; Mercy, 25 May 1676; and John, 29 Aug. 1677. On his est. admin. was gr. 23 Jan. 1707, when the wid. was call. Mary, and she soon aft. sold to the same John her share of the prop. Sarah m. 20 June 1684, John Shatswell.

YOUNGMAN, FRANCIS, Roxbury, m. 2 Dec. 1685, Ann, wid. of the third Isaac Heath of the same, had Jonathan, b. 9 Oct. 1686; Cornelius, 1 Sept. 1688; Ebenezer, 2 Nov. 1690; Ann, 1 Dec. 1695; Eliz. 17 Jan. 1699; and Leah, 4 May 1701, d. the same mo.; beside John, whose b. is not seen, but his d. is on the rec. 26 July 1711; as is also that of the f. 23 July of next yr.

YOUNGS, or YONGS, JOHN, Southold, L. I. a min. of St. Margarets, Co. Suff'lk. aged 35, with Joan his w. 34, and six ch. John, Thomas, Ann, Rachel, Mary, and Joseph, would have come to Salem in N. E. in the Mary Ann from Great Yarmouth, May 1637, with many other passeng. of wh. was the wid. of learn. William Ames, the Professor at Franequer, as is seen in a collect. of rec. at Westminster, with copy of wh. her majesty's keeper of those treasures favored me; and in the margin of this part is insert. "This man was forbyden passage by the Commissnrs. and went not from Yarmouth." Probably the scrivener had no idea of a negative pregnant, as the lawyers say, in his mind, when he made that entry, but may have suppos. that the power of the great archbp. the imperious and foolish Laud, would forever restrain that migrat. As the whole complication of ecclesiast. impolicy was overthrown three yrs. aft. the puritan's desire was then, if not earlier gratif. One report places him at New Haven 1638-40. I presume that Wood, in his Hist. of L. I. where he makes Y. a min. at Hingham, Eng. and to come to New Haven with part of his church in 1640, and to begin the settlem. of Southold, in Oct. of that yr. foll. tradit. of the neighb. and may be more trustworthy, as Farmer quotes him, where he says, he d. 1672, in his 74th yr. JOHN, Southold, L. I. eldest s. of the preced. (wh. is duly commemo. under Young), was, in 1681, under the governm. of the Duke of York, sheriff of the whole insular territo. as Wood tells, and d. in his 75th yr. 1698. JOSEPH, Southold, L. I. sen. and JOSEPH, jr. of the same, adm. freemen of Conn. 1662, were prob. br. and s. of the Rev. John, or possib. s. and gr.s. tho. less prob. ROBERT, York, k. by the Ind. betw. York and Kittery 16 or 22 Aug. 1690. THOMAS, Greenwich 1673, and of Oyster Bay, on the opposite coast of L. I. 1682, may have been s. of Rev. John, brot. from Eng.

ZECHARIAH, LEWIS, Ipswich 1675, is all that Mr. Felt can tell a. this person, whose surname may have changed places with the bapt. as Farmer found Merry Waters. Yet I have no acquaint. with Zechariah Lewis, not even so much as with Lewis Zechariah. The name of Daniel Zechary in Boston, turns up in 1706.

ZULLESH, DAVID, freem. of Mass. 18 May 1642, is the last name on the long list of that day's adm. as well as the latest in the labor of this Dictionary, wh. closes with regret that no further report of him can be afford. nor can any conject. be hazard. even for his resid. It hardly seems like an Eng. name, and f. mo. br. sis. w. or ch. are unkn. As approxim. to so unusual a surname, I have seen nothing but Mr. Zellick, a merchant at New Haven, 1647, only as a transient visitor, if even he were not far remote, whose goods of £200. value were attach. there by Mr. Pell, no doubt Thomas, one of the chief men there. I suppose he was a Dutchman from Manhattan; and that his name was by Boston folks turn. into Sellock.

MORE ADDITIONS AND CORRECTIONS

IN VOL. I.

P. 8. l. 11 from bot. aft. 1656; add, beside Eliz. wh. m. William Parkman.

P. 9. l. 5, aft. 1701; add, beside Daniel, Samuel, Benjamin, Joseph, and Thomas; and d. 1713, aged 61.

" l. 8, bef. *EDWARD, ins. EDWARD, Windsor, m. 25 May 1660, Eliz. Buckland, d. perhaps, of Thomas, had, says Stiles, Edward, wh. d. bef. his f. and Mary, 6 Aug. 1671, wh. m. John Matson, as Porter tells me.

P. 16. l. 3, for 1690 r. 1693 — also, aft. ch. add, Samuel, b. 1 Jan. 1678; and Abraham.

P. 22. l. 20, strike out, of the w.

P. 23. l. 7, aft. Alice, add, beside Ruth.

P. 33. l. 7 from bot. bef. JOSEPH, ins. JOSEPH, Salem, had w. Bethia, wh. had admin. of his est. 29 June 1682 for good of self and ch.

P. 40. l. 2, at the end, add, In 1697 he kept a shop at Hartford, had w. Lydia, ch. Edward, and Martha. But ano. EDWARD at H. m. Rachel, d. of James Steele, had John, b. 4 Mar. 1690; and Rachel, 20 Aug. 1694.

P. 41. l. 11, bef. 1691, ins. 7 July

" l. 11 from bot. aft. again, ins. 28

" l. 9 from bot. at the end, add, 17 Jan. 1686;

" l. 8 from bot. aft. Eliz. add, Nov. 1691; — also, aft. Esther, ins. 10 June 1697. — also, aft. 1707, add, or 1709

P. 43. l. 15, aft. m. ins. 3 Jan. 1684,

" l. 11 from bot. aft. Newberry. add, His s. Samuel d. 1648.

P. 45. l. 6 from bot. aft. 247. add, She d. unm.

P. 47. l. 2 from bot. for JOSEPHUS r. JOHANNES

P. 56. l. 11, aft. est. add, wh. was good.

P. 58. l. 7 from bot. for ds. r. d. — also, aft. Sarah, ins. b. a. 1622; — also, aft. and, ins. had — also, aft. Hannah, ins. b. a. 1625, at P.

" l. 2 from bot. aft. Susanna, ins. b. a. 1630;

" last l. aft. 315, ins. (where is error of a yr.) — also, at the end, add, or 22

P. 59. l. 1, aft. 1649; strike out all to Desire in l. 3, and ins. beside — also, in l. 3 erase, aft. 1653, all to the end of sent. in l. 6.

" l. 14, at the end, add, He d. 1678.

P. 63. l. 16 from bot. at the end, add, See Thompson, Hist. of L. I. I. 486, 90, and II. 13.

P. 67. l. 19 from bot. aft. childr. ins. John, Joseph, Eliz. Margaret, and Mary;

" l. 17 from bot. at the end, add, exc. the two s. of wh. Joseph went to Phila. and JOHN, of Nantucket, wh. m. 26 Feb. 1704, Mary, youngest d. of Eleazer Folger, had Keturah; Eunice, b. 29 Aug. 1706; Rhoda, 26 Nov. 1708; Persis, 17 Nov. 1710; Thomas, 8 Nov. 1712; Stephen, 2 Feb. 1715; and Priscilla, 2 Nov. 1718 He d. 1 Nov. 1719, and his wid. d. 7 Oct. foll.

P. 76. l. 10, aft. 1682, add, d. in few days.

" l. 12, aft. 1693, add, d. next yr.

P. 79. l. 3 from bot. for 1678 r. 1677

P. 89. l. 10 from bot. at the end, add, His first w. was Sarah, d. of John Charles.

P. 91. l. 15 from bot. aft. 1667. add, Hannah m. Thomas Walley, and next Rev. George Shove.

P. 98. l. 6, aft. John, ins. b. 31 Dec.

P. 106. l. 2, erase Mary, or

" l. 6, aft. Alling, ins. 21 Oct. 1684;

" l. 7, aft. Mercy; ins. Mary, bapt. 30 July 1693; — also, aft. Mabel, add, b. 1695.

" l. 8 from bot. aft. 1680; ins. a s. 12 Sept. 1681, d. soon; Dorothy, 10 Dec. 1682;

" l. 7 from bot. bef. Apr. ins. 5

P. 117. l. 8, strike out Plymouth a. 1660, and ins. Sandwich 1658, m. Jane, wid. of Anthony Bessey,

P. 120. l. 3, aft. 1679; add, beside Benjamin, Ebenezer, Timothy, and Abigail, all, or most bef. the preced.

" l. 5, bef. 3 May ins. 29 Apr. or

" l. 13, aft. *there* ins. had Martha, wh. m. William Rogers; Sarah, wh. m. James Skiff of N.; and Mary, wh. m. her cous. Nathaniel B. and he

P. 121. l. 18 from bot. aft. same, add, was a tanner, m. 16 Nov. 1669, Mercy Betts, had Hannah, b. 23 Dec. 1670; Thomas; John, 12 Jan. 1673; Nathaniel, 7 Nov. 1677; Israel, 22 Apr. 1680; Joanna, or Susanna, 16 Dec. 1682; and Benjamin, 24 Aug. 1692.

P. 122. l. 5 from bot. aft. 1676, ins. and his d. Mercy m. 20 Oct. or Dec. 1666, Bartholomew Jacobs.

P. 123. l. 1, aft. same, add, by w. Abigail — also, aft. b. ins. 21 Nov. 1679; Sarah, 17 Feb.

" l. 5, aft. 1711. add, The f. d. 1712.

" l. 3 from bot. for May r. Apr.

P. 136. l. 8, aft. Hingham, add, s. prob. youngest of the first William,

" l. 9, aft. Hobart, add, had Joseph, William, Elnathan, Jeremiah, Lydia, Ruth, and Eliz. and d. 1712.

" l. 10, aft. Joyce. add, He d. 16 Jan. 1710, in his will of six days preced. he ment. nine ch. then liv. whose names are not giv. Prob. he had sec. w. Hannah, wh. d. 1709, and it is uncert. wh. was mo. of the ch. respectiv.

" l. 12, at the end, add, He had Mary, b. 8 Mar. 1650, d. in few days.

" l. 21 from bot. aft. 1667. add, Other ch. beside a sec. William, were Nathaniel, Ruth, Jane, and Joseph.

" l. 14 from bot. bef. 1684, ins. 29 Aug.

" l. 12 from bot. bef. WILLIAM, ins. WILLIAM, Sandwich, s. of William the first, m.

Mary, d. of Hugh Burt the first of Lynn, had Mary, b. 21 Nov. 1654 ; and William, 1656 ; perhaps others, and d. 1670. Yet it may be, that the Lynn and the Sandwich William were the same.

P. 165. l. 13, at the end, add, He had Mary, b. 18 Sept. 1657 ; Joseph, 25 May 1659 ; Joanna, 25 July 1662 ; and five more, wh. d. young.

P. 170. l. 2, bef. EDWARD, ins. EBENEZER, Guilford, s. of Andrew, m. Abigail, d. of John Graves.

P. 172. l. 16, at the end, add, His wid. m. next. yr. George Barlow, and in her last will, 6 Aug. 1693, pro. 5 Oct. foll. names all the same ch. exc. Mary and David (wh. in that long interval may have d.) call. Ann Hallet, and Eliz. Bodfish ; but she adds to the list of ch. s. John, and d. Rebecca Hunter with ds. of said Rebecca, Alice, and Rebecca. Now this w. of Hunter was m. 17 Feb. 1671, and she was therefore b. bef. the m. of Barlow with her mo.

P. 189. l. 3 from bot. aft. Samuel, ins. m. Grace, d. of Moses Ventris,

P. 190. l. 7, aft. m. ins. 21 Dec. 1676, — also, bef. THOMAS, ins. SAMUEL, Woodbury, s. of the preced. m. 20 Nov. 1684, Sarah Kimberly, had Samuel, b. 28 Jan. 1686 ; Miriam, 2 May 1688 ; Jonathan, 6 Jan. 1691 ; Sarah, 8 Sept. 1692 ; Ann, 2 Dec. 1694 ; Mary, 16 Sept. 1696 ; James, 27 Apr. 1699 ; Mehitable, 31 Aug. 1702 ; and Tilley, 18 Mar. 1705. Of this list the first and last were b. at Roxbury, and the first six were bapt. Cothren says, in Aug. 1697.

P. 194. l. 13, aft. Hannah, ins. d. of Thomas Tolman, — also, aft. ch. add, had been w. of George Lyon,

" l. 14 for 90 r. above 87 yrs.

P. 195. l. 10 from bot. aft. 32. add, He m. 3 Dec. 1650, Hannah, d. of John Potter. Ano. EBENEZER of New Haven, perhaps s. of the preced. had Ebenezer and Hannah, tw. b. 4 Feb. 1685 ; Abigail ; Susanna, 21 May 1689 ; Grace, 1 Jan. 1694 ; Abraham, 15 Dec. 1695 ; and Isaac, 31 July 1703 ; and d. 24 Sept. 1735.

P. 220. l. 14 from bot. aft. 1685, add, had Hannah, b. 6 May 1677 ; and ano. d. 1680.

P. 226. l. 10, for Jan. 1662 r. 23 Jan. 1661

" l. 11, at the end, add, Bethia, w. of James

" l. 12, aft. Denison, ins. m. 25 Nov. 1662.

" l. 18 from bot. erase perhaps

P. 230. l. 14 from bot. at the end, add, SAMUEL, Branford, possib. s. of the preced. by his inv. of 10 Apr. 1694 left some est. and w. Sarah, ch. Samuel ; and Nathaniel, aged 15 yrs. both idiot. ; Mary, 8 ; and John, 3.

P. 232. l. 18, aft. Wiswall, of wh. the former h.'s name is not seen,

P. 234. l. 12, bef. PETER, ins. NATHANIEL, New Haven, youngest s. of the first William, m. 1688, Ruth, d. of Abraham Dickerman, had James, b. 12 Oct. of that yr. ; Ruth, 23 Jan. 1691 ; Miriam, 4 July 1698 ; and Nathaniel, 16 May 1701.

P. 237. l. 7, bef. had, ins. d. perhaps of William Ventris,

P. 248. last l. aft. 1644. He came, he says, with John Oldham, and calls him f.-in-law, but perhaps that means, that J. O. m. his mo. and yet he is not ment. by Bond, exc. very slight. p. 95, but not at all 861-4.

P. 249. l. 1, aft. Persis, ins. d. of Thomas Pierce of C.

" l. 2, aft. 1647. add, He is the same as the preced. and his wid. m. Mar. 1652, John Harrison.

" l. 16, bef. 1682 ins. 24 June

P. 252. l. 1, at the end, ins. perhaps sec. w.

P. 257. l. 1, bef. HENRY, ins. DANIEL, New Haven, s. of Henry, m. Esther Sperry, had Esther, b. 6 Feb. 1698 ; Eliz. 13 Aug. 1699 ; Ann, 12 Feb. 1701 ; Daniel,

15 Oct. 1702 ; Obedience, 7 Oct. 1704 ; Samuel, 8 Aug. 1706 ; and Richard, 18 Oct. 1708.

P. 257. l. 6, bef. RICHARD, ins. JOHN, New Haven, s. of the preced. had John, b. 4 Oct. 1686 ; Mehitable, 29 June 1688 ; and Joseph, 9 Aug. 1689.

P. 258. l. 8, aft. 1683 ; add, John, again, 13 Sept. 1686, d. at 23 yrs. ; Samuel, 8 Nov. 1691 ; and Benjamin, 28 May 1697, d. young ; — also, strike out prob. others. and ins. and d. 1720.

P. 260. l. 16 from bot. aft. Hannah, ins. wid. of Samuel

P. 261. l. 5, aft. 1666, ins. wh. m. 2 July 1688, William Baldwin

P. 266. l. 21, aft. Lydia. add, His wid. m. Nov. 1679, William Paine.

P. 273. l. 20 from bot. aft. *had* ins. ds. Eliz. Mary Hubbard, and Hannah Cogswell, beside John ; Nathan ; Jacob ; and

" l. 18 from bot. at the end of the sent. add, But devis. ld. giv. by his f. Dec. 1673, his will of 10 Oct. 1716 calls him of I.

P. 280. l. 12, bef. RICHARD, ins. JOHN, Farmington, s. of the preced. m. Sarah, d. of Moses Ventris, and took sec. w. 17 Apr. 1709, Mary, wid. of John Chatterton.

P. 284. l. 9 from bot. aft. uncle, Mr. Porter adds, that his ch. were Sarah, Ann, Ruth, Esther, Samuel, and Thomas ; that his will was of 6 Oct. 1692, his inv. of 2 Apr. 1700 ; and the inv. of his wid. 12 Sept. 1706.

" l. 8 from bot. aft. *had* ins. Hannah, wh. m. bef. 1655, Thomas Welch ;

" l. 7 from bot. aft. Boston. add, Perhaps his w. was Ann, outliv. him, and in her will, of 18 Mar. 1687, may instr. us, for she names ch. Daniel, Samuel, Thomas, d. Mary Parker, gr.ch. Ann, Mary Merwin, Thomas and Esther, ch. of her d. Hannah Welch, and Sarah Fowler.

P. 285. l. 12, at the end, add, b. 7 Aug. 1703,

" l. 13, at the end, add, Mr. Porter assures me, that he *was* s. of Thomas of Saybrook, and had, beside Joseph, wh. liv. to 29 Nov. 1760, Isaac, b. 25 Sept. 1700 ; and Ann, 12 Apr. 1706 ; wh. both d. young.

P. 292. l. 16 from bot. aft. 1692, ins. with eight more, of wh. one was her d. nam. Mary Withridge (see Essex Inst. II. 53),

P. 299. l. 16, bef. *Ann* ins. Eliz. m. Thomas Look ; Mary m. Stephen Coffin, — also, aft. Coleman ; add, and Martha m. 8 Oct. 1676, Stephen Hussey.

" l. 9 from bot. bef. 1712. ins. 26 June

P. 300. l. 5, erase perhaps

P. 307. l. 17, aft. Boston, ins. had, it is said, ten ch.

P. 312. l. 20, for Jemima r. Joanna

P. 316. l. 11, bef. NATHAN, ins. JOHN, Branford, as Porter suggests, wh. d. 9 Aug. 1680, had five ch. by the first w. and by Benedicta, the sec. w. had three more, but names are not giv. exc. of John, and Eliz. wh. m. the sec. Eleazer Stent. JOHN, Branford, s. of the preced. by w. Hannah had Hannah, call. 5 and ½ yrs. old, and John, 3 and ½, when the inv. d. of f. was brot. in, 20 Mar. 1691.

P. 323. l. 8 from bot. aft. His, ins. will of 25 May, pro. 18 June of that yr. is seen in Geneal. Reg. XVI. 159, and the

P. 327. l. 4 from bot. aft. Eliz. add Butler

" l. 2 from bot. aft. 1689 ; add, beside John, 1697 ; and d. 1719.

P. 328. l. 2, aft. 1703 ; add, beside Daniel, b. 1706 ; Daniel, again, 1710 ; and Elias, 1714. — also, bef. THOMAS, ins. SAMUEL, Hartford, s. of Thomas the first of the same, m. 16 Mar. 1708, Mary Clark, had Mary, b. 1708 ; Samuel, 1710 ; Eliz. 1713 ; Joseph, 1717 ; a d. 17 Sept. 1719, d. at ten days, and he d. 1725.

" l. 7, at the end, add, Mary m. Joseph Dickens ; Abigail m. 25 Mar. 1695, John

Church; Eliz. m. a. 1696, Samuel Breman the sec. of Wethersfield; and Hannah m. a Bliss of Springfield.

P. 328. l. 8, erase prob.

" l. 9, at the end, add, He had Thomas, bapt. 1689; Jonathan, 1694; James, 1697; Hannah, 1699; Moses, 1703; Lois, 1706; Aaron, 1710; and d. 1739.

" l. 14, erase perhaps

P. 331. l. 12, aft. Camp, ins. oft. Kemp.

" l. 15, erase prob.

" l. 17, at the end, for Jan. r. June

" l. 18, aft. Abigail, ins. 1696; and ano. — also, for 30 r. 31

P. 332. l. 17, aft. rem. add, His will, of 23 Feb, 1687, names ch. Thomas, wh. d. bef. his f. leav. w. Rebecca with ch. Thomas, and Rebecca; Jeremiah; Sarah Platt; Phebe Smith, w. of John; Eliz. Baldwin; Abigail Staples; Mary; Hannah; and Mehitable. The will of his wid. Phebe was made 28 July 1690.

P. 338. last l. aft. Newbury; add, and Ann m. 25 Nov. 1678, Thomas Putnam.

P. 339. l. 10, aft. 1640, ins. br. of George.

P. 343. l. 8, aft. Nantucket, ins. by w. Eliz. Trott, sis. of John, whose f. is unkn.

" l. 10, aft. 1705. add, His wid. d. 11 Oct. 1729. She was his sec. w. but wh. was the first is not told; yet the opin. at N. is that she bore Nicholas.

" l. 11, aft. *had* ins. by w. Orange, d. of William Rogers of the same,

P. 348. l. 6 from bot. aft. 58. add, By Porter I feel able to add, Jonathan, 1683, and Hannah, 1685.

P. 349. l. 4, aft. John, add, b. 1663,

" l. 13, at the end, ins. aged a. 78.

P. 360. l. 3, at the end, add, But in Geneal. Reg. XV. 356, such a trustworthy writer, as he wh. signs H. N. O. adds, Sarah, 3 Mar. 1658; Hannah, 23 Oct. 1662; Ebenezer, 6 Apr. 1664; Jonathan, 12 Feb. 1666; and Union, 23 Dec. 1669.

" l. 5, aft. Henry, add, b. 1 June 1666, d. young; Henry, again, 19 Mar. 1679; — also, aft. Benjamin, ins. 2 Feb. 1683; beside Sarah, 3 Mar. 1670; and Bethia, 19 Feb. 1673; — also, erase and two

" l. 8, bef. Thomas, ins. Sarah, 16 Mar. 1668; — also, aft. Thomas, ins. 10 or

" l. 9, aft. John, ins. 14 May 1674 — also, aft. Ebenezer, ins. 26 June 1677; Hannah, 21 June 1679, d. soon; Hannah, again, 18 July 1680; — also, for Daniel, r. David, 16 Nov. 1682 — also, aft. Jonathan, add, 20 Feb. 1685, d. at 1 yr.; Jonathan, again, 23 Sept. 1688; — also, strike out resid. of the sent.

" l. 20, aft. 1675. add, His wid. d. 8 Feb. 1683.

P. 364. l. 17, at the end, add, Other ch. are ment. as Mary, wh. m. 16 May 1651, Martin Tichenor; one d. w. of Jonathan Rose; ano. w. of John Peate; and Sarah m. William Backus. John, New Haven, s. perhaps of the preced. wh. d. 1705, by w. Hannah had Hannah, John, and Abraham.

P. 366. l. 13 from bot. bef. Michael, ins. John, New Haven, s. of William, m. 30 Apr. 1690, Mary Clemence, had three ch. and d. 1701. His wid. m. 17 Apr. 1709, John Brownson.

" l. 10 from bot. erase prob. — also, aft. Mary, add, d. of John Clark or of James C. of the same, — also, at the end, add, His ch. were, Sarah, b. 19 July 1661; Hannah, 4 Aug. 1663, d. at 3 mos.; Mercy, 22 Nov. 1664; Mary, 12 Dec. 1666, d. soon; John, 21 Feb. 1669; Samuel, 10 June 1671; Mary, again, 29 Nov. 1673; Joseph, 1 June 1676; Susanna, 17 Sept. 1678; and Hannah, 23 Jan. 1681;

P. 370. l. 12, erase prob.

P. 370. l. 21, aft. Sept. ins. 1650,

" l. 17 from bot. for many yrs. bef. perhaps, r. 12 Oct. — also, erase or 4

" l. 16 from bot. bef. William ins. 20 Oct. 1692,

" l. 13 from bot. at the end, add, d. of Jeremiah Hull,

" l. 10 from bot. aft. 1709, add, d. in one week

P. 372. l. 2 from bot. aft. Roxbury, ins. eldest s. of William,

P. 373. l. 11, aft. *more*, add, certain. Thomas, first b. beside William, Ellen, and Margaret, wh. in his will of good est. 30 Apr. 1667, are provid. for as the bef. nam.

" l. 15, erase or the first William,

P. 383. l. 19 from bot. bef. s. ins. eldest

" l. 18 from bot. bef. *had* ins. by w. Sarah — also, aft. *had* strike out to the end of the sent. and ins. Peter, b. 28 Aug. 1713, d. in two days; Mary, 14 Aug. 1714; John, 27 Feb. 1719; Lucretia, 24 June 1721; Lydia, 21 June 1723, d. in few ds.; and Margaret, 7 Mar. 1725, d. in few mos.; and he d. 5 Feb. 1729.

" l. 8 from bot. bef. RICHARD, ins. ‡

" l. 4 from bot. aft. 1702; strike out the rest of the sent. and ins. Richard, 18 Aug. 1685; Peter, 18 July 1687; and John, 15 Mar. 1690; the last two of wh. d. unm.

" l. 2 from bot. aft. had ins. Joseph, 14 July 1692; Mary, 18 Sept. 1694; Jonathan, 19 Sept. 1696; Grace, 14 Oct. 1698; Lydia, 10 Aug. 1701; Ruth, 26 Sept. 1705; Joanna, 19 Mar. 1707; and

" last l. aft. 1726. add, He was judge of Pro. and Assist. and left good est.

P. 384. l. 4, at the end, add, RICHARD, New London, s. of the first Richard, m. 14 Aug. 1710, Eliz. eldest d. of Gov. Saltonstall, had Richard, b. 29 July 1712; Eliz. 13 Sept. 1714; Mary, 17 Dec. 1716; Joseph, 30 Nov. 1722; and Catharine, 2 Jan. 1725.

P. 385. l. 17, aft. Mary, add, b. 17 Nov. 1656,

" l. 17 from bot. erase perhaps

P. 386. l. 15 from bot. aft. ch. add, His wid. d. 1690.

P. 388. aft. l. 5 ins. CHUZ, WILLIAM, Marblehead, is the form, 1664, of spell. one, perhaps of Fr. orig. but conject. may go wild in scrutiny of exactn.

P. 391. l. 18 from bot. bef. Fisher, ins. d. of Joshua,

P. 392. l. 19 and 18 from bot. for 4 Aug. 1664, r. or 14 Apr. 1654,

P. 394. l. 1, aft. June, ins. had Ebenezer, b. perhaps, 29 Nov. 1651; Susan, 1652; Samuel; James; and Mary;

P. 395. l. 6, aft. 1640; ins. Mary, wh. as Porter says, m. William Chatterton; — also, aft. 1646. add, His inv. was of 13 May 1648.

P. 396. l. 17, at the end, add, JOHN, New Haven, s. of the first John of the same, m. 1 Feb. 1662, Sarah Smith, had Sarah, b. 24 Dec. foll. d. soon; John, 23 Jan. 1663; Samuel, 20 Aug. 1666; Joseph, 27 Oct. 1668; Sarah, again, 24 Oct. 1671; Mary, and Abigail, tw. 19 July 1674. His w. d. six days aft. and he m. 28 May next, Mary Walker.

P. 398. l. 2 from bot. bef. 1663. ins. 27 Aug.

P. 400. l. 19, bef. SAMUEL, ins. SAMUEL, New Haven, s. of James the first, m. 7 Nov. 1672, Hannah, eldest d. of John Tuttle (wh. d. 21 Dec. 1706), had Samuel, b. 7 Aug. foll.; Daniel, 6 Mar. 1675; John, 23 Feb. 1677; Joseph, 20 Oct. 1678; Stephen, 24 Dec. 1680; Nathaniel, 20 Feb. 1683; Hannah, 6 Apr. 1685; Phineas, 27 June 1687; and Abigail, 6 Sept. 1689.

P. 403. l. 2 from bot. aft. 74. add, Hannah m. 26 Sept. or Nov. 1691, the first Thomas Rodman.

P. 406. l. 12, at the end, add, It may be suppos. he is the same as the Salem John, without final s.

P. 412. l. 5, aft. Sarah, add, wid. of Edmund Bridges the sec.

P. 415. aft. l. 17, ins. COCK, JOSEPH, Boston, m. 10 Nov. 1659, Susanna, d. of Nicholas Upshall. See Cox.

P. 418. l. 20 from bot. aft. Elsey, add, and d. 1702.

" l. 2 from bot. erase prob.

P. 419. l. 3, aft. 1713. add, But he had a former w. Love, d. of Richard Gardner, d. soon.

P. 425. l. 5 from bot. bef. DANIEL, ins. *

P. 430. l. 7, bef. 1661, ins. 14 June

" l. 9, bef. Dec. ins. 10 — also, aft. Sarah, ins. 25

" last l. aft. 1659, ins. m. 1663, Hannah, d. of John Porter,

P. 431. l. 20, for 83 r. 80.

" l. 9 from bot. at the end, add, He had right in Nantucket lds. but did not go there, perhaps, with his f. or even aft. his d.

P. 434. l. 7, for a. 1683 r. 9 May 1696

" l. 8, aft. Mehitable, add, b. 29 May 1697 ;

P. 436. l. 8 from bot. aft. m. ins. 1 Jan. — also, for Blanch Marrett r. Henry Morrill — also, aft. 1685, add, He had a d. b. 1670, whose name is not seen ; John, 10 Mar. 1673 ; William, 4 Mar. 1675 ; Daniel, 28 May 1677 ; Sarah, 31 Dec. 1679 ; Jonathan, 25 May 1682 ; and Nathaniel, 25 Jan. 1685.

P. 450. l. 15, for and a d. without name, r. Mary, 3 Mar. 1672 ;

P. 454. l. 18, aft. 1641, add, wh. m. 2 Dec. 1658, Abraham Dickerman ;

" l. 19, aft. Potter ; ins. John, bapt. 29, not, as rec. has it, 28, May 1642 ;

" l. 20, bef. 1662, ins. 23 Mar. — also, aft. *he* ins. aft. 1675 m. Jane, wid. of John Hall, and

" l. 19 from bot. aft. ano. ins. Rebecca, b. 29 Nov. — also, aft. Mary, ins. 15 Nov. 1669,

" l. 18 from bot. aft. 1671 ; ins. Sarah, 26 Apr. 1673 ; — also, aft. Samuel, for 3 r. 20 — also, aft. 1675 ; ins. Mary, 4 Sept. 1677 ; — aft. 1679 ; ins. Hannah, 10 Aug. 1681 ; Joseph, 11 Sept. 1683 ; and Rebecca, again, 1689.

P. 461. l. 19 from bot. at the end, add, They were m. 12 May 1657.

P. 462. l. 2, aft. Rowland, ins. or rather Roland

P. 466. l. 15 from bot. bef. JOHN, ins. * — also, aft. 1652, ins. rep. 1653 and 4,

" l. 14 from bot. aft. 1684 ; add, and ch. Samuel, b. 1639 (of wh. r. under COLE) ; — also, aft. JOHN, ins. 1641,

" l. 13 from bot. aft. m. ins. 22 Nov. 1668, — also, aft. Hartford ; ins. Hannah, 1644, wh. m. Caleb Stanley, and d. 1689 ; — also, erase Samuel of Farmington

" l. 12 from bot. for beside r. also he had — also, for one r. Sarah, bapt. 7 Feb. 1647,

" l. 11 from bot. aft. Hartford, add, but d. 1676 — also, for *ano. d.* r. 1649 — also, aft. Bull, add, and she d. at F. 1691 ; Mary, 1654, wh. m. as Porter writes, Nehemiah Dickinson ; and Eliz. wh. m. Richard Lyman.

" l. 8 from bot. aft. *e.* add, That John of Hatfield, sec. s. of the preced. had Hannah, b. 14 Nov. 1669 ; Jonathan, 1670 ; Samuel, 1673 ; John, 1676, d. young ; Abigail, 1679, d. young ; Sarah, 1681 ; Mary, 1683 ; and Esther, 1686.

P. 471. last l. aft. 1668, add, thence to Newark, N. J.

P. 474. l. 14, bef. DANIEL, ins. DANIEL, Salem, d. prob. Nov. 1681, for 29 of that mo. inv. was brot. by his wid. of the slender est. of 19s. 9d.

P. 483. l. 7, at the end, add, Eliz. b. 7 Oct. 1673 ; Ann, 15 May 1677 ; both d. soon ; and Eliz. again, 21 Aug. 1678.

P. 487. l. 4, bef. SAMUEL, ins. RICHARD, Wallingford, had three s. and a d. wh. m. Nathaniel Howe, but of the four, only Isaac is nam. The f. d. 17 Sept. 1681.

P. 493. l. 5, bef. JAMES, ins. DAVID, Boston, s. of John, the surg. had w. Ann, and two ch. whose names are not heard, d. 8 Oct. 1730.

P. 494. l. 4, bef. JOHN, ins. JOHN, Hingham, a surg. wh. chang. his name from John Demesmaker, m. 4 Jan. 1675, Mary, d. of Edward Cowell, had John, b. 6 Aug. 1676; Peter, 7 July 1679; Mary, 24 July 1682; Hannah, June 1685; Abigail, 1 Nov. 1687, d. in few mos.; David, 1 Nov. 1689; Ruth, 22 Feb. 1692; Eliz. 7 Sept. 1695; and Abigail, again, 30 May 1699, the last two at Boston, to wh. he rem. for perman. resid. and here d. 1717. His wid. had admin. of his good est. 30 Nov. of that yr. His eldest s. JOHN foll. the f's. profess. m. 21 Aug. 1716, Joanna, wid. of Thomas Richards, whose maid. name was Dodd, but had no issue.

" l. 15 bef. ROBERT, ins. PETER, sec. s. of Dr. John, had, by w. Ruth, Eliz. b. 22 Oct. 1707; Mary, 20 Dec. 1708; and John; and d. 1722.

" l. 17 from bot. aft. 1661; add, Sarah, 1666; Ruth, 1668; David, 1670; and Jonathan, 1678;

P. 498. l. 11, at the end, add — also, aft. *He* add, spell. his name Allin,

P. 499. l. 10, erase all the line.

P. 503. l. 23 from bot. at the end, add, ano. d. Ruth m. 1655, John Sprague.

" l. 17 from bot. at the end, add, a ch. b. 21 Sept. 1663;

" l. 15 from bot. at the end, add — also, at the end, ins. b. 28 Sept. 1660,

P. 512. l. 7 from bot. aft. 12 add from bot.

P. 514. l. 12 from bot. aft. Salem, ins. s. of Thomas,

P. 516. last l. aft. 15 add from the bot.

MORE ADDITIONS AND CORRECTIONS

IN VOL. II.

P. 9. l. 13 from bot. aft. 1639; ins. had Robert, b. at C. 1 Dec. 1641; and

P. 16. l. 8, bef. *He* ins. His w. and ch. John, aged 9, Mary, 4, and Eliz. 1, emb. at London, Apr. 1635, in the Elizabeth, to foll. him.

P. 30. l. 17 from bot. aft. 1669, add, but late in her days m. John Wing of Yarmouth

P. 36. l. 4, aft. DENISON, add, sometimes DENYSON,

P. 47. l. 20, aft. Hannah, ins. wh. m. 6 July 1693, Caleb Chedsey, as his sec. w.

P. 51. l. 8, erase or perhaps br.

" l. 9, erase it is thot. — also, aft. m. ins. Apr. 1663;

" l. 10, strike out 1654 and ins. Apr. 1664 — also, for 1656 r. 1666 — also, for 1658 r. 1668

" l. 11, for 1663 r. 1673 — also, for 1665 r. 1675 — also, erase and by sec. w. had

" l. 12, aft. Mehitable, ins. 1677 — also, for 1670 r. 1680 — also, for 1672 r. 1682.

P. 51. l. 13, for 1674 r. 1684 — also, aft. 9, add, but rem. to Mansfield, Conn. where his w. d. 8 May 1727, aged 81 ; and he d. 29 Oct. 1732. But his eldest s. Thomas

" l. 22, aft. 1641. add, He d. 1659, but the wid. was liv. 1683. — also, aft. w. ins. Ann,

P. 57. l. 11, erase perhaps

" l. 15, aft. 1670, ins. with Edward and Joseph excors.

P. 58. l. 17 from bot. for br. of the preced. r. s. of John, as is seen in Geneal. Reg. XV. 288,

P. 60. l. 1, aft. Eliz. ins. 12 Apr. — also, aft. Mary, ins. 22 Feb.

" l. 4, for Eliz. r. Abigail — also, aft. Moss, ins. d. of John, m. 2 July 1663.

" l. 5, bef. 1667, ins. 12 Feb. — also, bef. 1669. ins. 26 Feb.

P. 61. l. 7, for 1661 r. 15 or 26 Dec. 1662

" l. 8, bef. 1666 ins. 16 July — also, for 1667 r. 8 Jan. 1668 — also, bef. 1669 ins. 13 Dec. — also, a s. Aug. 1671, d. soon ;

" l. 9, bef. 1673 ins. 15 Oct. — also, for 1677 r. 1 Mar. 1676 — also, bef. 1680 ins. 12 May

" l. 10, aft. w. ins. m. 19 Sept. 1700, was Eliz. Bunnell, wid. prob. of Benjamin ; — also, bef. 1711 ins. 1 May

" l. 12, at the end, add, JOSEPH, New Haven, s. of Edmund, m. 24 Aug. 1693, Mary, d. prob. of William Wilmott.

P. 62. l. 21, aft. Cooke, add, wid. perhaps of Daniel Wilcox

P. 65. l. 5, bef. 1659, ins. 5 Mar.

" l. 6, bef. 1662 ; ins. 28 Oct. — also, bef. 1665 ins. 28 Jan. — also, bef. 1667 ins. 3 Apr.

" l. 7 bef. 1669 ins. 19 Apr. — also, bef. 1671 ins. 19 Jan. — also, bef. 1672 ins. 25 Nov. — also, bef. 1674 ins. 29 Aug.

" l. 8, bef. 1676 ins. 17 Dec. — also, bef. 1679 ins. 5 July.

P. 69. l. 21, at the end, add, b. 1651,

P. 76. l. 6, for 1689 r. Feb. 1690 — also, aft. Eng. add, but came back the same yr. with commiss. as Ch. Just. of Mass. — also, aft. *was* ins. aft.

P. 80. l. 1. bef. 1662, ins. 1660, at least was desir. by some inhabs. of Salisbury, wh. wish. to set. new town, now Amesbury

P. 81. l. 7, bef. had ins. m. Mary, d. of Roger Porter of Watertown.

P. 97. l. 2 from bot. aft. *but* add, did not please his f. and d. unm. 1707 ;

P. 103, l. 16, aft. He add, in 1653 was aged 60, and

P. 107. l. 6, bef. 1661, ins. 22 July

" l. 7, bef. 1663 ins. 21 Dec. — also, bef. 1666 ins. 29 July — also, bef. 1669 ins. 12 Apr.

" 8, at the end, add, THOMAS, New Haven, s. of the preced. m. Martha, eldest ch. and only d. of Samuel Munson. The name sometimes seems Elcote.

P. 113. l. 20, aft. 1667, ins. d. Jan. 1674

P. 114. l. 14, aft. Juda, ins. or Judith,

P. 122. l. 4, for *above twenty* r. near. ten. This error, point. out by a careful hand in Essex Inst. II. 228 deserves grateful acknowl. with an explanat. for slight. the other correct. by him offer. that it is not need.

" l. 14, at the end, add, Gov. Danforth, also, in his exact enumerat. of yrs. in wh. his friend E. had been Gov. makes the earliest of the *sixteen* to be 1644. See his valua. papers in 2 Mass. Hist. Coll. VIII. 52.

P. 126. l. 20, for 23 May r. 16 Sept.

P. 127. l. 18, aft. Susanna, ins. or Hannah,

P. 127. l. 19, at the end, add, wh. came to New Haven, and d. 1667.

P. 134. l. 8, for Dec. r. Feb.

P. 143. l. 6, aft. perhaps, ins. but not prob.

P. 149. l. 4 from bot. bef. came, ins. s. of David, wh. bot. ld. in M. 1655, yet that may not prove his personal com.

P. 150. l. 2, aft. m. ins. 30 July 1695,

P. 153. l. 19, at the end, add, to Conn. and had at Mansfield in that col. other ch. certain. Jacob, 1698, and Dorothy, 1700.

P. 162. l. 3, aft. Blake. ins. He had m. 14 Nov. 1663, as sec. w. Isabel, wid. of Edward Breck.

" l. 5, aft. Joanna, ins. wid. of his s. Anthony, — also, bef. div. ins. all b. in Eng.

" l. 7, aft. Norf. add, eldest s. of the preced.

" l. 15 and 16, erase the whole sent.

P. 163. l. 13, aft. Watertown, add, Eliz. b. 6 Feb. foll.

" l. 19, aft. f. ins. but prob. a br. of Anthony the first, — also, strike out perhaps as sec. w.

" l. 5 from bot. aft. he ins. was a lieut.

P. 164. l. 9, aft. Wrentham, ins. s. of Thomas the first of Dedham, — also, aft. Melatiah, add Snow — also, aft. had, ins. Samuel; Eliz.

" l. 10, aft. 1672; ins. Melatiah;

" l. 14, at the end, add, in Co. Suffk. had Thomas, Samuel, perhaps a d. was

" l. 15, aft. 1637, add, was engag. to build the meeting-ho. and d. 1638. His wid. Eliz. d. 21 Jan. 1651.

" l. 18, aft. 1678. add, He had six ds. no s.

" l. 19, bef. WILLIAM, ins. VIGILANCE, Medfield, s. of lieut. Joshua, m. 27 Nov. 1678, Rebecca Patridge, perhaps d. of John, had Lydia, b. 26 Aug. 1679; Samuel, 12 Dec. 1681; James, 4 Apr. 1686; Rebecca, 25 June 1688; David, 12 Nov. 1690, d. soon; and Abigail, 25 Aug. 1692. His w. d. 6 July 1694; and by sec. w. Hannah he had Benjamin, 29 Nov. 1697; Joseph, 28 Aug. 1699; Hannah, and Mary, tw. 29 Oct. 1702; and Ebenezer, wh. d. young. The f. d. 10 Apr. 1713.

P. 167. l. 10 from bot. aft. agreem. add, Prob. his wid. m. 3 Nov. 1661, Thomas Rix of S.

P. 177. l. 21 from bot. aft. Mary, ins. 14 Feb. 1684

" l. 19 from bot. aft. rem. ins. to Edgartown.

" l. 16 from bot. aft. Gibbs. ins. She outliv. by three yrs. at least this h. wh. d. a. 1660.

P. 181. l. 9, bef. Ward, ins. d. of the first Miles

P. 182. l. 2 from bot. aft. New Haven, ins. s. of Timothy,

P. 183. l. 17 and 18, for had w. r. m. 27 Jan. 1674,

" l. 18, aft. Eliz. ins. Hopkins,

" l. 7 from bot. for 1661 r. 1662

P. 197. l. 1, at the end, add, and he took, 16 Dec. foll. ano. w. Rebecca Wythe, wid. of Nicholas,

P. 217. l. 10 from bot. aft. 1643, add, m. Hannah Marsh, and had a child b. 1651.

P. 222. l. 11, aft. 1640, ins. m. Mary Castle,

" l. 13 from bot. aft. 1689. add, He d. 2 Aug. 1727, and his wid. d. 18 Aug. 1751.

P. 228. last l. aft. 1684; add, beside Mary, wh. m. 1706, Matthew Jenkins.

P. 229. l. 10 from bot. aft. more, add, but hear that she was first w. of James Coffin the sec. of N. and early d. without issue

P. 241. l. 16, bef. WILLIAM, ins. RICHARD, Gloucester 1665.

P. 244. l. 13 from bot. aft. him. add, TIMOTHY, New Haven, s. of William, m. Sarah Coe, had two ds. and d. under 30 yrs.

" l. 2 from bot. aft. Andrews; add, and Abigail m. 26 June 1683, John Goodyear.

P. 266. l. 22, for 16 r. 14

" l. 23, aft. yr. add, not 82d as in Geneal. Reg. XIV. 168

P. 268. l. 11, aft. 1658, ins. was aged 28 in 1653, and

P. 278. l. 7 and 6 from bot. erase wid. of to Lamberton inclus.

P. 289. l. 18 for Jehoadam r. Jehoadan

P. 290. l. 9 from. bot. bef. 1689 ins. 20 Mar.

" l. 6 from bot. aft. Ann, add, wh. m. 8 Jan. 1707, Moses Brackett; and the f. d. 10 Dec. 1719.

P. 294. l. 17, aft. Ventris, ins. prob. sis. of Moses the first,

P. 295. l. 17, aft. Stillwell, ins. had John, Joseph, Nathaniel, Sarah, Abigail, and Hannah, with good est. — also, bef. rep. ins. capt. deac.

" l. 18, aft. 1685 add, Prob. he d. 1694, for his inv. was brot. in 28 Apr. of that yr.

P. 298. l. 10, aft. Southworth. add, Thus is exposed a sad error in Geneal. Reg. XV. 12, whereby this Desire is made w. of Samuel Kent, wh. d. 8 Feb. 1762, aged a. 94 yrs. so that she must have been b. bef. her mo. was 17 yrs. and four yrs. bef. her m. with S.

P. 306. l. 18, aft. 1667. ins. Hannah m. 5 Nov. 1666, Joseph Richardson of Woburn.

P. 311. l. 4 from bot. aft. ord. ins. Oct.

P. 312. l. 19, aft. m. ins. 1649

P. 314. l. 11 from bot. aft. 1655, ins. SAMUEL, Derby, d. 14 July 1691, leav. w. Eliz. ch. Phebe, a. 6 yrs. and Eliz. 4.

P. 323. l. 16 from bot. bef. Fenn, ins. w. of the sec. Benjamin

P. 340. l. 17, aft. Eng. add, m. prob. Ann, d. of Anthony Bessey.

P. 353. l. 2, aft. 1695 ; ins. Judith, early in 1698 ; — also, aft. Eliz. for 1697 r. 4 Oct. 1699

" l. 3, aft. Huldah, ins. 10 Feb. 1709

" l. 4, for 1764 r. 1763

P. 358. l. 10 from bot. aft. Mary, ins. 7 Nov. — also, aft. 1680, ins. d. young — also aft. Leonard, ins. 5 June — also, aft. Richard, ins. 9 Aug.

P. 366. l. 20, aft. 1661 ; add beside Isaac, 18 June 1664.

" l. 5 from bot. aft. m. ins. a. 1656.

" l. 4 from bot. bef. 1657, ins. 1 Mar. — also, bef. 1658 ins. 13 Dec.

P. 370. l. 14, aft. 214. add, He m. Jan. 1670, Hannah Gilbert, had Peter, b. 10 Feb. 1671 ; David, 20 Sept. 1672 ; Hannah, 1 July 1674 ; John, 14 Apr. 1676 ; Mary, 25 Mar. 1678 ; and Sarah, 15 Apr. 1680. See Essex Inst. II. 152.

P. 377. l. 9 from bot. aft. yr. add, His will was of 17 Feb. 1680. He

P. 389. l. 14, aft. 1654. add, His will was of 27 Oct. 1646, and was pro. 11 July 1654

P. 399. l. 3 from bot. bef. 1662 ins. 20 Nov.

P. 400. l. 7, aft. New Haven, add, a cordwainer,

P. 403, l. 10 from bot. aft. mariner. add, In Remarka. Providences, by Incr. Mather, 27, is seen his rescue, Apr. 1681, of shipwreck. sailors in an open boat.

P. 408. l. 16, erase by first w.

" l. 18, aft. 1670 ; add, and d. 9 Nov. 1711. His wid. Mary d. 12 Mar. 1716.— also, strike out He and ins. JACOB, Dorchester, s. of the preced. brot. by his f. from Eng.

" l. 20, strike out Mary, &c. to the end of sent. and ins. d. 1691, without will, but his inv. was tak. 10 Sept.

P. 409. l. 16 from bot. at the end, add, By pervert. types in Geneal. Reg. XIII. 11, the name is giv. Titchburne

P. 411. l. 12, for *and in* r. 3 Feb.

" l. 14, aft. early, ins. John, b. 7 Nov. 1679; and Eliz. 26 Jan. 1681; — also, bef. 1683 ins. 26 Jan.

P. 415. l. 18, for perhaps r. much

P. 421. l. 11, bef. Abraham ins. Zechariah, b. 10 Nov. foll. acc. rec. Middlesex, and

P. 427. l. 7, aft. m. ins. 15 Oct.

" l. 9. aft. Barnabas, ins. b. 20 Feb. 1668; Sarah; Eliz. 29 Oct. 1671;

P. 428. l. 13 from bot. aft. 1674, ins. Matthias, 1 Apr. 1676;

P. 431. l. 15, for Wenslead r. Wenstead — also, aft. Essex, ins. a. 7 ms. from London,

P. 432. l. 2, aft. m. for 1686 r. prob. Dec. 1676,

P. 434. l. 19, aft. w. ins. Eliz.

" l. 22, aft. missionary; ins. and Dorothy, wh. was ano. m. 19 Apr. 1704, Daniel Mason.

P. 438. last l. but one, bef. *had* ins. by w. Eliz. Cleverly, m. 1642, — also, at the end, add, John, b. 1643; Samuel, 1645; James, 1647, wh. d. soon;

P. 439. l. 1, erase and perhaps ds. also. — also, aft. d. ins. 28 Dec.

P. 440. l. 21, aft. orphan, ins. Josiah,

" l. 10 from bot. bef. Nathaniel, ins. John, bapt. 7 Apr. 1667;

P. 443. l. 8, 9, and 10, erase by Experience, &c. to There inclus.

P. 455. l. 18 and 19 erase and Mary

" l. 21 from bot. bef. JOHN, ins. JAMES, Salem 1692, with w. Ruth, speak of John Proctor and his w. charg. with witchcr. as being good Xtians.

P. 475. l. 16 from bot. aft. Bethia, ins. or Bathshua,

" l. 15 from bot. strike out and perhaps others; and ins. was a mariner, trad. to W. I. and

P. 476. l. 14, aft. New Haven, ins. s. of Jeremy,

" l. 15, aft. 1660. ins. He had d. Eliz. b. 27 July 1666; a s. 20 Sept. 1669; ano. July 1671; but names of both and of w. are unseen.

P. 481. l. 19, aft. Newbury. add, Naomi m. 23 Mar. 1678, John Lovejoy, jr.

P. 486. l. 11, at the end, add, In the Hist. of the diabol. witchcr. delus. Essex Inst. II. 191, to one Eliz. H. is giv. the bad distinct. of being brot. as witness in more cases than others.

P. 491. l. 11 from bot. aft. sometimes ins. HURLBUT, or

P. 493. l. 3, aft. 1685, add, and d. 13 Jan. 1701.

P. 494. l. 6, aft. yr. add, But prob. he sat down first at Weymouth, where is seen by the rec. 12 June 1636, his right for 9 heads, i. e. 54 acres, being larger than any other share.

" l. 6 from bot. bef. *had* ins. perhaps br. of Andrew,

P. 496. l. 17 from bot. bef. 1651, ins. 19 Aug.

" l. 16 from bot. bef. 1653 ins. 7 Aug. — also, bef. 1655 ins. 13 Jan. — also, bef. 1656 ins. 19 Oct. — also, strike out "prob. Joan and other ch." and ins. ano. prob. John, and two ds. of wh. we kn. one, Abigail, was b. 17 May 1661; and he

" l. 15 from bot. for 1663 r. 16 Jan. 1664. His wid. m. 15 Dec. foll. Richard Little

" l. 14 from bot. aft. s. ins. as prob. also was JOHN of the same, wh. m. 10 Sept. 1685, Sarah, d. of John Tuttle, had John, b. 24 Oct. 1686; Lydia, 1 Apr. 1689; Sarah, and Mary, tw. 8 Apr. 1693; and James, 7 May 1696; and the f. d. the same yr. SAMUEL, New Haven, eldest s. of Henry, m. 21 Jan. 1678, Hannah, d. of John Johnson of the same, had Samuel, b. 1678; Hannah, 2 July 1680; Mary, 17 Jan. 1683; Matthew, 22 Nov. 1685; Nathaniel, 21 Sept. 1688; and Silence, posthum. 7 Feb. 1691, the f. d. 12 days bef. THOMAS, New Haven, prob. s. of Henry, m. 31 May 1694, Eliz. d. of the sec. Thomas Sanford, had Ebenezer, b. 14 Mar. foll; Eliz.; and Thomas, 3 May 1699; beside Joseph, 14 Nov. 1705. But it may be that this last was by sec. w. the wid. Esther Howe, of whose time of m. we are ign. as of the day or yr. of d. of the first. He d. Jan. 1716.

P. 500. l. 16, aft. 1682, add, H. C. 1700, min. of Dartmouth, d. 1730.

" l. 21 and 20 from bot. erase s. of the first Ephraim,

" l. 19 from bot. aft. 1678; add, and ano. d.

" l. 15 from bot. erase perhaps — also, bef. Ephraim, ins. the sec.

P. 502. l. 21 aft. fam. add, gave his little prop. to Sarah, w. of William Meaker, Mary, wid. of William Preston, and to Peter Mallory.

" l. 3 from bot. aft. Bearce, add, Alice, and Rebecca.

P. 514. l. 7 from bot. aft. 1671, ins. wh. prob. d. young

P. 523. l. 12 from bot. bef. WILLIAM ins. SAMUEL, Haddam, s. prob. of John, m. Sarah, wid. of William Lord, d. of Thomas Shaler.

P. 525. l. 16 from bot. aft. 1669, add, m. 12 Nov. 1668, Hannah, d. of Nathaniel Merriman, had John, b. 14 Nov. 1669; rem. to Wallingford, and d. 1682, leav. four other ch. His wid. m. the sec. Joseph Benham. — also, aft. 1685. add, He m. 2 Jan. 1673, Mary, d. of Thomas Yale, had Joseph, b. 17 Oct. foll.; Mary, 18 Oct. 1674, d. soon; Mary, again, 17 Mar. 1676; Samuel, 6 Nov. 1677; Matthew, 5 Mar. 1679; Lazarus, 19 Feb. 1681; Thomas, 22 Aug. 1683; Abigail, 17 Aug. 1685, d. soon; John, 18 Jan. 1687, d. soon; as did ano. ch. 1690; and Ebenezer, 6 Apr. 1692. Only six ch. outliv. him, wh. d. 4 Nov. 1694. His wid. d. 1710.

P. 530. l. 17 from bot. aft. 1660, ins. d. 23 Dec. foll.

P. 541. l. 19, aft. Mary, ins. d. prob. of John

" last l. at the end, ins. m. 1684, perhaps as sec. w. Mary, wid. of Abraham Ripley,

P. 542. l. 1, aft. Thomas, ins. prob. by earlier w.

" l. 2, bef. had ins. m. Sarah Gilbert,

" l. 20, bef. OBADIAH, ins. MATTHEW, Nantucket, s. of Peter, m. 9 Aug. or Oct. 1706, Mary Gardner, d. of Joseph, had Thomas, b. 29 Nov. 1707; Peter, 30 Apr. 1710; Joseph, 29 Mar. 1713; Benjamin, 15 Jan. 1717; Bethia, 25 Jan. 1719; Sarah, 24 Oct. 1722; and Mary, 15 May 1727. He d. 10 Nov. 1758.

" l. 22, bef. REGINALD ins. PETER, Edgartown 1670, had Joseph, Matthew, Thomas, and Sarah; but no dates of b. of ch. or of his own m. or d. are seen.

P. 544. l. 20, aft. 1639. add, But in the div. of lds. June 1646, six acres for ea. person over twelve yrs. and three for younger, eighteen acres fell to the sen. and 45 to the jun. for his fam.

P. 552. l. 12, at the end, add, A very remarka. paper, in Geneal. Reg. VIII. 360, calls his mo. Ann Meadows, d. of Robert of Stamford; and an orig. will, made by him 28 Apr. 1627, it is said, confirms the fact by refer. to his gr.f. Robert M.

P. 554. l. 15, aft. 1662, ins. had Thomas, b. 25 Apr. 1664; ano. ch. 1666; and Samuel, 8 Mar. 1671; perhaps rem. to Derby, had sev. more ch. and d. 1704.

" l. 4 from bot. aft. will, ins. of 22 Nov. that yr. calls hims. 63 yrs. old.

P. 555. l. 14, bef. JOHN, ins. JOHN, New Haven, by w. Hannah had Hannah, wh. m. 21 June 1677, Samuel Hummerstone; John, b. 27 Aug. 1661; Ruth, 3 Apr. 1667, wh. m. as is said, 10 Oct. 1698, Benjamin Dorman; Abigail, 7 Apr. 1670; Daniel, 21 Feb. 1672; beside Sarah, wh. m. 8 Feb. 1684, John Wolcott.

P. 555. l. 13, bef. Jonathan ins. JOHN, New Haven, s. of Robert, m. 2 Mar. 1684 or 5, Mabel Grannis, d. of Edward, had John, b. 3 Mar. 1687; Thomas, 12 June 1690; Ann, Feb. 1691; Sarah, 9 Apr. 1694; Daniel, 22 Apr. 1696; Joseph, 3 Dec. 1698; Benjamin, 9 Mar. 1701; Robert, 2 June 1703; James, 3 Sept. 1705; Mehitable, 29 Feb. 1708; and Hannah, 23 May 1710.

P. 556. last l. at the end, add, His wid. Adeline m. 7 Jan. 1663, Robert Hill; and next, 22 May 1666, John Scranton. Porter suppos. him to be s. of an earlier Robert, wh. was d. in 1641.

P. 558. l. 8, aft. 1657, ins. Abigail, b. 19 Jan. 1658, d. soon; Sarah, 2 Nov. 1659; — also, aft. Abigail, add, again, 14 June 1662. He m. sec. w. Sept. 1663, Frances Hitchcock, had Thomas, 11 July foll. and rem. to Newark, N. J.

P. 559. l. 11, aft. 1685. add, Ano. WILLIAM, New Haven, perhaps s. of the first John, had fourteen ch. but the mo. is unkn.; William; Abraham, b. 10 Mar. 1669; Abigail, 6 Dec. 1670; Isaac, 27 Oct. 1672; Jacob, 25 Sept. 1674; John, and Sarah, tw. 6 Nov. 1676; Samuel, 3 Sept. 1678; Mary, 1 Apr. 1680; Lydia, 7 Jan. 1682; Eliz. 11 Jan. 1684, d. next mo.; Hope, and Eliz. tw. 10 May 1685, of wh. Hope liv. but few days; and Ebenezer, 5 Apr. 1688; and the f. d. 1716.

" l. 20, bef. 1664, ins. Dec.

P. 561. l. 9 from bot. aft. 1704, add, d. at 4 yrs. — also, for 1706 r. 1707 — also, for 1708 r. 1709

" l. 8 from bot. for 1712 r. 1713

P. 563. l. 11, bef. JOHN, ins. JOHN, Newbury, mariner, s. of Thomas, made his will, bound on a voyage, 17 July 1676, pro. Nov. foll. giv. all his est. specify. ld. in Barbados, to his mo. Ann White, so that I presume his f. had d. some time bef.

P. 568. l. 6, aft. 1705. add, My New Haven correspond. makes her as bad or worse than he.

P. 578. l. 20 from bot. aft. 1673. add, This John d. June 1680, and to his wid. Ann admin. was giv. 1 July.

P. 579. l. 16 from bot. at the end, add, He was, I think, s. of the first Thomas.

P. 581. l. 5 from bot. aft. b. ins. 5 or

" l. 21, at the end, for . r. ;

" l. 23 from bot. aft. Apr. ins. — also, aft. Dec. ins. —

P. 584. l. 12, aft. Richard, ins. again,

P. 585. l. 9 from bot. at the end, add, by his first w. Margaret Fryer,

P. 588. l. 6 from bot. for 293 r. 296 and 7 — also, strike out, "the end of the sentence" and ins. 1662 in l. 2 of latter p.

" l. 3 from bot. aft. out, ins. Ano. ROBERT

P. 592. l. 17 from bot. at the end, add, d. of Thomas Pierce,

" l. 11 from bot. aft. m. ins. Jan. 1670, Harriet, — also, aft. Gilbert, add, had Peter, b. 10 Feb. 1671; David, 20 Sept. 1672; Hannah, 1 July 1674; John, 14 Apr. 1676; Mary, 25 Mar. 1678; and Sarah, 15 Apr. 1680;

" l. 7 from bot. aft. 21 ins. from bot.

" last l. may be struck out, for the matter is put better in Vol. III. 630.

P. 593. l. 10 from bot. bef. 6 ins. first

" l. 2 from bot. for aft. 1667, r. 24 Sept. 1668,

P. 596. l. 16 from bot. for Nathaniel r. NATHANIEL

" l. 12, 11, 10 and 9 from bot. may be erased, as the substance is giv. more careful. in Vol. III. 638.

P. 597. l. 3, 4, 5, and 6 are better express. in Vol. III. 639.

" l. 21 and 22 will appear better in Vol. III. 639.

P. 599. l. 16 for William r. WILLIAM

MORE ADDITIONS AND CORRECTIONS

IN VOL. III.

P. 2. l. 4 from bot. bef. EDWARD, ins. or KEILEY,

" l. 3. from bot. at the end, add, In his will, of 27 Sept. 1690, is nam. no w. nor ch. but legacies of his small prop. are seen to Nathan Andrews and two others.

P. 6. l. 12, aft. first, ins. m. 22 Sept. 1687, Sarah, d. of John Merrill,

" l. 13, aft. John, ins. 16 Dec. 1694 — also, aft. Isaac, ins. Jan. 1697 — also, aft. Jacob, ins. 17 Apr. 1699 — also, aft. Benjamin, ins. 1 Jan. 1702 ; — also, aft. Joseph, ins. 13 Apr. 1703 — also, aft. Daniel, ins. Apr. 1706 ; was deac. and d. 1717.

P. 7. l. 21, bef. JOHN, ins. DANIEL, s. of William, went to L. I. where the fam. name has spread.

" l. 20 from bot. for perhaps r. not

" l. 9 from bot. bef. 1650 ins. Feb.

" l. 6 from bot. at the end, add, Ano. WILLIAM, of Hartford, by w. Abigail had Abigail, b. 1694 ; Jonathan, 1696 ; Ruth, 1698 ; and he d. that yr.

P. 23. l. 6, bef. Mary ins. Hannah, b. 11 Jan. 1656 ; Sarah, bapt. July 1659, d. young ;

" l. 13, bef. THOMAS ins. NATHANIEL, New Haven, s. of Thomas, had Nathaniel, b. 4 Jan. 1667 ; Eliz. and two other ds. Apr. 1679, one without name, the other, Sarah.

" l. 16, erase bef. or aft. — also, aft. d. ins. 10 Oct.

" l. 17, aft. w. ins. Mary, wid. of William Preston,

P. 24. l. 9 from bot. aft. 1679, ins. d. next yr.

" l. 8 from bot. aft. 1685, ins. d. next yr. — also, aft. 1687 ins. d. soon, — also, aft. 1692. add, His w. was Eliz.

P. 30. l. 13, aft. 1668, ins. his will was of 31 July, and inv. tak. 4 Nov. of that yr. To s. of his br. Daniel, of Staplehurst in Kent, was giv. his est.

P. 32. l. 12 from bot. aft. yr. add, d. 5 Jan. foll.

" l. 5 from bot. aft. 1648, ins. wh. m. 20 Feb. 1666, Timothy Robinson

P. 36. l. 12, for 1699 r. 19 Apr. 1698 — also, for *that* r. next

" l. 13, bef. JACOB ins. His w. was Sarah Church, d. of John, and ch. were Sarah, b. 27 Apr. 1680, wh. m. as Porter writes, 25 Dec. 1699, George Saxton ; Love, 10

Sept. 1682, m. 20 Nov. 1702, Thomas Andrews; Ann, 6 Apr. 1688, m. 9 Dec. 1715, prob. as sec. w. Samuel Galpin; and Eliz. 13 Dec. 1690, m. 12 June 1707, Nathaniel Cole.

P. 38. l. 21 from bot. aft. 1668. ins. Perhaps Mary m. 5 June 1677, Daniel Ross.

P. 42. l. 2 from bot. aft. Wenham, ins. d. 8 Oct. 1684; by w. Sarah had William; Samuel; Joseph, b. 1651; and Nathaniel, 29 June 1658.

P. 43. l. 1, bef. br. ins. younger

" l. 3, aft. 1692, add, aged 70. He m. for sec. w. 17 May 1682, as is said, Mary Kimball.

P. 48. last l. aft. 1645; ins. beside Hope, George, and Hannah;

P. 49. last l. aft. 1645, add, d. 1686, unm.

P. 50. l. 1, aft. Windsor. ins. But he took sec. w. 6 Nov. 1663, Eliz. wid. of Henry Line, and d. in few wks. his posthum. s. Eleazer was b. 14 Aug. and his wid. m. John Morris, and liv. not long aft.

P. 54. l. 16, aft. least, ins. Joseph, b. 23 Mar. 1650.

" l. 10 from bot. erase perhaps

P. 55. l. 21 from bot. at the end, add, had prob. Sarah, and other ch.

" l. 20 from bot. aft. 1644, ins. br. of the preced.

P. 56. l. 18, at the end, add, The name is oft. mispr. interchang. with Langdon.

P. 64. l. 2, for luckily r. lucki.

P. 73. l. 5 from bot. bef. WALTER ins. THOMAS, Farmington, s. of John of the same, m. 11 Sept. 1707, Mary Camp, d. of John of Hartford, had Lydia, b. 22 June foll.; Mary, 2 Oct. 1709; Jared, bapt. 11 Nov. 1711; Joseph, 1713; John and Thomas, tw. b. 7 Dec. 1716; and by sec. w. Eliz. Hubbard, m. 1725, had Ebenezer, 1727.

P. 75. l. 1, bef. 1685 ins. and had fam.

" l. 9 from bot. for 1671 r. 7 Apr. 1670.

P. 76. l. 15, at the end, add, There was a fam. of this name at Bristol 1689; but bapt. name of the h. is not found.

P. 80. l. 8, aft. Eliz. ins. d. of John Lyman,

P. 81. l. 5 from bot. for got w. r. m. 23 Nov. 1674 — also, aft. Eliz. ins. Preston.

P. 89. l. 5, bef. *had* ins. by w. Hannah — also, aft. had ins. Edward, wh. d. 1662

P. 95. l. 21, for late in r. 29 Sept. — also, erase or early in 1661

" l. 22, for of this yr. r. foll.

" l. 16 from bot. aft. Norwalk, add, beside a s. wh. d. 8 Sept. 1660, prob. inf. His wid. Rosamond m. 15 Mar. 1664, Nathaniel Richards.

P. 96. l. 13 from bot. aft. 1685. ins. By w. Ann he had posthum. s. Benjamin, and d. 26 July 1689

" l. 9 from bot. at the end, add, 13 Jan.

" l. 8 from bot. aft. wid. ins. Eliz. wh. m. 6 Nov. foll. Thomas Lamson, and next, 29 Mar. 1667, John Morris.

" l. 5 from bot. for *perhaps* r. prob. not, as Porter writes, — also, aft. Samuel, ins. Apr. 1649, the

" l. 4 from bot. bef. 1652, ins. 18 July — also, bef. 1655 ins. Nov. — also, bef. 1659 ins. Dec.

" l. 3 from bot. aft. 1669, add, and d. 3 Sept. 1689.

P. 97. l. 1, erase perhaps — also, for had w. r. m. Nov. 1674,

" l. 10 from bot. at the end, add, Other ch. were Mary and Hannah. The s. had s. John, wh. took admin. of est. of gr.f. 23 July 1698, while that of the f.'s est. was 9 May 1684, so that I inf. the first John long outliv. his s.

P. 99. l. 15 from bot. at the end, add, m. 15 Dec. 1664, Joan, wid. of Henry Humiston, had Eliz. b. 4 Apr. 1666; Hannah, 21 Oct. 1667, d. young; Mary, 28 July 1669; Hannah, again, 30 Nov. 1671; and Martha, 29 Mar. 1677. He was

P. 99. l. 14 from bot. aft. 1685, add, and d. 1689, betw. 5 Sept. the date of his will, and 7 Nov. that of his inv.

P. 102. l. 21, bef. 1671 ins. , — also, aft. 1671 for , r. ; beside Ann, 1674 ;

P. 112. l. 2 from bot. aft. 1664; ins. Isaac, 10 July 1666;

P. 115. l. 21, at the end, add, He m. 22 Nov. 1678, Martha, d. of the first Richard Tozer, had Martha, b. 14 Oct. foll. ; Nathan, 13 May 1681 ; William, 20 Mar. 1683 ; Richard, 1 Mar. 1685 ; Judith, 29 Mar. 1687 ; Samuel, 14 June 1689 ; Mary, 29 July 1691 ; John, 18 Jan. 1693; Sarah, 28 Mar. 1696 ; Ann, 27 May 1697 ; and Abraham, 29 Oct. 1699.

" l. 14 from bot. for 1664 r. 17 May 1662

" l. 3 from bot. bef. 1685 ins. Nov.

" last l. for William r. John

P. 116. l. 1, for uncert. r. well sett.

" l. 22, for Annie r. Amie

" l. 18 from bot. aft. ascert. add, but it was a. 1667.

P. 117. l. 7, aft. yr. ins. and rec. more liberal than tradit. absurd. says, 97th.

" l. 15, after preced. ins. m. Sarah, prob. d. of Thomas Shaler, and

P. 125. l. 4, bef. 1670 ins. 14 Apr.

P. 127. l. 17 from bot. bef. HENRY, ins. EXPERIENCE, perhaps of Edgartown, s. of Henry, m. Eliz. d. of John Manter, had Zephaniah, b. 19 Feb. 1695 ; perhaps others, and d. 9 Jan. 1747, — also, aft. 1668. add, Prob. he rem. to the Vineyard, and by w. Remember had Experience, b. 7 Feb. 1673, perhaps others.

P. 128. l. 15 from bot. bef. 1676 ins. unm.

" l. 14 from bot. aft. m. ins. next yr. — also, for George r. John

" l. 11 from bot. for George r. John

P. 131. last l. at the end, for 1652. r. 1662, and had Hannah, b. 27 May 1665.

P. 134. l. 14, aft. 1658 ins. d. 1663

" l. 15, Ephraim should be Experience, as Mr. Porter assures me.

" l. 6 from bot. aft. wid. ins. bore that yr. posthum. s. — also, aft. m. ins. 1664,

P. 135. l. 5, for 1671 r. 1672

" l. 9, at the end, add, 1690,

P. 142. l. 22, aft. *His* ins. wid. d. 1706, aged 94 ;

P. 144. l. 10 and 9 from bot. aft. *and* strike out to the end, and ins. his wid. m. 7 June 1682, Thomas Rodman,

" l. 6 from bot. aft. Peter, ins. m. 30 Dec. 1636, Eliz. Kimberly

P. 145. l. 2, for May 1649 r. Mar. 1650 — also, bef. Oct. ins. 28

" l. 17, aft. 1687 ; add, beside Aaron, 10 Mar. 1690 ;

" l. 18 from bot. aft. John, ins. b. 6 June 1673 ;

" l. 15 from bot. aft. 1667, ins. mariner

" l. 14 from bot. aft. troop, ins. had w. Eliz. but d. 1701,

P. 147. l. 7, bef. GEORGE, ins. DENNIS, Nantucket, m. 1678, Catharine Innis, but wh. she was, is unkn. had Betty, b. 10 July 1679 ; James, 20 Jan. 1681 ; David, 2 Apr. 1683 ; Dorcas, wh. m. the sec. Nathaniel Barnard; William ; Benjamin ; Eunice, wh. m. Thomas Newcomb; Dinah, wh. m. 1717, William Stubbs; and Rebecca, wh. m. 1719, Joseph Mott of R. I.

P. 148. l. 15, aft. Harv. add, WILLIAM, Nantucket, s. of Dennis, m. 1726, Hannah, d. of Shubael Gorham of Barnstable, had David, and Phebe, and d. 20 July 1730.

P. 148. l. 11 from bot. bef. JOHN, ins. EBENEZER, New Haven, s. of Joseph, m. 20 Apr. 1710, Hannah Bassett, but Mr. Porter names no issue. JAPHET, New Haven, youngest s. of Joseph, m. 14 Jan. 1703, Hannah Bradlee.

P. 149. l. 8. bef. JOSEPH, ins. JONATHAN, New Haven, youngest ch. of Moses the first, m. 1 June 1708, Hannah, d. of the sec. John Alling, had a fam. but their names are unkn.

" l. 12, at the end, add, 6 Apr.

" l. 13, bef. 1660 ; ins. 18 Apr. — also, strike out, and perhaps others ; and ins. Mercy, 26 July 1662 ; Silence, 24 Oct. 1664 ; Eliz. 20 Sept. 1666 ; Comfort, 6 Dec. 1668 ; John, 8 Apr. 1671, d. at 19 yrs. ; Joseph, 27 Nov. 1673 ; Ebenezer, 6 Feb. 1678 ; and Japhet, 8 July 1681 ; and d. 15 Nov. 1692. His wid. Mary d. 1701.

" l. 20, aft. had ins. Abigail, b. 7 Feb. 1665 ; Mercy, 2 Apr. 1667 ; Hannah, 14 Mar. 1669 ; — also, aft. Samuel, ins. 31 Dec. 1671,

" l. 22, aft. f. add, perhaps Moses, 15 Aug. 1674 ; Sarah, 14 June 1677 ; Richard, 20 July 1680, d. at 1 yr. ; Bathshua, 1 Jan. 1683 ; and Jonathan, 15 Feb. 1686. He m. sec. w. 8 Nov. 1702, Margaret Prout, and had third w. Abigail, d. of the first Thomas Yale, and d. 3 Oct. 1703. His wid. d. 28 Feb. 1708. MOSES, New Haven, s. of the preced. was a mariner, had a fam. Mr. Porter tells me, but gives no names.

P. 155. l. 1, aft. f. ins. had John, b. 1668, and other ch.

" l. 15, for a ch. without a name r. Joseph

P. 175. l. 7 from bot. at the end, add, m. Mary, d. of Edward Adams.

P. 176. l. 11, bef. DANIEL, ins. CALEB, New Haven, s. of William, m. 13 Jan. 1702, Eliz. Hotchkiss, d. perhaps of Daniel.

" l. 20 from bot. strike out "prob. others ; and " for wh. ins. perhaps more ds. but certain. six more s. of wh. only John and Benjamin are nam. to me, the latter being youngest s. and progenit. of all wh. remain on the Cape, as Otis instr. us.

" l. 6 from bot. bef. JOHN ins. JOHN, Yarmouth, s. of James, by w. Sarah had only John, for he was k. 1676, at Rehoboth, by the Ind. His wid. bec. sec. w. of Joseph Rider.

P. 177. l. 16, at the end, add, WILLIAM, Branford, had Eliz. b. 27 Dec. 1672 ; Caleb ; Thomas ; and William ; and his will, of 14 Apr. 1684, ment. ano. ch.

" l. 10 from bot. bef. 1669 ins. 2 Mar.

P. 185. l. 20 from bot. erase Nantucket

" l. 18 from bot. for rem. to N. r. went to Eng.

" l. 11 from bot. for Sansom r. Sarson

P. 192. l. 15, for 1666 r. 1667

P. 199. l. 2 from bot. aft. had ins. w. Joan, and ch. John, wh. d. 26 Sept. 1651

" last l. at the begin. ins. 16 May — also, erase perhaps

P. 200. l. 1, for 1659, r. 1654 — also, aft. Mary, ins. 12 July 1657

" l. 3, aft. conject. ins. Samuel, b. 29 Sept. 1662 ; — also, aft. 1665 ; add, sons in 1667 ; and Eliz. again, 14 Sept. 1669.

" l. 6, aft. 80. add, Hannah m. 12 Nov. 1668, John Ives ; and Mary m. a Curtis.

" l. 18 from bot. aft. m. ins. 1663, — also, aft. John, ins. b. 1664,

P. 201. l. 18 from bot. bef. 1682, ins. 16 Dec.

P. 206. l. 9 from bot. for 1674 r. 1675

" l. 8 from bot. for 20 r. 10

" l. 7 from bot. aft. Joseph, add, 26 Oct. 1690.

P. 207. l. 19 from bot. aft. h. add, She d. 27 Jan. 1687, at Wallingford.

" l. 4 from bot. aft. m. ins. 20 Sept. 1681.

P. 208. l. 6, at the end, add, m. 3 Apr. 1665, Sarah, prob. d. of John Weston, had John, b. 8 Jan. 1669 ; and Mary, 22 Nov. 1670.

P. 215. l. 10 from bot. bef. s. ins. fourth

" l. 3 from bot. bef. s. ins. fifth

" l. 2 from bot. for prob. had w. r. m. 20 June of that yr.—also, aft. Hannah, ins. d. of James Avery, erase the rest of the l. and ins. had Ephraim, b. 22 June 1668 ; Thomas, 17 Dec. 1669, d. young ; Hannah, 20 Apr. 1671 ; Rebecca, Sept. 1672 ; Eliz. Apr. 1674, d. young ; Samuel, Dec. 1676, d. young ; Deborah, 13 Apr. 1677, unless the pub. fam. geneal. has a wrong fig. d. young ; Deborah, again, Apr. 1679 ; Samuel, again, Aug. 1681 ; James, Nov. 1682 ; Grace, Sept. 1683 ; and John, Apr. 1685 ; was freem. 1674

" last l. aft. 1676, add, but the d. of his dec. is not told.

P. 216. l. 10, for had w. r. m. 23 Oct. 1668,—also, aft. Mary, add, d. of James Avery, by wh. he had eight ch. and one more by sec. w. Bridget, wid. of William Thompson. They were Joseph, b. 19 Sept. 1669 ; Mary, 6 Oct. 1671 ; Benjamin, 25 June 1676 ; Deborah, and Sarah, perhaps tw. bapt. 30 Mar. 1679 ; Christopher ; Joanna ; Prudence ; and Bridget ; but I doubt sev. dates of the fam. geneal. and I gain neither dates of m. nor d. of sec. w. nor of his d.

" l. 11, bef. s. ins. seventh

" l. 12, aft. town, rem. to Stonington, m. 26 Sept. 1670, Lydia Moore, whose f. is not kn.

" l. 14, bef. THOMAS, ins. SAMUEL, youngest s. of Thomas, m. 1681, Mary Lord, and d. next yr.

" l. 19, aft. to ins. Saybrook, thence to

" l. 20, for if r. but

" l. 21, aft. Thomas, ins. b. 1638, d. young

" l. 21 from bot. aft. Manasseh, ins. 1647 —also, aft. Ephraim, ins. 1642 — also, aft. Joseph, ins. 1636 — also, aft. Judah, ins. 1644 — also, aft. Samuel, ins. 1652 — also, aft. Ann, ins. 1649 — also, aft. Eliz. add 1653, d. young

" l. 20 from bot. aft. Eunice, ins. if the true name be not Hannah, — also, aft. Mary, ins. 1655

" l. 15 from bot. aft. d. ins. 23 Oct. — also, aft. 83 ; add, and his w. d. the same yr. Hannah, the only d. that liv. to mid. age, m. 1677, Thomas Avery.

P. 221. l. 15 from bot. strike out, d. bef. him and ins. m. 5 Dec. 1672, Philip Alcock

" l. 13 from bot. for *only* r. other

P. 222. l. 16 from bot. aft. Wilmot, add, wh. d. 20 Aug. 1711

" l. 15 from bot. aft. Abigail, ins. 17 Apr. 1687 — also, aft. Mercy, ins. 16 Apr. 1691 — also, bef. Jan. ins. 21

P. 223. l. 7, bef. 1650 ; ins. 17 Mar. — also, bef. 1654 ; ins. 7 Feb.

" l. 8, at the end, add, This man is the same, Mr. Porter says, as William Meeker.

P. 233. l. 19, bef. 1650, ins. 9 Apr.

P. 235. l. 12 from bot. aft. Ann add Osborne

" l. 11 from bot. at the end, add, His wid. d. 10 Dec. 1726,

" l. 2 from bot. bef. perhaps ins. not — also, for *early* r. 4 Apr. 1664 — also, aft. m. ins. 29 Mar. 1666,

" last l. aft. John, ins. b. 16 Dec. foll.

P. 236. l. 1, bef. June ins. 19

" l. 3, bef. Apr. ins. 26

" l. 4, aft. 1687. ins. He d. 1718.

" l. 8, aft. 1705 ; add, and d. 1711.

P. 236. l. 11 from bot. strike out *soon*, and ins. next day, but Thomas liv. over 21 yrs. — also, aft. Joseph, ins. b. 25 Mar.

" l. 10 from bot. for w. r. wid. — also, for 1668 r. 1681

" l. 8 from bot. for 1652, r. 1662,

P. 237. l. 1, aft. 1690. add, He m. 21 Oct. 1687, Sarah, d. of William Jones, had Sarah, b. 7 July 1689; Margaret, 16 Aug. 1691, d. in few wks.; Ann, 4 Nov. 1693; Theophilus, 6 Jan. 1696; Margaret, again, 12 Aug. 1699; and Andrew. He d. early in 1703.

" l. 18 from bot. aft. 23 ins. or 25

" l. 4 from bot. for 1658 r. 1657.

P. 238. l. 11 and 12, strike out EZRA, Dedham 1639, &c. to end of the sent.

" l. 14, strike out, and d. 1697.

" l. 9 and 8 from bot. strike out, Dorcas, b. &c. to young; inclus.

" l. 3 from bot. strike out, *perhaps* — also, aft. rem. ins. to Dedham the same yr. — also, strike out yr. to Ipswich and ins. to Boston

P. 239. l. 1, aft. home, ins. Nov. 1654, and did not ret. — also, strike out *but*, and ins. JOHN, Dedham, s. of Samuel, went home, and — also, for may be r. was

" l. 2, aft. 1657 ins. It has caus. some confus. and much uncert. that the John of Dedham and he of Boston, both tailors, should both have gone home so near. in the same yr. both die near the same time, but one [which?] return. to die on our side of the water; yet it may be overcome by aid of the wills.

" l. 13, strike out "d. says the Genealog. in Apr. 1683, but," and ins. of wh.

" l. 19 from bot. aft. makes ins. erron.

" l. 7 from bot. erase *prob.*

" l. 5 from bot. erase Joshua, perhaps;

P. 240. l. 20 from bot. aft. here. add, That author makes the b. of the s. in the same yr. he tells me, wherein the f. d. 1667.

P. 241. l. 18, bef. ROBERT, ins. PETER, Newbury, br. of the first Anthony, prob. went with others to N. J. where they obtain. large gr. of ld. — also, erase *perhaps*

" l. 18 and 17 from bot. strike out, *perhaps* br. and ins. f.

" l. 13 from bot. aft. 1654. ins. Mr. Morse assures me, the true d. is 5 Dec.

" l. 5 from bot. for July 1654 r. Jan. 1655

P. 242. l. 21 from bot. aft. John, add, wh. liv. at Tiverton, — also, erase or — also, aft. Jonathan, ins. 1640,

" l. 19 from bot. aft. 69. add, He had also Joshua, and prob. William, as he is call. sen. All the fam. was scatter. by the witcher. virulence, some to R. I. some to Plym. and perhaps not a few in N. J. or further s. were spell. Moss.

P. 246. l. 9 from bot. aft. 1670. add, Abigail, m. 2 July 1663, Abraham Doolittle, as his sec. w.

P. 247. l. 1, aft. 1681; add, and d. 18 Mar. 1716.

P. 254. l. 5 from bot. at the end, add, His wid. m. Dennis Scranton, or Crampton; but I have not courage enough to adjudge the right.

P. 257. l. 20, aft. 1698; ins. beside Israel, 6 Mar. 1687;

" l. 22, for 1692 or 3 r. Dec. 1691

P. 261. l. 14, aft. 1642, ins. liv. much at Hartford,

" l. 17, bef. and, ins. Rebecca, 12 Mar. 1658; — also, at the end, add exc. Samuel, 3 Feb. 1664, wh. d. young;

P. 267. l. 10, aft. there, add, but was first of Yarmouth.

P. 272. l. 8 from bot. aft. Joseph, ins. bapt. — also, aft. Eliz. ins. 29 Nov. bapt.

P. 275. l. 17, aft. b. ins. 1 July

" l. 20, aft. sure, add, wh. prob. d. young

" l. 17 from bot. aft. 1646, ins. d. under 4 yrs. — also, strike out, bef. 1660 to the end of the sent. and ins. and was, 1657, a vintner in London.

P. 276. l. 20 from bot. bef. THOMAS, ins. SAMUEL, New Haven, s. of Richard, m. 15 Feb. 1688, Eliz. Rose of Branford, perhaps d. of the sec. Robert, and d. 1689, without ch. His wid. d. next yr. and the prop. fell to br. John and sis. Sarah.

P. 279. l. 15 from bot. erase CYPRIAN, &c. to capt. in next l. inclus.

" l. 14 from bot. erase James, &c. to perhaps in next l. inclus.

" l. 12 from bot. strike out the sent. His w. Helen, &c. and ins. He was b. a. 1642, and d. a. 1698.

" l. 11 from bot. aft. preced. ins. was a capt.

" l. 10 from bot. for a. 1703 r. 12 May 1702

" l. 8 from bot. for prob. r. five

P. 289. l. 21 from bot. aft. Thomas, ins. b. 30 June 1650 ; — also, aft. John, ins. 13 Mar. 1652 ; — also, at the end, add, 25 Dec. 1654.

P. 290. l. 13, aft. of ins. 1 Sept. — also, aft. yr. add, He m. I presume, Mary, d. of Francis Norton of Milford, had Joseph, Samuel, Jeremiah, and John. His wid. perhaps m. again, for in her will, so late as 26 Jan. 1683, she names her ch. Zophan, Daniel, William, and Mary, but none of those ment. by her h's. will.

" l. 13 from bot. bef. Zachary ins. 24 Sept. 1668

" l. 9 from bot. aft. N. ins. cous. John Nash, s. Joseph Northrop with his s. Jeremiah.

P. 291. l. 14, for Barker r. Barber

P. 292. l. 5 from bot. aft. her, add, and d. 1687. His wid. m. 1688, John Lamb.

P. 293. l. 9, aft. Weymouth, ins. by w. Eliz.

" l. 10, aft. 1644, ins. wh. d. unm. rem. to — also, strike out NICHOLAS, and all the sent. from Edgartown, and ins. Seven ds. and two more s. he had, Joseph, and Benjamin, and both, with first b. Isaac, are stocks of large tribes.

P. 307. l. 9, aft. His ins. will was of 1653, as in a Vol. of Hartford rec. late. by the happy dilig. of Mr. Hoadley recover. aft. many yrs. loss, is seen ; and the

" l. 14, aft. Thomas, ins. b. 1669 ;

P. 308. l. 20, at the end, add, We kn. only, that by a petitn. to our Gen. Ct. William Bridge, in 1644, sets forth that 21 yrs. bef. he came with J. O. his f.-in-law.

P. 310. l. 2, erase d. young

P. 312. l. 15, aft. Marvin, add, wh. d. 1708,

" l. 18, aft. br. ins. Richard — also, aft. sis. ins. Rebecca.

" l. 19, aft. first, ins. had Mary, Sarah, and Eliz.

" l. 21 bef. NEHEMIAH, ins. JOSEPH, Hartford, s. of Nicholas, was deac. and d. 1726, had Joseph, James, Eliz. Nicholas, Nehemiah, b. 1686 ; Rebecca, 1688 ; Hannah, 1690 ; beside Richard, and descend. are very num.

" l. 14 from bot. aft. Joseph, ins. b. 1655 ;

" l. 4 from bot. erase perhaps — also, erase prob. — also, aft. Thomas, ins. b. 1692 ; Stephen, 1694 ; Sarah, 1696 ; Rebecca, 1697 ; Damaris, 1699 ; Daniel, 1701 ; Hannah, 1704 ; and Jerusha, 1706 — also, strike out the rest of the sent. and ins. He had a former w. Martha.

P. 316. l. 14, at the end, add, NATHANIEL, Barnstable, a mason, came from Nantucket with w. Mary, but was prob. s. of George of Boston. He d. 23 Nov. 1696, had ds. Susanna, Deborah, b. 1 Apr. 1692 ; and Jane, 24 Oct. 1696, only the last two at B. and the youngest d. soon. His wid. m. 14 Oct. 1697, Samuel Sturgis, and had seven more ch.

P. 317, erase l. 17, 16, 15, and 14 from bot.

" last l. bef. 1652 ins. 3 May

P. 318. l. 3, aft. b. ins. 6 Oct. — also, aft. 1660; ins. Ann, 6 Apr. 1663;

" l. 7, aft. custom. add, That the three first nam. ch. belong to Jeremiah, is denied by Mr. Porter, but he gives two others, Joseph, 15 Dec. 1667; and Rebecca, 11 July 1673.

" l. 8. aft. 1685. ins. JEREMIAH, New Haven, s. of the preced. m. Sarah, wid. of Timothy Gibbard, had Sarah, b. 19 May 1689; and Jonathan, 29 Mar. 1692; and d. 4 Jan. 1713.

P. 325. l. 18 from bot. strike out " ano. stock " to the end of paragr. and ins. the first John, thro. five intermed. generat.

" at the end of last l. add, Prob. he d. early in 1691, for his inv. of 30 May names w. Frances, and ch. Hester; Amy; Frances, aged 22; Samuel, 19; Abigail, 17; Thomas, 14; and Dorothy, 11.

P. 328. l. 4 from bot. bef. Sears, ins. d. of Richard — also, aft. yr. ins. rather 91st (very remarka. as falling short of truth).

" l. 3 from bot. at the end, add, The ch. were Ichabod, b. 1661; Zechariah, 1664; Eliz. 1666; John, 1668; Robert, 1670; Joseph, 1674; Nathaniel, 1677; and Judah, 1681.

P. 330. bef. l. 6 ins. PAFFLYN, JOHN, odd as the name appears, is a grantee by Boston, 24 Feb. 1640, of eight acres in Braintree.

" l. 19, aft. 1667, add, made his will, 10 May 1688, and his inv. is of 17 June next yr. His w. was Sarah, wh. outliv. him sev. yrs. prob. for her inv. was of 25 Nov. 1695, and the ch. were Sarah, George, Hannah, Jonathan, aged 20; Nathaniel, 16; and Daniel, 13. — also, strike out, may be the same who, and ins. Ano. GEORGE

P. 333. l. 20, bef. had, ins. m. Eliz. d. of Josiah Belcher of Boston,

P. 334. l. 7 from bot. for 1679 r. 1 Jan. 1680

" l. 4 from bot. bef. Mary, ins. Martha, b. 24 Oct. d. 5 Nov. 1681;

P. 336. l. 11 from bot. bef. had ins. Ware

P. 338. l. 18, aft. 1669, add, had, by w. whose name is not seen, Mercy, wh. m. 9 June 1664, John Frost; Eliz. wh. m. 11 Oct. 1666, Thomas Sanford; and John, bef. ment. Late in life, he m. Nov. 1679, Mary, wid. of Francis Brown, and his inv. was of 11 Jan. 1685.

P. 341. l. 10 from bot. for MICHAEL r. MICAH

" l. 9 from bot. at the end, add, His will of 13 Nov. 1681, names ch. John, Daniel, Micah, and others, Mr. Porter tells me, but names of those are not seen.

P. 344. l. 17, aft. unm. add, when her sis. Mary, also, was unm.

" l. 18, aft. Abigail, ins. b. 1712

P. 346. l. 13 from bot. aft. 1690; ins. left. ch. Mary, aged 18; Joseph, 16; Nathaniel, 13; and Christopher, 8;

P. 350. l. 6, bef. Apr. ins. or 28

" l. 8, aft. 1666, ins. 6 Dec. — also, aft. 1667, ins. 2 May

" l. 9, for 671 r. 12 Jan. 1672.

P. 352. l. 7 from bot. for very likely had more r. had Eliphalet, Samuel, and Edward.

P. 359. l. 16 from bot. at the end, add WILLIAM, Nantucket, m. Eliz. d. of Alexander Adams of Boston, had Mary, b. 25 Feb. 1680; and no more can I hear.

" l. 9 from bot. aft. others. add, By his will of 23 Dec. 1684, and the distrib. of assets in 1688, we gain the names of Joshua, Caleb, Isaac, Hannah, Stephen, Job, Priscilla, and Joel.

P. 364. l. 7, aft. 1648, add, but his inv. in Essex Co. is of 6 Jan. 1651.

P. 372. l. 17 from bot. aft. 27 ins. bapt. 28 — also, aft. 10 ins. bapt. 14

P. 377. l. 9 from bot. aft. 1658, add, had w. Eliz.

P. 380. l. 11 from bot. erase prob.

" l. 10 from bot. aft. 1672 ; ins. John ; — also, aft. 1679 ; add Lydia ;

" l. 9 from bot. aft. 1684 ; ins. Desire, 26 Aug. 1687 ; and Mehitable, bapt. 1689 ; — also, erase aft. 1685. to the end of l.

" l. 6 from bot. aft. m. strike out to Hotchkiss in next l. inclus. and ins. 31 Oct. 1671, Mary, d. of William Bunnell

" l. 2 from bot. for 16 r. 6

P. 381. l. 7 from bot. aft. 1725 ; add, and he d. a. 1734.

P. 382. l. 19, aft. 1693 ; add, and d. 15 Apr. 1720.

P. 383. l. 17, aft. younger. add, For *Israel*, also, he read Isabel,

" l. 20, aft. correct. add, Ano. and younger stud. in this branch of hist. starts the conject. Geneal. Reg. XV. 60, that the name spell. Perk in the former vol. may be Park of Newton.

" l. 8 from bot. for 1672 r. 1674 — also, aft. *but* strike out, I know not whether he had, and ins. Porter says no.

" l. 7 from bot. erase, or wh. was —, also, aft. w. ins. was Eliz.

P. 384. l. 21 from bot. for June r. Jan.

P. 389. l. 5, aft. ch. ins. Mary m. 12 Apr. 1666, Jonathan Tompkins.

" l. 6, at the end, add, and rem. to Newark, N. J.

P. 394. l. 5 from bot. bef. 1650 ins. 20 Mar. — also, bef. 1651 ins. 18 Aug.

" l. 4 from bot. bef. 1652, ins. 21 Sept. — also, bef. 1653 ins. 12 Nov. — also, bef. 1656 ins. 3 Oct.

P. 405. l. 7, aft. yr. ins. ano. Joseph, whether by first or sec. w. is unkn.

P. 406. l. 16 from bot. aft. 1702 ; ins. but in fam. geneal. 1 May 1690.

P. 407. l. 20, bef. s. ins. youngest

" l. 12 from bot. strike out may well, &c. to man inclus. and ins. was of Porlock, Co. Somerset, on Bristol channel, few ms. from the edge of Devon,

" l. 11 from bot. erase tho. more prob. his f.

" l. 6 from bot. bef. had ins. by sec. w. Mary Dover, m. 1638, — also, bef. 1639 ins. 1 Sept. — also, bef. Mar. ins. 2

P. 408. l. 1, aft. 1682. add, He adopt. for s. Samuel Wilson, neph. of his w. and gave his prop. to him.

P. 429. l. 19 from bot. erase ment. by Babson to date, inclus.

P. 431. l. 17 from bot. aft. 1635, ins. brot. from Eng. d. Persis, wh. m. William Bridge, and next, John Harrison,

P. 432. l. 10 from bot. aft. Abigail, ins. b. 19 Sept. 1696 — also, aft. w. ins. m. 26 July

" l. 9 from bot. aft. Hooker, add, had James, 21 May 1699, Y. C. 1718 ; Samuel, 30 Dec. 1700, Y. C. 1718 ; Mary, 23 Nov. 1702 ; Joseph, 21 Oct. 1704 ; Benjamin, 18 July 1706, d. in few mos. ; Benjamin, again, 17 Oct. 1707, Y. C. 1726 ; Sarah, 9 June 1709 ; and Hezekiah, 1712.

" l. 3 from bot. aft. 1714. add, Against a foolish invent. of recent date, mak. this humble clerg. "descend. of the Duke of Kingston," the differ. of spell. in the surname, as the sound of both is the same, would be slight obstacle ; but we may be sure it is incredib. for our James's f. was b. many a long yr. bef. the *first* Duke of K.

P. 438. l. 18 from bot. for Mary r. Mercy

" l. 17 from bot. for Mercy r. Mary — also, aft. Abigail, add, and Experience ;

" l. 6 from bot. aft. Nantucket, ins. said to have come from Isle of Wight,

P. 438. l. 2 from bot. aft. 263. add, She was Mary, d. of Hon. James Coffin.

P. 440. l. 12 from bot. aft. Eliz. ins. b. 1720; — also, bef. d. ins. his s. Nathaniel — also, for wid. r. d. Eliz.

" l. 11 from bot. aft. and ins. he — also, for 20 yrs. aft. r. 1765.

P. 445. l. 7, aft. Comstock. add, Decent est. was seen in the inv. 13 Feb. foll.

" l. 14, at the end, add, and sometimes is writ. Plott.

P. 459. l. 9 from bot. bef. BENJAMIN ins. BENJAMIN, Farmington, youngest s. of Robert, d. young, without ch. and his wid. m. June 1689, Edmund Scott, and bore him eight ch.

P. 461. l. 7 from bot. bef. first ins. unm.

P. 462. l. 6 from bot. bef. 1644 ins. 7 Nov.

" l. 4 from bot. strike out young; and ins. without ch. soon aft. his f.

" last l. strike out a — also, aft. wid. ins. of Stephen of Newark,

P. 463. l. 1, erase his br. — also, aft. Thomas, ins. not his br. of Milford, — also, aft. Eliz. add, and Ann m. 1 Apr. 1685, John Brown of Middletown.

" l. 13, at the end, add, 1687,

" l. 7 from bot. aft. Stephen ins. b. 4

P. 466. l. 18, aft. John, ins. Hannah,

" l. 16 from bot. for Jan. r. June — also, aft. and ins. his w. d. 13 days aft.

" l. 15 from bot. aft. Abigail, ins. 23 Sept. foll.

" l. 8 from bot. aft. William, ins. b. in Eng. by w. Phebe had Joseph, b. 8 Oct. 1661; Rebecca, 26 May 1663; ano. d. Mar. 1668. He

" l. 7 from bot. aft. yr. add, and his wid. m. May 1670, John Rose, jr.

P. 467. l. 1, aft. 1661; add, but this must, prob. belong to Puffer.

" l. 2, aft. William, ins. m. 1 Apr. 1675, Eliz. Hawes, had large fam. as Porter writes, but gives no detail.

P. 468. l. 2 bef. Thomas ins. SAMUEL, New Haven, s. of John the first, m. 21 Nov. 1670, Hannah Russell, d. of William of the same.

" l. 14, aft. Nathaniel, ins. 22 Dec. 1644; — also, at the end, ins. b. 3 Oct. 1641

" l. 15, aft. Rebecca, ins. bapt. Jan. 1643. — also, erase but not prob.

" l. 21, aft. 247. add, Hope m. 3 Feb. 1664 Daniel Robinson; and Rebecca m. 27 Nov. 1667, Thomas Adams.

" l. 13, 12, 11, and 10 from bot. erase WILLIAM to 1644 inclus.

P. 470. l. 6, bef. 1681, ins. 3 Oct.

" l. 7, bef. 1666, ins. or as ano. acco. says, 22 May — also, at the end, add; and Mary m. 8 Nov. 1669, Ephraim Sanford

P. 471. l. 15 from bot. aft. Sarah, ins. wh. m. 1690, Timothy

" l. 14 from bot. aft. Rachel, ins. b. 1671, wh. m. 22 Feb. 1694, John

P. 483. l. 6 from bot. for Meckes or Mix r. Meeker

" l. 5 from bot. bef. He ins. His wid. Mary m. Thomas Kimberly.

P. 485. l. 7 from bot. at the end, add, to New Haven, there d. 11 Nov. 1710, had only one ch. wh. d. under age, and the wid. d. 1711.

P. 486. l. 4, bef. 1671, ins. 26 Jan.

P. 488. l. 15 from bot. aft. m. ins. 7 Dec.

" l. 14 from bot. bef. 1657 ins. 16 Mar. — also, aft. John, ins. 5 Oct. — also, aft. Mary, ins. 8 Mar. — also, aft. 1690; strike out and perhaps others, and ins Ebenezer, 10 Sept. 1661; Joseph, 11 June 1663; Jonathan, 7 June 1665, d. soon; Sarah, 19 Oct. 1666; Samuel, 15 Apr. 1668; Ebenezer, again, 7 June 1669; Hannah, 10 Mar. and Joanna, 2 Feb. 1673, d. in few mos.

" l. 13 from bot. erase wh. may have been a s. — also, add, His will was of 1689.

P. 490. l. 5 from bot. bef. had ins. was a sea capt. and d. 20 Sept. 1719;

P. 490. l. 4 from bot. aft. John, ins. 19 Nov. 1689, Y. C. 1708, Treas. of the coll. 49 yrs. ; beside Susanna, 8 May 1688, d. soon ; — also, aft. Mary, ins. 16 Apr. 1686 ;

P. 492. l. 3, aft. John ins. b. 9 Nov. 1645,

" l. 3 from bot. bef. JAMES, ins. GEORGE, Braintree, had gr. of ld. 24 Feb. 1641, for five heads, i. e. 20 acres.

P. 493. l. 9 from bot. at the end, add, WILLIAM, New Haven, s. prob. of the preced. m. 21 Apr. 1703, Hannah Brown, perhaps d. of Thomas of Stonington.

P. 494. l. 9, bef. Nicholas ins. 20 Oct. 1646,

P. 497. l. 14, bef. Carr ins. youngest d. of George

P. 501. l. 19, strike out for wid. and ins. with tender refer. to late decease (in Aug. preced.) of his w.

P. 506. l. 18 from bot. aft. 1676, ins. (but more prob. his f.) a —, also, at the end, add, d. of the first Richard Tozer,

P. 534. l. 21 from bot. aft. issue, add, He d. I find, 1662, at New Haven.

" l. 3 from bot. aft. Cutter, add, or Cutler

P. 540. l. 19 from bot. erase prob.

" l. 18 from bot. strike out William Lumpkin, and ins. John Gray, was a soldier of Gorham's comp. in Philip's war, but liv. in 1698. He had sec. w. in 1680, but the sheet of town rec. that nam. his fam. is lost.

" l. 15 from bot. bef. PHINEAS ins. JOHN, Yarmouth, s. of Samuel, d. 5 Jan. 1706, but his w. had d. 23 Oct. 1691. Full rec. of his fam. is lost, but he had s. Samuel, wh. d. 14 Aug. 1702, and from his will we find other ch. Ebenezer, John, b. 1664, Joseph, Hannah, Lydia, and Thankful. JOSEPH, Yarmouth, br. of the preced. of wh. the imperf. rec. shows ch. Joseph, b. 22 Dec. 1676 ; Hannah ; Eliz. ; Mary ; Sarah ; Rebecca ; and Esther ; was a man of esteem, left large est. and his branch of the fam. was extinct in his gr.s.

" l. 13 from bot. aft. Willis I. ins. His name is, in Hutch. Coll. 398, call. Hidar. — also, for 1643 r. 1638 — also, erase m. to Plymouth in next l. inclus.

" l. 11 from bot. aft. Cole ; add, beside Benjamin, John, and Samuel, some of wh. may have been b. in Eng. and Zechary, first male b. of white parents in the town ; and Joseph ; all nam. with w. Ann in his will. He was a lieut. but disfranch. 1655, for favor. Quakers ; d. 22 Dec. 1679, aged 78 ; and his wid. d. at Plymouth 1695. — also, at the end, add, w. I suppose, no ch.

" l. 10 from bot. bef. SAMUEL ins. SAMUEL, Plymouth, a cooper, s. of the preced. perhaps b. in Eng. m. 23 Dec. 1656, Sarah or Mary, d. of Robert Bartlett, had Samuel, b. 18 Nov. foll. and prob. others.

" l. 9 from bot. aft. Scituate. add, He is said to have had fourteen ch.

P. 541. l. 3, at the end, add, ZECHARY, Yarmouth, s. of the first Samuel, had gr. of ld. for the first male ch. b. in the town, by w. Mary had Zechariah and John, was k. by casual shot at a train. 5 Sept. 1685 ; and his wid. m. Edward Sturgis.

" l. 21 from bot. bef. s. ins. youngest

" l. 7 from bot. erase perhaps — also, erase a.

P. 544. l. 15 from bot. bef. or ins. RIZLEY

" l. 10 from bot. aft. fam. add, of ch. by w. Rebecca, d. of John Adams, certain. Richard, Samuel, John, perhaps others ; but his elder br.

P. 545. l. 15 from bot. aft. Brooks, add, d. 1689, and his wid. m. 10 Dec. 1692, Nathaniel Tharpe.

P. 548. l. 11, bef. WILLIAM, ins. *

" l. 12, aft. 1669, ins. was rep. 1689.

P. 550. l. 1, bef. DAVID, ins. DANIEL, New Haven, m. 3 Feb. 1664, Hope, d. of William Potter, had Mary, b. 14 Dec. foll.; and Daniel, 27 Nov. 1666.

P. 553. l. 2, bef. JOSEPH ins. JONATHAN, Guilford, br. of Thomas of the same, d. 1684.

P. 558. last l. bef. THOMAS, ins. JOHN, younger br. of Thomas, came, says tradit. from Barbados, bring. w. Mary; but no more is told of him, exc. that he had s. Thomas, rem. to Block isl. next to N. J. and d. at Flushing, L. I. SAMUEL, Newport, s. of Thomas, m. 17 Mar. 1723, Mary Willet, had Thomas, b. 29 Dec. foll.; Hannah, perhaps 22 July 1725, d. soon; Charity, 15 Nov. 1727, d. young; Samuel, 31 Jan. 1730, d. aft. 2 yrs.; William, 18 Jan. 1732; Eliz. 28 Mar. 1736; Ann; Mary; and John; and d. 27 Dec. 1748.

P. 559. l. 3, aft. Malins, ins. wid. of Robert, d. of that Peter Easton, wh. d. on her birth day, at the age of 35; — also, at the end, add, Whether he had ch. by the first w. I kn. not; but by Hannah came Hannah, b. 9 Sept. 1694; Clark, 29 Sept. 1698; John, 29 July 1701, d. in few mos.; Samuel, 23 May 1703; Patience, 5 Apr. 1706; and William, 12 Sept. 1708, wh. d. next yr.

P. 562. l. 18, aft. 1684. add, His will of 1 Dec. 1683, names ch. Eliezer, Jabez, Abigail, wh. was w. of Ephraim Stiles, John, and gr.ch. Ruth Beardsley.

P. 565. l. 21, bef. espe. ins. ,

P. 569. l. 9 from. bot. aft. Nantucket, ins. m. Martha, d. of Robert Barnard,

" l. 8 from bot. aft. 1676 add; Orange; Martha; and Mary; and d. 23 Mar. 1718.

" l. 4 from bot. aft. Lothrop, ins. had Robert, and three other ch. — also, aft. Wallingford, ins. d. 1681, — also, at the end, add 1690,

P. 572. l. 3 from bot. Porter directs me to erase perhaps

" last l. for 1667 r. 1666

P. 573. l. 19 from bot. aft. Porter; ins. and d. 18 Dec. 1739.

" last l. for Hartford r. Farmington

P. 574. l. 12, for 1668 r. 1669

P. 575. l. 9 from bot. bef. Nov. ins. 4

" l. 8 from bot. bef. Jan. ins. 9 — also, bef. Mar. ins. 5 — also, bef. Aug. ins. 12

" l. 7 from bot. aft. Joseph, ins. 11 — also, aft. John ins. 24.

P. 576. l. 6, at the end, add, neither being Sunday.

" l. 12, aft. 1667. add, He had m. the wid. of William Luddington in 1663, and d. in the spring of 1683, and Porter advises me, that the name should be Ross; and he adds to the issue, Eliz. b. 21 Dec. 1665; and Hannah, 24 Aug. 1668; but his ch. by former w. were Martha, wh. m. William Luddington; John; Mary, wh. m. a Bates; and Hannah, w. prob. of Edward Frisbie. In his will, of 18 Apr. 1683, these are all ment. as is gr.d. Eliz. Rose.

" l. 15, bef. JOHN ins. JOHN, New Haven, call. jr. m. Aug. 1670, Phebe, wid. of Joseph Potter, prob. had d. Eliz.

" l. 17, erase may have been — also, erase or br. — also, aft. same, ins. and m. a d. of John Charles, and d. 1684.

" l. 21, aft. went ins. ,

" l. 15 from bot. aft. 1650. ins. His will was of 25 Aug. 1664, and inv. of good est. 2 June foll. His w. was Rebecca, ch. Jonathan, Hannah, John, Mary, Eliz. and five others.

P. 577. l. 4, aft. Roose, add, sometimes Rawse,

" l. 13 from bot. bef. 1672 ins. 30 Sept.

P. 578. l. 15 from bot. aft. William ins. (but Porter denies it)

P. 579. l. 7, for may r. must

P. 579. l. 8 and 9, erase but to the end of sent.

" l. 12, aft. 1641, ins. bapt. 1 Oct. 1643 — also, bef. *and* ins. Lydia, Aug. 1644, d. soon; John, bapt. 19 July 1646; Mary, b. 23 Feb. 1650; Eliz. 19 June 1652, d. soon, — also, aft. d. ins. Sept.

" l. 14, bef. 1670, ins. 11 Dec. — also, aft. Hall, add, and next, 23 Aug. 1681, John Prout.

P. 580. l. 7 from bot. for Jan. 1651 r. 10 Aug. 1650 — also, aft. Daniel, ins. 4

" l. 6 from bot. for Nov. 1658 r. 20 Feb. 1659

" l. 5 from bot. aft. Aug. ins. but ano. acco. says 6 June

P. 587. l. 2 from bot. aft. 1711. add, Full relat. of his being struck by lightning, 1666, while driv. a team, of wh. the cattle were all k. is seen in Mather's Remarka. Providen. 78.

P. 590. l. 16 from bot. bef. 1673 ins. 21 Jan. — also, bef. 1674 ins. 21 Aug.

P. 592. l. 7, for 1670 r. 19 Mar. 1671 — also, bef. Sept. ins. 2 — also, aft. young, add, at sea

" l. 8, aft. 1679, add, or 1674, to ano. eyesight,

P. 593. l. 3 from bot. at the end, add, His wid. m. 29 Dec. 1679, John Potter.

P. 594. l. 16 from bot. for *first* d. r. b. 12 — also, aft. 1703, add, d. next yr. — also, bef. *sec.* d. ins. b. 19 Aug.

P. 595. l. 5 and 6, erase s. prob. &c. to the same inclus.

" l. 8, bef. 1653 ins. 10 Nov.

" l. 10, bef. 1664 ins. 3 Dec.

" l. 11, aft. m. for *a.* r. 21 Nov. 1670, Samuel

" l. 18, aft. mos. ins. WILLIAM, New Haven, s. of John of the same, d. 1700, at sea, but leav. ch. John and Hannah.

P. 598. l. 25, aft. preced. ins. m. 13 Sept. 1682, Abigail, d. of Moses Mansfield,

P. 600. last l. at the end, add, — also, erase br. of Daniel of the same.

P. 602. l. 1, at the end, ins. ; and perhaps was of Elizabethtown, N. J. 1685.

" l. 19 from bot. at the end, add, ISAAC, New Haven, s. perhaps eldest of the preced. by w. Joanna had Isaac, b. 20 Oct. 1680; Ebenezer, 24 Feb. 1683; Joanna, and Hannah, prob. tw. bapt. 1685; John, 1689; Abigail, and Abiah, tw. b. 25 Sept. 1693; and Jemima, 12 Dec. 1696; and he d. 1708. JOHN, New Haven, br. of the preced. by w. Eliz. had John, b. 9 Oct. 1671; Mary, 23 Feb. 1673; Eliz.; Joanna, 21 July 1677; Sarah; Jemima, 11 Feb. 1681; Joseph, 13 Feb. 1684; and Ebenezer, 12 Apr. 1686; and d. 1712.

P. 603. l. 5, at the end, for 1658 r. 1655, wh. d. 30 May 1667, by wh. he had John, b. 4 Nov. 1655, d. in few days; Sarah, 15 Sept. foll.; Mary, 10 Apr. 1660; Hannah, 8 Jan. 1662; and John, again, 15 Sept. 1664. By sec. w. he had Joseph, 9 June 1670.

" l. 19, at the end, add, Elder than him, prob. was that WILLIAM, Manchester, wh. d. 20 Nov. 1682, leav. w. Jane, ch. Moses, Aaron, Mary, beside gr.ch. John, Aaron, and Abigail Croc, whose f. is not of my acquaint. See Essex Inst. III. 231.

" l. 10 from bot. at the end, add ; and his s. John d. 1661, unm.

P. 604. l. 20 from bot. at the end, add, But he d. (as I infer) ten yrs. bef. for on 26 June 1682, his w. brot. inv. of his est. The d. Eliz. m. 16 Dec. 1698, Israel Shaw.

P. 605. l. 22, bef. and, ins. Daniel, 1680; Lydia, 28 Nov. 1685; Ebenezer, 9 Nov. 1689; Abraham, 9 Apr. 1693; and Esther, 14 May 1696; was deac.

" l. 23. aft. add, ins. Mary, 15 Apr. 1687; Desire, 19 Apr. 1690; Benjamin, 1 Oct. 1692; Abner, 6 Mar. 1696; and Caleb, 5 May 1700.

P. 607. l. 21 from bot. aft. Martha, ins. — also, aft. Samuel, ins. m. 26 Oct. 1665

" l. 18 from bot. aft. Sarah, ins. m. 23 May 1682

" l. 19 from bot. at the end, add, Porter writes me, that by w. Rebecca Mallory, wh. d. 12 Mar. 1691, he had Rebecca, b. 19 Jan. 1668, d. in a wk.; Rebecca, again, 11 Feb. 1669; Judith, 13 Apr. 1672; Benjamin, 4 Jan. 1676, d. in few days; Ann, 8 Jan. 1678, d. young; Benjamin, again, 29 Nov. 1679; Hezekiah, 23 Mar. 1682; Rachel, 16 Dec. 1683; Nathaniel, May 1686; Israel, 12 Mar. 1690; and his sec. w. Eliz. wid. of John Sperry, bore him Ann, 11 Oct. 1695; and his wid. m. 19 Sept. 1700, Edmund Dorman. NATHAN, New Haven, br. of the preced. m. 3 Jan. 1667, Susanna Whitehead, eldest d. of Isaac.

P. 608. l. 3, at the end, add, Rebecca, d. of Benjamin Bunnell, had Ann, b. 30 Dec. 1685; and eleven other ch. as Porter writes, without giv. the names.

" l. 17 from bot. at the end, add, and had Rebecca, b. 29 Dec. 1671; Hannah, 14 Nov. 1673; Zaccheus, 5 Jan. 1676; Samuel, 24 July 1678; Mary, 18 Feb. 1681; Desire, 20 Oct. 1686; and Abigail, Apr. 1689.

P. 609. l. 26, at the end, add, — also, aft. 1668, ins. m. 19 Apr. 1669, Lydia Haley, had Peter, and Samuel, tw. b. 29 Dec. 1678.

P. 610. l. 3, at the end, add, Perhaps she was mo. of all the ch. but he had 17 Oct. 1661, m. Ann, wid. of John Wakefield.

P. 611. l. 7 from bot. for aft. 1659 r. bef. LOT.

P. 612. l. 15 from bot. aft. 10 ins. from bot.

P. 613. l. 16 from bot. at the end, add, He had, also, Ephraim, wh. was admor. on est. Nov. 1682, tho. the wid. was then liv.

P. 614. l. 13 from bot. for John r. Jacob

P. 615. l. 24 from bot. for some r. Some

P. 619. l. 11, for Tomkins r. Tompkins

P. 620. l. 11 from bot. at the end, add, — also, aft. Joseph. ins. We may infer from the div. of est. under order of Ct. June 1680, to the first and last only of these ch. that both the other s. were d. bef. mid. age.

P. 622. l. 13 from bot. at the end, add, His wid. m. 6 Dec. 1677, John Shepard of Lynn.

P. 623. l. 23, aft. had ins. sec. — also, aft. Damaris ins. Shattuck, a wid. from Eng.

P. 624. l. 11, bef. 1668, ins. 26 Nov.

" l. 13, at the end, add, , m. 3 June 1673

" l. 15, erase had — also, for 1676 r. 1706

" l. 6 and 5 from bot. strike out "tho. neither," &c. to *he* inclus. and ins. m. 7 Dec. 1671, Joanna, d. of Stephen Daniel, and

P. 625. l. 2, at the end, add, was posthum. without doubt, for the f. d. in Oct. 1679.

" bef. l. 12 ins. " l. 6 from bot. aft. m. add, 1687,

" l. 15, for 1705 r. 1725

" l. 20, for Obadiah r. Obedience

" l. 9 from bot. for 14, aft. est. r. 12, bef. JOSHUA

P. 626. l. 3 from bot. at the end, add, of Newbury.

P. 627. l. 3, at the end, add, By his will of 19 May 1688 he gave prop. to cous. Abel. His wid. m. a Davis.

" l. 25, for June r. Jan.

P. 628. l. 13, aft. Marblehead, ins. 1674,

P. 629. l. 6, bef. Ebenezer, ins. Bethia, 7 Sept. 1658;

" l. 17 and 16 from bot. for Hawkins r. Howkins.

" l. 3 from bot. aft. add, ins. was rep. 1683,

P. 630. l. 7, for Mar. r. May

" l. 7 from bot. aft. ch. ins. to inf. inclus.

" aft. last l. add, " l. 9 from bot. aft. yr. add, His will of 17 Feb. 1680, made w. Ann extrix. provides for ch. of Eleazer, his s. wh. was d. viz. William, Samuel, and Abigail, for Sarah, wid. of his s. William, for a gr.ch. in Europe, if he come here, if not, then that gift to go to other gr.ch. i. e. two eldest s. of his d. Coker, w. I presume of Joseph.

P. 631. l. 26, at the end, add, He d. 16 Oct. 1712. His s. Seth and Theophilus had fams. as Porter writes, without specify. Abigail m. Dec. 1691, Ebenezer Atwater, and next, 27 Nov. 1712, John Gilbert.

P. 632. l. 10 from bot. for 1667 r. 20 Feb. 1668 — also, strike out, beside Eliz. 1672; and ins. 15 Sept. 1673; and Mary, 27 Mar. 1676;

P. 633. l. 17, at the end, add, So she sav. her life from that peril, but allow. the devil to seduce her to infernal revenge by accus. the mo. of the constab. wh. arrest. her for the same horrid or preposterous offence. See Essex Inst. II. 133.

P. 634. l. 8 from bot. at the end, add, In the will of Richard, f. of Ann Hathaway, w. of the immort. Shakespeare, made 1 Sept. 1581 at Stratford, he names Edward Hollyocke, as to him was due 20 shillings for wood; but tho. Warwicksh. and Staffordsh. adj. it must be large 30 ms. from Stratford to Tamworth, so that, if that Edward were f. of our Edward, he had earlier, without doubt, liv. nearer London.

P. 635. l. 25 from bot. for br. prob. eldest r. eldest br.

P. 636. l. 11, bef. Sept. ins. 17

" l. 23, at the end, add , but that he and brs. Isaac and Daniel d. 1690.

" l. 25 from bot. bef. m. ins. s. of Jeremy,

" l. 22 from bot. aft. Matthew, ins. 18 Nov. 1672 — also, for Sarah r. Samuel

P. 637. l. 7, at the end, add, Abigail m. Dec. 1680, Richard Blackleach of Stratford, and d. Mar. 1713.

" l. 13, at the end, add, , 27 Nov. 1677;

P. 638. l. 4, aft. br. ins. more prob. s.

" l. 6, aft. His ins. inv. was tak. 13 Nov. and the

" l. 26 and 27 may be eras. as the matter is better put in Vol. II. 596.

" l. 4 from bot. at the end, add, Always in old pr. or wr. the first two letters of this name are subj. to the variab. interchang. I for J, and J for I, U for V, and V for U.

P. 639. l. 6, for Mary r. Sarah

" l. 7, bef. kill. ins. attempt. at

" l. 23 from bot. bef. copy ins. later

" l. 15 from bot. with l. 14, 13, and 12 may be eras. as the matter is better seen on · p. 597 of Vol. II.

" aft. the last l. ins. " l. 15, aft. 1662, add, had Thomas, b. 25 Apr. 1664; a ch. 1666; and Samuel, 8 Mar. 1671; rem. perhaps, to Derby, had more ch. and d. 1704.

P. 640. bef. the first l. ins. P. 554. l. 4 from bot. aft. *will* ins. of 22 Nov. in that yr. call. hims. 63 yrs. old,

" l. 2, at the end, add, JOHN, New Haven, s. of Robert, m. 2 Mar. 1685, Mabel Grannis, had John, b. 3 Mar. 1687; Thomas, 12 Jan. 1690; Ann, Feb. 1691; Sarah, 9 Apr. 1694; Daniel, 22 Apr. 1696; Joseph, 2 Dec. 1698; Benjamin, 9 Mar. 1701; Robert, 2 June 1703; James, 3 Sept. 1705; Mehitable, 29 Feb. 1708; and Hannah, 23 May 1710.

P. 641. l. 24, at the end, add, for ano. w. he took, 3 Dec. 1680, Susanna, wid. prob. of Isaac Hyde,

P. 642. l. 10, erase or 5

P. 643. l. 1, aft. Mary ins. d. of John Reeves,

" l. 2, bef. 1 Feb. ins. but I suppose his name was John,

P. 645. l. 25, for the spell r. ill spell.

P. 647. l. 14, aft. Kensington, ins. physician,

P. 648. l. 12, aft. ins. add, His wid. m. 13 June 1692, deac. Thomas Bull, and d. 10 Jan. 1728.

P. 649. at the foot for VOL. II. r. VOL. III.

P. 650. l. 3, aft. 1681 ; add, beside Thomas, John, Richard, Jabez, and Mary ;

" l. 20, for by r. By

P. 652. l. 15, for elder r. older — also, aft. ins. add, Samuel, wh. d. prob. very young ;

" l. 25, at the end, add, ; and his d. Esther m. 10 June 1695, Daniel Willard, both parties hav. past mid. age.

P. 654. l. 3, at the end, add, He and his descend. always spell More.

P. 655. l. 12, at the end, for 1716 r. 1671

" last l. at the end, ins. ;

P. 656. l. 9, at the end, add, SAMUEL, New Haven, s. of Richard, m. 15 Feb. 1688, Eliz. Rose of Branford, perhaps d. of Robert the sec. and d. next yr. without ch. His wid. d. the yr. foll. and his br. John and sis. Sarah inherit. his prop.

P. 657. l. 15, for Eliz. Harrison r. Miriam Hannison

" l. 16, bef. wh. ins. aft. made Handerson, or Henderson,

" l. 17, aft. 1695, ins. d. in Feb. foll.

" l. 23, at the end, add, Their gr.mo. Eliz. Spooner, in her will of June 1677, drives me to suspect, that he is the same as the preced. and that Boston rec. is not trustworthy in date of b. of the first two chapters. See Essex Inst. II. 236.

" at the bot. add, He had John, b. 15 Aug. 1674 ; Abigail, 17 Mar. 1676 ; Eliz. 2 Oct. 1677 ; Josiah, 21 Sept. 1679, d. next yr. ; William, 24 Feb. 1681 ; Samuel, 27 Feb. 1683 ; Mary, 18 Sept. 1685, d. at 18 yrs. ; and James, 6 Apr. 1687. Sec. w. he took, 24 Mar. 1692, was Jemima, but no issue came of this m.

P. 658. l. 12 from bot. strike out Sept. and ins. bapt. 20

P. 659. l. 3, for Robert r. ROBERT

" l. 20 from bot. at the end, add, Prob. he had but one w. Porter adds to my list of ch. Mary, 20 Aug. 1692 ; Hannah, 19 Feb. 1694 ; Mabel, 28 Sept. 1696 ; Eliz. 22 Oct. 1699 ; and Esther, 24 May 1704 ; and prolongs the life of wid. to 1758, aged 96.

P. 660. l. 18, for 1638 r. 1683

" l. 14 from bot. aft. 3 ins. or 30 — also, at the end, add, He was a deac.

" l. 13 from bot. for Samuel r. SAMUEL

P. 663. l. 17, at the end, add, See the nuncup. will in Geneal. Reg. XV. 76.

ADDITIONS AND CORRECTIONS

IN VOL. IV.

P. 2. l. 6 from bot. aft. again. add, This name was writ. by Dr. Holmes in his Hist. of Cambridge, 1 Mass. Hist. Coll. VII. 10, Oakes, but that was more than 60 yrs. since, and he bec. as he grew older, better able to read ancient rec.

P. 5. l. 9 from bot. aft. preced. ins. by w. Freeborn had Hannah, b. 9 Sept. 1654; Mary, 2 Feb. 1659; — also, in that and next l. strike out, "prob. in June as" and ins. by drown. 8 Apr. and

P. 6. l. 7, bef. Mary ins. John, b. 9 May foll.

" l. 10, at the end, add, m. Oct. 1664, Remember, d. of Benjamin Felton, had Eliz.; Mary, b. 16 Mar. 1669; Susanna, 30 May 1670; George, 1 Mar. 1672, posthum. for the f. d. a. 12 Feb. preced.

" l. 11, aft. Newport add, 1669, had there a w. and was

" l. 12, bef. SAMUEL, ins. PETER, Salem, m. 4 June 1677, Ann Thompson, had Martha, b. 29 July 1679, d. in 3 mos.; Ann, 30 Aug. 1680; Peter, 1 July 1682; and Sarah, 18 Aug. 1683.

" l. 18, aft. Amesbury, ins. m. 30 Nov. 1669, Mary with surname very odd, had William, b. Apr. 1670

" l. 9 from bot. aft. 1674, add, m. perhaps, Ann, d. of Samuel Condy, and had sev. ch.

P. 12. l. 16 from bot. aft. Rebecca, ins. d. of James

" l. 6 from bot. aft. Mary, ins. of sec. Nathaniel

P. 17. l. 20 for SANSOM r. SARSON

" l. 22, at the end, add, ; had Samuel, and Mehitable.

P. 19. l. 11, for WILLIAM r. *WILLIAM.*

" l. 19, aft. Barnstable, ins. where he succeed. famous John Lothrop in the pulpit, and

P. 21. l. 20 from bot. aft. 1669. ins. JOHN, Salem, m. 5 Nov. 1661, Hannah Pickman, prob. d. of Nathaniel, had Hannah, b. 15 Mar. 1663, wh. d. at 9 yrs.; John, 22 Oct. 1665; James, 23 Sept. 1667; Nathaniel, 2 July 1670; Joseph, 21 Aug. 1673, d. next yr.; and Eliz. 28 Aug. 1678, had

P. 27. l. 18, aft. 1691. add, See 2 Mass. Hist. Coll. III. 256.

P. 31. l. 15, for WILLIAM r. SAMUEL

" l. 18, aft. 1681. add, WILLIAM, Ipswich, s. of the first William, rem. to Wells, by w. Sarah had Joseph, b. 14 Aug. 1678; Francis, 6 Mar. 1681; Daniel, 26 May 1683; Hannah, 9 Apr. 1685; and Ruth, 26 May 1687; and he d. 7 June 1718. His wid. d. Jan. 1734, aged 84.

P. 37. l. 8, for by w. r. m. June 1689, the wid. of Benjamin Porter,

P. 38. l. 2 from bot. aft. 1638. ins. ROBERT, Charlestown, adm. 1651, to inhab. there, came from Barbados.

P. 41. l. 1, aft. 1660, ins. m. Sarah, wid. of Nicholas Munger.

P. 42. last l. at the end, add, comp. with III. 142.

P. 45. l. 7, bef. ANDREW, ins. ALEXANDER, Salem, b w. Mary had Robert, b. 6 Aug. 1657; Mary, 22 Feb. 1660, wh. d. young; Abigail, wh. d. 16 Jan. 1663, prob. very young; and Alexander, 25 May 1664.

P. 45. l. 5 from bot. bef. WILLIAM, ins. THOMAS, Salem, by w. Damaris, had John, b. 30 Oct. 1666 ; Mary, 6 May 1668 ; and Thomas, 5 Aug. 1674.

P. 46, l. 11, aft. Daniel, ins. b. 1682 ; Richard, 1684 ;

" l. 12, erase prob.

" l. 13, aft. Scituate, ins. had Samuel, b. 1663 ; Paul ; John, 1677 ; beside sev. ds. whose names are not seen ;

" l. 14, aft. come, ins. with spell. of Sayer — also, aft. 30 ins. then aged 40,

" l. 16, aft. Dorothy, ins. m. 1632, it is said, in fam. geneal. with surname of Thacher, but wh. she was unkn.

" l. 17, aft. 1676. ins. His wid. d. 1680. She was younger than her h. — also, erase prob.

" l. 19, bef. Thomas ins. Silas ;

" l. 20, aft. ch. ins. presum. to be Richard, Joseph, Josiah, Eliz. and Dorothy ;

P. 51. l. 1, aft. debts. add, How his name was pervert. to Zullesh may be seen near the end of this vol.

P. 52. l. 20, at the end, add, He took sec. w. 11 Jan. 1661, Hannah, d. of Robert Read.

P. 53. l. 4, aft. Sewell, ins. or Seawell — also, aft. EDWARD, add, Salem, m. 3 July 1671, Sarah Hale, had Eliz. b. 27 June foll. ; and Edward, 14 July 1674 ; prob. rem. to

" l. 16 from bot. aft. 10 ins. or 19

P. 56. l. 5 from bot. aft. Robie. add, Aft. 1686 he liv. at Salem.

P. 58. l. 2 from bot. for in r. 12

P. 62. l. 17, for sec. r. first,

" l. 22, aft. but ins. her name was Grace, and

P. 64. l. 4, aft. him, add, exc. that he m. Eliz. Booth, and had Israel, b. 16 Dec. 1698 ; and Susanna, 29 Sept. 1703.

P. 67. l. 8, bef. Edward, ins. William, wh. d. in the pestilence of 1677 ; beside

" l. 9, aft. ign. add, and he d. 7 or 17 May 1713, aged 63.

" l. 10, aft. 70 ; add, but she must have been third w. for a sec. m. 2 Mar. 1703 was Eliz. wid. of John Pinney, d. of Thomas Rand.

" bef. l. 19 ins. SHEARMAN, JOHN, Dartmouth, of wh. he was among early sett. m. Sarah, d. of William Spooner, had ch. Timothy, Philip, Isaac, Ephraim, as is learn. from his will of 19 June 1720, pro. 21 May 1734, beside ds. Abigail Chase, and Hannah Shea, the h's. of wh. are unkn. to me. It made Philip and Timothy excors. and ment. his br. Peleg. But no informat. of the br. is obt. nor could I learn any thing of descend. of John, yet it is well kn. they have been num. Always have I suspect. that this name is the same as Sherman, even on our side of the water, but a large proportion of one branch being Quakers, the distinct. was easi. and harmless. made by insert. of the first let. of our alpha. JOHN, Marshfield, s. of the first William. But see Sherman, as comm. the name is writ.

P. 70. l. 3, bef. JOHN, ins. JOHN, Newport 1651.

P. 71. l. 3, aft. evil. add, One Susanna S. a girl of 18 yrs. perhaps d. of this man, was terrib. afflict. in the witcher. times, 1692, if one fourth of what she sw. was true.

P. 73. l. 8, for irresitab. r. irresistab.

P. 75. l. 5, aft. 1689. add, He m. 6 Dec. 1677, Rebecca, wid. of John Fuller of Lynn, d. of John Putnam.

P. 78. l. 9, bef. 1757 ins. 29 Dec.

P. 79. l. 15 from bot. to l. 11, strike out " Trinity " to " honors," and ins. Emanuel Coll. Cambridge Univ. where

P. 79. l. 6 from bot. strike out " to the contra. for " and ins. that

" l. 4, 3, and 2 from bot. strike out, "It is needless," &c. to "can be found," and ins. Too easi. was this man presumed to be our John, and aft. large investigat. the correctness of that part of Mather's relat. is establish. By suggest. of Rev. Hen. B. Sherman of Newark, N. J. I was led to obtain more minute and very curious details of THREE *other* John Shermans at Cambridge Univ. but very short time bef. or aft. this Watertown min. all by the acad. rec. made D. D. and one was even of Emanuel, and another of the three was from the same Essex Dedham beside; yet all were anti-puritan. He of Dedham was at Queens, tak. A. B. Jan. 1650, and aft. a fellow of Jesus, of wh. coll. he wrote a hist. was archdeac. of Salisbury, and d. 1671. The Emanuel scholar was a little earlier, A. B. 1642, had been matricul. 1638, four yrs. aft. the N. E. cry in the wilderness by his namesake began; but the Trinity divine, wh. misled me, matricul. Dec. 1626, of course, something too old for our John, was A. B. Jan. 1630; A. M. 1633; B. D. 1640; and D. D. 1660. He was eject. from his fellowsh. 1650 for refus. to sign the "Engagement," wh. was a contriv. by the Independ. or Cromwell party to put down the other. See Neal's Hist. of Pur. IV. 27, of Ed. 1796. But he was learn. and gave some of his skill to Walton's Polyglot, and my Newark benefactor says, he was of Ipswich, and d. 1663.

P. 86. l. 16 and 15 from bot. strike out aft. both, all to the end of the sentence, and ins. for his will of June 1657, pro. 4 June 1658, ment. s. John and Thomas, d. Mary, w. Sarah, and refers to other ds. without nam. them. His est. was good.

" l. 13 from bot. aft. 1672. ins. But his inv. of May 1676, ment. no w. or ch.

P. 88. l. 5, aft. w. add, Grace m. 19 Nov. 1679, the first Timothy Pratt.

P. 90. l. 3 and 4, strike out, prob. d. of Rev. and ins. eldest d. of Nathaniel Bacon, wid. of the sec.

" l. 8, aft. foll. ins. His mo. wh. had m. Richard Peacock of Roxbury, was bur. near 26 yrs. aft. from the ho. of her s.

P. 94. l. 8, for 1686 r. 1687

P. 97. l. 5 from bot. bef. 1655 ins. 4 June

P. 100. l. 10 from bot. aft. 1668, ins. m. 1 Aug. 1679, Hannah Wells, had Richard, b. 11 Dec. 1681; d. 19 Mar. foll. and to his wid. admin. of his little prop. was given 27 June 1682.

P. 103. l. 8, strike out the next, and ins. him wh. at Boston had, by w. Sarah, John, and John, again, b. 25 Apr. 1660. See SCATE. It may be the same person as the foll.

P. 104. l. 16 from bot. bef. FRANCIS ins. EPHRAIM, Salem, s. of the first Henry, m. Sept. 1671, Martha Mellard (if Essex Inst. III. 144 has correct spell.), had Hannah, b. 11 July foll.; Martha, 13 July 1674; and he d. 11 Oct. 1676.

" l. 15 from bot. aft. 1692. ins. His wid. d. 10 Aug. of the same yr.

" l. 8 from bot. aft. old, add, d. 12 Apr. 1697

" l. 7 from bot. aft. preced. ins. m. 9 Nov. 1665, Priscilla, d. of the first Henry Lunt, had Francis, b. 25 Nov. 1666; Ann, 14 June 1669; Priscilla, 13 July 1671; — also, at the end, add, d. 30 Aug. 1691; and his wid. Eliz. d. 6 Mar. 1693.

P. 105. l. 2, at the end ins. On 19 June 1667 he sign. contr. with Joanna, wid. of Nathaniel Baldwin, wh. had been wid. of Richard Westcoat, by wh. she should have power to devise her prop. to John, Daniel, Joanna, and Abigail, her ch. by said Richard W. and to Sarah, Deborah, and Samuel, her ch. by said Nathaniel B. she intend. to m. said Thomas S.

" l. 3, bef. JAMES ins. BENJAMIN, Chilmark 1676, m. 20 Feb. 1680, Hannah, whose surname may have been Merry. Of him I hear no more, but that in 1704 he and others were employ. by Gov. Dudley in an import. trust.

P. 105. l. 6, aft. Bourne. add, He took sec. w. 18 Nov. 1659, Eliz. Nabor. JAMES, Nantucket, prob. s. of the preced. m. Sarah, d. of Robert Barnard, had Nathaniel, Patience, Mary, Hannah, Beulah, and Sarah. He rem. to Tisbury. NATHAN, Tisbury, br. of the preced. m. Hepzibah Codman, perhaps d. of Robert, had James, b. 10 Mar. 1689; Benjamin, 29 Apr. 1691; Stephen, 26 May 1693; Mary, 20 May 1695; beside Eliz. of uncert. date. His sec. w. m. Feb. 1698, Mary Chipman, d. of John, had Sarah; Mary, 5 July 1701; Samuel, 24 Dec. 1703; John, 22 Aug. 1705; and Joseph, 18 Nov. 1707; and d. 19 July 1726, aged 70.

" l. 16 from bot. aft. Mary, ins. d. of Joseph Loomis

" l. 15 from bot. for JOHN r. John, wh.

P. 106. l. 15, at the end, add, Perhaps Catharine of L. was ano. sis.

P. 107. l. 1, aft. Hampton, ins. s. of Thomas, — also, for by w. r. m. 23 May 1682, — also, aft. Eliz. ins. Shaw — also, aft. had, ins. Eliz. of unkn. date

" l. 2, aft. 1686; add, Aaron, 23 July 1688; Joseph, and John, tw. 14 June 1690; Samuel, 1 Dec. 1692; Elisha, 9 May 1694; Hezekiah, 11 May 1696; Ebenezer, 18 May 1697, d. at one yr.; Jonathan, 17 Mar. 1699; Abigail, 17 Apr. 1700; Mehitable, 25 Apr. 1701; Ebenezer, again, 24 Apr. 1702; a d. 7 July 1704, d. soon; Mary, 21 May 1706; Ithamar, 15 Sept. 1708; and by w. Sarah, had Daniel, 9 May 1715; and Edward, 26 Oct. 1719; and d. 9 May 1732.

" l. 5, aft. but, ins. had liv. at H. 5 yrs. and

" l. 6, aft. Aaron, ins. b. 20 Feb. 1661; — also, aft. John, ins. 10 Feb. 1652; — also, aft. Eliz. ins. a. 1645,

" l. 7, aft. sec. add, beside Mary, 1647; Naomi, 15 Apr. 1655; Moses, of unkn. date; and Luther, 14 Nov. 1668, wh. d. under 2 yrs. — also, at the end, add, His wid. d. 5 Feb. 1703, aged 80.

P. 112. l. 5, aft. first John, ins. more prob. of Ralph the sec.

P. 119. l. 18, for JOHN r. *JOHN*

" l. 14 from bot. aft. them. add, He rem. to New York, but contin. there not long; was min. at Sandwich, and d. aft. 1690.

P. 121. l. 18, aft. Packard, ins. d. of Samuel the first,

" l. 12 from bot. aft. 203. ins. In his will of 20 Jan. 1679, it is seen, that he had two s. viz. George and Exercise, ds. Tamosin and Margaret, that his w. was sis. of Joshua Buffum, to wh. was giv. the s. Exercise, as was George to ano. of that peacef. sect.

P. 125. l. 18, aft. Dorothy, add, eldest

P. 129. l. 14, aft. there, ins. was constable 1660.

" l. 15, aft. 1654, ins. Samuel, older than her; Thomas; — also, aft. ch. add, His w. Grace with s. Samuel, had admin. of his est. 27 Oct. 1685.

P. 132. l. 16, aft. Eastham, ins. s. of Ralph, perhaps b. in Eng.

P. 138. l. 7 from bot. aft. Constance, ins. (by wondr. error in Geneal. Reg. XIV. 89, call. Eliz.)

P. 139. l. 17 from bot. aft. 1679. add, From Prob. Reg. we find, that his wid. had admin. that ch. were Eliz. w. of Joseph Lovett; Hannah, w. of John Trask; Martha, w. of Thomas Kilham; Abigail, w. of Mordecai Larcum; Mary, wh. m. John Edwards; Sarah, wh. m. Daniel Poole; Bethia; and Joseph, wh. last d. under age; that the wid. mo. of these ch. had m. Ezekiel Woodward, and was since dec.

" l. 12 from bot. aft. 1692. add, He m. 23 July 1693, Dorcas, d. of Nathaniel Coffin; and she m. 1736, it is said, Nathaniel Gorham.

P. 140. l. 8 from bot. at the end, add, exc. that their s. Joseph was b. 5 Jan. 1660.

P. 142. l. 14 from bot. bef. LAWRENCE ins. DANIEL, s. of Lawrence, m. 23 Feb. 1663, Esther, d. of Joseph Boyce, had Esther, b. 26 June 1665; Eliz. 24 June 1668; Daniel, 25 Mar. 1671; Elinor, 25 June 1674; and Hannah, 7 Aug. 1677. JOHN, Salem, eldest s. of Lawrence, m. Sarah, wid. of Samuel Tidd, had Sarah, b. June 1644; Mary, 10 Oct. 1646; and Samuel, 19 Feb. 1659. JOSIAH, Salem, br. of the preced. by w. Mary had Joseph, b. 3 Apr. 1662; Mary, Nov. 1664; Cassandra, Nov. 1667; and Ruth, 21 Feb. 1674.

P. 143. l. 6, for Constant, or Thomas, r. Edward,

" last l. for Constant r. Edward

P. 144. l. 3, aft. them. add, A very long l. of most val. public serv. in Mass. Conn. and N. Y. proves, that honors from the Ct. of Queen Eliz. were not need.

" l. 18, aft. Nathaniel, ins. ord. 12 June 1695,

P. 148. l. 11, aft. *first* d. ins. Audry or Susanna,

" l. 20, aft. m. ins. 7 Dec. 1671, — also, aft. Sweetman, add, had Rebecca, b. 4 Nov. 1673.

" l. 15 from bot. aft. first ins. of the same,

P. 150. l. 13 from bot. aft. 1656, ins. for this was the date of his inv.

P. 151. l. 1, aft. Bunnell; add, and next, 19 Sept. 1700, Edward Dorman;

" last l. for Marshfield r. Plymouth

P. 152. l. 19, at the end, add, ano. acco. says, 19 June

" l. 4 from bot. for 1670 r. 1660, — also, aft. Dartmouth, add, was a town offic. in 1663,

" l. 2 and 1 from bot. for whose name is not seen, r. Hannah Pratt, d. perhaps of Jonathan,

P. 162. l. 4, aft. 1642, ins. and d. Nov. 1679.

P. 170. l. 6 from bot. at the end, for *a* r. 24 Nov. 1650, Susanna

" l. 5 from bot. aft. Hollingsworth, ins. had Robert, Richard, and Susanna; and his w. d. 17 May 1665; — also, aft. capt. ins. m. 30 Dec. 1669, Mary Conklin, had Mary, b. 9 Oct. 1670; Sarah and Hannah, tw. 22 June 1673; and ano. ch.; — also, erase ROBERT, wh.

" l. 3 from bot. at the end, add, His s. Robert d. in two yrs.

" l. 2 from bot. for 25 r. 23

P. 171. l. 8, for or even with him r. 1636,

P. 172. l. 3, aft. ano. ins. with the same num. interchang.

" l. 15, bef. Eunice, ins. Barnabas; — also, bef. Hepzibah ins. Priscilla, 1676;

" l. 16, aft. 2, ins. or 7 — also, aft. 1680; ins. Ann;

P. 174. l. 8, bef. 20, ins. 10 or

P. 180. l. 15, aft. w. ins. m. 18 Oct. 1651, — also, for 1658 r. 1654

" l. 16, aft. Mary, ins. the eldest

" l. 6 from bot. aft. Sarah, ins. a. 1639 — also, bef. 23 ins. 22 or

" l. 5 from bot. aft. 1655 add or 6 — also, for Mary r. Mercy — also, erase perhaps

" l. 3 from bot. aft. Mary, ins. or Mercy,

P. 181. l. 4, aft. Hills, add, and d. Mary m. 24 Oct. 1670, John Thompson.

" l. 19, aft. 13 ins. or 30

" l. 21, aft. preced.; add, and his wid. d. 1702. He

P. 185. l. 19, aft. torn; ins. beside Erasmus.

P. 186. l. 2 from bot. bef. JOHN ins. JOHN, Salem, m. 2 July 1661, Love Holyroad, if Essex Inst. III. 142 give the true spell. had Mary, b. 1 May foll. d. soon; John, 1 June 1664; Joshua, 15 July 1666; and Mary, 13 Oct. 1675; and his w d. 7 Dec. foll.

P. 188. l. 17, aft. Salem, ins. where he m. 17 Dec. 1672, Rebecca, d. — also, aft. S. ins. had Samuel, b. Sept. foll. d. in few wks.; and Sarah, 8 May 1674 — also, at the end, add, wh. m. 28 Feb. foll. Simon Orne.

P. 192. l. 6 from bot. aft. yr. ins. A very dilig. inquir. in Essex Inst. II. 163, is confid. that he d. bef. June 1639, tho. he states that the inv. was not brot. in bef. Nov. 1663. Yet, as E. S. jr. appears in many appraisem. 1653 and aft. I doubt much.

P. 195. l. 3, aft. Boston. ins. But the Story of Stiles is far less prob.

P. 199. l. 21 from bot. for absurdly r. absurd.

P. 204. l. 3 from bot. bef. prob. ins. possib. not

P. 206. l. 3, bef. wid. ins. his

" l. 16, at the end, add, by wh. he had John, b. 25 Nov. 1654; and Samuel, 15 Nov. 1658.

P. 207. l. 8 from bot. for 1657 r. 23 Jan. 1658

" l. 7 from bot. aft. Robert, ins. 24 Jan. 1662 — also, aft. Benjamin, ins. 28 Feb. 1665 — also, aft. not. add, One was Sarah, 28 Feb. 1668.

" l. 2 from bot. for had w. r. m. 27 Aug. 1685, — also, aft. Hannah ins. Eager, had Eliz. b. 16 Aug. foll. d. in few mos.; and Robert, 4 Mar. 1688;

P. 209. l. 12, at the end, add, had Samuel, b. 15 Jan. 1685; Robert, 7 Jan. 1687; Eliz. 1 Feb. 1689; Catharine, 15 Apr. 1691; Mary, 21 Feb. 1693, wh. d. in few ds.

P. 224. l. 2 from bot. at the end, add, beside Benjamin, 18 Mar. 1689.

P. 228. bef. l. 10 from bot. ins. STROUD, ROBERT, Boston, by w. Mary had Mary, b. 11 Oct. 1659.

P. 229. l. 19, aft. ch. ins. and perhaps one was Edward,

" l. 18 from bot. aft. ch. ins. His d. Deborah m. James Redfield,

" l. 15 from bot. aft. Orris, ins. whose h. Nathaniel d. 23 Nov. preced.

P. 230. bef. l. 20 from bot. ins. SUMERTON, JOB, in Essex Inst. Coll. III. 50, but in Index Summerton, I must feel, is mispr. for Swinerton.

P. 233. l. 15 from bot. aft. Medfield, ins. m. 31 Jan. 1675, Hannah, eldest d. of John Plimpton, but I kn. no more, exc. that he was liv. in

P. 234. l. 18, at the end, add, wh. d. 9 May,

" l. 19 aft. Sarah. ins. But this was in Essex Co.

P. 235. l. 16, aft. Hannah; ins. Patience; and Mary; without dates, but the last nam. is thot. to be the eldest of all.

" l. 15 from bot. strike out in 1663 had sett. and ins. lost his w. in childb. 31 Oct. 1662,

" l. 11 from bot. aft. more; add, but rem. to N. J. where are descend. the nautical S. of Cape May.

P. 236. l. 19, at the end, add, JOHN, Newport 1651, as found by Stiles.

P. 237. l. 3 from bot. aft. Salem, ins. by w. Mary had Joseph, b. 13 Oct. 1653; Eliz. 1 Dec. 1655; Mary, 21 Apr. 1659; Abigail, 24 Jan. 1662; Samuel, 19 Aug. 1664; John, 30 Sept. 1666; and Stephen, a. 22 Sept. 1669 — also, erase the rest of that l. and half of the next, to ;

" l. 2 from bot. at the end, add, more prob. his wid.

" last l. at the end, add, JOSEPH, Salem, s. of the preced. m. 16 Oct. 1678, Eliz. Lambert, had Samuel, b. 14 Sept. 1682; Eliz. 20 May 1684; and Joseph, 20 Aug. 1685.

P. 238. last l. aft. Rachel. ins. JOSEPH, Boston, by w. Eliz. had Benjamin, b. 22 Jan. 1660,

P. 239. bef. l. 8 from bot. ins. SWETLAND, or SWEETLAND, WILLIAM, Salem, by w.

Agnes had Peter, b. 1 Sept. 1676 ; Grace, 8 Mar. 1680 ; John, 1 Sept. 1681 ; and Joseph, 5 Jan. 1684.

P. 242. l. 13, aft. SWINERTON, ins. SWIMERTON.

" l. 15 and 16 aft. had, strike out two s. and two ds. and ins. Jasper, b. 4 June foll. ; Joseph, 8 Feb. 1661 ; Eliz. 26 Feb. 1663 ; Ruth, 22 Mar. 1665 ; and Ruth, again, 17 May 1670 ; and his w. d. 5 days aft. He m. 2 Sept. 1673, Esther Baker.

" l. 21, aft. physician, ins. m. 8 Mar. 1680, Hannah Brown, a wid. whose former h. is beyond my discov. had Mary, b. 24 Dec. 1681,

" l. 22, at the end, add, JOSEPH, Salem, prob. s. of Job, but whether of the first or of the sec. of that name is unkn. by w. Mary had Mary, b. 22 Mar. 1693 ; Joseph, 1 Dec. 1694 ; Joanna, and Ruth, tw. 22 Nov. 1696 ; Sarah, 17 Jan. 1699 ; and Job, 30 Nov. 1701.

P. 245. l. 19 from bot. for Oct. r. Feb.

" l. 18 from bot. for 1670 r. 1671 — also, bef. Mar. ins. 6

" l. 17 from bot. aft. Benjamin ins. 7 Jan. 1685 — also, aft. Thomas, ins. 1 Apr. 1677 ; — also, aft. Joseph, ins. 20 Mar. 1682 — also, aft. Sarah, ins. 21 Feb. 1688

" l. 17 from bot. aft. again, ins. 29 Sept. 1679,

" last l. aft. jury. ins. JOHN, Salem, m. 3 Mar. 1690, Sarah, d. of John Waters, had John, b. 22 Mar. 1692.

P. 246. l. 7, for Deborah r. Dorothy

" l. 16, for ano: r. first

" l. 17, bef. 1645 ins. 10 Dec.

" l. 17 from bot. aft. Rebecca, ins. d. of Bennett Swayne of Salisbury, Co. Wilts,

" l. 14 from bot. for has r. had

P. 247. l. 3, aft. 1663 ; ins. and he d. 26 July 1675.

" l. 16 from bot. aft. yr. ins. at I. leav. large est. 21,

P. 248. l. 16, at the end, add, is prob. the same, seen at Bristol, 1689, call. Robert Taft, with w. and five ch.

P. 252. l. 15, aft. 1685. add, His wid. m. 14 Nov. 1695, Samuel Bishop.

" l. 16, aft. 1685, ins. m. 18 Nov. 1686, Abigail, d. of Hon. James Bishop.

P. 253. l. 17, for 1678 r. 1671

" l. 18, bef. JOHN ins. GILBERT, Salem, s. of the preced. m. 10 Apr. 1686, Lydia, d. of Thomas Small, had Mary, b. 4 Nov. 1689 ; Joseph, 30 July 1692 ; Lydia, 10 Mar. 1697 ; and Gilbert, 13 July 1699.

" l. 18 from bot. at the end, add, Sometimes the spell. is Topley.

P. 255. l. 4 from bot. aft. Salem, ins. m. 25 Oct. 1678, Mary Nurse, d. of that female victim of the saddest fanaticism and cruelty that ever raged in N. E. had John, b. 9 Aug. 1680 ; Mary, 3 Apr. 1688 ; Cornelius, 25 Mar. 1690 ; Jonathan, 21 Feb. 1692 ; Eliz. 22 Mar. 1694 ; and Sarah, 2 Oct. 1696, was

P. 256. l. 12, aft. John, ins. posthum. 20 July 1674

" l. 19, erase John, 20 July 1674 ;

" l. 17 from bot. aft. 8 ins. or 18

P. 258. l. 20, for 1686 r. 1682

" l. 21, aft. name ins. of John T.

P. 262. l. 9 from bot. aft. Marshfield, ins. youngest s. of Richard of Yarmouth,

P. 268. l. 8, bef. 1640 ins. 14 Dec. — also, bef. Thomas ins. Hannah, 15 Mar. 1642 ; Mary, 17 June 1644 ; — also, bef. 1648 ins. 16 July — also, aft. James, ins. 15 Aug.

P. 268. l. 11, bef. prob. ins. by w. Catharine — also, aft. 1640; ms. Eliz. 9 Apr. 1643; Mary, 24 Sept. 1646; Samuel, 6 Apr. 1650; and Sarah, 15 Apr. 1652;

P. 274. l. 15 from bot. aft. 1685. add, He m. 10 Dec. 1692, Sarah, wid. of Benjamin Robbins.

P. 277. l. 14 from bot. aft. *aft.* ins. He made complaint in Eng. against our Col. to wh. the answ. in Remonstrance of Braintree is one of the most curious papers in our annals. It may be read in 4 Mass. Hist. Coll. V. 104.

P. 280. l. 15, aft. Salem, erase 1688, and add, m. 28 Dec. 1667, Mary, d. of Richard Graves, had Richard, b. 6 Dec. 1668; George, 14 Apr. 1670; Mary, 3 Dec. 1671; Eliz. 4 Jan. 1673; Hannah, 6 June 1674; and Ruth, 8 Feb. 1676.

P. 285. l. 17 from bot. aft. 6. add, His d. Abigail m. first, Jonathan Curtis, next, Nicholas Huse, and d. 1731, wid. of Samuel Sherman.

" l. 3 from bot. at the end, add, He was m. by Gov. Endicot, at Boston, 4 Aug. 1656, to Ann Vicaris; but wh. the bride was, may be hard to find.

P. 289. l. 21 from bot. aft. 1648, add or 9.

P. 290. l. 20 from bot. for John r. JOHN

" l. 19 from bot. aft. 1603, add, and br. of Rev. Herbert, a prebend of Westminster,

" l. 14 from bot. aft. Eng. ins. there had Alice, and Martha, bapt. 10 Apr. 1669, then of ripe yrs.

" l. 11 from bot. for a. 1670, r. and was bur. 3 Nov. 1668 in the cloisters.

" l. 8 from bot. aft. preced. ins. was bapt. 18 Apr. 1663, aged a. 20 yrs. by the dean at Westminster Abbey,

P. 291. l. 1, bef. THOMAS, ins. SAMUEL, a soldier of Gallop's comp. 1690, for the mad expedit. against Quebec, acc. the list in Geneal. Reg. XIII. not in IX.

P. 292. l. 16, for in 1677 r. a. 1694

" l. 17, at the begin. ins. where his s. Thomas had in 1677 — also, for 13 r. 15

" l. 20 from bot. aft. Boston. ins. But the witness may have been his s. of the same name.

" l. 12 from bot. for 1647 r. a. 1650

P. 293. l. 1, aft. 1726, ins. bur. 22d.

P. 295. l. 16, bef. or ins. THORLA,

" l. 7 from bot. aft. him, add, and bore Lydia, 1 Apr. 1640; and John, 19 July 1644.

P. 300. l. 3, for TICKENOR r. TICHENOR

" l. 12 from bot. aft. Eng. add, may have liv. at Salem, by w. Sarah had Eliz. b. May 1642, and he soon d. for his wid. had m. John Southwick long eno. to bear him a d. June 1644.

" bef. l. 11 from bot. ins. TIDMARSH, RICHARD, Salem, m. 20 June 1659, Mary Felmingham, d. perhaps of Francis, had Richard, b. 12 July 1660.

P. 303. last l. aft. preced. ins. was prob. the soldier in Gallop's comp. 1690,

P. 306. l. 2, aft. 1652, ins. d. soon

" l. 16, aft. 1643, ins. apprent. of Timothy Hatherly, wh. had, July 1634, transfer. him to John Winslow, had gr. of ld. Aug. 1642, and ano. in Oct. foll. by w. of unkn. name, a d. of Peter Brown,

" l. 20, at the end, add, He was constable 1681, and propound. for freem. 1682.

P. 309. l. 19, bef. John, ins. Mehitable, b. 10 Jan. 1   ;

" l. 21, bef. 1668 ins. 26 Nov.

P. 311. l. 16, aft. 1651, ins. wh. m. 5 Nov. 1671, Nathaniel Silsbee. His w. Margaret d. 18 July 1672, and in Sept. 1673 he m. Mary Read, and d. 23 June 1681.

P. 311. l. 20, bef. JOHN ins. JOHN, Salem, s. of the preced. m. 26 June 1672, Rebecca Knight, had Margaret, b. 8 Mar. foll.; John, 3 Sept. 1674; Rebecca, 19 July 1676; Nathaniel, 20 Sep^t. 1678; Eliz. 14 Mar. 1681; Mary, 28 May 1686; Deborah, 8 Jan. 1688, when the w. d.

P. 312. l. 12, bef. NATHANIEL, ins. JOHN, and JOHN, jr. were soldiers in Gallop's comp. 1690.

" l. 9 from bot. at the end, add, In May 1692, one Roger, of Billerica, prob. this yearling of 1635, was arrest. for witcher. and he may have been guilty of perform. some unexpect. cure, clear. show. diabolic. aid.

P. 316. l. 8, aft. Benjamin, ins. b. 5 Nov. 1654

P. 319. l. 20 from bot. aft. Mass. add, and had prob. rem. from Ipswich.

P. 320. l. 22, aft. others; add, certain. Eliz. wh. m. Richard Randall, and Martha, wh. m. 22 Nov. 1678, Nathan Lord;

P. 321. l. 14, bef. 1668 ins. Nov.

P. 322. l. 15 from bot. aft. Elias, ins. had sec. w. Hannah, a d. of John Solart of Wenham,

" l. 4, at the end, add, he was a mariner, and in July 1659 gave evid. also call. his age 20 yrs.

P. 331. l. 20 from bot. bef. BERNARD ins. BENJAMIN, Nantucket, s. of John, m. 15 Jan. 1730, Eliz. d. of Jacob Norton, had Mary, b. 1730; Benjamin, d. soon; Rachel; John; Ann; Priscilla; and Dinah; and d. 8 Sept. 1776. His wid. d. 17 June 1780.

" l. 16 from bot. aft. had, ins. by w. Ann,

" l. 14 from bot. aft. John, ins. prob. tw.

" l. 12 from bot. aft. 1697, add, i. e. prob. 1698; beside Eliz.; and he d. 26 Apr. 1728. His will of 5 Jan. 1723, pro. 17 July 1728, ment. all the six ds. four s. but express. uncert. whether James and Joseph be liv. Tabitha m. John Frost, and next Joseph Brown; Rachel m. Thomas Gorham; Abigail m. Mar. 1720, George Brown, as his sec. w.; and Priscilla d. unm. 30 Dec. 1770.

P. 336. l. 17 from bot. aft. there ins. by w. Ellen had Hannah, b. 14 Feb. 1641; Judah, 3 June 1643; Ruth, 23 Apr. 1645; Joseph, 19 May 1647; — also, aft. Swan ins. had Abigail, 10 Dec. 1651, and

P. 345. l. 17, aft. Boston, ins. m. 30 Apr. 1670, Mary, d. of Habacuck Gardner, had Robert, b. 25 Apr. foll.; Mary, 25 Jan. 1673; and she d. 14 Oct. 1674, unless that date belong to the f.

P. 350. l. 2 from bot. aft. 1683. add, Hannah m. 7 Nov. 1672, Samuel Clark; and Sarah m. 10 Sept. 1685, John Hummerston.

P. 352. l. 6, aft. me, ins. exc. that he m. Sarah, d. of Richard Newman.

P. 362. l. 13 from bot. aft. blacksmith, ins. by w. Elinor had James, b. Sept. 1660; William, Mary, and Elinor, wh. three d. in 1663, but may not all have been younger, for ano. William was b. 10 June of this yr.; and Samuel, Oct. 1664; Isabel, 3 Jan. 1667; Ezekiel, Sept. 1668; Joseph, 9 Apr. 1670; and Francis, 1 July 1671.

P. 363. l. 9, for 1686 r. prob. Dec. 1676

P. 370. bef. l. 14 ins. VERDEN, JOHN, Marblehead, m. 2 Dec. 1669, a Masters, whether wid. or maid. is unkn. had Mary, b. 14 Nov. 1672; John, 5 Feb. 1674; and Eliz. 10 July 1675.

P. 371. l. 6, bef. Abigail ins. Sarah m. 9 Dec. 1673, Deliverance Parkman;

" l. 7 from bot. at the end, add 11 Nov.

P. 372. l. 15 from bot. for 1666 r. 1667 — also, for 1668 r. 1669.

P. 373. l. 4, bef. 1681 ins. 28 Mar.

P. 373. l. 5, aft. Thomas, ins. b. 25 May foll. acc. Essex Inst. III. 237.

P. 391. l. 9, bef. JOHN ins. JAMES, Lynn, d. Nov. 1682, was perhaps only trans. resid. for his inv. tak. 10 Jan. foll. by the constable, was only £2. 4s.

P. 401. l. 15, aft. me. add, Late. I have learn. that my conclus. of the m. of George Shove with d. of *first* Thomas, rather than wid. of the *sec.* was wrong. This sec. Barnstable Thomas, wh. by early d. bef. his f. led to the false infer. had m. Hannah, d. of Nathaniel Bacon, and she next m. as above said, Rev. George Shove of Taunton.

" l. 17 from bot. at the end, add, Only ch. Nicholas is ment. by wid. Eliz. when she took admin. June 1682.

P. 404. l. 19 from bot. aft. storehouse. add, In a London publicat. LITHOBOLIA, or the stone-throwing Devil, of wh. the Library of Harv. Coll. possess. an orig. copy as may be read, 1698, reprint. as the first article in New York Hist. Magaz. for Nov. 1861, the childish credul. of both f. and s. is outdone. Yet the incidents so exact. concur. and even the phraseol. of not a few of the tales so near. corresponds, that rashness will not be imput. to the surmise, of assist. by either Increase or Cotton in supervis. the MS. of this tract, for certain. one (if one, both) enjoy. perusal of it, soon aft. it came from the press ; and it was the proper nutrim. for their credulity.

P. 415. l. 12 from bot. aft. witchcraft. add, Under the paralysis of fear his moral power had yield. to the falsehood of confess. of guilt, but on the approach of execut. was happy eno. to recover sense, and retract the folly.

P. 454. l. 13, erase or 70, — also, aft. w. add, had Mary, b. 7 Jan. foll. ; Mehitable, 16 Oct. 1671 ; Sarah, 6 May 1674 ; Experience, 24 June 1677 ; Mercy, 24 Apr. 1679 ; Jonathan, 6 May 1681 ; Benjamin, 1 Apr. 1685 ; and Lydia, 30 Jan. 1688.

P. 456. l. 10 from bot. aft. Barbara, ins. 3 Oct. 1673 ; — also, aft. Eliz. ins. 28 Mar. 1675 ;

" l. 8 from bot. aft. 1668. add, At Salem, also, were b. Joseph, 1670, wh. d. soon ; Joseph, again, 1671, d. in few mos. ; Micherson, Apr. 1672, d. next yr.

P. 488. l. 20, aft. Richard, ins. had Samuel, b. 23 Mar. 1660 ; Joseph, 3 Sept. 1663 ; Benjamin, 1 Oct. 1665 ; and John, 9 Sept. 1667 ;

P. 494. l. 18, erase perhaps, — also, at the end, strike out d. 1701 and ins. m. 30 Jan. 1684, Ann, d. of Thomas Riggs, had Nathaniel, b. 1685 ; Rebecca, 1686 ; Mary, 1687 ; Charity, 1688, d. soon ; Thomas, 1689 ; Mary and Experience, tw. 1690 ; Hannah, 1691 ; Arthur, 1694 ; John, 1696 ; Patience, 1697, d. soon ; Abraham, 1699, d. young ; and Lydia, 1701 ; and his w. d. 17 Dec. of the same yr. He was liv. 1734

P. 504. l. 21, at the end, add, JOHN, Salem, prob. or some neighb. town, was one of the witness. in May 1692 to prove witcher. upon Rev. George Burroughs by the fact of holding a gun at arm's length.

P. 508. l. 13 from bot. erase Esther ;

P. 509. l. 2, aft. 16 ins. (but ch. rec. has, bapt. 14, wh. was Tuesday.)

P. 510. l. 4, bef. 1738. ins. 29 Mar.

" l. 14 from bot. bef. Daniel ins. John,

" l. 11 from bot. aft. ea. add, outliv. the last.

P. 512. l. 3, aft. John, ins. b. 26 Sept. 1689 — also, bef. 1695 ins. 26 Mar.

" l. 4, aft. Jonathan, ins. 18 Sept. — also, bef. 1708 ins. 14 Mar.

" l. 6, aft. 1733. add, He d. 13 Nov. 1750, aged 87.

" l. 18 from bot. aft. 1678, ins. had w. Remembrance.

P. 513. l. 8, at the end, add, few days aft. his w.

P. 514. l. 19, aft. N. E. add, Short abstr. of her will, 2 Apr. 1682, pro. June foll. is in Essex Inst. III. 189.

P. 516. l. 12 from bot. aft. N. J. ins. Susanna m. 3 Jan. 1667, Nathan Bunnill.

P. 533. last l. for br. of the preced. r. s. of Thomas,

P. 534. l. 3, aft. others; ins. of wh. Pelatiah, 1683, was youngest.

" l. 12, aft. said; ins. but it is not kn. that he was m.

P. 535. l. 16, aft. 1672, add, d. at 20 yrs.

" l. 20 from bot. aft. Daniel, ins. b. 31 July 1633

" l. 19 from bot. aft. Eliz. ins. perhaps b. in our country, 1641; — also, aft. Benjamin, ins. 1643

" l. 18 from bot. aft. Thomas, ins. 1645 — also, aft. Samuel, ins. 1647 — also, aft. Pelatiah, ins. 1650 — also, aft. Abraham, ins. 1655 or 6.

" l. 12 from bot. aft. Reading. add, Two ws. were nam. Sarah, and to the third, Hannah, bef. embarc. four ch. are assign. by tradit. wh. says, that six were b. on our side of the sea.

P. 536. l. 4, aft. order. ins. June 1682,

P. 541. l. 14 from bot. for S. r. s.

P. 557. l. 4, aft. W. add, But in comp. with Ashley he had come in the spring or 1630, and prob. was sent home on tempora. confidential business by his employer. That he was s. of Andrew, a D. D. of some celebr. with the Puritans, wh. d. Dec. 1621, is suggest. to me by Mr. Thornton. See Bradford's Hist. p. 259-60.

P. 574. l. 8, the yr. of Mary's b. was 1670

P. 576. l. 11 from bot. bef. Hannah ins. Obadiah, 5 Mar. 1686;

" l. 10 from bot. aft. 1694; ins. Ebenezer, 9 Apr. 1697;

" l. 8 from bot. at the end, add, b. 20 May 1639; Judith, 14 June 1641; Mary, 14 Apr. 1648, all at Sandwich, as the indefatig. Mr. Morse instructs me.

P. 579. l. 15 from bot. aft. Abigail, ins. 4 Apr. 1679 — also, aft. Sarah ins. 13 July 1684;

" l. 14 from bot. aft. S. ins. as were Eliz. 10 June 1687; and John, 11 Dec. 1688.

P. 588. l. 14, aft. imposts; ins. and d. prob. May 1681, for his inv. was tak. in May, and his w. Ann had admin. in June that yr.

P. 606. l. 20, aft. m. ins. aft. d. of her f. — also, aft. Jordan, add, wh. had admin. in 1648.

P. 618. l. 6, bef. 1702 ins. 17 Apr.

" l. 7, aft. Thomas, add, b. 1666; Henry, 1668; John, 1670; Samuel, 1672; and Joseph, 1676; by w. Sarah, d. of Morris Somes, wh. he m. 15 June 1665, and she d. 11 May 1689. He m. 23 Oct. 1691, Lydia Griffin, wh. outliv. him only few mos.

" l. 14, at the end, add, See WETHERIDGE. One Mary Witheridge of Salem vill. was arrest. in May 1692, as a witch (Essex Inst. III. 119); but I see no proof, that either the devil or the court prevail. to obt. convict.

P. 619. l. 9 from bot. aft. Mary, ins. wh. m. 6 June 1665, Samuel Stocker.

P. 624. bef. l. 7 from bot. ins. WOLLOND, or WOOLLEN, EDWARD, of wh. I kn. no more but that he was an appraiser on two est. 1679 and 80, in Essex Co. in one case call. sen. so as to make it prob. he had s. Edward.

P. 634. l. 21 from bot. aft. again, ins. but rec. says Sarah,

" l. 20 from bot. for 1667 r. 1666

P. 636. l. 8, aft. Plummer, ins. wh. was b. Mar. 1653 — also, aft. Abigail, ins. Aug. 1655;

" l. 10, aft. Nicholas, ins. 31 July 1657;

P. 637. l. 13 for one r. three

P. 642. l. 16 from bot. aft. 1678, ins. by w. Rebecca had Mary, b. 21 Apr. 1660; and his w. d. 2 June 1663, and he

P. 643. l. 2 from bot. aft. 1669. ins. He m. later, Sarah, wid. of John Solart of Wenham.

P. 647. l. 19, aft. Samuel, ins. b. 3 Oct. 1659 ; — also, aft. John, ins. 9 May 1665 ; — also, aft. Matthew, ins. 4 Dec. 1668 ; — also, aft. Mary, ins. 3 Feb. 1662 ; — also, aft. Margaret, ins. 4 Aug. 1671 ; — also, aft. Eliz. ins. 5 May 1674 ; — also, aft. Dorcas. ins. But Mary prob. d. young ; and he had Mary, again, 26 Nov. 1677.

" l. 18 from bot. aft. Samuel, ins. b. 14 Jan. 1685 ; Daniel, 17 Nov. 1697 ; and the f. d. in four days aft.

" l. 17 from bot. aft. John, ins. 2 July 1687 ; — also, aft. Gideon, ins. 30 Jan. 1689 ; — also, aft. Joseph, ins. 25 Sept. 1690 ; — also, aft. Benjamin, ins. 28 Dec. 1691 ; — also, for Daniel r. Jonathan, 5 Apr. 1693 ;

P. 652. l. 6, aft. had ins. by w. Miriam — also, aft. in ins. Oct. — also, aft. 1642, ins. Josiah, — also, aft. tradit. ins. false.

" l. 20, aft. 1683. add, One capt. with this *bitter* name testif. against Rev. George Burrows in 1692, to his diabolic. strength.

P. 662. l. 3 from bot. aft. 1658, ins. came from Scotland,

P. 663. l. 6, aft. belong. add, He d. 3 May 1693, aged 71, says gr.-st.

" l. 12, at the end, add, ROBERT, Charlestown, sec. s. of Edward, had, by w. Ruth, Robert and Timothy, and d. 14 Nov. 1709.   His wid. d. 26 Dec. 1742, aged 73. WILLIAM, Charlestown, youngest br. of the preced. m. 26 Oct. 1701, Eleanor, d. of Thomas Jenner of the same, had Thomas, b. 14 Oct. 1704; Edward, 8 July 1706 ; William, 11 July 1710 ; David, 24 Feb. 1712 ; and Eleanor, 14 July 1714 ; and he d. Feb. 1749.

P. 675. l. 10, at the end, add, His d. Ann m. sec. Andrew Hallet as sec. w.

END OF VOL. IV.

GENEALOGICAL NOTES AND ERRATA.

Communicated by Mrs. CAROLINE H. DALL.

GENEALOGICAL science stands at this disadvantage. When an error has been discovered, there seems no way of recording it, for the benefit of others, so that there shall be no possibility that any future student may be misled, by a wrong base, a wrong figure, or a worn-out tradition. Genealogical registers themselves, teem with long refuted assertions, and every inquirer has to begin at the beginning and work his way through the confusion.

I have for a long time thought of suggesting to this journal the propriety of publishing a couple of loose pages or more, quarterly, upon which, under the head of errata, old mistakes might be corrected and references might be given, and these pages, easily detached, might in time constitute an invaluable volume.

A great deal of matter would accumulate if those who are in the habit of using Savage's *Dictionary* would check the errors they detect, and forward them to the editor to be ranged under such a head.

No genealogist should be over-sensitive in such a matter. His work is of a kind that requires many auditors. Let him be never so careful, yet if he is human, he must now and then lose the thread of the old story, or may at any absorbed moment permit the misprint of a numeral, — which *he* knows so well, that he will instinctively *read* it right, however it is printed.

I wish now to draw attention to a few items, some of them errors, some of them discoveries which may be of value to other students, and which I have encountered at different times during the last few years.

Francis, Richard. Mr. Savage speaks of Richard Francis as once of *Dorchester.* The records of that town contain no allusion to any Francis who was a married man. At the age of 39, Richard is found in Cambridge, married to Alice (probably Wilcockes), in the year 1644. He had no son Richard in Cambridge. If he had a son by an early marriage in England, it might have been such a *son* Richard, who, living in Dorchester in 1661, signed a petition for the continuance of religious liberties after the restoration of the Stuarts. In 1669 the constables were ordered to look after sixteen young men, who could not prove an "orderly living." First on the list was Richard Francis, of Dorchester. This orderly living might be translated "constant employment." If a man remained unmarried he was a legitimate object of public concern. Savage gives an unmarried Richard Francis in Northampton in 1675. He "came from the East," and was clerk of Turner's company in King Philip's war. He wrote a very good hand, and if he was Richard, of Dorchester, would have been then 38 years old.

Richard Francis, of Cambridge, is afterward registered in Medford, and his will is proved in Boston. This does not prove that he changed his residence. William Heley, recorded first in Roxbury and then in Cambridge, seems to have lived, from the first, in Newton, near to what we now call Brook Farm. I have instances of families registered in Ipswich in 1638; in Rowley, 1660; Boxford, 1680, and Andover, 1700, who do not seem to have left the land they first settled on, in all that time.

Whittingham, John. This person, who married the sister of Hubbard, the historian, was in Ipswich at a very early date. Even Savage is found asserting that he was the son of *Baruch*, a posthumous child of the translator of the Geneva bible, and his wife Katharine, sister of John Calvin.

Surtees gives a careful pedigree of the Whittinghams, and another may be found in the publications of the Camden society.

No such person as Baruch is known, nor did John Calvin ever have a sister Katharine. John Calvin married a widow, Idolette Storder née DeBures. Idolette had a sister Katharine, daughter of Louis Jacqueman, of Orleans, heiress, in her mother's right, to the Lords of Turvyle and Gouteron. It was she who became the wife of William Whittingham, dean of Durham. The dean left two sons, Sir Timothy and Daniel, — the first the oldest, the other probably the youngest of a family of six children. Daniel, born Nov. 12, 1571, was living in 1590, and received estates under his mother's will in Kingsgate, Durham, which were probably those which the American family inherited. He was not married at that time, and is lost sight of in Durham. It must have been his son John who came with his mother to Ipswich, and did a man's duty there in 1640.

In the Rogers memoranda, in the fifth volume of the REGISTER, there is a confusion, easily cleared up, concerning the wife of the Rev. John Rogers. In January, 1687, John Rogers, *farmer*, was married in Ipswich to a Mrs. Martha Smith. Children were born to this pair many years after the Rev. John Rogers married Martha Whittingham; and his name is always entered *Mr.* John Rogers, farmer.

The names of Whittingham and Hubbard have been left in inextricable confusion by all the early chroniclers. It was so common for two or more children of one family to receive the same name in baptism, that only a full record will dissipate the obscurity. This has been gleaned chiefly from the probate court. William Hubbard, father of the historian, came to Massachusetts in the Defence in 1635, with his wife Judith, and two daughters, Martha and Margaret. His other children were: John, aged 15; William, aged 13; Nathaniel, aged 6; Richard, aged 4. Hubbard removed from Ipswich to Boston in 1662, and died in 1670. He is said to have sold his property in England for the advantage of the infant state, reserving only an income of £100 for himself and family.

About the same time, from Southerton, now Sutterton, in Lincolnshire, came John Whittingham, who married Martha Hubbard; and possibly a brother Thomas, who was lieutenant of the Ipswich company in 1645.

Their mother was the widow of Daniel Whittingham, the youngest of the six children left by William Whittingham, dean of Durham.

Daniel was born Nov. 12, 1571; he was living in 1590 and unmarried, inheriting property under his mother's will. There is no record of his marriage or death in Durham, but it is possible both might be found in Southerton. It is he whom Mrs. Partington has chosen to record as Baruch, but why she should describe him as a posthumous child is best known to herself.

John Whittingham married Martha, daughter of the first William Hubbard. Her sister Margaret was already married to Ezekiel Rogers, and Ezekiel's sister Margaret, the beloved daughter of the Rev. Nathaniel Rogers, subsequently married his brother by that marriage, the Rev. Wm. Hubbard, the historian.

John and Richard died unmarried in England, where they went to look after property, perhaps at Tendring Hundred in Essex.

As Nathaniel is never mentioned after his arrival, he probably died early.

William Hubbard, the historian, born in England in 1622, graduated in the first class at Harvard in 1642. He was invited to the Ipswich pulpit in 1656, and soon after married. He died Sept. 25, 1704, at the age of 83; having written more than any man in behalf of the colony, if we except Governor Winthrop, whose material he doubtless had leave to use as if it were his own.

Of Margaret Rogers Hubbard we hear little. She devoted herself to her father in his last illness, and with his dying breath, the Rev. Nathaniel Rogers blessed the three children of his only daughter. She had no children after 1655.

John Whittingham, the sole survivor of his family, married Martha Hubbard, and they had: John, *dead* before 1653; Martha, Richard, William, Elizabeth and Judith.

According to the testimony of their nephew Samuel Clarke, John, Richard, Elizabeth and Judith died without issue, and as John Whittingham himself died in 1649, his grandchildren seem never to have known his name, but to have taken it for granted that it was William.

The sole surviving daughter, Martha, married the Hon. John Clarke, about 1667. This Clarke was the oldest son of the famous old surgeon, lumber merchant and cattle dealer, who had married Martha Saltonstall, and came from Newbury to Boston in 1651, a man who excelled in everything, from trepanning a skull and cutting for the stone, to inventing economical wood stoves. As this second John Clarke was not made a freeman of Boston till 1673, he may have been educated abroad, and probably came from Newbury to Boston.

The Hon. John Clarke married Martha, daughter of John Whittingham and Martha Hubbard, about 1667. They had:

John, born 1668;

William, born 1670; married to Mary, dau. of Wm. Whittingham;

Samuel, born 1677, who wrote the Gordon and Hubbard legend, and inherited the Gordon tankard; and

Elizabeth, born 1680; married first-to a cousin "Hubbard" who was a mariner, and afterward the third wife of the Rev. Cotton Mather, who considered her "a great spoil!" In 1818 one of her descendants, Hannah Mather Crocker, dedicated to Hannah More some "Observations on the Rights of Women," probably the first book on that much vexed topic ever printed in America.

William Whittingham, brother of Martha Whittingham Clarke, married Mary, daughter of John Lawrence, who went from Ipswich to New-York in 1662. By her he had at Rowley, near Ipswich:

Martha, married March 4, 1691, to the Rev. John Rogers, of Ipswich;

Mary, married first, to the Hon. Wm. Clark, of Boston, a cousin on the Whittingham side; second, to the Hon. Gurdon Saltonstall, governor of Connecticut, a distant cousin of her first husband;

Elizabeth, married first, to the Hon. Samuel Appleton, of Ipswich; second, to the Rev. Edward Payson, of Rowley;

Richard, graduated at Harvard in 1689;

William, who died early in the West Indies.

It ought to be said here, that few of the families coming to Massachusetts Bay could properly be called puritans.

The Rogerses, Hubbards and Whittinghams were all what is called conformists, though some of them lived to repent of their conformity.

Further corrections in reference to the families of Rogers and Wise, I defer to a future article, but wish to record an interesting discovery made by myself recently in Ipswich, which affords a confirmation of the entry found by Col. Chester on the Candler MS. (*ante*, xxii. 47). Among the children of Nathaniel Rogers in this MS., Col. Chester finds this item:

"Mary married to Wm. Heley."

When this item was published, hardly a descendant of William Heley credited it. Nathaniel Rogers made no will proper, and no one knew that he ever had a daughter Mary. The Heley family had no associations with Ipswich. The item was doubted altogether.

Recently, in making some family investigations in Ipswich, connected with the name of Symonds, I determined to read every line of the records till I exhausted them, and I came unexpectedly upon the following entries.

Elizabeth Heley married Jonas Gregory, May 10, 1672.

Mary Heley married John Wood, May 1, 1676.

It will be observed that the spelling of this name is the same as in the Candler MS. The family have not preserved it, either in this country or in England.

These girls may have been brought up by their grandfather. At all events they appear to have been married from their uncle's house, that of the Rev. John Rogers, afterward president of Harvard College.

Although the descendants of William Heley, who bear his name, are now very few, there must be many persons interested in it, and as his various marriages have confused many investigations, I should like to conclude this article with an exhibit of recorded facts.

Genealogical Notes and Errata.

At some future time I wish to speak of the family registers ordered to be kept by the Massachusetts Company, and of some interesting matters relating to the posterity of Reginald Foster.

WILLIAM HELEY, b. 1613, probably in Devonshire; m. first, Grace, dau. of Miles Ives, of Watertown, 1643, and had :—

   i.   HANNAH, bap. July 7, 1644.
   ii.   SAMUEL, bap. Feb. 14, 1646 ; d. early.
   iii.   ELIZABETH, bap. Nov. 14, 1647.

Grace (Ives) Heley died in childbed, Nov. 8, 1649, and William Heley m. second, Mary, dau. of the Rev. Nathaniel Rogers, in 1650, and had :

   iv.   SARAH, bap. Feb. 2, 1651; d. Oct. 10, 1653.
   v.   WILLIAM, bap. July 11, 1652.

He m. third, Grace, dau. of Nicholas Buttrice, 14. 8. 1653, and had :

   vi.   GRACE, b. 1654.
   vii.   MARY, b. Nov. 4, 1657.
   viii.   NATHANIEL, bap. Feb. 5, 1659.
   ix.   MARTHA, bap. Sept. 9, 1660.

He m. fourth, Phœbe, dau. of Bartholomew Greene, 15. 6. 1661, and had:

   x.   SAMUEL, b. 16. 9. 1662.
   xi.   PAUL, b. April 3, 1664.
   xii.   MARY, b. Oct. 29, 1665.

He m. fifth, Nov. 29, 1677, widow Sarah Brown, of Hampton, the mother of the *Miss* Sarah Brown, married by his son William in 1682.

It will be seen that neither of the daughters married in Ipswich were the children of Mary Rogers. Nor does the circumstance that two Maries were born and named in 1657 and 1665, prove that either died. I shall at some time give some curious facts to show this.

The date of Mary Rogers's death is not known. She appears on the records simply as "wife Mary."

The elements of confusion in the above record are many ; but a copy of it may have this use—it may preach patience.

Students who found children born to William and Grace in 1647, to William and Mary in 1651, and to William and Grace again in 1654, naturally enough thought that there were two William Heleys, a delusion which only the probate record has dispelled.

Again, William Heley, 2d, who married Sarah Brown in Hampton in 1682, returned to Cambridge, where he died in 1689, and his children by " wife Sarah " have been imputed to William Heley, 1st, who died at the age of 70, in less than a year after his son's marriage.

I expect to find the pedigree of William Hele among the descendants of William de la Hele of South Hele in Devonshire.

He seems to have been an unfortunate man, perhaps an oldest son who had lost his inheritance in the civil wars.

He was evidently admitted to the best families, yet it is not uncommon to find his name recorded in the wills of the period, as one to whom "that deat that is in his hand" is remitted.

He was never very fortunate, but all his sons did well.

In 1679, the county court of Middlesex, Mass., issued an order requiring certain statistical returns from the several towns. In the Cambridge return we find : — "30. 1. 1680. For English, our school dame is Good-Wife Heley at present but nine scholars."

A

GENEALOGICAL

CROSS INDEX

OF THE

FOUR VOLUMES

OF THE

GENEALOGICAL DICTIONARY

OF

JAMES SAVAGE.

BY

O. P. DEXTER, M.A., LL.B.

PREFACE.

SOME years ago I discovered that there was in Savage's Dictionary a great deal more information about many families than could be found under the name, and that an index such as is now uniformly found in genealogical works would be of great use. In the preparation for the press of my family genealogy, I found that the maiden name of the wife of the only son of my first American ancestor still eluded my best endeavors; so, as I had not been able to induce any one else to do the work, I compiled the following index. It has been done very hurriedly, but, I hope, will be found reasonably free from errors.

The amount of additional information it lays open is very much more than even I expected; but my object is yet unattained. I still want the maiden name of

> Sarah, who married John Dexter, who died 1677; afterwards married William Boardman,[1] who died 1696; probably finally married Daniel Hichens.[2]

Any one who will help me to some enlightenment in the premises, will greatly oblige,

O. P. DEXTER,

May, 1884.   P. O. Box 193, New York City.

[1] Variously spelt Bordman and Boreman.

[2] Variously spelt Hitchens, Hitchings, etc.; perhaps even Hutchins.

INDEX.

8

10

See Burrill.
Busby, I. 328, 372. II. 319. III. 284. IV. 3.
Bush, I. 381. III. 141, 579. IV. 264.
Bushnell, I. 18 (2), 148 (2). II. 417, 429, 467, 522, 558, 565. III. 115, 164, 212, 222. 394, 550, 584. IV. 16, 41, 57 (3), 124, 379.
Bushrod, II. 351.
Busicot (or Bassaker). IV. 151, 205.
Buss, I. 230. II. 562, 563. IV. 502.
Buswell, I. 274. II. 254. IV. 192.
Butcher, III. 394.
Butler, I. 22, 27. 72, 134. 176 (3), 264, 328, 351, 419, 476 II. 247, 275, 378, 385, 451, 585. III. 20, 118, 217, 270, 295, 312, 327, 415, 654. IV. 23, 24, 75, 167, 181, 208, 209, 249, 363, 429, 446, 659, 676.
Butley, II. 358.
Butnam, III. 629.
Butterfield, I. 202. III. 408. IV. 436, 535.
Butters, IV. 221.
Butterworth, I. 336. II. 542. IV. 395.
Buttery, II. 34.
Buttolph, I. 142, 158, 180. II. 227, 276. IV. 15, 33, 555.
Button, II. 78, 509, 591. III. 28, 50, 84, 119. IV. 372, 497.
Buttress, II. 396.
Buttrick, (II. 373, 525 IV. 508.
Buttry.)
Buxton, I. 274, 329, 446. III. 34, 612.
Buzzell, II. 220.
Byam, IV. 611.
Byfield, I. 401. III. 83. 133.
Byles, I. 410. II. 310. III. 173, 368.
Byley, II. 77, 329. 334. IV. 216, 651.
Byram, II. 102 (2). III. 67. IV. 63, 524, 575.

Cable, I. 173.
Cabot, IV. 54.
Cadwell, III. 440, IV. 175, 588.
Cady, I. 126, 405. III. 16, 24, 34.
Cakebread, I. 316. II. 319. IV. 493.
Caldwell, II. 50. 189. IV, 399.
Calef, I. 134, 383. II. 408.
Call, I. 498. II. 306, 596. III. 15, 73, 126, 504. IV. 77 (3), 305.
Calley, II. 258.
Callum, I. 505.
Calverly, IV. 45.
Cammock, II. 570.
Camp, I. 104, 256. III. 602. IV. 15, 120, 283, 688.
Campbell, I. 221. III. 622.
Campfield, I. 105 III. 201. IV. 123, 326, 579.
Candee, III. 606.
Cane, III. 362.
Canney, II. 436. III. 519. IV. 299, 595.
Canning, III. 404.
Cannon, IV, 293.
Canterbury, I. 122. III. 446. IV. 642.
Capen, I. 61, 135. II. 189. III. 373 (2). IV. 241, 332, 361.
Caper, II. 259.
Card, I. 242. II. 379. IV. 257.
Carder, II. 282, 305, 445. III. 527. IV. 432.
Carew, II. 341.
Carlton, I. 86, 476. II. 598.
Carman, I. 417.
Carpenter, I. 64, 201, 231, 260, 280, 315. II. 469, 585. III. 244, 317, 400, 522, IV. 110, 125, 143, 239, 303, 308, 374, 454.
Carr, I. 94, 142, 255, 394, 408, 464. II. 94. III. 283, 437, 497, 641.
Carrier, II. 177.
Carrington, III. 632. IV. 154.
Carrow, III. 305.
Carter, I. 88, 113, 238. 266, 359, 444 (2), 466.

516. II. 19, 157, 158, 165, 192, 280, 283, 502, 566. III. 9, 143, 378, 504, 621 (2). IV. 123, 350, 413, 526, 559, 664.
Carteret, III. 63.
Carthrick, I. 251.
Carver, I. 194, 380. II. 71, 184. IV. 232.
Carwithee, II. 142. III. 253.
Cary, I. 35, 243 (2), 398. II. 266, 364, 546. IV. 482, 524.
Case, I. 24. II. 315, 422. III. 88, 113, 193, 406, 494, 659. IV. 150, 160, 342, 660.
Casewell, II. 466.
Cash, III. 190. IV. 253.
Casley, III. 288.
Cass, II. 71. III. 408, 409, 522.
Cassell, I. 405.
Castle, IV. 219, 220, 682.
Caswell, III. 81. IV. 294.
Cate, IV. 362.
Catlin, I. 103 (2), 459. II. 208. III. 158, 159, 289. IV. 280.
Caulkins, I. 105, 181. II. 469. III. 529, 546. 569, 570.
Cave, II. 87. III. 656.
Cecil, II. 67.
Center, IV. 658.
(See Senter)
Chadbourne, IV. 330, 579.
Chadderton, II. 552.
Chadwell, I. 475. II. 17, 280, 367, 526, 548, 566. III. 265.
Chadwick, I. 502. II. 197, 321, 416. IV. 532, 649.
Chaffin, I. 14.
Chalker, I. 294, 461. II. 417. III. 465. IV. 16.
Challis, IV. 19.
Chamberlain, I. 289. II. 19, 48, 295. III. 506. IV. 62, 68. 266 340, 458, 515.
Chambers, IV. 369.
Champernoon, I. 495. II. 109.
Champion, I. 167, 258.
Champlin, I. 86, 267. II. 579.
Champney, I. 126, 222, 248, 394, 444, 458. II. 205, 303, 373, 484. III. 217, 227, 454, 538, 591.
Chandler, I. 2 (2). 3, 5, 57, 188, 232. 309, 327, 409, 422, 423. II. 6 (3), 21, 63. 71, 412. III. 116, 126, 169, 360 (2), 401, 407, 536. IV. 86, 130.
Chantrel, III. 159.
Chapin, I. 13, 201, 432, 453. II. 251, 428. III. 160, 518. IV. 69, 282, 654, 655.
Chapleman, III. 655.
Chaplin, II. 263.
Chapman, I. 139, 147, 170, 202, 266, 292, 478, 504. II. 50, 250, 384, 520, 576, 590. III. 287, 474. IV. 50, 67, 172, 235, 246, 331, 640.
Chappel, II. 9. IV. 161.
Charles, IV. 300, 674, 698.
Charlet, II. 378.
Chase, I. 59, 85, 95 (2), 114, 180, 209, 338, 347. II. 178, 232. III. 42, 199, 258, 367, 395, 408, 409, 548. IV. 187, 497, 704.
Chatfield, III. 413.
Chatterton, IV. 676, 678.
Chauncy, I. 243, 290, 307. II. 440. III. 112, 280, 452, 633. IV. 227, 400.
Checkley, I. 12. II. 134, 246, 512. III. 109. IV. 40 (3), 503.
Chedsey, I. 41, 234. IV. 286, 680.
Cheeny, II. 442. III. 11, 19.
Cheesebrough, I. 103. II. 223. III. 342.
Cheever, I. 58. II. 270, 289, 591. III. 85, 89, 342.
Chenery, I. 226.
Chenevard, I. 150.
Cheney, I. 159. 316. II. 374, 384, 551. III. 271, 298, 403, 446 (2). IV. 3. 61, 639, 650, 651.

3

4

28

5